The Law of Administrators and Receivers of Companies

The Law of Administrators and Receivers of Companies

By

Sir Gavin Lightman
LLM (University of Michigan), LLB (Lond.)
*Formerly One of her Majesty's Justices and
Bencher and sometime Treasurer of Lincoln's Inn
Consultant with Winston & Strawn
Fellow of University College London*

And

Gabriel Moss
QC, MA, BCL (Oxon)
*Bencher of Lincoln's Inn
Visiting Professor in Corporate Insolvency Law at Oxford University
Visiting Fellow at St Catherine's College Oxford University*

With

Hamish Anderson
LLM, Hon. LLD
*Solicitor of the Senior Courts, Partner, Norton Rose LLP
Visiting Professor, Nottingham Law School, Nottingham Trent University
Visiting Fellow, Centre for Insolvency Law and Policy, Kingston University*

Ian F. Fletcher
MA, LLM, MCL, PhD, LLD
*Bencher of Lincoln's Inn
Professor of International Commercial Law, University College London*

Richard Snowden
QC, MA (Cantab.), LLM (Harvard)
Bencher of Lincoln's Inn

SWEET & MAXWELL   **THOMSON REUTERS**

First edition 1986
Second edition 1994
Third edition 2000
Fourth edition 2007

Published in 2011 by Sweet & Maxwell
100 Avenue Road, London NW3 3PF part of Thomson Reuters (Professional)
UK Limited (Registered in England & Wales, Company No 1679046.
Registered Office and address for service: Aldgate House, 33 Aldgate High
Street, London EC3N 1DL).

Typeset by LBJ Typesetting Ltd of Kingsclere
Printed in the UK by CPI William Clowes Ltd, Beccles, NR34 7TL

For further information on our products and services, visit
www.sweetandmaxwell.co.uk

No natural forests were destroyed to make this product; only farmed timber
was used and re-planted.

A CIP catalogue record for this book is available from the British Library.

ISBN 978-0-414-04536-1

To Naomi and Judith and Kirsti and
Letitia and Amanda

Preface to the Fifth Edition

Insolvency Law has continued to develop since the date of the fourth edition of this work. Administration, in its post-Enterprise Act form, is no longer a "new" procedure. As intended, it has substantially replaced administrative receivership as the procedure for dealing with insolvent companies with viable businesses. This trend is reflected in the case-law developments with many more new decisions being reported on administration than on receivership. Receivership nonetheless remains important and has been the procedure of choice for dealing with the collapse of some investment funds.

The structure of the book has been revised and the new table of contents reflects this remodelling. The book is now divided into seven parts (each dealing with both procedures). The first part is introductory and the second deals with matters affecting the choice of procedure. Then, following the natural sequence of events, there are parts dealing with the commencement of the chosen procedure, the conduct of the proceedings and closure. These are followed by discrete parts dealing with court appointed receivers and cross-border insolvency. We hope that this more logical presentation will commend itself to all users of the work. Finally, on the structure of this fifth edition, the opportunity has been taken to incorporate some smaller chapters from previous editions into other chapters whilst still retaining the overall coverage of the work.

As with the fourth edition, the new edition benefits from the expertise and commitment to the project of three managing editors, Richard Snowden QC, Professor Ian Fletcher and Mr Hamish Anderson and contributions (large and small) to individual chapters as indicated in the subsequent List of Contributors. We gratefully acknowledge their invaluable assistance. We would also like to thank Professor Sandra Frisby for her time case-updating and cross-referencing this edition, which has been immensely helpful.

We again thank our wives Naomi and Judith and the wives of the managing editors Kirsti, Letitia and Amanda (to whom this edition is dedicated) for once again patiently putting up with us when we have been detained and distracted by our work on this edition.

We have attempted to state the law as at July 31, 2011. In selecting materials for inclusion in the Appendices, it has been assumed that the reader will have access to copies of *Sealy & Milman: Annotated Guide to the Insolvency Legislation 2011*, 14th Edition, Volumes 1 & 2 or some equivalent compilation of the relevant statutory materials.

Sir Gavin Lightman
Gabriel Moss QC

STOP PRESS

Re Nortel GmbH [2011] EWCA Civ 1124

This text endeavours to state the law as at July 31, 2011, although some references to later developments have been included where possible. The text, and in particular Ch.4 dealing with "Expenses", includes references to the first instance decision of Briggs J. in *Re Nortel GmbH* [2011] B.C.C. 277 where on July 31, an appeal had been heard by the Court of Appeal but the outcome was not known. Judgment was delivered on October 14, 2011.

The case concerns the ranking of liabilities under financial support directions and contributions notices issued pursuant to the Pensions Act 2004 after the commencement of administration. Briggs J. had held that such liabilities would not be provable debts for the purposes of r.13.12 of the Insolvency Rules 1986 because they could not be said to have arisen out of a pre-administration liability and that they constituted an administration expense.

In view of the size of some pension deficits, the particular question of the ranking of pension liabilities is one which can be of profound significance in any given case. It is also an issue which exposes an anomaly between the ranking of the employer's own debt, which the Pensions Act provides shall be an ordinary unsecured liability, and the collateral obligations of others arising out of financial support declarations and contribution notices, where the legislation is silent and ranking has to be determined in accordance with general principles. It is the latter point which gives the case its wider significance and its principal interest for the purposes of this work; at issue is the question whether a liability which cannot be said to have arisen out of a pre-administration obligation can be other than a liability which enjoys the super-priority of an administration expense. This is the dichotomy which threatens to undermine the utility of administration as a procedure for business rescue.

In the Court of Appeal, Lloyd L.J. (with whom Rimer and Laws L.JJ. simply agreed) held that the case had been correctly decided at first instance—essentially for the reasons given by Briggs J. which are discussed elsewhere in this text. That means that the analysis of the issues remains the same subject to the very important consideration that post-Enterprise Act administration expenses are now the subject of a binding Court of Appeal authority The issue is ripe for early consideration by the Supreme Court and it is understood that, at the time of writing this short update, permission to appeal has been granted.

Contributors

Contents

Table of Cases

TABLE OF CASES

Table of Statutes

Table of Statutory Instruments

Table of European Union Treaties and Secondary Legislation

Table of International Treaties and Conventions

Abbreviations

The following abbreviations are used in this work:

BIS	Department of Business, Innovation and Skills
COMI	Centre of main interests
Cork Report	*Report of the Review Committee on Insolvency Law and Practice* (Cmnd.8558, 1982)
CPR	Civil Procedure Rules 1998
CVA	Company voluntary arrangement
DTI	Department of Trade and Industry
EC Regulation	EC Regulation on Insolvency Proceedings 2000
RSC	Rules of the Supreme Court 1965
TUPE Regulations	Transfer of Undertakings (Protection of Employment) Regulations 2006

Chapter 1

Introduction

1. INTRODUCTION

This book deals with the law concerning administrators, receivers and admin- **1–001**
istrative receivers of companies. Although the present-day law accords primacy
of importance to administration, this was historically the most recent development in the evolution of the procedures which are here discussed. It was only
with the entry into force of the Insolvency Act 1986 that the administration
procedure for companies first became available under English law whereas
receivership, in its various forms, has a far lengthier pedigree. In the present
chapter the respective procedures are introduced in reverse order to their listing
in the title of the book in its current edition. This is because many elements of
the administration procedure were modelled upon aspects of receivership, and
is also in the interests of providing a sequential account of the history of the
subject matter of this book.

2. THE RECEIVER AND MANAGER

The power of the Court of Chancery to appoint a receiver to safeguard equi- **1–002**
table interests is centuries old.[1] By comparison, the right of a mortgagee to
appoint a receiver out of court under the terms of the contract with the
mortgagor is of more recent origin. Prior to the development of the concept of
a floating charge in the latter part of the nineteenth century, security for a loan
or other indebtedness took the form of a fixed mortgage of specific items of
property. An important characteristic of such a fixed charge was that if the
mortgagee went into possession of the charged property he was subject to a
strict liability to account to the mortgagor both for what he had received and
for what he ought to have received from the property. In order to overcome this
disadvantage, mortgagees began to insist on the insertion of a provision in the
mortgage giving the mortgagee the right to call upon the mortgagor to appoint
a receiver of the charged property with the task of receiving any income (such
as rent) produced by the assets, to apply such income to the payment of interest
on the secured debt and to pay any surplus to the mortgagor. A significant
feature of the private appointment of receivers in this way was that they acted
as agents for the mortgagor, who was solely responsible for their acts and
omissions. This was the origin of one of the apparent paradoxes of receivership
in modern times, namely that a receiver whose function is to serve the interests

---

[1] See, e.g. *Hopkins v Worcester & Birmingham Canal Proprietors* (1868) L.R. 6 Eq. 437, 447,
per Giffard V.C. For receivers appointed by the court see below, Ch.29.

of the mortgagee by whom he has been appointed is expressly cast in the role of agent of the mortgagor, thereby reducing the potential liability of the mortgagee for any damaging consequences of the use of this procedure. In time the contractual powers given to receivers were extended and they were given powers to preserve, manage and sell the charged assets in the event of default by the mortgagor.[2]

1–003   This method of securing credit had two practical limitations. First, the fixed charge[3] froze and barred dealings with the property and accordingly could not be attached to assets such as stock in trade with which the borrower required to deal in the ordinary course of his business. Secondly, in the case of a charge by a business-owner, the sale of the charged assets piecemeal was likely to achieve less than a sale of the business as a going concern, for a charge over specific assets did not empower the mortgagee to sell the business as a going concern or to manage it as an interim measure pending sale.[4]

1–004   The concept of the floating charge was a late nineteenth century creation of equity which overcame these limitations, and reconciled the requirements of the borrower for freedom to carry on his business and of the lender to have the most ample form of security in the event of jeopardy to his repayment.[5]

> "The floating charge was invented by Victorian lawyers to enable manufacturing and trading companies to raise loan capital on debentures, offering a charge over the company's whole undertaking, without inhibiting its ability to trade."[6]

1–005   The floating charge is a form of charge over one or more classes of assets of a company which gives the company freedom to deal with the assets during the ordinary course of its business until a specified event occurs which causes

---

[2] See, e.g. the historical account of the development of the law and practice in relation to the appointment of receivers out of court in *Gaskell v Gosling* [1896] 1 QB 669 (CA), 691, per Rigby L.J., referred to in *Medforth v Blake* [2000] Ch. 86 (CA).

[3] On fixed and floating charges generally, see Ch.3.

[4] A mortgage of land can confer on a mortgagee the power to carry on business on the land without charging the existing business carried on there by the mortgagor, but in this case the mortgagee cannot sell the assets of the mortgagor's business or prevent the mortgagor closing, or selling the assets and goodwill of, the business: *Atkins v Mercantile Credit Ltd* (1985) 10 A.C.L.R. 153. A valuer in making a valuation for mortgage purposes must take this into account: *Coris and Investment Ltd v Druce & Co* (1978) 248 E.G. 315, 407, 504.

[5] Equity had also created the concept of the floating trust in the law of mutual wills which arose on the death of the first to die and crystallised on the death of the survivor: see *Birmingham v Renfrew* (1937) 57 C.L.R. 666 (High Court of Australia), cited in *Re Cleaver* [1981] 1 W.L.R. 939, 946.

[6] *Re Brightlife* [1987] Ch. 200, 214–215, per Hoffmann J. Subsequent legislation meant that property subject to a floating charge was no longer regarded as belonging wholly to the debentureholder: *Re Barleycorn Enterprises Ltd* [1970] Ch. 465 (CA), 474D, per Lord Denning M.R. (The Barleycorn case was overruled by the House of Lords in *Buchler v Talbot*; sub nom. *Re Leyland Daf Ltd* [2004] 2 A.C. 298 (HL). Although no longer good law on the actual point decided by the Court of Appeal in that case, the observations of the then Master of the Rolls concerning statutory incursions upon the proprietary entitlements of a floating charge-holder are correct as a matter of historical fact.) The effect of *Buchler v Talbot* was subsequently reversed by s.1282 Companies Act 2006, which inserted s.176ZA into the Insolvency Act 1986 with effect from April 6, 2008. See below, Ch.4.

the charge to "crystallise" and become a fixed charge, preventing any further dealing by the company with the charged assets. Traditionally the company granted fixed charges over assets with which it did not require to deal and a floating charge over the remainder.[7] Such a floating charge would normally include the whole (or substantially the whole) undertaking of a company. In a case where a floating charge is granted over the undertaking, the mortgagee is given the right to carry on and sell the business of the company as a going concern. To facilitate the exercise of this right, the floating charge ordinarily gives the mortgagee the powers to appoint a receiver to receive the income and preserve the assets pending sale, and to appoint the receiver or another person as manager of the subject matter of the floating charge, whose responsibility it is to carry on the business and sell it and the other assets charged in order to repay the mortgagee. These powers enable the mortgagee to take the management of the company's property out of the hands of the directors and entrust it to a person or persons[8] of his choice.[9] To enable the mortgagee to avoid responsibility for the receiver's management of the undertaking, the floating charge declares the receiver to be the agent of the company, which accordingly is solely liable for his acts and defaults.[10] An appointee with the dual role of receiver and manager accordingly becomes the new managing agent of the company.[11]

Although the concept of a receiver and manager was well established prior to 1986, the law relating to his powers and liabilities was often obscure and unsatisfactory. One of the primary aims of the Insolvency Act 1986 was to update and rationalise this area of the law. Another aim was to make suitable provision for cases in which there was no person who could appoint, or who was willing to appoint, a receiver and manager to a company so as to enable its business to be sold as a going concern rather than simply being put into **1–006**

---

[7] In recent times, in spite of the fact that chargor companies naturally wish to collect in and utilise the proceeds of their book debts to finance the conduct of their business, lenders have invariably insisted that companies grant what purport to be fixed charges over their book debts in an attempt to give the lenders security which will rank in priority to the claims of preferential creditors in a liquidation. The issue of whether and if so to what extent this can validly be achieved has given rise to considerable litigation over the last 25 years: see below, Ch.3.

[8] In the exercise of his powers, the mortgagee may appoint: (i) a receiver alone; (ii) a manager alone; (iii) different persons as receiver and as manager; (iv) a single person as receiver and manager; or (v) a receiver with power to employ a manager. In case (v), the receiver is treated as a receiver and manager if he exercises the power of appointment, for the manager is his agent, responsible to him: see *Parsons v Mather & Platt* [1977] 1 W.L.R. 855. In practice the mortgagee normally appoints the same person as receiver and manager.

[9] *Shamji v Johnson Matthey Bankers Ltd* [1986] F.T.L.R. 329 (CA), 330, per Oliver L.J.

[10] Under the modern legislation the deemed agency of an administrative receiver is the subject of a specific provision in s.44(1)(a) of the Insolvency Act 1986. It has been suggested that "The so-called 'agency' of the receiver is not a true agency, but merely a formula for making the company, rather than the debenture-holders, liable for his acts": per Peter Millett QC in "The Conveyancing Powers of Receivers After Liquidation" (1977) 41 Conv. (N.S.) 83 at 88. But "this agency of the receivers is a real one, even though it has some peculiar incidents": per Nicholls L.J. in *Re Offshore Ventilation* [1989] 1 W.L.R. 800 (CA), 807; see also *Ratford v Northavon RDC* [1987] Q.B. 357 (CA) and *Astor Chemical Ltd v Synthetic Technology Ltd* [1990] B.C.C. 97, 105, Vinelott J.

[11] *Re Mack Trucks (Britain) Ltd* [1967] 1 W.L.R. 780, 786.

liquidation.[12] These aims resulted in the creation by the 1986 Act of the new offices of the "administrative receiver" and the "administrator".

3.   THE ADMINISTRATIVE RECEIVER

1–007   The most important innovation of the 1986 Act in relation to receivership was to create and to invest with a special status a particular category of receivers or managers called "administrative receivers".

1–008   According to s.29(2) of the Insolvency Act 1986 an administrative receiver is:

> "(a)   a receiver or manager of the whole (or substantially the whole) of a company's property appointed by or on behalf of the holders of any debentures of the company secured by a charge which, as created, was a floating charge, or by such a charge and one or more other securities; or
>
> (b)   a person who would be such a receiver or manager but for the appointment of some other person as the receiver of part of the company's property."

1–009   Under the first alternative in s.29(2)(a), the requirements for classification as an administrative receiver are accordingly:

> (a)   the appointment as "a receiver or manager": either position is sufficient;
>
> (b)   "of the whole or substantially the whole of a company's property": this provision reflects the fact that a certain proportion of the company's property may be excluded[13] or released[14] from the charge created by the debenture or from the appointment. It is thought that the criterion of whether the subject of the receivership is of substantially the whole of a company's property is primarily value to the company[15] and that the judgment is to be made as at the date of the appointment so that the character of the office held is not altered by subsequent events, e.g. the disposal by the company of the excluded property or the release by the debenture-holder of charged property from the debenture.[16] Where a charge covers all of the assets of the company, present and future, and is not in form exclusively a fixed charge, the fact that at the time of creation of the charge the company does not have any assets, or any

---

[12] See below, para.1–012.

[13] Property held by the company as trustee for third parties will be excluded from the ambit of every floating charge.

[14] e.g. causes of action against the debenture-holder or receiver or onerous leases. But see *Scottish & Newcastle Plc, Petitioners* [1993] B.C.C. 634 (Court of Session) where the release was so extensive that the appointees were held receivers, and not administrative receivers.

[15] This would appear to be necessary if (for the purpose of the judgment to be made) like is to be compared with like.

[16] Each office has distinct legal responsibilities and privileges from inception until vacation.

assets which are not the subject of a fixed charge, does not prevent such a charge from falling within s.29(2).[17] "Company" in this context includes corporations incorporated abroad which can be wound up as an unregistered company under Pt V of the Insolvency Act 1986[18];

(c) "appointed by or on behalf of the holders of any debentures[19] of the company". Accordingly, receivers or managers appointed by the court are excluded[20];

(d) "secured by a charge which, as created, was a floating charge or by such a charge and one or more other securities": at least one of the charges under which the appointment is made must at the date of its creation have been a floating as opposed to a fixed charge (this being a test of substance, not form). For this purpose it does not matter if the charge has later crystallised, so long as it was a floating charge at the time of creation, irrespective of the length of the period before crystallisation. On a literal reading of the words of the provision it might be suggested that as long as the debenture under which the appointment is made is secured by a floating charge and one or more fixed charges, then an appointee under one or more fixed charges not appointed under the floating charge could still be an administrative receiver. This was clearly not what was intended by the legislature. The central concept of an administrative receiver involves a receiver who is appointed under a floating charge.[21] The words "or by such a charge and one or more other securities" simply provide for the usual modern situation where the debenture contains fixed as well as floating charges. It has been held that a receiver who could have been but was not appointed under a subsisting floating charge in a debenture but was appointed only under a fixed charge in the debenture could not be an administrative receiver and did not need to be qualified as such.[22]

Under the second alternative in s.29(2), an administrative receiver will be "a **1–010** person who would be such a receiver or manager but for the appointment of some other person as receiver of part of the company's property". This provision contemplates the appointment as receiver or manager of a person who would qualify under alternative (a) in s.29(2), but for the prior appointment of a receiver or receivers of a part or parts of the company's property where the

---

[17] *Re Croftbell Ltd* [1990] B.C.C. 781.
[18] *Re International Bulk Commodities* [1993] Ch. 77. The reasoning in that case was questioned in *Re Devon and Somerset Farmers Ltd* [1994] Ch. 57 but it is suggested that it is correct. An industrial society is not, however, a company for these purposes: see *Re Diary Farmers of Britain Ltd* [2010] Ch. 63. See also below, Ch.30.
[19] A mortgage, charge or other security issued by a company is called a debenture: *Downsview Nominees Ltd v First City Corporation Ltd* [1993] A.C. 295 (PC), 311D–E.
[20] See further, paras.29–009 at sub-para.(g).
[21] *A Revised Framework of Insolvency Law*, Cmnd. 9175, p.19; *Cork Report on Insolvency Law and Practice*, Cmnd., 8558 paras 495–498, 504, 508, 520.
[22] *Meadrealm Ltd v Transcontinental Golf Construction Ltd* Unreported November 29, 1991. The necessary qualifications for an administrative receiver are dealt with below, Ch.8.

part or parts in question are such that the remainder cannot fairly be regarded as substantially the whole of the company's property.

4. DISTINCTIONS BETWEEN ADMINISTRATIVE RECEIVERS AND OTHER RECEIVERS

1–011   Whether an appointee is or is not an administrative receiver is a question of law, and neither his description in the appointment nor the parties' intention is rarely if ever relevant. A receiver or manager who does not fulfil the statutory conditions (e.g. because he is appointed over specific assets only) will fulfil the role of receiver or manager largely unaffected by the Insolvency Act 1986. To a degree, such an "ordinary" receiver and manager might fairly be described as a lesser form of receiver or manager, for, unlike an administrative receiver:

(a) his appointment does not preclude the appointment of an administrator[23];

(b) he is not, and does not enjoy the privileges and investigatory powers of, an office-holder[24];

(c) his powers are strictly limited to those conferred by the debenture and are not deemed to be extended unless the contrary intent appears[25];

(d) a person dealing with him (but not with an administrative receiver), even if acting in good faith and for value, is concerned to inquire whether the receiver is acting within his powers[26] and whether there has been any defect in his appointment, nomination or qualifications[27];

(e) he is strictly liable to third parties if he seizes or disposes of their property, notwithstanding the absence of negligence and the existence of reasonable grounds for believing (as well as actual belief) that he is entitled to seize or dispose of the property[28];

(f) there is no statutory provision applicable to an ordinary receiver and manager equivalent to that whereby the court may, on application by an administrative receiver, order that a sale be made of property free of any charge, the charge instead being made to attach to the proceeds of sale[29];

(g) there is no statutory bar on the removal and replacement of an ordinary receiver or manager by his appointor at any time[30];

---

[23] See below, Ch.6.
[24] See below, Ch.8.
[25] As to the extensions of the powers of administrative receivers, see s.42(1) of and Sch.1 to the Insolvency Act 1986.
[26] cf. s.42(3) of the Insolvency Act 1986.
[27] cf. Insolvency Act 1986, s.232.
[28] cf. Insolvency Act 1986, s.234(3) and (4) and *Welsh Development Agency v Export Finance Co Ltd* [1992] B.C.C. 270 (CA).
[29] Insolvency Act 1986, s.43(1) and (7).
[30] As to the bar on the removal of an administrative receiver, see below, para.28–002.

(h) unlike an administrative receiver, an ordinary receiver or manager need not be qualified to act as an insolvency practitioner in relation to the company.[31]

5. THE ADMINISTRATOR

Before 1986 there was no procedure by which a company in financial diffi- **1–012**
culty could obtain a temporary breathing space from its creditors to see if it could be rehabilitated or reach a compromise or arrangement with its creditors. Further, if no person was entitled to, or was willing to, appoint a receiver and manager of the undertaking of the company, there was no mechanism by which the business and assets of the company could be realised as a going concern for the benefit of creditors. The Cork Committee[32] recommended that this gap be filled by conferring power on the court to appoint a judicial manager of an insolvent company upon application by legitimately interested persons. This proposal was given effect in Pt II of the Insolvency Act 1986 which introduced a new concept, company administration, and a new species of office holder, the administrator.[33] This part of this chapter briefly describes the position of administrators appointed under the 1986 Act before the amendments intro- duced by the Enterprise Act 2002 took effect. The position of administrators under the law currently in force is as described in the next part of this chapter and in the remainder of this work. For a detailed treatment of the previous law the reader is referred to the third edition of this work.

Under the legislation first introduced in 1986 an administrator was an **1–013**
insolvency practitioner appointed by the court for a limited period to manage the affairs of an insolvent company. This mission was undertaken with the benefit of a limited statutory moratorium on adverse acts by creditors and with the objective of restoring the company or part of its business to good health, or facilitating a compromise or arrangement with its creditors, or achieving a more advantageous realisation of its assets than would be achieved in a winding-up.[34]

As envisaged by the Cork Committee, the appointment of an administrator **1–014**
was an alternative to the appointment of an administrative receiver or a liquidator. Notice of the presentation of the petition for an administration order had to be given to any person who had appointed or may have been entitled to appoint an administrative receiver,[35] and an administrator could not be appointed if an administrative receiver had been appointed unless the court was satisfied either that the appointor had consented or that, if the administration

---

[31] Insolvency Act 1986, s.388(1).

[32] Cmnd. 8558, Ch.9 (paras 495–521).

[33] See, to this effect, *Bristol Airport v Powdrill* [1990] Ch. 744 (CA),756, per Brown-Wilkinson V.C.

[34] See below, Ch.2, paras 2–038 to 2–040 and Ch.6, paras 6–003 to 6–006.

[35] Insolvency Act 1986, s.9(2) (repealed). For the current provisions concerning the giving of notice to holders of floating charge security, see Insolvency Act 1986, Sch.B1, paras 12(2),15(1), 26(1),(2).

order were made, the charge or security by virtue of which the receiver was appointed would be liable to be released or discharged under ss. 238 to 240 or would be avoided under s.245 of the Act.[36] An administrator could not be appointed after the company had gone into liquidation.[37]

1–015   In many ways the administrator to be appointed pursuant to the Insolvency Act 1986 as originally enacted was similar to the administrative receiver (and this remains the case under the legislation as amended by the Enterpise Act 2002). The following points of similarity are especially noteworthy. An administrator is an office-holder and has many of the same rights and privileges given to an administrative receiver under the Insolvency Act 1986[38] together with some additional powers.[39] In common with an administrative receiver, the administrator acts as the agent of the company.[40] His appointment also displaces the powers of the company's directors to the extent that they might interfere with the proper exercise of his own powers.[41]

1–016   There has, nevertheless, always been an important conceptual difference between administrators and administrative receivers. An administrator is an officer of the court who has additional privileges and responsibilities by virtue of that status. In particular he is responsible for managing the company under his control for the benefit of all those interested in the insolvent estate, and must hold the balance fairly between all those parties. The administrative receiver, by contrast, owes his primary duties to the person who appointed him, and where the interests of the debenture-holder conflict with those of the other creditors of the company, he is entitled to put the interests of his appointor first.[42]

6. ADMINISTRATORS AND ADMINISTRATIVE RECEIVERS UNDER THE ENTERPRISE ACT 2002

1–017   The administration order procedure introduced by the Insolvency Act 1986 was intended as the central element of a new departure in terms of insolvency law and policy, aimed at providing a range of procedures to facilitate the rescue and rehabilitation of companies experiencing financial difficulties. Unfortunately, for a variety of reasons the new procedure proved unsuitable for use in a high proportion of cases, as demonstrated by the statistical evidence of the first ten

---

[36] Insolvency Act 1986, s.9(3) (repealed). For the current provision concerning the power of the court to make an administration order despite the fact that there is an administrative receiver of the company, see Insolvency Act 1986, Sch.B1, para.39.

[37] Insolvency Act 1986, s.8(4) (repealed). For the current provisions, which are to the same effect, see Insolvency Act 1986, Sch.B1, paras 8, 17, and 25 (see also para.37).

[38] e.g. the powers in Sch.1 to the 1986 Act, and the power to deal with charged property (formerly governed by s.15 (repealed), and currently governed by Sch.B1, paras 60–66, 70–72).

[39] Such as the power to remove directors: see Sch.B1, para.61(a) (formerly provided by s.14(2) (repealed)).

[40] s.14(5). The consequences of this agency are not identical: see, e.g. the different approaches to adoption of contracts in s.44 and in para.99(4)–(6) of Sch.B1 to the Act (formerly s.19(4)–(7) (repealed) of the Act) and the decision of the House of Lords in *Paramount Airways Ltd*; sub nom. *Powdrill v Watson* [1995] 2 A.C. 394 (HL).

[41] Again, the comparison between an administrator and an administrative receiver in this respect is not exact: see below, paras 2–031 to 2–034 and 2–037, and Ch.10 generally.

[42] *Medforth v Blake* [2000] Ch. 86 (CA).

years of its existence.[43] Successive studies and consultations conducted by
the Insolvency Service consistently arrived at the conclusion that reforms were
necessary.[44] A White Paper published in July 2001 contained proposals for
extensive reforms of both the administration order procedure and administrative receiverships, the declared intention being that there should be an almost
complete elimination of the latter procedure so that floating charge-holders
would in future lose the right to appoint an administrative receiver and would
instead be restricted to having recourse to a "streamlined version" of the
administration order procedure.[45] The legislative vehicle for implementation of
the proposed reforms, the Enterprise Bill 2002, was the subject of a vigorous
campaign by the financial and business community which was alarmed at the
negative implications for the future provision of corporate finance which were
predicted to ensue from a near-total emasculation of floating charge security.
The subsequent dialogue between government and the City resulted in a
number of important changes to the provisions eventually enacted by Pt 10 of
the Enterprise Act 2002, which inserted a new Sch.B1 to the Insolvency Act
1986 to replace Pt II of that Act. Although in the majority of instances the
granting of a floating charge by a company after the operative date when
the relevant sections of the Act were brought into force—September 15,
2003—no longer confers the right to appoint an administrative receiver, there
are a number of important exceptions to this proposition.[46] In addition to the
specific exceptions which apply to floating charges created by certain types of
company after the operative date, all floating charges which were created prior
to that date continue to confer upon the charge-holder the right to appoint an
administrative receiver.[47] Holders of floating charges benefiting from any of
the statutory exemptions from the effects of the prohibition imposed by
s.72A(1) of the Insolvency Act 1986 retain the right to appoint an administrative receiver as an alternative to invoking the administration procedure in its
amended form. It should also be observed that the revised administration
procedure differs in several ways from the proposals for the "streamlined"
administration procedure which were outlined in the White Paper of July 2001.
Where the latter would have retained the requirement of a court application for
the obtaining of an administration order in all cases, the procedure which is
now contained within Sch.B1 to the Insolvency Act confers upon certain

---

[43] Statistical information concerning the use made of administration orders, and of other forms
of insolvency procedures, can be viewed on the website of the Insolvency Service at: *http://www.
insolvencydirect.bis.gov.uk/otherinformation/statistics/insolvency-statistics.htm.*

[44] "Company Voluntary Arrangements and Administration Orders: A Consultative Document"
(October 1993); "Revised Proposals for a New Company Voluntary Arrangement Procedure"
(April 1995); "A Review of Company Rescue and Business Reconstruction Mechanisms"
(September 1999).

[45] Productivity and Enterprise: Insolvency—A Second Chance, Cm.5234 (July 2001). See especially paras 1.1, 1.7–1.9, 2.5, 2.6.

[46] See ss.72A to 72H of the Insolvency Act 1986, together with Sch.2A, inserted by s.250 of the
Enterprise Act 2002 together with related statutory instruments, notably SI 2003/1832. These
provisions are considered below in Ch.2.

[47] See the definition of "holder of a qualifying floating charge in respect of a company's property" supplied by s.72A(3) of the Insolvency Act 1986 together with para.14 of Sch.B1 to that Act,
as amended by the Enterprise Act 2002, ss.248–250 together with Sch.16.

parties—namely the company, or its directors, or the holder of a qualifying floating charge—the power to appoint an administrator directly without the need to apply to the court.[48] Although, as is explained in subsequent chapters of this book, the consequences resulting from the secured creditor's exercise of a right of direct appointment of an administrator cannot be regarded as fully equivalent to those resulting from the appointment of an administrative receiver, a number of not insignificant advantages, relative to the position of other interested parties, are enjoyed by a creditor who holds a qualifying floating charge in respect of a company's property. It may therefore be expected that this particular form of security will continue to feature in the practices associated with corporate borrowing and finance for the foreseeable future.

---

[48] Insolvency Act 1986, Sch.B1, paras 14, 22. Note that holder of a floating charge created before September 15, 2003 may also enjoy the power to appoint an administrator out of court, because the floating charge, although exempted by s.72A(4)(a) from the prohibition against appointing an administrative receiver, may nevertheless fulfil the requirements of being a "qualifying floating charge" as defined by para.14 of Sch.B1 (see previous footnote). If that is the case, the floating charge-holder has the options of appointing an administrative receiver pursuant to the terms of the charge, or of appointing an administrator under para.14(1) of Sch.B1, or of applying to the court under para.12(1)(c) of the Schedule for an administration order in respect of the company. See further, Ch.5 below.

Chapter 2

The Company in Financial Trouble

When a company falls into financial difficulties, control of the company and its   **2–001**
undertaking may pass from the board of directors to a receiver, an administrator or a liquidator and indeed successively from one to the other. During the
period of an administration, control may be shared between the administrator
and the board of directors, though in this case the board will have a limited role
and be very much the junior partner. Administrative receivership has some
similarities in this respect but, following the qualified prohibition of that form
of procedure introduced by the Enterprise Act 2002 reforms,[1] it is encountered
much less frequently in practice. Unlike administration, there may be concurrently a receivership (including an administrative receivership) and a
liquidation,[2] and in this case, though the liquidator has certain distinct functions, the receiver has the predominant role in preserving and realising assets.
In view of the overlapping functions and responsibilities of the board of directors, receivers, administrators and liquidators, an overview of their respective
roles and legal duties in the context of insolvency is called for.

1. THE RESPONSIBILITIES OF MANAGEMENT AT A TIME OF FINANCIAL DIFFICULTY

Directors confronting solvency issues still have all the general duties of direc-   **2–002**
tors specified in ss.170 to 177 Companies Act 2006, but their duty to promote
the success of the company is expressed to be subject to any enactment or rule
of law requiring directors to consider or act in the interests of creditors.[3]
Directors do not have a duty to ensure that the company does not trade at a loss
(in the sense of a duty which is enforceable as such and without more), but they
are at risk of both personal liability and subsequent disqualification from acting
as a director if they allow the company to trade when insolvent.[4] Continuing to
trade without due consideration for the consequences involves the risk of challenge, if the company does not survive, on the grounds of fraudulent or
wrongful trading or in disqualification proceedings brought by the Secretary of
State. In considering all these questions it is important to remember that any

---

[1] Insolvency Act 1986, s.72A.
[2] An administration cannot exist at the same time as either an administrative receivership or a
liquidation: see para.6–059.
[3] Companies Act 2006, s.172(3).
[4] *Re CS Holidays Ltd* [1997] 1 W.L.R. 407, 414. For public companies, consider also Companies
Act 2006, s.656 (duty of directors to call meeting on serious loss of capital), the Listing Rules and
the Disclosure and Transparency Rules (applicable to public companies listed on the London Stock
Exchange), and Financial Services and Markets Act 2000, ss.118, 118A (market abuse and supplementary provision about certain behaviour) and 397 (misleading statements and practices).

insolvency proceedings will relate to a specific company rather than a group. Directors who hold multiple directorships within a group must be astute both to recognise and address conflicts which may exist between different companies in the group and to make sure that their actions in respect of each company are justified by reference to the circumstances of each company. The conflicts of interest between a parent company and one or more of its insolvent subsidiaries may be particularly acute.

(a) Duties of directors to the company

2–003   In general, a company owes no duty of care in the conduct of its business to present or future creditors, and its directors likewise owe no duties to the present or future creditors of their company.[5] But if the company is insolvent, the directors owe a duty to the company to take care to protect the interests of its creditors.[6] This duty will be enforceable in the name of the company by a liquidator, administrator or administrative receiver. The time at which the directors' duties require them to have primary regard to the interests of creditors rather than the interests of shareholders is difficult to define with any precision.[7] It may be that as a company's financial situation worsens, the directors will be under a duty to pay greater attention to the interests of its creditors, and that duty will be reinforced if a potential transaction or proposed course of action carries a high level of risk and therefore of potential prejudice to creditors if it goes wrong[8] (particularly since, in performing their duty to promote the success of the company, they are required by statute to have regard

---

[5] per Dillon L.J. in *Multinational Gas and Petrochemical Co v Multinational Gas and Petrochemical Services Ltd* [1983] Ch. 258 (CA).

[6] See per Dillon L.J. in *Liquidator of West Mercia Safetywear v Dodd* (1988) 4 B.C.C. 30 (CA), referring with approval to *Kinsela v Russell Kinsela Pty Ltd* (1986) 4 N.S.W.L.R. 722 (New South Wales Court of Appeal); *New South Wales and Yukong Line Ltd of Korea v Rendsburg Investments Corp of Liberia* [1998] 1 W.L.R. 294, 312. See also *Colin Gwyer & Associates Ltd v London Wharf (Limehouse) Ltd* [2003] B.C.C. 885; *Nicholson v Permakraft (NZ) Ltd* [1985] 1 N.Z.L.R. 242 (New Zealand Court of Appeal) and the obiter dicta in *Spies v The Queen* (2000) 201 C.L.R. 603 (High Court of Australia). It is suggested that the obiter dictum of Lord Templeman in *Winkworth v Edward Baron Development Co Ltd* [1986] 1 W.L.R. 1512 (HL), 1516, which suggests that the duty is owed to creditors as well as to the company, does not accurately represent English law. Such a direct duty has, nevertheless, been held to exist in Ireland: see *Jones v Gunn* [1997] 3 I.R. 1 (High Court of Ireland). A director who acts in the interests of the general body of creditors, but inconsistently with the interests of a particular creditor, is not in breach of his fiduciary duty: see *Re Pantone 485 Ltd* [2002] 1 B.C.L.C. 266, 272. The rule against recovery of reflective loss applies to claims for breach of fiduciary duty and may apply to claims brought by creditors: see the obiter dictum of Neuberger L.J. in *Gardner v Parker* [2005] B.C.C. 46 (CA), 77.

[7] In *Facia Footwear Ltd v Hinchcliffe* [1998] 1 B.C.L.C. 218, 228, Sir Richard Scott V.C. held that the directors of a company which had been "in a very dangerous financial position" had been required to take account of the interests of creditors. See also, e.g, *Re Onslow Ditchling Ltd* [2011] EWHC 257 (Ch).

[8] See per Street C.J. in *Kinsela v Russell Kinsela Pty Ltd (In Liquidation)* (1986) 4 N.S.W.L.R. 722 (New South Wales Court of Appeal). See also *The Bell Group (In Liquidation) v Westpac Banking Corporation* (2008) 70 A.C.S.R. 1 (Supreme Court of Western Australia), 242: a director has a duty to act in the best interests of the company which is owed to the company and not to third parties, but in an insolvency context the duty entails or includes an obligation on the part of directors to take into account the interests of creditors.

to the likely long term consequences of their decisions[9]. Once it is the interests of creditors which are at stake, a ratifying resolution by shareholders will not protect the directors from the consequences of a breach of their fiduciary duty.[10]

(b) Fraudulent trading

If in the course of the winding-up of a company it appears that any business of **2–004** the company has been carried on with intent to defraud creditors[11] of the company or creditors of any other person, or for any fraudulent purpose, the court may on the application of the liquidator of the company declare that any persons who were knowingly parties to the carrying on of the business in such manner are to be liable to make such contribution (if any) to the company's assets as the court thinks proper.[12]

For the purpose of this section, the authorities establish the following propositions:

(a) for a person to be held liable for fraudulent trading, it must be established that he was personally dishonest, and the more improbable such personal dishonesty, the more compelling must be the evidence needed to satisfy the court on the balance of probability.[13] Dishonesty is an essential element. It is accordingly necessary to show that there was either an intent to defraud or a reckless indifference whether or not the creditors were defrauded[14];

(b) the carrying out of one transaction alone may be sufficient, for example, the acceptance of a deposit or the purchase price for goods in advance knowing that the goods cannot be supplied and the deposit or price will not be repaid[15];

---

[9] Companies Act 2006, s.172(1)(a).

[10] *Liquidator of West Mercia Safetywear v Dodd* (1988) 4 B.C.C. 30 (CA).

[11] The term "creditor" denotes one to whom money is owed, whether or not the debt is presently recoverable; in the context of the section the term includes both existing contingents and future creditors: see *R. v Smith* [1996] 2 B.C.L.C. 109 (CA), 122; and see *Cannane v J. Cannane* (1998) 192 C.L.R. 557 (High Court of Australia), 566.

[12] Insolvency Act 1986, s.213. The contribution is of a compensatory nature and ought not to include a punitive element: see the obiter dictum of Chadwick L.J. in *Morphitis v Bernasconi* [2003] Ch. 552 (CA), 579; *Re Overnight Ltd (No.2)* [2010] B.C.C. 796 and *Re Overnight Ltd (No.3) Ltd* [2010] B.C.C. 808. This section and s.214 (below) may be applicable to foreign companies operating in the UK: consider *Re A Company* [1988] Ch. 210. See also *Stocznia Gdanska v Latreefers Inc* [2001] B.C.C. 174 (CA).

[13] *Aktieselskabet Dansk Skibsfinansiering v Brothers* [2001] 2 B.C.L.C. 324 (Court of Final Appeal of Hong Kong), per Lord Hoffmann; *Re H (Minors)* [1996] A.C. 563 (HL), 586–587, per Lord Nicholls.

[14] *Hardie v Hanson* (1960) 105 C.L.R. 451 (High Court of Australia) and see also *Cannane v J. Cannane* [1998] 192 C.L.R. 557 (High Court of Australia), 565–567. See also *Bernasconi v Nicholas Bennett & Co* [2000] B.C.C. 921.

[15] *Re Gerald Cooper Chemicals Ltd* [1978] Ch. 262, 268 F–G, per Templeman J.: "[A] man who warms himself with the fire of fraud cannot complain if he is singed". See further *R. v Lockwood* (1986) 2 B.C.C. 99333 (CA). Query whether the provision requires the party to have been an accessory before, and not merely after, the fact, and therefore to have given some encouragement to the trading in question before it takes place.

(c) the defrauding of an individual creditor may be sufficient, but the section is not engaged in every case where an individual creditor has been defrauded. It must be shown that the business of the company has been carried on with intent to defraud[16];

(d) the mere giving or receipt of a preference over other creditors will not necessarily constitute fraudulent trading[17];

(e) to be a "party" to the impugned trading, there must be shown: (i) to have been fraud on the part of the company in the conduct of its business[18]; and (ii) that the individual concerned took some active step to promote such business on the part of the company. It is not sufficient that he failed to warn or advise against it or indeed failed to prevent it[19];

(f) it is not necessary that the individual should have had any power of management or control over or have assisted in the carrying on of the company's business. It is sufficient that he has knowingly[20] taken advantage of such trading, for example by accepting repayment of his debts from monies he knew to have been obtained by the company carrying on business in this way for the purpose of making the repayment[21];

(g) a company may be held liable for fraudulent trading, and an employee's knowledge of fraud may be attributed to his employer notwithstanding that the employee acts dishonestly, in breach of duty and in circumstances where he would not have passed on his knowledge to his employer[22];

(h) there is a sufficient intent to defraud if credit is obtained at a time when the person knows that there is no good reason for thinking that funds will become available to pay the debt when it becomes due or shortly thereafter. It is unnecessary to establish knowledge that funds will never become available.[23]

---

[16] *Morphitis v Bernasconi* [2003] Ch. 552 (CA).
[17] *Re Sarflax Ltd* [1979] Ch. 592; *R. v Grantham* [1984] Q.B. 675 (CA). The giving of a preference might, however, lead to disqualification proceedings.
[18] *Re Augustus Barnett & Son Ltd* (1986) 2 B.C.C. 98904.
[19] *Re Maidstone Building Provisions Ltd* [1971] 1 W.L.R. 1085.
[20] As to the meaning of "knowledge" in this context see *Morris v Bank of India* [2004] B.C.C. 404, [113]–[121], affirmed in [2005] B.C.C. 739 (CA), 752.
[21] *Re Gerald Cooper Chemicals Ltd* [1978] Ch. 262.
[22] *Bank of India v Morris* [2005] B.C.C. 739 (CA).
[23] *R. v Grantham* [1984] Q.B. 675 (CA). "A company incurs a debt when by its choice it does or omits to do something which, as a matter of substance and commercial reality, renders it liable for a debt for which it otherwise would not have been liable": *Standard Chartered Bank of Australia Ltd v Antico* (1995) 18 A.C.S.R. 1 (Supreme Court of New South Wales), 57. In this respect, the fraud of the company is the same as that of any customer for goods or services who obtains credit on the basis of an express or implied representation that he can and will pay in due course: see *DPP v Ray* [1974] A.C. 370 (HL).

The leading case on dishonesty in a commercial setting is *Royal Brunei Airlines* **2–005**
Sdn Bhd v Tan[24] in which Lord Nicholls stated,

"Honesty has a connotation of subjectivity, as distinct from the objectivity
of negligence. Honesty, indeed, does have a strong subjective element in
that it is a description of a type of conduct assessed in the light of what a
person actually knew at the time, as distinct from what a reasonable
person would have known or appreciated. Further, honesty and its counterpart dishonesty are mostly concerned with advertent conduct, not
inadvertent conduct. Carelessness is not dishonesty. Thus for the most
part dishonesty is to be equated with conscious impropriety. However,
these subjective characteristics of honesty do not mean that individuals
are free to set their own standards of honesty in particular circumstances.
The standard of what constitutes honest conduct is not subjective. Honesty
is not an optional scale with higher or lower values according to the moral
standards of each individual. If a person knowingly appropriates another's property, he will not escape a finding of dishonesty simply because he
sees nothing wrong in such behaviour . . .
. . . [it must be kept in mind] that honesty is an objective standard. The
individual is expected to attain the standard which would be observed by
an honest person placed in those circumstances. It is impossible to be
more specific. Knox J. captured the flavour of this, in a case with a
commercial setting, when he referred to a person who is "guilty of
commercially unacceptable conduct in the particular context involved":
see Cowan de Groot Properties v Eagle Trust Plc.[25] Acting in reckless
disregard of others' rights or possible rights can be a tell-tale sign of
dishonesty. An honest person would have regard to the circumstances
known to him, including the nature and importance of the proposed
transaction, the nature and importance of his role, the ordinary course
of business, the degree of doubt, the practicality of the trustee or the third
party proceeding otherwise and the seriousness of the adverse consequences to the beneficiaries. The circumstances will dictate which one or
more of the possible courses should be taken by an honest person . . .
. . . Likewise, when called upon to decide whether a person was acting
honestly, a court will look at all the circumstances known to the third
party at the time. The court will also have regard to personal attributes of
the third party, such as his experience and intelligence, and the reason
why he acted as he did."

The extent to which dishonesty is a subjective or an objective concept has been **2–006**
the subject of some debate.[26] For a time, it was thought that a greater degree of

[24] *Royal Brunei Airlines Sdn Bhd v Tan* [1995] 2 A.C. 378 (PC), 389–391.
[25] *Cowan de Groot Properties v Eagle Trust Plc* [1992] 4 All E.R. 700, 761.
[26] In *Grupo Torras SA v Al-Sabah* [1999] C.L.C. 1469, a case, inter alia, about dishonest assistance, Mance L.J. regarded dishonesty as essentially objective, yet he acknowledged that test of
dishonesty in *Tan* allowed some subjective considerations to be taken into account: "Ingredient
(iii) [dishonesty] was considered in *Royal Brunei Airlines Sdn. Bhd. v Tan*, where Lord Nicholls

subjectivity had been introduced into the concept of dishonesty by *Twinsectra Ltd v Yardley*.[27] One, widely-held, interpretation of the case was that in order to characterise a defendant as dishonest, he must have engaged in behaviour which was dishonest by objective standards, and he must have subjectively realised that his conduct was dishonest by those standards (or at least have been reckless as to the fact).[28] Lord Hoffmann, however, put a different interpretation on Twinsectra when giving the advice of the Privy Council in *Barlow Clowes International Ltd (in liquidation) v Eurotrust International Ltd*[29]:

"The judge stated that the law in terms largely derived from the advice of the Board given by Lord Nicholls of Birkenhead in Royal Brunei Airlines Sdn. Bhd. v Tan [1995] 2 A.C. 378. In summary, she said that the liability for dishonest assistance requires a dishonest state of mind on the part of the person who assists in the breach of trust. Such a state of mind may consist in knowledge that the transaction is one in which he cannot honestly participate (for example, a misappropriation of other people's money), or it may consist in suspicion combined with a conscious decision not to make inquiries which might result in knowledge: see Manifest Shipping Co Ltd v Uni-Polaris Insurance Co Ltd [2003] 1 A.C. 469. Although a dishonest state of mind is a subjective mental state, the standard by which the law determines whether it is dishonest is objective. If by ordinary standards a defendant's mental state would be characterised as dishonest, it is irrelevant that the defendant judges by different standards. The Court of Appeal held this to be a correct state of the law and their Lordships agree.

...

Their Lordships accept that there is an element of ambiguity in these remarks which may have encouraged a belief, expressed in some academic writing, that the Twinsectra case had departed from the law as previously understood and invited inquiry not merely into the defendant's mental state about the nature of the transaction in which he was participating but also into his views about generally acceptable standards of honesty. But they do not consider that this is what Lord Hutton meant. The reference to 'what he knows would offend normally accepted standards of honest conduct' meant only that his knowledge of the transaction had to be such as to render his participation contrary to normally acceptable standards of honest conduct. It did not require that he should have had reflections about what those normally acceptable standards were.

---

gave the advice of the Privy Council. The case establishes that dishonesty in the context of a knowing assistance claim is an objective standard: see at 389B–G. The individual is expected to attain the standard which would be observed by an honest person placed in the circumstances he was: at 390F. But those circumstances include subjective considerations like the defendant's experience and intelligence and what he actually knew at the time: at 389D and 391B".

[27] *Twinsectra Ltd v Yardley* [2002] 2 A.C. 164 (HL).

[28] See the speeches of Lord Hoffmann and Lord Hutton in *Twinsectra* [2002] 2 A.C. 164 (HL), [20] and [35]–[36] respectively.

[29] *Barlow Clowes International Ltd (in liquidation) v Eurotrust International Ltd* [2006] 1 W.L.R. 1476 (PC), [10], [15]–[16].

Similarly in the speech of Lord Hoffmann, the statement (in para.20) that a dishonest state of mind meant 'consciousness that one is transgressing ordinary standards of honest behaviour' was in their Lordships' view intended to require consciousness of those elements of the transaction which did not make participation transgress ordinary standards of honest behaviour. It did not also require him to have thought about what those standards were."

It is not easy to reconcile the Privy Council's "clarification" of the majority speeches in *Twinsectra* with the fact that Lord Millett dissented in that case on the question of the correct interpretation of Lord Nicholls' speech in Royal Brunei. In Lord Millett's opinion, dishonesty was a subjective concept insofar as account must be taken of considerations such as the defendant's experience and intelligence and his state of knowledge at the relevant time, but the question for the court was whether an honest person in those circumstances would appreciate that what he was doing was wrong or improper, not whether the defendant himself actually appreciated this.[30] It is suggested that although the Privy Council presented its judgment in *Barlow Clowes* as "clarification" of the majority judgments in *Twinsectra*, the effect of the decision in *Barlow Clowes* was in reality an affirmation of Lord Millett's dissenting judgment.   2–007

This apparent divergence of view between the Privy Council and the House of Lords[31] was considered by the Court of Appeal in *Abou-Rahmah v Abacha*.[32] The Court of Appeal decided, having considered the proper approach to precedent involving cases from the House of Lords and Privy Council, that the "interpretation" of *Twinsectra* given by the Privy Council in *Barlow Clowes* should be taken to represent the law of England and Wales.[33] Thus, a person is to be judged by an objective standard of honesty—he cannot set his own standard.[34] But in judging whether someone has attained this standard, the Court will take into account what he actually knew and intended, i.e. his subjective state of mind.[35]   2–008

---

[30] ". . . it is not necessary that he should actually have appreciated that he was acting dishonestly; it is sufficient that he was": see paras 121 and 122 and pp.408–409 respectively. See also *Barnes v Tomlinson* [2006] EWHC 3115 (Ch) and *Al-Khudairi v Abbey Brokers Ltd* [2010] P.N.L.R. 32.

[31] See *Conaglen and Nolan*, "Precedent from the Privy Council" (2006) 122 *Law Quarterly Review* 349.

[32] *Abou-Rahmah v Abacha* [2007] 1 All E.R. (Comm) 827 (CA). See *also Cunningham v Cunningham* [2009] J.L.R. 227 (Royal Court of Jersey); *Aerostar Maintenance International Ltd v Wilson* [2010] EWHC 2032 (Ch), [183]–[184] and *Aviva Insurance Ltd v Brown* [2011] EWHC 362 (QB).

[33] See *Abou-Rahmah*, [66]–[70], per Arden L.J.

[34] The relevant standard is the ordinary standard of dishonest behaviour. It may not be a universal standard and the existence of a body of opinion to the effect that the ordinary standard is too high will not preclude dishonesty: *Starglade Properties Ltd v Nash* [2011] Lloyd's Rep. F.C. 102 (CA).

[35] *Royal Brunei, Twinsectra* and *Barlow Clowes* were all cases on liability for dishonest assistance, but the Royal Brunei principles as clarified in *Barlow Clowes* are consistent with Lord Hoffmann's observations in the Court of Final Appeal of Hong Kong on the concept of dishonesty in fraudulent trading in *Aktieselskabet Dansk Skibsfinansiering v Brothers* [2001] 2 B.C.L.C. 324 (Court of Final Appeal of Hong Kong), 334.

2–009 Against this background, the real problem posed for management by the fraudulent trading rules is how far and how long the company can continue to incur credit when the directors realise that the outcome of future trading is uncertain and that there is a real risk that things may not improve so that creditors may not be paid. As set out above, although the test of dishonesty will involve a court inquiring into the subjective state of mind of the directors in order to ascertain what they actually knew and intended, the standard by which their conduct is judged to be honest or dishonest is an objective one. If by ordinary standards the directors' conduct in continuing trading is dishonest, they will not be able to escape liability by saying that they saw nothing wrong in what they did.

(c) Wrongful trading[36]

2–010 In contrast to the rules on fraudulent trading discussed above, where the principal focus is on the propriety of incurring new liabilities,[37] wrongful trading is concerned with the inevitability of an insolvent liquidation. In any case where directors[38] have been responsible for wrongful trading by the company which, by depleting its assets, has occasioned loss, s.214 of the Insolvency Act 1986 empowers the court to impose on those directors liability to contribute to the assets of the company for the benefit of its creditors. Two conditions have to be satisfied before that power can be exercised:

> (a) the company must have gone into insolvent liquidation (meaning liquidation at a time when its assets are insufficient for the payment of its debts and other liabilities and the expenses of winding up); and
>
> (b) at some time before the commencement of the winding-up of the company the person to be held liable was a director and either knew

---

[36] See *Re A Company* [1988] Ch. 210; *Re A Company* (1988) 4 B.C.C. 424; *Re Produce Marketing Ltd* (1989) 5 B.C.C. 569; *Re DKG Contractors Ltd* [1990] B.C.C. 903.

[37] It is possible (though relatively rare) that a company's business is carried on with intent to defraud existing creditors.

[38] The term "director" for this purpose includes (1) a de jure director; (2) a de facto director (i.e. a person who assumes the status and functions of a director although never or never validly appointed); (3) a "shadow director", i.e. a person (not claiming or purporting to be a director) in accordance with whose directions or instructions (but not on whose advice in a professional capacity) the directors are accustomed to act: Insolvency Act 1986, ss.214(7) and 251). It is sufficient that the shadow director has a real influence and it is unnecessary that the directors adopt a subservient role: see *Secretary of State v Deverell* [2001] Ch. 340 (CA). It is also sufficient that a governing majority of the board is accustomed to act accordingly: see *Ultraframe (UK) Ltd v Fielding* [2005] EWHC 1638 (Ch), [1272]. For a valuable analysis, see *Re Kaytech International Plc* [1999] B.C.C. 390 (CA). In that case, the Court of Appeal did not agree with the notion that the two concepts of a de facto director and a shadow director did not overlap, a view which had been espoused by Millett J. in *Re Hydrodan (Corby) Ltd* [1994] B.C.C. 161. See also Noonan and Watson, "The Nature of Shadow Directorship: Ad Hoc Statutory Intervention or Core Company Law Principle?" [2006] J.B.L. 763. A director of a corporate director is not, without more, a de facto director of the subject company: *Commissioners of Revenue and Customs v Holland* [2010] 1 W.L.R. 2793 (SC).

or ought to have concluded that there was no reasonable prospect that the company would avoid going into insolvent liquidation.[39]

It is not enough to say that, if the company had not still been trading, a particular loss would not have been suffered. There has to be a sufficient connection between the directors' misconduct and the company's losses.[40] However, in any case when these conditions are satisfied, the court may, on the application of the liquidator (and no one else), declare that such person is liable to make such contribution to the company's assets as the court thinks proper unless it is satisfied that after the date of such actual or constructive knowledge the person took every step with a view to minimising the potential loss to the company's creditors as he ought to have taken (assuming him to have known that there was no reasonable prospect that the company would avoid going into insolvent liquidation).[41] Accordingly, the burden of proof of "due diligence" is squarely placed on the director.

For the purpose of determining the extent of his constructive knowledge and   **2–011**
for the purpose of determining the propriety and sufficiency of the action taken, the standard is taken to be that of a reasonably diligent person having both:

"(a) the general knowledge, skill and experience that may reasonably be expected of a person carrying out the same functions as are carried out by or entrusted to that director in relation to the company; and

(b) the general knowledge, skill and experience that director has."[42]

Whether a company has a reasonable prospect of avoiding an insolvent liquidation cannot be determined on the basis of a snap-shot but must reflect rational expectations of what the future might hold. However, directors are not clairvoyant and their failure to foresee what subsequently happens does not necessarily mean that they are liable for wrongful trading.[43]

The following distinctions between fraudulent and wrongful trading   **2–012**
stand out:

(a) liability for fraudulent trading can attach to anyone, whatever his role in or relationship to the company; in the case of wrongful trading,

---

[39] Insolvency Act 1986, s.214(2)(b), (c). So long as he had the required knowledge whilst a director, it is not essential that he remained a director when the acts or omissions constituting wrongful trading took place.

[40] *Re Continental Assurance Co of London Plc* [2001] B.P.I.R. 733.

[41] Insolvency Act 1986, s.214(3). In *Re Produce Marketing Consortium Ltd (No. 2)* (1989) 5 B.C.C. 569 it was held that the jurisdiction was compensatory rather than penal and that the order should reflect the amount by which the company's assets had been depleted by the director's misconduct. In *Re DKG Contractors Ltd* [1990] B.C.C. 903, the court the court identified the date on which the directors should have recognised the inevitability of liquidation and assessed liability by requiring a contribution equal to the trade debts incurred after that date.

[42] Insolvency Act 1986, s.214(4) and (5), cf. *Department of Health and Social Security v Evans* [1985] 2 All E.R. 471.

[43] *Re Hawkes Hill Publishing Co Ltd* [2007] B.C.C. 937.

liability can extend only to directors (but including de facto and shadow directors)[44];

(b) liability in the case of fraudulent trading depends on some positive act, whilst liability for wrongful trading can attach in respect of an omission to act;

(c) in the case of fraudulent trading, the burden of proving fraud lies squarely on the complainant; but in the case of wrongful trading, once the two conditions for establishing liability are satisfied, the burden is upon the director to prove that he was diligent in attempting to avoid loss to the creditors;

(d) fraudulent trading involves primarily a failure to have proper regard to the interests of future creditors (i.e. those giving credit to the company); wrongful trading involves a failure to have regard to the interests of all the creditors as a class;

(e) for the purpose of fraudulent trading actual knowledge must usually be established of the company's actual or prospective inability to pay debts as they fall due; for the purpose of wrongful trading there need only be shown that the director ought to have known of the inevitability of insolvent liquidation.

It is at least theoretically possible, albeit unlikely in practice, for a director to incur liability for fraudulent trading in circumstances where he would not be liable for wrongful trading. This could happen where a director had a legitimate expectation that his company would escape liquidation through some form of restructuring but meanwhile caused the company to incur new debts that he knew would not be paid in full. For that reason, directors dealing with a possible insolvency have to consider their actions in the light of both potential statutory liabilities and not merely treat fraudulent trading as an aggravated form of wrongful trading.

(d)   Disqualification of directors for trading whilst insolvent

2–013   In cases under s.6 of the Company Directors Disqualification Act 1986, a ground of unfitness often relied upon is that the director concerned was responsible for the company trading whilst insolvent and that in so doing he took unwarranted risks with creditors' money. In *Re CU Fittings Ltd*[45] Hoffmann J. summarised the position as follows:

"directors immersed in the day-to-day task of trying to keep their business afloat cannot be expected to have wholly dispassionate minds. They tend to cling to hope. Obviously there comes a point at which an honest busi-

---

[44] *Re A Company (No.005009 of 1987)* (1988) 4 B.C.C. 424.
[45] *Re CU Fittings Ltd* (1989) 5 B.C.C. 210, 213.

nessman recognises that he is only gambling at the expense of creditors on the possibility that something may turn up".

Trading whilst insolvent is not, of itself, ordinarily sufficient to demonstrate unfitness; it has also to be shown that the director knew or ought to have known that there was no reasonable prospect of meeting creditors' claims.[46] Other matters to be taken into account in determining unfitness, in the case of an insolvent company, include responsibility for the causes of insolvency and responsibility for failure to supply goods or services which have been paid for.[47] Fraudulent trading and wrongful trading are free-standing grounds for disqualification under s.10 of the Company Directors Disqualification Act 1986.[48]

In *Secretary of State v Laing*,[49] Evans-Lombe J. referred to the importance in all such cases of the directors maintaining accurate financial records and management accounts in order to know the position of their company with a reasonable degree of accuracy at any particular time and stated, **2–014**

"where it can be demonstrated that a company has continued trading for a substantial period of time while it was insolvent and as a result has put the claims of existing creditors at unwarrantable risk and has incurred fresh creditors at the unjustifiable risk of not being able to pay them, it is not open to a director of the company to avoid responsibility by contending that he did not know at the material time that such was taking place. It is the duty of all directors to ensure that they have from time to time a reasonably clear picture of the financial state and trading profitability of their companies."[50]

In light of the above, once the directors appreciate that to continue trading will involve incurring further credit with no reasonable prospect of payment, they should not cause the company to trade at the risk of future creditors. It is important that all directors recognise that they have individual responsibilities in this respect and that even those with only a nominal or wholly non-executive role can face disqualification proceedings. Neither the directors nor the court can sanction further trading at the expense of future creditors. This would seem to be so even if the cessation of trading will damage the company and its current creditors, in particular by precluding a beneficial sale of the undertaking as a going concern. Continued trading is only legitimate if it is in the interests of creditors generally and either (a) the future creditors are warned **2–015**

---

[46] *Secretary of State v Creegan* [2004] B.C.C. 835 (CA); *Re CS Holidays Ltd* [1997] 1 W.L.R. 407 and *Re Uno Plc* [2006] B.C.C. 725.

[47] Company Directors Disqualification Act 1986, s.9 and Sch.1 Pt II.

[48] See, e.g., *Re Attorney General's Reference (Nos. 88, 89, 90 and 91 of 2006)* [2007] 2 Cr. App. R. (S.) 28 (CA).

[49] *Secretary of State v Laing* [1996] 2 B.C.L.C. 324, 342.

[50] See also *Re Galeforce Pleating Co Ltd* [1999] 2 B.C.L.C. 704. The corollary of the director's duty to maintain a clear picture of the company's finances is that the company should cease to trade if the directors do not have any such picture.

and agree to accept the risk of non-payment or (b) any further credit obtained is underwritten by somebody of sufficient substance.

2–016   If neither of these conditions is satisfied, closure of the business is probably inevitable unless:

> (a) there is a voluntary arrangement under s.1–7 of the Insolvency Act 1986 or a scheme of arrangement under Pt 26 of the Companies Act 2006; or
>
> (b) if permitted by the insolvency legislation, a debenture-holder appoints an administrative receiver (as he may be invited to do by the company); or
>
> (c) an administrator or interim manager is appointed by the court or by another person entitled to do so; or
>
> (d) on presentation of a petition for winding up a provisional liquidator is appointed and is authorised to continue the company's business; or
>
> (e) on a compulsory winding-up the liquidator is authorised to continue trading with a view to a beneficial realisation[51] or, on a voluntary liquidation, the liquidator decides to take this course.

These are all possible solutions which the directors should consider (doubtless with the benefit of professional advice). This work is primarily concerned with administration and receivership, but a brief description of the other options available to directors who have concluded that some formal process is required follows in order to put administration and receivership in context and to explain the effect on the business and the differing ongoing roles of the directors. Following the Enterprise Act reforms which introduced the possibility of directors appointing administrators without recourse to the court and the substantial curtailment of the power of debenture holders to appoint administrative receivers, the directors of an insolvent company now have a more important decision-making role in relation to the choice of procedure than was formerly the case.

2.   COMPANY VOLUNTARY ARRANGEMENTS AND SCHEMES OF ARRANGEMENT

2–017   In 1982 the Cork Committee proposed that the existing procedures for company voluntary arrangements were entirely unsuitable and suggested a new form of voluntary arrangement for companies which could be concluded without an order of the court but which would still be binding as between the company and its creditors.[52] Part I of the Insolvency Act 1986 gave effect to that proposal. The procedure was reformed by the Insolvency Act 2000, which also introduced for certain eligible companies an optional (but, as yet, little used) variant

---

[51] *Re General Service Co-operative Stores* (1891) 64 L.T. 228.
[52] Cmnd. 8558, paras 419–430.

of this procedure with the benefit of a moratorium while the proposal is being formulated and considered.[53] The principal feature of the legislation is that any voluntary arrangement to be voted upon by creditors will have been reviewed and endorsed and will be administered by an insolvency practitioner or other authorised person. The voluntary arrangement cannot affect the rights of secured creditors without their consent[54] (although the rights of secured creditors are restricted during the period of any moratorium in relation to an eligible company).

(a)   The moratorium for eligible companies

A moratorium comes into effect when the directors of an eligible company file   **2–018** certain documents with the court, which must include a document setting out the terms of the proposed voluntary arrangement. The qualifying conditions for a company to be eligible for a moratorium are prescribed by the legislation and primarily relate to small companies.[55] The company must not fall within one of the prescribed exceptions (relating mostly to the financial sector and structured finance transactions) and must not be subject to an existing voluntary arrangement (or have been subject to a moratorium within the previous year) or be in administrative receivership, administration or liquidation. The moratorium ends upon the arrangement becoming effective and, in any event, expires after 28 days (or earlier, upon the relevant meetings being held) unless it is extended. During the period of the moratorium, the directors' power to obtain credit for the company, pay its debts and dispose of its assets is restricted; creditors are prevented from enforcing certain rights; and special provisions apply to the disposal of assets subject to a security interest or hire-purchase arrangement.

(b)   The approval and implementation of a voluntary arrangement

For an eligible company for which a moratorium is being sought, a proposal   **2–019** for a voluntary arrangement is formulated by the directors. Otherwise, it is formulated by the directors if the company is not in administration or liquidation, or by the administrator or liquidator if it is. If it is formulated by the directors (whether in connection with a moratorium or not), a statement by the nominee that there is a reasonable prospect of the voluntary arrangement being approved and implemented must be submitted to the court. The nominee must be a qualified insolvency practitioner or other authorised person.

---

[53] In July 2010, the Insolvency Service published more wide-ranging proposals: *Proposals for a Restructuring Moratorium—a consultation*. However, a written ministerial statement in May 2011 recorded that responses had indicated that the problems were not as urgent as had been supposed and that the matter would be given further consideration.

[54] See further *Webb v MacDonald QC and Dakers Green Brett* [2010] B.P.I.R 503 (a case on the equivalent provisions in relation to individual voluntary arrangements).

[55] Insolvency Act 1986, s.1A and Sch.A1.

2–020   The proposal is voted upon by meetings of the company and its creditors and, to become effective, it must be accepted either at both of those meetings or at the creditors' meeting only (in the latter case, subject to no member of the company challenging the creditors' decision successfully by application to the court within 28 days after the meetings). If accepted, the arrangement will become binding upon all persons who in accordance with the rules were entitled to vote at the meeting (whether or not present or represented), or who would have been so entitled if they had had notice of it, as if they were parties to the voluntary arrangement.[56] This has been described as giving rise to a statutory hypothesis that the creditor was a party to the arrangement as if he had consented to it.[57] A person entitled to vote at the meeting (or a person who would have been so entitled if he had had notice of it) is entitled to challenge an arrangement by application made to the court within 28 days of the outcome of the meetings being reported to the court (or within 28 days of becoming aware that the creditors' meeting has taken place, if he had not had notice of it) on the grounds of either unfair prejudice or materiality irregularity in relation to the meetings, and the court has the power to revoke or suspend any decision which has taken effect and/or give a direction for the summoning of further meetings.[58]

2–021   If approved, the voluntary arrangement is thereafter administered by a supervisor who must be a qualified insolvency practitioner or other authorised person. The supervisor is not an officer of the company and has no power to act in the name of the company unless given authority to do so pursuant to the terms of the voluntary arrangement. The supervisor is subject to the supervisory control of the court, and both he and creditors who are dissatisfied with any act, decision or omission of his can apply to the court for directions.[59] It has been held in relation to the analogous case of an individual voluntary arrangement that a supervisor is not susceptible to an action for damages for breach of statutory duty or tort in relation to his supervision of the voluntary arrangement[60] although, in a subsequent case,[61] it was held that a nominee in respect of a debtor's proposal for an individual voluntary arrangement owed the debtor a duty of care in both contract and tort in respect of advice given during a short adjournment of the creditors' meeting, on the basis that he had reverted to acting in an advisory capacity (and not in his respective capacities as nominee and chairman of the meeting) during that period.[62]

---

[56] Insolvency Act 1986, s.5(2) and Sch.A1, para.37(2).

[57] *Johnson v Davies* [1999] Ch. 117 (CA); *Raja v Rubin* [2000] Ch. 274 (CA) (both cases dealing with individual voluntary arrangements).

[58] Insolvency Act 1986, s.6 and Sch.A1, para.38. See, e.g. *Revenue and Customs Commissioners v Portsmouth City Football Club Ltd* [2011] B.C.C. 149; *Mourant & Co Trustees Ltd v Sixty UK Ltd* [2010] B.C.C. 882.

[59] Insolvency Act 1986, s.7 and Sch.A1, para.39.

[60] *King v Anthony* [1998] 2 B.C.L.C. 517 (CA).

[61] *Prosser v Castle Sanderson Solicitors* [2003] B.C.C. 440 (CA). See also *Firth v Everitt* (2007) 104(39) L.S.G. 30 (Ch).

[62] More generally, as to the limitation on the ability of a creditor to maintain an action against an office-holder, see *A&J Fabrications (Batley) Ltd v Grant Thornton* [1998] B.C.C. 807; *Oldham v Kyrris* [2004] B.C.C. 111 (CA); *Re HIH Casualty & General Insurance Ltd* [2006] 2 All E.R. 671, [116]–[126] (the subsequent appeal to the House of Lords reported at [2008] 1 W.L.R. 852

The Insolvency Act 1986 contains no provision enabling a voluntary **2–022**
arrangement to be amended or varied, whether by vote of creditors,[63] or on an
application to the court for directions.[64] It is therefore usually desirable to
include in the scheme itself a procedure enabling amendments to be made.[65]
The question of whether the voluntary arrangement will end upon the making
of a winding-up order is determined partly by the terms of the arrangement
and, it seems, partly by the circumstances under which the winding-up petition
is presented.[66] However, the termination of an arrangement does not necessarily have the effect of terminating any trust constituted thereunder in respect
of the assets held by the supervisor.[67]

As an alternative to a company voluntary arrangement, it may be possible **2–023**
for a scheme of arrangement to be promoted and sanctioned under Pt 26 of the
Companies Act 2006 (formerly ss.425–427 of the Companies Act 1985).
Section 899 of the 2006 Act provides that a compromise or arrangement
which is proposed between a company and its members or creditors,[68] or
any class of them, is approved by a majority in number representing 75 per
cent in value of those present in person or by proxy at meetings of each class
of member[69] or creditor, and which is subsequently sanctioned by the
court, shall be binding upon all members or creditors, or upon the class of
members or creditors, and upon the company. Where a scheme involves a
reduction of capital, the statutory provisions in that regard must also be
complied with.[70]

The concept of a compromise or arrangement is a wide one.[71] Whilst the **2–024**
court will be slow to differ from the views of the statutory majorities of
members or creditors, the role of the court in deciding whether to exercise its
discretion to sanction a scheme is not simply to "rubber stamp" the decisions

---

does not affect this issue); *Lomax Leisure Ltd v Miller* [2008] 1 B.C.L.C. 262; *Hague v Nam Tai Electronics Inc* [2008] B.C.C. 295 (PC) and *Charalambous v B & C Associates* [2009] 43 E.G. 105 (C.S.).
   [63] *Raja v Rubin* [2000] Ch. 274 (CA).
   [64] *Re Alpa Lighting Ltd* [1997] B.P.I.R. 341 (CA).
   [65] *Horrocks v Broome* [2000] B.C.C. 257. For a similar approach in relation to a scheme of arrangement under s.425 Companies Act 1985 (now Pt 26 of the Companies Act 2006) see *Re Cape Plc* [2006] 3 All E.R. 1222.
   [66] See, e.g. *Re Arthur Rathbone Kitchens Ltd* [1998] B.C.C. 450; *Re Excalibur Airways Ltd* [1998] 1 B.C.L.C. 436; and *Re NT Gallagher & Son Ltd* [2002] 1 W.L.R. 2380 (CA).
   [67] Where a voluntary arrangement provides for money or other assets to be paid or transferred to or held for the benefit of creditors, the result is to create a trust for the creditors. The effect of liquidation of the debtor or failure of the arrangement on such a trust depends on the terms of the arrangement. If provision is made for that contingency, effect must be given to the provision. If no provision is made, the trust continues and must take effect according to its terms notwithstanding the liquidation or failure of the arrangement. The creditors of the arrangement can then prove in the liquidation for so much of their debt as remains after taking into account their rights under the trust: see *Re NT Gallagher & Son Ltd* [2002] 1 W.L.R. 2380 (CA).
   [68] Every person who has a pecuniary claim against the company, whether actual or contingent, is a creditor within the Act. This will, e.g. include a lessor of property to the company.
   [69] In *Re Uniq Plc* [2011] EWHC 749 (Ch) 85 per cent of the members had not voted but, since the company had an unusually high number of members with small shareholdings, this was not a matter of concern and the scheme was nonetheless sanctioned.
   [70] *Re White Pass Ry Co* [1918] W.N. 323.
   [71] See, e.g. *Re NFU Development Trust Ltd* [1972] 1 W.L.R. 1548.

of the relevant meetings.[72] Not only will the court decide whether the relevant class meetings have been held[73] and the procedures properly followed[74] and check that full and accurate information has been given to members and creditors,[75] but it will also decide "whether the proposal is such that an intelligent and honest man, a member of the class concerned and acting in respect of his interest, might reasonably approve".[76] This is an obvious difference to the court's role in relation to a company voluntary arrangement, which, in the absence of challenge from dissident creditors, is far more administrative in nature.

3. THE APPOINTMENT OF A RECEIVER

2–025 There is in most cases a world of difference between the value of a company's undertaking as a going concern and its scrap value. It is for this reason that, historically, creditors have sought floating charges on the undertaking as well as specific charges on certain assets of the debtor company. However, as a result of reforms introduced by the Enterprise Act 2002, regardless of the terms of the debenture, the holder of a floating charge created on or after September 15, 2003 may not appoint an administrative receiver of the debtor company unless the transaction falls within one of the statutory exceptions.[77] Accordingly, administrative receivership is now a much less significant procedure for rescuing the business of an insolvent company.

2–026 A debenture in the ordinary case provides for the appointment by the secured creditor, on the occasion of any default by the debtor or the occurrence of other

---

[72] See, e.g. *Re English, Scottish and Australian Chartered Bank* [1893] 3 Ch. 385 (CA), 398, 409; *Re National Bank Ltd* [1966] 1 W.L.R. 819, 829; *Re BTR Plc* [2000] 1 B.C.L.C. 740 (CA), 744; and *Re Hawk Insurance Company Ltd* [2002] B.C.C. 300 (CA), 310.

[73] The approach of the court to the composition of classes was set out by Bowen L.J. in *Sovereign Life Assurance Co v Dodd* [1892] 2 Q.B. 573 (CA), 583: "It seems plain that we must give such a meaning to the term 'class' as will prevent the section being worked so as to result in confiscation and injustice, and that it must be confined to those persons whose rights are not so dissimilar as to make it impossible for them to consult together with a view to acting in their common interest." The question of whether classes have been correctly constituted will depend upon the facts of each case: see *Re Osiris Insurance Ltd* [1999] 1 B.C.L.C. 182; *Re BTR Plc* [1999] 2 B.C.L.C. 675, [2000] 1 B.C.L.C. 740 (CA); *Re Anglo-American Insurance Company Ltd* [2001] 1 B.C.L.C. 755; *Re Hawk Insurance Company Ltd* [2002] B.C.C. 300 (CA), 309–310, in which, in his leading judgment, Chadwick L.J. referred to the test set out by Bowen L.J. in *Sovereign Life* (above) as "settled law"; *Re Telewest Communications Plc* [2005] B.C.C. 29 (CA); and *Re British Aviation Insurance Company Ltd* [2006] B.C.C. 14. The focus is on the effect of any differences in the creditors' rights against the company rather than differences in their individual interests: see *Re BTR Plc*, (above) and *Re Hawk Insurance* (above). Where a proposed scheme is in practical terms an alternative to a liquidation or administration, it is not wrong to consider, when determining the classes of creditors, how the creditors would have been treated in the liquidation or administration: see *Marconi Corp Plc v Marconi Plc* [2003] EWHC 663 (Ch), [20].

[74] See Practice Statement (Companies: Schemes of Arrangement) [2002] 1 W.L.R. 1345.

[75] See *Re Minster Assets plc* (1985) 1 B.C.C. 99299.

[76] See per Maugham J. in *Re Dorman, Long & Co Ltd* [1934] Ch. 635, 657. See also *Re National Bank Ltd* [1966] 1 W.L.R. 819, 829A–E; *Re Hellenic & General Trust Ltd* [1976] 1 W.L.R. 123; *Re Osiris Insurance Ltd* [1999] 1 B.C.L.C. 182, 188g–189g; *Re BTR Plc* [1999] 2 B.C.L.C. 675 (Ch), 680b–g, [2000] 1 B.C.L.C. 740 (CA).

[77] Insolvency Act 1986, s.72A. For the statutory exceptions, see Insolvency Act 1986, ss.72B–72H (inclusive). The appointment of an administrative receiver under s.72E (the fourth exception: project finance) was held invalid in *Feetum v Levy* [2006] Ch. 585 (CA).

specified events, of a receiver with power to carry on the company's business.[78] The appointment takes the management of the company's property out of the hands of the directors and places it in the hands of the receiver.[79] This power may be exercised either with a view to reviving the company or with a view to the beneficial sale of the undertaking as a going concern. The power to carry on the business of the company through an administrative receiver is deemed to be granted by the debenture except in so far as the existence of such power is inconsistent with any provision of the debenture.[80] The power to present or defend (and presumably by implication to support or not oppose) a petition to wind up the company is likewise deemed to be granted,[81] and if properly exercised must preclude any representation of the company at the instance of the directors.[82] A non-administrative receiver will only have such powers if conferred by the debenture.[83] The appointment of a receiver in no way precludes other creditors petitioning for winding up, and indeed unsecured creditors may be well advised to petition to protect their position in case a surplus exists after completion of the receivership and in order to preserve the "relation back" period for any challenge to the grant of the debenture to the secured creditor under ss.238 (preferences) and 245 (avoidance of floating charges) of the Insolvency Act 1986. The appointment of a receiver does not prevent time running for purposes of limitation[84] and the liquidator may exercise some supervision and restraining influence on the receiver.[85]

A creditor with the power to appoint a receiver has the choice whether to **2–027** make the appointment (if permitted to do so by the insolvency legislation, in the case of an administrative receiver).[86] Once the appointment is made, it is

---

[78] Although the power of appointment is a power of the secured creditor, there is no reason why directors who conclude that receivership is the best solution should not invite the creditor to exercise its power. In practice, creditors prefer to make receivership appointments by invitation in order to reduce the risks of an appointment being challenged.

[79] *Re Joshua Shaw & Sons Ltd* (1989) 5 B.C.C. 188, 190. The appointment does not terminate the office of director: *Re Barton Manufacturing Co Ltd* [1998] B.C.C. 827, 828; but the loss of control means that directors are unlikely to be able to act to safeguard the interests of creditors and therefore will not be held to be in breach of such duties to the company.

[80] Insolvency Act 1986, s.42(1) and Sch.I, para.14.

[81] Insolvency Act 1986, s.42(1) and Sch.I, para.21.

[82] *Bank of New Zealand v Essington Developments Pty Ltd* (1991) 5 A.C.S.R. 86 (Supreme Court of New South Wales), 89. The only course available to the directors if they oppose such action by the receiver will be an application to the court for a contrary direction to be given to the receiver, but such direction can only be expected if it can be shown that the receiver's proposed course of action would be unconscionable. cf. *Edwards v Singh* (1990) 5 N.Z.C.L.C. 66,770 (High Court of Auckland).

[83] In the case of such a receivership, if the power is not so conferred, the directors can authorise the company's defence to the petition: see *Re Reprographic Exports (Euromat) Ltd* (1978) 122 Sol. J. 400.

[84] *Re Cases of Taff's Well Ltd* [1992] Ch. 179; *Re Joshua Shaw & Sons Ltd* (1989) 5 B.C.C. 188.

[85] *Re Northern Developments (Holdings) Ltd* Unreported June 16, 1976, affirmed by the Court of Appeal Unreported March 1, 1977. Although not its usual practice, the Companies Court has the power to adjourn a winding-up petition for long periods if the interests of unsecured creditors so require (*Re Northern Developments*). For an example of the exercise of this power, see *Re Demaglass Holdings Ltd* [2001] 2 B.C.L.C. 633.

[86] *Raja v Austin Gray* [2003] B.P.I.R. 725 (CA), [55]; *Silven Properties Ltd v Royal Bank of Scotland Plc* [2004] 1 W.L.R. 997 (CA); *Meretz Investments NV v ACP Ltd* [2007] Ch. 197 (this point was not challenged on the appeal reported at [2008] Ch. 244 (CA)) and *Coomber v Bloom* [2010] EWHC 121 (Ch). See further below, Ch.7.

then for the receiver to decide whether to carry on the business with the objective of a rescue in the long term or of a beneficial sale as a going concern in the short term or to close the business and sell up.[87] There is no general duty on the creditor or the receiver to carry on business on the mortgaged premises in order to safeguard the company's goodwill or attempt to procure the most beneficial realisation.[88]

2–028   If the receiver does continue the company's business, five limitations on his freedom of action come into operation. First, the receiver will ordinarily be granted power and authority to carry on the company's business as agent of the company.[89] But though the power to carry on the business survives liquidation, the agency does not. Thereafter the receiver can only trade as principal or (with his debenture-holder's consent) as agent for his debenture-holder.

2–029   Secondly, the provisions of s.213 of the Insolvency Act 1986 will apply to the receiver in respect of the period of his carrying on business as agent for the company prior to liquidation, and accordingly if he is a party to fraudulent trading, he may be subject to a claim in a subsequent liquidation.[90] The wrongful trading provisions of s.214 of the Insolvency Act 1986 could also apply to him if he exercises such influence over the affairs of trading subsidiaries that the directors of those companies become accustomed to act on his directions or instructions but this risk will be avoided if the receiver merely causes the parent company to exercise its shareholder powers.[91]

2–030   Thirdly, in respect of certain aspects of his conduct he owes duties to the company and may be held liable in negligence or for acts which damage the company.[92] All his powers (statutory and otherwise) are exercisable only for the purposes for which he is appointed, i.e. the preservation, recovery and realisation of the assets subject to the charge in order to bring about a situation in which interest on the secured debt can be paid and the debt itself paid.[93]

2–031   Fourthly, the directors' powers of management of the undertaking are placed in suspense during the period of his appointment in so far as their exercise would be inconsistent with the exercise by the receiver of powers conferred on the debenture-holder under his debenture.[94] There is no kind of diarchy over the company's assets: the board has no power over assets in the possession or

---

[87] *Silven Properties Ltd v Royal Bank of Scotland Plc* [2004] 1 W.L.R. 997 (CA) and *Coomber v Bloom* [2010] EWHC 121 (Ch).

[88] See *Medforth v Blake* [2000] Ch. 86 (CA) and below, Chs 10 and 13.

[89] In the case of the administrative receiver the power and authority are deemed to be granted by the debenture in the absence of some inconsistent provision in the debenture: Insolvency Act 1986, s.42(1) and Sch.I, para.14. In the case of non-administrative receivers, they must be conferred by the debenture.

[90] See *Re Leyland DAF Ltd* [1994] 4 All E.R. 300, 311–312.

[91] See fn.38 above in relation to the meaning of "shadow director".

[92] See below, Chs 13 and 14.

[93] *Bank of New Zealand v Essington Developments Pty Ltd* (1991) 5 A.C.S.R. 86 (Supreme Court of New South Wales), 88 and *Medforth v Blake* [2000] Ch. 86 (CA), 102G.

[94] See Brightman J. in *Re Emmadart Ltd* [1979] Ch. 540, 544. "The receiver replaces the board as the person having the authority to exercise the company's powers", per Lord Hoffmann in *Village Cay Marina Ltd v Acland* [1998] B.C.C. 417 (PC), 422. See also *Capital Globe Investments Pty Ltd v Parker Investments Australia Pty Ltd* [2011] Q.S.C. 31 (Supreme Court of Queensland).

control of the receiver. The directors remain in office[95] and their powers remain exercisable so far as they are not incompatible with the right of the receiver to exercise the powers conferred on him.[96]

The law is unsettled as to the extent to which, independently of the receiver, **2–032** the directors have the right in the name of the company to bring proceedings on causes of action of the company. In *Newhart Developments Ltd v Cooperative Commercial Bank Ltd*,[97] Shaw L.J. stated that the appointment of the receiver:

"does not divest the directors of the company of their power, as the governing body of the company, of instituting proceedings in a situation where so doing does not in any way impinge prejudicially upon the position of the debenture-holders by threatening or imperilling the assets which are subject to the charge. . . . If in the exercise of his discretion [the receiver] chooses to ignore some asset such as a right of action, or decides that it would be unprofitable from the point of view of the debenture-holders to pursue it, there is nothing in any authority which has been cited to us which suggests that it is not then open to the directors of the company to pursue that right of action if they think it would be in the interests of the company. Indeed, in my view, it would be incumbent upon them to do so".

In line with this approach, the directors have been allowed in the name of the company to institute proceedings challenging the validity of the debenture or the appointment of the receiver, and, acting as monitors of the stewardship of the company's affairs by the receiver, to challenge his actions in the court[98] and to seek to enforce independent causes of action against the appointing

---

[95] *Independent Pension Trustee Ltd v L.A.W. Construction Co Ltd*, 1997 S.L.T. 1105 (Court of Session, Outer House).

[96] Their statutory duties to keep accounts under the Companies Act 2006, ss.386–389 continue (notwithstanding that the effect of the appointment of the receiver is to deprive them of access to the funds required to pay for the discharge of them), and they have a continuing right to require the receiver to provide information for this purpose: see para.13–069. See also *Gomba Holdings v Homan* [1986] 1 W.L.R. 1301 (the directors have no right to information from the receiver in order to prosecute an action where the provision of such information would be contrary to the interests of the debenture-holder); *Re Geneva Finance Ltd* (1992) 10 A.C.S.R. 415 (Supreme Court of Western Australia) (in a pre-receivership context, the directors have a right of access to the company's books and records without demonstrating a "need to know" but the appointment of a receiver alters the position to the extent necessary to recognise the receiver's pre-eminent position in realising assets for the benefit of the debenture-holder) and *Oswal v Burrup Holdings Ltd* [2011] FCA 609 (Federal Court of Australia) (because of the pre-eminent role of that receivers have to realise assets on behalf of the debenture-holder, the court should not facilitate inspection that may threaten the proper administration of the receivership and imperil the assets the subject of the charge by which the receivers have been appointed).

[97] *Newhart Developments Ltd v Cooperative Commercial Bank Ltd* [1978] Q.B. 814 (CA), followed in *Shanks v Central Regional Council* 1987 S.L.T. 410 (Court of Session, Outer House), which differed from the view expressed in *Imperial Hotels (Aberdeen) Ltd v Vaux* 1978 S.L.T. 113 (Court of Session, Outer House). See also Brightman J. in *Re Emmadart Ltd* [1979] Ch. 540, 544. But cf. the language of Danckwerts L.J. in *Lawson v Hosemaster Co Ltd* [1966] 1 W.L.R. 1300 (CA), 1315. See also *Gartner v Ernst & Young* (2003) 21 A.C.L.C. 560 (Federal Court of Australia). As an alternative the court may appoint a receiver ad litem: see below, Ch.29.

[98] *Hawkesbury Development v Landmark Finance* (1970) 92 W.N. (NSW) 199, 210 and see *Watts v Midland Bank Plc* [1986] B.C.L.C. 15 where Gibson J. held that the mortgagor company was entitled to sue the receiver in respect of an improper exercise of his powers.

debenture-holder. Indeed Shaw L.J. questioned whether the receiver can enforce claims against the debenture-holder, for such a step and any negotiations for compromise would involve such conflicts of interest on his part as to make it desirable that enforcement is left to the directors. Protection of the assets charged and the interests of the debenture-holders may require provision of an indemnity to the company against any liability for costs.[99]

2–033   In *Tudor Grange Holdings Ltd v Citibank NA*,[100] Sir Nicolas Browne-Wilkinson V.C. expressed substantial doubts whether the decision of the Court of Appeal in *Newhart Developments Ltd v Cooperative Commercial Bank Ltd* was correct, though he accepted that the decision bound him. He was of the view that the reasoning based on the embarrassment of the receiver deciding to sue his appointor could be met by an application by the receiver under s.35 of the Insolvency Act 1986 to the court for directions as to the course to be taken, a point apparently not drawn to the attention of the Court of Appeal; and that the decision ignored the difficulty which arose if two different sets of people, the directors and the receiver, who may have widely differing views and interests, both have power to bring proceedings on the same cause of action. He raised the question, in the situation where the directors bring proceedings and there is a counterclaim directly attacking the property of the company, as to who is to have the conduct of the counterclaim. Browne-Wilkinson V.C. insisted that in any event any action at the instance of the directors must be struck out until the company provides a complete indemnity in respect of any liability for costs.[101]

2–034   It is suggested that two different situations require to be considered:

> (a)   where both the receiver and the directors have power to represent the company, e.g. on a petition to wind up the company, if the receiver properly exercises his power, the power of the directors is suspended and is not exercisable. The exercise of such power by the receiver must be bona fide. On this ground a receiver's purported discontinuance of proceedings commenced by the directors in the name of the company for a declaration that the debenture was invalid as already cancelled and that the appointment of the receiver accordingly was invalid, was held capable of challenge[102];

---

[99] See *Tudor Grange Holdings Ltd v Citibank NA* [1992] Ch. 53; *Newhart Developments Ltd v Cooperative Commercial Bank Ltd* [1978] Q.B. 814 (CA), 819. Consider also *Fairholme and Palliser v Kennedy* (1890) 24 L.R. Ir. 498 (High Court of Ireland) (receiver permitted to sue in name of personal representatives on giving indemnity); and *Deangrove Pty Ltd v Commonwealth Bank of Australia* (2001) 37 A.C.S.R. 465 (Federal Court of Australia) (directors permitted to sue debenture-holder in name of company on giving indemnity) (reasoning adopted in *Gartner v Ernst & Young* (2003) 21 A.C.L.C. 560 (Federal Court of Australia)). See also *Enigma Technique Ltd v Royal Bank of Scotland* [2005] EWHC 3340 (Ch), where a director was ordered to compensate the company for its wasted costs in bringing an action against the receivers and, further, to meet the receivers costs in defending the action.

[100] *Tudor Grange Holdings Ltd v Citibank NA* [1992] Ch. 53 .

[101] For a "reconciliation" placing critical importance on the availability of the indemnity as to costs, see *L. Lascomme Ltd v UDT* [1994] I.L.R.M. 227 (High Court of Ireland).

[102] *Edwards v Singh* (1990) 5 N.Z.C.L.C. 66,770 (High Court of Auckland).

(b) where the company's cause of action is included in the debenture, it is thereby assigned to the mortgagee.

It is suggested that the solution to this quandary lies in the recognition that the relevant relationship is not between the directors and the company and the receiver and the company, but between the rights of the company and the debenture-holder respectively or mortgagor and mortgagee of the relevant chose in action. After the assignment has been effected by the charge, the assignee alone can seek to enforce the assigned right. Accordingly in respect of any cause of action charged to the debenture-holder, only the debenture-holder can sue. The only qualification is that in practice the receiver, without objection, sues in the name of the company, though technically the claimant should be the mortgagee.[103] The company itself by its directors can only sue (a) in respect of causes of action not assigned to the mortgagee or released by the mortgagee from the charge[104]; or (b) in respect of causes of action so assigned after redemption or perhaps with the consent of the debenture-holder.

Fifthly, as soon as the debenture-holder, preferential creditors, unsecured creditors (if applicable)[105] and all receivership costs, liabilities and expenses are or can be paid off, the receiver must in the absence of any provision to the contrary in the debenture cease to act and hand back to the directors the powers of management.[106]   **2–035**

Occasionally, but comparatively rarely, the court will appoint a receiver and manager of a company. Usually this is done on the application of a debenture-holder when the debenture for some reason does not enable him to make an appointment out of court or does not give the powers required to ensure a beneficial realisation of the company's undertaking in the interests of all to the company's creditors. An appointment may also be made if the validity of the debenture or of the appointment of a receiver out of court is challenged. A court-appointed receiver is an officer of the court and does not act as agent for the company or anyone else, but in so far as he carries on business he contracts and incurs liabilities personally. Such appointments are invariably short-lived, being designed to achieve an early sale as a going concern.[107]   **2–036**

Whichever the form of the appointment, if the company's fortunes improve, the receivership will give way to a resumption of management by the directors. If the receivership merely produces sufficient money to pay off the appointing debenture-holder, its conclusion may give rise to a further appointment of a different receiver by a subsequent encumbrancer, the appointment of an administrator or a liquidation.   **2–037**

---

[103] cf. below, Ch.13.
[104] All that is required for a release is a unilateral consent to the release: *Scottish & Newcastle plc, Petitioners* [1993] B.C.C. 634 (Court of Session, Outer House).
[105] See Insolvency Act 1986, s.176A.
[106] See below, Ch.28.
[107] See below, Ch.29.

4.   ADMINISTRATOR[108]

2–038   The office of administrator is the creation of statute, namely Part II of the Insolvency Act 1986 although the legislation currently in force is substantially changed and expanded from the original enactment.[109] An administrator may be appointed by the court, by the holder of a qualifying floating charge in respect of the company's property, by the company itself or by its directors.[110] However appointed, in performing his functions, the administrator must have regard to the interests of the creditors of the company as a whole.[111] An administrator must perform his functions with the objective of rescuing the company as a going concern, unless he thinks either that it is not reasonably practicable to achieve that objective, or that an alternative course of action would achieve a better result for the company's creditors as a whole than would be likely if the company were wound up (without first being in administration)[112], in which case he must perform his functions with the objective of achieving that result instead. If he thinks that it is not reasonably practicable to achieve either of those objectives, then he may pursue the objective of realising property in order to make a distribution to one or more secured or preferential creditors, but only if in doing so he does not unnecessarily harm the interests of the creditors as a whole.[113]

2–039   If on an application to the court for an administration order the applicant satisfies the court that the order is reasonably likely to achieve the relevant objective, the court has a discretionary power to make the order.[114] However, the court must be satisfied that the company is or is likely to become unable to

---

[108] For full consideration of this topic, see below, Chs 6 and 12. Only companies registered under the Companies Act 2006 in England and Wales or in Scotland and certain companies formed or incorporated outside the UK may enter administration: see Insolvency Act 1986, s.8 and Sch.B1 para.111(1A) and (1B). See also below, Ch.31. An entity incorporated under Luxembourg law which was a combination of a joint stock company and a limited partnership was held be be a "company" for these purposes in *Re Hellas Telecommunications (Luxembourg) II SCA* [2010] B.C.C. 295.

[109] This part of this chapter deals only with the regime under Pt II of the Insolvency Act 1986 as amended by the Enterprise Act 2002, s.249 and as applied to "ordinary" companies (different vintages of administration legislation are applied to an increasingly large number of special types of company, e.g. banks, utility and railway companies, all of which are outside the scope of this work).

[110] Insolvency Act 1986, s.8 and Sch.B1, para.2.

[111] The prudent administrator will have file notes to reflect his decision-making process, and this is particularly the case with so-called "pre-packaged" administrations where he will have to comply with the requirements of Statement of Insolvency Practice 16 which calls for an explanation of the administrator's decision to be given. (See also *Re Kayley Vending Ltd* [2009] B.C.C. 578 as to disclosure duties to the court.)

[112] Avoidance of statutory fees applicable in a compulsory liquidation was a relevant consideration in *Europcar Ltd v Top Marques Car Rental Ltd* [2005] All E.R. (D) 388 (Feb), but note that the relevant fee structures are now different.

[113] Insolvency Act 1986, Sch.B1, para.3. The "new" objectives were not met in *Doltable Ltd v Lexi Holdings Plc* [2006] B.C.C. 918, where the primary purpose of the administration application was to use the moratorium on enforcing a secured creditor's rights in order to attempt to achieve a higher sale price for some land.

[114] See, e.g., *Bank of Scotland Plc v Targetfollow Properties Holdings Ltd* [2010] EWHC 3606 (Ch).

pay its debts[115]; and a company or its directors giving notice of intention to appoint an administrator "out of court" must file with the court a statutory declaration confirming that this is the case. Inability to pay debts for these purposes means inability to pay debts as they become due or a deficiency of assets in relation to liabilities, either is sufficient.[116] Insolvency is not a prerequisite to an appointment by a qualifying floating charge-holder, nor to an appointment by the court on an application by a qualifying floating charge-holder, although the floating charge must be enforceable on the date of the appointment.

Once the appointment has taken effect, whether made by court order or out of court, there begins a period under the stewardship of the administrator in which to set the affairs of the company in order, to reorganise and repay its debts, or dispose of its business or assets for the benefit of creditors.[117] Administration is intended to be "only an interim and temporary regime"[118] which is not to remain in force for a long time[119] and which is "designed to revive, and to seek the continued life of the company if at all possible".[120] Though it is convenient to describe the breathing space afforded to the company as a moratorium, there is no authorisation to the company to postpone payment of its debts or discharge of its liabilities, but merely a limited immunity granted to the company against the enforcement of a number of legal rights and remedies (including various rights incidental to securities) without the leave of the court or the consent of the administrator.   **2–040**

Whilst the appointment of a receiver (administrative or non-administrative) can co-exist with that of a liquidator, the appointment of an administrator cannot co-exist with the appointment of an administrative receiver or liquidator.[121]   **2–041**

The court has no jurisdiction to appoint an administrator if there is an administrative receiver in office without the consent of his appointor, unless it thinks that the security under which the receiver was appointed can be challenged on specified grounds.[122] Once an administrator is appointed, no administrative receiver can be appointed throughout the administrator's period in office.   **2–042**

---

[115] "Likely" in this context means "more probable than not": *Re COLT Telecom Group Plc* [2003] B.P.I.R. 324.

[116] Insolvency Act 1986, s.123 as applied by Sch.B1 para.111(1).

[117] Examples are to be found in cases decided before the Insolvency Act 1986 of companies which went into liquidation but whose insolvency was only "temporary", e.g. *Re Rolls Royce Ltd* [1974] 1 W.L.R. 1584, and for the conversion of an insolvent into a solvent liquidation see *Re Islington Metal and Plating Works Ltd* [1984] 1 W.L.R. 14. The concept of a period of orderly stewardship following appointment, upon which the legislation was modelled, is somewhat at variance with the growing practice of pre-packaged administrations.

[118] *Re Atlantic Computer Systems Plc* [1992] Ch. 505 (CA), 528, per Nicholls L.J.

[119] *Re Arrows Ltd (No.3)* [1992] B.C.C. 131, 135. See now also Insolvency Act 1986, Sch.B1, para.76.

[120] *Re MTI Trading Systems Ltd* [1998] B.C.C. 400 (CA), 403, per Saville L.J.

[121] As to co-existence of administration and non-administrative receivership, see below, Ch.6.

[122] Insolvency Act 1986, Sch.B1 para.39; *Chesterton International Group Plc v Deka Immobilien Inv GmbH* [2005] B.P.I.R. 1103. See further below, Ch.6.

2-043   The administrator has extensive statutory powers and has power to continue the company's business as agent for the company.[123] He is given power to appoint and dismiss the directors,[124] and any powers of the directors which might interfere with the exercise by the administrator of his powers are exercisable only with his permission.[125] His appointment will cease to have effect after one year (although it may be extended for a limited period by court order or by consent of the creditors). Otherwise, once the administrator has fulfilled his role, or his role ceases to be capable of fulfilment, his appointment will cease to have effect, and either the board of directors (as reconstituted) will regain full power or the company will be wound up.[126]

2-044   Prior to the reform of Pt II of the Insolvency Act 1986 by the Enterprise Act 2002, there were substantial limitations on the effectiveness of this jurisdiction. Previously an administrator could not be appointed against the wishes of a debenture-holder if there was a floating charge under which the debenture-holder had appointed an administrative receiver, but the ability of a floating charge-holder to veto the appointment of an administrator has now been abolished except in the limited circumstances in which a floating charge-holder may still appoint an administrative receiver.[127] In addition, although previously, the jurisdiction was not exercisable in respect of a company which had already gone into liquidation, it is now possible for a liquidator or the holder of a qualifying floating charge to apply to the court for an administration order and accordingly to displace the liquidation.[128] It remains the case that there is no power to appoint a provisional administrator (although an interim manager may be appointed) and that the moratorium is of a strictly limited character (which does not restrict the exercise of contractual termination rights) but, as a result of these changes as well as the introduction of the ability for the company, its directors and qualifying floating charge-holders to appoint an administrator directly without application to the court, administration is a now the usual method of rescuing the business of a company, which is insolvent or approaching insolvency, where a formal procedure is required.[129]

---

[123] In *Re John Slack Ltd* [1995] B.C.C. 1116 it was held that an administrator had the power to pay off pre-administration debts in full out of the company's assets to ensure the survival of the company as a going concern but this decision should now be read subject to paras 65 and 66 of Sch.B1 of the Insolvency Act 1986. He should seek the guidance of the court where there is a substantial change in the circumstances which led to the making of the administration order, but should not seek the court's guidance as to the making of commercial decisions: *Re CE King Ltd* [2000] 2 B.C.L.C. 297; *Re T & D Industries Ltd* [2000] 1 W.L.R. 646.

[124] Insolvency Act 1986, Sch.B1, para.61.

[125] Insolvency Act 1986, Sch.B1, para.64. In Scotland, it has been held that para.64 does not prevent the directors of a company from causing the company to apply for the removal of an administrator: *Re Grant Estates Ltd* [2011] CSOH 119 (Court of Session, Outer House).

[126] As to ending administration generally, see the Insolvency Act 1986, Sch.B1, paras 76–86 (inclusive); and see also below, Ch.27.

[127] See above, para.2-025.

[128] Insolvency Act 1986, Sch.B1, paras 8, 37 and 38. A validation order under Insolvency Act 1986, s.127 may nonetheless be required, see *Re Albany Building Ltd* [2007] B.C.C. 591.

[129] The abolition of the right to appoint an administrative receiver had no retrospective effect. Even though, by virtue of the Insolvency Act 1986, s.72A and SI 2003/2095, the abolition does not affect powers under debentures created before September 15, 2003, it seems that such powers have

5.   PROVISIONAL LIQUIDATOR

At any time after the presentation of a winding-up petition, the court may   **2–045**
"appoint a liquidator provisionally".[130] A winding-up petition may be presented
by, inter alia:

(a) a creditor[131] on the ground that the company[132] is insolvent in that it
    is unable to pay its debts when due[133]; that it is just and equitable to
    wind up the company[134]; or that the period of a moratorium for the
    formulation and consideration of a voluntary arrangement has come
    to an end with no arrangement having become effective[135]; and/or

(b) a contributory, but only if there is a probability of surplus assets
    available to be returned to the contributories[136] (barring exceptional
    circumstances).[137]

Both conditions or one only may be satisfied at the same time, for a company
may have a surplus of assets over liabilities but the assets may not be liquid,

---

been increasingly rarely exercised. Useful statistical information illustrating the increasing importance of administration as the procedure of choice can be found in the Insolvency Statistics Archive
on the website of the Insolvency Service (*http://www.insolvencydirect.bis.gov.uk/otherinforma-
tion/statistics/insolvency-statistics.htm*).

[130] Insolvency Act 1986, s.135. The liquidator so appointed is referred to as a "provisional
liquidator".

[131] Exceptionally, in *Re Lafayette Electronics Europe Ltd* [2007] B.C.C. 890 former administrators petitioned as creditors on the basis of their own unpaid fees and were appointed as provisional
liquidators.

[132] The jurisdiction is exercisable in respect of a foreign company if: (1) there is a sufficient
connection with England and Wales; (2) there is a reasonable possibility of benefit to those
applying for the winding-up; and (3) one or more persons interested in the distribution of the
company's assets are subject to the jurisdiction of the court: *Re Latreefers Inc* [2001] B.C.C. 174
(CA) per Morritt L.J. delivering the judgment of the court at [17]–[34] but the jurisdiction to wind
up foreign companies is now subject to the constraints of Council Regulation 1346/2000/EC on
insolvency proceedings. In exercise of its jurisdiction to act in aid of a foreign court from which it
has received a letter of request pursuant to s.426 of the Insolvency Act 1986, the court has
appointed provisional liquidators without any winding-up petition having been issued: *Re HIH
Casualty and General Insurance Ltd* [2006] 2 All E.R. 671.

[133] Insolvency Act 1986, s.122(1)(f) A petition may be presented and an order made against a
substantial company which fails to pay an undisputed debt: *Cornhill Insurance Plc v Improvement
Services Ltd* [1986] 1 W.L.R. 114. If, however, the company disputes liability on some substantial
ground the petition will not be allowed to proceed: *Mann v Goldstein* [1968] 1 W.L.R. 1091, 1096.
The same usually applies where the company has a cross-claim which equals or exceeds the petition debt: *Re Portman Provincial Cinemas Ltd* [1999] 1 W.L.R. 157 (CA) and *Re Bayoil SA* [1999]
1 W.L.R. 147 (CA).

[134] Insolvency Act 1986, s.122(1)(g); *Re Dollar Land Plc* [1993] B.C.C. 823 (contingent
creditor).

[135] Insolvency Act 1986, ss.122(1)(fa) and 124(3A).

[136] *Re Chesterfield Catering Co Ltd* [1977] Ch. 373; *Re Commercial & Industrial Insulation Ltd*
(1986) 2 B.C.C. 98901. But cf. *Re DJH Consultants Ltd* Unreported Civil Appeals (No.164 of
1984) where the Court of Appeal of Hong Kong in a judgment delivered on November 29, 1984
questioned this rule of practice and its applicability in Hong Kong.

[137] See *Re Newman and Howard Ltd* [1962] Ch. 257. In the situation where relief is sought
against a number of companies, a separate petition ought to be presented in respect of each
company, at least when the companies are not included in any group or the subject of a common
holding company: *Re A Company* [1984] B.C.L.C. 307.

being assets which can only be realised over a relatively long time span; or the company's assets may be liquid but there may be a deficiency of assets to longer-term liabilities.

2–046   The right of an unpaid creditor to obtain a winding-up order is a class right to be exercised by the petitioner on behalf of the general body of creditors.[138] The court will ordinarily respect and give effect to the view of the majority in value of the independent creditors unconnected with the company and its directors as to what course of action best promotes their interests,[139] and the existence of a receivership is no bar.[140] The power of the court to adjourn petitions should be exercised with caution, for the effect is to prolong the period during which the company has to trade with the petition hanging over its head and the existence of the petition on the file effectively prevents other creditors presenting a petition.[141]

2–047   The company can itself petition at the instance of the directors if they are authorised by the articles of association to present a petition in the name of the company, or otherwise pursuant to a resolution of its members in general meeting.[142] The need for such authorisation has long since been removed in that directors now have locus to present a petition in their own names.[143] As long as the directors as a board have resolved that a petition should be presented, any one or more of their number may present the petition on behalf of all the directors.[144] Prior to the Insolvency Act 1986, a receiver could present a petition in the name of the company only if such a power could be inferred on the true construction of the debenture.[145] Such a power is deemed to be granted to an administrative receiver unless inconsistent with the terms of the debenture.[146]

2–048   The presentation of a winding-up petition does not affect the powers of the directors or the authority of the company's agents, but s.127 of the 1986 Act retrospectively invalidates dispositions of the company's property after the date of presentation of the petition if a winding up order is made on the petition. The purpose of the provision is to preserve the free assets in the insolvent

---

[138] *Re A Company* (No.0089 of 1894) [1894] 2 Ch. 349; *Re Crigglestone Coal Co* [1906] 2 Ch. 327 (CA); *Re A Company No. 001573 of 1983* (1983) 1 B.C.C. 98,937; *Re Southbourne Sheet Metal Co Ltd* [1991] B.C.C. 732; *Re Leigh Estates (UK) Ltd* [1994] B.C.C. 292; *Bell Group Finance (Pty) Ltd v Bell Group (UK) Holdings Ltd* [1996] B.C.C. 505, 513G–514A.
[139] *Re P & J Macrae Ltd* [1961] 1 W.L.R. 229 (CA) and *Re Demaglass Holdings Ltd* [2001] 2 B.C.L.C. 633.
[140] See below, para.15–007.
[141] *Re Boston Timber Fabrications Ltd* (1984) 1 B.C.C. 99052 (CA), 99056 per Oliver L.J. cf. *Re Demaglass Holdings Ltd* [2001] 2 B.C.L.C. 633.
[142] *Re Emmadart* [1979] Ch. 540. The view of Brightman J. that an article in the terms of art.80 in Table A (Companies Act 1948) was insufficient for this purpose has been rejected in New South Wales: *Spicer v Mytrent Pty Ltd* (1984) 8 A.C.L.R. 711 (Supreme Court of New South Wales), 720.
[143] Insolvency Act 1986, s.124.
[144] *Re Equiticorp International Plc* [1989] 1 W.L.R. 1010. See also *Minmar (929) Ltd v Khalatschi* [2011] B.C.C. 485.
[145] *Re Emmadart Ltd* [1979] Ch. 540.
[146] Insolvency Act 1986, s.42(1) and Sch.1, para.21.

estate for distribution to creditors in accordance with the statutory scheme.[147] The court has power to make validation orders.[148]

As noted above, the presentation of the petition is usually a condition precedent to the appointment of a provisional liquidator. At any time after the presentation of an effective petition,[149] the court may on application appoint a provisional liquidator to hold office.[150] The provisional liquidator has traditionally had the role of securing the company's property pending the outcome of the petition, of maintaining the status quo and of preventing any creditor gaining priority.[151] His powers may accordingly be limited by the order appointing him,[152] and he is discharged if the petition does not result in a winding-up order.[153] His position in the past has been similar to that of a receiver of property in dispute appointed pending determination of the dispute, and he has had to display independence and neutrality in areas of potential conflict between the company and its creditors, and between the creditors themselves. Thus, he was not able without the authority of the court (which was most unlikely to be forthcoming) to take proceedings to set aside a debenture (though this might be desirable from the point of view of the unsecured creditors)[154] or bring an end to the proceedings for winding up. **2–049**

The rescue culture now prevalent in insolvency has led to provisional liquidation being treated, where appropriate, in ways similar to administration. Examples of this have included the petition in relation to the Bank of Credit and Commerce International SA, in which provisional liquidators were appointed at once, but themselves took part in negotiating possible schemes and rescues and themselves made representations to the court in respect of adjournments of the petition.[155] In BCCI and other substantial recent **2–050**

---

[147] *Re Gray's Inn Construction Co Ltd* [1980] 1 W.L.R. 711 (CA), 717.

[148] For the treatment of transactions with banks, see *Coutts & Co v Stock* [2000] 1 W.L.R. 906; *Hollicourt (Contracts) Ltd v Bank of Ireland* [2001] Ch. 555 (CA) and *Rose v AIB Group (UK) Plc* [2003] 1 W.L.R. 2791. See also Practice Note: Validation Orders (ss.127 and 284 of the Insolvency Act 1986) [2004] B.P.I.R. 94.

[149] *Re A Company No. 00315 of 1973* [1973] 1 W.L.R. 1566.

[150] Insolvency Act 1986, s.135(1). The court may dispense with notice to other parties and hear the application immediately: *Re WF Fearman Ltd* (1988) 4 B.C.C. 139. See also *Re First Express Ltd* [1991] B.C.C. 782 and *Re Secure & Provide Plc* [1992] B.C.C. 405. The application must be made to the Companies Court judge who may hear the application in private: Practice Direction: Insolvency Proceedings (the updated text of which can be found at *www.justice.gov.uk*); and Practice Note: The Hearing of Insolvency Proceedings (the updated text of which can be found at *http://www.hmcourts-service.gov.uk*).

[151] *Re Dry Docks Corp of London* (1888) 39 Ch. D. 306 (CA).

[152] Insolvency Act 1986, s.135(5).

[153] If the petition is dismissed, the applicant for the appointment may be ordered to reimburse the company the provisional liquidator's remuneration and expenses: *Graham v John Tullis & Son (Plastics) Ltd* [1991] B.C.C. 398 (Court of Session, Inner House). But the Secretary of State for Trade and Industry, when applying without notice for the appointment of a provisional liquidator pending determination of a public interest winding-up petition is not required to give a cross-undertaking in damages.

[154] *Re Chateau Hotels Ltd* [1977] 1 N.Z.L.R. 381 (Supreme Court of New Zealand).

[155] See the judgments reported at [1992] B.C.C. 83 and Moss and Phillips: "Provisional Liquidators: New Uses for an Old Remedy" (1992) Insolv. Int. The passage in the text and the article were cited with approval by H.H. Judge Dean QC in *Smith v UIC Insurance Co Ltd* [2001] B.C.C. 11.

international insolvency and insurance cases, the powers of the provisional liquidators have been set out in wide terms in the order appointing them.[156]

2–051 The person appointed provisional liquidator in any ordinary case used to be the official receiver,[157] though in exceptional circumstances some other person could be chosen.[158] The "exceptional" cases have become more frequent in recent years in view of the exceptional size, complexity and specialised nature of some recent insolvencies. Private insolvency practitioners are now regularly appointed as provisional liquidators where there is a business or a specialised industry or where complicated investigation is required.[159] The provisional liquidator is bound to carry out such functions as the court may confer on him.[160] In any case where a company has gone into liquidation, or a provisional liquidator has been appointed, the liquidator or provisional liquidator may apply for the appointment of a special manager (such as a director)[161] to manage the business or property of the company with such powers as may be entrusted to him by the court.[162] The provisional receiver or special manager may be directed to carry on the company's business, and indeed the winding-up order itself may authorise or direct that the business be continued thereafter.[163]

2–052 An application for the appointment of a provisional liquidator may be made by, inter alia, the petitioner, a creditor, a contributory, the company itself, the Secretary of State or any person entitled to present a petition for winding up. The applicant must show sufficient ground.[164] The court has a general discretion whether or not to make an appointment of a provisional liquidator. Two factors have traditionally been taken into account:

---

[156] In *Re Daewoo Motor Co Ltd* [2006] B.P.I.R. 415, the court ordered the transmission of the proceeds of realisation of a Korean-incorporated company's assets in England and Wales by the company's provisional liquidators to a Korean receiver.

[157] *Re Mercantile Bank of Australia* [1892] 2 Ch. 204.

[158] *Re Croftheath, The Times*, February 18, 1975; *Re WF Fearman Ltd* (1988) 4 B.C.C. 139 (joint appointees).

[159] Apart from being authorised to act as insolvency practitioners (Insolvency Act 1986, ss.388 and 389), the critical requirement is independence, see *Re West Australian Gem Explorers Pty Ltd* (1994) 13 A.C.S.R. 104 (Federal Court of Australia), 109 (liquidators must be independent and be *seen* to be independent) and *Re Bank of Credit and Commerce International SA* [1992] B.C.C. 83.

[160] Insolvency Act 1986, s.135(4).

[161] As in *Re Mawcon Ltd* [1969] 1 W.L.R. 78.

[162] Insolvency Act 1986, s.177(1). In *Re Union Accident Insurance Co Ltd* [1972] 1 W.L.R. 640, the application was made without notice the day after the provisional liquidator was appointed. Although the special manager (in contrast to the provisional liquidator) need not be an authorised insolvency practitioner, his position is regulated by rr.4.206–4.210 Insolvency Rules 1986. See also *Re US Ltd* (1984) 1 B.C.C. 98985 (a case under the Companies Act 1948 and the Companies (Winding-Up) Rules 1949).

[163] *Re General Service Co-operative Stores* (1891) 64 L.T. 228. The appointment of a provisional liquidator can be made with a view to investigating the possibility of fraudulent or wrongful trading claims (*Re A Company (No.00359 of 1987)* [1988] Ch. 210, reported elsewhere as *International Westminster Bank Plc v Okeanos Maritime Corp*) and his powers can include the conduct, on the company's behalf, of other proceedings brought against it by the petitioning creditor (*Re Latreefers Inc* [1999] 1 B.C.L.C. 271, not affected as authority for this point by the appeal reported as *Stocznia Gdanska SA v Latreefers Inc (No.2)* [2001] B.C.C. 174 (CA)).

[164] Insolvency Act 1986, s.135 and Insolvency Rules 1986, r.4.25. In case of an application by the company the court will require to be satisfied that the directors should not retain control pending the outcome of the petition: *Re Tamaris Plc* Unreported November 9, 1999.

(a) The existence of a good prospect that the company will eventually be wound up,[165] at least if no more satisfactory exit, e.g. a scheme under Pt 26 of the Companies Act 2006, becomes available.

(b) The urgent need for relief pending the hearing of the petition, which is normally the safeguarding of assets within the jurisdiction which are in jeopardy, but in exceptional cases may extend to ascertaining the whereabouts and recovery, e.g. of a vessel abroad.[166]

The traditional aim and purpose of the appointment was usually to secure the assets of the company so that they may be available for equal distribution to creditors. Accordingly, obvious insolvency and jeopardy to assets are reasons for an appointment, but not the only reasons. Other reasons include the public interest in the protection of the public from the successful frauds of the company[167] and the need for an immediate vigorous investigation by a totally independent officer of the court.[168] The avoidance of a scramble by creditors for assets and the protection of the assets pending the putting forward of a Companies Act scheme of arrangement have been accepted in recent cases as good reasons for the appointment of provisional liquidators.[169]

The serious consequences for the company of the appointment of a provisional liquidator require a relatively high standard of proof in cases in which the appointment is not sought by the company itself. The greater the prospect of the eventual order for winding up being made, the lighter the requirement for the urgent grant of relief, and vice versa.[170] If the directors unreasonably cause the company to oppose the application, an order for costs may be made against them personally.[171]   **2–053**

The offices of liquidator and provisional liquidator are statutory and their powers derive solely from statute: the powers of the directors do not vest in them nor can they exercise powers vested in the board.[172] The order for the   **2–054**

---

[165] *Re Mercantile Bank of Australia* [1892] 2 Ch. 204 and *Re A Company (No.005287 of 1985)* [1986] 1 W.L.R. 281, 285, per Hoffmann J.

[166] *Re A Company* [1988] Ch. 210 (reported elsewhere as *International Westminster Bank Plc v Okeanos Maritime Corp*). It is not appropriate to use the jurisdiction to put the company in a better position against one of its creditors when an appointment is not necessary to maintain the status quo: *Re Namco UK Ltd* [2003] 2 B.C.L.C. 78.

[167] *Re Highfield Commodities Ltd* [1985] 1 W.L.R. 149, 159, per Megarry V.C.

[168] *Re Pinstripe Farming Co Ltd* [1996] B.C.C. 913 (where the company was already in voluntary liquidation, but the liquidators were not perceived to be sufficiently independent); *Re Latreefers Inc* [1999] B.C.L.C. 271 (this point is also not affected by the appeal reported as *Stocznia Gdanska SA v Latreefers Inc (No.2)* [2001] B.C.C. 174 (CA)); *Integro Fiduciaine SARL v Denito Ltd* Unreported March 10, 1997 noted at (1998) 11 Insolv. Int. 69 by F. Toube).

[169] This was almost invariably been the case in relation to insolvent insurance companies, before administration was available, and where knowledge of the potential insolvency of the company may have caused a scramble for assets and resulted in "short-tail" creditors receiving preferential treatment over "long-tail claimants": see *Re Andrew Weir Insurance Company Ltd* Unreported November 12, 1992 and *Re English & American Insurance Co Ltd* [1994] 1 B.C.L.C. 649, 650. Administration (with certain modifications) is now available to insurers: see SI 2002/1242.

[170] *Re Capital Expansion & Development Corp, The Times*, November 30, 1992.

[171] *Gamelstaden Plc v Bracklands Magazines* [1993] B.C.C. 194.

[172] *Butterell v Docker Smith Pty Ltd* (1997) 41 N.S.W.L.R. 129 (Supreme Court of New South Wales).

appointment operates to divest the directors of powers (and in particular the power of management) by conferring those powers hitherto exercisable by the directors on the provisional liquidator and it likewise operates to revoke the authority of agents appointed to act on behalf of the company by or under the authority of the directors and this includes the agency of a receiver for the company.[173] The gazetting of the appointment constitutes notice that the directors are no longer the company's authorised agents.[174] The displacement of the powers of the directors (unlike the displacement effected on the appointment of an administrator) is not the result of any express statutory provision, but an implication arising from the inconsistency between the statutory role of the provisional liquidator and the continued existence of the directors' powers. Accordingly, the displacement is not total and does not extend to powers which cannot reasonably have been intended to vest in the provisional liquidator. Thus, it does not extend to the power of the board in the name of the company to oppose the winding-up petition, to apply for the discharge of the provisional liquidator or to appeal from the making of a winding-up order.[175]

2–055   The provisional liquidator can of course revive the authority of agents of the company whose authority lapsed on his appointment.[176] The provisional liquidator is an officer of the court, and in no way the agent of the person who secures his appointment.

2–056   On the appointment of a provisional liquidator, as on the making of a winding-up order, no action may be proceeded with or commenced against the company except by leave of the court and subject to such terms as the court may impose.[177] The provisional liquidator is bound to take into his custody or under his control all the property and things in action to which the company is or appears to be entitled.[178]

2–057   The appointment will leave the contractual relations between a company and its employees unaffected if the petition does not result in a winding-up order,[179] and it is thought that a subsequent winding-up order will not alter the position retrospectively. Dismissal should only occur if the provisional liquidator exercises the power of dismissal or by reason of the winding-up order being made.

---

[173] *Pacific and General Insurance Co Ltd v Hazell* [1997] B.C.C. 400 not following *Re KVE Homes Pty Ltd* [1979] 1 N.S.W.L.R. 181 (Supreme Court of New South Wales). The appointment of a provisional liquidator was held not automatically to crystallise a floating charge (with reference to the specific wording of the mortgage debenture) in *Re Obie Pty Ltd (No.2)* (1983) 8 A.C.L.R. 574 (Supreme Court of Queensland), 581.

[174] *Re Mawcon Ltd* [1969] 1 W.L.R. 78.

[175] *Re Union Accident Insurance Co Ltd* [1972] 1 W.L.R. 640. But the directors cannot in the name of the company initiate proceedings.

[176] *Pacific and General Insurance Co Ltd v Hazell* [1997] B.C.C. 400.

[177] Insolvency Act 1986, s.130(2).

[178] Insolvency Act 1986, s.144(1). He may, however, be directed by the court not to spend scarce resources where it is not practical or cost-effective to pursue assets, e.g. where they are abroad in a jurisdiction which does not recognise the appointment.

[179] Consider *Re Dry Docks Corp of London* (1888) 39 Ch. D. 306 (CA).

If the provisional liquidator or the special manager continues the company's **2–058**
business, though he may be given wide powers, he carries on business as agent
of the company and usually incurs no personal liabilities.[180]

The provisional liquidator is not entitled to appear on the hearing of the peti- **2–059**
tion[181] but in exceptional cases the court may in fact allow him to appear and
to make representations in the interests of creditors.[182]

6. LIQUIDATOR[183]

The liquidator in the case of a winding-up by the court is an officer of the **2–060**
court,[184] but this is not so in the case of a voluntary liquidation.[185] This difference in status is reflected in the degree of autonomy conferred upon them. The
liquidator in the case of a winding-up by the court may, with the sanction of the
court or the liquidation committee, carry on the business of the company so far
as may be necessary for its beneficial winding-up but no such sanction is
required in the case of a voluntary winding-up.[186] If the voluntary liquidator,
after taking all proper advice, honestly and reasonably decides to carry on business he is not liable even if the decision turns out to be ill-fated.[187] It is,
however, advisable for the liquidator to seek the consent of the court if the
wisdom of carrying on business may be questioned later or if the period of such
continuation of business will be protracted.

The court will be very slow to interfere with the exercise by a liquidator of **2–061**
his powers in relation to the realisation of assets, which is essentially regarded
as a matter of commercial judgment.[188] So long as the liquidator acts only in
the name of the company and discloses that it is in liquidation, all debts and
liabilities incurred in the course of the carrying on of such business are liabilities of the company, and not the liquidator personally. Such liabilities rank as

---

[180] *Stead Hazel & Co v Cooper* [1933] 1 K.B. 840; *Smith v Lord Advocate*, 1978 S.C. 259 (Court
of Session, Inner House) and *Stewart v Engel* [2000] B.C.C. 741 (all cases involving liquidators,
as opposed to provisional liquidators, but the applicable principles are the same). Insolvency Rules
1986, r.4.30 provides that a provisional liquidator's remuneration and expenses shall be paid out
of the company's assets if no winding-up order is made and as an expense of the liquidation "in the
prescribed order of priority" if an order is made. The prescribed order is set out in r.4.218. (For
background before the relevant rules were in their present form, see *Re Grey Marlin Ltd* [2000] 1
W.L.R. 370 and *Smith v UIC Insurance Co Ltd* [2001] B.C.C. 11).
[181] *Re The General International Agency Co Ltd* (1865) 36 Beav. 1.
[182] *Re Bank of Credit and Commerce International SA* [1992] B.C.C. 83.
[183] On the making of a winding-up order, the Official Receiver, by virtue of his office, becomes
liquidator pending his replacement by an appointee capable of acting. In view of the temporary
nature of his tenure of office, prior to the Insolvency Act 1986, he was confusingly called a "provisional liquidator", though he enjoyed the full powers of a liquidator: see, e.g., *Re ABC Coupler
(No.3)* [1970] 1 W.L.R. 702, 715. Section 136(2) of the Insolvency Act 1986 now terms the official
receiver "liquidator", and the term "provisional liquidator" is accordingly no longer apposite in
this context.
[184] *Deloitte & Touche AG v Johnson* [1999] 1 W.L.R. 1605 (PC).
[185] *Re TH Knitwear (Wholesale) Ltd* [1988] Ch. 275 (CA).
[186] Insolvency Act 1986, Sch.4, Pt II, para.5.
[187] *Re Great Eastern Electric Co Ltd* [1941] Ch. 241.
[188] *Re Buckingham International Plc (No.2)* [1998] B.C.C. 943 (CA); *Re Edennote Ltd* [1996]
B.C.C. 718 (CA); *Mahomed v Morris* [2001] B.C.C. 233 (CA).

costs of the liquidation and in priority to the general debts and liabilities of the company.[189]

2–062   The making of the winding-up order operates by implication[190] to divest the directors of all powers the exercise of which is inconsistent with the powers intended to vest in the liquidator.[191]

2–063   In the case of a voluntary liquidation, on the appointment of the liquidator, statute expressly provides that the powers of the directors shall cease except as (in the case of a members' voluntary liquidation) the members in general meeting or the liquidator and (in the case of a creditors' voluntary liquidation) the liquidation committee or the creditors sanction their continuance.[192] The directors in a voluntary liquidation accordingly retain no residual powers which are exercisable of their own volition.

2–064   In both cases, the company's directors and employees continue to be under a duty not to disclose confidential information of the company, for this is as much the property of the company as any other asset.[193] The directors also become subject to a duty to comply with s.208(1) of the Insolvency Act 1986 which requires them to co-operate with the liquidator and pro-actively (rather than reactively) to disclose and deliver to the liquidator the company's property.[194]

2–065   Liquidation is in all ordinary cases the end of the road for the company,[195] though not necessarily for its undertaking and business. This is reflected in the principle of law enshrined in s.107 of the Insolvency Act 1986 that on the commencement of winding up the beneficial ownership by the company of its assets is terminated and such assets are thereafter held subject to a form of statutory trust for distribution to creditors and contributories according to their entitlement.[196] Thus:

---

[189] *Re S Davis and Co Ltd* [1945] Ch. 402.

[190] The statement of Shaw L.J. in *Newhart Developments Ltd v Cooperative Commercial Bank Ltd* [1978] Q.B. 814 (CA), 819, that there was a statutory provision to that effect, must be treated as having been made per incuriam. However, it has been accepted at least since *Re Oriental Inland Steam Company Ex p. Scinde Railway Co* (1874) 9 Ch. App. 557 (CA) that a winding-up order has the effect of bringing directors' powers to an end. Moreover, in *Measures Brothers Ltd v Measures* [1910] 2 Ch. 248 (CA) the court regarded a director's office (as opposed to the powers of that office) as having come to an end on the making of a winding-up order.

[191] It has been held that the directors retain the power to instruct solicitors and counsel in the name of the company to appeal against the order: *Re Union Accident Insurance Co Ltd* [1972] 1 W.L.R. 640. This exception has been followed in Scotland in *Re Grant Estates Ltd* [2011] CSOH 119 (Court of Session, Outer House) (dealing with administrators' powers) but has been superseded in Australia by a statutory provision (Corporations Act 2001 (Cth), s.471A) which has been held to require a director to obtain the approval of either the liquidator or the court to appeal against a winding-up order as an officer of the company: *Rock Bottom Fashion Market Pty Ltd v HR & CE Griffiths Pty Ltd* (1997) 25 A.C.S.R. 467 (Queensland Court of Appeal), 468–469.

[192] Insolvency Act 1986, s.91(2) (members) and s.103 (creditors). It is thought that the directors must nonetheless remain in office since any other conclusion would be difficult to reconcile with the express provision for them to continue to act if so sanctioned.

[193] *Re Country Traders Distribution Ltd* [1974] 2 N.S.W.L.R. 135 (Supreme Court of New South Wales), 139.

[194] *R. v McCredie* [2000] B.C.C. 617 (CA).

[195] In *Re MTI Trading Systems Ltd* [1998] B.C.C. 400 (CA), 402–403 Saville L.J. said that winding-up orders "bring the life of the company to an end". The life of the company can however be revived if the winding-up is stayed: see below.

[196] *Ayerst v C & K (Construction) Ltd* [1976] A.C. 167 (HL).

". . . on a winding-up . . . the statutory scheme for distribution of a company's assets among its creditors comes into operation ... once the company has gone into liquidation, the unsecured creditors are in the nature of cestui que trust with beneficial interests extending to all the company's property under that scheme. Realistically in view of [section 127 of the Insolvency Act 1986], the scheme relates back to the commencement of the winding-up."[197]

In the case of a compulsory or voluntary liquidation, the liquidator may sell **2–066** for cash the whole or any part of the company's undertaking.[198] In the case of a voluntary liquidation, he may (with the relevant sanction) sell or enter into a transaction whereby the whole or part of the undertaking is transferred to another company (or limited liability partnership) in return for benefits in the form of cash, shares, policies or other interests in the transferee company (or cash or membership in the transferee limited liability partnership) provided either to the transferor company or directly to its members.[199]

Even a winding-up order may be stayed and the company given a fresh lease **2–067** of life if, by reason of some turn of events, it is proved that the company is viable.[200] This jurisdiction is, however, to be exercised with the utmost caution and cogent reasons need to be demonstrated.[201] Prior to the Insolvency Act 1986, a stay was unlikely to be granted unless it was shown that:

(a) the creditors would, unless they consented, be paid off in full or otherwise satisfied, e.g. by means of a Companies Act scheme of arrangement;

(b) the liquidator would be safeguarded; and

(c) the members consented or payment of at least as much as they would receive on a winding-up was secured.[202]

A similar jurisdiction existed in respect of companies in voluntary liquidation and the same considerations applied.[203]

As noted above, the Insolvency Act 1986 provides that the liquidator himself **2–068** may now propose a company voluntary arrangement and/or apply to the court for an administration order. In the case of a proposal for a voluntary arrangement, the court may stay the winding-up proceedings pending the outcome of

---

[197] *R. v Registrar of Companies Ex p. Central Bank of India* [1986] Q.B. 1114 (CA), 1161–1162, per Dillon L.J. citing as authority Lord Brightman L.J. in *Victoria Housing Estates Ltd v Ashpurton Estates Ltd* [1983] Ch. 110 (CA), 123.

[198] Insolvency Act 1986, s.167 (compulsory), s.165 (voluntary) and Sch.4.

[199] Insolvency Act 1986, ss.110, 111.

[200] Insolvency Act 1986, s.147(1).

[201] *Re Lowston Ltd* [1991] B.C.L.C. 570. As an alternative, an application could be made for rescission of the winding-up order under Insolvency Rules 1986, r.7.47 but this jurisdiction is also only exercised very sparingly: *Re Piccadilly Property Management Ltd* [2000] B.C.C. 44 and *Re Metrocab Ltd* [2010] 2 B.C.L.C. 603.

[202] *Re Calgary & Edmonton Land Co Ltd* [1975] 1 W.L.R. 355.

[203] *Re Calgary & Edmonton Land Co Ltd* [1975] 1 W.L.R. 355. Such an application would now be made under the Insolvency Act 1986, s.112.

the meetings and, if the proposal is duly passed (in the case of a compulsory liquidation) rescind the winding-up order and (in the case of a voluntary liquidation) permanently stay the liquidation[204] to facilitate the implementation of the scheme or composition under the supervision of the supervisor. If the court makes an administration order on the application of a liquidator, any winding-up order in respect of the company must be discharged.[205]

[204] *Re Dollar Land (Feltham) Ltd* [1995] B.C.C. 740.
[205] Insolvency Act 1986, Sch.B1, paras 8 and 38.M

Chapter 3

Fixed and Floating Charges

1. GENERAL

Receivers over the property of a company are commonly appointed, where **3–001** such an appointment is still permitted, under the terms of a debenture containing a mixture of fixed and floating charges.[1] Strictly speaking, a debenture is merely a writing of a company creating or acknowledging a debt and may be secured by a charge or charges over the assets of the company or may be unsecured.[2] However, it is only a secured debenture which will normally provide for the appointment of a receiver by the holder of the debenture, for the right to appoint is in practice invariably an incident of the charge on property. In theory, an unsecured debenture or other contract could provide for the appointment of a receiver or manager, but this does not occur in practice.[3]

In the absence of a provision to the contrary, a debenture is freely assignable,[4] **3–002** but in so far as it is a chose in action, the assignee takes subject to all equities subsisting between the assignor and the company at the date that notice is

---

[1] Generally speaking, there is no need for the purposes of this work to distinguish between a "charge" and a "mortgage". "The technical difference between a 'mortgage' or 'charge', though in practice the phrases are used interchangeably, is that a mortgage involves a conveyance of property subject to a right of redemption, whereas a charge conveys nothing and merely gives the chargee certain rights over the property as security for the loan", per Slade J. in *Re Bond Worth* [1980] Ch 228. See also per Buckley L.J. in *Swiss Bank Corporation v Lloyds Bank Ltd* [1999] 2 W.L.R. 364, CA.

[2] See, e.g. *Austral Mining Construction Pty Ltd v NZI Capital Corp Ltd* (1991) 9 A.C.L.C. 651. Cf. "A security issued by a company is called a debenture" per Lord Templeman in *Downsview Nominees Ltd v First City Corp Ltd* [1993] A.C. 295 (PC), 311E. On the other hand a charge may be created where the chargor has no personal liability to make a payment: see *Re Conley* [1938] 2 All E.R. 127. Such a collateral security might take the form of a floating charge. Such a charge, though neither creating nor acknowledging a debt would, for practical legal purposes, be treated as a debenture.

[3] A debenture need not be executed as a deed, but it is desirable that it should be for at least two reasons. First, because certain statutory powers are only conferred on a mortgagee where the mortgage is created by deed, e.g. powers of sale and to appoint a receiver: s.101 of the Law of Property Act 1925. Secondly, although the common law rule that an agent cannot deliver a deed unless he is appointed under seal has been abolished by s.1(1)(c) of the Law of Property (Miscellaneous Provisions) Act 1989, that statute does not appear to have abolished the common law rule that an agent cannot execute a deed unless his authority to do so has been conferred under seal: see Harpum and Virgo, "Breaking the Seal, the New Law on Deeds" [1991] L.M.C.L.Q. 209. If a debenture is granted by a company under seal and contains a clause irrevocably appointing any receivers who might be appointed by the mortgagee to be attorneys for the company with power to execute deeds, this will satisfy the common law rule. Thus, receivers who were subsequently appointed only in writing could validly execute a deed: see *Phoenix Properties Ltd v Wimpole Street Nominees Ltd* [1992] B.C.L.C. 737.

[4] See, e.g. *Re Portbase (Clothing) Ltd* [1993] Ch. 388 for a suggestion that the benefit of a fixed charge might be assigned as part of an agreement as to priority between charge-holders.

given to the company, unless the debenture contains a provision that the assignor may transfer free of such equities.[5]

3–003   In *Re Bank of Credit and Commerce International SA (No.8)* Lord Hoffmann described a charge as a proprietary interest granted by way of security, and continued:

> "Proprietary interests confer rights in rem which, subject to questions of registration and the equitable doctrine of purchaser for value without notice, will be binding upon third parties and unaffected by the insolvency of the owner of the property charged. A proprietary interest provided by way of security entitles the holder to resort to the property only for the purposes of satisfying some liability due to him (whether from the person providing the security or a third party) and, whatever the form of the transaction, the owner of the property retains an equity of redemption to have the property restored to him when the liability has been discharged. The method by which the holder of the security will resort to the property will ordinarily involve its sale or, more rarely, the extinction of the equity of redemption by foreclosure. A charge is a security interest created without any transfer of title or possession to the beneficiary. An equitable charge can be created by an informal transaction for value (legal charges may require a deed or registration or both) and over any kind of property (equitable as well as legal) but is subject to the doctrine of purchaser for value without notice applicable to all equitable interests."[6]

3–004   There is a clear conceptual distinction between a charge and a trust, but in *Re Bond Worth Ltd*[7] Slade J. held that a debtor can create an equitable charge by declaring himself to be a trustee of property "by way of security" for the payment of a specified debt. The key to distinguishing a charge from a pure trust is to ask whether the equitable interest of the beneficiary in the subject-matter of the trust or charge is defeasible upon payment of the secured debt. However, the distinction is not always easy to draw. In *Squires v AIG Europe (UK) Ltd*,[8] the Court of Appeal considered a "non-competition" clause in a deed of indemnity under which a parent company had agreed with a third party provider of a commercial guarantee for the debts of its subsidiary, that the parent would not prove in the insolvency of the subsidiary until the third party had been paid in full. The deed went on to provide in the next clause that the parent would hold in trust for, and forthwith pay or transfer to the third party,

---

[5] *Hilger Analytical Ltd v Rank Precision Industries Ltd* [1984] B.C.L.C. 301. Such clauses are commonly inserted in debentures.

[6] *Re Bank of Credit and Commerce International SA (No.8)* [1998] A.C. 214 (HL), 226. See also the classic description of a charge by Atkin L.J. in *National Provincial and Union Bank of England v Charnley* [1924] 1 K.B. 431 (CA), 449–450. See also the discussion of the nature of equitable charges by Buckley L.J. in *Swiss Bank Corp v Lloyds Bank Ltd* [1982] A.C. 584 (HL), 594–596, the statements by Millett J. in *Re Charge Card Services Ltd* [1987] Ch. 150, 176 and Millett L.J. in *Re Cosslett (Contractors) Ltd* [1998] Ch. 495 (CA), 508–510 and the discussion by Blackburne J. in *Re TXU Europe Group Plc* [2004] 1 B.C.L.C. 519, [35].

[7] *Re Bond Worth Ltd* [1980] Ch. 228.

[8] *Squires v AIG Europe (UK) Ltd* [2006] Ch. 610 (CA).

any payment received by it contrary to the non-competition clause. It was suggested by the liquidators of the parent company that the latter clause was an unregistered charge over the debt due from the subsidiary to the parent because it applied to all payments that might be received by the parent, even in excess of those required to pay the surety in full. The Court of Appeal held, affirming Lloyd J., that whilst the latter clause did involve the creation of a property right in the monies that might be received by way of trust, on its true construction the subject matter of the obligation was limited to the amount due to the surety, so that it would create a trust and not a charge.

2. DISTINGUISHING BETWEEN FIXED AND FLOATING CHARGES

It is often critical to determine whether a particular charge over defined assets is fixed or floating. A fixed charge is generally the best type of security for the creditor as it gives the chargee priority over preferential creditors and other claims on the company's assets. Such other claims include the setting aside of a prescribed part of floating charge realisations for the benefit of unsecured creditors[9] and the payment of the expenses of a liquidation[10] or an administration.[11] The holder of a fixed charge cannot, however, appoint an administrator or administrative receiver (and there are restrictions on the type of floating charges that give such rights of appointment). If an administrative receiver or administrator is in any doubt as to the validity or character of the charge under which he has been appointed, he should investigate any material facts that may not be clear,[12] seek legal advice and, if necessary, seek the directions of the court.[13]   **3–005**

Conventionally, the character of a transaction, whether or not a charge and (if a charge) whether a fixed or floating charge, is to be determined by reference to the facts as they were or might be foreseen at the date of the transaction.[14] Resolution of the question of whether the charge in a particular case is fixed or floating may involve three separate issues.   **3–006**

---

[9] Pursuant to s.176A of the Insolvency Act 1986.

[10] Pursuant to s.176ZA of the Insolvency Act 1986, inserted by the Companies Act 2006 to reverse the decision of the *House of Lords in Buchler v Talbot* sub nom. *Re Leyland Daf Ltd* [2004] 2 A.C. 298 (HL).

[11] Pursuant to s.19(4) of, and para.99(3) of Sch.B1 to the Insolvency Act 1986.

[12] In the case of an administrative receiver or an administrator, and if it becomes necessary to do so, using his special powers under ss.235 and 236 of the Insolvency Act 1986; see Ch.8.

[13] Under s.35 (administrative receivers) or s.14(3) of, or para.63 of Sch.B1 to the Insolvency Act 1986 (administrators).

[14] See *Re Armagh Shoes Ltd* [1984] B.C.L.C. 405, referred to by Morritt J. in *William Gaskell Group Ltd v Highley* [1993] B.C.C. 200, 205. As Knox J. pointed out in *Re New Bullas Trading Ltd* [1993] B.C.C. 251, s.40 of the Insolvency Act 1986 determines the priority to be given to preferential debts by reference to whether a charge was, "as created", a floating charge. See also the comments of Lord Walker in *Re Spectrum Plus Ltd (In Liquidation)* [2005] 2 A.C. 680 (HL), [160] and *Re Harmony Care Homes Ltd* [2010] B.C.C. 358, [17]–[19]. See also *Bowesco Pty v Zohar* [2007] FCAFC 1 (Federal Court of Australia). On the construction of contracts, see generally *Mannai Investments Co Ltd v Eagle Star Life Assurance Co* [1997] A.C. 749 (HL); *Investors Compensation Scheme Ltd v West Bromwich Building Society* [1998] 1 W.L.R. 896 (HL); *Sirius International Insurance Co v PAI General Insurance Ltd* [2004] 1 W.L.R. 3251 (HL); *Att Gen of Belize v Belize Telecom* [2009] 1 W.L.R. 1988 (PC) (implied terms); *Chartbrook v Persimmon Homes* [2009] 1 A.C. 1101 (HL) (correction of mistakes by construction); and *Sigma Finance Corp* [2010] 1 All E.R. 571 (SC).

3–007   The first issue (which is only a live question in rare cases) involves consideration of whether, in so far as the debenture purports to create a fixed charge
on a particular asset, the provision in the debenture is susceptible of challenge
on the grounds that the debenture should be rectified or the specific provision
ignored as a sham. To establish a claim to rectification, it must be proved that
the parties to the debenture had a prior agreement or continuing common intention that the charge in respect of the particular asset should be a floating charge,
and that the debenture was intended to but did not give effect to that agreement
as a result of a common or, exceptionally, a unilateral mistake by the parties.[15]
To establish a sham, it is necessary to show that the parties to the debenture
actually agreed or both intended at the time of execution that the debenture
should not operate according to its terms, i.e. that notwithstanding the supposed
imposition of a fixed charge, the parties in fact intended that the company
should be free to deal with the property in question on some other basis and
without reference to the terms of the written document.[16] This necessarily
involves a degree of dishonesty.[17]

3–008   Once it is accepted that the documents genuinely represent the transaction
into which the parties have entered, the second issue involves the construction
of the terms of the charge documentation against the commercial background
and then the examination of those rights and obligations in order to ascertain
the true legal character of the transaction. In giving the judgment of the Privy
Council in the case of *Agnew v Commissioner of Inland Revenue*; sub nom. *Re
Brumark Investment Ltd* (*Agnew*).[18] Lord Millett described this inquiry as
follows[19]:

> "The question is not merely one of construction. In deciding whether a
> charge is a fixed charge or a floating charge, the Court is engaged in a
> two-stage process. At the first stage it must construe the instrument of

---

[15] For rectification generally, see *Swainland Builders Ltd v Freehold Properties Ltd* [2002] 2
E.G.L.R 71 (CA); *Homburg Houtimport v Agrosin Private* [2004] 1 A.C. 715 (HL); and *Chartbrook
v Persimmon Homes* [2009] 1 A.C. 1101 (HL). Rectification will generally not be permitted if it
would prejudice a bona fide purchaser of the legal estate for value who has acquired an interest in
the property dealt with in the instrument sought to be rectified without notice of the facts giving
rise to the right to seek rectification. The court may also refuse rectification of a debenture
following liquidation of the company on the grounds that it would prejudice unsecured creditors
who acquired an interest in the statutory trust that arises over the assets of the company upon
winding up: see *J.J. Leonard Properties Pty Ltd v Leonard (W.A.) Pty Ltd* (1987) 5 A.C.L.C. 838.
[16] *R. v Knightsbridge Crown Court Ex p. Marcrest Properties Ltd* [1983] 1 W.L.R. 300 (CA),
308, citing *Snook v London and West Riding Investments Ltd* [1967] 2 Q.B. 786 (CA), 802. See
also the dicta of the Court of Appeal in *Welsh Development Agency v Export Finance Co Ltd*
[1992] B.C.C. 270 (CA) and *Orion Finance v Crown Financial Management Ltd* [1996] B.C.C
621 (CA). For a discussion of sham arrangements, see *Conaglen, Sham Trusts* [2008] C.L.J. 176.
[17] *National Westminster Bank Plc v Jones* [2001] 1 B.C.L.C. 98, [39]–[40] per Neuberger J.,
(appeal dismissed on other grounds, [2002] 1 B.C.L.C. 55 (CA)). In *Orion Finance v Crown
Financial Management Ltd* [1996] B.C.C 621 (CA), Millett L.J. described a sham as "deceptive
language by which the parties have attempted to conceal the true nature of the transaction into
which they have entered".
[18] *Agnew v Commissioner of Inland Revenue*; sub nom. *Re Brumark Investment Ltd* [2001] 2
A.C. 710 (PC).
[19] *Agnew v Commissioner of Inland Revenue*; sub nom. *Re Brumark Investment Ltd* [2001] 2
A.C. 710 (PC).

charge and seek to gather the intentions of the parties from the language they have used. But the object at this stage of the process is not to discover whether the parties intended to create a fixed or a floating charge. It is to ascertain the nature of the rights and obligations which the parties intended to grant each other in respect of the charged assets. Once these have been ascertained, the Court can then embark on the second stage of the process, which is one of categorisation. This is a matter of law. It does not depend on the intention of the parties. If their intention, properly gathered from the language of the instrument, is to grant the company rights in respect of the charged assets which are inconsistent with the nature of a fixed charge, then the charge cannot be a fixed charge however they may have chosen to describe it."

In the case of a charge, the relevant background for the purposes of construing the documents will include the terms of the company's memorandum and articles of association, the nature of its business, the actual and anticipated relationship between the company and the chargee, and other contemporaneous banking documents such as any facility or overdraft agreement.[20] The approach to categorisation outlined by Lord Millett means that the court will have little, if any, regard to the label used by the parties,[21] but will consider the rights and obligations created in the light of the "touchstone" of whether the assets charged or their proceeds are available to the chargor without the specific consent of the chargee.[22] It is suggested that whilst the legal test is to be applied having regard to the commercial substance of the matter, the economic effect of a transaction is not a basis for characterizing a charge as either fixed or floating.[23]

A possible third issue, which may arise in some cases, is the result of a dictum of Lord Millett in *Agnew*. Lord Millett indicated that a valid fixed charge over book debts required payment of the proceeds into a "blocked account": this requirement is considered further below. Lord Millett added, however, that a provision for a blocked account would not be enough "if it is not operated as one in fact".[24] It would therefore seem that the court might have **3–009**

---

[20] See, e.g. *United Builders Pty Ltd v Mutual Acceptance Ltd* (1979) 33 A.L.R. 1 (High Court of Australia); *Boambee Bay Resort Pty Ltd v Equus Financial Services Ltd* (1991) 6 A.S.C.R. 532; (1992) 10 A.C.L.C. 56 (NSW CA); *Re GE Tunbridge Ltd* [1994] B.C.C. 563; *Re Cimex Tissues Ltd* [1994] B.C.C. 626; *Re Cosslett (Contractors) Ltd* [1998] Ch. 495 (CA); *Re Spectrum Plus Ltd (In Liquidation)* [2005] 2 A.C. 680 (HL), [55] and [56], per Lord Hope and [156]–[159], per Lord Walker; *Gray v GTP Group, Re F2G Realisations Ltd* [2011] 1 B.C.L.C. 313.

[21] The question is usually whether a charge which is described by the parties as a fixed or specific charge is, in law a floating charge. But the issue may (unusually) also arise the other way around: see *The Russell Cooke Trust Co Limited v Elliot* [2007] 2 B.C.L.C. 637.

[22] In accordance with the test set out in *Agnew* and in *Re Spectrum Plus Ltd (In Liquidation)* [2005] 2 A.C. 680 (HL) (see below). See also Moss, "Fictions and Floating Charges", Ch.1 in Getzler and Payne (eds), *Company Charges, Spectrum and Beyond*, (Oxford University Press, 2006) at pp.6–7.

[23] Moss, "Fictions and Floating Charges", Ch.1 in Getzler and Payne (eds), *Company Charges, Spectrum and Beyond* (Oxford University Press, 2006), pp.7–8. See also *Beconwood Securities Pty v ANZ Banking Group* [2008] FCA 594 (Federal Court of Australia).

[24] *Agnew v Commissioner of Inland Revenue*; sub nom. *Re Brumark Investment Ltd* [2001] 2 A.C. 710 (PC), [48].

some regard to the conduct of the parties after the execution of the charge, but Lord Millett did not explain on what basis this was to take place.

3–010   Unless Lord Millett was intending some radical departure from the ordinary principles of construction of documents that the nature of the charge is to be ascertained at the date upon which it was created,[25] his observation must have been intended to have effect in one (or more) of three ways: either as a reference to the cases on "sham" agreements, where the court can look at conduct after the execution of the charge as evidence in order to ascertain whether the parties genuinely intended to be bound by the document in question; or as a reference to cases in which the parties subsequently vary the character of their agreement; or cases where the chargee waives, or is estopped from asserting his right to a fixed charge.[26]

3–011   Sham agreements have been considered above. In the case of variation, the courts have usually been slow to infer that any fundamental change in the nature of the transaction has taken place merely because, in commercial practice, the parties have occasionally departed from the strict terms of the contract. For example, in *Lloyd's and Scottish Finance Ltd v Cyril Lord Carpets Sales Ltd*[27] the parties had set up a block-discounting arrangement. Although there had been "some inconsistency" with the contractual arrangements and "rough edges" in the way that business had been done, given the flexibility of the block-discounting agreement and the large number of transactions involved, the House of Lords was not prepared to conclude that the parties had abandoned the block-discounting agreement as the basis of their relationship. In the case of estoppel, a party seeking to establish the alleged estoppel would have to show a representation, or at least a common assumption, and reliance on that. Furthermore, an estoppel does not necessarily operate in favour of parties other than those who have relied on the representation or assumption, though it may do so.[28]

3–012   It remains to be seen whether Lord Millett's dictum gives rise to any greater willingness on the part of the courts to infer that a variation of the terms or effect of a fixed charge has taken place, whether by agreement or subsequent waiver or estoppel, so that the charge originally granted as a fixed charge has, in effect, become a floating charge. Such an approach would give rise to substantial problems in practice. There might well be issues as to whether, and

---

[25] A proposition that has been rejected in England *(Beam Tube Products* [2006] B.C.C. 615 and *Re Harmony Care Homes Ltd* [2010] B.C.C. 358) and in Australia *(Bowesco Pty v Zohar* [2007] FCAFC 1 (Federal Court of Australia)).

[26] See Moss, "Fictions and Floating Charges", Ch.1 in Getzler and Payne (eds), *Company Charges, Spectrum and Beyond* (Oxford University Press, 2006), pp.5–6. See also Berg, "The Cuckoo in the Nest of Corporate Insolvency: Some Aspects of the Spectrum Case" [2006] J.B.L. 22.

[27] *Lloyd's and Scottish Finance Ltd v Cyril Lord Carpets Sales Ltd* [1992] B.C.L.C. 609—a decision of House of Lords of March 29, 1979, also noted at (1979) 129 N.L.J. 366 and (1980) 130 N.L.J. 207. "A right is not diminished because for a period its existence or full extent is not appreciated", per Lord Morris in *Wickman Machine Tool Sales v Schuler* [1974] A.C. 235 (HL), 260, cited by Knox J. in *Re A Company (No.005009 of 1987)* (1988) 4 B.C.C. 424. See also the *Atlantic Computer Systems* case [1992] Ch. 505 (CA), 534 discussed below para.3–038.

[28] See, generally J. McGhee, *Snell's Equity*, 32nd edn (London: Sweet & Maxwell, 2010), Ch.12.

if so, when, the floating charge required registration under the Companies Act 2006. Problems might also arise given that (unless the context otherwise requires) the definition of a floating charge for the purposes of the Insolvency Act is a charge which "as created" or "on its creation" was a floating charge.[29]

Although it will be a question of construction and characterisation of the individual clause in each case, as a general proposition the courts have tended to construe charging clauses on an "all or nothing" basis. As such, a charging clause in a debenture which simply lists a number of different types of assets and purports to subject them to a fixed charge will not be held to have created a fixed charge over any of the assets unless all of the assets within the clause are properly subject to a fixed charge.[30]   **3–013**

(a)   Fixed charges

In the leading case of *Re Yorkshire Woolcombers Association* sub nom. *Illingworth v Houldsworth*, a fixed charge[31] was described as a charge that "without more fastens on ascertained and defined property or property capable of being ascertained and defined".[32] The fixed charge creates an immediate interest in the chargee, either at once in the case of existing property or, in the case of future property, at the point of acquisition of that property by the company.[33]   **3–014**

The concept of a fixed charge fits best where the charged asset is part of the enduring capital structure of the company, rather than where the charged asset is one which will come and go in the normal routine of business operations.[34] However, as a matter of law the assets which may be the subject of a fixed

---

[29] See s.251 of and para.111(1) of Sch.B1 to the 1986 Act. See also per Knox J. in *Re New Bullas Trading Ltd* [1993] B.C.C. 251, referring to the priority given to preferential debts by reference to whether a charge "as created" was a floating charge. The problems are similar to those discussed in relation to the re-flotation of crystallised floating charges in paras 3–081 to 3–085, below. See also Atherton and Mokal, "Charges over Chattels: Issues in the Fixed/Floating Jurisprudence" (2005) 26 Comp. Law. 10.

[30] In *Re ASRS Establishment Ltd (In Administrative Receivership and Liquidation)* [2000] 1 B.C.L.C. 727 at first instance, Park J. favoured the "all or nothing" approach. The point was left open on appeal: see [2002] B.C.C. 64 (CA). The "all or nothing" approach to construction was touched upon in the House of Lords decision in *Smith (Administrator of Cosslett (Contractors) Ltd) v Bridgend CBC* [2002] 1 A.C. 336 (HL), [44] in which Lord Hoffmann thought that it was not possible to construe the relevant clause of the debenture as creating a charge over the coal-washing machines that was different in nature from the charge over other plant and machinery included within the same clause. In *Re Beam Tube Products Ltd* [2006] B.C.C. 615, [33] Blackburne J. also favoured the "all or nothing" approach. Walton, "Fixed charges over assets other than book debts–is possession nine-tenths of the law?" (2005) 21(4) *Insolvency Law and Practice* 117 suggests that severance of such a clause may be possible but that a chargee would be well advised to draft separate charging clauses in a debenture, each relating to different types of asset.

[31] Sometimes referred to as a "specific" charge. In this context, the terms "fixed" and "specific" are interchangeable: see *Re ASRS Establishment Ltd* [2000] 1 B.C.L.C. 727, per Park J., whose decision was upheld on appeal, [2002] B.C.C. 64 (CA).

[32] *Re Yorkshire Woolcombers Association* sub nom. *Illingworth v Houldsworth* [1904] A.C. 355 (HL), 358, per Lord Macnaughten.

[33] *Tailby v Official Receiver* (1888) 13 App. Cas. 523.

[34] See *Re ASRS Establishment Ltd* [2000] 1 B.C.L.C. 727, 732 (above) per Park J.; *Arthur D. Little Ltd v Ableco Finance LLC* [2003] Ch. 217 (shares in subsidiary subject to a fixed and not a floating charge).

charge are not limited to any particular category or description.[35] It is conceptually possible to create a fixed charge over a specified class of assets, coupled with a limited licence to the chargor to deal with those charged assets. Nevertheless, even large assets or assets which are part of the company's capital structure may be held to be subject to a floating charge if the essential element of chargee control over the charged asset is missing (see below).[36]

(b) Floating charges

3–015 The floating charge is not a creature of statute, but, as indicated by Lord Scott in *Re Spectrum Plus Ltd (In Liquidation)* (*"Spectrum"*), it was "bred by equity lawyers and judges out of the needs of the commercial and industrial entrepreneurs" in the 1870s.[37] Lord Scott continued[38]:

> "By the middle of the 19th century industrial and commercial expansion in this country had led to an increasing need by companies for more capital. Subscription for share capital could not meet this need and loan capital had to be raised. But the lenders required security for their loans. Traditional security, in the form of legal or equitable charges on the borrowers' fixed assets, whether land or goods, could not meet the need. The greater part of most entrepreneurial companies' assets would consist of raw materials, work in progress, stock-in-trade and trade debts. These were circulating assets, replaced in the normal course of business and constantly changing. Assets of this character were not amenable to being the subject of traditional forms of security. Equity, however, intervened . . .
>
> *Holroyd v Marshall* (1862) 10 HLC 191 opened the way to the grant by companies of security over any class of circulating assets that the chargor company might possess. Acceptance that it was possible to do this became established by the 1870s . . .
>
> The two features mentioned by Gifford LJ in *In re Panama New Zealand and Australian Royal Mail Co* (1870) 5 Ch App 318 became the hallmark of the new form of security, namely, (1) a charge on the chargor company's assets, or a specified class of assets, present and future and (2)

---

[35] See, e.g. *State Bank of India v Lisbellow Ltd* [1989] 2 H.K.L.R. 604, per Godfrey J. (holding that a textile "quota" granted by the authorities in Hong Kong was capable of being the subject of a fixed charge). But the contract creating a chose in action may prohibit the assignment or charging of the chose: see *Linden Gardens Trust Ltd v Lenesta Sludge Disposals Ltd* [1994] 1 A.C. 85 (HL). In such a case, the charge would not attach to the non-assignable contractual rights: see *Re Turner Corporation Ltd* (1995) 17 A.C.S.R. 761, unless the charge was lawfully entered into before the contract creating the relevant chose in action was entered into: see *Foamcrete (UK) Ltd v Thrust Engineering Ltd* [2002] B.C.C. 221 (CA). A charge may still be created over a purportedly non-assignable right if there had been effective waiver of the prohibition on assignment, or if an estoppel precludes reliance on the prohibition: see *Orion Finance Ltd v Crown Financial Management Ltd* [1994] B.C.C. 897; [1996] B.C.C. 621 (CA).

[36] In *Smith (Administrator of Cosslett (Contractors) Ltd) v Bridgend CBC* [2002] 1 A.C. 336 (HL) a charge over two huge coal-washing machines was held to be a floating charge for this reason.

[37] For an account of the historical development of floating charges, see R.C. Nolan, "Property in a Fund" (2004) 120 L.Q.R. 108, 120–124.

[38] *Re Spectrum Plus Ltd (In Liquidation)* [2005] 2 A.C. 680 (HL), [95]–[97].

the right of the chargor company to continue to use the charged assets for the time being owned by it and to dispose of them for its normal business purposes until the occurrence of some particular future event. In *In re Colonial Trusts Corporation* (1879) 15 Ch D 465 Jessel MR referred to this form of security as a 'floating security' (see at pp 468, 469 and 472) and in *Moor v Anglo-Italian Bank* (1879) 10 Ch D 681, 687 he contrasted the new form of security with a 'specific charge' on the property of the company.

By the last decade of the 19th century this form of security, Jessel MR's 'floating security', had become firmly established and in regular use."[39]

The classic description of a floating charge is to be found in the decision of the Court of Appeal in *Yorkshire Woolcombers Association Ltd, Re Illingworth v Houldsworth*.[40] Romer L.J. set out three characteristics of a floating charge and indicated that if a charge has all these features it will be a floating charge. He also warned that these features were not an exact definition and need not all be present in a floating charge. The three features are: **3–016**

   (a) that it is a charge on a class of assets of a company present and future[41];

   (b) that the class is one which, in the ordinary course of the business of the company, would be changing from time to time; and

   (c) that it is contemplated that, until some future step is taken by the chargee, the company may carry on its ordinary course of business in respect of the class of charged assets.[42]

---

[39] Although most judicial statements refer to floating charges being granted by companies, there is nothing in the essential nature of the floating charge which means that it could not be granted by an individual or partnership. Nor is there anything in the scope of an individual's or partnership's legal capacity that deprives it of the ability to grant a floating charge where a company can do so. That point is illustrated by the fact that s.344 of the Insolvency Act 1986 expressly recognises that it is possible for an individual or partnership to grant a floating charge over present and future book debts provided that he or it complies with the registration requirements of the bills of sale legislation. There are, however, practical reasons why an individual, or a partnership which includes an individual, cannot grant a floating charge in the conventional form over the entirety of his or the partnership's undertaking and assets. The problem is the formal requirements of the bills of sale legislation which applies to disposals of chattels by individuals. A floating charge granted by an individual which purported to charge present and future property would not comply with the requirement that the charged property must be specifically identified in a schedule in statutory form, because the future property could not be listed. The bills of sale legislation does not, however, apply to companies: *Online Catering Ltd v Acton* [2011] Q.B. 204 (CA). See generally W.J. Gough, *Company Charges*, 2nd edn (London: Butterworths, 1996), pp.52–56; Fitzpatrick, "Why not a Partnership Floating Charge" [1971] JBL 18; J. Weisman, "Floating Charges on Assets of an Individual" (1986) 21 *Israel Law Review* 129; P. Giddins, "Floating mortgages by individuals: are they conceptually possible?" (2011) 26 BJIB&FL 125.

[40] *Re Yorkshire Woolcombers Association Ltd, Illingworth v Houldsworth* [1903] 2 Ch. 284 (CA), 295; and see the comments in *Re Bond Worth Ltd* [1980] Ch. 228, per Slade J.

[41] See also *Re Panama, New Zealand and Australia Royal Mail Co* (1870) L.R. 5 Ch. App. 318.

[42] It is implicit that if the company carries on its business in the ordinary way, it does so for its own account. For a discussion of the concept of "ordinary course of business" see paras 3–023 to 3–025 below.

In the same case, Vaughan-Williams L.J. took a similar approach, stating[43]:

> "I do not think that for a 'specific security' you need to have a security of a subject-matter which is then in existence. I mean by 'then' at the time of the execution of the security; but what you do require to make a specific security is that the security[44] whenever it has come into existence, and has been identified or appropriated as a security, shall never thereafter at the wish of the mortgagor cease to be a security. If at the wish of the mortgagor he can dispose of it and prevent it being any longer a security, although something else may be substituted more or less for it, that is not a 'specific security'."

3–017 The passages referred to above were cited in *Re Cosslett (Contractors) Ltd*[45] and Millett L.J. (as he then was) continued:

> "The essence of a floating charge is that it is a charge, not on any particular asset, but on a fluctuating body of assets which remain under the management and control of the chargor, and which the chargor has the right to withdraw from the security despite the existence of the charge. The essence of a fixed charge is that the charge is on a particular asset or class of assets which the chargor cannot deal with free from the charge without the consent of the chargee. The question is not whether the chargor has complete freedom to carry on his business as he chooses, but whether the chargee is in control of the charged assets."

3–018 In *Agnew*, Lord Millett also stressed the importance of Romer L.J.'s third characteristic, stating that[46]:

> "It is the third characteristic which is the hallmark of a floating charge and serves to distinguish it from a fixed charge. Since the existence of a fixed charge would make it impossible for the company to carry on business in the ordinary way without the consent of the charge holder, it follows that its ability to [do] so without such consent is inconsistent with the fixed nature of the charge."

Lord Millett also indicated that[47]:

> "in construing a debenture to see whether it creates a fixed or a floating charge, the only intention which is relevant is the intention that the

---

[43] *Yorkshire Woolcombers Association Ltd, Re Illingworth v Houldsworth* [1903] 2 Ch. 284 (CA), 295.

[44] In this context, "security" must mean the asset which is the subject of the charge.

[45] *Re Cosslett (Contractors) Ltd* [1998] Ch. 495 (CA), 510c.

[46] *Agnew v Commissioner of Inland Revenue*; sub nom. *Re Brumark Investment Ltd* [2001] 2 A.C. 710 (PC), [13].

[47] *Agnew v Commissioner of Inland Revenue*; sub nom. *Re Brumark Investment Ltd* [2001] 2 A.C. 710 (PC), [32].

company should be free to deal with the charged assets and withdraw them from the security without the consent of the holder of the charge; or, to put the question another way, whether the charged assets were intended to be under the control of the company or of the charge holder."

This emphasis was repeated by the members of the House of Lords in *Spectrum*. **3–019** Lord Scott said that he was inclined to think that if a security had Romer L.J.'s third characteristic, it would qualify as a floating charge and could not be a fixed charge. Lord Scott continued[48]:

"In my opinion, the essential characteristic of a floating charge, the characteristic that distinguishes it from a fixed charge, is that the asset subject to the charge is not finally appropriated as a security for the payment of the debt until the occurrence of some future event. In the meantime the chargor is left free to use the charged asset and to remove it from the security. On this point I am in respectful agreement with Lord Millett."

Lord Walker stated[49]:

"Under a fixed charge the assets charged as security are permanently appropriated to the payment of the sum charged, in such a way as to give the chargee a proprietary interest in the assets. So long as the charge remains unredeemed, the assets can be released from the charge only with the active concurrence of the chargee . . . under a fixed charge that will be a matter for the chargee to decide for itself.

Under a floating charge, by contrast, the chargee does not have the same power to control the security for its own benefit. The chargee has a proprietary interest, but its interest is in a fund of circulating capital, and unless and until the chargee intervenes (on crystallisation of the charge) it is for the trader, and not the bank, to decide how to run its business."

Accordingly, in construing the terms of the charge, it will be necessary to iden- **3–020** tify the nature of the class of charged assets and to ascertain whether the parties have agreed that the charged assets must be retained by the company as the subject of a specific charge, or whether it is intended that the company be at liberty to deal with the assets, free from the chargee's security. Any unfettered or significant commercial freedom in the chargor to deal with a fluctuating class of assets without the consent of the chargee will be inconsistent with the existence of a fixed charge over those assets. The critical issue is the nature and extent of the chargee's control of the assets in question. Resolution of this issue will therefore require an examination of the nature and extent of the

---

[48] *Re Spectrum Plus Ltd (In Liquidation)* [2005] 2 A.C. 680 (HL), [111].
[49] *Re Spectrum Plus Ltd (In Liquidation)* [2005] 2 A.C. 680 (HL), [138]–[139].

restrictions placed by the charge documents and any ancillary agreements upon the dealings by the company with the charged assets.

3–021   The emphasis placed upon the third of Romer L.J.'s characteristics and its elaboration in *Agnew* and *Spectrum* has reinforced a trend in the authorities under which the courts have been unwilling to characterise charges which permit the debtor to deal with a fluctuating class of charged assets in the ordinary course of business as fixed charges with a licence to deal. The tendency will now be to characterise such charges as floating charges and cases decided prior to *Agnew* or *Spectrum* must be regarded with some caution.[50]

3–022   An important issue which the cases currently leave unresolved is whether, in order to maintain a fixed charge, it is necessary for the consent by the chargee to be given on an item-by-item basis as and when the chargor seeks to remove the assets from the charge, or whether it is permissible that consent can be given in advance pursuant to some formula or mechanism. The issue is particularly likely to arise in relation to book debts and the operation of "blocked" accounts.[51]

In *Spectrum*, Lord Walker referred to the need, if there was to be a fixed charge, for the "positive" concurrence of the chargee.[52] The need for such positive steps might be seen as a function of the need to demonstrate that the chargee retains control over the charged assets. Whilst it will plainly be fatal to a fixed charge if the release operates by default unless the chargee intervenes (negative consent), it is suggested that there is nothing in principle that prevents an agreement that consent will be given by reference to specified criteria. However, given the overriding need for the chargee to demonstrate continuing control over the charged assets, the less precise the criteria for consent, and hence the greater the latitude given to the chargor to determine whether and when particular assets or amounts of fungibles or money can be released, the less likely the court will be to uphold the fixed nature of the charge. The court will also doubtless be astute to detect automatic arrangements which seek to achieve the same commercial effect as an unrestricted right for the chargor to deal with the charged assets or their proceeds.[53]

---

[50] See, e.g. the discussion in *R. in Right of British Columbia v Federal Business Development Bank* (1987) 65 C.B.R. 201 (CA) British Columbia and the comments in *Spectrum* by Lord Scott at [98] and by Lord Walker at [141] to the effect that there is a public interest which overrides unrestrained freedom of contract, namely to ensure that preferential creditors obtain the measure of protection which Parliament intended them to have when it gave them priority over floating charge assets. For a discussion of this topic from a historical perspective, suggesting that in principle it ought to be possible to have a fixed charge with a licence to deal as an alternative to a floating charge in relation to a fluctuating class of assets, see Gregory & Walton, "Fixed Charges over Changing Assets: The Possession and Control Heresy" [1998] C.F.I.L.R. 68. It is suggested that such historical analysis cannot be reconciled with the approach adopted in the more recent cases such as *Cosslett (Contractors)*, *Agnew* and *Spectrum*.

[51] See paras 3–030 to 3–039 below.

[52] *Re Spectrum Plus Ltd (In Liquidation)* [2005] 2 A.C. 680 (HL), [140].

[53] As indicated above, the approach taken in *Agnew* and *Spectrum* is to characterise charges which permit the debtor to deal with a fluctuating class of charged assets in the ordinary course of business as floating charges rather than fixed charges with a licence to deal.

As has been seen above, one critical concept under the approach set out in **3–023**
Re Yorkshire Woolcombers, as endorsed in *Agnew* and *Spectrum*, is the freedom
of a company which has granted a floating charge to deal with the charged
assets "in the ordinary course of business" of the company. This right is the
touchstone by which to distinguish floating charges from fixed charges.
However it should not be forgotten that it is only transactions that fall within
this concept that will be implictly permitted by a floating charge. The meaning
of this expression was considered by Etherton J. in *Ashborder BV v Green Gas
Power Ltd*.[54]

After a review of the authorities, Etherton J. indicated that it would be
unwise to attempt any particular or comprehensive formulation of the test
for determining whether a transaction fell within the ordinary course of a
company's business for the purposes of a floating charge. However, he ventured
some conclusions on the basis of the decided cases. Etherton J. said this was a
mixed question of fact and law, which it was convenient to approach in two
stages:

". . . first, to ascertain, as a matter of fact, whether an objective observer,
with knowledge of the company, its memorandum of association and its
business, would view the transaction as having taken place in the
ordinary course of its business, and, if so [. . .] second, to consider
whether, on the proper interpretation of the document creating the floating
charge, applying standard techniques of interpretation, the parties nonetheless did not intend that the transaction should be regarded as being in
the ordinary course of the company's business for the purpose of the
charge."[55]

Etherton J. also said that, subject to any special considerations resulting
from the proper interpretation of the charge document, there was no reason
why an unprecedented or exceptional transaction could not, in appropriate
circumstances, be regarded as falling within the ordinary course of business
of a company; nor did the mere fact that a transaction would, in a liquidation,
be liable to be avoided as a fraudulent or otherwise wrongful preference
or that it was made in breach of fiduciary duty by one or more directors
necessarily preclude it from doing so. Finally, he concluded that transactions
which are intended to bring to an end, or have the effect of bringing to an end,
a company's business are not in the ordinary course of its business.[56]

---

[54] *Ashborder BV v Green Gas Power Ltd* [2005] B.C.C. 634. See also the discussion in *Willmott
v London Celluloid Co* (1887) L.R. 34 Ch. D. 147; *Hamer v London City and Midland Bank Ltd*
(1918) 118 L.T. 571; *Re Cummins* (1986) 62 A.L.R. 129; *Re GE Tunbridge Ltd* [1994] B.C.C. 563;
and the dicta of Millett L.J. in *Re Cosslett (Contractors) Ltd* [1998] Ch. 495 (CA) referred to above
in para.3–017.
[55] *Ashborder BV v Green Gas Power Ltd* [2005] B.C.C. 634, [227].
[56] The expression "ordinary course of business" is also used in the New Zealand voidable preference provisions and in that context was considered by the Privy Council in *Countrywide Banking
v Dean* [1998] A.C. 338. The Privy Council suggested that the transaction must be such that it
would be viewed by an objective observer as having taken place in the ordinary course of business,
that the prior practices of the particular company are relevant as well as those of the commercial

3–024   In accordance with this approach, it is clear that the payment of trade debts and the sales of stock in trade[57] (including sales on hire purchase)[58] will usually be regarded as being in the ordinary course of business.[59] However, it is essential that such disposition be made with a view to the continuation of the company's business as a going concern.[60] Thus, for example, the transfer by a company of the whole of its stock back to its supplier in circumstances where the company was insolvent and there was no prospect of the company continuing to distribute the products would not be a transaction in the ordinary course of the company's business.[61] Similarly, the sale of assets or a part of the business of a company at an undervalue or on extended terms as to payment at a time when the company is insolvent or facing insolvency is unlikely to be regarded as a sale in the ordinary course of business.[62] Likewise, the transmission of funds by a provisional liquidator to various bank accounts in order to circumvent the freezing of the company's bank accounts is likely to be outside the usual course of the company's business.[63]

3–025   The grant of specific charges over some or all of a company's assets may be regarded as being in the ordinary course of its business,[64] as will the subsequent grant of a floating charge over some part of the same assets, even if it is expressed to rank in priority to the earlier charge.[65] However, the creation of a subsequent floating charge which is expressed to rank on an equal footing with an earlier floating charge over the same assets will apparently be regarded as inconsistent with the bargain with the earlier chargee under which the company was granted the freedom to deal with its assets in the ordinary course of its business.[66]

---

world in general, and that the focus must be on the operational activities of businesses as going concerns not in response to abnormal financial difficulties. See also *Waikato Freight v Meltzer* [2001] 2 N.Z.L.R. 541 and *Carter Holt Harvey v Fatupaito* (2003) 9 N.Z.C.L.C. 263. Compare also the approach of the Privy Council to the words "in the ordinary course of its [i.e. the particular company's] business" in the context of the then Australian law on financial assistance in *Steen v Law* [1964] A.C. 287 (PC).

[57] *Willmott v London Celluloid Co* (1887) L.R. 34 Ch. D. 147 (CA); *Hamer v London City and Midland Bank Ltd* (1918) 118 L.T. 571; *Re Old Bushmills Distillery Co* [1897] I.R. 488; *R. in Right of British Columbia v Federal Business Development Bank* (1987) 65 C.B.R. 201.

[58] *Dempsey v Traders' Finance Corp Ltd* [1933] N.Z.L.R. 1258.

[59] See also *Mac-Jordan Construction Ltd v Brookmount Erostin Ltd* [1992] B.C.L.C. 350, in which the Court of Appeal thought that the existence of floating charge would not, until crystallisation, have prevented a property development company from fulfilling its contractual obligations to create a trust fund into which to pay retention monies due to a builder.

[60] It has been said that a floating charge is founded upon what is taken to be the mutual assumption of the parties that the company's business will continue as a going concern: per Sheller J.A. in *Fire Nymph Products Ltd v The Heating Centre Pty Ltd* (1992) 7 A.C.S.R. 365, 376.

[61] *Fire Nymph Products Ltd v The Heating Centre Pty Ltd* (1992) 7 A.C.S.R. 365.

[62] *Torzillu Pty Ltd v Brynac Pty Ltd* (1983) 8 A.C.L.R. 52.

[63] *Re Bartlett Estates Pty Ltd* (1988) 14 A.C.L.R. 512.

[64] *Cox Moore v Peruvian Corp Ltd* [1908] 1 Ch. 604; *Reynolds Bros (Motors) Pty Ltd v Esanda Ltd* (1983) 8 A.C.L.R. 422; (1983) 1 A.C.L.C. 1, 1,333.

[65] *Re Automatic Bottle Makers Ltd* [1926] Ch. 412 (CA).

[66] *Re Benjamin Cope & Sons Ltd* [1914] 1 Ch. 800.

The precise conceptual nature of a floating charge has occasioned consider- **3–026** able academic[67] and judicial[68] debate. It is clear (not least from the wording of s.40(1) of the Insolvency Act 1986) that a floating charge, when executed, is a present security and not merely an agreement to create a future charge.[69] Accordingly, even whilst the charge is still floating, the debenture-holder may obtain an injunction to restrain the company from dealing with the assets other than in the ordinary course of business,[70] or may obtain the appointment by the court of a receiver where the security is in jeopardy.[71]

Differing views have been expressed (and continue to be expressed even **3–027** after *Agnew* and *Spectrum*) as to whether, and if so to what extent, a floating charge creates any form of *proprietary* interest in any particular assets covered by its terms before it crystallises. Whether or not the interest is regarded as proprietary for the purposes of any particular statutory definition will depend not just on the nature of the interest in question but also on the terms of the particular definition.[72] As a matter of general law, the importance of a proprietary interest is that it may entitle the holder of the interest to assert the

---

[67] See, e.g. J.H. Farrar (1980) 1 Comp. Law. 83; W.J. Gough, *Company Charges*, 2nd edn (London: Butterworths, 1996) pp.97–101; E. Ferran, "Floating Charges, The Nature of the Security" [1988] C.L.J 213 and Company Law and Corporate Finance (1999) at 509–512; S. Worthington, "Floating Charges: An Alternative Theory" [1994] C.L.J 81 and Proprietary Interests in Commercial Transactions (1996) p.74ff; R.C. Nolan, "Property in a Fund" (2004) 120 L.Q.R. 108; Goode, *Legal Problems of Credit and Security*, 4th edn (London: Sweet & Maxwell, 2008), paras 4–03 to 4–06; Gullifer and Payne, *Corporate Finance Law: Principles and Policy* (Hart Publishing, 2011), p.242ff; *Snell's Equity*, 32nd edn (London: Sweet & Maxwell, 2010) Ch.40 (R.C. Nolan).

[68] Cases which addressed the issue before *Agnew* and *Spectrum* include *Driver v Broad* [1893] 1 Q.B. 744 (CA); *Re Yorkshire Woolcombers' Association Ltd* [1903] 2 Ch. 284 (CA); *Illingworth v Houldsworth* [1904] A.C. 355 (HL), 358; *Evans v Rival Granite Quarries Ltd* [1910] 2 K.B. 979 (CA); *Re Dawson* [1915] 1 Ch. 626 (CA); *Re Manurewa Transport Ltd* [1971] N.Z.L.R. 909; *Cretanor Maritime Co Ltd v Irish Marine Management Ltd* [1978] 1 W.L.R. 966 (CA); *Landall Holdings v Caratti* [1979] W.A.R. 97; *United Builders Pty Ltd v Mutual Acceptance Ltd* (1980) 144 C.L.R. 673; *Hamilton v Hunter* (1982) 7 A.C.L.R. 295; *Re Margart Pty Ltd, Re Hamilton v Westpac Banking Corp* (1984) 2 A.C.L.C. 709; [1985] B.C.L.C. 314; *Tricontinental Corp Ltd v Federal Commissioner of Taxation* (1987) 5 A.C.L.C. 555; *R. in Right of British Columbia v Federal Business Development Bank* (1987) 65 C.B.R. 201; *Re Atlantic Computer Systems Plc* [1992] Ch. 505 (CA); *Fire Nymph Products Ltd v The Heating Centre Pty Ltd* (1992) 7 A.C.S.R. 365; *Re Atlantic Medical Ltd* [1992] B.C.C. 653; *Re New Bullas Trading Ltd* [1993] B.C.C. 251; [1994] B.C.C. 36 (CA); *Royal Trust Bank v National Westminster Bank Plc* [1995] B.C.C. 128 and [1996] B.C.C. 613 (CA).

[69] *Evans v Rival Granite Quarries Ltd* [1910] 2 K.B. 979 (CA), 999 per Buckley L.J.; *Re Cimex Tissues Ltd* [1994] B.C.C. 626, [30]. See also Goode, *Legal Problems of Credit and Security*, edited by Gullifer, 4th edn (London: Sweet & Maxwell, 2008), paras 4–03 to 4–06. In *Spectrum*, [107], Lord Scott appeared to hold that there was no difference in categorisation between the grant of a fixed charge expressed to come into existence on a future event in relation to a specified class of assets owned by the company at that time and the grant of a floating charge over the specified class of assets with crystallisation taking place on the occurrence of that event. It is respectfully suggested that this dictum should not be read as suggesting that a floating charge is not a present security. For a case which illustrates the importance of distinguishing between a present security and an agreement to create a future security, see *Rehman v Chamberlain* [20011] EWHC 2318 (Ch).

[70] *Hubbuck v Helms* (1887) 56 L.T. 232; *Re Woodroffes (Musical Instruments) Ltd* [1986] 1 Ch. 366, 378A, per Nourse J.; *Atkins v Mercantile Credit Ltd* (1985) 10 A.C.L.R. 153.

[71] *Edwards v Standard Rolling Stock Syndicate* [1893] 1 Ch. 574; *Re Victoria Steamboats Ltd* [1897] 1 Ch. 158; *Re London Pressed Hinge Co Ltd* [1905] 1 Ch. 576.

[72] *CPT Custodian Pty Ltd v Commissioner of State Revenue* [2005] HCA 53; (2005) 221 ALR 196 (High Court of Australia).

interest to defeat rival claims to the asset in question. So the issue may be important in resolving questions of priority between the chargee and third parties who acquire assets from the company prior to crystallisation of the charge, as well as when considering the question of whether a crystallised floating charge can be re-floated or de-crystallised.[73]

3–028   It is suggested[74] that a floating charge creates a species of immediate but limited equitable proprietary interest in favour of the chargee in the charged assets owned by the company and falling within the description in the charge.[75] That property interest does not confer an immediate entitlement on the part of the chargee to have recourse to any specific asset to satisfy the secured debt and does not prevent the company from exercising its right, as owner, to deal with and dispose of the particular assets within the class from time to time, provided that it does so in the ordinary course of its business. In other words, the chargee has equitable rights in the charged assets from the moment the floating charge is created, but until the charge crystallises, those rights are limited and subordinate to the powers of the company to deal with the assets consistently with the terms of the charge. The limited equitable interest created by a floating charge is, however, capable of taking priority over the claims of a third party who acquires property falling within the scope of the charge from the chargor company other than in the ordinary course of the company's business and if the third party has actual or constructive notice of the nature of the charge and is aware of the circumstances of transfer.[76]

---

[73] W.J. Gough, *Company Charges*, 2nd edn (London: Butterworths, 1996), takes the view that a charge has no property interest of any form until crystallisation. This view has received some judicial support in Australia: see *Lyford v Commonwealth Bank of Australia* (1995) 17 A.C.S.R. 211, 217–218; and *Wily v St George Partnership Banking Ltd* (1997) 26 A.C.S.R. 1, 5–10, which was, however, doubted on appeal, (1999) 30 A.C.S.R. 204, 209–214. It has, however, generally been rejected by academic writing in England. Gullifer and Payne, *Corporate Finance Law: Principles and Policy* (Hart Publishing, 2011), pp.245, following Goode, suggests that the chargee has a property interest in a fund (albeit not in any specific assets) and cites Lord Walker's dictum in *Spectrum* at [139] in support. However, the "property interest in a fund" analysis does not answer the underlying question of whether a property rights exists in any of the constituent elements of the fund, and the force of the point is somewhat diminished because Lord Walker also referred to Professor Worthington's analysis in *Proprietary Interests in Commercial Transactions* (1996) which had advanced the view that the floating charge was akin to a defeasible fixed charge, which does not sit entirely easily with the decision in *Spectrum* itself.

[74] The analysis in the text follows a similar line to that advanced by R.C. Nolan: see "Property in a Fund" (2004) 120 L.Q.R. 108; and *Snell's Equity*, 32 edn (London: Sweet & Maxwell, 2010), Ch.40.

[75] Equitable proprietary interests are very varied in their incidents, and it is wrong to assume that every such interest necessarily confers immediate access to the benefits from the assets in which it subsists, or that an interest cannot be proprietary if it does not confer such access. Equally, the legal owner of the assets in which an equitable proprietary interest subsists may well have powers to deal with the assets free of the interest, but that does not affect the description of the interest. See, generally, R.C. Nolan, "Property in a Fund" (2004) 120 L.Q.R. 108 and "Equitable Property" (2006) 122 L.Q.R. 232. So, for example, there is nothing remotely odd in conceiving a limited equitable proprietary interest that confers deferred or contingent rights to benefit from assets conjoined with present rights to control management of those assets if (and only if) their managers act beyond their powers: consider, for example, a remainder interest, or a contingent reminder interest under a trust to which the Trustee Act 2000 applies.

[76] See the discussion in paras 3–051 to 3–057 below. See also *Hamilton v Hunter* (1982) 7 A.C.L.R. 295; *Reynolds Bros (Motors) Pty Ltd v Esanda Ltd* (1983) 8 A.C.L.R. 422; (1983) 1 A.C.L.C. 1, 333.

Under this theory, the floating charge only becomes immediately enforceable in respect of any particular assets on the occurrence of a specified event or events, when it ceases to float (crystallises) and takes on the form of a fixed charge. This brings to an end the rights of the company to deal with the property which is the subject of the charge without the specific consent of the chargee and results in a fixed charge attaching to the particular assets within the scope of the charge at the moment of crystallisation.[77] Consequently, the company is no longer permitted to deal with the specific assets to which the charge has attached and the chargee's fixed security interest now entitles the chargee to have recourse to the assets to discharge the obligations secured by the charge.

In summary, before crystallisation the chargee has an equitable interest in   **3–029**
the assets subject to a floating charge, but this is an interest which is limited in its effect and enforceability because it is subordinated to the company's freedom to deal with its assets in the ordinary course of its business (for its own account). On crystallisation of the floating charge, the company's freedom to deal with the charged assets is ended and the effect and enforceability of the chargee's interest is no longer limited in the same way.

3. PARTICULAR PROBLEMS

(a) Book debts

Many of the reported cases concerning the distinction between fixed and   **3–030**
floating charges relate to charges over book debts and other receivables.[78] In the case of a trading company these may represent a very substantial proportion of the valuable assets of the company, and the issue of the debenture-holder's entitlement to existing and future book debts arising from any continued trading may be of the greatest importance in the receivership or the administration.

The expression "book debt" is not a specifically defined legal term, but is commonly thought to mean:

"a debt arising in the course of a business and due or growing due to the proprietor of that business that . . . would or could in the ordinary course

---

[77] *Illingworth v Houldsworth* [1904] A.C. 355 (HL), 358 per Lord Macnaughten; *Fire Nymph Products Ltd v The Heating Centre Pty Ltd* (1992) 7 A.C.S.R. 365, 373 per Gleeson C.J.

[78] In *Re ASRS Establishment Ltd* [2000] 1 B.C.L.C. 727, affirmed by the Court of Appeal, [2002] B.C.C. 64, the court proceeded on the basis that the same approach to construction of charges applied in the case of charges over other receivables as in the case of charges over book debts. In *Agnew* [2001] 2 A.C. 710 (PC), [38], Lord Millett commented that a charge on uncalled share capital leaves the chargor with the right to make calls, and this could properly be regarded as analogous to a right of a chargor to collect book debts, although he suggested that a charge on uncalled capital normally restricts the chargor's use of receipts. See on this point Walton, "Fixed charges over assets other than book debts—is possession nine-tenths of the law?" (2005) 21(4) I.L. & P. 117, who observes that there is in fact a degree of variation in the drafting of fixed charges over uncalled capital and contends that, following *Agnew* and *Spectrum*, to achieve a fixed charge, not only must the charge instrument impose express restrictions on the chargor's use of receipts, but such restrictions must be shown to be operated in fact.

of such a business be entered in well-kept books relating to that business
... whether it is in fact entered in the books of the business or not".[79]

Monies standing to the credit of the company at its bank (on either a current
"trading" account or a "non-trading" account) are unlikely to fall within the
terms of a charge on "book debts and other debts" which is commonly to be
found in debentures.[80] The normal business or accountancy treatment of such
monies is "cash at bank".[81] That is so even if the monies represent the proceeds
of collection of book debts. Whilst the nature of a charge over book debts will
require the court to have regard to restrictions on dealings with the proceeds of
those book debts, it is perfectly possible to express a charge as attaching solely
to monies once received without it being characterised as a charge over book
debts.[82] Further, the realisation of charged assets by way of a sale by a receiver
will not give rise to a "book debt".[83]

3–031   There is no doubt, at least in England, that there is no objection in principle
to a fixed charge being created over book debts, either existing or future.[84] It
has always been understood that in order to create a valid fixed charge over
book debts, it will be essential for the chargee to retain control over the uncollected book debts and for the company to be prevented from alienating such
receivables without the consent of the chargee, e.g. by factoring, discounting
or selling the same.[85] However, as explained above, as a result of the decisions

---

[79] Per Buckley L.J. in *Independent Automatic Sales v Knowles and Foster* [1962] 1 W.L.R. 974;
Re Falcon Sportswear Pty Ltd (1983) 1 A.C.L.C. 690, 695; *Coakley v Argent Credit Corp Plc*
Unreported June 4, 1998.
[80] *Re Brightlife Ltd* [1987] Ch 200; *Re Permanent Houses (Holdings) Ltd* (1989) 5 B.C.C. 151,
per Hoffmann J.; *Northern Bank Ltd v Ross* [1990] B.C.C. 883 (CA) (NI). See also the comments
of Lord Hoffmann in *Re B.C.C.I. S.A. (No.8)* [1998] A.C. 214 (HL). In the *Permanent Houses* case,
Hoffmann J. was at pains to point out that the issue is essentially one of construction of the terms
of the debenture.
[81] See Balance Sheet formats at Sch.4 to the Companies Act 1985; Sch.4 to the Small Companies
and Groups (Accounts and Directors' Report) Regulations 2008 and Sch.1 to the Large and
Medium-sized Companies and Group (Accounts and Reports) Regulations 2008. It was formerly
questioned whether it was conceptually possible for a book debt due to a company to be charged
in favour of the debtor itself. In *Re Charge Card Services Ltd* [1987] Ch. 150, Millett J. held that
this was not possible, but this was doubted by Dillon L.J. (obiter) in *Welsh Development Agency v
Export Finance Co Ltd* [1992] B.C.C. 270 (CA) and the possibility of such a "charge back" was
accepted by the House of Lords in *Re B.C.C.I. S.A. (No.8)* [1998] A.C. 214 (HL).
[82] In *Re SSSL Realisations (2002) Ltd (In Liquidation)*; sub nom. *Squires v AIG Europe (UK)
Ltd* [[2005] 1 B.C.L.C. 1, Lloyd J. considered whether, if the trust obligation in question had
constituted a charge, it was a charge over book debts. He concluded that in principle it would be
possible to create a charge over a sum of money held by a person once received, without also
creating a charge over the debt in respect of which it was paid. His decision was upheld by the
Court of Appeal: see [2006] Ch. 610 (CA), [122], per Chadwick L.J.
[83] See *Re Falcon Sportswear Pty Ltd* (1983) 1 A.C.L.C. 690.
[84] See *Spectrum* [2005] 2 A.C. 680 (HL), [80], [103] and [104], per Lord Scott; [136], per Lord
Walker; [52] per Lord Hope.
[85] The "rival lines of judicial authority" as to the correct categorisation of a charge over book
debts preceding the House of Lords decision in *Spectrum* [2005] 2 A.C. 680 (HL), were set out by
Lord Scott in [86]–[89] (inclusive) of his speech in that case. One line of authority was based both
on the judgment of Slade J. in *Siebe Gorman & Co Ltd v Barclays Bank Ltd* [1979] 2 Lloyd's Rep.
142, holding that a debenture in typical clearing bank format had created a fixed charge over the
chargor's book debts, as well as on the subsequent judgment of the Court of Appeal in *Re New
Bullas Trading Ltd* [1994] B.C.C. 36, upholding an attempt by a non-bank lender to employ the
conceptual distinction between an uncollected book debt and its proceeds so as to maintain a fixed

in *Agnew*[86] and *Spectrum*[87], it will not be enough for the charge simply to impose restrictions preventing the company from alienating the book debts before they are paid. To create a valid fixed charge it will also be necessary for the charge to contain restrictions on the manner in which the company is entitled to receive and deal with the monies arising on payment of the book debts. The company must be prohibited from dealing with such proceeds and withdrawing them from the charge without the consent of the charge-holder.[88] Merely requiring the chargor to pay the proceeds into its account with the chargee bank will not be sufficient if the chargor is able to draw on its account in the ordinary course of its business.[89]

The logic for this additional requirement in the case of book debts derives   **3–032** from the particular nature of those assets. Like other assets, the value of a book debt can be realised by sale or assignment. However, the value of a book debt can also be realised by collection, upon which the debt is extinguished and replaced by monies (proceeds) in the hands of the creditor. In *Agnew*, Lord Millett dismissed the authorities that had held that it was sufficient to create a fixed charge on book debts that the company should be prohibited from alienating them, whether by assigning, factoring or charging them, but had not sought to go further and also prohibit the company from collecting them and disposing of the proceeds. Lord Millett stated that this approach[90]:

> "makes no commercial sense because alienation and collection are merely different methods of realising a debt by turning it into money, collection being the natural and ordinary method of doing so. A restriction on disposition which nevertheless allows collection and free use of the proceeds is

---

charge on the former notwithstanding that the chargor was left free to deal with the latter. Both decisions were overruled by the House of Lords in *Spectrum*. Their Lordships preferred the second line of authority, which began with *Re Brightlife Ltd* [1987] Ch. 200. In that case, Hoffmann J. (as he then was) held the charge in question to be a floating charge because the chargor was able to collect debts which were subject to the charge, pay the proceeds into its bank account and draw on the account as it wished. Hoffmann J.'s approach was followed by Millett L.J. in *Re Cosslett (Contractors) Ltd* [1998] Ch. 495 (CA). A similar line of reasoning was taken in certain cases in New Zealand, leading to the decision of the Privy Council, on appeal from the Court of Appeal of New Zealand, in *Agnew* [2001] 2 A.C. 710, where the Privy Council held that the critical feature distinguishing a floating charge from a fixed charge was the chargor's ability, freely and without the chargee's consent, to control and manage the charged assets and withdraw them from the security.

[86] *Agnew v Commissioner of Inland Revenue*; sub nom. *Re Brumark Investment Ltd* [2001] 2 A.C. 710 (PC).

[87] *Re Spectrum Plus Ltd (In Liquidation)* [2005] 2 A.C. 680 (HL).

[88] It is an interesting question whether a valid second fixed charge can be taken over book debts if the charge simply permits the company to pay the proceeds of the book debts into its account with the first chargee, and control over drawings from the account vests solely in the first chargee. It is suggested that although the company does not have an unfettered right to deal with the proceeds because of the control exercised by the first chargee, the lack of control exercised by the second chargee should lead to the conclusion that the second charge is a floating charge only.

[89] See the comment of Lord Hope in *Spectrum* [2005] 2 A.C. 680 (HL), [60], that the ordinary relationship of banker and customer does not entitle the bank, without notice, to prevent the customer from operating a current account while it is in credit or within the limits of any agreed overdraft.

[90] *Agnew v Commissioner of Inland Revenue*; sub nom. *Re Brumark Investment Ltd* [2001] 2 A.C. 710 (PC), [36].

inconsistent with the fixed nature of the charge; it allows the debt and its proceeds to be withdrawn from the security by the act of the company in collecting it in."

Lord Millett continued[91]:

"While a debt and its proceeds are two separate assets, however, the latter are merely the traceable proceeds of the former and represent its entire value. A debt is a receivable; it is merely a right to receive payment from the debtor. Such a right cannot be enjoyed in specie; its value can be exploited only by exercising the right or by assigning it for value to a third party. An assignment or charge of a receivable which does not carry with it the right to the receipt has no value. It is worthless as a security. Any attempt in the present context to separate the ownership of the debts from the ownership of their proceeds (even if conceptually possible) makes no commercial sense."

3–033 Having thereby set out the conceptual basis for the requirement that a chargee must have control on dealings with the proceeds of book debts if a charge over them is to be a valid fixed charge, Lord Millett then set out how such control might be achieved in practice[92]:

"To constitute a charge on book debts a fixed charge, it is sufficient to prohibit the company from realising the debts itself, whether by assignment or collection. If the company seeks permission to do so in respect of a particular debt, the charge holder can refuse permission or grant permission on terms and can thus direct the application of the proceeds. But it is not necessary to go this far. As their Lordships have already noted, it is not inconsistent with the fixed nature of a charge on book debts for the holder of the charge to appoint the company as its agent to collect the debts for its account and on its behalf. Siebe Gorman and Re Keenan merely introduced an alternative mechanism for appropriating the proceeds to the security. The proceeds of the debts collected by the company were no longer to be trust moneys but they were required to be paid into a blocked account with the charge holder. The commercial effect was the same: the proceeds were not at the company's disposal. Such an arrangement is inconsistent with the charge being a floating charge, since the debts are not available to the company as a source of its cash flow. But their Lordships would wish to make it clear that it is not enough to provide in

---

[91] *Agnew v Commissioner of Inland Revenue*; sub nom. *Re Brumark Investment Ltd* [2001] 2 A.C. 710 (PC), [46]. See the very similar analysis in the third edition of this work at paras 3–036 to 3–038 referring to the decision of Millett L.J. (as he then was) in *Royal Trust Bank v National Westminster Bank* [1996] B.C.C. 613 (CA), 618. The same analysis was adopted by Lord Scott in *Spectrum* [2005] 2 A.C. 680 (HL), [110].

[92] *Agnew v Commissioner of Inland Revenue*; sub nom. *Re Brumark Investment Ltd* [2001] 2 A.C. 710 (PC), [48].

the debenture that the account is a blocked account if it is not operated as one in fact."

In *Spectrum*, Lord Scott agreed with Lord Millett's approach in *Agnew* and **3–034** decided that the categorisation depended on what, if any, restrictions there were on the chargor's ability to use the proceeds of collection of book debts by making use of "the credit to the account that reflects each payment in", and that it made no difference whether the account was in credit or in debit.[93]

Lord Hope also expanded upon Lord Millett's analysis in *Agnew* of the practical means by which a fixed charge over book debts might be achieved[94]:

"There are, as Professor Sarah Worthington has pointed out, a limited number of ways to ensure that a charge over book debts is fixed: 'An "Unsatisfactory Area of the Law"–Fixed and Floating Charges Yet Again' (2004) 1 International Corporate Rescue, 175, 182. One is to prevent all dealings with the book debts so that they are preserved for the benefit of the chargee's security. This is the only method which is known to Scots law which, as I have said, insists upon assignation of the book debts to the security holder and its intimation to the company's debtor as the equivalent of their delivery. One can, of course, be confident where this method is used that the book debts will be permanently appropriated to the security which is given to the chargee. But a company that wishes to continue to trade will usually find the commercial consequences of such an arrangement unacceptable. Another is to prevent all dealings with the book debts other than their collection, and to require the proceeds when collected to be paid to the chargee in reduction of the chargor's outstanding debt. But this method too is likely to be unacceptable to a company which wishes to carry on its business as normally as possible by maintaining its cash flow and its working capital. A third is to prevent all dealings with the debts other than their collection, and to require the collected proceeds to be paid into an account with the chargee bank. That account must then be blocked so as to preserve the proceeds for the benefit of the chargee's security. A fourth is to prevent all dealings with the debts other than their collection and to require the collected proceeds to be paid into a separate account with a third party bank. The chargee then takes a fixed charge over that account so as to preserve the sums paid into it for the benefit of its security."

Lord Hope then noted that the method used by the bank in *Spectrum* came closest to the third of these, and that the critical question was whether the restrictions imposed went far enough[95]:

"one must look, not at the declared intention of the parties alone, but to the effect of the instruments whereby they purported to carry out that

[93] *Re Spectrum Plus Ltd (In Liquidation)* [2005] 2 A.C. 680 (HL), [116]–[117].
[94] *Re Spectrum Plus Ltd (In Liquidation)* [2005] 2 A.C. 680 (HL), [54]–[55].
[95] *Re Spectrum Plus Ltd (In Liquidation)* [2005] 2 A.C. 680 (HL), [54]–[55].

intention. Was the account one which allowed the company to continue to use the proceeds of the book debts as a source of its cash flow or was it one which, on the contrary, preserved the proceeds intact for the benefit of the bank's security? Was it, putting the point shortly, a blocked account?"

3–035 However, important questions remain unanswered. As Lord Walker observed in *Spectrum*, the exact nature and requirements of the operation of the "blocked account" referred to by Lord Millett in *Agnew* and by Lord Hope in *Spectrum* have yet to be resolved.[96] The position of chargees is also not so clear in other situations, such as structured financing transactions, where the chargor company is often a special-purpose vehicle rather than a trading company with a cash-flow requirement, and the documentation creates charges over more specifically identified debts and may impose greater, although not necessarily complete, control in favour of the secured party over the proceeds of the debts.

3–036 So, for example, in the case of a trading company, what would be the result if the chargee bank required the company to pay the proceeds of the charged debts into an account from which no withdrawals were permitted, but simultaneously permitted the chargor company to draw upon a second account up to the balance on the first from time to time? Or if the bank put in place an automatic "sweep" mechanism which transferred any surplus monies in excess of a pre-determined amount from the blocked account to a second account from which the company could draw at will? In the Court of Appeal in *Spectrum*, Lord Phillips M.R. commented in a postscript to his judgment that[97]:

> "it would seem beyond dispute that a requirement to pay book debts into a blocked account will be sufficient restriction to render a charge over book debts a fixed charge, even if the chargor is permitted to overdraw on another account, into which from time to time transfers are made from the blocked account".

Lord Phillips M.R. had based his analysis of the restrictions upon the use of the proceeds of book debts upon the point that when proceeds are paid into a bank account they cease to exist as such and are replaced by a new asset—a debt owed by the bank to its customer. This approach was flatly rejected in the context of categorisation of charges by Lord Scott. Lord Scott described it as a "formalistic analysis of how the bank clearing system works" and instead indicated that one had to have regard to "the commercial nature and substance of the arrangement" and to the restrictions "on the use the chargor can make of the credit to the account that reflects each payment in".[98] Lord Walker also commented that[99]:

---

[96] *Re Spectrum Plus Ltd (In Liquidation)* [2005] 2 A.C. 680 (HL), [160].
[97] *Re Spectrum Plus Ltd (In Liquidation)* [2004] Ch. 337 (CA), [99].
[98] *Re Spectrum Plus Ltd (In Liquidation)* [2005] 2 A.C. 680 (HL), [116].
[99] *Re Spectrum Plus Ltd (In Liquidation)* [2005] 2 A.C. 680 (HL), [160].

"the expedient mentioned in the postscript to the judgment of the Master of the Rolls, although no doubt appropriate and efficacious in some commercial contexts, may not provide a simple solution in every case".

In light of these statements, it is suggested that the courts would be keen to detect the commercial purpose of the arrangements, and hence that it is likely that banking arrangements such as those described above which gave the chargor company automatic access to funds equivalent to any substantial part of the monies collected from the charged debts would be regarded as giving rise to floating charges only.

The position in relation to structured finance transactions may be less clear-cut. Conventionally, a portfolio of receivables may be transferred to a special-purpose vehicle, which issues bonds in order to finance the purchase and then charges the receivables in favour of a trustee to secure repayment of the bonds together with periodic interest. The charge and associated documentation will require all proceeds of collection of the receivables to be made into a designated bank account which itself will be charged in favour of the security trustee. Payments will only be permitted to be made from the designated bank account for limited purposes, including primarily the payment of interest and principal on the bonds. In order that the arrangements should be self-financing, the documentation (to which the security trustee is a party) also usually provides for the costs and expenses of the special-purpose vehicle (e.g. professional fees and bank charges) to be paid out of the receivables, together with the fees of other parties (such as the security trustee itself) which are involved in the arrangements. **3–037**

Such arrangements have little in common with the decided cases which have involved trading companies with variable cash-flow needs. In contrast, it is usually possible for the parties to structured finance arrangements to predict the liabilities and expenses of the special-purpose vehicle with a degree of precision and for the chargee to give its informed consent to the use of the proceeds of the book debts to pay those expenses, within realistic limits. Moreover, as the special-purpose vehicle is unlikely to incur any, or any substantial levels of, preferential and unsecured debt which would be prejudiced by recognition of the charge as a fixed charge, rather than a floating charge, the courts may feel less inclined for reasons of policy to adopt a restrictive approach to categorising the charge as a fixed charge.

Following *Agnew* and *Spectrum*, it is also doubtful that the decision of the Court of Appeal in *Re Atlantic Computer Systems Plc*[100] which was not expressly commented upon by the Privy Council or the House of Lords, remains good law. The Court of Appeal had to consider the nature of charges taken by the owners of numerous items of computer equipment which had been leased to a company. With the consent of the owners, the equipment had been sub-leased by the company to end-users. In the case of each sub-lease, **3–038**

---

[100] *Re Atlantic Computer Systems Plc* [1992] Ch. 505 (CA). The decision was somewhat surprisingly described as "non controversial" by Otton L.J. in *Re ASRS Establishment Ltd* [2002] B.C.C. 64 (CA).

and as security for the payment of the head-lease rentals relating to that equipment, the company assigned to the owners of the equipment all the benefit of the terms of the sub-lease, including all rental monies to which the company was or might in the future be entitled under or by virtue of the sub-lease. The charge did not require the sub-lease rentals to be paid direct to the owners of the equipment and, in practice, the sub-lease rentals were paid to the company and were used by it in the ordinary course of its business.

The company went into administration. Following the making of the order, the administrators collected in sub-lease rentals and paid them into designated bank accounts. The question arose as to whether the charges created by the assignments of the benefit of the sub-leases were fixed or floating charges. The Court of Appeal held, without reference to any cases such as *Siebe Gorman Co Ltd v Barclays Bank* or *Re Brightlife Ltd* that the charges were fixed charges. Giving the judgment of the court, Nicholls L.J. (as he then was) said:

> "The notable feature of the present case is that the charges were not ambulatory. The property assigned by the company was confined to rights to which the company was entitled under specific, existing contracts. The assignments consisted of the company's rights 'under or by virtue of' subleases each of which was already in existence at the time of the assignments and each of which was specifically identified in the relevant deeds of assignment. In each case the payments due to the company under a specific sublease were charged as security for the payments due by the company under the head lease relating to the same equipment. The company's right to receive future instalments from end users in due course pursuant to the terms of the subleases was as much a present asset of the company . . . as a right to receive payment of a sum which was immediately due . . .
>
> We have in mind that in practice sums payable by the end users under these subleases were paid to the company and utilised by it in the ordinary course of business. In so far as this is relevant, it may well be that this was what the parties intended should happen. The company was to be at liberty to receive and use the instalments until [the chargee] chose to intervene. We are unpersuaded that this results in these charges, on existing and defined property, becoming floating charges. A mortgage of land does not become a floating charge by reason of the mortgagor being permitted to remain in possession and enjoy the fruits of the property charged for the time being".[101]

3–039   It is difficult to reconcile the approach of the Court of Appeal with the earlier cases or with *Agnew* and *Spectrum*. A direct analogy can be drawn between the sub-leases and the rental payments in *Atlantic Computers* and the book debts and their proceeds in *Agnew* and *Spectrum*. As a result of the focus on Romer L.J.'s third criterion, it is difficult to see how the lack of control by the charge

---

[101] *Re Atlantic Computer Systems Plc* [1992] Ch. 505 (CA), 534.

over the proceeds of the charged sub-leases could be regarded as consistent with the maintenance of a fixed charge.

Nicholls L.J.'s analogy to a mortgage of land and the "fruits of the property charged" is also questionable. In *Agnew*, Lord Millett referred to the distinction between what had been termed a power of disposition and a power of consumption and appeared to recognise that it might not be inconsistent with a fixed charge to permit the chargor company to exploit the characteristics inherent in the nature of the charged property "so long as the destruction of the security is due to a characteristic of the subject matter of the charge and not merely to the way in which the charge is drafted".[102] Whilst the precise parameters of this distinction may be unclear, there would seem to be a difference in principle between a mortgagor who is prohibited from disposing or dealing with charged land nevertheless being entitled to continue to occupy the land and retain the incidental benefits of that land (on the one hand) and the chargor company which was entitled to continue to continue to receive and use the rental payments which were the very essence of the value of the sub-leases (on the other). When the company was using the sub-rental payments in its business on its own account, it was not simply enjoying the "fruits" of the charged property, but was actually consuming charged property itself.[103]

It is therefore suggested that the better view is that, notwithstanding the failure of the House of Lords expressly to overrule it in Spectrum, if the facts of *Atlantic Computer Systems* arose for decision in the future, the court would hold that the charge was a floating charge rather than a fixed charge.[104]

(b)   Stock in trade

By analogy with book debts, it might be thought legally possible to create a   **3–040**
fixed charge over stock in trade provided that the chargee was able to exercise sufficient control on both the stock and its proceeds of sale. However, in order to operate such a fixed charge, the company would have to seek the consent of the chargee to any disposal of such stock. As this is unlikely to be feasible in

---

[102] *Agnew v Commissioner of Inland Revenue*; sub nom. *Re Brumark Investment Ltd* [2001] 2 A.C. 710 (PC), [37].

[103] The distinction between the charged property and its fruits has also arisen in the case of charges over shares and receipts of dividends: see *Arthur D Little v. Ableco Finance LLC* [2003] Ch.217 (para.3–044 below).

[104] The decision in *Re Atlantic Computer Systems Plc* [1992] Ch. 505 (CA) was applied by Vinelott J. in *Re Atlantic Medical Ltd* [1992] B.C.C. 653 on the basis that the charging clauses were materially similar in the two cases. The learned judge held that it was not crucial that the charge in *Atlantic Medical* purported to be a specific charge not only over the company's right and interest in existing sub-leases (as had been the position in the *Atlantic Computers* case) but also over the rights and interest in any future sub-leases, since all sub-leases would relate to the same, existing chattels. In response to a submission that there was a distinction to be drawn between the nature of the charge over the sub-leases themselves and the charge over the rentals due under them, the learned judge held that such a distinction would be "unreal". However, the distinction between the sub-leases and the rentals arising under them was at the heart of the "land and fruits" analogy employed by the Court of Appeal in *Atlantic Computer Systems Plc*. Both cases are now widely regarded as being wrongly decided in light of *Agnew* and *Spectrum*: see Gullifer and Payne, *Corporate Finance La Principles and Policy* (Hart Publishing, 2011), p.252.

practice, it is suggested that a court is likely to construe any such charge as a floating charge rather than as a fixed charge.[105]

(c) Fixed and replaceable plant and machinery

3–041   In *Re Hi-Fi Equipment (Cabinets) Ltd*[106] Harman J. considered the ambit of the phrase "fixed plant and machinery" which appeared in a debenture as the subject of a fixed charge. Harman J. held that the expression was to be construed as containing a single item and that it connoted plant and machinery which was in some way firmly attached to the company's premises. A similar approach was adopted by Henry J. in the High Court of New Zealand in the case of *National Bank of New Zealand Ltd v Commissioner of the Inland Revenue*.[107] Henry J. held that a specific charge over "fixed plant and machinery" did not include computer software (source codes) which were accordingly only covered by a floating charge.

3–042   In *Re Cosslett (Contractors) Ltd*[108] (*"Cosslett"*) the Court of Appeal held that a power of sale and retention of proceeds arising in favour of a council under standard conditions of the Institution of Civil Engineers in respect of two coal-washing plants owned by a company in liquidation was a floating charge. In assessing whether the council, as chargee, had the requisite degree of control of the charged assets for the purposes of a fixed charge, the court took the view that: (a) the council's purpose in imposing a restriction on the company removing from the site the plant or materials required for completion of the works was not to protect its security but to ensure that the company would give proper priority to the completion of the works; and (b) the fact that the decision whether to consent to a request by the company to remove plant or materials if completion would not be prejudiced or delayed by the removal was left to the engineer showed that such a decision was to be made on operational grounds, and the engineer would not be permitted to refuse consent on the ground that the remaining plant would be insufficient security if the company were in default.

The Court of Appeal's decision on this point was upheld by the House of Lords,[109] where Lord Hoffmann expressly approved Millett L.J.'s reasoning and conclusion with reference to the (subsequent) decision of the Privy Council (given by Lord Millett) in *Agnew*. The coal-washing plants fell within a general charge on "constructional plant, temporary works, goods and materials on the

---

[105] See *R. in Right of British Columbia v Federal Business Development Bank* (1987) 65 C.B.R. 201 (CA) (British Columbia). A similar approach has been taken to shares in the context of a stockbroking business; *Re Lin Securities (Pte)* [1988] 2 M.L.J. 137; *Re E.G. Tan & Co (Pte)* [1990] 1 S.L.R. 1030 and Unreported November 13, 1992 (CA) (Singapore); and *Dresdner Bank v Ho Mun-Tuke Don* [1993] 1 S.L.R. 144 (CA). In *Agnew* [2001] 2 A.C. 710 (PC), [30], Lord Millett referred to trading stock as being just as much a part of a trading company's circulating capital as book debts, describing both as "the natural subjects of a floating charge".

[106] *Re Hi-Fi Equipment (Cabinets) Ltd* (1987) 3 B.C.C. 478. See also *Re GE Tunbridge Ltd* [1994] B.C.C. 563.

[107] *National Bank of New Zealand Ltd v Commissioner of the Inland Revenue* [1992] 1 N.Z.L.R. 250. The contrary decision of Jeffries J. in the earlier New Zealand case of *Tudor Heights Ltd v United Dominion Corp Finance Ltd* [1977] 1 N.Z.L.R. 532, in which it had been held that the phrase did not connote "fixtures" as that term is used in land law but merely connoted that the items would be expected to be retained by the company in its business, cannot be considered good law.

[108] *Re Cosslett (Contractors) Ltd* (CA) [1998] Ch. 495.

[109] *Smith (Administrator of Cosslett (Contractors) Ltd) v Bridgend CBC* [2002] 1 A.C. 336 (HL).

site" and in Lord Hoffmann's opinion it was not possible to construe the relevant provision as creating a charge over the coal-washing plants different in nature from that which it created over the other plant and materials brought on site.[110] Lord Hoffmann added[111]:

> "Although the washing plant was very large, it was not inconceivable that during the contract, just as it was found necessary to acquire a second plant, it might be found advantageous to replace one or both by a more efficient machine. In that case the [company] would have been entitled to withdraw the old machine from the site and the charge."

In short, as noted above, it may well be that fixed plant and machinery is more **3–043** amenable to being the subject of a fixed charge, but if the chargor has the power unilaterally to dispose of the item during its usable life, the charge may be floating.[112] Fine distinctions may also be required to be drawn in relation to other dealings with such charged assets. For example, it is not thought that it would be inconsistent with the existence of a fixed charge if the company was allowed to dispose of such plant and machinery when it became obselete, even without accounting for its scrap value: a fortiori if the terms of the charge required the company to acknowledge that the fixed charge extended to any scrap value and its replacement. But if the company is able to dispose of a charged asset during its usable life without the consent of the chargee, then even if it was obliged to replace it with another similar machine, or an improved model, for the reasons set out above, that might not be a fixed charge.[113] Similar questions may arise in relation to repairs to large composite items of plant and machinery. It is suggested that the freedom in a chargor to repair or renew parts of a larger non-obselete whole should not lead to a conclusion that what would otherwise be a fixed charge over the whole is in fact a floating charge. It is probably implicit that a chargee in such a case gives the chargor consent to effect necessary repairs and renewals to preserve the value of his security over the whole.[114]

---

[110] As to this "all or nothing" approach, see above, para.3–013.

[111] *Smith (Administrator of Cosslett (Contractors) Ltd) v Bridgend CBC* [2002] 1 A.C. 336 (HL), [44].

[112] In *Re Cimex Tissues Ltd* [1994] B.C.C. 626 the judge suggested that he would have been inclined to hold a charge over certain specific machinery and equipment to be fixed even if the chargor had had the power to dispose of the assets without reference to the chargee. In light of the subsequent cases these must be a question whether the case remains good law, even where the charge in question affects specifically identified assets

[113] The argument against the charge being floating would be that in this context the proceeds should not be identified with the asset, unlike the position in relation to book debts. Where the charge is only on a specific asset (unlike in *Coslett*) it would make more sense to hold that an otherwise effective fixed charge is not turned into a floating charge by a mere power of substitution of assets of equivalent or greater value.

[114] Atherton and Mokal suggest that power given to a chargor to substitute charged property for the purposes of maintenance, alteration or improvement is not necessarily inconsistent with a fixed charge, provided that the exercise of that power is subject to an explicit acknowledgment that the substituted assets fall within the ambit of the security: "Charges over chattels: issues in the fixed/floating jurisprudence" (2005) 26 Comp. Law. 10, 15ff. Walton suggests that any power of substitution, however limited, would seem now to make the charge float: "Fixed charges over assets other than book debts–is possession nine-tenths of the law?" (2005) 21(4) I.L. & P. 117.

(d)   Shares and other investments

3–044   In *Arthur D Little Ltd (in administration) v Ableco Finance LLC*[115] a charge granted by a Scottish company on the shares of its English subsidiary together with the related distribution rights was held to be fixed. The relevant provision in the debenture was drafted generically so as to purport to create a fixed charge on the shares of all subsidiaries of the chargor, although it included specific reference to the English subsidiary. The debenture contained a restriction on disposal, as well as an undertaking by the chargor to deliver all share certificates relating to its subsidiaries to the chargee promptly on execution of the debenture (although in fact the share certificates in relation to the English subsidiary were delivered some time after that). The debenture also provided that, until default, the chargor was entitled to receive and retain dividends and other distributions in relation to shares in subsidiaries, and to exercise all voting and other rights in a manner not prejudicial to the chargee's security.

The judge adopted Lord Millett's two-stage process of construction of the charge instrument from *Agnew* and held that, despite the generic reference to subsidiaries in the charging clause, the only shares intended to be charged at the time the debenture was made were the shares in the English subsidiary; that the chargor was not trading in shares; that the shares in the English subsidiary were not part of its circulating capital and it did not need to dispose of them or to substitute them in the ordinary course of its business; and that the shares were not permitted to be disposed of, and did not remain under the management and control of the chargor in a manner which meant the chargor was free to withdraw them from the security.[116]

The judge also held that it made no difference that the charge extended to the related distribution rights and that the chargor was permitted to retain any distributions for itself until default. The judge referred to the dictum of Lord Millet in *Agnew* and held that the receipt of dividends and the enjoyment of voting rights could be regarded as exploitation of an ancillary characteristic of the charged assets rather than a disposal of the charged assets (i.e. the shares).[117]

3–045   The *Arthur D Little* case dealt with the basic case of a charge over a single, identifiable shareholding in a subsidiary company which was, by its nature, not

---

[115] *Arthur D Little Ltd (in administration) v Ableco Finance LLC* [2003] Ch 217.

[116] In *Ashborder BV v Green Gas Power Ltd* [2005] B.C.C. 634, [183], a charge on shares was held to be floating because, despite the fact that the shares were not part of the chargor's circulating capital which it needed to sell in the ordinary course of its business, the parties had agreed an express provision permitting the chargor to dispose of any of its assets in the ordinary course of its business. Thus the chargee, in attempting to argue for a fixed charge, fell at the first hurdle of Lord Millett's two-stage test. As to the meaning of "ordinary course of business" in this context, see above, paras 3–023 to 3–025.

[117] The case was thus thought to be distinguishable from cases on book debts and their proceeds, and leases and rental payments, because dividends may not be regarded as the only or even the primary means of realising value from shares. For a discussion of the situation where a company charges its goodwill but is still permitted to receive and use income from any licences it may have given to third parties to take advantage of the company's reputation, see Walton, "Fixed charges over assets other than book debts–is possession nine-tenths of the law?" (2005) 21(4) I.L. & P. 117, 120.

a circulating fund of assets. Greater difficulties arise in relation to charges over portfolios of securities, where the composition of the portfolio is inherently likely to be changing. The problems can be illustrated by obiter dicta in two cases decided after *Agnew* but before *Spectrum* which each raised the impact of a right given to the chargor to withdraw the charged assets from the scope of the charge on terms that he reinvested the proceeds of their sale in other assets or provided substitute assets of equivalent value by way of security. In each case the court decided that the charge was a fixed charge, but doubts have been cast upon the decisions subsequently.

The first case was *Re TXU Europe Group Ltd*[118] where a portfolio of **3–046** shares owned by the defendant company was set aside or "ring-fenced" in order to provide a source out of which to provide top-up pension benefits to certain executives. The portfolio was managed by an investment manager who was answerable only to the company and who had the freedom to sell any of the securities and to reinvest the proceeds. The executives had no say in management of the portfolio. After the company became insolvent, the executives alleged that the portfolio was subject to an equitable charge in their favour.

On the facts, Blackburne J. held that notwithstanding that the portfolio had been set aside by the company as a source to fund pension top-ups for the executives, it had not been intended that the executives should have any enforceable charge over the fund to secure fulfilment of that purpose. The judge went on to consider, obiter, whether, if a charge had been created, it would in any event have been void as an unregistered floating charge. He held that it would have been a valid fixed charge:

"If the company has no right to apply the individual investments which together constitute the portfolio for any of its ordinary purposes but is obliged to hold them at all times subject to the charge in favour of the chargees, the charge is a fixed charge. It is none the less a fixed charge because, under the charge, there is a right in the chargor to convert the investment into cash or exchange it for other investments. If therefore the question had arisen, I would have held that the equitable charge was fixed rather than floating in nature."[119]

The decision has much to commend it in terms of commercial reality: it **3–047** treated the ring-fenced fund of investments as having an identity of its own and the constituent securities as fungible. If the condition under which certain investments are to be released from the security is that their proceeds are used to acquire other investments of exactly equivalent value which are made available as security, the commercial reality is that the charged assets

---

[118] *Re TXU Europe Group Ltd* [2004] 1 B.C.L.C. 519.

[119] *Re TXU Europe Group Ltd* [2004] 1 B.C.L.C. 519, [57]. Consider also *Russell Cooke Trust Co Ltd v Elliott* [2007] 2 B.C.L.C. 637, where a charge over certain assets described as floating in the documentation was held to be fixed on the basis of the chargor's inability to deal with the charged assets.

are not available for use by the company in the ordinary course of its business.

As has been indicated above, however, the emphasis of the judgments and speeches in *Agnew, Cosslett (Contractors)* and *Spectrum* was on the issue of control of the individual assets which fall within the description of the charged assets. Given that the executives who claimed the benefit of the charge had no say in the management of the portfolio at all, and that the investment manager who did was answerable only to the chargor company, it is difficult to reconcile Blackburne J.'s analysis with the statement of Vaughan-Williams L.J. in *Re Yorkshire Woolcombers* that "If at the wish of the mortgagor he can dispose of it and prevent it being any longer a security, *although something else may be substituted more or less for it,* that is not a 'specific security'"[120] (emphasis added) or the emphasis in *Agnew* and *Spectrum* on control by the chargee of the charged assets. Reference can also be made to the observations of Lord Hoffmann in *Cosslett*[121] that the freedom given to a chargor to replace a less efficient machine with a newer and more efficient one meant that the charge over the old one (as part of a general charge covering plant and machinery) could not be classified as a fixed charge.

3–048   The second case is *Queens Moat Houses Plc v Capita IRG Trustees Ltd.*[122] The company and its subsidiaries had purported to charge a portfolio of real properties by way of specific charge to secure an issue of debenture stock for which the defendant was the security trustee. The charge document permitted the company, until enforcement of the security and without reference to the chargee, to withdraw any items of property from the security without replacement if and in so far as the total value of the charged properties remaining exceeded 175 per cent of the amount of the outstanding debenture stock. It also permitted the company, until enforcement of the security, to withdraw any item of charged property from the security provided that it provided by way of security either a further item of property of equivalent value satisfactory to the chargee, or a sum of money of equivalent value to be held by the chargee as part of the security. To that end the charge contained a clause requiring the chargee to release any item of charged property upon receipt from the company of a certificate of value and any replacement security.

The issue arose as to whether the company was entitled to withdraw from the security, without replacement, a short leasehold which had been included in the charged property but which had a nil value under the special value rules in the charge. It was argued for the chargee that it could not have been intended that the company would have the right to require the chargee to agree to the removal of this asset, as this would have been inconsistent with the parties' expressed intention to create a fixed charge. Lightman J. rejected that argument holding that,

---

[120] *Re Yorkshire Woolcombers* [1903] 2 Ch. 284 (CA), 295.
[121] *Smith (Administrator of Cosslett (Contractors) Ltd) v Bridgend CBC* [2002] 1 A.C. 336 (HL), [44].
[122] *Queens Moat Houses Plc v Capita IRG Trustees Ltd* [2005] B.C.C. 347.

"the existence of a right unilaterally to require a chargee to release property from a charge does not render what is otherwise a fixed charge a floating charge. There is a critical difference between the right of a corporate chargor to deal with and dispose of property free from charge without reference to the chargee and the right of a corporate chargor to require the chargee to release the charged property from the charge . . . there is no inconsistency between the existence of a fixed charge and a contractual right on the part of the chargor to require the chargee to release property from the charge."

In so far as the decision suggests that there is a difference of substance between a unilateral right on the part of a chargor to deal with charged assets without reference to the chargee and a unilateral contractual right on the part of a chargor to require the chargee to release the property from the charge, the decision in *Queen's Moat Houses* cannot sit easily with the subsequent decision in *Spectrum*.[123] The House of Lords in *Spectrum* made it clear that the court must look at the commercial substance and not the legal form of the transaction. In neither situation identified by Lightman J. would the chargee be in a position to "decide for itself" whether to agree to the release of the asset in question as required by Lord Walker.

3–049

There is force in the suggestion that the requirement that securities are replaced by others of equivalent value will not be sufficient to uphold a fixed charge unless there is also a requirement that the replacement securities are of the same type (i.e. the same company and issue) or unless the charge retains the right to approve or dictate the identity of the replacement securities.[124] The position might also be different if the charge permitted the company to deal with the charged property free of the security on terms that it paid the proceeds of sale or the assessed value of the property (or even a specified proportion of those amounts) to the chargee absolutely in (partial) discharge of the secured debt. This might be regarded as a form of partial redemption of the charged property. But that was not the case, for example, in *Queens Moat Houses*: no money was payable to the chargee upon withdrawal of charged property with a nil value under the terms of the charge.

3–050

---

[123] *Queen's Moat Houses v Capita IRG Trustees Ltd* [2005] B.C.C. 347 was referred to by Vos J. in *Gray v G-T-P Group Ltd, Re F2G Realisations Ltd* [2011] 1 B.C.L.C. 313 and distinguished on the basis that it only concerned the question of whether, as a matter of construction, the property in question could be removed from the security. But Vos J. commented (at [38]) that had it been relevant to consider the characterisation point, the "very clear dicta" in *Spectrum* would have had to take precedence.

[124] See Antony Zacaroli QC, "Taking Security over Intermediated Securities" in Payne and Gullifer, *Intermediated Securities, Legal Problems and Practical Problems* (Hart, 2010), pp.174–180.

4. PRIORITIES BETWEEN CHARGES[125]

(a) As between fixed charges

3–051   A first fixed charge will generally prevail over any subsequent charge.[126] The only major exception is that a prior fixed equitable charge will be defeated by a subsequent purchaser of the legal title for value without notice.

3–052   In the absence of a clear contractual restriction imposed by the chargor, it is possible for two chargees to agree between themselves to vary their priority rights without the consent of the chargor.[127] However, care should be taken in drafting any priority agreement. In *Re Portbase (Clothing) Ltd*,[128] a fixed charge-holder had agreed with a subsequent floating chargeholder that, purely as a matter of contract, the fixed charge should be postponed to and should rank after the floating charge. Chadwick J. held that both chargees ranked behind the claims of the liquidator for his liquidation expenses and behind the preferential creditors.[129] The learned judge accepted, however, that it would be possible for two secured creditors to enter into an agreement by which they exchanged their rights under their respective securities, e.g. where the fixed charge-holder assigned to the holder of a subsequent floating charge some part or all of his rights to receive payment under the fixed charge.

(b) As between fixed and floating charges

3–053   As explained earlier, it is a feature of a floating charge that the company is permitted to deal with the charged assets in the ordinary course of its business as a going concern. This freedom will permit the subsequent grant of a specific mortgage or charge in the ordinary course of the company's business which will take priority over the earlier (uncrystallised) floating charge even if the

---

[125] See, e.g. Goode, *Legal Problems of Credit and Security*, 4th edn (London: Sweet & Maxwell, 2008), Ch.5. Questions of priority may also involve considerations of subrogation where monies are advanced by subsequent chargees to repay earlier indebtedness: see e.g. *Anfield (UK) Ltd v Bank of Scotland Plc* [2011] 1 W.L.R. 2414, referring to *Banque Financière de la Cité v Parc (Battersea) Ltd* [1999] 1 A.C. 221 (HL).

[126] In the case of two equitable charges, priority of time prima facie gives the better equity: *Abigail v Lapin* [1934] A.C. 491 (PC), 503–504, regarding as disapproved the rival formula in *Rice v Rice* (1854) 2 Drew. 73, 78, per Kindersley V.C. to the effect that, if the equities are in all other respects equal, priority of time gives the better equity.

[127] *Cheah Theam Swee v Equiticorp Finance Group Ltd* [1992] 1 A.C. 472 (PC); *Re Portbase (Clothing) Ltd* [1993] Ch. 388.

[128] *Re Portbase (Clothing) Ltd* [1993] Ch. 388.

[129] Relying on *Re Camden Brewery Ltd* (1911) 106 L.T. 598; *Re Robert Stephenson & Co Ltd* [1913] 2 Ch. 201 (CA) and the decision of Nicholson J. in the Supreme Court of Victoria in *Waters v Widdows* [1984] V.R. 503 in relation to the question of the priority to be accorded to the preferential claims; and upon *Re Barleycorn Enterprises Ltd* [1970] Ch. 465 (CA) and ss.115 and 175(2)(b) of the Insolvency Act 1986 in relation to the priority of the liquidation expenses. The House of Lords subsequently took the view that *Re Barleycorn Enterprises Ltd* had been wrongly decided: see *Re Leyland DAF Ltd* [2004] 2 A.C. 298 (HL), in which their Lordships held that costs and expenses of a company's liquidation were not payable out of a company's floating charge assets in priority to the holder of a floating charge. This decision does not affect Chadwick J.'s decision in so far as it related to priority over preferential debts. The decision in *Leyland DAF* has been reversed by legislation: see s.176ZA of the Insolvency Act 1986 (inserted by the Companies Act 2006).

subsequent chargee has notice of the earlier charge.[130] However, a specific charge granted outside the ordinary course of the company's business to a chargee with notice of the prior floating charge will be postponed to the floating charge.[131]

The freedom given in a floating charge to the company to deal with its assets **3–054** in the ordinary course of its business as a going concern will not permit the grant of a second floating charge over the same assets without the consent of the holder of the prior floating charge.[132] If the earlier floating charge permits the company to grant further charges over specified assets, the company may create a second floating charge on those assets ranking in priority to the earlier.[133]

5. RESTRICTIVE CLAUSES

As a result of the possibility that charges subsequently granted by a company **3–055** may obtain priority over earlier floating charges, modern debentures very frequently contain restrictions on the company's freedom to charge or deal with (and less frequently to create liens on) the assets covered by the floating charge ("negative pledge" clauses).[134] Such provisions are binding as between the company and the debenture-holder as contractual covenants, but are "mere" or "personal" equities only.[135] The questions thus arise as to whether, and if so in what circumstances, such clauses will be binding upon third parties who subsequently deal with the company.

At the date of preparation of this work, the short answer is that third parties **3–056** will be bound by the restrictions in a prior charge if they have actual notice of such restrictions.[136] Registration of a floating charge at the Companies Registry

---

[130] *Re Hamilton's Windsor Ironworks* (1879) L.R. 12 Ch. D. 707; *Re Colonial Trusts Corp* (1880) L.R. 15 Ch. D. 465, 472; *Wheatley v Silkstone & Haigh Moor Coal Co* (1885) L.R. 29 Ch. D. 715, 724; *Fire Nymph Products Ltd v The Heating Centre Pty Ltd* (1992) 7 A.C.S.R. 365, 377.

[131] *Re Hamilton v Hunter* (1982) 7 A.C.L.R. 295.

[132] *Re Benjamin Cope & Sons Ltd* [1914] 1 Ch. 800. In *Griffiths v Yorkshire Bank Plc* [1994] 1 W.L.R. 1427, a later floating charge was crystallised by notice before the earlier floating charge over the same property was crystallised by the appointment of a receiver. The second charge, which was first to crystallise, was held to have priority. This decision has been widely criticised: see, e.g., Walters, "Priority of the Floating Charge in Corporate Insolvency" (1995) 16 Comp. Law. 291. The decision in *Griffiths* on other matters (the application of the Insolvency Act 1986, s.40) has been doubted and was not followed in *Re H & K (Medway) Ltd* [1997] 1 W.L.R. 1422.

[133] *Re Automatic Bottle Makers Ltd* [1926] Ch. 412 (CA).

[134] It is too late to argue that such restrictions are inconsistent with the nature of a floating charge and are thus invalid: see Farrar, "Floating Charges and Priorities" (1974) 38 Conv. (N.S.) 315, 318.

[135] *Latec Investments Ltd v Hotel Terrigal Pty Ltd* (1965) 113 C.L.R. 265; *Landall Holdings Ltd v Caratti* [1979] W.A.R. 87; *Fire Nymph Products Ltd v The Heating Centre Pty Ltd* (1992) 7 A.C.S.R. 365, 377–378.

[136] *Re Valletort Sanitary Steam Laundry Co Ltd* [1903] 2 Ch. 654; *Wilson v Kelland* [1910] 2 Ch. 306 at 313; *Fire Nymph Products Ltd v The Heating Centre Pty Ltd* (1992) 7 A.C.S.R. 365, 377. Whilst the rationale for this rule is yet to be finally stated, it is suggested that dealing with the company in breach of such prior contractual restraints on the company constitutes a wrongful interference with the contractual relations between the company and the debenture-holder. The rule has been doubted in *Griffiths v Yorkshire Bank Plc* [1994] 1 W.L.R. 1427, 1435F. It is suggested that the extemporary comments of Morritt J., that the "negative pledge" has no effect on third parties, are obiter and probably incorrect: see Walters, "Priority of the Floating Charge in Corporate Insolvency" (1995) 16 Comp. Law. 291.

constitutes constructive notice of the particulars required to be registered and disclosed on the register to those persons who would reasonably be expected to search in the ordinary course of business.[137] However, the current requirements concerning registration of charges under the Companies Act 2006 do not allow for the application of concepts of constructive or implied notice of restrictive clauses so as to bind third parties because the legislation does not require details of any restrictive clauses to be mentioned on the appropriate form.[138]

The matter is more complex where the debenture-holder gives notice of the restriction on the registration form. It has been suggested that a cautious lender proposing to advance funds ought to search and, as part of the search, inspect the form lodged by the debenture-holder.[139] There is, however, no obligation to search in every case, and accordingly, even if a restriction is included on the registered form but no search is made, a subsequent chargee may not be bound.[140] There is, however, no direct authority on point. If the proposed lender sees the restriction on the registered form, he obtains actual notice and is bound by it. If he searches and yet fails to look at the form, it has been suggested that he might be bound by constructive notice,[141] but this surely cannot be the case since this is not a matter required to be registered and to allow it to bind third parties would be an undesirable extension of the application of the doctrine of constructive notice.[142] In any case, it is difficult to see why, if the creditor is

---

[137] A person who would not ordinarily be expected to search the register in the ordinary course of business should not be fixed by constructive notice: see Goode, *Legal Problems of Credit and Security*, 4th edn (London: Sweet & Maxwell, 2008), para.2–29 and Beale, Bridge, Gullifer and Lomnicka, *The Law of Personal Property Security* (Oxford University Press, 2007), paras 11.04–11.14.

[138] *Wilson v Kelland* [1910] 2 Ch. 306 (notice of a document is not notice of its contents); *Siebe Gorman Co Ltd v Barclays Bank* [1979] 2 Lloyd's Rep. 142; *Welch v Bowmaker* [1980] I.R. 251; *Swiss Bank Corp v Lloyds Bank* [1979] Ch. 548, 575; [1979] 2 All E.R. 853 at 874. Farrar, "Floating Charges and Priorities" (1974) 38 Conv (N.S.) 315, 319 argued that restrictions are now so common in floating charges that, even in the absence of any registration of a restriction or notice of the existence of a floating charge, a person will have what is tantamount to implied notice of a restriction, but this suggestion runs contrary to the statutory scheme.

[139] Salinger, *Factoring Law and Practice* (London: Sweet & Maxwell, 1991), p.156; Lingard, *Bank Security Documents*, 2nd edn (London: Butterworths, 1988), para.1.23. These suggestions are not repeated in the most recent editions of these works.

[140] See Goode, *Legal Problems of Credit and Security,* 4th edn (London: Sweet & Maxwell, 2008), pp.90–91.

[141] Reeday, *The Law Relating to Banking*, 5th edn (London: Butterworths, 1985), p.148.

[142] See per Lindley L.J. in *Manchester Trust v Furness* [1895] 2 Q.B. 539 (CA), 545: "as regards the extension of the equitable doctrines of constructive notice to commercial transactions, the Courts have always set their faces resolutely against it". See also *Panchaud Frères SA v Etablissements General Grain Co* [1970] 1 Lloyd's Rep. 53 (CA), 57, per Lord Denning M.R.: "our commercial law sets its face resolutely against any doctrine of constructive notice". Examples of the refusal of the courts to extend the doctrine of constructive notice to commercial transactions can be found in cases on knowing receipt such as *Re Montagu's Settlement Trusts* [1987] Ch. 264. A similar point was also made by Lord Neuberger MR (sitting in the Court of Final Appeal in Hong Kong) in *Kasikornbank v Akai Holdings Ltd* [2010] HKCFA 63, [51ff], holding that a claim of apparent authority should only be defeated if the third party was dishonest or irrational, rather than on the application of any doctrine of constructive notice (which he took to mean a failure to make the inquiries that a reasonable person would have made in the circumstances). In *Macmillan Inc. v Bishopsgate Investment Trust Plc (No.3)* [1995] 1 W.L.R. 978, 1000–1001 Millett J. suggested that the relevant question in determining whether the doctrines of constructive notice ought to apply was not whether the transaction was "commercial" or not, but whether there existed a "recognised procedure for investigating title" which the creditor ignored at his peril.

under no duty to search, he should be in a worse position because he undertakes a perfunctory or incomplete search than if he makes no search at all.

To address at least some of these issues, in August 2011 the government **3–057** published proposals for revisions to the scheme of registration under the Companies Act 2006 which would include in the statement of particulars required to be registered in the case of a floating charge, a tickbox to indicate whether the terms of the charge prevent the chargor from creating any further security that would rank equally with or ahead of the charge. If that proposal is implemented, third parties who would be expected to search the register of charges will be fixed with contructive notice of the existence of such restrictive clauses. Although there would still not be any obligation imposed upon lenders to search the register, it may be that the courts would more readily infer that such searches should be undertaken given the clear legislative intention behind making enhanced information available.

6. CRYSTALLISATION

(a) General

Floating charges are founded in contract. This being so, the circumstances in **3–058** which a charge may cease to float and become attached to specific property are also primarily a question of contract.[143] Following this principle, the courts have accepted the validity of "automatic crystallisation" clauses (see below). It would also appear to be possible for the debenture to make express provision for crystallisation to take place with respect to some class of charged assets and not others.[144] In the absence of such a provision the debenture-holder cannot restrict crystallisation to some, and not all, of the charged assets[145] and any action on his part will be ineffective to crystallise his floating charge unless it unequivocally terminates the company's licence to deal with the entire subject-matter of the floating charge.[146]

The events which may or may not cause crystallisation of a floating charge **3–059** can be considered under two headings: crystallisation by intervention (including crystallisation by the giving of notice) and automatic crystallisation.

(b) Crystallisation by intervention

The conceptual basis of crystallisation by intervention is that the company's **3–060** freedom to deal with the assets which are the subject of the floating charge in the ordinary course of its business is terminated by some form of external

---

[143] See per Hoffmann J. in *Re Brightlife Ltd* [1987] Ch. 200, 213H–215G; and per Gleeson C.J. in Fire *Nymph Products Ltd v The Heating Centre Pty Ltd* (1992) 7 A.C.S.R. 365, 371. For the historical development of crystallising events, see R.C. Nolan, "Property in a Fund" (2004) 120 L.Q.R. 108, 124.

[144] *Re Griffin Hotel Co Ltd* [1941] Ch. 129.

[145] *Evans v Rival Granite Quarries Ltd* [1910] 2 K.B. 979 (CA).

[146] *R. v Consolidated Churchill Copper Corp* (1978) 5 W.W.R. 652, per Berger J. (notice to company to terminate licence to carry on part, but not all, its business held ambiguous and ineffective to bring about crystallisation); *Evans v Rival Granite Quarries Ltd* [1910] 2 K.B. 979 (CA).

intervention.[147] Clearly, the appointment of a receiver, whether by the debenture-holder or by the court, will crystallise the floating charge.[148] The right to
intervene by the appointment of a receiver may be triggered by the happening
of any one or more of the events of default stipulated in the debenture. Examples
of circumstances giving rise to the right to appoint a receiver which are
frequently included in debentures include:

(a) if the company defaults in making the payments secured by the
     debenture[149];

(b) if an order is made or an effective resolution passed for the winding-
     up of the company;

(c) if a receiver or administrative receiver is appointed of the under-
     taking or assets of the company;

(d) if a petition is presented or other relevant step taken in relation to the
     appointment of an administrator;

(e) if a distress or execution is levied or enforced upon the property of
     the company;

(f) if the company stops payment or ceases or threatens to cease to carry
     on its business;

(g) if the company becomes unable to pay its debts within the meaning
     of s.123 of the Insolvency Act 1986[150]; and

(h) if the company makes an unauthorised disposal of charged assets.

3–061 The commencement of winding up will cause a floating charge to crystallise[151]
(even if the winding-up is merely for the purposes of reconstruction),[152] for the
company in liquidation no longer has the power to carry on its business other
than for the purposes of a beneficial winding-up. In the absence of a clause in
the debenture, however, the floating charge will not be crystallised by the mere

---

[147] A mere demand for payment does not constitute an intervention: *Evans v Rival Granite Quarries Ltd* [1910] 2 K.B. 979 (CA); *Chase Manhattan Bank v Circle Corp* (1986) 37 W.L.R. 160 (CA of Eastern Caribbean States).

[148] See, e.g. *Evans v Rival Granite Quarries Ltd* [1910] 2 K.B. 979 (CA), 1000–1001, per Buckley L.J.

[149] In the absence of a specific clause to this effect, default in payment of the secured debt will not be a crystallising event: see *Government Stock and Other Securities Investment Co Ltd v Manila Rwy Co Ltd* [1897] A.C. 81 (HL). Also, in the absence of a specific provision in the debenture, the debenture-holder cannot appoint a receiver because he considers that the security is in jeopardy. He must apply to the court: see *Cryne v Barclays Bank Plc* [1987] B.C.L.C. 548 (CA).

[150] As to the meaning of which see *Byblos Bank v Al-Khudhairy* (1986) 2 B.C.C. 99509 (CA); *Cheyne Finance Plc* [2008] 2 All E.R. 987; and *BNY Corporate Trustee Services Ltd v Eurosail-UK 2007–3BL Plc* [2011] 3 All E.R. 470 (CA). An appeal is pending to the Supreme Court in the *Eurosail* case.

[151] *Re Florence Land and Public Works Co* (1878) 10 Ch.D. 530; *Evans v Rival Granite Quarries Ltd* [1910] 2 K.B. 979 (CA), 1000, per Buckley L.J.

[152] *Re Crompton & Co Ltd* [1914] 1 Ch. 954.

presentation of a winding-up petition[153] or the appointment of a provisional liquidator[154] or the appointment by the court of a receiver at the instance of another creditor.[155]

Floating charges now normally contain a clause enabling a debenture-holder   **3–062** to appoint a receiver if a petition is presented or other relevant step is taken in relation to the appointment of an administrator. The appointment of an administrative receiver, in the limited range of circumstances in which this is now permitted by the insolvency legislation,[156] will generally block the appointment of an administrator.[157] Absent any such appointment of an administrative receiver, it is an open question whether the appointment of an administrator will cause a floating charge to crystallise. It is suggested that the better view is that the appointment of an administrator does not necessarily cause a crystallisation of the floating charge for, unlike a liquidator, an administrator will have the power to carry on the business of the company as a going concern and not merely for the purpose of winding up the company. If, however, the appointment of the administrator is by the holder of a qualifying floating charge who would (apart from the statutory prohibitions) have been entitled to appoint an administrative receiver, then it would seem implicit that such appointment must crystallise the floating charge.[158] In any event, the practical significance of this issue is substantially reduced by the power given to an administrator by para.70 of Sch.B1 to the Insolvency Act 1986 to deal with assets free of any charge which, as created, was a floating charge.

In *Re Brightlife Ltd*,[159] Hoffmann J. held that a floating charge which   **3–063** contained a clause enabling the debenture-holder to serve a notice on the company crystallising the floating charge was valid and effective and that there was no public policy reason to refuse to give effect to such a term of the contract between chargee and chargor. Hence, service of the notice constituted intervention by the debenture-holder which caused the crystallisation of the floating charge.[160]

(c)   Automatic crystallisation

There has been much debate over the question of whether it is possible or   **3–064** desirable to give effect to a clause in a debenture providing for automatic crystallisation of a floating charge on the happening of specified events without

---

[153] *Re Victoria Steamboats Ltd* [1897] 1 Ch. 158.
[154] *Re Obie Pty Ltd (No.2)* (1983) 8 A.C.L.R. 574.
[155] *Bayhold Financial Corp Ltd v Clarkson Company Ltd* (1991) 10 C.B.R. (3rd) 159 (Sup. Court. App. Div, Nova Scotia).
[156] See the Insolvency Act 1986, s.72A.
[157] Insolvency Act 1986, Sch.B1, paras 17, 25 and 39.
[158] See Goode, *Legal Problems of Credit and Security,* 4th edn (London: Sweet & Maxwell, 2008) para.4–37.
[159] *Re Brightlife Ltd* [1987] Ch. 200.
[160] See *Re Brightlife Ltd* [1987] Ch. 200, 215F. The point appears to have been conceded in *Re Woodroffes (Musical Instruments) Ltd* [1986] Ch. 366. See also *Re Griffin Hotel Co Ltd* [1941] Ch. 129.

any intervention by the debenture-holder.[161] However, much of the potential significance of automatic crystallisation has been reduced by the introduction of s.40(1) of the Insolvency Act 1986 which gives preferential creditors priority over the claims of the holders of charges which, *as created*, were floating charges, irrespective of whether or when such charge crystallised. In relation to "eligible" companies,[162] automatic crystallisation on a filing by a company's directors for a moratorium with a view to a voluntary arrangement, and automatic crystallisation on the occurrence of anything done with a view to obtaining such a moratorium, is prohibited.[163]

3–065   Other than in such circumstances, in spite of the Cork Committee having recommended that automatic crystallisation should be generally prohibited, it would seem to be accepted that there is no public policy preventing effect from being given to a clause providing for automatic crystallisation in the contract which has been made between the company and the debenture-holder.[164] Any such clauses will, however, be narrowly construed and only enforced if there is a well-defined crystallisation event.[165] This will promote commercial certainty and minimise the potential prejudice to third parties who might not have notice of crystallisation.[166]

3–066   The permissible conceptual limits of automatic crystallisation were tested in the Australian case of *Fire Nymph Products Ltd v The Heating Centre Pty Ltd*.[167] The clause in question sought to produce the effect that a floating charge automatically crystallised and became fixed "at the moment immediately prior to" any dealing with the charged property other than in the ordinary course of the company's business. The clear intent was to produce the consequence that the extraordinary dealing which resulted in crystallisation would not itself escape the consequences of that crystallisation. It was held that the clause could not operate so as to bring about a retrospective crystallisation but that it was possible for automatic crystallisation to occur contemporaneously with the crystallising event such that the assets passed to the disponee subject to a fixed

---

[161] Academic discussion includes articles by Farrar, (1976) 40 Conv (N.S.) 397 and (1980) 1 Comp. Law. 83; A.J. Boyle, [1979] J.B.L. 231; R. L. Dean, (1983) *Company and Securities Law Journal* 185. See also Gough, *Legal Problems of Credit and Security*, 4th edn (London: Sweet & Maxwell, 2008), Ch.11; Gough in Equity and Commercial Relationships (ed. P. Finn), p.239; Goode, *Legal Problems of Credit and Security*, 4th edn (London: Sweet & Maxwell, 2008), paras 4–53 to 4–56; *Palmer's Company Law*, paras 13.199.42–13.199.49; and Lingard, *Bank Security Documents*, 4th edn (London: Lexis Nexis, 2006), paras 9.26–9.32. See also the comments of the Review Committee on Insolvency Law and Practice (Cmnd. 8558), paras 1570–1582. Judicial analysis can be found in cases such as *Stein v Saywell* (1968) 121 C.L.R. 529; *Re Manurewa Transport Ltd* [1971] N.Z.L.R. 909; *R. v Consolidated Churchill Copper Corp Ltd* (1978) 5 W.W.R. 30; (1978) 90 D.L.R. (3d) 357; *Re Brightlife Ltd* [1987] Ch. 200; *Fire Nymph Products Ltd v The Heating Centre Pty Ltd* (1992) 7 A.C.S.R. 365. See also *Re Horne & Hellard* (1885) L.R. 29 Ch. D. 736; *Re Bond Worth* [1980] Ch. 228, 260D, per Slade J.; and *Re Woodroffes (Musical Instruments) Ltd* [1986] Ch. 366 (where Nourse J. treated crystallisation on cesser of business as a species of automatic crystallisation).
[162] Essentially small companies which are not banks or insurance companies.
[163] Insolvency Act 1986, Sch.A1, para.43.
[164] See *Re Brightlife Ltd* [1987] Ch. 200, 212, per Hoffmann J.; *Fire Nymph Products Ltd v The Heating Centre Pty Ltd* (1992) 7 A.C.S.R. 365, 371, per Gleeson C.J.
[165] *Covacich v Riordan* [1994] 2 N.Z.L.R. 502.
[166] See the comments at [1987] Ch. 213 and (1992) 7 A.C.S.R. 371.
[167] *Fire Nymph Products Ltd v The Heating Centre Pty Ltd* (1992) 7 A.C.S.R. 365 (CA NSW).

charge. How the third party disponee was affected by this state of affairs would depend upon the nature of the title which he acquired and whether he was aware of the crystallisation of the charge.[168]

(d) Cesser of business

A question which arose for decision in *Re Woodroffes (Musical Instruments)* **3–067** *Ltd*,[169] was whether, absent any clause to this effect in a debenture, cessation of business by a company would automatically crystallise a floating charge. In the case, the company in question had created two floating charges in similar terms over its undertaking and assets. The first had been granted to the company's bank; the second (which was created in breach of the restrictive provisions in the first charge and which was expressed to rank after the first) was in favour of one of the company's directors. Each debenture expressly permitted the debenture-holder to convert the floating charge into a fixed charge by giving notice to the company.

The second debenture-holder gave notice to crystallise the second floating **3–068** charge. The significance of this notice appears to have largely escaped the company which continued its business for a short time over a Bank Holiday weekend until the first debenture-holder made a demand under its debenture and appointed a receiver. The question primarily concerned priorities as between the first debenture-holder and the preferential creditors of the company. Priority as between the first debenture-holder and the preferential creditors depended upon whether the first floating charge had crystallised prior to the appointment of the receiver (the case pre-dated s.40(1) of the Insolvency Act 1986).

Nourse J. held that cessation of business, which necessarily put an end to the **3–069** company's capacity to deal with its assets, automatically caused a floating charge to crystallise, but that, on the evidence, such cessation of business was not made out. In reaching this conclusion, Nourse J. based himself upon a line of cases which had "to a greater or lesser extent" assumed that crystallisation took place on a cessation of business. The learned judge stated that on a cessation of business "That which kept the charge hovering has now been released and the force of gravity causes it to settle and fasten on the subject of the charge".[170] Although such a test may cause great factual uncertainties in ascertaining whether, and if so when, a company has ceased to carry on its business, the principle of automatic crystallisation on cesser of business would now appear to be established.[171] It should be noted that the decision is not authority

---

[168] See further below paras 3–074 to 3–079.

[169] *Re Woodroffes (Musical Instruments) Ltd* [1986] Ch. 366.

[170] *Re Woodroffes (Musical Instruments) Ltd* [1986] Ch. 366, 378B. See also the dictum of Gleeson C.J. in the *Fire Nymph* case that: "Part of the original idea of a floating charge was the freedom of a debtor company to carry on its business as a going concern and dispose of its assets in the ordinary course of business notwithstanding the existence of the charge. The corollary was that, if the company suspended trading, it should cease to be free to dispose of its assets."

[171] See *William Gaskell Group v Highley* [1993] B.C.C. 200; *B.C.C.I. v BRS Kumar Brothers Ltd* [1994] 1 B.C.L.C. 211, and *Re The Real Meat Co Ltd* [1996] B.C.C. 254. See also *Re Sperrin Textiles Ltd (In Receivership)* [1992] N.I. 323.

for the proposition that a floating charge will automatically crystallise on the company ceasing to trade profitably or upon it becoming insolvent.

(e) The effect of crystallisation of one floating charge upon other floating charges

3–070 On a second issue in *Re Woodroffes (Musical Instruments) Ltd*, Nourse J. held that, in the absence of any express provision in the first debenture, the crystallisation of the second floating charge did not result in the automatic crystallisation of the first floating charge over the same property. Nourse J. held that the contention that crystallisation of the later floating charge operated to crystallise the earlier charge "over the head" of the first charge-holder and "possibly contrary to its own wishes" was inconsistent with the contractual provisions which operated as between the company and the first debenture-holder. The learned judge held that there was neither an express nor an implied term in the bank's floating charge causing automatic crystallisation of that charge upon crystallisation of the later floating charge.

3–071   It is suggested that Nourse J. ought to have held that crystallisation of the second floating charge resulted in crystallisation of the first floating charge. The learned judge appeared to accept that "a fixed charge on the whole undertaking and assets of the company would paralyse it and prevent it from carrying on its business".[172] If this was so, then it is difficult to see why the crystallisation of the second floating charge into a fixed charge over the whole undertaking and assets of the company was not thought to paralyse the company and to prevent it from (lawfully) carrying on its business, resulting in the automatic crystallisation of the first charge.[173] Such a conclusion would also remedy the problem encountered in *Griffiths v Yorkshire Bank Plc*[174] of a second floating chargee gaining priority over the holder of a first floating charge.

(f) Problems of automatic crystallisation and the position of third parties

3–072 Apart from the problems of conflict between successive chargees referred to above, difficult questions may also arise as to the consequences for the debenture-holder of an unrecognised or unwanted automatic crystallisation. Whilst a debenture-holder may waive a provision for crystallisation before the event occurs, once the provision has been triggered, there may be irreversible consequences[175] and the process itself may be irreversible (see below).

3–073   Moreover, if steps are not taken by the chargee to prevent the company from continuing to trade and deal with its assets after crystallisation, there may well

---

[172] *Re Woodroffes (Musical Instruments) Ltd* [1986] Ch. 366, 377G–378C.
[173] The Cork Committee (Cmnd. 8558) acknowledged that it was uncertain whether a floating charge automatically crystallised on the appointment of a receiver under another charge held by another debenture-holder. It proposed that legislation ought to be enacted to specify that this was so: see paras 1573 and 1580 of the Report. The suggestion has not been taken up.
[174] *Griffiths v Yorkshire Bank Plc* [1994] 1 W.L.R. 1427.
[175] Contractual provisions may be triggered and leases may be rendered subject to forfeiture.

be the risk of claims by subsequent chargees that the debenture-holder has waived his right to rely upon the automatic crystallisation clause.[176]

So far as third parties are concerned, an obvious problem with automatic   **3–074** crystallisation or crystallisation on notice clauses is that there may be no means by which persons dealing with the company can determine with certainty whether or not crystallisation has occurred. Given the potentially far-reaching nature of some automatic crystallisation clauses, the making of inquiries of each registered debenture-holder or of the company on the occasion of each subsequent transaction can scarcely be practicable, is unlikely to be acceptable to the company and is not guaranteed to produce a reliable answer in any event.

It is suggested, however, that there is no overriding reason why automatic   **3–075** crystallisation clauses ought not to be given effect at least between the company and the chargee simply because of concerns about the position of third parties, because those third parties can be sufficiently protected under existing legal concepts. In the *Fire Nymph* case Gleeson C.J. stated[177]:

> "It is not sufficient objection to say that [automatic crystallisation clauses] could possibly be unfair to third parties. We are dealing with the operation of a contract, and there is nothing in legal theory that prevents parties from making a contract that might produce results adverse to third parties. In any event, the way in which third parties are affected will depend upon the rules as to priorities, often involving questions of notice, and those rules, generally speaking, operate in a fashion that gives practical effect (albeit in a somewhat formalised way) to considerations of fairness."

The analysis of this situation can be approached in two ways. The conventional   **3–076** approach focusses upon priority rules derived from the law of property to ascertain whether the third party acquired good title to the asset free of the claims of the holder of the floating charge. An alternative approach might be to approach the question from the perspective of whether the company had apparent authority to sell the asset free of the claims of the holder of the floating charge.

Approaching the question from the point of view of property rights, if a   **3–077** company disposes of its assets after a floating charge has crystallised, and the disposal appears to be in the ordinary course of the company's business, a purchaser in good faith who acquires legal title to the assets for value without notice of the crystallisation will take the assets free of the crystallised charge. Although the chargee would have acquired a fixed proprietary interest in the

---

[176] See *Campbell v Michael Mount PPB* (1995) 16 A.S.C.R. 296. Note also *Dovey Enterprises Ltd v Guardian Assurance Public Ltd* [1993] 1 N.Z.L.R. 540, 548–549, and Tan, "Automatic Crystallisation, De-crystallisation and Convertibility of Charges" [1998] C.F.I.L.R. 41, 47–48. Cf. *Re Atlantic Computer Systems Plc* [1992] Ch. 505 (CA) upholding a claim to a fixed charge, notwithstanding that the company was permitted to deal with charged assets until the chargee chose to intervene. Some of the risks of "overkill" in the drafting of automatic crystallisation clauses are well summarised in Goode, *Legal Problems of Credit and Security*, 4th edn (London: Sweet & Maxwell, 2008), paras 4–54 and 4–55. See also Beale, Bridge, Gullifer and Lomnicka, *The Law of Personal Property Security* (Oxford University Press, 2007), paras 4.58–4.60.

[177] *Fire Nymph Products Ltd v The Heating Centre Pty Ltd* (1992) 7 A.C.S.R. 365, 373.

specific assets covered by the charge at the moment of crystallisation, such interest was only an equitable interest, and hence, according to conventional doctrines, a bona fide purchaser of the legal title to the asset would take his title free of the prior equitable interest provided that he had no notice (actual or constructive) of it. The fact that the purchaser might be aware of the existence of the floating charge will be irrelevant if he does not know or have notice that it has crystallised. Actual or constructive notice (arising from registration) of the debenture does not constitute the required notice of the terms of the provision for crystallisation,[178] still less that the crystallising event has occurred.

The position of the third party may be more difficult if, as a result of a transaction which appears to be in the ordinary course of the company's business, he acquires not a legal title but only an equitable interest in the charged property, either as a result of the disposition which itself caused crystallisation (as in the *Fire Nymph* case) or after automatic crystallisation has occurred. If the matter was approached from a property perspective, in the case of two competing equities, prima facie the first in time prevails.[179] Consequently, it might appear that a debenture-holder whose charge crystallises before some third party acquires equitable rights in assets subject to the charge will have the prior and better right, even if the third party was unaware of the crystallising event and could not have discovered it.[180]

3–078 The alternative analysis is founded upon the fact that it is an essential feature of a floating charge that until the charge crystallises, the company has the power to deal with the charged assets in the ordinary course of its business free of the charge. If the basis of the company's power to dispose of assets free of a floating charge to which they are subject can be said to be a form of authority given by the charge to the company to make such disposals, then a third party dealing with the company is entitled to assume that this authority continues, unless and until he knows that it has determined. In such a situation the third

---

[178] Constructive notice of a document by reason of registration does not import constructive notice of its contents: *Siebe Gorman & Co Ltd v Barclays Bank* [1979] 2 Lloyd's Rep. 142, following *Wilson v Kelland* [1910] 2 Ch. 306 and *Re Standard Rotary Machine Co* (1906) 95 L.T. 829.

[179] In the *Fire Nymph* case, the court identified, but on the facts did not need to resolve, the "difficult question" of which of the two equities was prior in time when the crystallisation of the floating charge was held to have occurred contemporaneously with the disposal to the third party.

[180] It might be argued that even applying a property-based analysis, the principles of estoppel by representation ought to operate so as to ensure that the disponee without notice takes free of the crystallised charge. By the taking of a floating charge, the debenture-holder represents to the world that the company has the power to dispose of the charged property in the ordinary course of its business. Unless and until the debenture-holder takes some active step to displace the appearance of continued powers of management and dealing on the part of the company, he should be estopped from challenging the priority of the interest acquired by the third party. See W.J. Gough, *Company Charges*, 2nd edn (London: Butterworths, 1996), pp.255–256 referring, inter alia, to the dictum of Lord Shand in *Governments Stock and Other Securities Investment Co v Manila Rly Co* [1897] A.C. 81 (HL), 87–88 to the effect that "active interference" was required by the debenture-holders to make it known that the company's licence to deal had been determined. On the loss of priority through estoppel, see also Meagher, Gummow and Lehane, *Equity, Doctrine and Remedies*, 4th edn (Sydney: Butterworths, 2002), paras 8–050 to 8–055.

party will obtain rights to the assets in priority to those of the debenture-holder by operation of the doctrine of ostensible authority.[181]

One potential difference between the two approaches lies in the state of knowl- **3–079** edge of the third party which would be sufficient to prevent him from obtaining good title to the assets free from the claims of the chargee. If the question is approached as a matter of authority, then it would seem that only actual knowledge of the crystallisation, or a dishonest or irrational belief that the charge had not crystallised, would suffice.[182] If the matter is approached from the perspective of property rights, then conventional wisdom suggests that constructive notice (i.e. the information that would have been obtained if the third party had undertaken the inquiries which a reasonable man would have undertaken in the circumstances) might suffice. It is suggested that since in most cases the third party will be a commercial purchaser and there will be no established process for investigation of title to the assets, the law ought to lean in favour of the third party rather than extend the application of doctrines of constructive notice.[183]

(g) After-acquired property

When crystallisation has taken place, after-acquired property of the company **3–080** falling within the scope of the charge (e.g. income generated by trading by the receiver) becomes subject to the fixed charge arising on crystallisation.[184]

7. DE-CRYSTALLISATION OR RE-FLOTATION

The question arises: can a fixed charge resulting from a crystallised floating **3–081** charge be re-converted into a floating charge?[185] As illustrated above, the essential distinction between a fixed and a floating charge is that in the case of the floating charge the company has the freedom to deal with the charged

---

[181] See Goode, *Commercial Law*, 4th edn (London: Lexis Nexis, 2009), pp.734–735, referring to a previous edition of this work. In *Kasikornbank v Akai Holdings* [2010] HKCFA 63, in a case involving a lack of authority on the part of the Executive Chairman and Chief Executive Officer of a listed Hong Kong company to execute a charge, Lord Neuberger rejected a submission that the bank taking the charge should be unable to rely upon the doctrine of apparent authority if it had failed to make the inquiries that a reasonable person would have made in the circumstances (which he regarded as akin to constructive notice). Lord Neuberger held that a third party could rely upon apparent authority of a director (assuming it to exist) unless the third party's belief that the director had authority was dishonest or irrational (which included turning a blind eye and being reckless). On the facts, however, he held that the bank had acted irrationally in forming the view that the director had the necessary authority.

[182] *Kasikornbank v Akai Holdings* [2010] HKCFA 63, [62].

[183] See *Macmillan Inc. v Bishopsgate Investment Trust Plc (No.3)* [1995] 1 W.L.R. 978, 1000–1001 per Millett J.

[184] *Robbie NW & Co v Witney Warehouse Co* [1963] 1 W.L.R. 1324, 1330–1331, 1338; *Ferrier v Bottomer* (1972) 126 C.L.R. 597; *Mineral & Chemical Traders Pty Ltd v T. Tymczyszyn Ltd* (1994) 15 A.C.S.R. 398.

[185] See Grantham, "Refloating a Floating Charge" [1997] C.F.I.L.R. 53; and Tan, "Automatic Crystallisation, De-crystallisation and Convertibility of Charges" [1998] C.F.I.L.R. 41. See also Beale, Bridge, Gullifer and Lomnicka, *The Law of Personal Property Security* (Oxford University Press, 2007), paras 4.61–4.65; Goode, *Legal Problems of Credit and Security*, 4th edn (London: Lexis Nexis, 2009) paras 4–57 to 4–59; *Snell's Equity*, 32nd edn (London: Sweet & Maxwell, 2010), para.40–022.

assets in the ordinary course of its business and without reference to the charge. Can a debenture-holder whose floating charge has crystallised and become a fixed charge reach an agreement with the company to convert his fixed charge back into a floating charge and thereby revive the company's right to deal with the charged assets in the ordinary course of business free of the charge? This question is one of considerable practical importance, since it is not exceptional for a company's fortunes to revive after crystallisation of a floating charge or for the triggering default to prove a false alarm. The debenture-holder as well as the company may wish that the company be given a second chance.

3–082   It is clear that the debenture-holder and company can agree to replace a charge which has always been a fixed charge with a floating charge. However, such a substitution may have serious consequences for the debenture-holder:

(a) The newly created floating charge will require registration and may be vulnerable to attack if administration or liquidation follows within the statutory period; or

(b) The newly created floating charge will be postponed to charges created after the fixed or crystallised floating charge and before its own date.

3–083   In the case of a fixed charge arising from crystallisation of a floating charge, it is in the interests of the debenture-holder that the re-floated charge be treated not as a replacement for, but as a continuation of, the original charge. This possibility will be most likely to be accepted if the debenture contains provisions for "re-flotation" in certain circumstances and, accordingly, the seeds for its own regeneration.

3–084   However, although there might be some commercial advantages by way of flexibility if the concept can be embodied in a coherent legal doctrine, there are undoubtedly very real theoretical difficulties with the notion of a charge that can continue to exist through the processes of crystallisation and re-flotation.[186] Most commentators appear to favour allowing re-flotation to a greater or lesser extent, provided that no liquidator (or administrator) has actually been appointed, but as yet there has been little discussion of the issue and it remains to be seen whether the courts or the legislature (if and when regulations are enacted dealing with the registration of crystallisation are made) will adopt this approach.[187] It should be borne in mind, however, that, even if this approach is adopted if a

---

[186] One might, for example, consider the difficulties created by re-flotation of a charge in circumstances where a second floating charge has automatically crystallised. In such a case it would seem that the second debenture-holder would have to consent to the re-flotation of the first charge.

[187] See, e.g. Goode, *Legal Problems of Credit and Security*, 4th edn (London: Lexis Nexis, 2009), para.4–58; Picarda, *The Law Relating to Receivers, Manager and Administrators*, 4th edn (London: Bloomsbury Professional, 2006), p.56; Lingard, *Bank Security Documents*, 4th edn (London: Lexis Nexis Butterworths, 2006), para.9.31. De-crystallisation is statutorily recognised under Scottish law: see s.62(6) of the Insolvency Act 1986. Picarda takes the view that re-registration ought not to be required, as the charge is the same security interest as originally created but which has simply first attached and then detached. If regulations are brought into force requiring registration of crystallisation, provision will have to be made to permit notification of re-flotation so as preserve the accuracy of the register.

receiver has been appointed, he will have a positive statutory duty to pay preferential creditors out of assets reaching his hands before directly or indirectly making any repayment to the debenture-holder.[188] Also, if he is an administrative receiver, he cannot be removed other than by order of the court.[189]

Careful consideration should also be given to the terms of any guarantees **3–085** and the prior consent obtained (if possible) of any guarantors, for there may be a substantial risk that the release of the fixed charge over assets (involved in the replacement of the fixed by the floating charge) may prejudice the rights of the debenture-holder against guarantors. It is, however, thought that this course cannot give rise to any claim against the debenture-holder by subsequent mortgagees.[190]

8. THE VALIDITY OF CHARGES

Apart from non-registration (as to which see section 9 below), the charge under **3–086** which a receiver is appointed may be invalid or at least its validity may be challenged on a number of grounds. These include:

(a) illegality;

(b) lack of corporate capacity;

(c) lack of authority on the part of the directors to execute the charge;

(d) substantial property transactions;

(e) defect of form; and

(f) as a result of various statutory provisions taking effect on the liquidation or in the administration of the company.

These grounds are examined in the sections that follow. When considering **3–087** these principles, it should be borne in mind that the validity or invalidity of a debenture will generally be determined by reference to the law applicable at the time of its execution. The relevant law changed in certain respects on the coming into force of the Companies Act 1985 and again when the Companies Act 2006 came into force. An indication of the relevant law prior to and after the coming into force of the Companies Act 2006 is given below: care should, however, be taken to apply the relevant law.

(a) Illegality

The grant of the charge may have been illegal. An obvious example might be **3–088** the grant of a charge by a company as security for the discharge of a loan

---

[188] Insolvency Act 1986, s.40. See *IRC v Goldblatt* [1972] Ch. 498, per Goff J.

[189] Insolvency Act 1986, s.45.

[190] A debenture-holder may release assets from his charge as suits his interest: *Scottish & Newcastle plc, Petitioners* [1993] B.C.C. 634 (Court of Session, Outer House) (in that case there was a release against repayment of capital).

provided to a third party for the purposes of acquisition of the shares in the company or its holding company. Prior to the coming into force of the relevant provisions of the Companies Act 2006, such charge would, unless falling within one of the relevant exemptions, have amounted to the provision of unlawful financial assistance contrary to what was s.151 of the Companies Act 1985. That prohibition applied to the giving of assistance by all companies. However, after the coming into force of the relevant provisions of the Companies Act 2006 in October 2008 the prohibition applies only where the acquisition in question is an acquisition of shares in a public company. If the statute is contravened by the provision of security, the charge will be void and unenforceable.[191] If may, however, be possible to sever the lawful part of the transaction from the unlawful part and to enforce the lawful part.[192]

(b)   Lack of corporate capacity[193]

3–089   The law relating to corporate capacity (the ultra vires doctrine) underwent a major reformation as a result of the passing of the Companies Act 1989, which took effect from February 4, 1991. After that date, companies were permitted to adopt a clause in their memorandum stating that the object of the company was to carry on business as a general commercial company, as a result of which the company had the power to do all such things as were identical or conducive to the carrying on of any trade or business by it.[194] Moreover, s.35 of the Companies Act 1985 (as substituted by the Companies Act 1989) provided that the validity of an act done by a company should not be called into question on the ground of lack of capacity by reason of anything in the company's memorandum. In addition, s.35B of the Companies Act 1985 provided that a party to a transaction with the company would not be bound to enquire as to whether it was permitted by the company's memorandum.

3–090   Since the coming into force of s.31 of the Companies Act 2006 on October 1, 2009, unless the articles specifically restrict the objects of a company, the objects of a company are unrestricted. Further, s.39 of the 2006

---

[191] *Heald v O'Connor* [1971] 1 W.L.R. 497. The failure to comply with a substantive (as opposed to a procedural) requirement of the Companies Act 1985 may have a like consequence: see, e.g. *Precision Dippings Ltd v Precision Dippings Marketing Ltd* [1986] Ch. 447 (CA). A charge taken in contempt of an order of the court would also be void for illegality: *Clarke v Chadburn* [1985] 1 W.L.R. 78, 81C, per Megarry V.C.; but cf. *Chapman v Honig* [1963] 2 Q.B. 502 (CA) (holding valid a notice to quit given in contempt of court in order to victimise a witness). In BCCI *v BRS Kumar Brothers Ltd* [1994] 1 B.C.L.C. 211, it appeared that the plaintiff and the defendant had colluded in a tax avoidance scheme. This involved the payment to an offshore recipient of monies lent by the plaintiff to the defendant. The loan from the plaintiff to the defendant was secured by fixed and floating charges. On an interim application, the court held that the debenture deed was not void for illegality, and so BCCI could appoint a receiver under it. It was held that any illegality did not constitute "an affront to the public conscience", such that the charges were void. From the brief details given at p.222 of the report, it appears that the parties were in pari delicto. See also *Tinsley v Millligan* [1994] 1 A.C. 340 (HL) on the issue of the effect of illegality.

[192] *Carney v Herbert* [1985] A.C. 301 (PC).

[193] See generally Ferran, *Company and Law and Corporate Finance* (1999), Chs 4 and 5 and Griffiths, *Contracting with Companies* (Hart Publishing, 2005), pp.164–170.

[194] Companies Act 1985, s.3A.

Act provides that the validity of an act shall not be called into question on the ground of lack of capacity by reason of anything in the conpany's constitution. The result is that since 1991 and certainly since October 2009 a potential chargee has not needed to concern himself with the capacity of the company to grant the charge in his favour.[195]

(c)   The authority of corporate representatives[196]

At common law, a director or directors who execute a charge on behalf of a company may bind the company if he or they have actual authority (express or implied) to do so. Express actual authority needs little explanation.[197] The implied actual authority of a director derives from his appointment and will extend to his being authorised to perform such acts as are reasonably incidental to the proper performance of his duties or which fall within the usual scope of the office to which he has been appointed.[198]   **3–091**

It is, however, implicit that a director of a company only has actual authority to act in the interests of his company or in a way which is intended to promote the success of the company. If he acts for improper purposes[199] or in a manner which is contrary to the interests of his company, his actions will be without authority, and the agreement which he purports to make will not bind the company unless the third party can rely upon the doctrine of apparent authority.[200]

Even if the director has no actual authority to bind the company, the company may be estopped by reason of its conduct from denying that it is bound, on the basis that the director has "ostensible" or "apparent" authority to bind the company. Ostensible or apparent authority may derive either from a person being appointed to, or held out by the company as occupying a particular position, in which case he may be taken to have all the powers which it is usual for a person in that position to have. Alternatively it may derive from particular representations made by or on behalf of the company as to the authority of the person. In any case, it is the totality of the conduct of the company which must be examined to see what ostensible authority a person may have had.[201]   **3–092**

In either case, however, the estoppel can only operate if the holding out or representation was made to the third party and was relied upon by him.

---

[195] The pre-1991 law in relation to ultra vires was extensively reviewed by the Court of Appeal in *Rolled Steel Products (Holdings) v British Steel Corp Plc* [1986] Ch. 246 (CA).

[196] See generally *Criterion Properties v Stratford UK Properties LLC* [2004] 1 W.L.R. 1846 (HL).

[197] It may, however, be that resolutions of the board purporting to grant actual authority are defective by reason of some defect in compliance with provisions in the articles, for example in relation to the disclosure of interests by directors leading to an inquorate meeting or an invalid resolution.

[198] See, e.g., per Denning M.R. in *Hely-Hutchinson v Brayhead Ltd* [1968] 1 Q.B. 549 (CA), 583.

[199] See *Rolled Steel Products (Holdings)* [1986] Ch. 246 (CA), 295.

[200] See *Hopkins v TL Dallas Group Litd* [2005] 1 B.C.L.C. 543, [88]–[89] per Lightman J., referring to *Lysaght Bros & Co Ltd v Falk* (1905) 2 C.L.R. 421 and *Macmillan Inc v Bishopgate Trust (No 3)* [1995] 1 W.L.R. 978. See also *Re Capitol Films Ltd* [2011] 2 B.C.L.C. 359, 374.

[201] *Egyptian International Foreign Trade Co v Soplex Wholesale Supplies Ltd, The Raffaella* [1985] 2 Lloyd's Rep. 36 (CA). *Armagas Ltd v Mundogas SA* [1986] A.C. 717 (HL).

Accordingly, a third party will be unable to rely upon the apparent authority of a director (assuming it to exist) if he knows that the director does not have any authority.[202] The third party also cannot rely upon any representation made by the director himself as to his authority: the holding out must be by the company or by some person authorised to make such representations on its behalf.[203] A simple lack of authority can be cured by ratification by the company in general meeting.[204]

3–093   These common law principles of agency are supplemented in the case of companies by the rule in *Turquand's* case and by statute. The rule in *Turquand's* case states that unless there are facts putting him on inquiry, an "outsider"[205] dealing with the company will not be affected by irregularities in the internal procedures of the company.[206] The rule in *Turquand's* case, however, only allows a third party to overcome any deficiency in the company's normal

---

[202] If the counterparty knows that a director is acting contrary to the commercial interests of his company, he is unlikely to be able credibly to assert that he genuinely believed that the director had actual authority: see *Criterion Properties v Stratford UK Properties* [2004] 1 W.L.R. 1846 (HL) at [31] per Lord Scott. On the question of the level of knowledge required to prevent a third party from claiming the benefit of the doctrine of apparent authority, see also *Freeman and Lockyer (a firm) v Buckhurst Park Properties (Mangal) Ltd* [1964] 2 Q.B. 480 (CA); *Hely-Hutchinson v Brayhead* [1968] 1 Q.B. 549 (CA); *British Bank of the Middle East v Sun Life Assurance Co of Canada (UK) Ltd* [1983] B.C.L.C. 78 (HL); and *Armagas Ltd v Mundogas SA* [1986] A.C. 717 (HL). In *Kasikornbank v Akai Holdings* [2010] HKCFA 63 (Court of Final Appeal of Hong Kong), Lord Neuberger rejected a submission that a bank taking a charge should be prevented from relying on the doctrine of apparent authority because it had failed to make the inquiries that a reasonable person would have made in the circumstances (which he regarded as akin to constructive notice). Lord Neuberger held that a third party could rely upon the apparent authority of a director (assuming it to exist) unless the third party's belief that the director had authority was "dishonest or irrational (which includes turning a blind eye and being reckless)". The reference to dishonesty (to include recklessness and "blind-eye" ignorance) plainly connotes a subjective inquiry into the state of mind of the third party and is consistent with the roots of the apparent authority doctrine in principles of estoppel. The reference to irrationality is more difficult: whilst Lord Neuberger accepted that this was ultimately an objective test, he indicated that it was not intended to be synonymous with unreasonableness, but was intended to impose a higher burden for a company seeking to avoid the contract, because the word irrationality "tends to carry more pejorative overtones". Whilst a person who has an irrational belief in the authority of the director may find it difficult to persuade the court that his belief was genuinely held, in the final analysis it is respectfully suggested that a subjective test is to be preferred. See also the related test of "good faith" in s.40 of the Companies Act 2006 (below).

[203] *British Bank of the Middle East v Sun Life Assurance Co of Canada (UK) Ltd* [1983] B.C.L.C. 78 (HL); *Egyptian International Foreign Trade Co v Soplex Wholesale Supplies Ltd, The Raffaella* [1985] 2 Lloyd's Rep. 36 (CA); *Armagas Ltd v Mundogas SA* [1986] A.C. 717 (HL); *Kasikornbank v Akai Holdings* [2010] HKCFA 63. See also *First Energy (UK) Ltd v Hungarian International Bank* [1993] B.C.C. 533 in which the Court of Appeal held that although a regional bank manager did not have any apparent authority to decide to offer a loan to a third party, he did have apparent authority to communicate to the third party that such a loan had been approved by the bank's head office and to make an offer on that basis which was capable of acceptance.

[204] *Grant v United Kingdom Switchback Railways Co* (1889) L.R. 40 Ch. D. 135 (CA).

[205] An outsider is (broadly speaking) someone who is not in such a position within the company to enable him to know whether or not the proper internal procedures have been followed.

[206] *Royal British Bank v Turquand* (1856) 6 El & Bl 327; *Mahoney v East Holyford Mining Co* (1875) L.R. 7 HL 869; *Morris v Kanssen* [1946] A.C. 459 (HL), 474, per Lord Simonds; *Freeman and Lockyer (a firm) v Buckhurst Park Properties (Mangal) Ltd* [1964] 2 Q.B. 480 (CA); *Hely-Hutchinson v Brayhead Ltd* [1968] 1 Q.B. 549 (CA); *Broadlands Finance Ltd v Gisborne Aero Club Inc* [1975] 2 N.Z.L.R. 496. See also the extensive analysis of the indoor management rule in *Northside Developments Pty Ltd v Registrar-General* (1990) 170 C.L.R. 146 (High Court of Australia).

internal procedures such as defects in the giving of notice for, or the absence of a quorum at, a board meeting to authorise the execution of documents. It does not enable the third party to hold a company to a transaction where he could not have established that the director or other representative would have had the requisite authority (actual or ostensible) even if there had been no failure to comply with matters of internal procedure.[207] It also does not apply in the case of forged documents.[208]

So far as statute is concerned, the Companies Act 1989 altered the common **3–094** law relating to limitations on the authority of directors and others to bind a company with effect from February 4, 1991. The relevant provisions for transactions with third parties unconnected with the directors of the company were to be found in ss.35A and 35B of the Companies Act 1985 (as amended) and have now been replicated without substantive change in s.40 of the Companies Act 2006.

Broadly speaking, those sections seek to protect third parties who are unconnected with the directors and who deal with companies in good faith from arguments that the directors or other agents lacked authority by reason of non-compliance with technical requirements under company's constitution. There is a less favourable regime for transactions between the company and its directors and those connected or associated with them, which is considered further below.

So far as unconnected third parties are concerned, s.40(1) of the 2006 Act **3–095** provides that, in favour of a person dealing with a company in good faith, the power of the board of directors to bind the company, or to authorise others to do so, is deemed to be free of any limitations under the company's constitution.[209] Section 40(2) provides that, for these purposes, a person deals with a company if he is a party to any transaction or other act to which the company is a party.[210] In addition, a person is not to be regarded as having acted in bad faith by reason only of his knowing that an act is beyond the powers of the directors under the company's constitution; and a person is deemed to have acted in good faith unless the contrary is proved. Additionally, s.40(2) provides that a party to a transaction with a company is not bound to inquire as to any

---

[207] See, e.g. *Freeman and Lockyer (a firm) v Buckhurst Park Properties (Mangal) Ltd* [1964] 2 Q.B. 480 (CA), 496.

[208] See, e.g. *Ruben v Great Fingall Consolidated* [1906] A.C. 439 (HL); *Northside Developments Pty Ltd v Registrar-General* (1990) 170 C.L.R. 146 (High Court of Australia). See also The Law Commission, *The Execution of Deeds and Documents by or on behalf of Bodies Corporate* (Law Com. Report 253 (1998)), paras 5.34–5.37.

[209] The reference to limitations deriving from the company's constitution is extended by s.40(3) to include limitations deriving from resolutions of the shareholders or from shareholder agreements. The concept of limitations deriving from the company's constitution would include provisions in the articles which, for example, mean that directors cannot be counted in a quorum or vote on a transaction in which they are interested unless they have declared their interest.

[210] The reference to "other act" is designed to catch gratuitous transactions. Some transactions, such as the issue of bonus shares, or the operation of pre-emption provisions over shares, may not amount to a "dealing" within s.40. See *EIC Services Ltd v Phipps* [2004] 2 B.C.L.C. 589 (CA) at [34]–[38] and *Cottrell v King* [2004] B.C.C. 307. Such questions are unlikely to cause problems in the context of the grant or purported grant of a debenture.

limitation on the powers of the board of directors to bind the company or authorise others to do so.[211]

3–096   A key component in the statutory test is the requirement that the third party be acting "in good faith". This concept requires some elaboration. First, whilst the terms of s.40(2) mean that an allegation of lack of good faith cannot be substantiated solely by alleging that inquiries ought to have been made which the section states a person is not bound to make,[212] it does not mean that a failure to inquire cannot be a component part of an allegation of bad faith. Secondly, s.40(2)(b) makes it clear that a person will not be regarded as being in bad faith by reason only that he knew that the transaction was beyond the powers of the directors.[213] Thirdly, it is nowhere suggested that actual knowledge is a necessary prerequisite for a finding of bad faith. In other words, the section envisages that it is neither necessary nor sufficient to establish actual knowledge of a lack of authority.

It is, however, suggested that in most cases, if actual knowledge of lack of authority is established, little more will be required to show a lack of good faith. Alternatively, an allegation of bad faith is likely to be justified if the third party consciously chose not to make an inquiry as to whether the execution of a debenture was authorised because he strongly suspected that it was not, and did not want his suspicions confirmed (so-called "Nelsonian knowledge" or "turning a blind eye"). A fortiori if an inquiry was made, and a plainly unsatisfactory answer was not pursued by further inquiries.[214]

Understood in this way, it is suggested that a finding of a lack of good faith under s.40 essentially requires a finding of dishonesty.[215] This is a question of fact and which will depend upon the particular circumstances of each case.[216] A person will be acting dishonestly if he fails to attain the standard of behaviour to be expected from an honest person in the circumstances. That is an objective standard (in the sense that a defendant cannot set his own standards of honesty and dishonesty), but in judging whether someone has attained the standard of required behaviour, the court will take into account what the third party actually knew and intended rather than what a reasonable person would have known or appreciated. Accordingly, a failure to make enquiries, however

---

[211] For an example of a case involving consideration of s.40 see *Ford v Polymer Vision Ltd* [2009] 2 B.C.L.C. 160.

[212] See *TCB v Gray* [1986] Ch. 621.

[213] See *Barclays Bank Ltd v TOSG Trust Fund Ltd* [1984] B.C.L.C. 1, 18c–g.

[214] This is consistent with the approach to the requirement of "good faith" in s.9(1) of the European Communities Act 1972, a precursor of, though substantially differently worded to, ss.35A and 35B of the Companies Act 1985 and s.40 of the 2006 Act: see *Barclays Bank Ltd v TOSG Trust Fund Ltd* [1984] B.C.L.C. 1. The dictum of Lawson J. in *International Sales and Agencies Ltd v Marcus* [1982] 3 All E.R. 551, 559g, that good faith is entirely subjective cannot be supported.

[215] As to which the leading cases are now *Royal Brunei v Tan* [1995] 2 A.C. 378 (PC) and *Barlow Clowes v Eurotrust* [2006] 1 W.L.R. 1476 (PC). On the question of terminology, see e.g. *Medforth v Blake* [2000] Ch. 86 (CA), 103D "In my judgment, the breach of a duty of good faith should, in this area as in all others, require some dishonesty or improper motive, some element of bad faith, to be established" and *Three Rivers DC v Bank of England* [2003] 2 A.C. 1 (HL) noting that "bad faith" and "dishonesty" are often used interchangeably.

[216] *Aktieselskabet Dansk Skibsfinansiering v Brothers* [2001] 2 B.C.L.C. 324 (Court of Final Appeal of Hong Kong).

unreasonable, ought not amount to dishonesty unless it results from a suspicion that there is something wrong, together with an unwillingness to discover the truth. A failure to make inquiries because the person concerned was "an honest blunderer or stupid man"[217] ought not to amount to bad faith or dishonesty.[218]

Assuming good faith, the provisions of s.40 go a long way to protecting a **3–097** third party who intends to take a charge from a company.[219] They do not, however, provide complete protection in all circumstances for third parties, nor are they intended to do so. For example, whilst the statutory provisions are aimed at removing the effect of any constitutional limitations on the powers of the board of directors to bind the company or to authorise others to do so, they are not intended to operate so as to insulate third parties from the effects of dealing with directors who are acting for improper purposes or in breach of their fiduciary duties to the company.[220] Nor, by deeming the powers of the board to bind the company or authorise others to do so to be free of limitation under the company's constitution, do the statutory provisions actually deem such powers to have been exercised as a matter of fact. So, for example, s.40 would not operate to protect a third party who accepted a charge executed by a lone director or by a director and the company secretary, in a situation where the board had not purported to authorise the execution by those persons of a debenture at all. In such cases, the third party would be driven to rely upon the common law principles of agency as applied to companies, together with the rule in *Royal British Bank v Turquand*[221] (see above).

As indicated above, in addition to their status as "insiders" for the purpose **3–098** of Turquand's rule, directors and those connected or associated with them are subject to a different regime under the Companies Act 2006. First, there is the

---

[217] See *Jones v Gordon* (1876–77) L.R. 2 App. Cas. 616 (HL), 628–629.

[218] In *Aktieselskabet Dansk Skibsfinansiering v Brothers* [2001] 2 B.C.L.C. 324 (Court of Final Appeal of Hong Kong), 334, Lord Hoffmann stated, in the context of a fraudulent trading case, that "While I quite accept that a defendant cannot be allowed to shelter behind some private standard of honesty not shared by the community, I think that there is a danger in expressing that proposition by invoking the concept of the hypothetical decent honest man. The danger is that because decent honest people also tend to behave reasonably, considerately and so forth, there may be a temptation to treat shortcomings in these respects as a failure to comply with the necessary objective standard". It is unclear whether an "irrational" belief, which Lord Neuberger accepted as a ground for denying a claim of apparent authority in *Kasikornbank v Akai Holdings* [2010] HKCFA 63, will be sufficient to justify a finding of bad faith. On the question of subjective and objective approaches to good faith, see also the approach of the courts to the scope of a director's duty to act in good faith as described in *Ultraframe v Fielding* [2005] EWHC 1638 (Ch), 1292–1294, referring to *Regentcrest v Cohen* [2001] B.C.C. 494, [120] and *Hutton v West Cork Railway* (1883) L.R. 23 Ch. D. 654 (CA), 671.

[219] Most debentures are executed pursuant to a board resolution: in these cases, the chargee will normally be protected against subsequent allegations that the board exceeded its authority under the company's constitution. The position will be less clear where the charge is granted without a board resolution, but it is unlikely that many lenders would in practice be content to accept a charge executed in this way.

[220] The requirement not to act for improper purposes or in breach of fiduciary duty are requirements of general law and not "limitations under the company's constitution". The scope of the European First Company Law Directive (68/151/EEC) which gave rise to what is now s.40 was considered in *Coöperative Radobank v Minderhoud* [1998] 1 W.L.R. 1025. The European Court of Justice held that transactions where there was a conflict of interest so far as the director was concerned were outside the First Directive and remained therefore a matter for national laws.

[221] *Royal British Bank v Turquand* (1856) 119 E.R. 886.

question of whether the director is even within the scope of s.40 of the 2006 Act at all. This was considered by the Court of Appeal in *Smith v Henniker-Major and Co*.[222] It was held that a director might be "a person dealing with the company" for the purposes of s.40, but he was not necessarily so.[223] On the facts, the director in question was not within the scope of the section, and did not "deal with the company" for the purposes of the section when attempting to take an assignment of rights from it, because he was also the company's sole director and hence was the very person responsible for the company's failure to make a valid assignment in the first place.[224]

Secondly, even if a director does establish that he was a "person dealing with the company" for the purposes of s.40, that section is to be read subject to s.41, under which, subject to certain limitations, a transaction will be voidable at the instance of the company if the board of directors exceed any limitation on their powers under the company's constitution and one of the parties to the transaction is a director or a person connected with a director.

3–099   If the execution of the debenture is unauthorised, then as between the company and the chargee, the charge will be void and the chargee will have no right to sell the charged property. If the charge has already been enforced and the property in question has been sold, then if it is property capable of being converted, the company will have a claim for damages for conversion which will be measured by reference to the value of the property on the date of sale.[225]

As an unauthorised disposal of company property also amounts to a breach of fiduciary duty by the directors concerned, if the property or its traceable proceeds can still be identified in the hands of the receipient, the company may have a proprietary claim to recover it or it in specie. If the property or its proceeds are no longer identifiable, the chargee may be personally liable to account for knowing receipt if the circumstances of his receipt make it unconscionable for him to retain the benefit of the property.[226] In *Kasikornbank v Akai Holdings*, Lord Neuberger suggested that in determining whether the test of unconscionability was met, equity would follow the law. Accordingly, he held that it would be necessary for the recipient to have accepted the charged asset either dishonestly (including blind-eye knowledge or recklessness) or with an irrational belief in the authority of the directors to grant the charge, and that reliance on the apparent authority of the directors which was merely negligent would not normally amount to unconscionability.

---

[222] *Smith v Henniker-Major and Co* [2003] Ch. 182 (CA).

[223] *Smith v Henniker-Major and Co* [2003] Ch. 182 (CA), [44]–[52], per Robert Walker L.J.; [108]–[110], per Carnwath L.J. and [118], [123]–[126], per Schiemann L.J.

[224] Questions have also been raised as to whether a member dealing with a company in his capacity as such is a "person dealing with the company" for the purposes of s.40: *EIC Services Ltd v Phipps* [2005] 1 W.L.R. 1377 (CA). Such questions are very unlikely to arise in the context of a company granting, or purporting to grant, a debenture.

[225] *Kasikornbank v Akai Holdings* [2010] HKCFA 63 per Lord Neuberger at [123] referring to *BBMB Finance (Hong Kong) v Eda Holdings* [1990] 1 W.L.R. 409 (PC).

[226] *Kasikornbank v Akai Holdings* [2010] HKCFA 63 per Lord Neuberger, referring to *BCCI v Akindele* [2001] Ch. 437 (CA) and *Charter v City Index Ltd* [2008] Ch. 313 (CA). In the *BCCI* case, Nourse L.J. reconsidered the earlier authorities and stated that he had come to the view that there ought to be a single test of knowledge for knowing receipt and that "The recipient's state of knowledge must be such as to make it unconscionable for him to retain the benefit of the receipt."

Under an order for an account of property or money unconscionably received, the recipient will ordinarily have to repay the value of what was received, together with any identifiable accretions and interest, which may well be on a compound basis if the property or money has been invested in the meantime. The recipient ought not, however, to be required to make good losses that would in fact have been suffered by the company if the assets had been retained by the company, for that would be to treat the recipient as an express trustee (which it is not) and would give an unjustifiable windfall to the company.[227]

(d) Substantial property transactions

Although the grant of a debenture does not itself constitute the disposal of a non-cash asset,[228] the grant of a debenture to a director or a person connected with him as part of a wider arrangement may be voidable under s.190 of the Companies Act 2006, if the rights acquired by the director or connected person are of sufficient value to bring the arrangement as a whole within the scope of the section and the transaction did not have the approval of the company in general meeting.[229]   **3–100**

(e) Formalities

The Companies Act 1989 made a number of significant changes to the ways in which companies could execute documents under seal.[230] Further changes were made with effect from September 15, 2005 by the Regulatory Reform (Execution of Deeds and Documents) Order 2005 as regards instruments executed on or after that date.[231] That law has been largely restated and clarified by Pt 4 of the Companies Act 2006.   **3–101**

A company may enter into a contract[232] (a) in writing under its common seal, or (b) by its agent acting under its authority.[233] Traditionally, most debentures were entered into under the common seal of the company, which required the company's seal to be affixed in accordance with its articles. This method of   **3–102**

---

[227] See e.g. *Warman v Dwyer* (1995) 128 ALR 201 and *Ultraframe (UK) Ltd v Fielding* [2005] EWHC 1638 (Ch), [1579] to [1588] per Lewison J. It is respectfully suggested that this would be a better explanation of the decision in *Kasikornbank v Akai Holdings* [2010] HKCFA 63 where Lord Neuberger appeared to apply principles relating to the assessment of equitable compensation for loss to the fashioning of an account for unconscionable receipt, holding that there needed to be some form of causal connection between the breach of trust and the loss for which compensation was payable: see *Target Holdings v Redferns* [1996] A.C. 421 (HL).

[228] *MC Bacon Ltd (No.1)* [1990] B.C.L.C. 324, 340–341.

[229] See *Ultraframe v Fielding* [2005] EWHC 1638 (Ch), [1388]–[1393], referring to s.320 of the Companies Act 1985. In connection with the grant of a debenture, note the extended meaning of the "transfer or acquisition of a non-cash asset" in s.1163 of the 2006 Act.

[230] The changes took effect from July 31, 1990. See generally, The Law Commission, *The Execution of Deeds and Documents by or on behalf of Bodies Corporate* (Law Com. Consultation Paper No.143 (1996)); Law Com. Report 253 (1998).

[231] SI 2005/1906.

[232] The same considerations apply to the execution of a debenture.

[233] Companies Act 1985, s.36 (as amended), and s.43 of the Companies Act 2006.

execution is preserved by the provisions of s.44(1)(a) of the Companies Act 2006 and the remainder of s.44 provides an alternative method of execution of documents by companies which does not involve the use of a seal.[234] Under s.44(2), if a document is signed in behalf of the company by two authorised signatories or by a director in the presence of an attesting witness, then it has the same effect as if executed under the common seal of the company. "Authorised signatories" include every director of the company and any secretary of the company. Moreover, s.44(5) provides that in favour of a purchaser (an expression which includes a mortgagee), a document shall be deemed to have been duly executed by a company if it purports to be signed in accordance with s.44(2). These provisions remove the doubts as to what constituted sealing which existed under the old (pre-1989 Act) law,[235] facilitate the execution of documents by companies and provide a considerable measure of protection to third parties. But the sections are not without their uncertainties. For example, it is not clear whether the provisions of s.44 will assist a purchaser where the document is a forgery.[236]

3–103   At common law, execution under seal was not of itself sufficient to constitute a document as a deed: it needed to be executed with that intention and delivered as such.[237] Section 46 of the Companies Act 2006 provides that a document is executed by a company as a deed[238] if it is duly executed and if it is delivered as a deed, and that it shall be presumed, unless a contrary intention is proved, to have been delivered upon its being so executed.

Execution as a deed is not a necessary pre-condition for the validity of a debenture. To be enforceable if not under seal, however, the debenture must (like any other contract not under seal) be supported by consideration. It may also be possible for the court to treat signed but unsealed debentures which are supported by consideration as documents amounting to or evidencing an enforceable agreement to issue sealed debentures.[239] It is possible to stipulate for a power to appoint a receiver in a document not under seal.[240]

3–104   Contracts for a disposition of an interest in land (which will include the execution of a debenture containing a charge over land) must now be made in writing, must incorporate all the terms expressly agreed between the parties

---

[234] A company may have a common seal but need not have one: see s.45(1) of the Companies Act 2006.

[235] See, e.g. *Stromdale & Ball v Burden* [1952] Ch. 223, 229; *First National Securities v Jones* [1978] 1 Ch. 109 (CA); *TCB Ltd v Gray* [1986] Ch. 621, per Browne-Wilkinson V.C.; affirmed on other grounds [1987] Ch. 458 (CA).

[236] Earlier case law has held forged documents to be nullities: see, e.g. *Ruben v Great Fingall Consolidated Ltd* [1906] A.C. 439 (HL). See also the Law Commission Report No.253, (1988) op. cit., paras 5.34–5.37.

[237] As to the common law complexities of delivery and escrows, see, e.g. *Alan Estates Ltd v W. G. Stores Ltd* [1982] Ch. 511 (CA); *Venetian Glass Gallery Ltd v Next Properties Ltd* [1989] 2 E.G.L.R. 42, per Harman J.; *Longman v Viscount Chelsea* [1989] 2 E.G.L.R. 242 (CA).

[238] A suitable form of words for a company to use would be "executed as a deed".

[239] *Re Fireproof Doors Ltd* [1916] 2 Ch. 142, considered in *Byblos Bank SAL v Rushingdale Ltd SA* (1986) 2 B.C.C. 99509 (CA).

[240] *Byblos Bank SAL v Rushingdale Ltd SA* [1986] 2 B.C.C. 99509 (CA); *Halsbury's Laws of England*, 4th edn (London: Lexis Nexis Butterworths, 1991), Vol. 32, para.675.

and must be signed by or on behalf of both parties.[241] There are no such requirements in the case of charges over personality.

(f) Statutory provisions in a winding-up or administration

Charges granted by a company may be challenged by a liquidator or adminis-   **3–105**
trator subsequently appointed of a company and invalidated under a number of
provisions of the Insolvency Act 1986.[242]

9. REGISTRATION OF CHARGES

Most systems of law require a security interest to be perfected by some form of   **3–106**
public notice or other act to bring the existence of the security to the attention
of third parties. English law has operated a public registration system for
company charges since the beginning of the century.[243] The current legislation
is embodied in Pt 25 (ss.860–882) of the Companies Act 2006 which, in spite
of substantial criticism[244] and proposals for reform, largely restates the previous
law as existed under Pt 12 of the 1985 Act.[245] Section 894 of the 2006 Act did
provide the Secretary of State with power to alter the existing system, but the
government has taken the view that this does not provide the power to determine the relative priority of registered charges, and therefore does not provide
the power to introduce a notice-filing system or otherwise provide priority
rules.

The most recent proposals for change, were the subject of a consultation
paper in March 2010 and a further consultation with draft amendments to Pt 25
of the 2006 Act in August 2011. The following summary assumes that the law
as stated in the Companies Act 2006 remains unchanged, but, where possible,
notes the main changes proposed in August 2011.

---

[241] s.2 of the Law of Property (Miscellaneous Provisions) Act 1989, which came into force on
September 27, 1989, replacing s.40 of the Law of Property Act 1925. Section 40 (which will
continue to apply to charges granted before that date) had simply required that there be a note or
memorandum in writing signed by or on behalf of the company. See generally *Megarry and Wade,
The Law of Real Property*, edited by C. Harpum, 6th edn (London: Sweet & Maxwell, 1999),
pp.651–671.

[242] See paras 15–012 to 15–027. An example of a challenge to a floating charge using these
provisions is *Re Fairway Magazines Ltd* [1992] B.C.C. 924.

[243] See *Agnew v Commissioner of Inland Revenue* [2001] 2 A.C. 710 (PC), [10], per Lord
Millett.

[244] Criticisms listed in the BIS consultation of August 2011 were (i) the list of registrable
charges has not been revised in line with changes in the law and commercial practice; (ii) the
particulars on the public record may not accurately reflect the charge created; and (iii) the procedures for registration are cumbersome.

[245] The main reports suggesting change were the Review of Security Interests in Property,
chaired by Professor A.L.Diamond for the DTI in 1989; Modern Company Law for a Competitive
Economy: Final Report, the Company Law Steering Group (2001), Ch. 12; and the Law
Commission's Report, Company Security Interests (2005) Cmnd 6654. For academic criticism and
a detailed review of the history of the registration system and proposals for reform, see Professor
Gerard McCormack, *Registration of Company Charges*, 3rd edn (London: Lexis Nexis
Butterworths, 1993), Ch.2.

(a) Registrable charges

3–107 The type of charges[246] which must be registered are listed in s.860(7) of the Companies Act 2006[247]:

"(a) a charge on land[248] or any interest in land, other than a charge for any rent or other periodical sum issuing out of land,

(b) a charge created or evidenced by an instrument which, if executed by an individual, would require registration as a bill of sale,

(c) a charge for the purposes of securing any issue of debentures,

(d) a charge on uncalled share capital of the company,

(e) a charge on calls made but not paid,

(f) a charge on book debts of the company,

(g) a floating charge on the company's property or undertaking,

(h) a charge on a ship or aircraft, or any share in a ship,

(i) a charge on goodwill or on any intellectual property[249]."

3–108 The court will investigate whether a particular transaction gives rise to a registrable charge.[250] The classic indicia of a charge were identified in *Re George Inglefield Ltd*[251] as being:

(a) the right of the chargor to redeem the charge;

(b) the obligation on the chargee to account to the chargor for any surplus realisations; and

---

[246] Which expression includes mortgages: see s.396(4) of the 1985 Act. There is a critical distinction between trusts (which are not registrable) and charges (which are): see *Associated Alloys Pty Ltd v ACN* (2000) 117 A.L.R. 568, 571 (High Court of Australia). As to what may constitute a charge, see *National Provincial and Union Bank of England v Charnley* [1924] 1 K.B. 431 (CA), 449; *Lovell Construction Ltd v Independent Estates Plc* [1994] 1 B.C.L.C. 31; *Orion Finance Ltd v Crown Financial Management Ltd* [1996] B.C.C. 621 (CA). See also *Re TXU Europe Group Plc (In Administration)* [2004] 1 B.C.L.C. 519 and *Re SSSL Realisations (2002)* (In Liquidation) and *Save Group Plc (In Liquidation)* [2005] 1 B.C.L.C. 1 affirmed sub nom. *Squires v AIG* [2006] Ch. 610. A freezing order does not create a charge or security interest: *Flightline Ltd v Edwards* [2003] 1 W.L.R. 1200 (CA).

[247] If the changes proposed to Pt 25 in the August 2011 consultation paper are implemented, the list of charges requiring registration will be deleted and replaced by a requirement to register "any charge, including a charge on land or any interest in land" subject to a limited number of exceptions (e.g. under the Financial Collateral Arrangements (No.2) Regulations 2003, rent deposit deeds, charges created by corporate members at Lloyds, and (for the avoidance of doubt) pledges over documents or corporeal moveables.

[248] In addition to registration under the Companies Act, registration may also be required under the provisions of the Land Registration Act 2002 (registered title) or the Land Charges Act 1972 (charges and mortgages over registered title other than a first legal mortgage).

[249] "Intellectual property " is defined in s.861(4) to mean any patent, trade mark, registered design, copyright or design right; and any licence under or in respect of any such right.

[250] *Lovell Construction Ltd v Independent Estates Plc* [1994] 1 B.C.L.C. 31.

[251] *Re George Inglefield Ltd* [1933] Ch. 1 (CA), 27, per Romer L.J. See also *TXU Europe Group Plc* [2004] 1 B.C.L.C. 519, [31]–[35].

(c) the right of recourse which the chargee has against the chargor for any shortfall in the secured debt following realisation of the security.

In analysing any particular transaction, the court will not be bound by the description which the parties give to their agreement but will be concerned to ascertain the legal substance of the arrangement. If the parties have consciously chosen not to cast their agreement using words of charge, the court will not disregard the chosen language simply because the agreement contains provisions which give rise to the same economic result as would a charge. But if the rights created are legally consistent only with a charge, then the court will hold the document to be a charge irrespective of the language used.[252]

Category (b) arises because companies are not otherwise subject to the Bills of Sale Acts 1878 and 1882.[253] It is to be noted that not all documents registrable as bills of sale will be registrable under s.860. It is only transactions which constitute a charge to secure the repayment of money which fall within the section.[254] The precise definition of the nature of a registrable bill of sale is very complex.[255] It generally covers all assignments, transfers, declarations of trust without transfer and other assurances of personal chattels, all authorities or licences to take possession of personal chattels as security for debt and any agreement by which a right in equity to any personal chattel or to any charge or security thereon is conferred. It does not, however, include transfers of goods in the ordinary course of business.[256] **3–109**

The Bills of Sale Act 1878 only deals with written documents which are effective to pass a proprietary interest and thus does not cover possessory securities. As such, a pledge of goods whereby possession of the goods themselves is given to the creditor will not be caught,[257] nor will a "letter of trust" under which the lender hands back documents of title pledged to it to the borrower to

---

[252] *Welsh Development Agency v Export Finance Co Ltd* [1992] B.C.C. 270 (CA); *Orion Finance v Crown Financial Mangement* [1996] B.C.C. 621 (CA), 626; *Agnew* [2001] 2 A.C. 710 (PC), [32].

[253] *Online Catering v Action* [2011] Q.B. 204 (CA), approving *NV Slavenburg's Bank v Intercontinental Natural Resources* [1980] 1 W.L.R. 1076 and *Standard Manufacturing Co* [1891] 1 Ch. 627 (CA).

[254] *Stoneleigh Finance Ltd v Phillips* [1965] 2 Q.B. 537 (CA).

[255] In *Welsh Development Agency v Export Finance Co Ltd* [1992] B.C.C. 270 (CA), 286E–286F. Dillon L.J. stated that "this territory is bedevilled by law that is now very out of date". Similar observations were made in the Diamond Report on A Review of Security Interests in Property (1989). For a recent decision illustrating the uncertainties of the Bills of Sale Acts as regards the requirements for attestation in the context of personal oans secured over cars, see *Log Book Loans Ltd v OFT* [2011] UKUT 280 (AAC).

[256] s.4 of the Bills of Sale Act 1878. At first instance in *Welsh Development Agency v Export Finance Co Ltd* Browne-Wilkinson V.C. held that an agreement to sell future goods other than in the ordinary course of business would be registrable as a bill of sale if made by an individual: *Welsh Development Agency v Export Finance Co Ltd* [1990] B.C.C. 393, 410–411. The Court of Appeal did not express any view on this point. cf. *Thomas v Kelly* (1888) L.R. 13 App. Cas. 506 (HL), 512, 519.

[257] *Wrightson v McArthur and Hutchinsons Ltd* [1921] 2 K.B. 807. For a valid pledge there must be actual or constructive possession by the pledgee: see *Askrigg Pty Ltd v Student Guild of Curtin University* (1989) 18 N.S.W.L.R. 738.

facilitate sale of the goods.[258] Other types of security over chattels not amounting to a charge are also included, e.g. a retention of title clause[259] or a contractual lien.[260]

3–110 "Debentures" are defined in s.738 of the Companies Act 2006 to include "debenture stock, bonds and any other securities of a company, whether or not constituting a charge on the assets of the company". A debenture is a document which acknowledges or creates an existing debt or makes provision for repayment of a loan to be made thereafter.[261] The term has been held to include an ordinary mortgage,[262] or a security for payment of the price of shares under a contract the performance of which was postponed.[263] The expression "any issue of debentures" is not defined in the Act but it is thought that it does not connote the issue of a single debenture (for that would render the remainder of the section largely redundant) but is restricted to the aggregate of a number of debentures issued by the company.[264]

3–111 The classic description of a "book debt" as referred to in s.860(7)(f):

> "a debt arising in the course of a business and due or growing due to the proprietor of that business that . . . would or could in the ordinary course of such a business by entered in well-kept books relating to that business . . . whether it is in fact entered in the books of the business or not."[265]

Charges on future book debts are registrable.[266] However, it is only assignments of book debts which are intended to be by way of security which will require registration and not outright assignments.[267] In *SSSL Realisations (2002) Ltd*, a subordination agreement under which a junior creditor agreed not to prove for his debt until the amount owing by the insolvent company to the senior creditor had been paid in full, and further required the junior creditor to hold on trust for the senior creditor any amounts received contrary to that prohibition up to the amount required to pay the senior creditor, was held not to constitute a charge over the underlying debt payable to the subordinated creditor. Moreover, even if it did not constitute a charge, it was held that a distinction could validly be drawn between provisions that only purported to

---

[258] *Re David Allester Ltd* [1922] 2 Ch. 211.

[259] See below Ch.21.

[260] *Barker (George) (Transport) Ltd v Eynon* [1974] 1 W.L.R. 462 (CA).

[261] *Handevel v Comptroller of Stamps* (1985) 62 A.L.R. 204 (High Court of Australia). *Levy v Abercorris Slate and Slab Co* (1888) L.R. 37 Ch. D. 260.

[262] *Knightsbridge Estates Trust Co Ltd v Byrne* [1940] A.C. 613 (HL).

[263] *Handevel v Comptroller of Stamps* (1985) 62 A.L.R. 204 (High Court of Australia).

[264] See *Automobile Association (Canterbury) Inc v Australasian Secured Deposits Ltd* [1973] 1 N.Z.L.R. 425 and the Diamond Report at p.119.

[265] Per Buckley J. in *Independent Automatic Sales v Knowles and Foster* [1962] 1 W.L.R. 974; *Re Falcon Sportswear Pty Ltd* (1983) 1 A.C.L.C. 690, 695; *Re Brightlife Ltd* [1987] Ch. 200; *Northern Bank Ltd v Ross* [1990] B.C.C. 883 (CA NI); *Re BCCI S.A. (No. 8)* [1998] A.C. 214 (HL); *Coakley v Argent Credit Corp Plc* Unreported June 4, 1998.

[266] *Independent Automatic Sales v Knowles and Foster* [1962] 1 W.L.R. 974; *Siebe Gorman & Co Ltd v Barclays Bank Ltd* [1979] 2 Lloyd's Rep. 142; *Re Brightlife Ltd* [1987] Ch. 200.

[267] See, e.g. *Ashby Warner & Co Ltd v Simmons* [1936] 2 All E.R. 697; *Re Kent and Sussex Sawmills Ltd* [1947] Ch. 177; *Re Welsh Irish Ferries Ltd* [1986] Ch. 471; *Re Marwalt Ltd* [1992] B.C.C. 32.

apply to monies if and when received, and the debts from which they emanated, so that such a charge would not be a charge over the underlying book debts but only over the proceeds of such debts if and when received. Hence it was not registrable as a charge over book debts in any event.[268]

A contractual "lien" on subfreight has been held to be a registrable charge on book debts.[269] That conclusion was strenuously criticised by Lord Millett, speaking for the Privy Council in *Agnew*, but the opportunity has not been taken to clarify the position in the current legislation.[270] A charge over an insurance policy issued by the Export Credit Guarantee Department (E.C.G.D.) is not a charge over a book debt.[271] **3–112**

Section 861(3) provides that the deposit of a negotiable instrument to secure the payment of any book debts of a company is not to be treated as a charge on those book debts. In *Chase Manhattan Asia Ltd v Official Receiver and Liquidator of First Bangkok City Finance Ltd*,[272] a company which was owed a book debt had obtained a promissory note from the debtor and had assigned part of the book debt, agreeing with the assignee to repurchase the assigned debt at a specified date in the future. As a term of the assignment, the company had agreed to deposit the promissory note with the assignee to secure the repurchase. The company failed to deposit the promissory note, failed to buy back the assigned part of the book debt and was wound up as insolvent. The Privy Council held that the assignment created a charge in equity on the promissory note, the monies payable thereunder and the book debt owed by the debtor to the company. However, as the promissory note had not been deposited, the Hong Kong equivalent of s.861(3) did not protect the assignee from the consequences of non-registration. It was therefore unable to enforce its equitable charge over the promissory note. **3–113**

There are a number of important exceptions to the requirements for registration mentioned above. One exception is created by implementation in England and Wales of the EC Financial Collateral Directive (the "FCD")[273] by the Financial Collateral Arrangements (No.2) Regulations 2003 (the "FCAR").[274] The FCD **3–114**

---

[268] See *Re SSSL Realisations (2002) (In Liquidation) and Save Group Plc (In Liquidation)* [2005] 1 B.C.L.C. 1, [49] –[54], affirmed sub nom. *Squires v AIG* [2006] Ch. 610 (CA).

[269] *Re Welsh Irish Ferries Ltd* [1986] Ch. 471; *Annangel Glory Cia Naviera SA v Golodetz Ltd* (1988) P.C.C. 37.

[270] See *Agnew* at [39]–[41]. The Privy Council noted that an amendment was proposed to the list of registrable charges by the Companies Act 1989 which would have made it clear that a lien over sub-freights was not to be treated as a charge over book debts or as a floating charge, but that change was never brought into effect. In *Cosco Bulk Carrier Co v Armada Shipping* [2011] 2 All E.R. (Comm) 481, Briggs J. described the arguments at [26]–[29] in terms that suggested that he favoured the views of Lord Millett. However, he did not consider it appropriate to decide the point on the application before him, commenting instead that the matter was "plainly ripe for consideration at least by the Court of Appeal".

[271] *Paul & Frank v Discount Bank (Overseas) Ltd* [1967] Ch. 348.

[272] *Chase Manhattan Asia Ltd v Official Receiver and Liquidator of First Bangkok City Finance Ltd* [1990] 1 W.L.R. 1181 (PC).

[273] Directive 2002/47/EC on financial collateral arrangements (OJ L168, 27.6.02).

[274] See generally Goode, *Legal Problems of Credit and Security*, 4th edn (London: Lexis Nexis, 2009), paras 6–36 to 6–44; Beale, Bridge, Gullifer and Lomnicka, *The Law of Personal Property Security* (Oxford University Press, 2007), Ch.10; McCormack, *Registration of Company Charges* 3rd edn (Jordans, 2009), paras 4.10–4.15; and Antony Zacaroli QC, *Taking Security over Intermediated Securities, in Intermediated Securities, Legal Problems and Practical Issues*, ed. Gullifer and Payne (2010).

aims to give special treatment to certain types of arrangements in respect of "financial collateral"—which means cash or financial instruments—which are granted as part of operations in the financial markets. The FCD requires member states to reduce the formalities associated with the creation of such arrangements and to modify their insolvency law so as to ensure that certain of the rights created by such arrangements are unaffected by the insolvency of the chargor.

The FCAR define two types of financial collateral arrangements—a "title transfer financial collateral arrangement", and a "security financial collateral arrangement". Of these it is the second which is relevant for present purposes, because r.4(4) provides that ss.860 (charges created by a company) and 874 (consequence of failure to register charges) of the Companies Act 2006 do not apply in relation to a security financial collateral arrangement or any charge created or otherwise arising under such an arrangement.

A "security financial collateral arrangement" is defined as,

> "an agreement or arrangement, evidenced in writing, where:
>
> (a)   the purpose of the agreement or arrangement is to secure the relevant financial obligations owed to the collateral-taker;
> (b)   the collateral-provider creates or there arises a security interest in financial collateral to secure those obligations;
> (c)   the financial collateral is delivered, transferred, held, registered or otherwise designated so as to be in the possession or under the control of the collateral-taker or a person acting on its behalf; any right of the collateral-provider to substitute equivalent financial collateral or withdraw excess financial collateral shall not prevent the financial collateral being in the possession or under the control of the collateral-taker; and
> (d)   the collateral-provider and the collateral-taker are both non-natural persons".

A "security interest" means,

> "any legal or equitable interest or any right in security, other than a title transfer financial collateral arrangement, created or otherwise arising by way of security including:
>
> (a)   a pledge;
> (b)   a mortgage;
> (c)   a fixed charge;
> (d)   a charge created as a floating charge where the financial collateral charged is delivered, transferred, held, registered or otherwise designated so as to be in the possession or under the control of the collateral-taker or a person acting on its behalf; any right of the collateral provider to substitute equivalent financial collateral or withdraw excess financial collateral shall not prevent the financial collateral being in the possession or under the control of the collateral-taker; or
> (e)   a lien".

"Equivalent financial collateral" is tightly defined to mean, in relation to cash, a payment of the same amount and in the same currency, and in relation to financial instruments, financial instruments of the same issuer or debtor forming part of the same issue or class and of the same nominal amount or currency.

There has been considerable academic debate as to whether and if so how, a floating charge over financial collateral could fall within the exemption from the registration requirements and the consequences of non-registration.[275] Although the very mention of the floating charge in the definition of 'security interest' would suggest that it was intended that the exemption would apply in some way to floating charges, the difficulty arises because of the requirement for exemption that the financial collateral should be in the possession or under the control of the collateral-taker—i.e. the chargee. That will not normally be the case with a floating charge until after crystallisation, since it is the essence of the floating charge that until crystallisation the assets falling within the charge are available to be dealt with by the chargor company in the ordinary course of its business.

3–115

In *Re F2G Realisations Ltd, Gray v GTP Group Ltd*,[276] Vos J. held that in order to fall within the exemption in the FCAR, the collateral taker/chargee had to have the legal right to control the collateral in the sense of being able to prevent the company providing the collateral from being able to deal with the charged assets in the ordinary course of business. Hence Vos J. held that a floating charge, under which the chargor company had a right to draw freely on the monies paid into a nominated account until a default event occurred, was not exempted from the requirements of registration under the Companies Act and was accordingly void against the liquidators of the company for non-registration. If this decision is correct it is difficult to envisage the type of floating charge that might be exempt from the requirements for registration as a result of the FCAR.

A further important exclusion from the types of security covered by s.860(7) is the category of charges which are not "created by a company" but which arise in some other way, such as by operation of law (e.g. an unpaid vendor's lien[277] or a separate lien) or imposed by a court order.[278]

3–116

Brief mention should also be made of the position of overseas companies— that is, companies incorporated outside the United Kingdom. Such companies are required to register prescribed particulars with the registrar if they open a UK establishment (i.e. a branch or place of business in the United Kingdom). The Overseas Companies (Execution of Documents and Registration of Charges) Regulations 2009 which came into force on October 1, 2009 required

3–116A

---

[275] See the various commentaries referred to in fn.274 above.

[276] *Re F2G Realisations Ltd, Gray v GTP Group Ltd* [2011] 1 B.C.L.C. 313.

[277] *London & Cheshire Insurance Co v Laplagrene Property Co Ltd* [1971] Ch. 499.

[278] See *Associated Alloys Pty Ltd v ACN 001 452 106 Pty Ltd* (2000) 171 A.L.R. 568, 596 per Kirby J. A charge will be registrable if it is contractual in nature: see ibid. and *Re Wallis & Simmonds (Builders) Ltd* [1974] 1 W.L.R. 391, a case on the creation of a charge by deposit of title deeds. Note that since 1991 such a charge cannot be created over land in England by mere deposit of title deeds, because this will not satisfy the requirements for writing in s.2 of the Law of Property (Miscellaneous Provisions) Act 1989: see *United Bank of Kuwait plc v Sahib* [1997] Ch. 107 (CA). The August 2011 proposals explicitly accept that a charge resulting from the operation of law or imposed by a court order will not be registrable.

such companies to register charges created by them if the property subject to the charge was situated in the United Kingdom and if the charge was of a type requiring registration (which followed the equivalent provisions for English companies). This requirement was, however, abolished with effect from October 1, 2011 by the Overseas Companies (Execution of Documents and Registration of Charges) (Amendment) Regulations 2011. As a consequence, the only requirement for overseas companies is to maintain their own register of charges (fixed or floating) affecting property situated in the UK, to notify the registrar of the location of that register and to keep it available for inspection.

(b)   The required particulars

3–117   Under the Companies (Particulars of Company Charges) Regulations 2008, the prescribed particulars that are required to be submitted to the Registrar of Companies are (a) the date of creation of the charge, (b) a description of the instrument (if any) creating or evidencing the charge, (c) the amount secured by the charge, (d) the name and address of the charge, and (e) short particulars of the property charged. Although the requirement is also to submit the instrument itself, the primary purpose of the further particulars is to provide sufficient information in an easily accessible form on the company's record so that those inspecting the register can make an informed decision as to whether to review the (often voluminous) instrument itself.[279]

If the proposals made by the government in August 2011 are implemented, the particulars required will not require a statement of the amount secured or the property charged unless there is no instrument of charge (it apparently being thought that there is a risk of over-reliance on the brief particulars in this respect), but for the first time in England and Wales, the particulars will require it to be stated whether a floating charge contains any negative pledge clause preventing the chargor from creating any further security ranking equally with or ahead of the charge.

(c)   The consequences of non-registration

3–118   By virtue of s.874 of the Companies Act 2006, unless the prescribed particulars of the charge together with the document (if any) by which the charge is created or evidenced are delivered to or received by the Registrar of Companies for registration within 21 days of creation, most charges under which a receiver is likely to be appointed or which would give rise to the right to appoint an administrator will, so far as any security on the company's property or undertaking is conferred by it, be void against a liquidator,[280] an administrator and a

---

[279] See the BIS consultation document of August 2011, para.5.

[280] Note that the principle appears to apply whether the liquidation is an insolvent or a solvent liquidator: see *Re Oriel Ltd* [1984] B.C.L.C. 241. A solicitor may be held liable in negligence for failing to advise (and possibly) procure registration at the instance of a director who guaranteed the debt secured by charge: see *Re Foster* (1985) 129 S.J. 333.

creditor of the company. In addition, the avoidance of the charge for non-registration makes the monies secured immediately repayable: see s.874(2).

The concept of an unregistered charge being void against a liquidator, **3–119** administrator and a creditor of the company has been explored in a number of cases. It is clear that an unregistered charge will be void against secured creditors if the issue of priorities arises between them at any time, and it also cannot be asserted against a liquidator or administrator who brings proceedings in his own name to challenge the validity of the charge for the benefit of the other creditors of the company.[281] It is also clear that the section does not make an unregistered charge void as against the company itself whilst the company is a going concern.[282] A chargee can therefore enforce an unregistered charge against the company prior to liquidation or administration by seizing the charged property or receiving payment under charged debts.[283] Likewise, a receiver can be validly appointed prior to liquidation or administration under a unregistered charge and can act unless and until a challenge to the security is made by a person entitled to do so under s.874.[284]

In *Smith (Administrator of Cosslett (Contractors) Ltd) v Bridgend CBC*[285] the House of Lords held that an unregistered but registrable charge was void against the company in administration or liquidation, and not merely void against the liquidator or administrator with respect to any personal action which was vested in them. As Lord Hoffmann put it[286]:

"As in the case of liquidation, I consider that 'void against the administrator' means void against the company in administration or (another way of saying the same thing) against the company when acting by its administrator."

Yet, as has been noted, the charge is not void as against the company which created it for all purposes, so that the rights against the company outside administration or liquidation are wholly unaffected by the section. Consequently, if a company in administration or liquidation later turned out to be solvent (to some extent), so that the subject-matter of the charge (or its proceeds) eventually came back into ownership of the company outside of administration or liquidation, the company would still hold the assets in question subject to the

---

[281] *Re Ehrmann Bros Ltd* [1906] 2 Ch. 697 (CA), 708; *Re Monolithic Building Co Ltd* [1915] 1 Ch. 643 (CA); *Independent Automatic Sales Ltd v Knowles and Foster* [1962] 1 W.L.R. 974; *Bank of Scotland v TA Neilson & Co*, 1991 S.L.T. 8 (Court of Session, Outer House). A creditor cannot apply under the Insolvency Act 1986 for a declaration as to the invalidity of the charge against the liquidator or administrator: see *Re Ayala Holdings Ltd* [1993] B.C.L.C. 256, 261.

[282] *Re Monolithic Building Co Ltd* [1915] 1 Ch. 643 (CA), 667–668.

[283] See *Mercantile Bank of India Ltd v Chartered Bank of India* [1937] 1 All E.R. 231; *Slavenburg's Bank NV v Intercontinental Natural Resources Ltd* [1980] 1 W.L.R. 1076, 1090–1091; *Re Row Dal Constructions Pty Ltd* [1966] V.R. 249.

[284] *Burston Finance v Speirway* [1974] 1 W.L.R. 1648, 1657E, per Walton J. The receiver's position, however, is a precarious one and, if possible, the debenture-holder should be prevailed upon to seek leave to register the charge out of time under s.873 of the Companies Act 2006.

[285] *Smith (Administrator of Cosslett (Contractors) Ltd) v Bridgend CBC* [2002] 1 A.C. 336 (HL).

[286] *Smith (Administrator of Cosslett (Contractors) Ltd) v Bridgend CBC* [2002] 1 A.C. 336 (HL), [31].

charge, notwithstanding the failure to register it. An unregistered charge is not void or invalid against the chargor, and non-registration in advance of insolvency does not affect third parties, or debtors.[287]

3–120   It should be noted that s.860 does not require actual registration of the charge but merely the delivery of the prescribed particulars of the charge[288] to the Registrar of Companies. Thus, where the Registrar refuses to register a charge, s.860 is complied with simply by delivery of prescribed particulars.[289] Likewise, if the prescribed particulars are delivered but the Registrar neglects to register the charge, s.860 is complied with.[290] Conversely, a refusal to register a particular class of charges does not excuse such delivery if it is in fact required by the section. In *Slavenburg's Bank NV v Intercontinental Natural Resources Ltd*[291] it was shown that the Registrar was then in the habit of refusing to register particulars of charges created by foreign companies with an established place of business in England which had failed to register as an overseas company under the predecessor of the Companies Act 2006. Lloyd J. held that, notwithstanding that the Registrar would not have registered the charge in any event, a charge by a foreign company which then had an established place of business in England but had failed to register itself as an overseas company and had not delivered the prescribed particulars, was void as against the liquidator of the company.[292]

(d)   Priorities

3–121   The rules relating to priorities of charges apart from questions of non-registration have been discussed above.[293] Strictly speaking, the requirements of registration relate to perfection of security and not to questions of priorities which will be determined by reference to the common law and equitable principles discussed above. However, registration under s.860 affects the situation in two

---

[287] *Society of Lloyd's v Levy* [2004] 3 C.M.L.R. 56.

[288] It has been held that the statutory requirement is to deliver the prescribed particulars of the charge, not of the chargor, so that where a chargee made an error in completing the form as to the registered number of the chargor company, this was not a prescribed particular of the charge and hence did not result in the charge being invalidated: *Grove v Advantage Healthcare (T10) Ltd* [2000] B.C.C. 985. Lightman J. observed that a third party misled by the absence of the charge on the file of the company at the Companies Registry might have a claim against Registrar or the person submitting the charge for registration. Note, however, that the decision in *Grove* was doubted in *Clydesdale Bank Plc v Weston Property Co Ltd* [2011] EWHC 1251 (Ch). The position will change if the proposed August 2011 reforms are implemented: the prescribed particulars will then also include the registered name and number of the chargor company.

[289] *Slavenburg's Bank NV v Intercontinental Natural Resources* [1980] 1 W.L.R. 1076, 1086D, per Lloyd J.

[290] *National Provincial and Union Bank of England v Charnley* [1924] 1 K.B. 431 (CA), 447.

[291] *Slavenburg's Bank NV v Intercontinental Natural Resources Ltd* [1980] 1 W.L.R. 1076. See for the meaning of "established place of business in England", *Re Oriel Ltd* [1986] 1 W.L.R. 180 (CA); *Cleveland Museum of Art v Capricorn International* (1989) 5 B.C.C. 860; *Rakusens v Baser* [2002] 1 B.C.L.C. 104 (CA).

[292] This led to the practice of Companies House in maintaining a so-called Slavenburg index which listed companies which had submitted charges for registration in this way. The number of listings was large but it was not easy to search the index. The practice was abolished by the new regime introduced under the Companies Act 2006.

[293] See paras 3–051 to 3–057.

ways, first, because a subsequent chargee will be deemed to have constructive notice of an earlier registered charge, and, secondly, because unregistered charges will be rendered void as against subsequent chargees. It should also be noted that questions of priorities between registered charges depend upon the dates of creation of the respective charges and not on the dates of registration.

(e) Extension of time and rectification

Section 873 of the Companies Act 2006 provides that, if the court is satisfied **3–122** that the omission to register a charge within the time required or that the omission or mis-statement of any required particular was accidental or due to inadvertence or to some other sufficient cause or is not of a nature to prejudice the position of creditors or shareholders of the company or that on other grounds it is just and equitable to grant relief, then the court may, on the application of the company or a person interested, order that the time for registration shall be extended or the omission or mis-statement rectified.[294] In the light of the express statutory jurisdiction provided by s.873, the court has no inherent power of rectification of the register of charges.[295]

Prior to the company becoming insolvent, unsecured creditors have no suffi- **3–123** cient interest to oppose an application for late registration and no interest which ought to be protected if an extension of time is granted.[296] However, once the company has become insolvent, it would appear that such creditors have sufficient locus standi to be heard. The application should also be made promptly in any event.[297] The court will not look kindly at a chargee who delays in his application for late registration in order to pursue other ways of advancing his position, such as attempting to take a fresh charge.[298] The court can make an order under s.873 at an interlocutory stage if it can be satisfied of the requisite matters.[299] However, if the application is opposed and there is to be cross-examination on the affidavit evidence, then no interlocutory order will be made.[300]

In considering whether to accede to the application for late registration, the **3–124** underlying principle is that the court can exercise a wide discretion based upon what is just and equitable.[301] The imminence of liquidation or insolvency of the company is a relevant factor in the exercise of the discretion but, provided that the application is made before liquidation has actually occurred, the court may

---

[294] For an example of the use of the power to rectify the register to accord with a purposive interpretation of an incomplete charge document, see *Clydesdale Bank Plc v Weston Property Co Ltd* [2011] EWHC 1251 (Ch).

[295] *Igroup Ltd v Ocwen* [2004] 1 W.L.R. 451.

[296] *R. v Registrar of Companies Ex p. Central Bank of India* [1986] Q.B. 1114 (CA); *Re Chantry House Developments Plc* [1990] B.C.C. 646, 654, per Scott J.

[297] *Re Ashpurton Estates Lt*d [1983] Ch. 110 (CA), 131H, per Lord Brightman; *Re Fablehill Ltd* [1991] B.C.C. 590.

[298] *Re Telomatic Ltd* [1993] B.C.C. 404.

[299] *Re Chantry House Developments Plc* [1990] B.C.C. 646, 654, per Scott J.

[300] *Re Heathstar Properties Ltd* [1966] 1 W.L.R. 993; *Re Telomatic Ltd* [1993] B.C.C. 404.

[301] Per Hoffmann J. in *Re Braemar Investments Ltd* [1989] Ch. 54 referring to the dictum of Lord Hanworth in *Re M.I.G. Trust Ltd* [1933] Ch. 542 (CA), 560.

exercise its discretion in favour of an extension of time.[302] Once liquidation or administration has intervened, an order for an extension of time will only be made in exceptional cases.[303] Where liquidation is imminent, the order extending time should normally include a proviso based upon the decision in *Re LH Charles & Co Ltd*[304] giving liberty to any liquidator subsequently appointed to apply to the court within a specified period (usually 21 days) of liquidation to discharge the order.[305]

3–125   In granting an extension of time, it became common practice to insert a proviso into the order extending time to the effect that the order permitting late registration would be without prejudice to the rights of parties acquired prior to the time when the charge was actually registered.[306] In *Watson v Duff Morgan and Vermont (Holdings) Ltd*,[307] it was explained that this only protected charges created within the period between expiry of the 21 days for registration and the date of actual registration. Subsequently, the courts have generally adopted a form of wording which makes it clear that the protection is to extend to all charges created between the date of creation of the unregistered charge and the date of its actual registration (as extended). In certain cases, however, the courts have been willing to adopt modified versions of the proviso,[308] or to dispense with it altogether, as the justice of the case required.[309]

3–126   If such an extension is granted, it would appear to be open to the court in any order, if it is just and equitable, to reinstate the contractual date for repayment

---

[302] *Re Braemar Investments Ltd* [1989] Ch. 54.

[303] *Re Ashpurton Estates Ltd* [1983] Ch. 110 (CA); *Re RM Arnold & Co* [1984] B.C.L.C. 535; *Re Braemar Investments Ltd* [1989] Ch. 54; *Re Barrow Borough Transport Ltd* [1990] Ch. 227 (no extension when company in administration). See also *Top Marques Car Rental Ltd* (2006) 150 S.J.L.B. 264 in which, but for the erroneous grant of a certificate by the registrar, an extension of time for registration would have been set aside on the basis that the company was plainly insolvent. In *Re Fablehill Ltd* [1991] B.C.C. 590 and *Re Chantry House Developments Plc* [1990] B.C.C. 646 the financial postions of the respective companies were unsound, but the courts appear to have placed some weight on the fact that no winding-up petitions had actually been presented and no judgments had been entered in favour of creditors which remained unsatisfied. See also *Commercial Banking Co of Sydney Ltd v George Hudson Property Ltd* (1973) 131 C.L.R. 605; *Bloodstock v Roadrunner Equipment* (1985) 10 A.C.L.R. 36 (extension granted despite liquidation as there was no evidence that money had been paid or credit given on the basis that no charge had been registered during the hiatus period of two to three days); *J.J. Leonard Properties Pty Ltd v Leonard (WA.) Pty Ltd* (1987) 5 A.C.L.C. 838 (no rectification after liquidation had intervened). *Barclays Bank Plc v Stuart Landon Ltd* [2002] B.C.C. 917 (CA) (extension granted on terms even though imminent winding-up likely).

[304] *Re L.H. Charles & Co Ltd* [1935] W.N. 15.

[305] *Re Braemar Investments Ltd* [1989] Ch. 54; *Exeter Trust v Screenways Ltd* [1991] B.C.C. 477 (CA). See *Re Chantry House Developments Plc* [1990] B.C.C. 646 for a case where such a provision was not employed because it would have served little purpose. The rationale and practice of the court and registrar in relation to *Re Charles* orders was reviewed in *Top Marques Car Rental Ltd* [2006] EWHC 109 (Ch), [41]–43].

[306] *Re Joplin Brewery Co Ltd* [1902] 1 Ch. 79; *Re Ehrmann Bros Ltd* [1906] 2 Ch. 697 (CA); *Re Kris Cruisers Ltd* [1949] Ch. 138.

[307] *Watson v Duff Morgan and Vermont (Holdings) Ltd* [1974] 1 W.L.R. 450.

[308] *Re RM Arnold & Co Ltd* [1984] B.C.L.C. 535.

[309] *Re Fablehill Ltd* [1991] B.C.C. 590 (referring, to *Re S. Abrahams & Sons* [1902] 1 Ch. 695). See also *Confiance Ltd v Timespan Images Ltd* [2005] All E.R. (D) 224, where, allowing an application for registration out of time, the court did not defer the unregistered first charge to a registered second charge because allowing the application would cause no prejudice to the second chargee; the assets in question were more than adequate to satisfy all the debts owed by the company to the chargees.

of the secured debt in place of the accelerated date for repayment which is the statutory consequence of failure to register in time.[310]

It has been held that the power given to the court in the predecessors of s.873 **3–127** of the 2006 Act does not permit the whole registration of the charge to be deleted and that the court has no inherent power of rectification outside of the statute.[311]

(f) The Registrar's certificate

By s.869(6) of the Companies Act 2006, the Registrar's certificate of registra- **3–128** tion given under s.869(5) is conclusive evidence that the statutory require- ments of registration have been complied with as between the company and all persons other than the Crown. The authorities indicate that this even protects charges whose registrations are erroneous or misleading. Thus, for example, in *National Provincial and Union Bank of England v Charnley*,[312] the debenture charged both land and chattels. The prescribed particulars supplied to the Registrar stated that the property charged was the land: no reference was made to the chattels. Nonetheless, the Court of Appeal held that the Registrar's certificate was conclusive evidence that particulars of the charge on the chat- tels had been presented to the Registrar and entered on the register. Likewise, in *Re Mechanisations (Eaglescliffe) Ltd*[313] the Court of Appeal held that the Registrar's certificate was conclusive evidence that the prescribed particulars had been presented to the Registrar and that the maximum amount had been secured, when in fact a lower sum had been incorrectly stated in the particulars and on the register.

Equally, the Registrar's certificate is conclusive as to the date the charge was **3–129** created, even if in reality the 21-day rule was infringed. *Re Eric Holmes (Property) Ltd*[314] and *Re CL Nye Ltd*[315] show that a charge created outside the 21-day limit and left undated which is subsequently dated and registered within 21 days of the date used will be valid. The certificate is also conclusive as to the date of the application for registration. Thus, in *R. v Registrar of Companies Ex p. Central Bank of India*,[316] the debenture-holder submitted an incomplete application within the 21-day period and a complete application after its expi- ration. The Registrar's certificate that the complete application was made on the earlier date was held to be conclusive evidence to this effect.

A case which indicates the unwillingness of the courts to go behind the **3–130** Registrar's certificate is the decision of the Court of Appeal in *Exeter Trust Ltd v Screenways Ltd*.[317] In that case, a certificate had been obtained following a

---

[310] Companies Act 2006, s. 873(2).

[311] *Re C.L. Nye Ltd* [1971] Ch. 442 (CA); *Exeter Trust v Screenways Ltd* [1991] B.C.C. 477 (CA).

[312] *National Provincial and Union Bank of England v Charnle* [1924] 1 K.B. 431 (CA).

[313] *Re Mechanisations (Eaglescliffe) Ltd* [1966] Ch. 20.

[314] *Re Eric Holmes (Property) Ltd* [1965] Ch. 1052.

[315] *Re CL Nye Ltd* [1971] Ch. 442 (CA). Applied in *Clydesdale Bank Plc v Weston Property Co Ltd* [2011] EWHC 1251 (Ch).

[316] *R. v Registrar of Companies, ex p. Central Bank of India* [1986] Q.B. 1114 (CA).

[317] *Exeter Trust Ltd v Screenways Ltd* [1991] B.C.C. 477 (CA).

late registration which took place on the same morning but just prior to a liquidator being appointed to the company. Even though the liquidator subsequently
obtained an order setting aside the grant of the extension of time, the Court of
Appeal held that the Registrar's certificate was conclusive both as to the
delivery of the required particulars and also as to the fact that the order
extending time had itself been obtained.[318]

3–131   It would appear that the statutory provisions as to the conclusiveness of the
certificate does not bind the Crown, and accordingly the Attorney General can
challenge a certificate by way of judicial review on the grounds of error of law
or fact by the Registrar.[319] But no such right of challenge is available to any
other person, save possibly if fraud by the registering party is proved.[320] In case
of such fraud, alternative remedies may be available in the form of an action
against him preventing him taking advantage of the fraudulently obtained
certificate and "It may well be that . . . a creditor damaged by the fraud can take
proceedings in personam".[321] Proof of fraud in such situations is, of course,
notoriously difficult.

10. INQUIRY AS TO THE VALIDITY OF THE CHARGE, APPLICATIONS TO THE COURT FOR DIRECTIONS AND PROTECTION OF THIRD PARTIES IN CASES OF INVALIDITY

3–132   A receiver is bound to make due inquiry as to the validity of the charge under
which he is proposed to be or has been appointed. Not merely may he be criticised or prejudiced if he fails to make due inquiry[322] but, if the charge is invalid,
his appointment will be invalid, and he may become liable as a trespasser in
respect of his actions as a receiver or as a constructive trustee of the assets of
the company in his hands.[323] The exposure to a claim for damages by the
company can be immense. Though the *Jenkins Report* (para.306) recommended that the court be given jurisdiction to grant relief to the would-be
receiver in respect of such liability, this recommendation has not been implemented.[324] As it stands, his only protection is his own investigation, such
contractual right to an indemnity from the debenture-holder appointor as may

---

[318] The court followed an Australian decision, *Wilde v Australian Trade Equipment Co Pty Ltd*
(1981) 145 C.L.R. 590. *Exeter Trust* was itself applied in the unusual case of *Top Marques Car
Rental Ltd* (2006) 150 S.J.L.B. 264 in which the registrar had mistakenly issued a certificate
notwithstanding that a contested application to set aside the extension of time for registration was
pending.
[319] *R. v Registrar of Companies Ex p. Central Bank of India* [1986] Q.B. 1114 (CA).
[320] See also *Walton v Bank of New Zealand* (1997) 8 N.Z.C.L.C. 261, 455 referring to *Sun Tai
Cheung Credits Ltd v Attorney General of Hong Kong* [1987] 1 W.L.R. 948 (PC).
[321] *R. v Registrar of Companies Ex p. Central Bank of India* [1986] Q.B. 1114 (CA), 1177, per
Slade L.J.
[322] A receiver's failure to make such inquiries might form the basis of an allegation that he had
not accepted appointment to his office: see *Harris & Lewin Pty Ltd v Harris and Lewin (Agents)*
[1975] A.C.L.C. 28, 279 at 28, 293.
[323] *Rolled Steel Products (Holdings) Ltd v British Steel Corp* [1986] Ch. 246 (CA).
[324] Such a power was conferred in Scotland by s.23 of the Companies (Floating Charges and
Receivers) (Scotland) Act 1972 and re-enacted in s.479 of the Companies Act 1985. However, this
provision was abrogated by s.63 of the Insolvency Act 1986 which assimilated Scottish and
English law in this respect.

exist and the statutory right to apply for an indemnity conferred by s.34 of the Insolvency Act 1986.

Section 34 of the Insolvency Act 1986 confers on the court a discretionary **3–133** jurisdiction to order the "appointor" to indemnify the "appointee" in respect of any liability arising solely by reason of the invalidity of the appointment. Such liability may presumably be to a claim either by the company, (for example for conversion or trespass) or by a person with whom the receiver has dealt, (for example for breach of warranty of authority). The statutory language is not apposite to cover situations where the "receiver" contracted as such but assumed personal liability, in which case the invalidity would merely deprive him of his right to an indemnity out of the company's assets. The liability would not in this case arise solely by reason of the invalidity (the pre-condition to the statutory indemnity), though his loss would.

Section 35 of the Insolvency Act 1986 authorises a receiver or manager **3–134** appointed under powers contained in a debenture, and the debenture-holder himself, to apply to the court for directions in relation to any particular matter arising in connection with the performance of the receiver's functions.[325] On a strict construction of this section, it might be doubtful whether a receiver or debenture-holder could apply for directions to the court to determine the validity of the charge under which he was appointed, for the section would appear to stipulate that the applicant should be validly appointed.[326] But there would appear to be no good reason why the court should not determine this issue: it would have to do so if the appointment were challenged and there may be every reason to anticipate the challenge. The receiver would plainly be a person interested for this purpose, in view of his possible liabilities, his right to remuneration and his statutory claim to an indemnity.

As a condition of accepting the appointment or continuing to act, the receiver **3–135** may theoretically require the debenture-holder to seek a declaration as to the validity of the charge by action or, if there is a winding-up, by application.[327] The defendants or respondents should, in this case, include the company and any subsequent debenture-holder. The timescale involved in any such proceedings would however, normally preclude this course, since their desire to appoint would ordinarily postulate the need for immediate action by the receiver to protect the interests of the debenture-holder.

---

[325] The power to give directions should be interpreted liberally, but directions should not be sought on matters which are properly matters of commercial judgment: *Deputy Commissioner of Taxation v Best & Less* (1992) 10 A.C.L.C. 520; *Re T&D Industries Plc* [2000] 1 W.L.R. 646 and *Re T&N Ltd* [2004] 75 P.B.L.R., [22]. Guidance may be given on questions of the receiver's remuneration: *Re Therm-a-Stor Ltd* [1996] 1 W.L.R. 1338; *Munns v Perkins* [2002] B.P.I.R. 120. Under the Financial Services and Markets Act 2000, s.363(2), the FSA may be heard on an application concerning the receivership of an authorised person, an appointed representative or a person carrying on a regulated activity contrary to the general prohibition.

[326] Compare *Re Wood and Martin Ltd* [1971] 1 W.L.R. 293: an invalidly appointed liquidator cannot apply as "liquidator" for an order under s.651 declaring that the dissolution is void because the word "liquidator" in the section means a liquidator validly appointed before the dissolution. Nonetheless, within the meaning of the section he is a "person interested" and has a sufficient interest to seek the order in view of his potential claim for remuneration and the potential claim against him for intermeddling with property that was bona vacantia.

[327] *Re North Wales Produce and Supply Society Ltd* [1922] 2 Ch. 340.

3–136   With limited statutory exceptions, a person dealing with an administrative receiver is likewise concerned as to the validity of the charge and the appointment.[328] One exception is a person paying money to a receiver who is not concerned to inquire whether an event has occurred which enables the receiver to act.[329]

3–137   Section 42(3) of the Insolvency Act 1986 provides that a person dealing with the administrative receiver in good faith and for value shall not be concerned to inquire whether the administrative receiver is acting within his powers. But this section postulates dealing with a validly appointed receiver, and will be of no assistance if this proves not to be the case. Section 232 of the Insolvency Act 1986[330] validates acts of an administrative receiver notwithstanding defects in his appointment, nomination or qualifications.[331] Section 232 is designed "as machinery to avoid questions being raised as to the validity of transactions where there has been a slip in the appointment"[332] of the receiver, but does not apply "where the term of office . . . has expired", or "where the office has been from the outset usurped without the colour of authority", or where "there has been no genuine attempt to appoint at all".[333] Nor will this provision validate the acts of persons when the appointor had no power to make any appointment; the substantive power to make the appointment must exist.[334] In this situation, the party dealing with the purported receiver must be content (in default of ratification by the company) with a claim against the purported receiver for breach of warranty of authority, and it is suggested that a like claim should be available against the purported appointor as a joint tortfeasor.[335]

11.   STATUTORY POWERS OF APPOINTMENT[336]

3–138   Receivers appointed under statutory powers are often called "LPA receivers", since the principal relevant powers are contained in the Law of Property Act 1925, Pt 2. A specific mortgage or charge will often adopt and extend the statutory power in the 1925 Act to appoint a receiver in certain circumstances to

[328] The debenture may include a provision safeguarding a person dealing with the receiver from an invalidity of the appointment, but it is conceived that no such protection can be afforded in respect of the invalidity of the debenture itself.
[329] Law of Property Act 1925, s.109(4).
[330] As regards administrators, see Insolvency Act 1986, Sch.B1, para.104 for administrators appointed under that schedule, and in other cases (special administration regimes) see Enterprise Act 2002, s.249 and the Enterprise Act 2002 (Commencement No.4 and Transitional Provisions and Savings) Order 2003 (SI 2003/2093 (c.85)), art.3.
[331] The section validates "the acts", not the appointment: *Re Allison, Johnson & Foster Ltd Ex p. Birkenshaw* [1904] 2 K.B. 327.
[332] Per Lord Simmonds in *Morris v Kanssen* [1946] A.C. 459 (HL), 472 (considering the ambit of s.180 of the Companies Act 1948).
[333] *Morris v Kanssen* [1946] A.C. 459 (HL), 471.
[334] *Morris v Kanssen* [1946] A.C. 459 (HL), 472; *Woollett v Minister of Agriculture and Fisheries* [1955] 1 Q.B. 103 (CA).
[335] But in *Bank of Baroda v Panessar* [1987] Ch. 335, Walton J. held that if the purported appointment of the receiver is as agent of the company, and the receiver purports to act as agent for the company, the appointor is not responsible or liable for his acts.
[336] This subject is dealt with fully in *Kerr & Hunter on Receivers and Administrators*, 18th edn (London, Sweet & Maxwell), Ch.19.

enforce the security. Even where no express provision is made, s.101(1)(ii) of the 1925 Act provides for such a power in the case of any mortgage by deed.

The mortgage document will usually set out expressly the circumstances in **3–139** which the mortgagee's power of sale arises and in which a receiver can be appointed. Those circumstances are usually the same in each case and, unless the mortgage deed provides otherwise, a receiver cannot be appointed unless and until the power of sale arises.[337]

The statutory power of sale does not arise unless: **3–140**

(a) the principle monies secured have become due and notice has been served on the mortgagor[338] requiring repayment of the principal and default has been made for three month; or

(b) interest is two months in arrears; or

(c) there has been a breach of a provision in the mortgage deed not relating to repayments of principal or interest[339]; or

(d) the mortgage deed provides (as it does normally provide) for the power to arise without any of the foregoing occurring.

In the case of company charges, there is usually a provision permitting a receiver to be appointed as soon as the principal becomes repayable, or if interest is in arrears for a specified period, or if repayment of the principal or interest has been demanded and default made. If the chargee wishes to rely solely on a provision permitting appointment on the grounds of a winding-up, he must obtain the leave of the court.[340]

The statutory powers of an LPA receiver are very limited and do not extend **3–141** to running a business as receiver and manager. LPA receivers were therefore in practice only appointed where the charge in question covered land or (more recently) book debts and not a business. However, in some property developments the charges have given LPA receivers greatly extended powers, which have enabled them to complete or carry out very substantial construction works and to deal with the selling or letting of the completed property.[341]

---

[337] Law of Property Act 1925, s.109(1).

[338] In *Manton v Parabolic Pty Ltd* [1986] N.S.W.L.R. 361, it was held that: (1) the notice need only be served on the mortgagor, and need not be served on later mortgagees; and (2) if there was default in service of the notice and this was known to the purchaser, any conveyance to him by the mortgagee took effect subject to the mortgagor's equity of redemption, which continued to be enforceable against the purchaser.

[339] Law of Property Act 1925, s.103.

[340] Law of Property Act 1925, ss.110 and 205(1)(i).

[341] See e.g. the factual situation in *Re Kentish Homes Ltd* [1993] B.C.C. 212, 219.

Chapter 4

Expenses

4–001   Just as the correct differentiation of fixed and floating charges is fundamental to many of the issues which arise in connection with both administration and administrative receivership, so too the incidence of the expenses of insolvency proceedings affects many of the questions discussed in more detail elsewhere in this work. In general terms, the consequence of a debt or liability being characterised as an expense is that it will be paid in full, either from floating charge assets, or from the assets of the company not subject to a security in priority to other unsecured claims. For that reason, the incidence of expenses can also be a relevant factor in the choice of insolvency procedure by a secured creditor (where such a choice exists). It is therefore convenient to identify the issues relating to expenses in a discrete commentary before proceeding to those other questions.

In every case, the relevant questions are whether a debt or liability is an expense of the insolvency proceedings in question and, if so, from what assets it is to be paid and with what priority over other claims. In administration, the Act and rules make some provision for these matters[1]: assets subject to a floating charge are available to the administrator for the payment of administration expenses.[2] There is no equivalent legislation in respect of receivership expenses. As between the two, it is nevertheless the issues relating to administration expenses which have given rise to most of the uncertainties.

The contentious issues are largely a by-product of the amendments made to the Insolvency Rules 1986 in consequence of the Enterprise Act 2002 reform of administration, coupled with case law developments in connection with both floating charges and liquidation expenses. In short, r.2.67 now makes express provision for administration expenses (modelled upon the rules on liquidation expenses) and the House of Lords has successively ruled on the interpretation of the equivalent liquidation rule,[3] reversed 35 years' understanding of the incidence of liquidation expenses on floating charge realisations[4] (thereby introducing an anomalous distinction between administration and liquidation, but which has now been reversed by statute[5]) and,

---

[1] Insolvency Act 1986, Sch.B1 para.99 and Insolvency Rules 1986, r.2.67.
[2] Insolvency Act 1986, Sch.B1 para.70.
[3] *Re Toshoku Finance UK Plc (In Liquidation)* [2002] 1 W.L.R. 671 (HL).
[4] *Buchler v Talbot; Re Leyland DAF Ltd* [2004] 2 A.C. 298 (HL).
[5] Insolvency Act 1986, s.176ZA with effect from April 6, 2008 but subject to transitional provisions and savings in the Companies Act 2006 (Commencement No.5, Transitional Provisions and Savings) Order 2007 (SI 2007/3495).

lastly, characterised a common form of charge purporting to be a fixed charge on book debts as, in fact, being a floating charge.[6]

At the time of production of this work the decision of the Court of Appeal is **4–002** awaited in *Re Nortel GmbH*,[7] which is discussed below. However, as matters stand, further legislative intervention is needed to bring clarity and a more uniform approach to the issue of expenses across all insolvency procedures and in particular to resolve the continuing uncertainty as to the meaning and effect of para.99 of Sch.B1 and r.2.67 in administrations.[8] The need for legislative intervention is urgent because the uncertainties and lack of uniformity of the existing rules detract from the utility and attractiveness of administration as a rescue procedure.

1. LIQUIDATION EXPENSES

Subject to a number of important points of difference, the rules on liquidation **4–003** expenses provide the back-drop for the rules on expenses in administrative receivership and administration. One point of difference is that in an insolvent liquidation a liability that is neither a provable debt nor an expense will be a liability for which the law affords no remedy. This is not the case in administrative receivership where, even in the case of a liability incurred by the receiver as agent of the company and without personal liability, which does not fall to be paid or reimbursed from the floating charge assets, the creditor will be able to proceed against the company or prove his debt in a subsequent liquidation. Some liabilities incurred during the course of an administrative receivership where there is a concurrent liquidation, for example certain important tax liabilities, may even qualify as expenses of the liquidation.

The position in administrations is more complex. Until the changes brought about by the Enterprise Act 2002, administration was seen as a temporary regime, and there was thought to be no power in an administrator to make any distributions of assets to unsecured creditors.[9] The making of distributions was the exclusive preserve of the liquidator (unless the company entered into a company voluntary arrangement under the Insolvency Act 1986 or promoted a scheme of arrangement under what is now Pt 26 of the Companies Act 2006). The approach of the courts to the payment of expenses in such an administration reflected the practical needs of trading a struggling business for a limited period and involved an exercise in discretion, balancing the restrictions on the rights of the creditor to take steps to enforce his debt, and the efforts of the administrator to achieve a successful rescue of the company or parts of its business as a going concern. The courts were fortified in this pragmatic

---

[6] *Re Spectrum Plus Ltd (In Liquidation)* [2005] 2 A.C. 680 (HL). For a general review of the law on expenses in insolvency proceedings prior to all these changes, see Gabriel Moss and Nick Segal, "Insolvency Proceedings; Contract and Financing: the expenses doctrine in liquidation, administrations and receiverships" [1997] CFILR 1.

[7] The first instance decision is reported at *Re Nortel GmbH* [2011] B.C.C. 277. See STOP PRESS on the Court of Appeal decision after the preface to this work.

[8] Including in particular whether *Re Atlantic Computer Systems Plc* [1992] Ch. 505 (CA), the leading authority on administration expenses before the Enterprise Act 2002, remains good law.

[9] *Re St Ives Windings Ltd* (1987) 3 B.C.C. 634; but see *Re John Slack Ltd* [1995] B.C.C. 1116 (payment in full to unsecured creditors).

approach by the knowledge that if the company was restored to health by the administration or entered into a scheme or arrangement, it would pay the expenses of the administration in full; and if the company subsequently went into liquidation, any unpaid expenses would at least rank as unsecured debts in the liquidation.

The changes brought about by the Enterprise Act 2002 were far-reaching. For the first time the revised administration procedure included a power, with the consent of the court, to make distributions. The intent was that in an appropriate case, administration could operate as the only form of insolvency process for an insolvent company, and winding-up would be unnecessary. In such a case, a debt or liability which is not provable and does not rank as an expense could in theory go unpaid if the administrator exhausted the available funds in the estate through the exercise of his powers to make distributions. However, since, unlike the case in liquidations, distribution to unsecured creditors requires permission from the court, such a situation is unlikely to arise in practice because permission to distribute would probably be made conditional on justice being done. In policy terms, there is nevertheless a clear tension in a trading administration between (i) permitting an administrator, faced with a need to trade a struggling business, not to pay all debts and liabilities arising in the administration in full from limited resources, and (ii) ensuring that debts and liabilities that would be paid in full as expenses in a liquidation are paid or at least partly provided for.

(a) General

4–004   Rule 4.218 of the Insolvency Rules 1986 sets out a list of liquidation expenses and specifies the assets out of which they are to be paid.[10] In *Re Toshoku Finance UK Plc*[11] ("*Toshoku*"), Lord Hoffmann stated that such liquidation expenses are debts and liabilities incurred after the company went into liquidation and which cannot be proved. They are thus to be distinguished from debts or liabilities which had accrued due before the company went into liquidation,[12] or debts or liabilities to which the company becomes subject after that date by reason of an obligation incurred before that date. Those debts or liabilities can be proved: see rr.12.3(1) and 13.12(1).[13]

Lord Hoffmann also stated that r.4.218 was intended to be a definitive statement of what could qualify as an expense of the liquidation. He asserted that apart from any qualifications which could be discerned from the wording of the rule itself, and subject to r.4.220(2), the court had no discretion to disallow

---

[10] Insolvency Rules 1986, r.4.218 is supplemented by rr.4.218A–E regulating the payment of litigation expenses out of floating charge assets.

[11] *Re Toshoku Finance UK Plc (In Liquidation)* [2002] 1 W.L.R. 671 (HL).

[12] Which is the date upon which the order was made by the court or the resolution passed for the winding-up of the company.

[13] At [25] Lord Hoffmann gave, as an example of this category, debts arising out of a pre-liquidation contract, such rent reserved under a lease, which should generally be proved whether it accrued due before or after the liquidation. (The wording of both Insolvency Rules 1986, r.12.3(1) and r.13.12(1) has been amended since *Toshoku* but not so as to affect this point.)

any expenses falling within the wording of the rule.[14] As will be seen, this is a crucial aspect of the *Toshoku* decision when considering the application of the equivalent wording of r.2.67 in administrations.

However, Lord Hoffmann also described an exception to this approach under which a provable debt or liability arising out of obligations incurred before the winding-up may nevertheless be paid in priority to other creditors where the property to which the liability relates is retained and used by the liquidator for the benefit of the winding-up. The classic example is rent under a pre-liquidation lease which falls due during the winding-up in respect of a company's business premises which are occupied by the liquidator for the benefit of the winding-up. Such debt or liability may be treated *as if* it were an expense of the winding-up and accorded the same priority as a liquidation. Although originally founded in discretion, this approach has hardened into a well-settled principle which has come to be known as the *Lundy Granite* principle after the case of the same name.[15] As Lord Hoffmann explained, in *Re Oak Pits Colliery Co*[16] Lindley L.J. rationalised the principle on the basis that where a liquidator retained and used property in the liquidation, it would be just and equitable to treat the liability *as if* it were a debt contracted for the purpose of the winding up.

There has been some confusion in recent authorities as to whether the *Lundy*   **4–005**
Granite principle operates outside the list of liquidation expenses in r.4.218 and as an adjunct to it: or whether it is necessary for such a debt to qualify both under the *Lundy Granite* principle and under one of the heads in r.4.218 to be entitled to priority payment. In *Toshoku*, when examining Lindley L.J.'s rationale for the *Lundy Granite* principle, Lord Hoffmann observed that Lindley L.J. was not saying that a provable debt which was given priority, for example rent falling due in the liquidation under a pre-liquidation lease, had actually been incurred as an expense of the winding up, because "it plainly had not".[17] Lord Hoffmann also went on expressly to reject a submission that the grounds upon which post-liquidation debts count as expenses could be assimilated with the grounds upon which a continuing obligation under a pre-liquidation contract might be treated as a liquidation expense. He stated that "the two categories of expenses cannot be assimilated in this way."[18] That seemed clear enough, but Lord Hoffmann then also commented, in deciding that r.4.218 was intended to serve as an exhaustive list and rejecting a submission that the court had a discretion to decide what constituted an expense if the debt fell within r.4.218, that "The court will of course interpret rule 4.218 to include debts which, under the *Lundy Granite* principle, are deemed to be expenses of the

---

[14] *Toshoku* did not concern, and hence did not cast any doubt upon the cases under which the court retains the right to deprive a liquidator of payment of expenses which he has not properly incurred: see e.g. *Re Silver Valley Mines (Winding Up)* (1882) L.R. 21 Ch. D. 381 (CA); *Re Wilson Lovatt & Sons Ltd* [1977] 1 All E.R. 274; *Re MC Bacon Ltd (No.2)* [1990] 3 W.L.R. 646; *Mond v Hammond Suddards (No.2)* [2000] Ch. 40 (CA), 53; and *Re Floor Fourteen Ltd* [2001] 3 All E.R. 499 (CA).

[15] *Re Lundy Granite Co* (1870–1871) L.R. 6 Ch. App. 462 (CA).

[16] *Re Oak Pits Colliery Co* (1882) L.R. 21 Ch. D. 322 (CA).

[17] At [26]–[27].

[18] At [37].

liquidation. Ordinarily this means that debts such as rents under a lease will be treated as coming within paragraph (a), but the principle may possibly enlarge the scope of other paragraphs as well."[19] In obiter dicta in the administration case of *Re Lehman Brothers International (Europe), Lomas v RAB Market Cycles (Master) Fund Ltd*,[20] having held that the *Lundy Granite* principle applies to administration expenses, Briggs J. referred to this latter comment in *Toshoku* and seemed to conflate the two categories. A similar approach was taken by H.H.J. Purle QC in *Goldacre (Offices) Ltd v Nortel Networks UK Ltd*[21] who appeared to consider that it was necessary to fit a debt falling within the Lundy Granite principle into the list of administration expenses in r.2.67 as well. It is respectfully suggested that such an exercise is confusing and unnecessary if the *Lundy Granite* principle applies.

4–006   Two sub-paragraphs of r.4.218(3) are worthy of particular mention. Sub-paragraph (a)(ii) gives priority to expenses properly chargeable or incurred by the liquidator in preserving, realising or getting in any of the assets of the company or otherwise in preparing or conducting legal proceedings, whether in his own name or in the name of the company. If a liquidator were to enter into a fresh contract for such purpose (e.g. engaging solicitors to pursue a claim for recovery of assets), the debt or liability so incurred would be paid in priority to unsecured debts.

The second sub-paragraph worthy of particular note is subs.(m) which gives priority to "any necessary disbursements by the liquidator in the course of his administration".[22] *Toshoku* is an illustration of a "necessary disbursement", namely a sum which statute imposed upon the company in liquidation. In that respect, Lord Hoffmann adopted the "simple approach" of Brightman J. in *Re Mesco Properties Ltd*,[23] holding that since s.8(2) of the Income and Corporation Taxes Act 1988 expressly provides for a company to be chargeable to corporation tax on profits or gains arising in a winding-up, and because the tax was a post-liquidation liability it fell to be discharged by the liquidator as a "necessary disbursement" under what is now r.4.218(3)(m).[24] That approach applied even when, as in *Toshoku*, the tax liability did not arise from any act that benefited the liquidation.

4–007   Lord Hoffmann's reasoning in *Toshoku* in relation to "necessary disbursements" may well have gone further than reliance upon the wording of the relevant section of ICTA 1988. Lord Hoffmann expressly disapproved of the decision of Nicholls V.C. in *Re Kentish Homes Ltd*,[25] which had held that although a company was chargeable in respect of community charge on a block of flats in respect of the period during a winding-up, the court had a discretion to direct the liquidator not to pay the charge as a liquidation expense. Lord

---

[19] At [38].
[20] *Re Lehman Brothers International (Europe (In Administration)), Lomas v RAB Market Cycles (Master) Fund Ltd* [2009] EWHC 2545 (Ch).
[21] *Goldacre (Offices) Ltd v Nortel Networks UK Ltd (In Administration)* [2010] Ch. 455.
[22] "Necessary", in this context, means a legal not a commercial or moral necessity for payment.
[23] *Re Mesco Properties Ltd* [1979] 1 W.L.R. 558.
[24] At [42]. (The same provision was then Insolvency Rules 1986, r.4.218(1)(m).)
[25] *Re Kentish Homes Ltd* [1993] B.C.C. 212.

Hoffmann held in para.41 of his speech in *Toshoku* that there was no discretion about the application of what is now r.4.218(3)(m), and that since the company in *Kentish Homes* had been the chargeable person for the relevant period under the Local Government Finance Act 1988, the liquidator in that case ought to have been obliged to pay the community charge as a necessary disbursement.

The significance of this analysis is that, in contrast to Income and Corporation Taxes Act 1988, the Local Government Finance Act 1988 did not make any express reference to the company being in winding-up at all. Hence Lord Hoffmann appears to have thought that the mere fact that the company was the chargeable person under statute in respect of the period post-liquidation was sufficient to bring the community charge within the scope of what is now r.4.218(3)(m). Lord Hoffmann was also well aware that his decision might have the result that a wide class of liabilities imposed upon a company in liquidation might qualify for priority payment under that rule. He remarked that if this was thought unjust it was not because of the liquidation expenses principle, but because it might be unjust to impose certain liabilities on companies in liquidation. Whether this should be so was, he concluded, a legislative decision.[26]

In *Re Nortel GmbH* at first instance, Briggs J. took the view that Lord Hoffmann's reasoning did not depend upon whether the statutory language imposing the liability had expressly referred to it being payable by a company in liquidation: he decided that it was sufficient that the statute imposed liability on a company, whether or not in liquidation.[27]

In *Toshoku*, Lord Hoffmann did not appear to envisage that a company in liquidation could incur a liability to a third party that would neither be provable nor payable as an expense, and hence would fall into a "black hole". But it has been pointed out that this was not the ratio of his decision,[28] and subsequent cases have shown that this was a possibility.[29] It will, however, be a rare case in liquidations, and certainly not a result that a court would readily reach if the legislation made express provision for a liability to be payable by a company in liquidation.[30]

Against this background, subject to any judicial re-interpretation of Lord **4–008** Hoffmann's speech in *Toshoku*, for most purposes it would seem that the key

---

[26] Referring to the potential liabilities of a company in liquidation under environmental legislation: see [45]–[46]. The practical difficulty is that many statutes do not expressly consider the question of whether liabilities which they create should apply to a company in liquidation, administration or any other insolvency procedure.

[27] *Re Nortel GmbH* [2011] B.C.C. 277, [133]. See also STOP PRESS, after the preface to this work, on the Court of Appeal decision in *Nortel*.

[28] But see *Re Allders Department Stores Ltd* [2005] 2 All E.R. 122 and *Exeter City Council v Bairstow* [2007] 4 All E.R. 437, [77].

[29] In *Re T&N Ltd* [2006] 1 W.L.R. 1728, in the context of asbestos illnesses, David Richards J. held that on the construction of r.13.12(2), tort claims where the wrongful acts had occurred prior to liquidation but where the actionable loss had not been suffered until after the relevant date of winding-up (and hence where there was no accrued cause of action at the date of the winding-up) would not be provable debts. It was not (and could not sensibly be) suggested that such liabilities would be liquidation expenses either. This was seen as manifestly unjust and r.13.12(2) was promptly amended to reverse this position (see Insolvency (Amendment) Rules 2006, SI 2006/1272 as now further amended by the Insolvency (Amendment) Rules 2010, SI 2010/686).

[30] See *Toshoku*, [30] and *Nortel GmbH* [2011] B.C.C. 277, [68]. See also STOP PRESS, after the preface to this work, on the Court of Appeal decision in *Nortel*.

test for the identification of "necessary disbursements" in a liquidation will simply be whether the liability in question is one imposed upon the company by reason of events after the date of the winding-up order or resolution to wind-up, but which is not provable because it is not a debt or liability to which the company has become subject after the date of liquidation by reason of an obligation incurred before that date.

The extent to which debts or liabilities to which a company may become subject after liquidation may be provable because they arise by reason of an obligation incurred before liquidation has been considered in the context of set-off. In *Re Charge Card Services Ltd*,[31] Millett J. observed:

"By the turn of the [20th] century . . . the authorities showed that debts whose existence and amount were alike contingent at the date of the receiving order, and claims to damages for future breaches of contracts existing at that date, were capable of proof and, being capable of proof, could be set off under the section provided that they arose from mutual credits or mutual dealings. The only requirement was that they must in fact have resulted in quantified money claims by the time the claim to set off was made."

This comment was approved by Lord Hoffmann in *Secretary of State v Frid*,[32] where he observed[33]:

". . . It is sufficient [for set off] that there should have been an obligation arising out of the terms of a contract or statute by which a debt sounding in money would become payable upon the occurrence of some future events or events. The principle has typically been applied to claims for breach of contract where the contract was made before the insolvency date but the breach occurred afterwards . . . or claims for an indemnity by a guarantor where the guarantee was given before the insolvency date but the guarantor was called upon and paid afterwards . . .."

In *Frid*, Lord Hoffmann applied this principle by analogy to the obligations of the Secretary of State to make payment under ss.166 and 167 of the Employment Rights Act 1996 in respect of compensatory notice pay and redundancy payments due under ss.88 and 135 of the Employment Rights Act to former employees of a company in liquidation which had not made such payments. Lord Hoffmann did not distinguish between the two types of payment and held[34] that it made no difference that the contingent liability was created by statute. He also decided[35] that the statutory obligation of the Secretary of State

[31] *Re Charge Card Services Ltd (No.2)* [1987] Ch. 150.
[32] *Secretary of State for Trade and Industry v Frid* [2004] 2 A.C. 506 (HL).
[33] At [9].
[34] At [19].
[35] At [20].

under the Employment Rights Act was an exact analogy with a contractual guarantee. He therefore held[36]:

"The failure of the insolvent employer to pay is the contingency which crystallises the liability imposed upon the Secretary of State by sections 166 and 167 and the payment of those liabilities is in turn the contingency upon which the right of subrogation depends. But when it does become payable, it is a debt arising out of a statutory obligation which existed before the insolvency date."

Although the basic principle is relatively easy to state, its application has   **4–009** proved problematic, particularly in relation to debts and liabilities which are dependent upon the occurrence of a contingency, and debts and liabilities which arise from the exercise of some judicial or other discretion.

Although Insolvency Rule 12.3(1) proclaims that all claims by creditors are provable as debts against the company, whether they are present or future, certain or contingent, ascertained or sounding only in damages, that rule must be read together with the definition of "debt" in relation to winding-up in r.13.12. Insolvency Rule 13.12(1) defines debts so as to mean (a) any debt or liability to which the company is subject at the date upon which it goes into liquidation, and (b) any debt or liability to which the company may become subject after that date by reason of any obligation incurred before that date. In *T&N*[37] David Richards J. held that a claim which was subject to a contingency at the date of liquidation did not fall within (a), but was only provable if it fell within (b) because it arose from a pre-liquidation legal obligation. In so doing he followed the decision of the Court of Appeal in *Glenister v Rowe*[38] which was itself subsequently followed in *R. (Steele) v Birmingham CC*.[39] In *Re Nortel GmbH*, Briggs J. also commented that the need for the existence of a pre-liquidation legal obligation had also been emphasised by the High Court of Australia in *Foots v Southern Cross Mine Management*[40] and that this was now established short of a contrary decision of the Supreme Court.

Identifying a suitable obligation has not, however, proved straightforward. In *T&N*, David Richards J. held that the existence of a tortious duty of care or its breach would not amount to a pre-liquidation obligation for this purpose. But in *Haine v Day*[41] the Court of Appeal held that a pre-liquidation breach of an obligation to consult employees before making redundancies was sufficient to render the possibility of a protective award from an employment tribunal a provable contingent debt under r.13.12(1)(b).

As a separate issue, the courts have also excluded claims which, though originating from some events prior to liquidation, are still dependent upon the exercise of some form of discretion. In *Glenister* and *Steele* this was the

---

[36] At [21].
[37] *T&N* [2006] 1 W.L.R. 1728.
[38] *Glenister v Rowe (Costs)* [2000] Ch. 76 (CA).
[39] *R. (Steele) v Birmingham CC* [2006] 1 W.L.R. 2380 (CA).
[40] *Foots v Southern Cross Mine Management* [2007] B.P.I.R. 1498 (High Court of Australia).
[41] *Haine v Day* [2008] B.C.C. 845 (CA).

exercise of a judicial or administrative discretion to award costs or make an order for repayment of overpaid benefits respectively, and the resultant claims were held not provable. But in *Haine v Day*[42], the Court of Appeal was prepared to decide that where the exercise of the discretion in favour of the claimant was an inevitability, the claim was provable. The Court of Appeal also approved the old case of *Ex p. Edwards*,[43] in which an arbitrator's award of costs post-bankruptcy was held to be provable.

It is difficult to disagree with the views of Briggs J. in *Nortel GmbH* that the authorities are not entirely consistent. It is also difficult to avoid the observation that one approach seems to have underpinned the decisions in which a debtor is claiming that a particular liability was provable in his bankruptcy had hence that he was no longer subject to it after his discharge (*Glenister* and *Steele*) which another has been the foundation for the decisions in cases of corporate insolvency, where a finding that a debt was not provable might have resulted in the claim falling into a black hole (*Haine v Day*). That point was recognised overtly by Norris J. in *Unite v Nortel Networks UK Ltd*[44] and the suggestion made that the courts ought to lean in favour of provability in the case of claims by employees of insolvent companies. On any view, the area is in need of a coherent review at an appellate level.

(b)   Priorities in liquidation

4-010   As between themselves, liquidation expenses rank in the order of priority laid down by rr.4.218(3) and 4.219 which are subject to the residual jurisdiction of the court, under s.156 of the Insolvency Act 1986 and r.4.220, to vary priorities.[45]

Assets subject to a fixed or specific charge are treated as belonging in equity to the charge-holder from the outset and, as such, cannot be dealt with in any way by the company without the consent of the charge-holder. Hence, assets subject to fixed security have never been thought to be available for discharging the expenses of a liquidation which is conducted for the benefit of unsecured creditors of the company.[46]

However, in *Re Barleycorn Enterprises Ltd*[47] the Court of Appeal decided that in a liquidation, the equivalent of s.175 of the Insolvency Act 1986 meant that liquidation expenses took priority over the claims of the holder of a floating charge in the event of a deficiency of assets available for the payment of general creditors. The practical effect of this decision was diluted when, in

---

[42] *Haine v Day* [2008] B.C.C. 845 (CA).

[43] *Ex p. Edwards* (1886) 3 Morrell 179.

[44] *Unite v Nortel Networks UK Ltd* [2010] B.C.C. 706.

[45] As to the exercise of that jurisdiction, see *Re Linda Marie Ltd (In Liquidation)* (1988) 4 B.C.C. 463.

[46] If the charge-holder is not prepared to take possession of the charged assets or appoint a receiver to realise them, he may agree with the liquidator that the liquidator can sell the assets as his agent, deduct his fees and expenses, and pay the net proceeds to the charge-holder: see per Lord Hoffmann at [31] and Lord Millett at [62] and [63] of their speeches in *Buchler v Talbot; Re Leyland DAF Ltd* [2004] 2 A.C. 298 (HL).

[47] *Re Barleycorn Enterprises Ltd* [1970] Ch. 465 (CA).

Re Christonette International Ltd,[48] Vinelott J. held that where a floating charge had crystallised prior to the commencement of the winding-up (the passing of the resolution or the making of the winding-up order) this meant that the assets caught by that charge were no longer subject to a floating charge at the commencement of the liquidation, and hence were not available for payment of liquidation expenses. Vinelott J. followed the earlier decision of Bennett J. in *Re Griffin Hotel Ltd*[49] which was to the effect that pre-crystallisation of a floating charge meant that the assets covered by that (fixed) charge were not to be regarded as assets of the company available for payment of preferential creditors in the liquidation.

The Insolvency Act 1986 amended the definition of the floating charge to   **4–011** encompass a charge which "as created" was a floating charge. As Hoffmann J. indicated in *Re Brightlife Ltd*,[50] this plainly dealt with the possibility that the holder of a floating charge might attempt to "pre-crystallise" his charge without the appointment of an administrative receiver, thereby avoiding both the priority given by s.40 to receivership preferential creditors and the priority given to liquidation preferential creditors by s.175. This change was then held to have had more far-reaching consequences. In *Re Portbase Clothing Ltd*,[51] Chadwick J. applied the logic of *Barleycorn* and held that where a floating charge was pre-crystallised other than by the appointment of an administrative receiver, liquidation expenses as well as liquidation preferential creditors would have priority over the claims of the holder of the floating charge in the event of a deficiency of free assets.

In *Leyland DAF*,[52] the House of Lords held that *Barleycorn* was wrongly decided. The House of Lords' reasoning was that, in the case of a company that is in both administrative receivership and liquidation, its former assets are comprised in two separate funds, i.e. those subject to the crystallised floating charge, which belong beneficially to the debenture holder, and those not covered by the charge which are held in trust for the unsecured creditors, and each fund should bear its own costs of administering the fund. The fact that the legislature had intervened to give preferential creditors a claim in the debenture holder's fund in certain circumstances did not change the rule that the liquidation expenses are payable out of the company's fund and not the debenture holder's fund. However, the decision has now been reversed by statute (see below) and the history of decisions prior to that reversal is now primarily of interest because it helps to explain the current drafting of the rules.

Section 176ZA of the Insolvency Act 1986, introduced by the Companies   **4–012** Act 2006 following the decision of the House of Lords in *Leyland DAF*, provides that the expenses of a winding-up shall, where the unencumbered assets are insufficient to meet those expenses, be paid in priority to unsecured creditors, preferential creditors and the claims of floating charge holders. Section 176ZA also provides that rules could be made restricting

---

[48] *Re Christonette International Ltd* [1982] 1 W.L.R. 1245.
[49] *Re Griffin Hotel Ltd* [1941] Ch. 129.
[50] *Re Brightlife Ltd* [1987] Ch. 200.
[51] *Re Portbase Clothing Ltd* [1993] Ch. 388.
[52] *Buchler v Talbot; Re Leyland DAF Ltd* [2004] 2 A.C. 298 (HL).

its application, in such circumstances as might be prescribed, to expenses authorised by the holders of a floating charge, and by preferential creditors entitled to be paid in priority to them or by the court. This reflected the concern, which may have underlain the decision of the House of Lords in Leyland DAF, that the holders of a floating charge should not, in effect, be forced to write a "blank cheque" to cover expenses (e.g. for litigation in the interests of the unsecured creditors) in an amount over which they have no control and which are incurred by a liquidator who does not act in their interests.[53] The relevant rules are Insolvency Rules 1986, rr.4.218A–E.[54] The details of those rules are outside the scope of this work but, in short, they restrict a liquidator's recourse to floating charge assets for litigation costs to costs which have been authorised or approved by preferential creditors and floating charge holders whose floating charge recoveries would otherwise be diminished by the costs (or by the court in specified circumstances[55]).

(c)   Conclusion

4–013   The law on liquidation expenses may be summarised as follows. With the exception of debts and liabilities falling within the *Lundy Granite* principle applicable to property retained for the benefit of the winding-up, liquidation expenses are the expenses listed in r.4.218 which are incurred during the liquidation; the court has no discretion as to what is and what is not a liquidation expense if it falls within r.4.218. Liquidation expenses can be debited to floating charge realisations unless they are litigation expenses requiring authorisation or approval and which have not been approved or authorised. Because of this last point, and because floating charge realisations are always available to meet administration expenses,[56] the holder of a qualifying floating charge with the power to appoint an administrator, but no power to appoint an administrative receiver, may prefer to see the debtor company go into liquidation in order to have some power to prevent the dissipation of floating charge recoveries in payment of litigation expenses.

2.   ADMINISTRATIVE RECEIVERSHIP EXPENSES

(a)   General

4–014   The Act and Rules contain no rule dealing with administrative receivership in a manner equivalent to r.2.67 (administrations) or r.4.218 (liquidations). The

---

[53] Though ironically, in *Leyland Daf* itself, the majority of the liquidation expenses were actually liabilities to corporation tax incurred as a result of the activities of the administrative receivers: see para.4–011, above.

[54] Inserted by the Insolvency (Amendment) Rules 2008 (SI 2008/737).

[55] Insolvency Rules 1986, r.4.218E. The specified circumstances include the case where the person who is or is to be the defendant in proceedings, is the same person whose approval or authorisation would otherwise be needed.

[56] Insolvency Rules 1986, rr.4.218A–E are not replicated in the rules on administration expenses.

position in respect of the discharge of debts or liabilities incurred by administrative receivers is largely the product of case law.

Whatever uncertainties may have been raised about administration expenses by the introduction of r.2.67, the exposition of the principles applicable to administrative receivership in *Re Atlantic Computer Systems Plc*[57] (*"Atlantic Computers"*) remains the leading authority in relation to receivership expenses. Having first described the position in respect of liquidation (in terms which have been overtaken first by *Toshoku* and secondly by the ensuing legislation), Nicholls L.J., giving the judgment of the court, continued:

"The position now, with regard to administrative receivers, is set out in section 44(1) and (2) of the 1986 Act. Under that section an administrative receiver is personally liable on (a) any contract entered into by him in the carrying out of his functions, except in so far as the contract otherwise provides, and (b) on any contract of employment 'adopted' by him in the carrying out of those functions[58] . . . But even today an administrative receiver is not, in general, personally liable, and hence the statutory indemnity out of the assets of the company does not arise, in respect of contracts adopted by him in the course of managing the company's business, other than contracts of employment. With that one special exception, personal liability is confined, in general, to new contracts made by him. Thus he is not personally liable for the rent payable under an existing lease, or for the hire charges payable under an existing hire-purchase agreement. This is not a surprising conclusion. It does not offend against basic conceptions of justice or fairness. The rent and hire charges were a liability undertaken by the company at the inception of the lease or hire-purchase agreement. The land or goods are being used by the company even when an administrative receiver is in office. It is to the company that, along with creditors, the lessor and the owner of the goods must look for payment.

Nor is a lessor or owner of goods in such a case entitled to be paid his rent or hire instalments as an 'expense' of the administrative receivership, even though the administrative receiver has retained and used the land or goods for the purpose of the receivership. The reason is not far to seek. The appointment of an administrative receiver does not trigger a statutory prohibition on the lessor or owner of goods such as that found in section 130 in the case of a winding-up order. If the rent or hire is not paid by the administrative receiver the lessor or owner of the goods is at liberty, as much after the appointment of the administrative receiver as before, to exercise the rights and remedies available to him under his lease or hire-purchase agreement. Faced with the prospect of proceedings, an administrative receiver may choose to pay the rent or hire charges in order to retain the land or goods. But if he decides not to do so, the lessor or owner of goods has his remedies. There is no occasion, assuming that there is

---

[57] *Re Atlantic Computer Systems Plc* [1992] Ch. 505 (CA).
[58] Subsequently amended to restrict personal liability to "qualifying liability", see Ch.16.

jurisdiction, for the court to intervene and order the administrative receiver to pay these outgoings."[59]

4-015 An administrative receiver, even though acting as agent, may also incur personal liability under relevant legislation[60] and will, on general principles, be entitled to an implied indemnity out of the assets over which he has been appointed for all such liabilities properly incurred. Just as with the contractual liabilities considered in *Atlantic Computers*, any rights of indemnity enjoyed by a receiver are personal rights which do not give the third-party creditor any right to have the receivership assets, as such, applied in discharge of his claims.

The position is the same where, or to the extent that, s.109 of the Law of Property Act 1925 applies to the distribution of receivership realisations.[61] Creditors have no enforceable rights under s.109.[62]

In short, there is no concept of receivership expenses which is comparable to either liquidation or administration expenses. To the extent that the discharge of liabilities which otherwise might be thought to have the status of "expenses" is regulated at all, it is regulated through the imposition of personal liability. Outside the fields of employment contracts and new post-appointment contracts, personal liability is rarely encountered unless the receiver commits a tort.

4-016 It should not be overlooked that one consequence of the ability of an administrative receiver to create an undischarged liability on the part of the company is that, where he does so after the company has gone into liquidation, he may create a liquidation expense. This possibility was graphically illustrated by *Mesco Properties*[63] where various properties were sold during the course of a liquidation. Some were sold by receivers, some by mortgagees and some by the liquidator himself. It was common ground that neither the mortgagees nor the receivers had any liability for the tax on the chargeable gains resulting from the sales: the company alone was liable. Since the tax liability arose during the liquidation, it was not a provable debt; it was a "necessary disbursement" in the liquidation and thus a liquidation expense taking priority to the liquidator's own remuneration under the rules then in force.[64]

A similar situation arose in *Leyland DAF*.[65] Although not apparent from the short summary of the facts in the speeches in the House of Lords, it was apparent from the statement of facts before the House that most of the liquidation expenses at issue in the case did not comprise the professional costs or remuneration of the liquidators or derive from any of their activities in the liquidation. Well over half of the liquidation expenses comprised corporation tax on interest earned by the administrative receivers on the proceeds of sale of

---

[59] *Re Atlantic Computer Systems Plc* [1992] Ch. 505, 524–525.
[60] For examples of possible tax liabilities, see Ch.5.
[61] See below.
[62] *Yourell v Hibernian Bank Ltd* [1918] A.C. 372 (HL); *Liverpool Corp v Hope* [1938] 1 K.B. 751 (CA) and *Leicester Permanent Building Society v Butt* [1943] Ch. 308. See further Ch.28.
[63] *Re Mesco Properties Ltd* [1980] 1 W.L.R. 96 (CA).
[64] Insolvency Rules 1986, r.4.218(3)(m) and (p) now reverse this order of priority.
[65] *Buchler v Talbot; Re Leyland DAF Ltd* [2004] 2 A.C. 298 (HL).

assets by them in the administrative receivership. This charge to tax fell within what is now r.4.218(3)(p), namely "corporation tax on chargeable gains accruing on the realisation of any asset (without regard to whether the realisation is effected by the liquidator, a secured creditor, or a receiver or manager appointed to deal with a security)". In espousing the broad principle that the debenture holder's fund and the company's fund were separate, and that each should bear their own costs of administering the fund,[66] the House of Lords seemed to ignore the fact that the majority of the expenses which they decided should be borne by the company's fund was a corporation tax liability arising from interest earned on the proceeds of realisations of assets in the debenture-holder's fund made by the administrative receivers appointed by the debenture holder, even though this enabled the administrative receivers to treat the gross interest as a receivership realisation.

(b) Priorities in receivership

The absence of rules providing for the payment of administrative receivers' **4–017** expenses means that issues as to the priority and incidence of expenses do not arise in any way which corresponds to the issues arising in liquidation and administration. In practice, most questions as to the discharge of liabilities incurred during the course of an administrative receivership will be resolved by agreement between the receiver and his appointor.

Reference has already been made to a receiver's rights of indemnity and to s.109 of the Law of Property Act 1925. These matters are discussed in more detail in Ch.28. Where there is a right of indemnity out of charged assets, both fixed and floating charge assets are available to the receiver to satisfy his claims. Upon vacation of office, the receiver's right of indemnity is charged on and payable out of any property of the company then in his custody or control and the charge takes priority to the appointor's own security.[67]

Amongst other things, s.109 of the Law of Property Act provides for the payment of certain liabilities which would be regarded as expenses in a liquidation or in an administration. Although s.109 lays down an order of priority, it can be varied by agreement between the company and the mortgagee/debenture-holder at any time[68] and, in practice, a well drawn security will make express provision for distributions. Since the statute confers no rights on third parties, the position where there is a contractual variation is a fortiori and creditors can again have no rights to enforce payment.

Where s.109 applies, "rents, taxes, rates, and outgoings of whatever nature **4–018** affecting the mortgaged property" are payable in priority to remuneration. In *Re John Willment (Ashford) Ltd*,[69] the court appeared willing to accept that this normally conferred a discretion on the receiver as to whether or not to pay such sums but held that, where on the facts of the case non-payment of a tax liability

---

[66] See per Lord Millett at [62]–[63] and [89] (but note the subsequent legislative reversal described above under "Priorities in liquidation").
[67] Insolvency Act 1986, ss.37 and 45 and Sch.B1 para.41.
[68] Insolvency Act 1986, s.101(3) and *Yourell v Hibernian Bank Ltd* [1918] A.C. 372 (HL).
[69] *Re John Willment (Ashford) Ltd* [1980] 1 W.L.R. 73.

would cause the company to commit a criminal offence, the discretion could
only properly be exercised in favour of making payment. *Re John Willment
(Ashford) Ltd* has been applied by the Court of Appeal in *Sargent v Customs &
Excise Commissioners*.[70] This is notwithstanding that the criminal sanction
which persuaded Brightman J. in *John Willment* to hold that the receiver's
"discretion" could only be exercised in favour of accounting to C&E for
collected VAT no longer applied. However, according to Nourse L.J.:

> "The public policy argument now runs thus. The money having been
> demanded and collected from the tenants as VAT, they must be assumed
> to have paid it to the plaintiff in the expectation that he would account for
> it to the commissioners accordingly. Equally, it may be assumed that the
> tenants would not have paid the money to the plaintiff if they had known
> that he would be passing it on to the bank. It cannot possibly be right for
> the holder of a discretion to exercise it in such a way as to defeat the
> expectation of the tenants in circumstances such as these. The law does
> not allow the holder of a discretion to act so dishonourably."[71]

Sargent was in turn followed in relation to a provisional liquidator in *Re Grey
Marlin Ltd*.[72] See also consideration of this point in Ch.5.

If a receiver decides to pay an "expense" under s.109 of the Law of Property
Act, both fixed and floating charge realisations are available to him for the
purpose.[73] The discussion above on priorities makes no mention of non-
domestic rates, which, following the *Bairstow* case, feature quite prominently
in administration expenses. The basic position is that a receiver is not personally liable for non-domestic rates incurred during his period of office and is
protected in this regard by his status as agent of the company.[74] This brings
sharply into focus the different treatment in administration[75]—the administrator is also agent of the company, but the presence of a statutory scheme for
expenses, lacking in receivership, renders this fact irrelevant.

One further point is that the receiver's agency status will be lost if and when
the company enters into liquidation. Given the importance attached to the
agency status in *Ratford* and *Brown* the likelihood is that personal liability
would almost certainly follow and the receiver could rely on his indemnity.
There is then a complex question of the interplay between the fact that non-
business rates would be considered liquidation expenses (*Bairstow*), and so be
payable out of floating charge realisations, but also potentially payable by the
receiver who could then rely on his indemnity (and recourse to fixed charge
assets). At the date of publication no case has considered these issues.

---

[70] *Sargent v Customs & Excise Commissioners* [1995] 1 W.L.R. 821 (CA).

[71] *Sargent v Customs & Excise Commissioners* [1995] 1 W.L.R. 821 (CA), 829.

[72] *Re Grey Marlin Ltd* [2000] 1 W.L.R. 370.

[73] Having regard to the receiver's duties to preferential creditors under s.40, care must be taken
over apportionment between fixed and floating charge funds—see Statement of Insolvency
Practice 14.

[74] See *Ratford v Northavon DC* [1987] Q.B. 357 (CA); *Brown v City of London Corp* [1996] 1
W.L.R. 1070.

[75] Insolvency Act 1986, Sch.B1 para.99 and Insolvency Rules 1986, r.2.67.

(c) Conclusion

Where a choice of procedure exists, administrative receivership will usually be the procedure in which the treatment of expenses is most favourable to the holder of a qualifying floating charge because the absence of any statutory code dealing with expenses means that the discharge of liabilities to third parties will ordinarily be determined by commercial advantage rather than legal duty. Causing the company to incur debts or liabilities that might rank as liquidation expenses is of no concern to a receiver or his appointor unless and until the company is in liquidation, following which floating charge assets are available to the liquidator to meet those expenses. **4–019**

3. ADMINISTRATION EXPENSES

(a) General

Prior to the enactment of the Enterprise Act 2002, there was no statutory definition or list of administration expenses. Section 19(4) of the 1986 Act provided that, upon an administrator ceasing to hold office, the administrator's remuneration and any "expenses properly incurred by the administrator" were to be charged on and paid out of the property of the company in his custody or under his control in priority to any security which, as created, was a floating charge. In addition to this category of expenses, any sums payable in respect of debts or liabilities incurred, during the administration, under contracts entered into by the administrators in the carrying out of their functions, and any "qualifying liabilities" incurred under contracts of employment adopted by the administrators, enjoyed "super-priority" under ss.19(5) and 19(6). In addition to being charged on and paid out of the floating charge property, they also ranked ahead of the administrators' remuneration and expenses properly incurred by him as mentioned in s.19(4). In *Centre Reinsurance International Co v Freakley*[76] ("*Freakley*"), Lord Hoffmann[77] explained the distinction between s.19(4) and s.19(5) in the following terms: **4–020**

> ". . . subsection (4) deals with claims against the company by the administrator himself and subsection (5) deals with claims against the company by third parties. Claims by the administrator may be either for remuneration or expenses, that is to say, for goods and services supplied to the company for which the administrator has paid or chosen to make himself liable but for which he has not yet reimbursed himself out of the company's assets. Subsection (5) deals with debts and liabilities incurred by the administrator which have not been discharged and which were incurred under contracts entered into by the administrator "in the carrying out of his . . . functions . . ."

---

[76] *Centre Reinsurance International Co v Freakley* [2006] 1 W.L.R. 2863 (HL), [9].
[77] With whom the remainder of their Lordships simply expressed agreement.

Accordingly, debts arising in an administration from pre-administration contracts (such as rent or hire-purchase charges) did not automatically qualify for priority as administration expenses, and proceedings to enforce such debts could not be taken without the leave of the administrators or the court. The question of whether leave should be given depended upon a number of factors, including whether the property associated with the debt was being used by the administrators for the purposes of the administration, and whether the administration was for a limited period.

So, in *Atlantic Computers*[78] a company had acquired computer equipment on lease or hire-purchase from funders for subletting to end users. After the company went into administration, the administrators had required the end-users to continue to make payments to the company in respect of such equipment but had made no payments in respect of the larger sums due as head rentals to the funders. The Court of Appeal held that the funders were not entitled to be paid the rents due to them from the company as expenses of the administration, although it approved of the payment over of the smaller sub-rentals to the funders and would have ordered such payments as part of the court's power to give directions to its officers. The court emphatically rejected the application in administrations of the *Lundy Granite* principle that was applicable in liquidations, insisting instead upon a flexible approach, both as to what should be paid by administrators for the use of property and even as to when leave to take proceedings should be granted.

4–021   In *Freakley* the question was whether claims handling costs which a contract of re-insurance provided could be incurred by the re-insurers on behalf of the re-insured company would qualify for "super-priority" under s.19(5) as "debts or liabilities incurred, while he was administrator, under contracts entered into by him in the carrying out of his functions". The House of Lords held that they did not because the claim by the reinsurers to indemnity from the company arose under the terms of a pre-administration contract and the post-administration contracts had been entered into by the reinsurers and not by the administrators. Further, there was no policy reason why the claims should enjoy priority over other claims against the company. Lord Hoffmann went on to express the opinion that the court could in an appropriate case direct an administrator to authorise or ratify liabilities being incurred under pre-administration contracts and thereby bring them within s.(5).[79]

4–022   Section 19(3)–(10) of the 1986 Act were re-enacted with some apparently immaterial linguistic changes, as para.99 of Sch.B1. Paragraph 99(3) provides for payment of a "former administrator's remuneration and expenses" out of assets in the custody or control of the administrator in priority to any charge which, as created, was a floating charge. Paragraphs 99(4)–99(6) give "super-priority" to debts or liabilities arising out of contracts entered into by the

[78] *Re Atlantic Computer Systems Plc* [1992] Ch. 505 (CA).

[79] At [17]. In earlier first instance decisions it had been held that the court had jurisdiction to direct an administrator to pay liabilities falling outside s.19 both as an expense and in priority to s.19 liabilities: *Re Japan Leasing (Europe) Plc* [1999] B.P.I.R. 911; *Re A Company (No.005174 of 1999)* [2000] 1 W.L.R. 502.

administrators and (so long as they are qualifying liabilities) to debts and liabilities under adopted contracts of employment.

Paragraph 99 takes effect in conjunction with r.2.67 which, for the first time, provided a list of "the expenses of the administration" in "order of priority".[80] Rule 2.67 was patently modelled on the terms of r.4.218 which prescribe the categories and order of priority of expenses in a liquidation, and permit no discretion as to their payment: see *Toshoku* (above). The rule does not, any more than r.4.218 does for liquidations, itself identify the source of payment or any priority in respect of those expenses: the answers to those issues must be found (if at all) in para.99.

The purpose behind the introduction of r.2.67 was reasonably apparent. Because the Enterprise Act 2002 introduced for the first time a power for administrators, with the permission of the court, to make distributions, there was a concern that administrators should not be able to make distributions without paying the expenses (including in particular the tax liabilities) that would qualify for priority payment as an expense under r.4.218 when the company was wound-up. Hence r.2.67 was promulgated, based upon r.4.218, in order to provide a list of the expenses which qualify for priority payment.[81]

Issues soon arose over the new regime. Some concerned the drafting of the new provisions: the linkage between para.99(3) and the expenses which r.2.68(3)(c) requires must be paid before a distribution is made in an administration was not spelt out, and the reasons for the changes in wording between the old s.19 and the new para.99 were unclear. Other problems were more substantive, and arose out of the fact that the liquidation r.4.218 had been used as the template for the administration r.2.67 notwithstanding that administrations usually envisage that the company will continue to trade for a period under the control of the administrator, which is very rarely the case in a liquidation.   **4–023**

As to the first of these points, although there are minor differences in the wording of s.19 and para.99, there was no other discernible legislative intention in the Enterprise Act 2002 to make any substantive change to restrict the priority to be afforded to administration expenses. In particular, having enhanced the scope and importance of the administration procedure, there was certainly no evidence that Parliament intended substantially to change or restrict the scope of expenses that fell to be paid in full out of floating charge assets. The point was accepted by the Court of Appeal in *Re Huddersfield Fine*   **4–024**

---

[80] Insolvency Rules 1986, r.2.67(3) confers a power on the court to vary the order of priority which is comparable with that in r.4.220 (liquidations)—as to which see fn.29. In *Irish Reel Productions Ltd v Capitol Films Ltd* [2010] B.C.C. 588 the court declined to exercise the power so as to provide for the costs of a winding-up petition to be paid in priority to other administration expenses in the unlikely event of a deficiency. However, in *Re Nortel GmbH* [2011] B.C.C. 277, the court held that the jurisdiction could, in appropriate case, make a prospective order.

[81] David Richards J. doubted this analysis of the purpose of r.2.67 in *Exeter City Council v Bairstow* [2007] 4 All E.R. 437, [82] on the ground that the provisions also apply on vacation of office, but the status of expenses on vacation of office also arose under s.19 and is not a new issue under para.99. In this connection, it should be borne in mind that r.2.67(4) (establishing the linkage with para.99(3) was originally not part of r.2.67: it was introduced by way of amendment subsequently.

Worsteds Ltd[82] when considering whether any change had been intended to the "super-priority" categories in paras 99(5) and (6) of Sch.B1. The changes in language from the old s.19 were probably attributable to a legislative desire to modernise or simplify language, which is a characteristic of Sch.B1, rather than any intention to introduce any substantive limitation on the scope and priority to be afforded to administration expenses.

4–025   The second issue concerning the introduction of r.2.67 is more complex. The problem essentially arises because, apart from the ability to make distributions in both procedures, the nature of a liquidation in which r.4.218 applies is not by any means the same as the nature of an administration in which r.2.67 will apply. A liquidation is essentially a non-trading and terminal procedure, whereas administration is primarily aimed at rescuing the company or parts of its business as a going concern, and this will necessitate the continuation of trading, leading to substantial new liabilities being incurred.

Early decisions after the 2002 Act did not find the new statutory provisions easy to analyse in the context of trading administrations. In *Re Allders Department Stores Ltd*,[83] the issue was whether redundancy payments and unfair dismissal payments which would be incurred by administrators if they were to make employees redundant after the commencement of the administration would be payable in full as an expense by reason of para.99 and/or r.2.67, or would merely rank as unsecured claims. Lawrence Collins J. held that, as a matter of interpretation, paras 99(5) and (6) did not confer super-priority upon redundancy and unfair dismissal liabilities, because the statutory entitlements were not "wages or salary". In this, he (rightly) followed pre-Enterprise Act authority on s.19.[84] He also held that,

> "the position set out in paragraph 99 is not in my judgment affected by the general administration expenses provisions in the Insolvency Rules. The general provisions of rule 2.67 of the Insolvency Rules should not be construed to override the lex specialis of paragraph 99 in Schedule B1 of the 1986 Act."

In so far as that comment was intended to relate to "super-priority" under paras 99(5) and (6), it was undoubtedly correct.

Lawrence Collins J. also had to consider whether, by analogy with *Toshoku*, such payments might fall within r.2.67 and thereby qualify for "ordinary" priority as an expense of the administration. The learned judge held that they did not.[85] The main feature which influenced Lawrence Collins J.'s decision was the fact that there were already provisions giving certain other employee-related debts preferential status under Sch.6, and it would be contrary to that

---

[82] *Re Huddersfield Fine Worsteds Ltd* [2005] 4 All E.R. 886 (CA), [41]–[47].

[83] *Re Allders Department Stores Ltd (In Administration)* [2005] 2 All E.R. 122.

[84] *Powdrill v Watson* [1995] 2 A.C. 394 (HL); *Hughes v Secretary of State for Employment* Unreported December 13, 1995 (EAT).

[85] It is important to note that the case was decided on February 16, 2005. The Insolvency (Amendment) Rules 2005 were not made until March 8, 2005 and did not then take effect until April 1, 2005. Rule 2.67(4) was therefore not part of the provisions considered by the court.

statutory scheme if redundancy payments and unfair dismissal liabilities were intended, by a side-wind, to have greater priority. The judge also noted, quite correctly, that a contrary decision would have had such adverse policy consequences for the administration regime that it was impossible to conclude that such a result had been intended. If administrators had to pay in full as an expense redundancy and unfair dismissal liabilities for persons dismissed during the administration, there would be a perverse incentive for administrators to dismiss employees immediately rather than keep them on.

Although Lawrence Collins J. might have been right to observe that r.2.67 **4–026** was not intended to override the express "super-priority" provisions of paras 99(5) and (6),[86] and his decision undoubtedly avoided a serious threat to the future utility of administration, that was only half of the issue. The fact that the payments would not qualify for "super-priority" under paras 99(5) and 99(6) did not explain whether they might, by falling within r.2.67, qualify as expenses with (ordinary) priority under para.99(3). Lawrence Collins J. did not, however, venture to explain what might be encompassed within para.99(3). Nor, although he rejected a suggestion that the approach in *Toshoku* to "necessary disbursements" could apply to r.2.67(1)(f), did he explain what function r.2.67 (as it was then drafted i.e. without r.2.67(4)) had in the general scheme of administrations, or how it was supposed to relate (if at all) to para.99(3).

In 2005 doubts that had been raised about the relationship between para.99(3) **4–027** and r.2.67[87] led to r.2.67 being amended by the Insolvency (Amendment) Rules 2005[88] to include a new r.2.67(4):

"For the purposes of paragraph 99(3), the former administrator's remuneration and expenses shall comprise all those items set out in paragraph (1) of this Rule."

The accompanying explanatory statement described this as a miscellaneous amendment to "state expressly" the position. The linkage between r.2.67 and para.99(3) which is expressly established by r.2.67(4) precludes the restrictive interpretation of para.99(3) which might otherwise have been suggested by the decisions of Neuberger J. in *Re A Company (No.005174 of 1999)*[89] and, subsequently, the House of Lords in *Freakley*.[90] The intended consequence was on the face of it that any expenses falling within r.2.67 should qualify for priority payment from floating charge assets under para.99(3). Thus the distinction between s.19(4) and s.19(5) which was drawn by Lord Hoffmann in *Freakley*, confining s.19(4) to claims by the administrator against the company, and which is quoted in para 4–018 above cannot be applied to para.99(3), because

---

[86] A conclusion with which David Richards J. agreed in *Exeter City Council v Bairstow* [2007] 4 All E.R. 437, [77].

[87] For a résumé of the pre-Enterprise Act case law on the meaning and effect of s.19 and an analysis of new legislation before it had received any consideration by the court and before the addition of r.2.67(4), see Hamish Anderson, *Administration Expenses* (2003) 6 I.L.&P. 206.

[88] SI 2005/527.

[89] *Re A Company (No.005174 of 1999)* [2000] 1 W.L.R. 502.

[90] *Centre Reinsurance International Co v Freakley* [2006] 1 W.L.R. 2863 (HL).

r.2.67 manifestly covers a much wider range of claims.[91] It also raises doubts about whether Lord Hoffmann's obiter dictum[92] that the court could confer s.19(5) (now para.99(4)) priority on a liability under a pre-administration contract by directing the administrator to ratify or authorise it since that approach, under para.99, would apply to the new legislation so as to confer super-priority over all the r.2.67 expenses—a result which it is difficult to reconcile with policy where the administrator's para.99(3) "expenses" are no longer confined to his own claims for reimbursement from the company.[93]

4–028   After the introduction of r.2.67(4), in *Re Huddersfield Fine Worsteds Ltd*,[94] the Court of Appeal had to consider whether protective awards under the Trade Union Labour Relations (Consolidation) Act 1992 and payments in lieu of notice fell within para.99(5) and (6) (formerly s.19(6)–(10)). It was held that, as a matter of interpretation, but reinforced by practical and policy considerations, para.99 does not apply to protective awards[95] and that the law was thus unchanged in this respect. The practical and policy considerations were that a contrary decision would undermine the rescue culture by making it difficult for administrators to adopt contracts of employment and thereby impeding their ability to achieve the purpose of administration.

The judgment of the Court of Appeal did not, however, refer to r.2.67 and only referred in passing to para.99(3), which it misquoted, stating that it provided that a "former administrator's claim for remuneration and expenses" should generally have priority over other debts of the company. In so doing, the Court of Appeal appears to have assumed that the reference to a "claim for . . . expenses" in para.99(3) connoted no more than a former administrator's claim for out-of-pocket disbursements. Whilst this was consistent with the earlier decision of Neuberger J. in *Re A Company (No.005174 of 1999)*[96] (and also with the subsequent decision of the House of Lords in *Freakley*[97]) on s.19, it did not take account of r.2.67(4) which was, by then, law. The Court of Appeal did appear to accept, however, that what it termed "the expenses of the administration" have priority over most other debts.[98] Pumfrey J. followed *Huddersfield Fine Worsteds* in *Re Leeds United Association Football Club Ltd*[99] in holding that claims for wrongful dismissal subsequent to the adoption of a contract of employment did not enjoy super-priority under para.99(6), Sch.B1 Insolvency Act.[100]

[91] *Exeter City Council v Bairstow* [2007] 4 All E.R. 437, [49].
[92] At [17].
[93] At [6], Lord Hoffmann said: "Changes have since been made by the Enterprise Act 2002 but I say nothing about these because they were not in force at the relevant time."
[94] *Re Huddersfield Fine Worsteds Ltd* [2005] 4 All E.R. 886 (CA).
[95] It was also held that most, but not all, liabilities for payments in lieu fall outside para.99.
[96] *Re A Company (No.005174 of 1999)* [2000] 1 W.L.R. 502.
[97] *Centre Reinsurance International Co v Freakley* [2006] 1 W.L.R. 2863 (HL).
[98] See [5]–[7].
[99] *Re Leeds United Association Football Club Ltd* [2008] B.C.C.11.
[100] In *Re Nortel Networks UK Ltd* [2010] B.C.C. 706, Norris J., consistently with *Huddersfield Fine Worsteds*, held that various employee claims arising out of post-administration dismissals, including unfair dismissal and discrimination claims, were provable debts for the purposes of rr.12.3(1) and 13.12 (and thus, by implication, not expenses).

Various important questions thus remained unanswered in relation to **4–029** para.99(3) and r.2.67. First, how does r.2.67 operate in conjunction with para.99(3) during the course of an administration? Secondly, is r.2.67 intended, like r.4.218 in the context of liquidations, to be a definitive and mandatory list of expenses qualifying for priority payment in an administration? Thirdly, what is meant by "expenses properly incurred" in r.2.67(1)(a) and "necessary disbursements" in r.2.67(1)(f)? Fourthly, can any liabilities be incurred in the course of an administration which are not expenses? All these questions bear directly on whether or not the flexible approach adopted by the Court of Appeal in *Atlantic Computers* is still sustainable in respect of post-Enterprise Act administrations.

There have been a series of decisions at first instance since the publication of the last edition of this work, culminating in *Re Nortel GmbH*,[101] which have addressed these issues and which have exposed the gravity of the problems resulting from the way in which the administration expenses regime was introduced. At the time of production of the present edition, the Court of Appeal has heard an appeal in *Nortel* but has not yet delivered its judgment.[102] In view of that, and the possibility of a further appeal to the Supreme Court, the law cannot be regarded as settled.

As to the first question, it is thought that r.2.67 must have some effect on the conduct of the administration. If the authorities on s.19 are still reliable (except in so far as r.2.67(4) now provides to the contrary) then, although the para.99 charges are only stated to arise when the administrator ceases to act, they must inform the administrator's decisions as to the payment of money during the administration.[103] It would also follow that para.99(3) creates a statutory obligation, at the end of the administration, to pay as well as a charge on assets then remaining to secure the discharge of that obligation.[104] Indeed, in *Re Trident Fashions Plc*,[105] the Court of Appeal appears to have assumed that an expense payable pursuant to r.2.67 would be actionable at the suit of the expense creditor against administrators who had drawn remuneration in priority to such expense, although the judgment relates only to who should be parties to the proceedings and is very brief.

The issue has arisen in subsequent decisions but it has not yet been addressed either comprehensively or conclusively. In *Re Sports Betting Media Ltd*[106] questions arose as to the treatment of para.99(4) creditors in circumstances where earlier administrators had been replaced and new administrators applied for directions. Some post-administration creditors had been paid by the earlier administrators before they vacated office but others had not. It was held that the estate, for para.99(4) purposes, consisted only of the property in the custody

---

[101] *Re Nortel GmbH* [2011] B.C.C. 277.
[102] See STOP PRESS, after the preface to this work, on the Court of Appeal decision in *Nortel*.
[103] *Re Atlantic Computer Systems Plc (No.2)* [1990] B.C.C. 439, on appeal [1992] Ch. 505 (CA); *Powdrill v Watson* [1994] 2 B.C.L.C. 118 (CA), and [1995] 2 A.C. 394 (HL); *Re A Company (No.005174 of 1999)* [2000] 1 W.L.R. 502 and *Re Salmet International Ltd* [2001] B.C.C. 796.
[104] *Re Maxwell Fleet and Facilities Management Ltd (In Administration) (No.1)* [2001] 1 W.L.R. 323.
[105] *Re Trident Fashions Plc* [2007] 1 B.C.L.C. 491 (CA). *Trident* was an earlier round of the litigation which eventually led to *Exeter City Council v Bairstow* [2007] 4 All E.R. 437.
[106] *Re Sports Betting Media Ltd (In Administration)* [2008] B.C.C. 177.

or control of the earlier administrators when the new administrators were appointed and that the remaining claims should be paid pari passu without any prior payments being brought into account. All the claims were, however, subordinated to a claim for reasonable payment to the new administrators for executing the charge.[107] More pertinently, in *Goldacre (Offices) Ltd v Nortel Networks UK Ltd*[108] it was held that the status of a r.2.67 expense as such was not necessarily determinative of when it should be paid. There is no right to immediate payment. This decision was consistent with earlier authority but the matter did not require further consideration because the sufficiency of assets to pay all expenses was not in question. The *Goldacre* approach was followed by the Court of Session in *Cheshire West and Chester BC, Petitioners*, where it was held that the question of the remedy for a failure to pay a debt falling within r.2.67 during the administration was "entirely a matter of discretion".[109]

In *Re WW Realisation Ltd*[110] the court applied liquidation principles and gave directions to administrators enabling them to distribute funds in hand without reserving for possible expense liabilities in respect of which no claims had been received notwithstanding repeated invitations to lodge claims.

4–030   The second issue is complex. In deciding whether r.2.67 is a definitive code, two related issues arise. First, does the administrator have either a power or an obligation to make other payments in full, and, secondly, is there any room for discretion not to pay expenses falling within the statutory list.

It is probably easiest to begin with the question of whether the administrator has a power, if he wishes, to make payments in full which do not fall within r.2.67. Paragraph 66 expressly empowers the administrator to pay a creditor in full if he thinks it likely to assist achievement of the purpose of the administration and Sch.1 para.13 confers a separate power to make any payment which is necessary or incidental to the performance of his functions (which may include conferring other benefits for creditors). It is suggested that the wording of r.2.67 should not be taken to restrict the powers of the administrator derived from the primary legislation[111] and that this is a fundamental point which should also inform other aspects of the interpretation of r.2.67.[112]

---

[107] The provision of payment for the new administrators was an exercise of the court's jurisdiction established by *Re Berkeley Applegate (Investment Consultants) Ltd (No.1)* [1989] Ch. 32.

[108] *Goldacre (Offices) Ltd v Nortel Networks UK Ltd (In Administration)* [2010] Ch. 455.

[109] *Cheshire West and Chester BC, Petitioners* [2011] B.C.C. 174 (Court of Session, Outer House), [32].

[110] *Re WW Realisation 1 Ltd* [2011] B.C.C. 382.

[111] This interpretation is also consistent with pre-Enterprise Act law where it was held that the court retained a jurisdiction to direct administrators to pay sums falling outside s.19 and in priority to s.19 liabilities, see *Re Japan Leasing (Europe) Plc* [1999] B.P.I.R. 911 and *Re A Company (No.005174 of 1999)* [2000] 1 W.L.R. 502. In *Re Sixty UK Ltd* [2010] B.P.I.R. 1234 the court treated an agreement to pay rent as a legitimate exercise of the para.66 power which bound the administrators. See also *Re Lehman Brothers International (Europe)* [2009] EWHC 2545 (Ch) (the imposition by the court of a condition for the refusal of permission to enforce security may have the effect of converting a debt which would not otherwise be an administration expense into one that is).

[112] Consider, in this connection, the jurisdiction of the court to authorise payments to respect foreign priorities: *Re Collins & Aikman Europe SA* [2006] B.C.C. 861. See *Re MG Rover Espana SA* [2006] B.C.C. 599 (administrator could, by virtue of para.66, depart from the normal ranking of claims in order to facilitate achievement of the purpose of the administration).

The question of whether an administrator might be under an *obligation* to pay debts or liabilities falling outside the wording of r.2.67 is less clear.[113] The argument is that, in the same way as the *Lundy Granite* principle operates in liquidations as an addition to (or means of enlarging the meaning of) r.4.218, the use of similar words in r.2.67 indicates that there should be a similar principle in administrations, so that debts or liabilities arising under continuing pre-administration contracts in respect of property retained for use in the administration are required to be discharged in full in the administration.

This argument appears to have been accepted, at least at first instance. In *Re Lehman Brothers International (Europe), Lomas v RAB Market Cycles (Master) Fund Ltd*[114] Briggs J. accepted (obiter) that the *Lundy Granite* principle should be as applicable in administrations as in liquidations. A similar approach was taken by H.H.J. Purle QC in *Goldacre (Offices) Ltd v Nortel Networks UK Ltd*[115] in relation to the payment of rent under a pre-administration lease, and this was followed in Scotland in *Cheshire West and Chester BC, Petitioners*.[116] As indicated above, there would appear to be some uncertainty—traceable to para.38 of Lord Hoffmann's speech in *Toshoku*—as to whether a liability which would qualify for priority payment under the *Lundy Granite* principle need also fall within one of the sub-rules of r.2.67(1) as well, but the courts seem to have adopted a pragmatic approach to interpretation so that, for practical purposes, the real issue is whether the *Lundy Granite* principle applies.

In the *Lehman Brothers* case, Briggs J. was concerned with whether monies received in respect of securities which were held for customers of the bank pursuant to pre-administration custody agreements gave rise to debts to the customers which ranked for priority payment. He held that such monies were trust monies, so the question of priority payment of debts did not arise. But Briggs J. went on to express the view, obiter, that even though the *Lundy Granite* principle did not strictly apply because the securities had not been used for the benefit of the administration, nevertheless it was necessary "in fairness and justice" that such debts should be paid to avoid a windfall accruing to the unsecured creditors of the bank at the expense of the customers, and hence that the debts would have qualified as "necessary disbursements" under

---

[113] Except in the case of the costs of applications. In *Re Professional Computer Group Ltd* [2009] B.C.C. 323, following *Re Structures & Computers Ltd* [1998] B.C.C. 348 and *Re World Class Homes Ltd* [2005] 2 B.C.L.C. 1, held that it had jurisdiction to order that an opposing creditor's costs be paid as an administration expense (but declined to make the order) but the jurisdiction to make such orders is founded in r.2.12, not r.2.67. See also *Irish Reel Productions Ltd v Capitol Films Ltd* [2010] B.C.C. 588 where the court exercised the same jurisdiction to provide for payment as an administration expense of the costs of a dismissed winding-up petition where an administration order was made instead. Questions have also arisen in respect of pre-appointment costs and pre-packs—see *Re Kayley Vending Ltd* [2009] B.C.C. 578 and *Re Johnson Machine and Tool Co Ltd* [2010] B.C.C. 382. Those cases involved the general power of the court to make orders under Sch.B1, para.13(1)(f) and any such question should now be considered in the light of (the subsequently introduced) r.2.67A (pre-administration costs).

[114] *Re Lehman Brothers International (Europe), Lomas v RAB Market Cycles (Master) Fund Ltd* [2009] EWHC 2545 (Ch).

[115] *Goldacre (Offices) Ltd v Nortel Networks UK Ltd (In Administration)* [2010] Ch. 455.

[116] *Cheshire West and Chester BC, Petitioners* [2011] B.C.C. 174 (Court of Session, Outer House).

r.2.67(1)(f) in any event. Though a producing a meritorious result, such a broad approach to the interpretation of r.2.67 is difficult to justify logically, as it would enable a court to use the "necessary disbursements" head as a discretionary catch-all.

4–031   The question of whether r.2.67 is intended to be an exhaustive and non-discretionary list of liquidation expenses was considered by David Richards J. in *Exeter City Council v Bairstow*[117] ("*Exeter City*") where the council applied for declarations that non-domestic rates on occupied property were expenses within r.2.67(1)(a) or, alternatively, (f) and, in either eventuality, were within para.99(3).[118] It was held that they were necessary disbursements within r.2.67(1)(f) and para.99(3). Although the status of unoccupied property rates was not before David Richards J. in *Exeter City*, he was invited to express a view and responded that unoccupied property rates appeared indistinguishable.[119]

The argument for treating r.2.67 as a definitive (i.e. exhaustive and non-discretionary) code is based on Lord Hoffmann's decision in *Toshoku* that r.4.218 was a definitive code both as a matter of authority and construction. In *Exeter City*, David Richards J. concluded that it was inconceivable that Parliament could have intended that the provisions of r.2.67, which were obviously derived from the wording of r.4.218, should be interpreted any differently[120] Although Lawrence Collins J. in *Allders* sought to distinguish *Toshoku* on the grounds that administrations were not liquidations and that, in *Toshoku*, Lord Hoffmann was "justifying the treatment of certain debts as expenses, not offering a definition of what liabilities were disbursements", he did so in the context of deciding that employees' statutory entitlements were not "necessary disbursements" within the meaning of r.2.67(1)(f). He had already noted that, where r.4.218 applies, there is no room for discretion. The decisions in *Allders* and *Exeter City* were compatible in that respect.

4–032   The question of whether there is any discretion not to pay expenses falling within r.2.67 in full has also received consideration in subsequent cases. Although the application of the *Lundy Granite* principle was held to be subject to the exercise of an *Atlantic Computers*[121] discretion in *Re Sixty UK Ltd*,[122] the reverse was held to be the case in both *Goldacre* and *Cheshire West*.[123] The

---

[117] *Exeter City Council v Bairstow* [2007] 4 All E.R. 437. See also *Re TM Kingdom Ltd (In Administration)* [2007] B.C.C. 480, where a company was moved from administration into voluntary liquidation in order to avoid the liability.

[118] The narrow terms of the declarations sought in *Exeter City* meant that David Richards J. was not concerned with the first of the questions identified above, namely how r.2.67 and para.99(3) operate during the course of an administration. The judgment records, on two occasions, that he is not dealing with that issue—see [13] and [47].

[119] This was particularly serious because administrators, unlike liquidators, have no power to disclaim onerous property. However, with effect from April 1, 2008, the Non-Domestic Rating (Unoccupied Property) (England) Regulations 2008 (SI 2008/386) extended the relief from unoccupied property rates for companies in liquidation to companies in administration.

[120] See [79] and [80].

[121] *Re Atlantic Computer Systems Plc* [1992] Ch. 505 (CA).

[122] *Re Sixty UK Ltd (In Administration)* [2010] B.P.I.R 1234.

[123] Neither judgment refers to the earlier decision in *Re Sixty UK Ltd*. Discretion as to whether a liability ranks as an expense must be clearly distinguished from discretion as to enforcement—as to which, see para.4–023. In *Goldacre*, H.H. Judge Purle QC (sitting as a High Court judge) was able to distinguish the decision of the Court of Appeal in *Sunberry Properties Ltd v Innovate*

matter then received more extensive consideration in the judgment of Briggs J. in *Re Nortel GmbH*.[124] This case, where judgment in the Court of Appeal is now awaited,[125] raised the problems with the new administration expense rules in a particularly acute form. At issue was the ranking of liabilities resulting from the issue of financial support directions and contributions notices by The Pensions Regulator after the commencement of administration. After a detailed review of the previous authorities, Briggs J. first concluded that the liabilities were not provable debts for the purposes of r.13.12[126] because they could not be said to have arisen out of a pre-administration obligation. He also held that, following what he took to be the implication of Lord Hoffmann's speech in *Toshoku*,[127] that it is general rule that a statutory liability which is not a provable debt constitutes a necessary disbursement which is an administration expense within r.2.67(1)(f) (unless it falls within any other paragraph of the rule). Despite Briggs J.'s evident concern at the implications of his conclusions, he held that the decision in *Toshoku* precluded the exercise of any discretion.[128]

In support of the conclusion emerging from these decisions it might also be **4–033** argued that, if there is any discretion in whether or not to pay expenses falling within r.2.67 in full, it renders r.2.67 almost meaningless. This cannot have been intended, especially given that at least one (if not the main) purpose of the introduction of r.2.67 was to prevent administrators exercising their new powers to make distributions in such a way as to leave undischarged those (tax) liabilities which would be paid in full as an expense in the course of a liquidation. Notwithstanding the clear differences between liquidation and administration as insolvency procedures, rr.2.67 and 4.218 are two similar rules in the same statutory instrument dealing with the same type of subject matter. Both derive from the exercise of the power to make delegated legislation dealing with the costs of insolvency proceedings.[129]

That said, if r.2.67 does not involve any element of discretion, it is difficult to see why the administrator's power to distribute to creditors (other than secured and preferential creditors) should require the leave of the court under

---

Logistics Ltd [2009] B.C.C. 164 (CA) on that ground. In that case, administrators had allowed a third party into occupation of leasehold premises in breach of the tenant company's covenants and the landlords sought permission under Sch.B1, para.43 to commence proceedings. Permission was refused with the court holding that the question of rent was one in respect of which it had a wide discretion. However, the Court of Appeal did not consider the *Lundy Granite* principle or its implications.

[124] *Re Nortel GmbH* [2011] B.C.C. 277.

[125] See STOP PRESS, after the preface to this work, on the Court of Appeal decision in *Nortel*.

[126] The case also deals with a derivative point about proof of debt in a subsequent liquidation but the law in that respect, where a liquidation is immediately followed by administration, is now that the cut-off date is the date of the commencement of administration following amendments resulting from the Insolvency (Amendment) Rules 2010 (SI 2010/686).

[127] *Re Toshoku Finance Plc (In Liquidation)* [2002] 1 W.L.R. 671 (HL).

[128] In *Re Capitol Films Ltd* [2011] 2 B.C.L.C. 359, 401–402, the court refused to allow administrators to recoup the costs of proceedings even though such costs are capable of being an administration expense in an appropriate case. However, this is an example of the court's discretion as to whether administrators should have indemnity out of the estate which does not inform any consideration of whether, in cases where the right of indemnity is not in issue, there is any residual discretion to disallow payment as an administration expense. See further fn.14.

[129] Insolvency Act 1986 s. 411, Sch.8 paras 17 and 18.

para.65(3). The fact that such leave is required means that the court can require that all creditors are fairly treated having regard to what would happen if leave were refused and distribution had to be made instead through the medium of a liquidation (when the para.99 charges would apply).[130] If permission to distribute to unsecured creditors is sought, the administrator will have to explain and justify the proposed treatment of post-administration liabilities. Taking this premise it can be argued that r.2.67 can and should be interpreted more purposively and thus differently from r.4.218. The interpretation which would be most consistent with the rescue culture is that it is merely a priority provision which assumes that the expenses with which it is concerned are payable out of the company's assets and provides for their priority, but that of itself it confers no right to pay or be paid.[131] Earlier in his judgment in *Exeter City*, David Richards J. had accepted the need for a purposive construction which was consistent with the promotion of business rescue and that the automatic treatment of business rates as an expense would have adverse consequences in at least some cases.[132] Recognising an element of discretion would also be consistent with the administrator's express statutory powers, referred to above, to pay sums to unsecured creditors which may mean that funds will not be available for payment of the sums mentioned in r.2.67.

4–034   As to the interpretation of r.2.67 and, in particular, r.2.67(1)(a) and (f), in *Re Trident Fashions Plc*,[133] the Court of Appeal recognised the possibility that non-domestic rates arising after the commencement of the administration might constitute an expense of the administration for the purposes of either r.2.67(1)(a) or (f). On closer consideration in *Exeter City*, David Richards J. held that business rates (occupied or unoccupied) could not be "expenses properly incurred" for the purposes of r.2.67(1)(a) but were "necessary disbursements" for the purposes of r.2.67(1)(f).[134] The same conclusion was reached by Briggs J. in *Re Nortel GmbH* in respect of the pensions liabilities.[135] Setting aside the wider questions as the application of r.2.67 as a whole, this conclusion is plainly consistent with earlier authority on liquidation expenses. However, David Richards J.'s explicit agreement with Lawrence Collins J.'s decision in *Allders*, that the statutory entitlements of employees are not expenses with r.2.67, suggests that, whilst r.2.67 must be accorded like effect to r.4.218 (as a mandatory code) this does not necessarily, mean that everything that would be an expense in a liquidation will also be an expense in an administration. In this respect, it would appear that the rescue context may yet affect the meaning of the words used.

4–035   The fourth and wider question is whether there can be any liabilities incurred during an administration which are not expenses, bearing in mind that the

---

[130] David Richards J. in *Exeter City* was not persuaded by submissions to this effect, see [82].

[131] This interpretation would follow that accorded to s.115 by Millett J. in *Re MC Bacon Ltd (No.2)* [1991] Ch. 127.

[132] At [59] and [68]. Briggs J. also recognised the relevance of the rescue policy to the process of statutory construction in *Re Nortel GmbH*, [147]. See also STOP PRESS, after the preface to this work, on the Court of Appeal decision in *Nortel*.

[133] *Re Trident Fashions Plc* [2007] 1 B.C.L.C. 491 (CA).

[134] At [52] and [84].

[135] *Re Nortel GmbH* [2011] B.C.C. 277, [146] and [196].

creditor will be unable to prove for the liability in the administration[136] and the administrator may make distributions exhausting the available funds. Although, in *Allders*, Lawrence Collins J. held that it was not the ratio of *Toshoku* that a liability must be either a provable debt or payable as an expense (and David Richards J. agreed in *Exeter City*), as previously noted, that nonetheless appears to have been the implicit assumption of Lord Hoffmann in relation to liquidation and, on any footing, it will be true of the generality of the liabilities of a company in liquidation.

Briggs J. in *Nortel* carefully considered whether *Allders* and *Exeter City* stood in the way of what he concluded was the true principle established by *Toshoku*, namely that a statutory liability imposed on a company in liquidation was a "necessary disbursement" and concluded that they did not. However, he was careful to confine his conclusion to statutory liabilities. The extent to which the same approach is applicable in administration could yet be found to depend on whether the ability of the administrator to distribute the available funds without paying expenses is more than a theoretical possibility. It is suggested that in practice it will not happen because leave is required and that this affords a further ground for distinguishing *Toshoku* both in this respect and on the issue of discretion.

The full implications of these questions on the pre-Enterprise Act decision **4–036** in *Atlantic Computers* remain unclear—at least pending the outcome of the *Nortel* case on appeal.[137] However, it seems increasingly likely that the introduction of r.2.67 into delegated legislation will be found to have had the effect of reversing the interpretation reached in the *Atlantic Computers* case on the comparable provisions of the primary statute in relation to the application of the *Lundy Granite* principle. In this respect there are two obstacles to any contrary conclusion. First, such a contrary conclusion can only be avoided by according a different meaning and effect to r.2.67 to that accorded, on the highest authority, to r.4.218, and, secondly, the ostensible purpose of r.2.67. The latter can be overcome through using the court's discretion when leave to distribute is sought. Notwithstanding *Exeter City* and subsequent first instance decisions, it would seem that the differences between administration and liquidation could yet justify rr.2.67 and 4.218 being construed differently, but whether there are any limits in this respect and, if so, what they are, remains to be established by further authority or legislative clarification.

A solution to the policy tensions could still be found in the approach to be adopted to the grant of leave to distribute under para.65(3) identified above but this is untested and considerable uncertainty remains. This is a matter of fundamental importance to administrators and administration creditors.

(b) Priorities in administration

As has been discussed above, in an administration, assets subject to a floating **4–037** charge can be used to pay all the expenses of the administration and are charged

---

[136] Insolvency Rules 1986, r.2.72(3)(b)(ii).
[137] See STOP PRESS, after the preface to this work, on the Court of Appeal decision in *Nortel*.

with the payment of those expenses, in priority to the claims of the holder of a charge which, as created, was a floating charge (without any qualification as regards litigation expenses requiring approval or authorisation).[138]

(c) Conclusion

4–038 As can be seen from the above, the position of a floating charge-holder in relation to payment of expenses is therefore very different in an administrative receivership and in administration and different again in a liquidation.

Whatever the prevailing uncertainties as to the precise scope and effect of the rules on administration expenses, it is clear that from the point of view of the holder of a floating charge, administration is, at present, the least favourable procedure in terms of the payment of expenses out of floating charge realisations. There is, therefore, a perverse incentive for qualifying floating charge-holders with a choice to avoid it. This is flatly contrary to the policy objective which lay behind the Enterprise Act reforms of administration which were intended to make it the procedure of choice for the rescue of businesses and a constructive alternative to administrative receivership which would reduce the total number of companies going into liquidation.

---

[138] Insolvency Act 1986, Sch.B1 para.99.

Chapter 5

Taxation of Companies in Administration and Administrative Receivership[1]

1. INTRODUCTION AND OVERVIEW

Although the Enterprise Act 2002 reforms have been effective for over eight years there are still many areas where the interaction of tax law with insolvency law is uncertain. This unfortunate state of affairs has arisen because there was little appetite on the part of Her Majesty's Revenue and Customs (HMRC) to amend the law when the economy was growing and no time (and perhaps again little appetite) to amend it when the economy entered recession. Consequently, we are left with a situation where valuable time (and creditors' money) is spent resolving issues which should already have been clarified and with the possibility that similar cases are taxed in different ways because of the different views of those dealing with them. When the Enterprise Act administration procedure was introduced, the policy of the then Department of Trade and Industry (DTI) was that the choice between whether a company should go into administration or liquidation should not be affected by taxation considerations. In order to achieve this, the taxation of administrations was aligned as much as possible with that of liquidations. Consequently, this created a difference between administrations and administrative receiverships a more obvious choice of procedure for creditors. **5–001**

The taxation of pre-Enterprise Act administrations remains unchanged and readers are referred to the 3rd edition of this work for the taxation of such cases.[2] Notwithstanding there have been no new pre-Enterprise Act administrations for eight years, there are still such cases around with unresolved tax issues, not least of which is whether tax is an expense of such administrations.[3] **5–002**

The principal changes made to tax legislation to take account of the Enterprise Act 2002 were: on appointment an administrator becomes the proper officer of the company,[4] the appointment ends an accounting period for tax **5–003**

---

[1] This chapter does not attempt a comprehensive treatment of the taxation of administrations or administrative receiverships but focuses on particular problems which appear to be of legal interest, especially those arising through the interaction of the Enterprise Act 2002 and tax legislation.

[2] See Lightman & Moss, *The Law of Receivers and Administrators of Companies*, 3rd edn (London: Sweet & Maxwell, 2000), Ch.13.

[3] It is thought that the better view is that tax was not an expense.

[4] s.108(3), Taxes Management Act 1970 (as amended by Finance Act 2003).

purposes,[5] tax liabilities arising during appointment are expenses of the administration,[6] Crown preference for pre-appointment tax liabilities was abolished,[7] and the termination of the administration ends an accounting period.[8]

5–004   These changes do not apply to the appointment of an administrative receiver. Consequently, the first part of the chapter deals with administrators and the second with administrative receivers.[9]

5–005   There are few provisions of the Taxes Acts which refer specifically to the various insolvency procedures. Many of the tax provisions to be applied were drafted with solvent going concerns in mind and this leads to many uncertainties and ambiguities.[10] Often the resolution of these problems lies in negotiation with the HMRC Officer responsible for the particular company or group. This is an unsatisfactory state of affairs and one which can lead to inconsistency between different cases. There is also the tendency of HMRC to require specific tax provisions to cover matters that are already adequately covered under the general or insolvency law. An example of this is s.130, Finance Act 2008 which deals with set-off of tax debts (owing from and to HMRC) in an insolvency procedure and which does so in a way different to the Insolvency Rules. Being primary legislation and later than the Insolvency Rules the Finance Act 2008 has introduced a different regime for tax unbeknownst to most insolvency practitioners. It is thought that HMRC thought they were merely replicating the rules; however, the fact that s.130 applies in the same way to both liquidations and administrations, whereas the rules for liquidations and administrations under insolvency law are different, shows this was flawed from the outset. In practice, whether through ignorance or convenience, the Finance Act 2008 rules tend to be ignored. A number of these problems are discussed in the following pages; however, what emerges is the fact that tax law needs to be reformed if there is to be any certainty in the taxation of the administration procedure.

2.   TAX AS A DETERMINANT OF WHICH INSOLVENCY PROCEDURE TO ADOPT

5–006 Notwithstanding that as a result of the Enterprise Act reforms, the holder of a qualifying floating charge, in the majority of cases,[11] can no longer appoint an

---

[5] s.10(1)(i), Corporation Tax Act 2009 (formerly s.12(7ZA), Income and Corporation Taxes Act 1988).

[6] Insolvency Rules 1986 (SI1986/1925), 2.67(1)(f) and (j).

[7] Sch.6, Insolvency Act 1986: Category 1 abolished by s.251, Enterprise Act 2002 with effect from September 15, 2003.

[8] s.10(1)(j), Corporation Tax Act 2009 (formerly s.12(3)(da), Income and Corporation Taxes Act 1988).

[9] In the 3rd edn the two were dealt with together thus emphasising how the 2002 reforms created a fundamental difference between administrations and administrative receiverships for tax purposes.

[10] Although this can lead to flexibility and pragmatic solutions it can also lead to similar cases being taxed in different ways.

[11] For the narrow situations in which an administrative receiver may still be appointed see Chs 1 and 2.

administrative receiver[12] there still exist many pre-September 15, 2003 charges under which such a receiver can be appointed. Where a bank still has a choice of whether to appoint an administrator or an administrative receiver, the incidence of taxation may be a fundamental factor in the choice of appointment.

The point is best illustrated by way of a simple example.   **5–007**

A company trades from premises which it bought 10 years ago for £750,000. A bank has a fixed and floating charge over the premises and a floating charge over all other assets of the business. The company is now in financial difficulty and the bank wishes to enforce its security. The premises are valued at £1,500,000.

If the bank were to appoint an administrative receiver over the company's   **5–008** assets, the sale of the premises would realise a gain of some £750,000.[13] This gain would be liable to corporation tax on chargeable gains at, for example, 26 per cent and would give rise to a tax liability of some £195,000. This would be a liability of the company and would be an unsecured claim in any subsequent liquidation (alternatively one qualifying for payment as a liquidation expense ahead of other unsecured claims if the sale takes place once the company is in liquidation).

The appointment of an administrator followed by a sale of the property   **5–009** would result in a similar liability arising; however, by contrast, the tax would be an expense of the administration.[14] The administrator would have recourse to floating charge realisations in order to pay the expense.[15] The bank would therefore, in effect, finance the tax out of any floating charge realisations.

Depending upon the amount of the floating charge assets, the bank's posi-   **5–010** tion would therefore be worse by up to £195,000 by appointing an administrator. Each individual case needs to be examined on its own merits. For example, where the company is a holding company and owns freehold properties and shares in subsidiaries, there may be no floating charge assets in that company and any tax liability, although an expense, may go unpaid for insufficiency of funds.

Similarly, the company may own no assets on which there is a chargeable   **5–011** gain, and so this particular question becomes irrelevant although other tax issues may be relevant, for example, the availability of losses and the capital allowances position. Commercial considerations may also override the tax considerations. Two examples are: the existence of the moratorium in administration, and the risk that if the company is in administrative receivership and the company is wound up, the tax liability will become an expense of the liquidation and any tax advantage lost.[16]

---

[12] s.72A, Insolvency Act 1986, inserted by s.250, Enterprise Act 2002.
[13] Ignoring expenses and indexation.
[14] r.2.67(1)(j), Insolvency Rules 1986.
[15] paras 99 and 65, Sch.B1, Insolvency Act 1986 Act read in conjunction with s.175(2)(b), of that Act.
[16] As noted earlier, the administration provisions on expenses mirror those of liquidation.

3. ADMINISTRATION: APPOINTMENT

(a) Status of the administrator

5–012   Independent of becoming an agent of the company on appointment,[17] the administrator becomes the "proper officer" of the company[18] and is responsible for "[e]verything to be done by a company under the Taxes Acts".[19] This will include, amongst other things, the filing of tax returns, accounting for tax[20], ensuring that PAYE is accounted for and complying with the obligations to provide employees with information with regard to any benefits in kind.

5–013   Moreover, the breadth of s.108(1), Taxes Management Act 1970 means that the responsibility of the administrator as the proper officer of the company is not limited to post-appointment matters: he will have responsibility for matters that relate to pre-appointment periods as well. For example, a company's tax return does not need to be filed until 12 months after the end of the accounting period. If a company has a year end of December 31, 2010 and an administrator is appointed on June 30, 2011, the administrator will have to file a return for the period January 1, 2010 to December 31 2010 before December 31, 2011, a period for which there may be few reliable records due to the deteriorating financial position of the company. The administrator will need to sign a declaration that the return is correct to the best of his knowledge and belief and will therefore require some work to be done to enable such a declaration to be given.[21]

5–014   Where joint administrators are appointed, the proper officer is such one of them as they by notice specify and where no such notice is given such one or more of them as the Board of Revenue and Customs may designate.[22] In practice, where there are joint administrators they will have been given the same powers and returns will be signed by either of them.

(b) Liability for pre-appointment taxes

5–015   An administrator does not incur any personal liability for the taxes of a company accrued prior to appointment: that liability remains that of the company. Moreover, the duty to pay fiscal liabilities as preferential debts out of assets subject to a floating charge (as created) was abolished by the Enterprise Act 2002 with effect from September 15, 2003.[23]

[17] para.69, Sch.B1, Insolvency Act 1986.
[18] s.108(3), Taxes Management Act 1970.
[19] s.108(1), Taxes Management Act 1970.
[20] Although the administrator must account for the tax this does not create a personal liability, any such personal liability arises out of the fact that tax is an expense of administration and it will be as an unpaid expense that any personal liability might arise.
[21] In practice, the company's inspector may be prepared to accept a nil gain/nil loss position for this period; however, if the administrator wishes to use pre-administration losses or reclaim tax paid, a return will usually be required. Best practice is to contact the company's inspector on appointment to agree the way forward.
[22] s.108(4), Taxes Management Act 1970. Note that no such provision exists for joint liquidators.
[23] s.251, Enterprise Act 2002, except for levies on coal and steel production: para.15A (Category 6), Sch.6, Insolvency Act 1986.

An administrator is, however, liable to pay taxes incurred during the administration as an expense of the administration. These will normally include tax on interest, tax on rents receivable and tax on capital gains.[24] Any personal liability arises under insolvency law not tax law.   **5–016**

(c) Accounting periods

As mentioned above, the policy of the DTI was to remove any tax advantage   **5–017** from administrations and align the taxation of administrations, so far as possible, with that of liquidations. Tax was therefore made an expense of administrations in the same way as in liquidations.[25] In order to do this, it was necessary to determine the tax arising during the administration. Consequently, an accounting period ends,[26] and a new one begins, immediately before the day the company enters administration. An accounting period shall also end, and a new one shall begin, on the termination of the appointment.[27]

During the course of the administration, the normal rules for ending   **5–018** accounting periods will continue to apply, so an accounting period will also end if the company ceases trading[28] and also on the company's accounting reference date.[29]

This could lead to a number of short accounting periods all requiring the tax   **5–019** to be calculated. For example:

- A company has a year-end December 31, 2010. It is put into administration on April 1, 2011. The administrator sells the business and ceases trading on June 1, 2011. The company comes out of administration on February 1, 2012 by going into liquidation.

- An accounting period will end on December 31, 2010 (accounting reference date), March 31, 2011 (the day before it enters administration), June 1, 2011 (the date it ceases trading), December 31, 2011 (accounting reference date) and February 1, 2012 (the date it ceases to be in administration). Each period will require a separate return.

---

[24] r.2.67(1) (f) and (j), Insolvency Rules 1986 (SI 1986/1925). A failure to pay such taxes as an expense may lead to personal liability (by analogy with *Inland Revenue Commissioners v Goldblatt* [1972] Ch. 498).

[25] HMRC occasionally argue in respect of pre-Enterprise Act administrations that tax was always an expense, it is considered this view is wrong.

[26] ss.10(1)(i) and 10(2), Corporation Tax Act 2009 (formerly s.12(7ZA), Income and Corporation Taxes Act 1988).

[27] s.10(1)(j), Corporation Tax Act 2009 (formerly s.12(3)(da), Income and Corporation Taxes Act 1988).

[28] s.10(1)(d), Corporation Tax Act 2009 (formerly s.12(3)(c), Income and Corporation Taxes Act 1988). It should be remembered that, here, trading has its strict tax meaning not a commercial one.

[29] s.10(1)(b), Corporation Tax Act 2009 (formerly s.12(3)(b), Income and Corporation Taxes Act 1988). Notwithstanding the fact that the company is in administration, it would appear that there is still an obligation on the directors to prepare accounts although in practice Companies House do not require it. The company's accounting reference date will therefore remain and an accounting period will end. This has been confirmed with His Majesty's Revenue and Customs (HMRC). It would appear that this was not intended.

5–020   In the event that the period of the administration is extended beyond a year, this will have no effect on the accounting periods, which will continue to run to the usual dates.

5–021   The position in administration can be compared with that in liquidation where an accounting period ends immediately before the winding up starts[30] but then will not then end otherwise than on the expiry of 12 months or on the final dissolution of the company.[31] It is thought that the difference is based on the fact that administration was not normally expected to last more than 12 months and so it was thought that such a rule would be unnecessary. It has proved to be the case that in the larger and more complex administrations an extension has been needed, ironically sometimes to deal with tax issues. Furthermore, unlike a liquidation where the accounting period ends "immediately before the winding up starts" in administration it ends "immediately before the day the company enters administration". If, therefore an administrator is appointed at midday and decides that the company should cease trading there is the theoretical possibility of an accounting period lasting from midnight to midday. There seems no reason for this complication. In practice the difference is ignored; however, at what point does it become immaterial? What if the administrator causes the company to cease trading at the end of the day; the following day; a week later?

5–022   Where the company goes from administration to dissolution, an assessment may be made by the company during the accounting period notwithstanding that the accounting period has not ended.[32] In doing so, the administrator (who will of course, be making a self-assessment of the company's liability) may make an assumption as to the date on which the company will come out of administration for the purposes of determining when the accounting period will end.[33] If this assumption is wrong and the actual date is later, an accounting period is deemed to end on the assumed date and a new accounting period deemed to start.[34]

5–023   This provision is needed because, once a company comes out of administration, the administrator vacates office and is no longer the proper officer of the company and cannot be compelled to make a return. The administrator must, of course, account for any tax arising during the period in office as an expense of the administration, and there are special provisions which apply in case the rate of corporation tax changes to determine the rate which is to be applied in determining the company's liability to tax.[35]

---

[30] ss.12(2) and 12(3), Corporation Tax Act 2009 (formerly s.12(7), Income and Corporation Taxes Act 1988).

[31] s.12(4), Corporation Tax Act 2009 (formerly s.12(7), Income and Corporation Taxes Act 1988).

[32] s.631, Corporation Tax Act 2010 (formerly s.342A(6), Income and Corporation Taxes Act 1988).

[33] s.631, Corporation Tax Act 2010 (formerly s.342A(6), Income and Corporation Taxes Act 1988).

[34] s.10(1) Corporation Tax Act 2009 then applies as if the company had entered administration on the assumed date, see s.631(4)–(6), Corporation Tax Act 2010 (formerly s.342A(8), Income and Corporation Taxes Act 1988).

[35] s.630, Corporation Tax Act 2010 (formerly s.342A(2) to (4), Income and Corporation Taxes Act 1988).

The mechanism is fraught with difficulties. The section works by reference **5–024** to the "dissolution event"[36] (which used to be termed the "relevant event" under the pre-rewrite provisions). This is the date on which, under para.84(1) of Sch.B1 to the Insolvency Act 1986, the administrator sends a notice to the Registrar of Companies that he thinks the company has no property which might permit a distribution to its creditors. The administrator is allowed, in applying s.10(1) of Corporation Tax Act 2009 for the purpose of determining when an accounting period of the company ends, to make an assumption as to what the actual dissolution date will be.[37] This date is referred to in the legislation as the "assumed dissolution date". Paragraph 84(5) of Sch.B1 provides that, if such a notice is sent, the administrator shall, as soon as reasonably practicable, file a notice with the court and send a copy of the notice to each creditor of whose name and address he is aware; this will include HMRC. The Registrar upon receipt of the notice shall register it, upon which registration the appointment of the administrator shall cease to have effect. On the assumption that notice is given to creditors, which will include HMRC, at the same time as it is sent to the Registrar, the company is still likely to have come out of administration by the time it comes to HMRC's attention. There appears to be no power to reinstate the administration; there is only a power to extend the period before which the company is dissolved. This is a period during which there is no administrator and consequently no proper officer of the company. Officers of HMRC tend to show little interest in administrations and the first that will be known of the imminent dissolution will be receipt of the notice.[38] It is therefore highly unlikely that the Officer will ever be able to enquire into an assessment of a company in administration which is going into dissolution.[39]

Such provisions are not required if the company is not to go to dissolution **5–025** because either a liquidator will be appointed in which case the liquidator will become the proper officer, or the company will pass back into the hands of the directors in which case the company secretary will become the proper officer again.[40]

One of the consequences of an accounting period ending when the company **5–026** goes into administration is that trading losses arising pre-appointment can (unless carried back or set-off against other profits of the period in which they arose) only be carried forward and used against profits of the same trade.[41] Trading losses can only be set against capital gains of the same (and subject to

---

[36] s.626(4), Corporation Tax Act 2010 (formerly s.342A(1), Income and Corporation Taxes Act 1988).

[37] s.631, Corporation Tax Act 2010 (formerly s.342A(7), Income and Corporation Taxes Act 1988).

[38] In practice the administrator may seek formal clearance to end the administration.

[39] HMRC, as a creditor, can apply to court to extend the period before dissolution but it is difficult to see what effect for tax purposes this will have. Furthermore, if such an application is made, the administrator (as opposed to the former administrator) is to send a notice to the Registrar; however, there is no administrator in this period as the administrator vacates office on the Registrar registering the notice.

[40] s.108(3)(a), Taxes Management Act 1970.

[41] s.45, Corporation Tax Act 2010 (formerly s.393, Income and Corporation Taxes Act 1988).

certain limitations, earlier) accounting periods.[42] Consequently, those losses will not be available to an administrator to use against capital gains arising during the course of the administration, which are, of course, an expense of the administration.[43]

5–027   Furthermore, capital losses can only be carried forward over an accounting period and cannot be carried back.[44] This may be of relevance if the company's accounting reference date falls during the administration period.

5–028   For example, a company goes into administration on April 1, 2010. The company owns two properties, one of which is standing at a gain of £100,000 and one of which is standing at a loss of £100,000. The administrator sells the building standing at a gain on May 1. The company's year end is September 30. He sells the building standing at a loss on the October 15; because the year end falls on September 30, an accounting period will end and the loss cannot be carried back to use against the gain. Had he sold the building three weeks earlier, the loss could have been used against the gain. As a consequence, tax is payable which is an expense of the administration and payable out of the floating charge realisations. Had the order of sales been reversed, the losses could have been used because they could have been carried forward over the end of the accounting period and used against the gain. In fact, all other things being equal, in the example above it would pay the floating charge-holder to buy the asset at market value before September 30, as this would reduce the gain and therefore the expense payable out of floating-charge realisations and the charge-holder could sell the asset on to recoup the cash paid to the administrator for the asset.[45]

4. Administration: liabilities arising during appointment

5–029   Since the administrator is the proper officer of the company it is essential for the administrator to take tax advice in relation to any disposals made during the course of the administration. A failure to account for tax is a failure to account for the expenses of administration and may lead to personal liability if not properly accounted for.[46]

(a)   Tax on capital gains

5–030   Where on the sale of property by an administrator a chargeable gain arises, it is treated as having been made by the company.[47] Accordingly, the administrator is not personally liable in respect of the tax on such gain as tax.

---

[42] s.37, Corporation Tax Act 2010 (formerly s.393A, Income and Corporation Taxes Act 1988).
[43] This can be compared with administrative receiverships—see para.5–049.
[44] s.8(1)(b), Taxation of Chargeable Gains Act 1992.
[45] Obviously factors such as expenses of sale and stamp duty land tax, where applicable, would need to be taken into consideration.
[46] By analogy with *Inland Revenue Commissioners v Goldblatt* [1972] Ch. 498.
[47] ss.26 and 60, Taxation of Chargeable Gains Act 1992.

The tax will be an expense of the administration and must be discharged out   **5–031**
of any funds available for that purpose. The administrator may be personally
liable if this is not accounted for.[48]

It should be noted that the expenses are to be discharged before vacating   **5–032**
office. Where the company is rescued and is to be returned to the directors, tax
will, in practice,[49] be paid at the end of the accounting period instead of nine
months after the end of the accounting period as is usually the case.[50] There is
a cash flow disadvantage to such a company.[51] Furthermore, where the
company is returned to the directors, the directors may do things which alter
the amount of tax payable during the administration period, for example, by
disclaiming capital allowances that the administrator has claimed. In this way,
the amount of the "expense" may alter after the administration is over. It is
considered that provided the administrator accounts for the right amount of tax
when vacating office, subsequent alterations to that amount will not expose the
administrator to personal liability.

(b)   Tax on income

(i)   Trading income

The administrator will trade as agent of the company.[52] The trade receipts and   **5–033**
profits will therefore be those of the company and the company will be liable
for the corporation tax. As the proper officer of the company, the administrator
will be liable to account for the tax. During the course of the administration
HMRC will usually accept a trading account based on the Receipts and
Payments Account. This is in effect a cash basis of assessment. It would be
unusual for an administrator to draw up any more formal accounts.

Trading losses made prior to administration may be available to reduce any   **5–034**
taxable trading profit made during the course of administration. The quantum
of such available losses may be hard to justify, especially if the company's
records have not been kept up to date. It may be a matter of demonstrating that
the company had agreed losses carried forward from previous periods and to
agree to use these rather than calculate losses in the period immediately before
administration.

(ii)   Rental income

As with tax on trading income, only the company is liable to tax on rental income   **5–035**
received during the administration period. As proper officer of the company, the
administrator is liable to account for it as an expense of the administration.

---

[48] See fn.43.
[49] The practice of paying the tax before the end of the accounting period is derived from para.99,
Sch.B1, Insolvency Act 1986.
[50] s.59D(1), Taxes Management Act 1970.
[51] This is a theme which runs throughout the taxation of administrations; namely that a company
is in a worse tax position when it is being rescued than when it is not.
[52] para.69, Sch.B1, Insolvency Act 1986.

(iii)   Interest

5–036   Liability for tax on interest falls on the company; again, as proper officer the administrator is responsible for accounting for the tax on any such interest.

(iv)   PAYE and NIC

5–037   PAYE and NIC contributions arising during administration have super-priority in respect of both new employees and employees whose employment contracts have been adopted by the administrator.[53]

5.   ADMINISTRATION: GROUPS

5–038   Where an administrator is appointed to a company in a group this may affect the group structure for tax purposes. Unlike a liquidation, the appointment does not cause the company to lose beneficial ownership of its assets.[54] However, HMRC argue that the appointment of an administrator breaks the group relationship for the purposes of group relief above the company in administration.[55] This position is based on the argument that the company in administration and those above or beside it are no longer controlled by the same person or persons, with the result that there are "arrangements" in place by virtue of which a person or persons (i.e. the shareholders) have control of the latter companies but not of the company in administration. Whilst this argument superficially has some merit it is submitted that the legislation does not support it.

5–039   The relevant parts of the legislation provide:[56]

"154 Arrangements for transfer of member of group of companies etc

(1)   This section applies if, apart from this section, one company ('the first company') and another company ('the second company') would be members of the same group of companies.

(2)   For the purposes of this Part the companies are not members of the same group of companies if—

(a)   one of the companies has surrenderable amounts for an accounting period ('the current period'), and

(b)   arrangements within subs.(3) are in place.

---

[53] para.99, Sch.B1, Insolvency Act 1986.

[54] *Ayerst (Inspector of Taxes) v C&K (Construction) Ltd* [1976] A.C. 167 (HL).

[55] On the basis of s.154, Corporation Tax Act 2010 (formerly s.410 Income and Corporation Taxes Act 1988). It appears that the only public acknowledgement by HMRC that this is their position is to be found in their Company Taxation Manual at para.97760, in which they state that it is their view that "the appointment of an insolvency practitioner causes the previous owners of a company to lose control of it, breaking the group relationship".

[56] s.154 Corporation Tax Act 2010 (formerly s.410, Income and Corporation Taxes Act 1988).

(3) Arrangements are within this subsection if they have any of the following effects.

Effect 1
At some time during or after the current period, the first company or any successor of it—

(a) could cease to be a member of the same group of companies as the second company, and
(b) could become a member of the same group of companies as a third company (see subs.(4)).

Effect 2
At some time during or after the current period a person (other than the first or second company) has or could obtain, or persons together (other than those companies) have or could obtain, control of the first company but not of the second company.

Effect 3
At some time during or after the current period, a third company could start to carry on the whole or a part of a trade that at a time during the current period is carried on by the first company and could do so—

(a) as the successor of the first company, or
(b) as the successor of another company which is not a third company and which started to carry on the whole or a part of the trade during or after the current period.

(4) A 'third company' means a company that is not, apart from any arrangements within subs.(3), a member of the same group of companies as the first company."

The definition of "control" is that found in s.1124, Corporation Tax Act 2010,[57] which provides that:

"In relation to a body corporate ('company A'), 'control' means the power of a person ('P') to secure—

(a) by means of the holding of shares or the possession of voting power in relation to that or any other body corporate, or
(b) as a result of any powers conferred by the articles of association or other document regulating that or any other body corporate,

that the affairs of company A are conducted in accordance with P's wishes."

---

[57] As applied by s.1176(2), Corporation Tax Act 2010.

"Arrangements" here are defined as meaning arrangements of any kind whether in writing or not.[58]

5–040   The first of the three Effects in s.154 will be in point if the administrator has arranged to transfer shares in one group company to a company outside the group. This is straightforward and it ought to be apparent where this has occurred.

The application of the second Effect is more difficult. As mentioned HMRC are known to argue that control of the company in administration is lost by the shareholders, because they are no longer able to secure that the affairs of the company are conducted in accordance with their wishes. Thus, HMRC argue that, in the case of a two-company group where the subsidiary is in administration, the shareholders of the parent company can be said still to control the parent but not its subsidiary; accordingly, say HMRC, the group is severed above the level of the subsidiary.

But this argument, if correct, leads to arbitrary results. For example, if the parent company itself went into administration then (assuming that the parent and the subsidiary had the same administrator) Effect 2 in s.154 would not be in point because it would not be the case that the shareholders of the parent controlled that company but not its subsidiary; accordingly the two companies would still be grouped. Similarly, if the parent company owned not one but two subsidiaries, both of which were in administration with the same administrator, then again Effect 2 would not be in point as regards the two subsidiaries since the shareholders of the parent would not have control of either of them: thus they would remain grouped.

In addition, when one looks to the underlying purpose of the provisions it is apparent that they are designed to prevent taxpayers taking undue advantage of the group relief provisions, principally by means of transferring a loss-making company into a "temporary" group with a view to transferring it back to its original group once the requisite losses have been surrendered. The provisions are also wide enough to catch the more common situation where a "genuine" group reaches an agreement with a third party to sell one of the group companies. Whilst it is less easy to see the mischief in this situation, it is perhaps explicable on the basis that, at the point at which it is agreed that the target company will leave the group it is no longer to be viewed as part of the same economic unit for group relief purposes. But, it is very difficult to see why those provisions would be intended to apply simply on the occasion of the administration of one of the group companies since there is no avoidance element and, without more, the company in administration will not leave the economic group. Moreover, the history of the legislation concerned further indicates that it could not have been Parliament's intention, when enacting what is now s.154, Corporation Tax Act 2010, to preclude group relief in relation to companies in administration. That section began life in 1973 as s.29 (Group relief: effect of arrangements for transfer of company to another group, etc) of the Finance Act of that year, whereas the administration procedure was only introduced in the Insolvency Act 1985 (which was re-enacted in the Insolvency Act 1986) following the recommendations made in the report of the Cork Committee in 1982.

---

[58] s.156, Corporation Tax Act 2010.

There is, in addition, a more fundamental policy issue, namely that administration was intended to be a rescue procedure. On HMRC's analysis a group can surrender losses internally before administration, but on administration this facility is lost. Yet if the company survives, the ability is regained if the company is passed back to the directors. Accordingly, and somewhat perversely, the only time that losses cannot be surrendered is when the company is being rescued: arguably a time when group relief would be most valuable. It is submitted that this approach is squarely at odds with the policy that underlay the reforms effected by the Enterprise Act 2002.

However, whilst a purposive interpretation of the provisions would suggest **5–041** that HMRC's view is incorrect, it must be accepted that it is not a straightforward task to construe the words of the legislation so as to achieve that result. Even so, it is submitted that the key lies in the interpretation of the term "control" and that the shareholder of a company in administration ought to be considered as retaining "control" (as defined) of the company (albeit that that control is in abeyance pending the outcome of the administration) since the shareholder still holds the "power", by means of holding shares in the company, to secure that the affairs of the company are conducted in accordance with the shareholder's wishes. This is so notwithstanding that that "power" can be described as being temporarily inhibited during the currency of the administration.

This conclusion follows from the fact that, unless the shareholder has "control" it would seem that no-one does. This is because the administrator will not hold shares in or voting power in relation to the company. Moreover, the powers of control he does possess over the company do not emanate from the company's constitutional documents; rather they emanate from statute and perhaps also from a debenture, but neither of those is a "document regulating [the company]". The only other candidate for control would be the creditors of the company, who might be said to "control" the company by virtue of being able to vote in creditors' meetings. However, such an interpretation could give rise to odd results, not least that control of company could end up in the hands of HMRC in circumstances where they are the majority creditor.

Furthermore, it cannot be said that the administrator controls the company over which he is appointed because this requires him to be able to direct that the affairs of the company are carried on in accordance with his wishes. Although an administrator exercises commercial judgement, he is restricted in the exercise of his powers by statute and it cannot truly be said that the administrator by his actions carries out his wishes.

Accordingly it is submitted that the better interpretation is that "control" (as defined) is retained by the shareholder of the company during the currency of the administration and that s.154, Corporation Tax Act 2010 is not, therefore, triggered on entry of a group company into administration.

6. ADMINISTRATION: PRE-PACKS

The taxation of a pre-pack administration does not differ from that of any other **5–042** administration; however, tax planning can play an important role. As a pre-pack administration requires the appointment of an administrator and an immediate sale any tax arising will be an expense of the administration. It is therefore important to have ascertained what the tax liabilities will be and what tax assets i.e. losses and capital allowances will be available to shelter any potential tax charge, before the pre-pack takes place.

7.   ADMINISTRATIVE RECEIVERSHIP: APPOINTMENT

(a)   Status of the administrative receiver

5–043   On appointment an administrative receiver does not become the proper officer of the company. The duty to make returns continues to be that of the proper officer who will be the company secretary or such other person as may for the time being have the express, implied or apparent authority of the company to act on its behalf.[59] It is considered that an administrative receiver will normally have sufficient authority to act on behalf of the company to be able to sign a return and it is not necessary to seek any specific authority from the company. It should be remembered that in signing the return, the administrative receiver is declaring that the information contained in it is correct and complete to the best of his knowledge and belief.

5–044   HMRC have argued that administrative receivers automatically become the proper officer because they have authority to act as agent of the company. It is thought that this view is wrong. The introduction of agents into the definition of proper officer in 1993 was to protect the then Inland Revenue when they accepted claims from people who were not the proper officer but appeared to have the authority of the company. If the view of HMRC is correct, the practical effect is that a company may have more than one proper officer and consequently each would be obliged to make a return; this cannot be correct.

5–045   Where the company is in liquidation, the liquidator becomes the proper officer of the company.[60] Where an administrative receiver wishes to deal with tax matters in order to secure repayments of tax, it is not uncommon for a liquidator to require payment to secure his co-operation. Any such payments will be held for the benefit of the liquidation.

(b)   Liability for pre-appointment taxes

5–046   An administrative receiver does not incur any personal liability for taxes of a company accrued prior to appointment. The duty to pay fiscal liabilities as preferential debts out of assets subject to a floating charge (as created) has been abolished.[61] There are no expenses of administrative receivership, other than those incurred in realising the asset, which are payable out of the proceeds of realisation.

---

[59] s.108(1) and (3), Taxes Management Act 1970.

[60] s.108(3), Taxes Management Act 1970.

[61] By s.251, Enterprise Act 2002 effective September 15, 2003; however, there is an express exception for levies on coal and steel production, see para.15 (Category 6), Sch.6, Insolvency Act 1986.

(c)   Accounting periods

The appointment of an administrative receiver does not end an accounting   **5–047**
period by virtue solely of that appointment. Where, however, the administrative receiver takes the decision that the company should cease trading, an
accounting period will end on the company so ceasing to trade.[62] An accounting
period will also end on the company's accounting reference date[63] and also if a
liquidator is appointed.[64] If a liquidator is appointed, an accounting period will
not then end otherwise than on the expiry of a period of 12 months or on the
company being dissolved.[65]

8.   ADMINISTRATIVE RECEIVERSHIP: LIABILITIES ARISING DURING APPOINTMENT

Since the administrative receiver is not the proper officer of the company, it is   **5–048**
common practice for him to ignore taxation. There are two circumstances where
an administrative receiver may be liable: first, where he is appointed over the
UK branch of a foreign company; and secondly, where he is appointed by a
foreign bank over a UK asset and remits money overseas which comprises
interest or rental income, in which case there may be an obligation to withhold
tax unless a double tax treaty applies. Other than in these circumstances, generally an administrative receiver is not liable to tax, for the reasons set out below.[66]

(a)   Tax on capital gains

Where on the sale of an asset (e.g. a property or shares in a subsidiary),[67] a   **5–049**
chargeable gain arises, it is treated as having been made by the company.[68]
Accordingly, neither a mortgagee nor an administrative receiver is personally
liable in respect of the tax on such gain.[69]

Where, therefore, an asset is sold prior to liquidation by an administrative   **5–050**
receiver, the liability to tax will be an unsecured claim in any subsequent liquidation if not previously paid by the company.

Where, however, the asset is sold after liquidation, and if there are free assets   **5–051**
surplus to the receivership, the corporation tax liability will be payable as an
expense of the liquidation.

---

[62] s.10(1)(d), Corporation Tax Act 2009 (formerly s.12(3)(c), Income and Corporation Taxes
Act 1988).
[63] s.10(1)(b), Corporation Tax Act 2009 (formerly s.12(3)(b), Income and Corporation Taxes
Act 1988).
[64] ss.12(2), Corporation Tax Act 2009 (formerly s.12(7), Income and Corporation Taxes Act
1988).
[65] s.12(4), Corporation Tax Act 2009 (formerly s.12(7), Income and Corporation Taxes Act
1988).
[66] See also *Re Piacentini* [2003] Q.B. 1497.
[67] Gains on the sale of shares in a subsidiary may be exempt under Sch.7AC, Taxation of
Chargeable Gains Act 1992 (substantial shareholdings).
[68] ss.26 and 60, Taxation of Chargeable Gains Act 1992. See also *Re Piacentini* [2003] Q.B.
1497.
[69] *Re Mesco Properties Ltd* [1980] 1 W.L.R. 96 (CA), 99B.

5–052   It was formerly the case that, where receivership preceded liquidation but the sale took place after liquidation, the liquidation expenses were not payable out of floating charge realisations. However, this was changed with effect from April 6, 2008 in order to bring it in line with administrations.[70]

(b) Tax on income

(i) Trading income

5–053   Prior to liquidation, an administrative receiver will normally trade as agent of the company. The receipts and profits of the trade will therefore be those of the company and the company will be liable for corporation tax.

5–054   Where a receiver causes the company to trade after his agency is determined by liquidation, it is considered that any profits he makes will still be profits of the company and therefore the liability will remain that of the company. The reason for this is that regardless of the capacity in which the receiver is acting, the profits still accrue to the benefit of the company in reducing its indebtedness to the debenture-holder.[71]

(ii) Rental income

5–055   An administrative receiver is no more liable to tax on rental income received than to tax on trading receipts, for the reasons set out above.

(iii) Interest income

5–056   Liability for tax on interest received by an administrative receiver falls on the company.

(iv) Income after liquidation

5–057   Corporation tax on income arising after liquidation is a "necessary disbursement" of the liquidator which is payable as an expense ahead of the claims of preferential creditors. Such expenses also have priority over the claims of the holders of floating charges.[72]

(c) PAYE

5–058   The appointment of a receiver out of court does not, generally speaking, discharge employees[73] and therefore prior to winding up employees normally remain in the employ of the company. HMRC take the view that, when a company is in receivership, it is the receiver who is under an obligation to

---

[70] s.176ZA, Insolvency Act 1986, inserted by s.1282(1), Companies Act 2006.
[71] *Gosling v Gaskell* [1897] A.C. 575 (HL).
[72] See fn.66 above.
[73] See Ch.16.

account for and operate PAYE as agent for the paying company. The Revenue's argument may be correct, since it is frequently the case that (where both companies are in the same group) an employee is employed by company A but paid by company B as agent for company A and the PAYE regulations are presumably designed to fix the paying company B with the obligation of deducting and accounting for PAYE even if it is only acting as agent for the other company.[74]

9.   VALUE ADDED TAX

For all practical purposes, there is no difference between administration and administrative receivership for VAT purposes.   **5–059**

(a)   Status of an administrator or administrative receiver

For the purposes of VAT, it is not clear whether receivership or administration (as opposed to liquidation) gives the Commissioners of Customs and Excise the power to bring a VAT period to an end. That power depends upon the true construction of regs 25(3)[75] and 30 of the Value Added Tax Regulations 1995.[76] These apply, in the words of reg.30:   **5–060**

"Where any person . . . dies or becomes incapacitated and control of his assets passes to another person, being a personal representative, trustee in bankruptcy, receiver, liquidator, or person otherwise acting in a representative capacity".

Arguably, a company that has had a receiver appointed is not one that has become "incapacitated", and the reference to a receiver can be understood as a reference to a receiver of an incapacitated individual.[77] But it seems to be accepted in practice that the Commissioners do have such a power in the case of corporate receivership.[78]

(b)   Accounting for VAT

It was held in *Re John Willment (Ashford) Ltd*,[79] that a receiver had a discretion whether or not to account for VAT, but that because a failure to account would   **5–061**

---

[74] But see *Re Piacentini* [2003] Q.B. 1497.

[75] reg.25(3) provides that: "where for the purposes of this Part of these Regulations the Commissioners have made a requirement of any person pursuant to reg.30(a) then the period in respect of which taxable supplies were being made by the person . . . who became incapacitated shall end on the day previous to the date when . . . incapacity took place; and (b) a return made on his behalf shall be furnished in respect of that period no later than the last day of the month next following the end of that period".

[76] SI 1995/2518.

[77] Cf. *Re John Willment (Ashford) Ltd* [1980] 1 W.L.R. 73, 76H; *Sargent v Commissioners of Customs and Excise* [1995] 1 W.L.R. 821 (CA).

[78] SPI Technical Release 2 which states (para.4.1) that: "for VAT compliance purposes, the insolvency practitioner takes responsibility for the VAT accounting of the trader from the date of the appointment".

[79] *Re John Willment (Ashford) Ltd* [1980] 1 W.L.R. 73.

cause the company to commit a criminal offence, the receiver could only properly exercise that discretion in favour of HMRC.[80] The criminal sanction was removed in 1985.

5–062   An amendment to the VAT legislation in 1985[81] enabled regulations to be made for persons carrying on "a business" of a company "in . . . receivership" to be treated as taxable persons. Under what is now reg.9 of the VAT regulations 1995,[82] HMRC have the power to treat a receiver who is carrying on the business of the company as a taxable person. Regulation 9 does not use the words "the business", but the references to "his business" and "that business" suggest that the regulation deals with "the" business of the company, not "a" business of the company. This, and the reference to the company "going into receivership", particularly alongside references to liquidation and administration orders, suggested to the Court of Appeal in *Sargent v Customs and Excise Commissioners*[83] that reg.9 was dealing only with administrative receivership. However, when the amendment was introduced in 1985 administrative receivership was a new and untested procedure. Furthermore, the regulations introduced in 1985 did refer to "an administration order" in anticipation of the Insolvency Act 1986 being enacted, as this act also introduced the concept of the administrator it would have made sense for the regulations to have used that phrase had the new and narrower office of administrative receiver been intended. It is highly probable therefore the reference to receivership was to the concept as then understood which included all receiverships. On the court of Appeal's analysis the appointment of an LPA receiver[84] does not mean that the company has gone into receivership and an LPA receiver, whilst he may carry on "a" business of the company, will not be able to carry on "the" business of the company, since even if the company has at the time of his appointment no other business, it remains open to the directors to commence any other business that they can properly cause the company to carry on.

5–063   Regulation 9 raises a number of other problems. First, is it necessary that the person in question should be carrying on business on his own account? If it is, then the right of the Commissioners will not arise in the case of a receiver who carries on the business of the mortgagor company as its agent until such agency terminates on liquidation. The judgment in the *Sargent*[85] case, where there was no liquidation, assumes that reg.9 covers a receiver acting as agent for the company.

5–064   Secondly, reg.9 empowers HMRC to treat a person carrying on the business as "a" taxable person, not "the" taxable person. Therefore any liability arising prior to the commissioners notifying the receiver that he is to be treated as a taxable person would appear to remain the liability of the company. The form

---

[80] Brightman J. in that case left open questions relating to fraudulent trading and misrepresentation.

[81] Finance Act 1985, s.31, amending Value Added Tax Act 1983, s.31.

[82] SI 1995/2518.

[83] *Sargent v Customs and Excise Commissioners* [1995] 1 W.L.R. 821 (CA).

[84] So called since the principal relevant powers are contained in the Law of Property Act 1925, Pt 2.

[85] *Sargent v Customs and Excise Commissioners* [1995] 1 W.L.R. 821 (CA).

of notification[86] of claim states in the Notes on the reverse side of the form: "1. You are to be treated as the taxable person named overleaf under VAT Regulations, 1995 Regulations 9 and 30".[87] But since reg.9 does not appear to give HMRC the power to treat the receiver as the taxable person, such a notice appears to be invalid or ineffective as a notice under reg.9. At first instance in the *Sargent* case[88] it was assumed that a letter purporting to treat the receiver as "the taxable person" was effective under reg.9.

Thirdly, the Court of Appeal held in the *Sargent* case that notwithstanding   **5–065** that the receiver had a discretion whether to pay the VAT element to HMRC, for public policy reasons that discretion could only be exercised in favour of HMRC. This was so notwithstanding that the criminal sanction had been removed. It is unfortunate that tax should be levied on public policy grounds not least because this had led to difficulties in the mechanics of collection as there appears to be no statutory procedure. If the Court of Appeal had held that all receivers and not just administrative receivers were taxable persons such a decision would have been unnecessary.

Fourthly, it is not clear how far the exercise of HMRC's discretion under   **5–066** reg.9 has retrospective effect. In the *Sargent* case,[89] the letter from HMRC purported to treat the receiver as the taxable person "with effect from the date of his appointment". Although reg.9 gives HMRC a discretion which can be exercised from the date of appointment of the receiver, it is difficult to see how reg.9 can be construed as authorising the exercise of this discretion on a date subsequent to the appointment with retrospective effect. If reg.9 were read in that way a receiver could not safely pay over sums including a VAT element to a mortgagee until the relevant period of limitations ran out. This could not have been the intention of the legislation.

10. INTERNATIONAL MATTERS

Increasingly, administrators are seeking appointments over European compa-   **5–067** nies incorporated in other Member States of the European Union arguing that their Centre of Main Interest (COMI) is in the UK. In doing so there is a danger that they will assert that the management of the company was exercised in the UK. This may mean that they expose the company to arguments that it is tax resident in the UK. Although such tax would be an unsecured claim, it raises the issue of whether the directors and company secretary are guilty of an offence for not having previously accounted for UK corporation tax.

Arguably, the appointment of a UK administrator will make the company   **5–068** UK tax resident in the future. Decisions affecting the company should be made in the country of incorporation to prevent such arguments arising.

---

[86] VAT 157.
[87] In the *Sargent* case the Customs wrote a letter pursuant to what is now reg.9 purporting to treat the receiver as "the taxable person".
[88] *Sargent v Customs and Excise Commissioners* [1995] 1 W.L.R. 821 (CA).
[89] *Sargent v Customs and Excise Commissioners* [1995] 1 W.L.R. 821 (CA).

Chapter 6

Appointment of Administrators

1. INTRODUCTION

6–001 A number of legal systems have adopted legislation designed to achieve the rehabilitation of a company which has fallen on hard times, but which if afforded a form of moratorium, or an opportunity to enter into a scheme of arrangement with its creditors, has a reasonable prospect of recovery. A familiar characteristic is that the court is given jurisdiction to appoint an officer to manage the affairs of the company and to regulate or restrict the exercise by creditors of the company of their rights and remedies, as a temporary measure whilst the necessary steps are taken to safeguard its future. Such a jurisdiction was first introduced into English law by Pt II of the Insolvency Act 1986 in the form of administration orders. An administrator could only be appointed by order of the court. The original administration regime was little used and a new administration procedure with a much reduced role for the court, was introduced by s.248 of the Enterprise Act 2002, which inserted Sch.B1 into the Insolvency Act 1986. Schedule B1 came into force on September 15, 2003.[1]

6–002 The essential nature of administration as originally conceived was summarised by Nicholls L.J. giving the judgment of the Court of Appeal in *Re Atlantic Computer Systems Plc*,[2] where he said:

> "an administration is intended to be only an interim and temporary regime. There is to be a breathing space while the company, under new management in the person of the administrator, seeks to achieve one or more of the purposes set out in section 8(3). There is a moratorium on the enforcement of debts and rights, proprietary and otherwise, against the company, so as to give the administrator time to formulate proposals and lay them before the creditors, and then implement any proposals approved by the creditors. In some cases winding-up will follow, in others not."[3]

2. THE EARLY HISTORY OF ADMINISTRATION ORDERS— PART II OF THE INSOLVENCY ACT 1986

6–003 The original administration jurisdiction was little used for two reasons in particular. First, there was a key limitation on the use of the original administration

---

[1] Enterprise Act 2002 (Commencement No.4 and Transitional Provisions and Savings) Order 2003 (SI 2003/2093).
[2] *Re Atlantic Computer Systems Plc* [1992] Ch.505 (CA).
[3] *Re Atlantic Computer Systems Plc* [1992] Ch.505 (CA), 528.

jurisdiction. An administrator could not be appointed if a chargee under a floating charge had appointed an administrative receiver, unless the court was satisfied either that the appointor had consented or that, if the administration order had been made, the charge or security by virtue of which the receiver had been appointed would be liable to have been released or discharged under ss.238 to 240, or would be avoided under s.245 of the Insolvency Act 1986. The fact that most companies had provided full fixed and floating charge "debenture" security to their bankers meant that in the vast majority of cases there was no possibility of an administration order being made because of the strong preference of banks to secure the appointment of their chosen administrative receivers, whose primary duty would be to secure the best outcome for the appointing bank, in precedence to any duty owed to the company and, therefore, to unsecured creditors.

Secondly, the affidavit in support of a petition for the appointment of an admin- **6–004**
istrator under Pt II of the Insolvency Act 1986 had to exhibit an "independent report on [the] company's affairs" that might have been prepared pursuant to r.2.2 of the Insolvency Rules 1986 (the so-called "2.2 report"). Whilst a r.2.2 report was technically voluntary, its absence had to be explained in the affidavit,[4] so in practice it was nearly always included. Unfortunately, the practice developed of producing an extremely detailed 2.2 report with consequent expense and delay. Despite statements by the courts to the effect that r.2.2 reports should not prevent orders being made in appropriate cases,[5] administration was seen as more cumbersome and expensive than administrative receivership and consequently the latter procedure was invariably used in preference where it was available.

It is important to note that Pt II of the Insolvency Act 1986 has not been **6–005**
repealed and that it continues to apply in a limited range of circumstances. First, it governs the process of administration in the very small number of cases where the administration petition was presented before September 15, 2003.[6] Secondly, the Pt II procedure also applies where a "special administration regime" applies; essentially where an administration petition is presented in respect of utility, transport and public-private partnership companies and building societies.[7] However, the "new" Sch.B1 administration procedure may apply to certain types of public utility companies[8] so that the exclusivity of the "special administration regime" is not absolute.

3. THE NEW REGIME: SCHEDULE B1 TO THE INSOLVENCY ACT 1986

The modern regime, under Sch.B1 to the Insolvency Act 1986 has effected a **6–006**
significant relaxation of the conditions that need to be fulfilled before an

---

[4] Insolvency Rules 1986, r.2.3(6). References in this chapter to rules are to the Insolvency Rules 1986 (SI 1986/1925) unless indicated to the contrary.
[5] See in particular Practice Note (Administration Order Applications: Content of Independent Reports) [1994] 1 W.L.R. 160.
[6] See in particular Practice Note (Administration Order Applications: Content of Independent Reports) [1994] 1 W.L.R. 160, art.3(2).
[7] s.249, Enterprise Act 2002.
[8] See the Energy Administration Rules 2005 (SI 2005/2483).

administrator can be appointed (in particular, by relegating the role of the court in most cases to the purely administrative and by removing the need for the 2.2 report).

As under the previous regime, administration is a corporate insolvency procedure that is available to companies[9] registered in England and Wales under the Companies Acts, as well as to certain other registered and unregistered undertakings.[10] By reason of the EC Regulation on Insolvency Proceedings 2000, there may be a restriction on the ability to appoint administrators in respect of a company where the "centre of main interests" of that company is located in another EC state. This is considered in detail below.[11]

6–007   A person may be appointed as administrator of a company:

(a) by administration order of the court under para.10 of Sch.B1 to the Insolvency Act 1986;

(b) by the holder of a qualifying floating charge under para.14; or

(c) by the company or its directors under para.22.[12]

Importantly (b) and (c) above envisage an appointment out of court, to replicate the flexibility enjoyed by the traditional ability to appoint administrative receivers, albeit that notice of appointment needs to be filed with the court which would otherwise have made the appointment had an application been made. In practice, appointments under (c) above are by far and away the most common, because banks are reluctant to exercise their overriding power to appoint, as holders of qualifying floating charges, provided that those nominated by the directors to act as administrators are acceptable to the bank[13]. The acquiescent approach of banks in this regard in some measure reflects their preference, when making receivership appointments,[14] to do so "by invitation of the company's directors" so as to distance themselves from the stigma that sometimes follows the making of any insolvency appointment.

4.   STRATEGIC CONSIDERATIONS PRIOR TO THE APPOINTMENT OF AN ADMINISTRATOR

6–008   The timing and manner of the appointment will be governed in large part by the strategic considerations relating to the administration. The proposed administrator will ordinarily undertake an investigation of the company's affairs and

---

[9] See para.111(1A) of Sch.B1, Insolvency Act 1986 for the definition of "company", and see *Panter v Rowellian Football Social Club* [2011] EWHC 1301 (Ch) (no jurisdiction to make an administration appointment over an unincorporated organisation).

[10] See further para.30–022.

[11] See below, Ch.31. See in particular *Re Kaupthing Capital Partners II Master LP Inc* [2011] B.C.C. 338.

[12] para.2 of Sch.B1 to the Insolvency Act 1986 and references in this chapter to individual paragraphs are to Sch.B1 unless indicated to the contrary.

[13] As to competing choices of appointee in the context of administration applications to the court, see para.6–066 below.

[14] See Ch.7, below.

financial position and consequently offer advice before being appointed,[15] which will including advice on the timing and manner of appointment. Accordingly, it is important to consider first the purposes of administration and the relevant strategic considerations, before going on to consider the practicalities and methods of appointment. Whichever method of appointment is used, the statutory purpose of the administration[16] must in practice have been considered and determined upon by the prospective appointor and appointee[17] and should inform the strategy adopted by the administrator once the appointment is made.

Whilst there are now more numerous routes into administration, there remains a common purpose irrespective of the identity of the applicant and whether the appointment is made by the court or outside court. Schedule B1 places a direct obligation on the administrator to: **6–009**

"perform his functions with the objective of—

(a)   rescuing the company[18] as a going concern, or

(b)   achieving a better result for the company's creditors as a whole than would be likely if the company were wound up (without first being in administration),[19] or

(c)   realising property in order to make a distribution to one or more secured or preferential creditors."[20]

The effect of this hierarchical statutory purpose, which is comprised of distinct objectives, on the conduct of an administration and the duties and liabilities of administrators is considered later,[21] as are the duties and the liabilities of the administrator and the consequences that flow from the fact that an administrator is an officer of the court[22] as well as being an agent of the company.[23]

The relevance for present purposes of the statutory objective is that the putative administrator must form a view at the outset that the objective can be achieved as it is a requirement of his appointment that he states that in his opinion if he is appointed "it is reasonably likely that the purpose of the administration will be achieved".[24] Whilst the proposed administrator will need to   **6–010**

---

[15] The recovery of costs incurred by the administrator in this respect ("pre-appointment costs") are governed by rr.2.33(2A) and 2.67 Insolvency Rules 1986 (see below at para.6–035).

[16] See para.6–067, below.

[17] See para.6–010, below. In relation to administration applications to the court, see para.6–067, below.

[18] Despite much lobbying from the Association of Business Recovery Professionals (R3) and others, the Government was not prepared to accede to an amendment that the objective be focused on rescuing the underlying business, rather than the company.

[19] In *Re Logitext UK Ltd* [2005] 1 B.C.L.C. 326, Lindsay J. held that this could be satisfied where an applicant for an administration was prepared to fund the investigation and pursuit of an alleged transaction at an undervalue claim and see *Re Redman Construction* [2004] EWHC 3468, and *El-Ajou v Dollar Land (Manhattan) Ltd* [2007] B.C.C. 953.

[20] Sch.B1, para.3(1).

[21] See below, Ch.12.

[22] Sch.B1, para.5; this is the case whether or not the administrator is appointed by the court.

[23] Sch.B1, para.69.

[24] r.2.3(5)(C).

ensure that he has gathered and analysed sufficient information to form this opinion, and his own records must demonstrate that this is indeed the case, there is no requirement for this statement to be supported by published evidence; in particular there is no need to prepare anything similar to a 2.2 report. It is, however, important that the administrator appreciates that the identification of particular statutory purposes will determine the ambit of his functions and therefore the work that can properly be undertaken and paid for as an expense of the administration.[25] Whilst most appointments will be made by directors,[26] the selection of an insolvency practitioner and the timing and manner of the appointment will be governed to some extent by the directors' view of what would happen if the appointment were taken out of their hands and made by the holder of a floating charge (normally the company's principal bankers).

6–011   There must be some "proper" purpose so that administration will provide a real, as opposed to an unsubstantiated, benefit. So in *Doltable Ltd v Lexi Holdings Plc*[27] the court declined to make an administration order in respect of a Jersey company which owned development land within the jurisdiction that was already under the control of receivers appointed by a fixed chargee. Administration should not be used simply to prevent a chargee from enforcing its security and, if the company were concerned in this respect, other remedies were available. A court will therefore be concerned to see that one of the statutory purposes will be more likely than not be achieved by the administration, as opposed to some other strategy or insolvency procedure, and evidence to this effect should be produced in an administration application.[28] The motivation behind the administration will not normally affect the validity of the procedure. In *Re Dianoor Jewels Ltd*[29] the fact that an administration petition was presented by a husband in an attempt to avoid matrimonial claims was irrelevant so far as the validity of the administration was concerned. The interests of all creditors, including the wife, would be protected by the administration of an undoubtedly insolvent company.

6–012   Among the strategies to be considered by administrator for achieving the purposes of the administration may be:

   (a)   A disposal of the company's business as a going concern.[30]

   (b)   A hive-down of the company's business.

   (c)   A "prepackaged disposal" of all part of the company's business.

---

[25] *Freakley v Centre Reinsurance International Co* [2006] 1 W.L.R 2863 (HL). See further Ch.4.

[26] Normally appointments will be made by the directors, rather than by the company in general meeting, as this is more straightforward.

[27] *Doltable Ltd v Lexi Holdings Plc* [2006] B.C.C. 918.

[28] See, e.g. *Re Redman Construction* [2004] EWHC 3468 (Ch) (administration order made on the basis of projection evidence that the procedure would increase the creditors' dividend).

[29] *Re Dianoor Jewels Ltd (Set Aside)* [2001] 1 B.C.L.C. 450.

[30] As to which see Ch.11.

(d) Continued trading (either on an interim basis or, less commonly, with a view to "trading out").[31]

The key strategic considerations in relation to these options (which are neither exhaustive nor mutually exclusive) are considered below.

A sale as a going concern is probably the most commonly intended outcome. It is through such sales that "rescue culture" is said to benefit creditors (because a price can be achieved which reflects the goodwill in the business rather than merely its underlying physical assets) and society more generally (by keeping viable businesses running). There remains, however, debate as to how far the pursuit of this form of rescue culture has positive long-term effects, (especially where the going concern sale purchaser is an existing owner/manager of the insolvent company) and whether preserving a business in this manner may have detrimental and unfair effects on its competitors, their employees and their creditors. **6–013**

Such a sale frequently entails a transfer of employees' contracts under the Transfer of Undertakings (Protection of Employment) Regulations 2006[32] (TUPE). This accords with the "rescue culture" said to underlie the 1986 Act and is clearly socially desirable. In administration this is compatible with the obligation to act in the interests of creditors as a whole[33] or at least to avoid unnecessary harm to creditors[34] and in at least one case the court has said that it will be positively influenced by the saving of employees' jobs.[35]

Transfer of employees' rights to the purchaser of a business means the purchaser assumes a series of contingent liabilities and is likely to take account of that fact by offering a lower price. In circumstances where the contingent liabilities for employees on a going concern sale are very considerable, this may have the effect of depressing the price below that which could be achieved on a break-up sale. **6–014**

Regulation 8 of TUPE provides insolvency-related exceptions to the policy of transfer of employee rights. The extent of the applicability of reg.8 to a sale in administration has been controversial. Where the relevant insolvency proceedings are "insolvency proceedings which have been opened in relation to the transferor *not* with a view to the liquidation of the assets of the transferor and which are under the supervision of an insolvency practitioner",[36] then (subject to the limited protections for a purchaser afforded by reg.8(5)) there will be an automatic transfer of the employee's rights. **6–015**

In *OTG Ltd v Barke*[37], the Employment Appeal Tribunal clarified the uncertainty in relation to this test, holding that all administrations were to be treated **6–016**

---

[31] As to which see Ch.10.

[32] Transfer of Undertakings (Protection of Employment) Regulations 2006 (SI 2006/246).

[33] para.3(2) of Sch.B1.

[34] para.3(4)(b) of Sch.B1.

[35] *DKLL Solicitors v Revenue & Customs Commissioners* [2007] B.C.C. 908, [20].

[36] reg.8(6). See below, Ch.16, at para.16–031.

[37] *OTG Ltd v Barke* [2011] B.C.C. 608. The Tribunal declined to follow the decision in *Oakland v Wellswood (Yorkshire) Ltd* [2009] I.R.L.R. 250, the correctness of which was itself doubted by the Court of Appeal in *Oakland v Wellswood (Yorkshire) Ltd* [2010] B.C.C. 263.

as "not with a view to the liquidation of the assets of the transferor". The Tribunal's "absolute" approach brings welcome certainty,[38] but at considerable cost in terms of increasing the burden on purchasers (and so depressing the price of any sale and consequent returns to creditors). In certain cases it may scupper a sale altogether, or provide a reason to make the sale through a liquidation or receivership rather than administration.

The decision in *OTG v Barke* may be open to question and subsequent challenge. The Tribunal reached its conclusion on the basis that the primary purpose of the administration procedure is rescue of the company as a going concern. However, it is clear that very many administrations do involve a "liquidation of assets", that such a such a strategy is perfectly legitimate purpose of an administration under para.3(1) of Sch.B1, and that in many cases the administration will be commenced "with a view to" adopting precisely that course. It is far from clear, on the plain wording of the Regulation (which is lifted directly from the relevant EC Directive)[39] why an administration commenced on that footing is not "with a view to liquidation of the assets".

6–017   TUPE also imposes information and consultation obligations in relation to transfers.[40] These require both the provision of prescribed employee information by transferor to transferee and information to and consultation with employees' representatives. Liabilities are imposed for failure to meet these obligations.[41] The extent of the obligations and the timing requirements[42] relating to some of them may lead to significant compliance difficulties. The penalties for non-compliance are variously, liability to the transferee[43] and liability to the affected employees,[44] employee representatives or union representatives.

There are provisions for some of these liabilities to be joint and several with the transferee.[45] This raises issues of rights of contribution between transferor and transferee. Regulation 18 prohibits contracting out of TUPE except to the extent that TUPE permits an agreement to exclude or limit the operation of TUPE.

In cases where there are special circumstances which "render it not reasonably practicable" for the transferor to comply with reg.13(2) to (7) (the duty to inform and consult with affected employees), reg.13(9) requires the transferor to take all steps towards performing those duties as are reasonably practicable in the circumstances. Regulation 15(5) and (6) qualifies this relaxation.

6–018   A "hive-down" is the transfer of certain assets of the business of the company in administration or receivership to a new wholly-owned subsidiary controlled by the office-holder, but leaving behind the liabilities. Without the dead weight of the accumulated debts of the parent, the subsidiary may prove both profit-

---

[38] It was followed by the Employment Appeal Tribunal in *Pressure Coolers Ltd v Molloy* [2011] I.R.L.R. 630.
[39] Council Directive 2001/23/EC.
[40] regs 11, 13 and 14.
[41] reg.12 (but see regs 12(4), 15 and 16).
[42] regs 11(6), 13(2) and (7) (but see regs 13(g) and 14).
[43] regs 12(3), 15(1)(a) and (d), 15(1)(b) and 15(1)(c) respectively.
[44] reg.15(g).
[45] reg.15(9).

able and marketable.[46] Hiving-down has advantages for the receiver in that the business can be conducted through the subsidiary, thereby avoiding personal contractual liability, and for the administrator of insulating the company in administration from administration expense claims.[47]

The principal advantages relate to the preservation and realisation of the business itself[48]: hiving-down is often an important ingredient in preparing the business for an advantageous sale to a purchaser. The benefits of this course of action include the following: **6–019**

(a) the office-holder can choose the assets which are profitable or otherwise desirable to transfer;

(b) the more saleable assets can be combined with the carry forward of capital allowances and trading losses for use against future profits for tax purposes. The right to relief in respect of trading losses is not a chose in action, still less is it assignable by the insolvent company. It is only by means of a hive-down of substantially the whole of the business of the company to a subsidiary that such losses will be capable of transfer to the subsidiary to be set against future profits. Under Pt 22 of the Corporation Tax Act 2010, provided that the transfer is achieved at a time when the transferee is a subsidiary of the transferor, the transferee can take over the past trading losses of the transferor as if it had always carried on the trade.[49] The hive-down should be effected prior to the execution of any agreement for sale if the tax losses are to be utilised in this way. It may be too late to hive-down after an agreement is signed, since the beneficial interest in the shares in the subsidiary will have already passed to the purchaser[50];

---

[46] Hiving-down prior to administration may be difficult because it may open up the directors to challenges by a subsequent liquidator.

[47] But the administrator may take on the responsibilities of being a director or shadow director of the subsidiary—responsibilities which could extend, e.g. to personal liability for wrongful trading of the subsidiary if the business does not prosper. See above, para.2–010 et seq.

[48] Minimising the risk of distress for rates, VAT and taxes is no longer an advantage following the decision in *Re ELS (formerly English Lifestyle)* [1995] Ch. 11 to the effect that crystallisation of the floating charge takes floating charge assets beyond such distress. The decision of the House of Lords in *Re Toshoku Finance UK Plc* [2002] 1 W.L.R. 671 (HL) (see Ch.3 above) overruled *Re Kentish Homes Ltd* [1993] B.C.C. 212 so that in a liquidation context rates will fall into the "necessary disbursement" category of liquidation expenses. That category also now appears in the list of administration expenses in Insolvency Rules r.2.67(1)(f) but the substance of the old s.19 is also retained in para.99. In *Exeter City Council v Bairstow* [2007] 4 All E.R. 437 it was decided that the non-domestic rates of occupied premises were necessary disbursements in administration and therefore payable as an administration expense. It was also stated (obiter) that the same status applied to non-domestic rates of unoccupied premises.

[49] The amount of losses carried forward is reduced by the difference between "relevant liabilities" (liabilities of the transferor prior to hive-down which were not transferred) and "relevant assets" (the value of any assets of the transferor prior to hive-down which were not transferred and the value of the consideration paid by the transferee for the transfer). In practice, the restriction of the losses means that this is no longer the primary reason for hiving-down a business.

[50] See *IRC v Ufitec Group Ltd* [1977] 3 All E.R. 924; *Wood Preservation v Prior* [1969] 1 W.L.R. 1077 (CA) and *J. Sainsbury Plc v O'Connor (Inspector of Taxes)* [1991] 1 W.L.R. 963 (CA).

(c) the subsidiary will be "clean" in the sense of not being saddled with the old company's debts or any disadvantageous credit standing with suppliers[51];

(d) it ought to be easier to establish the profitability of the business of the subsidiary;

(e) trading can continue without interruption even if the parent company is wound up;

(f) Customs and Excise will not allow an office-holder to obtain a repayment of VAT where there are pre-receivership liabilities in respect of VAT. In the case of a business which generates repayments, a hive-down solves this problem in relation to prospective repayments because the subsidiary will be able to obtain separate VAT registration and will be able to claim refunds on its own account, thereby avoiding any claim of Crown set-off;

(g) section 233 of the Insolvency Act 1986 provides that an administrator can require gas, electricity and telecommunication services to be provided so long as he personally guarantees payment for supplies after the date of his appointment[52]: the supplier cannot as a condition of supply make it a condition that pre-appointment bills are paid.[53] A subsidiary will be a new customer and will be entitled to such supplies without payment of its parent's debts. Accordingly, whilst a hive-down is not necessary to secure continued supplies without paying off arrears, it does have the advantage that the administrator or receiver can thereby secure such supplies without being required to give a personal guarantee.

6–020 By virtue of para.60 of Sch.B1, paras 18 and 19 of Sch.1 to the Insolvency Act 1986, an administrator will have the power to establish subsidiaries of the company and to transfer to any such subsidiaries of the company the whole or any part of the business and property of the company. This power may be exercised for the purpose of a hive-down.

6–021 A third option is a "pre-packaged" sale ("pre-pack"), a process which has been judicially described as follows:[54]

"Pre-packs are increasingly common, and highly controversial. The term refers to a sale of all or part of the business and assets of a company . . . negotiated 'in principle' while it is not subject to any insolvency procedure, but on the footing that the sale will be concluded immediately after

---

[51] The hive-down may not solve all the problems in this regard: supplies may be cut off before the hive-down is effected.

[52] This is a rare example of a statutory provision for an administrator to incur personal liability.

[53] Other suppliers continue to be entitled to insist on payment of all sums outstanding as a condition of any supply: see above, paras 8–007 to 8–010.

[54] *Re Kayley Vending Ltd* [2009] B.C.C. 578.

the company has entered into such a procedure, and on the authority of the insolvency practitioner appointed."

It is estimated that over a quarter of administrations now involve a pre-pack of some kind.[55]

The pre-pack strategy has caused considerable controversy, as noted by the court in *Re Kayley Vending Ltd*.[56] There are obvious advantages to such sales, which explains their frequency. The principal advantage is continuity in the business—the effect of an immediate or almost-immediate sale greatly reduces uncertainty among employees, customers and suppliers. In the alternative situation, where the business is marketed in an administration, there is inevitably uncertainty as to whether and in what form it will survive, which hinders trading and is destructive of value. Second, a pre-pack provides certainty. The administrator, and any creditors consulted on the process, know what is likely to be realised by placing the company in administration. Third, it obviates or reduces the need to fund continuing trading during an administration.   **6–022**

Those may all be good strategic reasons for appointing an administrator with a view to a pre-packaged sale. However, there are also very real concerns about pre-packs. The first concern is a general economic one. The effect of agreeing a pre-pack is that the administrator will not have been able to expose the business to the market during the course of the sale process. Accordingly it will be important not only that he can justify the need for an immediate sale but also that he can justify the price achieved by reference to expert valuation advice and such pre-administration marketing as may have been undertaken by the company itself.[57]   **6–023**

Secondly, unlike ordinary administration proposals, a pre-pack will limit or exclude any consultation with creditors still less approval of the sale in a creditors' meeting. Having been presented with a *fait accompli*, they often have insufficient information to make it worthwhile investigating and challenging the decisions taken. With respect to unsecured creditors, there is often an element of "divide and rule"—even if there is general dissatisfaction no individual creditor may have sufficient financial interest to fund a challenge.[58]   **6–024**

In *Re T & D Industries Plc*[59] it was decided that an administrator had power, notwithstanding the provision in s.17(2)(a) of the Act for the court to give directions, to dispose of the company's businesses without directions. In *Re Transbus International Ltd*[60] the court held that the same power and policies applied under the current legislation.[61] Nonetheless an administrator should

---

[55] The Insolvency Service Reports on the Operation of SIP 16 for 2009 and 2010 estimate 27 per cent of administrations in 2009 and 27 per cent in 2010 involved pre-packaged sales. See below, para.6–025 et seq.

[56] *Re Kayley Vending Ltd* [2009] B.C.C. 578.

[57] See commentary regarding the Insolvency Service's proposals to further regulate pre-packs, at paras 6–031 to 6–032.

[58] Although this is not invariably the case: see, e.g. *Clydesdale Financial Services v Smailes* [2010] Lloyd's Rep. I.R. 577.

[59] *Re T & D Industries Plc* [2000] 1 W.L.R. 646.

[60] *Re Transbus International Ltd (In Liquidation)* [2004] 1 W.L.R. 2654.

[61] para.68(2) of Sch.B1.

where possible consult creditors on the disposal decision. If time is pressing there is power for the court to order a creditors' meeting at short notice.[62] If holding a creditors' meeting is impractical the administrator should consider consulting major creditors about his plans.[63] In a pre-packaged sale the administrator must be prepared to explain why there could be no consultation at all with creditors.

6–025   Thirdly, a very large number of pre-packs involve a disposal to a connected party of one or more persons previously involved in the ownership or management of the company. This is in part due to the fact that is unlikely to have been so widely marketed. In 2010, the Insolvency Service reported that 72 per cent of pre-packs involved connected parties.[64] There is an obvious potential for existing directors and shareholders to choreograph an arrangement in which a pre-pack is put in place allowing them to continue running the business post-administration, but which does not realise the best price ultimately available. Such an arrangement may be connived in, on grounds of convenience, by an insolvency practitioner and/or by the senior secured creditor (which has no incentive to insist on a price higher than the amount of its debt) at the expense of unsecured creditors.

6–026   Finally, as a matter of public interest, there is a concern that the use of pre-packs provides a vehicle for the so-called "phoenix phenomenon", whereby directors run a company into insolvency, then simply re-start the business using a new company. The use of a pre-pack to purchase assets and goodwill can facilitate this.

6–027   The gravity of these concerns was noted by the court in *Kayley Vending*, and has been noted elsewhere by respected figures in the insolvency world.[65]

It has been sought, with limited success, to ameliorate these concerns through the promulgation of Statement of Insolvency Practice 16 (SIP 16), which was designed to improve the transparency of the pre-pack process by improving the timing and quality of information which is provided to creditors.

6–028   SIP 16 identifies various points to be borne in mind by insolvency practitioners with respect to pre-pack processes. These are of vital importance in considering when and in what circumstances to accept an appointment:

   (a) It stresses the requirements of paras 3(2) and 3(4) of Sch.B1 and emphasises that administrators must consider the interests of unsecured creditors.

---

[62] *Re Harris Bus Co Ltd* [2000] B.C.C. 1151.

[63] *T & D Industries Plc* [2000] 1 W.L.R. 646. The decision in *Re DKLL Solicitors* [2007] B.C.C. 908 implies in the context of partnership administration, that if, in fact, the sale will lead to a better outcome for the creditors as a whole, even the opposition of the majority creditor may be disregarded.

[64] The Insolvency Service Reports on the Operation of SIP 16 for 2009 and 2010 estimate 79 per cent of pre-packs in 2009 and 72 per cent in 2010 involved sales to connected parties.

[65] Frisby, *A Preliminary Analysis of Pre-Packaged Administrations* (August 2007) at *http://www.r3.org.uk/media/documents/publications/press/preliminary_analysis_of_pre-packed_administrations.pdf*. See also Moulton, "The Uncomfortable Edge of Propriety—prepacks or just stitch ups?", *Recovery Magazine*, Autumn 2005.

(b) It notes that insolvency practitioners should be "clear about their relationship with directors", including being clear in that they are advising the company—and that the directors should take separate advice if they are considering acquiring assets in a pre-pack.

(c) It provides a long list of information which should be disclosed to creditors in all cases following the sale, in order to permit them to evaluate, and if appropriate challenge, the administrator's decision. It is made clear that commercial confidentiality is unlikely to outweigh the requirement to provide this information.

A competent administrator must satisfy himself before accepting the appointment that he will be able to provide the information specified in that list. The list itself may be taken as a useful checklist of matters to be considered by a proposed administrator, including: **6–029**

(a) Marketing activities;

(b) Valuations of the business or assets;

(c) Why it was not appropriate to "trade on" with the business and whether working capital was available;

(d) Consultation with major creditors;

(e) Connection between the purchaser and directors/shareholders or secured creditors of the company.

SIP 16 also notes that insolvency practitioners should be mindful of duties owed to creditors in the pre-appointment period. The requirement for preparation time prior to administration creates a difficulty for the putative administrator and the directors and others involved. New credit will usually be incurred. Procedures should be put in place to ensure that these creditors can be paid in full (or at least that their overall position is not worsened). If credit is incurred in the knowledge or expectation that it cannot be repaid in full this is likely to amount to fraudulent trading.[66] Liability for fraudulent trading is not limited to directors but extends to all participants including advisors such as the proposed administrator. There is also a risk of liability for wrongful trading under s.214. To engage the statutory defence under s.214(3), it is necessary to show that a director took every reasonable and practicable step with a view to minimising the potential loss to the company's creditors as, under the circumstances, he ought to have taken.   **6–030**

The success of these measures has been doubtful at best. The Insolvency Service's review suggests that in 2010 25 per cent of administrators' reports were not compliant with SIP 16, and 15 insolvency practitioners were referred to the professional bodies. Unease about pre-packs does not appear to have died down, and on March 31, 2011, the Department for Business, Innovation and Skills released a statement proposing further measures including: **6–031**

---

[66] See above, para.2–004.

(a) Administrators to be required to give notice to creditors where they propose to sell a significant proportion of the assets of a company or its business to a connected party, in circumstances where there has been no open marketing of the assets;

(b) SIP 16 statements to be included in administration proposals lodged at Companies House; and

(c) Administrators required to confirm that the sale price represents, in their view, best value for creditors.

6–032 These proposals are currently contained in the draft Insolvency (Amendment) (No.2) Rules 2011.[67] If, in particular, the latter requirement becomes law, it is likely that putative administrators will have to do further pre-appointment work (and exercise a more critical eye) before accepting an appointment, and conversely that directors or secured creditors proposing a pre-pack will have to produce a more detailed justification for their plans.

6–033 If there is to be a sale immediately following administration it will invariably require negotiation of the terms prior to administration. The putative administrator will be involved but not in office. His role will be advisory. The company may not have sufficient funds to pay his fees and expenses for this period, but if they are to be paid by a party other than the company, that creates a real risk of conflict.

6–034 Prior to April 2010, there was real uncertainty about whether an administrator's pre-appointment fees were payable as an expense of the administration, given that they did not arise "in the administration of the company".[68] It was apparent that the court could (but would not always)[69] approve the payment of costs using its general power under para.13(1)(f) of Sch.B1, but it was not clear how the matter should be approached in relation to out-of-court appointments.

6–035 From April 6, 2010 administrator's pre-appointment fees and costs are now dealt with by Insolvency Rules 2.33(2A) which defines "pre-administration costs" as fees charged and expenses incurred by the administrator (or another qualified insolvency practitioner) prior to entry into administration but "with a view to the company doing so".[70] The rule requires a statement of pre-administration costs to be made, and Insolvency Rule 2.67A sets out a process for approval of those costs by creditors or the court. Pre-administration costs are now specifically covered in the hierarchy of expenses set out in Insolvency Rule 2.67(1).[71]

6–036 Achieving the primary purpose of rescuing a company in administration will almost always require a period of trading. A rescue will usually involve some element of compromise with the company's existing creditors through a company

---

[67] At the time of writing, the Insolvency Service is undertaking further consultation on the provisions of the draft statutory instrument and, more broadly, the general question of the further regulation of pre-packs.
[68] Insolvency Rule 2.67(1).
[69] See *Re Johnson Machine and Tool Co Ltd* [2010] B.C.C. 382, discussed below at 6–070.
[70] *Re Johnson Machine and Tool Co Ltd* [2010] B.C.C. 382.
[71] Insolvency Rule 2.67(1)(h).

voluntary arrangement (CVA), and at least 14 days' notice is required to be given by the administrator for a meeting of creditors to consider a CVA.[72] The administrator will therefore need to take account of the likely outcome of trading in assessing whether rescue or an immediate disposal will achieve the best result for the creditors as a whole.[73] In considering the implications of trading, the administrator must take account of the expenses that will be involved.

Similarly, it is likely that (unless there is a pre-pack of the company's entire business) any disposal as a going concern, or possibly even on a break-up basis, will require trading in the interim in order to permit a sale at the best price. It is thus essential to consider prior to, or on appointment, the basis and strategy for ongoing trading.

To justify trading on in the long term there must be a prospect of: **6–037**

(a) trading out, i.e. into a position of solvency; or, more frequently;

(b) selling the business at a sum substantially greater than the break-up value of the assets.

An administrator pursuing a rescue strategy will need to involve the company   **6–038** in his thinking and, unless he proposes to refinance the secured debt, will need the concurrence of the debenture holder.[74] In considering whether to trade an administrator should consider his duty to the company's creditors as a whole,[75] or, if there will be no funds for them other than those set aside under s.176A of the Act, his duty not to harm the interests of unsecured creditors unnecessarily. In administration the benefit to the creditors as a whole or the avoidance of unnecessary risk to creditors may on occasion justify trading even though only a break-up sale is ultimately expected—the administrator must evaluate the risks and rewards of such a strategy in the particular context.

The administrator will also need to consider the funds available to fund   **6–039** trading. If the company has not granted security, his concern will be focused on the liquidity of the company's assets to meet the costs of trading. In the more usual circumstances when the company has granted debenture security his access to assets for trading expenses will be restricted to the pool of floating charge assets.[76]

Similar logic will apply to an administrator who thinks that a disposal in   **6–040** administration will only allow a distribution to one or more secured or preferential creditors.[77] The administrator will be obliged to carry out his functions so that he does not unnecessarily harm the interests of the creditors of the

---

[72] Insolvency Rule 1.11(1). In circumstances when the company has only a few creditors who agree to compromise their claims the company is likely to avoid administration altogether.

[73] para.3(3)(b) of Sch.B1.

[74] See s.4(3), para.73(i)(a) Sch.B1.

[75] See s.4(3), para.73(i)(a) Sch.B1, para.3(2) Sch.B1.

[76] para.70(1) of Sch.B1. Although it is likely that if the administrator realises fixed charge assets, at least with the secured creditor's consent, he will be entitled to the expenses of realisation: *Re Regent's Canal Iron Works Co* (1875) 3 Ch.D 411 (CA) affirmed in *Buchler v Talbot*; sub nom. *Re Leyland DAF Ltd* [2004] 2 A.C. 298 (HL).

[77] para.3(1)(c) of Sch.B1 to the Act.

company as a whole.[78] The administrator may find that it is the level of administration expenses, rather than the price obtainable from the company's business and assets, which leads to there being no funds available for the prescribed part under s.176A of the Act.

5.   OTHER PRACTICAL CONSIDERATIONS

6–041   Normally more than one insolvency practitioner will be nominated to act as administrator in order to ensure that the absence of one individual does not prejudice the management of the administration and to ensure continuity. The rules expressly provide for the appointment of more than one person as "administrator of a company" provided that the appointment specifies which functions are to be exercised jointly and which by any or all.[79] Provision is also made for a person to be appointed to act jointly or concurrently, as an additional administrator.[80]

6–042   In relation to groups of companies, consideration should be given as to the effect of administration or alternative insolvency procedures. A relatively common structure is for a lender to take security over a holding company's shares in its operating companies, and over the operating companies themselves. Enforcing the security over the shares may not always be an effective means of securing control over the group—for example, the benefit of certain agreements may not run with the shares. By contrast, putting the holding company into administration may permit it to retain the benefit of those agreements. That will depend on the wording of the relevant contracts. In other circumstances, it may be more effective to place the operating companies but not the holding company into administration.

6–043   Creditors and those advising them must also have regard to the provisions of the Financial Collateral Regulations[81] which provide that in certain situations, the administration moratorium will not apply to financial collateral given by the company. In some cases this will render administration impractical, or make it substantially more difficult.

6–044   Practical considerations may also impact upon the method of appointment. While, as explained below, directors and floating charge holders tend to prefer out-of-court appointments, questions of certainty sometimes justify an application to the court. For example, in *Re Kaupthing Capital Partners II Master LP Inc*[82], it was held that an appointment in relation to a foreign entity was invalid—on analysis, the relevant entity was best characterised as a partnership rather than a company, and the appointment should have been made on Form 1B rather than Form 2.10B. An application to court could have resolved this difficulty. Similar considerations may arise where there is an issue as to jurisdiction under the EC Regulation, or as to the validity of the floating charge under which the administrator is to be appointed.

---

[78] para.3(4)(b) of Sch.B1 to the Act.
[79] Sch.B1 para.100.
[80] Sch.B1 para.103.
[81] The Financial Collateral Arrangements (No.2) Regulations 2003.
[82] *Re Kaupthing Capital Partners II Master LP Inc* [2011] B.C.C. 338.

Practical matters may bear on the timing of appointment. Following the **6–045** decision in *Goldacre (Offices) Ltd v Nortel Networks Ltd*[83] that rent incurred on a particular quarter day by a company in administration should be treated as payable, in full, as an administration expense, it seems likely that in many cases, where practicable, an appointment may be delayed until shortly after the quarter day to avoid incurring this expense liability.

Finally, it is important to note that specialist treatment is given to particular **6–046** types of company, including particularly insurers and financial institutions, the detail of which is outside the scope of this chapter.[84] When dealing with companies of this type, it is essential that creditors and insolvency practitioners should understand the implications of those specialist regimes. Further, the decision in *Re M.T.B. Motors Ltd*[85] illustrates the necessity for a careful investigation as to whether any given company in fact falls to be dealt with under one of these specialist regimes.

6. METHODS OF APPOINTMENT—APPOINTMENT OF ADMINISTRATOR BY THE COURT

An application to court for the appointment of an administrator may be made by: **6–047**

(a) the company[86];

(b) the directors of the company[87];

(c) one or more creditors[88] of the company (which includes a contingent creditor and a prospective creditor)[89];

(d) the justices' chief executive for a magistrates' court in the exercise of the power conferred by s.87A of the Magistrates' Courts Act 1980 where a fine has been imposed on the company; or

(e) a combination of persons listed in paras (a) to (d).[90]

As far as applications by creditors are concerned, the position regarding such applications where the debt upon which standing is based is disputed appears to be similar to that in relation to the presentation of a petition for the winding

---

[83] *Goldacre (Offices) Ltd v Nortel Networks Ltd* [2010] Ch. 455—discussed in Ch.4.

[84] See *Banks (Administration Proceedings) Order 1989* (SI 1989/1276); Credit Institutions (Reorganisation and Winding Up) Regulations 2004 (SI 2004/1045); Insurers (Reorganisation and Winding Up) Regulations 2004 (SI 2004/353).

[85] *Re M.T.B. Motors Ltd* [2010] EWHC 3751 (Ch).

[86] See *Re Emmadart Ltd* [1979] Ch. 540 in connection with the power of the company to apply.

[87] If the application is made by the directors, then after it is made, it is treated for all purposes as the application of the company, r.3(2). See further *Re Equipcorp International Plc* [1989] 1 W.L.R. 101.

[88] As to the need to establish that the applicant is indeed a creditor, see *Re Simoco Digital UK Ltd* [2004] 1 B.C.L.C. 541.

[89] Sch.B1, para.12(4). See generally *Re British American Racing (Holdings) Ltd* [2005] B.C.C. 110 in respect of an application by a contingent creditor.

[90] Sch.B1, para.12(1).

up of a company. In *Hammonds v Pro-Fit USA Ltd*[91] it was held that an applicant would be a creditor for the purposes of para.12(1)(c) if he could establish "a good arguable case that debt of sufficient amount is owing to him".[92]

6–048   An application may also be made by:

    (a) the liquidator of a company[93];

    (b) the supervisor of a company voluntary arrangement[94]; and

    (c) in certain circumstances, the Financial Services Authority.[95]

In practice, many applications for the appointment of an administrator by the court are likely to be "hostile" applications by creditors who do not hold floating charge security and therefore lack the ability to make their own appointment out of court, although applications were also often made where an administrator needs to seek recognition in a foreign jurisdiction where a court order is likely to prove more persuasive.[96] Where the company and its directors wish to appoint administrators they will almost invariably make use of the procedure for appointment out of court, which is considered below.[97] Similarly, creditors with floating charge security will make use of the powers that they have by virtue of their security, although if there is some doubt as to the validity of the floating charge it may be that an application for an appointment by the court will be appropriate, as it would enable the issue to be decided before the administrator or his appointor have left themselves open to the possible claims that could arise following an invalid appointment. The court does not, however, have to rule on validity to make an appointment if it is not in issue, although it can treat any uncertainty as a factor to be taken into account when exercising its discretion to make an appointment. Once an application is made it cannot be withdrawn without the permission of the court.[98]

6–049   The application to the court must be made in Form 2.1B. The application must generally include a statement of the applicant's belief that the "company is, or is likely to become, unable to pay its debts". Exceptionally this is not required where the application is made by the holder of a "qualifying floating charge" who is making the application on the basis that the charge is [otherwise] enforceable, in which case sufficient details must be provided as to why

---

[91] *Hammonds v Pro-Fit USA Ltd* [2008] 2 B.C.L.C. 159.

[92] *Hammonds v Pro-Fit USA Ltd* [2008] 2 B.C.L.C. 159, [53]. See also *Europcar Ltd v Top Marques Car Rental Ltd* [2005] All ER (D) 388 and *Corbett v Nysir UK Ltd* [2008] EWHC 2670 (Ch).

[93] Sch.B1, para.38.

[94] Sch.B1, para.12(5) and s.7(4)(b) of the Insolvency Act 1986.

[95] s.359 of the Financial Services and Markets Act 2000, as amended by para.55 of Sch.17 to the Enterprise Act 2002.

[96] See para.32–003.

[97] Exceptions occasionally arise where there are doubts about the ability of the directors to make a valid appointment (for example because the company's centre of main interests is arguably abroad) and it is thought prudent to seek a court order. See 6–044 above.

[98] Sch.B1, para.12(3).

this is the case (e.g. details of a non-insolvency related default which means that the floating charge has become enforceable).[99] Where there is a hostile application, the applicant must show on the balance of probabilities (i.e. the normal civil standard of proof) that the company is or is likely to become unable to pay its debts; it is not sufficient to suggest that there is a real prospect that this may be the case.[100] The meaning of this phrase has recently been considered by the Court of Appeal in *BNY Corporate Trustee Services Ltd v Eurosail—UK 2007—3BL Plc*,[101] where the court made it clear that the "balance sheet" test in s.123(2) is not an exercise of simply assessing net assets or liabilities but instead entails deciding whether the company has reached the point of no return such that its use of its cash or other assets for current purposes would amount to a fraud on its future or contingent creditors.[102]

The application in Form 2.1B must have attached to it a statement in Form   **6–050** 2.2B by each of the proposed administrators stating:

(a) that he consents to accept appointment;

(b) details of any prior professional relationship(s) that he has had with the company to which he is to be appointed as administrator[103]; and

(c) his opinion that it is reasonably likely that the purpose of administration will be achieved.[104]

It should first be noted that the requirement now is for the opinion to be given by the prospective administrators, as opposed to an appropriate "independent person" as was previously the case. In practice this person would invariably be the proposed administrator, but it did not have to be and, indeed, on a hostile appointment the court has held that it would be inappropriate for the proposed administrator to prepare a 2.2 report recommending his own appointment given that there would be a conflict of interest.[105] Whilst the opinion is now sought from the proposed administrator alone, this does not mean that the requirement for objectivity has in any way diminished and, in forming and giving an opinion, the proposed administrator should be very aware of his status as an officer of the court in the event that he is appointed.[106] As noted above, once the administrator has formed his opinion, there is no longer any requirement for the reasoning and conclusions to be expressed in a 2.2 report

---

[99] r.2.4(1) and r.2.4(3).

[100] *Re Colt Telecom Group Plc (No.2)* [2003] B.P.I.R. 324.

[101] *BNY Corporate Trustee Services Ltd v Eurosail—UK 2007—3BL Plc* [2011] B.C.C. 399 (CA).

[102] See *BNY Corporate Trustee Services Ltd* [2011] B.C.C. 399 (CA) at [49] and [51], and also *Re Cheyne Finance Plc* [2008] 2 All E.R. 987.

[103] Whilst the existence of a conflict of interest might well provide grounds for complaint to the insolvency practitioner's recognised professional body, it should not normally affect the validity of the administration unless, so far as any company voluntary arrangement proposed by the administrator is concerned the existence of the conflict can be relied upon to support an allegation of unfair prejudice, see *Sisu Capital Fund Ltd v Tucker* [2006] B.C.C. 463.

[104] r.2.3(5).

[105] See *Re Colt Telecom Plc (No.2)* [2003] B.P.I.R. 324.

[106] See generally *Re Colt Telecom Plc (No.2)* [2003] B.P.I.R. 324.

as was the case under the old regime. This does not mean, however, that these issues should not be documented; prospective administrators should be aware of the power of the court to order disclosure and cross-examination.[107]

6–051   The application in Form 2.1B (attaching the proposed administrator's statement) must also be supported by an affidavit or witness statement sworn by or on behalf of the applicant for the administration order containing:

(a) a statement of the company's financial position, specifying (to the best of the applicant's knowledge and belief) the company's assets and liabilities, including contingent and prospective liabilities;

(b) details of any security known to be held by creditors of the company, and whether in any case the security is such as to confer power on the holder to appoint an administrative receiver or to appoint an administrator. If an administrative receiver has been appointed, that fact must be stated;

(c) details of any insolvency proceedings in relation to the company including any petition that has been presented for the winding-up of the company so far as is within the immediate knowledge of the applicant;

(d) where it is intended to appoint a number of persons as administrators, details of the functions that are to be exercised jointly or severally[108]; and

(e) any other matters which, in the opinion of those intending to make the application for an administration order, will assist the court in deciding whether to make such an order, so far as lies within the knowledge or belief of the applicant.[109]

Where, as will often be the case, the administration application is made by a creditor, it is likely that the creditor's knowledge of the company's affairs will be limited. It is submitted, however, that the creditor will still need to take reasonable steps to obtain publicly available information and to combine this with information derived from its trading or other relationship in order to present as full a picture as possible to the court. Clearly the creditor must be able to put forward some compelling evidence otherwise the order could not be made by the court.

6–052   In addition to the above, the evidence must also state whether in the opinion of the applicant the EC Regulation applies and, if so, whether the proceedings will be main proceedings or territorial proceedings.[110] There is a continuing duty on the applicant to notify the court in writing of any proceedings that he

---

[107] *Re Colt Telecom Group Plc (No.1)* [2002] B.P.I.R. 311.
[108] Sch.B1, para.100(2).
[109] r.2.4(2).
[110] r.2.4(4) and see generally Ch.31.

becomes aware of subsequently, whether these are proceedings under the EC Regulation or domestic proceedings.[111]

The application (together with all of the supporting documents referred to   **6–053** above) must be filed at court with copies for service and use.[112] The "court" for these purposes means the Chancery Division of the High Court[113] or a county court with jurisdiction to wind up the company.[114] The filed copies are sealed by the court office and endorsed with the date and time of filing;[115] they are also endorsed with the venue for the application to be heard.[116]

"As soon as is reasonably practicable after the making of the administration   **6–054** application" notice must be given by means of service of the application as issued by the court[117] (together with the attached documents and supporting evidence)[118] to:

(a) any person who has appointed an administrative receiver of the company;

(b) any person who is or may be entitled to appoint an administrative receiver of the company;

(c) any qualifying floating charge-holder, who is or may be entitled to appoint an administrator of the company in such capacity;[119]

(d) such other persons who may be prescribed. Currently these are:

(i) any administrative receiver who has been appointed;

(ii) the petitioner in respect of any pending winding-up petition (and also to the provisional liquidator, if any);

(iii) any Member State liquidator who has been appointed in main proceedings in relation to the company;

(iv) the person proposed as administrator;

---

[111] r.2.5(4). See further *Re Hans Brochier Holdings Ltd* [2007] B.C.C. 127, where administrators had been appointed out of court and *Re Hellas Telecommunications (Luxembourg) II SCA* [2010] B.C.C. 295. The leading case is *Re Stanford International Bank (In Receivership)* [2011] Ch. 33 (CA).

[112] r.2.5(1).

[113] Either the Central Registry or one of the district registries (normally the most convenient for the proposed administrator and his advisers) with chancery jurisdiction.

[114] s.251 of the Insolvency Act 1985 which incorporates the definition in s.744 of the Companies Act 1985, which in turn refers back to s.117 of the Insolvency Act 1986. Accordingly, an administration application can always be made in the High Court. If a company has a share capital of not more than £120,000, the county court with insolvency jurisdiction in which the company's registered officer was situated for the greater part of the preceding six months has concurrent jurisdiction.

[115] r.2.5(2).

[116] r.2.5(3).

[117] r.2.6(2).

[118] r.2.6(1).

[119] But see *Re OMP Leisure Ltd* [2008] B.C.C. 67, where it was held that there would be no obligation to give notice to such a chargeholder where the debenture in question was not merely currently unenforceable but should have been discharged.

(v) the company, if the application is made by anyone other than the company; and

(vi) any supervisor of a voluntary arrangement under Pt I of the Insolvency Act 1986 who has been appointed.[120]

In addition to the requirement formally to serve the above, the applicant must give notice of the fact that the application has been made to:

(a) any enforcement or other officer who to his knowledge is charged with an execution or other legal process against the company or its property; and

(b) any person who to his knowledge has distrained against the company or its property.[121]

Whilst there is no specific requirement in this respect,[122] it is suggested that the applicant should notify any of the above if their existence only comes to his attention at a later date.

6–055   Provision is made in the Insolvency Rules 1986 for the manner in which service of the application and accompanying documents is to be effected. Essentially, where service is required it must be effected by leaving the documents at, or sending them by first-class post to:

(a) the company at its registered office or, if this is not practicable, its last known principal place of business in England and Wales[123]; and

(b) any other person at his "proper address", being such address as he has previously notified as his address for service or if no address has been notified "his usual or last known address".

Specific provision is made where the applicant is obliged to serve an authorised deposit-taker who has appointed or may be entitled to appoint an administrative receiver or administrator, by virtue of the fact that it holds a qualifying floating charge. Where that person has not notified an address for service, the proper address is the office "where, to the knowledge of the applicant, the company maintains a bank account", or if the applicant is not aware of any such office then the registered office, or if there is no such office the usual or last known address.[124] In cases of difficulty, directions may be sought from the court.[125] In any event, once the application has been served this must be verified by an affidavit of service in Form 2.3B, with details of the date and manner

---

[120] Sch.B1 para.12(2) and r.2.6(3).

[121] r.2.7.

[122] cf. r.2.5(4) which provides that an applicant must notify the court if he becomes aware of proceedings under the EC Insolvency Regulation after the application has been filed.

[123] r.2.8(a) and r.2.8(3).

[124] r.2.8(5).

[125] r.2.8(2)(c).

of service.[126] This affidavit, with a sealed copy of the application exhibited, must be filed in court as soon as reasonably practicable and in any event not less than one day before the hearing of the application.[127]

The question of whether or not the court may dispense with service has **6–056** caused some difficulty in the past. In the early case of *Re Vosper Ship Repairers Ltd*,[128] it was held that the court could dispense with service if a person entitled to appoint an administrative receiver consented. However, doubts were expressed about the power to dispense with service in *Re Valarette Ltd*.[129] In *Re Cavco Floors Ltd*[130] Harman J. made an administration order in reliance on a solicitors' undertaking to present a petition, having been given evidence that the debenture-holder consented to an abridgment and to the proposed order. The judgment states that the requirement for service on the proposed adminis-trator can be waived. In *Re Chancery Plc*[131] Harman J. again dispensed with service but in the special circumstances of an administration petition in respect of an authorised institution under the Banking Act, presented by the bank's directors with the Bank of England having been notified and having agreed to short notice. In *Re Shearing & Loader Ltd*[132] an administration order was made on an undertaking to present a petition forthwith. However, in *Cornhill Financial Services Ltd v Cornhill Insurance Plc*[133] Dillon L.J. expressly approved earlier criticism by Harman J. of the practice of obtaining adminis-tration orders on such undertakings. Despite the criticism of this practice, it is considered that in special cases administration orders can and should continue to be made on undertakings.

Not only must the application and accompanying documents be served as **6–057** soon as practicable, they must also be served not less than five days before the date fixed for the application to be heard.[134] Whilst the court has power to abridge this time period, this raises similar issues to the question of whether it is appropriate to dispense with service.[135] In *Re A Company (No.00175 of 1987)*[136] (dealing with an "old law" Pt II petition) it was held that there was no power in the Act which could be read as impliedly restricting the power of the court to abridge time. Vinelott J. found it difficult to conceive of circumstances in which an order would be made without giving a debenture-holder time to decide whether or not to appoint an administrative receiver. Conversely, the court may be requested to adjourn a petition but, save in the most exceptional circumstances, it is not appropriate to adjourn or stand over a petition for a

---

[126] r.2.9(1).
[127] r.2.9(2).
[128] *Re Vosper Ship Repairers Ltd* Unreported February 17, 1987.
[129] *Re Valarette Ltd* Unreported October 15, 1987.
[130] *Re Cavco Floors* [1990] B.C.C. 589.
[131] *Re Chancery Plc* [1991] B.C.C. 171.
[132] *Re Shearing & Loader Ltd* [1991] B.C.C. 232; see also *Re Rowbotham Baxter Ltd* [1990] B.C.C. 113.
[133] *Cornhill Financial Services Ltd v Cornhill Insurance Plc* [1992] B.C.C. 818 (CA).
[134] r.2.8(1).
[135] See para.6–034 above.
[136] *Re A Company (No.00175 of 1987)* (1987) 3 B.C.C. 124; see also *Re Gallidoro Trawlers Ltd* [1991] B.C.C. 691.

substantial period.[137] Whilst the five day period of notice that was required in respect of petitions presented pursuant to Pt II of the Insolvency Act 1986 was routinely abridged, reflecting the fact that such petitions were normally presented by the company and its directors after the consent of the holder of any floating charge had been obtained, it is unlikely that the court will be prepared to abridge the notice period in anything other than an extreme case, where the company has not consented, given the serious effects which the appointment of administrators will have so far as the company is concerned.[138]

6–058   Where an application to the court is made by someone other than the holder of a qualifying floating charge, the qualifying floating charge-holder may nevertheless intervene by application to the court to appoint as administrator its choice of insolvency practitioner.[139] If such an application is made, the charge-holder must produce to the court:

    (a) the written consent of all holders of any prior qualifying floating charge;

    (b) a written statement in the Form 2.2B made by the specified person proposed by him as administrator; and

    (c) sufficient evidence to satisfy the court that he is entitled to appoint an administrator under paragraph 14 (i.e. that he is indeed the holder of a qualifying floating charge and that he is entitled to make the appointment under the terms of the charge).[140]

The effect of the foregoing is to preserve the right of a qualifying floating charge-holder to determine the identity of administrators even where an insolvency practitioner has been selected by another creditor or other permitted applicant. In these circumstances both the costs of the original applicant and the qualifying floating charge-holder who intervenes are, unless the court otherwise orders, paid as an expense of the administration.[141]

6–059   Where a company is already in liquidation it is generally not possible for an administrator to be appointed.[142] There are, however, two exceptions. First, if the holder of a qualifying floating charge could appoint an administrator but for the fact that there is a winding-up by the court (i.e. this does not apply if there is a voluntary winding-up), the charge-holder is still entitled to apply for the appointment of his choice of administrator.[143] In this case, the court may make an order discharging the winding-up order and dealing with consequential issues.[144] As well as dealing with the general matters referred to below, the

---

[137] *Re Chelmsford City Football Club (1980) Ltd* [1991] B.C.C. 133; *Re Kyrris (No.1)* [1998] B.P.I.R. 103.
[138] See *Re Colt Telecom Plc (No.2)* [2003] B.P.I.R. 324.
[139] Sch.B1, para.36.
[140] r.2.10(1).
[141] r.2.10(2).
[142] Sch.B1, para.8(1).
[143] Sch.B1, para.37(2).
[144] Sch.B1, para.37(3).

application by the charge-holder must contain sufficient evidence to satisfy the court of the charge-holder's power to appoint.[145] The second exception is that a liquidator of any company in liquidation (i.e. voluntary or compulsory) can apply to place the company in administration.[146] In this case, the court must discharge any existing winding-up order, or presumably stay any voluntary winding-up, as well as dealing with consequential issues.[147]

Where orders are made on the application of the holder of a qualifying floating charge or liquidator pursuant to the above provisions, the court has to include in the order:

(a) in the case of a liquidator appointed in a voluntary winding-up, an order confirming his removal from office;

(b) details concerning the release of the liquidator;

(c) provision for payment of the expenses of the liquidation;

(d) provisions regarding any indemnity given to the liquidator;

(e) provisions regarding the handling or realisation of any of the company's assets in the hands of or under the control of the liquidator;

(f) such provision as the court thinks fit with respect to matters arising in connection with the liquidation; and

(g) such other provisions as the court shall think fit.[148]

The making of an application gives rise to the power of the court "on hearing an administration application" (wording which is presumably wide enough to include hearings prior to the first formal hearing of the application) to: **6–060**

(a) make the administration order sought;

(b) dismiss the application;

(c) adjourn the hearing conditionally or unconditionally;

(d) make an interim order;

(e) treat the application as a winding-up petition and make any order which the court could make under s.125 of the Insolvency Act 1986;

(f) make any other order which the court thinks appropriate.[149]

Although it is difficult to conceive of a wider range of powers being available to the court, it is still expressly provided that an interim order may restrict the

---

[145] r.2.11(2).
[146] Sch.B1, para.38(1). For an example of an unsuccessful application by a liquidator, see *Re Q3 Media Ltd* Unreported May 22, 2006.
[147] Sch.B1, para.38(2).
[148] r.2.13.
[149] Sch.B1, para.13(1).

exercise of a power of the directors or make provision conferring a discretion on the court or on a person qualified to act as an insolvency practitioner in relation to the company.[150] Further, while an interim order can be made[151] a court cannot appoint an interim administrator.[152]

6–061   Despite the above, it is suggested that the Act does in fact build in certain limitations on this apparently unlimited jurisdiction, and in particular it cannot be exercised to prevent persons exercising rights recognised as subsisting irrespective of the making of the application. Thus, this provision cannot be used as a basis of jurisdiction to restrain the presentation of a petition to wind up[153] or the appointment of an administrative receiver or the exercise by such receiver of his powers (unless the charge under which he is appointed is open to challenge under ss.238 to 240 or 245 of the Act).[154] Nor can new positive obligations be foisted on creditors, e.g. to supply or lend money to the company, as opposed to the imposition of restrictions on the exercise of existing rights.[155] Subject to such built-in limitations, the court can impose on the company and its creditors any scheme for protecting and preserving its assets and its future as the circumstances require.

6–062   The court does have jurisdiction to appoint an administrator with retrospective effect. It is suggested that this power ought to be used very sparingly, but it was used in *Re Derfshaw Ltd*[156] where an earlier out-of-court appointment had been invalid. The court used its powers to regularise the appointment.

6–063   Any of the following may appear or be represented on the hearing of the administration application:

    (a) the applicant;

    (b) the company;

    (c) one or more of the directors;

    (d) any administrative receiver who has been appointed;

    (e) any person who has presented a petition for the winding-up of the company;

---

[150] Sch.B1, para.13(3).

[151] *Re Gallidoro Trawlers Ltd* [1991] B.C.C. 691.

[152] Sch.B1, para.13(2); *Re A Company (No.00175 of 1987)* (1987) 3 B.C.C. 124; *Re Gallidoro Trawlers Ltd* [1991] B.C.C. 691. In Scotland it has been held that there is power to appoint an interim administrator: *Air Ecosse Ltd v Civil Aviation Authority* (1987) 3 B.C.C. 492 (Court of Session, Inner House); *Re Avenel Hotel Ltd* Unreported March 1987. See also *Scottish Exhibition Centre Ltd, Noters* [1993] B.C.C. 529 (Court of Session, Outer House); *Scottish Exhibition Centre Ltd v Mirestop* [1994] B.C.C. 845 (Court of Session, Outer House); *Secretary of State for Trade and Industry v Palmer* [1994] B.C.C. 990 (Court of Session, Inner House).

[153] In *Re W.F. Fearman Ltd* (1988) 4 B.C.C. 139 the court refused to use the power which was then contained in s.9(4) of the Act to appoint a provisional liquidator but made an appointment under a pending winding-up petition instead.

[154] Sch.B1, para.39.

[155] With the statutory exception under s.233 supplies utilities, as to which see paras 8–007 to 8–010.

[156] *Re Derfshaw Ltd* [2011] B.C.C. 631. See also, *Re G-Tech Construction Ltd* [2007] B.P.I.R. 1275.

(f)   the person proposed for appointment as administrator;

(g)   any Member State liquidator who has been appointed in main proceedings in relation to the company;

(h)   any person who is the holder of a qualifying floating charge;

(i)   any supervisor of a voluntary arrangement under Pt I of the Act;

(j)   with the permission of the court, any other person who appears to have an interest justifying his appearance.[157]

Questions of the applicant's status normally need to be resolved before the final order is made, but liquidation principles do not apply since it would frustrate the purpose of the legislation if any such issue necessarily had to be decided before an order could be made.[158] Although there is no provision for contributories' petitions,[159] the interests of shareholders and management in not having the business of the company taken out of their hands and sold to a third party were taken into account in *Re Imperial Motors (UK) Ltd*.[160] However, in *Re Chelmsford City Football Club (1980) Ltd*,[161] the court applied the classic winding-up test[162] and held that, since the company was plainly insolvent, shareholders had no interests sufficient to justify them being heard.[163] Although the opposition of creditors who obtain leave is relevant to a consideration whether there is any real prospect[164] of the intended purposes of an administration being achieved, the court will not simply count heads.[165] The interests of secured creditors are relevant but less persuasive than the interests of other creditors.[166]   **6–064**

Similarly where creditors prefer an alternative proposal, as in *Re Dollar Land (Manhattan) Ltd*, [167] where the creditor preferred winding-up to administration, the court will take their views into account. In *DKLL Solicitors v HM*   **6–065**

---

[157] r.2.12(1). See also r.7.53 (right of attendance). The application will be listed to be heard by a judge in public in accordance with para.5.1(5) of the Practice Direction on Insolvency Proceedings. In an appropriate case the court may be persuaded to sit in private: see the terms of para.5.1(5) of the Practice Direction on Insolvency Proceedings and Pt 39.2 of the CPR. See also *Re Chancery Plc* [1991] B.C.C. 171.

[158] *Re MTI Trading Systems Ltd* [1997] B.C.C. 703, on refusal of leave to appeal [1998] B.C.C. 400 (CA). See also *Re Simoco Digital UK Ltd* [2004] 1 B.C.L.C. 541.

[159] *Re Land and Property Trust Co Plc* [1991] B.C.C. 446.

[160] *Re Imperial Motors (UK) Ltd* (1989) 5 B.C.C. 214.

[161] *Re Chelmsford City Football Club (1980) Ltd* [1991] B.C.C. 133.

[162] *Re Rica Gold Washing Co* (1879) L.R. 11 Ch. D. 36 (CA).

[163] The members were also creditors and were given leave to be heard in the latter capacity. In *Re K&H Options Ltd* Unreported February 17, 2000, the possibility that future realisations would result in a balance sheet surplus was held to give members a tangible interest in the outcome and leave was given under what is now r.2.12(1)(j). See also *Re Farnborough Aircraft.com Ltd* [2002] 2 B.C.L.C. 641, where Neuberger J. suggested that the court should be careful before concluding that shareholders had sufficient interest to be joined where a company appeared to be insolvent.

[164] See below, para.6–067.

[165] *Re Land and Property Trust Co Plc* [1991] B.C.C. 446; *Re Rowbotham Baxter Ltd* [1990] B.C.C. 113; *Re Arrows Ltd (No.3)* [1992] B.C.C. 131. See also *Re Genesis Technologies International (S) Pty Ltd* [1994] 3 S.L.R. 390, (High Court of Singapore); *Re Structures & Computers Ltd* [1998] B.C.C. 348.

[166] *Re Consumer & Industrial Press Ltd* (1988) 4 B.C.C. 68; *Re Imperial Motors (UK) Ltd* (1989) 5 B.C.C. 214 (a case where the petitioner was a secured creditor).

[167] *Re Dollar Land (Manhattan) Ltd* [2007] B.C.C. 953.

Revenue & Customs[168] the court has indicated that it may also take into account the views of other stakeholders (in particular, employees)—although it is not clear that there would be any justification for overriding the interests of creditors in order to protect other stakeholders.

6–066   Although the proposed administrators are nominated by the applicant in the application, the court may find itself required to consider an alternative nomination. Where that issue arises (and subject to conflict of interest considerations), the court is likely to favour the appointment of prospective administrators who are already familiar with the company's business. Such knowledge may derive, for example, from the investigation required in order for the prospective administrators to form the necessary view that the statutory purpose can be achieved, or from acting as investigating accountants.[169] In *Re Structures & Computers Ltd*,[170] the court made an administration order notwithstanding the opposition of a major creditor, which also applied for its nominee to be appointed as an additional administrator. Although the application failed, the court considered that creditors' views should be taken into account when exercising its discretion and where, as in the instant case, the creditor had highlighted serious concerns it could be allowed its costs as an expense of the administration. Where, however, there is no reason to believe that the company's nominated administrator was unlikely to be independent, it will normally be inappropriate to hold a headcount of creditors to decide between the company's choice and the applicant's choice of administrator,[171] and it will normally not be appropriate to make a joint appointment of insolvency practitioners from different firms as this would simply lead to an increase in costs.[172] In *Oracle (North West) Ltd v Pinnacle Services (UK) Ltd*[173] the court appointed the creditors' preferred administrator rather than make a joint appointment of "rival" insolvency practitioners.

6–067   In order for the court to make an administration order it must be "satisfied":

(a) that the company is or is likely to become unable to pay its debts; and

(b) that the administration order is reasonably likely to achieve the purpose of administration.[174]

This test is very similar to that applicable under Pt II of the Insolvency Act 1986 prior to the Enterprise Act reforms, which referred in the equivalent of para.(b) above, to the court concluding that it "considers" that one or more of the old statutory purposes was "likely" (now "reasonably likely") to be achieved. Despite the difference in language, it is submitted nothing turns on

---

[168] *DKLL Solicitors v HM Revenue & Customs* [2007] B.C.C. 908, [20].
[169] *Re Maxwell Communications Corp Plc (No.1)* [1992] B.C.C. 372; *Re Strand Libraries Ltd* Unreported May 20, 1996; cf. *GP Noble Trustees Ltd v Berkeley Berry Birch Plc* [2007] B.P.I.R. 1271.
[170] *Re Structures & Computers Ltd* [1998] B.C.C. 348.
[171] *Re World Class Homes Ltd* [2005] 2 B.C.L.C. 1.
[172] *Re Structures & Computers Ltd* [1998] B.C.C. 348.
[173] *Oracle (North West) Ltd v Pinnacle Services (UK) Ltd* [2009] B.C.C. 159.
[174] Sch.B1, para.11.

this and the test remains that there is a "real prospect" (as opposed to a mere hope or possibility) that the statutory purpose can be achieved.[175] Opposition to a creditor's petition by the company or its members on the ground that management could achieve the relevant purpose more cheaply is unlikely to be persuasive.[176]

In relation to a pre-pack administration, the evidence will contain details of **6–068** the proposed transaction. These will obviously be relevant to the court's evaluation of whether the administration order is reasonably likely to achieve the purpose of the administration. It has been emphasised that in most cases the information provided by SIP 16 should be provided in the evidence.[177] However, it is not the role of the court to substitute its judgment for that of the administrator. As Lewison J. explained in *Re Hellas Telecommunications (Luxembourg) II SCA*[178]:

"It is not entirely easy to see precisely where in the statutory structure the court is concerned with the merits of a pre-pack sale. It seems to me that in general the merits of a pre-pack sale are for the administrator to deal with; and the creditors, if sufficiently aggrieved, have a remedy in the course of the administration to challenge an administrator's decision. It may on the evidence be obvious that a pre-pack sale is an abuse of the administrator's powers, in which event the court could refuse to make the administration order or could direct the administrators not to complete a pre-pack sale. At the other end of the spectrum it may be that it is obvious that a particular pre-pack is on the evidence the only real way forward, in which case the court could give the administrators liberty to enter into the pre-pack, leaving open the possibility that a sufficiently aggrieved creditor could nevertheless challenge the administrator's decision ex post facto. But in the majority of cases the position may not be clear; in which event the making of an administration order, even in the context of a pre-pack should not be taken as the court's blessing on the pre-pack sale."

If an administration order is made, the costs of the applicant, and any other **6–069** person appearing whose costs are allowed by the court, are payable as an expense of the administration.[179] In an exceptional case, such costs can include

---

[175] *Re Harris Simons Construction Ltd* [1989] 1 W.L.R. 368; see also *Re Consumer & Industrial Press Ltd (No.1)* (1988) 4 B.C.C. 68; *Re Manlon Trading Ltd (Petition for Administration Order)* (1988) 4 B.C.C. 455; *Re Primlaks (UK) Ltd* (1989) 5 B.C.C. 710; *Re SCL Building Services Ltd* (1989) 5 B.C.C. 746; *Re Rowbotham Baxter Ltd* [1990] B.C.C. 113; *Re Chelmsford City Football Club (1980) Ltd* [1991] B.C.C. 133; *Re Land and Property Trust Co Plc* [1991] B.C.C. 446; *Re Arrows Ltd* [1992] B.C.C. 131; *Re Maxwell Communications Corp Plc* [1992] B.C.C. 372; *Re Dallhold Estates (UK) Pty Ltd* [1992] B.C.C. 394; *Re Lomax Leisure* [2000] Ch. 502; *Re AA Mutual International Insurance Co Ltd* [2005] 2 B.C.L.C. 8; *Re C.14net.com.Inc.* [2005] B.C.C. 277.
[176] See further *Re K&H Options Ltd* Unreported February 17, 2000. See also *Re Greek Taverna* [1999] B.C.C. 153.
[177] *Re Kayley Vending Ltd* [2009] B.C.C. 578, [24].
[178] *Re Hellas Telecommunications (Luxembourg) II SCA* [2010] BCC 295, [8].
[179] r.2.12(3). See also *Re Shearing & Loader Ltd* [1991] B.C.C. 232 and *Re Dallhold Estates (UK) Pty Ltd* [1992] B.C.C. 394. For a case where no administration order was made, see *Re Business Properties Ltd* (1988) 4 B.C.C. 684.

the costs of a party who has unsuccessfully opposed the order being made.[180] The applicant's costs are not protected by the statutory charges under para.99 of Sch.B1 to the Insolvency Act 1986, but will ordinarily rank ahead of those charges.[181] Where there was a pre-existing winding-up petition relating to the company which is overtaken by the making of an administration order, the petitioner's costs will ordinarily be ordered to be paid as an expense of the administration.[182]

6–070 In appropriate cases the court can use its discretion under para.13(1)(f) of Sch.B1 to order that the pre-appointment costs of the proposed administrator in a pre-pack administration be treated as an expense of the administration. This will be the case where the court is satisfied that the balance of benefit arising from the incurring of those costs was in favour of the creditors than in favour of the purchaser (who may often be one or more of the directors instructing the insolvency practitioner).[183] In *Re Johnson Machine and Tool Co Ltd*[184] it was observed that with connected purchasers it is "rarely possible to establish clearly that the balance of advantage is in the creditors' favour" and onus is on those seeking costs to do so.[185] It was held that such orders would ordinarily be limited to costs of application rather than general advice to directors/purchasers. This case was decided before rr.2.33(2A) and 2.67A took effect.

6–071 Directors are personally at risk in respect of the costs of an administration application. In *Re W.F. Fearman Ltd (No.2)*[186] it was held that directors should bear costs which they had incurred in respect of an administration petition notwithstanding what is now r.2.3(2) which provides that an administration petition presented by directors shall be treated as a petition of the company from and after presentation. However, in *Re Gosscott (Groundworks) Ltd*[187] where the court also had to deal with the costs of a failed administration petition (presented in good faith) and an unopposed winding-up order, it was ordered that the company's costs on the administration petition be paid as costs in the winding-up. In *Re Land and Property Trust Co Plc*[188] directors who persisted with an unrealistic company petition were ordered to pay the costs of opposing creditors personally. The order was subsequently discharged on appeal, but the jurisdiction to award costs against directors was expressly affirmed. In *Re Tajik Air Ltd*[189] it was held that the test is whether reason and justice require the directors to pay the costs and this will usually mean that it must be established that they have caused costs to be incurred for an improper

[180] *Re Structures & Computers Ltd* [1998] B.C.C. 348.
[181] Insolvency Rules 1986, r.2.67(1)(c).
[182] *Irish Reel Productions Ltd v Capitol Films Ltd* [2010] B.C.C. 588.
[183] See *Re Kayley Vending* [2009] B.C.C. 578.
[184] *Re Johnson Machine and Tool Co Ltd* [2010] B.C.C. 382.
[185] At [5].
[186] *Re WF Fearman Ltd (No.2)* (1988) 4 B.C.C. 141.
[187] *Re Gosscott (Groundworks) Ltd* (1988) 4 B.C.C. 372.
[188] *Re Land and Property Trust Co Plc* [1991] B.C.C. 446; on appeal [1993] B.C.C. 462 (CA) (see also [1991] 1 W.L.R. 601 (CA)).
[189] *Re Tajik Air Ltd* [1991] B.C.C. 446; on appeal, reported as *Re Land and Property Trust Plc (No.2)* [1993] B.C.C. 462 (see also *Re Land and Property Trust Plc (No.3)* [1991] 1 W.L.R. 601 (CA)).

purpose, e.g. if their aim was to achieve a private advantage at the expense of creditors.

If the court makes an administration order,[190] the court must as soon as reasonably practicable send two sealed copies to the applicant[191] who must in turn as soon as reasonably practicable send one of these copies to the person appointed as administrator.[192] In the event that the court makes an interim order or any other order that the court considers appropriate, directions must be given for service.[193] Following his appointment, the administrator must advertise the making of the order and lodge a formal notice at Companies House as well as writing to known creditors.[194]

6–072

7. METHODS OF APPOINTMENT—APPOINTMENT OF ADMINISTRATOR BY A QUALIFYING FLOATING CHARGE-HOLDER

Whilst a creditor has always had the ability to present a petition, or latterly make an application, for the appointment of an administrator, the Enterprise Act 2002 conferred a particular standing on the holder of a "qualifying floating charge in respect of a company's property"[195] (referred to below as a "qualifying floating charge-holder") to appoint an administrator out of court. This effectively replaced the power of the holder of a floating charge to appoint an administrative receiver and thereby to block the appointment of an administrator by another party. Although not abolished with retrospective effect, so that administrative receivers may still be appointed under floating charges that were created before September 15, 2003, most institutional lenders have pursued a policy of allowing the appointment of administrators rather than relying on their right to appoint administrative receivers. Indeed, it is now rare for such institutions to make any appointments at all, preferring to acquiesce in the appointment by the directors of a mutually acceptable insolvency practitioner as administrator who will have, as one of his objectives, the realisation of property "in order to make a distribution to one of more secured or preferential creditors".[196] It is only because floating charge-holders can ultimately appoint the administrators of their choice that they are prepared to relinquish this limited degree of control in most cases.

6–073

Following the approach taken in the Insolvency Act 1986 there is no attempt to define what a "floating charge" is, for these purposes.[197] There are, rather, two tests that must be applied to determine whether a floating charge confers the power to make an appointment out of court.[198]

6–074

---

[190] Which must be in Form 2.4B, r.2.12(2).

[191] Form 2.4B, r.2.14(1).

[192] r.2.14(2).

[193] r.2.14(3).

[194] Sch.B1, para.46.

[195] para.14(1).

[196] para.3(1)(c).

[197] See further Ch.3.

[198] If the floating charge does not qualify then the holder will still be entitled to apply to court for the appointment of an administrator.

6–075   First, there has to be a consideration of whether it was the parties' intention that the charge-holder should be entitled to appoint an administrator or administrative receiver. If so, the floating charge is deemed to "qualify" for these purposes. This will be the case if the floating charge is created by an instrument which states that para.14 of Sch.B1 applies to the floating charge, or if it purports to empower the holder of the floating charge to appoint an administrator or administrative receiver.[199] Secondly, there is a separate objective legal test in that an otherwise qualifying floating charge will only allow the holder to appoint an administrator if he holds:

"one or more debentures of the company secured—

(a) by a qualifying floating charge which relates to the whole or substantially the whole of the company's property;

(b) by a number of qualifying floating charges which together relate to the whole or substantially the whole of the company's property; or

(c) by charges and other forms of security which together relate to the whole or substantially the whole of the company's property and at least one of which is a qualifying floating charge."[200]

6–076   If a company has created more than one floating charge, the holder of the second or subsequent floating charge cannot appoint an administrator until either the expiry of two business days' notice to the prior charge-holder or the receipt of the written consent to the making of the appointment from the prior floating charge-holders.[201] For these purposes, a floating charge is treated as being prior to another if it was created first, or if it is treated as having priority in accordance with an agreement between the floating charge-holders.[202] Whilst the Act does not refer to the possibility of charges ranking pari passu, the prudent approach must be to serve the charge-holder with notice in any event. If served with notice, a prior chargee does not have the power to restrain the appointment but he may seek to make a prior appointment of his own nominee as administrator in the event that this cannot be agreed with the subordinate charge-holder. The prescribed form for the giving of notice is Form 2.5B,[203] and this form must be filed at court at the same time as being served on any prior floating charge-holders in order to obtain the benefit of an interim moratorium.[204] For these purposes the rules relating to the service of an administration application apply.[205]

---

[199] Sch.B1, para.14(2). The four sub-paragraphs in para.14(2) are disjunctive, so that only one need be satisfied for a chargeholder to make the appointment of an administrator: *Stephen, Petitioner* [2011] CSOH 119 (Court of Session, Outer House).
[200] para.14(3). See generally Ch.3.
[201] para.15(1).
[202] para.15(2).
[203] r.2.15(1).
[204] Sch.B1, para.44(2) and r.2.15(2).
[205] r.2.15(3).

In order for a qualifying floating charge-holder to appoint an administrator, **6–077** its charge must be "enforceable".[206] Essentially this means that there must be a default on the part of the company, or an event must have occurred which has given the charge-holder the right to make the appointment.[207] However, a charge-holder is not precluded from making an administration appointment where a question over whether the charge was enforceable remains in dispute.[208] An appointment based on a charge where signatures have been forged may still be valid if the company would be estopped from disputing the validity of the document.[209] An administrator cannot be appointed by a qualifying floating charge-holder, however, if a provisional liquidator has already been appointed by the court, an administrative receiver is in office[210] or an administrator has already been appointed.[211] The existence of an undisposed of winding up petition does not prevent the appointment of an administrator, that petition being suspended for the duration of the administration under para.40 of Sch.B1 Insolvency Act 1986.[212]

In order to appoint an administrator, a qualifying floating charge-holder **6–078** must file with the court:

(a)   three copies of a notice of appointment in Form 2.6B[213] identifying the proposed administrator, supported by a statutory declaration on the form to confirm that the appointor is the holder of an enforceable floating charge and that the appointment is in accordance with Sch.B1. This statutory declaration must be made not more than five business days before the form is filed with the court.[214] A person who makes a statutory declaration which contains a statement that is false and which he did not reasonably believe to be true, commits an offence[215];

(b)   the proposed administrator's written statement in Form 2.2B,[216] which requires the same matters to be confirmed and information to be provided as if the appointment had been made by the court[217];

(c)   evidence that the required period of notice to floating charge-holders has elapsed or that they have consented to the appointment.[218] Where notice of intention to appoint an administrator has been given and filed with the court,[219] this may be proved by the prior floating charge-holder completing and returning to the appointor a copy of

---

[206] Sch.B1, para.16.
[207] See further Ch.3 on the enforceability of charges.
[208] *BCPMS (Europe) Ltd v GMAC Commercial Financial Plc* Unreported February 21, 2006.
[209] *Re Carson Country Homes Ltd* [2009] 2 B.C.L.C. 196.
[210] Sch.B1, para.17.
[211] para.7.
[212] *Re J Smiths Haulage Ltd* [2007] B.C.C. 135.
[213] rr.2.16(1) and 2.17(1).
[214] Sch.B1, para.18(6) and r.2.16(3).
[215] para.18(7).
[216] para.18(3) and r.2.16(2)(a).
[217] See above, para.6–010.
[218] r.2.16(2)(b).
[219] para.18(1) and r.2.15(2).

Form 2.5B. Otherwise, his consent must be evidenced by a signed and dated document with prescribed details of both the prior floating charge-holder and the proposed appointment[220]; and

(d) where it is intended to appoint a number of persons as administrators, details of the functions that are to be exercised jointly or severally.[221]

The appointment of an administrator by a qualifying floating charge-holder will normally take effect when all of the above requirements have been complied with, i.e. at the time at which the relevant documents are filed with the court.[222] The court will then seal all three copies of the notice of appointment endorsed with the time and date of filing[223] and issue two copies to the appointor who must serve one of these on the administrator as soon as reasonably practicable.[224]

6–079   Exceptionally, it is possible for a qualifying charge-holder to appoint an administrator when the court office is closed. This is an attempt to replicate the absence of any temporal restriction on the appointment of an administrative receiver save, perhaps, for the fact that any demand for payment that precedes a hostile appointment must allow sufficient time when banks are open for business for the payment to be made.[225] It is accordingly provided that a qualifying floating charge-holder may file a notice of appointment by fax when the court office is closed. This is deemed to have the same effect for all purposes as a notice of appointment that is filed as a hard copy at court.[226]

6–080   The fact that this procedure is only available in exceptional circumstances is made clear from the fact that the court office must be closed[227]; it is not an alternative procedure that is available at other times. A separate Form 2.7B is to be used for this purpose and this must be signed and endorsed by the administrator who thereby certifies his consent to act, that he is of the opinion that the purposes of the administration are reasonably likely to be achieved, the nature of any prior professional relationships and that he is authorised as an insolvency practitioner. In addition the Form 2.7B contains the appointor's confirmation that the consent of any prior floating charge-holders has been obtained.[228] The appointor must attach to the notice a statement providing full reasons for the out-of-hours filing including "why it would have been damaging to the company and its creditors not to have so acted".[229]

6–081   The fax must be sent to a fax machine that is designated by the Court Service for this purpose with details of the fax number being published by the

---

[220] r.2.16(5).

[221] r.2.16(2)(c); para.100(2).

[222] Sch.B1, para.19. The date of the statutory declaration on the notice of appointment is not relevant for these purposes: *Fliptex Ltd v Hogg* [2004] B.C.C. 870.

[223] r.2.17(1).

[224] r.2.17(2).

[225] See Ch.13.

[226] r.2.19(2).

[227] r.2.19(1).

[228] See Form 2.7B.

[229] r.2.19(8).

Insolvency Service.[230] The appointor must ensure that a fax transmission report is obtained, which confirms the time and date of transmission and contains a copy (in whole or part) of the first page.[231] The administrator is appointed with effect from the date and time of the fax transmission[232] and there is a rebuttable presumption that this is the date and time shown on the appointor's fax confirmation.[233] As soon as reasonably practicable, the copy of the notice of appointment that was received by the central fax machine is to be forwarded to the court named on the form as having jurisdiction for the purposes of the administration, so that it can be placed on the court file.[234]

The appointor must take three copies of the faxed notice of appointment, **6–082** together with the transmission report and all necessary supporting documents listed on Form 2.7B, to the court on the next day when the court is open for business.[235] It is crucial to note that, if the appointor fails to comply with this requirement, the administrator's appointment ceases to have effect.[236] The copies are to be endorsed by the court with the date and time when, according to the fax transmission report, the notice was faxed and the date when the notice and accompanying documents were filed.[237] Two copies are issued to the appointor who must send one of the copies to the administrator as soon as reasonably practicable.[238] Following his appointment, the administrator must advertise the making of the order and lodge a formal notice at Companies House, as well as writing to known creditors.[239]

Where a qualifying charge-holder purports to appoint an administrator, but **6–083** the appointment is discovered to be invalid, the court may order the appointor to indemnify the purported administrator against liability which arises solely by reason of the appointment's invalidity.[240] However, since an act of the administrator of a company is deemed to be valid in spite of a defect in his appointment or qualification[241], it is not immediately apparent what liability could arise that would be the subject of such an indemnity.

8. METHODS OF APPOINTMENT—APPOINTMENT OF ADMINISTRATOR BY A COMPANY OR ITS DIRECTORS

As noted above, the vast majority of appointments are in fact made by a **6–084** company or its directors, albeit often in the knowledge that if they fail to do so

---

[230] r.2.19(3). The number is published on the Insolvency Service website.

[231] r.2.19(4).

[232] r.2.19(5).

[233] r.2.19(11).

[234] r.2.19(6).

[235] r.2.19(7).

[236] r.2.19(10).

[237] r.2.19(9).

[238] r.2.19(12).

[239] Sch.B1, para.46.

[240] para.21 see also the related power of the court where there is an invalid receivership appointment, s.34 of the Insolvency Act 1986.

[241] Sch.B1, para.104. Further, any acquiescence in the appointment may give rise to an estoppel: *Fliptex Ltd v Hogg* [2004] B.C.C. 870.

a qualifying floating charge-holder will appoint out of court or a creditor or other permitted applicant will apply to court. The fact that qualifying floating charge-holders have a superior right to appoint administrators, which essentially means the right to select the insolvency practitioners who will be appointed for this purpose, means that there has to be a two-stage process with the company or its directors first giving notice of intention to appoint administrators to qualifying floating charge-holders before any appointment can be made by the company or its directors. There is, however, no duty on directors to consult with creditors (as opposed to notifying qualifying chargeholders) before appointing administrators.[242]

6–085   As noted above separate provision is made for the appointment of an administrator by a company[243] and its directors.[244] In the case of an appointment by a company, this will require a valid shareholders' resolution, either at a meeting or in writing,[245] which will need to be attached to the notice of intention to appoint administrators.[246] By contrast where the appointment is by the directors, there simply needs to be a record of the decision taken by the directors,[247] a majority of the directors is sufficient for these purposes.[248] However, any such decision must be taken in accordance with the provisions of the company's articles of association relating to matters of internal management.[249] Unsurprisingly, appointments by directors or by written shareholder resolution are substantially more common than those by meeting of the shareholders.

6–086   An administrator cannot be appointed out of court by a company or its directors during the period of 12 months commencing with the date when a prior appointment by the company or its directors, or an appointment by the court on the application of the company or its directors, ceased to have effect.[250] This does not, however, preclude an application to court being made by either the company or its directors during this period. There is a similar restriction on the appointment of an administrator out of court during the period of 12 months following the end of a small company moratorium or, in the event that a voluntary arrangement that was approved during the period of the moratorium ends prematurely, the date when it so ends.[251] There is also a bar on the appointment of an administrator by a company or its directors out of court if

---

[242] *Re Super Aguri F1 Ltd* [2011] B.C.C. 452.

[243] Sch.B1, para.22(1).

[244] para.22(2).

[245] It appears that an ordinary resolution is sufficient for these purposes, although in practice unanimity or near unanimity will be required given that an extraordinary general meeting will normally have to be called at short notice to pass an ordinary resolution and this will requires the consent of 95 per cent of shareholders, or all shareholders will need to consent for a valid written resolution.

[246] r.2.22.

[247] r.2.22.

[248] Sch.B1, para.105, cf. the position under s.9(1) where it has been held that unanimity is required: *Re Instrumentation Electrical Services Ltd* (1988) 4 B.C.C. 301, in the absence of a formal resolution that will bind a dissentient minority: *Re Equiticorp International Plc* [1989] 1 W.L.R. 1010.

[249] *Minmar (929) Ltd v Khalatschi* [2011] B.C.C. 485.

[250] Sch.B1, para.23.

[251] para.24.

there is a pending petition or application for the winding-up or administration of the company respectively, or if an administrative receiver of the company is in office.[252]

If the company or its directors propose to appoint an administrator they must **6–087** give at least five business days' written notice to any person who is or may be entitled to appoint an administrative receiver of the company and any person who is or may be entitled to appoint an administrator of the company, i.e. a qualifying floating charge-holder.[253] A copy of this notice must also be given to:

(a) any enforcement officer who, to the knowledge of the person giving the notice, is charged with execution or other legal process against the company;

(b) any person who, to the knowledge of the person giving the notice, has distrained against the company or its property;

(c) any supervisor of a voluntary arrangement under Pt I of the Act; and

(d) the company, if the company is not intending to make the appointment.[254]

The notice of intention to appoint must be in the prescribed form, Form 2.8B,[255] which complies with the separate requirement that it must identify the proposed administrator.[256] For these purposes, the rules relating to the service of an administration application apply equally.[257] If, however, there is no qualifying floating charge-holder, an immediate appointment by the company or its directors is possible.[258]

In addition to serving copies of the notice of intention to appoint, the **6–088** following must be filed at court as soon as reasonably practicable:

(a) a copy of the notice of intention to appoint, supported by a statutory declaration on the form to confirm that the company is insolvent, not in liquidation and, so far as the appointor can ascertain, there is no other restriction on the ability to appoint.[259] This statutory declaration must be made not more than five business days before the form is filed with the court.[260] A person who makes a statutory declaration which contains a statement that is false and which he did not reasonably believe to be true, commits an offence[261]; and

---

[252] para.25. See *Chesterton International Group Plc v Deka Immobilien Inv GmbH* [2005] B.P.I.R 1103 so far as administrative receivership is concerned.

[253] Sch.B1, para.26(1).

[254] para.26(2) and r.2.20(2). See *Minmar (929) Ltd v Khalatschi* [2011] B.C.C. 485.

[255] para.26(3)(b).

[256] para.26(3)(a).

[257] r.2.20(3) applying r.2.8(2)–(6).

[258] See para.6–039.

[259] Sch.B1, para.27(2) and para.27(3).

[260] para.27(3) and r.2.21.

[261] para.27(4).

(b) a copy of the resolution of the company to appoint an administrator or a record of the decision of the directors to make the appointment.[262]

6–089 When the notice of intention to appoint is filed with the court, the company has the protection of an interim moratorium to protect the company's assets[263] until the administrator is appointed or the expiry of ten business days beginning with the date on which the notice of intention to appoint is filed.[264]

6–090 The position in relation to the filing of multiple notices of intention to appoint remains regrettably unclear. On a straightforward construction of the statutory provisions, there is an obvious opportunity for abuse by filing consecutive notices of intention to appoint an administrator, and so extending the interim moratorium indefinitely without ever entering administration. In *Re Cornercare Ltd*[265], it was clarified that a second or subsequent notice to appoint is ordinarily valid and that an administrator appointed pursuant to such a notice is validly appointed. H.H.J. Purle QC suggested that in a situation where persons were "engineering a continuing moratorium", then:

> "the court would have adequate power to treat that as an abuse and act accordingly. The court could restrain the lodgement of further notices of intention to appoint unless followed by an actual appointment. It could even, in an extreme case, vacate and remove from the file under its inherent jurisdiction any abusive notice of intention to appoint".

However, that approach appears to be untested.

6–091 Once notice of intention to appoint has been given to any qualifying floating charge-holder, the company or the directors must wait until the expiry of the five business-day notice period before they can proceed to make an appointment without the consent of the qualifying floating charge-holders.[266] If, all qualifying floating charge-holders have provided their written consent, the appointment can be made once that consent has been obtained.[267] The power to appoint must be exercised before the expiry of the period of ten business days beginning with the date on which the notice of intention to appoint is filed.[268]

6–092 In order to appoint an administrator, a company or its directors must file with the court:

(a) three[269] copies of a notice of appointment. This must be in Form 2.10B[270] unless it is not necessary to give notice of intention to appoint to a qualifying floating charge-holder, in which case it should

---

[262] r.2.22.
[263] Sch.B1, para.44(4), and see Ch.9, on the nature and extent of the moratorium.
[264] para.28(2).
[265] *Re Cornercare Ltd* [2010] B.C.C. 592.
[266] para.28(1)(a).
[267] para.28(1)(b).
[268] para.28(2).
[269] para.29(1)(1) and r.2.26(1).
[270] r.2.23(1).

be in Form 2.9B.[271] In either case, the form will identify the proposed administrator[272] and will be supported by a statutory declaration confirming that the appointor is entitled to make the appointment, that the appointment is in accordance with Sch.B1 and, where notice of intention to appoint has been given, that so far as the maker of the statement is able to ascertain, the statements made, and information given in the statutory declaration included in such notice remain accurate.[273] The statutory declaration in the notice of appointment must be made not more than five business days before the form is filed with the court.[274] A person who makes a statutory declaration which contains a statement that is false and which he did not reasonably believe to be true, commits an offence[275];

(b) the proposed administrator's written statement in Form 2.2B,[276] which requires the same matters to be confirmed and information to be provided as if the appointment had been made by the court[277];

(c) where notice of intention to appoint has been given, the prescribed Form 2.9B requires confirmation that either the period of five business days has elapsed or each person to whom the notice was sent has consented to the appointment.[278] Indeed, the appointment cannot be made until this condition has been satisfied[279]; and

(d) where it is intended to appoint a number of persons as administrators, details of the functions that are to be exercised jointly or severally.[280]

The appointment of an administrator by the company or its directors will **6–093** normally take effect when all of the above requirements have been complied with, i.e. at the time at which the relevant documents are filed with the court.[281] The court will then seal all three copies of the notice of appointment endorsed with the time and date of filing[282] and issue two copies to the appointor who must serve one of these on the administrator as soon as reasonably

[271] Where the wrong form is mistakenly filed, the appointment will be invalid. However, the court may validate it retrospectively under para.13(1) Sch.B1: *Re G-Tech Construction Ltd* [2007] B.P.I.R. 1275. The court may also make an administration order with retrospective effect (*Re Derfshaw Ltd* [2011] B.C.C. 631). It appears, however, that the same approach cannot be taken where the necessary consent to an extension of the administration has not been obtained, and it has thereby ended after a one year period: see *Re Frontsouth (Witham) Ltd* [2011] B.C.C. 635.
[272] para.29(3).
[273] para.29(2).
[274] para.29(6) and r.2.24.
[275] para.29(7).
[276] para.29(3) and r.2.23(2)(a).
[277] See above, para.6–010.
[278] See para.8 of Form 2.9B.
[279] Sch.B1, para.28(1).
[280] r.2.23(2)(c) and para.100(2).
[281] Sch.B1, para.31. The date of the statutory declaration is not relevant for these purposes: *Fliptex Ltd v Hogg* [2004] B.C.C. 870.
[282] r.2.26(1).

practicable.[283] Failure to do so without reasonable excuse is an offence.[284] Following his appointment, the administrator must advertise the making of the order and lodge a formal notice at Companies House, as well as writing to known creditors.[285] It has been held that electronic notification of creditors is in compliance with para.46 where creditors themselves have nominated email addresses to which communications can be sent.[286]

6–094   Just as with an invalid appointment by a charge-holder, where a company or its directors purport to appoint an administrator and the appointment is discovered to be invalid, the court may order the appointor to indemnify the person appointed against liability which arises solely by reason of the appointment's invalidity.[287] However, as in the case of a charge-holder appointment, since an act of the administrator of a company is deemed to be valid in spite of a defect in his appointment or qualification,[288] it is not immediately apparent what liability could arise that would be the subject of such an indemnity.

[283] Sch.B1, para.32(a) and r.2.26(2).
[284] para.32(b).
[285] para.46.
[286] *Gould v Advent Computer Training Ltd* [2011] B.C.C. 44, distinguishing *Re Sporting Options plc* [2005] B.C.C. 88.
[287] para.34.
[288] para.104. Further, any acquiescence in the appointment may give rise to an estoppel: *Fliptex Ltd v Hogg* [2004] B.C.C. 870.

Chapter 7

Appointment of Receivers Out of Court

1. QUALIFICATIONS

Prior to the changes introduced by the Insolvency Acts of 1985 and 1986, there **7–001** was no qualification required of a prospective appointee as receiver of a company or its property, save that he be of full age. In the case of an appointment out of court the only persons disqualified from appointment were a body corporate[1] or an undischarged bankrupt.[2] In the case of a court-appointed receiver (who traded on his own account and not as agent for the company or a debenture-holder) persons subject to restrictions on trading (such as beneficed clergymen and barristers) were also disqualified, as were persons immune from the ordinary remedies against a receiver, such as a Member of Parliament or a Peer of the Realm or someone resident outside the jurisdiction.[3] There was no requirement of a practical or professional qualification,[4] though there may have been a duty on the part of the appointor to take reasonable care not to appoint an incompetent.[5] There was apparently no objection to the debenture-holder appointing himself as receiver.[6]

The 1986 Act left the law unchanged in respect of receivers who are **7–002** not administrative receivers, but an administrative receiver "acts as an insolvency practitioner in relation to a company"[7] and only individuals (i.e. natural

---

[1] Insolvency Act 1986, s.30, formerly Companies Act 1985, s.489 and see *Portman Building Society v Gallwey* [1955] 1 W.L.R. 96. The position is similar in Australia (Corporations Act 2001 (Cth), ss.418(1)(d), 1279(1)), New Zealand (Receiverships Act 1993, s.5(2)) and Hong Kong (Companies Ordinance, s.297).

[2] Insolvency Act 1986, s.31, formerly Companies Act 1985, s.490. Similarly, Australia (Corporations Act 2001 (Cth), ss.418(1)(d), 206B(3), 1282(4)); New Zealand (Receiverships Act 1993, s.5(1)(e)); Hong Kong (Companies Ordinance, s.297A).

[3] See *Halsbury's Laws of England*, 4th edn, Vol.39(2), para.350. Walton J. (the long-time editor of *Kerr on Receivers*) apparently disregarded this rule when appointing a Member of Parliament a receiver in *Wiggin v Anderson* Unreported March 16, 1982. Members of Parliament and Peers are no longer immune from arrest in connection with the winding-up or insolvency of companies: Insolvency Act 1986, s.426C(1).

[4] See *Bagot v Bagot* (1841) 10 L.J. Ch. 116, 120; even illiteracy was held to be no bar in *Garland v Garland* (1793) 2 Ves. Jr. 137.

[5] *Shamji v Johnson Matthey Bankers Ltd* [1991] B.C.L.C. 36 (CA), 42, per Oliver L.J., affirming Hoffmann J. at first instance: [1986] B.C.L.C. 278, 283. See further below Ch.13.

[6] See *Mace Builders (Glasgow) Ltd v Lunn* [1987] Ch. 191 (CA), 197, per Donaldson M.R.

[7] Insolvency Act 1986, s.388. (Under the Insolvency Act 1986, s.388(6), the definitions of "acting as an insolvency practitioner" are limited so as to exclude acts (wherever done) in relation to insolvency proceedings under the EC Insolvency Regulation in a Member State other than the UK.) "Company" for the purpose of determining whether a person is acting as an insolvency practitioner is defined in s.388(4) as meaning a company:

persons)[8] who are qualified to act as such can now be appointed.[9] A brief outline of the qualifications necessary to be an insolvency practitioner is to be found in Ch.8. Although this chapter deals with the appointment of both administrative receivers and receivers who are not administrative receivers, it must be borne in mind throughout that the ability to appoint an administrative receiver is now severely restricted by s.72A(1) of the Insolvency Act 1986.[10]

2. MULTIPLE AND JOINT APPOINTMENTS

(a) Introduction

7–003   This subject has produced much confusion. For clarity it is first essential to distinguish between a number of different factual situations:

(a) a case where more than one receiver has been appointed over the same property, but under different debentures;

(b) a case where more than one receiver has been appointed over the same property under a debenture in favour of a number of lenders as a result of separate appointments by those different lenders; and

(c) a case where more than one receiver has been appointed over the same property at the same time under the same debenture.

In the first case, which is quite common, questions as to the respective powers and duties of the receivers will depend on identifying the assets over which the respective receivers have been appointed and, where there is an overlap, resolving the relationship between the receivers as a matter of priorities of the charges under which they were appointed.[11] The second situation is likely to be

---

(a) formed and registered under the Companies Act 2006 in England and Wales or Scotland; or

(b) a company which may be wound up under Pt V of the Insolvency Act 1986 as an unregistered company (a category which includes foreign corporations).

However that definition, which is part of the general provisions of the Act regulating eligibility to act as an office holder, is not the same as the definition of a company contained in s.28, which applies to determine whether a person is an administrative receiver under s.29(2). Section 28 omits para.(b) of the s.388(4) definition, thereby precluding administrative receivership of a foreign company (see further Moss, Segal and Fletcher [2010] 23 Insolv. Int. 57). See also *Re Dairy Farmers of Britain Ltd* [2010] Ch. 63 where it was held that an industrial and provident society is not a company for the purposes of s.29(2).

[8] Insolvency Act 1986, s.390(1).

[9] Insolvency Act 1986, ss.230, 389 and 390.

[10] See further para.1–017.

[11] For a case in which the court was asked to resolve a dispute between rival receivers who had been appointed by mortgagees under separate debentures over the same property, see *Bass Breweries Ltd v Delaney* [1994] B.C.C. 851. A deed of priority had been executed under which the two charges were expressed to rank equally. The court resolved the resultant conflict by appointing the two receivers as court-appointed receivers with a mandate to act jointly or to refer disagreements back to the court for directions.

very rare in practice, but arose in *Gwembe Valley Development Co Ltd v Koshy (No.2)*.[12]

The third situation is routine: it is very common for two partners in the same 7–004
firm (or occasionally different firms) of accountants to be appointed as
receivers by a debenture-holder. This situation does, however, give rise to a
number of further issues, such as:

(a) whether the receivers can only act jointly or whether they can also act
severally. This is essentially a question of construction of the debenture, but also involves consideration of the extent to which s.231 of
the Insolvency Act 1986 operates in this area;

(b) whether, if acting jointly, the receivers are jointly and severally liable
for their acts and defaults and, if acting severally, whether one
receiver will be liable for the acts or defaults of the other; and

(c) whether the receivers' tenure in office is joint in the sense that it will
terminate on the death or retirement of one of their number.

In considering these matters, it is of prime importance to distinguish whether
the question in issue is one relating to the manner of exercise of the power of
appointment by the debenture-holder, or to the manner in which the receivers
may exercise their powers under the appointment, or to the liability of the
receivers so appointed, or as to the tenure of the receivers in office.[13]

(b) Multiple appointments

It is a matter of construction of the terms of the debenture(s) and any deed of 7–005
priorities[14] whether there can be more than one receiver appointed by different
lenders over the same property at any one time. In *Gwembe Valley Development
Co Ltd v Koshy*,[15] Rimer J. and the Court of Appeal had to construe an unusual
debenture governed by Zambian law which had been granted by a Zambian
company to two lenders to secure separate loans made by them to the company.
Although Rimer J. was initially attracted by the idea that the terms of the
debenture only permitted joint appointment, neither party contended for that
result, and the learned judge held that in the event of disagreement between the
two lenders, the particular terms of the debenture permitted each lender to

[12] *Gwembe Valley Development Co Ltd v Koshy* [2000] B.C.C. 1127.
[13] Many of the cases in this area fail to make these distinctions: see the comments to this effect
by Gummow and Kirby JJ. in *Kendle v Melsom* (1998) 193 C.L.R. 46 (High Court of Australia),
65, referring to the second edition of this work "as has been pointed out, the judgments . . .
responded to submissions which apparently did not distinguish between a joint appointment of
receivers to their office, and the ability or capacity of joint receivers to exercise severally as well
as jointly the powers conferred upon them." And see also the observations of Hayne J. in the same
case: "It is not a question whether those appointed hold office jointly . . . Even if the office is held
jointly (and I need not decide if that is so) this would not mean that the appointment could not
provide for the *powers* of the office to be exercised jointly and severally".
[14] See, e.g. *Bass Breweries Ltd v Delaney* [1994] B.C.C. 851.
[15] *Gwembe Valley Development Co Ltd v Koshy* [2000] B.C.C. 1127.

appoint a receiver to hold office simultaneously. Rimer J. also held that the first appointment did not preclude the second, so avoiding any unseemly rush by each lender to make the first appointment so as to shut out the other.

7–006   In reaching this conclusion, Rimer J. rejected an argument that the existence of more than one receiver appointed by different lenders over the same property would be a recipe for conflict and chaos. He asserted that there was nothing unusual about the conduct of a receivership being in the hands of two or more receivers, that the receivers would each be professional men and that it should not be assumed that more than one appointment would lead to difficulties in practice. Rimer J. suggested that if difficulties arose the receivers could seek the directions of the court, and drew a parallel with the notion of adding an additional trustee to an existing body of office-holders under s.36(6) of the Trustee Act 1925 which confers a general power to appoint additional trustees to act in a trust.

7–007   When the matter reached the Court of Appeal,[16] the appellant sought to advance the argument that the debenture only permitted an appointment to be made by the debenture-holders jointly. That argument was addressed as a "pure question of construction" and the Court of Appeal allowed the appeal, holding that the terms of the debenture only envisaged the appointment of a receiver by the senior lenders acting jointly.

7–008   The problems encountered in the *Gwembe Valley* case could have been avoided if the debenture had been drafted clearly so as to provide that the power of appointment could only be exercised by the lenders jointly rather than severally. Certainly this would be the preferable approach so as to avoid the potential conflicts in the conduct of the receivership. Whilst appointment of two or more receivers from the same firm by the same debenture-holder is routine, the simultaneous appointment of two receivers over the same property by two different lenders who enjoy equal priority is highly unusual. In practice the efficacy of such a course may well depend upon whether the receivers so appointed are authorised to act only jointly or severally. The existence of two receivers empowered to act severally would be most likely to give rise to conflicts, a risk which would be reduced if the receivers were required to act jointly.[17]

7–009   However, even this course is not without considerable problems (see below) and in *Gwembe* in the Court of Appeal, Chadwick L.J. remarked that such difficulties themselves provided an additional reason for not attributing to the parties an intention that there should be several appointments rather than joint appointments.

7–010   It is also respectfully suggested that Rimer J.'s reliance on the professional status of the appointees and the opportunity to apply to the court for directions as a means of conflict resolution is unlikely to be a satisfactory solution. The

---

[16] *Gwembe Valley Development Co Ltd v Koshy* Unreported December 14, 2000 (CA).
[17] See the concerns to this effect in *Bass Breweries Ltd v Delaney* [1994] B.C.C. 851, 856. If the receivers are able to act severally, there will be the possibility that one receiver might, say, contract to sell a piece of property which the other wished to retain for receivership trading; or one receiver might institute proceedings on behalf of the company which the other thought were misconceived and agreed with the defendant to compromise.

two receivers might well disagree on the essentially commercial question of whether, and if so, how best to realise a particular charged asset. Such disputes could be difficult and cumbersome to resolve by application to the court, and a court might well be unwilling, or consider itself ill-equipped, to make a commercial choice between the different options.

It does not appear that either receiver in the *Gwembe Valley* case was an **7–011** administrative receiver under the Insolvency Act 1986.[18] In deciding matters as a pure question of construction of the debenture, the Court of Appeal made no reference to the Insolvency Act 1986 and instead simply remarked that the receivership in question "if conducted in this country" would have been an administrative receivership. This leaves open the question whether, had the same issue occurred in respect of a debenture over the assets of an English company, or where the assets in question were located in England, the court would have been likely to hold that any appointment could only occur jointly, or that if several appointments were permitted, whether it would only have been the first of the two appointees, or both appointees, who would have qualified as an administrative receiver invested with particular powers and duties under the Insolvency Act.[19]

It is a question of construction of the debenture whether any particular power **7–012** of appointment permits the appointment of more than one person to act as a receiver.[20] In the absence of some indication of a contrary intention, the singular in the debenture should be construed as including the plural[21] and accordingly the power to appoint a receiver should be construed as a power to appoint more than one receiver.[22]

(c) Power to act jointly or severally

The question whether joint receivers can act severally as well as jointly is one **7–013** of construction of the power of appointment given in the debenture and of the terms of the appointment itself.[23] Modern debentures may contain express

---

[18] At the time that the case was decided it was possible for an administrative receiver to be appointed over the assets of a foreign company under s.29 of the Insolvency Act 1986: see *Re International Bulk Commodities Ltd* [1993] Ch. 77. The subsequent amendment of s.28 introducing s.28(1) now precludes that possibility.

[19] See, e.g. the suggestion by F. Oditah, "Lightweight Floating Charges" [1991] J.B.L. 49 that there cannot be multiple concurrent administrative receivers.

[20] *Wrights Hardware Pty Ltd v Evans* (1988) 13 A.C.L.R. 631 (Supreme Court of Western Australia), 633 referring to the first edition of this work; *NEC Information Systems Australia Pty Ltd v Lockhart* (1991) 9 A.C.L.C. 658 (New South Wales Court of Appeal), 665, per Kirby P. and 667, per Meagher J.A. "[I]n each case the question must be answered by construing the particular clause in the mortgage instrument in question, and those clauses vary from case to case"; and *Gwembe Valley Development Co Ltd v Koshy* [2000] B.C.C. 1127.

[21] Law of Property Act 1925, s.61(c).

[22] *NEC Information Systems Australia Pty Ltd v Lockhart* (1991) 9 A.C.L.C. 658 (New South Wales Court of Appeal), 663, per Kirby P., citing, inter alia, the first edition of this work and noting that it will also be presumed that such persons will act jointly and not jointly and severally. The debenture itself may provide that words importing the singular are to include the plural: see, e.g. *Kendle v Melsom* (1998) 193 C.L.R. 46 (High Court of Australia).

[23] See, e.g. the cases referred to in fn.20 above, together with *Kendle v Melsom* (1998) 193 C.L.R. 46 (High Court of Australia). (Contrast Insolvency Act 1986, Sch.B1 paras 100–103 dealing with administrators.)

clauses giving the power to appoint a plurality of receivers who can act severally as well as jointly. In the absence of an express term authorising the appointment of multiple receivers with power to act severally, the court will be required to consider whether a term authorising the use of powers severally can be implied. Whilst there is some force in the observation that the strictness of traditional tests for the implication of terms in commercial documents would seem to mitigate against the implication of such a term,[24] in construing debentures, the courts have in fact shown themselves to be willing to further what they perceive to be the general commercial purpose of the power to make multiple appointments.

7–014   In *Gwembe Valley Development Co Ltd v Koshy (No.2)*[25] Rimer J. considered authorities on this issue from Australia and New Zealand[26] and concluded that there was nothing in the debenture in question which pointed to a conclusion that a plurality of receivers could only act jointly, and that a conclusion that receivers might act severally would be a convenient regime under which the duties of the receivership could be divided between them.[27] Rimer J. observed that the appointed persons would ordinarily be professional people and that if differences arose, they could seek directions from the court. This part of Rimer J.'s decision is, of course, to be distinguished from the earlier part of the judgment, where the learned judge relied upon similar reasoning to reach a conclusion that there could be several appointments by different lenders. In that respect, Rimer J. was reversed on appeal. However, so far as the potential for conflict and confusion is concerned, there is every difference as a matter of practice between the appointment of a plurality of receivers by

---

[24] O'Donovan, *Company Receivers and Managers*, 2nd edn, para.3.120 suggests that on basic contractual principles there would appear to be no basis for implying a term allowing a debenture-holder to appoint receivers with authority to act severally as well as jointly merely from a term giving a power to appoint multiple receivers. Objection is taken that on the basis of the traditional tests for implication of contractual terms as summarised by the Privy Council in *BP Refinery (Westernport) Pty Ltd v Shire of Hastings* (1977) 180 C.L.R. 266, 282–283, such a term would not fulfil the requirement of business efficacy because the debenture is effective without it. There is some force in this point, because although it may well be much less convenient for receivers to have to act jointly rather than having the power to act severally, it cannot be said that their appointment would be rendered wholly unworkable if they had to act jointly. However, the force of these objections has been weakened by Lord Hoffmann's revised formulation of the test for the implication of terms as a matter of fact in *Attorney General of Belize v Belize Telecom Ltd* [2009] 1 W.L.R. 1988 (PC), [21]. Lord Hoffmann, commenting on the officious bystander and business efficacy tests, stated that: ". . . these are not in the Board's opinion to be treated as different or additional tests. There is only one question: is that what the instrument, read as a whole against the relevant background, would reasonably be understood to mean?"

[25] *Gwembe Valley Development Co Ltd v Koshy (No.2)* [2000] B.C.C. 1127.

[26] *DFC Financial Services Ltd v Samuel* [1990] 3 N.Z.L.R. 156 (New Zealand Court of Appeal); *NEC Information Systems Australia Pty Ltd v Lockhart* (1991) 9 A.C.L.C. 658 (New South Wales Court of Appeal); and *Kendle v Melsom* (1998) 193 C.L.R. 46 (High Court of Australia). These cases distinguished earlier authorities where there was no express reference to more than one receiver being appointed, such as *RJ Wood Pty Ltd v Sherlock* Unreported March 18, 1988 (Federal Court of Australia); *Wrights Hardware Pty Ltd (Provisional Liquidator Appointed) v Evans* (1988) 13 A.C.L.R. 631 (Supreme Court of Western Australia) and *Kerry Lowe Management Pty Ltd v Isherwood* (1989) 15 A.C.L.R. 615 (New South Wales Court of Appeal).

[27] In so doing, Rimer J. agreed with the majority reasoning of Gummow and Kirby JJ. in *Kendle v Melsom* (1998) 193 C.L.R. 46 (High Court of Australia).

different debenture-holders, and the appointment of a plurality of receivers, usually from the same firm, by the same debenture-holder.[28]

Whilst accepting that the issue in any particular case will be one of construction, and that the cases do not appear to be entirely consistent with the conventional tests for implication of terms, the trend towards construing appointments as authorising responsible office-holders from the same firm to exercise their powers severally as well as jointly is to be welcomed as facilitating the efficient conduct of modern receiverships.   **7–015**

If, notwithstanding the apparent approach of the courts outlined above, no express or implied provision can be found in the debenture authorising the exercise of powers severally, unanimity will be required for the exercise of powers by joint receivers.[29] Where the debenture authorises only the appointment of receivers who must exercise their powers jointly, but an appointment is made purporting to authorise the receivers to exercise their powers jointly and severally, then the appointment should be construed as a valid appointment but with the receivers being limited to exercising their powers jointly.[30]   **7–016**

(d) Declarations under section 231(2) of the Insolvency Act 1986

If more than one administrative receiver is appointed, the appointment must declare whether any act required or authorised under any enactment to be done is to be done "by all or any one or more" of the appointees.[31] This is sometimes done by providing that the administrative receivers may act "jointly and severally", a phrase which appears to be used as shorthand for the ability of each receiver to act for the other. Having regard to the different ways in which that expression can be interpreted in this context,[32] and the uncertainties which this may introduce, it is preferable to follow the wording of the statute.   **7–017**

Section 231, which applies also to liquidators and provisional liquidators,[33] appears to have overlooked the fact that, strictly speaking, most of the acts of an administrative receiver (as opposed to those of a liquidator or provisional liquidator) are not required or authorised to be done under any enactment, but are required or authorised to be done under the terms of the debenture or the   **7–018**

---

[28] Rimer J.'s decision in this respect was not addressed in the judgment of the Court of Appeal, given that it had decided that only a joint appointment was permissible.

[29] See, e.g. the presumption that an authority given to two or more persons is given jointly: *Bowstead & Reynolds on Agency*, 19th edn (London: Sweet & Maxwell, 2010), art.11(1), referring to cases such as *Re Liverpool Household Stores* (1890) 59 L.J. Ch. 616.

[30] *NEC Information Systems Australia Pty Ltd v Lockhart* (1991) 9 A.C.L.C. 658 (New South Wales Court of Appeal); *Kerry Lowe v Isherwood* (1989) 15 A.C.L.R. 615 (New South Wales Court of Appeal), 618 per Priestley J.A.: "The deed by which the receivers were appointed separated the joint and several appointments in a way which . . . calls for the conclusion that if the power of appointment was only that of appointing one receiver or joint receivers, then the deed of appointment succeeded in achieving the latter; and that the further purported appointment of the receivers as several receivers effected nothing and should simply be disregarded.".

[31] Insolvency Act 1986, s.231(2).

[32] See, e.g. the judgments of the majority in *Kendle v Melsom* (1998) 193 C.L.R. 46 (High Court of Australia).

[33] Joint and concurrent appointments of administrators are now dealt with in the Insolvency Act 1986, Sch.B1, paras 100–103.

general law.[34] In terms of drafting, it would be best, therefore, if debentures, appointments and declarations made it clear that the ability of one receiver to act for the other or others is not restricted to acts required or authorised under any enactment but applies to all the acts of any receiver or receivers.

7–019   It is also considered that compliance with the terms of s.231 is not intended to be a condition precedent to the validity of an appointment of administrative receivers. Section 231(1) makes it a precondition to the application of the requirement in s.231(2) that there should be an appointment or nomination. Thus, it is the appointment or nomination that is the pre-condition of the required declaration and not the other way round.

(e)   Liability of multiple receivers[35]

7–020   In practice, the issue of whether multiple receivers are jointly, severally or jointly and severally liable for their acts or omissions rarely causes any difficulties. Multiple appointments usually involve the appointment of partners in the same firm of accountants. Even where they act severally as a matter of fact, such partners often nevertheless purport to contract on behalf of their fellow appointees, and will certainly tend to do so where they wish to take advantage of any exclusion clauses, for example, in contracts for sale of assets. Similarly, proceedings against such persons generally tend to join all the appointees from the same firm without regard to the question of which particular receiver acted in relation to the events in question. The point is generally not taken, because in practice any personal liability which one receiver might attract as a consequence of his actions will be a joint and several liability as a consequence of the fact that the receivers are partners in the same firm.

7–021   The issue may, however, arise in the future, because it is possible that receivers may be appointed to a company from more than one firm of accountants, with the express intention that they might be called upon to act severally in relation to different areas of the receivership. This may occur, for example, in cases where the firm whose partner is most suited to conduct the majority of the receivership is thought to have a potential conflict of interest in relation to a specific aspect of the receivership, or lacks the necessary expertise in a particular area of the business of the company, or where the debenture-holder acts for a syndicate of banks in which there is a divergence of interests with particular banks wishing to ensure that an office-holder of their choice is involved in the receivership.[36] The issue may also arise when insolvency practitioners have formed limited liability partnerships.

---

[34] See, e.g. s.42(1) of the Insolvency Act 1986 which expressly states that the powers conferred on an administrative receiver "by the debentures by virtue of which he was appointed" are deemed to include the powers in Sch.1 to the Act. If it had been intended to confer authority on the administrative receiver by statute, the section would simply have provided that the administrative receiver was to have the powers set out in the Schedule.

[35] As to the liabilities of receivers, see generally below, Ch.13.

[36] The appointment of insolvency practitioners from more than one firm of accountants is more widespread in liquidations and administrations where the interests of a wider variety of creditor groups may be involved: see, however, the comments of Browne-Wilkinson V.C. in rejecting an application for the appointment of an additional provisional liquidator in *Re Bank of Credit and Commerce International SA (In Liquidation) (No.2)* [1992] B.C.L.C. 579 (CA).

If receivers are empowered to act jointly and do so, their liability to their **7–022**
appointor or to third parties may be joint or joint and several.[37] Where receivers
are appointed and empowered to act severally, and one of their number commits
a breach of duty to the company or to his appointor, it is suggested that he will
be individually liable for his breach of duty or tort, and his co-receivers will not
be jointly or vicariously liable with him unless they participate in the misconduct in question. The co-appointees may become liable to the company or their
appointor if it is shown that they knew or were on inquiry as to their co-receiv-
er's misconduct and failed in their own separate duty to take steps to prevent
such acts.[38] So far as liability to a third party is concerned, a receiver will only
be liable in tort on the basis of an assumption of personal responsibility,[39] so
that there is no question of any joint liability arising purely by reason of the fact
that the appointment of receivers was a multiple appointment.

(f) Tenure of office in the case of joint appointments

As indicated below, s.33(1) of the Insolvency Act 1986 contains provisions **7–023**
dealing with the time from which the appointment of a receiver will be effective. Provided that the receiver accepts his appointment by the end of the next
business day following the receipt by him of the instrument of appointment,
his appointment will take effect from the time of receipt of the instrument of
appointment.[40] In the case of joint appointments, s.33(2) and r.3.1 of the
Insolvency Rules 1986 provide that each joint appointee must similarly accept
his appointment, and the appointment will only be effective from the time at
which the instrument of appointment was received by or on behalf of all the
appointees.

The Insolvency Act and Rules do not deal in any detail with the question of **7–024**
what happens in the event of the death, retirement, removal from office of, or
vacation of office by, one of a number of joint receivers. As a matter of principle, the issue must be resolved by an examination of the intention of the
parties to the debenture under which the joint receivers were appointed and
the terms of the appointment itself. The general presumption is that, even
where an appointment to an office is a joint appointment, the death, resignation, etc. of one of the office-holders does not bring an end to the tenure of
office of the other appointees, who will be entitled, as survivors, to continue to

---

[37] See, e.g. the dissenting judgment of Brennan C.J. and McHugh J. in *Kendle v Melsom* (1998)
193 C.L.R. 46 (High Court of Australia).
[38] See, by analogy with the law on directors, *Dovey v Cory* [1901] A.C. 477 (HL); *Re City
Equitable Fire Insurance Co Ltd* [1925] Ch. 407 (CA), 452–453, 459 and *Secretary of State for
Trade and Industry v Baker* [1999] 1 B.C.L.C. 433, 487–489 (Jonathan Parker J.); [2001] B.C.C.
273, 283 (CA).
[39] See, again by analogy, *Williams v Natural Life Health Foods Ltd* [1998] 1 W.L.R. 830 (HL)
and para.13–059 below.
[40] For the position prior to the 1986 Act, see *RA Cripps (Pharmaceutical) and Son Ltd v
Wickenden* [1973] 1 W.L.R. 944 referring to *Windsor Refrigerator Co Ltd v Branch Nominees Ltd*
[1961] Ch. 375 (CA). See also *NZI Securities Australia Ltd v Poignand* (1994) 14 A.C.S.R. 1
(Federal Court of Australia), 7 per Beaumont, Gummow and Carr JJ.: "a receiver is appointed
when the document of appointment is handed to the receiver by a person having authority to
appoint in circumstances in which may fairly be said that he was appointing the receiver and where
the receiver accepts the appointment", referring to *Cripps* and *Windsor*.

exercise the powers which are attached to the office in question.[41] This would appear to be the basis upon which the Insolvency Act 1986 is drafted.[42] Most modern debentures put the matter beyond doubt by providing that in the event of the death, retirement, etc. of one of a number of joint appointees, the remaining receivers will continue in office and will be entitled to exercise the powers given to them under the debenture. The debenture-holder will also be given the power of appointment to fill the vacancy which has arisen.[43]

3.   DEMAND AS A PREREQUISITE TO APPOINTMENT

7–025   The debenture may enable an appointment of receivers to be made at any time, on the happening of a specified event or on the occasion of a default by the company.[44] The burden is upon the debenture-holder and receiver to prove that the power of appointment has become exercisable: there is no presumption of a right to act.[45] An appointment for the wrong reason will be valid if a correct ground existed at the time of appointment.[46]

---

[41] On the survival of powers annexed to an office, see, e.g. *Crawford v Forshaw* [1891] 2 Ch. 261 (CA), 266 (executors) and *Re Smith* [1904] 1 Ch. 139, 144 (trustees).

[42] See, e.g. the reference to a "continuing administrative receiver" in s.46(2) of the Insolvency Act 1986.

[43] See, e.g. the power given in the debenture in *Kendle v Melsom* (1998) 193 C.L.R. 46 (High Court of Australia), 69, fn.70 which provided that "in case of the removal retirement or death" of a receiver, the bank "may appoint another in his place". The court has no power to appoint an administrative receiver to fill a vacancy, even following exercise of its power to remove an administrative receiver from office under s.45(1) of the Insolvency Act 1986: see *Re A&C Supplies Ltd* [1998] B.C.C. 708, 713A.

[44] See, e.g. *Aquachem Ltd v Delphis Bank Ltd* [2008] B.C.C. 648 (PC) where it was held under Mauritian law that a mortgagee could appoint a receiver under an uncrystallised floating charge even though it could not have exercised its mortgagee's power of sale without first crystallising the charge.

[45] *Kasofsky v Kreegers* [1937] 4 All E.R. 374. In *Tricontinental Corp v HDFI Ltd* (1990) 21 N.S.W.L.R. 689 (New South Wales Court of Appeal) it was said that a strict approach was required to the question of whether conditions precedent to the liability of a surety had been satisfied. In *Pan Foods Co Importers & Distributors Pty Ltd v Australia and New Zealand Banking Group Ltd* (2000) 170 A.L.R. 579 (High Court of Australia), the court was faced with the different issue of whether the conditions precedent to the appointment of receivers in a loan agreement had been satisfied. The court held clearly that they had, and Kirby J. (at 584) took the opportunity to reiterate his dissenting view in the *Tricontinental* case to the effect that commercial agreements between a bank and a company "should be construed practically, so as to give effect to their presumed commercial purposes and so as not to defeat the achievement of such purposes by an excessively narrow and artificially restricted construction". Whatever the position in relation to suretyship, the approach of Kirby J. may well be more justifiable in cases dealing with the appointment of receivers. The issue of whether the right to appoint has arisen should be distinguished from the separate issue of whether the appointment has been properly made as a matter of form, as to which there may be a presumption of regularity: see *NZI Securities Australia v Poignand* (1994) 14 A.C.S.R. 1 (Federal Court of Australia).

[46] *Rushingdale S.A. v Byblos Bank S.A.L.* (1986) 2 B.C.C. 99509 (CA); *McMahon v State Bank of New South Wales* (1990) 8 A.C.L.C. 315 (New South Wales Court of Appeal), 319 per Meagher J.A. "the correct legal position is that a party who takes a step pursuant to a contract is entitled to justify the taking of that step if the objective facts which justify the taking of that step existed at the relevant time even though that party at the time that step was taken did not know of these facts"; *Retail Equity Pty Ltd v Custom Credit Corp Ltd* (1991) 9 A.C.L.C. 404 (Supreme Court of Western Australia); *Brampton Manor (Leisure) Ltd v McLean* [2007] B.C.C. 640.

The directors of the company commonly have an express power under the **7–026**
debenture document to invite the debenture-holder to appoint a receiver and
waive any outstanding condition for the making of an appointment. This course
may afford an opportunity for a beneficial realisation of the company's undertaking or some viable part of it as a going concern and thus safeguard the
interests of creditors and employees.

When, and if so upon what terms, the repayment of a loan can be demanded **7–027**
and a receiver appointed in default of repayment will be determined by the
terms of the agreement between the parties. Standard-form debentures often
provide that the debenture-holder must make a demand for payment before the
right to appoint a receiver arises (unless acting at the request of the company).[47]
In the absence of any express or implied term to the contrary, an overdraft will
be repayable on demand.[48] The right to demand repayment of other types of
loans will be a matter of construction of the terms of the facility and the associated security documents.[49] If a loan is made for a fixed term, a provision will
not be implied entitling the lender to require earlier repayment or to appoint a
receiver for cause on the ground that his security is in jeopardy.[50]

Where the making of a demand is an express or implied condition precedent **7–028**
to an appointment, the right to make the appointment must have accrued at the
date of acceptance of the appointment by the receiver if the appointment is to
be valid and effective. If the right accrues later, this will not "feed" the appointment nor validate the acts of the receiver, but merely justify a fresh appointment.[51] If a first invalid appointment is made and acted on, a second valid
appointment cannot be made until after the appointor has restored the company
to possession of its assets and renewed its demands.[52] If a fresh appointment is

---

[47] See, e.g. *Encyclopaedia of Forms and Precedents*, 5th edn, Vol.10(2), form 26, cl.11.1;
Lingard, *Bank Security Documents*, 4th edn (London: LexisNexis Butterworths, 2006), p.467
(Specimen Debenture, cl.6.01). Contrast the terms of the debenture at issue in *Pan Foods v
Australia and New Zealand Banking Group* (2000) 170 A.L.R. 579 (High Court of Australia)
which provided in part: "[t]he moneys hereby secured shall at the option of the Bank (notwithstanding anything hereinbefore contained) immediately become due and payable and the security
hereby created shall immediately become enforceable without the necessity for any demand or
notice . . . upon the happening of any one or more of the following events . . ."

[48] See, per Ralph Gibson J. in *Williams & Glyn's Bank Ltd v Barnes* [1981] Com. L.R. 205. In
Lloyd's Bank Plc v Lampert [1999] B.C.C. 507 the Court of Appeal held that although a bank and
its customer envisaged that an overdraft facility might be in place for some time, it was not inconsistent with that expectation for a bank to retain an express entitlement to "payment on demand".
See also *Hall v Royal Bank of Scotland plc* [2009] EWHC 3163 (QB).

[49] So a term requiring payment on demand might be held repugnant to the main purpose of an
overdraft facility which was expressed to be for a fixed term of 12 months: see *Titford Property Co
Ltd v Cannon Street Acceptances Ltd* Unreported May 22, 1975.

[50] *Cryne v Barclays Bank plc* [1987] B.C.L.C. 548 (CA), 556, per Kerr L.J., distinguishing a
dictum of Ralph Gibson J. in *Williams & Glyn's Bank Ltd v Barnes* [1981] Com. L.R. 205, on the
ground that the facility in the earlier case was granted in the context of a rescue operation accompanied by a moratorium of the creditors. Jeopardy in this situation is, however, a ground for the
appointment of a receiver by the court, see below, Ch.29.

[51] *RA Cripps (Pharmaceutical) and Son Ltd v Wickenden* [1973] 1 W.L.R. 944, 956–957;
R. Jaffe Ltd v Jaffe (No.2) [1932] N.Z.L.R. 195 (New Zealand Supreme Court).

[52] *RA Cripps (Pharmaceutical) and Son Ltd v Wickenden* [1973] 1 W.L.R. 944. Compare the
position where a freezing order is obtained without notice in breach of the duty to make full disclosure and the order is discharged, so as to ensure that the applicant cannot benefit from his own
wrong, before any fresh application is made: *Bank Mellat v Nikpour* [1985] F.S.R. 87 (CA). In

made or could at any time have been made, whilst the actions of the first receiver may be unlawful, it may be difficult for the company to prove that any loss has been occasioned by the initial premature appointment.[53]

7–029   As to the form of demand, it is usual for a debenture to require a demand to be in writing and traditionally many debentures also require a demand to be under the common seal of the bank or under the hand of any duly author-ised officer of the bank. Consideration should be given to the question whether the terms of the debenture are wide enough to cover modern forms of commu-nication. For example, a demand by telex would not be a demand "under hand".[54]

7–030   As to the quantum of the demand, unless the debenture states otherwise, the demand need not specify the amount due.[55] If the terms of a debenture require that a demand be made for the exact sum due or, for example, that a breakdown of the debt be given, then it is unclear whether a demand for a sum which exceeds the actual sum owed, or which fails to provide the specified particu-lars, will constitute a valid demand.[56] It is suggested that the ordinary principle

---

Bank of Baroda v Panessar [1987] Ch. 335, Walton J. (obiter at 351) took the view that this neces-sary hiatus period between an invalid appointment and a subsequent fresh demand and valid appointment did not preclude the application of the doctrine of estoppel barring the debtor from challenging the validity of the original appointment when the debtor had dealt with the receiver as validly appointed and the debenture-holder had accordingly refrained from serving a fresh demand and making a new appointment.

[53] See *Maredelanto Compania Naviera SA v Bergbau-Handel GmbH (The Mihalis Angelos)* [1971] 1 Q.B. 164 (CA).

[54] *Re A Company* [1985] B.C.L.C. 37, 43. To meet this point, a modern form of debenture may well permit a demand to be made by fax. The use of facsimile machines to serve court documents is now well established where the party to be served has indicated his willingness to be served in this way: see CPR Pt 6.3(1)(d) and 6.20(1)(d) and para.4.1 of Practice Direction 6A. It remains to be seen whether debentures in general use will provide for service of demands by email, and if so, what conditions may be attached to such provisions so as to ensure that delivery of the demand can be verified and comes to the attention of the relevant person: see, e.g. the additional requirements for service by email in para.4.2 of Practice Direction 6A, and Personal Property Securities Act 1999, s.189 (New Zealand).

[55] *Bank of Baroda v Panessar* [1987] Ch. 335 ("all moneys due"); *Bunbury Foods Pty Ltd v National Bank of Australasia Ltd* (1984) 153 C.L.R. 491, 503–504 (High Court of Australia) (however, the High Court went on to note at 504 that "the debtor must be allowed a reasonable opportunity to comply with the demand before the creditor can enforce or realise the security . . . In determining whether the debtor has had such an opportunity it will be relevant to take account of the debtor's knowledge, lack of knowledge and means of knowledge of the amount due and of the information which the creditor has provided in that respect, including the response which he has made to any enquiry by the debtor"; *Australia and New Zealand Banking Group Ltd v Pan Foods Co Importers & Distributors Pty Ltd* [1999] 1 V.R. 29 (Victorian Court of Appeal). The word "demand" need not be used: *Re Colonial Finance, Mortgage, Investment and Guarantee Corp Ltd* (1905) 6 S.R.N.S.W. (Supreme Court of New South Wales), 6, 9, per Walker J., approved by the Court of Appeal in *Bank of Credit and Commerce International SAO v Blattner* Unreported November 20, 1986. A demand for a sum due will be valid despite being accompanied by an offer to accept payment in instalments: *NRG Vision Ltd v Churchfield Leasing Ltd* (1988) 4 B.C.C. 56, 66.

[56] Knox J. specifically left open this point in *NRG Vision Ltd v Churchfield Leasing* (1988) 4 B.C.C. 56, 66. See also the split decision of the Court of Appeal of Victoria in *Australia and New Zealand Banking Group v Pan Foods* [1999] 1 V.R. 29 on the issue of whether a demand was bad for failing to give an accurate breakdown of the amount demanded. The point was not dealt with on appeal, because the High Court of Australia decided that no demand was necessary at all as a pre-condition to the appointment of a receiver: see (2000) 170 A.L.R. 579. The only judge who expressly dealt with the matter in the High Court of Australia (Callinan J.) agreed with Winneke P.'s judgment in the Court of Appeal of Victoria to the effect that it was the substance and not the

should be that a demand will be a valid demand even if the sum claimed exceeds the sum in fact due.[57] An analogy might be drawn with the well-established principle that a notice served by a mortgagee prior to exercise of a power of sale is not void merely on the ground that it demands more than is due. There may, however, be a qualification to this principle if the mortgagee expressly or impliedly refuses to accept less than the amount demanded.[58] Moreover, as Walton J. observed in *Bank of Baroda v Panessar*,[59] with the complexities of modern trade and bank facilities, in many cases it may be difficult for the chargee to ascertain the precise amount of money due at any point in time, especially if this has to be done very quickly.[60] If, as in the vast majority of cases, the company will not be in a position to pay the debt in any event,

form of the notice which was important. According to Callinam J., the declaration specified in the relevant clause of the debenture required simply "a clear expression of the reaching of a state of satisfaction of the mind of the respondent bank that a relevant event of default has in fact occurred" (at 592).

[57] *Deverges v Sandeman, Clark & Co* [1902] 1 Ch. 579 (CA), 597, per Cozens-Hardy M.R. (distinguishing *Pigot v Cubley* (1864) 15 C.B. (N.S.) 701); *Stubbs v Slater* [1910] 1 Ch. 632 (CA), 647, per Buckley L.J.; *Bank of Baroda v Panessar* [1987] Ch. 335, approving *Bunbury Foods Pty Ltd v National Bank of Australasia Ltd* (1984) 153 C.L.R. 491 (High Court of Australia). See also *Triodos Bank NV v Dobbs* [2004] N.P.C. 63, [233]–[234], citing *Bank of Baroda* and *Bunbury Foods*. See also per Malcolm C.J. in *Hassgill Investments Pty Ltd v Newman Air Charter Pty Ltd* (1991) 5 A.C.S.R. 321, 339 (Supreme Court of Western Australia), citing *Bunbury Foods* and *Clarke v Japan Machines (Australia) Pty Ltd* [1984] 1 Qd. R. 404 (Full Court, Supreme Court of Queensland). Under Canadian law, a demand for payment will nonetheless be effective if the amount of the demand is incorrect: *Bennett on Receiverships*, 3rd edn (Thomson Reuters Canada, 2011), p.118 citing, inter alia, *Four-K Western Equip v CIBC* (1983) 46 C.B.R. (N.S.) 146 (Supreme Court of British Columbia).

[58] See the cases referred to in *Bunbury Foods Pty Ltd v National Bank of Australasia Ltd* (1984) 153 C.L.R. 491 (High Court of Australia), 503–504 and in *Hassgill v Newman Air Charter* (1991) 5 A.C.S.R. 321 (Supreme Court of Western Australia), 339 (a case dealing with the service of a statutory demand as a precursor to winding-up proceedings). Some limited guidance may also be obtained from cases on the effect of over-statement of the amount due in statutory demands served on companies or as a pre-condition to the presentation of a bankruptcy petition. In England, where it is clear that a certain sum is owing, the mere over-statement of the amount in a statutory demand served on a company will not invalidate the demand provided that the company was in a position to know exactly what it ought to pay: see *Cardiff Preserved Coal & Coke Co v Norton* (1866–67) L.R. 2 Ch. App. 405; *Re A Company (No.003729 of 1982)* [1984] 1 W.L.R. 1090; *Re A Debtor (No.10 of 1988)* [1989] 1 W.L.R. 405, 406. Statutory demands in bankruptcy cases are also not liable to be set aside merely by reason of the over-statement of the amount of the debt: see *Re A Debtor (No.1 of 1987)* [1989] 1 W.L.R. 271 (CA); *Re A Debtor (No.490/SD/1991)* [1992] 1 W.L.R. 507. After considerable judicial differences of opinion, in Australia prior to 1992 it would seem that the view was also taken that a mere over-statement did not render a statutory demand served on a company invalid: see *Hassgill v Newman Air Charter* referring, inter alia, to *Re Fabo Pty Ltd* (1988) 14 A.C.L.R. 518 (Full Court, Supreme Court of Victoria). Since 1992 the position in Australia has been dealt with by statute, pursuant to which a defect does not automatically invalidate a demand, but the court is given the power to set aside a statutory demand if: there is a genuine dispute about the existence of the debt (Corporations Act 2001 (Cth), s.459H(1)(a)); the company has an offsetting claim (s.459H(1)(b)); there is a defect in the demand and substantial injustice will be caused if the demand is not set aside (s.459J(1)(a)); or there is some other reason why the demand should be set aside (s.459J(1)(b)); see *Topfelt Pty Ltd v State Bank of New South Wales Ltd* (1993) 12 A.C.S.R. 381 (Federal Court of Australia) and *Chains & Power (Aust) Pty Ltd v Commonwealth Bank of Australia* (1994) 15 A.C.S.R. 544 (Federal Court of Australia), 548–551.

[59] *Bank of Baroda v Panessar* [1987] Ch. 335.

[60] See to similar effect the dictum of Winneke P. in the *Australia and New Zealand Banking Group v Pan Foods* [1999] 1 V.R. 29 (Victorian Court of Appeal), 40.

there would seem to be little commercial sense in invalidating a demand merely
for inadvertent overstatement of the precise amount due.[61]

7–031   Conflicting considerations are relevant to the issue of the period of time
which the law ought to allow for repayment of a loan in response to a demand
by the debenture-holder before the right to appoint a receiver arises. The
company might contend that it ought to be given a reasonable opportunity to
find alternative sources of finance and to raise the sum required. Claims might
be made for additional time for legal and administrative reasons (such as
holding board meetings to authorise the release of funds for repayment or to
obtain any necessary third party or regulatory approval to such repayment). On
the other hand the holder of the security may need to take immediate and urgent
action if his security is to be safeguarded and to avoid the inherent risk of delay
(such as the disappearance of charged assets or their seizure by other
creditors).[62]

7–032   Different legal systems have adopted differing approaches to this issue.
Under English law, a series of first instance decisions have determined that a
debenture-holder in respect of an "on demand" facility need not give the
company a reasonable time to pay before appointing a receiver.[63] The company
is merely to be allowed the necessary time during banking hours to implement
the mechanics of payment by collecting or arranging for the transfer of the
money from its bank or some other "convenient place".[64] The company is not
entitled to time to raise such money either from its bank or from other sources[65]
unless such a right is expressly conferred or must necessarily be implied to

---

[61] This problem is often met by inclusion of a provision in the debenture that a statement of the
indebtedness in a particular form (usually a certificate) by the creditor is conclusive. A statement
pursuant to such a provision has been held to be conclusive unless some lack of good faith in its
preparation can be shown: *Bache & Co (London) Ltd v Banque Vernes et Commerciale de Paris
SA* [1973] 2 Lloyd's Rep. 437 (CA) but see now also *North Shore Ventures Ltd v Amstead Holdings
Inc.* [2011] 3 W.L.R. 628 (CA); *ANZ Banking Group (NZ) Ltd v Gibson* [1981] 2 N.Z.L.R. 513
(New Zealand High Court); *Dobbs v National Bank of Australasia Ltd* (1935) 53 C.L.R. 643 (High
Court of Australia), 652, where Rich, Dixon, Evatt and McTiernan JJ. held that such a clause is not
void as being against public policy because "[a] clear distinction has always been maintained
between negative restrictions upon the right to invoke the jurisdiction of the Courts and positive
provisions giving efficacy to the award of an arbitrator when made or to some analogous definition
or ascertainment of private rights upon which otherwise the Courts might have been required to
adjudicate".
[62] See *ANZ Banking Group (NZ) Ltd v Gibson* [1981] 2 N.Z.L.R. 513 (New Zealand High
Court), 519, per Holland J.
[63] *Brighty v Norton* (1862) 3 B. & S. 312, per Blackburn J: "a debtor who is required to pay
money on demand . . . must have it ready, and is not entitled to further time in order to look for it".
This statement of the law was approved by Goff J. in *RA Cripps (Pharmaceutical) and Son Ltd v
Wickenden* [1973] 1 W.L.R. 944 and by Walton J. in *Bank of Baroda v Panessar* [1987] Ch. 335 in
which the appointment of the receiver was upheld despite it taking place only one hour after the
demand.
[64] This has come to be known as the "mechanics of payment" test: see, e.g. *Moore v Shelley*
(1882–83) L.R. 8 App. Cas. 285 (PC), 293; *Bank of Baroda v Panessar* [1987] Ch. 335, 348B;
Sheppard & Cooper Ltd v TSB Bank Plc (No.2) [1996] 2 All ER 654, 657–658; and *Lloyd's Bank
plc v Lampert* [1999] B.C.C. 507, 512. In *Lloyd's Bank* the Court of Appeal declined to be drawn
into what Kennedy L.J. described as "the interesting academic question" as to whether the
mechanics of payment test should now be affirmed or rejected at appellate level, because on the
evidence there was no prospect of the company finding the money to make repayment so that,
whatever the test, the bank was entitled to appoint the receivers when it did.
[65] *Titford Property Co Ltd v Cannon Street Acceptances Ltd* Unreported May 22, 1975, Goff J.

give business efficacy to the loan agreement.[66] The personal circumstances of the borrower or officers of the company will not be taken into account unless so provided in the debenture.[67] On the other hand, it has been held that notwithstanding the objective nature of the mechanics of payment test, no time at all need be given if the borrower has by a director indicated that it cannot pay.[68]

In Canada a slightly more liberal approach has prevailed, requiring lenders **7–033** to give a borrower a reasonable time to make repayment of a demand loan before enforcing the security. Unless the circumstances are exceptional, the debtor must be given some notice on which he might reasonably expect to be able to act.[69] The Canadian courts have not generally been willing to extend very lengthy periods of time to debtors to find the money to make repayment. It has been pointed out that the cases which have given rise to the requirement of reasonable notice dealt with notices of an hour or less, and that whilst what constitutes reasonable notice will depend upon the facts of the particular case,[70] it is unlikely to encompass anything more than a few days.[71]

Since 1992, the Canadian Bankruptcy and Insolvency Act has required ten days' notice in a prescribed manner by a secured creditor who intends to enforce a security on all or substantially all of an insolvent debtor's inventory, accounts receivable or other property.[72] Whilst this statutory minimum is strictly only applicable to a narrow set of circumstances, it may also inform a court's view of a reasonable notice period in a broader range enforcements. However given the development of the common law of Canada prior to the enactment of this measure, required notice will rarely exceed the statutory minimum.

---

[66] *Williams & Glyn's Bank Ltd v Barnes* [1981] Com. L.R. 205, where the view was expressed by Ralph Gibson J. that under the facility agreement in question, business efficacy required that sufficient notice be given by the bank to permit the company to explore the possibility of actions such as borrowing elsewhere or selling sites or parts of its undertaking. The judge remarked, obiter, that he would be very surprised if such period would have exceeded one month.
[67] See *Oakdown Ltd v Bernstein & Co* (1985) 49 P. & C.R. 282, 293, per Scott J. who stated (rejecting a claim to be excused from completion pursuant to a notice to complete a contract for sale of land on the grounds that the tenets of Jewish law prohibited compliance on the date stipulated which was the Festival of Passover): "If parties wish to excuse themselves on religious grounds from discharging on specific days the contractual obligations which would otherwise lie upon them, they must in my judgment expressly so stipulate in their contracts." Query whether such a stipulation might be implied in the case of a contract between two devout adherents of the same faith, and what might be the effect of assignment upon any such term.
[68] *Sheppard & Cooper Ltd v TSB Bank plc (No.2)* [1996] 2 All E.R. 654, criticised in *Rowlatt on Principal and Surety*, 5th edn (London: Sweet & Maxwell, 1999), p.116 and fn.46.
[69] *Ronald Elwyn Lister Ltd v Dunlop Canada Ltd* (1982) 135 D.L.R. 1 (Supreme Court of Canada) referring to *Massey v Sladen* (1868–69) L.R. 4 Ex. 13, 19. See also *Royal Bank of Canada v W Got & Associates Electric Ltd* (1999) 178 D.L.R. (4th) 385 (Supreme Court of Canada), 391–392.
[70] Relevant considerations have been said to include: (1) the amount of the loan; (2) the risk to the creditor of losing his money or security; (3) the length of the relationship between the debtor and the creditor; (4) the character and reputation of the debtor; (5) the potential ability to raise the money demanded in a short period; (6) the circumstances surrounding the making of the demand; and (7) any other relevant factors: see per Linden J. in *Mister Broadloom Corp (1968) Ltd v Bank of Montreal* (1979) 101 D.L.R. (3rd) 713, 723, referred to with approval in *Royal Bank of Canada v W Got & Associates Electric* (1999) 178 D.L.R. (4th) 385 (Supreme Court of Canada), 391.
[71] See *Whonnock Industries Ltd v National Bank of Canada* (1987) 42 D.L.R. (4th) 1 (British Columbia Court of Appeal).
[72] Bankruptcy and Insolvency Act, R.S.C. c.B-3, as amended, s.244.

7–034   In Australia, the decision of the High Court of Australia in 1984 in *Bunbury Foods Pty Ltd v National Bank of Australasia Ltd* also appeared to adopt a requirement that a debtor who was liable to repay a debt "on demand" must be allowed a reasonable time to meet the demand before the creditor could take steps to appoint a receiver. The High Court stated that what would constitute a reasonable time would vary according to the facts, including the relationship between the parties, the knowledge of the debtor as to the amount due and the information provided by the creditor in the demand.[73] Subsequently, in *Bond v Hongkong Bank of Australia Ltd* the majority of the Court of Appeal of New South Wales referred to the "reasonable time" requirement in *Bunbury Foods* and held that an amount of time sufficient to cater for the necessary mechanics of payment (within the formulation expressed in *Bank of Baroda v Panessar*) was sufficient and that an alternative conclusion had never been reached by the High Court.[74]

7–035   In New Zealand the courts have adopted the "mechanics of payment" test. In *ANZ Banking Group (New Zealand) Ltd v Gibson*[75] the Court of Appeal rejected the approach in the Canadian cases, preferring to adopt an objective test which did not depend upon any matters personal to the parties so as to promote certainty in commercial matters. Richardson J. suggested that although no one would expect the borrower to have large cash sums immediately on hand, all that was required was that the debtor be given a reasonable time to convert resources presently available to him into immediate cash or to utilise them within the same time to obtain financial cover with which to make the repayment. Further time to negotiate a loan with a third party was not comprehended within the concept of a reasonable time.[76]

7–036   One point which is made in many of the cases referred to on this topic is that in most situations the question of the precise legal test to be applied will be entirely academic. The factual position will usually be that the company will be

---

[73] *Bunbury Foods Pty Ltd v National Bank of Australasia Ltd* (1984) 153 C.L.R. 491 (High Court of Australia).
[74] *Bond v Hongkong Bank of Australia Ltd* (1991) 25 N.S.W.L.R. 286 (New South Wales Court of Appeal), 295, 318–319. Kirby J. noted (at 318) in relation to the mechanics of payment test:

"It is a test which minimises the area of uncertainty for it confines the question of "reasonableness" to the mechanical issue of how long it would take a party (if otherwise entitled to do so) to secure the funds necessary to discharge the obligation once demand has been made. If considerations as to the means of the parties, the viability of the guarantor, the amount at stake, etc, have to be taken into account, the words "on demand" are neutered and each case where the obligation to pay "on demand" has been assumed will be diverted into an exploration of what was, or was not, "reasonable" in the circumstances and financial means of the parties. Such exploration would give rise to protracted litigation and a great deal of commercial uncertainty."

Note also the comments of Gleeson C.J. at 295 that it was necessary to put aside "any suggestion that the appellant was entitled to be given time to try to borrow the necessary funds from some third party."
[75] *ANZ Banking Group (NZ) Ltd v Gibson* [1986] 1 N.Z.L.R. 556 (New Zealand Court of Appeal).
[76] In *Housing Corp of New Zealand v Maori Trustee (No.2)* [1988] 2 N.Z.L.R. 708 (New Zealand Court of Appeal) the *ANZ* case was cited with approval, but in rejecting the claim that an unreasonably short period of time had been given the court curiously referred to the fact that the mortgagor had long been in default, time had been given and promises made but not kept. These factors would seem to be irrelevant to the objective test of the reasonable time to convert presently available resources into immediate cash with which to make payment.

unable to make repayment, or prove that it had any realistic prospect of doing so, in the period of time which would be permitted by either test. In *Bunbury Foods Pty Ltd v National Bank of Australasia Ltd*, a responsible officer of the debtor company informed the bank that the company could not pay and so there was "no question of allowing Bunbury any further time in which to get the money and the Bank was accordingly entitled to appoint the receiver and manager immediately."[77] It is important not to lose sight of the fact that the issues discussed above relate to demand liabilities, and it will be a very rare case indeed in which the debtor company has no warning of the bank's intention to take steps to call in its loan and enforce its security. Most companies in financial trouble are in regular contact with their bankers and have sufficient opportunity to take steps to seek alternative finance long before the final demand is served.

If the demand for payment specifies a date but not a time for payment, there is no default until midnight.[78] **7–037**

To avoid the appointment of the receiver or the exercise of any of the creditor's other rights under the debenture, the company must either tender or pay into court the sum claimed to be due[79] or (if the sum claimed is on the face of the mortgage excessive) the sum actually due.[80] **7–038**

If the debtor makes or tenders payment, an injunction will be granted restraining the debenture-holder from enforcing his security.[81] The company will be temporarily excused from making any tender or payment as a condition of its right to prevent the debenture-holder enforcing his security if the debenture-holder alone has knowledge of the sum secured and he fails to specify it in his demand.[82] **7–039**

If the company,[83] with knowledge of the facts which invalidate an appointment of a receiver, acquiesces in the receiver exercising his powers by, for example, continuing to run the company's business, it may be estopped from subsequently challenging the validity of the appointment.[84] It is unnecessary **7–040**

---

[77] *Bunbury Foods Pty Ltd v National Bank of Australasia Ltd* (1984) 153 C.L.R. 491 (High Court of Australia), 504–505.

[78] *Afovos Shipping Co SA v R Pagnan & Fratelli (The Afovos)* [1983] 1 W.L.R. 195 (HL).

[79] *Macleod v Jones* (1883) L.R. 24 Ch. D. 289 (CA). The company cannot unilaterally discharge the security without payment by appropriating a cross-claim: see *Samuel Keller Holdings Ltd v Martins Bank Ltd* [1971] 1 W.L.R. 43 (CA) and *Ashley Guarantee Plc v Zacaria* [1993] 1 W.L.R. 62 (CA). On the other hand, if the mortgagee undoubtedly owes monies to the mortgagor, the mortgagor appears to be able to "redeem" the mortgage by giving notice to the mortgagee to appropriate the debt due to the mortgagor in repayment of the mortgage: *Parker v Jackson* [1936] 2 All E.R. 281, 290. See also *National Westminster Bank Plc v Skelton* [1993] 1 W.L.R. 72 (CA); *Ashley Guarantee Plc v Zacaria* [1993] 1 W.L.R. 62 (CA) and below, para.22–005.

[80] *Hickson v Darlow* (1883) L.R. 23 Ch. D. 690 (CA).

[81] *Duke v Robson* [1973] 1 W.L.R. 267 (CA); *Inglis v Commonwealth Trading Bank of Australia* (1972) 126 C.L.R. 161 (High Court of Australia) where it was noted by Walsh J. at 166 that neither the existence of disputes as to the correct amount of the debt nor a claim by the debtor for damages was a ground for preventing the mortgagee from exercising its rights.

[82] Consider *Albemarle Supply Co Ltd v Hind & Co* [1928] 1 K.B. 307 (CA) (a case of lien). A mortgagor is entitled to know how much he is liable to pay and how that sum is arrived at: *Cityland and Property (Holdings) Ltd v Dabrah* [1968] Ch. 166, 172–173.

[83] Acting for this purpose by its directors.

[84] *Bank of Baroda v Panessar* [1987] Ch. 335, 353; *Village Cay Marina Ltd v Acland* [1998] B.C.C. 417 (PC), 422G. In *Australia and New Zealand Banking Group v Pan Foods* [1999] 1 V.R. 29, 58–59 in the Supreme Court of Victoria, Buchanan J.A. appeared to treat the matter as one of

for this purpose that the company should know that these facts give rise to a right to challenge the validity of the appointment.[85]

4. METHOD OF APPOINTMENT[86]

7–041   If the power to appoint a receiver has become exercisable, the debenture-holder owes no duty of care to the company or to its unsecured creditors or to any guarantor in deciding whether to exercise it, provided he acts in good faith.[87]

7–042   A receiver must be appointed in accordance with the terms of the debenture. If the debenture merely requires an appointment "by writing" an appointment is sufficient if under hand and need not be under seal.[88] Non-administrative receivers may, but do not need to, be appointed by deed to execute any deed as agent for the company (e.g. a conveyance or transfer or lease).[89] In the case of administrative receivers, on the other hand, their implied power to use the company's seal and to execute deeds and other instruments in the name and on behalf of the company is in no way dependent on the form of their appointment.[90]

7–043   An instrument of appointment may be executed in anticipation of a default and subsequent use.[91] Section 33 of the Insolvency Act 1986 provides that an appointment of a receiver or manager shall only be effective if it is accepted by the nominee before the end of the business day next following that on which the instrument of appointment is received by him or his behalf. The appointment is then deemed to have been made at the time at which the instrument of appointment was received by the nominee. Section 33 also applies to the appointment of two or more persons as joint receivers or managers of a company's property under powers contained in an instrument, in which case the appointment must be accepted by all the nominees and will be effective from

---

estoppel in the strict sense. He referred to the *Bank of Baroda* case but rejected a claim that the company and its directors were estopped from disputing the validity of the receiver's appointment, because the bank's view as to the validity of the appointment was based upon its construction of the debenture in question as a matter of law, and there was no evidence that such belief had been induced by any conduct or factual representation by the company and its directors. In contrast, Buchanan J.A. noted that in *Bank of Baroda v Panessar*, it could be said that the debtor, in failing to protest that the bank had not allowed enough time to collect money and pay it before the appointment of the receiver, had misled the bank as to a matter of fact.

[85] *Peyman v Lanjani* [1985] Ch. 457 (CA).

[86] For court-appointed receivers, see below Ch.29.

[87] *Shamji v Johnson Matthey Bankers Ltd* [1991] B.C.L.C. 36 (CA); *Re Potters Oils (No.2)* [1986] 1 W.L.R. 201; *Medforth v Blake* [2000] Ch. 86 (CA); *Coomber v Bloom* Unreported 26 January, 2010. See further below, Ch.13.

[88] *Windsor Refrigerator Co Ltd v Branch Nominees Ltd* [1961] Ch. 375; *RA Cripps (Pharmaceutical) and Son Ltd v Wickenden* [1973] 1 W.L.R. 944, 953–954.

[89] See *Phoenix Properties Ltd v Wimpole Street Nominees Ltd* [1992] B.C.L.C. 737. See further below, Ch.11.

[90] Insolvency Act 1986, s.42(1) and Sch.1, paras 8 and 9.

[91] *Windsor Refrigerator Co Ltd v Branch Nominees Ltd* [1961] Ch. 375; *RA Cripps (Pharmaceutical) and Son Ltd v Wickenden* [1973] 1 W.L.R. 944, 953–954. The appointment is effective as against creditors: *Re Zurich Insurance Co and Troy Woodworking Ltd* (1984) 45 O.R. (2d) 343; *MacKay and Hughes (1973) Ltd v Martin Potatoes Inc* (1984) 9 D.L.R. (4th) 439 (Ontario Court of Appeal).

the time at which the instrument of appointment was received by or on behalf of all the appointees.[92]

5.   SCOPE OF THE APPOINTMENT

The appointment will normally extend to the whole of the subject matter of the charge. But on occasions it may be appropriate to exclude from the appointment valueless[93] or onerous[94] property. It should be considered whether the extent of any property excluded may be such as to prevent the receiver being receiver of substantially the whole of the company's property, in which case he will not qualify as an administrative receiver[95] or, conversely, whether it is necessary deliberately to restrict the scope of the appointment so as to avoid a breach of the prohibition of the appointment of administrative receivers under s.72A(1) of the Insolvency Act 1986.   **7–044**

6.   VALIDATION OF ACTS WHERE THERE ARE DEFECTS IN APPOINTMENT OR QUALIFICATIONS

Section 232 of the Insolvency Act 1986 provides that the acts of an office-holder (meaning a liquidator, provisional liquidator, administrator or administrative receiver) shall be valid notwithstanding any defect in his appointment, nomination or qualifications. The defects in question are limited to defects in the form of or procedure for appointment, and do not extend to validating the acts of a person in a case where the appointor had no right or power to make any appointment[96] or where there has been no genuine attempt to appoint at all.[97]   **7–045**

7.   DURATION OF APPOINTMENT

Prior to the Insolvency Act 1985, the appointor could (subject to the provisions of the debenture and appointment) remove and replace a receiver and a manager at will. This continues to be the case in relation to non-administrative receivers. Under the Insolvency Act 1986 the appointor has no power to remove or replace the administrative receiver and any provision to this effect in the debenture or appointment will be void. This change in the law is designed to enhance the independence and standing of the administrative receiver,   **7–046**

---

[92] Insolvency Act 1986, s.33(2). See Insolvency Rules 1986, r.3.1 (as amended).

[93] *Re Griffin Hotel Co Ltd* [1941] Ch. 129 (hotel subject to prior charge excluded).

[94] Such as unproductive property exposing the receiver to liability for rates.

[95] See above, para.1–007 et seq.

[96] A distinction is drawn in the Act between an invalid appointment (s.34) and a defect in appointment (s.232). In *Woollett v Minister of Agriculture and Fisheries* [1955] 1 Q.B. 103 (CA), 121, 128 and 137, the Court of Appeal held that a similarly worded validating provision in the Agriculture Act 1947 validated the decisions of an agricultural lands tribunal where two of its members, who were eligible to sit, were wrongly appointed by the secretary of the tribunal instead of the Minister.

[97] *Morris v Kanssen* [1946] A.C. 459 (HL).

reflecting the professional status of the insolvency practitioner and his official powers and duties as an office-holder.[98]

7–047   An administrative receiver will remain in office unless and until:

    (a) he ceases to be qualified to act as an insolvency practitioner in relation to the company[99];

    (b) he is removed by order of the court[100];

    (c) he resigns[101]; or

    (d) the receivership is concluded.

The removal, resignation, termination and discharge of a receiver are dealt with in detail in Ch.28.

8. PRACTICAL PRECAUTIONS[102]

7–048   Before making or accepting appointment as administrative receiver and then acting as such, inquiries ought, in so far as circumstances permit, to be made so that appointor and appointee are satisfied as to the following matters.

(a) Validity of Debenture[103]

7–049   If the debenture is void ab initio, so must be the appointment, and the receiver is at risk of being held liable as a trespasser and the appointor as a joint tortfeasor.[104] Further, both the appointor and the appointee may be held liable as constructive trustees or to account for property which comes into their hands, given actual or constructive knowledge of the invalidity.[105] Section 34 of the Insolvency Act 1986 gives the court a discretionary jurisdiction to require the

---

[98] See below, Ch.8.

[99] Insolvency Act 1986, s.45(2). The vacation of office is immediate and automatic: consider *Re AJ Adams (Builders) Ltd* [1991] B.C.C. 62.

[100] Insolvency Act 1986, s.45(1).

[101] Insolvency Act 1986, s.45(1).

[102] A good practical guide to the issues which confront any person intending to make or take up an appointment is contained in Chs 5–9 of Samwell, *Corporate Receiverships; A Practical Approach*, 2nd edn (1988).

[103] See also above, para.3–086 et seq.

[104] *Ford & Carter Ltd v Midland Bank Ltd* (1979) 129 N.L.J. 543 (HL). See also *Re Jaffe Ltd v Jaffe (No. 2)* [1932] N.Z.L.R. 195 (New Zealand Supreme Court) and *Harold Meggitt Ltd v Discount & Finance Ltd* (1938) 56 W.N. (N.S.W.) 23 (Supreme Court of New South Wales), 24: the appointor was responsible because whatever the receiver did "was done on the instructions and with the approval and assent" of the appointor (Owen J.). Note also *OBG Ltd v Allan* [2005] Q.B. 762 (CA), affirmed [2008] 1 A.C. 1 (HL) in relation to possible liability for procuring a breach of contract.

[105] In *Rolled Steel Products (Holdings) Ltd v British Steel Corp* [1986] Ch. 246 (CA), the appointor and receiver had actual notice of the invalidity of the debenture under which the receiver was appointed; this being so, they were accountable to the plaintiff company as constructive trustees. It was not argued, given the facts, that a receiver should be liable only if he had actual knowledge. In principle, constructive knowledge is sufficient to found liability but the law as to what constitutes constructive knowledge is unclear: see further *Bank of Credit and Commerce International (Overseas) Ltd v Akindele* [2001] Ch. 437 (CA) and the cases cited therein.

appointor to indemnify the appointee against liabilities arising from the invalidity of the appointment. Equally, on appointment, the appointee may reasonably require the appointor to accept the risk of any invalidity and to provide a deed of indemnity.

If the debenture is valid at the date of the appointment but potentially flawed, **7–050** such as being susceptible to intervening invalidity by reason of non-registration or avoidance as a preference on a subsequent liquidation, the appointment is valid and the receiver continues entitled so as to act until the happening of the invalidating event.[106]

(b) Title to the debenture

An assignee of the debenture can only make an appointment pursuant thereto **7–051** once the assignment has been completed.[107]

(c) Enforceability of charge and validity of the form of the appointment

The conditions for appointment of a receiver must have been satisfied and the **7–052** appointment properly made.[108] If the appointment would be an appointment of an administrative receiver, the applicability of the general prohibition of such appointments under s.72A(1) of the Insolvency Act 1986 must be checked.[109] Administration is a further impediment. Under the original Pt II of the Insolvency Act 1986 (where still applicable) an administrative receiver cannot be appointed if an administrator has been appointed by the court under s.8 of the Insolvency Act 1986.[110] A receiver (other than an administrative receiver) cannot be appointed in those circumstances without the consent of the administrator or the leave of the court.[111] Under Sch.B1, the position is substantially the same despite the different methods by which an administrator can now be appointed. An administrative receiver cannot be appointed if the company is already in administration and a receiver (other than an administrative receiver cannot be appointed without either the consent of the administrator or the permission of the court.[112]

---

[106] *Burston Finance Ltd v Speirway Ltd* [1974] 1 W.L.R. 1648, 1657, per Walton J., and see paras 15–011 to 15–027 below.

[107] *Harris & Lewin Pty Ltd v Harris v Lewin (Agents)* (1975) C.L.C. 40–216 (Supreme Court of Victoria) and consider *Lever Finance v Needleman's Trustee* [1956] Ch. 375.

[108] See above, paras 7–025 to 7–040.

[109] See further *Feetum v Levy* [2006] Ch. 585 (CA). See also *Re Dairy Farmers of Britain Ltd* [2010] Ch. 63 on the inapplicability of Insolvency Act 1986, s.29(2) to industrial and provident societies.

[110] See s.11(3)(b) (in its original form). Note that the prohibition on appointment of an administrative receiver only arises on the making of the order and not on presentation of the petition (s.10(2)(b) in its original form).

[111] Insolvency Act 1986, s.11(3)(c) (in its original form), and see *Re Rosshill Properties Ltd (In Administration)*; sub nom. *Sinai Securities Ltd v Hooper* [2004] B.C.C. 973.

[112] Sch.B1, para.43(2) and (6A). Note that the prohibition on the appointment of receivers under the interim moratorium under para.44 does not prevent or require the permission of the court for the appointment of an administrative receiver or the carrying out of his functions but the administrative receiver will automatically vacate office under para.41(1) upon an administration order taking effect.

(d) Scope of the charge and existence of prior charges

7–053 Checks ought to be made to ascertain the precise scope of the property covered by the charges and the nature of the charges themselves. It will be important to identify whether a charge is a fixed or a floating charge. In relation to certain assets (such as book debts and other receivables) this may be far from simple.[113] It should also be established whether there are prior charges in favour of other parties over any of the assets covered by the charge. These will not prevent the appointment of a receiver, but the existence of a prior charge may affect the commercial viability of the receivership. Prior chargees may have the right to appoint a superior receiver who will be able to call for control of the charged assets and the existence of other claims having priority to monies realised from charged assets will have to be taken into account when dealing with charged property.

9. NOTICE OF APPOINTMENT

(a) To the registrar of companies

7–054 A person who appoints a receiver (including an administrative receiver) or manager of a company's property under the powers contained in an instrument, or obtains an order for the appointment of a receiver or manager by the court, is under a statutory duty to give notice of the fact to the Registrar of Companies within seven days of the appointment or order. This fact is then entered on the register of charges of the company.[114] Where a person appointed as a receiver and manager under an instrument ceases to act, he is obliged to give notice to the Registrar, who will enter notice of this fact on the register of charges.[115] In the case of an administrative receiver who vacates office (otherwise than by death), such notice must be given within 14 days after his vacation of office.[116]

(b) To creditors, the public and the company

7–055 After the receiver has been appointed, every invoice, order for goods or business letter, being documents upon which the company's name appears, and all of the company's websites, must contain a statement that the receiver has been appointed.[117]

7–056 On appointment, an administrative receiver is also duty bound:

   (a) forthwith to send to the company and to advertise in the prescribed manner a notice of his appointment; and

---

[113] See, e.g. above, Ch.3.
[114] Companies Act 2006, s.871.
[115] Companies Act 2006, s.871.
[116] Insolvency Act 1986, s.45(4).
[117] Insolvency Act 1986, s.39(1).

(b) within 28 days after his appointment, unless the court otherwise
directs, to send a notice to all creditors of the company so far as he is
aware of their addresses.[118]

The duty does not extend to an administrative receiver appointed to act with an
existing administrative receiver, nor does it extend to an administrative receiver
appointed in place of an administrative receiver dying or ceasing to act, save to
the extent that the predecessor has failed fully to comply with the duty.[119]

If the company is being wound up, the same duty exists, though the liquidator and administrative receiver may be the same person.[120]

There is no duty on the debenture-holder to give prior notice of the appoint-   **7–057**
ment to the company.[121]

---

[118] Insolvency Act 1986, s.46(1). The content of this notice is prescribed by the Insolvency
Rules 1986, r.3.2.
[119] Insolvency Act 1986, s.46(2).
[120] Insolvency Act 1986, s.46(3).
[121] *Rushingdale Ltd S.A. v Byblos Bank S.A.L.* (1986) 2 B.C.C. 99509 (CA).

Chapter 8

Office-Holders

1. INTRODUCTION

8–001   The Insolvency Act 1986 created the concept of the "office-holder", a novel status carrying special statutory privileges and responsibilities, which was conferred upon administrative receivers, liquidators (including provisional liquidators) and administrators.[1] A person holding any of these offices (unless an official receiver) is required to be qualified to act as an insolvency practitioner in relation to the company.[2] The requirement for a professional qualification in part reflects the far-reaching nature of an office-holder's special statutory privileges and responsibilities. These are designed to secure the beneficial management of the company's undertaking and the proper investigation of the company's affairs, to which the office-holder will usually be a stranger.

8–002   It is important to distinguish between the statutory concept of an "office-holder", and the different concept of an "officer of the court". Historically, officers of the court[3] have been persons appointed by the court who are subject to its general supervisory jurisdiction.[4] In accordance with the rule in *Ex p. James*,[5] officers of the court are obliged to act not only lawfully, but fairly and honourably.[6] Interference with their functions may be a contempt.[7] Court-appointed receivers and administrators have always been officers of the court. Somewhat curiously, but no doubt to ensure uniformity, administrators appointed out of court following the changes introduced by the Enterprise Act 2002 have also been accorded the status of officers of the court.[8] However, even though administrative receivers may seek the directions of the court in relation to matters arising in the administrative receivership,[9] they are not

---

[1] Insolvency Act 1986, s.233(1).

[2] Insolvency Act 1986, s.230 in relation to administrative receivers, liquidators and provisional liquidators, and para.6 of Sch.B1 in relation to administrators.

[3] Such as court-appointed receivers, administrators, provisional liquidators and liquidators in a compulsory liquidation.

[4] See, e.g. *Re Atlantic Computer Systems Plc* [1992] Ch. 505 (CA).

[5] *Ex p. James* (1874) 9 Ch. App 609 (CA in Chancery).

[6] See the consideration of the doctrine in *Re T&N Ltd* [2004] O.P.L.R. 343; *Re Agrimarche Limited* [2010] B.C.C. 775; and *Re Alitalia Linee Aeree Italiane SpA* [2011] 1 W.L.R. 2049. Liquidators in creditors voluntary liquidations are not officers of the court and are therefore not subject to the same principle: see *Re TH Knitwear (Wholesale) Limited* [1988] Ch. 275 (CA).

[7] *Re Mead* (1875) L.R. 20 Eq. 282.

[8] Insolvency Act 1986, Sch.B1, para.5.

[9] Pursuant to an application under s.35 of the Insolvency Act 1986. The list of persons who can apply to the court under s.35 is limited, and it is an unresolved question whether there is a general right in other interested parties to apply to the court for directions to be given to a receiver appointed out of court.

officers of the court subject to the general control of the court, they are not susceptible to the rule in *Ex p. James*, and they are not protected by the principles of contempt of court.[10]

2.   INSOLVENCY PRACTITIONERS

Only an individual, i.e. a natural person, can be qualified to act as an Insolvency   **8–003** Practitioner. In order to be qualified,[11] an individual must be:

(a)   authorised by a professional body recognised under s.391 and permitted so to act under its rules; or

(b)   authorised by a competent authority (the Secretary of State) under s.393[12]; or

(c)   authorised by the Department of Enterprise, Trade and Investment for Northern Ireland under art.352 of the Insolvency (Northern Ireland) Order 1989.

The individual must also have security in force for the proper performance of his functions.[13]

In addition, there are six disqualifications under the 1986 Act.[14] A person is   **8–004** not qualified to act as an insolvency practitioner if:

(a)   he is an undischarged bankrupt;

(b)   a moratorium period under a debt relief order applies to him;

(c)   he is subject to a disqualification order made, or a disqualification undertaking accepted, under the Company Directors Disqualification Act 1986,[15] or the Company Directors Disqualification (Northern Ireland) Order 2002;

---

[10] *Re Hill* [1896] 1 Ch. 947; *Re Magic Aust Pty Ltd* (1992) 10 A.C.L.C. 929.

[11] Insolvency Act 1986, s.390(2).

[12] The future of the Secretary of State's function in granting authorisations is under review—see The Insolvency Service, *Consultation on Reforms to the Regulation of Insolvency Practitioners*, February 2011.

[13] Insolvency Act 1986, s.390(3), in Scotland a caution.

[14] Insolvency Act 1986, s.390(4) and (5).

[15] Insolvency Act 1986, s.390(4)(b). The provisions of the Company Directors Disqualification Act 1986 (as amended): (i) give the court a discretion to make a disqualification order (an order disqualifying a person for a specified period from being a director of a company or receiver of its property or being concerned in any way in the promotion, formation or management of a company or from acting as an insolvency practitioner) if a person is found guilty of an indictable offence in connection with the promotion, formation, management or liquidation or striking off of a company, or with the receivership of a company's property or with being an administrative receiver of a company, or for persistent default in relation to specified provisions of the Companies Act; (ii) impose on the court a duty to make a disqualification order against a director or former director of a company which has gone into insolvent liquidation or administration or into administrative receivership and whose conduct as a director of that company (or of that and other companies) makes him unfit to be concerned in the management of a company (see, e.g. *Re Sevenoaks Stationers (Retail) Ltd* [1991] Ch. 164 (CA)); and (iii) permit the Secretary of State to accept a disqualification undertaking in lieu of applying to the court for a disqualification order for unfitness.

(d) he is a patient within the meaning of s.329(1) of the Mental Health (Care and Treatment) (Scotland) Act 2003 or has had a guardian appointed under the Adults with Incapacity (Scotland) Act 2000 (asp 4);

(e) he lacks capacity (within the meaning of the Mental Capacity Act 2005) to act as an insolvency practitioner; or

(f) a bankruptcy restrictions order or a debt relief restrictions order is in force in respect of him.

The Secretary of State is given power to make regulations (inter alia) prohibiting persons from acting as insolvency practitioners where a conflict of interest will or may arise.[16] The power has never been exercised but there is a very detailed Insolvency Code of Ethics which has been adopted by all the recognised professional bodies.[17] The Code includes five fundamental principles: integrity, objectivity, professional competence and due care, confidentiality and professional behaviour. It sets out a framework that practitioners can use to identify actual or potential threats and to determine what safeguards may be available to meet them. In particular, it deals with when an insolvency practitioner cannot properly accept appointment.[18]

8–005 Most insolvency practitioners have obtained authorisation from one of seven recognised professional bodies.[19] The requirements for the small minority of insolvency practitioners who are authorised by the Secretary of State as the "competent authority" are ostensibly more prescriptive because they are laid out in s.393(2) and the Insolvency Practitioners Regulations 2005,[20] which deal with whether the applicant is a fit and proper person and has met the requisite standards of education and training (the latter, in practice, meaning that they have passed the examinations set by the Joint Insolvency Examination

[16] Insolvency Act 1986, s.419(2)(b).

[17] The Code can be found on the Insolvency Service website along with a short Background and Overview paper. See http://www.insolvencydirect.bis.gov.uk/guidanceleaflets/conductethics/conductethics.htm. Adoption by the various recognised professional bodies may be subject to minor modifications to achieve compatibility with other ethical guidance.

[18] *Sheppard & Cooper Ltd v TSB Bank Plc* [1996] B.C.C. 653 (CA) was an unusual case in which the court granted an injunction to prevent two insolvency practitioners from the same firm from being appointed as administrative receivers of a company. Their firm had previously been engaged to investigate the financial affairs of the company on terms that, to avoid any conflicts of interest, the firm "would not undertake any responsibility for the management of the company's affairs either now or in the future". The Court of Appeal stated that the receivers "were not appointed individually" but "were appointed jointly". This statement should be read in the context of the issue which was whether they, as partners of the firm for the time being, were bound to abide by the terms of the earlier contract. Whatever the position as a matter of commercial reality, as a matter of law it is only individuals who can be appointed as office-holders under the Insolvency Act 1986, not firms or partnerships: see, e.g. *Re Sankey Furniture Ltd Ex p. Harding* [1995] 2 B.C.L.C. 594, 600–601.

[19] The Secretary of State has recognised for this purpose the following professional bodies: The Insolvency Practitioners Association, The Chartered Association of Certified Accountants, The Institute of Chartered Accountants in England & Wales, The Institute of Chartered Accountants in Ireland, The Institute of Chartered Accountants of Scotland, The Law Society and The Law Society of Scotland. See the Insolvency Act 1986, ss.391, 419 and the Insolvency Practitioners (Recognised Professional Bodies) Order 1986 (SI 1986/1764).

[20] SI 2005/524.

Board). However, the recognised professional bodies are all required to exercise their delegated powers of authorisation in accordance with Memorandums of Understanding which are directed to ensuring that the same standards will be applied to their members.

If an unqualified person acts as an insolvency practitioner when he knows or **8–006** has reasonable cause to suspect that he is not qualified, he commits a criminal offence punishable on conviction by imprisonment or a fine or both.[21] But his acts as such insolvency practitioner are valid notwithstanding the defect in his qualification or appointment.[22]

3. SUPPLIES BY UTILITIES

Prior to the current insolvency legislation, public utilities (like any other cred- **8–007** itor-supplier) could require the payment of all arrears as a condition of continued or resumed supply to the company in receivership or liquidation, and thus, by the exercise of their monopoly position in the market, obtain a preference in respect of their unsecured debts over the debts due to preferential creditors and, indeed, a debenture-holder.[23] But unlike any other creditor-supplier, public utilities could not refuse supplies to a new occupier of property. A mortgagee of a company in difficulties therefore had a choice. He could appoint a receiver as agent of the company, in which case the company continued in occupation and payment or security could be demanded by the utility. Or the mortgagee could take possession as a new occupier, in which case payment or security could not be demanded.[24] If, as was usually the case, the mortgagee decided to appoint a receiver, there was an advantage in a receiver hiving down the company's business to a subsidiary which, as a new occupier, could require supplies without any responsibility for past arrears.[25]

This continues to be the position where a company property is the subject of **8–008** a receivership other than an administrative receivership though, in practice, such receivers are not so often concerned with the continuation of the

[21] Insolvency Act 1986, s.389.

[22] Insolvency Act 1986, s.232. In the absence of such a validating provision, the appointment would be a nullity: see *Portman Building Society v Gallwey* [1955] 1 W.L.R. 96. Section 232 does not apply to administrators, but para.104 of Sch.B1 to the Insolvency Act 1986 validates acts of a defectively appointed or qualified administrator.

[23] The courts recognised no restriction on the right of a creditor to insist upon a collateral advantage, or a condition of continuing supplies, if the creditor possessed the legal right to cut off supplies: *Husey v London Electricity Supply Corp* [1902] 1 Ch. 411 (CA), 421 (court-appointed receiver). See also *Wellworth Cash & Carry (North Shields) Ltd v North Eastern Electricity Board* (1986) 2 B.C.C. 99265, where the threatened use of the Electricity Board's power to cut off electricity needed by a voluntary liquidator to keep food frozen, unless the pre-liquidation debt to the Board was paid in full, was "deplored". Nevertheless, the Board was held to be entitled to exercise such power. Creditors other than utilities can still withhold supplies unless pre-receivership debts are paid in full, and this does not amount to an abuse of a dominant position within art.86 of the EEC Treaty: *Leyland DAF Ltd v Automotive Products Plc* [1993] B.C.C. 389 (CA).

[24] *North American Trust Co v Consumer Gas Co* (1997) 147 D.L.R. (4th) 645.

[25] For hive-downs, see Ch.6; cf. the technique available to a liquidator appointed by the court to seek an order vesting the property in the liquidator himself, who thereby becomes a new occupier: *Re Fir View Furniture Co Ltd*, *The Times*, February 8, 1971, per Brightman J.; and see the Insolvency Act 1986, s.145(1).

company's business, and are therefore less vulnerable to the withdrawal of supplies. The position is different in the case of an administrative receiver, administrator, liquidator, provisional liquidator, nominee or supervisor of a company voluntary arrangement.[26] Section 233 of the Insolvency Act 1986 provides that, where a request is made by or with the concurrence of an office-holder for supplies of gas, electricity, water or telecommunication services, the utility[27] may not, as a condition of supply, require the payment of charges for supplies provided prior to the "effective date".

8–009   Where an administrative receiver is the only office-holder in relation to a particular company, the "effective date" is the date on which he was appointed or the date on which the first of his predecessors in office was appointed.[28] In the case of an administration, it is the date when the company entered administration.[29] Questions arise as to the effective date where there are two dates potentially available, e.g. in the case of a concurrent administrative receivership and liquidation. Is the effective date that of the appointment of the administrative receiver or the date of the liquidation? And, where there are concurrent office-holders, is it relevant which of the office-holders requests or concurs in the request for supplies? It is suggested that the effective date is that relating to the appointment of the office-holder in question, save that, where a composition or scheme is approved after the date of his appointment, the effective date is the date of such approval.[30]

8–010   The legitimate interests of the supplier in getting paid are protected, in that the utility may make it a condition of giving a supply that the office-holder personally guarantees the payment of any new charges.[31] To this extent, a hive-down still carries the advantage that no guarantee by the office-holder can be required. But a hive-down is unlikely to be worthwhile if undertaken simply for this reason and in practice an office-holder will always see to it that the post-hive-down debts of the subsidiary are paid, if only to avoid the risk of facing an allegation of fraudulent trading by himself or wrongful trading by the subsidiary's directors.

4. DELIVERY AND SEIZURE OF PROPERTY

8–011 Under s.234 of the Insolvency Act 1986 an administrative receiver or administrator, can apply to the court[32] for an order that any person[33] who has in his possession any property, books, papers or records to which the company

---

[26] All of whom are designated "office-holders" in this context: s.233(1) Insolvency Act 1986.

[27] See Insolvency Act 1986, s.233(3) and (5) for a description of the relevant utilities whose services are covered by the section.

[28] Insolvency Act 1986, s.233(4)(b).

[29] Insolvency Act 1986, s.233(4)(a).

[30] For the effective date in the case of administrations and company voluntary arrangements see s.233(4)(a), (ba) and (c).

[31] Insolvency Act 1986, s.233(2)(a).

[32] See Insolvency Rules 1986, Pt 7, on the detailed procedure for an application by an office-holder.

[33] This may include a liquidator appointed prior to an administrative receiver: *Re First Express Ltd* [1991] B.C.C. 782.

appears to be entitled should give those items up to the officer-holder. No specific sanctions are prescribed in the Act to deal with non-compliance. The office-holder has a lien on the property or proceeds of sale for expenses incurred in connection with the seizure or disposal.[34]

The section applies both to items actually belonging to the company and also to those that are the subject matter of a dispute as to ownership.[35] The court can, in proceedings under this section, decide questions of title.[36] The court will only make an order under this section if the items involved are being sought in order to enable the office holder to carry out his functions as such. In the case of an administrative receiver, this will be in order to protect and realise the mortgaged property for the benefit of the company and its creditors and will not be in order to assist the debenture holder in litigation against third parties.[37] This will generally mean that the items involved will have to fall within the property charged,[38] are needed to support the debenture-holder's title or are otherwise required by the administrative receiver to carry out his duties and functions.   **8–012**

Where an office-holder has reasonable grounds for believing that he is entitled to seize or dispose of any property and does so, he has special statutory protection under s.234(4) of the Insolvency Act 1986. If it turns out that the property seized or disposed of did not belong to the company, the office-holder will not be liable to any person in respect of any loss or damage resulting from the seizure or disposal except in so far as it is caused by his negligence. This applies whether or not the office-holder has acted following a court order under s.234(2). The protection afforded by these provisions is limited to tangible property, although the office-holder may have recourse to other defences in any action for wrongful interference with contractual relations.[39]   **8–013**

Applications under s.234 should be made in the name of the office-holder, rather than the company.[40] Applications should normally be made on notice, and an application without notice can only be justified if two conditions are met: **8–014**

---

[34] Insolvency Act 1986, s.234(4)(b).

[35] See *Re London Iron & Steel Co Ltd* [1990] B.C.C. 159, where the court held that it had power to deal with an application under s.234 for an order that property be handed over to an administrative receiver even though there was a dispute as to its ownership which could have been the subject of separate legal proceedings. It now appears that the courts are readily prepared to address questions of disputed ownership on an application under s.234: see *Euro Commercial Leasing Ltd v Cartwright & Lewis* [1995] B.C.C. 830 (a solicitors' lien); *Re Cosslett (Contractors) Ltd* [1998] Ch. 495 (CA) (plant on a construction site). The court has no power to determine ownership where the question of ownership is to be resolved by a foreign court: *Re Leyland DAF Ltd* [1994] B.C.C. 166.

[36] *Re London Iron & Steel Co Ltd* [1990] B.C.C. 159.

[37] *Sutton v GE Capital Commercial Finance Limited* [2004] 2 B.C.L.C. 662 (CA).

[38] See *Re First Express Ltd* [1991] B.C.C. 782.

[39] See *Welsh Development Agency v Export Finance Co Ltd* [1992] B.C.C. 270 (CA), 287–288 where the court rejected the receivers' defence to an action for wrongful interference on the basis that s.234(3) and (4) were inapplicable to choses in action but held that the receivers' conduct as agents of the company was immune on the basis of the rule in *Said v Butt* [1920] 3 K.B. 497. The Court of Appeal concluded that the references to seizure meant that s.234(3) and (4) only applied to tangibles.

[40] *Smith (Administrator of Cosslett (Contractors) Ltd) v Bridgend CBC* [2002] 1 A.C. 336 (HL). In the case of documents, since they will be the property of the company, it will be for the office-holder to determine whether to disclose them to the relevant authorities: see *Walker Morris v Khalastchi* [2001] 1 B.C.L.C. 1.

    (i)   notice to the respondent would be likely to cause injustice to the applicant as a result of delay or because of action that would be taken before the hearing; and

    (ii) any damage that the respondent might suffer can be compensated by a cross-undertaking or the risk of loss to the respondent which cannot be compensated is clearly outweighed by the risk of injustice to the applicant.[41]

Section 234 only allows an office-holder to gain possession of an item in specie. It does not form the statutory basis for an action in conversion by the office-holder.[42]

5.   CO-OPERATION FROM DIRECTORS, ETC.

8–015   Under s.235(2) of the Insolvency Act 1986, an office-holder may require, without a court order, that directors and certain others attend upon him and/or give him such information about the company as he may reasonably require. The persons subject to the requirements of this provision include not only all present and past officers of the company, but also certain promoters, and certain persons "in the employment of" the company.[43] The term "employment" is given an expanded definition by s.235(3)(c), so as to include "employment under a contract for services". This will accordingly include professional advisers to the company.

8–016   Section 235 does not provide any guidance as to how a court should determine the reasonableness of any requirement by the office-holder. By analogy with cases decided under s.236 (see Pt 6 of this Chapter, below), it is suggested that what may reasonably be required must involve a consideration of what is required for the efficient conduct of the insolvency process in question. The test is what is "reasonably required" not what is "necessary", and the onus of showing that a requirement is a reasonable one will be on the office-holder. In most cases the views of the office-holder will be entitled to a good deal of weight.[44] The interviewee can only be compelled to answer questions relating to the affairs of the company of which they were an office-holder or employee; however this includes questions which may shed light on the affairs of another company of which they were not an officer or employee.[45]

---

[41] See *Re First Express Ltd* [1991] B.C.C. 782, 785E.

[42] *Re Cosslett (Contractors) Ltd* [1998] Ch. 495 (CA), [24].

[43] Insolvency Act 1986, s.235(3), (4).

[44] In the context of s.236 of the Insolvency Act 1986, see, e.g. *Sasea Finance Ltd v KPMG* [1998] B.C.C. 216, 220F and *Re Atlantic Computers Plc* [1998] B.C.C. 200, 209D, per Robert Walker J. The further proceedings in the *Sasea Finance* case at [1999] B.C.C. 103 indicate limits on the possible use of s.236 for tactical purposes in litigation (see para.8–036 below).

[45] *Re Bernard L Madoff Investment Securities LLC* [2010] B.C.C. 328. In that case, which involved allegations of complex international fraud, Lewison J. said "the trustee would not, in my judgment, be entitled to attend a meeting to ask questions about the American company. The office-holder would, of course, be entitled to ask questions about the English company which may shed light on the dealings and affairs of the American company, but s.235 is not, as I see it, a shortcut to an application by the American trustee in bankruptcy under art.21 [in Sch.1 to] the Cross-Border Insolvency Regulations 2006 (SI 2006/1030)."

Failure to heed the office-holder's request without reasonable excuse is a **8–017** criminal offence punishable by the imposition of a fine.[46] A failure to respond can also be the subject of an application to the court to compel compliance,[47] or can be a ground for an application under s.236.[48] Failure by a director of an insolvent company to co-operate with an office-holder who is attempting to exercise their powers under s.235 may be relevant on an application for a disqualification order under s.6 of the Company Directors Disqualification Act 1986.[49] An unreasonable request by an administrator may be the subject of an application to the court to exercise its supervisory jurisdiction to order the request to be withdrawn. But as an administrative receiver is not an officer of the court, there would not appear to be any obvious mechanism for the recipient of an unreasonable request under s.235 from an administrative receiver to seek an order that the request be withdrawn. A claim for a declaration that the request was unreasonable may be the only remedy. However, the office-holder's unreasonable conduct in making a request will be a defence to any application to enforce the request or to a criminal charge.[50]

A person who is subject to a request under s.235 would have no defence to **8–018** an application to enforce compliance or to criminal liability under the section if he refused to respond to questions simply because he feared that he might incriminate himself by his answers. This is because s.235 implicitly abrogates the privilege against self-incrimination.[51] Such criminal liability for non-disclosure would not itself infringe the European Convention on Human Rights,[52] but the later use of information obtained might do so.[53]

The proper functions of an office-holder in an insolvency proceeding include **8–019** an investigation into the causes of the company's failure and as to whether any criminal offences have been committed.[54] An office-holder has a duty to report to the Secretary of State on the conduct of the company's directors if the company has become insolvent.[55] Accordingly, the office-holder can make a request under s.235 aimed solely at determining the responsibility of the directors for the collapse of the company and with a view to assisting the Secretary of State to determine whether disqualification proceedings should be brought

---

[46] Insolvency Act 1986, ss.235(5) and 430 and Sch.10.

[47] See Insolvency Rules 1986, r.7.20 and *Re Wallace Smith Trust Co Ltd* [1992] B.C.C. 707.

[48] See e.g. *Miller v Bain* [2002] B.C.C. 899 and *Hunt v Renzland* [2008] B.P.I.R. 1380.

[49] *Re Brampton Manor (Leisure) Ltd* [2009] EWHC 1796 (Ch).

[50] See Insolvency Act 1986, s.235(5) where liability depends on failure to meet the office-holder's request "without reasonable excuse".

[51] *Bishopsgate Investment Ltd v Maxwell* [1993] Ch. 1 (CA).

[52] See *Al-Fayed v United Kingdom* (1994) 18 E.H.R.R. 393 (ECtHR) and *Saunders v United Kingdom* [1997] B.C.C. 872 (ECtHR) on investigations under Pt XIV of the Companies Act 1985. The *Saunders* case was followed in *Kansal v United Kingdom* (2004) 39 E.H.R.R. 31 (ECtHR).

[53] *Saunders v United Kingdom* [1997] B.C.C. 872 (ECtHR) See also the Insolvency Act 1986, s.433, as amended by the Youth Justice and Criminal Evidence Act 1999, s.59, Sch.3, para.7, the scope of which was considered in *R v Sawtell* [2001] B.P.I.R. 381 (CA).

[54] *Re Pantmaenog Timber Co Ltd* [2004] 1 A.C. 158 (HL); *R. v Brady* [2004] 1 W.L.R. 3240 (CA).

[55] Company Directors Disqualification Act 1986, s.7(3).

against the directors concerned.[56] The office-holder can also disclose information or documents obtained under s.235 to the relevant prosecuting authorities, in order that they might decide whether to bring criminal charges.[57]

8–020   The Secretary of State also has powers to compel disclosure of information acquired by an office-holder.[58] This is so even if the office-holder has given an assurance that information or documents will only be used for the office-holder's own, limited, purposes.[59] So while an office-holder may, in his discretion, give undertakings of confidentiality in respect of information obtained or to be obtained by him under s.235, he cannot be required to give such undertakings,[60] and he cannot give an assurance that information will be withheld from anyone to whom he must report the information, or anyone who can by law require the information of him.[61]

6. Examination on Oath of Directors, etc

8–021   Section 236 of the Insolvency Act 1986 confers on an office-holder "an extraordinary power to assist him in obtaining information about the company's affairs",[62] a power also described as "drastic and far-reaching".[63] This work is principally concerned with applications made by administrators or receivers, but it should not be forgotten that they might be the object of such an application.[64] Under the section, an office-holder[65] may seek an order from the court for the attendance of any officer of the company, any person known or suspected of having any property of the company or supposed to be indebted to it, or any person the court thinks capable of giving information concerning the promotion, formation, business, dealings, affairs or property of the

---

[56] *Re Pantmaenog Timber Co Ltd* [2004] 1 A.C. 158 (HL).

[57] *R. v Brady* [2004] 1 W.L.R. 3240 (CA).

[58] Company Directors Disqualification Act 1986, s.7(4).

[59] See *Re Polly Peck International Plc* [1994] B.C.C. 15. The case concerned an administrator, rather than an administrative receiver, but the reasoning is equally applicable to an administrative receiver, being based on the duties and responsibilities of office-holders in general under the Company Directors Disqualification Act 1986.

[60] *Re Barlow Clowes Gilt Managers Ltd* [1992] Ch. 208; *McIsaac, Petitioners; Joint Liquidators of First Tokyo Index Trust Ltd* [1994] B.C.C. 410 (Court of Session, Outer House).

[61] In *Re Arrows Ltd (No.4)* [1995] 2 A.C. 75 (HL), 102–103, per Lord Browne-Wilkinson.

[62] In *Re Castle New Homes Ltd* [1979] 1 W.L.R. 1075, 1080G, per Slade J., referring to s.268 of the Companies Act 1948, one of the statutory predecessors to s.236 of the Insolvency Act 1986. See also *Joint Administrators of British & Commonwealth Holdings Plc v Spicer & Oppenheim* [1993] A.C. 426 (HL), 439D, per Lord Slynn.

[63] *Re Rolls Razor Ltd (No.2)* [1970] Ch. 576, 583D, per Megarry J., addressing s.268 of the Companies Act 1948. For a summary of the development of the powers of the courts to order private examinations, see the judgment of Lord Millett NPJ in *The Joint & Several Liquidators of Akai Holdings Limited v The Grande Holdings Limited* [2006] HKCFA 113 and the judgment of Bokhary PJ in *Akai Holdings Limited v Ernst & Young* [2009] HKCFA 14.

[64] See, e.g. *Re Trading Partners Ltd* [2002] 1 B.C.L.C. 655 and *Re Delberry Ltd* [2008] B.C.C. 653.

[65] The court may, in recognising a foreign insolvency office-holder under the Cross-Border Insolvency Regulations 2006, confer upon him the powers accorded to his UK counterparts under s.236 where there exists a sufficient connection with the United Kingdom and the order would facilitate the purpose of the overseas insolvency procedure: see *Re Phoenix Kapitaldienst GmbH* [2008] B.P.I.R. 1082.

company.[66] Also under the section, such a person may be ordered to submit an affidavit to the court containing an account of his dealings with the company or to produce any books, papers or records in his possession or under his control relating to the company or to its promotion. An order for production of documents may be made even if the person in possession of the documents holds a valid lien,[67] although any order for production will be without prejudice to the lien. A person summoned under this procedure can also be examined in private on oath, either orally or by interrogatories.[68]

Section 237(3) of the Insolvency Act 1986 provides that the court may order **8–022** a person to be examined in any part of the United Kingdom where he may be for the time being, or in any place outside England and Wales. In a few cases, an examination overseas may be more convenient than requiring the proposed examinee to attend in England and Wales, with travelling and hotel expenses and the possible need for an interpreter.[69] It is not clear whether the court may, under ss.236 and 237, order someone who is abroad to be examined in the United Kingdom.[70] Where a potential respondent is abroad, a possible alternative to an application under s.236 is to request the court to issue letters

---

[66] The jurisdiction under s.236 extended, in the unusual case of *Cowlishaw v O&D Building Contractors Ltd* [2009] N.P.C. 112, to order for production of documents held by building contractors to enable the liquidator to ascertain the state of completeness of a property development. In that case the respondent was not an officer or employee of the company, nor was it in a contractual relationship with the company. Nor did the company own the documents or have any entitlement to inspect them. However the application failed in part because of the indiscriminate nature of the request for documents.

[67] *Re Aveling Barford Ltd* [1989] 1 W.L.R. 360, 364–365: according to Hoffmann J. a lien was irrelevant in an action by the administrative receiver for production as between himself and the solicitor since the lien could not affect third parties and s.236 had conferred third party status on an administrative receiver ("a solicitor's lien is simply a right to retain his clients' documents as against the client and persons representing him" per Lord Lindley M.R. in *Re Hawkes* [1898] 2 Ch. 1, 7). Although administrative receivers, unlike other office-holders, cannot rely on s.246 of the Insolvency Act 1986 to render the lien unenforceable, the availability of an order for possession effectively renders the solicitor's lien substantially worthless.

[68] Insolvency Act, s.237(4). Insolvency Rules 1986, r.9.4 set down the procedure for hearings. In particular, a full transcript must be provided and approved by the person giving evidence. cf. Insolvency Act 1986, s.133, which involves a public examination of officers or others before the court.

[69] Insolvency Rules 1986, r.12A provides that service out of jurisdiction is governed by Pt 6 of the Civil Procedure Rules. The court's jurisdiction in relation to persons residing abroad is discussed below in Chs 30 and 31. In *McIsaac, Petitioners; Joint Liquidators of First Tokyo Index Trust Ltd* [1994] B.C.C. 410 (Court of Session, Outer House) the court rejected a submission than an order under s.236 for oral examination and the production of documents could not be made against a person resident in New York. See also *Re Casterbridge Properties Ltd (No.2)* [2002] B.C.C. 453 (esp. [37] et seq., noting the criticism, at [43], of the *First Tokyo Index Trust* case), on appeal [2004] 1 W.L.R. 602 (CA), and *Miller v Bain* [2002] B.C.C. 899. In addition, it is clear that the court has jurisdiction to make an order under s.236 for the production of documents relating to an overseas company which is being wound up in England, even though the documents are held abroad by a third party. However, in the exercise of its discretion under the section, the court will be mindful of: (i) the possibility that disclosure might expose the respondent, or its officers or employees, to liability under foreign law; (ii) the need to respect the sovereignty of other jurisdictions; and (iii) whether the order is likely to be effective. See *Re Mid East Trading Ltd* [1998] 1 All E.R. 577 (CA).

[70] *Re Casterbridge Properties Ltd (No.2)* [2002] B.C.C. 453. See also the comments, obiter, of Lord Mance in the House of Lords in *Masri v Consolidated Contractors International (UK) Ltd and others (No.4)* [2010] 1 A.C. 90, [20]–[23].

rogatory, addressed to a foreign court, seeking the assistance of that court for the purposes of examining the respondent or acquiring documents.[71]

It is unclear whether a court may on a s.236 application order the disclosure by a public body of information obtained from a foreign authority pursuant to a letter of request under the Crime (International Co-operation) Act 2003, where guarantees have been given to the foreign authority that the information provided would be used for a limited purpose only. In *XYZ v Revenue and Customs Commissioners*[72] such orders were given by consent of the foreign authorities in circumstances where the HMRC was both the requesting authority and the sole creditor of the insolvent company.

8–023 Where a person summoned to appear under s.236 fails to do so without reasonable excuse or where there are reasonable grounds for believing that he is about to abscond, or has absconded, with a view to avoiding an appearance before the court, the court may issue a warrant for that person's arrest and for the seizure of any books, papers, records, money or goods in that person's possession.[73] Express provision is made in the Insolvency Rules 1986 for the tender of conduct money to a proposed examinee,[74] and it may presumably be a reasonable excuse for non-appearance that no conduct money has been tendered.

8–024 Where it appears to the court from any evidence obtained under this provision that "any person" has in his possession any property of the company or is indebted to the company, the court may order delivery up of the property or payment of the sum involved to the administrative receiver as office-holder.[75] This part of this provision appears to have been derived from s.25 of the Bankruptcy Act 1914. In practice, such summary orders are rare and should only be made against the examinee himself on the basis of a clear admission.[76] The court should not use this provision to determine title to an asset without giving a hearing to anyone making an adverse claim to that asset. To do otherwise might constitute a breach of the provisions of the European Convention on Human Rights (the right to peaceful enjoyment of possessions, subject to due process of law and the right to a fair trial), which the courts must now uphold under ss.3 and 6 of the Human Rights Act 1998.

8–025 The court's powers under s.236 of the Insolvency Act 1986 are very wide, and even bind the Crown, so that information may be obtained under the section from government officials.[77] Nevertheless, the powers are limited by other statutory obligations of confidentiality and non-disclosure. So, in *Re*

---

[71] *Re Anglo American Insurance Co Ltd* [2002] B.C.C. 715.
[72] *XYZ v Revenue and Customs Commissioners* [2010] B.P.I.R. 1297.
[73] Insolvency Act 1986, s.236(4) and (5). The court may even, in a serious case, seek to restrain a person from leaving the jurisdiction under the powers in the Senior Court Act 1981, until he has complied with his obligations: *Re Oriental Credit Ltd* [1988] Ch. 204 and *Morris v Murjani* [1996] 1 W.L.R. 848 (CA). In an appropriate case, for example, where a prospective examinee had previously failed to co-operate with the liquidators of the company concerned, the court may require security from the examinee as a condition that he be allowed to leave the country, even though he is not a British national: see *Re BCCI (No.7)* [1994] 1 B.C.L.C. 455.
[74] Insolvency Rules 1986, r.9.6(4).
[75] Insolvency Act 1986, s.237(1) and (2).
[76] See *Re A Debtor (No.26 of 1982)* (1983) 126 S.J. 783.
[77] *Soden v Burns* [1996] 1 W.L.R. 1512.

Galileo Group Ltd,[78] Lightman J. held that the court's jurisdiction to order disclosure under s.236 of the Insolvency Act 1986 was implicitly limited by s.82 of the Banking Act 1987, which requires that information received for the (regulatory) purposes of the Banking Act be kept confidential, unless the relevant consents to disclosure are obtained. He therefore held that the court could not order disclosure of documents containing information within the scope of s.82, and that while the court had jurisdiction to order disclosure of redacted copies of the documents from which the confidential information had been excised,[79] it was inappropriate to exercise that jurisdiction in the circumstances, given that: (i) making such an order might undermine the protection afforded by s.82 and thereby prejudice the free flow of information to the Bank of England, which was vital for the performance of the function which it then had as regulator of the banking system; (ii) framing and performing such an order might well be very difficult; (iii) there was a risk that failure to remove all embargoed material might constitute a criminal offence; and (iv) there was a risk that the redacted document might prove misleading.

7. THE APPROACH OF THE COURTS TO MAKING ORDERS UNDER SECTION 236

The position under s.236 was explained by Buckley J. in *Re Rolls Razor Ltd (No.1)*,[80] in a passage subsequently approved by the Court of Appeal in *Re Esal (Commodities) Ltd (In Liquidation)*,[81] and by the House of Lords in the leading case of *British & Commonwealth Holdings Plc (Joint Administrators) v Spicer & Oppenheim*[82]:   **8–026**

"The powers conferred by section [236] are powers directed to enabling the court to help a liquidator to discover the truth of the circumstances connected with the affairs of the company, information of trading, dealings, and so forth, in order that the liquidator may be able, as effectively as possible, and, I think, with as little expense as possible to complete his function as liquidator, to put the affairs of the company in order and to carry out the liquidation in all its various aspects, including, of course, the getting in of any assets of the company available in the liquidation."

In the same case the House of Lords rejected a suggestion that had arisen in earlier cases that the powers of the court under s.236 might be limited to   **8–027**

---

[78] *Re Galileo Group Ltd* [1999] Ch. 100.
[79] In this case, any redaction would have been undertaken by the recipient of information, because of its duties in relation to the information. Note also *Soden v Burns* [1996] 1 W.L.R. 1512, 1532C, per Robert Walker J., where, in the absence of such duties, any redaction was to be undertaken at the behest of the examinee in question, rather than by the recipient of the information.
[80] *Re Rolls Razor Ltd (No.1)* [1968] 3 All E.R. 698, 700.
[81] *Esal (Commodities) Ltd (In Liquidation)* (1988) 4 B.C.C. 475 (CA), 480.
[82] *British & Commonwealth Holdings Plc (Joint Administrators) v Spicer & Oppenheim* [1993] A.C. 426 (HL). See also the summary of principles by Lord Millett NPJ in *The Joint & Several Liquidators of Akai Holdings Limited v The Grande Holdings Limited* [2006] HKCFA 113, [22]–[30].

assisting the office-holder to reconstitute the state of knowledge of the company.[83]

> "The wording of the section contains no express limitation to documents which can be said to be part of a process of reconstituting the company's state of knowledge. The words are quite general ... nor do I see any support in earlier judgments which may have been cited to us relating to the predecessors of section 236 or to comparable sections for such a limitation to 'reconstituting the company's knowledge'."[84]

The Official Receiver may make an application under s.236(1) even where the Official Receiver is not the liquidator of the company, and in those circumstances the scope of s.236 is extended to include the investigatory functions of the Official Receiver, and not merely to the efficient conduct of the winding up of the company.[85]

8–028   Before making any order under s.236, the office-holder will need to prove to the satisfaction of the court that the information he seeks under the proposed order is in fact reasonably required.[86] In the usual case his views will be given great weight, and he is under no duty to make out the requirement in such detail as would be expected in, for example, an application for specific disclosure in the context of ongoing litigation.[87]

8–029   When considering the exercise of its discretion under s.236, the court may also be interested in the steps taken by the office-holder before applying to the court. Unless there are factors negativing this (for instance, cases of great urgency), an office-holder ought in most cases to seek co-operation under s.235 of the Insolvency Act 1986 where a proposed examinee comes within that section, and in other cases may be well advised to submit a questionnaire seeking written answers. Although under the old bankruptcy and winding-up provisions information was often sought first by means of a questionnaire, it is entirely a matter for the court's discretion whether the office-holder is required to submit a questionnaire before being granted an order for an affidavit or an examination on oath.[88] In practice, persons of whom misconduct is suspected, usually directors or other insiders, will often not be allowed the advance notice of inquiries that a questionnaire would give, whereas parties who have no

---

[83] See, e.g. *Re Rolls Razor Ltd (No.2)* [1970] Ch. 576, 591–592, per Megarry J. and *Cloverbay Ltd v Bank of Credit and Commerce International* [1991] Ch. 90 (CA), 102, per Browne-Wilkinson V.C.

[84] *British & Commonwealth Holdings Plc (Joint Administrators) v Spicer & Oppenheim* [1993] A.C. 426 (HL), 437B–D, per Lord Slynn.

[85] *Re Pantmaenog Timber Co Ltd* [2004] 1 A.C. 158 (HL).

[86] The test is one of "reasonable requirement", not "absolute need": see *Re Atlantic Computers Plc* [1998] B.C.C. 200 and *Joint Liquidators of Sasea Finance Ltd v KPMG* [1998] B.C.C. 216; *Re XL Communications Group Plc* [2005] EWHC 2413 (Ch). See also *The Joint & Several Liquidators of Akai Holdings Limited v The Grande Holdings Limited* [2006] HKCFA 113, [30] per Lord Millett NPJ.

[87] In relation to the matters stated in this paragraph, see *Re John T. Rhodes Ltd* (1986) 2 B.C.C. 99284, per Hoffmann J.; Insolvency Rules 1986, r.9.2(1), and *Joint Liquidators of Sasea Finance Ltd v KPMG* [1998] B.C.C. 216.

[88] *Re Norton Warburg Holdings Ltd* (1983) 1 B.C.C. 98907 and *Re Embassy Art Products* (1987) 3 B.C.C. 292.

likely motive for concealing information will often only be requested to answer a questionnaire, and may only be examined if the answers to the questionnaire prove unsatisfactory.[89]

As s.236(2) confers a general discretion on the court,[90] any question **8–030** concerning the exercise of that discretion will involve the court in a balancing exercise.[91] On the one hand, the court will wish to help the office-holder discharge his functions efficiently, expeditiously and in the interest of creditors, recognising that the office-holder is usually a stranger to the relevant events. On the other, the courts have long been aware of the potential for oppression in the use of such powers,[92] and have sought to limit that potential through their approach to the exercise of discretion under the section.

In each case, the court will take into account several factors when exercising **8–031** its discretion in relation to what is an extraordinary power. For example, the case for making an order against an officer of the company will usually be stronger than against a third party because of the fiduciary duties and the statutory duty under s.235(2)(a) owed by the former.[93] Similarly, the court will take into account the width of the order sought and the amount of work involved in complying with the order.[94] The court will not generally require the applicant to specify the documents which are required to be produced with great precision, because the applicant is ordinarily a stranger to the company and to do so would reduce the utility of the section. But, the width of description of the documents to be produced will be treated as a matter going to the discretion of the court to make the order.[95]

---

[89] See *Re Norton Warburg Holdings Ltd* (1983) 1 B.C.C. 98907 (detailed written questions were required since the examinees had indicated that they would provide all reasonable assistance) and *Re Embassy Art Products* (1987) 3 B.C.C. 292 (where no prior notice of questioning was required). cf. *Re Rolls Razor (No.2)* [1970] Ch. 576 (no need for prior questioning where suspicious circumstances existed) and *House of Spring Gardens Ltd v Waite (No.1)* [1985] F.S.R. 173 (CA) (cross-examination in proceedings for a freezing injunction as to assets without prior notification of area of questioning).

[90] *British & Commonwealth Holdings Plc v Spicer and Oppenheim* [1993] A.C. 426 (HL), 437A–440A, per Lord Slynn. See also Lord Woolf's judgment in the Court of Appeal in the same case [1992] Ch. 342 (CA), 392–393.

[91] The need for a balancing exercise is repeated in numerous cases: see, e.g. *Cloverbay Ltd v Bank of Credit and Commerce International* [1991] Ch. 90 (CA); *British & Commonwealth Holdings Plc v Spicer and Oppenheim* [1993] A.C. 426 (HL); *Re BCCI (No.7)* [1994] 1 B.C.L.C. 455; *Re Bishopsgate Investment Management Ltd (No.2)* [1994] B.C.C. 732; *Re Maxwell Communications Corp Plc* [1994] B.C.C. 741; *Re BCCI (No.12)* [1997] B.C.C. 561; *Re Atlantic Computers Plc* [1998] B.C.C. 200; *Joint Liquidators of Sasea Finance Ltd v KPMG* [1998] B.C.C. 216.

[92] Such powers date back to s.115 of the Companies Act 1862: see, e.g. *Re North Australia Territory Co* (1890) 45 Ch. D. 87 (CA), 93, per Bowen L.J.; and *Re Castle New Homes Ltd* [1979] 1 W.L.R. 1075, 1089G, per Slade J.

[93] See *Re Cloverbay Ltd (No.2)* [1991] Ch. 90 (CA), 102G and 108D; *Re RBG Resources Plc* [2003] 1 W.L.R. 586 (CA), [35] and *Re Westmead Consultants Ltd* [2002] 1 B.C.L.C. 384.

[94] See *British & Commonwealth Holdings Plc v Spicer and Oppenheim* [1993] A.C. 426 (HL), 440H–441A, per Lord Slynn: whilst recognising that the order placed an extensive and inconvenient burden on the auditors and may lay them open to further claims, he stated that these were only factors in the balancing exercise. The auditors' argument that such an order would result in a flood of similar applications was dismissed. In any event, it was not disputed that the examinee was entitled to an order for the costs of compliance.

[95] *The Joint & Several Liquidators of Akai Holdings Limited v The Grande Holdings Limited* [2006] HKCFA 113, [35]–[45], referring to *Re Cloverbay* (1989) 5 B.C.C. 732 and *Re Mid East Trading* [1998] 1 All E.R. 577 (CA).

8–032   Although in many cases the reasonable requirements of the office-holder will not extend beyond that contained in the company's records and the knowledge of its officers, in some cases the interest of creditors will be substantial (particularly in the case of a large-scale corporate failure) and the reasonable requirements of the office-holder will be treated as extending to information which the company itself may never have possessed.[96] The production of such documents will be ordered where this will enable the office-holder to perform his functions properly.[97] It is, however, not appropriate for an office-holder to use s.236 for the purposes of obtaining documentation from a creditor for the purposes of adjudicating upon his proof of debt.[98]

8.   SECTION 236 AND PENDING LITIGATION

8–033   One particularly important aspect of the balancing exercise the court undertakes when faced with an application under s.236 is ensuring that the section "is not to be used for giving a litigant (just because he is an office-holder) special advantages in ordinary litigation".[99] Such an unfair advantage is regarded as one of the main forms of oppression to which an order under s. 236 may give rise.[100] The court will have regard both to the reasonable requirements of the office-holder to carry out his task, and to the need to avoid making an order which is unnecessary, unreasonable or oppressive to the person who is the subject of the order, because it would give the office-holder an unfair advantage over him in litigation.

8–034   Under the pre-1986 winding-up provisions, these restrictions usually meant that, where a liquidator had either begun or made a firm decision to begin proceedings against the proposed examinee, it would be rare for him to obtain an order for examination.[101] This approach was known as the "Rubicon Test": "a rule of thumb under which relief under section 236 would be withheld if office-holders had already commenced proceedings against, or definitely decided (mentally crossed the Rubicon) to proceed against the proposed witness [i.e. examinee]".[102] An order might have been granted, however, if the examination avoided questions connected with the proceedings.[103]

8–035   Subsequently, in proceedings brought under the current legislation, the Court of Appeal has recognised that a firm decision by an office-holder to bring an action against the person to be examined is not a bar to the grant of an

---

[96] See *Re Brook Martin & Co (Nominees) Ltd* [1993] B.C.L.C. 328.

[97] See per Woolf L.J. in the Court of Appeal in *British & Commonwealth Holdings Plc v Spicer and Oppenheim* [1992] Ch. 342 (CA), 390: "the reason for the existence of the powers was to assist office holders to achieve the relevant administrative purposes identified in s.8(3) of the Act".

[98] *Bellmex International Ltd v British American Tobacco* [2001] B.C.C. 253.

[99] *Re Atlantic Computers Plc* [1998] B.C.C. 200, 208F–209A, per Robert Walker J., citing *Re North Australian Territory Co* (1890) 45 Ch. D. 87 (CA); *Re Bletchley Boat Co Ltd* [1974] 1 W.L.R. 630; *Re Castle New Homes Ltd* [1979] 1 W.L.R. 1075 and *Re Esal (Commodities) Ltd (No.2)* [1990] B.C.C. 708. See also *Cloverbay Ltd v BCCI* [1991] Ch. 90 (CA), 102E, per Browne-Wilkinson V.C.

[100] *Re BCCI (No.12)* [1997] 1 B.C.L.C. 526.

[101] *Re Castle New Homes Ltd* [1979] 1 W.L.R. 1075, per Slade J.

[102] *Re Atlantic Computers Plc* [1998] B.C.C. 200, 208E, per Robert Walker J.

[103] *Re Franks, Ex p. Gittins* [1892] 1 Q.B. 646, per Vaughan Williams J.

order, although it may be an important factor to take into account on the question of discretion.[104] The court will primarily be concerned to understand the purpose for which the application is made. Accordingly, an application which is shown to be for the primary purpose of enabling the office-holder to understand the affairs of the company and to recover its assets may be granted, even though the information obtained may incidentally bear on, or expand the scope of, existing civil proceedings by the company against its ex-directors.[105] In *Re RBG Resources Plc*, Peter Gibson L.J. summarised the position as follows[106]:

> "It is oppressive to require a defendant accused of serious wrongdoing to provide what amount to pre-trial depositions and to prove the case against himself on oath. But that oppression may be outweighed by the legitimate requirements of the liquidator."[107]

Nevertheless the old "Rubicon Test" had at least a "germ of truth" in it,[108] and the courts remain wary of making orders under s.236 if the office-holder of the company in question might thereby gain an unfair advantage in current or imminent litigation.[109]

The principles can be illustrated by reference to the *Sasea Finance* case. In **8–036** *Joint Liquidators of Sasea Finance Ltd v KPMG*,[110] the liquidators made an application under s.236 against the former auditors of the company, seeking disclosure of documents. By the time of their application, the liquidators had issued a "protective writ" against the auditors, to stop limitation periods running, alleging professional negligence. Robert Walker J. (as he then was) held that, although there was some prejudice to KPMG in granting the liquidators' application, because it might give information to the liquidators earlier than otherwise, the balance weighed in favour of making the order sought, as there was considerable public interest in ascertaining the truth about a very

---

[104] *Cloverbay v BCCI* [1991] Ch. 90 (CA); *Re John T Rhodes Ltd* [1987] B.C.L.C. 77. Browne-Wilkinson V.C. in *Cloverbay* specifically noted that the subjective nature of the office-holder's precise intentions was an inappropriate basis for determining whether an order should be available. The court consequently recommended a more "case-by-case", empirical approach to making orders under s.236.

[105] *Re RBG Resources Plc* [2003] 1 W.L.R. 586 (CA).

[106] *Re RBG Resources Plc* [2003] 1 W.L.R. 586 (CA), [39]. See also *Daltel Europe Ltd (in liquidation) v Makki (No.1)* [2005] 1 B.C.L.C. 594.

[107] See also *Daltel Europe Ltd (in liquidation) v Makki (No.1)* [2005] 1 B.C.L.C. 594, where an order was made notwithstanding pending proceedings for fraud and dishonesty.

[108] *Re Bishopsgate Investment Management (No.2)* [1994] B.C.C. 732, 739E, per Hoffmann J.; *Re BCCI (No.12)* [1997] B.C.C. 561, 571–572, per Robert Walker J.; *Re Atlantic Computers Plc* [1998] B.C.C. 200, 208F, per Robert Walker J.

[109] *Re Atlantic Computers Plc* [1998] B.C.C. 200, 208F–209A, per Robert Walker J., citing *Re North Australian Territory Co* (1890) 45 Ch. D. 87 (CA); *Re Bletchley Boat Co Ltd* [1974] 1 W.L.R. 630; *Re Castle New Homes Ltd* [1979] 1 W.L.R. 1075 and *Re Esal (Commodities) Ltd (No.2)* [1990] B.C.C. 708. See also *Cloverbay Ltd v BCCI* [1991] Ch. 90 (CA), 102E, per Browne-Wilkinson V.C. In *RBG Resources Plc* [2003] 1 W.L.R. 586 (CA), [56], Mance L.J. observed that for liquidators to seek an examination under s.236 to gain advantage or to ascertain whether or not they have a claim in current civil litigation "seems bound to offend against elementary fairness.

[110] *Joint Liquidators of Sasea Finance Ltd v KPMG* [1998] B.C.C. 216.

substantial corporate collapse. Of significance to the court in making its decision were the facts that the litigation was still at a very early stage, and that only negligence, and not fraud or dishonesty, had been alleged against KPMG. The fact that the examination could render the evidence of the examinee open to scrutiny at an earlier point in time than would be the case in normal litigation was a factor, but not an overriding factor, to be taken into account in determining whether or not the order would be oppressive.

When, however, a further application was made later in the same proceedings,[111] by which the office-holders sought an order that the respondents answer interrogatories, Scott V.C. refused the application. He deplored the office-holders' tactic of issuing a protective writ and then seeking to use s.236. He also indicated that trying to use s.236 to extract explanations or justifications for known facts in the context of pending litigation, rather than to discover facts, was an unacceptable tactic, and any such application would be refused. Hence if the office-holder has the benefit of extensive disclosure of documents in connection with an action already commenced, the court may decline to grant an order under s.236.

8–037   The mere fact that proceedings had already been successfully taken against a person involved with the company will not of itself make an examination oppressive, vexatious or unfair. Nor does the principle against being sued twice about the same matter apply in these circumstances since the grant of an order does not necessarily mean that the office-holder will be commencing further proceedings.[112]

8–038   Documents (including the transcripts of the examinations) obtained by the use of s.236 in order to assist an office-holder to decide whether or not to commence proceedings (or to continue proceedings in respect of which a protective writ had been issued) may be covered by legal professional privilege in the hands of the office-holders if the sole or dominant purpose of conducting such examinations was to obtain legal advice as to the merits of the proposed proceedings. If so, such documents will not be required to be disclosed to the other parties to such proceedings.[113]

9.   OTHER FORMS OF PROTECTION FROM OPPRESSION UNDER SECTION 236

8–039   As well as giving a proposed examinee protection from oppression by carefully considering whether an order under the section should be made at all, a court may also choose the particular type of order it makes with a view to minimising any prejudice. The courts regard an order for oral examination as the most potentially oppressive order they can make under s.236. An order to swear an affidavit deposing to the affairs of the company in question is less likely to be oppressive,[114] and least likely to be oppressive is an order

---

[111] *Re Sasea Finance Ltd (in liquidation)* [1999] B.C.C. 103.
[112] *Re John T Rhodes Ltd* [1987] B.C.L.C. 77.
[113] *Akai Holdings Limited v Ernst & Young* [2009] HKCFA 14.
[114] *Soden v Burns* [1996] 1 W.L.R. 1512, 1531D–E, per Robert Walker J.

for the production of documents relating to the dealings or affairs of the company.[115] Consequently, a court may be more willing to make an order for the production of documents than for oral examination.[116] Furthermore, the court has jurisdiction to order disclosure of redacted documents, where ordering disclosure of the unedited document would be unlawful or undesirable.[117] The court may also direct the staged disclosure of documents, where the bulk of the documents to be disclosed is very great, in order to minimise the risk of oppression and prejudice by disruption, stress or expense. When considering such factors, the court will have regard to the respondent's resources, as well as the requirements of the office-holder.[118]

Further, where the court is considering an application under s.236 for an **8–040** order directing disclosure of evidence previously given by some third party to the person who is the subject of the proposed order, either the court can refuse to make the order without first hearing objections from the third party, or it can impose a condition that the third party be notified of the order and given the opportunity to object to disclosure within a specified time.

So, in *Morris v Director of the Serious Fraud Office*,[119] Nicholls V.C. indi- **8–041** cated that, save in exceptional cases, an office-holder was not entitled to use s.236 to obtain documents from the Serious Fraud Office, which the SFO had obtained from a third party, without giving the third party (in that case, a firm of accountants) an opportunity to object to the production of those documents on the basis that such production would be oppressive.

In *Soden v Burns*,[120] inspectors had been appointed by the Department of **8–042** Trade and Industry under s.432 of the Companies Act 1985 to investigate the collapse of Atlantic Computers Plc, and they had received evidence from third parties. The administrators of Atlantic applied under s.236 for disclosure of the transcripts of that evidence, which they admitted they might use in pending civil litigation. The court ordered disclosure of the transcripts, but not of documents mentioned in them, on condition that each witness who had given evidence was notified of such disclosure, and was given the opportunity to apply to set aside the order in so far as it affected him. The court also considered what might be done about citations in a transcript, which were attributed or attributable to some other person than the person giving evidence. If the citations were important, the person cited should be asked for his views about disclosure. If the citations were less important, they might be obliterated, or certified unimportant by counsel for the DTI Inspectors.

---

[115] *Cloverbay Ltd v BCCI* [1991] Ch. 90 (CA), 103C, per Browne-Wilkinson V.C.; *Re British & Commonwealth Holdings Plc* [1992] B.C.C. 165 (CA), 185, per Ralph Gibson L.J. See also *The Joint & Several Liquidators of Akai Holdings Limited v The Grande Holdings Limited* [2006] HKCFA 113, [30].

[116] See *Re JN Taylor Finance Pty Ltd* [1999] B.C.C. 197.

[117] *Re Galileo Group Ltd* [1999] Ch. 100.

[118] *Re BCCI (No.12)* [1997] B.C.C. 561.

[119] *Morris v Director of the Serious Fraud Office* [1993] Ch. 372.

[120] *Soden v Burns* [1996] 1 W.L.R. 1512.

10.   THE PARTICULAR POSITION OF ADMINISTRATIVE RECEIVERS
AND ADMINISTRATORS

8–043   The present s.236 of the Insolvency Act 1986 is largely based upon similar powers formerly only applying in the case of bankruptcy[121] and winding up.[122] In argument on the exercise of the court's discretion, reference is frequently made to authorities dealing with those earlier provisions. It is questionable whether applications by administrative receivers and administrators under s.236 should always be treated in exactly the same way as similar applications in relation to a company by its liquidators. This is because although an administrative receiver is an office-holder under the insolvency legislation, with all that implies, the fact remains that an administrative receiver acts principally for the benefit of the debenture-holder who appointed him. His position is to be contrasted with the role of a liquidator who acts for the general body of unsecured creditors, and with the role of an administrator under the revised regime following the Enterprise Act 2002, who may be appointed by the holder of a qualifying floating charge but is under a statutory duty to act for the benefit of all the creditors of the company.[123]

8–044   In winding-up cases under the statutory forerunners of s.236, a party other than a liquidator who sought an examination of this kind had to show that it would be for the general benefit of the winding-up, rather than for the personal advantage of the applicant.[124] Equally, in the old bankruptcy cases, the applicant was said to be required to show some probable benefit to the creditors.[125] An administrative receiver (or even an administrator) may well wish to use s.236 for the particular benefit of his appointor, for example by using the section to obtain information which is then to be disclosed to his appointor. This issue arises frequently, and is often compounded by the fact that (at least in the early days of the receivership) the same firm of solicitors will often act for both the administrative receiver or administrator and the debenture-holder who appointed him.[126]

8–045   Before the concept of the administrative receiver was created, and the powers under s.236 were conferred on him as an office-holder, it was said that

---

[121] Bankruptcy Act 1914, s.25.

[122] Companies Act 1985, s.561.

[123] See para.3 of Sch.B1 to the 1986 Act (as amended).

[124] *Re Imperial Continental Water Corp* (1886) 33 Ch. D. 314 (CA) and *Re Embassy Art Products Ltd* (1987) 3 B.C.C. 292.

[125] *Ex p. Nicholson, Re Willson* (1880) 14 Ch. D. 243 (CA).

[126] Even if the debenture-holder is content that it should not receive confidential information, the examinee may not be happy that an assurance to this effect from the solicitor is workable in practice. Moreover, if information disclosed in the examination is obtained by the debenture-holder from another source, it may be difficult for the solicitor to disprove the suspicions that will inevitably arise. It is not a satisfactory solution to try to erect a "Chinese wall" by designating one partner in a firm to deal with the s.236 application by the administrative receiver, and designating another partner to advise the debenture-holder: see *Re A Firm of Solicitors* [1992] Q.B. 959 (CA); *Re Solicitors* [1997] Ch. 1; and *Bolkiah v KPMG* [1999] 2 A.C. 222 (HL). Similar concerns and issues may arise in practice where administrators are appointed by the debenture-holder under a qualifying floating charge notwithstanding that the administrator so appointed is under a statutory duty to use his powers in the interests of the creditors of the company as a whole.

a debenture-holder was entitled, as against the receiver appointed by him, to be put in possession of all information concerning the receivership which was available to the receiver.[127] It is highly unlikely that this statement would be regarded as applicable to information obtained by an administrative receiver (and still less by an administrator) as an office-holder using his powers under s.235 or 236.

Instead, the overriding principle is that disclosure of information obtained **8–046** under s.235 or 236 by an administrative receiver or an administrator to a debenture-holder will only be permissible where such disclosure will assist the beneficial conduct of the receivership or administration (as the case may be).[128]

A particularly glaring example of the improper disclosure of documents **8–047** obtained by receivers under s.235 or 236 occurred in *Sutton v GE Capital Commercial Finance Ltd*.[129] The administrative receivers of a company had obtained documents from the company's ex-solicitors on the ostensible grounds that they required them for the purposes of their investigations into the affairs of the company. On receipt, the receivers immediately handed the documents over to a solicitor acting for their appointor, which was in litigation with the principal backer of the company to enforce a personal guarantee which the backer had given for the company's debts.[130] The receivers did not even retain copies of the documents and the evidence showed that they had given no consideration to whether it was appropriate that they should disclose information obtained under ss.235 and 236 to their appointor. The Court of Appeal held that such disclosure, which did not confer any benefit on the receivership, had been improper,[131] and that the company's confidence in, and any legal privilege attaching to, the documents had not been waived.

Although this was not the case in *Sutton*, in other situations, an administra- **8–048** tive receiver or administrator might claim that the receivership or administration would be assisted by his disclosing such information to the debenture-holder, either for the purposes of securing additional funding for the conduct of litigation by the company against the directors of the company or its professional advisers, or in order to facilitate the making of a direct claim by the debenture-holder against such persons,[132] in the hope that such a claim might reduce the claim of the debenture-holder against the company, with a possible knock-on effect for the benefit of unsecured creditors. Such issues have been

---

[127] See per Fox L.J. in *Gomba Holdings UK Ltd v Minories Finance Ltd (No.1)* [1988] 1 W.L.R. 1231, 1233H.

[128] See [2004] 2 B.C.L.C. 662 (CA), per Chadwick L.J., referring to the dictum of Lord Millett in *Re Pantmaenog Timber Co Ltd (In Liquidation)* [2004] 1 A.C. 158 (HL), [64]. See also, by analogy to liquidations, per Millett J. in *Re Barlow Clowes Gilt Managers* [1992] Ch. 208, 217G and per Dillon L.J. in *Re Headington Investments Ltd* [1993] Ch. 452 (CA), 494G–495B.

[129] *Sutton v GE Capital Commercial Finance Ltd* [2004] 2 B.C.L.C. 662 (CA).

[130] The solicitor for the appointor was a partner in the same firm that acted for the receivers.

[131] For the duties of receivers in relation to the exercise of their powers for the purposes of the receivership, see Ch.13.

[132] The position often arises that the lender believes that it may have its own claims against the directors of the company in fraud or misrepresentation arising out of the statements made to obtain the loan to the company. Or the administrative receiver may obtain information which suggests that, if the lender knew of these facts, it could bring such a claim.

raised in two decisions, one in England and one in Scotland, with differing results.

8–049   Chronologically, the first case is the decision of Harman J. in *Re A Company (No.005374 of 1993)*.[133] In that case, administrative receivers sought leave to disclose to their appointor bank information obtained under s.236 which appeared to show that a director of the company had misappropriated a VAT refund in breach of his duties to the company. Harman J. held that he had a discretion to grant leave on two grounds: first, if the disclosure was "for the purposes of the office which the office-holders hold" or secondly, if disclosure is "otherwise justified by the balance of considerations of how justice is properly to be attained". He permitted disclosure, but it is not clear on which ground. Harman J. held that the claims that the bank might bring were "closely analogous to the claims by the company and might lead to the company being relieved of liability" and that "there appear to be dealings here of such a nature that, in my view, justice can only properly be achieved if the information is made available to the bank which lent the money".

8–050   Harman J. clearly based his reasoning on the earlier decision of Millett J. in *Re Esal (Commodities) Ltd (No.2)*,[134] that being the only case referred to in his judgment. In *Esal*, the company concerned was in liquidation, and a member of the committee of inspection had applied for access to information gathered by the company's liquidator under s.236. The applicant wished to obtain the documents for use in a fraudulent trading action which he had already brought against the company's bank. Millett J. held that, save in exceptional circumstances, access to the information sought should be allowed by the court only if the use proposed to be made is within the purpose of the statutory procedure, that is to say, that the use proposed to be made of the material is to assist the beneficial winding-up of the company.[135] In the circumstances, therefore, disclosure could not be said to be for the purposes of the beneficial winding-up of the company. In spite of this, Millett J. held that this was an exceptional case which justified the grant of leave. He gave as his reasons the fact that the third party's claim was "closely related to the liquidation"; that the third party's allegations, if true, disclosed a major banking scandal that ought not to be hushed up; that the material was already to some extent in the public domain and would increasingly come into the public domain in the course of the litigation; and that the third party's counsel said that he could plead his case without the documents but in such a way that he could get them on discovery.

8–051   It is suggested that Harman J.'s reasons do not stand close scrutiny. It is far from clear what the bank's claim against the director would be, and even more difficult to see how advancement of any such claim could assist the beneficial

---

[133] *Re A Company (No.005374 of 1993)* [1993] B.C.C. 734.

[134] *Re Esal (Commodities) Ltd (No.2)* [1990] B.C.C. 708.

[135] Note that this statement of the reasons for disclosure of information would now be regarded as too narrow: see *Re Arrows Ltd (No.5)* [1995] 2 A.C. 75 (HL), 102E–G, per Lord Browne-Wilkinson, and *Re Pantmaenog Timber Co Ltd* [2004] 1 A.C. 158 (HL), per Lord Millett, because an office-holder can lawfully make disclosure to public authorities to whom he is obliged or permitted to give information concerning the collapse of the company and the conduct of its directors.

realisation of the bank's security. Further, Millett J. did not hold that there was an overriding discretion to order disclosure when the judge's view of the interests of justice requires it. Millett J. had commented that "the proper administration of justice would be better served by the grant of leave than by its refusal", but only in the context of permitting advance disclosure of documents which would in any event come into the third party's hands on discovery. He did this as a practical matter to prevent repeated applications to amend and arguments as to whether what was pleaded had come from the documents (which had already been seen by the third party in his capacity as a member of the committee of inspection).

In *Sutton v GE Capital Commercial Finance Ltd*,[136] Chadwick L.J. referred   **8–052**
to Harman J.'s decision in support of the proposition that disclosure could be made or authorised by the court where that would further the purposes of the receivership or otherwise be in the interests of the company in receivership. He did not indicate that there was any wider power to permit disclosure in the interests of justice.

A different approach to that of Harman J. was taken by Lord Cameron of   **8–053**
Lochbroom in a Scottish case arising out of the Maxwell saga, *Re First Tokyo Index Trust Ltd*.[137] In that case, the liquidators of a company applied for leave to disclose documents obtained under s.236 to a bank. Rather unusually, the company had no creditors of any significance. Instead the bank had become the sole shareholder of the company as a consequence of enforcing a charge over the shares from the company's parent to secure a loan from the bank on which the parent had defaulted. The bank had then appointed the liquidators. In this sense the case had close parallels with the situation which arises in receiverships in which the party principally interested in the outcome of the insolvency was the bank which appointed the office-holder. Over a period of a year or more, the bank had spent very substantial sums of money funding an inquiry by the liquidators of the company into the circumstances surrounding the disposal of the assets of the company. Apparently it had been intended that the company's assets should have been pledged to secure the loan from the bank, but the assets were in fact sold elsewhere and the proceeds used to support other Maxwell companies.

The liquidators made it clear to the court that the company intended to   **8–054**
commence proceedings against certain of the persons who had given the information under s.236 and who had been the custodians of the company's assets. The bank also indicated that it was considering commencing its own proceedings against the same persons, but on different and distinct grounds from those of the company, such as misrepresentation. The liquidators, supported by the bank, sought orders permitting wholesale disclosure of all of the information obtained to the bank on two grounds:

    (a) that in the particular circumstances where the bank was the only party having a substantial interest in the liquidation of the company,

---

[136] *Sutton v GE Capital Commercial Finance Ltd* [2004] 2 B.C.L.C. 662 (CA).
[137] *Re First Tokyo Index Trust Ltd* [1996] B.P.I.R. 406 (Court of Session, Outer House).

the "purposes of the liquidation" extended to attempting to obtain redress for the bank;

(b) that as the bank would be funding the litigation by the company, disclosure was necessary to demonstrate to the bank that the proceedings would be likely to be successful and to keep it informed of progress.

8–055   Lord Cameron rejected these arguments. He held that the crucial point in the case which distinguished it from the *Esal* case was that the claim of the bank would proceed on separate and distinct grounds to the claim of the company, and there was in any event no such claim yet pleaded by the bank. In contrast, in *Esal* the information had been obtained to found a fraudulent trading claim by the liquidators, which was precisely the same claim which the third party had also brought and had been able to formulate. Lord Cameron applied the dictum of Dillon L.J. in the case of *Re Headington Investments Ltd*[138]:

> "Cases where persons other than prosecution or regulatory authorities seek disclosure or inspection of transcripts may raise a variety of different considerations. In some cases, disclosure will clearly be justified because, to adopt the words of Millett J. in *Re Barlow Clowes Gilt Managers Ltd*, 'the use proposed to be made of the material is to assist the beneficial winding up of the company;' . . .
>
> But the mere fact that the transcript is wanted for use in proceedings, whether civil or criminal, is not enough. The process of private examination does not leave the Court with a pool of information to be made available to any third party who may want to go fishing to see what he can find that might be helpful in civil or criminal proceedings, e.g. as material for cross-examination if a witness gives evidence in such proceedings which might be thought inconsistent with what he had said on examination under section 236 of the Act of 1986, or as material to anticipate discovery."

8–056   On the facts, Lord Cameron was also not impressed by the argument that the bank needed to have access in order to determine whether to continue funding the litigation by the company. The bank had already spent considerable sums and had undertaken to support the commencement of proceedings. Given that the bank presumably had confidence in the solicitors and counsel employed by the liquidators, at that stage the bank did not need access to further information. In other cases, however, where an appointing bank is not already committed to providing support for litigation in the receivership or administration, it is suggested that the court might be prepared to permit limited disclosure, subject to suitable undertakings being given to ensure confidentiality was preserved, in order to enable the office-holder to persuade the appointor to provide such funding.

---

[138] *Re Headington Investments Ltd* [1993] Ch. 452 (CA), 494G–495B: see also per Megarry J. in *Re Spiraflite Ltd* [1979] 1 W.L.R. 1096, 1100.

In the event that a receiver or administrator forms the view that it would be **8–057** in the interests of the receivership or administration (as the case may be) to make disclosure of confidential or even privileged information obtained under s.235 or 236 to a debenture-holder, he ought to apply for permission from the Companies Court on notice to the person from whom the information was obtained. That person could then appear to assert its confidentiality or privilege and put forward argument as to why the disclosure should not be permitted.[139]

Conversely, where the office holder in the exercise of his discretion has decided not to seek documents or information pursuant to s.236, a disgruntled creditor cannot use Civil Procedure Rule 31.17, which permits orders for disclosure against third parties to proceedings, as a back door to seek documents which the office-holder did not obtain under s.236.[140]

11. SELF-INCRIMINATING INFORMATION

The importance attached to ensuring that the office-holder can perform his **8–058** functions in an effective and expeditious manner has meant that persons subject to duties under s.235, whether obliged to provide information under that section or under s.236, cannot, as a matter of English domestic law, invoke the privilege against self-incrimination.[141] The courts have recognised that the task of the office-holder would be incapable of proper performance if the examinee could invoke such a privilege.

The abrogation of the privilege against self-incrimination in inquisitorial **8–059** proceedings, such as those under s.236, is compatible with the European Convention on Human Rights. Article 6 of the Convention provides in part that:

"In the determination of his civil rights and obligations or of any criminal charge against him, everyone is entitled to a fair and public hearing within a reasonable time by an independent and impartial tribunal established by law."

Article 6 does not appear to apply to an investigation under s.236, since in essence it is not a determination of civil or criminal rights.[142] This is so notwith-

---

[139] See *Sutton v GE Capital Commercial Finance Ltd* [2004] 2 B.C.L.C. 662 (CA). cf. *Re PNC Telecom Ltd* [2004] B.P.I.R. 314, where Evans-Lombe J. refused to give administrators directions about how they might use information which had come into their hands independently of statutory processes.

[140] *Rubin v Coote* [2011] B.P.I.R. 536.

[141] See *Re Arrows Ltd (No.4)* [1995] 2 A.C. 75 (HL); *Bishopsgate Investment Management Ltd v Maxwell* [1993] Ch. 1 (CA). In the latter case, Stuart-Smith L.J. at 46 noted that Insolvency Rules 1986, r.9.4(7) permits written records taken under s.236 to be used as evidence against a respondent of any statement made by him in the course of the examination: cf. *Re Keypak Homecare Ltd (No.2)* [1990] B.C.C. 117, which related to the position under the old winding-up provisions. Note also *Re Arrows Ltd (No.2)* [1992] B.C.C. 446; *Re A E Farr Ltd* [1992] B.C.C. 150 and *Re Jeffrey Levitt* [1992] Ch. 457.

[142] Other articles of the European Convention on Human Rights will affect the conduct of examinations under s.236 of the Insolvency Act 1986.

standing that there is in s.237(1) a summary but separate power to order delivery up of the company's property on the basis of evidence obtained under s.236.

8–060   This distinction is demonstrated by *Al-Fayed v United Kingdom*[143] and *Saunders v United Kingdom*.[144] Both cases concerned a challenge to the activities of Department of Trade and Industry inspectors who had been appointed under Pt XIV of the Companies Act 1985 to examine the affairs of various companies, and in their reports had made adverse findings against respectively Mr Fayed and Mr Saunders. The activities of the inspectors were held not to fall within the scope of art.6, being investigations rather than adjudications: the reports themselves did not determine any legal right or obligation so as to fall within art.6.

8–061   In *Saunders v United Kingdom*, the European Court of Human Rights also held that self-incriminating information lawfully obtained from a person under compulsion or threat of compulsion could not, under art.6, be used against him in his trial on criminal charges. As a result of the incorporation of the Human Rights Convention into domestic law by the Human Rights Act 1998, such material would therefore have to be excluded from evidence in any criminal trial.[145] While the *Saunders* case concerned information obtained by Department of Trade and Industry inspectors, appointed under Pt XIV of the Companies Act 1985, there is no reason why the case should not apply equally to information obtained by the use, or threatened use, of s.236, or under s.235, which is itself backed by criminal sanctions.[146]

8–062   The Human Rights Act 1998 will, however, probably have less impact on the use in subsequent civil proceedings, for example by the administrative receiver, of information obtained under these sections, or by threat of an application for an order under s.236.

8–063   In *Official Receiver v Stern*,[147] the Court of Appeal held that proceedings under the Company Directors Disqualification Act 1986 were not criminal proceedings, and it was not in breach of the respondents' rights to a fair trial under the European Convention for the Official Receiver to use against them information he had received pursuant to s.235 of the Insolvency Act 1986.

8–064   The relevant factors relied on by the court in coming to this conclusion were: (i) disqualification proceedings are not criminal proceedings, but are

---

[143] *Al-Fayed v United Kingdom* (1994) 18 E.H.R.R. 393 (ECtHR).
[144] *Saunders v United Kingdom* [1997] B.C.C. 872 (ECtHR), followed in *Kansal v United Kingdom* (2004) 39 E.H.R.R. 31 (ECHR).
[145] See also Insolvency Act 1986, s.433, as amended by the Youth Justice and Criminal Evidence Act 1999, s.59, Sch.3, para.7, the scope of which was considered in *R. v Sawtell* [2001] B.P.I.R. 381 (CA).
[146] In *Rottmann v Brittain* [2010] 1 W.L.R. 67 the Court of Appeal applied the decision of the Privy Council in *Brannigan v Davison* [1997] A.C. 238 and held that the privilege against self-incrimination did not apply in the case of an examination of a bankrupt who was accused of a criminal offence in another country. The judge hearing the examination could exercise his discretion to permit or exclude incriminating questions, and it would be for the court conducting the criminal trial in the other country to control the use to which the examinee's answers could be put.
[147] *Official Receiver v Stern* [2000] 1 W.L.R. 2230 (CA), affirming the decision of Scott V.C., 1999 WL 1805552, December 20, 1999. See also *R. v Secretary of State for Trade & Industry Ex p. McCormick* [1998] B.C.C. 379 (CA).

regulatory proceedings primarily for the protection of the public, even though the proceedings often involve serious allegations and almost always carry stigma for a person disqualified; (ii) there are various degrees of coercion involved in the different investigative procedures available in corporate insolvency, which may therefore give rise to different degrees of prejudice if the information obtained is sought to be used in disqualification proceedings; and (iii) it is generally best for questions of fairness to be decided by the trial judge rather than in advance.

It is likely that ordinary civil proceedings instituted by an office-holder, for example for breach of duty against a director, will be even less likely to incline a trial judge to exclude material obtained by compulsion under s.235 or 236, because such proceedings do not carry the "stigma" of disqualification. **8–065**

In the context of civil litigation, the right to a fair hearing under art.6 of the European Convention also requires compliance with the principle of "equality of arms"[148]: "As regards litigation involving opposing private interests,[149] 'equality of arms' implies that each party must be afforded a reasonable opportunity to present his case—including his evidence—under conditions which do not place him at a substantial disadvantage vis-à-vis his opponent".[150] The English courts already strive to ensure that no unacceptable "inequality of arms" results from an order under s.236 by means of the limitations on the section examined above, such as the limitations on when an order will be made, or what type of order might be made. If anything more need be done in the context of civil litigation to protect "equality of arms", it is likely that it will be achieved through the exclusion of prejudicial evidence at trial.[151] **8–066**

It seems that an examinee can, save possibly in exceptional circumstances,[152] still refuse to provide the requested information if it is protected by legal professional privilege,[153] though no privilege can be asserted by solicitors in respect of documents in their possession but which belonged to the company itself.[154] **8–067**

---

[148] *Neumeister v Austria* (1979–80) 1 E.H.R.R. 91 (ECtHR); *X v Federal Republic of Germany* (1963) 6 Y.B. 520 (ECtHR), 574.

[149] This is how the English courts clearly understand litigation by a liquidator for the benefit of the company and those "interested" in its assets: see *Cloverbay Ltd v BCCI* [1991] Ch. 90 (CA), 108D, per Nourse L.J.

[150] *Dombo Beheer v Netherlands* (1994) 18 E.H.R.R. 213 (ECtHR), 229–230. See also *Feldbrugge v Netherlands* (1986) 8 E.H.R.R. 425 (ECtHR), 436–437, and *Van de Hurk v Netherlands* (1994) 18 E.H.R.R. 481 (ECtHR).

[151] The civil courts now have a discretion under CPR, r.32.1 to exclude evidence where its prejudicial effect outweighs its probative value: *Grobbelaar v Sun Newspapers Ltd*, *The Times*, August 12, 1999 (CA). The preferred practice of the courts in both criminal and regulatory cases is to leave the question of fairness to the trial judge (see respectively *Re Arrows Ltd (No.4)* [1995] 2 A.C. 75 (HL) and *Official Receiver v Stern* [2000] 1 W.L.R. 2230 (CA), affirming the decision of Scott V.C., 1999 WL 1805552, December 20, 1999). It therefore seems likely that this practice would be followed in the context of civil litigation.

[152] See dicta of Vinelott J. in *Re Brook Martin & Co (Nominees) Ltd* [1993] B.C.L.C. 328, 336–337.

[153] See the Australian decision of *Re Compass Australia Pty Ltd* (1992) 10 A.C.L.C. 1380 and *Re Highgrade Traders Ltd* [1984] B.C.L.C. 151 (CA).

[154] *Re Brook Martin & Co (Nominees) Ltd* [1993] B.C.L.C. 328. See also *Hooper v Duncan Lewis (Solicitors) Limited* [2010] B.P.I.R. 591.

12. PROCEDURE

8–068   The detailed procedures relating to court applications are set out in the Insolvency Rules 1986, rr.9.1 to 9.6. The application is made by the office-holder in question.[155] An order granted to that office-holder ceases to have effect if he ceases to hold office.[156]

8–069   Rule 9.2(4) provides that the application may be made without notice. Such an application used to be the common way of seeking an order under s.236. That approach has now been rejected, and an application on notice is the normal procedure.[157] Where the respondents are thought to have been involved in large scale fraud against the company, and have been uncooperative in response to requests for information and assistance, this may justify an ex parte application.[158] Where a person is to be ordered to disclose confidential information or documents belonging to a third party, the general rule is that the third party must be joined.[159] In making an application for an examination on oath, the applicant must disclose all material facts to the court. This appears to apply as much to an application on notice as to an application without notice.[160] The fact that full disclosure must be made does not, however, justify the revelation of "without prejudice" materials to the court.[161]

8–070   Rule 9.2(1) provides that the application shall specify the grounds on which it is made. Formerly r.9.2(1) required the application to be accompanied by a separate statement setting out those grounds, which was in the form of a sworn affidavit. It is now sufficient to provide an unsworn statement. The statement remains, as under the former rules, confidential.[162] Formerly, these reports were not filed and were not disclosed to the examinee, so as to allow the office-holder to explain his position fully to the court without putting the proposed examinee on notice of facts which could be used to the detriment of the insolvency administration.[163] In *Re British & Commonwealth Holdings Plc*,[164] the Court of Appeal indicated that office-holder reports will now be available to the proposed examinee, or to the person whose documents are sought to be inspected, if such disclosure is necessary to enable the

---

[155] *Re Maxwell Communications Corp Plc* [1994] B.C.C. 741.

[156] *Re Kingscroft Insurance Co Ltd* [1994] B.C.C. 343. Since the examination is by the court, it is questionable whether this result should follow.

[157] *Re Maxwell Communications Corp Plc* [1994] B.C.C. 741, 747 and 752, per Vinelott J.; *Re PFTZM Ltd* [1995] B.C.C. 280; *Re Murjani (a bankrupt)* [1996] 1 W.L.R. 1498, 1509D (a case under s.366 of the Insolvency Act 1986).

[158] *Hill v Van der Merwe* [2007] B.P.I.R. 1562.

[159] *Re Murjani (a bankrupt)* [1996] 1 W.L.R. 1498, 1510H.

[160] *John T Rhodes (No.2)* (1987) 3 B.C.C. 588, 593.

[161] *Re Anglo American Insurance Co Ltd* [2002] B.C.C. 715. (However, entirely different considerations will apply to the disclosure to the Companies Court of "without prejudice" communications between a liquidator and the defendant to a claim brought by him if an application is made to the Companies Court for directions as to the future conduct of the litigation by the liquidator: see *Re Transocean Equipment Manufacturing and Trading Limited* [2006] B.P.I.R. 1055.)

[162] *Re Aveling Barford Ltd* [1989] 1 W.L.R. 360.

[163] See *Re Gold Co* (1879) L.R. 12 Ch. D. 77 (CA).

[164] *Re British & Commonwealth Holdings Plc* [1992] B.C.C. 165 (CA). See also *Re British & Commonwealth Holdings Plc (No.2)* [1993] A.C. 426 (HL) and *Re Bishopsgate Investment Management Ltd (No.2)* [1994] B.C.C. 732.

court fairly to dispose of an application to resist or set aside an order under s.236.[165] This might well be the position where it is not clear from the affidavits what the case is that the proposed examinee, or person whose documents are sought, has to meet. If such a need arises, it shifts the burden on to the office-holder to prove that the material needs to be kept confidential.[166] Best practice should be to separate any confidential information in respect of which disclosure is to be resisted from the rest of the report and to place it in one or more confidential annexes.[167]

Section 236 of the Insolvency Act 1986 confers powers on the court, **8–071** although in practice an examination under the section is conducted by, or on the instructions of, the applicant office-holder. In such circumstances, only he, or a solicitor or counsel instructed by him, may put questions to an examinee, subject to one exception. That exception is the rare case where there are two office-holders in respect of a company, and an order for examination has been made on the application of one of them. In such a case, the other office-holder might, with leave of the court and if the applicant did not object, attend and question the examinee, but only through the applicant.[168]

When conducting an examination under s.236, the office-holder will be a **8–072** "public authority", subject to the provisions of the Human Rights Act 1998. This is because he will be a "person certain of whose functions are functions of a public nature" (s.6(3)(b) of the 1998 Act), and he will not fall within the exception to that definition (s.6(5)) which provides that "[i]n relation to a particular act, a person is not a public authority by virtue only of subsection (3) (b) if the nature of the act is private". An examination under s.236, which takes place under threat of coercion, and is undertaken by a court, or by an office-holder as its nominee, is undoubtedly a "public" act.[169]

In consequence, an office-holder conducting an examination under s.236 must **8–073** not infringe any of the rights guaranteed by the European Convention on Human Rights and imported into English law by the 1998 Act. For present purposes, the right most likely to be of importance is the right to respect for private and family life (art.8 of the Convention).[170] Nevertheless, action necessary in the interests of the economic well-being of the country, or the protection of the rights of others, does not infringe this right (art.8(2)). Any intrusion into an individual's privacy or family life will therefore have to be justified by reference to the office-holder's need for information to protect national economic interests, or the rights of others. Furthermore, the principle of proportionality means that a more serious intrusion will require a more compelling justification.

If an office-holder proposes to take steps which would violate rights **8–074** guaranteed by the Convention, or in fact has taken such steps, he will be open

---

[165] For a case where disclosure was refused, see *Re Anglo American Insurance Co Ltd* [2002] B.C.C. 715.

[166] See, e.g. *Re Murjani (a bankrupt)* [1996] 1 W.L.R. 1498, 1507D–1509A.

[167] See, e.g. *Re Bishopsgate Investment Management Ltd (No.2)* [1994] B.C.C. 732.

[168] *Re Maxwell Communications Corp Plc* [1994] B.C.C. 741.

[169] See *R (Hafner) v Westminster Magistrates Court* [2009] 1 W.L.R. 1005.

[170] See e.g. the argument made by the intervener in relation to the production of correspondence in *Warner v Verfides, Re Rivkin (deceased)* [2009] B.P.I.R. 153.

to an action under s.8 of the 1998 Act for an injunction, damages or other remedy.

8–075   Any transcript obtained following an examination is not available for inspection, without a court order, by any person other than the office-holder who made the original application or any person who could have made a similar application.[171] Similarly, the court may give directions as to the custody and inspection of any documents obtained under this procedure.[172]

8–076   As indicated above, an office-holder will generally only be entitled to use any information or documents obtained under the procedure for the purposes of the insolvency, and he should seek leave of the court if he proposes to use any of them for any other purpose.[173] An office-holder is also subject to an implied, qualified duty of confidentiality in respect of information obtained under s.236.[174] The duty does not prevent him from using information obtained by means of s.236 in the performance of his tasks,[175] and he can disclose it to State bodies when required or authorised to do so.[176] The court can also relieve him of this duty of confidentiality.[177]

8–077   The office-holder may, in his discretion, give undertakings of confidentiality in respect of information obtained or to be obtained by him under s.236, or under the threat of the section, though such undertakings cannot be required of him.[178] He cannot give an assurance that information will be withheld from anyone to whom he must report the information, or anyone who can by law require the information of him.[179] Third parties who are concerned that the office-holder may breach any previous assurances about confidentiality or legal professional privilege may seek an order of the court restraining disclosure,[180] although this may not be forthcoming in the context of criminal investigations.[181]

8–078   There is no public interest immunity to prevent the disclosure of transcripts of evidence made under s.236 to prosecuting or regulatory authorities.[182]

---

[171] Insolvency Rules 1986, r.9.5(2).

[172] Insolvency Rules 1986, r.9.5(4).

[173] See *Re Esal Commodities Ltd (No.1)* [1989] B.C.L.C. 59 (CA); *Re Esal (Commodities) Ltd (No.2)* [1990] B.C.C. 708 and *Re ACLI Metals (London) Ltd* (1989) 5 B.C.C. 749 for instances of disclosure permitted in circumstances not directly related to the office-holder's duties.

[174] See *Re Arrows Ltd (No.4)* [1995] 2 A.C. 75 (HL), 102–103, per Lord Browne-Wilkinson, indicating that the limits on disclosure indicated by Millett J. in *Re Esal (Commodities) Ltd (No.2)* [1990] B.C.C. 708 and *Re Barlow Clowes Gilt Managers Ltd* [1992] Ch. 208 are too tightly drawn, as they would apparently (and incorrectly) preclude the office-holder from disclosing information obtained by him under s.236 to persons to whom he may, or must, by law divulge that information. See also *Re A Company (No.005374 of 1993)* [1993] B.C.C. 734 and *Soden v Burns* [1996] 1 W.L.R. 1512.

[175] The tasks of an office-holder include taking and defending proceedings: *Soden v Burns* [1996] 1 W.L.R. 1512, 1524, per Robert Walker J.

[176] *Re Arrows Ltd (No.4)* [1995] 2 A.C. 75 (HL), 102–103, per Lord Browne-Wilkinson.

[177] *Re A Company (No.005374 of 1993)* [1993] B.C.C. 734.

[178] *Re Barlow Clowes Gilt Managers Ltd* [1992] Ch. 208; *McIsaac, Petitioners; Joint Liquidators of First Tokyo Index Trust Ltd* [1994] B.C.C. 410 (Court of Session, Outer House).

[179] *Re Arrows Ltd (No.4)* [1995] 2 A.C. 75 (HL), 102–103, per Lord Browne-Wilkinson.

[180] See *Re Barlow Clowes Gilt Managers Ltd* [1992] Ch. 208 and *Dubai Bank Ltd v Galadari* [1990] Ch. 98 (CA).

[181] *Re Arrows Ltd (No.4)* [1995] 2 A.C. 75 (HL).

[182] *Re Headington Investments Ltd* [1993] Ch. 452 (CA).

Furthermore, the person who might be the object of the possible criminal or regulatory proceedings cannot compel concurrent disclosure to himself.[183]

The court has a discretion to award any person attending on examination any **8–079** other costs incurred by him (save for the costs of a solicitor and/or counsel employed to attend any examination).[184] In practice, it is unlikely that an examinee will be able to obtain an order for costs.[185] In certain circumstances, an order for costs may be made against the examinee.[186]

---

[183] *Re Headington Investments Ltd* [1993] Ch. 452 (CA).

[184] Insolvency Rules 1986, r.9.4(5).

[185] But see *Morris v Bank of America National Trust and Savings Association* Unreported February 6, 1997, Robert Walker J., discussing *Re Aveling Barford* [1989] 1 W.L.R. 360 and the apparently contrary decision of Vinelott J. in *Re Cloverbay Ltd (No.1)* (1989) 5 B.C.C. 732.

[186] Insolvency Rules 1986, r.9.6(1) and (2). See *Miller v Bain* [2002] B.C.C. 899 and *Hunt v Renzland* [2008] B.P.I.R. 1380.

Chapter 9

Administrators and the
Statutory Stay

1. INTRODUCTION

9–001 By means of a statutory stay[1] on the enforcement of rights and claims by third parties, a company in administration[2] is afforded a "breathing space"[3] while the administrator carries out his functions.[4] The moratorium is procedural in nature, suspending the power to enforce rights but not extinguishing such rights.[5] Accordingly, the moratorium does not alter the order of priority existing between creditors at the date of the commencement of the administration and should not be used by administrators as a bargaining tool in negotiations designed to restructure interests in the company's pool of assets.[6] The statutory provisions provide that most aspects of the moratorium can be relaxed at the discretion of the administrators or the court in order to alleviate the effects of the moratorium in appropriate circumstances[7].

9–002 The purpose of the moratorium is to "give the administrator time to formulate proposals and lay them before the creditors, and then implement any

---

[1] Although the statutory stay provisions discussed in this chapter are commonly referred to as the administration moratorium, and shall be so labelled in this book, strictly speaking there is no moratorium (i.e. a legal authorisation to a debtor to postpone payment for a certain time) since the debts and liabilities remain payable, but only a quasi-moratorium affecting remedies for non-payment.

[2] Where steps have been taken to implement administration in respect of a company, an "interim moratorium" may apply before the company has gone into administration. See para.9–021.

[3] Per Nicholls L.J. in *Atlantic Computer Systems Plc* [1992] Ch. 505 (CA), 528.

[4] paras 40–44 of Sch.B1 and, in relation to administrations commenced by petition presented to court prior to September 15, 2003 or relating to certain types of public utility companies and building societies, ss.10 and 11 of the Act.

[5] *Barclays Mercantile Business Finance Ltd v Sibec Developments Ltd* [1992] 1 W.L.R. 1253, 1257, per Millett. J; *Re Olympia & York Canary Wharf Ltd (No.1)* [1993] B.C.C. 154; *Re David Meek Plant Ltd* [1993] B.C.C. 175. Thus, for example, a creditor with a right to repossess goods in the company's possession continues to enjoy an immediate right to possession despite the administration. Where the effect of declining permission to enforce security would be to destroy the rights enjoyed by the creditor, the courts will take steps to ensure that the creditor's priority is preserved: see *Bristol Airport Plc v Powdrill* [1990] Ch. 744 (CA), [17].

[6] *Re Atlantic Computer Systems Plc* [1992] Ch. 505 (CA), 528.

[7] See paras 9–022 to 9–025.

proposals approved by the creditors."[8] In *Re Olympia & York Canary Wharf Ltd (No. 1)*[9], Millet J. said[10]:

"[The moratorium provisions] are intended to impose a moratorium upon the creditors of the company in order to assist the administrator in his attempts to achieve the statutory purpose for which he was appointed. They are couched in procedural terms and are designed to prevent creditors from depriving the administrator of the possession of property which may be required by him for the purpose of the administration."

In the early years of the administration process the judiciary quickly embraced **9–003** the new regime and the "rescue culture" it sought to facilitate. Decisions as to the scope of the moratorium and the circumstances in which it should be relaxed were greatly influenced by public policy considerations as the courts attempted to strike an appropriate balance between private rights and collective interests within the context of the new insolvency culture. In *Bristol Airport Plc v Powdrill*, Browne-Wilkinson V.C. encapsulated this balancing exercise when setting out the approach to be taken to construction of the moratorium provisions. He said[11]:

"In my judgment in construing [the administration provisions] it is legitimate and necessary to bear in mind the statutory objectives with a view to ensuring, if the words permit, that the administrator has the powers necessary to carry out the statutory objectives, including the power to use the company's property. On the other hand, however desirable it may be to construe the 1986 Act in a way calculated to carry out the Parliamentary purpose, it is not legitimate to distort the meaning of the words Parliament has chosen to use in order to achieve that result. Only if the words used by Parliament are fairly capable of bearing more than one meaning is it legitimate to adopt the meaning which gives effect to, rather than frustrates, the statutory purpose."[12]

---

[8] Per Nicholls L.J., *Re Atlantic Computer Systems Plc* [1992] Ch. 505 (CA), 528. See also Browne-Wilkinson V.C. in *Bristol Airport Plc v Powdrill* [1990] Ch. 744 (CA), 759 where he set out the justification for the moratorium as follows: ". . . the statutory purpose [of administration] is to install an administrator as an officer of the court, to carry on the business of the company as a going concern with a view to achieving one or other of the statutory objectives mentioned in section 8(3). It is of the essence of administration . . . that the business will continue to be carried on by the administrator. Such continuation of the business by the administrator requires that there should be available to him the right to use the property of the company, free from interference from creditors and others during the usually short period during which such an administration continues. Hence the restrictions on the rights of creditors and others introduced by sections. 10 and 11 of the 1986 Act."

[9] *Re Olympia & York Canary Wharf Ltd (No.1)* [1993] B.C.C. 154.

[10] *Re Olympia & York Canary Wharf Ltd (No.1)* [1993] B.C.C. 154, 157–158

[11] *Bristol Airport Plc v Powdrill* [1990] Ch.744 (CA), 758.

[12] For an example of the purposive approach to interpretation being applied see Nicholls L.J. in *Re Atlantic Computer Systems Plc* [1992] Ch. 505 (CA), 532, and Judge Weeks QC in *Re David Meek Plant Ltd* [1993] B.C.C. 175 (see further at [19]). For an example of the limits of the purposive approach, see *Re Lomax Leisure Ltd* [2000] Ch. 502 in which Neuberger J. held "with regret" that the exercise by a landlord of the right of forfeiture by way of peaceful re-entry against a company in administration was effective notwithstanding the lack of prior consent or permission (see further at [22]).

9–004 In *Re Olympia & York Canary Wharf,* Millett J. stressed that to the extent that the moratorium represents an interference with private rights, it should go no further than is required to support the ability of the administrator to carry out his functions.[13] Although the moratorium provisions in Sch.B1 do not replicate precisely those under Pt II of the Act,[14] the differences are largely a matter of format[15] and case law relating to Pt II of the Act is apposite.[16]

The moratorium does not apply beyond the company and its property. Thus, directors, other company officers (including administrators) and sureties derive no protection from the statutory moratorium. However, the position of administrators is protected at common law: whilst in office they are officers of the court and, as such, any person wishing to sue them must first obtain leave of the court.[17]

Breach of the moratorium is a contempt of court[18] and may give rise to a claim in damages if loss results.[19] Proceedings begun without leave are stayed until consent or leave is granted.[20] The effect of a breach of the moratorium on the validity of steps taken with regard to other forms of prohibited action is rather less clear and is likely to depend on the particular circumstances of the case. There is a risk that such steps could be void.[21]

9–005 The imposition of a moratorium on the enforcement of claims when a company goes into administration does not, of itself, stop time running against affected claims for the purposes of the Limitation Act 1980.[22] Where administrators are aware that a limitation issue has arisen in relation to a claim or

---

[13] *Re Olympia & York Canary Wharf Ltd (No.1)* [1993] B.C.C. 154, 158.

[14] ss.10 and 11 of the Act.

[15] See the discussion in relation to "legal process" at [30].

[16] *Hudson v The Gambling Commission* [2010] Bus. L.R. 1608, [37].

[17] *Re Botibol* [1947] 1 All E.R. 26; *Re Maidstone Palace of Varieties* [1909] 2 Ch 283.

[18] *Re Atlantic Computer Systems Plc* [1992] Ch. 505 (CA); *Re Sabre International Products Ltd* [1991] B.C.C. 694; *Henry Pound v Hutchins* (1889) 42 Ch. D. 402 (CA). However, detention of chattels pursuant to a lien or right of detention pending the hearing of an application to court for permission is not contempt of court. See further [17].

[19] *Euro Commercial Leasing Limited v Cartwright & Lewis* [1995] B.C.C. 830.

[20] *Carr v British International Helicopters* [1993] B.C.C. 855; *Re Saunders (a bankrupt)* [1997] Ch.60.

[21] In *Re AGB Research Plc* [1995] B.C.C. 1091 a landlord purported to forfeit a lease against a company in administration without consent or permission. The landlord then sought to argue that the forfeiture was ineffective and the lease still in existence, relying on its own failure to obtain consent or permission. Vinelott J. held that the landlord could not succeed: however, he said: ". . . the administrators when they learned of the lease, could have relied upon the failure to obtain their consent or an order of the court as a ground for claiming that the [original] lease had not been forfeited . . ." See also *Unite the Union v Nortel Networks UK Ltd (in administration)* [2010] B.C.C. 706 in which former employees began proceedings against the company without the consent of the joint administrators and without permission of the court. Norris J. noted that the joint administrators did not assert that the proceedings were a nullity.

[22] *Re Leyland Printing Co Ltd* [2011] B.C.C. 358; *Re Cosslett (Contractors) Ltd* [2004] EWHC 658 (Ch); *Re Maxwell Fleet and Facilities Management Ltd* [2001] 1 W.L.R.323; *Re Cases of Taffs Well Ltd* [1992] Ch.179. Time stops running against claims in a liquidation because those claims are subject to the statutory scheme for distribution. Prior to the Enterprise Act 2002, administration could not be used as a distribution process and, therefore, the courts held that there was no basis upon which to hold that time stops running. This position may be reviewed in cases where the administration is or becomes a distribution process. Either way, the imposition of a moratorium has no bearing on the debate.

claims, they ought to consider lifting the moratorium in order to allow a protective claim to be issued, or otherwise seek directions from the court[23].

Although not expressing a concluded view, in *Bloom v Harms Offshore*   **9–006**
GmbH & Co[24] the Court of Appeal expressed the view that in light of the long line of authorities beginning with *Re Oriental Inland Steam Co Ex p. Scinde Railway Co*[25] the administration moratorium was not intended to have extra-territorial effect.[26] However, the court may take steps to prevent a creditor from taking advantage of proceedings taken in a foreign court, despite the existence of the English moratorium, in order to protect the assets of the company in administration, in circumstances where the creditor's conduct was oppressive, vexatious or otherwise unfair or improper.[27]

2.   THE SCOPE OF THE MORATORIUM

(a)   Winding up

Where a winding up petition is pending at the time the company goes into   **9–007**
administration that petition will be either dismissed (if the administrator is appointed by order of the court[28]) or suspended (if the administrator is appointed by the holder of a floating charge under para.14 of Sch.B1[29]). There is no mandatory suspension of a pending winding up petition where an administrator is appointed by the company or the directors under para.22 of Sch.B1. This omission serves to ensure that the progress of the petition comes within the provisions relating to "legal process"[30] which can, where appropriate, be lifted by the court, thus providing some protection against misuse of the para.22 appointment procedure.

Similarly, although there is no specific statutory provision applying the moratorium to a winding up petition presented during an administration, it is submitted that prior consent or permission would be required on the basis that the presentation of the petition at such a time would constitute the "institution" of a "legal process".[31]

---

[23] *Re Cosslett (Contractors) Ltd* [2004] EWHC 658 (Ch); *Re Condon, ex p.James* (1873–74) L.R. 9 Ch. App. 609 (CA).
[24] *Bloom v Harms Offshore GmbH & Co* [2010] Ch.187 (CA).
[25] *Re Oriental Inland Steam Co Ex p. Scinde Railway Co* (1873–74) L.R. 9 Ch. App. 557 (CA).
[26] But in *Banque Indosuez SA v Ferromet Resources Inc* [1993] B.C.L.C. 112, Hoffmann J., as he then was, appeared to assume that the stay would have extra-territorial effect as a matter of English law.
[27] See *Bloom v Harms Offshore GmbH & Co* [2010] Ch. 187.
[28] para.40(1)(a) of Sch.B1.
[29] para.40(1)(b) of Sch.B1. If the winding up petition was presented under s.124A of the Act (public interest) or s.367 of the Financial Services and Markets Act 2000 (petition by Financial Services Authority) then no such suspension occurs (para.40(2) of Sch.B1). Section 127(2) of the Act provides that where a petition is suspended in these circumstances s.127(1) of the Act shall have no effect in respect of anything done by the administrator.
[30] para.43(6) of Sch.B1. See *Re Synthetic Technology Ltd* [1990] B.C.L.C. 378, 381; *Re a Company (No.001992 of 1988)* [1989] B.C.L.C. 9; *Re a Company (No.001448 of 1989)* (1989) 5 B.C.C. 706; *Re International Tin Council* [1987] Ch. 419.
[31] para.43(6) of Sch.B1.

When a company is in administration, no resolution may be passed[32] or order made[33] for the winding up of the company save in respect of an order made on a winding up petition presented under s.124A of the Act or s.367 of the Financial Services and Markets Act 2000[34].

(b) Receivership

9–008 Administration and administrative receivership are mutually exclusive. If an administration order is made while an administrative receiver is in office, the administrative receiver must vacate office.[35] Where an administrative receiver is in office no administrator may be appointed by either of the "out-of-court" routes[36]. No administrative receiver may be appointed while a company is in administration[37].

A receiver of part only of a company's property appointed prior to the company going into administration must vacate office if, when the company goes into administration, the administrator requires him to do so.[38] Any attempt to appoint such a receiver after the company has gone into administration would require consent or permission on the basis that it is a step taken to enforce security.[39]

When an administrative receiver or receiver vacates office in accordance with para.41(1) or 41(2), his remuneration shall be charged on and paid out of any property of the company which was in his custody or control immediately before he vacated office.[40] However, enforcement of such charge is subject to the moratorium and so would require consent of the administrator or permission of the court to be enforced prior to the end of the administration.[41]

---

[32] para.42(2) of Sch.B1.

[33] para.42(3) of Sch.B1.

[34] para.82 of Sch.B1 provides that where a winding up order is made in respect of a company which is in administration on a petition presented under s.124(A) of the Act or s.367 of the Financial Services and Markets Act 2000 the court shall order that the appointment of the administrators shall cease to have effect or continue to have effect. If the latter, the court may also specify which powers are to be exercisable by the administrator and modify the operation of Sch.B1 in relation to the Administrator. Thus, in the event of a concurrent liquidation and administration the court will demarcate the responsibilities of the two office holders.

[35] para.41(1) of Sch.B1.

[36] paras 17(b) and 25(c) of Sch.B1.

[37] para.43 (6A) of Sch.B1.

[38] para.41(2) of Sch.B1. This provision does not apply if the receiver was appointed under a "market charge", a "system-charge", a "collateral security charge" or a charge created or otherwise arising under a financial collateral arrangement—see s.175(1A) of the Companies Act 1989, reg.3 of the Financial Markets and Insolvency Regulations 1996, reg.19 of the Financial Markets and Insolvency (Settlement Finality) Regulations 1999 and reg.8 of the Financial Collateral Arrangements (No.2) Regulations 2003 respectively.

[39] para.43(2) of Sch.B1. See paras 9–009 to 9–011.

[40] para.41(3) of Sch.B1.

[41] para.41(4)(c) of Sch.B1.

(c) Enforcement of security

During the administration of a company, "no step may be taken to enforce **9–009** security over the company's property except with the consent of the administrator or permission of the court."[42]

Under s.248 of the Act, ". . . except in so far as the context otherwise requires security means . . . any mortgage, charge, lien or other security".[43] The meaning of "other security" was first considered in *Bristol Airport Plc v Powdrill*.[44] Bristol and Birmingham Airports, both of which had pre-administration claims against Paramount Airways (in administration), sought to exercise their statutory right of detention under s.88 of the Civil Aviation Act 1982 against Paramount's aircraft located within their airports. At first instance[45], Harman J. held that enforcement of the statutory right of detention required permission of the court and he declined to grant such permission. Before the Court of Appeal, it was submitted that the detention of the aircraft did not require leave or permission under the moratorium because it was not the enforcement of a "lien or other security" within s.248 of the Act. Browne-Wilkinson V.C. held that the statutory right of detention was "other security", applying the natural meaning of those words, despite its special features.[46] He held that those features were not unique and there was no authority for the proposition that non-consensual security imposed by statute should not be subject to the statutory insolvency regime.

In subsequent cases the courts went further, holding that "other security" **9–010** could encompass commercial arrangements having an effect equivalent to security[47] but more recently this policy-driven approach has been firmly rejected. It is now generally accepted that, in the context of the moratorium, "other security" is limited to security, consensual and non-consensual, in the strict legal sense.[48]

It was further submitted in *Bristol Airport Plc v Powdrill* that the moratorium did not apply because: (i) the aircraft were leased by Paramount Airways and, therefore, not its "property"; (ii) detention of the aircraft against the administrators was not a "step" taken to enforce security but rather a step taken

---

[42] para.43(2) of Sch.B1. This provision does not apply to security in the form of a "market charge", "system-charge" (to a limited extent) or "collateral security charge", or any security interest created or otherwise arising under a "financial collateral arrangement"—see s.175 Companies Act 1989, regs 3, 6 and 7 of the Financial Markets and Insolvency Regulations 1996, reg.19 of the Financial Markets and Insolvency (Settlement Finality) Regulations 1999, and reg.8 of the Financial Collateral Arrangements (No.2) Regulations 2003 respectively.

[43] s.248 of the Act.

[44] *Bristol Airport Plc v Powdrill* [1990] Ch. 744 (CA).

[45] *Bristol Airport Plc v Powdrill* [1990] Ch. 744 (CA).

[46] It was, therefore, unnecessary for him to come to a concluded view on the question of whether the statutory right was strictly a lien.

[47] *Exchange Travel Agency Ltd v Triton Property Trust Plc* [1991] B.C.C. 341; *Re Olympia & York Canary Wharf Ltd (No.1)* [1993] B.C.C. 154; *March Estates Plc v Gunmark Ltd* [1996] 2 B.C.L.C. 1. In these cases a landlord's right to forfeit a lease by peaceable re-entry was held to be "other security" for the purposes of the moratorium.

[48] *Re Lomax Leisure Ltd* [2000] Ch. 502; *Razzaq v Pala* [1997] 1 W.L.R. 1336; *Clarence Cafe Ltd v Comchester Properties Ltd* [1999] L.& T.R. 303 drawing on Lord Millett in *Re Park Air Services Plc* [2000] 2 A.C.172 (HL) and Shaw L.J. in *Ezekiel v Orakpo* [1977] QB 260 (CA).

to create security; and, (iii) if the moratorium were to apply to rights based on the retention of possession, the holder of such rights would lose his priority, contrary to the intended effect of the moratorium. Browne-Wilkinson V.C. rejected these submissions and held that: (i) the definition of property under s.436 of the Act[49] was wide enough to include the equitable interests that arose in favour of Paramount Airways under the aircraft leases[50]; (ii) if it was correct to say that the act of detention *created* the security interest, this did not prevent it also being a step taken to *enforce* that interest[51]; and (iii) whilst it is agreed that it "cannot be right that the appointment of an administrator has the effect of turning a secured into an unsecured creditor"[52] the difficulty said to be posed by application of the moratorium to possessory security had little force in practice. The holder of such security was entitled to retain possession pending a prompt application to court for permission to enforce his security[53] and, further, in the event that the application for permission was denied the court would impose such terms as were considered necessary to protect the applicant's priority.[54]

9–011   The moratorium will apply to the enforcement of a lien against the company's property regardless of whether the administrator himself demands delivery up of the chattels. In *London Flight Centre (Stansted) Ltd v Osprey Aviation Ltd*[55] the moratorium was held to apply to the enforcement of a repairer's lien despite the fact that the immediate demand for possession was made by receivers of the aircraft in circumstances where the receivers had agreed to deliver up the aircraft to the administrators under the terms of the company's voluntary arrangement.

Whether the service of a demand or notice in accordance with the terms of a security instrument as a precondition to enforcement is itself a step taken to enforce security remains moot.[56] However, it is suggested that the better view

---

[49] "Property includes money, goods, things in action, land and every description or property wherever situated and also obligations and every description of interest, whether present or future or vested or contingent, arising out of, or incidental to, property."

[50] On Browne-Wilkinson V.C.'s analysis, an equitable proprietary interest arose in the aircraft because the rights under the leases would have been susceptible to an order for specific enforcement, each of the aircraft having unique features. This aspect of his reasoning has been criticised (see, e.g. Sir Roy Goode, *Principles of Corporate Insolvency Law*, 3rd edn, pp.355–356) and also begs the question as to whether this part of the moratorium would apply in favour of a lessee of non-unique chattels.

[51] See also *Re Sabre International Products Limited* [1991] B.C.C. 694 in which Harman J. held that retaining possession of goods against an administrator was a step enforcing a carrier's lien.

[52] *Bristol Airport Plc v Powdrill* [1990] Ch.744 (CA), 762.

[53] See the analysis of Woolf L.J. at *Bristol Airport Plc v Powdrill* [1990] Ch.744 (CA), 768: it is only an *unqualified* refusal to hand over possession that constitutes a step to enforce the security.

[54] Equivalent security may be provided by the administrator to avoid an application to court, but it is not the task of the administrator to suggest ways in which a lien holder should arrange his affairs so as to achieve this end: *Re Sabre International Products Ltd* [1991] B.C.C. 694.

[55] *London Flight Centre (Stansted) Ltd v Osprey Aviation Ltd* [2002] B.P.I.R. 1115.

[56] In *Re Olympia & York Canary Wharf Ltd (No.1)* [1993] B.C.C. 154, Millett J. said that nothing in his decision concerning the service of contractual notices should be taken as directed to this question. In *Re David Meek Plant Ltd* [1993] B.C.C. 175, Judge Weeks QC also declined to answer this question.

is that a preparatory demand or notice which does not of itself involve the exercise of a power over the charged asset is not within the moratorium.[57]

(d) Repossession of goods

"No step may be taken to repossess goods in the company's possession under a hire purchase agreement except with the consent of the administrator or with the permission of the court".[58] "Hire purchase agreement" includes a conditional sale agreement, a chattel leasing agreement and a retention of title agreement.[59] Thus, seizure of goods pursuant to the terms of a retention of title clause requires consent or permission.   **9–012**

Goods which are no longer in the company's possession having been subleased to a third party are nevertheless said to be in the company's possession for the purposes of the administration moratorium.[60] Termination of the hire purchase agreement under which the goods came into the possession of the company does not mean that the goods are no longer in the company's possession "under a hire purchase agreement".[61]

Goods which have been sold by the Administrators on terms that the buyer will retain them for a reasonable period of time and honour any valid retention of title claim by a supplier brought within that period are unlikely to be found to be in the company's possession after a reasonable period of time has elapsed. In *Fashoff (UK) Limited v Linton*,[62] the court left open the possibility that such goods may be held to be in the company's possession on a constructive basis before the expiry of such period.   **9–013**

(e) Forfeiture of premises

"A landlord[63] may not exercise a right to forfeiture by peaceable re-entry in relation to premises let to the company except with the consent of the   **9–014**

---

[57] In *Re Jones Ex p. National Provincial Bank* [1932] 1 Ch. 548, Clauson J. held that the acceleration of a secured loan and the threat to repossess and sell the charged property did not constitute the enforcement of the charge and that enforcement did not occur until after an agent had been appointed to sell the property. *Lonsdale Nominees Pty Ltd v Southern Cross Airlines Ltd* (in liquidation) (1993) 10 A.C.S.R. 739 (Supreme Court of Victoria) and *Re Scandees Danish Home Ice Cream Pty Ltd* (1995) 16 A.C.S.R. 777 (Supreme Court of Queensland) support the view that a demand or letter involving no immediate invocation of compulsive power in relation to the charged property is better regarded as a step taken with a view to subsequent enforcement of the charge rather than a step to enforce the charge. Contrast with *Re 21st Century Sign Company Pty Ltd* (1992) 9 A.C.S.R. 77 in which the letter in issue purported to crystallise the charge, vest the assets in the chargee and appoint a sale agent. In such circumstances, the letter was held to be a step to enforce the charge.

[58] para.43(3) of Sch.B1. This provision does not apply in relation to a "market charge" or a "system-charge"—see s.175(1) of the Companies Act 1989 and reg.3(1) of the Financial Markets and Insolvency Regulations 1996 respectively.

[59] para.111(1) of Sch.B1. The terms "chattel leasing agreement" and "retention of title agreement" are defined in s.251 of the Act. The terms "conditional sale agreement" and "hire-purchase agreement" are defined in s.436 of the Act by reference to s.189(1) of the Consumer Credit Act 1974.

[60] *Re Atlantic Computer Systems Plc* [1992] Ch 505 (CA). The decision of Ferris J. at first instance was overruled on this point.

[61] *Re David Meek Plant Ltd* [1993] B.C.C. 175.

[62] *Fashoff (UK) Limited v Linton* [2008] B.C.C. 542.

[63] "Landlord includes a person to whom rent is payable": para.43(8) of Sch.B1.

administrator or permission of the court".[64] In its original form, the Act failed to provide expressly that the exercise of such a right by a landlord required consent or permission. This omission was eventually rectified by s.9 of the Insolvency Act 2000[65] but not before the courts had attempted to cure the lacuna by finding that a landlord's exercise of a right of forfeiture by peaceable re-entry was either the commencement of a legal process or a step taken to enforce security. Ultimately, these decisions were held to be unsustainable.[66]

(f) Legal process

9–015   "No legal process (including legal proceedings, execution, distress and diligence) may be instituted or continued against[67] the company or property of the company except with the consent of the administrator or permission of the court."[68] The wording is slightly different from the equivalent provision under Pt II of the Act (s.11(3)(d)) which provides that "no other proceedings and no execution or other legal process may be commenced or continued and no distress may be levied, against the company or its property except with the consent of the administrator or leave of the court". The key term under the new wording is "legal process", of which "legal proceedings" has become a sub-category.

9–016   To understand the construction of the term "legal process" adopted by the courts in the context of s.11(3)(d), it is helpful to consider first how the courts construed "other proceedings" for the purposes of that sub-section. At first instance in *Bristol Airport Plc v Powdrill*,[69] Harman J. held that the words "other proceedings" covered "every sort of step against the company, its contracts or its property, which may be taken ...". In the Court of Appeal,[70] Browne-Wilkinson V.C. considered that this construction was too wide, leading to unacceptable uncertainty, and ignored the fact that the proceedings in question were required to be capable of being "commenced or continued". He concluded that Parliament intended "other proceedings" to mean "legal proceedings or quasi legal proceedings, such as arbitration".[71]

[64] para.43(4) of Sch.B1.
[65] In force from April 2, 2001.
[66] *Exchange Travel Agency Ltd v Triton Property Trust Plc* [1991] B.C.C. 341; *Re Olympia & York Canary Wharf Ltd (No.1)* [1993] B.C.C. 154; *March Estates Plc v Gunmark Ltd* [1996] 2 B.C.L.C. 1; *Razzaq v Pala* [1997] 1 W.L.R. 1336; *Clarence Cafe Ltd v Comchester Properties Ltd* [1999] L. & T.R. 303; *Re Lomax Leisure Ltd* [2000] Ch. 502. See the discussions at [16] and [28].
[67] An application to the Rail Regulator under s.17 of the Railways Act 1993 (*Re Railtrack Plc (in administration) (No.2)* [2002] 1 W.L.R. 3002 (CA)) and an application for late registration of a charge under s.404 of the Companies Act 1985 (*Re Barrow Borough Transport Ltd* [1990] Ch. 227) were held to be excluded from the ambit of the moratorium on the basis, inter alia, that they were not proceedings *against* the company or its property.
[68] para.43(6) of Sch.B1. This provision (indeed the whole of paras 42 and 43 of Sch.B1) does not apply to any action taken by an exchange or clearing house for the purpose of its default proceedings—see s.161(4) of the Companies Act 1989.
[69] *Bristol Airport Plc v Powdrill* [1990] Ch. 744 (CA).
[70] *Bristol Airport Plc v Powdrill* [1990] Ch. 744 (CA).
[71] *Bristol Airport Plc v Powdrill* [1990] Ch. 744 (CA), 765.

Applications for an award before an industrial tribunal,[72] the revocation of a patent before the Patents Court,[73] and an adjudication pursuant to s.108 of the Housing Grants Construction and Regeneration Act 1996[74] have been held to be "other proceedings" applying the test laid down in *Bristol Airport Plc v Powdrill*.[75]

The term "other proceedings" is not limited to proceedings commenced by creditors of the company[76], nor is it limited to civil proceedings.[77]   **9–017**

Whether or not regulatory proceedings, or determinations by regulators, fall within the ambit of the moratorium will depend on the circumstances[78]. If the regulator is taking a strategic decision which obliges him or her to take into account considerations of a public nature which may be of little or no concern to the parties then his or her role may be distinguished from that of a judge or arbitrator, and the moratorium may not apply.[79] If, by contrast, the proceedings instituted by the regulator are adversarial in nature and the regulator (or a tribunal appointed by the regulator) acts in the manner of a judge or arbitrator then they may come within the scope of the moratorium.[80] For example, if a regulatory decision is subject to appeal rather than judicial review, that may indicate that such decision (or the process out of which it arises) should be subject to the moratorium.

In *Exchange Travel Agency Ltd v Triton Property Trust Plc*[81] Harman J.   **9–018** considered that the term "legal process" should be distinguished from "other

---

[72] *Carr v British International Helicopters Ltd* [1993] B.C.C. 855.

[73] *Biosource Technologies Inc v Axis Genetics Plc* [2000] B.C.C. 943.

[74] In *A Straume (UK) Ltd v Bradlor Developments Ltd* [2000] B.C.C. 333, 336, per Judge Behrens (cited without disapproval by Lord Woolf CJ in *Re Railtrack Plc (in administration) (No.2)* [2002] 1 W.L.R. 3002 (CA) the court had little doubt that the adjudication procedure in question was a form of arbitration, within the classification of "other proceedings" adopted by the Court of Appeal in *Bristol Airport Plc v Powdrill*, despite the fact that "the arbitrator has a discretion as to the procedure that he uses, and albeit that the full rules of natural justice do not apply." The adjudicator's decision was binding on the parties but not final, in that either party was free to refer the dispute to court or arbitration for resolution, and it was enforceable through the courts by means of the summary judgment procedure. There is no authority as yet on expert determinations but it is submitted that an expert determination sharing the relevant features of the adjudication in *Straume* would, by analogy, be "other proceedings" or a "legal process" within 43(6).

[75] In the context of the liquidation moratorium, the term "proceedings" has been held to include interpleader proceedings (*Eastern Holdings Establishment of Vaduz v Singer & Friedlander Ltd* [1967] 1 W.L.R. 1017) and a counterclaim exceeding the company's claim (*Langley Constructions (Brixham) Ltd v Wells* [1969] 1 W.L.R. 503 (CA)).

[76] See *Re Rhondda Waste Disposal Company Ltd* [2001] Ch. 57 (CA); *Biosource Technologies Inc v Axis Genetics Plc* [2000] B.C.C. 943; *Carr v British International Helicopters Ltd* [1993] B.C.C. 855. For a contrary view, see *Air Ecosse Ltd v Civil Aviation Authority* (1987) 3 B.C.C. 492 (Court of Session, Inner House) and *MSF v Parkfield Casting* Unreported April 14, 1992 (IT).

[77] In *Re Rhondda Waste Disposal Co Ltd* [2001] Ch.57 (CA) the Court of Appeal held that criminal proceedings under the Environmental Protection Act 1999 were subject to the moratorium.

[78] There is no principle of public policy that regulatory proceedings or decisions should not come within the moratorium in certain circumstances—*Hudson v The Gambling Commission* [2010] Bus. L.R. 1608, [49].

[79] *Re Railtrack Plc (in administration) (No.2)* [2002] 1 W.L.R. 3002 (CA); *Air Ecosse Ltd v Civil Aviation Authority* (1987) 3 B.C.C. 492 (Court of Session, Inner House). Enforcement of a decision by a regulator would, however, be caught by the moratorium to the extent that it required an application to court: see *Re Railtrack Plc (in administration) (No.2)* [2002] 1 W.L.R. 3002 (CA).

[80] *Hudson v The Gambling Commission* [2010] Bus. L.R. 1608.

[81] *Exchange Travel Agency Ltd v Triton Property Trust Plc* [1991] B.C.C. 341.

proceedings" as defined by the Court of Appeal in *Bristol Airport Plc v Powdrill* and held that "legal process" included the exercise by a landlord of a right of forfeiture by way of peaceable re-entry. Harman J.'s reasoning was plainly influenced by policy considerations[82] and in *Re Olympia & York Canary Wharf*[83] Millett J. declined to follow him on this issue. Millett J. held that the term "legal process" was limited to a "process which requires the assistance of the court"[84]. Accordingly, he found that neither the service on the company of a contractual termination notice or of a notice making time of the essence for the purposes of a contract was the "commencement or continuation" of a "legal process".

9–019 The meaning of "legal process" was considered in *Hudson v The Gambling Commission*[85] in the context of the post-Enterprise Act wording. Norris J. said:

"I think the word "process" suggests something with a defined beginning and an ascertainable final outcome and which, in the interim, is governed by a recognisable procedure. I think the word "legal" indicates that the process must in some sense invoke the compulsive power of law and it suggests that the procedure must be "quasi-legal in nature". One indicator of that might be that the process results in an appeal rather than, for example, reconsideration by means of judicial review . . ."

9–020 It is submitted that, applying the approach taken in *Re Olympia & York Canary Wharf* and *Hudson v The Gambling Commission*, the exercise of set-off is not within the moratorium.[86]

3. THE INTERIM MORATORIUM

9–021 In circumstances where steps have been taken in order to place a company in administration, but before it goes into administration, an interim moratorium may have effect.[87] The interim moratorium applies during the following periods:

---

[82] "It would be astonishing, in my mind, if Parliament has plainly prevented a landlord from issuing a writ for forfeiture or taking steps in the courts to effect a forfeiture and a re-entry but has left entirely open and untouched the right to effect a peaceable re-entry. It must be obvious to all that the better realisation of the company's assets than in a winding up cannot be achieved if in a winding up peaceable re-entry is barred but in an administration peaceable re-entry is not barred." *Exchange Travel Agency Ltd v Triton Property Trust Plc* [1991] B.C.C. 341, 346 per Harman J.

[83] *Re Olympia & York Canary Wharf Ltd (No.1)* [1993] B.C.C. 154.

[84] *Re Olympia & York Canary Wharf Ltd (No.1)* [1993] B.C.C. 154, 157. Millett J.'s analysis of "legal process" in *Re Olympia & York* has been followed in subsequent cases, see e.g. *Clarence Cafe Ltd v Comchester Properties Ltd* [1999] L. & T.R. 303, and, in the context of s.252 of the Act, *McMullen v Cerrone* [1994] B.C.C. 25. Millett J.'s approach would appear to exclude from the scope of the moratorium the service of a demand required as a pre-requisite to the institution of proceedings, a question left open by the same judge in *Barclays Mercantile Business Finance Ltd v Sibec Developments Ltd* [1992] 1 W.L.R. 1253, 1258.

[85] *Hudson v The Gambling Commission* [2010] Bus. L.R. 1608.

[86] See *Electro Magnetic(s) Ltd v Development Bank of Singapore Ltd* [1994] 1 S.L.R. 734.

[87] para.44 of Sch.B1.

(i)   from the making of an application for an administration order until an administration order takes effect or the application is dismissed[88] (save that where an administrative receiver is in office when the application is made, the interim moratorium shall not come into effect until the person who appointed the administrative receiver consents to the making of the administration order[89]);

(ii) from the time when a copy of a notice of intention to appoint an administrator under para.14 or para.27(1) of Sch.B1 is filed with the court (the former must be in the prescribed form) until the appointment of the administrator takes effect or the period of five business days (in the case of a filing under para.14) or 10 business days (in the case of a filing under para.27(1)) beginning with the date of filing expires without an administrator having been appointed[90].

The provisions of paras 42 and 43 of Sch.B1 apply[91] during the period of the interim moratorium save that these provisions shall not prevent or require permission of the court in respect of: (i) the presentation of a petition under s.124A of the Act (public interest) or s.367 of the Financial Services and Markets Act 2000 (petition by Financial Services Authority)[92]; (ii) the appointment of an administrator under para.14 of Sch.B1; (iii) the appointment of an administrative receiver of the company; or (iv) the carrying out by an administrative receiver (whenever appointed) of his functions.[93]

4.   LIFTING THE MORATORIUM

The Act provides no guidance as to when the administrator or the court should allow the moratorium to be lifted in favour of a particular claim. But case law **9–022**

---

[88] para.44(1) of Sch.B1.

[89] para.44(6) of Sch.B1.

[90] paras 44(2) (3) and (4) and 28(2) of Sch.B1.

[91] Subject to the exceptions set out above in relation to default proceedings by an exchange or clearing house (s.161 of the Companies Act 1989) and enforcement of or under "market charges", "system-charges", "collateral security charges", and any security interest created or otherwise arising under a "financial collateral arrangement"—see s.175 Companies Act 1989, regs 3, 6 and 7 of the Financial Markets and Insolvency Regulations 1996, reg.19 of the Financial Markets and Insolvency (Settlement Finality) Regulations 1999, and reg.8 of the Financial Collateral Arrangements (No.2) Regulations 2003 respectively.

[92] Contrary to the interim moratorium under s.10(2)(a) of the Act there is no specific provision saving the presentation of an ordinary winding up petition from the effect of the moratorium. Thus, it is submitted that a winding up petition cannot be presented during the period of the interim moratorium without permission of the court, on the basis that it would be the institution of a "legal process" within para.43(6) of Sch.B1.

[93] para.44(7) of Sch.B1. Where the interim moratorium has come into effect and, during its continuance, an administrative receiver is appointed, the administrative receiver may perform his functions with the benefit of the interim moratorium, pending its expiry in accordance with the provisions set out above. This would not appear to be consistent with the purpose of the interim moratorium but, nevertheless, the court will not grant an application for permission to proceed as a matter of course: see Re Nuthall Lighting Ltd Unreported November 3, 1998 where permission to levy distress was refused.

provides guidance as to the principles to be applied and an administrator is at risk if he fails to exercise his discretion in accordance with such principles.[94]

The correct approach depends upon the nature of the claim being asserted by the applicant, but two principles may be said to apply across the board. First, it is for the applicant to make the case for the moratorium to be lifted.[95] Secondly, an applicant seeking an order lifting the stay will need to demonstrate that its underlying claim is seriously arguable.[96]

9–023　　In relation to claims to an interest in property and claims which are regarded as being equivalent to a proprietary claim,[97] the leading case is *Re Atlantic Computer Systems Plc*.[98] Atlantic Computers leased computers from finance houses and on-leased them to end users. It became unable to pay its debts and an administration order was made for the purpose of a more advantageous realisation of assets than would be achieved in a winding up. The administrators improperly sought to use the moratorium on repossession as a bargaining counter in negotiations with the finance houses and, in the circumstances, the Court of Appeal exercised its discretion to permit the finance houses to repossess their goods. At the conclusion of his judgment, Nicholls L.J. made a number of general observations[99] as to the factors that ought to be applied by administrators and the courts when deciding whether to lift the moratorium. In broad summary:

(i)　　the burden is on the applicant to make the case for permission to proceed;

---

[94] See para.38.

[95] *Re Atlantic Computer Systems Plc* [1992] Ch. 505 (CA).

[96] In *Re Polly Peck International Plc (In Administration) (No.5)* [1998] 3 All E.R. 812 (CA) the Court of Appeal held that the claimant did not have a seriously arguable case for the grant of a remedial constructive trust against the insolvent company in administration and on that basis denied the claimant permission to commence its claim. However, in *Hammonds v Thomas Muckle & Sons Ltd* [2006] B.P.I.R. 704, Judge Langan QC granted a firm of solicitors permission to commence proceedings against a company in administration under s.73 of the Solicitors Act 1974 seeking a declaration that certain of the company's property was subject to a charge in favour of the firm of solicitors. The Judge was satisfied that there was a seriously arguable case and that the order sought would not undermine the purpose of the administration.

[97] In *Somerfield Stores Limited v Spring (Sutton Coldfield) Ltd* [2010] 2 B.C.L.C. 452, the court held that a tenant's right to a new tenancy under the Landlord and Tenant Act 1954 was equivalent to a proprietary right and in *Magical Marking Ltd v Phillips* [2008] F.S.R. 36, the court regarded a claim for an injunction to restrain the misuse of confidential information and infringement of copyright as having, in essence, a "proprietary foundation". In both cases, therefore, the court followed the guidelines set out in Atlantic Computers in deciding whether to lift the moratorium. See also *Astor Chemicals v Synthetic Technology* [1990] B.C.C. 97 in which an application for injunctive relief to prevent the company in administration acting in breach of contract would appear to have been treated as equivalent to a proprietary claim.

[98] *Re Atlantic Computer Systems Plc* [1992] Ch. 505 (CA)

[99] Nicholls L.J. stressed that these "*observations*" should not fetter the wide discretion available to the courts and to administrators to decide each case on its own particular facts. However, they are commonly cited and applied, for example by Judge Weeks QC in *Re David Meek Plant Ltd* [1993] B.C.C. 175. The guidelines have continued to be followed in the case of administrations conducted under the new administration regime post-Enterprise Act 2002.

(ii) subject to the particular circumstances, permission should normally be granted if the proposed step is unlikely to impede achievement of the purpose of the administration[100];

(iii) if granting permission is likely to impede the achievement of the purpose of the administration, the private interests of the applicant must be weighed against the collective interests of the general body of creditors taking into account all the circumstances;

(iv) great weight should be given to proprietary interests and where an administration order is made in lieu of a liquidation it should not be used to benefit the unsecured creditors at the expense of those with proprietary rights;

(v) if significant loss[101] is likely to be caused to the applicant by the continued suspension of his rights then permission should be granted unless substantially greater loss would be caused to the general body of creditors by the grant of permission[102];

(vi) in carrying out this balancing exercise, all the circumstances must be taken into account,[103] including the conduct of the parties. Therefore,

---

[100] e.g. see *Euro Commercial Leasing v Cartwright* [1995] B.C.C. 830 in which a solicitor holding a lien over a sum of money in his client account in respect of unpaid bills was granted leave to enforce the lien by applying the money toward satisfaction of the bills.

[101] For these purposes, loss must be assessed in light of all the circumstances and "comprises any kind of financial loss, direct or indirect, including loss by reason of delay, and may extend to loss which is not financial." Per Nicholls L.J., *Re Atlantic Computer Systems Plc* [1992] Ch.505 (CA), 542.

[102] When the court is considering an application in the context of an administration the purpose of which is to effect a realisation of property in order to make a distribution to one or more secured or preferential creditors pursuant to para.3(1)(c) of Sch.B1, the court will be slow to allow the moratorium to be used to improve the position of the secured creditor at the expense of a third party with proprietary or quasi-proprietary rights: see *Somerfield Stores Ltd v Spring (Sutton Coldfield) Ltd* [2010] 2 B.C.L.C. 452, [13], [17].

[103] e.g. the result in *Re Atlantic Computers* can be contrasted with that in *Re David Meek Plant Ltd* [1993] B.C.C. 175. A further example is provided by the different decisions reached in *Metro Nominees (Wandsworth) (No.1) Ltd v Rayment* [2008] B.C.C. 40 (County Court) and *Innovate Logistics Ltd (in administration) v Sunberry Properties Ltd* [2009] B.C.C. 164 (CA). In both cases, the court considered circumstances in which, shortly after the appointment of an administrator, a company had allowed a third party to take possession of leased premises in breach of the lease. The landlords subsequently sought permission to enforce their rights. In *Metro Nominees*, the unsecured creditors had received the consideration for the tenancy and derived no further benefit from the third party's occupancy. The court found that giving permission to the landlord to pursue proceedings to enforce its contractual right of re-entry was unlikely to impede the achievement of the purpose of the administration. Even if it did, the court was persuaded that applying a balancing exercise would lead to the same conclusion, since the unsecured creditors would be entirely unaffected by giving permission to the landlord to proceed. By contrast, in *Innovate Logistics*, the Court of Appeal refused to grant permission to the landlord to proceed in circumstances where the occupancy of the premises by the third party was shown to have an ongoing benefit to the unsecured creditors by allowing the business to continue to trade and book debts to be collected. See also *NYK Bulkship (Atlantic) NV v Britannia Bulk Plc (in administration)* Unreported November 14, 2008, in which permission to commence an arbitration to determine the status of a lien on sub-freights was denied, on the basis that the validity of the lien was properly to be determined by the Companies Court upon an application for directions by the administrators.

applicants should make their position clear at the outset and bring their application for permission promptly[104];

(vii) in order to do justice between the parties, permission may be granted or refused on terms[105]; and

(viii) where the applicant claims to be secured but the security is disputed, the court must be satisfied that the applicant has a seriously arguable case that it is secured.[106]

9–024   When the applicant's claim is an ordinary money claim against the company, a balancing exercise as between the interests of the applicant and the interests of the general body of creditors may be undertaken,[107] but it will be only in exceptional cases that the court will lift the moratorium.[108] In most cases, the administrators will submit, broadly, that prejudice to the applicant, if any, is outweighed by the prejudice that would be suffered by the general body of creditors if the moratorium were lifted, as a result of the diversion of the

---

[104] In *Bristol Airport Plc v Powdrill* [1990] Ch. 744 (CA), the court declined to lift the moratorium in circumstances where the airport authorities had taken the benefit of the continuation of the company's business during the administration and were only in a position to create the security interest which they sought to enforce as a result of having agreed at the outset to continue to allow the company's aircraft to use their airports. See also *Fashoff (UK) Litd v Linton* [2008] B.C.C. 542 for an example of delay tipping the balance against the applicant.

[105] e.g. (i) permission to recover possession of leased property may be refused but only on condition that rent accruing during the administration is paid as an administration expense; (ii) when refusing permission to enforce a possessory security interest, the courts should make provision to ensure that the security holder is protected by equivalent security following his loss of possession (see para.17); (iii) when refusing permission to enforce a charge by the appointment of a receiver, the administrator may be required to return to court after a short period, on notice to the charge holder, to report on his progress with the realisation of assets (see *Re Meesan Investment Ltd* [1988] 4 B.C.C. 788 and *Royal Trust Bank v Buchler* [1989] B.C.L.C. 130).

[106] In *Funding Corp Block Discounting Ltd v Lexi Holdings Plc (in administration)* [2008] 2 B.C.L.C. 596, both sets of counsel agreed that this test was equivalent to the "real prospect" test applicable to summary judgments under CPR Pt 24.

[107] In some cases the courts have disposed of the application on the basis that there was no force in the applicant's submissions that it would in fact be prejudiced by the maintenance of the stay, rendering the balancing exercise unnecessary—*Re Divine Solutions (UK) Ltd* [2004] B.C.C. 325; *Unite the Union v Nortel Networks UK Ltd (in administration)* [2010] B.C.C. 706.

[108] *AES Barry Limited v TXU Europe Energy* [2005] 2 B.C.L.C. 22, [24], per Patten J.: ". . . it will be in exceptional cases that the Court gives a creditor whose claim is simply a monetary one, a right by the taking of proceedings to override and pre-empt that statutory machinery". Approved and followed in *Unite the Union v Nortel Networks UK Ltd (in administration)* [2010] B.C.C. 706. Where complex litigation involving other parties is already well underway by the time the moratorium comes into force, there may be some support for the view that, in some circumstances, the proceedings should be allowed to continue as against the party in administration. In *New Cap Reinsurance Corp Ltd v HIH Casualty & General Insurance Ltd* [2002] 2 B.C.L.C. 228 (CA) the court lifted the stay on the continuation of proceedings against a company in provisional liquidation (such stay arising under s.130(2) of the Act) in circumstances where the claimant was itself being sued and it was desirable that both sets of claims should be tried at the same time because common factual and legal issues would arise. Along similar lines, in *Magical Marking Ltd v Phillips* [2008] F.S.R. 36, the court allowed pre-existing proceedings to be continued against the company in administration in circumstances where the trial of the action was imminent, the action would continue in any event as against the other defendants and postponing the action as against the defendant in administration would lead to a serious duplication of costs. This was not a case determined under the test set out in *AES Barry*, the claim having a "proprietary foundation" (see fn.106), but it is submitted that the same factors may be persuasive in relation to monetary claims.

administrators' resources away from the fulfilment of their statutory functions and the risk that they could be swamped by other similar claims. In the absence of exceptional circumstances, such factors are likely to prevail.

When the applicant is a public or regulatory body seeking to continue legal process of a public nature, or there are issues of public policy involved, the courts have indicated that they will, as a rule, prefer the interests of the general public over the interests of the general body of creditors[109] although a balancing exercise must still be undertaken.[110]

In response to a request for consent to proceed, administrators must act reasonably, responsibly and speedily and must not use the moratorium as a bargaining counter.[111] If they fail to act appropriately in refusing consent, administrators may be ordered to pay the costs of any resulting application to court. Administrators who are found to have wrongfully refused to consent to the lifting of the moratorium may, furthermore, be at risk of a claim in damages. In *Barclays Mercantile Business Finance Ltd v Sibec Developments Ltd*[112] the administrators refused to give consent to the repossession of certain cars and computer equipment leased to the company. Most of the goods were not in use by the company during the administration. The owner sought leave to repossess and also sought damages from the administrators personally for wrongful interference with the goods. Just before the hearing the administrators agreed to allow repossession. When the administrators later applied for their release the owner of the goods applied for such release to be stayed pending resolution of its claim against the administrators. The court agreed to stay the administrators' release. Millett J. held[113]:

9–025

> "In my judgment the administrators remain exposed to the claim so long as they have not been released, whether they committed the tort of conversion or not. That is because [they] are officers of the court and at all times subject to the court's direction. If they wish to make use of another's property for the purposes of the administration and cannot agree terms,

---

[109] See *Re Rhondda Waste Disposal Ltd (In Administration)* [2001] Ch. 57 (CA), 70–71 and 74 in which the Court of Appeal permitted criminal proceedings to continue on the grounds that the gravity of the offence and the safety of the public outweighed the interests of the creditors. See also *Carr v British International Helicopters Ltd* [1993] B.C.C. 855 for an example of a case in which the pursuit of the claims was not found to be likely to interfere with the administrators' functions and where public policy considerations also appear to have been in the mind of the court. Lord Coulsfield said: ". . . the employment protection legislation is designed in the main, for the protection of employees. One of the principal objects of the legislation is to secure the speedy presentation and disposal of employees claims, and it is very hard to see that in the ordinary case, it is likely to be really prejudicial to the administration of the company that such matters should be so dealt with."

[110] See *Hudson v The Gambling Commission* [2010] Bus. L.R. 1608 in which the court held that the prejudice to the Gambling Commission if the moratorium was not lifted was so slight as to be outweighed by the interests of the general body of creditors.

[111] *Re Atlantic Computers Plc* [1992] Ch. 505 (CA); *Bristol Airport Plc v Powdrill* [1990] Ch. 744 (CA); *Barclays Mercantile Business Finance Ltd v Sibec Developments Ltd* [1992] 1 W.L.R. 1253; *Re David Meek Plant Ltd* [1993] B.C.C. 175.

[112] *Barclays Mercantile Business Finance Ltd v Sibec Developments Ltd* [1992] 1 W.L.R. 1253.

[113] *Barclays Mercantile Business Finance Ltd v Sibec Developments Ltd* [1992] 1 W.L.R. 1253, 1259.

they can seek the directions of the court. If administrators wrongly retain goods otherwise than for the proper purposes of the administration, for example to use them as a bargaining counter, the owner can apply to the court to direct the administrators to hand over the goods without the need for action, and to pay compensation for having retained them in the meantime."

Plainly, in cases of doubt, administrators should seek directions.

Chapter 10

Continuation of Trading

RESCUE AND REALISATION

1. ADMINISTRATION

An administrator is obliged to consider the rescue of the company as his **10–001** primary objective unless it is not reasonably practical, or a better return for the creditors as a whole can be achieved in another way. Usually, a rescue during administration will involve a company voluntary arrangement under Pt I of the Act or, more unusually, a scheme of arrangement under the Companies Act 2006. Often this will require a period of trading, following administration, while the relevant approval mechanisms take place.

If a better outcome can be achieved through a disposal, a period of trading is also likely to be needed to allow for marketing of the business and assets and negotiation of the sale contract, unless (as is frequently the case) the sale can be consummated immediately on the administrator's appointment (a "pre-packaged sale").

In the case of a pre-packaged sale of an operating company there will also usually be a period of trading prior to administration while buyers are sought and the sale contract is negotiated. This trading will be under the control of the directors. But they are likely to trade under the guidance of the prospective administrator. Trading during this period will usually require further credit to be incurred by the company.

The pre-packaged sale will invariably leave the company insolvent. The taking of credit in the knowledge it cannot be repaid, or recklessly as to whether it can be repaid, is fraudulent trading. It is both a criminal offence[1] and, in the event that the company is later wound up, a circumstance in which liability can be imposed under s.213 of the Act. The court may order any persons knowingly party of carrying on business in such a manner to contribute such amount to the company's assets as the court thinks fit.[2] The prospective administrator (and indeed other professional advisers and financiers involved in the trading strategy) should therefore take care to ensure that adequate funding is available to meet the cost of credit taken during the pre-administration marketing and negotiation period.[3]

---

[1] Companies Act 2006, s.993.
[2] Companies Act 2006, s.213(2).
[3] See *Re Leyland DAF Ltd* [1994] 4 All E.R. 300 and para.2–029, above. See also Statement of Insolvency Practice 16, para.6

2. RECEIVERSHIP

10–002 A receiver does not have a statutory requirement to consider rescue. Similar questions relating to trading will arise in the case of a receivership as in an administration. Indeed, the absence of a moratorium in receivership may make it more likely that the sale is conducted on a pre-packaged basis.

CONTINUATION OF TRADING

1. ADMINISTRATION

10–003 Achieving the primary purpose of rescuing a company in administration will almost always require a period of trading. A rescue will usually involve some element of compromise with the company's existing creditors through a company voluntary arrangement and at least 14 days' notice is required to be given by the administrator for a meeting of creditors to consider a CVA.[4] The administrator will therefore need to take account of the likely outcome of trading in assessing whether rescue or an immediate disposal will achieve the best result for the creditors as a whole.[5] In considering the implications of trading, the administrator must take account of the expenses that will be involved. The introduction into the Insolvency Rules relating to administration of a list of expenses very similar to that which has long existed in liquidation.[6] This raised questions about whether the approach to expenses in administration should more closely mirror that taken in liquidation. Paragraph 99 of Sch.B1 sets out the general priority of certain categories of expenses. It is in similar form to s.19 of the Act in the legislation previously applicable. The purposes of administration and liquidation being largely dissimilar, it had been argued that the similarity of wording between the rules applicable to administration and liquidation did not impose the same approach. This question has now been largely resolved in favour of the liquidation approach to administration expenses.[7] Accordingly, an administration must anticipate that post-appointment administration expenses will be assessed in the same way as those

---

[4] Insolvency Rule 1.11(1). In circumstances when the company has only a few creditors who agree to compromise their claims the company is likely to avoid administration altogether.

[5] para.3(3)(b) of Sch.B1.

[6] See Insolvency Rule 2.67(1) and Insolvency Rule 4.218(1). See generally, Ch.4, above.

[7] See *Exeter City Council v Bairstow* [2007] 4 All E.R. 437 (non-domestic rates); revised as to unoccupied non-domestic property by the Non-Domestic Rating (Unoccupied Property) (England) Regulation 2008 (SI 2008/386); the Non-Domestic Rating (Unoccupied Property) (Scotland) Regulations 2008 (SSI 2008/83) and the Non-Domestic Rating (Unoccupied Property) (Wales) Regulations 2008 (SI 2008/2499 (W217)); *Goldace (Offices) Ltd v Nortel Networks UK Ltd (In Administration)* [2010] Ch. 455; *Sixty UK Ltd (In Administration)* [2010] B.P.I.R. 1234; *Cheshire West and Chester BC, Petitioners* [2011] B.C.C. 174 (Court of Session, Outer House) and *Re Nortel GmbH* [2011] B.C.C. 277. See STOP PRESS, after the preface to this work, on the Court of Appeal in decision *Nortel. Re Allders Department Stores Ltd (In Administration)* [2005] 2 All E.R. 122 held that statutory liabilities for redundancy and unfair dismissal payments were not administration expenses under either r.2.67(1) (a) (expenses properly incurred) or 2.6.7.1 (f) ("necessary disbursements"). The *Allders* decision sits somewhat uncomfortably with the more recent decisions on administration expenses.

applicable to liquidation. The case law on administration expenses under the pre-Enterprise Act administration regime[8] now appears to be of only historic relevance

The administrator will also need to consider the funds available to fund trading and administration expenses. If the company has not granted security, his concern will be focused on the liquidity of the company's assets to meet the costs of trading. In the more usual circumstances when the company has granted debenture security his access to assets for trading expenses will be restricted to the pool of floating charge assets.[9] Following the decision of the House of Lords in *Re Spectrum Plus Ltd (In Liquidation)*[10] on the requirements for the creation of a valid fixed charge on book debts, there has been increased commercial incentive for companies to raise working capital by selling their book debts rather than borrowing money on the security of them. In those circumstances the debts are no longer assets of the company. The pool of assets available for administration trading may then be limited to stock which is not subject to valid retention of title. This limitation on funding goes some way to explaining the decline of trading administrations in favour of pre-packaged sales.

10–004

2. RECEIVERSHIP

Historically, in a receivership the primary purpose and advantage of a floating charge over the undertaking as distinct from a fixed charge over specific assets was that the creditor was afforded as part of his security the right on crystallisation (1) to continue the company's business and to do so through an individual (the receiver) who in the eyes of the law (until winding up) acts as agent for the company; and (2) to sell either the undertaking and business so continued as a going concern or simply to sell the assets charged. Following the amendments to the Act effective from September 15, 2003 those advantages are likely to be limited to appointment of administrative receivers under charges granted before September 15, 2003 and under charges granted after that date in circumstances when the prohibition on appointment of administrative receivers in s.72A of the Act does not apply.[11]

10–005

---

[8] *Re Atlantic Computer Systems Plc (No.1)* [1992] Ch. 505 (CA) (see for instance the *Goldacre* decision, [25] pointing to the rejection of the *Atlantic Computers* approach by the House of Lords in *Re Toshoku Finance UK Plc (In Liquidation)* [2002] 1 W.L.R. 671 (HL)).

[9] para.70(1) of Sch.B1. Although it is likely that if the administrator realises fixed charge assets, at least with the secured creditor's consent, he will be entitled to the expenses of realisation: *Re Regent's Canal Iron Works Co Ex. p. Grissell (No.2)* (1875) L.R. 3 Ch. D 411 (CA) affirmed in *Buchler v Talbot*; sub nom. *Re Leyland DAF Ltd* [2004] 2 A.C. 298 (HL).

[10] *Re Spectrum Plus Ltd (In Liquidation)* [2005] 2 A.C. 680 (HL) (and the earlier Privy Council decision in *Re Brumark Investments Ltd*, sub nom. *Agnew v Inland Revenue Commissioners* [2001] 2 A.C. 710 (PC)).

[11] See ss.72B to 72H of the Act. It is still possible to trade a company in receivership in cases outside these exceptions, provided the debenture gives sufficient powers to the receiver and the receiver is not appointed over substantially the whole of the assets (s.29(2)). The test appears to be whether the receiver is appointed under the floating charge rather than the scope of the charge itself: *Meadrealm v Transcontinental Golf Construction* Unreported November 29, 1991. Where a foreign incorporated company with a centre of main interests outside the EC for the purposes of Council Regulation (EC) No.1346/2000 on insolvency proceedings [2000] OJ L160/1 and the Cross-Border Insolvency Regulations 2006 (SI 2006/1030), has a business located in England and

3. POWERS TO TRADE

(a) Legal considerations

10–006   Debentures have for many years included provisions expressly conferring upon the receiver the power to carry on the company's business and the right to do so as agent of the company. These provisions are designed to enable the mortgagee to enjoy the advantage of his nominee, the receiver, displacing the mortgagor from control of the mortgaged property and from receipt of the income derived from it whilst at the same time avoiding assuming the liabilities of a mortgagee in possession.[12] A debenture-holder appointing an administrator achieves the same result since the Act provides that an administrator acts as agent of the company.[13] In the case of an administrative receiver, the Act deems the power to carry on the company's business and right to do so as agent of the company to be conferred on the receiver in the absence of some inconsistent provision in the debenture.[14] In any case where the power and right are conferred, in the absence of some clearly indicated intention to the contrary, the receiver will be deemed to be exercising the power to trade (and accordingly to enter into contracts) as agent of the company unless and until the company goes into liquidation.[15] Liquidation does not terminate the receiver's right to carry on the company's business, but the receiver cannot thereafter carry on business as agent of the company. Exceptionally, if authorised by the debenture-holder, the receiver may carry on business as agent for the debenture-holder, or (if the circumstances so require) he will carry on business as principal. On liquidation, only one of the last two courses is available and the latter is the usual. These issues are not relevant in administration since a company cannot be in administration and liquidation at the same time.

10–007   The purpose of appointing the receiver to be agent of the company is "simply in order to free the debenture-holders who appointed him from responsibility for his acts".[16] The powers of management of the directors are suspended and the receiver has complete control of the company's affairs. The relative

---

has granted a debenture a position very close to administrative receiverships may be achieved by utilising powers under a debenture. The prohibition under s.72A of the Act does not appear to apply to such companies—see s.28(1) of the Act. It is suggested that the decision in *Re International Bulk Commodities Ltd* [1993] Ch. 77 is no longer good law on this point. Such a "quasi" administrative receivership would not of course be subject to or have the benefit of statutory provisions applying to the de jure administrative receivers. The position would akin to a pre-1986 receiver and manager.

[12] *Medforth v Blake* [2000] Ch. 86 (CA), 93–94.

[13] para.69 of Sch.B1.

[14] s.42(1) and Sch.1, para.14. In the case of non-administrative receivers, the law continues to be that such receiver has no power to carry on business unless the power is conferred by the debenture: *Bompas v King* (1886) L.R. 33 Ch. D. 279 (CA). If a receiver is given power both to trade and to borrow, he is authorised to purchase on credit terms: *Ross v Taylor* [1985] S.L.T. 387 (IH (1 Div)).

[15] Insolvency Act 1986, s.44(1)(a) (administrative receivers) and *Thomas v Todd* [1926] 2 K.B. 511.

[16] Per Cross J. in *Lawson (Inspector of Taxes) v Hosemaster Machine Co* [1965] 1 W.L.R. 1399, 1410; reversed [1966] 1 W.L.R. 1300 (CA).

positions of the receiver and the directors appear clearly from the judgment of Brightman J. in *Re Emmadart*[17]:

"... the appointment of a receiver for debenture-holders suspends the powers of the directors over the assets in respect of which the receiver has been appointed so far as it is requisite to enable the receiver to discharge his functions[18] ... The authority of a receiver is not however, co-terminous with the authority of the board of directors. The powers of the receiver stem from (i) the powers contained in the memorandum and articles of association of the company to create mortgages and charges, coupled with (ii) the particular powers which have been conferred on a duly appointed receiver pursuant to the due exercise of the company's borrowing powers."[19]

In administration the directors' powers and those of the company are not exercisable save to the extent that the administrator authorises their continuation.[20]

Prior to the Insolvency Act 1986, one limitation was recognised on the powers which could be conferred on a receiver. A receiver appears to have been limited in the scope of his activities as agent of the company by the powers contained in the company's memorandum and articles.[21] There is nothing in the Act which would appear to remove this limitation on the powers of the administrative receiver.[22] The same position applies to administrators.[23] However, a person dealing with an administrator or administrative receiver in good faith and for value is no longer concerned to inquire whether the office-holder is acting within his powers,[24] and accordingly is not prejudiced if the transaction is ultra vires. The sole effect of a transaction during receivership being ultra vires will be to expose the receiver to liability to his appointor or the company if damage results. In administration the liability of the administrator would be to the company, although the administrator may be appointed by the debenture-holder his obligations are owed to the company and, through

10–008

---

[17] *Re Emmadart* [1979] Ch. 540. The agency also separates the receiver from liability for the acts of the company (unless he fails to exclude the effect of s.44(1)(b) or in cases where ss.44(1) (employees) and 232(2)(a)(utilities) apply). This facilitates the acceptance of the appointment by the receiver. The statutory agency of an administrator may have been designed with this purpose in mind.

[18] At 544, citing *Lawson (Inspector of Taxes) v Hosemaster Machine Co*, above and *Newhart Developments Ltd v Co-operative Commercial Bank Ltd* [1978] Q.B. 814 (CA). The power extends to control over the rights and powers of the company at least in so far as they have commercial value or significance: *Independent Pension Trustee Ltd v Capital LAW Construction Co Ltd*, 1997 S.L.T. 1105 (Court of Session, Outer House).

[19] *Re Emmadart* [1979] Ch.540, 547. See also above, para.2–026.

[20] para.64(1) of Sch.B1.

[21] *Lawson (Inspector of Taxes) v Hosemaster Machine Co* [1966] 1 W.L.R. 1300 (CA), 1315.

[22] s.42(1) reads into a debenture the powers specified in Sch.1 unless inconsistent with its provisions: it does not deal with the question whether the powers purportedly conferred on the receiver are ultra vires.

[23] See *Re Home Treat Ltd* [1991] B.C.C. 165.

[24] Insolvency Act 1986, s.42(3). Paragraph 59(3) of Sch.B1 "Good faith" means a belief that everything is being rightly and properly done: see *Mogridge v Clapp* [1892] 3 Ch. 382 (CA).

it, to the general body of creditors.[25] The apparent limitation on powers of the receiver as agent of the company, however, should not apply to the debenture-holder when exercising his powers as mortgagee or to the receiver when exercising, as agent of the mortgagee or as principal, powers delegated to him by the mortgagee.[26] One further limitation may exist where a receiver proposes to enter into a transaction for which statute requires the consent of the shareholders.[27]

(i) New contracts

10–009 A receiver (administrative[28] or non-administrative[29]) may if so authorised prior to any liquidation enter into contracts in the name and on behalf of the company, and if he does so and stipulates that he will not be personally liable, then the company alone will be liable and the receiver will not be. The stipulation need not be express: it may be implied.[30] An administrator is not subject to the equivalent personal liability in contracts entered into by him during the administration. However liabilities under such contracts are expenses of the administration with higher priority than the administrator's own remuneration.[31] It is not clear whether, and to what extent, this priority can be excluded or waived.[32]

(ii) Prior contracts

10–010 In the case of contracts made prior to his appointment, the office-holder generally has a free choice whether and for how long the company should give effect to them. He may decide that the contract shall continue in force so long as the company fulfils its obligations thereunder, or at any time may decide to

---

[25] It would follow that if damage resulted from the administrator acting in a way which was ultra vires, he would prima facie be liable for breach of statutory duty.

[26] In the case of companies incorporated under the Companies Acts the purpose of the ultra vires rule is to protect creditors and shareholders against misapplication of funds by the directors: *Trevor v Whitworth* (1887) L.R. 12 App. Cas. 409 (HL), 414–415. A mortgagee of the undertaking can be subject to no restriction beyond those imposed by the debenture and by equitable duties with regard to the realisation of the mortgaged property (discussed above in Ch.13). It might be possible to achieve the same result in administration if the administrator or the court gives the secured creditor permission to enforce its security (para.43(2) of Sch.B1).

[27] *Demite Ltd v Protec Health Ltd* [1998] B.C.C. 638: see below, paras 11–028 to 11–030. When considering the applicability of the Companies Act 1985, s.320 it is the company's equity of redemption that is relevant: *UltraFrame (UK) Ltd v Fielding* [2005] EWHC 1638 (Ch). Companies Act 2006, ss.190–196 reverse the effect of the *Demite* case in respect of administrators.

[28] Insolvency Act 1986, s.44(1)(b).

[29] Insolvency Act 1986, s.37.

[30] *Hill Samuel & Co Ltd v Laing* (1988) 4 B.C.C. 9 (Court of Session, Outer House), 20–21, not following the dictum of Cross J. to the contrary at first instance in *Lawson (Inspector of Taxes) v Hosemaster Machine Co* [1965] 1 W.L.R. 1399, 1410–1411. In the case of distributions in administration, liabilities arising out of post administration contracts will not be provable.

[31] para.99(4) of Sch.B1.

[32] It is possible for a creditor of a company to agree contractually to exclude its right to prove (*Re SSSL Realisations (2002) Ltd* [2006] Ch. 610 (CA)) or to subordinate it to other creditors (*Re Maxwell Communications Ltd* [1993] 1 W.L.R. 1402). These principles have not yet been tested in the context of administration expenses. In principle there seems no reason why an expense creditor should not be able to waive such a right. However, if the expense in question arose post administration it is difficult to see how it could rank with pre-administration creditors for dividend.

repudiate and bring the contract to an end. The decision in *Goldacre Offices Ltd v Nortel Networks UK Ltd*[33] shows that, in the case of administration at least, the office holder is not able to decide to take part of the benefit of a contract (in that case a lease) at part of the cost if the effect of doing so disadvantages the creditor as to the balance of the subject matter of the contract.

If and when a receiver decides that the company shall repudiate the contract, **10–011** the other party is left with his remedy in damages against the company and a claim as an unsecured creditor and has no claim against the receiver or his appointor, notwithstanding the receiver's interim adoption of the contracts in the course of managing the company's business. This does not offend against basic conceptions of justice and fairness. The liability has been undertaken by the company at the inception of the contract and the benefit accrues to the company even when the receiver is in office. The other contracting party (like other creditors) must look to the company for payment. During the receivership the other contracting party is in no way inhibited from exercising his contractual rights and remedies.[34]

To this general rule there are two exceptions. First, the receiver cannot effect **10–012** the discharge of contracts entered into by the company which are binding on the appointing debenture-holder and are specifically enforceable, e.g. for the sale or lease of property.[35] Secondly, if the receiver has adopted any contract of employment in the course of carrying out his functions, though his freedom of action in respect of a repudiation of the contract is unchanged, he is personally liable on the contract to the other contracting party.[36] The receiver should also bear in mind that his treatment of employees can give rise to liabilities which will pass on to a purchaser of the business and therefore have an impact on the price that may be obtained.[37]

The position of an administrator is different. He is not personally liable in **10–013** respect of adopted employee contracts.[38] Case law on the legislation applicable prior to September 15, 2003 indicated that the court had a discretion as to which pre-administration liabilities would be accorded priority as administration expenses and that the exercise of the discretion in administration was subject to different considerations from those which applied in relation to liquidation expenses.[39] The current legislation contains a priority list of expenses[40] which closely resemble those applicable in liquidation.[41] The House of Lords has ruled on the latter in the context of tax charges arising during

---

[33] *Goldacre Offices Ltd v Nortel Networks UK Ltd* [2010] Ch. 455.

[34] *Re Atlantic Computer Systems Plc* [1992] Ch. 505 (CA), 526–527.

[35] See below, Ch.13. See also *Cater-King Pty Ltd v Westpac Banking Corp* [1989] 7 A.C.L.C. 993.

[36] In the case of administrative receivers under the Insolvency Act 1986, s.44(1)(b), and in the case of other receivers under Insolvency Act 1986, s.37(1)(a). For discussion of extent of liability, see below, Ch.28.

[37] See below, para.11–063.

[38] See para.99(5) of Sch.B1, contrast s.44(1)(b). An administrator may be personally liable for breach of statutory duty if he fails to accord expense claims their statutory priority.

[39] *Re Atlantic Computer Systems Plc (No.1)* [1992] Ch. 505 (CA).

[40] Insolvency Rule 2.67(1).

[41] Insolvency Rule 4.218(1).

liquidation.[42] That decision has been distinguished in an administration context to exclude its application to certain employee claims arising during administration.[43] It now appears that the restrictive approach to the treatment of employee claims as expenses is not indicative of a general attitude to the treatment of post-administration liabilities. It arises primarily from the specific statutory limitations applicable to employee claims.[44] In a non-employment context non-domestic rates and rents payable for periods of occupation by administrators have been held to be expenses, as have financed support directions under the pensions legislation.[45] The pre-2003 case law on administration expenses now appears to be largely irrelevant and it would be prudent for administrators to provide fully for post-administration liabilities. Administrators should also assume that where the benefit of pre-administration contracts has been taken for the purposes of the administration the discretion of the court to treat liabilities on such contacts as expenses, will be exercised in favour of the other contracting party on a similar basis as would be the case in liquidation.

(iii) Ratified contracts

10–014 An office-holder can ratify a contract purportedly made on behalf of the company by an agent of the company without authority before or after the date of the receivership, and indeed, if the contract is advantageous, the office-holder may be in default of his duty if he refuses to do so.[46] In relation to receivers, a contract made during an earlier receivership may be ratified by a later receiver or (when all or any receiverships are discharged) by the company itself. The only bar to such ratification is an earlier repudiation of the contract by a prior receiver or the acquisition of rights by third parties in respect of any property in question between the date of the purported contract and ratification.[47] Such ratification does not operate to impose any personal liability on any earlier receiver during whose receivership the purported contract was made or the later receiver who ratified it.[48] The ratification does not constitute "the entering into" of a contract for the purposes of s.44(1)(b) of the Insolvency Act 1986 so as to require the receiver when ratifying to disclaim personal liability.[49]

Re Toshoku Finance UK Plc (In Liquidation) [2002] 1 W.L.R. 671 (HL).

[43] See Re Allders Department Stores Ltd (In Administration) [2005] 2 All E.R. 122 (redundancy and unfair dismissal payments) and Re Huddersfield Fine Worsteds Ltd (Krasner v McMath), Re Ferrotech Ltd and Re Granville Technology Group Ltd [2005] 4 All E.R. 886 (CA) (payments in lieu of notice and protective awards). See also Re Leeds United Association Football Club Ltd [2008] B.C.C. 11 (damages for wrongful dismissal).

[44] See para.99(5) and (6) and the previous history of statutory intervention to limit the extent to which employee claims are administration expenses (Insolvency Act 1994).

[45] See the cases referred to in fn.7. It is suggested that these, particularly Re Nortel GmbH [2011] B.C.C. 277, sit uncomfortably with the restrictive approach to employee claims.

[46] Lawson (Inspector of Taxes) v Hosemaster Machine Co [1966] 1 W.L.R. 1300 (CA), 1314.

[47] Lawson (Inspector of Taxes) v Hosemaster Machine Co [1966] 1 W.L.R. 1300 (CA), 1316.

[48] Lawson (Inspector of Taxes) v Hosemaster Machine Co [1966] 1 W.L.R. 1300 (CA), 1316.

[49] This is implicit in Lawson (Inspector of Taxes) v Hosemaster Machine Co [1966] 1 W.L.R. 1300 (CA). The alternative view would preclude any ratification without assuming personal liability. For such ratification would involve either the unilateral imposition of a new term by the receiver (i.e. his exemption from personal liability) or (if the other party agreed to this term) the making by the parties of a new contract between the parties incorporating this term.

Nor does ratification of a contract of employment necessarily involve adoption of the contract by the receiver within the meaning of the section if the ratification takes place within 14 days of the appointment of the receiver.[50]

The position is different in administration. The ratification of a pre-adminis- **10–015** tration contract by an administrator is very likely to give post administration liabilities under the contract expense status. The effect of para.99(1) of Sch.B1 is to preserve expense status for the contracts entered into by a former administrator. It is suggested that the same will apply if a contract ratified by the former administrator has been accorded expense status.

(iv) Indemnity as to contracts

An administrator has a statutory right of indemnity out of floating charge assets **10–016** for his remuneration and expenses.[51] If he realises fixed charge assets for the benefit of the debenture-holder he is entitled to deduct the costs of doing so from the proceeds.[52]

If the receiver trades in his own name, then he must rely on either his statutory **10–017** right to an indemnity out of the assets of the company[53] or his contractual indemnity (if any) from his debenture-holders. Many institutional appointors are reluctant to give indemnities at the time of appointment. Commercial pressures usually result in receivers accepting such appointments without indemnities.[54]

(b) Commercial considerations

In the short term, excellent reasons for carrying on trading may include: **10–018**

    (a) enabling work in progress to be completed so as to realise a higher sale price or to guard against set-offs in respect of book debts. It is

---

[50] Insolvency Act 1986, ss.37(2) and 44(2).

[51] para.99(3) of Sch.B1.

[52] By virtue of the salvage principle (see *Re Regent's Canal Ironworks Ex p. Grissell (No.2)* (1875) L.R. 3 Ch. D. 411 (CA) followed in *Re Buchler v Talbot, Leyland DAF Ltd*; sub nom. (above); also see para.71(3)(a) of Sch.B1).

[53] Insolvency Act 1986, ss.37(1)(b) and 44(1)(c). It is suggested that this right of indemnity is not confined to floating charge assets. In the case of a non-administrative receiver it is likely that his appointment will only relate to fixed charge assets. Also, the word "assets" in s.37(1)(a) is not qualified by "of the company". In the case of an administrative receiver the indemnity is so qualified (s.44(1)(c)) but it is difficult to see why a receiver appointed over fixed charge assets should be entitled to an indemnity from those assets but a receiver appointed over both fixed and floating charges assets should be limited to an indemnity from floating charges assets. See also s.45(3) which charges the right of indemnity on the property of the company in the hands of the receiver at the time of his vacation of office in priority to "any" security held by his appointor. The provisions of s.109 of the Law of Property Act (where not contractually excluded) may in practice reinforce the ability to recourse to the fixed charge. In circumstances when a receiver has a statutory obligation to pay expenses and a statutory indemnity it seems likely that the expenses creditors concerned will be subrogated to that indemnity (see *Powdrill v Watson* [1995] 2 A.C. 394).

[54] A solicitor who fails to advise the receiver to obtain an indemnity may be liable in negligence: *RA Price Securities Ltd v Henderson* [1989] 2 N.Z.L.R. 257 (NZCA). It is suggested that in the case of insolvency practitioners taking appointments from large financial institutions, the well understood commercial position referred to above would limit the requirement to advise on the need for an indemnity to circumstances of unusual risk.

increasingly common for companies to sell their book debts under discounting or factoring agreements. Trading will nonetheless often benefit the company by improving the collectibility of the debts thereby making good the company's claim to the price for which they were sold.[55]

When there is no effective retention of title on stock the officeholder is able to obtain the existing stock and work in progress without payment which makes it easier to trade out at a profit. Where, as is often the case, much of the stock is identifiable by the supplier[56] and subject to retention of title provisions which are not limited to stock supplied under unpaid invoices, the officeholder may face greater difficulties.

A receiver may be able to recover the gross profit margin of sale price over purchase price for the stock by agreeing with the retention of title creditor to dispose of them subject to an undertaking to remit the value of the outstanding invoices.[57]

An administrator has a statutory right to dispose of floating charge assets as it they were not subject to security.[58]

In relation to stock subject to retention of title, the administrator is in a different position to an administrative receiver since he can seek an order of the court to dispose of the stock.[59] Nonetheless in recent years there has been a significant decrease in the proportion of businesses entering administrative receivership and administration which are traded and a corresponding increase in pre-packages sales. The increased prevalence of discounting and factoring of receivables and wide retention of title provisions may be significant contributory factors to this development;

---

[55] It is common for the officeholders to enter into an amendment agreement with the receivables financier governing the terms on which the discounting or factoring agreement will operate during the insolvency.

[56] Either as a result of increased supplier awareness of the importance of retention of title or as a by-product of other requirements for traceability, for instance in the food supply industry.

[57] A supplier with a wide retention of title clause may be entitled to insist on the whole of the proceeds of sale but the cost of the supplier removing the goods may give the receiver the commercial leverage to agree the retention of the gross profit on sales.

[58] para.70(1) Sch.B1. This does not discharge the security since the priority of the floating charge holder attaches to the property acquired as a result of the disposal (para.72(2) Sch.B1). The effect of this provision has not been much explored in case law. The reference to "priority" may mean that it is the charge holder's common law priority position as a fixed charge holder that is preserved, subject to the statutory invasions of that position.

[59] para.72(1) Sch.B1. The retention of title creditor is entitled to have the sums due under the retention of title agreement satisfied out of the net proceeds of sale of the goods. The usual situation is that there are separate contracts for the supply of goods. Each contract retains title until all sums due in respect of goods, whenever supplied, have been paid. It is not usual for each contract to provide that sums due but unpaid under previous contracts are liabilities under the later contact. It is suggested therefore that the sum payable to the retention of title creditor will usually be limited to the invoice price of the goods sold (see para.72(3)). The power of the court to order the sale of secured assets in administrative receivership does not extend to assets subject to retention of title (see s.43).

(b) enabling the office-holder to make inquiries and make better informed decisions as to future trading; and

(c) providing time to market the business for sale as a going concern.

To justify trading on in the long term there must be a prospect of: **10–019**

(a) trading out, i.e. into a position of solvency; or, more frequently,

(b) selling the business as a going concern at a sum substantially greater than the break-up value of the assets.[60]

For any trading to be feasible, the office-holder must have access to: **10–020**

(a) employees able and willing to carry on the work;

(b) unencumbered supplies of any materials required or agreement with retention of title creditors[61];

(c) finance, normally only obtainable from trading cash flow, by agreement with the receivables financier when discounting or factoring agreements exist or (in the case of receivership) loans from the appointing debenture-holder[62];

(d) an available market for the finished product.

The office-holder is under a duty not to diminish the assets available to preferential creditors and he must have this in mind when considering the assets available for trade[63]. In the (perhaps rare) case where the company has at the commencement of the administration or receivership a fund of money available to discharge liabilities to preferential creditors, the office-holder should **10–021**

---

[60] In administration the benefit to the creditors as a whole or the avoidance of unnecessary risk to creditors may on occasion justify trading even though only a break-up sale is ultimately expected.

[61] Clauses in supply contracts providing for termination of contracts on insolvency are effective (subject to limited statutory exceptions). Where the office-holder is prepared to give an undertaking to meet the cost of new supplies this can improve the supply position in the business as the office-holder's commitment may be seen as a more reliable guarantee of payment than that which the company was able to provide when on the brink of insolvency.

[62] para.3 of Sch.1 and para.70(1) of Sch.B1 to the Act would appear to give an administrator power to borrow from any party and grant security over the floating charge assets of the company. However, the reference in para.70(2) of Sch.B1 to the preservation of the existing floating charge holder's priority in relation to the acquired assets (the new loan) gives rise to an argument that the loan would be subject to a fixed charge in favour of the existing debenture holder whose floating charge has crystallised. It is thought that this argument would be resolved in favour of the administrator since the priority of the existing debenture holder over the assets caught by the crystallised floating charge is subject to the administrator's right to deal.

[63] It is less clear whether directors have a duty to preserve the pool of floating charge assets for preferential and unsecured creditors (via the prescribed part) during trading prior to a pre-packaged sale. The duty under s.214 of the Act to minimise the loss to the company's creditors and the case law on that provision contains no guidance whether directors should act to mitigate loss or improve recovery for particular bodies of creditors. In practice a pre-packaged sale will usually reduce or eliminate preferential creditors.

not count on using these funds, for their loss may expose him to personal liability to the preferential creditors who have first call on such funds.[64] Following the introduction of the "prescribed part" of floating charge realisations for unsecured creditors[65] the same logic applies to the rights of the unsecured creditors in relation to the prescribed part. However, by analogy to the position in winding up, it may be possible to ask the court for directions to enable the office-holder to use these funds without risk, joining the preferential creditors as parties if they refuse to consent.[66] In principle, the same duty applies where the company has unrealised assets such as stock or work in progress. Subject to the expenses of the administration or receivership property chargeable to floating charge realisations, the preferential and (to the extent of the prescribed part) the unsecured creditors have first call on their realisable value.[67] But their value if the office-holder decides not to trade is likely to be very low indeed, and trading may be essential if any beneficial realisation is to be achieved.[68] If the office-holder decides that he should prudently trade on, he will inevitably use such assets, and this method of realisation should not ordinarily expose the office-holder to liability if the initial decision can reasonably be justified in the interests of the preferential creditors and unsecured creditors, even if in fact (notwithstanding the exercise of all reasonable diligence and expertise)[69] the endeavour fails to produce additional funds for them.

10–022   In case of doubt as to the wisdom of trading on, a receiver is probably safer in simply realising assets than in attempting to trade on, since he can have no duty to trade on if the results are speculative.

10–023   There is a difference of emphasis between administrators and receivers in respect of the decision to trade on. In many circumstances trading on will be required to effect a rescue of the company as a going concern or a better outcome for the creditors as a whole than would be likely in a liquidation.[70] If

---

[64] *Westminster Corp v Haste* [1950] Ch. 442 and see below, Chs 27 and 28. It is unclear to what extent the primary obligation of an administrator to seek to rescue the company permits him to resort to funds otherwise available to preferential creditors with lower risk of liability that would apply to a receiver. It seems likely that more flexibility would be allowed to an administrator as his activities seek to benefit creditors generally.

[65] Insolvency Act 1986, s.176A.

[66] Insolvency Act 1986, s.35 (receivership); para.63 of Sch.B1 (administration). Note that the introduction into liquidation of statutory priority for liquidation expenses over floating charge assets does not give a voice to potential beneficiaries of the prescribed part on the question of litigation expenses even though those expenses will have priority to their claims.

[67] Following the decision in *Re Toshoku Finance UK Plc (In Liquidation)* [2002] 1 W.L.R. 671 (HL) and the introduction of the list of expenses to administration through Insolvency Rule 2.67(1) and the decision in *Exeter City Council v Bairstow* [2007] 4 All E.R. 437 on non-domestic rates, it is clear that tax expenses generated by fixed charge disposals in administration have priority over preferential creditors and impact on the size or availability of the prescribed part for unsecured creditors. The legislation provides little guidance as to whether it is appropriate for an administrator to make a distribution to preferential or (with leave of the court) unsecured creditors in circumstances where future fixed charge disposals may give rise to significant tax charges. It is suggested that the administrator should make a prudent reserve for future expenses (see *WW Realisation 1 Ltd (In Administration)* [2011] B.C.C. 382 for the power of the court to direct the administrators to set a bar date for expense claims. It is not thought this power could be exercised to bar claims which might arise from future actions of the administrator).

[68] Unless a pre-packaged sale is possible.

[69] See *Medforth v Blake* [1999] 3 W.L.R. 922 (CA) in this respect.

[70] para.3(1)(a) and (b) of Sch.B1.

the administrator is not to pursue either of those aims he must first reach a conclusion that their achievement is not reasonably practicable.[71] A receiver has no such obligation.

The office-holder is not required by law to take into account, or indeed enti-   **10–024** tled, at the expense of the creditors as a whole (in the case of an administration) or of the debenture-holder or company (in the case of a receiver), to promote, the interests of employees in any decision he makes, such as continuing business so as to mitigate the hardship of unemployment. The duty to take into account the interests of employees is imposed on directors by s.172 of the Companies Act 2006. The duty does not, however, extend to office-holders and accordingly cannot justify or legitimise any action taken by an office-holder which is not otherwise justifiable on purely commercial grounds.[72]

There may be a commercial justification for an administrator to seek to improve the position of employees through trading. He may judge that the value of employee claims that would follow a cessation of trading will have a greater effect on the outcome of the administration for the creditors than the costs of trading on to achieve a going concern sale. In such a sale the employees are usually transferred and their claims are thereby extinguished or much reduced.

Concern for his public image and humanitarian considerations may impel   **10–025** the appointor to encourage the officeholder to trade on, but neither an administrator (whose duty is to the creditors as a whole) nor a receiver should be bound by these considerations. In any event, before acceding to any such requirement of the appointor not justifiable on commercial grounds the office-holder should seek an indemnity for his own protection and, in the case of an administrator, to protect the interests of the creditor body.[73]

In order to equip himself to make a decision whether to trade on, the office-   **10–026** holder will first obtain valuations on the alternative "going concern" and "break-up" bases and expert advice as to the prospects, methods and time-scales for such sales. The officeholder must then exercise his judgment as to whether the anticipated benefits justify the risks and greatly increased costs of trading on.

In reaching a decision, the officeholder will evaluate the following factors   **10–027** and information:

(a) in administration, the likelihood of a rescue of the company and its business being achieved and of that producing the best outcome for creditors;

(b) the attitude of preferential and secured creditors towards trading on and, in receivership, the risk that secured, hire purchase, lease or

---

[71] para.3(4)(a) of Sch.B1.

[72] There may be such commercial grounds if a going concern transfer is contemplated, as failure to consult employees properly may give rise to liabilities which pass to the purchaser and so depress the price that he is prepared to pay.

[73] The appointor should also be careful that he does not seek to direct the actions of the receiver so that the receiver does not become the appointor's agent: see below, para.13–066.

retention of title creditors will enforce their rights so as to frustrate continued trading;

(c) financial information as to past and current trading sales and profit forecasts and the marketability of the product or service;

(d) inventory and valuation of stock and work-in-progress;

(e) assessment of retention of title claims;

(f) value and usefulness of intellectual property and the effect of the insolvency on any intellectual property licences necessary for the continuation of the business;

(g) position as to debtors and, in particular, whether discounting or factoring arrangements are in place and, if so, whether continuation of those arrangements can be assured or they can be replaced;

(h) investments in subsidiaries and any interdependence with them;

(i) rights of occupation of premises and possible relocation;

(j) availability of customers and suppliers and any alternative sources of supply and customers;

(k) availability and capability of the workforce and co-operation of any trade unions involved;

(l) availability and reliability of plant and machinery (including any intellectual property necessary for its operation);

(m) control over overheads in relation to planned production;

(n) (on rare occasions) availability of European Union, United Kingdom and local authority grants;

(o) ability of management;

(p) product liability and insurance for same;

(q) taxation consequences (particularly in relation to administration);

(r) prospects and consequences of liquidation.

10–028 Before considering whether to trade, the officeholder should have in mind the distinct duties he owes in respect of his decision whether or not to continue to trade and (if he decides to trade) in respect of the manner of trading. A decision whether or not to continue trading and if so for how long does not require the consent of the company or the debenture-holder, but a cautious receiver will, if practicable, consult the debenture-holder.

An administrator pursuing a rescue strategy will need to involve the company in his thinking and, unless he proposes to refinance the secured debt, will need the concurrence of the debenture holder.[74] In considering whether to trade an

---

[74] See s.4(3), para.73(i)(a) Sch.B1.

administrator should consider his duty to the company's creditors as a whole,[75] or, if there will be no funds for them other than those set aside under s.176A of the Act, his duty not to harm the interests of unsecured creditors unnecessarily.

A receiver owes a duty of care to the debenture-holder in respect of such a decision,[76] and whilst he owes a duty of care to the company not to trade if this course is calculated neither to enable repayment of the secured debt and interest thereon nor to promote or safeguard the value of the equity of redemption, he owes to the company no duty to trade, however damaging this course may be to the company.[77] The consent of the debenture-holder and the company will preclude subsequent complaint by them. Even if such consent is not forthcoming, for the receiver to show that he elicited and gave due consideration to their views or objections before acting goes a long way to displacing any charge of negligence. As a matter of practice, a receiver is unlikely ever to ignore the debenture-holder's wishes, for this would (in the case of a non-administrative receiver) ordinarily lead to his removal and (in the case of either type of receiver) lead to a refusal of any indemnity. But the debenture-holder and the receiver must take care that no directions are given by the debenture-holder and that the decision is genuinely that of the receiver alone, for otherwise the receiver may be held to be acting as agent of the debenture-holder[78] and if the decision leads to loss to the company and is challenged as negligent, the debenture-holder may become liable to the company or lose rights against guarantors.[79]

The officeholder has a right to apply to the court for directions on the question of whether to continue trading,[80] but the court will not ordinarily decide questions involving commercial judgment which is the responsibility of the officeholder.[81]

If the receiver does decide to carry on trading, he is under a duty to take **10–029** reasonable steps in order to do so profitably and accordingly (for example) obtain available discounts.[82] It is likely that these considerations are equally applicable to an administrator. And if the mortgagee instructs the receiver to carry on the business in a manner that is in breach of the receiver's duty to the mortgagor, the mortgagee will likewise incur liability to the mortgagor.[83] The same position would be likely to obtain in circumstances where the purpose of the administration was that in para.3(1)(c) of Sch.B1 and the administrator traded, at the request of the secured creditor, without good reasons, and with

---

[75] See s.4(3), para.73(i)(a) Sch.B1, para.3(2) Sch.B1.
[76] *RA Price Securities Ltd v Henderson* [1989] 2 N.Z.L.R. 257 (NZCA).
[77] See below, para.11–03 et seq.
[78] *American Express International Banking Corp v Hurley* [1985] 3 All E.R. 564, applied in *Barclays Bank Plc v Kingston* [2006] 1 All E.R. (Comm) 519.
[79] *Standard Chartered Bank v Walker* [1982] 1 W.L.R. 1410 (CA).
[80] Insolvency Act 1986, para.68(2) Sch.B1 (administrators) s.35 (receivers).
[81] *MTI Trading Systems Ltd v Winter* [1998] B.C.C. 591, 595; *Re Osmosis Group Ltd* [2000] B.C.C. 428; *T&D Industries Plc* [2000] 1 W.L.R 646; *Re Transbus International Ltd (In Liquidation)* [2004] 1 W.L.R. 2654.
[82] *Medforth v Blake* [2000] Ch. 86 (CA), 93.
[83] *Medforth v Blake* [2000] Ch. 86 (CA), 95.

the result that sums which would have been available to unsecured creditors under s.176A of the Act were dissipated.

4. DUTY TO TRADE

The duty of an administrator is not expressed in terms of a duty to trade but, if the company is to be rescued as a going concern[84] or a better result achieved for creditors as a whole than would be likely if the company had been wound up without a pre-packaged sale,[85] a period of trading may well be required. Since an administrator must assess the purpose of the administration by forming opinions on the practicality or effect on creditors of the particular purposes in para.3 of Sch.B1 being achieved, this may in practice amount to an obligation to trade unless he thinks the purpose which would require trading is not achievable or will not produce the best outcome for creditors.

An administrator trading to produce realisations for secured or preferential creditors[86] should be mindful of his duty not unnecessarily to harm the interests of the creditors as a whole by trading which diminishes or extinguishes the funds available under s.176A of the Act, unless he can clearly demonstrate that doing so will enhance realisations for secured or preferential creditors.

10–030   The law is clear in recognising a duty on the part of a receiver appointed by the court (where this is practicable) to preserve the goodwill of the company's business and for this purpose to carry on its business and (where necessary for this purpose) pay debts incurred in the course of its business even if this course is not in the interests of the holder of the crystallised floating charge. This duty arises from the special role of the court-appointed receiver who has the responsibility of holding the scales evenly between the company and the chargee and must not sacrifice the interests of the one to the other.[87]

10–031   The position of the receiver appointed out of the court is quite different. He has a primary duty to deal with or realise the security in the best interests of the chargee and in particular to try to bring about a situation in which interest on the secured debt can be paid and the debt itself repaid.[88] He has only a secondary duty to the company to exercise care to prevent avoidable loss. Such a receiver will only be required to protect the interests of the company where means are available and may be given effect consistently with the performance of his primary duty.

10–032   The question accordingly arises whether this secondary duty to the company can in any circumstances require the receiver to continue the company's business and preserve its goodwill, e.g. by fulfilling outstanding contracts.

---

[84] para.3(i)(a) Sch.B1.
[85] para.3(i)(b) Sch.B1.
[86] para.3(i)(c) Sch.B1.
[87] For the position of such receivers, see below, Ch.29. They are rarely appointed in practice because of the availability and advantages of an appointment out of court. However, where trading is required and foreign recognition of the officeholder would be an advantage but administration is not possible (e.g. because COMI is not in the UK), a court appointed receiver may more easily gain recognition than one appointed out of court.
[88] *Medforth v Blake* [2000] Ch. 86 (CA), 102.

The authorities in this field prior to the *Downsview* case[89] are not particu- **10–033**
larly helpful either because they fail to have regard to the differing roles of the
two types of receiver or because they were decided before the law recognised
that a mortgagee and receiver owed to the mortgagor a duty not merely to be
honest but to be careful.

Thus, in *R. v Board of Trade*,[90] where the Divisional Court equated the two **10–034**
receiverships for the purpose of determining whether their management could
be the subject of an investigation of the affairs of the company under ss.164
and 165 of the Companies Act 1948 (now ss.431 and 432 of the Companies Act
1985), Phillimore J.[91] obiter, and in the form of a rhetorical question, suggested
that there was in each case a like duty to preserve goodwill, without noting the
distinct roles of the receivers. Winn J. did not expressly advert to the question,
but cited the dictum of Buckley L.J. in *Re Newdigate Colliery Ltd*[92] which
distinguished the role and duty of the court-appointed receiver to preserve
goodwill from that of a receiver appointed by a debenture-holder who is not,
and referred to *Re B. Johnson*[93] which held that the receiver appointed out of
court had no such duty. It may therefore be thought (by implication at least)
that Winn J. disagreed with Phillimore J.; Lord Parker C.J. enthusiastically (but
confusingly) agreed with both judgments.

In *Airlines Airspares v Handley Page*[94] the question arose whether a receiver **10–035**
appointed by debenture-holders can hive-down the undertaking to a newly
formed subsidiary in anticipation of the sale of such subsidiary, notwithstanding that such action must put it out of the power of the company to fulfil
an outstanding contract with the plaintiff. The cases on the duty of court-
appointed receivers to protect the company's goodwill were cited and relied
on, but the distinction was not drawn between the two types of receiver, nor
was *Re B. Johnson* cited. Graham J. upheld the right of the receiver to proceed
with his hive-down,[95] stating as the relevant principle that a receiver can repudiate a contract if the repudiation will not adversely affect the realisation of the
assets or seriously affect the trading prospects of the company in question, if it
is able to trade in the future. This formulation and its application is difficult to
fault as a statement of the principles applicable to court-appointed receivers,
but overstates the restrictions on the powers of a receiver appointed out of
court.

On the other side, there is the decision in *Re B. Johnson*[96] where the Court **10–036**
of Appeal (in unreserved judgments) laid down in emphatic terms the absence
of the duty on the part of a receiver appointed by debenture-holders to carry on
business. Unfortunately the court equally emphatically laid down the absence
of any duty of care on the part of the debenture-holder or receiver, holding that

---

[89] *Downsview Nominees v First City Corp Ltd* [1993] A.C. 295 (PC).
[90] *R. v Board of Trade* [1965] 1 Q.B. 603.
[91] *R. v Board of Trade* [1965] 1 Q.B. 603, 613.
[92] *Re Newdigate Colliery Ltd* [1912] 1 Ch. 468 (CA), 478.
[93] *Re B Johnson* [1955] Ch. 634 (CA), as to which see Ch.10.
[94] *Airlines Airspares v Handley Page* [1970] Ch. 193.
[95] As to hive-downs see below, paras 11–081 to 11–090.
[96] *Re B Johnson* [1955] Ch. 634 (CA), (but compare the approach of the Court of Appeal in
Lawson (Inspector of Taxes) v Hosemaster Machine Co Ltd [1966] 1 W.L.R. 1300 (CA), 1314).

the duty is limited to acting honestly, a view repeated as late as 1965 by Cross J. in *Lawson v Hosemaster*[97] and affirmed, with limited qualifications, by the Privy Council in *Downsview Nominees Ltd v First City Corporation Ltd*.[98] The difficulty is that these two holdings, if not mutually dependent, are at least mutually supportive, and the second proposition was subsequently decisively rejected by the Court of Appeal in *Cuckmere Brick v Mutual Finance*[99] and *Standard Chartered Bank v Walker*[100] and by the Privy Council in *Tse Kwong Lam v Wong Chit Sen*.[101] The fate of the second proposition must indicate that there are doubts as to the validity of the first, doubts which can only have increased with the rejection of *Downsview* by the Court of Appeal in *Medforth v Blake*.[102]

10–037   The Court of Appeal in *Medforth v Blake* held that in exercising his powers of management, (subject to his primary duty to try to secure payment of the sum due to secured creditors) a receiver owes a duty to manage the secured property with due diligence; that due diligence does not oblige him to continue to carry on a business on the mortgaged property previously carried on by the mortgagor; but that if he does carry on business, due diligence requires reasonable steps to be taken in order to do so profitably.

10–038   Accordingly in the present state of the law in the absence of a specific provision to the contrary in the debenture it would seem that there can be imposed on the mortgagee and receiver no duty to trade. It is suggested that there is much to be said for imposing such a duty if:

(a) the company has the necessary funds (as the court will not require the debenture-holder or receiver to dip into his own pockets[103] or to risk a charge of fraudulent trading);

(b) this course is necessary to secure a beneficial realisation of the company's undertaking as a going concern;

(c) a sale as a going concern in the short term is likely; and

(d) a cesser of business would lead only to a disadvantageous sale for a reduced break-up value.

---

[97] *Lawson (Inspector of Taxes) v Hosemaster Machine Co* [1966] 2 All E.R. 944 (CA), 951.

[98] *Downsview Nominees v First City Corp Ltd* [1993] A.C. 295 (PC).

[99] *Cuckmere Brick v Mutual Finance* [1971] Ch. 949 (CA), applied by the Court of Appeal in *Bishop v Bonham* [1988] 1 W.L.R. 742 (CA). See also *Parker-Tweedale v Dunbar Bank Plc* [1991] Ch. 12 (CA).

[100] *Standard Chartered Bank v Walker* [1982] 1 W.L.R. 1410 (CA); see also *American Express International Banking Corp v Hurley* [1985] 3 All E.R. 564; *Knight v Lawrence* [1991] B.C.C. 411.

[101] *Tse Kwong Lam v Wong Chit Sen* [1983] 1 W.L.R. 1349 (PC).

[102] *Medforth v Blake* [2000] Ch. 86 (CA).

[103] *Re B. Johnson* [1965] Ch. 634 (CA), 662.

Chapter 11

Disposals, Conveyances and Transfers

1. DISPOSALS

(a) The disposal decision

(i) Administration

Rescue of the company as a going concern, and not disposal, is the primary purpose of administration.[1] It is only if the administrator thinks that it is not reasonably practicable to rescue the company, or that a better result would be achieved for the creditors as a whole by a strategy other than rescue, or that neither objective is reasonably practicable, that the primacy of rescue as an objective gives way.[2]   **11–001**

In many circumstances a rescue of the company as a going concern will involve a corporate voluntary arrangement under Pt 1 of the Act. Deciding whether such an arrangement will deliver a better result for creditors as a whole than a strategy that sought to improve on the liquidation outcome[3] will not always be easy. It will necessarily involve a judgment by the insolvency practitioner on the likely structure of any proposed corporate voluntary arrangement and an estimation of the likely outcome of a disposal.   **11–002**

In practice it may be easier to determine that a rescue of the company as a going concern is not reasonably practicable. It will commonly be the case that the company will have created debenture security over all its assets. In that case, a voluntary arrangement will require the concurrence of the secured creditor[4] or the availability of alternative finance sufficient to repay the existing secured creditor, in circumstances where the new financier is willing to structure the voluntary arrangement so as to improve the position for creditors as a whole.[5]   **11–003**

If the administrator concludes that it is not reasonably practicable to achieve a rescue or that disposal is likely to achieve a better result than a rescue, there is a further level of analysis he should go through before he decides on a   **11–004**

---

[1] para.3(1)(a), 3(3) and 3(4) of Sch.B1 to the Insolvency Act 1986. Although as seen below that primacy may be more apparent than real in many cases.

[2] para.3(3)(a) and (b) of Sch.B1 to the Act.

[3] para.3(3)(b) and 3(1)(b).

[4] s.4(3) of the Act.

[5] To ensure that para.3(3)(b) is not fulfilled. Following the decision in *Re Spectrum Plus Ltd (In Liquidation)* [2005] 2 A.C. 680 (HL), it may be less likely that alternative finance would provide a better outcome for the creditors as a whole. The effect of bank security over book debts being re-categorised as floating charge security will be to swell the pool of assets in the floating charge and therefore the size of the prescribed part set aside under s.176A of the Act.

particular disposal strategy. He must first consider whether the disposal would achieve a better result for the company's creditors as a whole than would be likely if the company were wound up (without first being in administration).[6] This objective includes consideration of whether an amount would be available to unsecured creditors by virtue of s.176A if a disposal was to take place in administration.[7]

11–005   Prior to the effective reversal of the decision of the House of Lords in *Re Leyland Daf Ltd* by the introduction of s.176ZA of the Act, liquidation expenses had no priority over floating charge assets.[8]

11–006   Accordingly, if the disposal of the company's business took place in liquidation, taxation on chargeable gains will not operate to reduce the net property of the company for the purpose of calculation of the prescribed part for unsecured creditors under s.176A of the Act. Therefore, before considering the disposal in administration, the administrator needed (in recognition of his obligation under para.3(2) of Sch.B1 to consider the interests of the creditors as a whole) to examine whether a better result would be achieved for creditors if the disposal of the company's business were to take place in a creditors' voluntary liquidation following immediately upon the discharge of the administration. Now that there is priority for expenses in both administration and liquidation, these considerations no longer apply.[9] Liquidation argues for much of the negotiation of the terms of sale to take place during administration where the costs will be an expense having priority over floating charge creditors.

11–007   Assuming that the administrator has concluded that a disposal in administration is the appropriate step to benefit the company's creditors as a whole, he must then consider whether it is appropriate to seek the sanction of a creditors' meeting to his proposal. He will not be required to do so if he thinks that the price generated by the disposal will only enable funds to be available for unsecured creditors under the terms of s.176A of the Act[10] or where a disposal will not generate funds for unsecured creditors at all.[11] If the administrator thinks that the disposal will generate funds for unsecured creditors otherwise than by virtue of s.176A of the Act he will need to consider further whether there are reasons why in the interests of the creditors as a whole he should not lay his disposal proposals before a meeting with the creditors called under para.51 of Sch.B1 to the Act.[12]

---

[6] para.3(3)(b) of Sch.B1 to the Act.

[7] Contrast para.3(1)(b) and (3)(1)(c) of Sch.B1. See also para.52(1)(b) and (c) which impliedly limits objective 3(1)(c) to circumstances where no prescribed part will be available.

[8] *Buchler v Talbot*; sub nom. *Re Leyland DAF Ltd* [2004] 2 A.C. 298 (HL).

[9] It is possible that a liquidation disposal may still have benefits in avoiding TUPE transfer liabilities. The disposal would have to take place promptly following liquidation since the liquidator's powers to trade are limited (see Sch.4, Pt (II), para.5 to the Act). Such a disposal could also have significant implications for the status of employee contracts following the sale (see paras 11–055 to 11–069).

[10] para.52(1)(b).

[11] para.52(1)(c).

[12] See para.11–016, below.

(ii) Receivership

Receivers are not required to carry out the analysis required of administrators **11–008** before making a decision on disposal. Receivers are appointed primarily to effect the recovery as far as possible of the debt owed by the company to the debenture-holder. It may be possible to achieve this through the collection of rents from the company's properties or the collection of book debts arising from or made good by continued trading. Most commonly however, disposal of the company's assets is required.

(iii) The manner of disposal

Once the decision to dispose of the business or assets in administration is taken **11–009** the manner of disposal is likely to closely resemble that of a disposal in receivership. But an administrator, unlike a receiver, has a duty to creditors.[13] This imposes on him an obligation to consider the effect of the manner of disposal on those creditors. A purchaser of a business as a going concern may assume responsibility for certain liabilities of the company[14] which reduce the size of the creditor body in the administration. The administrator should therefore always consider both the price being achieved for the company's assets and the effect of the sale on the level of the company's liabilities. This is so even where there will be no funds available under s.176A as the administrator then has a duty to avoid unnecessarily harming the creditors as a whole. To the extent that he can obtain terms which assist creditors without affecting the price he should do so.

Sales of companies' assets in receivership involve a degree of tension **11–010** between the duty of the receiver in equity to take reasonable care to obtain a proper price[15] and the legitimate objective of the receiver to sell on terms which require him to retain only the minimum prudent level of reserves against potential liabilities (in particular under the sale contract) before making any distribution to his appointor. A similar logic applies in administration. The obligation to obtain a proper price arises from the administrator's duty to creditors as a whole and, where assets are subject to fixed security, by the requirement for the administration to make up any deficiency in the price defined below market value from other assets.[16] Distribution of sales proceeds to creditors will not be assisted if the administrator has to retain substantial funds to

---

[13] paras 3(2) and 3(4)(d) of Sch.B1.

[14] For instance under the Transfer of Undertakings (Protection of Employment) Regulations 2006 (SI 2006/246) or by the buyer arranging to fulfil the company's obligations on executory contracts to realise the value of work in progress purchased by the buyer. A receiver may also consider the effect of the Transfer Regulations if a sale of the business will reduce or extinguish preferential claims and thereby enhance the floating charge realisations available to the debenture holder.

[15] *Downsview Nominees Ltd v First City Corp* [1993] A.C. 295 (PC) applied in *Raja v Lloyds TSB Bank Plc* [2001] Lloyd's Rep. Bank. 113 (CA) and see below, paras 11–014 to 11–017; *Re B Johnson & Co (Builders) Ltd* [1955] Ch. 634 (CA); *Cuckmere Brick Co v Mutual Finance Ltd* [1971] Ch. 949 (CA).

[16] para.71(3)(b) of Sch.B1.

cover contingent liabilities arising under the sale contract. This objective results in sale contracts being drafted so as to provide the maximum permissible exclusion of warranties and liabilities, in contrast with the position in a solvent business sale where the terms typically provide considerable protection for the purchaser. At first sight, the form of contract would appear to conflict with the obligation to obtain a proper price. However, the conflict may be more apparent than real since the vendor company will invariably be insolvent. This will mean that any warranties, which it might have given, will be of little commercial value to the purchaser. In practice therefore it will usually be difficult to demonstrate that the absence of warranties has depressed the price.

(b) Sale as a going concern

11–011   Sale of the business and assets of the company as a going concern will, where it is possible, tend to fetch a higher price than the sale of assets on a break-up basis. There are a number of reasons for this: the costs of removal and transportation of the assets are avoided; the utilisation of the assets in the business can proceed without interruption; the continuity of the business activity (although not of the corporate structure) makes it more likely that the goodwill of the company can be maintained; the skills and knowledge of the company's employees can be preserved; and, commonly, such a transaction will qualify as a going concern transfer for VAT purposes, avoiding the need for the purchaser to pay VAT.[17]

11–012   A sale as a going concern frequently means a transfer of employees' contracts under the Transfer of Undertakings (Protection of Employment) Regulations 2006[18] (TUPE). This accords with the "rescue culture" said to underlie the 1986 Act and is clearly socially desirable. In administration this is compatible with the obligation to act in the interests of creditors as a whole[19] or at least to avoid unnecessary harm to creditors.[20] TUPE in its current form seems to be aimed at encouraging sales in administration (and other collective insolvency processes) by provisions which reduce the extent of transfer of accrued employee rights in those circumstances.[21] There is little support for a going concern sale as an end in itself in the receivership regime, which is not in the main a collective process.[22] The transfer of employees' rights to the purchaser of a business means the purchaser assumes a series of contingent liabilities and

---

[17] Value Added Tax (Special Provisions) Order 1995 (SI 1995/1268), art.5.

[18] SI 2006/246. If the transfer took place before April 6, 2006 the applicable provisions are the Transfer of Undertakings (Protection of Employment) Regulations 1981 (SI 1486/1794) (TUPE81).

[19] para.3(2) of Sch.B1.

[20] para.3(4)(b) of Sch.B1.

[21] See para.16–031 et seq. The "adoption" in TUPE of the phrase "insolvency proceedings instituted not with a view to the liquidation of the assets of the transferor" from the underlying European directive (Council Directive 2001/23/EC of March 12, 2001) caused some difficulty. It now seems likely, following the decision of the Employment Appeals Tribunal in *OTG Ltd v Barke* [2011] B.C.C. 608 not following *Oakland v Wallswood (Yorkshire) Ltd* [2009] I.R.L.R. 250, that administration sales will give rise to a transfer for the purpose of the TUPE.

[22] ss.40 and 42–49 of the 1986 Act are collective in approach. However, the emphasis on "insolvency proceedings" in the insolvency related provisions of TUPE casts doubt on whether an out of court receivership qualifies for the flexibility accorded to other insolvency regimes.

is likely to take account of that fact by offering a lower price. In circumstances where the contingent liabilities for employees on a going concern sale are very considerable, this may have the effect of depressing the price below that which could be achieved on a break-up sale. There is no authority in the legislation which permits a receiver to achieve the socially desirable object of preserving jobs by taking a lower price than could otherwise be achieved.[23] Accordingly it is purely fortuitous that in most circumstances going concern values of assets are sufficient to offset the depressive affect of TUPE transfers.

In many circumstances a going concern sale will only be achievable, if at all, **11–013** some time after the appointment of the administrator or receiver and the office-holder will therefore continue the company's business to keep its goodwill alive in the hope of achieving such a sale.[24] In other circumstances the continuation of the company's business after the appointment will not be a practical possibility. This may be so for a variety of reasons. The value of the business may be dependent upon a number of key people who may be likely to leave during the period of uncertainty that invariably follows an administrator's or a receiver's appointment. The business may involve complex ongoing contracts and there may be real fears that the customer will choose to exercise termination rights in those contracts if administrators or receivers are appointed without a successor to the business immediately being in place. Following the decisions in *Brumark*[25] and *Spectrum Plus*[26] there has been a movement from secured overdraft lending to financing through sales of receivables. This limits the extent of floating charge assets available to fund administration trading.[27] In those circumstances it is not uncommon for the details of a going concern sale to be negotiated on insolvency terms prior to the administrator's or receiver's appointment so that the office-holder is in a position to effect the sale immediately after appointment. This minimises disruption and uncertainty and preserves value. Such a sale is commonly known as "pre-packaged".

---

[23] The criticisms of the receivers' failure to consult employees in *Kerry Foods Ltd v Creber* [2000] I.R.L.R. 10 resulted in a protective award which was payable by the purchaser of the business not by the vendor company. Even if the liability for the award had not transferred (because the dismissals were for an economic, technical or organisational reason) the case does not suggest that the award would have ranked other than as an unsecured claim in the liquidation of the vendor. See also *Re Allders Department Stores Ltd* [2005] 2 All E.R. 122; *Re Huddersfield Fine Worsteds Ltd* [2005] 4 All E.R. 886 (CA) and another (in administration). *Krasner v McMath* [2005] 4 All E.R. 886 (CA) establishes that such a protective award will not be an administration expense. But, now that it has been established that liability for failure to consult can fall on the purchaser (the liability is now expressly provided for (TUPE, reg.15(9))), the prospect of purchasers seeking price reductions to offset the liability may provide commercial justification for receivers fulfilling consultation obligations. Where a business is disposed of in a pre-packages sale there will usually be no realistic possibility of consulting employees.

[24] He must take reasonable steps in doing so to try to run the business profitably: *Medforth v Blake* [2000] Ch. 86 (CA), applied *Raja v Austin Gray (a firm)* [2003] B.P.I.R. 725 (CA).

[25] *Re Brumark Investment Ltd*; sub nom. *Inland Revenue Commissioners v Agnew* [2001] 2 A.C. 710 (PC).

[26] *Re Spectrum Plus Ltd (In Liquidation)* [2005] 2 A.C. 680 (HL).

[27] para.70 of Sch.B1. There are increasing signs that the courts will apply the *Brumark* and *Spectrum* requirements for control by the lender over disposal of the charged assets to be the mark of a fixed charge to the other asset classes such as plant and machinery (see *Fanshawe v Re Amav Industries Ltd* [2006] B.C.C. 615 but these assets are less liquid than receivables and are less suitable to support administration trading.

11–014   Whenever contemplating a sale the office-holder must be mindful of his duty to take reasonable care to obtain a proper price. This will usually mean that he will seek expert advice on the value of the company's assets.[28] In a traditional business this may involve valuations of land and plant and machinery. In other businesses it may extend to valuations of income streams, intellectual property or permissions granted by public authorities. Valuations serve two purposes; they give the office-holder an idea of the values he might expect to achieve and, if a sale at that level can be negotiated, they protect him from claims that he has not achieved a proper price.[29]

11–015   In many cases initial valuations will have been obtained prior to the administrator or receiver's appointment as part of an Independent Business Review (which in general now replaces the former Investigating Accountants Report) which is often commissioned jointly by the company and its lenders prior to the appointment so as to assess the options available when the company's difficulties become apparent.

11–016   If a pre-packaged sale is effected the office-holder will not have been able to expose the business to the market (although the company may previously have done so) and accordingly it will be important not only that he can justify the need for an immediate sale but also that he can justify the price achieved by reference to expert valuation advice and such pre-receivership marketing as may have occurred.[30] The administrator should also be aware that a "prepackaged" sale will limit or exclude any consultation with creditors still less approval of the sale in a creditors' meeting. In *Re T&D Industries Plc*[31] it was decided that an administrator had power, notwithstanding the provision in s.17(2)(a) of the Act for the court to give directions, to dispose of the company's businesses without directions. In *Re Transbus International Ltd*[32] the court held that the same power and policies applied under the current legislation.[33] Nonetheless an administrator should where possible consult creditors on the disposal decision. If time is pressing there is power for the court to order a creditors' meeting at short notice.[34] If holding a creditors' meeting is impractical the administrator should consider consulting major creditors about his plans.[35] In a pre-packaged sale the administrator must be prepared to explain why there could be no consultation at all with creditors. In addition since January 1, 2009 all administrators completing pre-packages sales have been subject to the requirements to make subsequent disclosure to creditors and to

---

[28] See below, para.11–015.

[29] This protection does not extend to circumstances in which the valuation is negligent see *Raja v Austin Gray (a firm)* [2003] B.P.I.R. 725 (CA) citing the passage now at para.13–043 with approval.

[30] This is particularly important since pre-packaged sales are frequently to management and creditors will understandably be concerned to know that a proper price had been obtained.

[31] *Re T&D Industries Plc* [2000] 1 W.L.R. 646.

[32] *Re Transbus International Ltd (In Liquidation)* [2004] 1 W.L.R. 2654.

[33] para.68(2) of Sch.B1.

[34] *Re Harris Bus Co Ltd* [2000] B.C.C. 1151.

[35] *Re T&D Industries Plc* [2000] 1 W.L.R. 646 The decision in *Re DKLL Solicitors* [2007] All E.R. (D) 68 (Mar) implies in the context of partnership administration, that if, in fact, the sale will lead to a better outcome for the creditors as a whole, even the opposition of the majority creditor may be disregarded.

the Insolvency Service set out in Statement of Insolvency Practice 16 (SIP16) issued by their Recognised Professional Bodies. The disclosure is required to enable creditors to be satisfied that the administrator has acted with due regard to their interests.[36] The administrator must disclose such of the following information of which he is aware after making appropriate enquiries:

- The source of the administrator's initial introduction.

- The extent of the administrator's involvement prior to appointment.

- Any marketing activities conducted by the company and/or the administrator.

- Any valuations obtained of the business or the underlying assets.

- The alternative courses of action that were considered by the administrator, with an explanation of possible financial outcomes.

- Why it was not appropriate to trade the business, and offer it for sale as a going concern, during the administration.

- Details of requests made to potential funders to fund working capital requirements.

- Whether efforts were made to consult with major creditors.

- The date of the transaction.

- Details of the assets involved and the nature of the transaction.

- The consideration for the transaction, terms of payment, and any condition of the contract that could materially affect the consideration.

- If the sale is part of a wider transaction, a description of the other aspects of the transaction.

- The identity of the purchaser.

- Any connection between the purchaser and the directors, shareholders or secured creditors of the company.

- The names of any directors, or former directors, of the company who are involved in the management or ownership of the purchaser, or of any other entity into which any of the assets are transferred.

- Whether any directors had given guarantees for amounts due from the company to a prior financier, and whether that financier is financing the new business.

- Any options, buy-back arrangements or similar conditions attached to the contract of sale.[37]

[36] SIP16 para.8.
[37] SIP 16 para.9.

The information should be disclosed in all cases unless there are exceptional circumstances in which case the reason why the information is not provided should be stated. Where the sale is to a connected party, SIP 16 states that it is unlikely that considerations of commercial confidentiality would outweigh the need for creditors to be provided with this information.[38]

The disclosure requirements of SIP 16 are subject to any limitations on an administrator's disclosure authorised under the Act.[39]

SIP 16 requires[40] that the information should be provided with the first notification to creditors, and that where a pre-packaged sale has been undertaken, the administrator should hold the initial creditors' meeting as soon as possible after his appointment. Where no initial creditors' meeting is to be held it is impracticable to provide the information in the first notification to creditors it should be provided in the statement of proposals of the administrator which should be sent as soon as practicable after his appointment. The increased preference of pre-packaged sales, particularly those to connected parties has led to political pressure to imposed legislation controls on such sales. At the time of writing the government is consulting on draft regulations to require, among other things, prior notice to be given to creditors of pre-packages sales to parties which are connected or associated within the meaning of the Act.

11–017   If there is to be a sale immediately following administration it will invariably require negotiation of the terms prior to administration. The putative administrator will be involved but not in office. His role will be advisory. The company may not have sufficient funds to pay his fees for this period. Prior to April 6, 2010 it was unclear whether they could be approved at a later date since they were not remuneration of the administrator "for his services as such".[41] With effect from April 6, 2010 a formal regime for pre-administration costs[42] was introduced.[43] The administrators proposals are now required to provide a statement of pre-administration costs[44] containing among other things: details of pre-administration costs charged, both paid and unpaid at the date of administration; details of work done and arrangements under which fees were charged; and an explanation of why the work was done pre-administration and how it furthered the achievement of the purposes of administration. There is also a requirement to state that unpaid pre-administration costs are subject to approval under Insolvency Rule 2.67A separately to the approval of the administrators proposals.[45] Insolvency Rule 2.67A provides a mechanism for the determination as to whether and to what extent pre-administration costs are approved for payment. The requirement for preparation time prior to administration creates another difficulty for the putative

---

[38] SIP 16 para.10.

[39] SIP 16 para.12.

[40] SIP 16 para.11.

[41] Insolvency Rule 2.106(1).

[42] Defined by Insolvency Rule 2.33(2A)(a) as fees charged and expenses incurred by the administrator or another person qualified to act as insolvency practitioner before the company entered administration but with a view to its doing so.

[43] By the Insolvency (Amendment) Rules 2010.

[44] Insolvency Rule 2.33(2)(ka).

[45] See Insolvency Rule 2.33(2B) for the full requirements for the statement.

administrator and the directors and others involved. New credit will usually be incurred. Procedures should be put in place to ensure that these creditors can be paid in full (or at least that their overall position is not worsened). If credit is incurred in the knowledge or expectation that it cannot be repaid in full this is likely to amount to fraudulent trading.[46] Liability for fraudulent trading is not limited to directors but extends to all participants including advisors such as the proposed administrator.

In circumstance where a going concern sale is looked for some time after **11–018** appointment the office-holder will prepare a sales pack describing the assets and business for sale to prospective purchasers. He will also generally advertise the business for sale. Care should be taken to ensure that the advertisements appear in publications most likely to come to the attention of prospective purchasers for the particular business and that wherever possible sufficient time is allowed to enable prospective purchasers to make enquiries and negotiate a sale.[47] There will be cases where time is short, for instance where the company is incurring substantial trading losses or where uncertainty is likely to lead to a very immediate fall-off of new business. In these circumstances the comprehensiveness of the sales pack assumes an increased importance since the purchaser will have very limited time for due diligence. The absence of warranties makes purchaser due diligence particularly important in administration and receivership sales. The sales pack should include a description of the nature of the business, giving details of its structure and organisation and referring, where appropriate, to brochures and advertising materials. In addition, the document ought to include lists of assets (tangible and intangible) which have been offered for sale. In giving information to potential purchasers, the office-holder will almost invariably be dependent upon using information and figures produced by the company's directors and employees. As this is likely to be the case the office-holder should (where possible) quote specific sources and always expressly disclaim personal responsibility of liability of himself, his staff or agents.

Where the sale document offers for sale any shares in the company (e.g. if **11–019** there has been a "hive-down" of part of the assets and business of the company in receivership into a subsidiary which is then offered for sale) the office-holder must take care to comply with the restriction on the communication of "financial promotions" under the Financial Services and Markets Act 2000.[48]

---

[46] See above, para.2–004 et seq. See also SIP 16 para.6.

[47] *Standard Chartered Bank v Walker* [1982] 1 W.L.R. 1410 (CA), applied *Barclays Bank v Kingston* [2006] 1 All E.R. (Comm) 519. See also para.11–032, below.

[48] Broadly speaking no person may communicate a financial promotion in the United Kingdom in the course of business unless either the communication of the financial promotion falls within one of the exemptions contained in the Financial Services and Markets Act 2000 (Financial Promotion) Order 2005 (SI 2005/1529), or the person is authorised by the Financial Services Authority, or the content of a financial promotion is approved by such an authorised person: see s.21 of the Financial Services and Markets Act 2000. A detailed exposition of this topic lies outside the scope of this book and reference should be made to T. Little, *Financial Promotion—A Practitioner's Guide* (City & Financial Publishing London, 2004). Article 62 of the Financial Services and Markets Act 2000 (Financial Promotion) Order 2005 provides that the restriction in s.21 of the Financial Services and Markets Act 2000 shall not apply to the communication of a financial promotion on behalf of a body corporate, partnership, individual or group of connected

11–020   Any marketing process will inevitably lead to the disclosure to prospective purchasers of commercially sensitive or confidential information to a greater or lesser extent. An office-holder should naturally exercise care and discretion in deciding what confidential information concerning the affairs of the company to make available to the prospective purchasers. Often the persons who might be most interested in acquiring the business and assets will be trade competitors of the insolvent company. Also the amount of information that a potential purchaser will wish to know will increase, as he becomes more serious in his intentions to acquire the business.

11–021   It had been held in Australia that a receiver acting bona fide will not be restrained from disclosing confidential information relating to business contracts to a proposed purchaser, even though there was a risk that the proposed purchaser would use the information to harm the company.[49] It is likely that a similar approach would be taken to administrators. Notwithstanding this, the office-holder should take care to reveal confidential information on strict undertakings as to preservation of that confidentiality so as to minimise the risk inherent in revealing details which could damage the company's business in the event that no sale is concluded. He may wish to take a layered disclosure approach, releasing material of particular sensitivity only to those potential purchasers who have demonstrated their financial qualifications and commitment to buying the business during the initial negotiation process.

11–022   The office-holder should bear in mind that the availability of contractually enforceable confidentiality undertakings from unsuccessful bidders for the business may be important to the successful purchaser, who will wish to prevent misuse of confidential information which had been disclosed during the sale process.

11–023   Care should be taken during the negotiation process to be reasonable in any assertions regarding the possibility of rival offers. Over-zealousness can result in damages for fraudulent misrepresentation.[50] Exclusion clauses will not protect the company or, to the extent of his responsibility for the fraudulent misrepresentations, the office-holder from liability.

11–024   Legal advice should be taken in drawing up the contracts and dealing with the other legal formalities of the sale. In the sale of a solvent business the usual practice is for the purchaser's solicitors to prepare the first draft sale contract. In an insolvency sale it is the office-holder's solicitors who prepare the draft. This is probably the practical consequence of the office-holder's need so far as possible to exclude warranties and liability in the sale documentation.

---

individuals if the communication relates to a transaction to acquire or dispose of "shares" in a body corporate, other than an open-ended investment company, where the "shares" consist of or include 50 per cent or more of the voting shares in the company calculated either separately or with the shares of the person making the acquisition. In order to take advantage of the exemption, the acquisition or disposal must be between parties each of whom is a body corporate, partnership, individual or group of connected individuals. This might well exempt many sales of subsidiaries from the restriction of s.21.

[49] *Re Neon Signs (Australasia) Ltd* [1965] V.R. 125.
[50] *Smith New Court Securities v Scrimgeour Vickers (Asset Management) Ltd* [1997] A.C. 254 (HL).

(c) The sale contract

The administrator or receiver will wish to ensure that the sale that is achieved **11–025**
creates the minimum practical exposure to risk and liability on his part and, in
the case of receivership, on the part of his appointing lender. The content of the
draft sale contract will reflect these concerns. The extent to which the office-
holder can achieve his object will depend on the commercial strength of his
position in the case. Nonetheless the core aim of minimising liabilities to
achieve a clear fund for distribution to creditors, or, in the case of receivership,
to the secured lender, will usually be adhered to.

(i) The parties

The insolvent company should be the vendor. The assets of the company do not **11–026**
vest in the office-holder. It should be made clear that the administrator or
receiver is acting only as agent of the company and that personal liability of the
receiver is excluded.[51] The office-holder, in the case of receivership, will also
be a party in his own right to take the benefit of the exclusions, limitations and
indemnities in his favour which the contract will contain. The Contracts (Rights
of Third Parties) Act 1999 will, unless excluded by a sale contract made on or
after May 11, 2000, have the effect of allowing an office-holder to sue on the
benefit of exclusions and indemnities in his favour even if he is not a party.[52]
There are many circumstances in which an office-holder will not necessarily
wish to give other third parties rights to sue under an insolvency sale contract.
It is also not yet clear how the Act will work in practice. It is, therefore, likely
that the effect of the Act will be excluded in most sale contracts for the immediate future and the office-holders will continue to be parties.[53]

The purchaser will often be a new company incorporated or activated for the **11–027**
purpose of acquiring the business. Although administrators and receivers avoid
deferred consideration wherever possible, there will usually be contractual
obligations imposed upon the purchaser in favour of the office-holder and the
insolvent company under the sale contract. The financial standing of the
purchaser should, therefore, always be considered and where appropriate, a
suitable guarantor of its obligations should be found. This will often be a parent
company. If an appropriate guarantor cannot be provided, the office-holder
should seek to bolster the purchaser's obligations by some form of cash cover
in the agreement. His ability to do this will, of course, depend on the extent of

---

[51] The receiver will be personally liable in the absence of an exclusion (s.44(1)(b) of the 1986
Act). The administrator will not be personally liable (although it is common to exclude liability in
any event) but it should be remembered that para.99(4) of Sch.B1 makes liabilities under the sale
contract a priority expense payable out of floating charge assets ahead of the administrator's remuneration and expenses (see para.99(3)(b)). It is not clear that this priority for liabilities arising out
of administration contracts can be excluded. Care should therefore be taken to reduce to a minimum
the extent to which the company assumes liability under the contract.
[52] See further above, para.13–050.
[53] Where the disposal is by one member of an insolvent group consideration should be given to
whether any other group members would benefit from being able to enforce provisions of the sale
contract.

his bargaining position. His need to do so will depend on his commercial judgment of the potential value of the purchaser's post-contractual obligations.

11–028   It is often the case that a director or directors of the vendor company or its holding company will be the purchaser or, more commonly, that the purchaser will be a company associated with such a director within the meaning of s.320 of the Companies Act 2006. It was held in *Demite Ltd v Protec Health Ltd*[54] a case on the equivalent section of the Companies Act 1985, s.320 that when, in those circumstances, the receiver was selling as agent of the company (and therefore the vendor was the company) and the transaction was a substantial property transaction, it was subject to that section. The sale was therefore voidable by the vendor company, in that case acting by its provisional liquidator. The same logic seems to apply to sales in administration The difficulty arose because the statutory predecessor of s.320 pre-dated the reforms contained in the Insolvency Act 1986 and went back to a period when a receiver could have been a director or someone connected with a director and acting in league with him. This was overlooked when the Insolvency Act 1986 was passed: the exemption for liquidators should have been broadened to include other officeholders, including administrators and administrative receivers. This was largely remedied in the Companies Act 2006. Sections 190–196 (inclusive) of the Companies Act 2006, replaced ss.320–322 of the Companies Act 1985. Section 193 provides that members' approval shall not be required for substantial property transactions in the case of a company that is being wound-up (other than a members' voluntary winding-up) or that is in administration. The *Demite* decision will remain an issue for administrative receivership sales.

11–029   A resolution of the vendor company (and, where the director is a director of the holding company, of that company) affirming the transaction will authorise it. However, practical difficulties may arise in obtaining such a resolution. If a majority of members in favour of the transaction cannot be secured the receiver may have to request that the debenture-holder join in the sale to exercise its own power of sale.[55] Alternatively, the receiver could apply to the court for a sale by the court, with conduct given to the office-holder.

11–030   Even where the requisite majority of members is available timing will be an issue if an opposing minority refuse to consent to the meeting to verify the transaction being held at short notice.[56] In such a case it may be appropriate for the receiver to arrange at point of sale for the meeting of members to be called to ratify the sale, and to take irrevocable powers of attorney[57] from the consenting members to vote their shares when the meeting is held. Another alternative is for the director concerned to resign his office, but the receiver will be concerned to ensure that there is no prospect of the resignation being

---

[54] *Demite Ltd v Protec Health Ltd* [1998] B.C.C. 638. The decision in *Demite* was upheld in *Ultraframe (UK) Ltd v Fielding* [2005] EWHC 1638 (Ch). In that case it was also held (para.1409) that s.320 had no application in circumstances where the size of the secured debt meant that there was no possibility of a surplus from the sale proceeds being available to the company.

[55] If registered land is involved this will not be effective unless the debenture is registered. It was also suggested in *Demite* that directions of the court could be sought. It is difficult to see how, in a receivership sale, these could override the provisions of s.193 of the Companies Act 2006.

[56] See Companies Act 2006, s.307.

[57] Powers of Attorney Act 1971, s.4(1).

viewed as a device to avoid compliance with s.193. This is a particular difficulty if the sale is pre-packaged and the director in question is in office until
the company goes into administration.

(ii) Recitals

The recitals in the sale contract will usually be brief. The appointment of the   **11–031**
administrator or the receiver will usually be recited and referenced, in the case
of the administrator, to the dates and manner of his appointment and, in the
case of the receiver to the debentures or other security documents under which
he is appointed. An office-holder will usually wish to avoid warranting the
validity of his appointment.[58]

Recitals will also often set out the position that the purchaser is proceeding   **11–032**
relying on his own investigation of the assets and in the knowledge that he
bears the full risk of title to the assets not passing to him and that that is a
reasonable risk since the company is in administration or receivership. The
purpose of such a recital is to bolster the case for enforceability of the wide
exclusions which will be in the body of the contract.

(iii) Definitions

In general, the aim will be to limit clearly the definitions of those assets being   **11–033**
disposed of. This may be by reference to description and by reference to schedules or location. The assets should also be defined as those of the vendor so as
to avoid any suggestion that third party assets are being sold. This approach
also serves to limit the chances of valuable assets of which the office-holder
was unaware passing under wide, generic definitions. Conversely, where the
definitions relate to areas where the purchaser is to assume liabilities (such as
employees) or provide indemnities (such as third party stock or third party
assets held in the business), the office-holder will wish to have as wide a definition as possible to take account of the fact that his knowledge of the business
may be incomplete.

In a going concern sale, the framework for the definition of the assets sold   **11–034**
will usually be a definition of the business to which they relate. In circumstances where different businesses are operated under the same corporate
structure and there are several disposals, care will be needed to ensure that
there is no overlap, particularly in the area of shared facilities and access to
records of the business. Where the businesses are not all disposed of at the
same time the draftsman should seek to preserve flexibility so that negotiation
of the later sale is not unduly circumscribed.

(iv) The sale and title

The usual formula is for the company to sell whatever right, title and interest   **11–035**
(if any) it may have in a list of assets of the business (as defined). The primary

---

[58] Validity of the appointment is dealt with in Chs 6 and 7.

purpose of this formulation is to ensure that the purchaser cannot sue if the title is defective or absent.[59] The formulation also has the effect of providing the vendor and office-holder with a degree of protection against an action for conversion if it should prove any of the assets "sold" did not belong to the vendor company.[60]

11–036   The assets sold will vary according to the purchaser's requirements but will commonly include the business equipment, the stock (including any interest of the vendor in retention of title stock) and work in progress, the company's contracts, intellectual property, the goodwill and the business premises. For the avoidance of doubt, there will generally be a provision stating that no assets other than those listed are being sold and (without limitation to that provision) specifically listing assets which are not included in the sale. Some of these items are those which the company has a duty to retain, such as its records and statutory books. Others will be items which the office-holder may find it difficult to value correctly at the point of the sale such as potential damages claims against third parties, rights to refunds of taxes (such as VAT) and the rights that the vendor may have in respect of the company's pension fund. The vendor will also wish to make it clear that he is not disposing of assets used in the business which belong to third parties such as leased equipment or third parties' tooling held in the business. Finally, there will be assets such as cash in bank or book debts which will or may not realise any greater value if sold to the purchaser than if collected by the vendor. Even if book debts are not sold, there may be provisions in the contract for the purchaser's assistance in collection.

(v)   The price

11–037   The sale contract will apportion the price between the assets sold. Where land is included in the sale, this will be important for SDLT purposes. In the case of other assets, the apportionment is more likely to be relevant to the division between fixed and floating charge realisations, although the extent to which plant and machinery are fixtures, and are therefore part of the land, is relevant for SDLT purposes. The purchaser will have its own views on how it would like the assets apportioned. This should not stop the office-holder taking valuation advice relating to the apportionment of the price. This will ensure that he is not exposed to criticism from the various persons interested in the level of floating charge realisations.[61]

---

[59] But see *Nottingham Patent Tile and Brick Co v Butler* [1885–86] L.R. 15 Q.B.D. 261 and *Faruqui v English Real Estates Ltd* [1979] 1 W.L.R. 963 in relation to property sales; these cases suggest that the formulation will not protect the vendor if the defects are known to the vendor but not disclosed at the time of the sale.

[60] *Port v Auger* [1994] 1 W.L.R. 862, 872.

[61] See Statement of Insolvency Practice, June 14, 1999, para.3.6 for best practice recommendations on this point. Parties interested in the apportionment of the sale price to floating charge realisations will include administration expense creditors, preferential creditors, unsecured creditors (in relation to the prescribed part) and the debenture-holder.

(vi) Payment and completion

Wherever possible an office-holder will look for immediate payment. If for any reason consideration has to be deferred, he will usually look for adequate assurance of payment either by a guarantee deposit or through taking debenture security. Occasionally, there may be assets of the worth of which neither the purchaser nor the office-holder is certain but which can only be realised in the process of running the business. These might include some new process or product. In those situations, if the office-holder feels he is unable to achieve a price from the purchaser at the point of sale which adequately reflects the potential for future income, he may look for additional consideration based on future earnings. **11–038**

Where the sale clearly falls within HM Customs and Excise criteria for transfer as a going concern,[62] the sale will usually be completed without payment of VAT. But there will always be a clause requiring the purchaser to pay VAT should it later prove that VAT was, in fact, due on the sale. Particular care needs to be taken with regard to property. The grant of a fee simple in a new or unfinished commercial building or civil engineering work is standard rated for VAT purposes. "New" basically means that the building or engineering work is up to three years old. Alternatively in the case of "old" buildings it is also possible that an election has been made in the past to waive the exemption (also known as the option to tax) under Sch.10, para.2 to the Value Added Tax Act 1994. This has the effect of making all future dealings relating to the building by the party who exercised it taxable at the standard rate. The office-holder should make enquiries to ascertain the age of the building and any alterations and also whether the company has opted to tax. **11–039**

In both these situations VAT will be chargeable on the sale of the property unless the conditions for a transfer as a going concern are met. These conditions require the purchaser to use the property for the same purpose as it was used by the vendor and if the vendor had opted to tax the property the purchaser will do likewise. **11–040**

The requirements for a going concern transfer relating to property must be in place before contracts are exchanged. The office-holder should therefore ensure that he has details of the purchaser's VAT registration and any application to opt together with HM Customs and Excise's acknowledgement before exchange. Where the purchaser is a newly incorporated company the sale contract should include a clear commitment for the purchaser to register for VAT without delay. **11–041**

Where the sale is of only a limited part of the company's assets more akin to a break-up sale, payment of VAT will usually be provided for in the consideration. In hybrid cases where there is perceived to be a significant risk that VAT may be payable, or where there are concerns that the purchaser's covenant to pay VAT that is due may not be substantial, a VAT deposit may be taken to abide by Customs and Excise determination on the point. **11–042**

---

[62] Value Added Tax (Special Provisions) Order 1995 (SI 1995/1268), art.5.

(vii)   Property and risk

11–043   The office-holder will generally wish to pass risk to the purchaser immediately the purchaser takes over the business and will wish to retain title until he has been paid in full. This is particularly so if there is an element of deferred consideration. The practical enforcement of such a title retention will depend upon the particular assets over which title is retained. In practice, it will be more effective against fixed plant than stock or work in progress.

(viii)   Third party assets

11–044   Invariably a business will hold some third party assets. There has been an increasing trend in recent years towards asset-backed financing. The office-holder will not purport to sell these items. The vendor company's obligation will generally be limited to an obligation to assign the benefit of contracts where that is permissible and a limited obligation to assist with the novation of contracts where it is not. The purchaser will often wish to take possession of these assets and to use them in the business. From the office-holder's point of view, this may either be a practical necessity, because the assets are essential in the business, or be desirable because the value of outstanding payments due on the contracts may be less than their value to the purchaser. The purchaser may therefore be prepared to enhance his price for the business for the chance of acquiring them.

11–045   If negotiations with the third party owners can be concluded before the sale, there will be little difficulty. However, not infrequently, the sale will precede completion of discussions with the finance companies.[63] The office-holder will not be protected by s.234(3) of the Insolvency Act in relation to the disposal of property which he knows not to be the property of the company. Excluding those items from the sale is one line of defence against a claim from the true owner. By including them in the sale the company will have given up possession and will thereby have disabled itself from complying with any demand that the owner might make for return of the equipment. There is, also, a risk of a claim by the owner for damages for conversion.[64] To protect the company

---

[63] See *Transag Haulage Ltd (IAR) v Leyland DAF Finance Plc* [1994] B.C.C. 356; *On Demand Information Plc (In Administrative Receivership) v Michael Gerson (Finance) Plc* [2003] 1 A.C. 368 (HL) (applied *Governor of the Royal Bank of Scotland v Neath Port Talbot County Council* [2006] All E.R. (D) 61 (Aug)) for the importance of the office-holder seeking relief against forfeiture and an order for interim sale under CPR r.25.1(c)(v) before sale if he agrees to pass title to the purchaser. In *Celestial Aviation Trading 71 Ltd v Paramount Airways Private Ltd* [2011] 1 All E.R. (Comm) 259 held that the power to grant relief against forfeiture was not applicable in circumstances where the lessee's possessory right did not extend for substantially the whole of the economic life of the asset i.e. to operating leases rather than finance leases.

[64] *Martindale v Smith* (1841) 113 E.R. 1181. For a House of Lords decision on the scope of damages for conversion see *OBG Ltd v Allan* [2008] 1 A.C. 1 (HL); *Douglas v Hello* [2001] Q.B. 967 (CA). See also *Sandu (Ha Isher Fashions UK) v Jet Star Retail Ltd* [2011] EWCA Civ 459 for a case where a conversion claim for goods subject to retention of title failed because the authority of the purchaser to sell did not under the terms of the contract, terminate on administration and had not been terminated subsequently by the seller.

and the office-holder[65] from such claims, the sale contract will generally include an obligation on the purchaser to redeliver third party equipment on demand from the owner and indemnities in favour of the company and the office-holder for any loss suffered by them as a result of the purchaser's failure so to do.

(ix) Third party stock

Third party stock is similar to other third party assets with the important prac- **11–046** tical difference that generally speaking it has been supplied to the company for consumption or resale. The owner is therefore generally more interested in being paid the invoice price for the goods rather than recovering them. It is now established that an undertaking from an office-holder to pay the invoice price of goods, if it should prove that the retention of title claim is good, will prevent the supplier obtaining an injunction against their sale.[66]

The purchaser will usually wish to be able to dispose of or consume the **11–047** stock in the course of business. The purchaser may also be concerned to ensure that the office-holder does not antagonise the suppliers of the business in the process of seeking proof of their retention of title claims. The purchaser may also feel himself in a better commercial position to negotiate a favourable settlement of retention of title claims as he may be offering further business to the suppliers in question. It is therefore not unusual for the purchaser to agree to acquire all the stock, including the stock subject to third party rights, at a price discounted to take into account likely payments required for third party suppliers and to assume liability for those payments.[67]

Where there is considerable uncertainty about the number of retention of **11–048** title claims or their validity, there may be a retention from the purchase price to meet the claims. Unless the office-holder is very confident about the level of retention of title claims that will have to be met, he will be unlikely to agree that the vendor company will bear a risk of them without some limitation as to the quantum of liability and the time within which the claims must be made. To take on any open-ended liability would be inconsistent with his aim of providing clear funds for distribution to the creditors or the debenture-holder. In an administration sale it would also create uncertainty as to the level of administration expenses.

In any event, since the stock subject to third party claims may not be the **11–049** property of the company unless the office-holder, unusually, agrees to retain the responsibility of the claims, the sale contract will provide that the purchaser must deliver up the stock on demand or indemnify the vendor and the office-holder company for damages. There may also be provision for the purchaser to

---

[65] See *Clerk and Lindsell on Torts*, 19th edn (London: Sweet & Maxwell, 2009), p.640 and *Re Samuel (No.2)* [1945] Ch. 408 (CA) for the liability of agents assisting in wrongful disposals. This is an instance of where is it possible for an administrator to become personally liable notwithstanding his agency status.

[66] *Lipe Ltd v Leyland DAF Ltd (In Administrative Receivership)* [1993] B.C.C. 385 (CA).

[67] In these circumstances the financial standing of the purchaser and any available guarantor of the purchaser's obligations will be important.

conduct defence of the claims in the name of the company subject to indemnities for costs in the company's favour.

(x)   Intellectual property

11–050   Intellectual property is a field in which third party rights abound. It can be both a problem and an opportunity for an office-holder. The company may own valuable intellectual property rights which should be identified, protected and realised. It is likely to be prudent for the office-holder to take advice concerning this. On the other hand, the company's assets may be severely devalued because of the absence or termination of intellectual property rights. The company's business may be reliant on the use of computer software under licences which may be terminable on administration or receivership or a company may have costly equipment for the production of products which can only be sold if the licence to manufacture and sell is maintained. Without those rights, the equipment may be valuable only as scrap. The owners of these rights will often be in a position of considerable commercial strength. Relief against forfeiture is not available as (except perhaps in the area of commissioned works) the rights of the company as licensee can probably not be classified as either proprietary or possessory.[68]

11–051   Aside from the trading issues, the office-holder has the difficulty in simply identifying third party intellectual property much of which does not have to be registered anywhere. For that reason, any sale of intellectual property will usually exclude intellectual property of third parties and will be subject to any third party consent that may be required. The office-holder will usually also wish to impose upon the purchaser an obligation not to use the intellectual property without obtaining consent and will always look for an indemnity for any damage that might be suffered through unauthorised use.

(xi)   Apportionment of pre-payments and liabilities

11–052   As with any other business sale, there should be a clear point in time from which the purchaser assumes obligations for the ongoing liabilities of the business. As the company is likely to be insolvent it is common for the sale contract to provide that as to past liabilities not assumed by the purchaser, the company remains responsible for them but is under no obligation to the purchaser to discharge them. The office-holder will usually try to resist giving credit for pre-payments, particularly those made before his appointment, unless they are clearly represented in the value which the purchaser is paying for the business.

---

[68] See *Sport International Bussum BV v Inter-Footwear* [1984] 1 W.L.R. 776 (HL) and *On Demand Information Plc (In Administrative Receivership) v Michael Gerson Plc* [1999] 2 All E.R. 811, 821, not reversed on this point on appeal: [2003] 1 A.C. 368 (HL). Regulation 14 of the Investment Bank Special Administration Regulations 2011 provides for continuity of supply of hardware and software used by the investment bank in connection with the trading of securities and derivatives. "Investment Bank" has the meaning in s.232 of the Banking Act 2009 and will encompass many investment firms.

(xii)   Records

The company will have to hand over to the purchaser VAT records unless HM   **11–053**
Customs and Excise agree otherwise.[69] Where the records are handed over the
office-holder will wish to retain access to them both to account for VAT for the
administration or receivership trading and to pursue any claim that there may
be for VAT refunds.

The office-holder will wish to retain for the liquidator the statutory books of   **11–054**
the company and the ownership of the general company books and records.[70]
The office-holder will also have a practical need to consult these documents
for the collection of book debts and for dealing with preferential creditors. The
office-holder will, however, usually wish to avoid the trouble and expense
of removal and storage of the records.[71] Fortunately, the purchaser will generally require access to the records for the purposes of the ongoing business. The
sale contract will, therefore, frequently provide that ownership of the records
is retained by the company and that the company may allow the purchaser
possession of them.[72] Such a clause should also provide that the purchaser
must hold the records for six years and must allow the office-holder and any
liquidator access to them and deliver them up at their request. There are
frequently also conditions requiring the provision of office facilities for office-
holders' staff.

(xiii)   Employees

This subject is dealt with in detail in Ch.16. The framing of the contract in   **11–055**
respect of employees will depend upon whether the office-holder has dismissed
employees before embarking on the sale process or whether the employees
remain in the business at the point of sale.

The law relating to the effect on employees of business transfers has been   **11–056**
altered from April 6, 2006 by the Transfer of Undertakings (Protection of
Employment) Regulations 2006 (SI 2006/246) (TUPE). The Regulations in
force prior to that date (TUPE81)[73] did not expressly provide exceptions for
transfers by companies in insolvency processes.[74] TUPE now provides insolvency-related exceptions to the policy of transfer of employee rights. The
provisions applicable depend upon whether the transfer of employees takes

---

[69] See Value Added Tax Act 1994, s.49 and Sch.11, para.6.

[70] See *Engell v South Metropolitan Browning and Bottling Company* [1892] 1 Ch. 442 for a case
where the court compelled a court appointed receiver to deliver records to a liquidator against
suitable undertakings.

[71] Such an approach may not now constitute best practice (Statement of Insolvency Practice,
August 1, 1997, para.16).

[72] Retention of ownership of records or an extensive period of access are important since, if
disputes or litigation arise during the insolvency, including any subsequent liquidation, they may
take years to resolve and the company's records may be vital to the resolution of the dispute or for
disclosure in litigation.

[73] Transfer of Undertakings (Protection of Employment) Regulations 1981 (SI 1981/1794).

[74] The decision in *Abels v Administrative Board of the Bedrijfsvereniging Voor de Metaal-
Industrie en de Electrotechnische Industrie* [1985] E.C.R. 469 was that a sale in a terminal insolvency process such as liquidation was not within the Dutch equivalent of those regulations.

place in "bankruptcy proceedings or any analogous proceedings which have been instituted with a view to the liquidation of the assets of the transferor under the supervisions of an insolvency practitioner"[75] or "insolvency proceedings which have been opened in relation to the transferor not with a view to the liquidation of the assets of the transferor and which are under the supervision of an insolvency practitioner".[76]

11–057   Following the decision of the Employment Appeal Tribunal in *OTG v Barke*[77] it seems (absent a contrary decision at a higher level) that administration business sales will be regarded as insolvency in proceedings opened "not with a view to the liquidation of the assets".

11–058   The distinctions between transfers that fall within the full provisions of TUPE, those that fall within reg.8(6) and those within reg.8(7) are very substantial. For transfers outside regs 8(6) and 8(7) the full effect of TUPE will apply as it would to a solvent transfer. Where reg.8(6) applies employees who transfer (or would have transferred but for a transfer-related dismissal for a reason that is not an economic, technical or organisational reason (ETO) entailing changes in the workforce)[78] will be paid the amounts due to them under the relevant statutory schemes[79] by the Secretary of State as if their employment had terminated on the transfer date.[80] Liabilities above those limits will pass to the transferee. If the employees have been made redundant before the transfer for a transfer-related reason which is an ETO, the Secretary of State will in addition pay redundancy pay and notice pay. If the employees have been dismissed for a transfer-related reason which is not an ETO redundancy payments and notice pay will not be paid by the Secretary of State. It will be open to the employees to claim for unfair dismissal and damages for breach of their contractual notice provisions.[81] If reg.8(7) applies the effect is that there is no transfer of the employees' contracts and the provisions relating to automatic unfair dismissal do not apply.[82]

11–059   The other change applicable to transfers which fall within reg.8(6) is the ability for the transferor (or its insolvency practitioner) or the transferee to agree variations to the contracts of employment with employee representatives.[83] The variations must be solely by reason of or connected with the transfer and must be designed to safeguard employment opportunities by ensuring the survival of the transferring business.[84] This relaxation is likely to be the most commercially beneficial insolvency change in TUPE.

11–060   It is more doubtful whether receivership disposals benefit from either of the two insolvency requirements introduced by the new regulation. It is difficult to

---

[75] reg.8(7).
[76] reg.8(6). See below, Ch.16, at para.16–031.
[77] *OTG v Barke* [2011] B.C.C. 608 (EAT).
[78] regs 8(2) and 7(1).
[79] See reg.8(4) for the definition (save those dismissed for ETO reasons).
[80] These liabilities will not transfer (reg.8(5)).
[81] This is a policy decision: Redundancy Payments Directorate Mailshot, April 2006.
[82] regs 4 and 7 do not apply.
[83] reg.9.
[84] reg.9(7).

view the appointment of a receiver as the opening of insolvency proceedings[85] Receivership disposals may therefore fall to be governed by the same rules as those applicable to solvent disposals.[86]

The Redundancy Payments Directorate of the Insolvency Service have **11–061** issued to insolvency practitioners a statement of their policy concerning TUPE pending judicial clarification.[87] For the purposes of payments by the Secretary of State they intend to apply reg.8(6) to all transfers which have occurred as a matter of fact irrespective of the type of insolvency process applicable to the transferor.[88]

Whatever the factual situation, it is unlikely that the office-holder will be **11–062** prepared to permit the company to give any indemnity to the purchaser against the prospect that dismissed employees may transfer or in relation to the application of reg.8(6).[89]

The contract may take one of two forms. The contract will either state that **11–063** the employees have been dismissed or state that they are transferring; but in either case the office-holder will wish to make it clear that the purchaser will have no recourse should it prove that employees other than those expected to transfer do, in fact, transfer. Indeed in relation to those employees who are expected to transfer the office-holder will wish to impose an express obligation upon the purchaser to employ them so as to guard against voluntary and unfair dismissal claims if for any reason they do not transfer by operation of law. If commercial pressures force him to do so, the office-holder may be prepared to provide a retention out of the purchase monies to be applied towards claims from "unexpected" transferring employees made within the defined period. The office-holder will be concerned as to the manner in which the company's obligations to consult employees about the transfer have been carried out. Under TUPE81 liability for failure to consult transferring employees fell upon the purchaser.[90]

TUPE now imposes new information and consultation obligations in rela- **11–064** tion to transfers.[91] These require both the provision of prescribed employee

---

[85] At least in the usual circumstance of an out of court appointment. Applications within a receivership, e.g. for directions under s.35 of the Act, would be insolvency proceedings (Insolvency Rule 13.7) but they would not have "opened" or "instituted" the receivership. Arguably creditors' voluntary liquidation is not an insolvency proceeding. See the EC Regulation on Insolvency Proceedings 2000, Annexes A and B where references to confirmation by the court were inserted to bring creditors' voluntary liquidation within the definitions of insolvency proceedings (art.2(a)) and winding-up proceedings (art.2(b)). Receivership is not within the definitions of insolvency proceedings for the purposes of that regulation.

[86] This is at odds with the latest DTI guidance note (this note is only in draft at the time of writing) and (possibly) the Redundancy Payments Directorate Mailshot.

[87] Redundancy Payments Directorate Mailshot (above).

[88] The DTI are considering the issue of replacement guidelines as to the insolvency processes that are within regs 8(6) and 8(7) which may conflict with this policy approach.

[89] The office-holder should bear in mind that even when dismissing employees for an economic, technical or other reason the manner of dismissal itself may none the less be unfair: reg.7(3)(b)). If so the liability for damages for unfair dismissal will not transfer but will remain with the company; it seems they will not be treated as an administration expense: *Re Allders Department Stores Ltd* [2005] 2 All E.R. 122.

[90] *Kerry Foods Ltd v Creber* [2000] I.R.L.R. 10 (EAT).

[91] regs 11, 13 and 14.

information by transferor to transferee and information to and consultation with employees' representatives. Liabilities are imposed for failure to meet these obligations.[92] The extent of the obligations and the timing requirements[93] relating to some of them may lead to significant compliance difficulties. The penalties for non-compliance are variously, liability to the transferee[94] and liability to the affected employees,[95] employee representatives or union representatives.

11–065   In cases where there are special circumstances which "render it not reasonably practicable" for the transferor to comply with reg.13(2) to (7) (the duty to enforce and consult with affected employees), reg.13(9) requires the transferor to take all steps towards performing those duties as are reasonably practicable in the circumstances. Regulation 15(5) and (6) qualifies this relaxation.

11–066   There are provisions for some of these liabilities to be joint and several with the transferee.[96] This raises issues of rights of contribution between transferor and transferee. Regulation 18 prohibits contracting out of TUPE except to the extent that TUPE permits an agreement to exclude or limit the operation of TUPE.

11–067   Regulation 12(4)(b) requires the tribunal, in assessing the compensation that is just and equitable to have regard to loss sustained by the transferee and any contractual obligation in the business sale agreement for the transferor to pay an amount to the transferee in respect of failure to comply with the provision of employee information.[97] It is suggested that the business sale contract should provide for such a sum to be paid to the transferor (perhaps by way of deduction from the agreed price) as an agreed liquidated sum for any failure to provide the required employee information. The contract could also usefully recite the acknowledgment of the transferee that in view of the insolvency practitioner's limited knowledge of the business and the disorder in the company and the urgent need to secure a sale so as to ensure survival of the business it is fair and reasonable to limit the liability of the transferor for failure to provide prescribed employee information to that amount.

11–068   In relation to the joint and several obligations under reg.15(9) it is suggested that since the liabilities between the transferor and the transferee are not dealt with in that regulation (the parties are jointly and severally liable to the affected employees) it should be legally permissible for the transferee to indemnify the transferor in respect of the liability to employees and to waive any right of contribution it may have against the transferor. The same logic applies to the joint and several liability under reg.17(2).[98]

---

[92] reg.12 (but see regs 12(4), 15 and 16).
[93] regs 11(6), 13(2) and (7) (but see regs 13(g) and 14).
[94] regs 12(3), 15(1)(a) and (d), 15(1)(b) and 15(1)(c) respectively.
[95] reg.15(g).
[96] reg.15(9).
[97] reg.11.
[98] Where there has been no or no effective consultation of employees before the sale, as will almost invariably be the case in pre-packaged sales, the value of potential claims argues strongly for a guarantor of the purchaser where it is a Newco.

It should be noted that pension arrangements relating to employees do not **11–069** normally transfer.[99] The purchaser will have to make separate arrangements for future pension entitlements of the employees.[100] Where the transferor company maintained an occupational pension scheme there are now requirements for the purchaser of the business to make minimum replacement provisions for trans-ferring employees.[101]

(xiv) Contracts

The office-holder will wish to provide that the purchaser takes the benefit and **11–070** burden of existing contracts for supplies to and by the company. There will be provisions for the vendor to provide limited assistance with novation. In addi-tion, there will be provision for assignment of those contracts capable of assignment together with an indemnity in favour of the company and the office-holder in relation to the burden of the contracts. There may also be a specific provision for the purchaser to deal with warranty claims. The obliga-tion for the purchaser to perform contracts and to deal with warranty claims can be important to minimise practical and legal resistance to the office-holder's collection of pre-sale book debts. Also, while the receiver is not liable for pre-receivership contracts which have been continued during the trading period or post-receivership contracts where he has excluded liability, he will wish so far as possible to ensure that he has provided for the liabilities incurred during the receivership trading period both as a matter of professional reputation and to avoid any suggestion of fraudulent trading.[102] In administration, post-adminis-tration contract liabilities will be an administrative expense. The administrator will therefore wish to ensure that they are met in full. In practice too, the office-holder may have been commercially obliged to give to important suppliers undertakings to procure the company's fulfilment of its payment obligations during the administration or receivership trading period and he will wish to ensure that these are adequately covered either by the price paid by the purchaser or by collateral indemnities in the contract.

(xv) Book debts

The office-holder may wish to obtain the purchaser's assistance with the **11–071** collection of book debts. If, as is frequently the case, the purchaser will change its name following the sale or trade under a name similar to that previously used by the vendor, there is a risk of confusion amongst the creditors of the business. Accordingly, it is sensible to provide a trust and accounting obliga-tion on the purchaser in respect of payments received by it for pre-sale book debts. It may also be wise to provide that, where customers do not make it clear

---

[99] reg.10.

[100] reg.10. Personal pension plans, however are sometimes provided as part of the employment contract and the employees' obligation to make contributions may therefore transfer. For a detailed consideration see below, Chs 16 and 17.

[101] Pensions Act 2004, ss.257 and 258.

[102] See above, para.2–004 et seq.

to which debts particular payments relate, those payments should be appropriated to the earliest outstanding book debts due from the customer in respect of
the business. This will be particularly important in those circumstances where
the purchaser is acting as the vendor's agent in the collection of book debts.

11–072   It is increasingly common for financiers of the company which has become
insolvent to own the company's book debts under the terms of a factoring or
discounting agreement. This will usually provide for the assignment of all
debts as they are created. Although there is some uncertainty as to the effect of
such provisions on debts created during the administration or receivership[103] in
practice it is common for the office-holder to negotiate continuation of the
receivables financing during the insolvency trading period. In those circumstances the arrangements with any purchaser of the business relating to book
debts will be influenced by the receivables financier's wishes.

(xvi)   Goodwill

11–073   The sale of the goodwill will carry with it the right to use the trade names of
the company. The office-holder will not be able to agree to change the vendor's
name unless he also controls the vendor's holding company. It should also be
made clear that the right to use the company name is made available to the
purchaser only in so far as the vendor is able lawfully to do so. The office-
holder will wish to retain the right to use the vendor's name in relation to the
completion of the statutory requirements in the administration or receivership
and in the realisation of any retained assets.

11–074   Where the purchaser wishes to retain the director of the vendor company in
a managerial position or where the purchaser is a management buy-out team
and the purchaser wishes to trade under the same or a similar name as the
vendor, the purchaser will have to have regard to ss.216 and 217 of the
Insolvency Act 1986 and the need to seek leave of the court unless the circumstances fall within the three cases prescribed in the Insolvency Rules.[104] These
provisions are dealt with in more detail below, but it should be remembered
that, where two or more businesses operated by the company in receivership
are sold separately, none of the purchasers is likely to be a purchaser of substantially the whole of the business and this will limit the purchaser's avenues for
excluding the operation of s.216 without leave of the court.[105]

---

[103] See *Salinger on Factoring*, 4th edn (London: Sweet & Maxwell, 2005), paras 11.23–11.25
and the cases referred to.
[104] Insolvency Rules 1986, rr.4.228–4.230. See *First Independent Factors and Finance Ltd v
Churchill* [2007] B.C.C. 45 (CA) for a ruling that, in the context of a liquidation sale at least,
r.4.228 (as it was then drafted) could only be invoked before the director has become a director of
the Company with the prohibited name. The Insolvency (Amendment) Rules 2007 effective from
August 6, 2007, amended r.4.228 to provide that a contravention of s.216 will not occur when the
whole or substantially the whole of the insolvent business is acquired from a liquidator, administrator, administrative receiver or supervisor of an arrangement under Pt I of the Act provided that
notice is given by the person intending to act in advance of acting to the auditors. The prescribed
form of notice is Form 4.73.
[105] Insolvency Rules 1986, r.4.228.

(xvii) Exclusions

The office-holder will wish to exclude in respect of himself and the company **11–075** all warranties as to title, description and fitness for purpose. He will also wish to obtain the purchaser's acknowledgment that the purchaser is relying on his own enquiries and specialist advice and not on any representations of the vendor, the office-holder or his staff or agent. The purchaser will be asked to acknowledge that this is reasonable on the grounds that the company is in administration or receivership and the office-holder does not have full knowledge of its affairs. It is important to bolster the reasonableness of the exclusions in the light of the provisions in ss.2(2) and 11(1) of the Unfair Contract Terms Act 1977.

In addition to the general exclusions there should be included a specific **11–076** statement that the receiver is not personally liable on the sale contract whether under s.44(1) of the Insolvency Act or otherwise, that he contracts as agent of the company[106] and that he is party to the contract in his own name only for the purpose of taking the benefit of the exclusions, indemnities and other rights in his favour which the contract contains.[107]

(xviii) Properties

Conditions relating to the sale of land whether leasehold or freehold are gener- **11–077** ally very detailed. It is common practice to provide for them in a separate schedule. Care should be taken to ensure that the definitions in the contract are compatible with the definitions in any standard sale conditions subject to which the property is sold, albeit with appropriate modifications for an insolvency sale. The property should be sold without full or limited title guarantee. Generally, the terms of the contract will exclude the right of the purchaser to raise requisitions as to title. It is generally convenient for the completion of the property sale to occur at the same time as the completion of the sale of the business.

Where a landlord's consent is required for the assignment of leaseholds, it **11–078** should if possible be obtained prior to the sale. If this cannot be done and the purchaser goes into occupation on completion of the business sale, it will invariably be a breach of the terms of the lease and the purchaser should indemnify the vendor for any damage suffered. The licence should also provide for payments by the purchaser which equates with the rent and other outgoings

---

[106] Assuming there is no liquidation: see Ch.15.

[107] It is common to have a similar exclusion in administration business sale contracts although there is no statutory provision for an administrator to be generally personally liable on contracts entered into during administration. Sale contracts sometimes also seek to limit the extent to which liabilities will be administration expenses but it in unclear to what extent it is permissible to contract out of the effects of para.99(4) of Sch.B1. A more robust formulation would be to exclude liability of the company in respect of identified matters. A blanket exclusion of liability on the part of the company could call the enforceability of the whole contract into question (*Suisse Atlantique Société d'Armement Maritime SA v NV Rotterdamsche Kolen Centrale* [1967] 1 A.C. 361 (HL)).

that the company will have to pay.[108] Unless the property is let at below the current market rent, the landlord is likely in practice to be happier to have a solvent assignee rather than an insolvent tenant.

11-079　　Difficulties can arise where the purchaser wishes to occupy the company's premises on a short-term basis only following the sale. This may be to complete existing contracts or to allow time for the removal of plant and machinery. Occasionally, the purchaser's occupation will be under a licence. If the purchaser has exclusive occupation the licence may be construed as a tenancy.[109] If there is a tenancy at will, there should be no difficulty in obtaining possession as such a tenancy is outside the Landlord and Tenant Act 1954, Pt II.[110] Often a purchaser will require a definite period of occupation. Where a tenancy of business premises is for a period exceeding six months, the tenant will have security of tenure under Pt II of the Landlord and Tenant Act 1954 unless the landlord has first served a warning notice on the tenant and the tenant has made a declaration to the notice in response or the tenant has made a statutory declaration confirming that the security of tenure provisions are excluded.[111] It is not always sufficient merely to provide that the tenancy should be for six months or less. Section 43(3)(b) of the Landlord and Tenant Act 1954 provides that, where the tenant carries on the same business as the previous occupier, the tenant will have security if his period of occupation aggregated with that of the previous occupier exceeds 12 months. It will frequently be the case that the purchaser will be conducting the same business from the premises of that previously carried on by the vendor. It is often assumed that the problem of aggregation of the periods of occupation only arises when the vendor company was in occupation of the premises as a tenant and the purchaser will become a successor to that lease. In fact, s.43(3)(b) of the Landlord and Tenant Act 1954 appears to address the continuity of the business and not the continuity of the tenancy. Accordingly, previous occupation by the vendor as a freeholder would seem to be sufficient to trigger security provided there is continuity in the business carried on.[112]

11-080　　It is therefore frequently the case that occupation by the purchaser of the premises even for only a short period will require the parties to contract out of

---

[108] This is particularly important in administration since the introduction, following the Enterprise Act 2002, of a comprehensive expenses regime closely modelled on that of liquidation (Insolvency Rules r.2.67(1)). It now seems settled that the occupation of premises for the benefit of the administration will encourage the court to treat lease obligations as an administration expense (see *Re Atlantic Computer Systems Plc (No.1)* [1992] Ch. 505 (CA); *Re Toshoku Finance UK Plc (In Liquidation)*; sub nom. *Inland Revenue Commissioners v Kahn* [2002] 1 W.L.R. 671 (HL); *Goldacre (offices) Ltd v Nortel Networks UK Ltd (In Administration)* [2010] Ch. 455; *Sixty UK Ltd (In Administration)* [2010] B.P.I.R. 1234 (Ch); *Cheshire West and Chester BC, Petitioners* [2011] B.C.C. 174 (Court of Session, Outer House).

[109] *Street v Mountford* [1985] A.C. 809 (HL). The Landlord & Tenant Act 1954, Pt II applies to tenancies at no rent; see *Woodfall on Landlord and Tenant*, (London: Sweet & Maxwell) Vol. 2, para.22–023.

[110] This is so whether the tenancy at will arises by operation of law or by express agreement: *Wheeler v Mercer* [1957] A.C. 416 (HL) and *Manfield and Sons v Botchin* [1970] 2 Q.B. 612.

[111] Landlord and Tenant Act 1954, Pt II, s.43(3).

[112] This point was argued in *Cricket Ltd v Shaftesbury Plc* [1999] 3 All E.R. 283, 287 but expressly left open by Neuberger J.

the Landlord and Tenant Act. With effect from June 1, 2004 the procedure for landlords and tenants to contract out of the security of tenure provisions in the Landlord and Tenant Act 1954 has been greatly simplified as a result of amendments to the Act brought in by the Regulatory Reform (Business Tenancies) (England and Wales) Order.[113] Parties can now agree to contract out of the security of tenure provisions: (1) by the landlord serving a warning notice on the tenant in the prescribed form[114] at least 14 days before the tenant becomes contractually bound by the agreement, and the tenant making a declaration in the statutory form[115] confirming that it accepts the consequences of the notice; or (2) by the tenant making a statutory declaration in the prescribed form waiving the 14-day notice period and confirming that it accepts such consequences. Court orders obtained under s.38(4) of the Landlord and Tenant Act 1954 and agreements to enter into leases conditional upon obtaining such orders which were made prior to June 1, 2004 will remain valid, and in the case of the latter will be taken to refer to the new procedures.[116]

(d) Hive-down

(i) The concept

A "hive-down" is the transfer of certain assets of the business of the company **11–081** in administration or receivership to a new wholly-owned subsidiary controlled by the office-holder, but leaving behind the liabilities. Without the dead weight of the accumulated debts of the parent, the subsidiary may prove both profitable and marketable.[117] Hiving-down has advantages for the receiver in that the business can be conducted through the subsidiary, thereby avoiding personal contractual liability, and for the administrator of insulating the company in administration from administration expense claims.[118]

The principal advantages relate to the preservation and realisation of **11–082** the business itself[119]: hiving-down is sometimes an important ingredient in

---

[113] SI 2003/3096 and s.38A, Landlord and Tenant Act 1954.

[114] Landlord and Tenant Act 1954, Sch.1.

[115] Landlord and Tenant Act 1954, Sch.2.

[116] Landlord and Tenant Act 1954, art.29(2) and (3).

[117] Hiving-down prior to receivership may be difficult because it may open up the directors to challenges by a subsequent liquidator.

[118] But the office-holder may take on the responsibilities of being a director or shadow director of the subsidiary—responsibilities which could extend, for example, to personal liability for wrongful trading of the subsidiary if the business does not prosper. See above, para.2–010 et seq.

[119] Minimising the risk of distress for rates, VAT and taxes is no longer an advantage following the decision in Re ELS Ltd [1995] Ch. 11 to the effect that crystallisation of the floating charge takes floating charge assets beyond such distress. The decision of the House of Lords in Re Toshoku Finance UK Plc (above) overruled Re Kentish Homes Ltd [1993] B.C.C. 212 so that in a liquidation context rates will fall into the "necessary disbursement" category of liquidation expenses. That category also now appears in the list of administration expenses in Insolvency Rules r.2.67(1)(f) but the substance of the old s.19 is also retained in para.99. In Exeter City Council v Bairstow [2007] 4 All E.R. 437 it was decided that the non-domestic rates of occupied premises were necessary disbursements in administration and therefore payable as an administration expense. Non-domestic rates of unoccupied premises are subject to a legislative exception (see para.19–009 et seq., below).

preparing the business for an advantageous sale to a purchaser. The benefits of this course of action include the following:

(a) the office-holder can choose the assets which are profitable or otherwise desirable to transfer;

(b) the more saleable assets can be combined with the carry forward of capital allowances and trading losses for use against future profits for tax purposes. The right to relief in respect of trading losses is not a chose in action, still less is it assignable by the insolvent company. It is only by means of a hive-down of substantially the whole of the business of the company to a subsidiary that such losses will be capable of transfer to the subsidiary to be set against future profits. Under Pt 22 of the Corporation Tax Act 2010, provided that the transfer is achieved at a time when the transferee is a subsidiary of the transferor, the transferee can take over the past trading losses of the transferor as if it had always carried on the trade.[120] The hive-down should be effected prior to the execution of any agreement for sale if the tax losses are to be utilised in this way. It may be too late to hive-down after an agreement is signed, since the beneficial interest in the shares in the subsidiary will have already passed to the purchaser[121];

(c) the subsidiary will be "clean" in the sense of not being saddled with the old company's debts or any disadvantageous credit standing with suppliers[122];

(d) it ought to be easier to establish the profitability of the business of the subsidiary;

(e) trading can continue without interruption even if the parent company is wound up;

(f) Customs and Excise will not allow an office-holder to obtain a repayment of VAT where there are pre-receivership liabilities in respect of VAT. In the case of a business which generates repayments, a hive-down solves this problem in relation to prospective repayments because the subsidiary will be able to obtain separate VAT registration and will be able to claim refunds on its own account, thereby avoiding any claim of Crown set-off;

---

[120] The amount of losses carried forward is reduced by the difference between "relevant liabilities" (liabilities of the transferor prior to hive-down which were not transferred) and "relevant assets" (the value of any assets of the transferor prior to hive-down which were not transferred and the value of the consideration paid by the transferee for the transfer). In practice, the restriction of the losses means that this is no longer the primary reason for hiving-down a business.

[121] See *IRC v Ufitec Group Ltd* [1977] 3 All E.R. 924; *Wood Preservation Ltd v Prior* [1969] 1 W.L.R. 1077 (CA) and *J Sainsbury Plc v O'Connor (Inspector of Taxes)* [1991] 1 W.L.R. 963 (CA).

[122] The hive-down may not solve all the problems in this regard: supplies may be cut off before the hive-down is effected.

(g) section 233 of the Insolvency Act 1986 provides that an administrator or receiver can require gas, electricity and telecommunication services to be provided so long as he personally guarantees payment for supplies after the date of his appointment[123]: the supplier cannot as a condition of supply make it a condition that pre-receivership bills are paid.[124] A subsidiary will be a new customer and will be entitled to such supplies without payment of its parent's debts. Accordingly, whilst a hive-down is not necessary to secure continued supplies without paying off arrears, it does have the advantage that the administrator or receiver can thereby secure such supplies without being required to give a personal guarantee.

(ii)   Legality

By virtue of para.60 of Sch.B1, in the case of an administrator, s.42(1), in the **11–083** case of a receiver and in both cases paras 18 and 19 of Sch.1 to the Insolvency Act 1986, and unless the powers are inconsistent with any provisions of the debenture, an administrator or administrative receiver will have the power to establish subsidiaries of the company and to transfer to any such subsidiaries of the company the whole or any part of the business and property of the company. This power may be exercised for the purpose of a hive-down. The hive-down cannot prejudice third party property rights. Legal and equitable interests in the company's property must be respected and will not be prejudiced.[125] But purely contractual obligations may be converted into mere monetary claims in damages against the company. Prior to the Insolvency Act 1986, the legality of hive-downs had been challenged as involving the wholesale repudiation of contractual obligations by the company. Objection was taken on the basis that the company was divesting itself of its undertaking, thereby making it impossible to fulfil contractual duties. The challenge failed in the case of hive-downs by receivers appointed by debenture-holders on the ground that the receiver is entitled (whilst the company is not) to repudiate outstanding contracts of the company. This was thought necessary to achieve a beneficial realisation for the debenture-holder.[126] There may be a difference depending upon whether the receiver is acting as agent for the company or as principal, since if acting as agent for a contracting party he may be exempt from a claim in tort for interfering with the contractual relations between the company and the third parties, but may not be exempt if he is acting as principal.[127] If there is such a distinction, then the receiver appointed out of court will be exposed

---

[123] This is a rare example of a statutory provision for an administrator to incur personal liability.

[124] Other suppliers continue to be entitled to insist on payment of all sums outstanding as a condition of any supply: see above, paras 8–007 to 8–010.

[125] *Freevale v Metrostore (Holdings) Ltd* [1984] Ch. 199 and *Telemetrix v Modern Engineers of Bristol (Holdings) Plc* (1985) 1 B.C.C. 99417.

[126] *Airline Airspares v Handley Page* [1970] Ch. 193. "The lemon may, so to speak, be squeezed dry": per McPherson J. in *Re Diesels & Components Pty Ltd* (1985) 9 A.C.L.R. 825, 828.

[127] Consider *Re Botibol* [1947] 1 All E.R. 26, 28; *Telemetrix v Modern Engineers of Bristol (Holdings) Plc* (1985) 1 B.C.C. 99417 and *Welsh Development Agency v Export Finance Co Ltd* [1992] B.C.C. 270 (CA).

once winding up has commenced, since his agency thereupon terminates.[128] Where a mortgagee acquires his rights without notice of the rights of another party under a subsisting contract, the tort of wrongful interference with contract cannot preclude the mortgagee from enforcing his rights or remedies on the basis of his superior title.[129] If no complaint can be made against the mortgagee in such a case, surely none can be made against the receiver whether acting as agent of the mortgagee or as principal in right of the mortgagee. A receiver appointed by the court is always potentially exposed, since he never acts as agent for the company. He should seek the directions of the court before proceeding with a hive-down and the order will afford him protection.

11–084   There is no case law specifically applicable to creditor rights on hive-downs by administrators, but since the actions of administrators are carried out for the benefit of creditors as a whole it is suggested that a challenge would be unlikely to succeed.[130]

(iii) Method

11–085   The hive-down company will ideally be a newly formed company or possibly a subsidiary which has never traded. The office-holder should take care to ensure that suitable directors are appointed, usually the office-holder himself and/or members of his staff. The hive-down company may now have only one issued share,[131] held by the insolvent company. The office-holder should also ensure that the subsidiary keeps statutory books and proper books of account and that the requirements of Pt XV of the Companies Act 2006 are complied with, e.g. as to auditors and accounts; that all proper insurances are taken out; and that separate VAT registration is taken up.

11–086   The assets transferred will usually consist of plant, machinery, office furniture, equipment, vehicles, stock, work in progress and goodwill (including the right to use any trading name as the successor to the business carried out by the insolvent company) and the benefit of trading contracts. Initially, any interest in land (freehold or leasehold), trade marks, patents, licences, copyrights, rights in designs, cash and book debts are left in the parent. There is usually no advantage in incurring expense in transferring the land and intellectual property rights in the initial hive-down when it is not known for certain either that the subsidiary company will be able to trade successfully or that a buyer will be found. In due course, these assets can be sold to the subsidiary or to a purchaser together with the shares of the subsidiary. The liabilities of the parent company are of course left with the parent company.

---

[128] *Gosling v Gaskell and Grocott* [1897] A.C. 575 (HL). The same issues do not apply to administrators who always act as agents (para.69 of Sch.B1).

[129] See *Edwin Hill & Partners v First National Finance Corp* [1989] 1 W.L.R. 225 (CA); *Swiss Bank Corp v Lloyds Bank* [1979] Ch. 548, 571–572: the reversal on appeal ([1982] A.C. 584 (HL)) does not affect the authority of the judgment on this point. See also below Ch.13.

[130] Unless perhaps on the facts of a specific case it was possible to demonstrate that a hive-down to improve realisations for secured or preferential creditors had unnecessarily harmed the interests of creditors as a whole (para.3(4)(b) of Sch.B1).

[131] Note that, since July 15, 1992, it is possible to have a subsidiary which has only one share: see the Companies Act 2006, s.38.

It is important that the price for the assets to be hived-down is fixed so as to **11–087**
equate to the price attributed to those assets when the subsidiary company is
sold, thus giving rise to no profit or loss on the transaction. This is achieved by
providing in the hive-down contract for the transfer of the trading assets to the
subsidiary for a consideration to be certified either by an independent valuer or
by the office-holder's firm. The purchase price is left outstanding on inter-
company loan. When the subsidiary is sold to a purchaser, either a supplementary agreement is made between the insolvent company and its subsidiary,
removing the requirement for the valuer's certificate and inserting a figure for
the price which equates to the price at which the hived-down assets have been
valued for the purposes of the sale of the subsidiary; or a certificate will be
issued at the appropriate price. The purchaser of the shares of the subsidiary
will agree to discharge the inter-company loan so that, on completion, the
insolvent company will receive the purchase price for the assets sold.[132]

(iv)   Employees

The usual practice before the Insolvency Act 1986 was that employees were **11–088**
left with the parent and their services subcontracted to the hive-down subsidiary. The parent would invoice the subsidiary for the labour and pay the
employees itself to avoid any suggestion that contracts of employment had
been novated. The idea, of course, was to leave liabilities in respect of contracts
of employment with the parent as far as possible and enhance the value to a
purchaser of the hive-down company or business. Following the Insolvency
Act 1986, the basic practice is still the same in that employees are generally
retained in the parent company and not re-hired by the hive-down subsidiary.
The legal position has, however, been affected by the provisions of s.44 of the
Insolvency Act 1986[133] and in the case of hive-down by the interpretation
placed by the House of Lords on TUPE81. This approach is preserved under
TUPE.

Potential liability under s.44(1) of the Insolvency Act 1986 is discussed in **11–089**
detail in Ch.26.

TUPE provides that, where there is a relevant transfer of an undertaking or **11–090**
business,[134] contracts of employment shall not be terminated by the transfer
but shall have effect after the transfer as if originally made between the
employee and the transferee.[135] In effect, there is an automatic transfer of all of
the transferor's rights, powers, duties and liabilities under or in connection
with employment contracts (except in respect of an occupational pension
scheme) to the transferee of the undertaking. There was a special exception in

---

[132] The price paid by the purchaser for the shares will be equal to the net value of the subsidiary
after taking account of the inter-company loan. Note that the potential charge under s.179 of the
Taxation of Chargeable Gains Act 1992 will be relevant and a purchaser would normally expect to
be indemnified against it or to reduce the price offered to take account of it.
[133] Now amended by the Insolvency Act 1994 as a consequence of the decision of the Court of
Appeal in *Re Paramount Airways (No.3)* [1994] 2 All E.R. 513 (CA).
[134] reg.3 specifies the nature of the 1981 Regulations.
[135] reg.4 but see the discussion on the insolvency exceptions at paras 11–055 to 11–069.

the case of insolvency hive-downs from the effect of TUPE 81.[136] This was abolished by TUPE.[137] The practice of dismissing employees a short time before hive-down in an attempt to avoid the ultimate operation of reg.4 and thus to obtain a higher price for the sale of the subsidiary was largely rendered ineffective under TUPE 81 by the decision of the House of Lords in *Litster v Forth Dry Dock & Engineering Co Ltd*[138] and that approach continues in TUPE. Accordingly, except in cases when reg.8(7) applies or regulation 8(6) mitigates the position[139] the office-holder will have to deal with the potential purchaser of the hive-down business on the basis that the liabilities relating to the existing employees will be transferred with the hive-down company. For a detailed account of the position of employees in a transfer of the understanding, see Ch.16, at paras 16–024 to 16–035.

(e)   Prohibitions on re-use of company names

11–091   When a business is sold, either as a going concern or as part of a hive-down, it may often be the case that a purchaser will wish to retain any goodwill attaching to the name of the old company or its products and for that purpose may wish to acquire the rights to use the old company's name in its business. It is also frequently the case that the purchaser wishes to employ a director of the old company in a managerial position in the new business because he has a particular expertise and will be able to ensure a degree of continuity during the period of transition. Management buy-outs from office-holders will almost invariably exhibit these features. In such cases, it will be important to have regard to the provisions of ss.216 and 217 of the Insolvency Act 1986 which provide for restrictions on the re-use of the name of an insolvent company.[140]

11–092   Section 216 of the 1986 Act applies to a person where a company has gone into insolvent liquidation and the person was a director or shadow director of the company at any time in the 12 months before liquidation. In such cases, except with the leave of the court[141] or in certain prescribed circumstances, for a period of five years the ex-director cannot be a director of or in any way be concerned in the promotion, formation or management of any other company which is known by the same name as the company in liquidation or which is

---

[136] reg.4 of TUPE81.

[137] reg.20(1) of TUPE.

[138] *Litster v Forth Dry Dock & Engineering Co Ltd* [1990] 1 A.C. 546 (HL). See further below, at Ch.16, para.16–027 et seq. See also *Longden v Ferrari Ltd and Kennedy International* [1994] B.C.C. 250 (EAT).

[139] See paras 11–056 to 11–062, above for a full discussion of applicability.

[140] The section was introduced to deal with the prevalence of the "phoenix company" syndrome. The Cork Committee had noted (at para.1813): "there is widespread dissatisfaction at the ease with which a person trading through the medium of one or more companies with limited liability can allow such a company to become insolvent, form a new company, and then carry on trading much as before, leaving behind him a trail of unpaid creditors, and often repeating the process several times. The dissatisfaction is greatest where the director of an insolvent company has set up business again using a similar name for the new company and trades with assets purchased at a discount from the liquidator of the old company."

[141] The court will only grant leave with reference to the use of the name by specified companies and not generally: see *Re Lightning Electrical Contractors* [1996] B.C.C. 950.

known by a name which is so similar as to suggest an association with that company.[142] Contravention of the section is an offence and will result in both the director of the old company and any other person who acts on his instructions knowing him to be in breach of s.216 being personally liable with the new company for any debts which it incurs during the period of prohibition.[143]

These provisions contain a number of traps for the unwary, particularly if the **11–093** old company goes into liquidation sooner than might have been contemplated at the time of purchase of the business. In order to mitigate the potential effects of these sections in appropriate cases, and to provide a means by which a director can avoid the need to make a formal application to the court for leave at a later stage, the Insolvency Rules 1986 provide for three "excepted cases" in which the prohibitions will not operate.[144]

The first excepted case applies, inter alia, where a company acquires the **11–094** whole or substantially the whole of the business of the insolvent company under arrangements made with its office-holder[145] If, within 28 days of completion of the arrangements[146] the purchasing company gives a notice in the statutory form to all the creditors of the insolvent company of whose address it is aware, then any director of the old company named in the notice will be permitted to be a director of or concerned in the management, etc. of the purchaser company.[147] It is suggested, that if the purchaser of a business from an administrator or receiver wishes to use what might become a prohibited name and also wishes to engage a director of the old company, it would be prudent for him to give a notice under the rules in respect of that director. Similarly, if the office-holder wishes to employ a director of the old company to manage a similarly named subsidiary into which the business of the parent company has been hived-down, he should consider issuing such a notice.

---

[142] References to the name by which a company is known are to the name of the company itself or any name under which it carries on business. See *Ricketts v Ad Valorem Factors Ltd* [2004] 1 All E.R. 894 (CA); *Revenue & Customs Commissioners v Walsh* [2006] B.C.C. 431 (CA); *Revenue & Customs Commissioners v Benton-Diggins* [2006] B.C.C. 769.

[143] See *Thorne v Silverleaf* [1994] B.C.C. 109 (CA), applied *Ricketts v Ad Valorem Factors Ltd* [2004] 1 All E.R. 894 (CA).

[144] See rr.4.228–4.230 of the Insolvency Rules 1986. See also the decision in *First Independent Factors and Finance Ltd v Churchill* [2007] B.C.C. 45 (CA) and fn.104 to para.11–074, above.

[145] In *Re Bonus Breaks Ltd* [1991] B.C.C. 546, 547D–547F, Morritt J. expressed some surprise (obiter) at the view reported to be widely held in the insolvency profession that this "first excepted case" only applied where there was a sale of both assets and liabilities by an insolvency practitioner. The learned judge thought it clearly arguable that the statutory notice could have been given where there was a sale of the whole or substantially the whole of the business without the purchaser taking on any of the liabilities of the old company. It is thought that this interpretation is commercially sound and in line with the scheme of the Insolvency Rules. It should be noted that this exception is unlikely to apply where there are separate sales of businesses operated on a divisional basis by one corporate entity.

[146] This somewhat vague phrase is not defined. It is thought that it would include the completion of the hive-down transfer even though the price would not have been paid at that time.

[147] Curiously there does not appear to be any mechanism for the creditors of the old company to do anything in response to the receipt of such a notice. If the notice is correctly given in accordance with the Rules, permission to act follows automatically. Insolvency Rule 4.228A was amended with effect from August 6, 2007 to overcome difficulties with the rule highlighted by the decision in *First Independent Factors & Finance Ltd v Churchill* [2007] B.C.C. 45 (CA).

11–095   The second excepted case provides temporary but automatic protection for up to six weeks pending determination of a formal application to the court for leave to act, provided that the application is issued "not later than" seven days from the date on which the company went into insolvent liquidation. The time limits prescribed in this case seem to have little or no logic to them. In many cases where liquidation follows an administration or receivership, directors of the old company may not have been kept regularly informed of the state of the old company and may not learn of its liquidation until several weeks after it has occurred. In these cases, notwithstanding that the rules provide for the application to be made "not later than" seven days after liquidation, the court may be persuaded to exercise its discretion to extend this time limit so that the application for leave is treated as having been made in time and the automatic six-week protection period will begin to run (albeit without prejudice to any acts which have been done in the interim).[148] Additionally, the period of protection of six weeks bears little resemblance to the period which it may take for an application for leave to be heard and determined if the court decides to call for a report from the liquidator of the company.[149] Although there does not appear to be the jurisdiction to extend the six-week period referred to in the Insolvency Rules, in such cases the court may be prepared to make an "interim order" permitting the director to continue acting pending final determination of his application.[150]

11–096   The third excepted case provides simply that leave is not required where the new company has been known by the prohibited name for 12 months before the old company went into liquidation and it has not been dormant during that period.[151]

11–097   If advantage cannot be taken of the first or third "excepted cases", an application to the court for leave to act will have to be made. On such an application, the court will be concerned to examine the reasons for the demise of the previous company and the responsibility of the director for that demise, the circumstances surrounding the sale of the business (and in particular the fairness of the price paid), together with the role which the director is to have in the management of the new company.[152]

(f) Sale of property subject to a security

11–098   Although a mortgagee exercising a power of sale can transfer charged property free of interests postponed to his charge,[153] in the ordinary case a receiver who

[148] *Re Evans Hunt Scott Ltd* Unreported June 24, 1991 in which reference was made to the factors relevant to the exercise of the discretion to extend time by analogy to the principles applied in the case of *Re Virgo Systems Ltd* (1989) 5 B.C.C. 833. Mummery J. also observed in argument that the correct rule under which to extend the time limits was r.4.3 of the Insolvency Rules 1986, not r.12.9 and RSC, Ord.3, which applied only to questions of computation of time.

[149] Under r.4.227 of the Insolvency Rules 1986.

[150] See, e.g. *Re Oasis Marketing Ltd* Unreported June 18, 1988.

[151] *First Independent Factors and Finance Ltd v Mountford* [2008] B.C.C. 598 for a decision where the excepted case and not apply.

[152] See *Re Oasis Marketing Ltd* Unreported June 18, 1988; Harp, "What's in a prohibited name?" (1998) 1 Insolv. Int. 65; and *Re Bonus Breaks Ltd* [1991] B.C.C. 546.

[153] See, e.g. *Duke v Robson* [1973] 1 W.L.R. 267 (CA) and ss.2(1) and 104(1) of the Law of Property Act 1925.

acts as agent for the company in receivership cannot transfer a better title to property than could be transferred by the company itself. An administrator is in the same position save that he can deal with floating charge assets as if they were not subject to security.[154] Paragraph 71 of Sch.B2 to and s.43(1) of the Insolvency Act 1986 respectively give the court jurisdiction on an application by the administrator and administrative receiver to authorise them to dispose of property, which is subject to a charge having priority over the charge of their appointor, free of such charge. It must be a condition of any such order that the net proceeds of sale, and (where those proceeds are less than such amount as may be determined by the court to be the net amount that would be realised on a sale of the property in the open market by a willing seller) such sum as may be required to make good any deficiency, shall be applied towards discharging the security. If there is more than one security, the condition must require application of the net proceeds and further sum (if any) towards discharging these securities in the order of their priorities.[155] The jurisdiction of the court can only be exercised if the court is satisfied, in the case of an administrator's application, that the sale would be likely to promote the purpose of administration in relation to the company,[156] and in the case of an administrative receiver's application, that the disposal (with or without other assets) would be likely to promote a more advantageous realisation of the company's assets than would otherwise be effected and if the property in question is property of which the administrative receiver is or, but for the appointment of some other personal receiver of part of the company's property, would be the receiver and manager.[157] A copy of the order must be sent by the office-holder to the Registrar of Companies within 14 days under penalty of a fine.[158]

(g) Reconstructions and schemes

As an alternative to a sale of the business, it may be possible for a scheme of arrangement to be promoted and sanctioned under ss.895–901 of the Companies Act 2006. There is also the possibility of a company voluntary arrangement

11–099

---

[154] para.70(1) of Sch.B1. The charge-holder has the same priority in the assets (which presumably include proceeds of sale) acquired as a result of the disposal: para.70(2).

[155] para.71(3)(b) of Sch.B2 to and s.43(4) of the Insolvency Act 1986. Curiously, the Act does not make express provision for what is to happen if a sale has to be made at a time when there is doubt about the validity of any charge or if an application has been made to set aside a charge or if there is a dispute as to priorities between chargees. In *Re Newman Shopfitters (Cleveland) Ltd* [1991] B.C.L.C. 407 the court held, in relation to the similar power to order sale in administrations applicable at that time (s.15(2) of the 1986 Act), that there was no power within the section to order that the proceeds be retained pending the outcome of a dispute as to the validity of the security. If an application to challenge the security was already on foot such an order might be sought as interim relief in that action. See *On Demand Information Plc v Michael Gerson (Finance) Plc* [2003] 1 A.C. 368 (HL), for the effectiveness of interim sale orders to preserve the position of the parties in a forfeiture relief context.

[156] para.71(2)(b) of Sch.B1. In *Re Capital Films Ltd, Rubin v Cobalt Pictures Ltd* [2011] B.P.I.R. 334 an administrator who acted unreasonably in applying for an order under the paragraph was ordered to pay the costs personally on an indemnity basis.

[157] Insolvency Act 1986, para.71(2)(b) of Sch.B1 and s.43(7).

[158] Insolvency Act 1986, para.7(5) of Sch.B1 and s.43(5).

under Pt I of the 1986 Act.[159] The terms of s.895 of the Companies Act 2006 would not appear to allow an administrator or receiver to make the application to the court for sanction of the scheme in his own name and he would have to apply in the name of the company. He would also have to be satisfied that the promotion of the scheme was in the interests of the administration or receivership and, in the case of receivership, fell within his powers under the debenture, including those imported by s.42 of and Sch.1 to the Insolvency Act 1986 and in the case of administration, was within Sch.1 or that the course of action was one of the administrator's proposals approved by creditors under para.53 of Sch.B1. As a practical matter it will be essential for the office-holder to hold informal consultative meetings with members and creditors, who will be able to indicate informally whether they will vote in favour of the proposals.

(h) Forced sale of assets

11–100   Where the business cannot be sold as a going concern or hived-down, and no scheme is possible, the office-holder will have to sell on a "break-up" or "gone concern" basis. In the case of freehold or leasehold interests in land, he should employ reputable agents. In the case of plant, machinery and vehicles, he should consult reputable valuers and auctioneers specialising in the type of articles in question. In the case of intellectual property, the office-holder will need the advice of patent agents and other specialists. In all cases, a record should be kept of attempts to sell. The question of an administrator's and receiver's duties and potential liabilities on sale are dealt with in detail in Chs 12 and 13 respectively.

11–101   In the absence of a going concern sale the cash flow impact of the requirement for the purchaser to pay VAT on the assets may have a further depressive effect on the price.

(i) Sales at valuation

11–102   A regular feature of many administrations and receiverships (as of many liquidations) is the sale of certain assets "at a valuation", i.e. not at a price expressly agreed between the parties but at a price to be fixed by a third party valuer. This practice is particularly prevalent in the case of a sale including stock, but it also has its place and advantages when the conclusion of a contract for sale cannot sensibly or properly await the required valuation. The practice is well established and recognised.

11–103   Nonetheless there are two old authorities which affirm the proposition that a fiduciary (a term which includes administrators, receivers and liquidators as well as trustees) cannot sell at a valuation, since this involves a delegation to the valuer of the power to fix the price, and such a delegation can only be permissible if authorised by provision in the instrument appointing him or some applicable statutory provision.[160]

---

[159] See above, paras 2–017 to 2–022.
[160] *Peters v Lewes and East Grinstead Ry Co* (1880–81) L.R. 18 Ch. D. 429 (CA); and *Re Earl of Wilton's Settled Estates* [1907] 1 Ch. 50. This proposition has been accepted as current law in

It is suggested, however, that these authorities reflect thinking at a time **11–104** before valuation became more of a scientific exercise and when in both theory and practice the valuer exercised very much a personal judgment applying such subjective standards as he thought fit. In such a situation, the identity of the valuer in the case of any valuation was a matter of prime importance, for the valuation necessarily reflected his particular predispositions. It is hardly surprising that against such a background the court would not allow fiduciaries to substitute the judgment of a valuer for their own judgment as to the market or proper price. The professional qualifications of valuers, and the principles of valuation, evolved in the nineteenth century, and with them has grown the recognition of valuation as a form of science. The competent expert is expected to determine objectively the market value or at least approximate to it. With the substitution of objective standards by qualified experts for subjective standards by amateurs, the objection to the use of valuers to fix a price has gone. The fiduciary has sufficiently discharged his duty by selecting the purchaser and the formula for the valuation. The function of the valuer in working out the value gives scope for the exercise by him of professional judgment. The recognition of the developments in valuation and their implications in the law of contract may be found in the judgment of the House of Lords in *Sudbrook Trading Estate Ltd v Eggleton*.[161] Similar reasoning applies with equal force in the field of "fiduciaries" and there can be little doubt that, if the opportunity arises, the two authorities in question should be overruled so that the law can catch up with modern practice.[162]

(j)   Grant of leases

The conduct of the insolvency may require the grant by the administrator or **11–105** receiver of leases of the company's property. A debenture is deemed to give an administrative receiver the power to grant leases in the name of the company unless such power is inconsistent with any of the provisions of the debenture.[163] In administration the Sch.1 powers have the same effect. Leases may be granted by the debenture-holder as mortgagee but more usually they are granted by the administrator or administrative receiver in the name and on behalf of the company. The latter course, however, can only be adopted and a good title passed to the prospective lessee if there are no charges over the property precluding the exercise of the power of lease by the company or if

---

some leading textbooks: see, e.g. *Emmett on Title*, 19th edn (London: Sweet & Maxwell, 1986), para.13.004; *Halsbury's Laws of England*, 4th edn (London: Lexis Nexis), Vol. 42, paras 94 and 827; *Wolstenholme and Cherry*, Vol. 3, pp.139 and 219; *Lewin, The Law of Trusts*, 6th edn (London: Sweet & Maxwell), pp.511 and 585; *Farrand, Contract and Conveyance*, 4th edn, pp.251 and 309.

[161] *Sudbrook Trading Estate Ltd v Eggleton* [1983] 1 A.C. 444 (HL). See also *Jones v Sherwood Computer Services Plc* [1992] 1 W.L.R. 277 (CA); *Alstom Signalling Ltd v Jarvis Facilities Ltd* (2004) 95 Con. L.R. 55; *Cream Holdings v Stuart Davenport* [2010] EWHC 3096 (Ch).

[162] See G. Lightman, "Sales at Valuation by Fiduciaries" [1985] Conv. 44.

[163] Insolvency Act 1986, s.42(1) and Sch.1, para.15.

such chargees consent.[164] In the case of a lease by the administrator or administrative receiver as agent of the company, there is no limitation on the nature, length or terms of the lease that might be granted so long as the company has the power to grant such a lease and is not precluded from so acting, e.g. by the terms of its own head-lease[165].

11–106   The company and the debenture-holder may by agreement (whether or not contained in the debenture) restrict or extend the statutory powers of leasing conferred on mortgagees.[166] In practice, the debenture frequently confers on the debenture-holder the unlimited powers of leasing of a beneficial owner. Subject to any such provision in the debenture, the statutory powers of leasing will be applicable. These powers are subject to limitations:

(a) they are only exercisable after the mortgagee has taken possession (and thus rendered himself liable to account as a mortgagee in possession on the basis of wilful default)[167] or after he has appointed a receiver of the income of the property;

(b) the lease must be made to take effect in possession not later than 12 months after its execution;

(c) the lease must reserve the best rent reasonably obtainable without any fine being taken;

(d) the lease must contain a condition of re-entry in the event of rent being in arrears for a period not exceeding 30 days; and

(e) the term of lease must not exceed, in the case of agricultural and occupation leases, 50 years and, in the case of building leases, 999 years.[168]

11–107   In any case where these conditions are not satisfied, and the lease is not authorised by some express power conferred by the debenture, the lease will not bind the company after redemption unless the company has given its consent, which

---

[164] The powers in Sch.1 are managerial; they do not extend the ability of the company to deal with its assets. If consent is refused the officer-holder may seek an order of the court under para.71 of Sch.B1 (in the case of administration) or s.43 (in the case of receivership).

[165] The grant of an under lease by an administrator means that the lessor's obligations in so far as they are monetary or capable of sounding in damages, will be liquidation expenses. Given the limited duration of administration, underleases are unlikely to be attractive in most circumstances.

[166] Law of Property Act 1925, s.99(14). In any event the court has a discretion under the Law of Property Act 1925, s.91(2) to order a sale where the exercise of leasing powers at a rental substantially less than the ongoing interest payable on the loan would unfairly prejudice the borrower: see *Palk v Mortgage Services Funding Plc* [1993] Ch. 330 (CA). That case concerned the exercise of the power by a mortgagee but in principle it would seem to be applicable also to a receiver. In the case of an administration different logic applies because of the administration duty to the creditors as a whole.

[167] See below, paras 13–011 to 13–014.

[168] Law of Property Act 1925, ss.99(2) and 100(2).

it may do informally.[169] The like consent will in such a case be required of any subsequent mortgagees, if the lease is to bind them.

If the lease is granted in the name of the company, unless expressly authorised **11–108** by the debenture, no covenant may effectively be included on the part of the company other than the usual qualified covenant for quiet enjoyment.[170] Any such express authority would, it seems, determine on winding up. Thereafter, in any case where the acceptance of covenants by the landlord is essential to an advantageous letting, the office-holder may achieve this result by exercising (where not excluded by the debenture) his statutory power to establish a subsidiary,[171] granting a lease imposing no covenants on the company to the subsidiary and then causing the subsidiary to grant an underlease in whatever terms are desired. In certain cases, e.g. the disposal of flats in a block, the office-holder may, at the same time or subsequently, divest himself of the subsidiary or its reversion on the sub-lease by a transfer to the sub-tenants.

The question arises whether the office-holder or mortgagee can grant a lease, **11–109** not at a fixed rent, but at a rent to be determined by a valuer according to a formula, e.g. the formula laid down as an essential requirement for the grant of a valid lease by a mortgagee, namely the best rent reasonably obtainable.[172] Whilst the law cannot be said to be entirely clear, the balance of authority certainly favours an affirmative answer,[173] and this view is reinforced by considerations of convenience and accepted common practice. Indeed, if the answer were otherwise, an office-holder or mortgagee could not grant leases containing rent review clauses. Since the inclusion of such clauses is essential to maintain the value of the reversion in the case of anything other than a short-term lease, the limitation on the powers of the office-holder and mortgagee would operate most harshly on them, on the company, on other chargees and indeed on the ordinary creditors of the company.

2. CONVEYANCES AND TRANSFERS

General

The detailed requirements for dealings in land under statute and case law and **11–110** the existence of common form sale conditions lead to the aspects of business sales which deal with land, whether leasehold or freehold, being dealt with in a separate schedule or annex to the sale contract. This treatment also facilitates negotiation of the terms between property specialists largely independent of the negotiation of the terms of the balance of the sale contract. For this reason it is important to take care that contradictory provisions do not exist in the two parts of the contract and to provide clearly for where terms of general application to one part should not apply to the other.

---

[169] *Chapman v Smith* [1907] 2 Ch. 97, 102.

[170] Law of Property Act 1925, s.8(1).

[171] See the Insolvency Act 1986, Sch.1, para.15.

[172] Law of Property Act 1925, s.99(13).

[173] *Lloyd's Bank v Marcan* [1973] 1 W.L.R. 339 and [1973] 1 W.L.R. 1387 (CA), 1391H, per Russell L.J.

11–111   In any case where an administrator or a receiver (whether administrative or not) wishes to execute a conveyance or transfer of premises (or any form of property for which an instrument of transfer is required), questions will arise as to the form, content and execution of that instrument.[174]

Where the office-holder has already entered into a contract for the sale of the asset in question, such questions will, or should have been, anticipated in the contract. Those questions are more complicated in receivership than in administration but the starting point is powers that are common to both administration and administrative receivership.

(a)   Statutory powers

11–112   Administrators and administrative receivers share a number of specific powers in Sch.1 Insolvency Act 1986 that are relevant to the conveyance and transfer of the company's property:

    (a) the power to sell or otherwise dispose of the property of the company by public auction or private contract . . . (para.2);

    (b) the power to use the company's seal (para.8);

    (c) the power to do all acts and to execute in the name and on behalf of the company any deed, receipt or other document (para.9); and

    (d) the power to do all such things (including the carrying out of works) as may be necessary for the realisation of the property of the company (para.12).

There is also a power to do all other things that are incidental to the exercise of these powers (para.23).

The acts of both an administrator and an administrative receiver are valid despite any defect in their appointment or qualification.[175]

Warranties and covenants for title are another subject on which there will be a common starting point. Office-holders should, as a general rule, avoid giving any warranties; and covenants for title should also, as a general rule, be excluded. The interest of the office-holder in not assuming any personal liability is obvious and it is thought that it is generally inappropriate for the office-holder to cause an already insolvent company to assume any new ongoing liabilities. In a case where the office-holder finds it impossible to avoid giving some form of supporting assurances, then he should take care that they are limited to a specified time period within which claims must be advanced or in some other way which minimises the need to retain funds to cover any resultant liabilities.

---

[174] General guidance in respect of land transfers can be obtained from Land Registry Practice Guide 36: Administration and receivership (October 2005).

[175] s.232 and Sch.B1 para.104. There must, however, have been some purported appointment: *Morris v Kanssen* [1946] A.C. 459 (HL). The protection should not be relied upon by persons who are on notice of defects.

(b) Administrators

(i) General

An administrator, in exercising his power to transfer or convey property, is **11–113** deemed to act as the company's agent.[176] Therefore contracts entered into in an administration are made by an administrator as agent for the company and are binding on the company but not the administrator personally, save where the contract provides otherwise.

Third parties contracting with a company in administration need not inquire whether an administrator is acting within his powers if they are dealing in good faith and for value.[177]

Any contractual obligations of a company in administration resulting from an administrator's disposal will be charged on the assets in the administrator's custody or under his control immediately before the cessation of the administration.[178]

(ii) Over-reaching

An administrator has the power to dispose of or take action relating to property **11–114** which is subject to a floating charge as if it were not subject to such a charge.[179] No prior court order is necessary and the purchaser requires no evidence of release from the security.[180] Where property is disposed of in this way, the holder of the floating charge shall have the same priority in respect of any property that directly or indirectly represents the property disposed of.[181] Thus the priority enjoyed in relation to property disposed of carries through to what is termed in the Act as "acquired property".[182]

With respect to property that is subject to a security other than a floating charge, the court may by order enable an administrator to dispose of or take action relating to such property as if it were not subject to such a security.[183] An application for an order should, where time permits, be supported by valuation evidence, since such evidence is critical to the exercise of the court's discretion.[184] In the event of a dispute as to valuation, it is not appropriate for the

---

[176] Sch.B1 para.69.

[177] Sch.B1 para.59(3).

[178] Sch.B1 para.99(4).

[179] Sch.B1 para.70(1).

[180] As to Land Registry requirements for the removal of notice of the floating charge from the register, see Land Registry Practice Guide 36: Administration and receivership (October 2005).

[181] Sch.B1 para.70(2).

[182] This section does not apply to the enforcement of "market charges" as defined in s.173(1) of the Companies Act 1989 or collateral security as defined by the Financial Markets and Insolvency (Settlement Finality) Regulations 1999, which implements the EU Directive on Settlement Finality in Payment and Securities systems or charges created or arising under a financial collateral arrangement within the meaning of the Financial Collateral Arrangements (No.2) Regulations 2003.

[183] Sch.B1 para.71(1). See also, para.11-098 above.

[184] See *Re ARV Aviation Ltd* (1988) 4 B.C.C. 708, 713, dealing with similar wording in s.15 of the Insolvency Act 1986.

court to fix a valuation midway between the two sums.[185] The jurisdiction extends to authorising the disposal of goods held under hire-purchase agreements.[186] The court must be satisfied that the disposal would be likely to promote the purpose of the administration in respect of the company.[187] This requires balancing the prejudice that would be felt by the secured creditor (were an order made) against the prejudice that would be felt by those interested in the promotion of the purpose of the company (were it not).[188]

11–115   An order for sale is subject to the condition that certain monies be applied towards "the sums secured by the security"[189] and, if more than one charge, the sums secured by those charges or securities in the order of their priorities.[190] The condition is that the amount to be applied towards the sums secured by the security must be equivalent to the net amount that would have been realised on a sale of the property at market value. Therefore if the net proceeds of the disposal of the property are below this amount, additional money is required to be paid to discharge the sums secured by the security to satisfy the condition.[191] It is thought that, in computing the net proceeds, credit must be given for any sum required to be paid to obtain the redemption of a security which has priority to that to which the order relates and whose holder agrees to accept redemption upon completion of the sale.

It was originally thought that a question might arise as to whether a security-holder whose security is to be over-reached could artificially raise the net market value of the charged property by making an unrealistically high offer to buy in the property at a price approaching the secured debt outstanding but this does not appear to have materialised as a problem in practice.

---

[185] *Stanley J Holmes & Sons Ltd v Davenham Trust Plc* [2007] B.C.C. 485 (CA).

[186] Sch.B1 para.72. A "Hire-purchase agreement" is defined to include a conditional sale agreement, a chattel leasing agreement and a retention of title agreement; see Sch.B1 para.111(1).

[187] Sch.B1 para.71(2). See with regard to the meaning of this expression, *Re Harris Simons Construction Ltd* [1989] 1 W.L.R. 368; *Re Consumer & Industrial Press Ltd (No.1)* (1988) 4 B.C.C. 68; *Re Manlon Trading Ltd (Petition for Administration Order)* (1988) 4 B.C.C. 455; *Re Primlaks (UK) Ltd* (1989) 5 B.C.C. 710; *Re SCL Building Services Ltd* (1989) 5 B.C.C. 746; *Re Rowbotham Baxter Ltd* [1990] B.C.C. 113; *Re Chelmsford City Football Club (1980) Ltd* [1991] B.C.C. 133; *Re Land and Property Trust Co Plc* [1991] B.C.C. 446; *Re Arrows Ltd* [1992] B.C.C. 131; *Re Maxwell Communications Corp Plc (No.1)* [1992] B.C.C. 372; *Re Dallhold Estates (UK) Pty Ltd* [1992] B.C.C. 394; *Re Structures & Computers Ltd* [1998] B.C.C. 348; *Re Lomax Leisure Ltd* [2000] Ch. 502 on the construction of similar words in s.8. For a consideration of the position under Sch.B1, para.3, see *Notoriety Films v Revenue and Customs Commissioner* [2006] EWHC 1998 (Ch).

[188] *Re ARV Aviation Ltd* [1989] B.C.L.C. 664, 667h–668c per Knox J.

[189] These are the words used in Sch.B1 para.71(3). These sums include not only capital but ongoing interest and (subject to the court's over-riding discretion) costs which can be added to the security under the general law or under the terms of the instrument: see *Re ARV Aviation Ltd* (1988) 4 B.C.C. 708, dealing with similar wording in s.15. For circumstances in which the court will refuse to make an order authorising disposal of property of the company free from a security to which it is subject see *Re Newman Shopfitters (Cleveland) Ltd* [1991] B.C.L.C. 407.

[190] Sch.B1 para.71(4).

[191] Sch.B1 para.71(3). The "market value" is defined in para.111(1) as "the amount which would be realised on a sale of the property in the open market by a willing vendor". On the question of valuation, see *Stanley J Holmes & Sons Ltd v Davenham Trust Plc* [2007] B.C.C. 485 (CA).

(c) Receivers pre-winding up

In any case where a receiver wishes to sell and convey or transfer property of **11–116** the company, he must first consider whether the sale should be made:

    (a) by the receiver as agent for the company;

    (b) by the debenture-holder as mortgagee; or

    (c) pursuant to an order of the court.

(i) General

In the ordinary case, the desire of the debenture-holder to avoid being a party **11–117** to any transaction (as well as considerations of convenience) results in all transactions being entered into by the receiver as agent for the company when-ever this is practicable, the only participation of the debenture-holder being the release of its charge on completion.[192]

For the non-administrative receiver, the use of the company's seal requires the co-operation of the board of directors and this can create difficulties.

The non-administrative receiver is normally nowadays expressly given by the debenture a power of attorney enabling him to convey or transfer on behalf of the company. Provided that the debenture has been executed as a deed,[193] the non-administrative receiver can make use of statutory powers of conveying by signing the name of the company in the presence of at least one witness who attests the signature, such execution taking effect as if the company had executed the conveyance[194] even if the instrument of appointment is not executed as a deed.

In any other case, common law rules as to the execution of deeds mean that **11–118** a non-administrative receiver, in order to be able to transfer or lease land by deed as agent of the mortgagor, must have been appointed by deed executed by the mortgagor.[195] The one qualification is that, where the mortgagor has signed

---

[192] See further Land Registry Practice Guide 36: Administration and receivership (October 2005).
[193] In *Phoenix Properties Ltd v Wimpole Street Nominees* Ltd [1992] B.C.L.C. 737, per Mummery J., preferred the view in the first edition of this work at p.49 to the views of *Kerr on Receivers*, 17th edn (London: Sweet & Maxwell, 1992), pp.228–229, and *Halsbury's Laws of England*, 4th edn (London: Lexis Nexis), para.804. The contrary appears to have been assumed in *Re Wood's Application* [1941] Ch. 112 and in *Sowman v Samuel (David) Trust Ltd (In Liquidation)* [1978] 1 W.L.R. 22, 30–31. While the views in the most recent edition of Kerr, which is *Kerr and Hunter on Receivers and Administrators*, 19th edn (London: Sweet & Maxwell, 2005) now accord with those expressed here, *Halsbury's Laws*, 4th edn, states that the appointment needs be made by deed only if the receiver is appointed attorney and that it need not be made by deed if the mortgage contains an express delegation to seal and convey in the name of the mortgagor; see para.305.
[194] See s.74(3) of the Law of Property Act 1925, as amended by the Law of Property (Miscellaneous Provisions) Act 1989 s.4, Sch.2 (to delete the former requirement of sealing by the agent) and Regulatory Reform (Execution of Deeds and Documents) Order 2005 (SI 2005/1906).
[195] See also s.1(1) Powers of Attorney Act 1971.

and sealed the transfer or lease, an agent can be authorised to deliver the deed without any authorisation by deed.[196]

In the case of administrative receivers, their implied power to use the company's seal and to execute deeds and other instruments in the name and on behalf of the company is in no way dependent on the form of their appointment.[197]

Although the administrative receiver does not require the co-operation of the directors of the company, it may nonetheless be advantageous for him to obtain that co-operation and concurrence (if possible) since this may preclude a subsequent challenge to the transaction. The directors' concurrence with the transaction is particularly valuable if the directors, as often happens, are also guarantors to whom the receiver owes a duty of care in connection with the sale.[198] Receivers who as agent of the company sell the company's business (or any significant asset) to a new company controlled by one or more directors of the vendor company are required to obtain a requisite resolution of the vendor company's members.[199]

11–119   The practical limitation on the utility of a sale by the receiver in the name of the company is that, as the sale is by the company (as on any sale by the company whether in receivership or not), the sale is subject to all outstanding charges whether prior or subsequent to the charge of the debenture-holder, save to the extent that the chargees agree to release their charges on completion of the sale.[200] To obtain the concurrence of such chargees in a sale may be impracticable. A sale by the debenture-holder will be free of all charges postponed to his charge, but subject to any prior charges.[201] Accordingly, a sale by the debenture-holder is appropriate when his charge is a first charge and there are subsequent chargees who will not concur in a sale by the receiver on behalf of the company.

(ii)   Over-reaching

11–120   Section 43 provides that an administrative receiver may apply to the court for an order authorising him to dispose of any property of the company free from a security to which it is subject and which ranks in priority to the charge held by the appointing debenture-holder. The jurisdiction to authorise sale under s.43 is comparable with the jurisdiction to authorise administrators' sales under Sch.B1 para.71 which is discussed in the commentary in the earlier part of this chapter and to which reference should be made. However, it should be noted that the s.43 jurisdiction does not apply to the security under which the administrative receiver has been appointed, to other securities to which the appointment security takes priority or to hire purchase agreements. The court may

---

[196] The Law of Property (Miscellaneous Provisions) Act 1989 provides in s.1(1)(c) for the abolition of any rule which "requires authority by one person to another to deliver an instrument as a deed on his behalf to be given by deed".

[197] s.42 and Sch.1, paras 8 and 9.

[198] See Ch.13.

[199] Companies Act 2006, s.190; see *Demite Ltd v Protec Health Ltd* [1998] B.C.C. 638; *Ultraframe (UK) Ltd v Fielding* [2007] 2 All E.R. 983 (CA). See also para.15–045.

[200] *Re The Real Meat Co Ltd (In Receivership)* [1996] B.C.C. 254.

[201] Law of Property Act 1925, s.101.

make an order if satisfied that the disposal (with or without other assets) would be likely to promote a more advantageous realisation of the company's assets than would otherwise be effected. The court must as a condition of such an authorisation require that the net proceeds of sale plus any sum by which the net proceeds fall short of the net proceeds on a realisation of the property on the open market by a willing vendor shall be applied towards discharging the sums secured by the security[202] and, if more than one charge, the sums secured by those charges or securities in the order of their priorities.

(iii)   Sales by the court

Situations arise when no sale can be achieved without an order for sale by the court. Examples include: **11–121**

(a) where the validity or continued subsistence of the debenture is challenged[203];

(b) where there is a dispute as to priority between the debenture-holder and another chargee and no agreement can be reached as to sale;

(c) where the charge is not made by deed (in which case the statutory power of sale does not apply)[204];

(d) where the charge is equitable only and either:

    (i) there is no power of attorney empowering the chargee to convey the legal estate[205]; or

    (ii) no declaration of trust by the mortgagor in favour of the mort-gagee authorising the mortgagee to appoint himself or his nominee trustee in place of the mortgagor; or

    (iii) there has been a deposit of the deeds.[206]

In any such case, the court has a discretionary power to make an order for sale,[207] and in the exercise of this power may authorise the debenture-holder to

---

[202] The court has no power to order that a receiver's costs, expenses and remuneration be paid in priority to the sums secured under prior charges (other than receivers appointed by the court); see *Choudhri v Palta* [1992] B.C.C. 787 (CA).

[203] *Greendon Investments v Mills* [1973] 226 E.G. 1957.

[204] See Law of Property Act 1925, s.101(1)(i); Megarry and Wade, *The Law of Real Property* 7th edn (London: Sweet & Maxwell, 2008), para.25–043; *Re Hodson & Howes Contract* (1887) 35 Ch. D. 668 (CA); contrast *Re White Rose Cottage* [1965] Ch. 940 (CA), 951, per Lord Denning M.R.

[205] In cases (d)(i) and (d)(ii) there is doubt whether the mortgagee can convey legal title. The position of the mortgagee in this situation may be analogous with that of one of several executors who has power to contract to sell land, but cannot complete a conveyance, without the concurrence of his co-executors or an order of the court: Snell, *The Principles of Equity*, 31st edn (London: Sweet & Maxwell, 2004), paras 38–44 et seq.

[206] Since September 27, 1989, it has no longer been possible to create charges by the deposit of title deeds, see Law of Property (Miscellaneous Provisions) Act 1989 s.2; *United Bank of Kuwait Plc v Sahib* [1997] Ch. 107 (CA).

[207] Law of Property Act 1925 s.91, as amended by SI 1991/724, art.2(8), Sch.1.

proceed with and complete a conditional contract or intended sale. Incidental to the exercise of this power, the court may direct that entries which have been made by parties to the action in the Land Registry or Land Charges Registry and whose continued subsistence would preclude completion should be vacated.[208]

(iv)   Warranties

11–122   It has already been suggested that a receiver should avoid giving warranties and thereby he will avoid the need to retain funds to cover potential liability under the warranty and so delay remission of proceeds to the debenture-holder.[209] However, if he nonetheless does so, he should ensure that he is covered by a completely satisfactory indemnity from an undoubtedly solvent debenture-holder or that there is sufficient security provided for him in some other manner, e.g. by bank bond, to enable him to close the receivership in due course and pay over all remaining monies.

A request for warranties can sometimes be countered if the debenture or charge contains provisions to the effect that:

(a)   a purchaser of the charged assets need not inquire as to whether any default under the charge has occurred or notice required by the charge has been given;

(b)   in favour of a purchaser, a sale by the receiver should be deemed to be within the power of sale granted by the charge despite any impropriety or irregularity; and

(c)   the company's remedy in the event of any irregularity or impropriety would be restricted to damages.[210]

This type of provision can provide protection for a purchaser[211] as long as such purchaser has no actual knowledge of an irregularity and any irregularity is not obvious, e.g. on the face of the documents.[212]

(d)   Receivers post winding up

11–123   Winding-up will not prevent the receiver disposing of assets the subject of the charge over which he is appointed or the debenture-holder exercising powers of disposition as mortgagee.[213] The debenture-holder can execute conveyances and transfers in the name of the company if the debenture includes a power of attorney granted to the debenture-holder: such a power survives

---

[208] *National Westminster Bank v Hornsea Pottery* Unreported May 11, 1984 (CA).
[209] See paras 11–075 to 11–076, above.
[210] O'Donovan, *Company Receivers and Managers*, 1st edn, p.104.
[211] *Dicker v Angerstein* (1876) L.R. 3 Ch. D. 600.
[212] *Selwyn v Garfit* (1888) L.R. 38 Ch. D. 273 (CA).
[213] *Gaskell v Gosling* [1896] 1 Q.B. 669 (CA), per Rigby L.J. whose judgment was upheld in the House of Lords; *Sowman v Samuel (David) Trust Ltd (In Liquidation)* [1978] 1 W.L.R. 22, 30, per Goulding J.; *Barrows v Chief Land Registrar, Times*, October 20, 1977, per Whitford J.

liquidation.[214] It is more questionable whether a non-administrative receiver can still execute such a conveyance or transfer on behalf of the company. On balance, it is thought that the receiver does retain such power, most particularly if the debenture confers a power of attorney on him.[215] Any doubts as to such power on the part of an administrative receiver are removed by the express powers conferred on him by the Act.[216]

[214] *Sowman v Samuel (David) Trust Ltd (In Liquidation)* [1978] 1 W.L.R. 22, 30; *Barrows v Chief Land Registrar*, The Times, October 20, 1977.

[215] See the discussion in *Sowman v Samuel (David) Trust Ltd (In Liquidation)* [1978] 1 W.L.R. 22 and *Kerr and Hunter on Receivers and Administrators*, 19th edn (London: Sweet & Maxwell, 2005), paras 25–6 to 25–10. See further the article by Peter Millett QC, "The Conveyancing Powers of Receivers After Liquidation" (1977) 41 Conv (N.S.) 83 and *Re Leslie Homes* (1984) 8 A.C.L.R. 1020 where McLelland J. held that whilst only the liquidator could affix the company's seal, the receiver could execute a contract or transfer on behalf of the company under his own hand and seal.

[216] s.42 and Sch.1, paras 2, 8 and 9.

Chapter 12

Duties and Liabilities
of Administrators

1. STATUS AND ROLE OF ADMINISTRATOR

12–001 The governance of formal insolvency procedures and, in particular, the accountability of insolvency office-holders to creditors and other stakeholders are matters which have attracted heightened public scrutiny in the wake of the recent global financial crisis. This chapter provides an overview of one aspect of office-holder governance and accountability in English law, namely the duties and liabilities of administrators appointed to deal with the affairs of insolvent companies under the statutory framework of the Insolvency Act 1986, Sch.B1.

12–002 The administrator's principal legal duties and liabilities derive from his capacity as (variously): a professionally qualified statutory functionary and office-holder; an officer and agent of the company to which he is appointed; and an officer of the court. The relationships between these various capacities and the extent to which each is a source of entirely discrete categories of duty and liability are not matters that policy makers or the courts have yet felt any powerful practical need to address. The capacities are best regarded for practical purposes as overlapping as well as distinct. Thus, for example, the content and standard of the administrator's duty of care as an officer and agent of the company are clearly informed by the administrator's overlapping status as a professionally qualified statutory functionary.[1]

(a) Professionally qualified statutory functionary and office-holder

12–003 First and foremost the administrator is a creature of statute: a statutory functionary appointed under the machinery of the Insolvency Act 1986, Sch.B1 who is tasked with a statutory purpose, has extensive statutory powers directed towards achieving that purpose and is subject to statutory avenues of accountability. A person may be appointed as administrator of a company only if he is qualified to act as an insolvency practitioner in relation to the company.[2] Accordingly, appointments may only be taken by professionally qualified

---

[1] See further para.12–040, below.
[2] Insolvency Act 1986, ss.388(1)(a), 390 and Sch.B1, para.6. In the footnotes to this chapter references to sections are to sections of Insolvency Act 1986, references to paragraphs are to paragraphs of Sch.B1, and references to rules are to Insolvency Regulations 1986, unless the context otherwise admits.

insolvency practitioners licensed and regulated under the statutory framework set out in the Insolvency Act 1986, Pt XIII. The point is significant in the present context because the courts have generally been reluctant to engage in intrusive review of an administrator's conduct, especially as regards the formulation and execution of the administrator's general strategy, deferring instead to the professional and commercial judgment of the insolvency practitioner.[3]

The administrator is also an office-holder for the purposes of Insolvency Act 1986 and Insolvency Rules 1986 who is vested with the special powers and privileges conferred by Insolvency Act 1986, ss.230–241 and 244–246, which include information gathering powers and powers to challenge certain antecedent transactions such as unlawful preferences, transactions at undervalue and late floating charges.[4]   **12–004**

(b) Officer and agent of company

The administrator acts as the company's agent,[5] and is required, upon appointment as such agent, to take custody or control of all of the property to which he thinks the company is entitled, and to manage the company's affairs.[6] It follows that as a person undertaking responsibility to act on behalf of the company and entrusted as such with its management and property, the administrator owes the company fiduciary duties and a duty to act with reasonable care and skill.[7] It follows also that he does not normally incur personal liability on the contracts to which he commits the company, and that he can claim an indemnity from the company's assets for the liabilities that he does incur. These implications of the administrator's status as the company's agent are considered in para.12–050.   **12–005**

(c) Officer of the court

Regardless of the manner of his appointment,[8] the administrator is an officer of the court.[9] In this respect, he is no different from a liquidator in a compulsory   **12–006**

---

[3] See paras. 12–008 to 12–014, below.

[4] See further Ch.15. The various powers and privileges conferred by Insolvency Act 1986, ss.230–237 are shared with liquidators and administrative receivers, who are also "office-holders" for the purposes of those provisions. The avoidance powers conferred by Insolvency Act 1986, ss.238–241 and 244–246 are shared with liquidators alone.

[5] para.69.

[6] paras 67 and 68.

[7] For useful judicial accounts of fiduciary obligations and the facts that give rise to them see *Bristol & West Building Society v Mothew* [1998] Ch. 1 (CA), 16–18; *Peskin v Anderson* [2001] B.C.C. 874 (CA), [34]. It seems to have been accepted at first instance in *Kyrris v Oldham* [2003] 2 B.C.L.C. 35, [79]–[80] that an administrator (like a director or liquidator) owes fiduciary duties to the company. Moreover, Sch.B1 clearly assumes that the administrator owes fiduciary duties to the company: see para.75(3)(c). See further 12–035 to 12–041 and 12–063 to 12–065.

[8] An administrator may be appointed by court order or out of court by a qualifying floating charge holder or the company or its directors: see paras 11, 14 and 22. On the appointment of administrators generally, see Ch. 6.

[9] para.5. See also *Re CE King Ltd* [2000] 2 B.C.L.C. 297, 303a; *Re Atlantic Computer Systems Plc* [1992] Ch.505 (CA), 529e.

winding-up, a court-appointed receiver or indeed a solicitor.[10] This status confers upon him certain privileges. Thus, he is protected by the law of contempt from deliberate and unjustifiable interference with his management of the company's affairs.[11] He also has a general right of access to the court for directions.[12] This right of access exists alongside statutory powers, and, in some circumstances, duties to seek such directions contained in Sch.B1.[13] While the court's inherent jurisdiction to give directions to its officers is apparently not ousted by these statutory powers and duties, it is perhaps best regarded as a residual jurisdiction as, in most cases, the court will plainly have power under the statute to give the directions and make the orders sought.[14] It goes without saying that the administrator has a duty both as an officer of the court and by statute to obey directions that he is given.

12–007   The administrator's status as an officer of the court also places him under special obligations. He is required to be candid with the court,[15] and he is bound by the so-called rule in *Ex p. James*.[16] The administrator must also be, and be seen to be, independent and impartial in his management of the company, its property and its affairs.[17] This duty would appear to be coterminous with one aspect of his fiduciary obligations.[18] Finally, he is also under a duty to act speedily and responsibly.[19] The first facet of this duty mirrors his statutory duty in Sch.B1, para.4 to perform his functions as quickly and efficiently as is reasonably practicable.[20] The duty to act responsibly probably mirrors and, in practice, adds little to his duty to the company to act with reasonable care and skill.[21] It is suggested, as a general proposition, that the court's supervisory jurisdiction plays a rather more residual role than it once did. This reflects the fact that administrators are licensed professionals operating within a detailed statutory framework. Nevertheless, there may be cases where the administrator's behaviour qua officer of the court is relevant to

---

[10] On the like position of court-appointed receivers see Ch.31. In contrast, a liquidator in a voluntary winding-up is not an officer of the court: see *Re TH Knitwear (Wholesale) Ltd* [1988] Ch. 275 (CA).
[11] See further *Bristol Airport Plc v Powdrill* [1990] Ch. 744 (CA), 764e; *Re Sabre International Products Ltd* [1991] B.C.C. 694.
[12] The court will, however, usually defer to the administrator's commercial judgment and will not expect to be asked to give directions on what amount to commercial decisions. See, e.g. *MTI Trading Systems Ltd v Winter* [1998] B.C.C. 591 and paras.12–008 to 12–014, below.
[13] See generally paras 63 and 68(2) and, as regards duties to seek directions in specified circumstances, paras 12–047 to 12–049.
[14] *Re Collins & Aikman Europe SA* [2006] B.C.C. 861, [18]–[20], [37]–[40]. It was suggested by Lewison J. in *Re Hellas Telecommunications (Luxembourg) II SCA* [2010] B.C.C. 295, [8], that the court could direct an administrator not to complete a pre-pack sale. Presumably such a direction could be given under para.68(2).
[15] See further para.12–046.
[16] *Re Condon, Ex p. James* (1874) L.R. 9 Ch. App. 609 (CA in Chancery), discussed below in paras 12–044 to 12–045.
[17] See, e.g. by analogy, *Re Contract Corp* (1872) L.R. 7 Ch. App 207 (CA in Chancery), 211.
[18] The duty to act impartially as between all creditors, discussed below in para.12–040.
[19] *Re Atlantic Computer Systems Plc* [1992] Ch. 505 (CA), 529–530. See also *Re Sabre International Products Ltd* [1991] B.C.C. 694 on the administrator's duty to act reasonably and to respond promptly to requests, e.g. from the holders of security.
[20] Discussed in paras 12–031 and 12–043, below.
[21] Discussed in para.12–042.

questions of how particular claims and assets are to be treated or to questions of costs.[22]

(d)   The court's deference to the administrator's commercial judgment

The general attitude of the court when: (i) considering the strategies proposed **12–008** by the prospective administrator in support of administration applications under Sch.B1, para.12; or (ii) considering or reviewing decisions, acts and transactions of the administrator undertaken within the scope of his extensive statutory powers, is one of deference to the commercial judgment of insolvency practitioners as experts and regulated professionals. This reflects a broad judicial understanding of the nature of the administrator's task and the challenges that he faces on appointment; an appreciation, in particular, that the administrator will invariably be operating at pace in difficult and urgent circumstances which dictate the need for quick decision-making, often based on less than perfect information, if value is to be preserved and the purpose of administration achieved. It also reflects an institutional judgment that licensed professionals are better placed than the court to formulate and implement commercial strategy according to the circumstances in which they find themselves.

Accordingly, the exercise of the administrator's wide powers, inter alia, to **12–009** manage the company's business and realise its assets are regarded as matters for the commercial judgment of the administrator, rather than as appropriate matters for directions by the court. In the words of David Richards J., the court "would not normally give directions to an administrator as to the means by which he should market assets, any more than as to which particular deal to make."[23] Consistent with this approach, the court will not usually be prepared to review the commercial strategy that the administrator wishes to pursue in advance. Thus, the court will not generally interfere where the administrator wishes to dispose of the company's assets speedily, in order to preserve goodwill that may otherwise rapidly diminish, before creditors have received his proposals or have had the opportunity to consider and approve them formally at the initial creditors' meeting.[24]

This is not to say that the insolvency practitioner's decisions are immune to **12–010** challenge. While the court will generally defer beforehand to the administrator as to the commercial merits of his chosen strategy, it remains open after the event to aggrieved creditors or members to pursue a remedy for maladministration under Sch.B1, para.74 and to various parties (including a creditor, a contributory or a subsequently appointed administrator or liquidator) to bring

---

[22] *Re Japan Leasing (Europe) Plc* [1999] B.P.I.R. 911; *Re Sabre International Products Ltd* [1991] B.C.C. 694.

[23] *Re T&N Ltd* [2005] 2 B.C.L.C. 488, [76]. In a similar vein, see *MTI Trading Systems Ltd v Winter* [1998] B.C.C. 591; *Re Lehman Brothers International (Europe) Ltd* [2009] B.C.C. 632.

[24] *Re T&D Industries Plc* [2000] 1 W.L.R. 646; *Re Transbus International Ltd* [2004] 1 W.L.R. 2654; *Re Kayley Vending Ltd* [2009] B.C.C. 578, [16].

proceedings under Sch.B1, para.75 to remedy misconduct.[25] An administrator may also be removed from office by order of the court on cause shown.[26] Nevertheless, when reviewing the administrator's conduct after the event, the court will not question the administrator's commercial judgment unless it is based on a wrong appreciation of the law or is conspicuously unfair to a particular creditor[27] or is otherwise impeachable on grounds of breach of duty.[28] Thus, the court can generally be expected to proceed carefully when assessing with hindsight decisions taken by administrators in good faith and in challenging circumstances, whether under the statutory gateways to relief in Sch.B1, paras 74–75, under the statutory jurisdiction to remove the office-holder, or under the general supervisory jurisdiction in relation to its own officers.

12–011   Judicial deference to the administrator's commercial judgment and strategy is somewhat more qualified in relation to so-called "pre-pack" sales. The term "pre-pack" denotes "a sale of all or part of the business and assets of a company negotiated in principle while it is not subject to any form of insolvency procedure, but on the footing that the sale will be concluded immediately after the company has entered into such a procedure, and on the authority of the insolvency practitioner appointed."[29] Thus, in the classic pre-pack a deal for the sale of the insolvent company's business is reached before the company goes into administration, with the sale then being completed immediately after the administrator has been appointed. Pre-packs should therefore be distinguished from accelerated sales, which are also concluded before the initial creditors' meeting but have been negotiated and agreed only after the administrator's appointment.[30]

12–012   The commercial justification for pre-packs is that, in practice, they may often afford the only available means of achieving an effective going concern realisation of the insolvent company's assets and business. As pre-pack sales are agreed before the administrator's appointment and executed speedily thereafter, they can be useful in preserving value and, in particular, goodwill that would otherwise quickly diminish once the administrator's appointment becomes public knowledge and the company's financial plight is widely

---

[25] On remedies for maladministration or misfeasance, see further paras 12–056 to 12–065.

[26] The court has a general power to remove the administrator under para.88 but can also order removal by way of relief on an application under para.74: see *SISU Capital Fund Ltd v Tucker* [2006] B.C.C. 463, [88]; *Clydesdale Financial Services Ltd v Smailes* [2009] B.C.C. 810, [15]. Although the power in para.88 is apparently unlimited, it is trite law that there must be a good ground for removing an administrator: see *SISU Capital Fund Ltd v Tucker* [2006] B.C.C. 463, [87]–[88]; *Clydesdale Financial Services Ltd v Smailes* [2009] B.C.C. 810, [14], [30]; *Re St Georges Property Services (London) Ltd* [2011] B.C.C. 64, [7]–[9] affirmed by the Court of Appeal [2011] EWCA Civ 858; *Re Edennote Ltd* [1996] B.C. C. 718 (CA) (by analogy in relation to the statutory powers to remove a liquidator from office). On the question of how questions of costs should be determined on an application for removal, see *Coyne v DRC Distribution Ltd* [2008] B.C.C. 612 (CA).

[27] *Re C E King Ltd* [2000] 2 B.C.L.C. 297, 303a; *BLV Realty Organization Ltd v Batten* [2010] B.P.I.R. 277, [20], [22]. Along similar lines, see also *Re Lehman Brothers International (Europe) Ltd* [2009] B.C.C. 632.

[28] See paras 12–025 to 12–043.

[29] *Re Kayley Vending Ltd* [2009] B.C.C. 578, [2].

[30] For examples of accelerated sales which were not "pre-packs", see *Re T&D Industries Plc* [2000] 1 W.L.R. 646; *Re Transbus International Ltd* [2004] 1 W.L.R. 2654.

STATUS AND ROLE OF ADMINISTRATOR

known. Despite these advantages, pre-packs have aroused considerable controversy and public concern especially where the company's assets and business are sold to connected parties. Concerns have been expressed, especially from an unsecured creditor perspective, about lack of transparency, lack of marketing of the assets, lack of creditor consultation and influence in the process leading up to the sale, the risk that the sale may have been at an under-value and the perceived conflict of interest arising where the insolvency practitioner who advised the company to pursue a pre-pack strategy subsequently takes up the appointment thereby assuming a wider obligation to act in the interest of creditors as a whole and not merely in the interests of those who procured his appointment.[31] In order to assuage these concerns, the recognised professional bodies and the Insolvency Service, which together license and regulate the entire insolvency practitioner community, issued Statement of Insolvency Practice 16 (SIP 16) with effect from January 1, 2009. SIP 16 is one of a number of best practice standards binding on insolvency practitioners as a matter of professional obligation. To meet the point that pre-pack sales deprive the unsecured creditors of the opportunity to consider the proposed sale of the assets or business before it is consummated, SIP 16 requires extensive information to be disclosed to creditors about the circumstances and terms of the sale.[32]

It has become the practice in some cases where a pre-pack is proposed that is likely to give rise to dispute for the parties supporting the proposal to favour the court route to appointing the administrator even where it would have been open to them to procure an out-of-court appointment under Sch.B1, paras 14 or 22.[33] On occasions, the court route will be mandatory because the existence of a pending winding-up petition prevents the company or its directors from making an out-of-court appointment.[34] Thus, while the majority of appointments are now made out of court in line with the legislative policy underlying the changes to the administration regime introduced by Enterprise Act 2002 and now embodied in Sch.B1,[35] there are cases where the court is invited to scrutinise and approve a pre-pack at the outset. To date, the court has granted

12–013

---

[31] For further elaboration of these concerns, see *Re Kayley Vending Ltd* [2009] B.C.C. 578, [6]–[12]; *Clydesdale Financial Services Ltd v Smailes* [2009] B.C.C. 810, [6]; The Insolvency Service, *Improving the transparency of, and confidence in, pre-packaged sales in administrations* (March 2010). See also, in the context of a pre-pack disposal effected in an administrative receivership, *Re Delberry Ltd* [2008] B.C.C. 653.

[32] In March 2011, the Government announced that it proposed to introduce legislation requiring administrators to give notice to creditors where they intend to sell a significant proportion of the assets or business to a connected party in circumstances where there has been no open marketing. See now The Insolvency (Amendment) (No.2) Rules 2011 (Draft SI 2011/000). At the time of writing, the Insolvency Service is undertaking further consultation on the provisions of the draft statutory instrument and, more broadly, the general question of the further regulation of pre-packs. See, further, Ch.2, above.

[33] In *Re Super Aguri F1 Ltd* [2011] B.C.C. 452, [23], the court summarised the position as follows: "that however desirable it may be in any given case, there is no statutory duty on directors to consult with the company's creditors before appointing an administrator; that they are not obliged to abide by the creditors' expressed preference for a creditors' voluntary liquidation; that they are not obliged to seek the directions of the court before making the appointment; and that they are not obliged to convene a meeting of creditors before they embark on their duties as administrators."

[34] para.25(a). *Re DKLL Solicitors* [2007] B.C.C. 908 and *Re Kayley Vending Ltd* [2009] B.C.C. 578 are cases in point.

[35] *Re Kayley Vending Ltd* [2009] B.C.C. 578, [3].

administration orders facilitating pre-packs in a number of such cases, some-times in the teeth of creditor opposition.[36] Where the sale would involve an obvious abuse of the administrator's powers, the court may refuse to make an administration order or, having appointed the administrator, direct him not to complete it.[37] However, in the majority of cases where the court is called upon to consider a pre-pack before the event, the general propositions outlined above will hold good. In other words, the court will be reluctant to interfere with the insolvency practitioner's assessment of the commercial merits of the pre-pack as long as there has been adequate disclosure[38] and there is no obvious abuse. Nevertheless, this will not preclude aggrieved creditors from challenging the administrator's conduct and decisions after the event through the statutory gateways in Sch.B1, paras 74–75. Thus, in making an administration order which authorises the administrator to complete a pre-pack sale, the court will not be immunising the sale against future creditor challenge.[39] In reserving the right to intervene, the court has recognised that pre-packs do not easily map onto the statutory framework which contemplates that the administrator will usually seek creditor approval for proposals formulated after his appointment.[40] At the same time, there is an acknowledgment that the legislative policy behind the changes implemented by the Enterprise Act 2002 were designed to reduce the involvement of the court in the initiation of administrations[41] and to rein-force the court's non-interventionist approach, before the event, to the exercise of the administrator's powers.[42] It follows that cases where an administration application is refused to prevent implementation of a pre-pack or the adminis-trator is directed not to complete the sale are likely to be rare.

12–014   This prevailing understanding of the respective roles of the insolvency practitioner and the court provides an important context for the account of the

---

[36] *Re DKLL Solicitors* [2007] B.C.C. 908, [10], [18]–[21]. See also *Re Kayley Vending Ltd* [2009] B.C.C. 578; *Re Hellas Telecommunications (Luxembourg) II SCA* [2010] B.C.C. 295, [8]; *Re Cornercare Ltd* [2010] B.C.C. 592; *Re Halliwells LLP* [2011] B.C.C. 57. The administration application in *Hellas Telecommunications* was motivated in part by the desirability, in practice, of having the court open main insolvency proceedings under art.3 of Council Regulation (EC) 1346/2000 of May 29, 2000 on Insolvency Proceedings [2000] OJ L160/1 in relation to a foreign registered company and supplement its order with a judicial ruling affirming the English court's jurisdiction to open such proceedings for the purposes of international recognition.
[37] *Re Hellas Telecommunications (Luxembourg) II SCA* [2010] B.C.C. 295, [8].
[38] r.2.4 provides that the witness statement in support of an administration application must contain prescribed information and obliges the applicant to disclose any additional matters which, in his opinion, will assist the court in deciding whether or not make an administration order, so far as lying within the applicant's knowledge or belief. While it is for the applicant to identify what information is likely to assist the court, and that information may not be limited to the matters identified in SIP 16, it is generally expected that the information the insolvency practitioner is required to disclose to creditors under SIP 16 will be included in the application insofar as it is known or ascertainable at the date of the application: see *Re Kayley Vending Ltd* [2009] B.C.C. 578, [24]; *Re Cornercare Ltd* [2010] B.C.C. 592, [15].
[39] *Re Hellas Telecommunications (Luxembourg) II SCA* [2010] B.C.C. 295, [8].
[40] *Re Hellas Telecommunications (Luxembourg) II SCA* [2010] B.C.C. 295, [8]
[41] *Re Kayley Vending Ltd* [2009] B.C.C. 578, [3]. See also *Re Cornercare Ltd* [2010] B.C.C. 592. Legislative policy appears broadly supportive of pre-packs at least insofar as properly disclosed pre-administration costs incurred with a view to administration are now recoverable as administration expenses: see rr.2.33(2)(ka), (2A), (2B), 2.67A, introduced with effect from April 6, 2010 by the Insolvency (Amendment) Rules 2010 (SI 2010/686).
[42] *Re Transbus International Ltd* [2004] 1 W.L.R. 2654, [14].

administrator's various legal duties which follows. The critical point to be borne in mind is that the court will generally allow the administrator a wide measure of independence and latitude in the performance of his functions having regard both to the statutory framework which vests the management of the company's affairs in him and to the commercial exigencies that he faces.[43]

2. THE STATUTORY DUTY TO SELECT THE PURPOSE OF ADMINISTRATION

Under the old law set out in the former Pt II of Insolvency Act 1986, the court **12–015** could make an administration order for one or more of the following alternative purposes: (i) the survival of the company, and the whole or any part of its undertaking, as a going concern; (ii) the approval of a corporate voluntary arrangement under Pt I of Insolvency Act 1986; (iii) the sanctioning of a scheme of arrangement under (what was then) Companies Act 1985, s.425; (iv) a more advantageous realisation of the company's assets than would be effected on a winding up. The purpose of administration is now set out in Insolvency Act 1986, Sch.B1, para.3. This replaced the old four purposes of administration with a single purpose which subdivides into three objectives.[44] However, the three objectives are not equal-ranking alternatives. They are structured as a hierarchy of objectives.[45]

The starting point is Sch.B1, para.3(1), which provides that the adminis- **12–016** trator must perform his functions with the objective of: (i) rescuing the company as a going concern; or (ii) achieving a better result for the company's creditors as a whole than would be likely if the company were wound up (without first being in administration); or (iii) realising property in order to make a distribution to one or more secured or preferential creditors. The first objective—rescuing the company as a going concern—is the primary objective. This much is clear from para.3(3), the effect of which is to oblige the administrator to perform his functions with the objective of rescuing the company as a going concern in the first instance. Thus, Parliament clearly intended to prioritise the rescue of the company, or at least its business, over piecemeal realisation of the company's assets for the benefit of secured creditors. It is for this reason that the power to pursue lower priority objectives is made available to the administrator only if an appropriate combination of the conditions listed in paras 3(3)(a) and (b) and (4)(a) and (b) are satisfied.

The pursuit of the primary "company rescue" objective could involve any or a **12–017** combination of the following: (i) a restructuring of the company's debts (e.g. by means of a debt-for-equity swap, where the creditors become shareholders of the rescued entity); (ii) a rescheduling of the company's debts (e.g. through renegotiation of the due dates and other terms of repayment); (iii) the approval by the prescribed majorities of creditors of a corporate voluntary arrangement under

---

[43] See, e.g. *Re Lehman Brothers International (Europe) Ltd* [2009] B.C.C. 632, [45], [47].

[44] Sch.B1, para.111.

[45] For the legislative history relating to the para.3 hierarchy see, in particular, Hansard, H.L. Deb. July 2, 2002, cols 188–189; July 29, 2002, cols 764–769; October 21, 2002, cols 1100–1105 (Lord McIntosh of Haringey).

Insolvency Act 1986, Pt I or a scheme of arrangement under Companies Act 2006, Pt 26; or, less plausibly, (iv) the administrator deciding to trade the company out of its financial difficulties during the period of the administration.[46]

12–018   According to para.3(3), the administrator must perform his functions with the objective of rescuing the company as a going concern unless he thinks either: (i) that it is not reasonably practicable to achieve that objective; or (ii) that pursuit of the second objective in the hierarchy would achieve a better result for the company's creditors as a whole. It follows that the administrator is not obliged to pursue the primary objective of rescuing the company at any cost. If he makes the judgment that rescuing the company is not practicable (e.g. because there is no funding available to support continued trading) or that an immediate sale of the company's business and assets will produce a better result for creditors, it is legitimate for him to opt to pursue the second objective.[47] The obvious example of a "better result for creditors" under the second objective would be a going concern sale of all or part of the company's assets and business pursued in circumstances where the administrator forms the view that the only practical alternatives are either a sale which preserves going concern value or a piecemeal realisation of the assets on a break-up basis in a winding-up.[48] This will most often be the case where the statutory moratorium against secured creditors would allow (much of) the distressed company's business to be sold as an operational unit, thus preserving any going concern value. Alternatively, the second objective would be fulfilled if the protection of the administration moratorium allowed the company to "trade out" its existing contracts.[49] The administrator's judgment that pursuit of the first objective is "not reasonably practicable" is ground alone for the administrator to pursue the second objective. This is because the phrase "either . . . or" is used in para.3(3). In practice, lack of available funding will often dictate that the administrator is entitled to form the view that his options are limited to pursuing a rescue of the business by way of going concern disposal rather than a rescue of the company. Notwithstanding the noble, if misguided, legislative emphasis on rescuing the company, it may be inferred that lack of funding is one of the major reasons why, in practice, the administration regime functions as a mechanism for the facilitation of business rather than corporate rescue.[50]

---

[46] For judicial consideration of what is meant by "rescuing the company as a going concern", see *Doltable Ltd v Lexi Holdings Plc* [2006] B.C.C. 918, [33]–[42].

[47] Subject to his being under a duty to explain the choice he makes: see paras 12–021 and 12–024 below.

[48] See further Hansard, H.L. Deb. July 29, 2002, col.768 (Lord McIntosh of Haringey): "Rescuing businesses is exactly the kind of outcome that the second objective is . . . intended to recover [sic]. If it is not reasonably practicable to rescue the company, selling the constituent businesses as going concerns will almost always be the next best thing . . . the effect of the provision as drafted will be to cover and give priority to business rescues."

[49] See, e.g. J. Armour and R. Mokal, "Reforming the Governance of Corporate Rescue" [2005] L.M.C.L.Q. 32, 42. Generally on the second objective, see *Re Logitext UK Ltd* [2005] 1 B.C.L.C. 326; *Re British American Racing (Holdings) Ltd* [2005] B.C.C. 110, [47]–[52]; *BLV Realty Organization Ltd v Batten* [2010] B.P.I.R. 277, [11]–[12].

[50] For evidence suggesting that corporate as distinct from business rescue is rarely the outcome of administration, see Insolvency Service, *Enterprise Act 2002—Corporate Insolvency Provision: Evaluation Report* (January 2008), pp.85–99.

Paragraph 3(4) states that the administrator may perform his functions with   **12–019**
the third objective (realising property in order to make a distribution to one or
more secured or preferential creditors) but only if: (i) he thinks that it is not
reasonably practicable to achieve either the first or second objectives; and
(ii) he does not unnecessarily harm the interests of the creditors of the company
as a whole. Thus, as the explanatory notes to the Enterprise Act 2002 make
clear, if the administrator concludes that the company is distressed to such an
extent that its business is not saleable, he may nevertheless realise the assets on
a piecemeal basis for the benefit of secured or preferential creditors, subject to
the proviso that he does not cause "unnecessary harm" to the other creditors.[51]
The third objective facilitates enforcement of a floating charge-holder's security in circumstances where the charge-holder is now unable to appoint an
administrative receiver because of the prohibition in Insolvency Act 1986,
s.72A. While, at first sight, para.3(4) may therefore appear to be a gateway to
a quasi-receivership, the effect of the para.3(4) proviso is that the duty of an
administrator as regards the sale of the assets is wider than that of an administrative receiver. An administrative receiver is under a duty to take reasonable
care to obtain the best price reasonably obtainable for the assets but is free to
choose when to sell. He is not obliged to delay a sale in anticipation of a rising
market or to take active steps that may prove to be value-enhancing in the full-
ness of time.[52] Once an administrator has selected the third objective, his
primary duty is to secured and preferential creditors. This is clear from
para.3(2), which expressly states that the administrator's duty to perform his
functions in the interests of the company's creditors as a whole[53] is subject to
para.3(4). However, as Professor Sir Roy Goode QC has correctly observed,
the para.3(4) proviso means that the administrator "must avoid causing harm
which is not necessary for the protection of the creditors for whom his realisations are intended."[54] Thus, an administrator who performs his functions in
pursuit of the third objective is not free to realise the assets at a time of his
choosing if, in all the circumstances, a better price could be obtained were they
to be sold at some other time. Paragraph 3(4) therefore obliges the administrator to take reasonable steps, including delaying realisation, to obtain the best
price that circumstances permit, as failure to take steps that would improve the
position of unsecured creditors without in any way prejudicing the interests of
secured or preferential creditors causes unsecured creditors "unnecessary
harm".[55] This is in keeping with the overall policy of Enterprise Act 2002,

---

[51] See the hypothetical examples, which are based on the explanatory notes, in J. Marshall,
"Enterprise Act: Corporate Insolvency Aspects" (2003) 14(4) PLC 33.

[52] *Cuckmere Brick Co Ltd v Mutual Finance Ltd* [1971] Ch. 949 (CA); *Silven Properties Ltd v
Royal Bank of Scotland Plc* [2004] 1 W.L.R. 997 (CA); *Bell v Long* [2008] 2 B.C.L.C. 706. See
further paras 13–014 to 13–043, below.

[53] See further paras 12–025 to 12–026, below.

[54] Principles of Corporate Insolvency Law, 4th edn (London: Sweet and Maxwell, 2011),
pp.11–27.

[55] To this extent para.3(4) imposes on the administrator a duty coterminous with the administrator's general duty of care the contours of which were first established by Millett J. in *Re Charnley
Davies Ltd (No.2)* [1990] B.C.C. 605. See further para.12–042, below. In a different context, see
Re Halliwells LLP [2011] B.C.C. 57 (payments made from sale proceeds preferring some creditors
and members not unnecessarily harmful to the interests of creditors as a whole).

which was designed to restrict usage of administrative receivership as a mechanism for the enforcement of security on the premise that administrative receivers had insufficient legal incentives to maximise asset realisations, especially in circumstances where their appointor's security exceeded the value of the secured debt.[56]

12–020   In the process leading up to the company entering administration, the administrator must state in writing that "in his opinion the purpose of administration is reasonably likely to be achieved."[57] In order to be in a position properly to make this statement, the administrator merely needs to be satisfied, in his considered opinion, that administration is reasonably likely to achieve at least one of the three statutory objectives. He is required only to give a general indication at this stage and does not have to specify which of the three objectives he intends to pursue. As the administrator will rarely have complete information at the time the procedure is initiated, the requirement for a general statement rather than a precise pre-selection of the objective which will ultimately form the purpose makes sense. Otherwise, the proposed administrator would have to undertake a detailed investigation of the company's affairs before accepting appointment. This could delay entry into administration and appears to be contrary to the policy behind the changes implemented by Enterprise Act 2002, namely to streamline entry into administration, making it quicker and more cost-effective.[58] For the purpose of making the statement, an administrator appointed out of court is entitled to rely on information supplied by the company's directors (unless he has reason to doubt its accuracy).[59]

12–021   Once appointed, the administrator is then bound to consider which objective will form the purpose of administration. The administrator is required to send creditors a statement of proposals before the end of the period of eight weeks beginning with the day on which the company entered administration.[60] In the statement, the administrator must set out how it is envisaged that the purpose of the administration will be achieved.[61] Where he chooses to pursue either the second or third objective, he must also explain why he thinks that a higher

---

[56] DTI, Productivity and Enterprise: Insolvency—A Second Chance, Cm 5234 (2001), 2.1–2.3.

[57] Sch.B1, paras 12, 18(3), 29(3); rr.2.3(5), 2.16(2)(a), 2.23(2)(a) and Form 2.2B.

[58] DTI, Productivity and Enterprise: Insolvency—A Second Chance, Cm 5234 (2001), 2.7–2.10.

[59] Sch.B1, paras 18(4), 29(4).

[60] Sch.B1, para.49. The general scheme of Insolvency Act 1986 is that creditors whose individual rights of enforcement are suspended by the statutory moratorium should be told what the administrator is proposing to do as soon as possible once he has formed a view on the objective to be pursued and the means of pursuing it. Albeit the case was decided under the statutory framework as it stood before the Enterprise Act 2002 changes, there are passages in the judgment of Harman J. in *Re Charnley Davies Business Services Ltd* (1987) 3 B.C.C. 408 which carry the implication that the administrator should not wait to the end of the statutory eight-week period if he has already decided what to do.

[61] r.2.33(2)(m). It is clear from guidance issued by the Insolvency Service via the "Dear Insolvency Practitioner" letters that administrators should not simply include all three objectives in their proposals without making any attempt to identify which objective forms the purpose of administration: see *http://webarchive.nationalarchives.gov.uk/+/http://www.insolvency.gov.uk/insolvencyprofessionandlegislation/dearip/dearipindex.htm* (Chapter 1: Administration proceedings). Equally, however, the courts will interpret the requirements dynamically rather than statically allowing for the possibility that the administrator could pursue the first objective initially but move down the hierarchy as circumstances unfold: see *Hammonds v Pro-Fit USA* [2008] 2 B.C.L.C. 159, [20].

ranking objective cannot be achieved.[62] His proposals, including (where the first objective is not being pursued) his explanation of why he has chosen a lower ranking objective, must be placed before the initial creditors' meeting.[63] In the case of a pre-pack, the requirement to explain in timely fashion is supplemented by the professional obligation to disclose further information to creditors imposed on the administrator by SIP 16.

In reviewing an administrator's decision to pursue the second or third objectives, the court is required to consider the administrator's thought process. On the wording of para.3(3), the administrator is entitled to descend from the first to the second objective if *he thinks* either: (i) that it is not reasonably practicable to achieve the first objective; or (ii) that the second objective would achieve a better result for creditors as a whole than would be likely if the company were wound up. It is accordingly clear that the court must focus on what the administrator thought was "reasonably practicable" or "better for creditors as a whole", and not what the court, with hindsight, thinks may have been "reasonably practicable" or "better for creditors as a whole". The test to be applied in reviewing an administrator's "thinking" is likely to resemble closely the test which the court has regularly applied when reviewing decisions taken in the exercise of their powers by company directors[64] and liquidators.[65] It would appear then that the administrator's decision to pursue the second objective will only be open to challenge if it was made in bad faith or was clearly perverse in the sense that no reasonable administrator could possibly have thought that the first objective could not be achieved or that pursuit of the second objective would produce a better result for creditors.[66] This is a more deferential standard of review than an objective test framed in positive terms which asks whether the administrator has done what a reasonable

12–022

---

[62] Sch.B1, para.49(2)(b).

[63] The administrator is not obliged to call a creditors' meeting if he thinks the company has insufficient property to enable a distribution to be made to unsecured creditors other than out of the prescribed part which an administrator is required to set aside by s.176A, or if he thinks neither of the two higher ranking objectives can be achieved: para.52(1). However, he must summon a meeting if requested to do so by creditors holding at least ten per cent of the company's debt: para.52(2).

[64] See *Re Smith & Fawcett Ltd* [1942] Ch. 304 (CA); *Charterbridge Corp Ltd v Lloyds Bank* [1970] Ch 62; *Regentcrest Plc v Cohen* [2001] B.C.C. 494; *Extrasure Travel Insurances Ltd v Scattergood* [2003] 1 B.C.L.C. 598; *Colin Gwyer & Associates Ltd v London Wharf (Limehouse) Ltd* [2003] B.C.C. 885; *Ultraframe (UK) Ltd v Fielding* [2005] EWHC 1638 (Ch), [1292]–[1295], [1300]–[1302].

[65] *Re Edennote Ltd* [1996] B.C.C. 718 (CA); *Mahomed v Morris (No.2)* [2001] B.C.C. 233; *Abbey Forwarding Ltd v Hone* [2010] B.P.I.R 1053.

[66] Compare *Unidare Plc v Cohen* [2006] Ch. 489, [71], where, in response to a submission by counsel that an administrator's thinking for the purposes of para.83 must be based on reasonable grounds or at least not lead to conclusions that no reasonable administrator could have reached, Lewison J. observed somewhat delphically "that the process of thinking involves a rational thought process, and in that sense must be reasonable" but refused to accept that what the administrator "thinks" is subject to any form of test by reference to an objective standard. He nevertheless went on to find that the administrator had arrived at his decision to move the company from administration to creditors' voluntary liquidation on reasonable grounds: [72], [74]. Furthermore, the observation needs to be read in the light of *Re Trident Fashions Plc (No.2)* [2004] 2 B.C.L.C. 35, [39], where, in dismissing an application made under Insolvency Act 1986, s.6, the same judge said: "It seems to me that the court should only interfere if a judgment made by the administrator ... was a judgment to which no reasonable insolvency practitioner could come. That judgment should I think be made on the basis of the material available to the administrator at the time and not with the benefit of hindsight."

administrator would have done in all the circumstances. Consistent with what was said earlier in paras 12–008 to 12–014, the law therefore allows considerable latitude to administrators having regard to the difficult circumstances they will commonly face. It allows for a spectrum of disagreement between reputable practitioners as to the right way to proceed as long as the view formed by the administrator is not so perverse, irrational or absurd that no reputable practitioner could have arrived at it. Accordingly, the court will be slow to second-guess the administrator's commercial judgment as regards the purpose of administration where it is exercised in good faith and without caprice.[67]

12–023   The third objective can be pursued only if: (i) the administrator *thinks* that it is not reasonably practicable to pursue the first or second objectives; *and* (ii) pursuit of the third objective does not occasion unnecessary harm to the interests of the creditors of the company as a whole. Again, it is for the administrator to decide whether or not it is reasonably practicable to pursue either of the higher ranking objectives, subject to the standard of review outlined in the previous paragraph. However, the question of "unnecessary harm" does not turn on what the administrator thinks but is instead a matter for objective evaluation by the court. Paragraph 3(4) is not altogether happily drafted. The words "only if" and the word "and" linking the requirements in sub-paras 3(4)(a) and (b) suggest that the administrator may only select the third objective if the selection itself does not (objectively viewed) inflict "unnecessary harm". This unhelpfully elides the commercial judgment which the administrator has to make as regards what can practicably be achieved and the course he chooses to follow in order to implement that commercial judgment. It is therefore preferable to read para.3(4) as meaning that once the administrator has made the commercial decision to pursue the third objective (to which the court will generally defer), he has a wider duty in relation to realising security than would an administrative receiver.[68] In any event, little turns on the point as, if it could be established on an application under either para.74 or para.75 that an administrator who has pursued the third objective could have achieved a better result for creditors as a whole by some means other than piecemeal realisation without in any way prejudicing the interests of secured and preferential creditors, "unnecessary harm" would surely be made out.

12–024   It was seen in para.12–021 above that an administrator who selects either the second or third objective is under a statutory duty to explain why he thinks that a higher ranking objective cannot be achieved in the statement of proposals.

---

[67] For the relevant legislative history which supports the view expressed in the text, see Hansard, H.L. Deb. July 29, 2002, col.768: "The present wording would mean that if the administrator's view were then to be tested, it would be subject to a 'rationality' test—that is, his decisions would be subject to successful challenge if it could be shown that no reasonable administrator would have acted in such a way in the particular circumstances of a case. As I said, we do not think that the courts should or will second-guess the administrator's professional or commercial judgment in exercising his or her duties. The administrator is best placed to determine what is appropriate . . . without prejudice to the rights under para.74 of creditors or members to challenge the administrator's decision where that decision has unfairly prejudiced his or her interests." See also October 21, 2002, col.1105: "If necessary, we would expect the courts to assess whether the office-holder, in this case the administrator, has been rational in his decision. We are not seeking to apply any other test."

[68] See para.12–019 above.

What if he offers no (or no satisfactory) explanation? There is no specific sanction in para.49 for failure to comply with the duty to explain. Of course, in the absence of any or any adequate explanation, the creditors may decide not to approve the administrator's proposals at the initial creditors' meeting, in which case he would be obliged to seek directions from the court under para.55. Aggrieved creditors could also theoretically seek to enforce compliance by means of an application for relief under para.74.[69] The duty to explain is part of the legislative rebalancing that was effected by Enterprise Act 2002. In shifting the emphasis away from administrative receivership (which was significantly downgraded) and towards a streamlined collective administration regime designed to serve the interests of creditors as a whole, Enterprise Act 2002 sought to enhance transparency and accountability from the perspective of unsecured creditors.[70] This rebalancing has prompted one commentator to suggest that the effect of the duty to explain his selection of objective is to transfer the onus onto the administrator to demonstrate that his selection was rational.[71] It is not clear that the duty to explain per se gives rise to such a shift in the burden of proof. In the spirit of collectivity and transparency, it does, however, oblige the administrator to provide creditors with "sufficient information to allow them to participate in the proceedings in a meaningful way"[72] and more will be expected in this regard where he takes steps to achieve the purpose of administration before circulating his proposals and convening the initial creditors' meeting. Thus, in the case of pre-packs, the duty to explain is reinforced by SIP 16 which demands that creditors "are provided with a detailed explanation and justification of why a pre-packaged sale was undertaken, so that they can be satisfied that the administrator has acted with due regard for their interests."

3. THE ADMINISTRATOR'S GENERAL STATUTORY DUTY

As a general rule, the administrator must perform his functions in the interests of the company's creditors as a whole.[73] The only exception is where he forms the view that the first and second objectives are not achievable and elects to pursue the third objective for the benefit of secured or preferential creditors (albeit even then he must not unnecessarily harm the interests of the company's creditors as a whole). As individual creditors will have different interests and different priority rankings, the duty can only be meaningfully understood as a duty to act so as to maximise the total expected net recoveries of creditors as a whole.[74] In other words, the focus of the duty is on aggregate outcomes and

12–025

---

[69] See further paras 12–057 to 12–062 below.

[70] DTI, Productivity and Enterprise: Insolvency—A Second Chance, Cm 5234 (2001), 2.1–2.21.

[71] R. Mokal, *Corporate Insolvency Law—Theory and Application* (Oxford: Oxford University Press, 2005), pp.244–245.

[72] See "Dear IP", Chapter 1 on Administration Proceedings: *http://www.insolvency.gov.uk/ ukgwacnf.html?url=http://www.insolvency.gov.uk/insolvencyprofessionandlegislation/dearip/ dearipindex.htm.*

[73] Sch.B1, para.3(2), subject to sub-para.(4).

[74] For an extended discussion, see J. Armour and R. Mokal, "Reforming the Governance of Corporate Rescue" [2005] L.M.C.L.Q. 32, 42–49.

overall consequences. The upshot is that the administrator may act in ways that promote general creditor welfare at the expense of the welfare of individual creditors. A further corollary is that breach of the duty gives rise to a class remedy and is not actionable by individual creditors. The statutory moratorium in Sch.B1, para.43, which is strictly enforced as regards monetary claims,[75] further reinforces the collective nature of the administration regime.

12–026   In *BLV Realty Organization Ltd v Batten*[76] a company that had been formed to carry out a property redevelopment made a contract with another company (BLV) pursuant to which BLV managed the redevelopment and co-ordinated the various site contractors. The company defaulted on its banking facilities and subsequently entered administration. The administrators terminated the company's contract with BLV on the basis of a series of alleged irremediable breaches. Their decision to do so was premised on evidence that the site contractors had no confidence in BLV to complete the redevelopment on time or in budget. BLV applied under Sch.B1, para.74 seeking, inter alia, what amounted to its reinstatement as development manager on the ground that the administrators had wrongfully terminated the contract in breach of their duty to perform their functions in the interests of the creditors as a whole and/or in a manner unfairly harmful to BLV's interests. In the course of dismissing the application, Norris J. made the following useful observations on the scope of the general duty:[77]

> "[A]dministration is a form of class remedy. The obligation of the administrators is to perform their functions in the interests of 'the creditors as a whole'. That does not mean that the obligation falls to be performed in an identical way in relation to each and every constituent of the class. It may be in the interests of the creditors as a whole that one particular contract with one particular creditor is terminated (even wrongfully): for example if the administrators thought that a particular service could be provided more cheaply or to a higher standard than was currently being done by a creditor with a continuing contract for a service necessary to ongoing trading, with a beneficial result to the creditors as such. Or it may be that whilst in general ongoing contracts with creditors were being terminated (even wrongfully), one particular contract (e.g. to maintain the principal asset) was kept in being, with a beneficial result to the creditors as such. It would in each case be the interests of the creditors as a whole that would have to prevail over the particular interest of individual creditors: and that might result in different treatment."

The general duty is therefore best viewed as one that is designed to protect the creditors' collective interest and to provide a collective remedy in respect of misconduct or mismanagement which impacts on the overall value of the business and assets (such as a sale of assets at a manifest undervalue or negligent

---

[75] *Re Nortel Networks UK Ltd (In Administration)* [2010] B.C.C. 706.
[76] *BLV Realty Organization Ltd v Batten* [2010] B.P.I.R. 277.
[77] *BLV Realty Organization Ltd v Batten* [2010] B.P.I.R. 277, [20].

acts or omissions that cause the assets to diminish in value).[78] This is not to say that the administrator can wholly ignore the sectional interests of individual creditors. He must also act impartially and seek to maintain a fair balance between what may often be competing interests.[79] However, claims to the effect that the administrator has acted unfairly as between different creditor constituencies are properly framed as claims for relief from unfair harm rather than as claims for breach of the general duty.

4. OTHER SPECIFIC STATUTORY DUTIES

The following specific duties derive from the statutory framework set out in Insolvency Act 1986 and Insolvency Rules 1986 and from other legislation which imposes statutory obligations on administrators.[80] **12–027**

(a) Notification of appointment

As soon as reasonably practicable after being appointed, the administrator is required to send a notice of his appointment to the company, and to publish a notice to the same effect in the prescribed manner.[81] Further, and again as soon as reasonably practicable after being appointed, he must obtain a list of the company's creditors and send a notice of his appointment to each creditor of whose claim and address he is aware.[82] Within seven days of his appointment, he must also send a notice of his appointment to the registrar of companies and to any other prescribed person.[83] Failure to comply with these duties without reasonable excuse is an offence.[84] **12–028**

The administrator must also ensure that every invoice, order for goods or services, and business letter issued by or on behalf of the company or the administrator states the latter's affairs, business and property are being managed by him. If, without reasonable excuse, the company, any of its officers, or the administrator (as appropriate) authorise or permit a contravention of this requirement, they commit an offence.[85] It is thought that such a default may also expose them to personal liability for any loss occasioned to the person dealing with the company in ignorance of it having entered administration. **12–029**

---

[78] Accordingly, in the case of accelerated sales and pre-packs where the administrator implements proposals in advance of the creditors' meeting, he should seek the endorsement of as many of the creditors as he is able to consult in the time available: *Re T&D Industries* [2000] 1 W.L.R. 646.

[79] See further para.12–040, below.

[80] The list is not necessarily exhaustive.

[81] Sch.B1, para.46(2); r.2.27.

[82] Sch.B1, para.46(3).

[83] Sch.B1, para.46(4), (5). The seven-day period starts to run from the date of the administration order, or if the appointment is made out of court, from the date at which the administrator himself receives notice of his appointment: para.46(6). For prescribed persons to whom notice of appointment must be sent, see r.2.27(2).

[84] Sch.B1, para.46(9).

[85] Sch.B1, para.45. It appears, by analogy, however that the document in question is not deprived of legal effect: *Moon Workshops v Wallace & Phillips* [1947–51] C.L.Y. 736 (County Court) (failure by claimants to disclose appointment of receiver in letter as required by Companies Act 1948, s.370 did not prevent them from relying on letter as valid acceptance of defendant's offer).

This reflects the purpose of the duty which is to protect persons dealing with the company. Since the powers of the directors while the company is in administration are only exercisable by them with the consent of the administrator,[86] the directors will not be held to have authorised or permitted a contravention if they merely take no action to prevent it, since they do not permit that which they have no power to prevent.[87]

(b)   Custody and control of assets

12–030   The administrator is under a duty to take into his custody or under his control all the property to which he thinks the company is entitled.[88] The duty is analogous to that of a trustee on his appointment to lose no time in placing the trust property in a state of security.[89] The duty will not preclude the exercise of ordinary judgement as to whether the taking control of any particular asset will cost more than the asset is worth. If in doubt in this respect, the administrator may seek directions from the court. The administrator may apply to the court for orders for the restoration to the company of assets disposed of at an undervalue or as a voidable preference under Insolvency Act 1986, ss.238–239. In such proceedings, the administrator is personally a party and security for costs will not ordinarily be appropriate. But where the administrator brings proceedings in the name of the company with a view to recovering assets under the general law, security can be ordered.[90] Since, however, an order for security gives a successful defendant priority as regards adverse costs over the general costs of the insolvency proceeding, this may be a factor weighing against an order for security in the exercise of the court's discretion.[91]

(c)   Duty to perform functions quickly and efficiently

12–031   The administrator is enjoined by Sch.B1, para.4 to perform his functions as quickly and efficiently as is reasonably practicable. This duty is perhaps best viewed as part of a series of provisions that were designed to reduce delay, cost and formality in the administration process. As well as streamlining entry into administration through the introduction of out-of-court appointments, the Enterprise Act 2002 shortened the time in which the administrator is required to circulate his statement of proposals from three months to eight weeks and made provision for the automatic termination of the administrator's

---

[86] Sch.B1, para.64.

[87] *Sefton v Tophams (No.2)* [1967] 1 A.C. 50 (HL).

[88] Sch.B1, para.67. See also Insolvency Act 1986, s.234, which provides a summary remedy obtainable by an office-holder (meaning an administrator, administrative receiver, liquidator or provisional liquidator) to enable him to carry out his functions and collect property to which the company appears to be entitled for the purposes of the administration without necessarily involving any determination of title: *Smith (Administrator of Cosslett (Contractors) Ltd) v Bridgend CBC* [2002] 1 A.C. 336 (HL).

[89] See *Snell's Equity*, 32nd edn (Sweet & Maxwell, 2010), para.29–004.

[90] CPR r.25.13(2)(c).

[91] *Smith v UIC Insurance Co Ltd* [2001] B.C.C. 11, a case concerning a provisional liquidator. See further G.Moss, "Losing can Damage your Wealth: The Estate Costs Rule" (2000) 13(7) Insolv. Int. 49.

appointment after one year subject to extension by the creditors or the court.[92] Seen in this wider context, para.4 appears to be of relatively limited effect and to serve primarily an exhortative function.[93] Nevertheless, it appears that failure to act as quickly or as efficiently as is reasonably practicable is actionable per se without any requirement to show that it caused unfair harm.[94] Presumably, it would also be actionable under para.75 where it amounts to a breach of the statutory duties in Sch.B1, paras 3–4 and/or a failure to exercise reasonable care and skill which occasions loss to creditors as a whole.

(d) Duty to manage the company's affairs

The administrator is required to manage the company's affairs, business and property in accordance with any proposals duly approved by creditors (including subsequent revisions), and in accordance with any directions given by the court.[95] The administrator's duty to manage is correlative to the administrator's wide general power to "do anything necessary or expedient for the management of the affairs, business and property of the company" and sets outer parameters on the exercise of that power.[96]

12–032

(e) Other duties in Insolvency Act 1986 and Insolvency Rules 1986 governing the conduct of the administration

Under Insolvency Act 1986 and Insolvency Rules 1986, the administrator must also do as follows:

12–033

(i)   as soon as reasonably practicable after being appointed, require a statement of the company's affairs in prescribed form to be provided to him by the officers of the company or other relevant person or persons as defined[97];

(ii)   as soon as reasonably practicable and, in any event before the end of eight weeks beginning with the day on which the company enters administration, make and send to creditors, members and the

---

[92] Sch.B1, paras 49, 76.

[93] Note also *Re Atlantic Computer Systems Plc* [1992] Ch.505 (CA), 529F–H, where the Court of Appeal referred to the administrator's duty as an officer of the court to make decisions speedily and responsibly and to state his reasons for making decisions adverse to a party (in the context of the administrator's discretion to give consent to the enforcement of security over the company's property under what is now Sch.B1, para.43(2)(a)).

[94] See, in particular, Sch.B1, para.74(2).

[95] Sch.B1, para.68. The court's power to give directions is limited by para.68(3). See further paras 12–047 to 12–049, below.

[96] Sch.B1, para.59(1). See also para.60, which confers on the administrator all of the powers in Sch.1 to Insolvency Act 1986, including, inter alia, powers to get in and sell the company's property and to trade the business.

[97] Sch.B1, para.47; rr.2.28–2.32. The statement of affairs must be filed with the registrar of companies and the court: r.2.29(7). If the statement of affairs has not been filed with the court, a creditor has the right to require the responsible insolvency practitioner to furnish him with a list of the company's creditors and the amounts of their respective debts: r.12A.54.

registrar of companies, a statement in prescribed form setting out proposals for the achievement of the purpose of administration[98];

(iii) summon a meeting of creditors as soon as reasonably practicable and, in any event within ten weeks beginning with the date on which the company enters administration, to consider the administrator's proposals[99];

(iv) where the initial creditors' meeting has approved his proposals but he now proposes what he thinks is a substantial revision to those proposals, summon a further creditors' meeting and send a statement of the proposed revision to each creditor[100];

(v) summon a further creditors' meeting if requested to do so by those holding at least ten percent of the company's debt, or if directed to do so by the court[101];

(vi) where a creditors' committee is established, attend on the committee at any reasonable time of which he is given at least seven days' notice and provide the committee with information about the exercise of his functions as required[102];

(vii) prepare and send to creditors, the court and the registrar of companies a progress report, including a receipts and payments account, for the period of six months commencing on the date that the company entered administration, and every subsequent period of six months[103];

(viii) where he makes or proposes to make a distribution to any class of creditors, notify this to creditors[104];

(ix) where he thinks the purpose of administration cannot be achieved in relation to the company, or he thinks the company should not have entered administration, or he is required to do so by a creditors' meeting, apply to the court for his appointment to be terminated[105];

---

[98] Sch.B1, para.49; r.2.33. See further paras 12–021 and 12–024, above.

[99] Sch.B1, para.51; r.2.34. Notice of the result of the meeting must also be sent to creditors and filed with the court as soon as reasonably practicable after the meeting's conclusion: para.53(2); r.2.46. The requirement to summon a meeting is relaxed where the statement of proposals states that the administrator thinks that the company has sufficient property to enable each creditor to be paid in full, or that there is insufficient property to enable a distribution to be made to unsecured creditors other than from the prescribed part (see Insolvency Act 1986, s.176A(2)(a)), or that neither of the first two objectives can be achieved: para.52(1). But the administrator must nevertheless call a meeting if requested to do so by creditors holding at least 10 per cent of the company's debt: para.52(2).

[100] Sch.B1, para.54; rr.2.35(1)(c), 2.45–2.46.

[101] Sch.B1, para.56; rr.2.35(1)(d), 2.37.

[102] Sch.B1, para.57; r.2.62.

[103] r.2.47. For further circumstances in which the administrator is required to produce a progress or final report, see rr.2.47(3)(b), 2.110.

[104] r.2.68. On the provisions which must be made in the calculation and distribution of a dividend, see r.2.70.

[105] Sch.B1, para.79(2); r.2.114.

(x) in the case of an administration commenced by court order, apply to the court for his appointment to be terminated where he thinks that the purpose of administration has been sufficiently achieved[106];

(xi) where he thinks the company has no property which might permit a distribution to its creditors, send a notice to this effect to the registrar of companies, the court and the creditors[107];

(xii) in any case where the court makes an order under Sch.B1 terminating the appointment, send a copy of the order to the registrar of companies within the period of 14 days beginning with the date of the order[108]; and

(xiii) vacate office if he ceases to be qualified to act as an insolvency practitioner in relation to the company, and notify his appointor and the registrar of companies of this fact.[109]

(f) Other statutory duties affecting the conduct of administration

There are several other legislative provisions outside Insolvency Act 1986 and Insolvency Rules 1986 which impose obligations directly on administrators in defined circumstances. By way of example, the administrator must also do as follows: **12–034**

(i) maintain a record of the case containing specified information and ensure that there is a bond in force to secure the honest performance of his functions[110];

(ii) if it appears to him that the conduct of someone who is or has been a director (including a shadow or de facto director) of the company makes that person unfit to be concerned in the management of a company, report this forthwith to the Secretary of State[111];

(iii) if he thinks that the company is carrying on or has carried on a regulated activity in contravention of the general prohibition in Financial Services and Markets Act 2000, report to the Financial Services Authority without delay[112];

---

[106] Sch.B1, para.79(3); r.2114.

[107] Sch.B1, para.84. This triggers the termination of the appointment by administrative means followed by the dissolution of the company without further procedure.

[108] Sch.B1, para.86; r.2.116.

[109] Sch.B1, para.89; r.2.123.

[110] Insolvency Practitioners Regulations 2005 (SI 2005/524).

[111] Company Directors Disqualification Act 1986, ss.6(1), 7(3); The Insolvent Companies (Reports on Conduct of Directors) Rules 1996 (SI 1996/1909). See further A. Walters and M. Davis-White QC, *Directors' Disqualification and Insolvency Restrictions*, 3rd edn (London: Sweet and Maxwell, 2010).

[112] Financial Services and Markets Act 2000, ss.19, 22, 361(2).

(iv) where the company is a sponsoring employer of an occupational pension scheme, give notice to the Board of the Pension Protection Fund, the Pensions Regulator and the trustees or managers that the company has entered administration within 14 days beginning with the later of the date of entry into administration or the date he became aware of the existence of the scheme[113]; and

(v) if requested to do so by a person claiming against the company in relation to a matter where any liability of the company is insured pursuant to a contract of insurance, provide to that person specified information insofar as he is able for the purpose of establishing whether the rights of the company under the contract have transferred to that person pursuant to the Third Parties (Rights Against Insurers) Act 2010.[114]

5. GENERAL DUTIES GOVERNING THE ADMINISTRATOR'S DECISION-MAKING AND CONDUCT OF THE ADMINISTRATION

(a) The administrator as a fiduciary

12–035   Insolvency Act 1986 expressly stipulates that, in exercising his functions under Sch.B1, the administrator of a company acts as its agent.[115] As an agent who undertakes to act on behalf of his principal, it is beyond doubt that the administrator can be regarded in equity as occupying the position of a fiduciary in relation to the company. It accordingly follows that the exercise of the administrator's wide ranging statutory powers is controlled by fiduciary as well as statutory duties, with the aim of protecting the company as principal. Another way to make the same point is to say that the administrator's powers, although deriving from statute rather than a contract, trust or security instrument, are properly regarded as fiduciary in nature as they are exercised by the administrator on behalf of another in his capacity as a statutory office-holder.

12–036   In *Bristol & West Building Society v Mothew*[116] Millett L.J. (as he then was) provided the following general account of fiduciary obligations:

> "The distinguishing obligation of a fiduciary is the obligation of loyalty. The principal is entitled to the single-minded loyalty of his fiduciary. This core liability has several facets. A fiduciary must act in good faith; he must not make a profit out of his trust; he must not place himself in a position where his duty and his interest may conflict; he may not act for his own benefit or the benefit of a third person without the informed

---

[113] Pensions Act 2004, s.120; Pension Protection Fund (Entry Rules) Regulations (SI 2005/590). As regards a scheme that is eligible to be assessed in order to determine whether the Pension Protection Fund should assume responsibility for it, the administrator must also notify the Pension Protection Fund as to the status of the scheme: see further, Pensions Act 2004, ss.122, 123 and 148.

[114] Third Parties (Rights Against Insurers) Act 2010, s.11 and Sch.1.

[115] Sch.B1, para.69.

[116] *Bristol & West Building Society v Mothew* [1998] Ch. 1 (CA).

consent of his principal. This is not intended to be an exhaustive list, but it is sufficient to indicate the nature of fiduciary obligations."[117]

We saw in para.12–025 above that Insolvency Act 1986 directs the administrator, as a general rule, to perform his functions in the interests of the company's creditors as a whole. Thus, in exercising his powers as agent, the administrator must act with "single-minded loyalty" so as to promote the interests of creditors collectively (it being they who hold the economic interest in the company) over his own interests.[118] While we can expect fiduciary obligations insofar as they are applied to administrators to be flexed and moulded to reflect the administrator's role and functions and the statutory and regulatory framework within which he operates, there are two initial points flowing from the obligation of loyalty that can be made with confidence. First, the administrator must not allow any conflict to arise as between his duty and his personal interest, unless he acts with the informed consent of the creditors collectively.[119] Secondly, he must not make an unauthorised profit from his position.[120] On the face of it, these aspects of the core fiduciary obligation of loyalty would appear to flow equally from the administrator's general statutory duty in Sch.B1, para.3(2) to perform his functions in the interests of the company's creditors as a whole. As a practical matter, it is no doubt sensible to formulate the claim against the administrator as one for breach of the para.3(2) duty and/

---

[117] *Bristol & West Building Society v Mothew* [1998] Ch. 1 (CA), 18. Millett L.J.'s immediate purpose was to demonstrate that a claim for negligence against a solicitor could not be recharacterised as a claim for breach of fiduciary duty merely because the solicitor occupied a fiduciary position in relation to the claimant.

[118] This gives way where the administrator chooses to perform his functions with the objective of realising property in order to make a distribution to one or more secured or preferential creditors (the third objective). In these circumstances, the secured or preferential creditors (as appropriate) in effect become the principal subject to the duty to avoid unnecessary harm to the interests of the company's creditors as a whole: Sch.B1, para.3(2), (4); para.12–023, above.

[119] See, by analogy with the position in relation to liquidators, *Silkstone and Haigh Moor Coal Co v Edey* [1900] 1 Ch. 167; *Re Corbenstoke Ltd (No.2)* (1989) 5 B.C.C. 767, 769. Where the administrator or his firm have acted in the past as auditors of the company or its parent or subsidiary, the question is one of balancing the degree of risk that a conflict would arise against the possible cost savings of allowing someone who is already familiar with the company's affairs continuing in office; see *Re Maxwell Communications Corp Plc* [1992] B.C.C. 372; *Re World Class Homes Ltd* [2005] 2 B.C.L.C. 1. Similarly, in the context of group insolvencies, the court has recognised the need for a pragmatic approach involving effective management of conflicts rather than a rigid requirement to avoid them at all costs: see *SISU Capital Fund Ltd v Tucker* [2006] 1 All E.R. 167, especially [91]–[132].

[120] This extends to the administrator's remuneration, which may only be drawn insofar as it has been authorised in principle under Insolvency Rules 1986: see *Re R Gertzenstein Ltd* [1937] Ch. 115. As to fixing of the administrator's remuneration under Insolvency Rules 1986, see rr.2.106 2.109. Insolvency Rules 1986 are further supplemented by a 2004 Practice Statement, "The fixing and approval of the remuneration of appointees" ("the Practice Statement"), and by detailed professional standards: see Statement of Insolvency Practice 9 (Remuneration of Insolvency Office Holders). When the court fixes the remuneration of an administrator for his services at an ex parte hearing, as is usually the case where the application is unopposed, it is important that the written evidence addresses all of the matters set out in para.5.2 of the Practice Statement, because that will be the only evidence before the court. Where, because the application is opposed, it is dealt with at an inter partes hearing, any failure to address all of the matters set out at para.5.2 of the Practice Direction in the written evidence is less important, because any matters not dealt with in the written evidence can be fleshed out in the oral evidence: see *Re Super Aguri F1 Ltd* [2011] B.C.C. 452, [28].

or breach of fiduciary duty where equitable relief is sought through the statutory "misfeasance" gateway in Sch.B1, para.75.[121]

12-037   The rules against self-dealing and unauthorised profits are not the only controls on the exercise of powers vested in fiduciaries. There are also controls that define the scope and extent of the powers. While these controls have been developed primarily in cases concerning the powers of express trustees and company directors,[122] they apply mutatis mutandis to insolvency office-holders. Accordingly, an administrator must: (i) act within his powers[123]; (ii) exercise his powers in good faith; and (ii) exercise his powers for a proper purpose. The "proper purposes" control on the exercise of office-holder powers derives from the "fraud on a power" doctrine in trusts law and its variant in corporate law, the duty of a company director to exercise powers for the purpose for which they are conferred, now codified in Companies Act 2006, s.171(b).[124] Its effect is to prohibit the administrator from exercising his powers for a purpose, or with an intention, beyond their scope.[125] It follows that the administrator must not act perversely or irrationally or for irrelevant or extraneous reasons as, properly understood, in doing so he would be abusing his powers by acting beyond their scope.[126] As an office-holder, he must also take reasonable steps to acquire information relevant to his decisions, including, if appropriate, taking relevant professional advice.[127] If the administrator seeks advice (in general or specific terms) from apparently competent advisers as the implications of the course he is considering taking, and follows the advice so obtained, then it would appear that the administrator would not be in breach of his fiduciary duty for failure to have regard to relevant matters if the failure occurs because it turns out that the advice given to him was materially wrong.[128]

---

[121] On which see further paras 12–063 to 12–065, below.

[122] For a helpful restatement of the various forms of control, see R. Nolan, "Controlling Fiduciary Power" [2009] C.L.J. 293.

[123] Which includes acting within the scope of the company's powers: see *Re Home Treat Ltd* [1991] B.C.C. 165. A person who deals with an administrator in good faith and for value need not inquire whether the administrator is acting within his powers: Sch.B1, para.59(3).

[124] R. Nolan, "Controlling Fiduciary Power" [2009] C.L.J. 293, 297. See also *Duke of Portland v Topham* (1864) 11 H.L. Cas. 32 (HL); *Vatcher v Paull* [1915] A.C. 372 (PC); *Howard Smith Ltd v Ampol Petroleum Ltd* [1974] A.C. 821 (PC). The same applies to receivers: see *Downsview Nominees Ltd v First City Corp Ltd* [1993] A.C. 295 (PC), 314.

[125] R. Nolan, "Controlling Fiduciary Power" [2009] C.L.J. 293, 297.

[126] R. Nolan, "Controlling Fiduciary Power" [2009] C.L.J. 293, 297, citing *Re Manisty's Settlement* [1974] Ch. 17, 26.

[127] "The existence of the fiduciary duty on the part of trustees governing the exercise of their fiduciary powers requires trustees to inform themselves of the matters which are relevant to the decision", per Lightman J. in *Abacus Trust Co (Isle of Man) v Barr* [2003] Ch. 409, [16], citing *Scott v National Trust for Places of Historic Interest or Natural Beauty* [1998] 2 All E.R. 705, 717. In the latter case, Robert Walker J. also stated that such relevant matters "may not be limited to simple matters of fact but will, on occasion (indeed, quite often) include taking advice from appropriate experts." The approach taken by Lightman J. in *Abacus Trust Co (Isle of Man) v Barr* [2003] Ch. 409 was followed by Lloyd L.J. in *Pitt v Holt* [2011] 3 W.L.R. 19 (CA), [127], where he stated that "[t]he trustees' duty to take relevant matters into account is a fiduciary duty . . ." In relation to insolvency office-holders in particular, see also, e.g. *Re Hans Place Ltd* [1992] B.C.C. 737, 745–746; *Re Edennote Ltd* [1996] B.C.C. 718 (CA), 722; *Faryab v Smith* [2001] B.P.I.R. 246 (CA), 252–253, 255.

[128] Applying by analogy the position of a trustee as set out by Lloyd L.J. in *Pitt v Holt* [2011] 3 W.L.R. 19 (CA).

When called upon to review the exercise by insolvency office-holders of **12–038** their powers, the court has said that in the absence of fraud it "will only interfere . . . if [they have] done something so utterly unreasonable and absurd that no reasonable man would have done it."[129] The question is not whether the court would have acted in the same way or would have reached the same conclusion as the insolvency practitioner. Nor will the resulting transaction be set aside where it is established merely that a reasonable practitioner may have acted differently or reached a different conclusion as long as the course of action pursued by the administrator was one that a reasonable practitioner could reasonably have contemplated. The legal basis for interference is the office-holder's perversity or irrationality. To this extent, it can be said that, in exercising his powers for their proper purposes, the administrator is under a duty to act rationally.[130]

Where Sch.B1 refers to what the administrator "thinks" as the trigger for a **12–039** statutory duty or discretion,[131] it is suggested that the court will similarly only intervene where the administrator has either formed a view that no reasonable practitioner would have formed or avoided a conclusion that no reasonable practitioner could possibly have avoided. On the basis of the presumption that a word or phrase is not to be taken as having different meanings within the same instrument unless the intention is evident, the court can be expected to apply the same standard of review to all of the provisions in Sch.B1 which refer to the administrator's "thinking".[132]

As well as being under a general duty to act in the interests of creditors as a **12–040** whole, the fiduciary character of the administrator's status as agent and office-holder means that he must act impartially and even-handedly as between different creditors and different classes of creditor. In this respect, his position is analogous to a trustee who is required to hold the balance fairly between income and capital beneficiaries.[133] Thus, the administrator cannot unduly

---

[129] *Re Edennote Ltd* [1996] B.C.C. 718 (CA), 722. See also *Mahomed v Morris (No.2)* [2001] B.C.C. 233 (CA); *Abbey Forwarding Ltd v Hone* [2010] B.P.I.R 1053. In *Re Trident Fashions Plc (No. 2)* [2004] 2 B.C.L.C. 35, [39], Lewison J. referred to "the reasonable insolvency practitioner", rather than "the reasonable man."

[130] For detailed expositions of the administrator's duty to act rationally deriving support from the wider law relating to fiduciaries and laying particular emphasis on the rule in *Re Hastings Bass* [1975] Ch. 25 (CA), see: R. Mokal, *Corporate Insolvency Law—Theory and Application* (Oxford: Oxford University Press, 2005), Ch.7; J. Armour and R. Mokal, "Reforming the Governance of Corporate Rescue: The Enterprise Act 2002" [2005] L.M.C.L.Q. 32. Note, however, that the rule in *Re Hastings Bass* has since been comprehensively restated and clarified: see *Pitt v Holt* [2011] 3 W.L.R. 19 (CA), especially [94], [96], [127] and [222] (Lloyd L.J.).

[131] See paras 3(3), 3(4), 49, 52, 66–67, 79(2), 80, 83 and 84. On the duty to select the objective of administration in para.3, see further paras 12–015 to 12–024, above. On the question of whether the administrator's thought process should be judged by asking whether another reputable administrator could have reasonably arrived at the same result or, more demandingly, by reference to a test based on a body of reputable practitioners, see M. Simmons QC, "Enterprise Act and plain English" (2004) 17(5) Insolv. Int. 76.

[132] F. Bennion, *Understanding Common Law Legislation* (Oxford: Oxford University Press, 2001), p.108. See also *Re National Savings Bank Association* (1866) L.R. 1 Ch. App 547 (CA in Chancery), 549–550; *Madras Electric Supply Corporation v Boarland (Inspector of Taxes)* [1955] A.C. 667 (HL), 685.

[133] *Re Barton's Trust* (1868) L.R. 5 Eq. 238; *Re Smith* [1971] 2 O.R. 541 (Ontario Court of Appeal). See also *Cowan v Scargill* [1985] Ch.270, 287.

favour one creditor or one class of creditors over another and in the formulation
of his proposals he cannot be seen to side with any particular constituency.[134]
The duty as it applies to trustees is often animated by the need for intergenera-
tional equity as between income and capital beneficiaries or present and future
retirees in the case of pension funds. In an administration it will be relevant
wherever there are competing inter-creditor interests and, in this context, the
court does not simply defer to the administrator's commercial judgment
provided that it is exercised rationally, but instead will decide for itself how to
balance the competing interests.[135] An administrator is not prevented from
preferring the interests of some creditors over others—for example, by making
payments to key suppliers—where this is necessary in order to achieve the
statutory purpose. Such departures from the ordinary rules of priority and
distribution applicable on winding-up fall within the scope of the administrator's powers and are consistent with his general duty to act in the interests of
creditors as a whole.[136] However, where an administrator makes decisions that
are adverse to a particular party, such as refusing to consent to a secured creditor enforcing his security, he must explain his reasons.[137] Moreover, a failure
to act impartially in balancing competing interests will put the administrator at
risk as to costs if an affected party subsequently challenges his conduct.[138]
Where the administrator acts in a manner that unfairly harms the interests of a
creditor or a particular class of creditors, an application for relief may be
brought under Sch.B1, para.74.[139] Indeed, it is suggested that any attempt to
unravel an administrator's decisions on the ground that he has not acted impartially or even-handedly should generally proceed under para.74 and will fall to
be determined by reference to the statutory language. Depending on all the
circumstances, lack of impartiality may also provide grounds for the removal
of the administrator under Sch.B1, paras 74(3), 74(4)(d) or 88[140], and may be

---

[134] Particular care is needed where the practitioner has advised the board or acted as investigating accountant on the instructions of a major creditor prior to accepting the appointment. For
two salutary cases, see *Mourant & Co Trustees Ltd v Sixty UK Ltd (In Administration)* [2010]
B.C.C. 882 and *Clydesdale Financial Services Ltd v Smailes* [2009] B.C.C. 810. Threats to office-
holder independence and objectivity are also regulated by professional standards: see, e.g.
Statements of Insolvency Practice 3, 13, 16 and the Insolvency Code of Ethics. As the reception of
SIP 16 by the court in *Re Kayley Vending Ltd* [2009] B.C.C. 578 illustrates, it can be expected that
professional standards (which are agreed upon by all of the insolvency practitioner licensing
bodies) will influence the court's approach where breach of the administrator's duties is alleged.
[135] *Mitchell v Buckingham International Plc (In Liquidation)* [1998] B.C.C. 943 (CA), 961; *Re
Capitol Films Ltd* [2011] B.P.I.R. 334, [84].
[136] Sch.B1, para.66. See further *Re TXU (UK) Ltd* [2003] 2 B.C.L.C. 341; *Re Rover Espana SA*
[2006] B.C.C. 599; *Re Re Aikman Europe SA & Collins* [2006] B.C.C. 861; *Re MG Rover Belux
SA/NV* [2007] B.C.C. 446; *Re HPJ UK Ltd* [2007] B.C.C. 284. By analogy, see also *Edge v
Pensions Ombudsman* [2000] Ch. 602 (CA), 627E.
[137] See *Re Atlantic Computer Systems Plc* [1992] Ch.505 (CA), 527G–530A, 542A–544B; *Re
Sabre International Products Ltd* [1991] B.C.C. 694. For a modern application of the principles in
Atlantic Computer, see *Re Capitol Films Ltd* [2011] B.P.I.R. 334. See also *BLV Realty Organization
Ltd v Batten* [2010] B.P.I.R. 277, [22].
[138] *Coyne v DRC Distribution Ltd* [2008] B.C.C. 612 (CA); *Re Capitol Films Ltd* [2011] B.P.I.R.
334.
[139] See further paras 12–057 to 12–062, below.
[140] *Coyne v DRC Distribution Ltd* [2008] B.C.C. 612 (CA); *Clydesdale Financial Services Ltd
v Smailes* [2009] B.C.C. 810.

brought into focus on an application by a creditor under Sch.B1, para.43 for relief from the statutory moratorium or an application by an administrator under Sch.B1, para.71 to dispose of assets the subject of fixed charge security.[141]

Although, as we have seen, the court will generally defer to the administrator's commercial judgement and, in the words of David Richards J., will "not normally give directions to an administrator as to the means by which he should market assets, any more than as to which particular deal to make",[142] it is nevertheless strongly advisable for the administrator to seek and act under court directions where the exercise of his powers may impact on the treatment of competing claims.[143] This is particularly so where there are doubts about how a particular claim should be treated, for example, because it may or may not have proprietary effect[144] or is potentially time-barred[145] or susceptible to challenge under the office-holder's avoidance powers[146] with the consequence that the administrator's decision how to treat the claim will impact directly on other creditors.

12–041

(b) Duties to exercise reasonable skill and care, and to act with speed and efficiency

The administrator owes to the company a duty to exercise reasonable skill and care in the performance of his functions. The standard by which he will be judged is not that of the "most meticulous and conscientious member of his profession" but that of the "ordinary, skilled practitioner" or the "reasonably skilled and careful practitioner."[147] What the duty requires of the administrator in a given case is also shaped by his statutory obligations, notably the requirement in Sch.B1, para.3 that he perform his functions in the interests of creditors as a whole. Should the administrator decide to continue trading in an attempt to turn around the company's fortunes, or in the hope of generating value by "trading out" its existing contracts, or to provide an opportunity for a company voluntary arrangement or scheme of arrangement to be approved, he must exercise due care both in making the decision and in carrying on the

12–042

---

[141] *Re Atlantic Computer Systems Plc* [1992] Ch. 505 (CA), 527G–530A, 542A–544B; *Re Capitol Films Ltd* [2011] B.P.I.R. 334.

[142] *Re T&N Ltd* [2005] 2 B.C.L.C. 488, [76]. See generally paras 12–008 to 12–014, above.

[143] See, by analogy with the position of a liquidator, *Mitchell v Buckingham International Plc* [1998] B.C.C. 943 (CA), 961. See also *Re T&N Ltd* [2005] 2 B.C.L.C. 488; *Twizell v Entrust* [2010] S.T.C. 37 (CA); J. Armour and R. Mokal, "Reforming the Governance of Corporate Rescue: The Enterprise Act 2002" [2005] L.M.C.L.Q. 32, 51–54.

[144] *Re Japan Leasing (Europe) Plc* [1999] B.P.I.R. 911; *Re Farepak Food and Gifts Ltd* [2008] B.C.C. 22; *Re Lehman Brothers International (Europe)(In Administration) v RAB Market Cycles (Master) Fund Ltd* [2009] EWHC 2545 (Ch); *Lehman Brothers International (Europe) v CRC Credit Fund Ltd* [2011] Bus. L.R. 277 (CA); *Re Lehman Brothers International (Europe (In Administration)) v Lehman Brothers Finance SA* [2010] EWHC 2914 (Ch); *Lomas v JFB Firth Rixson Inc* [2011] 2 B.C.L.C. 120; *Re Lehman Brothers International (Europe) (In Administration)* [2011] EWHC 1233 (Ch).

[145] *Re Leyland Printing Co Ltd* [2011] B.C.C. 358.

[146] *Unidare Plc v Cohen* [2006] Ch. 489; *Re Parkside International Ltd* [2010] B.C.C. 309; *Re St Georges Property Services (London) Ltd* [2011] B.C.C. 64.

[147] *Re Charnley Davies Ltd (No.2)* [1990] B.C.C. 605, 618.

company's business itself.[148] Alternatively, should he decide to sell off the company's business as a whole or its constituent assets piecemeal, the "administrator as agent for the company owes a duty of care to the company in the choice of the time to sell and (by parity of reasoning) in the decision whether to take the appropriate available advantageous pre-marketing steps which are calculated to achieve the best price."[149] Breach of the duty of skill and care will give rise to a misfeasance claim under Sch.B1, para.75.[150]

12–043　　The administrator's statutory duty in Sch.B1, para.4 to perform his functions as quickly and efficiently as is reasonably practicable and to act with as much speed and efficiency as reasonably practicable overlaps with the common law duty to exercise reasonable skill and care. As indicated above in para.12–031, dilatoriness on the part of an administrator could be actionable under para.75 where it causes loss to creditors as a whole as a breach of Sch.B1, paras 3–4 and/or the duty to exercise reasonable skill and care.

6. DUTIES OF ADMINISTRATOR IN HIS CAPACITY AS OFFICER OF THE COURT

(a) Duty not to act dishonourably: the rule in *Ex parte James*

12–044　　As an officer of the court,[151] the administrator is under a duty not to act dishonourably or unfairly. He must "behave as honestly as other people" and "in an honourable and high-minded way."[152] and "act in accordance with standards of fairness over and above what may be required by the strict application of law".[153] This, the so-called rule in *Ex p. James*,[154] is said to derive from the court's reluctance to allow its officer to take advantage of the strict legal position in a way which is unfair, dishonest or dishonourable.[155] While the administrator is not required to be generous at the creditors' expense, he should, if occasion demands, temper the insistence on his strict legal and equitable rights with a respect for justice and honest dealings.[156] Some have argued that the rule is part of the law

---

[148] *Re Centralcrest Engineering Ltd* [2000] B.C.C. 727.

[149] *Silven Properties Ltd v Royal Bank of Scotland Plc* [2000] B.C.C. 727, [25] (Lightman J., obiter, on behalf of a unanimous Court of Appeal). See also *Re Charnley Davies Ltd (No.2)* [1990] B.C.C. 605, 618. In this regard, the position of an administrator contrasts with that of an administrative receiver, who is free to choose when he sells but, when he does sell, must take care to obtain the best price reasonably obtainable: see *Silven Properties Ltd v Royal Bank of Scotland Plc* [2004] 1 W.L.R. 997 (CA), [21]–[29].

[150] See paras 12–063 to 12–065, below.

[151] Sch.B1, para.5.

[152] *Re TH Knitwear (Wholesale) Co Ltd* [1988] Ch.275 (CA), 288B–C.

[153] *Miller v Bayliss* [2009] B.P.I.R. 1438, [97]. See also *Gresham International Ltd (In Liquidation) v Moonie* [2010] Ch. 285 [57].

[154] *Re Condon, Ex p. James* (1873–74) L.R. 9 Ch. App. 609, CA in Chancery.

[155] See, e.g. *Re Multi Guarantee Co Ltd (No.3)* [1987] B.C.L.C. 257 (CA); *Re Mark One (Oxford Street) Plc* [1999] 1 W.L.R. 1445; *Re Japan Leasing (Europe) Plc* [1999] B.P.I.R. 911; *Re CE King Ltd* [2000] 2 B.C.L.C. 297; *Re Farepak Food and Gifts Ltd* [2008] B.C.C. 22.

[156] *Re Condon Ex p. James* (1873–74) L.R. 9 Ch. App. 609 (CA in Chancery); *Re Tyler* [1907] 1 K.B. 865 (CA); *Re Thelluson* [1919] 2 K.B. 735 (CA); *Re Wigzell* [1921] 2 K.B. 835 (CA); *Re Wyvern Developments Ltd* [1974] 1 W.L.R. 1097; *Re Clark* [1975] 1 W.L.R. 559; *Re Byfield* [1982]

of restitution for unjust enrichment.[157] Indeed, there is some suggestion in the authorities that it may be confined to cases where the assets available for distribution are increased as a result of a mistake of law or fact or where advantage is taken of payments made by a third person without giving credit for them.[158] However, the rule has been applied in other circumstances.[159]

The rule in *Ex p. James* has an uncertain ambit, is seen as creating **12–045** uncertainty,[160] "has long been recognised as difficult to apply and anomalous",[161] and will only be applied "with the greatest caution."[162] Attempts to broaden the rule's ambit—for example, to extend it to voluntary liquidators who are not officers of the court, but who perform the same function as compulsory liquidators who are officers of the court[163]—have generally been unsuccessful. Although the principled basis of the rule remains elusive, it will not be applied to effect "palm tree justice"[164], nor does it prevent the administrator from taking steps, in the interests of the general body of creditors, to prevent a possible liability from accruing to the company in the future.[165] Where the administrator makes a distribution to creditors,[166] the rule may not be invoked by a creditor who is entitled to submit a proof except in the most unusual circumstances.[167] However, the rule can be invoked to permit an administrator, in appropriate circumstances, to honour assurances made to creditors as regards the distribution of realisations, where the assurances had been given with a view to benefiting creditors as a whole and had, in fact, led to such an outcome, but only so far as the honouring of the assurances would not expressly or by necessary implication be inconsistent with statutory provisions.[168]

Ch. 267; *Re John Bateson & Co Ltd* (1985) 1 B.C.C. 99378. See also *Powdrill v Watson* [1994] 2 All E.R. 513 (CA); *Donaldson v O'Sullivan* [2009] 1 W.L.R. 924 (CA).

[157] See *Goff and Jones: The Law of Restitution*, 7th edn (Sweet & Maxwell, 2009), 5–012 to 5–016; I. Dawson, "The Administrator, Morality and the Court" [1996] J.B.L. 437.

[158] *Re T&N Ltd* [2004] O.P.L.R. 343, [18], per David Richards J. (obiter) citing *Re TH Knitwear (Wholesale)* [1988] Ch. 275 (CA), 290; *Re Clark* [1975] 1 W.L.R. 559; *Re Japan Leasing (Europe) Plc* [1999] B.P.I.R. 911; *Patel v Jones* [2001] B.P.I.R. 919 (CA). To similar effect, see *Government of India v Taylor* [1955] A.C. 491 (HL), 512–513. Restitution for unjust enrichment seems also to have constituted the rationale for the application of the rule on the facts in, e.g. *Re Condon Ex p. James* (1873–74) L.R. 9 Ch.609 (CA in Chancery) itself and *Powdrill v Watson* [1994] 2 All E.R. 513 (CA), 144.

[159] See, e.g. *Re Byfield* [1982] Ch. 267.

[160] *Re Wigzell* [1921] 2 K.B. 835 (CA).

[161] *Re T&N Ltd* [2004] O.P.L.R. 343, [16]. For one thing, it may operate to the detriment of the company's creditors as a whole by preventing the uninhibited enforcement of the company's rights: see, e.g. *Re John Bateson & Co Ltd* [1985] 1 B.C.C. 99378, 99381.

[162] *Re Sandiford (No.2)* [1935] Ch. 681, 691.

[163] *Re TH Knitwear (Wholesale) Ltd* [1988] Ch. 275 (CA). See also *Re Agrimarche Ltd* [2010] B.C.C. 775, [25], where it was suggested obiter and without deciding the point that the rule perhaps should apply where the company moves from administration into creditors' voluntary liquidation, particularly where there is no change in the identity of the office-holder.

[164] *Re Farepak Food and Gifts Ltd* [2008] B.C.C. 22.

[165] *Re T&N Ltd* [2004] O.P.L.R 343.

[166] See Sch.B1, para.65.

[167] See, by analogy, *Re Clark (A Bankrupt)* [1975] 1 W.L.R. 559.

[168] See *Re Aikman Europe SA & Collins* [2006] B.C.C. 861, [17], a case in which the court authorised distributions to foreign creditors according to local laws in a pro tanto departure from ordinary English law rules of distribution where the administrators had given assurances that local law priorities would be respected as a means of persuading those creditors not to open local insolvency proceedings.

(b) Duty to be candid with the court

12–046   As an officer of the court, the administrator is required to be entirely candid with the court.[169] It is thought that this obligation applies even before the insolvency practitioner assumes office. So, for example, where he is required to provide a statement in support of an application for an administration order to the effect that he is of the opinion that the proposed administration is reasonably likely to achieve its purpose,[170] he acts as an expert and is subject accordingly to the duties set out in CPR Pt 35.[171] A further corollary is that the court has the power under its supervisory jurisdiction to require an administrator to disclose all relevant material, including in rare instances, privileged material, where without it, the court would be unable to resolve outstanding issues in the administration.[172]

7. COURT DIRECTIONS AND PERMISSIONS

12–047   The administrator is under specific duties to seek directions from or the permission of the court in the following circumstances:

> (i) where he becomes aware that a petition was presented prior to his appointment[173] or during the administration[174] to wind up the company either in the public interest under Insolvency Act 1986, s.124A, or by the Financial Services Authority pursuant to Financial Services and Markets Act 2000, s.367;
>
> (ii) where he finds that his proposals, or any revisions to them, are not approved at a creditors' meeting[175];
>
> (iii) where he wishes to make a distribution to a creditor who is neither a secured nor a preferential creditor[176];
>
> (iv) where he wishes to dispose of the company's property subject to a security interest other than one which, as created, was a floating charge[177];

---

[169] *Re Ah Toy* (1986) 10 F.C.R. 356 (Federal Court of Australia).

[170] r.2.3(5)(c).

[171] *Re Colt Telecom Group Plc (No.2)* [2003] B.P.I.R. 324, [80].

[172] *Expandable Ltd v Rubin* [2009] B.C.C. 443, [41]–[42].

[173] Sch.B1, para.40(3).

[174] Sch.B1, para.42(5).

[175] Sch.B1, para.55.

[176] Sch.B1, para.65(3). On the scope of the court's power under para.65(3), see and compare *Re GHE Realisations Ltd* [2006] 1 W.L.R. 287; *Re Rover Espana SA* [2006] B.C.C. 599; *Re Aikman Europe SA & Collins* [2006] B.C.C. 861; *Re MG Rover Belux SA/NV* [2007] B.C.C. 446. For a useful summary of the legal position as regards distributions in pre-Enterprise Act 2002 administrations, see *Re Crompton's Leisure Machines Ltd* [2007] B.C.C. 214.

[177] Sch.B1, para.71. No permission is required in order for the administrator to dispose of any of the company's property subject to a floating charge: Sch.B1, para.70.

(v) where he wishes to dispose of goods in the company's possession under a hire-purchase agreement[178];

(vi) where he wishes to prolong the duration of his appointment beyond one year[179];

(vii) where he thinks that the administration should come to an end, on the basis that the purpose of the administration cannot be achieved or that the company should not have entered into administration, or if a creditors' meeting requires him to make such an application, or, where the administration was initiated pursuant to an administration order, that the purpose of administration has been achieved[180];

(viii) where he thinks that disclosure in whole or part of the statement of the company's affairs would prejudice the conduct of the administration and wishes to apply for an order of limited disclosure[181]; and

(ix) where he considers that the remuneration fixed for him by the creditors' committee (where one is established), or by resolution of the creditors, is insufficient in amount or rate.[182]

More generally, the administrator is entitled under Insolvency Act 1986[183] and by virtue of his status as an officer of the court[184] to apply to the court for directions. However, as a rule of thumb, he should only seek directions where there is a serious question to be resolved.[185] As the current set up of the administration regime reflects a conscious policy to reduce the involvement of the court where possible, the court will be reluctant to provide guidance on administrative matters or those involving the exercise of commercial judgment.[186] Therefore, where a course of action (such as a sale of the assets in advance of the initial statutory creditors' meeting) is squarely within the administrator's wide powers to manage the company's affairs, business and property,[187] the court will regard this as matter which he must resolve for himself having sought professional advice where he considers it necessary to do so.[188] Put another way, the administrator is under no duty to seek directions and it is not necessarily improper for him to act without directions[189], although he must **12–048**

---

[178] Sch.B1, para.72.
[179] Sch.B1, para.76(2)(a).
[180] Sch.B1, para.79.
[181] r.2.30(1).
[182] r.2.108(1).
[183] Sch.B1, paras 63, 68(2).
[184] *Re Rovor Espana SA* [2006] D.C.C. 599, [18], and the authorities there cited.
[185] *RAB Capital Plc v Lehman Brothers International (Europe)* [2008] B.C.C 915. See also *Re PNC Telecom Plc* [2004] B.P.I.R. 314.
[186] *Re NS Distribution Ltd* [1990] B.C.L.C. 169; *Re T&D Industries Plc* [2000] 1 W.L.R. 646, 656–657; *Re Transbus International Ltd (In Liquidation)* [2004] 1 W.L.R. 2654, [14].
[187] Sch.B1, para.59 and Insolvency Act 1986, Sch.1. See also Sch.B1, paras 60–72.
[188] On the court's reluctance to second-guess the administrator's commercial judgment see, e.g. *MTI Trading Systems Ltd v Winter* [1998] B.C.C. 591; *Re CE King Ltd* [2000] 2 B.C.L.C. 297 and paras 12–008 to 12–010, above.
[189] *Unidare Plc v Cohen* [2006] Ch. 489, [71]–[74]. In contrast to a liquidator, an administrator's powers are therefore exercisable without the sanction of either the creditors' committee (where one is established) or the court.

comply with any directions he is given. Suitable issues for directions are questions of law which affect the adjudication and treatment of particular claims, such as: whether the administrator has power to make payments to foreign creditors in excess of their entitlement under English law[190]; whether a claim is proprietary or personal[191]; whether a claim amounts to a provable debt, a non-provable debt or an administration expense[192]; or whether a claim is susceptible to challenge under statutory avoidance powers.[193] In appropriate (albeit rare) circumstances, the court may also direct the administrator to disregard otherwise mandatory requirements of Insolvency Act 1986 and Insolvency Rules 1986 where it is necessary to ensure the convenient, economical and sensible management of the company's affairs.[194] However, the court may not give directions that authorise or require the administrator to act inconsistently with any proposals approved at the statutory creditors' meeting, unless there has been a material change in circumstances and directions are required in order for the administrator to respond appropriately, or if the court considers that directions are desirable because of a misunderstanding about the approved proposals.[195] The court should be particularly cautious before sanctioning an administrator to bring hostile litigation with an uncertain outcome.[196]

12–049   The comfort that the administrator may obtain from a direction will depend on the degree of disclosure made to the court, whether any other relevant party was notified of the administrator's intention to approach the court, and whether the direction was made after a contested hearing. Instead of seeking directions, the administrator might derive some comfort in adopting a course of action by obtaining the informed consent of, or even an indemnity from, relevant creditor groups, or, more doubtfully, by seeking to limit or exclude his liability by agreement.

8.   THE ADMINISTRATOR'S LIABILITIES

12–050   Schedule B1, para.69 states that in the exercise of his functions the administrator acts as the company's agent. The effect of this provision is that he is not personally liable on any contract or other obligation he enters into on the company's behalf and, as an agent, he will also usually be entitled to an indemnity out of the company's assets for obligations that he incurs. Although the parties may contract

---

[190] *Re Rover Espana SA* [2006] B.C.C. 599; *Re Aikman Europe SA & Collins* [2006] B.C.C. 861; *Re MG Rover Belux SA/NV* [2007] B.C.C. 446.

[191] *Re Japan Leasing (Europe) Plc* [1999] B.P.I.R. 911; *Re Farepak Food and Gifts Ltd* [2008] B.C.C. 22; *Lehman Brothers International (Europe) v RAB Market Cycles (Master) Fund Ltd* [2009] EWHC 2545 (Ch); *Lehman Brothers International (Europe) v CRC Credit Fund Ltd* [2011] Bus. L.R. 277 (CA); *Lehman Brothers International (Europe) v Lehman Brothers Finance SA* [2010] EWHC 2914 (Ch).

[192] *Bloom v Pensions Regulator* [2011] B.C.C. 277, and see *Re Nortel GmbH* [2011] B.C.C. 277 and STOP PRESS, after the preface to this work.

[193] *Unidare Plc v Cohen* [2006] Ch. 489; *Re Parkside International Ltd* [2010] B.C.C. 309; *Re St George's Property Services (London) Ltd* [2011] B.C.C. 64.

[194] *Gould v ITMO Advent Computer Training Ltd* [2011] B.C.C. 52.

[195] Sch.B1, para.68(3).

[196] See *Re Ciro Citterio Menswear Plc* [2002] B.P.I.R. 903, [35], where Pumfrey J. stated that it would be ". . . surprising if in the context of an administration that the administrator should have an unqualified right to recoup his costs by virtue of an order made a priori upon a partial assessment of the merits of the proposed litigation."

around the agency so that personal liability arises,[197] it will be rare for a well-advised administrator to enter into a contract on such terms. Counterparties dealing with the administrator are protected in two ways. First, a person dealing with the administrator in good faith and for value need not inquire whether the administrator is acting within his powers.[198] Secondly, once the administrator ceases to be in office, a sum payable in respect of a debt or liability arising out of a contract entered into by him before cessation is charged on and payable out of property of which he had custody and control immediately before cessation, and has "super priority": that is, it ranks in priority ahead both of any claims secured by a floating charge and of the administrator's remuneration and expenses.[199] Similarly, any liability for wages or salary arising under a contract of employment after it was adopted by the administrator is also charged on and payable out of such property.[200] For these purposes, statutory redundancy and unfair dismissal payments are not "wages or salary". They therefore do not have statutory "super priority" over floating charge claims and the administrator's remuneration and expenses.[201] The position is the same as regards protective awards made pursuant to s.189 of the Trade Union and Labour Relations (Consolidation) Act 1992 in respect of a failure by the employer in accordance with the requirements of that Act to consult in advance of making redundancies[202] and in respect of claims for wrongful dismissal arising from steps taken by the administrator subsequent to the adoption of the relevant contracts of employment.[203] However, where an employer gives proper notice of termination to his employee and does not require him to continue working until the end of the notice period, but instead pays him a lump sum in lieu of wages for the remainder of the notice period, this sum constitutes "wages" within the normal meaning of that word.[204]

As for liability in tort, an administrator who commits a tort while acting **12–051** as administrator is personally liable for it.[205] It is no defence to say that he

---

[197] *Stewart v Engel* [2000] B.C.C. 741.

[198] Sch.B1, para.59(3).

[199] Sch.B1, para.99(3), (4). On administration expenses generally, see Ch.4. paras 4–020 to 4–036, above.

[200] Sch.B1, para.99(5).

[201] Nor would such payments be "necessary disbursements" or "remuneration or emoluments of any person who has been employed by the administrator in the course of the administration" for the purposes respectively of rr.2.67(1)(f) and 2.67(1)(g): see *Re Allders Department Stores Ltd* [2005] 2 All E.R. 122. They therefore rank as unsecured claims provable in the administration: see *Re Nortel Networks UK Ltd (In Administration)* [2010] B.C.C. 706; *Bloom v Pensions Regulator* [2011] B.C.C. 277, [126]–[148] and see STOP PRESS, after the preface to this work, on the Court of Appeal decision in *Nortel*.

[202] On the basis that a protective award does not fall within the ambit of Sch.D1, para.99(6)(d), and is therefore not "wages and salary" within para.99(5)(c): see *Re Huddersfield Fine Worsteds Ltd* [2005] 4 All E.R. 886 (CA). Remuneration under a protective award does, however, rank as a preferential claim in the administration or a subsequent liquidation: Sch.B1, para.65(2); s.386 and Sch.6, para.13(2)(d).

[203] *Re Leeds United Association Football Club Ltd* [2008] B.C.C. 11.

[204] And so within Sch.B1, para.99(5)(c): *Re Huddersfield Fine Worsteds Ltd* [2005] 4 All E.R. 886 (CA), [14], [49], following *Delaney v Staples* [1992] 1 A.C. 687 (HL).

[205] *Rainham Chemical Works Ltd v Belvedere Fish Guano Co* [1921] 2 A.C. 465 (HL); *Performing Right Society Ltd v Ciryl Theatrical Syndicate Ltd* [1924] 1 K.B. 1 (CA); *C Evans & Sons Ltd v Spritebrand Ltd* [1983] Q.B. 310 (CA); *Williams v Natural Life Health Foods Ltd* [1998] 1 W.L.R. 830 (HL); *MCA Records Inc v Charly Records Ltd* [2002] B.C.C. 650 (CA); *Standard Chartered Bank v Pakistan National Shipping Corp* [2003] 1 A.C. 959 (HL).

was acting in the course of his duties as administrator. The company might also be liable as his principal on ordinary agency principles. Further, if the administrator intends, procures and shares a common design for the commission of a tort by the company, he could be made liable as a joint tortfeasor.[206] An administrator would not be liable as a joint tortfeasor with the company if he does no more than carry out his statutory role in the governance of the company. However, if he chooses to exercise control otherwise than through the constitutional organs of the company and the circumstances are such that he would be liable were he not a statutory office-holder, he might be liable with the company as a joint tortfeasor.[207] Where the administrator has wrongfully withheld consent to a creditor or owner of goods in the company's possession enforcing its security or repossessing its goods respectively,[208] and the court has been persuaded to direct the administrator to pay damages in conversion to the wronged party, the administrator may in an appropriate case be prevented from recouping himself from the company's assets.[209] Before dealing with third party assets which are in the possession of the company in administration, the administrator should seek an order of the court under the statutory overreaching provision in Sch.B1, para.72. Without the protection of such an order, the administrator is exposed to a claim in conversion.[210]

12–052   As regards personal liability in tort for unlawful interference in the company in administration's contractual relations with its counterparties, it appears that the rule in *Said v Butt*[211]—which holds that a servant or agent acting bona fide within the scope of his authority is not liable if he procures or causes the breach of a contract between his principal and a third party—confers immunity on the administrator. However, it is unlikely that the *Said v Butt* immunity would extend to encompass unlawful interference by an administrator in a contract to which the company in administration is not party.[212] In any event, it is open to doubt whether the rule in *Said v Butt* does or should give rise to an absolute immunity. Although, by a majority, the Court of Appeal in *Welsh Development Agency v Export Finance Co Ltd*[213] exonerated administrative receivers who had been appointed to manage the affairs of a company from tortious liability for interference with a master agreement to which it was party, considerable reservations were expressed about the reasoning in *Said v Butt*.[214] There is accordingly no reason in principle why an administrator should not be exposed to liability for unlawfully interfering with the contracts of a company in admin-

---

[206] *MCA Records Inc v Charly Records Ltd* [2002] B.C.C. 650 (CA), [29]–[53].

[207] *MCA Records Inc v Charly Records Ltd* [2002] B.C.C. 650 (CA), [50].

[208] Sch.B1, para.43(2), (3).

[209] *Barclays Mercantile Business Finance Ltd v Sibec Developments Ltd* [1992] 1 W.L.R. 1253, 1259–1260.

[210] *Hachette UK Ltd v Borders (UK) Ltd* [2009] EWHC 3487 (Ch).

[211] *Said v Butt* [1920] 3 K.B. 497. For a useful discussion, see R.Stevens, "Why do agents 'drop out'?" [2005] L.M.C.L.Q. 101.

[212] *SCI Games Ltd v Argonaut Games Plc* [2006] Info.T.L.R. 175.

[213] *Welsh Development Agency v Export Finance Co Ltd* [1992] B.C.C. 270.

[214] *Welsh Development Agency v Export Finance Co Ltd* [1992] B.C.C. 270, 289–290 (Dillon L.J.); 297–298 (Ralph Gibson L.J.); 305 (Staughton L.J.).

istration.[215] However, any unlawfulness would have to be judged in the light of the purpose of administration and the administrator's statutory powers. So, for example, there may be circumstances where it is in the interests of creditors as a whole that the administrator causes the company in administration to breach a contract with one particular creditor.[216] In such circumstances it is difficult to see how an action could lie against the administrator, even assuming that he is not protected by the rule in *Said v Butt*.

An administrator, like a receiver, is within the scope of the fraudulent trading provision in Insolvency Act 1986, s.213 in respect of any period of trading after his appointment commences.[217] Accordingly, he may be held liable where the company subsequently goes into liquidation. He will only be held liable if he was knowingly party to the carrying on of the business with intent to defraud creditors. His conduct must therefore be dishonest.[218] An administrator is not exposed to liability for wrongful trading under Insolvency Act 1986, s.214 in respect of the company in administration, as he is not a director or shadow director of the company. As s.213 applies to "any person" knowingly party to fraudulent trading, there is a question whether an insolvency practitioner who advises on a pre-pack sale could be liable as regards any period of trading which takes place between the parties agreeing the pre-pack and the company entering administration. On the face of it, where the insolvency practitioner facilitates a strategy pursuant to which the company continues to incur trade credit on usual terms that it will not be able to repay once the sale of its assets is consummated, there may be a case to answer. However, insofar as pre-packs are now regarded as a legitimate rescue tool, it may be difficult for a liquidator to establish that the insolvency practitioner acted dishonestly.

12–053

Where in distributing the company's assets pursuant to the powers in Sch.B1 paras 65–66 the administrator fails to pay an unsecured claim of which he is aware, it appears that the creditor has a personal right of action against the administrator for breach of statutory duty.[219] Similarly, it appears that pref-

12–054

---

[215] "Since the agent or employee is normally personally liable for any tortious acts he does to third parties in the course of his agency or employment, I would not find any conceptual difficulty in holding that an employee or agent who, in the course of his employment or agency, wrongfully causes a breach of a contract between his employer or principal and a third party is liable in tort to the third party for his tortious act of wrongfully causing a breach of contract, notwithstanding that the liability of his employer or principal for the agent's wrongful acts lies in breach of contract rather than in tort": *Welsh Development Agency v Export Finance Co Ltd* [1992] B.C.L.C. 148, 173, per Dillon L.J. (obiter).

[216] *BLV Realty Organization Ltd v Batten* [2010] B.P.I.R. 277. Similarly, a receiver who, in furtherance of his duty to a mortgagee or debenture holder, interferes with contracts to which the company in receivership is party should not be liable in tort: *Welsh Development Agency v Export Finance Co Ltd* [1992] B.C.L.C. 148, 173, per Dillon L.J. Thus, it is suggested that an administrator is entitled to give priority to the collective interests of creditors in much the same way as a receiver is entitled to give priority to the interests of the mortgagee or debenture holder. Compare, however, *Astor Chemical Ltd v Synthetic Technology Ltd* [1990] B.C.C. 97.

[217] See, by analogy, *Powdrill v Watson* [1995] 2 A.C. 394 (HL), 408c.

[218] *Morris v Bank of India* [2005] B.C.C. 739 (CA); *Brown v City of London Corp* [1996] 1 W.L.R. 1070; *Re Overnight Ltd (In Liquidation)* [2010] B.C.C. 796. On the test for dishonesty in this context, see also *Barlow Clowes International Ltd v Eurotrust International Ltd* [2006] 1 W.L.R. 1476 (PC) and *Aerostar Maintenance International Ltd v Wilson* [2010] EWHC 2032 (Ch), [183]–[184] (Morgan J.).

[219] *Pulsford v Devenish* [1903] 2 Ch.625, 632–633; *James Smith & Sons (Norwood) Ltd v Goodman* [1936] Ch. 216 (CA).

erential creditors also have a right to have their claims paid or provided for in accordance with the requirements of Insolvency Act 1986, a right which is enforceable by means of a personal action against the administrator for breach of statutory duty.[220] The authorities are somewhat equivocal as to the circumstances in which a personal claim for a misapplied distribution can be maintained by an individual creditor directly against the administrator. The Court of Appeal decision in *Oldham v Kyrris* suggests that an individual creditor will only have a direct cause of action against an office-holder in respect of a misapplied distribution once the company has been dissolved.[221] However, at first instance in *Re HIH Casualty and General Insurance Ltd*, David Richards J. suggested that a creditor will have a personal claim for damages against an office-holder for breach of statutory duty if he distributes assets without regard to a claim for which the creditor has proved in time and which has not been rejected and there are insufficient assets left over to make good the default.[222] On this view, while the procedure for seeking redress may therefore differ depending on whether the company has been dissolved, the underlying right is a personal right of the individual creditor to have his claim treated in accordance with the statutory scheme.[223] The two decisions are reconcilable insofar as an individual creditor has a right to apply to the court in a liquidation or a distributing administration for an order directing the office-holder to distribute the assets in accordance with his statutory duty.[224] However, no action lies against a liquidator or administrator for a dividend, there being no direct relation of debtor and creditor between the office-holder and the person entitled to prove and participate in the distribution.[225] It follows that a personal action against the administrator will only generally arise once the company has been dissolved.

12–055   As an officer of the company, an administrator is subject to a wide range of directly imposed statutory liabilities. These include potential criminal liability for breaches of health and safety and other employment legislation which will be of particular relevance where the administrator decides to continue trading.[226]

---

[220] *Inland Revenue Commissioners v Goldblatt* [1972] Ch. 498. By extension, the same applies to claims which fall to be treated as administration expenses payable in accordance with Sch.B1, para.99.

[221] *Oldham v Kyrris* [2004] B.C.C. 111, [154]–[160] (Jonathan Parker L.J.). See also *Lomax Leisure Ltd (In Liquidation) v Miller* [2008] B.C.C. 686 (CA), [34].

[222] *Re HIH Casualty and General Insurance Ltd* [2006] 2 All E.R. 671, [116].

[223] *Re HIH Casualty and General Insurance Ltd* [2006] 2 All E.R. 671, [120]. The relevant passages ([116]–[126]) distinguishing between personal claims by individual creditors for breach of statutory duty and class claims brought on behalf of unsecured creditors as a whole survive the subsequent decision of the House of Lords (reported at [2008] 1 W.L.R. 852), which reversed the decisions of the lower courts.

[224] r.2.70(3); 4.182(3).

[225] r.2.70(3); 4.182(3). See further *Spence v Coleman* [1901] 2 K.B. 199 (CA); *Lomax Leisure Ltd (In Liquidation) v Miller* [2008] B.C.C. 686 (CA).

[226] See further D.Pollard, "Personal Liability of an Insolvency Practitioner for Employee Discrimination Claims" (2007) 20(10) Insolv. Int. 145.

9. STATUTORY MECHANISMS FOR REVIEWING
THE ADMINISTRATOR'S CONDUCT AND
REMEDYING BREACHES OF DUTY

As a general rule, the administrator's duties are owed to the company (meaning, **12–056** in substance, we suggest, those who collectively have an economic interest in its business and assets). The corollary under the general law is that individual creditors have no direct cause of action against the administrator for breach of duty unless on the facts there is a special relationship between the administrator and a creditor which is capable of giving rise to a personal action.[227] That said, individual creditors do have standing under Sch.B1, para.75 to pursue a collective remedy for breach of duty on behalf of creditors as a whole.[228] Where the claim relates to negligent advice given to a party by an insolvency practitioner before he is appointed administrator, that party will have a conventional professional indemnity claim based on breach of a duty of care.[229] However, there may be cases where it is difficult to draw a line between pre-appointment conduct and conduct as an office-holder[230], with the consequence that the claim may not be susceptible to being struck out before trial.

(a) Challenges based on unfair harm

Paragraph 74 of Sch.B1 to Insolvency Act 1986 is headed "Challenge to **12–057** administrator's conduct of company". Paragraph 74(1) provides that a creditor or member of a company in administration may apply to the court on the basis that the administrator is acting, has acted or proposes to act so as unfairly to harm the interests of the applicant (whether alone or in common with some or all other members or creditors). The concept of "unfair harm" is identical to that of "unfair prejudice" in the former s.27 of Insolvency Act 1986 in force before the insertion of Sch.B1 by Enterprise Act 2002.[231]

Under the former s.27(1) the applicant was required to show that there was **12–058** unfair prejudice to the interests of the company's "creditors or members generally, or of some part of its creditors or members (including at least [the applicant] himself)." It was not sufficient to show that the rights of the applicant alone had been infringed.[232] In contrast, under para.74(1) the basis of the

---

[227] See, e.g. *Mahomed v Morris (No.2)* [2001] B.C.C. 233 (CA), [29] (Peter Gibson L.J.); *Kyrris v Oldham* [2004] B.C.C. 111 (CA), [141]–[163] (Jonathan Parker L.J.); *Clydesdale Financial Services Ltd v Smailes* [2009] B.C.C. 810, [49]; *Re Newscreen Media Group Plc* [2009] 2 B.C.L.C. 353.

[228] See further paras 12–063 to 12–065, below.

[229] See, e.g. *Griffin v UHY Hacker Young* [2010] P.N.L.R. 20.

[230] See *Prosser v Castle Sanderson* [2003] B.C.C. 440 (CA) and, in the context of a pre-pack, *Clydesdale Financial Services Ltd v Smailes* [2009] B.C.C. 810, [52].

[231] The change from "prejudice" to "harm" was intended to "modernise" the language; see Hansard, H.L.Deb July 2, 2002, col.84 (Lord McIntosh of Haringey). The phrase "unfair prejudice" was transplanted from what was then Companies Act 1985, ss.459–461 and is now Companies Act 2006, ss.994–996.

[232] See *Re A Company (No. 008699 of 1985)* (1986) 2 B.C.C. 99024, 99029; *Re Charnley Davies Ltd (No.2)* [1990] B.C.C. 605, 624–625.

complaint may be unfair harm to the interests of the applicant alone, or to his interests in common with those of some or all other members or creditors (as appropriate). A further requirement of the former s.27(1) was that the unfair prejudice had to stem from the manner in which the administrator had managed the company's affairs, business and property. Thus, conduct which did not amount to management of the company's affairs, business and property was not sufficient to give rise to a claim.[233] Paragraph 74(1) has no such restriction and simply requires that the administrator's acts or proposed acts have resulted or will result in unfair harm. This is wide enough to include (among other things) the administrator's decision as to which of the statutory objectives to pursue.[234] Nevertheless, the acts or proposed acts about which complaint is made must have caused, or be capable of causing, unfair harm.[235]

12–059   The harm to the applicant must be to his "interests". It is well established that "interests" is a wider concept than "rights".[236] The harm to the applicant must also be to his interests as a creditor or member rather than to his interests in some other capacity. Thus, where an administrator terminates an ongoing contract for services the counterparty cannot claim relief under para.74 as it is his interests as a contractor after the date of administration that are harmed rather than his interests as an unsecured creditor in respect of outstanding pre-administration fees.[237] Demonstrable harm to the applicant's interests is not enough unless the harm is also "unfair".[238]

12–060   The issue of fairness as between creditors or members under para.74 is closely linked to the administrator's duty to act impartially and even-handedly.[239] While the concept of "unfair prejudice" in what is now Companies Act 2006, s.994 may provide useful guidance on the meaning of "unfair harm",[240] what is fair or unfair must be judged in the particular context of administration and in the light of the administrator's wide powers to manage the company's business and affairs in the interests of creditors as a whole and with a view to achieving the statutory purpose.[241] Unequal or differential treatment is not necessarily unfair treatment.[242] It is not unfair for the administrator to act in a manner that is harmful to the interests of one creditor or a particular class of creditors where to do so is consistent with the administrator's general duty to act in the interests of creditors as a whole.[243]

---

[233] See *Re Charnley Davies Ltd (No.2)* [1990] B.C.C. 605, 624–625.
[234] See J. Armour and R. Mokal, "Reforming the Governance of Corporate Rescue" [2005] L.M.C.L.Q. 32, 55.
[235] *Unidare Plc v Cohen* [2006] Ch. 489, [66]; *Re Lehman Brothers International (Europe) Ltd* [2009] B.C.C. 632, [34].
[236] See, e.g. *Re Sam Weller & Sons Ltd* [1990] Ch. 682, 690; *Re Charnley Davies Ltd (No.2)* [1990] B.C.C. 605, 624.
[237] *BLV Realty Organization Ltd v Batten* [2010] B.P.I.R. 277, [24]. See further 13–026 above.
[238] *Re Lehman Brothers International (Europe) Ltd* [2009] B.C.C. 632, [37].
[239] See para.12–040 above.
[240] See, e.g. *O'Neill v Phillips* [1999] 1 W.L.R. 1092 (HL). See also *Re Charnley Davies Ltd (No. 2)* [1990] B.C.C. 605, 624–625.
[241] *Re Lehman Brothers International (Europe) Ltd* [2009] B.C.C. 632, [38].
[242] *BLV Realty Organization Ltd v Batten* [2010] B.P.I.R. 277, [22].
[243] *Re Lehman Brothers International (Europe) Ltd* [2009] B.C.C. 632; *BLV Realty Organization Ltd v Batten* [2010] B.P.I.R. 277.

In such circumstances, the administrator is merely complying with his statutory duty. As is the case on applications to set aside an approved company voluntary arrangement on the "unfair prejudice" ground in Insolvency Act 1986, s.6, there is no single and universal test for judging unfairness.[244] Whether conduct is unfairly harmful will therefore depend on all the circumstances of the case, including the alternatives available to the administrator and the practical consequences of the court's decision to grant or withhold relief.[245] The court will also consider whether any imbalance in treatment is proportionate and justifiable. So, for example, where it is necessary for the administrator to pay essential suppliers and service providers in order to secure the continuation of the company's business and the achievement of the statutory purpose, the differential treatment is not unfair to other creditors under para.74.[246]

Paragraph 74(2) of Sch.B1 to Insolvency Act 1986 provides that a creditor   **12–061**
or a member of a company in administration may apply to the court claiming the administrator is not performing his functions as quickly or as efficiently as is reasonably practicable. This second ground of challenge in para.74 has no statutory antecedent and corresponds to the administrator's duty in Sch.B1, para.4 to act as quickly and efficiently as is reasonably practicable, which duty is considered at paras 12–031 and 12–043, above.

Having heard an application under para.74, the court may grant relief,   **12–062**
dismiss the application, adjourn the hearing conditionally or unconditionally, or make an interim or any other order it thinks appropriate.[247] Such an order might regulate the administrator's exercise of his functions, require the administrator to do or not to do a specified thing, require a creditors' meeting to be held for a specified purpose, or provide for the administrator's appointment to cease to have effect.[248] The court may make an order whether or not the action complained of was within the administrator's statutory powers, and even if the action complained of was the disposal of property in the administrator's control which is subject to fixed charge security or a hire-purchase agreement pursuant to a court order under Sch.B1 para.71 or para.72.[249] But no order can be made pursuant to para.74 which would impede or prevent the implementation of a company voluntary arrangement, a compromise or scheme of arrangement, or any proposals approved at a creditors' meeting more than 28 days before the day on which the application for the order under para.74 was made.[250] In addition, relief may be withheld where it would affect the

---

[244] *Inland Revenue Commissioners v Wimbledon Football Club* [2004] D.C.C. 638 (CA), [23] (Lightman J.); *SISU Capital Fund Ltd v Tucker* [2006] B.C.C. 463, [71]; *Prudential Assurance Co Ltd v PRG Powerhouse Ltd* [2007] B.C.C. 500, [71]–[96]; *Mourant & Co Trustees Ltd v Sixty UK Ltd* [2010] B.C.C. 882, [64]–[71].

[245] *Inland Revenue Commissioners v Wimbledon Football Club* [2004] B.C.C. 638 (CA), [23].

[246] See, by analogy, *Prudential Assurance Co Ltd v PRG Powerhouse Ltd* [2007] B.C.C. 500, [90].

[247] Sch.B1, para.74(3).

[248] Sch.B1, para.74(4).

[249] Sch.B1, para.74(5).

[250] Sch.B1, para.74(6).

rights of third parties who have dealt with the administrator in good faith and for value.[251]

(b) Misfeasance

12–063   Pursuant to para.75 of Sch.B1 to Insolvency Act 1986, the court may, on the application of the Official Receiver, the administrator, the liquidator, a creditor or contributory of the company, examine the conduct of an administrator (including someone who purports or has purported to act as an administrator).[252] As is the case with Insolvency Act 1986, s.212, which applies where companies are being wound up, para.75 does not create a new head of liability but instead provides a summary method by which the administrator may be rendered accountable for misconduct and breach of duty.[253] The application must allege that the administrator has misapplied or retained money or other property of the company, has become accountable for money or other property of the company, has breached a fiduciary or other duty in relation to the company,[254] or has been guilty of misfeasance. Even when pursued by a creditor or contributory, an application under para.74 is a class claim to remedy wrongdoing suffered by the insolvent company and therefore by all of the creditors.[255]

12–064   Applications pursuant to para.75 cannot be used to enforce contractual debts.[256] Nor can they be used to circumvent statutory requirements that must be met in order to enforce particular claims created by Insolvency Act 1986.[257] Since the claim arises in respect of breaches of duty owed to the company which the company itself could have enforced, the fruits of a successful action are capable of being caught by an appropriately worded charge,[258] and can be assigned by the administrator.[259] The administrator may not set off against his obligation to make a payment under para.75 any debts owed to him by the company.[260]

---

[251] As regards acts ultra vires the administrator's powers see Sch.B1, para.59(3). Otherwise, the point rests on general equitable principles.

[252] An application in respect of a former administrator who has been discharged in accordance with Sch.B1, para.98 may only be made with the permission of the court: see Sch.B1, para.75(6).

[253] Re Continental Assurance Company of London Plc [2001] B.P.I.R. 733, [393]; Re Eurocruit Europe Ltd [2007] B.C.C. 916, [24]; Parkinson Engineering Services Plc v Swan [2010] Bus. L.R. 857 (CA). An administrator who wishes to commence proceedings for breach of duty against a former administrator of the same company has no standing under s.212: see Irwin v Lynch [2011] 1 W.L.R. 1364 (CA).

[254] This includes the common law duty of care: see Re D'Jan of London Ltd [1993] B.C.C. 646; Re Westlowe Storage and Distribution Ltd [2000] B.C.C. 851; Re Continental Assurance Company of London Plc [2001] B.P.I.R. 733, [393].

[255] Oldham v Kyrris [2004] B.C.C. 111 (CA), [77], [141]–[163] (Jonathan Parker L.J.).

[256] Re Etic Ltd [1928] Ch. 861.

[257] e.g. a preference claim under Insolvency Act 1986, s.239: see Re Continental Assurance Company of London Plc [2001] B.P.I.R. 733, [420].

[258] See, e.g. Re Anglo-Austrian Printing & Publishing Union [1895] 2 Ch. 891.

[259] See, e.g. Re Oasis Merchandising Services Ltd [1998] Ch.170 (CA).

[260] Re Anglo-French Co-operative Society Ex p. Pelly (1882) L.R. 21 Ch. D 492, CA; Manson v Smith (liquidator of Thomas Christy Ltd) [1997] 2 B.C.L.C. 161 (CA).

If the application succeeds, the court may order the administrator to repay, **12–065** restore or account for money or property; to pay interest; or to contribute a sum to the company's property by way of compensation for breach of duty or misfeasance. As an officer of the company, he is entitled to invoke Companies Act 2006, s.1157 (formerly Companies Act 1985, s.727) so as to seek relief from liability if he acted honestly and reasonably and ought fairly to be excused.[261] The requirement on the administrator to demonstrate that his conduct was "reasonable" as well as "honest" means it will often be difficult in practice to obtain relief.

10. THE ADMINISTRATOR AS A PUBLIC AUTHORITY UNDER THE HUMAN RIGHTS ACT 1998

Section 6 of the Human Rights Act 1998 (HRA 1998) makes it unlawful for a **12–066** "public authority" to act in a way which is incompatible with a Convention right unless precluded from acting differently by one or more provisions of, or made under, primary legislation. "Public authority" for this purpose includes any person certain of whose functions are functions of a public nature: his acts are "acts of a public authority" if the nature of the acts is not private. A "victim" of an act of a public authority committed after October 2, 2000 made unlawful by Human Rights Act 1998, s.6 may bring proceedings against the public authority[262] claiming any relief that is just and appropriate, and this includes damages where damages are necessary to afford just satisfaction.[263] The victim may also rely on a Convention right in any legal proceedings.[264]

As a statutory office-holder and an officer of the court an administrator is **12–067** clearly a "public authority" in that at least some of his functions are of a public nature for the purposes of human rights legislation. He is a creature of statute (and not merely someone subject to statutory regulation) who exercises statutory powers and discharges statutory responsibilities.[265] As an officer of the court, he undertakes functions on behalf of the court. He is invested with special investigative functions as an office-holder, e.g. the investigatory powers under Insolvency Act 1986, ss.235 and 236. He also has reporting obligations under the company director disqualification legislation, compliance with which may lead to the state commencing disqualification proceedings against the directors of the insolvent company.[266] The term "victim" requires

---

[261] *Re Home Treat Ltd* [1991] B.C.C. 165. In *Rawnsley and Canal Dyeing Company Ltd v Weatherall Green & Smith North Ltd* [2010] B.C.C. 406, HH Judge Behrens (sitting as a High Court Judge) considered it to be seriously arguable that a liquidator is outside the ambit of s.1157 (see at [66]). It appears, however, that his attention had not been drawn to the decision in Home Treat.

[262] Human Rights Act 1998, s.7.

[263] Human Rights Act 1998, s.8.

[264] Human Rights Act 1998, s.7(1)(b).

[265] See above, paras 12–003 to 12–004, and compare *YL v Birmingham City Council* [2008] 1 A.C. 95 (HL), [26], [28], [29], [31], [102], [116], [134] and [167].

[266] Company Directors Disqualification Act 1986, ss.6, 7(3); *Re Pantmaenog Timber Co Ltd* [2004] 1 A.C. 158 (HL).

more than that the person in question is interested in the compliance by the "public authority" with the Convention right: in the ordinary case he must be directly affected by or threatened with non-compliance, though in some cases substantial indirect effect may be sufficient.[267] Depending on the facts and circumstances, a company director, officer, creditor or shareholder may qualify as a victim.[268]

---

[267] See, e.g. *Marckx v Belgium* (1979–80) 2 E.H.R.R. 330 (ECtHR), [27].

[268] On the impact of human rights legislation on insolvency practice, see generally C. Gearty and S. Davies QC, *Insolvency Practice and the Human Rights Act 1998* (Bristol: Jordans, 2000); M. Simmons QC and T. Smith, "The Human Rights Act 1998: The Practical Impact on Insolvency" (2000) 16(5) *Insolvency Law & Practice* 167; W. Trower, "Bringing Human Rights Home to the Insolvency Practitioner" (2000) 13(6) Insolv. Int. 41 and (2000) 13(7) Insolv. Int. 52; W. Trower, "Human Rights: Article 6—The Reality and the Myth" (2001) *Insolvency Lawyer* 48.

Chapter 13

Duties and Liabilities of Receivers and their Appointors

In a work on receivers, it is appropriate to consider the duties and liabilities **13–001** both of the receiver and of the debenture-holder who appoints the receiver, for there is a mutual interest on the part of both the receiver and his appointor that the other shall not be unnecessarily exposed to claims. For this purpose it is essential that each should know the extent of the other's duties and liabilities to third parties.[1] The similarity (though not identity) of their duties and liabilities to third parties suggests that they should be considered together in Part I of this chapter. In Pt II there will be a consideration of the duties and liabilities of the receiver and his appointor inter se.

PART I—DUTIES AND LIABILITIES OF DEBENTURE-HOLDER AND RECEIVER TO THIRD PARTIES

1. PRELIMINARY

It is of the essence of a security[2] that the chargor gives the chargee rights and **13–002** powers over the chargor's property, and agrees to the chargee using those rights and powers in his own interests to achieve repayment of the debt which

---

[1] As will become apparent in the following discussion, the extent to which a receiver has been recognised as owing duties to parties other than the mortgagor who has appointed him is limited. Following the reforms introduced by Enterprise Act 2002, the holder of a qualifying floating charge created on or after September 15, 2003 may not appoint an administrative receiver except where the appointment is made in connection with a select few categories of transaction such as a capital market arrangement or a public-private partnership: see Insolvency Act 1986, ss.72A–H. This curtailing of the right to appoint a receiver was motivated by concerns that administrative receivership provided inadequate incentives for the maximisation of economic value and an unacceptable level of transparency and accountability to the range of stakeholders interested in a company's affairs: see DTI, *Productivity and Enterprise: Insolvency—A Second Chance*, Cm 5234 (2001), 2.2–2.6. For further discussion of the policy arguments see R. Mokal, *Corporate Insolvency Law—Theory and Application* (Oxford: Oxford University Press, 2005), pp.208–219.

[2] The difference between a mortgage and a charge, the two forms of security with which this chapter is concerned, is that the former involves the transfer of title to the collateral from the debtor to the creditor, whereas the latter does not; see e.g. *Re Cosslett (Contractors) Ltd* [1998] Ch. 495 (CA), 508. The similarity between the two forms of security is that, in both cases, beneficial ownership of the collateral remains vested in the debtor, represented in the case of the chargor by his title, and in the case of the mortgagor by his equity of redemption (which includes the right to reclaim title to the collateral: *Kreglinger v New Patagonia Meat and Cold Storage* [1914] A.C. 25 (HL), 48; see, e.g. *Casborne v Scarfe* (1783) 1 Atk. 603 (HL), 605; *Re Sir Thomas Spencer Wells* [1933] Ch. 29 (CA), 52; *Quennell v Maltby* [1979] 1 W.L.R. 318, 324. For ease of exposition and unless the contrary is indicated by the context, the terms "charge" and "mortgage" are used interchangeably in this chapter, and the term "equity of redemption" is used expansively to refer to the debtor's interest in the collateral, regardless of the nature of the security.

he is owed.[3] But recognising that a mortgage is merely a security for the payment of a debt or performance of an obligation, and with the intention of ensuring that the mortgagee or receiver acts fairly, equity affords certain protections to the mortgagor and any other persons who are interested in the equity of redemption.[4] What equity's "core value" of fairness requires will naturally vary depending on the circumstances and the particular relationship between the parties.[5] Invariably equity will require a mortgagee[6] or receiver to act in good faith and to use the powers conferred upon him for proper purposes. In appropriate circumstances, equity may also impose upon a mortgagee or receiver a duty to exercise due diligence or a duty to take reasonable care. Such duties may be owed to the mortgagor and to others interested in the equity of redemption,[7] including any guarantor of the secured indebtedness.[8] In the event of breach of these duties, equity may require the mortgagee or receiver to make good (or provide compensation for) any consequent loss in value of the equity of redemption, and in particular to give credit for that loss in the taking of accounts between the mortgagee and the mortgagor. The damage suffered by subsequent mortgagees is to be measured by reference to the quantum of their respective interests in the property subject to the mortgage.[9]

13–003   The relatively strict duties of a mortgagee "in possession", and the basic duties of a receiver or of a mortgagee who is not in possession, namely to act in good faith and for proper purposes, are long established. But there has been an acute conflict in the authorities as to whether a receiver or a mortgagee who is not in possession are under any further duties, such as a general duty of care or even a general duty to act fairly to the mortgagor and others interested in the equity of redemption.

13–004   It is proposed to consider first the duty of a mortgagee and receiver to act in good faith and for proper purposes; secondly, the duties of the mortgagee if he

---

[3] See, e.g. per Lord Hoffmann in *Re Bank of Credit and Commerce International S.A. (No.8)* [1998] A.C. 214 (HL), 226.

[4] *Burgess v Auger* [1998] 2 B.C.L.C. 478; *Medforth v Blake* [2000] Ch. 86 (CA), 102A–B.

[5] *Parker Tweedale v Dunbar Bank Plc* [1991] Ch. 26 (CA); *Downsview Nominees Ltd v First City Corp* [1993] A.C. 295 (PC); *Medforth v Blake* [2000] Ch. 86 (CA).

[6] The duties are the same in the case of a legal and an equitable mortgagee: *Leech v National Bank of New Zealand* [1996] 3 N.Z.L.R. 707.

[7] For example, subsequent mortgagees, but not beneficiaries under trusts of the mortgaged property: *Parker Tweedale v Dunbar Bank Plc* [1991] Ch. 26 (CA); *Raja v Austin Gray* [2003] B.P.I.R. 725 (CA), [27]–[28], [55]. The cause of action created by any breach of the duty of good faith is, however, trust property, and the trustee holds this property for the beneficiaries of the trust. A tenant at will also has no interest in the equity of redemption: *Jarrett v Barclays Bank* [1947] Ch. 187 (CA).

[8] *ENT Pty Ltd v McVeigh* (1996) 6 Tas. R. 202 (Supreme Court of Tasmania); *Skipton Building Society v Stott* [2001] Q.B. 261 (CA); *Barclays Bank Plc v Kingston* [2006] 1 All E.R. (Comm) 519, [17]–[23]. The liability to guarantors is based on the ground of their interest in the equity of redemption, and not on the existence of any common law duty of care as held in *Standard Chartered Bank v Walker* [1982] 1 W.L.R. 1410 (CA) and *American Express International Banking Corp v Hurley* [1985] 3 All E.R. 564. It is because general creditors, contributories, officers, employees and members of the debtor company are not so interested that no duty is owed to them: see *Burgess v Auger* [1998] 2 B.C.L.C. 478.

[9] *Meretz Investments NV v ACP Ltd* [2007] Ch. 197, [292]. Although the decision in *Meretz Investments* was reversed in part on appeal (see [2008] Ch. 244 (CA)), the decision of the Court of Appeal has no bearing on this point.

takes possession; and thirdly, how far there may be other duties imposed upon a mortgagee not in possession or upon a receiver, such as a general duty of care or a duty to act fairly.

2. DUTY TO ACT IN GOOD FAITH AND FOR PROPER PURPOSES

A mortgagee and a receiver both owe a duty in exercising their powers to do so   **13–005**
in good faith for the purpose of preserving, exploiting[10] and realising the assets comprised in the security and obtaining repayment of the sum secured.[11] A want of good faith or the exercise of powers for an improper purpose will suffice to establish a breach of duty.[12] It is proper for the mortgagee to exercise his powers in order to protect his security, and the exercise of the power is not bad because it is motivated by several purposes, as long as one of the purposes is a proper one, for example to recover the secured debt or to protect the security.[13]

A mortgagee is at all times free to consult his own interest alone in deciding   **13–006**
whether and if so when to enforce his security or exercise any of the powers conferred on him as mortgagee.[14] His decision to exercise or refrain from exercising such powers is not constrained by reason of the fact that the exercise or non-exercise of the powers will occasion damage or loss to the mortgagor. The mortgagee is entitled to sell the mortgaged property in the state in which he finds it, and is under no obligation to improve or increase its value.[15] Provided he acts in good faith, he is entitled to subordinate any conflicting interest of the mortgagor (as well as those of creditors and third parties)[16] to what he genuinely perceives to be his own interest in securing repayment.

Provided he acts in good faith, when deciding whether and, if so, how to   **13–007**
exercise powers vested in him, a receiver is likewise entitled and indeed obliged to give priority to the interests of the mortgagee in securing repayment.

---

[10] This extends to exploiting a "ransom strip" or exploiting the dependence of customers who have no contractual right to the on-going supply of products and no alternative source for the products produced by the charged business by demanding a high price for that land or for those products: see *Re Transtec Automotive (Campsie) Ltd* [2001] B.C.C. 403. See also *Medforth v Blake* [2000] Ch. 86 (CA); *Freeguard v Royal Bank of Scotland Plc* [2004] EWHC 3258 (Ch).

[11] *Bank of New Zealand v Essington* (1991) 9 A.C.L.C. 1039 (Supreme Court of New South Wales); *Medforth v Blake* [2000] Ch. 86 (CA), 102G.

[12] *Downsview Nominees Ltd v First City Corp* [1993] A.C. 295 (PC), 317; *Yorkshire Bank Plc v Hall* [1999] 1 W.L.R. 1713 (CA), 1728E; *Medforth v Blake* [2000] Ch. 86 (CA), 102A–B.

[13] *Nash v Eads* (1880) 25 Sol.J. 95 (CA); *Belton v Bass* [1922] 2 Ch. 449; *Meretz Investments NV v ACP Ltd* [2007] Ch. 197, [314]. Although the decision in *Meretz Investments* was reversed in part on appeal (see [2008] Ch. 244 (CA)), the decision of the Court of Appeal has no bearing on this point.

[14] See, e.g. *Raja v Austin Gray* [2003] B.P.I.R. 725 (CA), [55].

[15] *Silven Properties Ltd v Royal Bank of Scotland Plc* [2004] 1 W.L.R. 997 (CA), [16]–[17]. Even if the mortgagee has embarked upon the process of increasing the value of the property, e.g. by making a planning application, he remains free at any time to halt such efforts and proceed immediately to a sale: [2004] 1 W.L.R. 997 (CA), [17]. However, in order to obtain a proper market price, the mortgagee is under a duty to take reasonable steps to advertise any development potential inherent in the property: [2004] 1 W.L.R. 997 (CA), [20]. See too *Raja v Austin Gray* [2003] B.P.I.R. 725 (CA).

[16] *Grosvenor (Mayfair) Estate v Edward Erdman Property Investment Ltd* [1996] E.G. 83 (C.S.).

He is no more required to take steps to increase the value of the property subject to the security interest than is the mortgagee in possession.[17]

13–008   Breach of the duty of good faith involves something more than negligence or even gross negligence: it requires some dishonesty, or improper motive, some element of bad faith, to be established. Reckless indifference to the rights or interests of others or shutting one's eyes deliberately to the consequences of one's actions may suffice to establish dishonesty or bad faith.[18] In judging whether the mortgagee or receiver was acting in good faith in deciding how best to serve the interests of the mortgagee, it would be inappropriate to apply any "Wednesbury" type test of reasonableness, but if the decision lay outside the range which the court thought might be arrived at by a reasonable commercial man, this might provide some evidence that the decision was not taken in good faith.

13–009   The use of powers for improper purposes will extend to the exercise of powers for the purposes of the advancement of the interests of the debenture-holder other than as mortgagee (e.g. as a competitor of the mortgagor) or (whether by pressure or otherwise) to obtain a collateral advantage unprovided for by the debenture (e.g. to inhibit proceedings by the mortgagor against the debenture-holder or anyone else).[19]

13–010   So, for example, a first debenture-holder and the receiver appointed by it were held liable for breach of duty where the receiver was appointed and the receivership conducted for the purpose of disrupting an existing receivership under a second debenture and preventing enforcement of the second debenture. Damages were awarded reflecting the loss occasioned by such appointment and receivership.[20]

3.   MORTGAGEE IN POSSESSION

13–011   In the absence of an agreement or statutory provision to the contrary, a mortgagee is entitled to possession for the purpose of protecting or enforcing his

---

[17] *Silven Properties Ltd v Royal Bank of Scotland Plc* [2004] 1 W.L.R. 997 (CA), [28], approving the first instance decisions in *Meftah v Lloyds TSB Bank Plc* [2001] 2 All E.R. (Comm.) 741, 744, 766, *Garland v Ralph Pay & Ransom* [1984] 2 E.G.L.R. 147, 151 and *Routestone Ltd v Minories Finance Ltd* [1997] B.C.C. 180, 195c–d. For further discussion see K.Loi, "Receivers' Power of Sale and Duty of Care" [2010] Conv. 369. Loi argues that the (lack of) liability of a mortgagee as regards the timing of sale rests on the general rule of private law that there is no liability for nonfeasance whereas a receiver owes a duty to the mortgagor but one which is subject to his overriding duty to the mortgagee and so does not oblige the receiver to delay or expedite a sale in anticipation of a rising or falling market.

[18] *Medforth v Blake* [2000] Ch. 86 (CA), 103D. On the meaning of dishonesty in commercial matters, see *Royal Brunei Airlines v Tan* [1995] 2 A.C. 378 (PC); *Twinsectra Ltd v Yardley* [2002] 2 A.C. 164 (HL); *Barlow Clowes International Ltd (in liquidation) v Eurotrust International Ltd* [2006] 1 W.L.R. 1476 (PC); and the useful summary of the meaning of "dishonesty" by Morgan J. in *Aerostar Maintenance International Ltd v Wilson* [2010] EWHC 2032 (Ch), [183]–[184]. See, too, *Starglade Properties v Nash* [2011] Lloyd's Rep. F.C. 102 (CA); *Cunningham v Cunningham* [2009] J.L.R. 227 (Royal Court of Jersey), [40]. See also the comments of Lord Hoffmann on the dangers inherent in the concept of the "hypothetical decent honest man" in *Aktieselskabet Dansk Skibsfinansiering v Brothers* [2001] 2 B.C.L.C. 324 (Court of Final Appeal of Hong Kong).

[19] *Speed Seal Ltd v Paddington* [1985] 1 W.L.R. 1327 (CA); and see also *Quennell v Maltby* [1979] 1 W.L.R. 318.

[20] *Downsview Nominees Ltd v First City Corp* [1993] A.C. 295 (PC).

security as soon as the mortgage is granted, whether or not the mortgagor is in default[21] and whether or not the mortgagor has a cross-claim against the mortgagee.[22] This is to be contrasted with the right to appoint a receiver, which only arises when the conditions for making such an appointment specified in the mortgage are satisfied. The appointment of a receiver as agent of the mortgagor and taking possession are alternative remedies: such an appointment cannot remain in force once the mortgagee takes possession, whereupon the receiver becomes the agent of the mortgagee.[23] The intention to take possession is not sufficient to constitute a mortgagee in possession: the intention of the mortgagee must be accompanied by an unequivocal act of taking possession. Thus, for example, the collection of rents is not conclusive of this issue.[24]

By taking possession the mortgagee becomes the manager of the charged property.[25] The authorities establish that a mortgagee in possession is accountable to the mortgagor for his possession and management[26] of the charged property on the basis of "wilful default":   **13–012**

"If a mortgagee takes possession of the mortgaged property, he is liable to account for rent on the basis of wilful default; he must keep the mortgaged premises in repair; he is liable for waste. Those duties are imposed to ensure that a mortgagee is diligent in discharging his mortgage and returning the property to the mortgagor."[27]

The precise content of the liability for "wilful default" has not been clearly defined.[28] Although "wilful default" has often been said to be a "strict" liability,[29] in fact the majority of cases appear to have treated "wilful default" as synonymous with a failure on the part of the mortgagee to exercise "due diligence".[30] So it has been said that the mortgagee must account not only for all he receives, but also for all he ought to have received had he managed the property with due diligence.[31] But other than indicating that liability will attach even though the default of the mortgagee is not "wilful" in the sense of being   **13–013**

[21] See, e.g. *Ropaigealach v Barclays Bank Plc* [2000] Q.B. 263 (CA).
[22] *TSB Bank Plc v Platts* [1998] 2 B.C.L.C. 1, 10 (CA).
[23] *North American Trust Co v Consumer Gas Co* (1997) 147 D.L.R. (4th) 645 (Ontario Court of Appeal).
[24] *North American Trust Co v Consumer Gas Co* (1997) 147 D.L.R. (4th) 645 (Ontario Court of Appeal), citing *Noyes v Pollock* (1886) L.R. 32 Ch. D. 53, CA.
[25] *Silven Properties Ltd v Royal Bank of Scotland Plc* [2004] 1 W.L.R. 997 (CA), [13] (CA); *Kendle v Melsom* [1998] 193 C.L.R 46 (High Court of Australia), 64.
[26] Where a mortgagee exercises his power of sale, different considerations have traditionally been applied: see paras 13–015 to 13–017, below.
[27] *Downsview Nominees Ltd v First City Corp* [1993] A.C. 295 (PC), 315A, per Lord Templeman.
[28] See the discussion by Stannard in "Wilful Default" [1979] Conv. 345 and the summary by Frisby in "Making a silk purse out of a pig's ear" (2000) 63 M.L.R. 413, 418–419.
[29] See, e.g. *Yorkshire Bank Plc v Hall* [1999] 1 W.L.R. 1713 (CA), 1728E–F, per Robert Walker L.J.; and C. Harpum, S. Bridge and M. Dixon, *Megarry and Wade: The Law of Real Property*, 7th edn (London: Sweet & Maxwell, 2008), para.25–026.
[30] *Sherwin v Shakspear* (1854) 5 De G.M. & G. 517, 537, per Turner L.J.
[31] See, e.g. the discussion in *Megarry and Wade: The Law of Real Property*, 7th edn (Sweet & Maxwell, 2008) (above) and *Medforth v Blake* [2000] Ch. 86 (CA), 92G.

deliberate, the "due diligence" formulation is of itself no help in indicating the precise level of "diligence" (i.e. care) which will be regarded as "due". Some older authorities tended to indicate that more than mere negligence (i.e. a failure to take reasonable care) might be required,[32] but recent authorities have tended to assimilate the "due diligence" standard with a duty to take reasonable care.[33] So it has been said that the duty requires the mortgagee in possession to be active in protecting and exploiting the security, maximising the return but without taking any undue risks.[34] The mortgagee is under no obligation to take steps to increase the value of the property subject to the security.[35]

4. OTHER DUTIES

13–014   The question arises whether and (if so) in what circumstances the general duty of the mortgagee or receiver to act in good faith and for proper purposes is supplemented by other duties, such as a duty to exercise powers with reasonable care or a duty to act fairly.

13–015   Three general principles can be stated. First, as mentioned above, the powers conferred on a mortgagee are conferred on him for his own benefit: he is not a trustee of them for the mortgagor. Accordingly, the mortgagee can act in his own interests in making any decision as to whether or not, and if so, when to exercise his powers.[36] Secondly, a receiver can also give priority to the interests of his appointor in deciding whether, and if so when and how he should exercise the powers vested in him. But unlike a mortgagee, a receiver, once appointed, cannot simply remain passive: he has a duty to preserve and protect the charged assets.[37] And thirdly, it has long been established that if a mortgagee or a receiver decides to exercise a power of sale, he will generally owe a duty of care to the mortgagor in respect of the manner in which he does so.[38] This is usually expressed as an obligation to obtain the best price reasonably obtainable at the time of sale.[39]

13–016   At common law, no duty of care on the exercise of a power of sale was recognised, because in the view of the common law the mortgagee was the legal owner exercising the power of sale of his own property for his own

---

[32] See, e.g. *Hughes v Williams* (1806) 12 Ves. 493; *Brandon v Brandon* (1862) 19 W.R. 287.

[33] See, e.g. *Palk v Mortgage Services Funding Plc* [1993] Ch. 330 (CA), 338; *Medforth v Blake* [2000] Ch. 86 (CA). See also *Leech v National Bank of New Zealand* [1995] 2 N.Z.L.R. 30.

[34] *Palk v Mortgage Services Funding Plc* [1993] Ch. 330 (CA), 338A, per Nicholls V.C. See also *Hughes v Williams* (1806) 12 Ves. 493.

[35] *Silven Properties Ltd v Royal Bank of Scotland Plc* [2004] 1 W.L.R. 997 (CA), [16]–[20].

[36] *China and South Sea Bank Ltd v Tan Soon Gin* [1990] 1 A.C. 536 (PC).

[37] See below, para.13–030. See also K. Loi, "Receivers' power of sale and duty of care" [2010] Conv. 369.

[38] See, e.g. *Cuckmere Brick v Mutual Finance Ltd* [1971] Ch. 949 (CA); *Downsview Nominees Ltd v First City Corp* [1993] A.C. 295 (PC), 315; *Yorkshire Bank Plc v Hall* [1999] 1 W.L.R. 1713 (CA), 1728E–F; *Medforth v Blake* [2000] Ch. 86 (CA), 98H–99A.

[39] See, e.g. *Cuckmere Brick v Mutual Finance Ltd* [1971] Ch. 949 (CA); *Tse Kwong Lam v Wong Chit Sen* [1983] 1 W.L.R. 1349 (PC); *Downsview Nominees Ltd v First City Corp* [1993] A.C. 295 (PC); *Medforth v Blake* [2000] Ch. 86 (CA); *Raja v Austin Gray* [2003] B.P.I.R. 725 (CA); *Silven Properties Ltd v Royal Bank of Scotland Plc* [2004] 1 W.L.R. 997 (CA); *Bell v Long* [2008] 2 B.C.L.C. 706. See further para.13–033, below.

benefit.[40] By contrast, equity looked at substance and not at form. It insisted on seeing through the conveyancing device of the transfer of title involved in the creation of a mortgage, and recognised the commercial reality of the transaction as a means of conferring security rather than ownership on the mortgagee. It therefore accepted the mortgagor's equity of redemption as constituting beneficial ownership of the property subject to the security.[41] Consistently with this, the Court of Chancery recognised a duty of care on sale on the part of the mortgagee in the case of *Wolff v Vanderzee*,[42] and the existence of this duty was affirmed by the Privy Council in *McHugh v Union Bank of Canada*.[43] At least in the normal case, if the mortgagor and (as appropriate) others to whom this duty is owed have agreed with the mortgagee the terms on which the property is to be sold, and if the mortgagee subsequently sells according to those terms, no complaint can lie against him.[44]

This equitable duty of care has on occasion been equated with and expressed **13–017** in terms of the tort of negligence, but this has been said to be wrong.[45] Nor should contractual duties be implied.[46] Whether expressed as a common law duty or as a duty in equity, the ambit of the duty is the same,[47] and as with the common law duty, the equitable duty of care may be modified, and accordingly enlarged or reduced, by contract.[48] A breach of the duty may give rise to a claim to equitable set-off against any sums claimed by the mortgagee under the

---

[40] *Gilligan & Nugent v National Bank Ltd* [1901] 2 I.R. 513. For the perpetuation of this approach in precluding a claim for loss of title deeds, see *Browning v Handiland's Group* (1976) 35 P.C.C.R. 345. For the analogous application in the case of resale by a vendor on default by a purchaser, see *Sullivan v Darkin* [1986] N.Z.L.R. 214.

[41] See, e.g. *Casborne v Scarfe* (1783) 1 Atk. 603, 605; *Re Sir Thomas Spencer Wells* [1933] Ch. 29 (CA), 52; *Quennell v Maltby* [1979] 1 W.L.R. 318, 324.

[42] *Wolff v Vanderzee* (1869) 20 L.T. 353, 354. See also *Tomlin v Luce* (1889) L.R. 41 Ch. D. 573 (reversed in part (1890) L.R. 43 Ch.D. 191 (CA)) and *Nash v Eads* (1880) 25 Sol.J. 95 (CA).

[43] *McHugh v Union Bank of Canada* [1913] A.C. 299 (PC), 311: "It is well settled law that it is the duty of a mortgagee when realizing the mortgaged property by sale to behave in conducting such realization as a reasonable man would behave in the realization of his own property, so that the mortgagor may receive credit for the fair value of the property sold". See also *Movitex v Bulfield* (1986) 2 B.C.C. 99403.

[44] *Apple Fields Ltd v Damesh Holdings Ltd* [2004] 1 N.Z.L.R. 721 (PC), 728, [21] (a decision on s.103A of the New Zealand Property Law Act 1952, which codifies the general equitable duty; see *Apple Fields Ltd v Damesh Holdings Ltd* [2004] 1 N.Z.L.R. 721 (PC), 728, [22]).

[45] *Downsview Nominees Ltd v First City Corp* [1993] 2 A.C. 295 (PC), 315. It can be no objection that the breach of an equitable duty gives rise to a claim in damages: see, e.g. *Bristol and West Building Society v Mothew* [1998] Ch. 1 (CA). But there have been suggestions that the imposition of such a duty of care has no foundation in traditional equitable principles in the absence of a fiduciary relationship: see the comment by Sealy in "Mortgages and receivers—a duty of care resurrected and extended" [2000] Camb. L.J. 31, 33. In *Medforth v Blake* [2000] Ch. 86 (CA), 102E, Scott V.C. demonstrated obvious irritation at such debate over the precise source of the duty of care: "I do not, for my part, think it matters one jot whether the duty is expressed as a common law duty or a duty in equity. The result is the same." But it is suggested that the issue may well be of some significance given the limited application of the Unfair Contract Terms Act 1977, which only applies to common law duties of care: see below, paras 13–054 to 13–055.

[46] *Yorkshire Bank Plc v Hall* [1999] 1 W.L.R. 1713 (CA), 1728D.

[47] *Medforth v Blake* [2000] Ch. 86 (CA), 102D–E.

[48] But it should be noted that the potential application of the Unfair Contract Terms Act 1977 may be different: see below, paras 13–054 to 13–055.

mortgage.[49] The limitation period is the same for a breach of a common law duty of care and an equitable duty of care.[50]

13–018   The more contentious issue is whether there should be any general duty of care or fairness owed by a mortgagee or receiver in circumstances other than when a power of sale is exercised.

(a)   A general duty of care?

13–019   In 1955, in an extemporary judgment, the Court of Appeal in *Re B Johnson & Co (Builders) Ltd*[51] overlooked the earlier authorities relating to the duty arising in the exercise of a power of sale and held that the only duty of a receiver and manager was to act in good faith and in accordance with the powers given to him under the debenture, but that in no circumstances did he owe to the mortgagor a duty of care. In 1971 the equitable duty of care on a sale was revived by the Court of Appeal in *Cuckmere Brick v Mutual Finance*[52] and was later reinforced by the decision of the Privy Council in 1983 in the case of *Tse Kwong Lam v Wong Chit Sen*.[53] The like duty on the part of a receiver was recognised by the Court of Appeal in 1982 in the case of *Standard Chartered Bank v Walker*.[54]

13–020   In *Downsview Nominees Ltd v First City Corp Ltd*[55] (*Downsview*) the Privy Council affirmed that a mortgagee who was not in possession or a receiver and manager appointed by him who decided to exercise a power of sale owed a duty to take reasonable care to obtain the best price reasonably obtainable, but held that neither a mortgagee nor a receiver owed a general duty of care in any other circumstances. In *Yorkshire Bank Plc v Hall*[56] (*Yorkshire Bank*), Robert Walker L.J. also rejected a suggestion that a general equitable duty of care should be imposed upon a mortgagee simply because in the circumstances there was no conflict between his interests and those of the mortgagor, stating that such a principle would "be fraught with uncertainty and difficulty" and that he could "find no warrant for it in the authorities".[57]

---

[49] *TSB Bank Plc v Platts* [1998] 2 B.C.L.C. 1 (CA), and see below, Ch.22. A breach of contractual duty owed by a creditor to a guarantor, if repudiatory, may operate to discharge the guarantor from all liability, but a breach of the equitable duty (and in particular the duty on sale to obtain the best price reasonably obtainable) does not have this effect and instead merely reduces pro tanto the amount of the guarantor's liability: *Skipton Building Society v Stott* [2001] Q.B. 261 (CA).

[50] *Raja v Lloyd's TSB Bank Plc* [2000] Lloyd's Rep. Bank. 377.

[51] *Re B Johnson & Co (Builders) Ltd* [1955] Ch. 634 (CA), 651, per Evershed M.R. and 662, per Jenkins L.J.

[52] *Cuckmere Brick v Mutual Finance* [1971] Ch. 949 (CA). *Re B Johnson* was not cited or referred to in *Cuckmere Brick*. In *American Express International Banking Corp v Hurley* [1985] 3 All E.R. 564, Mann J. held that the law was as stated in *Cuckmere Brick* and not *Re B Johnson*.

[53] *Tse Kwong Lam v Wong Chit Sen* [1983] 1 W.L.R. 1349 (PC).

[54] *Standard Chartered Bank v Walker* [1982] 1 W.L.R. 1410 (CA), followed in *American Express International Banking Corp v Hurley* [1985] 3 All E.R. 564; and in Ireland in *McGowan v Gannas* [1983] I.L.R.M. 516.

[55] *Downsview Nominees Ltd v First City Corp Ltd* [1993] 2 A.C. 295 (PC).

[56] *Yorkshire Bank Plc v Hall* [1999] 1 W.L.R. 1713 (CA).

[57] *Yorkshire Bank Plc v Hall* [1999] 1 W.L.R. 1713 (CA), 1729A–C.

The view expressed in *Downsview*, circumscribing so narrowly the circum- **13–021**
stances in which a mortgagee who was not in possession or a receiver might
owe a duty of care, was the subject of detailed criticism in an earlier edition
of this work and was subsequently rejected by the Court of Appeal in *Medforth
v Blake*[58].

In *Medforth*, Scott V.C. did not differ from Robert Walker L.J.'s views in the **13–022**
Yorkshire Bank case, but indicated clearly that he regarded the views expressed
by Lord Templeman in *Downsview* as being too narrow. Scott V.C. found that
it "does not seem to me to make commercial sense nor, more importantly, to
correspond with the principles expressed in the bulk of the authorities" that a
duty of care should be owed when a power of sale was exercised, but not when
a power to manage a business was being exercised. Scott V.C. also founded
himself heavily upon what was conceded to be the duty of a mortgagee in
possession to exercise due diligence in the management of the charged
property.

Scott V.C. expressed the view that equity should be flexible in adjusting the **13–023**
duties owed according to the "requirements of the time" and that the extent and
scope of any duty additional to a duty of good faith would depend upon
the particular facts of the particular case.[59] He then held that subject to what he
acknowledged was a receiver's primary duty to bring about a situation in which
interest on the secured debt can be paid and the debt itself repaid, a receiver
who exercises his powers to manage charged property owes a duty to the
mortgagor and to those interested in the equity of redemption to do so with
due diligence.[60]

Although the decision in *Medforth* has not commanded universal support, **13–024**
and might be criticised for the methods by which Scott V.C. sought to distinguish some of the contrary authorities, it has generally been welcomed as
bringing the law into line with good commercial practice.[61] As Scott V.C.
acknowledged, receivers must be free to put the interests of the debenture-
holder first in making any decision in good faith as to the course which the
receivership will take. But subject to that overriding requirement, there will
usually be no good reason why, in implementing their decisions in relation
both to management and to disposal of charged assets, receivers should not
be required to use reasonable skill and care and be answerable to the mortgagor
if they do not.[62]

---

[58] *Medforth v Blake* [2000] Ch. 86 (CA).
[59] *Medforth v Blake* [2000] Ch. 86 (CA), 102B–D.
[60] *Medforth v Blake* [2000] Ch. 86 (CA),102F–H.
[61] See, e.g. R.J. Mokal, "The Floating Charge—An Elegy", in S. Worthington (ed.), *Commercial Law and Commercial Practice* (Oxford: Hart Publishing, 2003), pp.479, 496–498. For a contrary view from Australia, to the effect that Medforth not only is inconsistent with *Downsview* but also "shows a limited understanding of the historical genesis of receiverships", see J. O'Donovan, *Company Receivers and Administrators*, 2nd edn (Sydney: LBC, 1992), para.11–260, referring, inter alia, to *Expo International Pty Ltd v Chant* [1979] 2 N.S.W.L.R. 820.
[62] See the comment by Frisby in (2000) 63 M.L.R. 413, 420–421 to the effect that what is being targeted is careless behaviour rather than a deliberate course of conduct that will benefit the mortgagee to the detriment of the mortgagor. Properly analysed and applied, *Medforth* does not overturn the balance of power between mortgagee and mortgagor.

13–025   It is suggested that the approach to the imposition of equitable duties in *Medforth* will necessarily require in each case an examination of whether there is any conflict between the interests of the mortgagee and the mortgagor. If there is such conflict, then the receiver will not be liable to the mortgagor if he chooses to put the interests of the mortgagee first, in accordance with his principal duty.

13–026   Where the interests of the mortgagee and mortgagor are not in conflict, then it is suggested that as a matter of principle the courts should be ready to impose a duty of care upon a mortgagee or receiver in the absence of some relevant countervailing consideration. In other words, the existence of a coincidence of interests is a strong pointer to the existence of a duty of care, but it will not invariably bring such a duty into existence.

13–027   Where the interests of the mortgagee and mortgagor are not in conflict, a further pointer to the existence or absence of a duty of care may also be whether the exercise of the power in question involves the incurring of risks or liabilities or the expenditure (or foregoing) of money which would otherwise be available for the potential repayment of the mortgage.

13–028   An example of the existence of a conflict between the interests of chargor and chargee so as to exclude a duty of care is to be seen in the exercise of the contractual power of appointment of a receiver. The very appointment of a receiver involves an inherent conflict of interest, involving as it does the replacement of the directors, as managers of the mortgagor's property, by the debenture-holder's chosen appointee. In such a situation, in the absence of some qualification in the debenture, the debenture-holder is entitled to look only to his own interests. So long as he acts in good faith, if he considers that the appointment will serve his best interests he is under no duty to refrain from doing so because such an appointment will frustrate advanced negotiations to re-finance the company or will cause loss to the company or its unsecured creditors.[63]

13–029   But whilst a mortgagee may owe no duty of care in making the decision whether and if so when to appoint, if the power to appoint a receiver is exercised, it is in the interest of both mortgagee and mortgagor that care should be taken to ensure that a competent and qualified person is appointed. Hence a duty of care may be owed to ensure the appointment of a competent professional.[64]

13–030   As indicated above, a mortgagee has no duty at any time to exercise his powers as a mortgagee, to take possession or to appoint a receiver and preserve the security[65] or its value[66] or to realise or exploit his security, e.g. by selling securities before they become valueless.[67] The mortgagee is free to exercise the

---

[63] *Re Potters Oils Ltd (No.2)* [1986] 1 W.L.R. 201.
[64] *Shamji v Johnson Matthey Bankers Ltd* [1991] B.C.L.C. 36 (CA), 42. The requirement that an administrative receiver has to be a qualified insolvency practitioner to be eligible for appointment under the Insolvency Act 1986 suggests that this duty will usually be satisfied by the appointment of such a person.
[65] *AIB Finance v Debtors* [1998] 2 All E.R. 929 (CA).
[66] *Yorkshire Bank Plc v Hall* [1999] 1 W.L.R. 1713 (CA).
[67] *China and South Sea Bank Ltd v Tan Soon Gin* [1990] 1 A.C. 536 (PC).

rights and remedies available to him "simultaneously or contemporaneously or successively or not at all".[68] But once the decision has been taken by the mortgagee to exercise his power to appoint a receiver, then, provided that action would not damage the interests of the debenture-holder,[69] the receiver has no right to remain passive if this would damage the interests of the company as mortgagor.[70] The receiver has the power to manage independent of the power to sell[71] and provided that the debenture-holder is not prejudiced, the receiver must be active in the protection and preservation of the charged property over which he has been appointed. Accordingly, the receiver of a reversion upon a lease may be liable at the instance of the mortgagor and the mortgagee for the respective loss occasioned to them by failure to inspect the lease and to trigger a rent review clause in due time.[72] But the receiver is not obliged to carry on the company's business either at the expense of the debenture-holder or at the mortgaged premises.[73]

A mortgagee is not a trustee of his power of sale and accordingly can be under no duty to the mortgagor to exercise that power.[74] A receiver is likewise under no general duty to exercise a power of sale,[75] but may be obliged to do so if a failure to do so would cause loss to the mortgagee and mortgagor (e.g. by the goods in question perishing).   **13–031**

Having determined to exercise a power of sale, subject to one qualification, the mortgagee and receiver are entitled to choose their own time for that sale.[76] This means that they are not obliged to defer a sale until an expected rise in the market is realised[77] or until after the company has had the opportunity to redeem the mortgage,[78] or until after making an application for planning permission[79] or until after the outcome of such an application is known. The one qualification is that apart from cases where there is a need for an urgent   **13–032**

---

[68] *China and South Sea Bank Ltd v Tan Soon Gin* [1990] 1 A.C. 536 (PC), 545, quoted with approval by Callinan J. in *Pan Foods v ANZ Bank* (2000) 170 A.L.R. 579, 592, [61].

[69] The debenture-holder may, of course, be required to give his consent as holder of security to disposals by the receiver of charged assets.

[70] *Silven Properties Ltd v Royal Bank of Scotland Plc* [2004] 1 W.L.R. 997 (CA), [23], approving a statement to this effect in the third edition of this book.

[71] *Medforth v Blake* [2000] Ch. 86, 103A (CA).

[72] *Knight v Lawrence* [1991] B.C.C. 411, cited with approval in *Medforth v Blake* [2000] Ch. 86 (CA), 99F.

[73] *Medforth v Blake* [2000] Ch. 86 (CA), 102G–H; *Expo International Pty Ltd v Chant* [1979] 2 N.S.W.L.R. 820, 841–842.

[74] *Bishop v Bonham* [1988] 1 W.L.R. 742 (CA), 749, citing *Cuckmere Brick v Mutual Finance* [1971] Ch. 949 (CA), 965–966.

[75] *Routestone Ltd v Minories Finance Ltd* [1997] B.C.C. 180, 187G.

[76] *Silven Properties Ltd v Royal Bank of Scotland Plc* [2004] 1 W.L.R. 997 (CA); *Cuckmere Brick v Mutual Finance* [1971] Ch. 949 (CA), 965G–966A; *Reliance Permanent Building Society v Harwood-Stamper* [1944] Ch. 362, 372; and *Bank of Cyprus (London) Ltd v Gill* [1980] 2 Lloyd's Rep. 51 (CA). Compare the analogous duty of a vendor who sues for damages for breach of contract to mitigate damages, a duty which does not extend to nursing the land as a speculative builder and to sell it off gradually: see *Keck v Faber Jellett and Keeble* (1915) 60 Sol.J. 378.

[77] *Cuckmere Brick v Mutual Finance* [1971] Ch. 949 (CA); *China and South Sea Bank Ltd v Tan Soon Gin* [1990] 1 A.C. 536 (PC). See also *Henry Roach (Petroleum) Pty Ltd v Credit House (Vic) Pty Ltd* [1976] V.R. 309, 313, and *Pendlebury v Colonial Mutual Life Assurance Society Ltd* (1912) 13 C.L.R. 676, 701.

[78] *Routestone Ltd v Minories Finance Ltd* [1997] B.C.C. 180.

[79] *Silven Properties Ltd v Royal Bank of Scotland Plc* [2004] 1 W.L.R. 997 (CA).

sale (e.g. where the goods are perishable) they must fairly and properly expose the property to the market or sell at a price which is based upon such exposure.[80] It has been suggested that elementary common sense and fairness may require them to avoid selling at the worst possible moment for the mortgagor,[81] though it is doubtful whether this is consistent with the authorities discussed above. The position would be otherwise where the sale was conducted under such adverse market conditions as to suggest the existence of bad faith, particularly when postponing the sale would have caused no appreciable harm to the mortgagee's interests.

13–033   Where there is a market for the asset in question, the duty to take reasonable care to obtain the best price reasonably obtainable[82] will usually require a sale to be made at the current market value.[83] The mortgagee or receiver is accordingly obliged to make reasonable and proper arrangements to expose the property to the market and to achieve the sale itself. While mortgagees and receivers have a degree of latitude not only as to the timing of the sale but also the method of sale to be employed, the asset must be properly marketed in whatever way is appropriate to that method of sale.[84] The duty to take care to obtain the best price reasonably obtainable may be breached, for example, where the condition of the property is not assessed in an appropriate way as a prelude to advertising,[85] if advertisements for the property are placed too late,[86] or in an obscure newspaper, or omit the fact that the property has the benefit of a valuable planning permission, or that its value could be increased by obtaining planning permission or by granting a lease,[87] or if inquiries from interested parties are not responded to in an appropriate manner.[88] Likewise the duty may

---

[80] *Predeth v Castle Phillips Finance Co Ltd* [1986] 2 E.G.L.R. 144 (CA), 148D, per Ralph Gibson L.J. Similarly, while mortgagees and receivers are given a degree of latitude as to the method of sale to be employed, once the method of sale is chosen the property must be properly marketed in whatever way is appropriate to the method of sale: see *Bell v Long* [2008] 2 B.C.L.C. 706, [17], where Patten J. held that the receivers were not in breach of duty for electing to sell four properties as a portfolio and to discontinue marketing each property for sale on an individual basis.

[81] Per Lord Denning M.R. in *Standard Chartered Bank v Walker* [1982] 1 W.L.R. 1410 (CA). This may be particularly important where there are drastic seasonal fluctuations in price, as in some agricultural situations. In *McGowan v Gannas* [1983] I.L.R.M. 516, Carrol J. posed, but left unanswered, the question whether a receiver, who knows that the market is very bad, is entitled to go ahead and sell at a bargain price.

[82] *Cuckmere Brick v Mutual Finance* [1971] Ch. 949 (CA).

[83] *China and South Sea Bank Ltd v Tan Soon Gin* [1990] 1 A.C. 536 (PC), 545, cited with approval in *Palk v Mortgage Services Funding Plc* [1993] Ch. 330 (CA), 337. See further s.420A(1) of the Australian Corporations Law and s.19 of the New Zealand Receiverships Act 1993, which reflect the distinction between market value and the best price reasonably obtainable. For an illustration of circumstances in which the market was not tested, but where the best price reasonably obtainable was secured, see *Re Blastclean Services Ltd* (1985) 2 N.Z.C.L.C. 99,282.

[84] *Bell v Long* [2008] 2 B.C.L.C. 706, [17]. In that case, the defendant receivers were held not to have breached their duty where they had elected to sell four properties as an investment portfolio having previously marketed each property for sale on an individual basis.

[85] *Dean v Barclays Bank Plc* [2007] EWHC 1390 (Ch) (no breach of duty found on the facts).

[86] See, e.g. *Bishop v Blake* [2006] 17 E.G. 113 (C.S.), particularly [105] et seq.

[87] *Silven Properties Ltd v Royal Bank of Scotland Plc* [2004] 1 W.L.R. 997 (CA), [20].

[88] See, e.g. *Silven Properties Ltd v Royal Bank of Scotland Plc* [2004] 1 W.L.R. 997 (CA); *American Express International Banking Corp v Hurley* [1985] 3 All E.R. 564; *Commercial & General Acceptance Ltd v Nixon* (1981) 152 C.L.R. 491 (High Court of Australia); *Davy v Nathan Securities Ltd* (1989) 4 N.Z.C.L.C. 65,321.

be broken if the receiver or mortgagee selects an inappropriate method of sale by private treaty rather than some form of public auction or following a public tender process. Where the property in question is a cause of action, the receiver would be well advised before selling it to invite bids for the cause of action from the party against whom it may lie, since in the ordinary case this is likely to be fairer and more advantageous to all those interested in the debtor company's undertaking.[89] The question whether appropriate value has been obtained for the property is a commercial one, to be viewed in practical commercial terms, so that, for example, if a side-benefit is being procured for the mortgagor which is additional to the stated price, that is part of the commercial context against which the question must be answered.[90]

In *Palk v Mortgage Services Funding Plc*[91] (*Palk*) the Court of Appeal left **13–034** open the question whether a mortgagee can, instead of selling, lease the property in such a way that the accruing interest exceeds the rent and substantially increases the burden on the mortgagor. It is suggested that, as was evident on the facts of that case, the interests of mortgagor and mortgagee in such a case may well be in conflict. The mortgagor would wish there to be an order for sale of his house in order to stop interest accruing on most of the mortgage debt, but the mortgagee might not wish the house to be sold until the property market improved. If such a conflict exists, it is suggested that a decision not to sell could only constitute a breach of duty by the mortgagee if it is so improvident as to be indicative of a lack of good faith on his part. But where a mortgagee intends to act in such a way that the refusal to sell exposes the mortgagor to a risk of loss disproportionate to any gain to the mortgagee, the court may, in its discretion, order the sale of the property at the suit of the mortgagor pursuant to s.91(2) of the Law of Property Act 1925 (which expressly applies to actions for foreclosure, redemption or sale). This is not the same as imposing an independent duty upon the mortgagee which would give rise to a reduction in the secured debt or in an obligation to pay compensation in equity.

(b)   A general duty of fairness?

In the Court of Appeal in *Palk*, Nicholls V.C. made a number of observations, **13–035** obiter, as to the duties which a mortgagee owes to a mortgagor. He stated:

> ". . . in the exercise of his rights over his security the mortgagee must act fairly towards the mortgagor. His interest in the property has priority over the interest of the mortgagor, and he is entitled to proceed on that footing. He can protect his own interest, but he is not entitled to conduct himself in a way which unfairly prejudices the mortgagor. If he takes possession, he might prefer to do nothing and bide his time, waiting indefinitely for an improvement in the market, with the property empty meanwhile. That

---

[89] *Hopkins v TL Dallas Group Ltd* [2005] 1 B.C.L.C. 543, particularly [105] (a case concerning a liquidator).
[90] *Apple Fields Ltd v Damesh Holdings Ltd* [2004] 1 N.Z.L.R. 721 (PC), [24].
[91] *Palk v Mortgage Services Funding Plc* [1993] Ch. 330 (CA).

he cannot do. He is accountable for his actual receipts from the property. He is also accountable to the mortgagor for what he would have received but for his default. So he must take reasonable care of the property. Similarly if he sells the property; he cannot sell hastily at a knockdown price sufficient to pay off his debt. The mortgagor also has an interest in the property and is under a personal liability for the shortfall. The mortgagee must keep that in mind. He must exercise reasonable care to sell only at the proper market value . . ."

13–036   Nicholls V.C. then expressed the view, again obiter, that the mortgagee's duties in and about the exercise of his powers of letting and sale should not be confined to the duty to obtain a proper market rent or a proper market price, and concluded:

". . . quite apart from section 91(2) there is a legal framework which imposes some constraints of fairness on a mortgagee who is exercising his remedies over his security."

13–037   Reference can also be made to similar comments by Scott V.C. in his judgment in *Medforth*. Scott V.C. did not refer to the decision in *Palk*, albeit that it was cited to the Court of Appeal, but he did make a passing reference to the fact that the equitable duties which were imposed upon a mortgagee were "introduced in order to ensure that a mortgagee dealt fairly and equitably with the mortgagor."

13–038   It is suggested that when read in context, the remarks of Nicholls V.C. in *Palk* and Scott V.C. in *Medforth* were not intended to establish a free-standing duty upon a mortgagee to act fairly to a mortgagor in all circumstances, or a new basis upon which a mortgagor could seek to challenge the conduct of a mortgagee or receiver on the grounds of "unfair prejudice" to his interests. Were there to be such a free-standing duty to act fairly, it would subsume (and render redundant) the established free-standing duties to act in good faith and to act with due care. The remarks in *Palk* and *Medforth* are to be understood as setting out the core aim of Equity of achieving a fair balance between the interests of the mortgagor and mortgagee. Equity achieves this result: (1) by imposing the free-standing duty to act in good faith; (2) (where to do so does not interfere with the right of the mortgagee to have regard exclusively to his own interests) by imposing the free-standing duty to act with due care and regard for the interests of the mortgagor; and (3) by requiring the court to take into account the question of fairness when any question arises as to the exercise of a discretion, e.g. whether to order a sale of mortgaged property at the instance of the mortgagor against the wishes of the mortgagee.

5.   THE CONTENT OF THE DUTY OF CARE

13–039   A mortgagee or receiver is only to be adjudged negligent if he has acted as no mortgagee or receiver of ordinary competence acting with ordinary care and (where appropriate) on competent advice would act. In deciding whether he has fallen short of his duty, the facts must be looked at broadly and he will not be adjudged to be in default unless he is plainly on the wrong side of the line. Thus, if two or more alternative courses of action are available, there is no negligence if the course taken might have commended itself to a competent mortgagee or receiver, even though subsequent events show that it was in fact the "wrong" course.[92] However, the receiver or mortgagee would not escape liability simply by showing that some other receivers or mortgagees would have acted as he has. Rather, the receiver or mortgagee must have acted consistently with a practice that is respectable, responsible and reasonable, and which has a logical basis.[93]

No allowance will be made for lack of experience or expertise on the part of the mortgagee or receiver.[94] But the failure to seek expert advice may in certain circumstances constitute negligence.[95] Thus, the sale of sound and lighting equipment for use at concerts of popular music, being of a specialist nature, has been held to require specialist advice from a person knowledgeable about the popular music industry.[96] Equally, in the case of a sale of land it is likely to be appropriate for a mortgagee or receiver to obtain and pay due regard to expert professional advice.   **13–040**

What is the position if proper care is taken to select and instruct such an expert, the advice of such expert is obtained and quite reasonably accepted and acted on, but such advice is subsequently found to be both wrong and negligent? Is the mortgagee or receiver liable to the mortgagor despite the absence of any personal fault? Who should bear the risk of such negligence?   **13–041**

The question whether the mortgagee is liable in these circumstances was long a subject of some uncertainty. It was considered by the members of the Court of Appeal in the case of *Cuckmere Brick*, but only decided by Cross L.J. who in his judgment said as follows: **13–042**

"[Counsel for the mortgagee] further submitted that even if we should be of opinion that a mortgagee was liable to account to the mortgagor for loss occasioned by his own negligence in the exercise of his power of sale, it was not right that he should be liable for the negligence of an agent reasonably employed by him ... I do not accept the submission. In

---

[92] Consider *Maynard v West Midland Regional Health Authority* [1984] 1 W.L.R. 634 (HL), 638.

[93] This paragraph in the previous edition of this work was described as "an accurate and succinct statement of the law" by Kenneth Parker J. in *R. (on the application of Glatt) v Sinclair* [2011] Lloyd's Rep. F.C. 140, [9]. See *Bolitho v Hackney Health Authority* [1998] A.C. 232 (HL); and see further, A. Dugdale and M. Jones, *Clerk & Lindsell on Torts*, 19th edn (London: Sweet & Maxwell, 2006), para.15–63, as supplemented (2009).

[94] See A. Dugdale and M. Jones, *Clerk & Lindsell on Torts*, 19th edn (London: Sweet & Maxwell, 2006), Ch.10, as supplemented (2009).

[95] "It may well be right that in most cases for a liquidator to sell an asset of the company without a proper valuation would amount to negligence, but I do not think that that is something which can be laid down as a general rule": per Nourse J. in *Pitman & Co v Top Business Systems (Nottingham) Ltd* [1984] B.C.L.C. 593, 597d–597e.

[96] *American Express Banking Corp v Hurley* [1985] 3 All E.R. 564, where Mann J. held the receiver negligent in failing: (1) to obtain such advice; and (2) to advertise the sale in publications concerning the popular music industry.

support of it, counsel pointed out that a trustee is not liable for the default
of an agent whom it is reasonable for him to employ. But the position of a
mortgagee is quite different from that of a trustee. A trustee has not, qua
trustee, any interest in the trust property,[97] and if an agent employed by
him is negligent his right of action against the agent is an asset of the trust.
A mortgagee, on the other hand, is not a trustee and if he sues the agent
for negligence any damages which he can recover belong to him.[98] Of
course in many cases the mortgagee may suffer no damage himself by
reason of the agent's negligence because the purchase price, though less
than it should have been, exceeds what is owing to the mortgagee. In
such circumstances it may be that nowadays the law would allow the
mortgagor to recover damages directly from the agent although not in
contractual relations with him; but that was certainly not so 100 years ago
when *Wolff v Vanderzee*[99] was decided. In those days the only way to
achieve justice between the parties was to say that the mortgagee was
liable to the mortgagor for any damage which the latter suffered by the
agent's negligence and to leave the mortgagee to recover such damages,
and also any damage which he has suffered himself, from the agent. I do
not think that we can say that the mortgagee used to be liable to the mortgagor for the negligence of his agent, but that that liability disappeared at
some unspecified moment of time when the law had developed enough to
allow the mortgagor to sue the agent himself. In my judgment, therefore,
if either the [defendant mortgagees] or [the agents] were guilty of negligence in connection with the sale, the defendants are liable to compensate
the plaintiffs [mortgagors] for any damage they have suffered by reason
of that negligence."[100]

The other members of the court found it unnecessary to decide the question,
because in the court below the mortgagees had conceded that they were liable
for any negligence of their agents. But Salmon L.J.[101] did say that the argument
against liability "certainly could not be squared with Cotton L.J.'s judgment in
Tomlin v Luce" and Cairns L.J.[102] stated that, if the point were open to the
defendants, "I should need more argument to satisfy me that Kekewich J. and
Cotton L.J. [in *Tomlin v Luce*][103] were wrong".

---

[97] i.e. beneficial interest. A trustee has of course his right to a trustee's lien.

[98] Whilst the mortgagee cannot claim more than his own loss (see per Aickin J. in *Commercial
& General Acceptance Ltd v Nixon* (1981) 152 C.L.R. 491 (High Court of Australia)), his loss
includes any liability to the mortgagor, and accordingly the imposition of a strict liability on the
mortgagee ensures that the full difference between the price obtained and the price that should
have been obtained is recovered.

[99] *Wolff v Vanderzee* (1869) 20 L.T. 350. In that case, Stuart V.C. held that a mortgagee was
accountable to the mortgagor for the loss in purchase price occasioned by the auctioneer describing
the property as let at £150 per annum when in fact it was let at £182.

[100] *Cuckmere Brick Co Ltd v Mutual Finance Ltd* [1971] Ch. 949 (CA), 973.

[101] *Cuckmere Brick Co Ltd v Mutual Finance Ltd* [1971] Ch. 949 (CA), 969.

[102] *Cuckmere Brick Co Ltd v Mutual Finance Ltd* [1971] Ch. 949 (CA), 980.

[103] Kekewich J. at *Tomlin v Luce* (1889) L.R. 41 Ch. D. 573 held that a first mortgagee was
liable to account for the loss occasioned to the second mortgagee by the auctioneer misdescribing
the roads on the property as completely kerbed, which led to the allowance of compensation to the

The approach adopted by Cross L.J. creates a form of strict liability on the **13–043**
mortgagee. His duty of care to sell at the best price reasonably obtainable is not
delegable in the sense that he can avoid or perform his duty merely by
appointing a reputable agent to conduct the sale, but extends to ensuring that
reasonable care is taken by any agent or professional adviser employed by him
in the sale. The extension of his duty may be an accident of history, but it
promotes justice for the mortgagor who is thereby saved from the invidious,
and often difficult, task of apportioning blame between the mortgagee and his
agents and can also claim credit for any loss when settling accounts with the
mortgagee.[104] Moreover, the mortgagee can be assumed to be better placed to
know the facts relating to a claim against the agent[105] and is frequently in a
better financial position to pursue the claim, and ultimately it must be remembered that it was the mortgagee who chose the agent who was later negligent.[106] Once the special rule applicable to mortgagees is accepted, there is no
sufficient reason to distinguish the position of the mortgagee and that of the
receiver,[107] and it would therefore appear that a receiver is subject to a like
strict liability in respect of disposals.[108] The logic of the Court of Appeal's
decision in *Medforth* dictates that similarly strict principles also be applied to
the negligence of agents in situations other than disposals of the charged
property.[109]

---

purchaser. His judgment was challenged, not on liability, but on quantum. The challenge was
successful, but the Court of Appeal proceeded on the basis that the finding of liability was correct:
Tomlin v Luce (1890) L.R.43 Ch. D. 191 (CA). The judgment of the Court of Appeal was referred
to with apparent approval in *Downsview* at 312 and *Medforth* at 934D–E as deciding that a mortgagee is liable for the loss occasioned by a misstatement by his appointed auctioneer. The judgment of Kekewich J. drew a distinction between errors in matters of detail (for which a mortgagee
was not liable) and serious blunders (for which he was liable), but it is suggested that the proper
distinction is between errors that amount to negligence and errors that do not: see per Gibbs C.J.
in *Commercial & General Acceptance Ltd v Nixon* (1981) 152 C.L.R. 491 (High Court of
Australia), 497 and per Aickin J., 511.

[104] This is the approach adopted in relation to an equivalent statutory duty in *Commercial &
General Acceptance Ltd v Nixon* (1981) 152 C.L.R. 491 (High Court of Australia).

[105] "For a mortgagor to sue an agent in circumstances where there has been no prior relationship
between them and he cannot know the instructions that were given by the mortgagee could be an
exercise fraught with difficulty": per Wilson J. in *Commercial & General Acceptance Ltd v Nixon*
(1981) 152 C.L.R. 491 (High Court of Australia), 520 and see per Mason J., 505.

[106] This factor was adverted to as relevant to the question whether the duty was "delegable" or
not by Lord Radcliffe in *Riverstone Meat v Lancashire Shipping* [1961] A.C. 807 (HL), 863. For a
consideration of the scope of delegable and non-delegable duties in tort, see, e.g. J. Murphy, *Street
on Torts*, 12th edn (Oxford: Oxford University Press, 2007), pp.599–602. The alternative would be
to liken the liability of the mortgagee to that of a solicitor who does not abdicate all responsibility
by acting on the advice of counsel, but is normally protected if he does: *Davy-Chiesman v Davy-
Chiesman* [1984] Fam. 48 (CA). A similar strict duty is imposed by statute on building societies
(see *Reliance Permanent Building Society v Harwood-Stamper* [1944] Ch. 362, 372) and on all
mortgagees in Queensland: see *Commercial & General Acceptance Ltd v Nixon* (1981) 152 C.L.R.
491, above. Consider also *Austin Securities Ltd v Northgate and English Stores Ltd* [1969] 1
W.L.R. 529 (CA) (liquidator cannot shelter behind mistakes of solicitor).

[107] The receiver may readily be assumed to be protected by an insurance policy covering such a
claim, as to the potential relevance of which see *Smith v Eric S. Bush* [1990] 1 A.C. 831 (HL),
858–859.

[108] *Medforth* [2000] Ch. 86 (CA), 99F, citing *Tomlin v Luce* (1890) L.R. 43 Ch. D. 191 (CA).

[109] This paragraph in a previous edition of this work was approved in *Raja v Austin Gray* [2003]
B.P.I.R. 725 (CA), [34]–[35] by Clarke L.J., with whom the other members of the Court of Appeal
agreed. See further at [62], per Peter Gibson L.J.; *Francis v Barclays Bank Plc* [2005] P.N.L.R. 18

6. THE SELF-DEALING AND FAIR-DEALING RULES

13–044   These two rules impose constraints upon sales (and other dealings) by a mort-gagee and receiver. Mortgagees and receivers both owe fiduciary duties.[110] A trustee (a term which includes a trustee for debenture-holders)[111] is subject to a very strict "self-dealing" rule to the effect that he will not be allowed to enter into a transaction in which he has a personal interest which may conflict with his duty unless he has the informed consent of all of the beneficiaries or the leave of the court.[112] A receiver is subject to a like duty and is accordingly disqualified from purchasing charged property from the mortgagee[113] and (in the case of a receiver appointed by trustees for debenture-holders) from purchasing debentures from debenture-holders without the leave of the court. Mortgagees are, however, subject to less severe restrictions[114]:

(a) a strict but very limited "self-dealing" rule whereby a mortgagee may not sell to himself or to a trustee for himself[115]; and

(b) a "fair dealing" rule whereby a conflict of interest makes a sale void-able (or the subject of a claim to damages) unless it can be shown (the onus being on the mortgagee or purchaser) that the sale was at full market value.

It is considered that where a receiver sells as agent of the mortgagor to a company in which the mortgagee has an interest: (1) the self-dealing rule does not apply, since there are two real parties to the transaction; and (2) the fair dealing rule is applicable on the basis that the receivership sale involves the exercise of the mortgagee's remedies. To be absolutely safe in such a case, the mortgagee can seek a sale by the court.

13–045   The case of *Tse Kwong Lam v Wong Chit Sen*[116] is illuminating as to the application of these rules and the nature and extent of the duties of a mortgagee and the remedies available to a mortgagor. The mortgagee sold the mortgaged property at auction at an undervalue to a company of which he was a director and shareholder and of which the remaining directors and shareholders were his wife and children. The mortgagor sought to set aside the sale and in the alternative claimed damages. The Privy Council held that:

---

and *Bell v Long* [2008] 2 B.C.L.C. 706, 709, [5], [7]. In *Bell v Long* the defendant receivers sought to protect themselves against possible liability by issuing a claim for indemnity under CPR Pt 20 against the selling agents.

[110] *Watts v Midland Bank* (1986) 2 B.C.C. 98961, 98967.

[111] *Re Magadi Soda Co* (1925) 94 L.J. Ch. 217.

[112] *Tito v Waddell (No.2)* [1977] Ch. 106; *Re Thompson's Settlement* [1986] Ch. 99.

[113] *Nugent v Nugent* [1908] 1 Ch. 546 (CA) (purchase from mortgagee).

[114] *Farrar v Farrar's Ltd* (1888) L.R. 40 Ch. D. 395 (CA); *Tse Kwong Lam v Wong Chit Sen* [1983] 1 W.L.R. 1349 (PC); *Movitex v Bulfield* (1986) 2 B.C.C. 99403; *Mortgage Express v Mardner* [2004] EWCA Civ 1859; *Bradford & Bingley Plc v Ross* (2005) 102(19) L.S.G. 34.

[115] There is, however, no general rule that a company in which a mortgagee is interested cannot purchase the mortgaged property on a mortgagee sale: *Apple Fields Ltd v Damesh Holdings Ltd* [2004] N.Z.L.R. 721 (PC), [25].

[116] *Tse Kwong Lam v Wong Chit Sen* [1983] 1 W.L.R. 1349 (PC).

(a) whilst a mortgagee cannot validly sell to himself, or a trustee for himself, a sale to a company in which he is interested is not necessarily invalid; but in view of the conflict of interest and duty involved, the ordinary rules regarding burden of proof are reversed, and in order to sustain the transaction and avoid a claim in damages the mortgagee and his company must affirmatively prove that reasonable care was taken to obtain the best price;

(b) the mortgagee had failed in his duty to take all reasonable steps to obtain the best price reasonably obtainable;

(c) the mortgagee was not excused from this duty or the consequences of his breach by a provision in the mortgage excluding liability for selling without first complying with the requirements as to the existence of default by the mortgagor or giving prior notice to the mortgagor;

(d) the ordinary remedy for the breach in such a case (where the purchaser was related in this way to the mortgagee) was an order setting aside the sale;

(e) such remedy was precluded by the delay of the mortgagor in seeking such a remedy, since the purchaser had meanwhile incurred substantial expenditure on the property and the grant of such a remedy would be inequitable; and

(f) damages should be awarded representing the difference between the true market value at the date of the auction and the price in fact paid.

Lord Templeman stated the law relating to the relevant duties thus: **13–046**

"The mortgagee and the company seeking to uphold the transaction must show that the sale was in good faith and that the mortgagee took reasonable precautions to obtain the best price reasonably obtainable at the time. The mortgagee is not, however, bound to postpone the sale in the hope of obtaining a better price or to adopt a piecemeal method of sale which could only be carried out over a substantial period or at some risk of loss."[117]

7.   EXCLUSION OR LIMITATION OF LIABILITY

The question arises how far (if at all) it is possible to exclude or limit a duty or   **13–047**
liability of the mortgagee or receiver. As seen above, the duty or liability will ordinarily be owed to the mortgagor and to all persons interested in the equity of redemption, including any guarantor. Although seeking and obtaining the informed consent of each member of the class affected will no doubt preclude subsequent challenge, in most cases it is unlikely to be possible to obtain such

---

[117] *Tse Kwong Lam v Wong Chit Sen* [1983] 1 W.L.R. 1349 (PC), 1355.

unanimous consent. It is a sensible precaution (where practicable) to give members notice of a proposed transaction, and thus afford an opportunity to them to make representations, but a failure to object prior to the transaction does not preclude any challenge to the transaction after it has been completed. Accordingly, it will in most cases be necessary to look at whether provisions in the mortgage or guarantee are effective to limit the duty or liability of the mortgagee or receiver.

(a) Privity of contract

13–048 A mortgage or guarantee may contain express provisions limiting the duty or liability of the mortgagee.[118] When considering whether, and if so to what extent, the mortgage or guarantee may limit the duty or liability of the receiver, who is not a party to the contract, it is necessary to have regard to the position both at common law and under statute.

13–049 At common law, whilst the mortgagee may obtain protection for himself, the established principles of privity of contract[119] continue to preclude the conferment of any direct exemption on third parties, e.g. any prospective receiver.[120] They equally preclude the recognition by English law of any doctrine of vicarious immunity, i.e. that an agent performing a contract for his principal is entitled to any immunity from liability which the contract confers on the principal.[121] But the law of contract recognises at least four possible indirect methods of securing the protection of the receiver which may be reflected in a provision in the mortgage or guarantee[122]:

   (a) the mortgagee expressly contracting as agent for any such receiver (an agency which may be previously authorised or subsequently ratified) may exact from the mortgagor or guarantor a term limiting the duty or liability of the receiver[123];

---

[118] *Bishop v Bonham* [1988] 1 W.L.R. 742 (CA), 752. An exemption clause in a mortgage exempting a mortgagee from liability for a receiver's default will not bind a guarantor under a separate instrument: *McManus v Royal Bank* (1983) 47 C.B.R. (N.S.) 252, 257.

[119] Which may not survive in their current form if reviewed by the Supreme Court and Privy Council: see *The Mahkutai* [1996] A.C. 650 (PC), 664–665.

[120] See H. Beale, *Chitty on Contracts*, 30th edn (London: Sweet & Maxwell, 2008), Vol.1, para.14–042. The common law position is, however, affected by s.3 of the Contracts (Rights of Third Parties) Act 1999.

[121] *Scruttons v Midland Silicones* [1962] A.C. 446 (HL). A contract may confer immunity against claims in tort by third parties in exceptional circumstances: *Leigh & Sillivan Ltd v Aliakmon Shipping Co Ltd* [1985] Q.B. 350 (CA), 397, approved in *White v Jones* [1995] 2 A.C. 207 (HL), 239, per Steyn L.J.; *Southern Water Authority v Carey* [1985] 2 All E.R. 1077; *Norwich City Council v Harvey* [1989] 1 W.L.R. 828 (CA), 837.

[122] See generally J.Beatson, *Anson's Law of Contract*, 29th edn (Oxford: Oxford University Press, 2010), pp.645–651.

[123] See J. Beatson, *Anson's Law of Contract*, 29th edn (Oxford: Oxford University Press, 2010), pp.647–649. In *Expo International Pty Ltd v Chant* [1979] 2 N.S.W.L.R. 820, Needham J. held that such a provision was ineffective if the identity of the receiver was unknown at the date of the mortgage. Consider, however, *Port Jackson Stevedoring Pty Ltd v Salmond & Spraggon (Australia) Pty Ltd* [1981] 1 W.L.R. 138 (PC).

(b) the mortgagor or guarantor may agree with the mortgagee not to sue the receiver (which agreement the mortgagee can enforce for the benefit of the receiver)[124];

(c) (in a case where the mortgagee assumes an obligation to indemnify the receiver) the mortgagor or guarantor may agree to pay over all the proceeds of a claim against the receiver to the mortgagee; or

(d) the mortgage or guarantee may contain a provision expressly authorising the mortgagee acting as agent for the mortgagor or guarantor to agree with the receiver as a term of his appointment that, in consideration of his acceptance of the appointment, the duty or liability of the receiver to the mortgagor or guarantor shall be restricted.

English common law was fundamentally changed by the Contracts (Rights of Third Parties) Act 1999, which came into force on November 11, 1999 and applies to contracts entered into at least six months after that date (i.e. after May 11, 2000) or (if entered into earlier) which expressly provide for the application of the Act. Section 1 of the Act provides that a person not a party to a contract (a "third party") may in his own right enforce a term of the contract if the contract expressly provides that he may or (unless on a proper construction of the contract it appears that the parties did not intend the term to be enforceable by the third party) the term purports to confer a benefit on him.[125] The third party must be expressly identified in the contract by name, as a member of a class or as answering a particular description, but need not be in existence when the contract is entered into. Accordingly, protection can be conferred both on the mortgagee and on any receiver if and when appointed by the mortgagee. **13–050**

(b) Construction of exemption clause

Once it is clear that an exemption provision on which the mortgagee or receiver is entitled to rely has been included in the instrument, the next question is whether, as a matter of construction, the provision covers the breach of duty.[126] If the language of the agreement reasonably admits of two constructions, one giving a wider and the other a narrower scope for application of the exemption clause, the contra proferentem rule will be applied and the construction adopted **13–051**

---

[124] *Snelling v John G. Snelling Ltd* [1973] Q.B. 87. See also *The Elbe Maru* [1978] 1 Lloyd's Rep. 206; and *The Chevalier Roze* [1983] 2 Lloyd's Rep. 438, 443 (need for real possibility of prejudice to mortgagor or guarantor).

[125] For a full consideration of the provisions of the Contract (Rights of Third Parties) Act 1999, see H. Beale, *Chitty on Contracts*, 30th edn (London: Sweet & Maxwell, 2008, and the 2nd Cumulative Supplement to the 30th edn, 2011), Vol.1, paras 18–088 to 18–120; E.Peel, *Treitel on the Law of Contract*, 12th edn (London: Sweet & Maxwell, 2007), paras 14–095 to 14–127; J. Beatson, *Anson's Law of Contract*, 29th edn (Oxford: Oxford University Press, 2010), pp.624–635.

[126] For the general principles governing the construction of exemption clauses, see H. Beale, *Chitty on Contracts*, 30th edn (London: Sweet & Maxwell, 2008, and the 2nd Cumulative Supplement to the 30th edn, 2011), Vol.1, paras 14–005 to 14–058.

giving the narrower scope. In other words, the exemption clause will only be effective if the words are clear and fairly susceptible of one meaning only.[127]

13–052   Hence a clause exempting a mortgagee from responsibility for loss occasioned to the mortgagor on exercise of the power of sale will not exonerate a mortgagee from liability for negligence to the mortgagor; an exclusion of liability for negligence must be expressly conferred.[128] A clause giving protection against liability for sales made before the power of sale has become exercisable will not extend to claims in respect of a failure to exercise due care to obtain the best price obtainable.[129] And a provision that the receiver shall be deemed the agent of the mortgagor who shall be solely responsible for his defaults will not exclude liability of the mortgagee for defaults of the receiver occasioned by the directions of the mortgagee.[130]

13–053   The contra proferentem rule applies both to clauses excluding liability and to clauses limiting the amount of damages recoverable (albeit less strictly in the latter case).[131] However, it is not permissible to adopt a strained construction to prevent a party in default relying on either type of clause, and such a clause may afford protection if sufficiently widely drawn, even in the case of a fundamental breach of contract.[132]

(c)   Unfair Contract Terms Act 1977 (UCTA 1977)

13–054   Unfair Contract Terms Act 1977 imposes two limitations on the ability to exclude or restrict liability by means of contract terms. First, it limits the extent to which civil liability for "negligence" can be avoided by means of contract terms. "Negligence" is defined as the breach of any obligation, arising from the express or implied terms of the contract or from any common law duty to take reasonable care or exercise reasonable skill. Secondly, it limits the extent to which a person who has contracted on his written standard terms of business can exclude or restrict liability for breach of contract or render a contractual performance substantially different from that which was reasonably expected of him.

13–055   At the date of an earlier edition of this work, the view that mortgagees and receivers owed common law duties of care was in the process of being displaced by recognition of the duties as equitable. The opinion was expressed that for this reason UCTA 1977 had no application, but as a matter of caution, in case this view proved wrong, there was some detailed consideration of UCTA 1977.

---

[127] The same strict construction is applicable to indemnity clauses: *R. v Canada Steamship Lines* [1952] A.C. 192 (PC), 208.

[128] *Bishop v Bonham* [1988] 1 W.L.R. 742 (CA), 752–756 (power to sell without liability for loss howsoever arising only authorised sale within limits of duty of care imposed by the general law and, accordingly, did not exempt from liability for loss arising from failure to take care to obtain proper price).

[129] *American Express International Banking Corp v Hurley* [1985] 3 All E.R. 564; *Bishop v Bonham* [1988] 1 W.L.R. 742 (CA).

[130] *Tse Kwong Lam v Wong Chit Sen* [1983] 1 W.L.R. 1349 (PC), 1360.

[131] *Standard Chartered Bank v Walker* [1982] 1 W.L.R. 1410 (CA).

[132] *Ailsa Craig Fishing v Malvern Fishing* [1983] 1 W.L.R. 964 (HL); *George Mitchell (Chesterhall) Ltd v Finney Lock Seeds Ltd* [1983] 2 A.C. 803 (HL).

The displacement of the earlier view is now complete[133], and it is now abundantly clear that the duties are equitable and do not arise at common law or from the express or implied terms of any contract.[134] Accordingly, it would seem clear that UCTA 1977 has no application to such clauses.[135]

8.   WRONGFUL INTERFERENCE WITH CONTRACT

Knowingly to procure or induce a party to break his contract to the damage of the other contracting party without reasonable justification or excuse is a tort.[136] The tort covers dealings with the contract-breaker which the third party knows to be inconsistent with the contract. The question raised is how far this tort has application to actions of a validly appointed receiver or a debenture-holder in repudiating contracts of the company.[137] The relevant principles would appear to be as follows: **13–056**

(a) Notwithstanding the grant of the charge or the appointment of the receiver, in the ordinary case the contract continues in force between the parties to the contract and the other party is free to bring proceedings against the company to protect or enforce the contract by way of injunction[138] or an order for specific performance of the company's obligation,[139] e.g. to buy[140] or to sell.[141] Any order so made is binding

---

[133] See above, para.13–017.

[134] See, e.g. per Robert Walker L.J. in *Yorkshire Bank Plc v Hall* [1999] 1 W.L.R. 1713 (CA), 1728D–E.

[135] Likewise it has been held that a provision in trust deeds entitling trustees to charge remuneration is not contractual: see *Re Duke of Norfolk's Settlement Trusts* [1982] Ch. 61 (CA), 77A; and that there is no statutory restriction on the breadth of exoneration clauses contained in trust deeds: see *Armitage v Nurse* [1998] Ch. 241 (CA) and Lightman J., "The Chancery Approach to Trustees' Liability" (1999) 5(1) *Journal of Pensions Management* 11–17. In her article at [2000] 63 M.L.R. 413, Frisby expresses a view that the courts might be persuaded to deal with the matter by a "de facto application of UCTA principles". It is suggested that this is unlikely given the approach adopted in relation to exoneration clauses and express trustees.

[136] *OBG Ltd v Allan* [2008] 1 A.C. 1 (HL), [39]–[44]. The following principles may be derived as to this tort: (1) the defendant must have actual subjective knowledge that he is procuring a breach of contract; (2) knowledge includes Nelsonian knowledge, that is, knowledge of facts to which one has deliberately turned a blind eye; (3) there must be an intention to procure a breach of contract; intention is present if the breach is either the defendant's end or a means to his end, but not if a breach is merely a foreseeable consequence of his actions; and (4) there must be an actual breach of contract. For discussions of this tort pre-dating the House of Lords' decision in *OBG v Allan*, see A. Dugdale and M. Jones, *Clerk & Lindsell on Torts*, 19th edn (London: Sweet & Maxwell, 2006), Ch.25, as supplemented (2009) and *Law Debenture & Trust Corp v Ural Caspian Oil Corp Ltd* [1995] Ch. 152 (CA).

[137] See *Re Botibol* [1947] 1 All E.R. 26, 28 and *Airlines Airspares v Handley Page* [1970] Ch. 193. For an account of the chapter of accidents which explain the decision in Airline Airspares, see Lightman J., "The Challenges Ahead" [1996] J.B.L. 113, 114. For the position of invalidly appointed receivers, see *OBG Ltd v Allan* [2008] 1 A.C. 1 (HL), particularly [86]–[93].

[138] *Ash & Newman Ltd v Creative Devices Research Ltd* [1991] B.C.L.C. 403 (protecting right of pre-emption).

[139] Where there is a subsisting contractual obligation capable of enforcement by an order for specific performance in the form of a mandatory injunction, the appointment of a receiver does not of itself preclude the making of an order for specific performance which otherwise ought to be made: *Land Rover Group Ltd v UPF (UK) Ltd* [2003] 2 B.C.L.C. 222.

[140] *AMEC Properties v Planning Research & Systems* [1992] B.C.L.C. 1149 (CA).

[141] *Freevale v Metrostore (Holdings) Ltd* [1984] Ch. 199.

on the company and the receiver to the extent that he acts as agent of the company, but unless the contract or obligation bound the chargee this order made enforcing the contract or obligation does not prejudice the rights of the chargee in respect of the enforcement of his security.

(b) If a person is granted a charge on property which he knows to be subject to a contractual obligation, he can be restrained from exercising his rights under the charge in such a way as to interfere with the performance of that contractual obligation.[142] The essential feature is the attachment of the contractual obligation to a specific asset or specific assets as opposed to the mere imposition of a requirement to fulfil an obligation (e.g. to make a payment or set up a fund out of the general funds of the company).[143]

(c) In the absence of such knowledge, the chargee and the receiver are free (vis-à-vis the third parties) to cause the company to repudiate or ignore its outstanding contractual obligations to third parties as long as the chargee's title is equal to or superior to the third party's rights,[144] though this course may give rise to a claim in respect of the loss occasioned by the company if involving an unnecessary and unreasonable exercise of the chargee's powers.[145]

(d) The receiver as agent for the company is equally free of liability to third parties for causing the company to breach its contracts with them,[146] for no person can be liable for the tort of interference with contractual relations if he acts as agent for one of the contracting parties.[147] A receiver appointed by the court may not

---

[142] *Swiss Bank Corp v Lloyd's Bank Ltd* [1979] Ch. 548, 571–572. See, however, *MacJordan Construction Ltd v Brookmount Erostin Ltd* [1992] B.C.L.C. 350 (CA); see also *Astor Chemical Ltd v Synthetic Technology Ltd* [1990] B.C.C. 97 and *Edwin Hill & Partners v First National Finance Corp Plc* [1989] 1 W.L.R. 225 (CA).

[143] In *MacJordan v Brookmount Erostin Ltd* [1992] B.C.L.C. 350 (CA), Scott L.J. suggested that if the grant of a floating charge will not interfere, but the grant of a fixed charge will, the relief may not be available against the grantee of a floating charge who thereafter crystallises his floating charge. This suggestion cannot be correct: the result must be the same whether the grant of the fixed charge is a one- or two-stage exercise. See also the discussion of the limits of the tort in *Law Debenture & Trust Corp v Ural Caspian Oil Corp Ltd* [1995] Ch. 152 (CA).

[144] *Edwin Hill & Partners v First National Finance Corp Plc* [1989] 1 W.L.R. 225 (CA); *Astor Chemical Ltd v Synthetic Technology Ltd* [1990] B.C.C. 97; *The Kaliningrad* [1997] 2 Lloyd's Rep. 35, 39.

[145] *Airlines Airspares v Handley Page* [1970] Ch. 193. The receiver has the power to repudiate pre-receivership contracts with impunity unless the power is exercised dishonestly or recklessly: *Re Diesels & Components Pty Ltd* (1985) 9 A.C.L.R. 825, 828, per McPherson J.

[146] *Lathia v Dronsfield Bros* [1987] B.C.L.C. 321, so long as he acts in good faith and within the scope of his authority.

[147] *Welsh Development Agency v Export Finance* [1992] B.C.C. 270 (CA). The Court of Appeal based the immunity of the receiver on English, Australian and New Zealand authority dealing with directors acting as agents of a company: *Said v Butt* [1920] 3 K.B. 497; *Scammell v Hurley* [1929] 1 K.B. 419 (CA); *DC Thomson & Co Ltd v Deakin* [1952] Ch. 646 (CA), 680–681; *O'Brien v Dawson* (1942) 66 C.L.R. 18 (High Court of Australia), 32, per Starke J. and 34, per McTiernan J.; *Rutherford v Poole* [1953] V.L.R. 130 (Court of Appeal of Victoria), 135–136; *Official Assignee v Dowling* [1964] N.Z.L.R. 578 (Supreme Court of New Zealand), 580–581. The Court of Appeal in

enjoy this exemption from liability, since he is not the agent of the company.[148]

(e) Neither the receiver nor the debenture-holder can interfere with the existing equitable rights of third parties over property of the company having priority to the charge.[149] The reason for this is that the charge attaches only to property in which the company has a beneficial interest and to the extent of that beneficial interest.[150] A threat of such action may be restrained by injunction, and it has been suggested that such action if implemented may constitute a tort and accordingly give rise to a claim in damages.[151] But this can only be so where the debenture-holder or receiver acted with notice of the existence of the relevant equitable rights.[152]

9. TRESPASS AND BREACH OF WARRANTY OF AUTHORITY

The debenture-holder and his receiver will be liable to the company in tort for **13–057** damages for the acts of the receiver in interfering with the possession of the company or dealing with its property, if the receiver is invalidly or improperly appointed.[153] The receiver will also ordinarily be liable to third parties if in the course of his receivership he takes possession of or deals with property that

---

Welsh Development Agency laid to rest doubts as to the application of such agency principles to the "unusual" agency of a receiver which had been expressed by Peter Gibson J. in *Telemetrix Plc v Modern Engineers of Bristol* (1985) 1 B.C.C. 99,417, 99,420; see also Lightman J.'s analysis of the "peculiar incidents" of the receiver's agency in *Silven Properties Ltd v Royal Bank of Scotland Plc* [2004] 1 W.L.R. 997 (CA), [27]–[28]. In *Einhorn v Westmount Investments Ltd* (1969) 6 D.L.R. (3d) 71 (affirmed (1970) 11 D.L.R. (3d) 509), it was held that directors who prevented a company from performing its contract by diverting its assets to an associated company might be liable for the tort. It is unclear whether the basis of this decision was that *Said v Butt*, above, was wrong or that the immunity of agents did not extend to directors who are in reality the masters rather than the agents of the company or that the special facts akin to sharp practice justified piercing the corporate veil. But directors are surely agents for the purpose: see *Northern Counties v Jackson & Steeple* [1974] 1 W.L.R. 1133, 1144. See also *Mancetter Developments v Garmanson* [1986] Q.B. 1212 (CA), 1223, per Kerr L.J., and *De Jetley Marks v Greenwood* [1936] 1 All E.R. 863, 872 (liability of directors in conspiracy). For the argument that "there is no general principle of agency law by which an agent is treated by the law as the alter ego of his principal . . . so that he will automatically 'drop out' and escape liability", see R. Stevens, "Why do agents 'drop out'?" [2005] L.M.C.L.Q. 101.

[148] *Telemetrix Plc v Modern Engineers of Bristol* (1985) 1 B.C.C. 99,417, explaining *Re Botibol* [1947] 1 All E.R. 26. This may also be the position of a receiver whose agency for the company has ceased on winding-up and who thereafter acts as principal.

[149] *Freevale v Metrostore* [1984] Ch. 199.

[150] *Sharp v Woolwich Building Society* [1998] B.C.C. 115 (HL).

[151] *Telemetrix Plc v Modern Engineers of Bristol* (1985) 1 B.C.C. 99,417, where Peter Gibson J. granted injunctions restraining a receiver from assigning to third parties options over land already agreed by the company to be assigned to the plaintiffs after threats by the receiver to assign to the third party.

[152] *Competitive Insurance Co Ltd v Davies Investments Ltd* [1975] 1 W.L.R. 1240.

[153] *Ford & Carter Ltd v Midland Bank Ltd* (1979) 129 N.L.J. 543 (HL); *Pollnow v Garden Mews-St. Leonards Pty Ltd* (1985) 9 A.C.L.R. 82 (Supreme Court of New South Wales). See also *OBG Ltd v Allan* [2008] 1 A.C. 1 (HL). Insolvency Act 1986, s.232, even if it applies to validate the actions taken, is unlikely to protect an administrative receiver in this context: see *OBG Ltd v Allan* [2008] 1 A.C. 1 (HL), 40–41, [89]–[91].

does not belong to the company.[154] But Insolvency Act 1986, ss.234(3) and (4) confer upon an administrative receiver exemption from such liability if, at the date of seizure or disposal, he believes and has reasonable grounds for believing that he is entitled to seize or dispose of the property and is not negligent. The provision only applies to physical property which can be seized and does not apply, for example, to book debts.[155]

13–058   Liability may also arise for breach of warranty of authority where the receiver in his dealings with a third party has purported to act as agent for the company when such agency never arose (because the receiver was never validly appointed) or has terminated (because of supervening liquidation or the appointment of a receiver by the court).[156]

10.   LIABILITY FOR OTHER TORTS

13–059   A director is not liable for torts committed by the company merely because it is his acts which are sufficient to make the company liable in tort: the mere carrying out of the duties of a director do not render a director liable. It is necessary either that he himself (and not the company through his agency) committed the tort; or that he assumed personal responsibility (not merely responsibility on behalf of his company) to the claimant for the acts constituting the tort; or that he ordered or procured the commission of tortious acts by the company.[157]

13–060   In each case, the degree of participation of the director in question must be examined and, in cases of torts containing a mental element, the state of mind and knowledge of the director must also be investigated. Accordingly a director may be liable for a breach of copyright[158] or the tort of waste[159] where the act in question was carried out on his instructions. A director will only be liable in negligence for the negligent advice given by the company if he assumed personal responsibility for that advice and the claimant relied on that assumption of responsibility.[160]

13–061   The same considerations apply in the case of claims to hold a receiver liable for torts committed by the company during his receivership. If the conduct of the receiver falls within one of the three categories above, and he has so acted at the instance of the debenture-holder, the debenture-holder will be equally liable.

---

[154] See *Re Goldburg (No.2)* [1912] 1 K.B. 606. The third party has the option of treating the receiver as his agent in order to obtain an account of profits in relation to the receiver's dealings with the third party's property: see *Re Simms* [1934] Ch. 1 (CA).
[155] *Welsh Development Agency v Export Finance Co* [1992] B.C.C. 270 (CA).
[156] *Starkey v Bank of England* [1903] A.C. 114 (HL).
[157] *Williams v Natural Life Health Foods Ltd* [1998] 1 W.L.R. 830 (HL), and see the valuable discussion in R. Grantham and C. Rickett, "Directors' Tortious Liability" (1999) 62 M.L.R. 133. However, where a director commits fraud the fact that he did so or purported to do so on behalf of the company is no defence to an action against him personally in the tort of deceit: see *Standard Chartered Bank v Pakistan National Shipping Corp (No.2)* [2003] 1 A.C. 959 (HL), [20]–[22] and [34]–[41].
[158] *C Evans & Sons Ltd v Spritebrand Ltd* [1983] Q.B. 310 (CA), 323–324, per Slade L.J.
[159] *Mancetter Developments v Garmanson* [1986] Q.B. 1212 (CA), 1217A, per Dillon L.J.
[160] *Williams v Natural Life Health Foods Ltd* [1998] 1 W.L.R. 830 (HL).

11. BREACH OF STATUTORY DUTY

Various statutory duties are imposed specifically on the debenture-holder and **13–062** the receiver. Thus, the receiver is under a duty to pay preferential creditors out of certain assets coming to his hands in priority to the debenture-holder,[161] and is personally liable to the preferential creditors if he fails to do so.[162] If in breach of this duty the receiver pays the debenture-holder, the debenture-holder comes under a statutory duty to pay the preferential creditors.[163] Other statutory duties are imposed on the company, and though a receiver is not ordinarily liable for breach of these,[164] he may be if he deliberately puts the company into breach. Any available discretion on his part ought normally to be exercised to avoid a breach which constitutes a criminal offence (e.g. non-payment of VAT).[165] Certain statutory duties are imposed on the party fulfilling a particular description, e.g. the occupier of property, and if the receiver assumes the role, then he will fall subject to the statutory duty and be liable for breach.[166]

12. THE HUMAN RIGHTS ACT 1998 (HRA 1998)

Human Rights Act 1998, s.6[167] makes it unlawful for a "public authority" to act **13–063** in a way which is incompatible with a Convention right unless precluded from acting differently by one or more provisions of, or made under, primary legislation. "Public authority" for this purpose includes any person certain of whose functions are functions of a public nature: his acts are "acts of a public authority" if the nature of the acts is not private. A "victim" of an act of a public authority committed after October 2, 2000 made unlawful by s.6 may bring proceedings against the public authority[168] claiming any relief that is just and appropriate, and this includes damages where this is necessary to afford just

---

[161] See *Standard Chartered Bank v Walker* [1982] 1 W.L.R. 1410 (CA); *American Express International Banking Corp v Hurley* [1985] 3 All E.R. 564; *HM Commissioners for Revenue and Customs v Royal Bank of Scotland Plc* [2008] B.C.C. 135 (CA).

[162] *Inland Revenue Commissioners v Goldblatt* [1972] Ch. 498; *Re H & K Medway Ltd* [1997] 1 W.L.R. 1422. See further below, para.28–040.

[163] *Woods v Winskill* [1913] 2 Ch. 303; *Westminster Corp v Haste* [1950] Ch. 442 (the period of limitation for this statutory liability runs from the date when the receiver has sufficient sums to pay the preferential creditors); *Inland Revenue Commissioners v Goldblatt* [1972] Ch. 498.

[164] e.g. the duty of an owner to maintain means of escape in case of fire in good condition: *Solomons v R Gertzenstein Ltd* [1954] 2 Q.B. 243 (CA).

[165] *Re John Willmont (Ashford) Ltd* [1980] 1 W.L.R. 73, 78A–78B; and see *Sargent v Customs and Excise Commissioners* [1995] 1 W.L.R. 821 (CA).

[166] *Meigh v Wickenden* [1942] 2 K.B. 160, a case exemplifying "the peculiar results produced by the Factories Acts": per Danckwerts L.J. in *Lawson v Hosemaster* [1966] 1 W.L.R. 1300 (CA), 1315. cf. *Liverpool Corp v Hope* [1938] 1 K.B. 751 (CA) (no liability for non-payment of rates); *Brown v City of London Corp* [1996] 1 W.L.R. 1070.

[167] For a full consideration of Human Rights Act 1998, see Lester, Pannick and Herberg, *Human Rights Law and Practice*, 3rd edn (London: LexisNexis, 2009), Beatson, Grosz, Hickman, Singh and Palmer, *Human Rights: Judicial Protection in the United Kingdom* (London: Sweet & Maxwell, 2008), and Harris, O'Boyle and Warbrick, *Law of the European Convention of Human Rights*, 2nd edn (Oxford: Oxford University Press, 2009).

[168] Human Rights Act 1998, s.7.

satisfaction.[169] The victim may also rely on a Convention right in any legal proceedings.[170]

13–064   An officer of the court[171] is clearly a "public authority" for this purpose, and it is thought that a receiver might also be a public authority in so far as he exercises certain functions as an office-holder, e.g. the investigatory powers under Insolvency Act 1986, ss.235 and 236.[172] The term "victim" requires more than that the person in question is interested in the compliance by the "public authority" with the Convention right: in the ordinary case he must be directly affected by or threatened with non-compliance, though in some cases substantial indirect effect may be sufficient.[173] Depending on the facts and circumstances, a company director, officer, creditor or shareholder may qualify as a victim. So could an innocent third party whose assets are tied up in some way with the defendant and from whose assets the receiver's lien entitles him to recover his costs and expenses[174]: given the potential injustice of the operation of this principle, it is possible that in an appropriate case art.1 of the First Protocol of the European Convention for the Protection of Human Rights and Fundamental Freedoms could limit the costs and expenses recoverable by the receiver from an innocent third party.[175]

13.   FRAUDULENT AND WRONGFUL TRADING

13–065   A receiver is subject to the law of fraudulent trading[176] in respect of the period prior to liquidation when he trades as agent for the company and may be held liable on a subsequent liquidation.[177] He will only be held liable if his personal conduct can be categorised as dishonest.[178] A receiver is not exposed to liability for wrongful trading in respect of the company of which he is the receiver, for he is not a director of the company; but if there is a hiving-down, a receiver may be at risk in respect of the subsidiary if he is a director of the subsidiary or the directors of the subsidiary act on his instructions.[179]

---

[169] Human Rights Act 1998, s.8.

[170] Human Rights Act 1998, s.7(1)(b).

[171] Such as a provisional liquidator, a liquidator in a winding-up by the court and an administrator.

[172] See above, Ch.8, paras 8–015 to 8–025.

[173] See, e.g. *Marckx v Belgium* (1979–80) 2 E.H.R.R. 330 (ECtHR), [27].

[174] *Sinclair v Glatt* [2009] 1 W.L.R. 1845 (CA), [39] (Elias L.J.).

[175] *Sinclair v Glatt* [2009] 1 W.L.R. 1845 (CA), [42] (Elias L.J., obiter).

[176] See above, Ch.2, paras 2–004 to 2–009.

[177] *Powdrill v Watson* [1995] 2 A.C. 394 (HL), 408.

[178] *Morris v Bank of India* [2005] B.C.C. 739 (CA); *Re Sobam BV* [1996] 1 W.L.R. 1070; *Re Overnight Ltd* [2010] B.C.C. 796. On the test for dishonesty in this context, see also *Barlow Clowes International Ltd v Eurotrust International Ltd* [2006] 1 W.L.R. 1476 (PC) and *Aerostar Maintenance International Ltd v Wilson* [2010] EWHC 2032 (Ch), [183]–[184].

[179] For hive-down see Ch.11 on Disposals at para.11–081 et seq. For an analysis of the concept of a shadow director, see *Secretary of State v Deverell* [2001] Ch.340 (CA) and A. Walters and M. Davis-White QC, *Directors' Disqualification and Insolvency Restrictions*, 3rd edn (London: Sweet & Maxwell, 2010), paras 3–44 to 3–69A.

14.   LIABILITY OF DEBENTURE-HOLDER FOR ACTS OF RECEIVER

In the case where the receiver is acting as agent of the debenture-holder, the   **13–066**
debenture-holder will be liable for the acts of the receiver as his agent in accordance with ordinary agency principles. If a receiver is appointed to act as agent
for the mortgagor, the exercise of the power of appointment does not of itself
render the appointor liable for the receiver's acts or omissions.[180] Accordingly,
the mortgagee is not liable if such a receiver sells at an undervalue.[181] But even
if the receiver is appointed and acts as agent of the mortgagor, the mortgagee
will be liable and responsible for the receiver's acts and defaults if the mortgagee gives directions to or puts pressure on the receiver or so interferes with
the conduct of the receivership as to prevent the exercise of independent judgment by the receiver.[182] In this case, any provision in the debenture excluding
liability of the receiver will be of no avail to the mortgagee, for the mortgagee
will be held liable personally in respect of the impugned acts as his own acts,
and not merely vicariously in respect of a liability of the receiver.

The debenture-holder has no duty to supervise the receiver and, save perhaps   **13–067**
in the case of actual knowledge or suspicion of misconduct, has no obligation
to intervene in the receivership.[183]

15.   LIABILITY OF RECEIVER IN CONTRACT

A receiver will be personally liable under contracts entered into by him except   **13–068**
in so far as the contract otherwise provides and under contracts of employment
adopted by him.[184] The statutory liability of the receiver is not analogous to
the contractual liability of a guarantor, and is not discharged by conduct
which would discharge the liability of a surety, e.g. the giving of time to the
company.[185]

16.   LIABILITY TO ACCOUNT AND PROVIDE INFORMATION

(a)   During the receivership

A non-administrative receiver is, during the receivership, under a statutory   **13–069**
duty under Insolvency Act 1986, s.38 to send accounts of receipts and payments

---

[180] The legal position is on all fours with that of a shareholder who exercises a power to appoint
a director unless he interferes with company's affairs by giving instructions to the appointee. No
liability attaches if the mortgagee merely acquiesces or with full knowledge has the opportunity to
intervene: active intervention is required: *National Bank of Greece S.A. v Pinios Shipping Co No.1*
[1990] 1 A.C. 637 (HL), 648–649, per Lloyd L.J.
[181] *Commonwealth Bank of Australia v Muirhead* [1997] 1 Qd.R. 567 (Supreme Court of
Queensland).
[182] *Medforth v Blake* [2000] Ch. 86 (CA), 95B.
[183] *National Bank of Greece S.A. v Pinios Shipping Co No.1* [1990] 1 A.C. 637 (HL), 661–662,
per Nicholls L.J.; *Downsview Nominees Ltd v First City Corp* [1993] A.C. 295 (PC), 317D–E;
Medforth v Blake [2000] Ch. 86 (CA), 94C.
[184] See below, Ch.16.
[185] See *British Airways Board v Parish* [1979] 2 Lloyd's Rep. 361 (CA).

to the Registrar of Companies. An administrative receiver has a duty under Insolvency Act 1986, s.48 to send a report to the Registrar of Companies and all creditors and (unless the court otherwise directs) to lay a copy of his report before a meeting of the company's unsecured creditors. Both types of receiver are also under an equitable duty to the company, enforceable in the name of the company by the directors or the liquidator,[186] to supply information required by the directors or liquidator to enable them to perform their duties, e.g. to file accounts and to enable the company to redeem, if it bona fide intends to do so,[187] but the equitable duty stops short of requiring the receiver to supply any information which in his judgment would be prejudicial to the debenture-holder for him to supply.[188]

(b) End of receivership

13–070   At the close of the receivership, the receiver is under a general duty to account.[189]

17. LIABILITY AS CONSTRUCTIVE TRUSTEE

13–071   If the directors of a company grant a debenture in breach of their fiduciary duties to the company and the grantee appoints a receiver, the grantee and the receiver may in certain circumstances become liable "as constructive trustees" for dishonest receipt in respect of all assets which come into their hands.[190] The current test appears to be whether the debenture-holder or receiver respectively had knowledge of such facts as would make it unconscionable for him to retain the assets received.[191]

PART II—DUTIES AND LIABILITIES OF DEBENTURE-HOLDER AND RECEIVER TO EACH OTHER

1. LIABILITY OF RECEIVER TO APPOINTOR

(a) Contract

13–072   The offer and acceptance of the appointment as receiver constitutes a contract between the appointor and the appointee. The terms of the contract may be fully set out in a written agreement which fully regulates the relationship

---

[186] *Re Photosprint Australia Pty Ltd* (2004) 212 A.L.R. 517 (Federal Court of Australia), [6].
[187] *Downsview Nominees Ltd v First City Corp* [1993] A.C. 295 (PC).
[188] *Gomba Holdings (UK) Ltd v Homan* [1986] 1 W.L.R. 1301, per Hoffmann J. To like effect. see *The Irish Oil and Cake Mills Ltd v Donnelly* Unreported March 27, 1983 (High Court of Ireland) and *Re Photosprint Australia Pty Ltd* (2004) 212 A.L.R. 517 (Federal Court of Australia), [6]. For an administrative receiver's position, see Insolvency Act 1986, s.48.
[189] *Smiths Ltd v Middleton* [1979] 3 All E.R. 842.
[190] See *Rolled Steel Products (Holdings) Ltd v British Steel Corp* [1986] Ch. 246 (CA) and above, at para.7–049.
[191] *Bank of Credit and Commerce International (Overseas) Ltd v Akindele* [2001] Ch. 437 (CA).

between the parties and defines the duties and liabilities of the receiver. There may, on the other hand, be no written document beyond the appointment itself.

In the absence of any indication to the contrary, there will be implied an **13–073** obligation on the part of the receiver to act with all reasonable skill and care.[192] This obligation subsists whether the receiver acts as agent for the mortgagor or agent for the mortgagee or in a personal capacity.[193] Any carelessness by the receiver will constitute a breach of contract entitling the appointor to sue for damages. The measure of damages will be the full loss occasioned and will not be limited to the sum required to pay off the mortgage: but if the appointor is liable to the mortgagor for the negligence of the receiver, the mortgagor will be entitled to an indemnity against this liability also. The limitation period will run from the date of the careless act or omission. In any case where the receiver is acting as agent for the appointor, and the appointor is held liable for the default of the receiver (in the absence of any express exclusion in the contract of agency), he will be entitled under an implied term of the contract of agency to an indemnity from the receiver.[194]

(b) Tort

A co-extensive duty and liability to the contractual duty of skill and care may **13–074** exist under the tort of negligence.[195] In this case, the limitation period will run from the date of damage sustained by the appointor. This will ordinarily, but not necessarily, be the same date as the act of negligence.[196]

(c) Fiduciary duty

A receiver, whether he acts as agent for the company, as agent for the deben- **13–075** ture-holder or as principal, owes to his appointor fiduciary duties in relation to the realisation of the charged assets, although he is not a full trustee of the charged assets.[197] He is duty-bound to keep the debenture-holder fully informed about the receivership.[198]

---

[192] This passage was cited with approval by the New Zealand Court of Appeal in *RA Price Securities v Henderson* [1989] 2 N.Z.L.R. 257, 261, which held that a receiver's primary duty is to recover the sums due under the debenture, a duty which the receiver was held to have overlooked in his concern to continue trading. A nominee director owes a like duty to the person nominating him: *Kuwait Asia Bank E.C. v National Mutual Life Nominees Ltd* [1991] 1 A.C. 187 (PC), 221–222.

[193] Invariably the receiver will be appointed or (in the case of an administrative receiver) be deemed to be appointed as agent of the mortgagor until liquidation.

[194] *American Express International Banking Corp v Hurley* [1985] 3 All E.R. 564.

[195] *National Bank of Greece SA v Pinios Shipping Co No.1* [1990] 1 A.C. 637 (HL), 650, 662.

[196] See the discussion in *UBAF v European American Banking Corp* [1984] Q.B. 713 (CA), referring to *Forster v Outred & Co* [1982] 1 W.L.R. 86 (CA); and *Pirelli General Cable Works Ltd v Oscar Faber & Partners* [1983] 2 A.C. 1 (HL).

[197] *Visbord v Federal Commissioner of Taxation* (1943) 68 C.L.R. 354 (High Court of Australia); *Re Magadi Soda Co* (1925) 94 L.J. Ch. 217.

[198] *Gomba Holdings v Minories Finance* (1987) 3 B.C.C. 643, 644–645; *Re Magadi Soda* (1925) 94 L.J. Ch. 217. But see above, para.8–015 et seq. in respect of information obtained under Insolvency Act 1986, ss.235 and 236.

2.   LIABILITY OF APPOINTOR TO RECEIVER

13-076   A contract collateral to the appointment may expressly confer rights on the receiver in respect of (for example) remuneration or an indemnity. The indemnity will not extend to losses or liabilities incurred as a consequence of the receiver's own negligence or default unless the appointor consented to such a breach of duty,[199] nor will it extend to conduct of the receiver which he knows constitutes a tort.[200] In default of an express provision regulating the position, the court will readily infer a warranty on the part of the appointor of his authority to make the appointment. Insolvency Act 1986, s.34, in addition, confers on the court a discretionary jurisdiction to order the appointor or person on whose behalf the appointment is made to indemnify a person appointed receiver or manager against any liability arising solely by reason of the invalidity of the appointment.[201] Further, the appointor may be liable to indemnify the receiver in respect of any liability to the company or third parties incurred by the receiver in acting pursuant to the instructions of his appointor.[202]

PART III—WAIVER AND RELEASE

13-077   Rights of and against a receiver and his appointor may be waived or released. Whilst the equitable doctrine of waiver (or acquiescence) requires knowledge of the right which is being waived (or the wrong which is being acquiesced in) the effect of a release made for consideration is entirely a matter of construction of the release and does not depend on knowledge of the claim in question.[203] Equity may preclude reliance on a release if such reliance is unconscionable.[204]

---

[199] *RA Price Securities Ltd v Henderson* [1989] 2 N.Z.L.R. 257 (such implication may more readily be made where the receiver acts in accordance with the directions of the appointor).

[200] *W Cory & Son v Lambton and Hetton Collieries* (1916) 86 L.J.K.B. 401.

[201] See above, para.7–045.

[202] *Re B Johnson & Co (Builders) Ltd* [1955] Ch. 634 (CA), 647–648, per Evershed M.R., cited in *RA Price Securities Ltd v Henderson* [1989] 2 N.Z.L.R. 257.

[203] *Village Cay Marina Ltd v Acland* [1998] B.C.C. 417 (PC), 423, per Lord Hoffmann.

[204] *Bank of Credit and Commerce International SA v Ali* [2000] 3 All E.R. 51 (CA) (affd. [2002] 1 A.C. 251 (HL)) (although the majority in the House of Lords preferred to rest the outcome on ordinary principles of construction rather than on unconscionability).

Chapter 14

Receivers and Unsecured Creditors

One set of problems facing a receiver concerns the special rights of creditors **14–001** other than the debenture-holder. Local authorities (in respect of rates), land-lords (in respect of rents) and preferential creditors are dealt with elsewhere in this work.[1] This chapter concerns a variety of other unsecured creditors who may claim priority over the debenture-holder's charges.

1. EXECUTION CREDITORS

(a) Third party debt orders

One method of enforcement of a judgment is for an unsecured creditor to seek **14–002** an order that a third party who owes money to the company should pay it directly to the creditor. Such an order does not constitute a charge on the monies, nor does it operate as an assignment of the company's rights to the creditor.[2] A debenture-holder may therefore be able to intervene and success-fully assert title provided he does so at an appropriate time. In *Robson v Smith*,[3] Robson was the holder of a debenture containing a floating charge. The company defaulted. Robson obtained judgment and levied execution by fieri facias, but failed to recover the whole sum due. Trade creditors also obtained judgments and obtained a garnishee order nisi (the old name for an interim third party debt order) in respect of a sum due from a third party. The next day Robson obtained a similar order. The trade creditors obtained garnishee orders absolute (the old name for a third party debt order) and Robson obtained a similar order the next day, expressed to rank behind the orders obtained by the trade creditors. The third party paid the sums under the orders in the manner directed. Robson then launched an action against one of the trade creditors claiming the sum paid over to that creditor. Romer J. rejected this claim on the grounds that, when the third party had paid the money over, the floating charge had not crystallised: "No receiver had been appointed at the instance of a

---

[1] See below, Ch.19, for rates, Ch.18, for rent and Chs 27 and 28 for preferential creditors.
[2] *Re Combined Weighing and Advertising Machine Co* (1889) L.R. 43 Ch. D. 99 (CA); though cf. dicta apparently to the contrary in *Galbraith v Grimshaw & Baxter* [1910] 1 K.B. 339 (CA), 343 where Farwell L.J. states that whilst the order does not operate as a transfer of the property in the debt, it is an "equitable charge" on it (in the limited sense that debtors cannot safely pass anyone else). The House of Lords affirmed the decision of the Court of Appeal without mentioning this point: [1910] 1 A.C. 508 (HL). For a contrary view (albeit acknowledging that the law is as stated in the text) see *Palmer's Company Law*, Vol.3, para.13–199.80; and see also *N Joachimson (a Firm) v Swiss Bank Corp* [1921] 3 K.B. 110 (CA), 131, per Atkin L.J.; *Fraser v Oystertec Plc* [2006] 1 B.C.L.C. 491, [5].
[3] *Robson v Smith* [1895] 2 Ch. 118.

debenture-holder, nor had the plaintiff taken any step, as against the company, to enforce his security or to prevent the company from carrying on business". The evidence showed that "the company continued for some time afterward to carry on business", so that crystallisation did not take place as a result of cesser of business. Whilst the charge remained floating, the debenture-holder could not single out a particular debt due to the company and require it to be paid to him. Moreover, although the debenture contained a restriction on further charges, Romer J. held that this could not be material since "garnishee proceedings [i.e. third party debt proceedings] are only a form of execution, and do not lead to any 'charge', in the true sense, being created by the company".

14-003   *Robson v Smith* was followed by the Court of Appeal in *Evans v Rival Granite Quarries*.[4] The debenture-holder had demanded payment under the debenture but had taken no steps to enforce the security when another creditor obtained a garnishee order nisi in respect of a bank account. The debenture-holder contested the creditor's application but the court made the order absolute.

14-004   The court rejected the idea that the mere existence of a floating charge over the debt prevented it from being taken in execution.[5] That would have been inconsistent with the company's freedom to carry on business, which had to be subject to the processes of law if the company did not pay its debts.[6] The notion that the debenture-holder could crystallise the floating charge over a single debt was also rejected,[7] and the court held that, in order to attain priority, the floating charge had to have crystallised.

14-005   Unfortunately, the court did not clearly indicate what events might be sufficient to bring about such crystallisation. Vaughan Williams L.J. considered that there had to be some action by the debenture-holder to appoint a receiver to enforce his security or some intervention by the debenture-holder to terminate the company's licence to carry on business. Fletcher Moulton L.J. stated that the charge would only crystallise when the company ceased to trade or when the debenture-holder intervened. Buckley L.J. agreed that the debenture-holder "must do something to turn his security from a floating to a fixed charge", but also alluded to the possibility that crystallisation would occur automatically on the occurrence of an event defined in the debenture.[8] An automatic crystallisation clause in a debenture may therefore be effective to defeat execution.[9]

---

[4] *Evans v Rival Granite Quarries* [1910] 2 K.B. 979, CA.

[5] cf. *Re London Pressed Hinge Co Ltd* [1905] 1 Ch. 576 where neither *Robson v Smith* nor *Robinson v Burnell's Bakery* [1904] 2 K.B. 624 (below, fn.18) was cited. The case law is discussed by the Federal Court of Australia in *Wily v St George Partnership Banking Ltd* [1999] B.P.I.R. 1030.

[6] *Evans v Rival Granite Quarries* [1910] 2 K.B. 979 (CA), 995, per Fletcher Moulton L.J.

[7] This is certainly the case in the absence of an express provision for partial crystallisation. On crystallisation generally, see above, Ch.3.

[8] See also *Davey & Co v Williamson* [1898] 2 Q.B. 194 and the discussion of automatic crystallisation in Ch.3, above.

[9] See, e.g. *Gough on Company Charges*, 3rd edn (London: LexisNexis Butterworths 2011).

Norton v Yates[10] indicates that, if a receiver is appointed before payment of **14–006** monies to the creditor pursuant to an interim third party debt order, then the debenture-holder will gain priority. As has been seen, *Robson v Smith*[11] is authority for the proposition that actual payment over will defeat any subsequent action by the debenture-holder. But what is the significance of the making of a garnishee order absolute? *Evans v Rival Granite Quarries Ltd*[12] might be taken to imply that such an order will itself defeat the claim of a debenture-holder, but it is suggested that this cannot be correct. A third party debt order is simply a means of execution and not a charge capable of transforming an unsecured creditor into a secured one.[13] As such, though the judgment contains confusing references to garnishee orders as "charges", the decision of Walton J. in *Cairney v Back*[14] is probably right: the appointment of a receiver after a final order but before payment over was held to be sufficient to gain priority for the debenture-holder's charge.

The analysis above only applies to floating charges over debts. A fixed **14–007** charge over book and other debts will, if valid, obviate this problem, but gives rise to another. If the creditor has actual notice that the company's debt is the subject of a fixed charge, he cannot properly obtain payment without the consent of the debenture-holder. If the creditor does not have this notice, then he can properly obtain a third party debt order and accept payment. If the company's debtor does not have actual notice of the fixed charge, he can and must pay in accordance with the third party debt order; but if he is aware of the fixed charge, then by payment to the execution creditor he obtains no discharge from his liability to pay the debenture-holder, and accordingly is at risk of having to pay twice.

Debentures now frequently contain provisions enabling holders of floating **14–008** charges to crystallise the floating charge over individual assets, thereby reversing the actual outcomes in *Robson v Smith* and *Evans v Rival Granite Quarries Ltd* discussed above.

(b) Writs of fieri facias

The writ of fieri facias requires a sheriff to seize and sell goods of a debtor to **14–009** meet the creditor's claim. When seizure is made, the goods can be left in the physical possession of the debtor by agreement, the sheriff taking constructive possession only. None of these processes gives any charge over the goods.[15]

---

[10] *Norton v Yates* [1906] 1 K.B. 112. Compare also *Fraser v Oystertec Plc* [2006] 1 B.C.L.C. 491 where a creditor sought a final third party debt order against a credit balance at the debtor's bank. The bank had the benefit of a prior charge over the credit balance and a prior right of contractual set-off. The court refused to make a final third party debt order. The judgment contains confusing references to a third party debt order creating a charge over the credit balance: see fn.2 above.

[11] *Robson v Smith* [1895] 2 Ch. 118.

[12] *Evans v Rival Granite Quarries Ltd* [1910] 2 K.B. 979 (CA).

[13] See *Robson v Smith* [1895] 2 Ch. 118, per Romer J. and see fnn.3 and 11, above.

[14] *Cairney v Back* [1906] 2 K.B. 746.

[15] In *Re A Debtor (No.10 of 1992)* [1995] B.C.C. 525, M.E. Mann QC, sitting as a Deputy Judge of the High Court, decided that a creditor who had executed under a writ of fieri facias was a secured creditor within the meaning of s.258(4) of the 1986 Act, the security being "not unlike a

14–010   Despite earlier cases which appeared to give undue weight to the mere existence of a debenture,[16] it is now clear that the creditor has priority if execution is completed by payment prior to crystallisation.[17] A debenture-holder can, it is submitted, obtain priority if he intervenes to crystallise his security before the execution is completed by payment of monies over to the execution creditor.

14–011   The case of *Robinson v Burnell's Bakery*[18] illustrates an alternative approach on somewhat unusual facts. The sheriff seized goods subject to a floating charge, but before the debenture-holder could intervene the company agreed to make periodic payments out of earnings in consideration of the suspension of the execution proceedings. A receiver was subsequently appointed and he claimed these sums from the sheriff. Channell J. found that the sheriff had made the agreement with the company as agent for the creditor, that the execution had not of itself determined the company's licence to trade and, as such, the sums paid were simply repayments of the company's debt in the ordinary course of its business.[19] The creditors were thus entitled to the monies, for the debenture-holder had not intervened to crystallise his security in time.

14–012   The learned judge did not give any opinion as to what might have been the case if the goods had been sold and the proceeds held or paid over by the sheriff. It is suggested that the proceeds would have the same status as the goods, i.e. they would be the property of the company subject to the floating charge and therefore susceptible to being taken by the debenture-holder or receiver upon crystallisation. If, however, the proceeds are actually paid over to creditors prior to, or without notice of, crystallisation, it is suggested that the creditors acquire legal title to the money free of the debenture-holder's equity.

2.   CHARGING ORDERS

14–013 By virtue of the Charging Orders Act 1979 the court may, as part of the execution of a judgment, impose a charge on the property of a debtor. In practice, this tends not to cause a problem in receiverships since a charging order will typically relate to land, and any land owned by the company will almost certainly be subject to a prior fixed charge in favour of the debenture-holder.

---

lien". It is, however, thought that this is not correct. The contrary view is supported by *Relwood Pty Ltd v Manning Homes Pty Ltd (No.2)* [1992] 2 Qd. R. 197, 200, lines 5–40, where the references to security in some of the earlier case law, including that relied on in the *Re A Debtor* case, were explained as being founded on an ambiguity of language, so that the references to security did not connote any proprietary interest in goods seized in execution.

[16] See particularly *Re Standard Manufacturing Co* [1891] 1 Ch. 627 (CA); *Re Opera Ltd* [1891] 3 Ch. 260 (CA).

[17] *Palmer's Company Law*, Vol.3, para.13.199.78. Palmer suggests that the execution creditor is entitled to the proceeds of sale even if the floating charge crystallises after sale, but before the enforcement officer makes payment. The dicta in *Evans v Rival Granite Quarries Ltd* [1910] 2 K.B. 979 (CA) were expressed to relate to priorities in cases concerning seizure by sheriffs. cf. *Lochab Brothers v Kenya Furfural* [1985] L.R.C. (Comm.) 737 where the majority of the Court of Appeal of Kenya held that execution was completed on sale, and accordingly prior to payment of the proceeds to the execution creditor.

[18] *Robinson v Burnell's Bakery* [1904] 2 K.B. 624.

[19] The case and this analysis were followed and applied to very similar facts by Salter J. in *Heaton & Dugard v Cutting Bros* [1925] 1 K.B. 655; cf. *Taunton v Sheriff of Warwickshire* [1895] 2 Ch. 319 (CA).

In the unlikely event of the charging order affecting an asset over which **14–014** there is a floating charge, the position is not at all clear. Lord Brightman indicated in *Roberts Petroleum Ltd v Bernard Kenny Ltd*[20] that a charging order nisi (now called an interim charging order, and which is obtained without notice) is a defeasible right that only becomes indefeasible on being made absolute (i.e. final). As such and by analogy to the other types of execution discussed above, it is suggested that, in order to secure priority, the debenture-holder would have to intervene to bring about a crystallisation of his security before the charging order is made absolute.[21] Alternatively, crystallisation pursuant to an automatic crystallisation clause could probably prevent the charging order being made absolute.

It may sometimes be possible for a debenture-holder or receiver acting on **14–015** his behalf to apply to set aside a charging order which has been made absolute by applying under s.3(5) of the Charging Orders Act 1979, which provides that the court by which a charging order was made may at any time, on the application of the debtor or of "any person interested in any property to which the order relates", make an order discharging or varying the charging order. In circumstances where the rights of debenture-holders are not in issue, a charging order will not be made absolute after the winding-up of the judgment debtor company has commenced, whether by presentation of a winding-up petition or by the passing of a resolution for a voluntary winding-up. Where such formal insolvency proceedings have not yet commenced, but the judgment debtor company is in financial difficulties, it appears that whether a final order should be made lies in the discretion of the court. If a final order is made, and both the court and the judgment creditor were unaware of the debtor company's financial difficulties at the time of making that final order, then absent special circumstances the order ought not to be set aside on application under s.3(5) of the Charging Orders Act 1979 since the judgment creditor has obtained the benefit of the charge in good faith and without notice of any financial difficulties. It is possible that a final order might be set aside where, for example, the judgment creditor was aware of the financial circumstances of the judgment debtor company but failed to bring these to the attention of the court. In this regard it may be noted that the standard form applications for charging orders over land or securities, Forms N 379 and N 380, require the judgment debtor to state whether or not he knows of any other creditors of the judgment debtor, and if he does, to give their names and addresses, nature and amount of debt, if known.

If an application under s.3(5) is feasible, it seems that a debenture holder **14–016** will be "a person interested in any property to which the order relates" so as to give standing under that sub-section. For these purposes, a person will only be interested in property to which the charging order relates if that person has a

---

[20] *Roberts Petroleum Ltd v Bernard Kenny Ltd (In Liquidation)* [1983] 2 A.C. 192 (HL). See also *Clarke v Coutts & Co* [2002] B.P.I.R. 916 (CA).

[21] The case actually decided that the intervention of the statutory scheme brought into effect by a resolution to wind up the company was sufficient reason for a refusal to make a charging order absolute. The House was concerned not to elevate one unsecured creditor to secured status in the winding-up.

proprietary interest in the property, or something akin to that "in the sense that they are a person who at least has some interest such that their legal rights or liabilities are directly affected by the charging order".[22] A debenture holder plainly has such an interest by virtue of his charge.

3. FREEZING INJUNCTIONS

14–017 A receiver may discover upon his appointment that a party claiming to be an unsecured creditor has frozen all or some of the charged assets of the company pending the resolution of that creditor's claim. This was the situation considered by the Court of Appeal in *Cretanor Maritime Co v Irish Marine Management Ltd*.[23] There, the company had become the charterer of a vessel and subsequently had executed a debenture containing a floating charge. During a dispute with the company, the owners of the vessel obtained a freezing injunction[24] restraining the company from taking out of the jurisdiction assets which might be required to meet the owners' claim. The Court of Appeal appears to have accepted that subsequently the company impliedly bound itself by contract not to remove the monies. A receiver was appointed over the company's assets, who applied for the release of certain sums from the injunction. It was held that a receiver who was the company's agent was bound by the injunction and could not apply for its release, but the debenture-holder was entitled to apply. The injunction did not confer any sort of lien or proprietary right over the property in question but merely safeguarded it to await an eventual execution after judgment. Upon the appointment of the receiver, the floating charge crystallised and the debenture-holder had a fixed charge over the assets of the company. This would prevail over any future execution. Although the application at first instance had been made by the receiver, the Court of Appeal was prepared to treat it as if it had been made by the debenture-holder and simply added him as party to the summons. Moreover, the debenture-holder was entitled to apply without becoming a party to the action.

14–018 The *Cretanor* case was distinguished by Harman J. in *Capital Cameras Ltd v Harold Lines Ltd*.[25] Harman J. pointed out that in the *Cretanor* case the receiver had been applying as agent of the company in a situation where the company was restrained by contract from removing the money from the jurisdiction. The receiver was therefore seeking an order for the release of monies so that he could cause the company to breach a pre-receivership contract. He

---

[22] *Banque Nationale de Paris Plc v Montman Ltd* [2000] 1 B.C.L.C. 576, 581, referring to *Harman v Glencross* [1986] Fam. 81 (CA), where the property concerned was a house in respect of which the applicant wife had a right of occupation.

[23] *Cretanor Maritime Co v Irish Marine Management Ltd* [1978] 1 W.L.R. 966 (CA). cf. *Zealcastle Ltd v Galadari* Unreported July 28, 1986. See also *Industrial Diseases Compensation Ltd v Marrons* [2001] B.P.I.R. 600; *Nationwide Building Society v Wright* [2010] Ch.318 (CA).

[24] The freezing injunction was traditionally known as a "Mareva" injunction, being a shorthand of the name of the case in which the type of injunction was first reported. The new terminology was introduced by the Civil Procedure Rules: see CPR Pt 25, and the accompanying Practice Direction.

[25] *Capital Cameras Ltd v Harold Lines Ltd* [1991] 1 W.L.R. 54.

could not be allowed to do this as agent for the company.[26] In the *Capital Cameras* case, there were no contractual terms binding the company in relation to the assets subject to the freezing injunction and thus Harman J. rejected the argument of two of the defendants to the effect that the company by its administrative receivers (as opposed to the debenture-holder) was the wrong party to have applied to court for variation of the injunction. He went on to point out that the appointment of authorised insolvency practitioners would probably mean that the assets were no longer in jeopardy and that the injunction could be varied to allow the receiver to deal with the assets.

Even where the release of the freezing injunction was with a view to a breach   **14–019** of an agreement binding the company but not a debenture-holder, it may well be possible as a practical matter to persuade the party who has obtained a freezing injunction to agree to an application being made by the receiver alone in order to save costs.

The standard form freezing injunction provides for the injunction to cease to   **14–020** have effect if the respondent to the order provides security by making a payment into court, or otherwise makes provision for security by agreement with the applicant's solicitors.[27] In *Technocrats International Inc v Fredic Ltd*[28] the respondent paid monies to their solicitors to be held on terms which, in effect, followed the standard form of injunction relating to payments into court. The respondent company was subsequently placed into administration, and an issue arose between the holders of a debenture over the company's undertaking, the administrators, and the applicant, as to whether the applicant had security in the form of a charge over the monies held by the solicitors. Jack J. applying the principles in the *Cretanor* case, held that the provision for security in the standard form freezing injunction did not give the applicant any proprietary right in respect of the monies. Rather, "security" meant security against the risk of dissipation or removal.

Often, parties will agree to the release of a freezing injunction on terms that   **14–021** provide for "security" to be provided by the respondent to the applicant. In such cases, whether such security is subject to a proprietary interest in favour of the applicant depends ultimately on the legal effect of what the parties have agreed. If, as a matter of construction, the parties agreed, or embodied in a consent order, terms to similar effect as those in the standard form freezing injunction, then no proprietary rights will be created—as in the Technocrats case. The same result was reached by the Court of Appeal in *Flightline Ltd v Edwards*,[29] where the effect of the parties' agreement was less clear. The Court of Appeal held that for the monies to be subject to security, there had to be an obligation on the respondent to pay the debt out of the monies which

---

[26] A receiver can as agent for the company but using the priority of the debenture-holder cause the company effectively to repudiate purely contractual agreements: see above, Ch.13.

[27] See para.11(4) of the standard form freezing injunction purportedly appended to Practice Direction—Interim Injunctions of CPR Pt 25, but in fact found in the "Miscellaneous Forms" section of the Civil Procedure Forms, Form FI, and also as Appendix 5 of the Admiralty and Commercial Courts Guide.

[28] *Technocrats International Inc v Fredic Ltd* [2005] 1 B.C.L.C. 467.

[29] *Flightline Ltd v Edwards* [2003] 1 W.L.R. 1200 (CA).

constituted the "security". There was no such obligation expressed in the agreement reached by the parties in that case, and hence the applicant had no proprietary right in the monies. However, the creation of an equitable charge does not necessarily depend on there being an express provision to pay a debt out of a specific fund. The reasoning of Neuberger J. at first instance,[30] where he followed the analogy of cases relating to monies paid into court to await the verdict of litigation is more convincing. A payment into court (or instead into a joint bank account) of monies to await the outcome of litigation implies an agreement that any judgment debt will be paid in whole or in part out of those monies. Monies paid into court have long been regarded as secured.[31]

4. DISTRESS FOR TAXES

14–022 Distress is a primitive but legal form of self-help which entitles one party to seize property of another to enforce payment of the other's liability to the seizer. Statute has provided for distress in the case of a number of taxes.[32]

14–023 There is no reported case law concerning the priority of authorities who have distrained for taxes on a "person" as opposed to taxes charged on property.[33] The question arises: at what point in the process of distraining upon and selling goods does the distraining tax authority become entitled to keep possession of goods and sell them (or receive and keep the proceeds of sale, as the case may be), where a receiver has been appointed? The answer to this question depends upon whether distress by tax authorities is analogous to distress for rates or to execution.[34]

14–024 The use of the word "distress" by Parliament would seem to suggest that distress for taxes is analogous to other forms of distress. But it is sometimes said that distress for taxes is a statutory remedy more analogous to execution than to distress for rent.[35] The importance of the distinction is that when a person distrains for rent, he takes a pledge of the goods by taking possession of the goods in question.[36] The distrainor thus takes security over the goods seized, and this security interest could take priority over the interest of a debenture-holder having a floating charge.[37] Where goods are seized by

[30] *Flightline Ltd v Edwards* [2002] 1 W.L.R. 2535.

[31] *Re Ford* [1900] 2 Q.B. 211; *Sherratt v Bromley* [1985] Q.B. 1038 (CA).

[32] See *Halsbury's Laws of England*, 4th edn (London: LexisNexis Butterworths, 2007 reissue), Vol.13, para.1127. As a result of the Tribunals, Courts and Enforcement Act 2007, an inclusive definition of "distress" has for the first time been prospectively included in the Insolvency Act 1986, s.436(1), at a date to be appointed.

[33] Though see *Re Modern Jet Support Centre Limited* [2005] 1 W.L.R. 3880, discussed further at para.14–028, below.

[34] See also Samwell, *Corporate Receiverships* 2nd edn (London: Institute of Chartered Accountants in England and Wales, 1988), p.80.

[35] See *Halsbury's Laws of England*, 4th edn (London: LexisNexis Butterworths, 2007 reissue), Vol.13, para.1127.

[36] In the case of the common law of distress for rent, by taking possession of the goods, the distrainor becomes a pledgee: see *Halsbury's Laws of England*, 4th edn (London: LexisNexis Butterworths, 2007 reissue), Vol.13, paras 901 and 902.

[37] This is the basis upon which the Inland Revenue (now Her Majesty's Revenue and Customs–HMRC) themselves argue (or at least, have argued in the past) that they have priority over debenture-holders in relation to goods seized prior to crystallisation of the floating charge. For an

execution creditors pursuant to a writ of fieri facias,[38] the creditor takes no pledge of the goods seized.[39] The creditor thus has no security interest which can take priority over the security of the debenture-holders. Seizure of the goods is merely a step towards selling the goods and, thus, being paid.

In a number of cases, the courts have distinguished between distress for taxes and distress for rent.[40] However, those cases deal with rather different issues, such as whether the category of goods upon which distraint can be levied is the same in the case of statutory distress as under the common law.[41]   **14–025**

The law in relation to execution creditors is far from clear, and few principles emerge which could be applied by analogy.[42] Certain of the authorities in that area are treated as decisions on the priority of execution creditors as against floating charge-holders, yet the judgments in the cases do not address the issue of priorities.[43] If the right of the tax authorities to sell goods distrained upon or to keep the proceeds of sale depends on the priorities of secured creditors, little guidance is to be found on this point in the cases on execution creditors.   **14–026**

The authority which bears most closely on this issue appears to be *Herbert Berry Ltd v IRC*.[44] That case concerned the power of the Inland Revenue to sell goods which they had seized under their power of distraint prior to the voluntary liquidation of the debtor company. The Inland Revenue had kept constructive possession of the goods under a walking possession agreement.[45] The House of Lords decided that the Inland Revenue could sell the goods and keep the proceeds. It is implicit in the decision that the Inland Revenue had become   **14–027**

---

account of the position of the Inland Revenue, see *Tolley's Taxation in Corporate Insolvency*, 5th edn (London: Butterworths Tolley Ltd), para.4.5.

[38] In fact, the person distraining under the purely common law right of distraint for rent would not take a "pledge" of the goods in the sense in which the word is normally used, as the common law gave the "pledgee" no right of sale: *Halsbury's Laws of England*, 4th edn (London: LexisNexis Butterworths, 2007 Reissue), Vol.13, para.902.

[39] See above, para.14–009.

[40] See *Halsbury's Laws of England*, Vol.13, 4th edn (London: LexisNexis Butterworths, 2007 reissue), para.904, fn.4 and the cases cited there. Surprisingly, the *Herbert Berry* case (see below, para.14–027) is not listed; nor is the *Modern Jet Support* case.

[41] The case of *Potts v Hickman* [1941] A.C. 212 (HL) concerns the detailed wording of s.1 of the Landlord and Tenant Act 1709; but see the more general statements of Viscount Maugham and Lord Wright, at 235 and 241 respectively. The cases discussed in *Hickman* generally concerned the issue whether the limitations of the categories of goods which could be distrained upon at common law should apply to statutory distraint: see per Lord Wright, 241; also *Swaffer v Mulcahy* [1924] 1 K.B. 608; *Hutchins v Chambers* (1758) 1 Burr. 579; *MacGregor v Clamp* [1914] 1 K.B. 288.

[42] For a criticism of the case law in relation to execution creditors, see R.J. Calnan, "Priorities Between Execution Creditors and Floating Charges" (1982) 10 N.Z.U.L.R. 111; D.M. Hare and D. Milman, "Debenture Holders and Judgement Creditors–Problems of Priority" [1982] L.M.C.L.Q. 57.

[43] e.g. *Re Standard Manufacturing Co* [1891] 1 Ch. 627 (CA); *Opera Ltd, Re* [1891] 3 Ch. 260 (CA). In particular, it is implicit in the cases that a floating charge is a fixed charge coupled with a licence to deal, a view of the floating charge which was rejected by the Court of Appeal in this area in *Evans v Rival Granite Quarries Ltd* [1910] 2 K.B. 979 (CA).

[44] *Herbert Berry Ltd v IRC* [1977] 1 W.L.R. 1437 (HL).

[45] On the nature and effect of walking possession agreements, see *National Commercial Bank of Scotland v Arcam Demolition and Construction Ltd* [1966] 2 Q.B. 593 (CA), 599, per Lord Denning M.R.; and *Halsbury's Laws of England*, 4th edn (London: LexisNexis Butterworths, 2007 Reissue), para.1018; cf. *Peck v Craighead* [1995] B.C.C. 525.

secured creditors of the debtor company upon taking possession of the goods.[46] Unless the Inland Revenue had acquired a security interest in the goods prior to the creditors' voluntary liquidation, the goods or their proceeds would have fallen to be distributed on a pari passu basis. Thus, the Inland Revenue must have become pledgees of the goods upon taking possession. If this is correct, where distress for taxes is levied (that is, possession taken of the goods) but not completed by sale prior to the crystallisation of a floating charge, the debenture-holder's interest will nevertheless be postponed to the interest of the distrainor.[47]

14–028   In *Re Modern Jet Support Centre Ltd*[48], the issue was whether the process of distraint against goods for unpaid taxes under s.61 of the Taxes Management Act 1970 was an "execution" within the meaning of s.183 of the Insolvency Act 1986. Section 183 prevents a creditor from retaining the benefit of such execution unless it is completed before the commencement of the winding-up: and in that case, the revenue authorities had the benefit of a walking possession agreement over certain chattels of the company in liquidation, but had not completed the process of distraint. In the course of his judgment, Warren J. considered the nature of distraint for taxes, and quoted the general legal meaning of distress and distraint from Halsbury's,[49] to the effect that distraint is a summary remedy by which a person is entitled without legal process to take into his possession the chattels of another person, to be held as a pledge. After referring at length to the *Herbert Berry* case, in particular the judgment of Templeman J. at first instance[50], Warren J. commented that a distress levied (but not completed by sale) was in effect a pledge as security for the debt, and hence the insolvent company's assets available for distribution to the general unsecured creditors were limited in the same way as if the distrainor had the benefit of a fixed charge[51]. The reasoning strongly supports the view that if distress is levied by the taking of possession over assets subject to an uncrystallised floating charge, the distrainor has priority to the floating charge holder in respect of such assets.

14–029   Prior to September 15, 2003, debts owing to Crown creditors were often preferential, in whole or in part. Such preferential status has now been removed.[52] When the Crown creditors had preferential status, their status as

---

[46] cf. *Roberts Petroleum Ltd v Bernard Kenny Ltd (In Liquidation)* [1983] 2 A.C. 192 (HL): see above, para.14–014.

[47] The issue of the priority of the distrainor was not specifically addressed in *Herbert Berry*. However, at least one of the judges (see Buckley L.J. in the Court of Appeal in [1977] 3 All E.R. 729 (CA), 733, where he refers to over-riding rights) appears to acknowledge that the issue rests on priority of securities. On the other hand, the courts' affirmation of *Re Great Ship Co Ltd* (1863) 4 De G.J. & S. 63 suggests that the courts were simply unaware of any policy justification for enforcing pari passu distribution.

[48] *Re Modern Jet Support Centre Ltd* [2005] 1 W.L.R. 3880.

[49] *Re Modern Jet Support Centre Ltd* [2005] 1 W.L.R. 3880, [15]; the passage quoted is from vol.13 of the earlier reissue, para.601; in the 2007 Reissue, it is now Vol.13, para.901.

[50] *Herbert Berry Ltd v IRC* [1976] 1 W.L.R. 783.

[51] *Herbert Berry Ltd v IRC* [1976] 1 W.L.R. 783, [26].

[52] Preferential status was accorded by virtue of s.386 of the Insolvency Act 1986 and Categories 1, 2 and 3 of Sch.6 to the 1986 Act. Those categories were repealed by s.251 of the Enterprise Act 2002 with effect from September 15, 2003.

secured or unsecured creditors would often make little difference, save where the assets of the company were insufficient to pay such creditors in full. Their status is now of greater importance.

When a receiver is appointed, he comes under a statutory duty to pay prefer- **14–030** ential creditors out of floating charge assets.[53] Where distress has been levied but not completed over such assets at the time of appointment, it may be that a receiver is entitled to an injunction restraining completion of the distress to the extent that it interferes with payment of the preferential creditors.[54]

If the receiver or debenture-holder launches a compulsory winding-up peti- **14–031** tion to try to combat distress that has been put in but not completed by sale, the court is unlikely to restrain the sale unless there are special reasons (such as unconscionable conduct or delay) which would render sale inequitable.[55] Compulsory winding up may provide some relief for preferential creditors in that, if a winding up order is secured within three months after the completion of the distress, the proceeds are divided rateably so that "the list of preferential creditors will have added to it the [distrainor's] claim and the creditors then on the list will be paid pari passu from the distress fund".[56]

Where the relevant chattels are subject to a fixed charge, even if subsequent **14–032** distress for taxes were to create a pledge, this would rank behind the fixed charge.

[53] See below, Ch.28.
[54] See *Re ELS Ltd* [1995] Ch.11, 26–27, a rates case discussing *Taggs Island Casino Hotel Ltd v Richmond-upon-Thames BC* [1967] R.A. 70.
[55] See *Re Memco Engineering Ltd* [1986] Ch.86.
[56] *Re Memco Engineering Ltd* [1986] Ch.86, 98E–F, see Insolvency Act 1980, s.176.

Chapter 15

Receivers and Winding-Up

15–001   Whilst receivership is in essence a remedy for a debenture-holder, winding-up involves the administration of the company's property for the benefit of all the company's creditors. The receiver appointed out of court is the choice of the debenture-holder, whereas the liquidator is in effect the choice of the unsecured creditors. Generally speaking, during the period of any receivership of a company in liquidation, the receiver's administration takes precedence and a liquidator has a secondary role. This is the case whether the receiver is appointed before or after the commencement of winding-up.[1] The liquidator's special responsibilities are threefold:

    (a)   the liquidator alone can invoke certain statutory remedies, e.g. in respect of preferences;

    (b)   the liquidator has the right and duty to scrutinise the security of the debenture-holder and conduct of the receiver[2];

    (c)   the liquidator has the right to all assets which lie outside the charge and to any surplus of assets after discharge of the secured debt.

1.   CAN A RECEIVER PETITION?

15–002   A non-administrative receiver can petition in the name of the company in order to preserve or protect its assets.[3] The debenture-holder can petition if he can

---

[1] See *Re Potters Oils Ltd* [1986] 1 W.L.R. 201 where Hoffmann J. (as he then was) affirmed the right of a debenture-holder to appoint a receiver after liquidation if it thought that its best interests would be served by such an appointment. This was so despite the fact that the receiver's remuneration would he paid out of funds otherwise available to the unsecured creditors. If the receiver is appointed after a winding-up, he requires the court's leave to take possession from the liquidator, an officer of the court, but he is entitled to leave as of right (*Re Potters Oils Ltd* [1986] 1 W.L.R. 201, 206). The receiver, if appointed after the liquidation, is entitled to require the liquidator to transfer to him the assets of the company to enable the receiver to pay off the secured and preferential creditors: *Manley, Petitioner* [1985] S.L.T. 42 (Court of Session, Outer House).

[2] In Australia, by statute the receiver has a duty to the liquidator to do whatever is reasonably required by the liquidator to help the winding-up: *Re Photosprint Australia Pty Ltd* (2004) 212 A.L.R. 517. There is also general equitable duty to account and to provide information other than that which may be injurious to the creditor: *Re Photosprint Australia Pty Ltd* (2004) 212 A.L.R. 517 citing *Gomba Holdings (UK) Ltd v Homan* [1986] 1 W.L.R. 1301, 1307.

[3] *Re Emmadart Ltd* [1979] Ch. 540 (winding-up order saved company from liability for unoccupied property rate); *Re Roisnob Ltd* Unreported October 25, 1983 (group tax relief under an arrangement with the Inland Revenue became available on liquidation); and see *Bank of New Zealand v Essington Developments Pty Ltd* (1990) 5 A.C.S.R. 86, 88; (1991) 9 A.C.L.C. 1039, 1041.

show that a benefit to him would accrue from the winding-up.[4] The Insolvency Act 1986, Sch.1, para.21, gives an administrative receiver "power to present ... a petition for the winding-up of the company". Although no limitation is placed upon the exercise of the power, since the administrative receiver is deemed to be the agent of the company until liquidation, it is thought that he should petition in the name of the company.[5]

Where a petition is by the receiver in the name of the company, the company need not be served under the Insolvency Rules 1986.[6] The court may expect the directors and secretary to be made respondents and served where practicable, in case they wish to oppose, although this is not required by the 1986 Rules.[7]   **15–003**

Unlike a creditor, a receiver is not entitled to a winding-up order ex debito justitiae: the court will exercise its discretion whether to make such an order.[8]   **15–004**

Whether a receiver can call the requisite meetings of members and creditors to wind up the company voluntarily depends on whether the receiver is given such a power, explicitly or implicitly, by the terms of the debenture under which he is appointed.[9]   **15–005**

2.   CAN A RECEIVER RESIST A PETITION?

Nothing in the 1949 Rules required a winding-up petition to be served on a receiver and, prior to the Insolvency Act 1986, he appears to have had no locus standi to appear in his own right.[10] Now, however, any petitioner for a winding-up order who knows that an administrative receiver has been appointed in relation to a company must send a copy of the petition to the receiver.[11] Further, para.21 of Sch.1 to the Insolvency Act 1986 expressly empowers an administrative receiver to defend a petition. It is thought that this power should be exercised in the name of the company, and not in the receiver's own name.[12]   **15–006**

---

[4] *Re Borough of Portsmouth Tramways Co* [1892] 2 Ch. 362. In *Re Emmadart Ltd* [1979] Ch. 540, the debenture-holder appeared as a supporting creditor on the receiver's petition. See also *Re Anvil Estates Ltd* Unreported 1993 discussed by Pugh and Ede in (1994) 10 *Insolvency Law and Practice* 47.

[5] See, e.g. *Re Television Parlour Plc* (1988) 4 B.C.C. 95, 98. The general rule is that a receiver has no locus standi to sue in his own name, save in respect of rights to which he is personally entitled: *Robertson v Oskar* (1984) 8 A.C.L.R. 570.

[6] Insolvency Rules 1986, r.4.8.

[7] See *Re Emmadart Ltd* [1979] Ch. 540, 548; *Re Roisnob Ltd* Unreported October 25, 1983.

[8] *Re Emmadart Ltd* [1979] Ch. 540, 547–548.

[9] See *Valorum Ltd v Rickett* Unreported December 2, 1999, where receivers purported to call a meeting of the members of the company ultimately with a view to placing the company into voluntary liquidation. The receivers argued that they had power under the debenture to call such a meeting, specifically under a clause which provided that the receivers could "do all such other things as may from time to time be considered by such receivers to be conducive to the exercise of his or their functions as receivers". The argument was rejected, since the receivers had advanced no reasons as to why they wished to call the meeting.

[10] He could, however, cause the company to appear to oppose the petition.

[11] Insolvency Rules 1986, r.4.10 (2). The *Cork Report*, at para.468, suggested that the receiver should be given notice.

[12] Compare above, fn.5. A voluntary liquidator who appears on a petition in order to assist the court does so in his own name *Re Medisco Equipment* (1983) 1 B.C.C. 98,944) but the positions of the voluntary liquidator and the receiver are not analogous.

15–007   The mere fact that all the company's available assets are charged to their full value by the debenture cannot of itself bar a winding-up order.[13] A winding-up order has been made where there was a receivership in progress and the majority of creditors opposed the making of such an order.[14] But, the right of an unpaid creditor to obtain a winding-up order is a class right and, if the majority of the class consider that they have a better chance of getting paid if a winding-up order is not made, then the court may well give effect to the wishes of those opposing creditors and refuse a winding-up order.[15] Moreover, whilst it is not the usual practice of the Companies Court to grant lengthy adjournments, a very lengthy adjournment has been granted where an ongoing receivership gave rise to a reasonable prospect of a return for unsecured as well as secured creditors.[16]

15–008   Receivers might well have cause to oppose the making of a winding-up order, at least where the receivers are trading all or part of the company's business with the aim of achieving going concern values for its business or assets. In such circumstances, the effect of a winding-up order is to terminate the contracts of employment of employees, whose continued employment might be necessary to continued trading.[17] A winding-up order further terminates the receiver's authority to act as the company's agent, and whilst a receiver can, nonetheless, carry on the business of the company, he might be unwilling to do so as principal, or agent of the debenture-holder (see para.15–043 below).

15–009   *Re Demaglass Holdings Ltd*[18] concerned a company in receivership where the receivers continued to trade the business so as to realise glassware manufactured by the company at going concern values. A trade creditor petitioned for winding-up. The receivers opposed the making of an immediate winding-up order on the basis that the business would then be shut down by reason of the termination of the employees' contracts and sought an adjournment of the

---

[13] Insolvency Act 1986, s.125(1).

[14] *Re Clandown Colliery* [1915] 1 Ch. 369. In that case, however, there were rather special circumstances in that the chairman of the company had in reality been carrying on business in the company's name and this was a state of affairs which was not reasonable or proper in the interests of innocent unsecured creditors. Furthermore, the opposing creditors gave no reason for their opposition.

[15] *Re Crigglestone Coal Co Ltd* [1906] 2 Ch. 327 (CA), 331–332. The opposing creditors should give notice to the petitioning creditor, file evidence and appear by counsel at the hearing if the opposition is to be effective. See also *Re Macrae* [1961] 1 W.L.R. 229 (CA); *Re JD Swain* [1965] 1 W.L.R. 909 (CA). In *Re Leigh Estates (UK) Ltd* [1994] B.C.C. 292, the court held that in evaluating the strength of support or opposition to a petition, secured creditors were to be treated as unsecured creditors to the extent of any deficiency, and drew an analogy between the class rights of creditors on the hearing of a winding-up petition and in relation to voting on a scheme of arrangement under s.425 of the Companies Act 1985 (now Companies Act 2006, Pt 26, s 895). Where there are no assets in the estate, the court must ask itself whether it is just and equitable to wind up the company, for example to promote an investigation: *Bell Group Finance (Pty) Ltd (In Liquidation) v Bell Group (UK) Holdings Ltd* [1996] B.C.C. 505. Debenture-holders and receivers will not be able successfully to oppose a winding-up petition where the object of their opposition is to prevent an investigation of the validity of the debenture (*Bell Group Finance*). The court will pay much more attention to the views of creditors who are wholly independent of the company: *Re Southard* [1979] 1 W.L.R. 1198 (CA), 1205, per Buckley L.J.

[16] *Re Northern Developments (Holdings) Ltd* Unreported June 16, 1976 affirmed on appeal, March 1, 1977 (CA).

[17] See para.16–005, below and *Re Demaglass Holdings Ltd* [2001] 2 B.C.L.C. 633, discussed in para.15–009, below.

[18] *Re Demaglass Holdings Ltd* [2001] 2 B.C.L.C. 633.

petition for some ten weeks. The adjournment was granted. Neuberger J. (as he was then) set out the principles applicable, as follows. First, the foundation of the court's jurisdiction to deal with a winding-up petition was its discretion under s.125(1) of the 1986 Act. Secondly, the petitioner had to establish the possibility of the prospect of some sort of benefit from a winding-up. Thirdly, an unpaid creditor was entitled to a winding-up order virtually as of right in the absence of a good reason as to why the order should not be made. Fourthly, where some creditors supported and some opposed a winding-up order, an order would ordinarily be made if the majority of creditors supported the petition and would only be refused if the majority were against it. Fifthly, in considering the views of creditors the court will give little weight to the views of secured creditors (at least in so far as they are secured) and will give greater weight to the views of independent creditors rather than those connected with the company. The exercise of the court's discretion will not normally be dependent on mathematical niceties. Sixthly, the fact that a majority of creditors oppose winding-up is not sufficient: the court must be satisfied that they have a good reason to oppose. Seventhly, where the court is satisfied that the opposition to a winding-up is supported by a majority and is justified but the petitioner's desire for an order is also justified the court must then carry out a balancing exercise, and no general principles could be laid down. These principles were said to apply where a petitioner seeks a winding-up order and opposing creditors seek the dismissal of the petition; the judge held that where the opposing creditors sought merely an adjournment of the petition, the principles applicable were not wholly dissimilar, though the fact that the petitioner's remedy was, ultimately, not being opposed was a relevant factor, depending on the length of the adjournment sought.

The receiver's control over the company may not prevent the directors from **15–010** causing the company to oppose a petition, if the receiver does not wish to reserve to himself the power to represent the company on the petition.[19]

3. INVALIDITY OF CHARGES

(a) Non-registration

In practice, all charges over any property of a company registered in England **15–011** and Wales under which receivers are likely to be appointed are registrable, and unless registered within 21 days after the date of creation, are void as against a liquidator, administrator or creditor.[20] The position is the same in respect of charges on property in England and Wales created by companies incorporated

---

[19] *Re Reprographic Exports (Euromart) Ltd* (1978) 122 S.J. 400; *Bank of New Zealand v Essington Developments Pty Ltd* (1990) 5 A.C.S.R. 86; (1991) 9 A.C.L.C. 1039; and see above, para.2–026.

[20] See above, Ch.3. The references in s.395 of the Companies Act 1985 (see now Companies Act 2006, s 874(1)) to the charge being void as against a liquidator or administrator mean void as against the company in liquidation or the company in administration, as the case may be: *Smith (Administrator of Cosslett (Contractors) Ltd) v Bridgend CBC* [2002] 1 A.C. 336 (HL). In the case of companies registered in England or Wales, registration is required of charges created over property within or outside the UK.

outside Great Britain which, at the date of creation of the charge, have an established place of business in Great Britain.[21] The effect of non-registration within the requisite period is to make the monies secured immediately payable.[22]

(b) Floating charges

15–012 A floating charge created in favour of a person not connected with a company (if duly registered) is not invalidated by the subsequent liquidation of the company or the making of an administration order against it, provided that the company was solvent at the time of creation and did not become insolvent as a consequence of the transaction creating the charge.[23] But subject thereto, a floating charge created:

> (a) in favour of a person connected to the company[24] within two years of the commencement of winding-up (the onset of insolvency); or
>
> (b) in favour of any other person within one year of these dates; or
>
> (c) in either case between the making of an administration application in respect of the company and the making of an administration order on that application[25] or between the filing with the court of a copy of notice to appoint an administrator[26] and the making of an appointment thereunder;

is invalid except to the extent of the aggregate of

> (i) the value of the consideration for the creation of the charge that is paid or supplied to the company at the same time as or after the creation of the charge; and
>
> (ii) the interest (if any) agreed to be payable on these amounts.[27]

For the purposes of this provision, the value of any goods or services supplied shall be the amount in money which could reasonably have been expected to be obtained for supplying the goods or services in the ordinary course of business at that time on the same terms (apart from the consideration) as those on which they were supplied to the company.[28]

15–013 The phrase "at the same time as" in s.245(2)(a) and (b) of the 1986 Act replaces "at the time of" in s.617 of the Companies Act 1985. The old phrase

---

[21] *Re Oriel Ltd* [1986] 1 W.L.R. 180 (CA), and see above, Ch.3.

[22] Companies Act 2006, s 874(3).

[23] Insolvency Act 1986, s.245(4).

[24] For the definition of a person connected with a company, see Insolvency Act 1986, ss.249 and 435.

[25] That is, under Insolvency Act 1986, Sch.B1, paras 12, 35, 37 or 38.

[26] That is under Insolvency Act 1986, Sch.B1, paras 14 or 22.

[27] Insolvency Act 1986, s.245(1), (2).

[28] Insolvency Act 1986, s.245(5).

was interpreted very loosely in favour of lenders where money was lent on the faith of a promise to execute a debenture but the execution was delayed by the borrower.[29] Monies paid some considerable time before the execution of the debenture were held to be secured. Although the legislature, in altering the wording, did not intend any change in the law, the Court of Appeal[30] has held that the previous decisions were: (a) not binding, because they were based on different wording; and (b) erroneous. They held that monies paid prior to execution were not secured unless the interval was de minimis (such as a coffee break) or unless there was a prior binding agreement which amounted to an equitable charge.[31]

Under the previous law, the courts were very indulgent to chargee banks in applying the rule in *Clayton's Case*[32] and in treating withdrawals subsequent to the charge as being cash advanced after and in consideration of the charge.[33] A similar approach may be expected to be taken under s.245 of the Insolvency Act 1986.   **15–014**

Such cash advances must, however, benefit the company, and not merely be a means of substituting a secured for an unsecured debt (or a better for an existing security) to the benefit of one creditor at the expense of another.[34] Underhand conduct on the part of the chargee is not pre-requisite to the operation of s.245.[35] The new wording in s.245(2)(b) has clarified the fact that the discharge or reduction of a debt is as good as cash. It is still the case therefore that in a genuine business transaction designed to benefit the company's business, the discharge of a debt will validate a floating charge even if the result is to make a formerly unsecured creditor secured under the floating charge.[36] In each case, the court looks at the substance of what is happening.[37]   **15–015**

The invalidation of the floating charge only takes effect as at the date of commencement of the winding-up or (where the section applies by reason of an administrator being appointed) the making of the application for the administration order, the filing of intention to appoint an administrator, or otherwise when the appointment of the administrator takes effect and only invalidates the security element in the floating charge. The invalidation has no retrospective effect, and accordingly any realisation of the security by the debenture-holder   **15–016**

---

[29] See *Re Columbian Fireproofing Co Ltd* [1910] 2 Ch. 120 (CA) (11 days); *Re F & E Stanton Ltd* [1929] 1 Ch. 180 (two separate advances: 5 and 54 days).

[30] *Re Shoe Lace Ltd* [1993] B.C.C. 609 (CA), affirming on different grounds the judgment of Hoffmann J. (as he then was) [1992] B.C.C. 367. See also *Re Fairway Magazines Ltd* [1992] B.C.C. 924 (though note that in relation to the two payments of £10,000, the judgment does not consider the possible application of s 245(2)(b) of the 1986 Act).

[31] *Re Shoe Lace Ltd* [1993] B.C.C. 609 (CA), 619F–619H.

[32] *Clayton's Case* [1814–23] All E.R. Rep. 1.

[33] *Re Yeovil Glove Co Ltd* [1965] Ch. 148 (CA); *Re Thomas Mortimer Ltd* [1965] Ch. 186.

[34] *Re Fairway Magazines Ltd* [1992] B.C.C. 924; *Re GT Whyte & Co Ltd* [1983] B.C.L.C. 311, applying *Re Matthew Ellis Ltd* [1933] Ch. 458 (CA).

[35] *Re Fairway Magazines Ltd* [1992] B.C.C. 924; *Re GT Whyte & Co Ltd* [1983] B.C.L.C. 311, 317.

[36] See, under the old wording, *Re Matthew Ellis Ltd* [1933] Ch. 458 (CA) (loan made by chairman of company used to pay debts to firm of which he was partner in order to secure further supplies on credit and thereby to be able to continue the business); cf. *Re Destone Fabrics Ltd* [1941] Ch. 319 (CA).

[37] *Re Matthew Ellis Ltd* [1933] Ch. 458 (CA), 474, 478.

or the receiver prior to that date is unaffected, and any payment made prior to that date cannot be recovered under s.245 by the liquidator.[38] For this purpose, the commencement of a compulsory winding-up is the presentation of the petition to wind up.[39]

(c) Transactions at an undervalue and preferences[40]

15–017 Sections 238–241 afford to liquidators and administrators extensive rights of recovery in respect of transactions at an undervalue or preferences. The object is to secure the distribution of an insolvent company's assets equally amongst its body of creditors.

15–018   Sections 238–241 provide that a liquidator or administrator may apply to the court to set aside a transaction, to release or discharge (in whole or in part) any charge or security given by a company or to direct payment by a person to the office-holder of such sums as the court shall think fit in respect of benefits received if the transaction was entered into "at a relevant time" by the company: (i) for no consideration or for a consideration the value of which was significantly less than the value of the consideration provided by the company; or (ii) with a creditor of the company or guarantor of any of its debts or liabilities, and has the effect (and the decision by the company to enter into it was influenced by a desire to produce the effect) of placing that person in a better position in a liquidation than he would have been in if the transaction had not been entered into.[41] A "relevant time" as defined by s.240 of the Insolvency Act 1986 is one at which the company was unable to pay its debts within the meaning of s.123 of the Insolvency Act 1986 or became so unable by reason of the transaction or preference; and if also that time was either:

(a) (in the case of a preference given to person not connected with the company[42]) within six months; or

(b) (in the case of a transaction at an undervalue or a preference given to a person so connected) within two years of the commencement of the winding-up or (where the section applies by reason of a company going into liquidation by virtue of art.37 of the EC Regulation, or

---

[38] *Mace Builders (Glasgow) Ltd v Lunn* [1987] Ch. 191 (CA). That was a decision on the wording prior to the Insolvency Act 1986. The section has been completely rewritten, but there does not appear to have been any intention of altering the law so as to make the invalidity retrospective.

[39] *Re Shoe Lace Ltd* [1993] B.C.C. 609 (CA).

[40] The concept of a preference presupposes knowledge on the part of the company that the company's assets are insufficient to pay all creditors: see *Re Sarflax* [1979] Ch. 592, 602, per Oliver J. But a belief that creditors would all be paid eventually is insufficient to preclude a preference where it is known that all creditors cannot be paid in full at the time the preferential payment is made: *Re FP & CH Matthews Ltd* [1982] Ch. 257 (CA). It is thought that the propositions expressed in these cases remain valid, notwithstanding Millett J.'s denial of the utility of cases decided before the 1986 Act in *Re MC Bacon Ltd* [1990] B.C.C. 78, 87.

[41] Insolvency Act 1986, s.238(4).

[42] For the definition of a connected person, see Insolvency Act 1986, ss.249 and 435. For the purpose of ss.239 and 241, a person is not to be treated as a connected person by reason only of his being an employee of the company.

when the appointment of the administrator ceases to have effect) the date on which the company entered administration (or, if relevant, the date on which the application for the administration order was made or copy of notice of intention to appoint was filed); or (where an administration order has been made) the date of the administration application; or (where an administrator has been appointed by the company or the holder of a qualifying floating charge by filing of a notice of intention to appoint), the date of such filing; or (where an administrator has otherwise been appointed) the date on which the appointment takes effect; or

(c) between the making of an administration application in respect of the company and the making of an administration order thereon, or at a time between the filing with the court of a copy of notice to appoint an administrator[43] and the making of an appointment thereunder.

Payments made to a holder of a valid debenture prior to the commencement of the liquidation will rarely be liable to be set aside as a preference within the meaning of s.239. Under s.239(4)(b) of the 1986 Act, a hypothetical liquidation is posited, taking effect immediately after the transaction which is sought to be impugned, and the court must examine whether the debenture-holder's position is better, by reason of the payment being made, than it would otherwise have been.[44] Normally, the debenture-holder's position would not be any better than in the hypothetical liquidation, since the debenture-holder would be entitled to payment by virtue of his charge in any event.[45] However, there are situations where the debenture-holder's position might be improved by such payments, e.g. if the charge is liable to challenge on any of the grounds set out in the text, or if the debenture-holder receives more than the total of any secured debt, or (in the case of a crystallised floating charge) if the result of the payment is that creditors who were preferential as at the date of the hypothetical liquidation go unpaid in whole or in part. **15–019**

The grant of relief under ss.238 and 239 is discretionary.[46] Relief in respect of a transaction at an undervalue is precluded if the company entered into the transaction in good faith and in the ordinary course of its business and if, at the time it did so, there were reasonable grounds for believing that the transaction would benefit the company.[47] In any event, it is unlikely that the grant of a debenture could successfully be challenged as a transaction at an undervalue.[48] Further, the interests acquired by purchasers from the holder of a debenture **15–020**

---

[43] That is, under Insolvency Act 1986, Sch.B1, para.14 or para.22.

[44] There can be no voidable preference unless the party in question is actually preferred: *Lewis v Hyde* [1998] 1 W.L.R. 94 (PC).

[45] In Australia, it has been held that an essential element of any alleged preference is that it should decrease the property available for distribution in the liquidation, and hence that there can be no preference where payment is made to a debenture-holder who would have been entitled to payment within a liquidation in any event: *Wily v St George Partnership Banking Ltd* [1999] B.P.I.R. 1030 (Federal Court of Australia (Full Court)).

[46] *Re Paramount Airways Ltd (in Administration)* [1993] Ch. 223 (CA).

[47] Insolvency Act 1986, s.238(5).

[48] See para.15–024 below.

potentially voidable under these provisions, or from a receiver appointed thereunder, are not open to challenge if their acquisition was in good faith, for value and without notice[49] of the circumstances rendering the debenture open to challenge on the grounds of undervalue or preference.[50] The protection extends to any "interest in property which was acquired from a person other than the company",[51] an expression which should surely include in this context a receiver as well as the debenture-holder who appointed him, even where the receiver is acting as the "deemed agent" of the company, for in substance, if not in form, the acquisition is from the debenture-holder.

15–021   For a transaction to fall within s.238(4)(b) of the 1986 Act, the transaction must be: (i) entered into by the company; (ii) for a consideration; (iii) the value of which measured in money or money's worth; (iv) is significantly less than the value; (v) also measured in money or money's worth; (vi) of the consideration provided by the company. This requires a comparison to be made between the value obtained by the company for the transaction and the value of the consideration provided by the company. Both values must be measurable in money or money's worth and both must be considered from the company's point of view.[52]

15–022   The first issue for the court is to define the relevant "transaction" which is sought to be impugned. "Transaction" is defined in s.436 of the 1986 Act as including a "gift, agreement or arrangement, and references to entering into a transaction shall be construed accordingly". These are wide words, which will doubtless be given a broad interpretation by the courts.[53] Difficulties can arise where two or more persons have entered into a number of different

---

[49] As to the question of good faith and the absence of notice, see Re Sonatacus Ltd [2007] B.C.C. 186 (CA).

[50] Insolvency Act 1986, s.241(2), (2A), (3), (3A), (3B) and (3C). Similar protection was given under the predecessor, s.320 of the Companies Act 1948, because s.44(2) of the Bankruptcy Act 1914 was read into the Companies Act 1948: see Mace Builders (Glasgow) Ltd v Lunn [1986] Ch. 459, 469, Scott J. (and in [1987] Ch. 191 (CA), 199, per Lord Donaldson M.R.).

[51] Insolvency Act 1986, s.241(2)(a).

[52] Re MC Bacon Ltd [1990] B.C.L.C. 324, 340, per Millett J. (as he then was); approved subsequently by the Court of Appeal in National Bank of Kuwait v Menzies [1994] 2 B.C.L.C. 306 (CA), 319–320 and described by Lord Scott as a "useful breakdown" in Phillips v Brewin Dolphin Bell Lawrie Ltd [2001] 1 W.L.R. 143 (HL), 151F–G. It is not a necessary pre-condition to the grant of relief under the section that the consideration moving from and to the company be capable of assessment with precision, provided that the court can be satisfied that the incoming value is, on any view, significantly less than the outgoing value: Re Thoars (deceased) (No.2) [2005] 1 B.C.L.C. 331 (CA). Where able to do so, the court should arrive at precise figures, if only to make the process of assessing any monetary compensation easier (Re Thoars).

[53] Despite the protean nature of this inclusive definition, it has been held that, save possibly in respect of a gift, a "transaction" will be something which involves at least some element of dealing between the parties to the transaction: Re Taylor Sinclair (Capital) Ltd (In Liquidation) [2001] 2 B.C.L.C. 176, 184h (payment to a creditor of a third party held not to be a transaction); see also Clarkson v Clarkson [1994] B.C.C. 921 (CA), 928 (appointment under a trust of a life insurance policy held not to be a transaction); cf. National Bank of Kuwait [1994] 2 B.C.L.C. 306 (CA), and sub nom. Re Ayala Holdings Ltd [1993] B.C.L.C. 256 (letter of instruction to a bank as to the destination of proceeds of an insolvent company held to be a transaction). In Feakins v DEFRA [2007] B.C.C. 54 (CA), [78], Jonathan Parker L.J. pointed out that "transaction" included "arrangement", and was thus apt to include an agreement or understanding between parties, whether formal or informal, oral or in writing. The wide definition of "transaction" was said to be entirely consistent with the statutory objective of remedying the avoidance of debts under s.423. The same definition applies in the context of s.238, where the statutory objective is different.

arrangements. In *Phillips v Brewin Dolphin Bell Lawrie Ltd*,[54] the Court of Appeal decided that the relevant transaction had to be identified by reference to the person with whom it was entered into and only the elements of the transaction and that person could be taken into account. The company in liquidation had sold the shares in a subsidiary (which had been incorporated for the purposes of a hive-down) to X, and further agreed to sub-lease certain equipment to X's parent company, Y. The two contracts were entered into simultaneously. On an application by the liquidator of the company that the sale of the shares in the subsidiary was a transaction at an undervalue, X argued that the "transaction" for the purposes of s.238 included the sub-lease agreement, so that the consideration payable by X's parent under the sub-leases had to be taken into account. The Court of Appeal rejected this argument, since the two contracts had been entered into with different persons, i.e. X and its parent and had been deliberately kept separate. On appeal, the House of Lords approached the issues differently. The question was not to identify the relevant transaction, but to identify the consideration payable under the transaction as a matter of fact. Hence, in evaluating the consideration payable under the share sale agreement, the court would take into account not only the consideration moving under that agreement, but also the consideration moving under the sub-lease agreement entered into at the same time. Lord Scott pointed out that the wording of s.238(4)(b) did not stipulate by whom the relevant consideration was to be provided, and hence such person did not have to be a party to the transaction in issue (see at [20].)

At [26], Lord Scott indicated that regard might be had to events subsequent to the transaction in question in valuing the consideration. However, the Phillips case concerned the value of a covenant which was inherently precarious: and regard was had to subsequent events to show that its value was merely speculative at the time of the transaction, and hence that no value could properly be ascribed to it. In *Stanley v TMK Finance Ltd*[55] David Richards J. held that the use of "hindsight" to determine valuation was limited to such circumstances. Nonetheless, where property had been disposed of, and then subsequently sold in the market, the value paid in that subsequent sale was, in principle, evidence from which the market value of the property might be inferred at the earlier date of the transaction.

The Court of Appeal in *Barclays Bank v Eustice*[56] agreed for the purpose of s.423 of the Insolvency Act 1986 to treat three related transactions alleged to amount to an undervalue as one transaction consisting of three parts. This was done at the invitation of the parties but was described by the court as "realistic". **15–023**

A grant of a debenture by a company may, it seems, be a transaction at an undervalue by reason of s.238(4)(a) of the Insolvency Act 1986 if no consideration at all is given for the grant of the debenture.[57] Whether the grant of a **15–024**

---

[54] *Phillips v Brewin Dolphin Bell Lawrie Ltd* [1999] 1 W.L.R. 2052 (CA).

[55] *Stanley v TMK Finance Ltd* [2011] B.P.I.R. 876.

[56] *Barclays Bank v Eustice* [1995] 1 W.L.R. 1238 (CA). See also *Feakins v DEFRA* [2007] B.C.C. 54 (CA).

[57] *Hill v Spread Trustee Ltd* [2007] 1 W.L.R. 2404 (CA), a case decided under s.423 Insolvency Act 1986, per Arden L.J. at [93], where she distinguished the case before her from MC Bacon on

debenture could be set aside as a transaction at an undervalue under s.238(4)b), hence on the basis that the consideration moving to the company granting the debenture is significantly less than the value of the consideration moving from the company (i.e. the debenture itself), is unclear.

In *Re M.C. Bacon Ltd*,[58] the grant of the debenture was held not to be a transaction at an undervalue since, first, the charge by the grantor company of its assets did not deplete those assets, and secondly, the loss, by reason of the debenture, of the grantor's right to apply the proceeds of its assets otherwise than in satisfaction of the debt secured by the debenture was not something capable of valuation "in money or money's worth" within the meaning of s.238(4)(b). The reasoning in M.C. Bacon was accepted by the Court of Appeal in *Feakins v DEFRA*,[59] without, it appears, contrary argument. In *Hill v Spread Trustee Ltd*,[60] Arden L.J. doubted the reasoning in M.C. Bacon on the basis a grant of security does involve the disposition of a proprietary right by the grantor.[61]

Arden L.J. does not expressly address the second reason given in M.C. Bacon, namely that the grant of a debenture was not something capable of valuation in monetary terms, considered from the grantor's point of view. Since it is not necessary to place a specific value on those rights, provided that the disparity in consideration can be seen to be significant,[62] it is considered that, in principle, the grant of security may be capable of valuation in monetary terms.

15–025   The meaning of "consideration" in s.238 has yet to be fully clarified by judicial decisions. Identification of the consideration is a question of fact.[63] Section 238(4)(b) does not specify or limit the person from whom the relevant consideration must move, and thus, for example, where the company agrees to sell an asset to A on terms that B enter into a collateral agreement with the company, the consideration will be the sum of the consideration moving from A to the company under the relevant transaction, and that moving from B under the collateral agreement.[64]

---

the basis that whereas in Bacon forbearance from calling in a previous loan constituted consideration moving from the grantee of the debenture, there was no such consideration in *Hill* (see *Re MC Bacon Ltd* [1990] B.C.L.C. 324, 340f, per Millett J.).

[58] *Re MC Bacon Ltd* [1990] B.C.L.C. 324, 340f–341d.

[59] *Feakins v DEFRA* [2007] B.C.C. 54 (CA), [72], per Parker L.J. See also *Ultraframe (UK) Ltd v Fielding* [2005] EWHC 1638 (Ch), [1388]–[1389]. The issue in that case was whether the grant of a debenture could constitute the acquisition of a "substantial non-cash asset" within the meaning of Companies Act 1985, s.320 (see now Companies Act 2006, s.190). Lewison J., following *MC Bacon*, held that it could not, since the company parted with nothing of value when it granted the debenture, and the consideration it received was incapable of being valued in money or money's worth.

[60] *Hill v Spread Trustee Ltd* [2007] 1 W.L.R. 2404 (CA).

[61] *Hill v Spread Trustee Ltd* [2007] 1 W.L.R. 2404 (CA), [138] Arden L.J. refers to *Buchler v Talbot* [2004] 2 A.C. 298 (HL), [29] and [51]. Arden L.J. refers to the fact that the security in *Hill v Spread Trustee* consisted of legal mortgages, but on the basis of her reliance on the passages in *Buchler v Talbot*, it appears that her reasoning would apply equally in the context of mere equitable fixed or floating charges. This part of the judgment is obiter.

[62] *Re Thoars (deceased) (No.2)* [2005] 1 B.C.L.C. 331 (CA).

[63] *Phillips v Brewin Dolphin Bell Lawrie Ltd* [2001] 1 W.L.R. 143 (HL), [20].

[64] Where consideration provided would be challengeable as a preference under s.239, it will not amount to consideration for the purposes of s.238, see *Barber v CI Ltd* [2006] B.C.C. 927.

Even where, as between transferor and transferee, full consideration is **15–026** apparently given, there may still be a transaction at an undervalue if the interests of a third party are prejudicially affected by the transaction. In *Agricultural Mortgage Corp Plc v Woodward*,[65] a husband entered into a lease of his agricultural holding in favour of his wife at what was assumed to be a full market rent, the purpose of the lease being to prevent the claimant mortgagee taking vacant possession of the land. Since the loss of vacant possession reduced the value of the land from over £1 million to less than £500,000, the wife was placed in a "ransom position" vis-à-vis the mortgagee. Since that ransom position had not been reflected in the rent, the lease was held by the Court of Appeal to be at an undervalue. It was also argued by the mortgagee in Woodward that the mere detriment to the husband in reducing the value of his land by virtue of the lease could constitute "consideration", but the Court of Appeal expressly left the point open for later decision.

(d) Extortionate credit transactions

Under the 1986 Act, a liquidator or administrator may apply for relief in respect **15–027** of any extortionate credit transaction entered into by the company within the period of three years before the company went into liquidation or entered administration.[66] The section applies to transactions which, having regard to the risk accepted by the creditor, require grossly exorbitant payments to be made (whether unconditionally or in certain contingencies) in respect of the provision of credit, or which otherwise grossly contravene ordinary principles of fair dealing. The court is given power to set aside the whole or any part of any obligation created by the transaction, vary the terms of the transaction or the terms on which any security is held or require the surrender of any security. The powers conferred by the section are exercisable concurrently with any powers exercisable in relation to that transaction as a transaction at an undervalue under s.238.

(e) Commencement of winding-up

A compulsory winding-up is deemed to commence on the date of presentation **15–028** of the petition on which the order is made.[67] Accordingly, the order has retrospective effect and will invalidate all charges created by the company after the date of the petition unless the court otherwise orders.[68]

---

[65] *Agricultural Mortgage Corp Plc v Woodward* [1994] B.C.C. 688 (CA), which was decided under s.423 of the 1986 Act, the wording of which is, for the purpose of the point in the text, the same as s.238.

[66] Insolvency Act 1986, s.244; and see *White v Davenham Trust Ltd* [2011] B.C.C. 77 (where an attempt by a debtor to invoke s.244 in applying to set aside a statutory demand was dismissed).

[67] Insolvency Act 1986, s.129. When the court makes a winding-up order by virtue of para.13(1) (e) of Sch.B1 to the Insolvency Act 1986, the winding-up is deemed to commence on the making of the order: Insolvency Act 1986, s.129(1A).

[68] Insolvency Act 1986, s.127. A transaction contravening s.127 is unlikely to be validated unless it was in the ordinary course of business or for the company's benefit: see *Re TW Construction* [1954] 1 W.L.R. 540; *Re Operator Control Cabs* [1970] 3 All E.R. 657; *Re Gray's Inn Construction Co* [1980] 1 W.L.R. 711 (CA); *Re SA & D Wright Ltd* [1992] B.C.C. 503 (CA). Where cheques are drawn on a company's account after presentation of a petition, whether the

15–029   A voluntary winding-up commences on the date of the resolution to this effect. Receivers have been held to have standing to apply under s.127 of the 1986 Act, on the basis that the statute imposes no limitation on who might apply.[69] Property recovered as a result of a void disposition of a company's property is caught by a debenture if that debenture would have covered the property prior to the disposition. Since such dispositions are void, the character of the property disposed of does not change.[70]

4.   CONSEQUENCES OF INVALIDITY OF CHARGES

15–030   Where a charge under which a receiver has been appointed is invalid, so also is his appointment, and he is a trespasser in respect of all assets of which he takes possession.[71] A receiver may therefore be liable for damages for trespass (in respect of land and chattels) and for conversion (in respect of chattels), but will not be liable for conversion in respect of any interference by him with intangible assets, such as contractual rights of the company, as the tort of conversion applies to tangibles only.[72] In *OBG Ltd v Allen* receivers were appointed under an invalid debenture, and took control of the business away from its board of directors. The receivers purported to manage the contractual rights of the company but did not intend to procure any breach or other actionable wrong, or hinder or prevent performance of the company's contracts. The House of Lords held that the tort of interference with contractual relations provided the company (now in liquidation) with no remedy.

15–031   In the case of a charge void for non-registration (where the charge is valid as against the company as a going concern, i.e. not in liquidation or administration[73]) it seems that:

    (a)   a receiver may act safely until liquidation except in so far as (d) applies[74];

    (b)   if the sums due under the charge are repaid before either (i) liquidation or (ii) subject to (d) below, a challenge, the chargee cannot be

---

account is in credit or overdrawn, the amounts so paid are not recoverable from the bank, but only from the payees of the cheques: *Hollicourt (Contracts) Ltd (In Liquidation) v Bank of Ireland* [2001] Ch. 555 (CA) (where certain broad dicta in *Gray's Inn Construction* were disapproved). In *Re Dewrun Ltd* [2002] B.C.C. 57 the court validated a sale of property to a third party solely to the extent necessary to validate the security granted by the purchaser to the funder of the transaction. The same problem does not arise in the case of a voluntary liquidation (not followed by a compulsory winding-up), since the winding-up commences at the date of the resolution and there is no question of any retrospective operation: Insolvency Act 1986, s.86.

[69] *Merton v Hammond Suddards* [1996] 2 B.C.L.C. 470. See also *Re Argentum Reductions (UK) Ltd* [1975] 1 W.L.R. 186; *Re Dewrun Ltd* [2002] B.C.C. 57 (where the application was made by a secured creditor). A creditor of a shareholder in the applicant company has been permitted to be heard: *Re Rescuepine Ltd* [2003] 1 B.C.L.C. 661.

[70] *Merton v Hammond Suddards* [1996] 2 B.C.L.C. 470.

[71] *Re Goldburg (No.2)* [1912] 1 K.B. 606.

[72] *OBG Ltd v Allen* [2008] 1 AC 1 (HL).

[73] *Re Monolithic Building Co* [1915] 1 Ch. 643 (CA). *Smith (Administrator of Cosslett (Contractors) Ltd) v Bridgend CBC* [2002] 1 A.C. 336 (HL), [21], per Lord Hoffmann, and [65]–[67], per Lord Scott.

[74] Dictum of Walton J. in *Burston Finance Ltd v Speirway* [1974] 1 W.L.R. 1648, 1657E.

required to repay such sums unless the repayment is voidable as a fraudulent preference[75];

(c) prior to such challenge the receiver can validly sell assets of the company[76];

(d) where the receiver or chargee with notice of the relevant facts receives monies caught by another charge having priority, the receiver or chargee holds such monies as constructive trustee for the other chargee.[77] Where a floating charge is avoided by the special provisions relating to floating charges in a subsequent winding-up, sums repaid under the charge prior to the commencement of the winding-up do not have to be repaid.[78]

In all the above-mentioned situations, at the time of the action taken by the receiver or repayment, the security is perfectly valid against the company and has not been challenged by the parties who presently or in the future may have locus standi to do so. **15–032**

In a case where the invalidity of the charge arises only from the invalidity of the guarantee secured by the charge, the House of Lords has held that the receiver should only be treated as a trespasser from the date that a writ is served on him claiming damages.[79] **15–033**

Where a receiver has been appointed under an invalid charge, but his management of the company has incontrovertibly benefited that company, the receiver might be entitled to remuneration on a quantum meruit basis.[80] **15–034**

5. APPOINTMENT AFTER WINDING-UP

A winding-up does not prevent the appointment of a receiver,[81] though an administration, whether by court order or by direct appointment by a qualified party, does.[82] Paragraph 43(6A) of Sch.B1 to the Insolvency Act 1986 provides that an administrative receiver of the company may not be appointed to a **15–035**

[75] *Re Parkes Garage* [1929] 1 Ch. 139; *Re Ehrmann Bros Ltd* [1906] 2 Ch. 697 (CA), 708, per Romer L.J.; *Welsh Development Agency v Export Finance Co Ltd* [1990] B.C.C. 393, 412B–412C (not reversed on this point on appeal). Likewise if the charge-holder seizes the charged assets prior to the liquidation: *Mercantile Bank of India v Chartered Bank* [1937] 1 All E.R. 231, 241, per Porter J., relying on the pledge case of *Wrightson v McArthur & Hutchisons* [1921] 2 K.B. 807; *Re Row Dal Constructions Property Ltd* [1966] V.R. 249; *NV Slavenburg's Bank v Intercontinental Ltd* [1980] 1 W.L.R. 1076, 1090–1091.
[76] *Royal Bank of Canada v First Pioneer Investments* (1980) 106 D.L.R. (3d) 330.
[77] *Welsh Development Agency v Export Finance Co Ltd* [1990] B.C.C. 393, 412. It proved unnecessary on appeal to deal with the suggestion that the charge-holder with superior rights needed to intervene positively to assert his rights to the monies: [1992] B.C.C. 270, 286G, per Dillon L.J. and 304E–304F, per Staughton L.J.
[78] *Mace Builders (Glasgow) Ltd v Lunn* [1987] Ch. 191 (CA).
[79] *Ford & Carter v Midland Bank* (1979) 129 N.L.J. 543 (HL). The receiver appeared to have been acting as such prior to that date with the company's consent.
[80] *Monks v Poynice Pty Ltd* (1987) 8 N.S.W.L.R. 62.
[81] *Re Henry Pound Son & Hutchins* (1889) L.R. 42 Ch. D. 402 (CA); *Strong Carlyle Press* [1893] 1 Ch. 268 (CA); *Re Northern Garage Ltd* [1946] Ch. 188.
[82] See above, Ch.7.

company in administration. Where a receiver is appointed after a winding-up order, he will need the leave of the court to take possession of the charged assets, but such leave will be given as a matter of course.[83]

15–036 So far as the costs of the winding-up are concerned, in relation to voluntary liquidations, s.115 of the Insolvency Act 1986 provides that "all expenses properly incurred in the winding-up, including the remuneration of the liquidator, are payable out of the company's assets in priority to all other claims". In both compulsory and voluntary winding-up, r.4.218 of the Insolvency Rules 1986 lists in order of priority a number of categories of fees, costs, charges and other expenses of the liquidation which are to be regarded as expenses of the liquidation.

15–037 Prior to the Insolvency Act 1986, it was well understood that the expression "the company's assets" in the forerunner of s.115 included assets which were the subject of a floating charge which had not crystallised at the moment of winding-up.[84] Thus where a receiver was appointed after the making of a winding-up order, the costs of the liquidator in the winding-up were payable prior to the preferential creditors out of the assets subject to the floating charge. On the other hand, where the receivership preceded the making of a winding-up order (even if after the date of presentation of the petition) or the passing of a resolution for the voluntary liquidation of the company, so that the floating charge had crystallised prior to liquidation, it had been held prior to the 1986 Act that the costs of the liquidator were postponed to the claims of the preferential creditors and those of the debenture-holder.[85] Following the 1986 Act, and as a result of the new definition of "floating charge" under s.251 of that Act, it had been held that the costs of a liquidator in a winding-up were payable in priority to preferential creditors, and hence the holders of the floating charge, even where the appointment of receivers pre-dated the commencement of the winding-up.[86]

15–038 The law as set out in the previous paragraph was then wholly overturned by the decision of the House of Lords in *Buchler v Talbot*.[87] In that case, administrative receivers were appointed by the holder of a floating charge and the company was subsequently placed in voluntary liquidation. The expenses of the liquidation (including the liquidator's remuneration) far exceeded any realisations of uncharged assets of the company. The issue was whether the expenses of the liquidation should be paid out of floating charge realisations in priority to all other claims. At first instance and in the Court of Appeal, the courts applied the reasoning in the decision in *Barcleycorn*, as extended by

---

[83] *Re Henry Pound Son & Hutchins* (1889) L.R. 42 Ch. D. 402 (CA); *Re Potters Oils Ltd (No.2)* [1986] 1 W.L.R. 201, 206, per Hoffmann J.

[84] *Re Lewis Merthyr Consolidated Collieries* [1929] 1 Ch. 498 (CA); *Re Griffin Hotel Company* [1941] Ch. 129; *Re Barleycorn Enterprises Ltd* [1970] Ch. 465 (CA); *Buchler v Talbot* [2004] 2 A.C. 298 (HL), where the speeches give a full historical account of the relevant statutory provisions and case law decided thereunder.

[85] *Re Christonette International Ltd* [1982] 1 W.L.R. 1245; see *Buchler v Talbot* [2004] 2 A.C. 298 (HL), [85], per Lord Millett.

[86] See in particular *Re Portbase Clothing Ltd* [1993] Ch. 388; and *Mond v Hammond Suddards* [2000] Ch. 40 (CA). For a further discussion and criticism of the law as understood prior to the discussion of the House of Lords in *Buchler v Talbot*, see the 3rd edn of this work, paras 11–032 to 11–033.

[87] *Buchler v Talbot* [2004] 2 A.C. 298 (HL).

Portbase and *Mond v Hammond Suddards*, holding that the liquidation expenses should be paid in priority out of floating charge realisations.

These decisions were reversed by the House of Lords, which held that liqui-   **15–039**
dation costs had no priority over the net realisations of the floating charge assets, and hence *Barcleycorn* was explicitly overruled, whilst the reasoning in *Portbase* and *Mond v Hammond Suddards*, in so far as it adopted and extended that in *Barcleycorn*, was implicitly disapproved. The House of Lords identified two different funds of assets, namely: (i) assets and their realisations subject to a floating charge; and (ii) those not so subject. As to the former category, the relevant priority was: (i) the costs of preserving and realising of assets; (ii) the receiver's remuneration and the proper costs and expenses of the receiver-ship; (iii) the debts which are preferential in the receivership; (iv) the principal and interest secured by the floating charge; (v) the company. As to the latter category, the relevant priority was: (i) the costs of preserving and realising the assets; (ii) the liquidator's remuneration and the proper costs and expenses of the winding-up; (iii) the debts which are preferential in the winding-up; (iv) the charge-holder to the extent that the preferential debts have been paid out of assets subject to the floating charge; (v) the general body of creditors.

With regard to floating charges created after September 15, 2003 (the coming   **15–040**
into force of s.176A of the Insolvency Act 1986) these priorities are altered by the effect of the "prescribed part" of the assets subject to the floating charge made available to unsecured creditors in priority to the floating charge-holder.

Parliament intervened to overturn, in large part, the *Buchler* decision by   **15–041**
enacting s.176ZA of the Insolvency Act 1986[88]. The broad effect of s.176ZA (1) is that the expenses of the winding-up once more have priority over the claims of the debenture-holder and any preferential creditors entitled to be paid out of floating charge assets (though not over any amount to be made available as the "prescribed part" under s.176A). However, the priority for expenses created by s.176ZA(1) is subject to rules made pursuant to s.176ZA(3), i.e. rr.4.218A–4.218E of the Insolvency Rules 1986. These rules permit the use of floating charge assets to pay "litigation expenses" (as defined in r.4.218A(1)) only where the necessary approval or authorisation has been given by those with an interest in the charged assets. Rules 4.218B–4.218E set out detailed provisions on how such approval or authorisation must be obtained. These rules recognise that, in respect of litigation costs, those with a right to look for payment out of the charged assets have a special interest in those assets, so that a liquidator should not have power, unilaterally, to spend such assets on litigation.

6. END OF RECEIVER'S AGENCY/CONTINUATION OF POWERS

(a) Termination of agency

The winding-up order or resolution for winding-up terminates the receiver's   **15–043**
agency for the company.[88] The powers given by the debenture to exploit the

---

[88] Insolvency Act 1986, s.44(1)(a) (administrative receivers), *Gosling v Gaskell* [1897] A.C. 575 (HL); *Barrows v Chief Land Registrar, The Times*, October 20, 1977, per Whitford J.

company's undertaking and assets, however, continue unaffected, save only that they cannot be exercised so as to create any new debt or fresh liability.[89] The receiver can, therefore, carry on the business of the company,[90] get in and realise the company's assets[91] and take proceedings in the name of the company to recover assets.[92] He may do so either as agent for the debenture-holder or as principal: "If the receiver continues to act, he does not automatically become the agent of the mortgagee but he may become so if the mortgagee treats him as such."[93] For the receiver to become the agent of the debenture-holder it will have to be shown that the relationship of principal and agent has been constituted between them.[94] Ordinarily, the receiver carries on the business and exercises his other surviving powers as principal,[95] incurs personal liability[96] but claims a right of indemnity out of any assets in his hands.[97]

15–044   As a principal, the receiver will not be bound by any restriction on the powers of the company. Where the receiver acts as agent of the company, the company, and hence the receiver, will be bound by statutory and other restrictions on the company's actions.[98]

(b)   Realisation and disposal of assets

15–045   The termination of the receiver's agency does not prevent the receiver from realising the assets charged.[99]

(winding-up order); *Thomas v Todd* [1926] 2 K.B. 511; and see *Re Beck Foods Ltd* [2002] 1 W.L.R. 1304 (CA), [76]. The appointment of provisional liquidators of a company appears similarly to terminate the agency: see above, para.2–045.

[89] Winding up merely determines the receiver's power to pledge the company's credit: per Needham J. in *Mercantile Credit Ltd v Atkins* [1985] 1 N.S.W.L.R. 670, 679, affirmed 10 A.C.L.R. 153.

[90] *Gosling v Gaskell* [1897] A.C. 575 (HL).

[91] *Re Henry Pound Son & Hutchins* (1889) L.R. 42 Ch. D. 402 (CA).

[92] *Goughs Garage v Pugsley* [1930] 1 K.B. 615. This sentence and that which immediately precedes it were approved as correctly stating the law by the Court of Appeal in *Re Beck Foods Ltd* [2002] 1 W.L.R. 1304 (CA); see [76], per Parker L.J. The receiver will personally be at risk as to costs: see below, para.15–049. The requirement on the receiver not to render the company liable for costs is analogous to the requirement placed on directors suing in the name of the company during a receivership to indemnify the company against any liability for costs: see above, Ch.7.

[93] Per Mann J. in *American Express International Banking Corp v Hurley* [1985] 3 All E.R. 564, 568 (citing *Re Wood* [1941] Ch. 112); *Edmonds v Westland Bank Ltd* [1991] 2 N.Z.L.R. 655.

[94] *Royal Bank of Scotland v O'Shea* Unreported February 3, 1998, per Morritt L.J.

[95] *Gaskell v Gosling* [1896] 1 Q.B. 669 (CA), 699, per Rigby L.J. (dissenting) whose judgment was upheld on appeal by the House of Lords. The *Cork Report*, para.461 suggested that legislation was appropriate to clarify the receiver's position after the termination of his agency, but this was not included in the Insolvency Act 1985.

[96] *Sowman v David Samuel Trust* [1978] 1 W.L.R. 22, 26; *Gaskell v Gosling* [1896] 1 Q.B. 669 (CA).

[97] Insolvency Act 1986, s.44(1)(c) (administrative receivers); Insolvency Act 1986, s.37(1) (non-administrative receivers).

[98] See, e.g. *Demite Ltd v Protec Health Ltd* [1998] B.C.C. 638: receivers, as agents of the company, sold the business of the company in receivership to a party connected with a former director of the company, without obtaining the approval of the members of the company in general meeting. The sale was held to be voidable at the election of the company, under s.320 of the Companies Act 1985 (now Companies Act 2006, s.190). See also *Ultraframe (UK) Ltd v Fielding* [2005] EWHC 1638 (Ch). Whilst there are exceptions when the company is in winding-up or (now) administration, there is no exception where the company is in receivership: Companies Act 2006, s.193.

[99] *Gaskell v Gosling* [1897] A.C. 575 (HL), per Rigby L.J.; *Sowman v David Samuel Trust Ltd* [1978] 1 W.L.R. 22; *Barrows v Chief Land Registrar*, *The Times*, October 20, 1977: *Re Sobam BV*

Although s.127 of the Insolvency Act 1986 prevents valid dispositions of the **15–046** company's property after the commencement of the winding-up, this does not apply to dispositions by a receiver of property contained in a relevant charge.[100] Despite the winding-up, the receiver is entitled to continue or take legal or other action[101] in the name of the company.[102]

Despite the winding-up, the receiver may take possession of the property **15–047** subject to the charge.[103] The receiver will require the leave of the court to take possession of the company's assets if a court-appointed liquidator has possession of those assets. The need to obtain leave in such a case is based on the fact that the court-appointed liquidator in a compulsory winding-up is an officer of the court.[104] It follows that leave is also required where a provisional liquidator has possession and refuses to deliver up, but not in the case of a voluntary liquidator. Leave is given "as of right".

(c) Costs of action

The right of a receiver to take or continue proceedings in the name of the **15–048** company to preserve its assets is part of the debenture-holder's security and accordingly survives winding-up.[105]

Where, after a winding-up order or resolution to wind up, the receiver is **15–049** suing in the name of the company, he does so as a principal in the exercise of the powers granted by the debenture, so that costs may be ordered against him personally or to be payable as expenses of the receivership.[106] The costs of

---

[1996] 1 W.L.R. 1070. Nor does it prejudice his lien securing his entitlement to an indemnity against liabilities properly incurred prior to termination out of the assets of the company: *Hill v Venning* [1979] 4 A.C.L.R. 555.

[100] *Sowman v David Samuel Trust Ltd* [1978] 1 W.L.R. 22, 30C, per Goulding J.; *Re Henry Pound Son & Hutchins* (1889) L.R. 42 Ch. D. 402 (CA), 421, per Cotton L.J.; *Re Landmark Corp Ltd* (1968) 88 W.N. (Pt.1) (N.S.W.) 195; *Re Otway Coal Co Ltd* [1953] V.L.R. 557, 565, per O'Bryan J.; *Sheahan v Carrier Air Conditioning Pty Ltd* (1996) 189 C.L.R. 407 (High Court of Australia). *Re Clifton Place Garage Ltd* [1970] Ch. 477 (CA) does not suggest the contrary. The monies sought (unsuccessfully) to be recovered as void dispositions in that case were monies of a subsidiary and were not charged under the debenture: see the facts set out at 479–480 and *Re Margart Pty Ltd* [1985] B.C.L.C. 314, 319.

[101] *Bacal Contracting Ltd v Modern Engineering (Bristol) Ltd* [1980] 2 All E.R. 655.

[102] *Gough's Garages Ltd v Pugsley* [1930] 1 K.B. 615 (application for new lease in exercise of statutory rights); *Newhart Ltd v Co-op Commercial Bank* [1978] Q.B. 814 (CA). To the opposite effect, see the dictum of Cotton L.J. in *Re Henry Pound Son & Hutchins* (1889) L.R. 42 Ch. D. 402 (CA), 421, although his view may simply have been based on the construction of the particular debenture in question: see the explanation of the dictum in *Kelaw Pty Ltd v Catco Development Pty Ltd* (1989) 15 N.S.W.L.R. 587, 592, per Brownie J.

[103] *Re Henry Pound Son & Hutchins* (1889) L.R. 42 Ch. D. 402 (CA), 422–423; *Re Potters Oils Ltd (No.2)* [1986] 1 W.L.R. 201, 206A–206B, per Hoffmann J.; *Re Landmark Corp Ltd* (1968) 88 W.N. (Pt.1) (N.S.W.) 195, 196–197, where Street J. suggests that unless the liquidator challenges the receiver's right to possession, leave need not be sought.

[104] *Re Henry Pound Son & Hutchins* (1889) L.R. 42 Ch. D. 402 (CA), 422; *Re Potters Oils Ltd (No.2)* [1986] 1 W.L.R. 201.

[105] *Goughs Garages Ltd v Pugsley* [1930] 1 K.B. 615; *Newman Bros v Allum* [1934] N.Z.L.R. 694.

[106] *Bacal Contracting Ltd v Modern Engineering (Bristol) Ltd* [1980] 2 All E.R. 655; *S & M Hotels v Family Housing Association* Unreported Transcript 1979/132 (CA). See also *Kelaw Pty Ltd v Catco Developments Pty Ltd* (1989) 15 N.S.W.L.R. 587 and C. de Kerloy, "The Personal Liability of Liquidators and Administrative Receivers for the Costs of an Unsuccessful Action" (2000) 4(1) R.A. & L.Q. 13.

defending an action adopted by a receiver after the defendant company has gone into liquidation may similarly be payable by the receiver.[107]

The case law is discussed in *Dolphin Quay Development Ltd v Mills*,[108] where the issue was whether a third party costs order should be made against administrative receivers who had unsuccessfully pursued litigation on behalf of the company in receivership. The company was not in liquidation. The Court of Appeal held that prior to liquidation, the receiver acted as agent of the company, and hence was in a position analogous to that of a director or liquidator (para.82), so that no third party costs order would ordinarily be made. The defendant's remedy was to seek security for his costs. Once the company had gone into liquidation, the receiver was the "real party" and hence a third party costs order might be made.

(d)   Leases

15–050   Any authority to impose on the company obligations, other than the usual qualified covenant for quiet enjoyment, by a grant of a lease would probably be determined on a winding-up.[109]

7.   EFFECT ON RECEIVER'S REMUNERATION

15–051   In a winding-up, the liquidator has a statutory power to apply to the court to fix the remuneration of a receiver.[110] The court has power to fix such remuneration in relation to a period prior to the application, even where the receiver has died or ceased to act prior to the application. In special circumstances, the court may require repayment of all or part of the remuneration paid for any period prior to the making of the order. The court will, however, only interfere where the remuneration can clearly be seen to be excessive.[111]

8.   CUSTODY OF BOOKS AND DOCUMENTS

15–052   Despite an order or resolution to wind up, the receiver will be entitled to documents necessary to support the debenture-holder's title to assets charged.[112]

---

[107] *Anderson v Hyde* [1996] N.I. 304 (Northern Ireland CA).

[108] *Dolphin Quay Development Ltd v Mills* [2008] 1 W.L.R. 1829 (CA).

[109] See above, para.11–108.

[110] Insolvency Act 1986, s.36.

[111] *Re Potters Oils Ltd (No.2)* [1986] 1 W.L.R. 201. The same test was applied by the court in *Munns v Perkins* [2002] B.P.I.R. 120, which concerned an application by a debenture-holder under s.35 of the Insolvency Act 1986 to reduce the remuneration charged by a receiver appointed by him. In principle, it appears that the "Practice Statement—The Fixing and Approval of the Remuneration of Appointees (2004)", issued by the Chief Registrar on July 15, 2004, applies to applications under Insolvency Act 1986, s.36. It is doubtful, however, whether the provisions of the statement could apply at least with their full rigour. The remuneration of a receiver is, in essence, a matter of contract between the receiver and the debenture-holder, and thus differs fundamentally from remuneration earned by insolvency practitioners in other types of insolvency process. It is thus considered that the decision in *Potters Oils* remains, essentially, good law. For court-appointed receivers, see below, para.29–017.

[112] *Re Landmark Corporation Ltd* (1968) 88 W.N. (Pt.1) (N.S.W.) 195.

A liquidator will be entitled to documents relating to the management and business of the company in so far as they are not needed to support such title.[113]

Although there is authority to the effect that a court-appointed receiver can **15-053** be compelled to deliver documents to a liquidator entitled to them on receipt of an undertaking to produce them to the receiver on request,[114] there is no such authority with respect to other receivers. However, general practice supports the proposition that delivery up in return for an undertaking and subsequent production on request should occur and could be compelled in respect of non-administrative receivers.[115]

Under s.234 of the Insolvency Act 1986, an administrative receiver can **15-054** apply as an "office-holder" to the court to compel "any person" to deliver to him books, papers or records "to which the company appears to be entitled". The phrase "any person" is wide enough to cover a liquidator.[116] The application should be made by the office-holder in his own name[117] and should normally be made on notice.[118] Questions of disputed ownership will now normally be decided by the courts on such an application,[119] but not where this issue falls for decision by a foreign court.[120] Likewise under s.234, a liquidator can apply as an "office-holder" for delivery up of papers and documents except in so far as they are needed to support the debenture-holder's title to the charged assets, since these latter documents would not be ones to which the company (as against the debenture-holder) would "appear to be entitled".

Whilst both administrative receivers and liquidators have the ability to seek **15-055** orders for the production of documents held subject to a lien under s.236 of the 1986 Act,[121] receivers do not have the additional assistance of s.246, which makes unenforceable liens over documents as against, inter alia, liquidators and provisional liquidators to the extent that the enforcement of the lien would deny possession of the books, papers, etc. The special assistance to liquidators does not extend to "documents which give title to property and are held as such".[122]

9. ACCOUNTS

By statute[123] a liquidator may require a receiver to render accounts of receipts **15-056** and payments and pay over any sums payable to the liquidator.

---

[113] *Kerr and Hunter on Receivers and Administrators*, 19th edn (London: Sweet & Maxwell, 2009), para.25–17 at p.622.

[114] *Engel v South Metropolitan Brewing Co* [1892] 1 Ch. 442.

[115] See *Kerr and Hunter on Receivers and Administrators*, 19th edn (London: Sweet & Maxwell, 2009), fn.8, para.25–17 at p.622.

[116] *Re First Express Ltd* [1991] B.C.C. 782.

[117] *Smith (Administrator of Coslett Contractors) Ltd v Bridgend CBC* [2002] 1 A.C. 336 (HL), [32], per Lord Hoffmann.

[118] *Smith (Administrator of Coslett Contractors) Ltd v Bridgend CBC* [2002] 1 A.C. 336 (HL) and see above, Ch.8.

[119] *Re London Iron and Steel Co Ltd* [1990] B.C.C. 159; and see *Coslett Construction Ltd* [1998] Ch. 495 (CA).

[120] *Re Leyland DAF Ltd* [1994] B.C.C. 166 (CA).

[121] *Re Aveling Barford Ltd* [1989] 1 W.L.R. 360 and see above, Ch.8.

[122] s.246(3). The meaning (or lack of meaning) of the words "held as such" is discussed in *Re SEIL Trade Finance Ltd* [1992] B.C.C. 538.

[123] Insolvency Act 1986, ss.38 and 41.

10.   CALLS ON CAPITAL

15–057   As between a non-administrative receiver and a liquidator, calls after a winding-up order or resolution can only be made by the liquidator.[124] If the liquidator fails or neglects to make a call, the non-administrative receiver can apply to the court for an order requiring the liquidator to make the call or authorising the receiver to use the liquidator's name to make the call.[125] Although the Insolvency Act 1986 gives administrative receivers an apparently unrestricted power to make calls on uncalled capital,[126] it is suggested that the power should be construed as exercisable only until a liquidation in accordance with the rules that govern other receivers. It is unlikely that the legislators intended that, after a liquidation, both the liquidator and the receiver should have concurrent powers to make calls: it is sufficient that the administrative receiver can compel the liquidator to exercise his power.

11.   VOIDABLE PREFERENCE AND MISFEASANCE

15–058   Prior to the Insolvency Act 1986, where a liquidator recovered sums of money in respect of a "fraudulent preference"[127] the recovery was held to be designed to benefit unsecured creditors and so fell outside assets charged by a debenture.[128] The position is the same under the 1986 Act.[129] If the subject-matter of the preference was not money, but specific and identifiable property, the subject of the floating charge, on its recovery this probably fell within the property charged by the debenture.[130] In any case, where the recoveries fell outside the charge, they constituted "assets of the company available for payment of general creditors". Again, it is suggested that the position is the same under the 1986 Act.

---

[124] *Fowler v Broad's Patent Night Light Co* [1893] 1 Ch. 724. The rationale for the rule is "that the moment you have got a liquidation, the call-making power is limited to the statutory power of making calls in a winding up", 730, per Vaughan Williams J.

[125] *Fowler v Broad's Patent Night Light Co* [1893] 1 Ch. 724; *Re Westminster Syndicate Ltd* (1908) 99 L.T. 924; *Re South Australian Barytes Ltd* (1977) 3 A.C.L.R. 52, 63.

[126] Insolvency Act 1986, s.42 and Sch.1, para.19.

[127] Under the Companies Act 1948, s.321, replaced by the Companies Act 1985, s.615.

[128] *Re Yagerphone* [1935] Ch. 392; *Re MC Bacon Ltd* [1991] Ch. 127, 137; see also *Re Quality Camera Co Pty Ltd* (1965) 83 W.N. (Pt.1) (N.S.W.) 226; [1965] N.S.W.R. 1330.

[129] *Re Oasis Merchandising Services Ltd (In Liquidation); Ward v Aitken* [1998] Ch. 170 (CA); *Re Exchange Travel (Holdings) Ltd (No.3)*; sub nom. *Katz v McNally* [1997] B.C.C. 784 (CA); *Re Floor Fourteen Ltd* [2001] 3 All E.R. 499 (CA). However, it appears that in *Ciro Citterio Menswear Plc (In Administration) v Thakrar* Unreported July 10, 2002, Neuburger J., whilst acknowledging that he was bound by the decision of the Court of Appeal in *Floor Fourteen Ltd*, stated in an obiter dictum that had he to decide what order it would have been appropriate to make to reverse the effects of a preferential payment, he would have made an order to the benefit of, in effect, a floating charge-holder, rather than giving the ordinary unsecured creditors a windfall by ordering that the proceeds of the preferential payment be held on trust for the unsecured creditors: see P. Fleming, "Sharing the Spoils of a Preference Action" (2003) 16(5) Insolv. Int. 33, 33–35.

[130] See *NA Kratzmann Pty Ltd v Tucker (No.2)* (1968) 123 C.L.R. 295 (High Court of Australia); *Ross v Taylor* [1985] S.L.T. 387 (Court of Session, Inner House); *Bank of New Zealand v Essington Developments Pty Ltd* (1990) 5 A.C.S.R. 86, 89–90, per McLelland J.

The debenture-holder or receiver has no right to bring proceedings to recover **15–059** property invoking the statutory voidable preference provisions.[131] This can only be done by the liquidator (or by an administrator), and he should not do so, if the property recovered falls within a charge, unless:

(a) the debenture-holder agrees to give up his claim on the property recovered for the benefit of all the creditors[132]; or

(b) (it is thought) the interests of the unsecured creditors require that this action be taken (e.g. because the recovery will produce a surplus of secured assets over secured liabilities, leaving a balance available for unsecured creditors).[133]

The same reasoning is equally applicable to recoveries by the liquidator under the Insolvency Act 1986 in respect of "transactions at an undervalue"[134] and "extortionate credit transactions".[135]

In case of such recoveries by an administrator, it is thought that the same **15–060** principle applies during the period of administration or if the administration is immediately followed by a liquidation. But (in the absence of some provision in a scheme of arrangement precluding this result) if the administration comes to an end and liquidation does not immediately follow, the recovery may fall within the scope of a charge created by a debenture whether prior or subsequent to the recovery.

Recoveries by a liquidator in respect of wrongful trading claims under s.214 **15–061** of the Insolvency Act 1986 are not caught by a charge over the company's assets, since such claims are special statutory rights in liquidation designed to benefit unsecured creditors[136] and therefore the same considerations apply as in the case of voidable preference recoveries. The same applies to fraudulent trading claims under s.213.[137]

---

[131] Insolvency Act 1986, s.239. It is considered that the change in the wording of the preference provisions has made no difference in this regard. In *Re MC Bacon Ltd* [1991] Ch. 127, 137, Millett J. rejected the argument that, since s.239(3) empowered the court to restore the position to what it would have been had the preference not been given (when the assets given in order to prefer the creditor would have been subject to the charge), the proceeds of a successful s.239 action would belong to the debenture-holder.

[132] *Ex p. Cooper* (1875) L.R. 10 Ch. App. 510 (CA in Chancery), 511; *Willmott v London Celluloid Co* (1887) L.R. 34 Ch. D. 147 (CA in Chancery). See also *Albert Gregory Ltd v C Niccol Ltd* (1916) 16 SR. (N.S.W.) 214; *Couve v J Pierre Couve Ltd* [1933] 49 C.L.R. 486.

[133] Any recovery for the secured creditor may benefit the unsecured creditors by reducing the amount of his unsecured indebtedness, in respect of which he will compete with the unsecured creditors. On the other hand, the effect of a successful claim under s.239 might be to make the respondent an unsecured creditor in a sum similar to the reduction in the secured creditor's unsecured claim. Nevertheless, unsecured creditors might benefit where, for example, the value of property given in discharge of a debt has increased significantly since the discharge.

[134] Insolvency Act 1986, s.238.

[135] Insolvency Act 1986, s.244.

[136] *Re MC Bacon Ltd* [1991] Ch. 127, 136–138, per Millett J. *Re Oasis Merchandising Services Ltd* [1998] Ch. 170 (CA). Knox J. in *Re Produce Marketing Consortium Ltd (No.2)* [1989] B.C.L.C. 520, 554a stated that the fruits of successful s.214 proceedings would go to the debenture-holders, though it is not clear whether any argument was addressed on the point and no relevant cases were cited.

[137] See *Oasis Merchandising Services Ltd* [1998] Ch. 170 (CA).

15–062   Recoveries by a liquidator for "misfeasance" (breach of duty) against directors and others will usually fall within the property charged.[138]

15–063   Following the decision of the Court of Appeal in *West Mercia Safetyware
Ltd v Dodd*,[139] it seems that many proceedings under the fraudulent trading,
wrongful trading, voidable preference and undervalue provisions[140] could
instead (or in the alternative) be based on misfeasance. Given the obvious
advantage to the debenture-holder of the proceedings being brought in misfeasance, the receiver should ensure that the liquidator agrees in such cases to
make a misfeasance claim and agrees a fair method of appropriating recoveries
between different heads of claim. Failing such agreement, the receiver should
consider whether he should mount concurrent proceedings in the name of the
company and seek to have those heard with the liquidator's proceedings.

12.   RATES

15–064   The position upon liquidation in relation to rates is dealt with in Ch.19.

13.   RECEIVER'S INDEMNITY UPON HANDING OVER ESTATE TO LIQUIDATOR

15–065   It is sometimes convenient for a receiver to hand over the estate of the company
to a liquidator without fully carrying out the administration required in the
receivership. In such a situation, a suitable indemnity should be taken.[141]

14.   EFFECT ON CONTRACTS OF EMPLOYMENT AND OTHER CONTRACTS

15–066   As a general rule, liquidation of a company, whether voluntary or compulsory,
does not itself operate to determine subsisting contracts between the company
and third parties, although there is an exception in the case of contracts which

---

[138] *Re Anglo-Austrian Printing Union (No.3)* [1895] 2 Ch. 891; s.212 of the Insolvency Act
1986. This section (unlike the Insolvency Act 1986, ss.214, 238–239) does not create a right or
remedy but merely a special procedure for recovery. Thus, whereas the cause of action which is the
subject of a misfeasance summons may exist prior to the winding-up of the company, and thus can
be subject to the floating charge, rights of action under ss.214, 239–240 exist solely by virtue of
the winding-up of the company and cannot exist before such winding up. See also *Re Asiatic
Electric Co Pty Ltd* (1970) 92 W.N. (N.S.W.) 361, 362, per Street J.; [1970] 2 N.S.W.R. 612, 613.
[139] *West Mercia Safetyware Ltd v Dodd* (1988) 4 B.C.C. 30 (CA). See also *Facia Footwear Ltd
(In Administration) v Hinchcliffe* [1998] 1 B.C.L.C. 218; *Berg Sons & Co Ltd v Mervyn Hampton
Adams* [1992] B.C.C. 661. The breach of fiduciary duty is actionable by the company, and not at
the suit of any individual creditor: *Yukong Line Ltd of Korea v Rendsburg Investments Corp of
Liberia* [1998] 1 W.L.R. 294. In *Knight v Frost* [1999] 1 B.C.L.C. 364, 382 Hart J. decided that in
order for a preference to be actionable as a misfeasance, the breach of duty must have taken place
within the time limits imposed in relation to voidable preferences by the 1986 Act. The mere fact
that a payment would be recoverable as against the recipient under s.239 of the 1986 Act does not
necessarily mean that the directors of the company which authorised the payment are ipso facto
liable for misfeasance: *Re Brian D Pierson (Contractors) Ltd* [1999] B.C.C. 26, where it was held
obiter that misfeasance would not be found where s.239 was satisfied only on the basis of a statutory presumption as to desire.
[140] Insolvency Act 1986, ss.213, 214, 239 and 240.
[141] Since each situation is different, legal advice should preferably be obtained in each case.

by their express terms or by necessary implication cannot survive liquidation. Hence arises the need for the statutory provision for disclaimer of unprofitable contracts.[142] Special rules have developed in the case of contracts of employment.[143]

15.   PUBLIC EXAMINATION OF THE RECEIVER

Where the company is being wound up by the court, the Official Receiver may, **15–067** at any time before dissolution of the company, apply to the court for the public examination (amongst others) of any person who has acted as an administrator or receiver or manager, and (unless the court otherwise orders) shall make such an application if he is requested to do so by: (a) one-half in value of the company's creditors; or (b) three-quarters in value of the company's contributories.[144]

---

[142] Insolvency Act 1986, s.178(3).
[143] See below, paras 16–003 to 16–006.
[144] Insolvency Act 1986, s.133.

Chapter 16

Employees

16–001   One of the most important resources of a business over which an administrator or receiver is appointed is likely to be the employees. The relationship of the company with its labour force imports a host of problems from employment law, some of which create a danger of personal liability for administrators or receivers.[1] The greatest danger of personal liability arises from changes set out in the Insolvency Act 1985 and consolidated in the Insolvency Act 1986.

There is some authority that an administrator or receiver owes a general duty of care to employees of the company to act reasonably in taking decisions which affect them[2] but this is inconsistent with the established principles governing the ambit of duties owed by such office holders.[3]

1.   CONTRACTS OF EMPLOYMENT

(a)   Survival of existing employment contracts

(i)   Pre-liquidation

16–002   *Administrators.*   The appointment of an administrator operates as the appointment of a managing agent of the company and accordingly does not terminate contracts of employment. The usual case of an appointment of an administrator for the company does not affect the personality of the employer, and accordingly contracts of employment,[4] for services and of agency[5] are unaffected, unless they expressly or impliedly provide to the contrary or could no longer be performed consistently with the appointment and role of administrator. The

---

[1] For a fuller treatment of these aspects of employment law see Sweet & Maxwell's *Encyclopaedia of Employment Law*; Grunfeld, *The Law of Redundancy* (London: Sweet & Maxwell, 1990); J. Bowers, *A Practical Approach to Employment Law* 8th edn (Oxford: Oxford University Press, 2009); D. Pollard, *Corporate Insolvency; Employment and Pension Rights*, 3rd edn (Tottel Publishing, 2007).

[2] *Larsen v Henderson*, 1990 S.L.T. 498 (Court of Session, Outer House). This is a Scottish decision the authority of which is undercut by the fact that the decisions which it purports to follow do not on analysis support the proposition.

[3] See *Burgess v Auger* [1998] 2 B.C.L.C. 478 and above, para.13–002.

[4] *Re Foster Clark Ltd's Indenture Trusts* [1966] 1 W.L.R. 125; *Re Mack Trucks (Britain) Ltd* [1967] 1 W.L.R. 780; *Griffiths v Social Services Secretary* [1974] Q.B. 468; *Deaway Ltd v Calverley* [1973] 3 All E.R. 776; *James Miller Holdings v Graham* (1978) 3 A.C.L.R. 604.

[5] *Re Peek Winch & Tool Ltd* [1979] C.A.T. 190 (CA); and see *Reigate v Union Manufacturing Co (Ramsbottom) Ltd* [1918] 1 K.B. 592 (CA), 606, per Scrutton L.J.

most obvious example is the managing director of the company who may no longer have any substantial functions to perform.[6]

Court-appointed receivers. The general rule is that the appointment by the **16–003** court of a receiver of the undertaking of a company does not affect existing contracts of the company but, as an exception to this rule, it does operate as a dismissal of the company's employees.[7] The theory is that the appointment effects a change in the personality of the employer from the company to the receiver, because the court-appointed receiver cannot contract as agent for the company, and any such change must operate as a dismissal.

There may be a distinction between capacity to enter into a contract and capacity to continue to fulfil the obligations under an existing contract. The fact that a company in receivership may not be able to enter into a contract of employment with a third party does not necessarily mean that that all existing contracts of employment by that company are terminated. Yet that appears to be the logic behind the holding that the appointment of the receiver terminates all contracts of appointment.

There is a contrast to be made with the appointment by the court of the receiver of a company[8] (as opposed to its undertaking): such an appointment will not terminate contracts of employment, because such a receiver is constituted as the managing agent of the company in place of its directors, and there is accordingly no change in the personality of the employer. There is no logical reason why the appointment of a receiver of the undertaking of a company should have this impact on contracts of employment and not on other continuing contracts which survive the court order. The likely explanation (as for similar principles applicable in case of compulsory liquidation[9]) is a tenderness towards employees.

Receivers of undertaking appointed by debenture-holders. The rare case of **16–004** an appointment by debenture-holders of a receiver to act as agent for the debenture-holders or as principal has the same effect as a court appointment in substituting the receiver for the company as the employer and therefore terminating contracts of employment. Such an appointment will only occur in practice in the rare case where the debenture does not provide that the receiver

---

[6] In *Re Mack Trucks (Britain) Ltd* [1967] 1 W.L.R. 780, 786c, Pennycuick J. instanced as a contract whose terms are inconsistent with the appointment "of a new managing agent" a contract for employment of a manager. By contrast, in *Griffiths v Social Services Secretary* [1974] Q.B. 468, the appointment of a receiver and manager was held not to effect dismissal of the managing director, because his contract of employment placed him strictly under the control of the board of directors and the receiver would have limited involvement in the running of the company's business.

[7] *Reid v Explosives Co* (1887) L.R. 19 QBD 264 (CA); *Re Foster Clark Ltd's Indenture Trusts* [1966] 1 W.L.R. 125, 132; *Nicoll v Cutts* [1985] B.C.L.C. 322 (CA). cf. the dicta of the Privy Council in *Parsons v Sovereign Bank of Canada* [1913] A.C. 160 (PC), 167 and 171 (a case concerning a contract for the supply of goods); *South Western of Venezuela (Barqisiment) Railway Co* [1902] 1 Ch. 701 and *Sipad Holding DDPO v Popovic* (1996) 12 A.C.L.C. 307, 309. See further para.29–009 below.

[8] See below, para.29–009, et seq.

[9] See below, para.16–005.

shall be agent for the company[10] and the receiver is not an administrative receiver.[11]

(ii) Post-liquidation

16–005 *Compulsory liquidation.* The generally accepted principle is that a compulsory liquidation operates (as from the date of publication of the order) as a dismissal of all the company's employees. For this principle to apply it is unnecessary that the company is insolvent: the position is the same if the liquidation occurs on a creditor's or contributory's petition. The principle is based on the premise that the order for winding up automatically terminates the company's business.[12] The premise, whatever its validity in practice in the nineteenth century when the principle was established, is now unsustainable, most particularly in today's rescue culture when the closure of the business is far from inevitable on the making of the order. An alternative explanation or justification for the principle is that it affords (as an act of tenderness to employees) special treatment of contracts of employment which is designed to crystallise their position at the earliest possible moment and enable them immediately to seek employment elsewhere free of all fetters to a doomed company.[13] It is, however, doubtful whether this alternative basis can justify a rule of law so out of line with other accepted principles of law. But the principle must be treated as established law until reviewed by an appellate court. Accordingly, if a compulsory liquidation follows the appointment of an administrative receiver, the contracts of employment which survive the receivership will immediately be terminated.

16–006 *Voluntary liquidation.* A voluntary liquidation does not necessarily result in the dismissal of a company's employees. There was some early authority that the position in the case of a voluntary liquidation was the same in the case of a compulsory winding-up.[14] But it is now reasonably clear that voluntary liquidation only operates as notice of dismissal if it involves the positive step of termination of the employee's employment by the company.[15] For this purpose, it is necessary to have regard to the facts of the particular case, and relevant

---

[10] See, e.g. *Re Vimbos* [1900] 1 Ch. 470; *Robinson Printing Co v Chic Ltd* [1905] 2 Ch. 123.

[11] Under s.44(1)(a) of the Insolvency Act 1986, an administrative receiver is deemed to be an agent of the company until liquidation. There is no express qualification that the deeming provision is subject to provisions to the contrary in the debenture, but it is thought that such a qualification should be implied. Nonetheless, it is difficult to conceive why a debenture should ever contain a provision to the contrary.

[12] *Re English Joint Stock Bank Ex p. Harding* (1867) L.R. 3 Eq. 341; *Re General Rolling Stock Co Chapman's Case* (1865–66) L.R.1 Eq. 346; *Fox Bros (Clothes)Ltd v Bryant* [1979] I.C.R. 64. It is thought that a winding-up order is effective to dismiss employees, even though the order is wrongly made and is subsequently discharged on appeal, and that the discharge of the order on appeal does not effect a reinstatement.

[13] McPherson, *The Law of Company Liquidation*, 3rd edn, p.174, fn.29.

[14] *Re Imperial Wine Co v Shirreff's Case* (1872) L.R. 14 Eq. 417.

[15] *Midland Counties Bank v Attwood* [1905] 1 Ch. 357; *Gerard v Worth of Paris Ltd* [1936] 2 All E.R. 905 (CA); *Fox Bros (Clothes)Ltd v Bryant* [1979] I.C.R. 64. See McPherson, *The Law of Company Liquidation,* 3rd edn, pp.174–175.

factors include whether the company is solvent[16] or insolvent[17]; whether the company has previously intimated to the relevant employee that his employment is likely to terminate on liquidation[18]; whether the liquidation involves the immediate cessation of the company's business; whether the employee's continuation in office is inconsistent with the role of the liquidator, e.g. the case of the managing director[19]; and whether a receiver has been appointed who has not adopted the contract of employment. In a doubtful case, an employee may seek clarification of the liquidator's intentions, and so prompt the service of a notice of dismissal. Frequently the passing of a resolution for winding up has the effect that the company in fact ceases to trade.

(b) Dismissal

Where the appointment of the receiver brings about a dismissal, the dismissal **16–007** is in law the act of the company, and not of the receiver. In the case of contracts which survive the receivership, the receiver has the option to continue them or to treat them as discharged. In the latter case, the company is in law again treated as having dismissed the employee. Whether the dismissal is effected by the appointment of the receiver or by the receiver as agent of the company, the employee may have a claim for breach of the contract of employment against the company and will have the rights afforded by statute in the case of dismissal by an insolvent employer.[20]

Where an employee's contract is terminated, the employee and the trustees of his occupational pension schemes (if any) have rights to certain payments from the Secretary of State for Business, Innovation and Skills, who becomes subrogated to the employee's and trustees' rights against the company.[21] Thus, subject to a statutory limit (at present £310 per week), the employee can claim up to eight weeks' arrears of pay, sums in lieu of notice, holiday pay and a redundancy payment or the basic award (but not compensatory award) in respect of unfair dismissal.[22]

---

[16] *Gerard v Worth of Paris Ltd* [1936] 2 All E.R. 905 (CA).

[17] *Fowler v Commercial Timber Co* [1930] 2 K.B. 1 (CA); *Reigate v Union Manufacturing Co* [1918] 1 K.B. 592 (CA).

[18] *Fowler v Commercial Timber Co* [1930] 2 K.B. 1 (CA); *Reigate v Union Manufacturing Co* [1918] 1 K.B. 592 (CA).

[19] *Fowler v Commercial Timber Co* [1930] 2 K.B. 1 (CA), 16.

[20] Employment Rights Act 1996, ss.182–190.

[21] This does not apply where the receiver is appointed over the book debts only: *Secretary of State for Employment v Stone* [1994] I.C.R. 761.

[22] *Benson v Secretary of State for Trade and Industry* [2003] I.C.R. 1082 raised non-contractual guarantee payments in excess of the statutory scheme. For the detailed provisions see the Employment Rights Act 1996, s.183(3). The relevant forms and booklets can be obtained by the receiver from Job Centre Plus. It should be noted that the payment must be at the rate of at least the national minimum wage which is currently for most purposes £3.60 an hour pursuant to the National Minimum Wage Act 1998. Failure to pay the minimum wage is a criminal offence and under s.32 directors and other officers may commit an offence if the employer company does so and the same is with their consent, connivance or neglect.

(c) Direct government payment

16–008 The Employment Rights Act 1996 builds on earlier legislation to offer these further ways of ensuring that the employee's position is protected to some degree where:

(a) an individual has been declared bankrupt or has made a composition or arrangement with his creditors;

(b) an individual's estate is being administered in accordance with an order under s.421 of the Insolvency Act 1986;

(c) a company is wound-up by a shareholders' resolution;

(d) a company is in administration for the purposes of the Insolvency Act 1986; or

(e) if a voluntary arrangement proposed in the case of the company for the purposes of Pt I of the Insolvency Act 1986 has been approved under that part of that Act; and in certain similar aspects of limited liability.

(i) National Insurance Fund

Speedy and safe recourse may be made to the Government's National Insurance Fund in the case of the following debts[23]:

(a) up to eight weeks' wages including guarantee pay, medical suspension pay, union duties pay, ante-natal care pay, statutory sick pay and protective award,[24] up to a maximum of £400 per week;

(b) minimum pay during notice under s.86 of the Employment Rights Act 1996 or damages for failure to give such notice,[25] but not including the appropriate holiday pay during notice according to the EAT in *Secretary of State for Employment v Jobling*[26];

(c) up to six weeks' accumulated holiday pay during the last 12 months preceding the relevant date[27];

(d) basic award made by an employment tribunal for unfair dismissal[28];

(e) reimbursement of premiums or fees paid for apprenticeship or articles of clerkship.[29]

---

[23] Employment Rights Act 1996, s.182.
[24] Employment Rights Act 1996, s.184(1)(a).
[25] Employment Rights Act 1996, s.184(1)(b).
[26] *Secretary of State for Employment v Jobling* [1980] I.C.R. 380.
[27] Employment Rights Act 1996, s.184(1)(c).
[28] Employment Rights Act 1996, s.184(1)(d).
[29] Employment Rights Act 1996, s.184(1)(e).

Item (d) may be reclaimed in full, but the other payments are subject to a maximum of £40 per week, for, it would appear, each type of payment.[30] The sum is to be index-linked to the retail prices index[31] and must be uprated every September. In the unusual case where the employer has a cross-claim against the employee, for example in respect of a loan, this may be set-off.[32] This maximum is subject to reduction if the employee earns from another source or receives state benefits during the period of his notice. In *Westwood v Secretary of State for Employment*[33] the House of Lords also decided that the employee need only account for net benefits received during the period of unemployment. This had an important effect in the case of Mr Westwood who had been unemployed for more than a year and was entitled to a refund based on the loss arising from exhaustion of unemployment benefit after a year. This was, however, cleared up by the Social Security (General Benefit) (Amendment) Regulations 1984 (SI 1984/1259) which provide that days which are covered by payments made under the insolvency provisions do not count in establishing eligibility to what was then known as unemployment benefit, now Jobseekers Allowance.[34]

The important timing for claims is that they arise on the "relevant date" which is defined by statute as the latest of the following dates: when the employer becomes insolvent; when employment came to an end; and where the debt is a basic award for unfair dismissal or a protective award for failure to consult the union over redundancies, the date when the award was made[35].

(ii) Pensions

The right to unpaid employer's pension contributions from the Department for Business, Innovation and Skills extends to:

(a) arrears accrued within 12 months prior to insolvency;

(b) arrears certified by an actuary to be necessary to pay employees' benefits on dissolution of the scheme;

(c) 10 per cent of the last 12 months' payroll for the employees covered by the scheme.

The maximum in each case is the lowest of these various figures. The Secretary of State must be satisfied that "an employer has become insolvent and that at the time he did so there remained unpaid relevant contributions falling to be paid by him to the scheme". Again, the Department for Business, Innovation and Skills defers until a trustee or liquidator is appointed before paying, and recourse is to an employment tribunal in the event of a dispute.[36]

---

[30] Employment Rights Act 1996, s.186(1).
[31] Employment Relations Act 1999, s.34.
[32] *Secretary of State for Employment v Wilson and BCCI* [1997] I.C.R. 408.
[33] *Westwood v Secretary of State for Employment* [1985] A.C. 20 (HL).
[34] See also *Secretary of State for Employment v Cooper* [1987] I.C.R. 766 (CA).
[35] Employment Rights Act 1996 s.185.
[36] ss.124 and 125 Pension Schemes Act 1993.

(iii)   Redundancy payments

An employee can claim a redundancy payment direct from the National Insurance Fund where he is entitled to such a payment from his employer in the usual way, and he has taken all reasonable steps to obtain payment besides resorting to legal proceedings, or the employer is insolvent as defined in s.166(5) of the Employment Rights Act 1996. The employee then receives his normal redundancy payment less any payment in fact already made towards it by the employer. The employee's rights and remedies are taken over by (subrogated to) the Secretary of State,[37] who may take proceedings against the employer, while disputes over these payments may be referred to an employment tribunal.[38]

(iv)   Maternity payments

There are similar provisions for a claim from the Maternity Fund save that the employer need not be insolvent,[39] and the employee is entitled to her maternity pay even though the employer is put into liquidation in the course of her absence.[40]

(d)   Continuance and adoption

(i)   Prior to the Insolvency Act 1986

16–009   Prior to the Insolvency Act 1986, it was clearly established that if the receiver, as agent for the company, continued the employment of the company's employees, the company alone was liable for salary accrued due after as well as before the date of the receivership and for any damages or other award made on the subsequent dismissal of such employees.

In *Nicoll v Cutts*,[41] the employee, prior to receivership, had been the only working director of a company and had been in charge of the day-to-day running of the business. Before the receivership the employee was hospitalised as a result of a road accident. The receiver did not immediately cause the company to dismiss the employee, but discussed the company's business with him as though he were an employee and obtained his assistance from his bed in hospital. Three weeks after his appointment the receiver terminated the employee's contract of service by one month's notice, and sold the business of the company as a going concern. The employee claimed from the receiver the amount of his salary in respect of the period after the date of the receiver's appointment. His claim to prove for this sum in the subsequent liquidation of

---

[37] Employment Rights Act 1996, s.167.
[38] s.170.
[39] Statutory Maternity Pay (General) Regulations 1986 (SI 1986/196), regs 7 and 30.
[40] *Secretary of State for Employment v Cox* [1984] I.C.R. 867.
[41] *Nicoll v Cutts* [1985] B.C.L.C. 322 (CA), considered in *Re Atlantic Computer Systems Plc* [1992] Ch. 505 (CA) and in *Powdrill v Watson* [1995] 2 A.C. 394 (HL), 440–441.

the company would have been worthless in view of the company's insolvency. The employee argued:

> "that it makes no sense that an employee, whose service contract is continued by the bank's receiver in order to assist in realising the company's assets to the best advantage, should, qua payment of his remuneration for the period of that continuation of his service contract, get nothing (save from the State's Redundancy Fund[42]) and be postponed to the bank getting payment in full".[43]

Nevertheless the Court of Appeal was unable to find any legal basis for the employee's claim because: **16–010**

(a) section 369(2) of the Companies Act 1948 (subsequently s.492(3) of the Companies Act 1985) did not assist since it only made the receiver personally liable for contracts entered into by him, i.e. *after* the commencement of the receivership, whereas the employee was employed under a pre-existing contract[44];

(b) the receiver was not obliged to pay to the employee the sum claimed as part of the costs and expenses of the receivership; that concept only covered sums actually paid by the receiver or sums which he was liable to pay.

The receiver had a discretion whether or not to pay, and such discretion was to be exercised taking into consideration whether the interests of the debenture-holder and the company in the beneficial realisation of the charged assets were served by making the payment.[45] The receiver had properly exercised his discretion not to pay the employee.

(ii)   From the Insolvency Act 1986 to the Insolvency Act 1994

The decision in *Nicoll v Cutts* prompted Parliament to enact ss.44(1)(b) and (2)   **16–011**
of the Insolvency Act 1986.[46] Sections 44(1)(b) and (2) provides that:

> "[The administrative receiver] is personally liable on any contract entered into by him in the carrying out of his functions (except in so far as the contract otherwise provides) and to the extent of any qualifying liability on a contract of employment adopted by him in the carrying out of those functions . . . [but] the administrative receiver is not to be taken to have

---

[42] Now the National Insurance Fund.
[43] *Nicoll v Cutts* [1985] B.C.L.C. 322 (CA), 324, per Dillon L.J.
[44] See also above, Ch.14.
[45] cf. the similar approach to an ex gratia payment by the liquidator in *Re Banque des Marchands de Moscou (Koupetschesky) (No.2)* [1953] 1 W.L.R. 172.
[46] See *Re Atlantic Computer Systems Plc* [1992] Ch. 505 (CA) and *Powdrill v Watson* [1995] 2 A.C. 394 (HL), 441.

adopted a contract of employment by reason of anything done or omitted to be done within 14 days after his appointment."

A similar amendment was enacted to impose the same liability towards employees by receivers of companies who are not administrative receivers.[47] An analogous provision was introduced by s.19 in respect of administrators but instead of imposing personal liability on the administrator, it instead confers entitlement on the employees to priority payment. This is now contained in Sch.B1 as inserted by the Enterprise Act 2002.

The statute raised three particular problems: (1) it left unclear the legal significance of the 14-day period; (2) it contained no definition of the term "adopt" and accordingly left open the question whether a receiver or administrator adopted a contract only if he became a party to it by way of novation or whether it was sufficient that he treated it as continuing in force; and (3) what was the extent of a receiver's liability "on" an adopted contract of employment. These questions were resolved by the House of Lords in the combined appeals in *Powdrill v Watson* and in, *Re Leyland DAF* (*Powdrill*).[48]

16–012 *The 14-day period.* The House of Lords held that the proviso to the sections is designed to give the receiver or administrator 14 days in which to decide upon their attitude to outstanding contracts of employment. Their freedom of choice is not to be limited by any interim arrangements which they make in respect of the 14-day decision period. If the receiver or administrator makes a final decision to adopt the contract before the 14-day period has expired, his decision is not binding unless and until continued after the 14 days. He may, however, within the 14-day period contract to adopt the contracts after expiration of the 14-day period or to assume immediately the obligations imposed by adoption, and such a contract will have full legal effect.

16–013 *The meaning of "adoption" in ss.19 and 44.* In *Powdrill*, the House of Lords held that the concept of "adoption" in ss.19 and 44 does not mean "novate", for the legislation was clearly intended to alter, and not confirm, the legal position established in *Nicoll v Cutts*. The legislation was directed at curing the mischief of a receiver or administrator making use of an employee's services without giving full payment to that employee. The House of Lords held that the concept of "adoption" in ss.19 and 44 connotes some conduct by a receiver or administrator which amounts to an election to treat a contract of employment as giving rise to a separate liability in the receivership or administration. It was further held that if a receiver or administrator caused the company to continue the employment for more than 14 days after his appointment, this would inevitably be conduct amounting to such an election, and the contract of employment would thus have been "adopted" for the purpose of ss.19 and 44. The House of Lords indicated that it was not possible to pick and choose between different liabilities under the contract, so that if a contract of employment is

---

[47] Insolvency Act 1986, s.37(1).
[48] *Powdrill v Watson* [1995] 2 A.C. 394 (HL).

adopted, it is adopted as a whole.[49] It is implicit in the decision that conduct by a receiver or administrator amounting to an adoption of the contract of employment will be treated as such, irrespective of any purported notification to the employee that the contract of employment is not being adopted.[50]

The extent of an administrative receiver's liability under an adopted contract. **16–014** At first instance in *Re Leyland DAF*, Lightman J. held that if an administrative receiver adopted a contract of employment, the literal wording of s.44 meant that the administrative receiver would be personally liable for all liabilities whenever incurred of whatever kind under the adopted contract.[51] The House of Lords noted that this would have resulted in an administrative receiver becoming personally liable for "imponderable" past and future liabilities and would have made the task of the administrative receiver in considering whether to continue to employ staff to trade the business of a company almost impossible. Because these results were considered to be inimical to the rescue culture which the 1986 Act was designed to promote, the House of Lords adopted what it acknowledged to be a "forced construction" of s.44, holding that the liability of an administrative receiver on any adopted contract must be subject to the same temporal restriction as applies to contracts adopted by an administrator under s.19, namely that it is restricted to liabilities incurred under the adopted contract while he was the receiver.[52]

(iii)   After the Insolvency Act 1994

Administrators.   Parliament was thus alerted to the potential impact of ss.19 **16–015** and 44 of the 1986 Act upon administrative receivers and administrators by the decision of the Court of Appeal in *Powdrill*.[53] It acted swiftly and without waiting for the decision of the House of Lords, by passing the Insolvency Act 1994 to limit the scope of these sections. The 1994 Act amended the provisions of ss.19 and 44 in so far as they applied to contracts of employment adopted on or after March 15, 1994. The technique used by Parliament was to amend the 1986 Act so as to restrict the scope of liabilities which would attract priority under s.19(5) in the case of administrations, and for which an administrative receiver would be personally liable under s.44, to so-called "qualifying liabilities". Such "qualifying liabilities" are liabilities for wages, salary or contributions to an Occupational Pension Scheme in respect of services rendered *after* adoption of a contract of employment. The position is now governed by Sch.B1,

---

[49] *Powdrill v Watson* [1995] 2 A.C. 394 (HL), 448–450, per Lord Browne-Wilkinson.

[50] The House of Lords in effect overruled the decision of Harman J. in *Re Specialised Mouldings Ltd* Unreported February 13, 1987, and affirmed the decision of the Court of Appeal that standard-form letters to employees purporting to avoid adoption would be of no effect if the contract was in fact continued for more than 14 days after appointment: see *Powdrill v Watson* [1994] 2 All E.R. 513, 521f–g (CA), 141c–d.

[51] *Powdrill v Watson* [1995] 2 A.C. 394 (HL), 413–415.

[52] For a comment on the case, see Mr. Justice Lightman, "The Challenges Ahead" [1996] J.B.L. 113 at 121–122. See also *Lindop v Stuart Noble & Sons Ltd* [1999] B.C.C. 616 (Court of Session, Outer House).

[53] *Powdrill v Watson* [1994] 2 All E.R. 513 (CA).

para.99(5) of the Insolvency Act 1986 as amended by the Enterprise Act 2002.[54] Where an administrator is appointed he will be taken to have adopted the contract of employment of an employee if he maintains that employment for 14 days and "no account shall be taken of a liability which arises, or in so far as it arises, by reference to anything which is done or which occurs before the adoption of the contract of employment". If adoption occurs para.99(5) gives priority to "wages or salary". This phrase has an extended definition by para.99(6) to include holiday pay, sick pay, payment in lieu of holiday, sums treated as earnings for the purposes of social security and contributions to an occupational pension scheme.

16–016   *Administrative receivers.* In addition, in the case of administrative receivers, s.44(2B) of the 1986 Act (as amended) provides that where an administrative receiver is personally liable in respect of a qualifying liability for services rendered partly before and partly after the adoption of the contract, his liability shall only extend to so much of the sum as is payable in respect of the services rendered after the adoption of the contract.

16–017   *The consequences.* The most important consequence of the amendments made in 1994 is to prevent the administrative receiver from being personally liable to an employee who is dismissed without notice in a receivership for sums which would have been payable under his adopted contract of employment in lieu of notice, or for damages for wrongful dismissal. Equally, such sums will not qualify for priority payment from the assets of a company in the case of an administration. The 1994 Act enacts the decision of Evans-Lombe J. at first instance in *Powdrill*[55] that statutory compensation for unfair dismissal does not qualify for priority in an administration or result in personal liability for an administrative receiver, because such liabilities are not liabilities "under" or "on" a contract of employment.[56]

Notwithstanding the changes introduced by the 1994 Act, difficult issues may still arise over when a particular liability is incurred for the purposes of ss.19 and 44 and whether it amounts to a qualifying liability.[57] So, for example, in *Re Company (No.005174 of 1999)*[58] Neuberger J. (as he then was) held that for the purposes of s.19(9) of the 1986 Act (as amended), which deems wages or salary payable in respect of a period of holiday to be wages or salary in respect of services rendered during the period by reference to which the holiday

---

[54] This took effect on September 15, 2003.

[55] *Powdrill v Watson* [1994] 2 B.C.L.C. 118 (CA), 132e.

[56] See also *Albion Automotive Ltd v Shaw* Unreported EAT 523/94.

[57] Difficult issues of limitation may also arise. In *Re Maxwell Fleet and Facilities Management Ltd* [2001] 1 W.L.R. 323 it was held that in an administration where contracts of employment had been adopted prior to the changes introduced by the 1994 Act, the employees' contractual claims for wrongful dismissal under their adopted contracts accrued when they were dismissed. This would also be the case in an administrative receivership in relation to the administrative receiver's personal liability for breach of contract. It was further held that in an administration, a separate statutory obligation to pay employee's claims arises under s.19(5) of the 1986 Act on the discharge of the administration order, which attracts a six year limitation period. The enforcement of the statutory charge created by s.19(5) is subject to a separate limitation period of 12 years under s.20 of the Limitation Act 1980.

[58] *Re Company (No.005174 of 1999)* [2000] 1 W.L.R. 502.

entitlement arose, the effect of the adopted contract of employment for a number of teachers was that they accrued holiday entitlement for the period after the relevant term worked. As a result their holiday pay for the summer holidays after the school year ended was a qualifying liability. Neuberger J. indicated that the proper approach to the question of whether a particular liability falls within the definition of qualifying liabilities is that "one should look primarily at the terms of the contract of employment" and "take into account all surrounding circumstances known or reasonably capable of being known to the parties at the time, but also looking at the nature of the liability and the factual circumstances in which it falls to be paid."[59] In early 2005 administrators were appointed over Allders department stores and the question was posed whether claims for statutory redundancy and unfair dismissal payments were payable as administration expenses under r.2.67(1)(f) of the Insolvency Rules 1986. Lawrence Collins J. answered in the negative in an unreported decision. This was further considered by the Court of Appeal in the later set of combined decisions known as *Re Huddersfield Fine Worsteds Ltd.*[60] Paragraph 99(5)(c) requires that the sum is a "liability arising under a contract of employment" and that the relevant sum is "wages or salary" and the Court of Appeal did not consider that a protective award for failing to inform and consult over redundancies arose *under* a contract of employment".[61] Thus the protective award was not given super priority.

The Court of Appeal also commented that it would undermine the rescue culture if protective awards and payments in lieu of notice did have such super priority.

There are indeed many different categories of payments in lieu of notice. The relevant categories of payments in lieu delineated by the House of Lords in *Delaney v Staples*[62] as considered in *Huddersfield* were: (a) payments at the end of the employment when employer and employee agree that the employment is to terminate forthwith on payment of a sum in lieu of notice; and (b) where without the agreement of the employee, the employer summarily dismisses the employee and tenders a payment in lieu of proper notice.

In *IRC v Lawrence*,[63] the Court of Appeal had to consider whether PAYE and national insurance contributions which were deducted at source by administrators enjoyed priority and payment under s.19(5) and (6) Insolvency Act 1986. It was held that they did because they were part of the salary itself and the liability only arose where a salary payment was made to an employee. It would be artificial and wrong to split the contractual liability into two.

Non-administrative receivers. Non-administrative receivers are in the worst **16–018** possible position in relation to adoption. They are not covered by the changes introduced by the 1994 Act, although no convincing reason has been given for their exclusion. Such receivers will only be safe from personal liability if they cause the company to dismiss all employees whom they are able to cause it to

---

[59] *Re Company (No.005174 of 1999)* [2000] 1 W.L.R. 502, 508.
[60] *Re Huddersfield Fine Worsteds Ltd* [2005] 4 All E.R. 886 (CA).
[61] See also para.4–028, above.
[62] *Delaney v Staples (t/a De Montfort Recruitment)* [1992] 1 A.C. 687 (HL).
[63] *IRC v Lawrence* [2001] B.C.C. 663 (CA).

dismiss within the initial 14-day period. Thereafter, and subject to the validity of "contracting out" (see below), they may be forced to seek to negotiate new contracts with such employees as they wish to employ to run the business, but on terms which exclude their personal liability. The relevant debenture may authorise the receiver to pay such employees as a cost of the receivership in priority to the other creditors of the company.

16–019   *Contracting out.* Whilst the decision in *Powdrill* has settled that it is not possible to "contract out" of adoption itself, the Insolvency Act 1986 left open the question of whether, following adoption, it is possible for an employee and a receiver to "contract out" of the employee's personal claims against the receiver. It is also an open question as to whether it is permissible for a receiver to dismiss employees during the initial 14-day period and then to re-engage them on new contracts of employment incorporating the same terms as the old, but expressly excluding any personal liability on his part. Following the changes enacted in the 1994 Act, these issues are only likely to arise in relation to non-administrative receiverships, because it is unlikely that there would be any practical incentive for employees and administrative receivers to contract out of liability for the limited "qualifying liabilities". The issue is essentially one of policy, and at first instance in both *Powdrill*[64] and *Leyland DAF*[65] it was accepted that there are no public policy reasons to prevent such agreements being reached between receivers and employees.[66] The policy of the original statute, now confirmed by the amendments introduced by the 1994 Act, is indeed to prevent receivers encouraging expectations of payment for work, and then disappointing them. Absent any questions of sham amendments or duress of employees, an agreed variation of an adopted contract or a dismissal and re-engagement on terms excluding personal liability, are not of themselves objectionable. Indeed they may operate to the benefit of the employee if the only alternative is dismissal. As discussed below, any such agreement must be clear and unequivocal to be effective, and a unilateral statement by the receivers coupled with a failure to object on the part of the employee will not be sufficient.[67]

(e) Re-employment and new employees

16–020   The administrator or receiver, as agent for the company, has power to enter into new contracts of employment, whether re-employing former employees or employing new employees. As indicated above, where a contract is adopted, the receiver incurs personal liability on it, and the same is true of new contracts entered into after his appointment unless he takes avoiding action. If the administrator or receiver is to avoid personal liability under such contracts, he

---

[64] *Powdrill v Watson* [1994] 2 B.C.L.C. 118 (CA), 129f–130b.

[65] *Powdrill v Watson* [1995] 2 A.C. 394 (HL), 411D–F.

[66] The point was raised in argument in relation to administrators in *Powdrill* in the Court of Appeal, but the Court of Appeal did not consider it necessary to determine the issue: see [1994] 2 B.C.L.C. 118 (CA), 141. The point did not arise in the House of Lords.

[67] See, e.g. the approach of Evans-Lombe J. to the wording of the relevant letter in *Powdrill* [1994] 2 B.C.L.C. 118 (CA), 130.

must ensure that the contracts contain express provisions to this effect.[68] Therefore, as noted above, a receiver can by dismissing and subsequently re-employing them, avoid incurring personal liability by retaining the existing workforce and thereby adopting their contracts of employment.

If the administrator or receiver requires employees under existing contracts to agree to new terms, depending upon the significance of the new term this may amount to:

(a) a variation of the old contract of employment which will have been adopted so that the receiver will be personally liable; or

(b) a new contract, under which the receiver will be personally liable.

If the receiver seeks to impose a new term to which the employee does not agree, and the variation is sufficiently serious to be a repudiatory breach, the employee may treat this conduct as constructive dismissal by the company.[69]

Once a compulsory liquidation supervenes, all existing contracts of employ- **16–021**
ment come to an end, as does the receiver's agency for the company. This will also ordinarily (though not necessarily) happen once a voluntary liquidation supervenes. Thereafter the receiver can only employ either as principal or (where so authorised and so stated in the contract) as agent for his appointor. If he employs as principal, he will be personally liable under the contract, but then will be entitled to an indemnity out of the charged assets.

Where there has been a dismissal and re-employment by the administrator or receiver in whatsoever capacity, there will be no common law right to damages for wrongful dismissal if in every respect the employment remains the same, since the employee will have suffered no loss by reason of the dismissal. Likewise, there will not be any entitlement to a redundancy payment, since re-engagement on the same terms of employment by the receiver, whether as agent of the company or not, will lead the employee to being regarded as not having been dismissed.[70] Accrued statutory continuity rights are transferred to this new employment.[71]

(f) Consultation with trades unions or elected representatives over redundancies

Upon commencement of the administration, the administrator should notify **16–022**
the employees immediately of the position.[72] If he considers that 20 or more redundancies are necessary and there are one or more unions recognised by the company, he must consult with officials of any such trade unions as soon as

---

[68] The receiver was held personally liable because this provision was omitted in *Re Mack Trucks (Britain) Ltd* [1967] 1 W.L.R. 780.

[69] See in particular *Western Excavations(ECC) Ltd v Sharp* [1978] Q.B. 761 (CA) and *Hogg v Dover College* [1990] I.C.R. 39.

[70] Employment Rights Act 1996, ss.138, 145.

[71] As to continuity of employment see *Lassman v Secretary of State for Trade and Industry* [2000] I.C.R. 1109 (CA).

[72] The phrase "an employer proposing to dismiss as redundant" includes cases where the employer is in administration and the administrator proposes the dismissals: *Re Hartlebury Printers Ltd (In Liquidation)* [1992] I.C.R. 559, 569h.

possible after the proposal to dismiss has been made and (in the absence of a recognised union), with elected representatives of the workforce. There are minimum periods for consultation: where 100 or more are to be made redundant at one establishment[73] within a period of 90 days or less, at least 90 days must be allowed for consultation before the first of those dismissals takes effect. At least 30 days must be given where between 20 and 99 employees are to be made redundant.

Where no union is recognised the employer must consult with employee representatives who have already been appointed or elected by the affected employees for other purposes (e.g. a works or staff council) or if this has not occurred, the employer must arrange for an election by affected employees.[74] The employer may choose whether to consult an already appointed works council or alternatively arrange for a special election procedure to take effect, but if the union is recognised that is the sole channel for consultation.

At the commencement of the consultation, the employer must disclose in writing to the union or elected representatives the following information[75]: the reason for the loss of jobs; the number, although not necessarily the names of those to be dismissed; the total number of workers employed and the proposed method of selection. This consultation must take place "with a view to reaching agreement" which in effect means that it must take place in good faith.[76]

16–023 The mere fact of the insolvency of the company on the appointment of the receiver does not in itself relieve the company of its obligations with regard to consulting unions or elected representatives about proposed redundancies so as to absolve the employer from liability.[77]

Rather, there must be "special circumstances" for this liability to be avoided and ". . . to be special the event must be something out of the ordinary, something uncommon. . ." A "sudden disaster" would qualify as being "special".[78]

A breach of the consultation procedures may enable a recognised trade union or elected representatives (as relevant) to claim a protective award from an employment tribunal. That award is a sum which is "just and equitable in all the circumstances having regard to the employer's default" subject to a maximum of 90 days' pay.[79]

A receiver may also possibly be subject to criminal liability if he fails to notify the Secretary of State for Business Innovation and Skills of impending redundancies.[80]

---

[73] "Establishment" has a technical meaning: see *Barratt Developments Ltd v UCATT* [1978] I.C.R. 319; *Green & Son (Castings) Ltd v ASTMS and AUEW* [1984] I.C.R. 352.

[74] Trade Union and Labour Relations (Consolidation) Act 1992, s.188(1B)(b)(ii).

[75] Trade Union and Labour Relations (Consolidation) Act 1992, s.188(4).

[76] Trade Union and Labour Relations (Consolidation) Act 1992, s.188(6).

[77] *Clarks of Hove Ltd v Bakers' Union* [1978] 1 W.L.R. 1207 (CA). See also *Angus Jowett & Co Ltd NUTGW* [1985] I.C.R. 646; *APAC v Kirvin Ltd* [1978] I.R.L.R. 318; *Hamish Armour v ASTMS* [1979] I.R.L.R. 24; *USDAW v Leancut Bacon Ltd* [1981] I.R.L.R. 295; *Re Hartlebury Printers Ltd* [1992] I.C.R. 559, 570e; *GMB v Rankin & Harrison* [1992] I.R.L.R. 514.

[78] *Clarks of Hove v Bakers Union* [1978] I.C.R. 1076 (CA), 1085, per Geoffrey Lane L.J.; *Susie Radin v GMB* [2004] 2 All E.R. 279 (CA).

[79] Trade Union and Labour Relations (Consolidation) Act 1992, ss.189 and 190.

[80] Trade Union and Labour Relations (Consolidation) Act 1992, s.194(3). The liability is extended to "any director manager secretary or other similar officer of the body corporate, or any

2. TRANSFER OF THE UNDERTAKING[81]

(a) The general principle

At common law the transfer of the business of the company would in almost all **16–024** cases terminate contracts of employment.[82] The position was radically altered by The Transfer of Undertakings (Protection of Employment) Regulations 1981[83] which was introduced to put into effect the EU Acquired Rights Directive.[84]

"The general scheme of the Regulations is directly contrary to the pre-existing law. The general rule is that on the transfer of a business the employees of that business are transferred with it, i.e. the employees' contract of employment . . . undergoes a statutory novation"[85]

The new Transfer of Undertakings (Protection of Employment) Regulations 2006 (SI 2006/246) came into force on April 6, 2006 and were a complete replacement of the 1981 Regulations.

(b) What is a transferred undertaking?

The Regulations apply to transfers of an "undertaking". This term is not **16–025** precisely defined but includes "any trade or business". The economic entity (defined as an organised grouping of resources which has the objective of pursuing an economic activity,[86] whether or not that activity is central or ancillary) must retain its identity for there to be a transfer in the paradigm sense.[87] Alternatively since the 2006 amendments there may be a service provision change whereby:

---

person who was purporting to act in such capacity": these latter words may possibly "catch" the receiver. cf. *Re B Johnson & Co (Builders) Ltd* [1955] Ch. 634 (CA).

[81] See generally P. Elias QC and J. Bowers, *Transfer of Undertakings: The Legal Pitfalls,* 5th edn (Longmans, 1994); J. Bowers QC et al., *Transfer of Undertakings Encyclopaedia* (London: Sweet & Maxwell, 2010). See also above, Ch.11, at paras 11–055 to 11–069 and 11–088 to 11–090.

[82] *Brace v Calder* [1895] 2 Q.B. 253 (CA): *Re Foster Clark Ltd's Indenture Trusts* [1966] 1 W.L.R. 125.

[83] SI 1981/1794 ("Transfer Regulations"). The Regulations are intended to implement EC Directive 77/187: [1977] O.J. L61/26 (the so-called "Acquired Rights Directive") as amended.

[84] EC Directive 77/187 as now amended by Directive 98/50. The Acquired Rights Directive is compulsorily applicable to insolvency proceedings whose object is to effect a corporate rescue to keep the business intact but not to proceedings the purpose of which is to liquidate the assets of the transferor. This is because art.1(1) limits its scope to transfers made "as a result of a legal transfer or merger" (*Abels v Administrative Board of the Bedrijfsvereniging Voor de Metaal-Industrie en de Electrotechnische Industrie* [1985] E.C.R. 469; *D'Urso v Ercole Marelliu Elettromeccanica Generale SpA* (C-362/89) [1991] E.C.R. I-4105; *Jules Dethier Equipement SA v Jules Dassy* (C-319/94) [1998] All E.R. (EC) 346).

[85] *Premier Motors (Medway) Ltd v Total Oil Great Britain Ltd* [1984] 1.W.L.R. 377.

[86] This does not apply to activities concerned wholly or mainly of the supply of goods for the client's use; reg.3(3)(b).

[87] reg.3(1)(a) and (2).

"(i)   activities cease to be carried on by a person (a client) on his own behalf and are carried on instead by another person on the client's behalf (a contractor);

(ii)   activities cease to be carried on by a contractor on a client's behalf . . . and are carried on by another person (a subsequent contractor) on the client's behalf; or

(iii) activities cease to be carried on by a contractor or a subsequent contractor on a client's behalf . . . and are carried out instead by the client on his own behalf".[88]

Tribunals must consider the substance and not the form in deciding whether there is an undertaking and whether there has been a transfer of that undertaking.[89] A transfer "may take place whether or not any property is transferred to the transferee by the transferor". The Regulations also apply to the transfer of *part* of an undertaking and the question in such a case is whether the part transferred is a self-contained, separate and severable part of the whole and whether there is an economic entity which retains its identity after transfer.[90] The factors to be taken into account in determining this question derive from the European Court of Justice case of *Spijkers*[91] and include whether assets or staff were transferred and whether the undertaking was carried on in the same or a similar way. The factor of whether the majority of staff are transferred is one amongst many to be considered.[92]

(c)   The consequences of a transfer of undertaking

16–026   There is a general provision that a relevant transfer shall not in itself terminate employment contracts.[93] Quite the contrary, contracts of employment will have effect "as if originally made" between the employee and the transferee of the business. The transferee thus takes over all "rights, powers, duties and liabilities of or in connection with any such contract" of employment.[94] However, occupational pensions and criminal liabilities[95] are expressly excluded from the scope of the liabilities which are transferred.

As a result of the Regulations, the employees of the company[96] will generally become the employees of the transferee of the business. This is so even where the transferee makes it clear from the start that he has no intention of

---

[88] reg.3(1)(b).
[89] reg.3(1).
[90] *ECM (Vehicle Delivery Service) Ltd v Cox* [1999] 4 All E.R. 669 (CA).
[91] *Spijkers v Benedik* (24/85) [1986] E.C.R. 1119.
[92] See also *Betts v Brintel Helicopters Ltd (t/a British International Helicopters)* [1997] 2 All E.R. 848 (CA); *Whitewater Leisure Management Ltd v Barnes* [2000] I.C.R. 1049; *ECM (Vehicle Delivery Services) Ltd v Cox* [1999] 4 All E.R. 669 (CA).
[93] reg.4(1).
[94] reg.4(1) and (2).
[95] reg.4(6) and 10.
[96] Or in some cases the employees of the debenture-holder or the receiver.

actually keeping in employment the employees so transferred.[97] Where there is a substantial change in an employee's working conditions to his detriment, the employee has a right to terminate his contract of employment without notice. The mere fact that there is a new employer is not a "substantial change" unless the employee shows that in all the circumstances the change of employers is a "significant change" to the employee's detriment.[98]

Any purported variation of a contract of employment is void if the sole or principal reason is the transfer itself or a reason connected with the transfer which is not an economic, technical or organisational reason entailing changes in the workforce.[99]

There is an exception from the principle of automatic transfer if an employee "informs the transferor or transferee that he objects to becoming employed by the transferee" but this does not amount to a dismissal.[100]

(d) Application of the regulations only to those employed "immediately before the transfer"

Regulation 4(3) provides that the Regulations only apply in respect of those **16–027** employed "immediately before the transfer".[101] This is often highly material in the context of the receivership. Authoritative guidance on the meaning of those words was given by the House of Lords in *Litster v Forth Dry Dock & Engineering Co Ltd*.[102] Their Lordships decided that in order that the manifest purpose of the Regulations might be achieved and effect be given to the clear (but inadequately expressed) intention of Parliament, certain words must be read into them by necessary implication. This principle justified not taking a narrow approach to the phrase "a person employed immediately before the transfer". To do so would render the Regulations "capable of ready evasion through the transferee arranging with the transferor for the latter to dismiss its employees a short time before the transfer becomes operative", said Lord Keith. Lord Oliver[103] thought that it was necessary to remember in this regard that the purpose of the Directive and the Regulations was to "safeguard" the rights of employees on transfer and that there was a mandatory obligation to "provide remedies which are effective and not merely symbolic to which the Regulations are intended to give effect. The remedies ... in the case of an insolvent transferor are largely illusory unless they can be exerted against the transferee as the Directive contemplates". It was thus the duty of the court to

[97] *Premier Motors (Medway) Ltd v Total Oil* [1984] I.C.R. 58, 62.
[98] reg.4(9). See *University of Oxford v Humphreys* [2000] 1 All E.R. 996 (CA). See also *Hope v PGS Engineering Ltd* Unreported March 18, 2005.
[99] reg.4(4).
[100] reg.4(7) and (8).
[101] See, e.g. differing conclusions in *Alphafield Ltd (t/a Apex Leisure Hire) v Barratt* [1984] 1 W.L.R. 1062; *Secretary of State for Employment v Anchor Hotel (Kippford)* [1985] I.C.R. 724; *Secretary of State for Employment v Spence* [1987] Q.B. 179 (CA) and, subsequent to *Litster* (see fn.102, below), see *Brook Lane Finance Co Ltd v Bradley* [1988] I.C.R. 423. The European Court of Justice considered the matter in *P Bork International A/S v Foreningen af Arbejdsledere i Danmark* [1988] E.C.R. 3057 (101/87).
[102] *Litster v Forth Dry Dock & Engineering Co Ltd* [1990] 1 A.C. 546 (HL).
[103] 576G.

give to reg.5 a construction which accords with the decisions of the European Court of Justice on the corresponding provisions of the Directive. Regulation 5(3) had to be construed on the:

"footing that it applies to a person employed immediately before the transfer or who would have been so employed if he had not been unfairly dismissed before transfer for a reason connected with the transfer".[104]

Lord Oliver stated that the sequence of events in the transfer in question could not be rationally explained otherwise than on the basis that the dismissal of the workforce was engineered to prevent any liability attaching to Forth Estuary Engineering Ltd (the solvent transferee). On the other hand:

"Where, before the actual transfer takes place, the employment of an employee is terminated for a reason unconnected with the transfer, I agree that the question of whether he was employed 'immediately' before the transfer cannot sensibly be made to depend on the temporal proximity between the two events, except possibly in a case where they are so closely connected in point of time, that it is, for practical purposes, impossible realistically to say that they are not precisely contemporaneous."[105]

16–028 There may be complex and uncertain situations where a transferor negotiates with several different purchasers in order to be in a position to gain the best price, and the actual transferee is not identifiable until the day of contract and completion. In such a situation it has been much debated whether the *Litster* principle applies before the specific transferee to whom the transfer eventually is made has been precisely identified, so that anyone dismissed before that time would not be employed immediately before the transfer and thus not transferred.[106] It is the better view that transfer takes place at the moment of completion rather than on exchange of contracts.

While the *Litster* approach may make sense in a solvent situation, it may not be so in a receivership or administration. In the latter type of case, the aim of selling the business as a going concern and saving as many jobs as can be saved often requires the shedding of some staff prior to the sale. Purchasers often will not or cannot accept all the existing employees into their employment. The effect of *Litster* in such situations may be to prevent one or more sales that may have saved some jobs or may be to encourage the shedding of employees at a stage when it is not clear how many employees would be accepted by a purchaser.

---

[104] Per Lord Templeman, 554H.
[105] 575D.
[106] *Harrison Bowden Ltd v Bowden* [1994] I.C.R. 186; *Ibex Trading Co v Walton* [1994] B.C.C. 982; *Morris v John Grose Group Ltd* [1998] I.C.R. 655.

(e) The voidable transfer

Another problem which arises from time to time is that the contract to transfer **16–029**
the business is itself voidable, e.g. because the directors acted in breach of their
duties and the transferee had notice of such breach (particularly where the
transferee is controlled by these directors or persons connected with them). In
the event that the transfer is avoided, e.g. as a result of action taken by a
receiver of the transferor, the position of the employees appears to be in doubt.
The Regulations make no specific provision for the reverting of contracts of
employment to the transferor in such cases. Logic suggests that, in cases where
employees' contracts follow the business, the avoidance of a transfer of the
business should indeed revest the contracts in the transferor, and this conclusion has been reached by the European Court of Justice as the proper construction of the relevant Directive.[107]

(i) Special Insolvency Provisions

The Acquired Rights Directive 2001 introduced new freedoms in relation to **16–030**
insolvency proceedings and transfers of undertakings. The scope of the procedures is, however, controversial.[108]

The TUPE Regulations 2006 for the first time makes use of these provisions
and applies them to any employee of the transferor whose contract "is terminated if the sole or principal reason is the transfer itself or a reason connected
with the transfer which is not an economic, technical or organisational reason
entailing changes in the workforce".[109]

(ii) The scope of the provisions

Article 5(1) of the Acquired Rights Directive 2001 refers to "the transferor [as] **16–031**
the subject of bankruptcy proceedings or any analogous insolvency proceedings which have been insolvency proceedings which have been instituted with
a view to the liquidation of the assets of the transferor and under the supervision of a competent public authority". This applies in effect to anything other
than terminal insolvency.[110] The TUPE Regulations in effect copy this out so
that relevant insolvency provision means such as "have been opened in relation
to the transferor not with a view to the liquidation of the assets of the transferor
and are under the supervision of an insolvency practitioner".[111]

---

[107] *Berg v Besselsen* [1988] E.C.R. 2559 (144/87).

[108] See *R3 Technical Bulletin*, Issue 77, November 2006. See also the DTI "Dear IP" letter, Issue 26, March 2006.

[109] reg.8(1) and see para.16–034, below.

[110] See, e.g. differing conclusions in *Alphafield Ltd (t/a Apex Leisure Hire) v Barratt* [1984] 1 W.L.R. 1062; *Secretary of State for Employment v Anchor Hotel (Kippford)* [1985] I.C.R. 724; *Secretary of State for Employment v Spence* [1987] Q.B. 179 (CA) and, subsequent to *Litster* (see above, paras 16–027 to 16–028), see *Brook Lane Finance Co Ltd v Bradley* [1988] I.C.R. 423. The European Court of Justice considered the matter in *P Bork International A/S v Foreningen af Arbejdsledere i Danmark* [1988] E.C.R. 3057 (101/87).

[111] reg.8(6).

Article 5(4) of Directive 2001/23 obliges Member States to take "appropriate measures with a view to preventing misuse of insolvency proceedings in such a way as to deprive employees of the rights provided for" in the Acquired Rights Directive although there is no specific implementation of this in the TUPE Regulations. In five conjoined appeals under the title *OTG Ltd v Barke*, [2011] I.R.L.R. 272, UKEAT/0320/09 the EAT decided that TUPE does apply to employee. This was because administration proceedings could not be regarded as "instituted with a view to liquidation of the assets of the company" within reg.8(7) TUPE. The EAT considered that administrations (including pre-pack schemes) can never fall within reg.8(7). It thus departed from its previous decision in *Oakland v Wellswood (Yorkshire) Ltd* [2009] I.R.L.R. 250. It wished to give certainty to this area by an absolute rule. This case closes the route for purchasers who wished to avoid inheriting employee liabilities under TUPE by a pre-pack route. The EAT in *OTG* did, however, point out that employees who have already been dismissed by an administrator by the time of transfer are likely to fall in a significantly weaker position.

(iii)   No transfer to transferee

16–032   There are two consequences of this liberalisation of TUPE which may assist the rescue culture. The first is that reg.8(5) prevents the normal operation of reg.4 (the automatic transfer of employee liabilities[112]) which operates to transfer liability for unpaid sums due to transferring employees as long as there are sums reimbursable by the Secretary of State under "relevant statutory schemes". These would primarily cover ss.166–170 and 182–190 of the Employment Rights Act 1996.[113]

Debts not covered by these schemes or the excess over any applicable statutory limits are still inherited by the transferee under reg.4.

(iv)   Changes to terms

16–033   Further the transferor or transferee or an insolvency practitioner may agree to a variation in the contract of employment of an assigned employee[114] where "the sole or principal reason is the transfer itself or a reason connected with the transfer which is not an economic, technical or organisational reason entailing changes in the workforce and it is designed to safeguard employment opportunities by ensuring the survival of the undertaking business or part of the business that is the subject of the relevant transfer".[115]

Regulation 8(7) provides that the normal provisions of TUPE on unfair dismissal do not "apply to any relevant transfer where the transferor is the

---

[112] See discussion in para.16–024, above.

[113] See reg 8(5), and see also para.16–008, above. This applies, e.g. to arrears of pay for up to eight weeks; notice pay; holiday pay; and the basic award of unfair dismissal compensation pursuant to s.184(1) Employment Rights Act 1996.

[114] Note that this is different to "affected employee" which governs other features of transfer law such as information and consultation.

[115] reg.9(1) and (7).

subject of bankruptcy proceedings or any analogous insolvency proceedings which have been instituted with a view to the liquidation of the assets of the transferor and under the supervision of an insolvency practitioner".

This is in effect a copy out of the Acquired Rights Directive. In the Insolvency Act 1986 Pt XIII capacities in which an insolvency practitioner may act include liquidator, administrative receiver, administrator and supervisor of a voluntary arrangement.[116]

The appropriate representatives of transferring employees may validly agree such contractual changes. This means representatives of any recognised unions or those appointed as workforce representatives either elected in accordance with the relevant requirements for the purpose or having the requisite authority to act in such matters.[117] Such changes in terms may only, however, be made in respect of assigned employees, that is "those assigned to the organised grouping of resources or employees that is the subject of the relevant transfer".[118]

Where trade union representatives are not involved, special formality is required for such changes in that:

(a) the agreement recording the permitted variations must be in writing and signed by each of the employee representatives who have made it or, where that is not reasonably practicable, by a duly authorised agent of that employee representative.

(b) The employer must before the agreement is made available for signature provide all employees to whom it is intended to apply on the date on which it is to come into effect with copies of the agreement and "such guidance as those employees might reasonably require in order to understand it fully".[119]

Regulation 9(6) states that a permitted variation "shall take effect as a term or condition of the assigned employee's contract of employment in place where relevant of any term or condition which it varies".

A further curiosity is that the Regulations give no scope for employees to object to the decision of their representatives to reach an agreement. This is indeed one of the few areas where a contract may be amended without the consent of the employee.

(f) Transfers and unfair dismissal

If either before or after a relevant transfer an employee is dismissed and if the   **16–034**
principal reason for the dismissal is the transfer or a reason connected with it,

---

[116] The Government's view in the TUPE Consultation Document, paras 58 and 64, was that reg.8(7) applied "in particular to compulsory winding-up and bankruptcy".
[117] reg.9(2).
[118] reg.9(7).
[119] reg.9(5)(b).

the employee is treated as having been dismissed unfairly,[120] unless the principal reason for the dismissal is "an economic, technical or organisational reason entailing changes in the workforce of either the transferor or the transferee . . .".[121] In that case, the employer is treated as having demonstrated some other potentially fair reason for dismissal within s.98(1)(b) of the Employment Rights Act 1996. The question still remains in such a case of economic, technical or organisational reason whether the dismissal was in fact fair for the purposes of unfairness as defined by s.98(4) of the 1996 Act.[122] It is important to note that any such reason must entail "changes in the workforce". A desire by the new employers to whom the business had been transferred to put all their employees on the same footing by reducing the pay of employees taken over did not entail "a change in the workforce" so that an employee who had his pay reduced had been automatically unfairly dismissed.[123] On the other hand, it has been decided that the dismissal of the entire workforce by a receiver prior to a transfer necessarily entailed "a change in the workforce".[124] The cases are by no means easy to reconcile on this point.[125]

To qualify as an economic reason, the reason for dismissal must be connected with the conduct or running of the business itself and not be merely a desire to achieve a better price for the entity transferred.[126] Where the reason does qualify and the employee is held to have been fairly dismissed because of a change in the workforce, he may still be entitled to a redundancy payment.[127]

(g)   Information and consultation over transfers

16–035   The "employer" has a duty to give advance warning of a relevant transfer and (amongst other things) of its "legal economic and social implications . . . for the affected employees . . ." to representatives of any recognised independent trade union.[128] Where measures are to be taken which will affect employees, there must be consultation with the recognised union(s) if unions are recog-

---

[120] Transfer Regulations, reg.7(1).
[121] Transfer Regulations, reg.7(1)(a) and (2).
[122] *Berriman v Delabole Slate Ltd* [1985] I.C.R. 546 (CA); *McGrath v Rank Leisure Ltd* [1985] I.C.R. 527; *Crawford v Swinton Insurance Brokers Ltd* [1990] I.C.R. 85; *Whitehouse v Charles A Blatchford & Sons Ltd* [2000] I.C.R. 542 (CA); *Kerry Foods Ltd v Creber* [2000] I.C.R. 556; *London Metropolitan University v Sackur* Unreported August 17, 2006.
[123] See above, paras 16–027 to 16–028.
[124] *Anderson v Dalkeith Engineering (In Receivership)* [1985] I.C.R. 66.
[125] "Workforce" means the workforce as an entity separate from the individuals who make up that workforce. The issue under the Transfer Regulations is whether the reason for dismissal involved a change in that workforce. There could be such a change even if the same people were retained but were given different jobs by the transferee: *Crawford v Swinton Insurance Ltd* [1990] I.C.R. 85; *Porter and Nanayakkara v Queens Medical Centre* [1993] I.R.L.R. 486.
[126] *Wendelboe v LJ Music ApS* [1985] E.C.R. 457 (19/83); *Gateway Hotels Ltd v Stewart* [1988] I.R.L.R. 287; *Wheeler v Patel* [1987] I.C.R. 631.
[127] *Meikle v McPhail* [1983] I.R.L.R. 351; *Canning v Niaz* [1983] I.R.L.R. 431 (no claim possible); *Gorictree Ltd v Jenkinson* [1985] I.C.R. 51 and *Anderson v Dalkeith (In Receivership)* [1985] I.C.R. 66 (claim possible).
[128] Transfer Regulations, reg.13. The original restriction to recognised unions was in breach of the Acquired Rights Directive according to the European Court of Justice in *Commission of the European Communities v United Kingdom* (C-382/92) [1994] E.C.R. I-2435. See *Institute of Professional Civil Servants v Secretary of State for Defence* [1987] I.R.L.R. 373.

nised "with a view to seeking their agreement".[129] In the absence of a recognised union the employer must inform and consult (if necessary) with employee representatives already appointed or elected by the affected employees for another purpose or arrange for such representatives to be appointed by way of the procedure laid down in the Regulations.[130]

Failure to comply with this duty can lead to an award of compensation being made against the "employer" of up to 13 weeks' pay,[131] unless the "employer" shows:

"(a) that there were special circumstances which rendered it not reasonably practical for him to perform the duty; and

(b) that he took all such steps towards its performance as were reasonably practicable in those circumstances".[132]

Such an award of compensation may well rank as a preferential debt and thus affect the receivership.[133] Liability in a transfer situation passes to the transferee.[134]

---

[129] reg.13(6) inserted by the Trade Union Reform and Employment Rights Act 1993, s.33.

[130] reg.13(3).

[131] reg.16(3).

[132] Transfer Regulations, reg.15(2). As to what might constitute "special circumstances" in such a case. cf. *BakersUnion v Clarks of Hove Ltd* [1978] 1 W.L.R. 1207 (CA); *Armour v ASTMS* [1979] I.R.L.R. 24; *APAC v Kirvin Ltd* [1978] I.R.L.R. 318; *USDA W v Leancut Bacon Ltd* [1981] I.R.L.R. 295; *GMB v Rankin and Harrison* [1992] I.R.L.R. 514 (all decided on the basis of similar wording in the Employment Protection Act 1975).

[133] Insolvency Act 1986, Sch.6, paras (9)(b) and 13(2)(e) and see below, Chs 27 and 28. The maximum is only two weeks' pay and it may be set off against a protective award for failure to consult about redundancies or damages for breach of contract: reg.11(7).

[134] *Kerry Foods Ltd v Creber* [2000] I.C.R. 556; *Alamo Group (Europe) Ltd v Tucker* [2003] I.C.R. 829. cf. *Angus Jowett v NUTGW* [1985] I.C.R. 646.

Chapter 17

Pensions

1. INTRODUCTION

17–001 In recent years, the increasing importance of pensions in the financial affairs of companies and their employees, together with the increased legislative intervention in the treatment of pensions in corporate insolvencies, have made this area of particular practical importance for administrators and other insolvency practitioners.[1]

A key aspect of company pension schemes is that their assets are almost invariably held in trust, kept separate from the company's assets, and administered by the trustees of the schemes. Formerly, such schemes were required to be established under irrevocable trusts in order to qualify for valuable tax exemptions; nowadays, there is a statutory requirement for such schemes to be set up under trust in order for the trustees to be able to accept contributions.[2] The practice of providing pension schemes under trust is intended to ensure that the assets of the scheme remain separate from the assets of the company, and consequently protected from use by the administrator for the benefit of the company's creditors.

However, there are several ways in which the company's pension scheme may impact upon the assets of the company, and will therefore remain a concern of the administrator.

2. EFFECTS OF ENTRY INTO ADMINISTRATION

17–002 From the insolvency practitioner's point of view, an immediate important impact of administration of a company which sponsors a pension scheme is that it triggers various overlapping notification obligations:

> (a) He must as soon as reasonably practicable give notice to: (a) the Pensions Regulator; (b) the Pension Protection Fund; and (c) the trustees of the scheme that he has begun to act as an insolvency practitioner in relation to the employer in relation to the scheme.[3]

---

[1] For detailed introductory treatment of pensions law generally, see Bell, Jones et al, *Pensions Law Handbook*, 9th edn (Bloomsbury Professional, 2009) and for an introduction to the treatment in insolvency law, see the Pension chapter in the fourth edition of this work.

[2] s.252(2) of the Pensions Act 2004: certain exceptions to this requirement are provided for in reg.2 of the Occupational Pension Schemes (Trust and Retirement Benefits Exemption) Regulations 2005 (SI 2005/2360).

[3] s.22 of the Pensions Act 1995.

(b) He must within 14 days of the insolvency date or of becoming aware of the existence of the pension scheme (whichever is the later), give a notice to the effect that the insolvency event has occurred in relation to the employer to (a) the Pension Protection Fund, (b) the Pensions Regulator and (c) the trustees of the scheme.[4] Details of what needs to be included in the notice are to be found in regulations.[5]

This is a specific statutory provision, additional to the general duty of the employer, to notify the scheme trustees within one month of the occurrence of an event relating to the employer which there is reasonable cause to believe will be of material significance in the exercise by the trustees or their advisers of any of their functions.[6] Non-compliance with this obligation may render him subject to a civil penalty imposed by the Pensions Regulator.[7]

(c) The administrator should also be aware of notification requirements under s.69 of the Pensions Act 2004 and the Pensions Regulator (Notifiable Events) Regulations 2005 (SI 2005/900), even though his appointment is not itself a notifiable event for the purposes of that section.

(d) Furthermore, the administrator must provide the trustees of the scheme, as soon as practicable after the receipt of the request, with any information which the trustees may reasonably require for the purposes of the scheme.[8]

(e) In addition, the administrator may be subject to a request by the Pensions Regulator to provide any document or information which is relevant to the exercise of the Pensions Regulator's functions.[9]

The Pension Protection Fund referred to above is a statutory lifeboat that in **17–003** many cases has a significant impact on the course of an administration. Further information on the Pension Protection Fund is provided at para.17–018, below. For an introduction to the insolvency practitioner's responsibilities as regards the Pension Protection Fund, reference should also be made to the Pension Protection Fund's Guidance for Insolvency Practitioners and Official Receivers.[10]

Subject to the potential effect of the legislation relating to the Pension Protection Fund, administration may also impact on the status of pension schemes, in terms of the winding-up of the scheme and its "contracted-out status": see 17–007 and 17–009 below.

---

[4] s.120 of the Pensions Act 2004 and reg.4 of the Pension Protection Fund (Entry Rules) Regulations 2005.
[5] reg.4(2) of the Pension Protection Fund (Entry Rules) Regulations 2005.
[6] s.47(9) of the Pensions Act 1995 and reg.6(1)(b) of the Occupational Pension Schemes (Scheme Administration) Regulations 1996 (SI 1996/1715).
[7] s.10 of the Pensions Act 1995.
[8] s.26 of the Pensions Act 1995.
[9] s.72 of the Pensions Act 2004.
[10] Available at: *http://www.pensionprotectionfund.org.uk/DocumentLibrary/Documents/insolvency_guidance.pdf*.

17–004   An administrator or receiver should also be aware that, after his appointment, the Pensions Regulator has power to appoint an independent trustee
of the scheme.[11] This is normally implemented by the Regulator where,
for example, the existing trustees are no longer in a position to act, or are
unwilling to act, or are in an inappropriate position to act, perhaps because
their position is compromised. After such appointment, any power which the
scheme confers on the employer and which is exercisable by him at its discretion but only as trustee of the power may be exercised only by the independent
trustee.[12]

3.   THE COMPANY'S OBLIGATIONS TO THE SCHEME

17–005 An administrator will be concerned to identify the potential claims over the
company's assets which the scheme may generate.

Obligations to provide funds to a company's pension scheme can arise from
a number of sources:

(a)   the express terms of the scheme requiring contributions from the
      employer;

(b)   the statutory provisions requiring employers to fund scheme liabili-
      ties, i.e. Pt 3 of the Pensions Act 2004 and s.75 of the Pensions Act
      1995; and

(c)   the "moral hazard" provisions of the Pensions Act 2004 requiring
      employers and other persons to make contributions to pension
      schemes in certain circumstances.

(a)   Express contribution obligations

17–006 Most final-salary pension schemes will include terms requiring the company to
pay the balance of the cost of funding members' benefits, to the extent that the
existing assets are insufficient for that purpose. How the entry of the company
into administration affects such provisions depends upon their precise wording:
it is possible that the occurrence of an insolvency event in respect of the
company automatically terminates both the accrual of future benefits and
the obligation of the employer to contribute to those benefits; alternatively, the
obligation to contribute may continue, perhaps subject to a term allowing
the company to terminate its contribution liability. In the latter situation, the
administrator may consider it to be in the best interests of the company to cause
it to terminate the payment of contributions to the scheme, even if this does not
automatically occur on the entry of the company into administration.[13]

---

[11] s.23(1) of the Pensions Act 1995; see also *The Pensions Regulator, Changes to our trustee
register*, May 2010.

[12] s.25 of the Pensions Act 1995.

[13] There may, however, be constraints imposed upon the termination of future accrual by the
employment contracts of the affected members of the scheme, although that will not be of practical
concern to either an administrator, who is not personally liable in respect of adopted contracts (see

However, in most cases, the commencement of an administration or the appointment of an administrative receiver will cause the cessation of further ongoing contributions to the scheme, at least temporarily, as those events will trigger an "assessment period" for the purposes of the Pension Protection Fund,[14] during which time generally no further benefits may accrue under the scheme and no contributions not already due as at that date may be made to it.[15] If the scheme does not qualify for entry into the Pension Protection Fund, there are provisions for the recommencement of benefit accrual and contribution payments, which are retrospective back to the commencement of the assessment period.[16]

In whichever way contribution liability is terminated, such termination will normally only operate to end the company's obligation to make contributions in respect of *future* benefit accrual; it will not normally prevent the trustees from seeking to impose a liability on the company to pay any deficit in the scheme caused by *past* service benefit accrual, calculated as the cost of securing such benefits by the purchase of annuities (the so-called "buy-out basis") which is nowadays usually very expensive.[17] Thus, if the termination provision requires a period of time to elapse between service of the notice and the effective date of termination, the trustees may well seek a lump sum contribution from the company to meet the additional costs of securing all the scheme benefits; and even if there is no prescribed time period, a term may be implied in the notice provision requiring a reasonable time to elapse so as to enable the trustees to seek such a contribution.[18]

Members of the company scheme may be "contracted-out" of the state **17–007** second pension scheme, which causes the company's National Insurance contributions to be reduced in return for the provision by the scheme of benefits which reflect the state pension provision. Termination of contributions may cause the scheme's contracting-out certificate to cease, and the National Insurance contributions of the company to increase.

As to how past service contribution obligations rank in priority terms, **17–008** because the basis of the company's obligation to pay contributions to the scheme is contractual in nature,[19] any obligation imposed by the terms of the scheme will generally rank as an unsecured debt in the insolvency of the company. However, preferential debt status is accorded to the following unpaid

---

para.99(5) of Sch.B1 to the Insolvency Act 1986), or an administrative receiver, whose personal liability under employment contracts applies only in respect of services rendered wholly or partly after the adoption of the contract (Insolvency Act 1986, s.44(2A)).

[14] As to which, see 17–018 below.

[15] s.133(3)(5) of the Pensions Act 2004.

[16] Pensions Act 2004, s.150(5)(6); reg.20 of the Pension Protection Fund (Entry Rules) Regulations 2005 (SI 2005/590).

[17] For examples of such claims by trustees, see *McClelland v Unisys (NZ) Ltd* [2002] P.L.R. 87 (High Court of New Zealand); and *Pinsent Curtis v Capital Cranfield Trustees Ltd* [2005] 4 All E.R. 449 (CA).

[18] *Pinsent Curtis v Capital Cranfield Trustees Ltd* [2005] 4 All E.R. 449 (CA), [32], per Smith L.J.

[19] *Air Jamaica Ltd v Charlton* [1999] 1 W.L.R. 1399 (PC),1408, per Lord Millett.

arrears of pension contributions outstanding at the commencement of the insolvency[20]:

(a) any employee contributions deducted from earnings during the four months immediately prior to insolvency;

(b) in relation to contracted-out salary-related schemes, company contributions payable in the 12 months prior to insolvency;

(c) in relation to contracted-out money-purchase schemes, sums owed on account of a company's minimum payments falling to be made in the 12 months prior to insolvency;

(d) sums (known as "state scheme premiums") payable in respect of the reinstatement to the state second pension of an employee formerly in contracted-out employment.

In addition, the company will be liable to the Secretary of State for any contributions arrears payable by the Secretary of State to the scheme trustees, although any such debt is unsecured and non-preferential.[21]

17–009   A further consequence of the termination of the company's liability to contribute to a scheme may be to trigger a winding-up of the scheme; indeed, a winding-up may be triggered automatically by the occurrence of an insolvency event in respect of the company. Winding up a scheme involves the trustees using the assets of the scheme to secure the benefits of the scheme, and gives rise to a statutory debt on the company, discussed in 17–012 below. Certain regulatory issues arise on a winding-up.[22]

It is often in the interests of the company to avoid a winding-up being triggered by the size of that debt, and many schemes will provide a discretion on the part of the trustees or the company to defer the winding-up and continue the scheme as a "closed scheme", with no new members being admitted and no more benefits accruing.[23] Another benefit of the scheme being continued as a closed scheme is the continuing availability of the power of amendment,[24] which is not available where the scheme is in winding-up.[25]

---

[20] See paras 8 and 9 of Sch.6 to the Insolvency Act 1986 and Sch.4 to the Pension Schemes Act 1993.

[21] s.124 of the Pension Schemes Act 1993.

[22] See the Pension Regulator's Guidance on Winding-up issued in June 2008, which provides useful suggestions on how to effect an efficient and timely winding-up, which is available at: *http://www.thepensionsregulator.gov.uk/guidance/guidance-winding-up.aspx*.

[23] In the absence of such a power, s.38 of the Pensions Act 1995 confers such a power on the trustees, although there are some significant exclusions from its scope: see reg.10 of the Occupational Pension Schemes (Winding Up) Regulations 1996 (SI 1996/3126).

[24] *Re Edward Jones Benevolent Fund* Unreported March 8, 1985 (John Chadwick QC), and see Inglis-Jones, *The Law of Occupational Pension Schemes* (Sweet & Maxwell, looseleaf).

[25] *Thrells v Lomas* [1993] 1 W.L.R. 456.

(b)   Statutory liabilities

There are two main sources of statutory liability of an employer to contribute   **17–010**
to a company pension scheme:

(a)   while the scheme is ongoing, pursuant to Pt 3 of the Pensions Act
2004; and

(b)   where an insolvency event occurs in respect of the employer, pursuant
to s.75 of the Pensions Act 1995.

(i)   Part 3 of the Pensions Act 2004

By Pt 3 of the Pensions Act 2004,[26] employers of defined benefit pension   **17–011**
schemes are obliged to fund the scheme to ensure it meets the "statutory
funding objective" of ensuring that the scheme has sufficient and appropriate
assets to meet its liabilities (known as "technical provisions"), calculated on a
basis agreed by the employer and trustees and certified by the scheme actuary.
This legislation also provides for statements of funding principles, schedules
of contributions and, if necessary, recovery plans to be agreed between the
employer and the trustees.[27] Failure to pay contributions under the legislation
gives rise to a statutory debt on the part of the employer.[28]

These provisions expressly override any of the terms of the scheme, to the
extent that there is a conflict.[29] Thus, whilst any provision in the scheme which
would operate to reduce the employer's contributions obligations below those
imposed by Pt 3 of the Pensions Act 2004 is to be disregarded, it is likely that
any such provision which imposes greater obligations than those required
by the legislation will continue to apply.[30]

The cessation of the contribution obligations of an employer triggered by the
commencement of a Pension Protection Fund assessment period, referred to in
17–006 above, applies equally to any contributions due under Pt 3 of the
Pensions Act 2004.

(ii)   Section 75

The commencement of an administration or the appointment of an administra-   **17–012**
tive receiver in respect of the company constitutes the occurrence of an "insolvency event" for the purposes of s.75 of the Pensions Act 1995. Where the
company is the sole employer of the scheme concerned, it will owe the scheme

---

[26] Introduced to comply with the EU Directive 2003/41/EC on the activities and supervision of
institutions for occupational retirement provision.

[27] See ss.223, 226 and 227 of the Pensions Act 2004.

[28] Pensions Act 2004, s.228(3): there is no suggestion in the legislation that this debt is anything
other than unsecured and non-preferential.

[29] Pensions Act 2004, s.306.

[30] In *PNPF Trust Co Ltd v Taylor* [2010] Pens. L.R. 261, [714], Warren J. confirmed the former
principle, and [764] expressed an inclination towards the latter principle, without definitively
deciding the matter.

trustees a debt equivalent to the deficit of the scheme at that time. Where the insolvent company is one of a number of employers of the scheme, it will be liable for a proportionate share of the deficit.[31]

In the latter situation, unless the scheme rules provide otherwise, the debt is apportioned pro rata between the companies by reference to their share of the liabilities.[32]

Companies which participated in a scheme some years previously and have ceased to do so, (e.g. because they have been sold out of the group) may remain liable for a share of a scheme deficit, depending upon whether any s.75 debt existed at the time of their cessation of participation and how that debt was then dealt with.[33]

The s.75 debt is calculated on the (usually expensive) buy-out basis,[34] and is therefore likely to represent a significant proportion of the total liabilities of the company in administration. However, the practical effect of this debt is mitigated on the insolvency of the company by the fact that it is to be treated as unsecured and non-preferential.[35]

The liability of the employer to meet the s.75 debt is not affected by the commencement of any Pension Protection Fund assessment period.

Where a s.75 debt is triggered by an insolvency, the scheme trustees are entitled under s.15 of the Trustee Act 1925 to agree a compromise of their claim to that debt with the administrator.[36] However, care must be taken when considering such a compromise, as the Pensions Regulator must be notified of such a compromise,[37] and may require the company or its associates to inject further funds into the scheme pursuant to a contribution notice.[38] This, together with the possibility that such a compromise may jeopardise the entry of the scheme into the Pension Protection Fund,[39] means that no such compromise should be entered into without the involvement of both the Pensions Regulator and the Pension Protection Fund.

(c)   "Moral hazard" provisions

17–013   Part 1 of the Pensions Act 2004 provides the Pensions Regulator with two means of requiring contributions to be made to the scheme by an employer or

---

[31] s.75A of the Pensions Act 1995; regs 6–8 of the Occupational Pension Schemes (Employer Debt) Regulations 2005 (SI 2005/678).

[32] Occupational Pension Schemes (Employer Debt) Regulations 2005 (SI 2005/678), reg.6(2). There are several alternative methods of dealing with the s.75 debt other than immediate payment: see Occupational Pension Schemes (Employer Debt) Regulations 2005, regs 6B, 6C, 7, 7A and 16.

[33] see Occupational Pension Schemes (Employer Debt) Regulations 2005, reg.9.

[34] Occupational Pension Schemes (Employer Debt) Regulations 2005, reg.5(11).

[35] s.75(8) of the Pensions Act 1995.

[36] *Bradstock Group Pension Scheme Trustees Ltd v Bradstock Group Plc* [2002] I.C.R. 1427.

[37] reg.2 of the Pensions Regulator (Notifiable Events) Regulations 2005 (SI 2005/900).

[38] As to which, see para.17–014, below. The Pensions Regulator has issued guidance on how it expects trustees to approach such compromises: May 2007 Guidance on Abandonment of Defined Benefit Pension Schemes. This is available at: *http://www.thepensionsregulator.gov.uk/guidance/guidance-abandonment.aspx*.

[39] reg.2(2) of the Pension Protection Fund (Entry Rules) Regulations 2005.

an associated or connected person, such as other companies within the same group: contribution notices and financial support directions.

(i) Contribution notices[40]

A contribution notice can be issued where an employer, or a connected or associated person,[41] is a party to an act, omission or course of conduct one of whose main purposes was to prevent the recovery of all or part of a s.75 debt, to prevent such a debt becoming due, or to compromise or otherwise settle or reduce the amount of such a debt. In addition, the act or omission (or the first act or omission in a series) must have occurred on or after April 27, 2004, or the effect of the act, omission or course of conduct was materially detrimental to members' interests and the act, omission (or at least one act or omission in a series) occurred on or after April 14, 2008. In addition, the act or failure to act must have occurred within a six year period prior to the date of issue of the contribution notice, and the Pensions Regulator must be of the opinion that it is reasonable to impose liability.

17–014

A contribution notice can require the employer or it's associate or connected person to pay all or part of the s.75 debt, and is enforceable as a debt by the trustees or by the Pensions Regulator, except during a Pension Protection Fund assessment period, when it is enforceable solely by the Pension Protection Fund Board.[42]

The Pensions Regulator will determine whether it is reasonable to impose a contribution notice on a particular person having regard, where relevant, to its relationship with the employer and the scheme, its degree of involvement in the act complained of, its financial resources, whether there was any failure to report to the Pensions Regulator, all the purposes of the act or failure to act including whether a purpose was to prevent loss of employment, the value of any benefits received by that person from the employer, the likelihood of creditors being paid, and the financial circumstances of the person.[43]

A clearance procedure allows parties to request the Pensions Regulator to confirm in advance whether any proposed action will give rise to a contribution notice. If the Pensions Regulator gives clearance to a particular transaction, it is binding on it unless the facts are materially different to those presented to it.[44]

As to the relationship between the contribution notice and any outstanding s.75 debt: the Pensions Regulator has the power to prevent the trustees from recovering the s.75 debt pending recovery of the contribution notice debt; any sum paid under the contribution notice is treated as reducing the s.75 debt; and the recipient of a contribution notice may ask the Pensions Regulator to reduce

---

[40] ss.38–42 of the Pensions Act 2004
[41] Defined respectively in ss.249 and 435 of the Insolvency Act 1986: such persons do not include insolvency practitioners acting in accordance with their functions: s.38(3)(c) of the Pensions Act 2004.
[42] s.40(3)–(5) of the Pensions Act 2004.
[43] Pensions Act 2004, s.38(7).
[44] Pensions Act 2004, s.42.

the amount to be paid under a contribution notice if any payment is made in respect of the s.75 debt.[45]

To date only one contribution notice has been issued by the Pensions Regulator. In May 2010, the Pensions Regulator issued a notice against the holding company of an employer, following a restructuring of the group involving a "pre pack" administration and resale of the employer. The Pensions Regulator held that that was an exercise designed to avoid liability under the scheme for a s.75 debt, and required the holding company to pay the sum necessary to take the scheme up to solvency on the statutorily-prescribed "PPF calculation" basis. The target company sought a review of the decision from the Upper Tribunal,[46] which sent the case back to the Pensions Regulator for reconsideration of a number of issues, in particular relating to the quantum of the contribution, which the Tribunal ruled should be based on the amount by which the target company's actions had actually reduced the s.75 debt that the employer would have paid.

(ii)   Financial support directions[47]

17–015 A financial support direction can be issued where the Pensions Regulator thinks it is reasonable and the employer is either a service company (as defined), or is "insufficiently resourced", i.e. its resources are less than 50 per cent of the estimated s.75 deficit, and the resources of a connected or associated person (or group of such persons) would, when added to the employer's resources, be 50 per cent or more of that deficit.

In determining whether it is reasonable to impose a financial support direction, the Pensions Regulator is required to take account, where relevant, of the relationship which the target person has or has had with the employer, the value of any benefits received directly or indirectly by that person from the employer, any connection or involvement which the person has or has had with the scheme, and the financial circumstances of the person.[48]

A financial support direction involves the Pensions Regulator directing the employer or a connected or associated person to put financial support in place for the scheme within a specified time. The person issued with the direction may put in place a variety of arrangements, including making all group companies jointly and severally liable for the employer's pension liabilities, making a holding company (which satisfies prescribed requirements) liable for the employer's pension liabilities, or making additional financial resources (which satisfy prescribed requirements) available to the scheme.[49]

If a financial support direction is not complied with, the Pensions Regulator may issue a contribution notice to any of the persons to whom the direction

---

[45] Pensions Act 2004, s.41.
[46] *Michel Van De Wiele NV v Pensions Regulator* [2011] Pens. L.R. 109.
[47] ss.43–51 of the Pensions Act 2004.
[48] Pensions Act 2004, s.43(7).
[49] Pensions Act 2004, s.45.

was issued, which is treated as a debt in the same way as for a contribution notice.[50]

As with the contribution notice provisions, there is a clearance procedure under which the Pensions Regulator can be asked to confirm in advance whether a person would be potentially liable to provide financial support and, if so, whether it considers it reasonable to impose such a liability. The clearance statement is binding on the Regulator unless the facts are materially different to those presented to it.[51]

The relationship between a contribution notice issued following a financial support direction and any outstanding s.75 debt is dealt with in the same terms as the corresponding provision for s.38 contribution notices.[52]

Where some or all of the members of a pension scheme in relation to which a financial support direction could have been issued are transferred to other schemes, the Pensions Regulator may issue a financial support direction in relation to any transferee scheme.[53]

To date there have been three determinations to issue financial support directions, all of which have been targeted at companies within the relevant group, some or all of which were in domestic or overseas insolvency processes. It is notable that the Pensions Regulator has determined that the insolvency of the particular target supports the issue of a financial support direction.

A key point is where any liability imposed pursuant to a financial support direction is to rank in the insolvency of the company. The administrators of some of the target companies concerned with two of the determinations to issue financial support directions sought directions on the issue, and in *Bloom v The Pensions Regulator*,[54] Briggs J. held as follows:

(a) if the Pensions Regulator issues a financial support direction *before* the company enters a formal insolvency process, any subsequent liability arising in connection with that financial support direction (including any subsequently-issued contribution notice) will be a provable debt against the company and rank as an unsecured creditor claim in the company's insolvency;

(b) if the Pensions Regulator issues a financial support direction *after* the company enters a formal insolvency process, any liability arising in connection with that financial support direction (including any subsequently-issued contribution notice) will rank as an expense of the insolvency process; and

(c) although an expense of the insolvency process during which it was issued, a liability arising from a contribution notice issued for non-compliance with a financial support direction issued in one

---

[50] Pensions Act 2004, ss.47–49.
[51] Pensions Act 2004, s.46.
[52] Pensions Act 2004, s.50: see 17–014 above.
[53] Pensions Act 2004, ss.43A and 43B.
[54] *Re Nortel GmbH; Bloom v The Pensions Regulator* [2011] B.C.C. 277, and see, on the Court of Appeal decision at [2011] EWCA Civ 1124 (CA), STOP PRESS after the preface to this work.

insolvency process (e.g. an administration) will be a provable debt (and consequently rank as an unsecured claim against the company) in any successive insolvency process (e.g. a liquidation), provided that the first insolvency process commenced before April 6, 2010: the revisions to the Insolvency Rules 1986 that came into effect on that date mean that, for insolvency processes commencing after that date, such liability will rank as an expense of the second process.

The ranking of debts arising from a financial support direction as an expense of the insolvency gives the Pensions Regulator the power to impose a very significant "super-priority" liability if it issues such a direction in the course of an administration. This has caused considerable disquiet in the insolvency industry, as it may hinder the implementation of restructuring strategies for companies with significant pension deficits and for other companies in the same corporate group. Shortly before publication of this work Briggs J.'s decision was upheld by the Court of Appeal: [2011] EWCA Civ 1124. Permission to appeal to the Supreme Court has been given.[55]

4.　The Statutory Pensions Lifeboats

17–016　There are three statutory pensions lifeboats: the Financial Assistance Scheme, the Pension Protection Fund and the Fraud Compensation Fund (operated by the Pension Protection Fund).

(a)　The Financial Assistance Scheme

17–017　The Financial Assistance Scheme was announced by the Government in May 2004 and introduced in July 2005. It was originally administered by the Department for Work and Pensions though, in 2009, responsibility transferred to the Pensions Protection Fund.

The rules of the Financial Assistance Scheme have evolved over time.[56] The basic idea is that it provides a top-up, subject to a cap, to the pensions of defined benefit occupational pension scheme members where the scheme is unable to provide more than 90 per cent of those benefits, and where the sponsoring employer is insolvent (or to be treated as insolvent) and the scheme began to wind up between January 1, 1997 and April 5, 2005 (or have started to wind up after April 5, 2005 but be ineligible for help from the Pension Protection Fund because of the date on which the employer became insolvent).

Because of the eligibility criteria, the Financial Assistance Scheme will typically be of limited relevance to companies entering administration.[57]

---

[55] See *Bloom v The Pensions Regulator* [2011] EWCA Civ 1124 (CA) and STOP PRESS after the preface to this work.

[56] For the current position see ss.286–286A of the Pensions Act 2004 and the numerous regulations made under s.286.

[57] For more information on the Financial Assistance Scheme, see: *http://www.pensionprotectionfund.org.uk/FAS/Pages/fas.aspx*.

(b) The Pension Protection Fund

The Pension Protection Fund is a statutory fund, created by the Pensions Act **17–018**
2004. In certain circumstances it assumes responsibility for the payment of
members' salary-related pension scheme benefits if a company becomes
insolvent—which includes going into receivership—and the value of the
scheme's assets is less than the value of the protected liabilities on a prescribed
basis.[58] In broad terms, pensioners are protected to 100 per cent of their income
and others receive up to 90 per cent, subject to a maximum payment, with
provisions for limited increases to pensions in payment.[59]

Where a company goes into receivership or an administrator is appointed,
the receiver or administrator must give a written notice in a prescribed form to
that effect within a prescribed period to the Pensions Regulator, the Pension
Protection Fund and the trustees of the scheme.[60]

The receiver or administrator must then ascertain whether or not it is possible
to effect a "scheme rescue", which occurs either:

- where there has been a rescue of the employer's business as a going
  concern and the employer retains responsibility for the scheme and
  the full amount of the debt arising under s.75 of the Pensions Act
  1995; or

- where someone else has assumed responsibility for the employer's
  liabilities under the scheme.[61]

When a scheme rescue has occurred, or where it is not possible to rescue the
scheme, the receiver or administrator must notify the Pensions Regulator,
Pension Protection Fund and the trustees.[62]

The Pension Protection Fund must formally approve any notice given by the
receiver or administrator for it to be binding.[63] If the receiver or administrator
fails to issue this notice, the Pension Protection Fund must do it itself.[64]

On the issue of a notice that a scheme rescue is not possible (known as a
"scheme failure notice"),[65] and if the scheme remains in deficit, the Pension
Protection Fund assumes responsibility for the scheme.[66] A notice of the

---

[58] ss.126–181 of the Pensions Act 2004. See also Pensions Protection Fund, Guidance for insolvency practitioners and official receivers, September 2005, available at: *http://www.pensionprotectionfund.org.uk*.

[59] Sch.7 of the Pensions Act 2004.

[60] Pensions Act 2004, s.120.

[61] reg.9(1)(a) of the Pensions Protection Fund (Entry Rules) Regulations 2005 (SI 2005/590).

[62] ss.120–122 of the Pensions Act 2004. Further details about the information the receiver or administrator needs to provide to the Pension Protection Fund are in the Pension Protection Fund (Provision of Information) Regulations 2005 (SI 2005/674) as amended by the Pension Protection Fund (Provision of Information) (Amendment) Regulations 2006 (SI 2006/ 595).

[63] s.123 of the Pensions Act 2004.

[64] Pensions Act 2004, ss.124–125.

[65] Pensions Act 2004, s.130(2): a copy of the notice must be sent to, amongst others, the receiver or administrator.

[66] Pensions Act 2004, ss.127(2), 161.

transfer of such responsibilities must be given to (amongst others) the receiver or administrator.[67]

While the scheme is being assessed for entry into the Pension Protection Fund, the scheme may not go into wind-up and no liabilities may be discharged.[68] Any attempted contravention of this prohibition is void, save to the extent that it is validated by the Pension Protection Fund, notice of which is sent to (amongst others) the receiver or administrator.[69]

The Pension Protection Fund becomes a creditor of the company in relation to any debt owed to the scheme, whether pursuant to s.75 of the Pensions Act 1995 or otherwise.[70]

The Pension Protection Fund has powers of enquiry, disclosure and search for the purposes of exercising its functions, all of which may be directed at the receiver or administrator.[71]

(c) The Fraud Compensation Fund

17–019 The Fraud Compensation Fund (FCF) was established under the Pensions Act 2004 to provide compensation to occupational pension schemes, with insolvent employers, that suffer a loss that can be attributable to an offence involving dishonesty. The Fraud Compensation Fund became operational on September 1, 2005 and replaces the former Pensions Compensation Board. It applies to most defined benefit and defined contribution occupational pension schemes. It does not apply to state retirement pensions.

Full details on the basis on which fraud compensation can be paid are set out in the Pensions Act 2004 and regulations made under it the Occupational Pension Schemes (Fraud Compensation Payments and Miscellaneous Amendments) Regulations 2005, and the predecessor provisions in the Pensions Act 1995 and the Occupational Pension Schemes (Pensions Compensation Provisions) Regulations 1997.

The FCF is a statutory fund run by the Board of the Pension Protection Fund (the Board), a statutory corporation established under the Pensions Act 2004.

5. RECOVERY OF PENSION CONTRIBUTIONS FROM THE SCHEME

17–020 The administrator may be interested in whether it is possible to recover any contributions wrongfully made to the scheme in the following circumstances:

(a) Such payments may be ultra vires the company. Thus, while there is inherent power to make pension contributions for employees, there

---

[67] Pensions Act 2004, s.160(6).
[68] Pensions Act 2004 s.135.
[69] Pensions Act 2004, ss.135(10), 136.
[70] Pensions Act 2004, s.137.
[71] Pensions Act 2004, ss.190–194.

must be a specific power in the articles of association to permit such contributions for directors.[72]

(b) Pension contributions made by a director for his own benefit may be so excessive as to constitute a breach of his fiduciary duty to the company.[73] In such circumstances a claim for repayment does not depend upon the company being insolvent or near insolvency at the time of the payment.[74]

(c) The Pensions Regulator can issue a restoration order where there has been a transaction at an undervalue (i.e. significantly less than money or money's worth) involving the assets of the scheme, and where the transaction was entered into no more than two years prior to the employer becoming insolvent.[75] The Pensions Regulator may in such circumstances make such order as it thinks fit to restore the position to what it would have been if the transaction had not been entered into.[76] However, no order may be made which prejudices any interest in property acquired in good faith and for value.[77] Where a party fails to comply with a restoration order, the Regulator may issue a contribution notice.[78]

6.   DEALING WITH SCHEME SURPLUSES

Given recent economic circumstances and other factors affecting pension schemes, it is unlikely that a company's scheme will be over-funded at the commencement of the administration, and it is much more likely that it will be in substantial deficit. However, if there are any surplus assets in the scheme, the administrator will be interested in securing some or all of the surplus for the benefit of the company's creditors, but there are significant obstacles to substantial recovery by the administrator.   **17–021**

(a) A surplus will only usually emerge when a scheme is wound up and will depend upon there being money left in the scheme after all other liabilities have been secured. The winding-up of the scheme might not commence during the administration and, even if it does, it may take some time for other liabilities to be dealt with.

(b) Recovering the surplus may be contrary to the governing provisions of the scheme, and changing those provisions may prove difficult,

---

[72] See, e.g. *Normandy v Ind Coope & Co Ltd* [1908] 1 Ch. 84. Where there is such a power, there is no need for the company to prove that the grant of the pension benefited the company: the payment of such a pension is an independent object in its own right provided it is in the memorandum: *Re Horsley & Weight Ltd* [1982] Ch. 442 (CA).

[73] *Re Horsley & Weight Ltd* [1982] Ch. 442 (CA), 455, per Templeman L.J.

[74] *Bednash v Hearsey* Unreported February 15, 2001 (Nicholas Stewart QC), application for permission to appeal refused [2002] 14 P.B.L.R. (CA).

[75] s.52(2) of the Pensions Act 2004.

[76] Pensions Act 2004, s.52(3).

[77] Pensions Act 2004, s.53(3).

[78] Pensions Act 2004, s.55.

even though an application to the Pensions Regulator may be made to do so.[79]

(c) There are several procedural requirements which must be satisfied before any surplus can be paid to the employer, including the requirement that the trustees must be satisfied that the payment is in the interests of the scheme members.[80]

(d) Because of changes made to the surplus regime, any power in the provisions of the scheme to make surplus payments to employers which existed prior to April 6, 2006 will be lost unless the trustees pass a resolution to retain the power by April 5, 2011.[81]

(e) Trustees are often given a discretion in the winding-up provisions of the scheme to improve benefits using surplus before any of it is returned to the company.[82]

(f) All surplus payments are subject to a 35 per cent tax charge.[83]

[79] s.69(3)(a) of the Pensions Act 1995.

[80] Pensions Act 1995, s.37 (ongoing schemes); Pensions Act 1995, s.73 (schemes in winding-up). No refunds can be made from an ongoing scheme unless the scheme actuary has certified that the scheme is in surplus on the buy-out basis: reg.5 of the Occupational Pension Schemes (Repayment to Employers) Regulations 2006 (SI 2006/802).

[81] s.251 of the Pensions Act 2004. Clause 21 of the Pensions Bill 2011 will, if passed, extend the deadline to April 5, 2016.

[82] Indeed, some schemes require members' benefits to be augmented to the maximum permitted by HMRC before any assets can be returned to the company: see, e.g. *Harwood-Smart v Caws* [2000] Pens. L.R. 101.

[83] s.207(4) of the Finance Act 2004.

Chapter 18

Leases

1. LEASES AS SECURITY

The receiver, or the administrator, may be appointed in relation to a company **18–001** which is the lessee of one or more properties. At one level, the appointment of a receiver, or an administrator, as the agent of the company does not change the relationship between the landlord and the company as tenant; the company can continue to enjoy its rights as tenant, acting through the agency of the receiver or the administrator. At another level, the fact of the appointment of the receiver, or the administrator, may give the landlord rights which it did not enjoy against the company prior to the appointment of the receiver or the administrator. Further, the receiver, or the administrator, is likely to be appointed at a time when the company is in financial difficulties and its difficulties may have led to its failing to pay the rent due under the lease or committing other breaches of the lease. Further, a company in administration will have the benefit of restrictions on the action which its landlord can take against it. Accordingly, this chapter will consider the various landlord and tenant issues that may confront a receiver or administrator of a company tenant either as a result of the appointment of the receiver or administrator or, more generally, because of the financial position of the company at the time of the appointment. In this chapter reference to the "charge" is a reference to the charge or holder of the charge under which a receiver or an administrator is appointed.

(a) The questions which are likely to arise

The questions which are likely to arise include the following: **18–002**

(i) Remedies of landlord for breach of covenant or condition:
    (a) Was the grant of the charge a breach of the terms of the lease?
    (b) Was the appointment of the receiver, or the administrator, a breach of the terms of the lease?
    (c) Is the landlord entitled to seek forfeiture of the lease by reason of the grant of the charge or the appointment of the receiver or the administrator?
    (d) Is the landlord entitled to seek forfeiture of the lease by reason of non-payment of rent or other breaches of covenant?

(ii) Other issues relating to the company's lease:
    (e) Will the company be able to obtain relief from forfeiture?

(f)   Will the chargee be able to obtain relief from forfeiture?
(g)   Is the landlord entitled to distrain for unpaid rent or seek payment as an expense of the administration?
(h)   Is the landlord entitled to intercept rent otherwise payable to the company tenant by its sub-tenants?
(i)   When should the chargee release the lease from the charge?

(iii) Questions arising in respect of assigning the lease or subletting the premises:
(j)   Does the receiver, or the administrator, have any personal liabilities?

Although this chapter will focus on cases where the company (in relation to which the receiver or administrator is appointed) is the tenant, the chapter will also include brief remarks which are relevant where the company is a landlord.

(b)   Was the grant of the charge a breach of the terms of the lease?

18–003   In the absence of an express provision to the contrary in the lease, the lessee is free to assign, underlet, part with possession of the premises and to charge the lease.[1] It is common for commercial leases to include a covenant controlling the lessee's ability to assign, underlet, part with possession of the demised premise or charge the lease. The reference to charging the lease plainly includes the grant of a fixed charge over the lease. There is no decided case as to whether a covenant against charging a lease prohibits the grant of a floating charge in respect of the company which is the lessee. This may be because the typical charge will include both a fixed and a floating charge. Based on the analysis of the nature of a floating charge set out in Ch.3, it is arguable that the grant of a floating charge alone in relation to the company, without there being a fixed charge of the lease, will not necessarily result in the subsequent creation of a charge of the lease and so is not contrary to the lease. However, when the floating charge crystallises, the result will be a charge over the lease; nonetheless, the floating charge may have crystallised without any specific conduct on the part of the lessee company and it may be argued by the tenant that it has not acted contrary to the terms of the lease.[2]

If the lease does not expressly prohibit "charging" the lease, but does prohibit assignment or subletting or parting with possession, it will be necessary to consider whether the grant of a charge involves any of these transactions. The grant of a charge is not an assignment of the lease or of the premises. The grant of a charge is generally considered not to involve a subletting; rather,

---

[1] See *Woodfall on Landlord and Tenant* (looseleaf Ed.), Vol.1, para.11–113.
[2] As to the distinction between a floating and fixed charge, see in particular the decision of the House of Lords in *Re Spectrum Plus Ltd (In Liquidation)* [2005] 2 A.C. 680 (HL).

by statue, the chargee has the same protection, powers and remedies as if there were a mortgage by sub-demise.[3] If the mortgage, somewhat unusually, is in the form of an actual sub-demise, then such a mortgage is a subletting within the meaning of the covenant.[4] The grant of a charge does not itself involve a parting with possession.[5] The covenant may contain an absolute prohibition on some or all of those things but, more usually, the covenant will be a qualified covenant which provides that the landlord's consent is needed to the proposed transaction. The express terms of a qualified covenant are subject to statutory modifications. First, where licence is required to a mortgage by sub-demise, such licence is not to be unreasonably withheld.[6] Further, more generally, a covenant in a lease against assigning, under-letting, charging or parting with the possession of the demised premises or any part thereof is subject to a proviso to the effect that such consent is not to be unreasonably withheld.[7] If the landlord unreasonably withholds consent to the charge, then his consent ceases to be required and the lessee can grant the charge without such consent and without committing a breach of the lease. A prospective chargee should carefully check the terms of any lease before accepting a charge over it to ensure that the grant of the charge will not involve a breach of covenant and that all the requirements of the lease are complied with.[8] It should also check whether the subsequent taking of possession or the appointment of a receiver will trigger a right to forfeiture on the part of the landlord.

---

[3] Law of Property Act 1925, s.87(1); and see *Gentle v Faulkner* [1900] 2 Q.B. 267 (CA); *Grand Junction Co v Bates* [1954] 2 Q.B. 160, 168, per Upjohn J.; *Belgravia Insurance Co v Meah* [1964] 1 Q.B. 436 (CA), 443, per Lord Denning M.R.; *Regent Oil Co Ltd v Gregory (JA) (Hatch End)* [1966] Ch. 402 (CA), 431, per Harman L.J. Land Registration Act 2002 s.23(1)(a) excludes from the owner's powers in relation to a registered estate the power to mortgage by (sub-) demise, but these are now very rare and s.23(1)(a) does not impact on s.87(1). Land Registration Act 2002, s.133 inserted Law of Property Act 1925, s.87(4).

[4] *Serjeant v Nash Field & Co* [1903] 2 K.B. 304 (CA).

[5] *Megarry and Wade: The Law of Real Property*, 7th edn (London: Sweet & Maxwell, 2008), para.24–036, fn.90 suggests that there will be a breach of a covenant against parting with possession when the mortgagee takes possession. For the latest consideration of what does and does not amount to a parting with possession, see *Clarence House v National Westminster Bank Plc* [2010] 1 W.L.R. 1216 (CA).

[6] Law of Property Act 1925, s.86(1).

[7] Landlord and Tenant Act 1927, s.19(1). For the case law as to what amount to reasonable grounds for refusal of consent, see *Woodfall on Landlord and Tenant* (looseleaf Ed.), para.11–138 et seq. As to the duty on the landlord to consider and respond to an application by the tenant for consent and not to withhold consent unreasonably, see the Landlord and Tenant Act 1988, s.1. The operation of the 1988 Act was considered in *Go West Ltd v Spigarolo* [2003] Q.B. 1140 (CA). In a case where the tenancy is affected by a mortgage and the mortgagee proposes to exercise his statutory or express power of sale, references in the 1988 Act to "tenant" include the mortgagee: s.5; *Meretz Investments NV v ACP Ltd* [2008] Ch. 244 (CA). Damages are payable for breach of this duty: s.4. The court may in a proper case award exemplary damages: *Design Progression v Thurloe Properties Ltd* [2005] 1 W.L.R. 1.

[8] A grant in breach of condition or covenant is effective, although it may render the lease liable to forfeiture: see *Old Grovebury Manor Farm Ltd v W. Seymour Plant Sales and Hire Ltd (No.2)* [1979] 1 W.L.R. 1397 (CA) (a case of assignment in breach of covenant).

(c)   Was the appointment of the receiver, or the administrator, a breach of the terms of the lease?

18–004   In the absence of an express provision to such effect, the appointment of a receiver or administrator in relation to a company tenant will not place the company in breach of its lease. Furthermore, it would be unusual for a lease to contain an express covenant that has that effect. But it is a separate matter whether the lease contains a forfeiture clause that permits the landlord to claim a forfeiture of the lease in the event of the appointment of a receiver, or an administrator, in relation to the company lessee. Such a clause is very common in modern commercial leases: see below.

(d)   Is the landlord entitled to seek forfeiture of the lease by reason of the grant of the charge or the appointment of the receiver, or the administrator?

18–005   The standard forfeiture clause in a commercial lease will permit forfeiture of the lease in the event of any breach by the tenant of its obligations contained in the lease. Thus, if the grant of, or the existence of, the charge involved a breach of the lease, then the landlord is entitled to seek to forfeit the lease on that account. It is also commonplace in modern commercial leases for the forfeiture clause to contain a condition entitling the landlord to forfeit in the event of the appointment of a receiver or administrator in relation to the company tenant. In such cases, the landlord is not exempted from the requirement to serve a statutory forfeiture notice before seeking to re-enter[9].

(e)   Is the landlord entitled to seek forfeiture of the lease by reason of the non-payment of rent or other breaches of covenant?

18–006   The standard form of forfeiture clause in a commercial lease will permit forfeiture in the event of non-payment of rent or breach by the tenant of its obligations contained in the lease. The entitlement to forfeit usually arises once rent is unpaid for 14 or 21 days, and no statutory forfeiture notice is required.

(f)   Other questions arising in relation to a possible forfeiture

18–007   The first question that arises is whether the alleged breach has been committed or the alleged event which may give rise to a forfeiture has occurred. This has been addressed above. The second question is whether the right to forfeit has been waived by the landlord. This question is principally important in relation to once and for all breaches as compared with continuing breaches, and is addressed in the next paragraph. The third question is whether the landlord has

---

[9]   Law of Property Act 1925, s.146(1),(9),(10). See para.18–009, below.

complied with any statutory formalities before being able to seek forfeiture.[10] The statutory formalities usually require the tenant to be given the opportunity to remedy the breach (if the breach is remediable) so as to avoid forfeiture. The fourth question is whether the landlord has effected a forfeiture (subject to the possibility of relief from forfeiture). The last question is whether the tenant or the chargee will be able to obtain relief from forfeiture. These questions will be considered with particular reference to the factual situations most likely to occur as a result of, or at the same time as, the appointment of a receiver or administrator of the company.[11]

(g) Waiver

The law of waiver is an example of the general principles relating to election between inconsistent rights. A landlord is held to have waived a right to forfeit which has arisen (whether by reason of a previous breach of covenant or by reason of some other specified event entitling the landlord to forfeit) when the landlord, with knowledge of the breach or the event giving rise to the forfeiture, does some act which unequivocally recognises the continuing existence of the lease at a time after the right to forfeit has arisen. Knowledge in this context is knowledge of the facts which constitute the breach or the event entitling the landlord to forfeit rather than knowledge of the law as to whether the facts amount to a breach or not.[12] The act in question must be communicated to the tenant. The most usual act relied on is the demand for or the acceptance of rent.[13] A demand for rent will cause a waiver in law irrespective of the subjective intention of the landlord, and waiver occurs though the demand was inadvertent.[14] A demand for, or an acceptance of, rent due prior to the breach will not indicate a waiver.[15] In the case of a once and for all breach, waiver of the right to forfeit for that breach means that the right to forfeit for that breach is forever gone; in the case of a continuing breach, waiver of the right to forfeit by recognising the existence of the lease up to a certain date, will not prevent the landlord forfeiting for a continuation of the breach after

18–008

---

[10] para.18–009, below.

[11] para.18–011, below.

[12] *David Blackstone Ltd v Burnetts (West End) Ltd* [1973] 1 W.L.R. 1487. The authorities are reviewed in *Cornillie v Saha* (1996) 72 P. & C.R. 147 (CA). This is the traditional view in the law of landlord and tenant in respect of waiver of the contractual right to forfeit. In *Peyman v Lanjani* [1985] Ch. 457 (CA), in the context of the waiver of the equitable right to rescind, the Court of Appeal held that a party should not be taken to have elected to affirm or rescind a contract unless he has knowledge, not only of the facts, but also of the right to elect. This reasoning has been criticized by Handley at (2006) 122 L.Q.R. 82. The Privy Council has stressed that waiver requires an informed choice and the information which is relevant includes knowledge of the legal ability to object: *Millar (David Cameron) v Dickson* [2002] 1 W.L.R. 1615 (PC) (a case concerning art.6 of the Human Rights Act 1998). It has been recognised that the requirements for waiver of forfeiture are less strict (and more favourable to the tenant) than is the case with the principles of election in other contexts: *Ballard (Kent) Ltd v Oliver Ashworth (Holdings) Ltd* [2000] Ch. 12 (CA), 30E.

[13] *Expert Clothing Service & Sales Ltd v Hillgate House Ltd* [1986] Ch. 340 (CA).

[14] *Central Estates (Belgravia) Ltd v Woolgar (No.1)* [1972] 1 Q.B. 48 (CA).

[15] *Re Debtor (No.13A-IO-1995)* [1995] 1 W.L.R. 1127. For the position where post-breach rent is accepted, see *Thomas v Ken Thomas Ltd* [2007] Bus. L.R. 429 (CA).

that date.[16] If the grant of a charge is a breach of a covenant in the lease, such breach will be committed when the charge is granted and will be a once and for all breach. If the event of forfeiture is the appointment of a receiver, or an administrator, that event occurs when the receiver or administrator is appointed and is a once and for all event, even though the receiver's, or the administrator's, appointment continues to be effective. The distinction between once and for all breaches and continuing breaches is a completely different distinction from that between remediable and irremediable breaches.

(h)   Remedying the breach

18–009   A right of forfeiture of a lease (by reason of matters other than non-payment of rent) is not enforceable, by action or otherwise, unless and until the landlord serves on the tenant a notice specifying the particular breach complained of, requiring the tenant to remedy the breach (if the same is capable of remedy) and requiring the tenant to make compensation in money for the breach.[17] Further, the right of forfeiture is not exercisable unless the tenant fails within a reasonable time of the notice to remedy the breach (if the same is capable of remedy) and to make reasonable compensation in money, to the satisfaction of the landlord, for the breach.[18] The landlord need not serve the notice on a mortgagee of the lease even when the mortgagee is in possession.[19] No such notice is needed in the case of forfeiture for non-payment of rent and the landlord need not wait a reasonable time for the tenant to pay the rent after the time allowed by the forfeiture provision for payment of rent.[20] A s.146 notice is needed where the right to forfeit arises by reason of the appointment of a receiver, or an administrator, even though such an event is not separately a breach of covenant.[21] The general test for remediability is whether the harm

---

[16] A breach of a covenant to carry out and complete building works "as expeditiously as possible" was a once and for all breach: *First Penthouse v Channel Hotels & Properties (UK) Ltd* [2004] L. & T.R. 27 (CA).

[17] Law of Property Act 1925, s.146(1). The requirement that the breach intended to be relied upon is sufficiently "specified" was not satisfied in *Akici v LR Butlin Ltd* [2006] 1 W.L.R. 201 (CA). It is mandatory for the notice to require remedy: see, e.g. *Savva v Houssein* [1996] 2 E.G.L.R. 65 (CA). By contrast, despite the apparently mandatory language, it has been held that the notice is not bad for not requiring compensation in money: *Lock v Pearce* [1893] 2 Ch. 271 (CA). The landlord's right to serve a notice in respect of a breach by a tenant of a covenant or condition in the long lease of a dwelling is restricted by Commonhold and Leasehold Reform Act 2002, ss.167–172; for further restrictions on forfeiture of a tenancy of a dwelling (for non-payment of service charge), see Housing Act 1996, s.81. Pursuant to Commonhold and Leasehold Reform Act 2002, s.171 the national authority may regulate the right of re-entry or forfeiture for a breach of a covenant or condition in a long lease of an unmortgaged dwelling. There are exceptional cases where a s.146 notice is not required where the ground of forfeiture is the bankruptcy or liquidation of the lessee: Law of Property Act 1925, s.146(9), 205(1)(i); and see *Hockley Engineering Co v V&P Midlands* [1993] 1 E.G.L.R. 76.

[18] Law of Property Act 1925, s.146(1).

[19] *Smith v Spaul* [2003] Q.B. 983 (CA).

[20] Law of Property Act 1925, s.146(11). It is usual for the forfeiture provision in the lease to give the tenant some time, usually 14 or 21 days, before the right to forfeit for non-payment of rent arises.

[21] See *Halliard Property v Jack Segal* [1978] 1 W.L.R. 377 (right to forfeit in the event of insolvency of a surety); and see *Ivory Gate Ltd v Spetale* [1998] 2 E.G.L.R. 43 (CA).

that has been done to the landlord by the relevant breach is, for practical purposes, capable of being retrieved within a reasonable time.[22] The Court of Appeal has held that the grant of a sub-lease in breach of a covenant against sub-letting is an irremediable breach[23] and the reasoning in this case would indicate that the grant of a charge in breach of covenant will be held irremediable. It is suggested that the appointment of a receiver which gives rise to a right to forfeit would be capable of remedy by removing the receiver.[24] It is further suggested that the appointment of an administrator would be capable of remedy by ending the administration. Although a breach may be held irremediable for the purposes of s.146(1) of the Law of Property Act 1925, this does not mean that the court does not have power to grant relief against forfeiture in relation to that breach.

(i) The forfeiture

In general, where the demised premises do not comprise or include a dwelling-house, a landlord may seek to forfeit the lease by action or by peaceable re-entry.[25] There are certain cases where a landlord needs the leave of the court to bring a claim for forfeiture and possession against a tenant. These are: **18–010**

(a) between the presentation of an administration application and the making of the order or the dismissal of the application or between the filing of a notice of intention to appoint an administrator and the appointment of the administrator or the expiry of five business days from the notice without any such appointment having been made[26];

(b) while the company is in administration[27];

(c) when a winding up order has been made or a provisional liquidator has been appointed[28];

---

[22] *Savva v Houssein* [1996] 2 E.G.L.R. 65 (CA). See, e.g. *Courtney Lodge Management Ltd v Blake* [2005] 1 P. & C.R. 17 (landlord did not afford tenant sufficient "reasonable" time before issue of proceedings); the question of remedy within a reasonable time was considered in *Akici v LR Butlin Ltd* [2006] 1 W.L.R. 201 (CA).
[23] *Scala House & District Property Co v Forbes* [1974] Q.B. 575 (CA) and see *Expert Clothing Service & Sales Ltd v Hillgate House* [1986] Ch. 340 (CA) which affirmed as the ratio decidendi of the *Scala* case that a breach of a covenant against assignment or sub-letting was irremediable, but held that a breach of a covenant to give notice of a grant of a charge was remediable. The authorities have now been reviewed and it has been held that an underletting or (it seems) an assignment in breach of covenant is irremediable but a parting with or a sharing of possession in breach of covenant is remediable: *Akici v LR Butlin Ltd* [2006] 1 W.L.R. 201 (CA).
[24] In the case of an administrative receiver, who can only be removed by the court, this would seem to be an unlikely option.
[25] For a case involving mixed premises and the restriction on peaceable re-entry, see *Patel v Pirabakaran* [2006] 1 W.L.R. 3112 (CA).
[26] Insolvency Act 1986, s.8 and Sch.B1 para.44.
[27] Insolvency Act 1986, s.8 and Sch.B1 para.43. For the approach to be adopted by the court, see *Re Atlantic Computer Systems* [1992] Ch. 505 (CA). Leave was given in *Scottish Exhibition Centre v Mirestop* [1993] B.C.C. 529 (Court of Session, Outer House) and in *Metro Nominees (Wandsworth) (No.1) v Rayment* [2008] B.C.C. 40.
[28] Insolvency Act 1986, s.130(2).

(d) where an interim order is in force (i.e. as a preliminary to a voluntary arrangement)[29];

(e) after the making of a bankruptcy order and before the bankrupt is discharged[30];

(f) where an interim receiver has been appointed.[31]

There is in general no need to obtain the leave of the court to forfeiture by peaceable re-entry, but permission is needed for such a re-entry where the case falls within paras (a), (b) or (d) above.[32] In the case of (b), company in administration, consent to re-enter may be given by the administrator instead of by the court. There is no requirement that the landlord obtain the leave of the court before commencing proceedings or before peaceably re-entering where the ground of forfeiture is the appointment of a receiver over the company tenant.[33] Where the landlord brings proceedings against the tenant for possession of residential property based on a forfeiture of the lease, the landlord must state in the particulars of claim the name and address of any underlessee or mortgagee entitled to claim relief against forfeiture of whom he knows and must file a copy of the particulars of claim for service on such persons.[34] In the light of these provisions, it should be normal practice for a chargee of a lease of residential premises to inform a landlord of the existence of the charge.[35]

The forfeiture of a headlease will also determine any underleases. The landlord is entitled to mesne profits quantified by reference to the letting value of the property for the duration of the period for which he is kept out of possession; irrespective of any vesting order which is made in favour of the underlessees under the Law of Property Act 1925 s.146(4).[36]

---

[29] Insolvency Act 1986, s.252(2).

[30] Insolvency Act 1986, s.285(3); *Ezekiel v Orakpo* [1977] Q.B. 260 (CA); *Harlow DC v Hall* [2006] 1 W.L.R. 2116 (CA).

[31] Insolvency Act, s.286(6).

[32] Insolvency Act 1986, s.8 and Sch.B1 paras 43 and 44, as substituted by Enterprise Act 2002; these cases are therefore exceptions to the general position in relation to peaceable re-entry in an insolvency context which is considered in *Re Lomax Leisure* [2000] Ch. 502 (where the authorities are reviewed); in the case of an interim order, see Insolvency Act 1986 s.252(2), as amended by Enterprise Act 2002.

[33] For the procedure relating to possession claims brought by landlords, former landlords, licensors or former licensors, and to claims by tenants seeking relief against forfeiture, see the Civil Procedure Rules 1998 Pt 55.2–55.10 (added by SI 2001/256 and amended subsequently by SIs 2002/2058, 2008/2178 and 2009/3390) and Practice Direction—Possession Claims PD 55A.

[34] CPR 55A PD para.2.2 and 2.4. The former rules of court were considered in *Rexhaven v Nurse* (1996) 28 H.L.R. 241 and *Croydon (Unique) Ltd v Wright* [2001] Ch. 318 (CA).

[35] See *Megarry and Wade: The Law of Real Property*, 7th edn (London: Sweet & Maxwell, 2008), para.18-035. Also, note the restrictions on forfeiture of long leases of residential property referred to in para.18–009, fn.17, above.

[36] *Viscount Chelsea v Hutchinson* [1994] 2 E.G.L.R. 61 (CA); *Inverugie Investments Ltd v Hackett* [1995] 1 W.L.R. 713 (PC).

(j)   An application for relief from forfeiture by the tenant

In the event of a forfeiture, the tenant will wish to consider applying for relief **18-011** from forfeiture. It is necessary to consider separately the provisions dealing with relief from forfeiture where the ground of forfeiture is breach of covenant or other event (but not non-payment of rent) and relief from forfeiture where the ground of forfeiture is non-payment of rent. In the former case, the tenant may apply for relief from forfeiture under s.146(2) of the Law of Property Act 1925 and relief is discretionary. In the latter case, the tenant may obtain automatic relief from forfeiture under s.212 of the Common Law Procedure Act 1852 (in the case of proceedings for forfeiture brought in the High Court) or under s.138 of the County Courts Act 1984 (in the case of proceedings for forfeiture brought in the county court). The automatic effect of relief from forfeiture applies where the tenant pays off the arrears of rent and costs in accordance with the time limits laid down in those statutory provisions. In addition, the tenant is entitled to apply for discretionary relief from forfeiture for non-payment of rent under ss.210 of the Common Law Procedure Act 1852 and/or s.38 of the Supreme Court Act 1981 (in the High Court) and under s.138 of the County Courts Act 1984 (in the County Court). A receiver has no locus standi in his own right to apply for relief from forfeiture but he will normally be able to act as agent for the company tenant and make such an application in the name of the company.[37] An administrator can make an application for relief from forfeiture, in the name of the company.[38] Where the tenant obtains automatic relief or where the court grants relief to the tenant, the lease is retrospectively revived without the need for any further lease to be granted. The right to seek relief is an assignable chose in action and may be assigned by the company (acting through its receiver) to a purchaser of the right.[39]

(k)   An application for relief from forfeiture by the chargee

By s.87 of the Law of Property Act 1925, a chargee of a lease has the same **18-012** protection powers and remedies as if it had a sub-term less by one day than the term of the lease vested in the chargor. This enables a chargee to claim relief from forfeiture of the lease in the same way as an underlessee could claim such relief. The protection does not extend to an equitable chargee; however, the chargor's implied obligation which is owed to the chargee to take reasonable steps to preserve the equitable chargee's security will enable the equitable chargee to bring an indirect claim for relief from forfeiture by joining the chargor as a party to the claim and claiming relief in the shoes of the chargor.[40] There are

---

[37] *Goughs Garages v Pugsley* [1930] 1 K.B. 615; the receiver's authority to act in this way will survive a subsequent liquidation.
[38] By reason of Insolvency Act 1986 (as amended by Enterprise Act 2002), Sch.B1, paras 59, 60 and 69 and Sch.1, paras 1, 5 and 12.
[39] *Howard v Fanshawe* [1895] 2 Ch. 581. The same will apply in principle to an administrator.
[40] *Bland v Ingram's Estates Ltd (No.1)* [2001] Ch. 767 (CA). The court considered the terms on which relief will be granted in such circumstances in *Bland v Ingrams Estates Ltd (No.2)* [2002] Ch. 177 (CA).

two ways in which a chargee can claim relief from forfeiture. The first is by
relying on the statutory powers which confer on the tenant the right to automatic
relief or the right to seek relief. In a series of decisions, the Court of Appeal has
held that the references to "lessee" in s.138 of the County Courts Act 1984, s.38
of the Supreme Court Act 1981 and s.146(2) of the Law of Property Act 1925 all
include an "underlessee" and therefore a chargee.[41] Where the forfeiture is on a
ground other than non-payment of rent, and relief is obtained by a chargee under
s.146(2) of the Law of Property Act 1925, the relief is retrospective to the date
of forfeiture.[42] The same applies where the forfeiture is for non-payment of rent
and relief is granted in the first way described above.[43] The second way in which
a chargee can seek relief from forfeiture is pursuant to s.146(4) of the Law of
Property Act 1925; this provision applies whether the forfeiture is for non-
payment of rent or on another ground. The chargee can apply under this provision even in those exceptional circumstances[44] where the lessee cannot seek
relief.[45] The grant of relief operates by way of an order vesting the premises in
the chargee as a lessee. The court has power to impose conditions on the grant
of the vesting order. The court is likely to require the chargee to covenant with
the landlord to perform the covenants in the forfeited lease.[46] The making of the
vesting order is not retrospective so that there is likely to be a gap between
the date when the former lease ended as a result of the forfeiture and the date of
the vesting order.[47] During this period the landlord is prima facie entitled to
damages for trespass from persons in possession of the premises.[48] Whether the
chargee obtains relief by way of retrospective reinstatement of the lease or by
way of a vesting order, he holds the lease as substitute security subject to an
equity of redemption in favour of the chargor.[49] The chargee's preference as to
the mode by which relief from forfeiture is obtained will normally be, first, the
grant of relief to the lessee, second, the grant of relief to the chargee under

[41] *United Dominions Trust v Shellpoint Trustees Ltd* [1993] 4 All E.R. 310 (CA) and the cases
together reported as *Escalus Properties v Robinson* [1996] Q.B. 231 (CA), applied in *Bank of
Ireland Home Mortgages v South Lodge Developments* [1996] 1 E.G.L.R. 91.

[42] *Dendy v Evans* [1910] 1 K.B. 263 (CA).

[43] Either as a result of the statutory provisions expressly so providing or as a result of *Dendy v
Evans* [1910] 1 K.B. 263 (CA).

[44] Law of Property Act 1925, s.146(8), (9) and (10).

[45] Law of Property (Amendment) Act 1929, s.1. See also *Rexhaven Ltd v Nurse* (1996) 28
H.L.R. 241 (court has jurisdiction to grant a mortgagee relief from forfeiture after execution of a
judgment for possession, although jurisdiction will be exercised only in exceptional
circumstances).

[46] *Gray v Bonsall* [1904] 1 K.B. 601 (CA), 608; *Official Custodian for Charities v Parway
Estates Developments Ltd (In Liquidation)* [1985] Ch. 151 (CA), 164. A chargee would normally
be reluctant to take on this obligation. Before the coming into force of the Landlord and Tenant
(Covenants) Act 1995 on January 1, 1996, such a covenant as original lessee (as the chargee would
be) would have endured for the remainder of the term of the lease; now the original lessee will be
released from the covenant from the date of a lawful assignment: see ss.5 and 11; but, the original
lessee may be required to enter into an "authorised guarantee agreement" under s.16 of the 1995
Act in relation to the liability of the first assignee.

[47] *Cadogan v Dimovic* [1984] 1 W.L.R. 609 (CA).

[48] *Official Custodian for Charities v Mackey* [1985] Ch. 168 and *Official Custodian for
Charities v Mackey (No.2)* [1985] 1 W.L.R. 1308.

[49] *Chelsea Estates Investment Trust Co Ltd v Marche* [1955] Ch. 328 and *Official Custodian for
Charities v Parway Estates Developments Ltd (In Liquidation)* [1985] Ch. 151 (CA), 164.

s.146(2) and third, the grant of a vesting order to the chargee. Under the first of these, the chargee avoids taking on direct liability under the covenants in the lease; under the first and second of these, relief is retrospective so that there is no gap between forfeiture and the reinstatement of the lease; under the third mode of obtaining relief, the chargee will usually have to give a direct covenant to the landlord and there will be a gap between forfeiture and the grant of the vesting order which has consequences as regards the payment of damages for trespass and the effect on derivative interests.[50]

(l) The time for applying for relief

The tenant or the chargee is entitled to apply for relief from forfeiture under **18–013** s.146(2) of the Law of Property Act 1925 while "a lessor is proceeding" to enforce its right of forfeiture. Similarly, a chargee is entitled to apply for relief under s.146(4) of the 1925 Act while a lessor is so proceeding. A landlord begins to proceed to enforce his right of forfeiture as soon as he serves a s.146 notice and an application for relief may thereupon be made.[51] Where the lessor has brought court proceedings claiming possession as a result of a forfeiture, the lessor is proceeding to enforce the right of forfeiture until the lessor executes a judgment for possession obtained in those proceedings.[52] Upon execution of the judgement, the tenant or chargee loses the right to seek relief under s.146(2) or s.146(4). In some circumstances the tenant or chargee may have proper grounds to have the judgment set aside.[53] Where the lessor has sought to enforce his right of forfeiture by peaceable re-entry without court proceedings, it has been held that the lessor does not cease to proceed to enforce his right of forfeiture on the taking of possession and the court retains jurisdiction under s.146(2) and s.146(4) to grant relief from forfeiture.[54] The time limits for seeking relief from forfeiture for non-payment of rent differ depending on whether the landlord is enforcing the right of forfeiture in the High Court or in the county court, or by peaceable re-entry.[55]

---

[50] See the difficulties in *Hammersmith and Fulham LBC v Top Shop Centres Ltd* [1990] Ch. 237.

[51] *Pakwood Transport v 15 Beauchamp Place* (1978) 36 P. & C.R. 112 (CA).

[52] *Rogers v Rice* [1892] 2 Ch. 170 (CA).

[53] *Rexhaven v Nurse* (1996) 28 H.L.R. 241; in that case the judgment was not set aside to allow a mortgagee to apply for relief from forfeiture because the mortgagee had been notified under the rules of court of the proceedings for forfeiture and had neglected to intervene and seek relief until after a judgment for possession had been executed. The judgment was set aside in *Croydon (Unique) v Wright* [2001] Ch. 318 (CA): this case concerned forfeiture for non-payment of rent and County Courts Act 1984, s.138.

[54] *Billson v Residential Apartments* [1992] 1 A.C. 494 (HL).

[55] In summary, the position is: in the High Court, following an order for possession, within six months of execution: Common Law Procedure Act 1852, s.210; in the High Court, following peaceable re-entry, no statutory time limit but a period of six month is used by analogy as a guide; in the county court, following an order for possession, within six months after execution: County Courts Act 1984, s.138(9A)–(9C); in the county court, following peaceable re-entry, within six months of the re-entry: County Courts Act 1984, s.139(2). If the application for relief is made by the chargee under s.146(4) of the Law of Property Act 1925, the application must be made while "the lessor is proceeding", as to which see the main text. For a full treatment, see *Woodfall on Landlord and Tenant* (looseleaf Ed.), Vol. 1 at paras 17–178 to 17–195.

(m) The court's discretion to grant relief from forfeiture

18–014 The court has a wide discretion in relation to the circumstances in which, and the terms on which, it will be prepared to grant relief from forfeiture. It is possible to state some general principles which guide the approach of the court. In the case of forfeiture for non-payment of rent, equity regarded the right of forfeiture as security for payment of the rent, with the result that if the arrears of rent were paid off and the landlord was reimbursed his costs and expenses, it was normally considered just to grant relief from forfeiture; save in exceptional cases, the court would not have regard to other breaches of covenant.[56] In the case of forfeiture on other grounds, an applicant for relief was normally required to remedy, that is undo the consequences of, the breach, make compensation for any damage caused and make it clear that the covenants would be performed in the future. In such circumstances, a court would be minded to grant relief from forfeiture. The court would consider the conduct of the tenant, the nature and gravity of the breach and the value of the property being forfeited.

Different views have been expressed as to the relevance of the fact that the breach was deliberate or wilful. It has been said that wilful breaches should only exceptionally be relieved against because sound principle required that the landlord should not be forced to remain in a relationship of landlord and tenant with a person in deliberate breach of his obligations.[57] However, the more recent approach is to hold that relief from forfeiture in the case of a wilful breach is not to be confined to exceptional cases, although the court should not in exercising its discretion encourage the belief that parties to a lease can ignore their obligations and buy their way out of any consequential forfeiture.[58] Where the breach consists of doing something, e.g. the grant of a charge without first asking for the landlord's consent, it will be relevant to ask whether such consent could have been unreasonably withheld. The above principles will therefore apply where the breach alleged is the grant of a charge of the lease in breach of covenant. Where the event which gives rise to the forfeiture is the appointment of a receiver or an administrator, the court is likely to consider whether the landlord suffers any prejudice by reason of the appointment of the receiver over and above the prejudice suffered by reason of any financial weakness of the company tenant. It is unlikely that a court would refuse relief from forfeiture where the only matter complained of was the appointment of a receiver, or an administrator, and the lease had a value which the company acting through its receiver, or administrator, wished to realise.

As indicated above, the chargee will normally prefer that relief be granted to the tenant rather than to the chargee direct. This reluctance is matched by the

---

[56] *Gill v Lewis* [1956] 2 Q.B. 1 (CA). It was suggested in *Re Naaem* [1990] 1 W.L.R. 48 that where the landlord as creditor was bound by a voluntary arrangement which restricted the landlord's ability to recover in full the arrears of rent, relief might be granted on terms that the tenant only paid off part of the arrears in accordance with the voluntary arrangement but this suggestion has since been doubted: *March Estates v Gunmark Ltd* [1996] 2 B.C.L.C. 1.
[57] *Shiloh Spinners v Harding* [1973] A.C. 691 (HL).
[58] *Southern Depot v British Railways Board* [1990] 2 E.G.L.R. 39.

consideration that it will probably be more difficult, against the wishes of the landlord, to obtain an order vesting the premises in the chargee as compared with obtaining a grant of relief to the tenant itself; this is because the court will be more cautious about forcing on the landlord the relationship of landlord and tenant with someone whom the landlord has not freely accepted. Of course, the landlord may positively prefer the making of a vesting order in favour of the chargee rather than the grant of relief to the tenant because the making of a vesting order may provide the landlord with a better covenant (that of the chargee rather than the lessee) and there may be the consequential advantages that the landlord may be able to claim damages for trespass in relation to the gap between the forfeiture of the lease and the making of the vesting order. Relief may be refused where the landlord has acted reasonably in re-letting the premises following the forfeiture.[59]

(n)   Relief against forfeiture for breach of a condition against liquidation

Although generally speaking the jurisdiction to grant relief, whether to the **18–015** company tenant or to the chargee, is unlimited, in the case of breach of a condition against the winding-up of the tenant or the taking of the lease into execution, relief cannot be granted to the lessee where the lease is of:

(a)   agricultural or pastoral land;

(b)   mines or minerals;

(c)   a public house or beershop;

(d)   a furnished dwelling-house;

(e)   property with respect to which the personal qualifications of the tenant are of importance for the preservation of the value or character of the property or on the ground of neighbourhood to the landlord or any person holding under him.[60]

Further, in all other cases of a breach of this condition, the court cannot grant any relief to the tenant unless either the landlord takes steps to forfeit and the tenant applies for relief, or the lease is sold within one year.[61] In default of such application or sale, relief both under statute and under the inherent jurisdiction of equity is barred.[62] The existence of a specifically enforceable contract for sale is sufficient for this purpose.[63] In the case where such a sale takes place,

---

[59] *Silverman v AFCO (UK)* [1988] 14 E.G. 67 (CA); *Fuller v Judy Properties* [1992] 1 E.G.L.R. 75 (CA); and *Bank of Ireland Home Mortgages v South Lodge Developments* [1996] 1 E.G.L.R. 91. cf. *Bland v Ingram's Estates_Ltd (No.1)* [2001] Ch. 767 (CA).

[60] Law of Property Act 1925, s.146(9). For the application of this sub-section see, *Hockley Engineering v V&P Midlands* [1993] 1 E.G.L.R. 76.

[61] Law of Property Act 1925, s.146(10).

[62] *Official Custodian for Charities v Parway Estates Ltd (In Liquidation)* [1985] Ch. 151 (CA).

[63] *Harry Lay v Fox* (1963) 186 E.G. 15.

the court, in the exercise of its discretion whether to grant relief, considers whether the lessor is secure in respect of the future performance of the covenants of the lease, and for this purpose the standing and trustworthiness of the purchaser may be relevant. If the purchaser is of good standing and trustworthy, the court will incline to grant relief, for to refuse to do so would involve giving the value of the lease to the lessor at the expense of the lessee.[64]

18–016   But neither the statutory exclusion nor the restriction of the grant of relief to the lessee has application to a claim for relief by a mortgagee.[65] Nor will the court impose, as a condition of the grant of relief, a requirement that the mortgagee sells the lease whether within a fixed period or at all, for "any requirement which might prejudice a mortgagee's security or interfere with his choice of remedies is at odds with the principle on which relief is granted".[66]

(o)   Is the landlord entitled to distrain for unpaid rent?

18–017   A landlord's right to distrain for rent[67] is unaffected by the creation or crystallisation of a floating charge over the tenant company.[68] It may be in the interests of the receiver and debenture-holder that the subject matter or proceeds of the distress be applied in payment of preferential creditors rather than the landlord, and in the following circumstances it may be possible to achieve this result. In a case where the lessee was in liquidation, a liquidator was held entitled to restrain distress on the ground that the company's assets were insufficient to pay preferential creditors, notwithstanding that the company's assets were charged to secure a sum far exceeding their value.[69] Kerr suggests that on his appointment, even in the absence of a liquidation, the receiver might equally apply for such relief in the name of the company or (if so authorised) of a preferential creditor.[70] Alternatively the receiver has power to petition for a winding-up[71] so as to lay the basis for an application by the liquidator to restrain distress.

The landlord may not distrain without the leave of the court in the following cases:

---

[64] *Harry Lay v Fox* (1963) 186 E.G. 15.

[65] Law of Property (Amendment) Act 1929, s.1 amending s.146(4) of the Law of Property Act 1925, and see *Official Custodian for Charities v Parway Estates Ltd (In Liquidation)* [1985] Ch. 151 (CA).

[66] Per Nourse J. in *Official Custodian for Charities v Mackey (No.2)* [1985] 1 W.L.R. 1308, 1317H.

[67] s.71 of the Tribunals, Courts and Enforcement Act 2007 abolishes the common law right to distrain for arrears of rent and replaces it with a "commercial rent arrears recovery" procedure, as provided for in ss.72–84 and Sch.12 of the Act. The Act received Royal Assent on July 19, 2007, but s.71 has not been brought into force.

[68] *Re Roundwood Colliery Co* [1897] 1 Ch. 373 (CA), 393 and see *Purcell v Queensland Public Curator* (1922) 31 C.L.R. 220. *Metropolitan Life v Essere Print Ltd* (1990) N.Z.C.L.C. 66, 775 (Jeffries J.); [1991] 3 N.Z.L.R. 170, (NZ CA) contrasts the common law position with the result of the New Zealand Statute Reforms in 1908, which have the effect of preventing such distress. See also below, para.19–022.

[69] *Re South Rhondda Colliery Co* [1928] W.N. 126. See also Insolvency Act 1986, s.176.

[70] *Kerr & Hunter on Receivers and Administrators*, 17th edn (London: Sweet & Maxwell, 1989), p.204, fn.86.

[71] See above, Ch.15.

(a) between the presentation of an administration application and the making of the order or the dismissal of the application or between the filing of a notice of intention to appoint an administrator and the appointment of the administrator or the expiry of 5 business days from the notice without any such appointment having been made[72];

(b) while the company is in administration[73];

(c) after the commencement of a compulsory winding up.[74]

The landlord's promise to accept a lesser sum in settlement of the full rent will bind the landlord notwithstanding the absence of consideration, where the promise was: (i) intended to be binding; (ii) intended to be acted upon; and (iii) in fact acted on, at least until the landlord gives reasonable notice revoking his promise.[75]

The tenant under a long lease of a dwelling is not liable to make a payment of rent under the lease unless the landlord has given notice, in the prescribed form, of the payment due by the tenant.[76]

In principle, a tenant may set-off cross-claims against its liability to pay rent in accordance with the settled principles as to legal and equitable set-off.[77] However, a right of set-off is now regularly excluded by the terms of the lease.[78] Where the reversion on the tenancy has been assigned, then even where a right of set-off is in principle available, the tenant may not set-off against rent accruing due after the assignment of the reversion cross-claims which are only available against the assignor of the reversion.[79]

(p)   Release of the lease from the charge

Unlike a liquidator, neither a receiver nor an administrator has a right to disclaim a lease. But the chargee may at any time release from its charge any property and the effect is to restore the powers of the directors of the chargor to deal with the asset. This may be done because the property in question is not of any value, or not of sufficient value to merit efforts at realisation, or because it attracts liability for unoccupied property rates on the part of the receiver.[80] A decision whether or not to release frequently has to be taken in regard to leases.

18–018

---

[72] Insolvency Act 1986, s.8 and Sch.B1 paras 44(5) and 43(6), as substituted by Enterprise Act 2002.

[73] Insolvency Act 1986, s.8 and Sch.B1 para.43(6) as substituted by Enterprise Act 2002.

[74] Insolvency Act 1986, s.128(1).

[75] *Central London Property Trust Ltd v High Trees House Ltd* [1947] K.B. 130; applied in *Smith v Lawson* (1998) 75 P. & C.R. 466 (CA).

[76] Commonhold and Leasehold Reform Act 2002, s.166; SI 2002/1912, SI 2004/3056. In Wales, the provision is in force by virtue of SI 2002/3012 and SI 2005/1353.

[77] *British Anzani (Felixstowe)Ltd v International Marine Management (UK) Ltd* [1980] Q.B. 137.

[78] See e.g. *Unchained Growth III Plc v Granby Village (Manchester) Management Co Ltd* [2000] 1 W.L.R. 739 (CA), and compare *Connaught Restaurants Ltd v Indoor Leisure Ltd* [1994] 1 W.L.R. 501 (CA).

[79] *Edlington Properties Ltd v J H Fenner & Co Ltd* [2006] 1 W.L.R. 1583 (CA).

[80] See below, Ch.19.

Care must be taken to ensure that the release of the lease from the charge does not inadvertently release a guarantor in respect of the debt which was secured by the charge.[81]

(q)　Disclaimer of the lease

18-019　A liquidator of a lessee company, notwithstanding the fact that it has charged its lease as security, may, subject to the requirements of the section, disclaim the lease as onerous property under s.178 of the Insolvency Act 1986. The effect of disclaimer is to determine, as from the date of the disclaimer, the rights, interests and liabilities of the company in or in respect of the property disclaimed; but it does not, except so far as is necessary for the purpose of releasing the company, affect the rights and liabilities of any other person.[82] A chargee may, as a "person claiming an interest in the disclaimed property" under s.181 of the Act, apply to the court for a vesting order within three months of becoming aware of the disclaimer or of receiving a copy of the liquidator's notice of disclaimer, whichever is the earlier.[83] A court cannot make a vesting order on the application of a chargee except on terms that the chargee is made subject to the same liabilities to which the company was subject at the commencement of the winding-up, alternatively subject to the same liabilities as there would have been if the chargee had taken an assignment at the commencement of the winding-up.[84]

(r)　Personal liability of receiver or administrator

18-020　The receiver is not personally liable under the covenants in the lease, or for an occupation rent in respect of the period that the company under his receivership continues in beneficial occupation,[85] unless he agrees with the lessor to assume such liability.[86] Such agreement is on occasion a method of reconciling the interests of the lessor in securing the due performance of the covenants

---

[81] The relevant principles are summarised in *Chitty on Contracts*, edited by H.G. Beale, 30th edn (London: Sweet & Maxwell, 2008), Vol. 2, para.44–105; see also *Chitty on Contracts* edited by H.G. Beale, 30th edn, paras 44–107 to 44–108 as to the responsibility owed by a secured creditor to a surety in relation to the realisation of the security; and see also *Skipton Building Society v Stott* [2001] Q.B. 261 (CA).

[82] Insolvency Act 1986, s.178(4). The effect of this provision was analysed in detail in *Hindcastle Ltd v Barbara Attenborough Associates Ltd* [1997] A.C. 70 (HL); see, in particular, 89, where the position of a third party such as an underlessee or chargee is discussed. In *Hindcastle*, the House of Lords overruled *Stacey v Hill* [1901] 1 Q.B. 660 (CA) to hold that the liability of a surety of the rent will continue notwithstanding that the lessee is no longer primarily liable. See too *Christopher Moran Holdings Ltd v Bairstow* [2000] 2 A.C. 172 (HL), and *Doleman v Shaw* [2009] Bus. L.R. 1175 (CA).

[83] Insolvency Rules 1986, r.4.194; the period may be extended pursuant to r.4.3.

[84] Insolvency Act 1986, s.182(1).

[85] *Hand v Blow* [1901] 2 Ch. 721 (CA); *Re Westminster Motor Garage Co* [1915] 84 L.J. Ch. 753; *Re British Investment Development Pty Co Ltd* [1979] A.C.L.C. 31, 100; *Rangatira Pty Ltd v Viola Hallam Ltd* [1957] N.Z.L.R. 1188, 1190.

[86] *Hay v Swedish Ry* (1892) 8 T.L.R. 775; *Consolidated Entertainments Ltd v Taylor* [1937] 4 All E.R. 432; *Central London Electricity Ltd v Berners* [1945] 1 All E.R. 160. The agreement between lessor and receiver may limit the receiver's liability to assets in his hands as receiver.

with the interests of the receiver in having an opportunity, without interference or legal action by the lessor, to secure a beneficial realisation to a respectable and responsible assignee. No liability will attach to the receiver and no agreement for personal liability will be inferred merely because the receiver continues, as agent of the company, to pay rent. Further, a receiver who pays rent in his own name will not be liable as tenant by estoppel unless the landlord has been induced by such payment to believe that the lease had been assigned to the receiver.[87] Although the onset of a winding-up deprives the receiver of his agency for the company, continued beneficial occupation thereafter by the receiver, whether as principal or as agent of the mortgagee, still does not render him (or the mortgagee) liable for rent: a contract to pay must be established. The distinction to be drawn is between the receipt of benefits of a subsisting contract between the landlord and the company (in which case the receiver, whether appointed by or out of court, is under no liability) and the receipt of benefits under a contract to which the receiver personally is a party (in which case he may be exposed to liability).[88]

If the receiver decides not to perform the terms of the lease, he will render the tenant liable for breach. The receiver will not, however, be liable for the tort of inducing the tenant to breach its contract, although he may be liable if he acts in bad faith or outside his authority.[89]

Under s.109(8)(i) of the Law of Property Act 1925, which applies in the case of statutory appointments and which is often incorporated by reference into debentures, there is an "obligation" on the part of the receiver to pay (inter alia) rents out of monies coming into his hands. It has, however, been held with regard to other sums payable under s.109(8) that the prospective payee has no locus standi to enforce payment and that the obligation is owed to the mortgagee and mortgagor alone.[90] A failure to make such payment out of receipts may expose the receiver to liability at the instance of the mortgagor or mortgagee if such failure occasions loss to either of them.[91]

An administrator is an officer of court.[92] He acts as the agent of the company.[93] He similarly is not without more liable under the covenants of the lease, though the rent and other sums due may become payable as expenses of the administration even where the lease was made, and so the liabilities were incurred, before the start of the administration.[94] An administrator is subject to the possibility that his conduct may be examined by the court where there is an allegation that he: (a) has misapplied or retained money or the property of the

---

[87] *Rangatira Pty Ltd v Viola Hallam Ltd* [1957] N.Z.L.R. 1188; *Re British Investment Pty Ltd* [1979] A.C.L.C. 31.

[88] *Consolidated Entertainments Ltd v Taylor* [1937] 4 All E.R. 432.

[89] *Lathia v Dronsfield Bros Ltd* [1987] B.C.L.C. 321; *Welsh Development Agency v Export Finance Co Ltd* [1992] B.C.C. 270 (CA) (counterclaim).

[90] *Liverpool Corp v Hope* [1938] 1 K.B. 751 (CA); *Re John Willment (Ashford) Ltd* [1980] 1 W.L.R. 73. See below, Ch.19.

[91] *Visbord v Federal Commissioner of Taxation* (1943) 68 C.L.R. 354, 385.

[92] Insolvency Act 1986, Sch.B1, para.5.

[93] Insolvency Act 1986, Sch. B1, para.69.

[94] *Goldacre (Offices) v Nortel Networks UK* [2010] Ch. 455, and see Ch.4, above. An administrator cannot be required himself to stand as surety on an assignment of the company's lease: see *Legends Surf Shops v Sun Life Assurance Society* [2006] B.C.C. 204.

company; (b) has become accountable for money or other property of the company; (c) has breached a fiduciary or other duty in relation to the company; or (d) has been guilty of misfeasance or is liable for misfeasance.[95]

(s) Personal liability of the receiver: trespass

18–021 There is an open question whether a receiver, appointed by a mortgagee of a lease, who continues to act as such and causes or permits the mortgagor to continue in occupation or to receive rent from sub-lessees during the period between the service of proceedings for forfeiture by the lessor and an order for possession in favour of the lessor, may be liable as a trespasser for mesne profits.[96] The lessor is certainly entitled to mesne profits in respect of this period during which he has been deprived of possession by the lessee and the sub-lessee. This is a type of damages for trespass.[97] The quantum of mesne profits is generally assessed according to the letting value of the property for the time that the landlord is excluded, though a landlord may elect for a restitutionary measure, based on the value of the property to the lessee.[98] Mesne profits are awarded regardless that a vesting order may be granted to underlessees under the Law of Property Act 1925 s.146(4).[99]

If the receiver has personally authorised the trespass, in principle he may be held liable as a joint tortfeasor.[100] A distinction might be drawn between the positive act of authorising continued occupation (occasioning personal liability) and the passive act of accepting rent from sub-lessees, but this distinction is tenuous, for the receipt (even if not anticipated by a demand for payment) is equivalent to an endorsement of the continued occupation of the sub-lessees.

(t) Head-landlord's right to rent under sub-lease

18–022 In a case where the receiver is being paid rent by sub-lessees of the company but is not causing the company to pay rent to the lessor, the lessor can serve notice[101] on the sub-lessees in any case where the lessee's rent is in arrears, requiring future payments of rent, whether already accrued due or not, to be paid to the lessor until the arrears specified in the notice have been paid in full.[102] The effect of such a notice is to transfer from the company in receiver-

---

[95] Insolvency Act 1986, Sch.B1, para.75.

[96] See *Official Custodian for Charities v Mackey (No.2)* [1985] 1 W.L.R. 1308, where the lessors were held estopped from making such a claim by obtaining judgment for mesne profits against the lessees in a sum equivalent to the rent under the forfeited lease and satisfaction of such judgment by the receivers out of rents received from the sub-lessees.

[97] See *Woodfall's Law of Landlord and Tenant* (looseleaf Ed.), Vol. 1, para.20–012.

[98] *Ministry of Defence v Ashman* (1993) 66 P. & C.R. 195 (CA); *Ministry of Defence v Thompson* [1993] 2 E.G.L.R. 107 (CA).

[99] *Viscount Chelsea v Hutchinson* [1994] 43 E.G. 153 (CA); *Inverugie Investments Ltd v Hackett* [1995] 1 W.L.R. 713 (PC).

[100] See above, Ch.13.

[101] The notice may be served by registered post, recorded delivery or personally: *Jarvis v Hemmings* [1912] 1 Ch. 462 and Recorded Delivery Service Act 1962, s.1.

[102] Law of Distress Amendment Act 1908, s.6.

ship to the lessor the benefit of the obligation of the sub-lessees to pay rent until the specified arrears are paid off. An immediate relationship of landlord and lessee is deemed to be established between the head landlord and the sub-lessee.[103] Following service of the notice, the lessor may recover the rent payable by the sub-lessees by action or distress; moreover, he is not thereby precluded from proving in the liquidation for any balance of the arrears due from the head lessee.[104] The sub-lessee may, however, deduct any sums paid to the head lessor from the amount due to his immediate landlord.[105]

There is no authority as to whether these provisions are also generally available in the case of a company lessee in administration. It could be said that a lessor seeking to exercise this right to receive the sub-rents is instituting a legal process (which phrase includes a distress) against the property of the company (the right to receive the sub-rents), and if so, the lessor would require the consent of the administrator or the permission of the court.[106]

In *Re Rhodes v Allied Dunbar Pension Services Ltd; Offshore Ventilation Ltd*,[107] the question arose whether a landlord who had served a notice under s.6 after he had had notice of the appointment of receivers under a debenture thereby gained priority over the receivers. The debenture was in a usual form, with a charge by way of legal mortgage over the lessee's interest and a fixed charge over debts, as well as a floating charge. Harman J. at first instance treated the matter as one of priority between competing assignments, namely, an equitable assignment of the right to receive the under-rents effected by the crystallisation of the floating charge and the statutory assignment of the same right effected by the service of a notice under s.6. He held that the debenture-holder had priority because the landlord had notice of the debenture-holder's assignment when the landlord gave notice.

The Court of Appeal held that on the facts there was no equitable assignment to the debenture-holder and the question of competing assignments therefore did not arise. On the true construction of the debenture, the entitlement to the under-rents as between the debenture-holder and the company was governed by the charge by way of legal mortgage and not by the fixed charge on debts or the general floating charge; the company remained entitled to the under-rents unless and until the debenture-holder went into possession, which it had not. The appointment of receivers made no material difference to this analysis, since they were deemed to be the agents of the company and received the under-rents as such. Moreover, even if the debenture-holder had gone into possession, s.6 would still have been available to the landlord, since the debenture-holder's sub-term would have been subject to the rights conferred on the superior landlord under the Act

The result of the Court of Appeal's decision is that, in a case involving the common type of debenture employed in *Rhodes v Allied Dunbar*, the lessor can   **18–023**

---

[103] Law of Distress Amendment Act 1908, s.3.
[104] See *Woodfall's Law of Landlord and Tenant* (looseleaf Ed.), Vol. 1, paras 9–083 to 9–084.
[105] *Woodfall's Law of Landlord and Tenant* (looseleaf Ed.), Vol. 1, para.9–085.
[106] See the restrictions imposed by Insolvency Act 1986, Sch.B1, paras 43 and 44.
[107] *Rhodes v Allied Dunbar (Pension Services) Ltd; Offshore Ventilation Ltd* [1987] 1 W.L.R. 1703; [1989] 1 W.L.R. 800 (CA).

obtain priority by serving notice on sub-lessees. Debenture-holders will no doubt consider re-drafting their charges so as to cover the right to under-rents expressly. In that event, the question of competing assignments will have to be considered once again.

The construction of the debenture by the Court of Appeal excluding rentals from the scope of the fixed charge on debts has been questioned.[108] An assignment by a landlord to a third party of the right to the rents payable under a lease is an assignment of an interest in land.[109]

2. GRANT AND ASSIGNMENT OF LEASES

18–024 The terms of any lease held by the company must be carefully considered before any commitment is assumed whether to assign, sub-let or part with possession. Invariably, leases contain provisions regulating these matters; but the provisions vary in their content between absolute prohibitions and provisions merely requiring subsequent notification to the lessor. But the common form provision requires the prior written consent of the lessor, such consent not to be unreasonably withheld.[110]

The advantage of an assignment is, of course, that the tenant company may be able to realise any value there may be in the lease. Further, in relation to "new tenancies", that is tenancies granted on or after January 1, 1996, an assignment which is permitted by the covenants in the lease will result in the benefit and burden of all leasehold covenants being transmitted.[111] The assignee tenant becomes bound by the covenants to the extent that they bound the assignor prior to the assignment, and conversely is entitled to the benefit of the landlord covenants.[112] The assignor is released from any liability as original tenant or under a direct covenant which would otherwise endure for the remainder of the term.[113] If the assignor assigns only part of the premises, he is released from his liability under those covenants in proportion to the extent that the covenants are to be complied with in relation to the demised part.[114]

---

[108] Moss and Segal, "Insolvency and Leases" in (1992) *Blundell Memorial Lectures*, paras 11–004 and 11–008.

[109] *IRC v John Lewis Properties* [2002] 1 W.L.R. 35, [6]–[16]; the point was not considered by the Court of Appeal in that case: [2003] Ch. 513 (CA).

[110] If the lease requires the tenant to obtain the landlord's consent to the assignment or underletting but does not expressly state that such consent is not to be unreasonably withheld, a proviso to this effect is implied by statute: see Landlord and Tenant Act 1927, s.19(1)(a), amended in respect of assignments in relation to covenants in "qualifying leases" (essentially commercial leases granted on or after January 1, 1996) by the Landlord and Tenant (Covenants) Act 1995. For the case law as to what amount to reasonable grounds for refusal of consent, see *Woodfall's Law of Landlord and Tenant* (looseleaf Ed.), paras 11–139 et seq. A landlord owes a statutory duty to consider and respond to an application for consent to assignment or underletting: Landlord and Tenant Act 1988, s.1, as to which see above, para.18–003 and fn.7. If the sale is by the mortgagee in exercise of its power of sale, then any licence required for such sale is not to be unreasonably withheld: Law of Property Act 1925, s.89(1).

[111] Landlord and Tenant (Covenants) Act 1995, s.3(1).

[112] Landlord and Tenant (Covenants) Act 1995, s.3(2), (3).

[113] Landlord and Tenant (Covenants) Act 1995, s.5(2).

[114] Landlord and Tenant (Covenants) Act 1995, s.5(3).

Under the provisions above, the assignor tenant prima facie ceases to be liable at all under the lease, including in respect of rent; and the landlord cannot claim the same alleged debt from both assignor and assignee.[115] However, the tenant company may be required as a condition of the assignment to enter into an "authorised guarantee agreement", which guarantees to the landlord the obligations of the assignee during the period that the lease is vested in the assignee.[116] If an assignor remains liable under leasehold covenants subsequent to and irrespective of the assignment, the assignor (and any relevant guarantor of the assignor) are to be promptly informed of their obligations in the event of default by the assignee tenant.[117] Where the terms of the lease are varied after the assignment, such persons are protected from liability to pay any sum to any extent that is referable to the variation, provided that the landlord had an absolute right to refuse the variation when it was made.[118]

If the assignor is in receivership, or in administration, and its covenant is not **18–025** of substantial value, the landlord may choose to dispense with the requirement of an authorised guarantee agreement, though it is entitled to require one if the lease so provides and is not entitled to a guarantee from the receiver or administrator himself.[119] The covenant against assignment or sub-letting may sometimes contain an express proviso to the effect that the landlord's consent is not required in the case of an assignment or sub-lease to a subsidiary or associated company.[120] In a case where the lease contains such a proviso, and no other applicable restriction,[121] there is afforded to the receiver an opportunity to escape from the covenant, for he may with impunity assign or sub-let to a subsidiary or associated company (if necessary, acquired or incorporated for the purpose) and then freely dispose of the company.

The effect on the liability of an original tenant of a voluntary arrangement entered into between the landlord and an assignee of the tenancy turns upon the true construction of the voluntary arrangement. The question is whether the landlord has released the debt or has reserved the right to proceed against the original tenant. There is no rule of law to the effect that such a voluntary arrangement, to which the original tenant is not a party, cannot release the original tenant.[122]

[115] *Contrast Commercial Union Life Assurance Co Ltd v Moustafa* [1999] 2 E.G.L.R. 44: action against original tenant for arrears of rent, service charge and insurance premiums; tenancy began before January 1, 1996.
[116] Landlord and Tenant (Covenants) Act 1995, s.16.
[117] Landlord and Tenant (Covenants) Act 1995, s.17; considered in *Scottish & Newcastle v Raguz* [2008] 1 W.L.R. 2494 (HL), in a case where there was a long delay between a rent review date and the determination of the amount of the reviewed rent.
[118] Landlord and Tenant (Covenants) Act, s.18.
[119] *Legends Surf Shops Plc (In Receivership) v Sun Life Assurance Society Plc* [2006] B.C.C. 204.
[120] This is no longer usual; at the present time it is more usual to find a covenant which only permits the tenant to share occupation with an associated or subsidiary company.
[121] e.g. precluding disposal of shares in any assignee of the lease.
[122] *Johnson v Davies* [1999] Ch. 117 (CA).

3. REVERSIONS AS SECURITY

18–026 The powers of leasing of a mortgagor and of a mortgagee are considered above, at para.11–078 et seq. A mortgagee will be bound by a lease granted by the mortgagor before the grant of the mortgage. A mortgagee will also be bound by a lease granted by the mortgagor after the grant of the mortgage provided that the mortgagor has acted within its powers of leasing and obtained any necessary consent from the mortgagee. Where the mortgagee is bound by such a lease, the mortgagee of the reversion also takes subject to any statutory rights of the lessee (or of a sub-lessee holding under such lessee) to the grant of a new lease[123] or to purchase the reversion,[124] and to any like contractual rights so long as these rights are duly protected by registration or (in the case of registered land) subsist as overriding interests.[125] Of course, the mortgagee and any receiver may be principally concerned with the right to enjoy the benefits of the reversion and, in particular, the right to receive the rent payable under the lease. The mortgagee may benefit from these rights by taking possession of the rents or by appointing a receiver, who will receive the rents as agent for the mortgagor. A problem can arise where the mortgagor has bargained with the lessee for the payment by the lessee of "rent" substantially in advance of the due dates for payment of rent under the lease. Although this will not commonly occur, it may happen for cash flow reasons (possibly with a discount given by the mortgagor to the tenant) or for tax reasons or because there is a connection between the landlord and the tenant.[126] It is necessary to analyse the effect of such an agreement as between the mortgagor and the tenant and then to consider the extent to which a receiver or a mortgagee is bound by it.

Such an advance payment (over and above what is required by way of advance payment by the terms of the lease) is not a fulfillment of the obligation to pay rent; it is an advance to the landlord with an agreement that on the day when the rent becomes due such advance will be treated as a fulfillment of the obligation to pay rent.[127] This agreement will bind the landlord and the landlord's agent such as a receiver. Such an agreement has also been held to create an equitable interest in the property capable of binding third parties.[128] Whether

---

[123] The Landlord and Tenant Act 1954, Pt II provides for the circumstances in which business tenants are entitled to continue and/or to renew their leases; see s.36(4) dealing with powers of leasing and s.67 dealing with mortgagees in possession. See also the right to extended leases or new leases for residential long lessees under the Leasehold Reform Act 1967 and the Leasehold Reform, Housing and Urban Development Act 1993, Pt I, Ch.II; see, in particular, ss.12, 13 of the 1967 Act and s.58 of the 1993 Act.

[124] For the powers of long lessees to acquire the freehold see the Leasehold Reform Act 1967 and the Leasehold Reform, Housing and Urban Development Act 1993, Pt I, Ch.II and, in particular ss.12, 13 of the 1967 Act and s.5 of the 1993 Act. For the operation of both the 1967 Act and the 1993 Act, see *Hague on Leasehold Enfranchisement*, 5th edn (London: Sweet & Maxwell, 2011) and, for the special provisions relating to mortgagees of the reversion, see Chs 13, 28–18, 32–10 and 34–13.

[125] See, e.g. *London and Cheshire Insurance Co Ltd v Laplagrene Property Co Ltd* [1971] Ch. 499 and the Land Registration Act 2002.

[126] These suggestions were put forward in *Dibeek Holdings Pty v Notaras* [2000] A.C.T.S.C. 1.

[127] *De Nicholls v Saunders* (1870) L.R. 5 C.P. 589; *Cook v Guerra* (1872) L.R. 7 C.P. 132.

[128] *Green v Rheinberg* (1911) 104 L.T. 149; *Grace Rymer Investments v Waite* [1958] Ch. 831 (CA); *Dibeek Holdings v Notaras* [2000] A.C.T.S.C. 1.

such an equitable interest will bind third parties, such as the mortgagee, will depend on the sequence of events and the doctrine of notice (for unregistered conveyancing) and the principles of land registration (for registered conveyancing). The position will also be affected in the case of leases granted on or after January 1, 1996 by the Landlord and Tenant (Covenants) Act 1995. If the sequence is that the landlord grants a lease, then makes an agreement for an advance payment of rent, then mortgages the reversion, the mortgagee will in most circumstances be bound by the agreement because it will be held to have constructive notice of it (unregistered land) or the equitable rights of the tenant will be an overriding interest binding the mortgagee under the subsequent mortgage (registered land).[129] The same result was reached where the sequence was that the landlord granted a mortgage, then granted a lease which was initially not binding on the mortgagee, then made an agreement with the tenant for an advance payment of rent, then obtained the consent of the mortgagee to the lease; the lease was binding on the mortgagee by reason of its consent and the equity arising out of the advance payment agreement was binding because the mortgagee had actual or constructive notice of it.[130] In the case of a lease granted on or after January 1, 1996, the agreement made by the landlord would appear to qualify as a landlord covenant[131] and, accordingly, will be enforceable by the tenant against a mortgagee in possession of the reversion who is entitled to the rents and profits.[132] If the sequence is that the landlord grants the lease, then mortgages the reversion, then makes an agreement with the tenant for advance payment of rent, that agreement does not bind the mortgagee.[133]

---

[129] *Green v Rheinberg* (1911) 104 L.T. 149; *Grace Rymer Investments v Waite* [1958] Ch. 831 (CA).

[130] *Dibeek Holdings v Notaras* [2000] A.C.T.S.C. 1.

[131] As defined in s.28(1) of the 1995 Act; see also the definition therein of "covenant" and "collateral agreement".

[132] Landlord and Tenant (Covenants) Act 1995, s.15(2).

[133] *De Nicholls v Saunders* (1870) L.R. 5 C.P. 589. This is subject to any argument that the agreement between the landlord and the tenant (even after the grant of the mortgage) is a landlord covenant which will bind a mortgage who subsequently takes possession: see s.15(2) of the Landlord and Tenant (Covenants) Act 1995.

Chapter 19

Rates

1. NATURE OF RATES

19–001 Rates fall into two categories: occupied property rates and unoccupied property rates. Both are a direct levy by way of taxation made in relation to land within a local government area as a means of defraying local government expenses, and both constitute a personal charge, in the former case on the occupier of the property, and in the latter case on the person entitled to possession of the property.[1]

In the case of occupied property rates, in case of default in payment, an action for payment did not lie prior to 1989: the only available remedies were either (so long as the defaulter remained in occupation) distress on the defaulter's goods on the property, or (in the case of an individual) bankruptcy proceedings[2] or (in the case of a company) a winding-up petition.[3] As a result of the Non-Domestic Rating (Collection and Enforcement) (Local Lists) Regulations 1989,[4] however, the local authority may now sue[5] or seek a liability order from a magistrates' court[6] and then distrain[7] or seek a winding-up order or a bankruptcy order.[8]

From 1897[9] to 1986 rates were a preferential debt payable (pari passu with other preferential debts) out of assets in the hands of a receiver subject to a floating charge in priority to the claims of the debenture holders. As a result of the recommendations of the Cork Committee on Insolvency,[10] rates are, under the provisions of the Insolvency Act 1986, no longer preferential in either a receivership or liquidation. Rates have never been preferential in an administration.

This chapter considers the nature of a company's liability for rates in the context of that company's administration or receivership, as well as the potential personal liability of an administrator or receiver for the company's liability

---

[1] For a general account, see *Ryde on Rating and the Council Tax* (London: Butterworths, 1995).

[2] *Re McGreavy* [1950] Ch. 269 (CA).

[3] *Re North Buckinghamshire Furniture Depositories* [1939] Ch. 690.

[4] SI 1989/1058, made pursuant to the Local Government Finance Act 1988 and in force from July 21, 1989.

[5] reg.20.

[6] reg.12.

[7] reg.14.

[8] reg.18.

[9] Preferential Payments in Bankruptcy Amendment Act 1897.

[10] (1982) Cmnd. 8558, para.1427.

for rates, and the rights of local authorities to distrain on the property of a company in administration or receivership.

2. OCCUPIED PROPERTY RATES

There are four necessary ingredients for rateable occupation[11]:

19–002

(a) there must be actual occupation, in the sense of some actual use or enjoyment, however slight[12];

(b) the occupation must be exclusive in the sense that a person using it may prevent others using it in the same way[13];

(c) the occupation must be beneficial in the sense of being of some value or benefit to the occupier[14]; and

(d) the occupation must have some degree of permanence, and not be entirely transient or intermittent.[15]

Rateable occupation is a question of fact, namely whether the required occupation exists, and does not depend upon legal title.[16]

(a) Liability of administrators for occupied property rates

It is a general principle of rating law that where an agent is required to occupy a hereditament in order to secure the better performance of his duties as agent, his occupation is for rating purposes ordinarily treated as that of his principal. If, on the other hand, an agent occupies his principal's property otherwise than in his capacity as agent, the occupation will be treated as his own for rating purposes.[17]

19–003

This principle will ordinarily apply to administrators, because an administrator is expressly deemed by statute to be the company's agent in exercising

---

[11] *John Laing & Son Ltd v Assessment Committee for Kingswood Assessment Area* [1949] 1 K.B. 344 (CA), 350, per Tucker L.J.

[12] *R. v St Pancras Assessment Committee* (1876–77) L.R. 2 Q.B.D. 581, 588, per Lush J.; *Mayor, Aldermen and Councillors of the City of Westminster v Southern Rly Co Ltd* [1936] A.C. 511 (HL), 529, per Lord Russell of Killowen. See also *Re Briant Colour Printing Co Ltd (In Liquidation)* [1977] 1 W.L.R. 942 (CA).

[13] *Cory v Bristow* (1876–77) L.R. 2 App. Cas. 262 (HL), 276, per Lord Hatherley. See also *Peak v Burley Golf Club* [1960] 1 W.L.R. 568 (CA) and *John Laing & Son Ltd v Assessment Committee for Kingswood Assessment Area* [1949] 1 K.B. 344 (CA).

[14] *Hare v Putney Overseers* (1880–81) L.R. 7 Q.B.D. 223 (CA), 233–234, per Brett L.J.; *Winstanley v North Manchester Overseers* [1910] A.C. 7 (HL), 15, per Lord Atkinson.

[15] *Mayor, Aldermen and Councillors of the City of Westminster v Southern Rly Co Ltd* [1936] A.C. 511 (HL), 529, per Lord Russell of Killowen. See also *LCC v Wilkins (Valuation Officer)* [1957] A.C. 362 (HL); *Field Place Caravan Park Ltd v Harding* [1966] 2 Q.B. 484 (CA) and *Cinderella Rockerfellas Ltd v Rudd* [2003] 1 W.L.R. 2423 (CA).

[16] *Assessment Committee v Halkyn Drainage* [1895] A.C. 117 (HL), 125, per Lord Herschell.

[17] *Ratford and Hayward v Northavon DC* [1987] Q.B. 357 (CA), 371, per Slade L.J. See also *Exeter City Council v Bairstow* [2007] 4 All E.R. 437.

his powers,[18] a provision the main object of which is to ensure that the administrator will not ordinarily incur personal liability in the course of carrying on the company's business. By analogy with the principles that have been established in the case of receivers (see 19–005 below) an administrator will accordingly not incur personal liability, provided his occupation is in order to secure the better performance of his duties as agent of the company, pursuant to his statutory duty to seek to achieve the purposes of the administration. The actions of an administrator in, for example, managing the company's business from the company's premises will not, without more amount to rateable occupation of those premises by him. Nor does it mean that the company has ceased to occupy the premises for rating purposes.

19–004   It has been suggested[19] that an administrator is a rateable occupier because he has a duty to take the company's property into his custody or control.[20] However, the mere fact that an administrator has a duty to take possession of the company's premises does not mean that the character of his occupation is other than that of an agent.[21]

The position may be different, on the other hand, if the administrator inadvertently took possession of premises which were not in fact owned by the company (something which is expressly contemplated by para.67 of Sch.B1 of the Insolvency Act 1986, which provides that the administrator shall "take custody or control of all the property to which he thinks the company is entitled"). Such an action could be regarded as the dispossession of the true owner, with the result that the administrator's occupation of the premises would be rateable. Similarly, if the administrator occupies the company's premises otherwise than as agent (circumstances which are difficult to imagine in practice) then his occupation is likely to be regarded as his own for rating purposes, as opposed to occupation on behalf of the company.

(b) Liability of receivers for occupied property rates: pre-liquidation

19–005   In most cases the appointment and the debenture will provide for the receiver to be deemed to be the agent of the company. Therefore the actions of a receiver and manager in managing the company's business will not, without more, amount to rateable occupation of the company's premises by the receiver and manager. Receivers who are appointed as agents for a company will not fall to be treated as being in rateable occupation of the company's premises unless they are shown to have occupied the company's premises otherwise than in

---

[18] See para.69 of Sch.B1 of the Insolvency Act 1986.

[19] Anderson, *Administrators* (1987), pp.79–80, referring to s.17(1) of the Insolvency Act 1986 as originally enacted.

[20] This provision, which was originally contained in s.17(1) of the Insolvency Act 1986 as originally enacted, is now located in para.67 of Sch.B1 of the Insolvency Act 1986 (as inserted by s.248(2) of the Enterprise Act 2002 with effect from September 15, 2003 pursuant to SI 2003/2093).

[21] A similar proposition was accepted by Jonathan Parker L.J. *Rees v Boston BC* [2002] 1 W.L.R. 1304 (CA), 1321B–D in respect of the liability of a receiver.

their capacity as agents for the company.[22] The mere fact that a receiver enters upon a company's premises for the purpose of managing and carrying on its business does not mean that the company has ceased to occupy the premises for rating purposes or that the receiver has dispossessed the company.[23]

The leading case on the pre-liquidation liability of receivers is *Ratford and Hayward v Northavon District Council*,[24] in which receivers and managers were appointed under a debenture which included a "deemed agency" clause. The receivers decided to carry on the company's business and by letter they notified the rating authority of this decision. Thereafter they managed the business and from time to time had representatives at the company's premises, which they subsequently caused the company to sell. The justices granted the rating authority a distress warrant against the receivers as rateable occupiers.

At first instance, Kennedy J. held that the letter to the rating authority was **19–006** prima facie evidence that the receivers were in rateable occupation, and that the burden was on them to show that there was no change in rateable occupation. He further held that it was open to the justices (even if the burden of proof was on the rating authority to prove a change of rateable occupation) to find that on the above facts the receivers were the rateable occupiers.

The Court of Appeal reversed his decision. Slade L.J. held[25] that:

(a) the burden of proof at least in the first instance was upon the receivers to show that no change of rateable occupation had taken place;

(b) the receivers had prima facie discharged this burden by showing that they had been appointed on terms which, though empowering them to do so, did not oblige them to take possession and provided that, in carrying out their activities, they should be deemed to be the agents of the company;

(c) the onus then shifted to the rating authority to show that the receivers had dispossessed the company or, to put it another way, to show that the quality of any possession of the premises which the receivers might have enjoyed was not that of mere agents;

(d) the facts showing that the receivers managed and controlled the company's business and assets and had a presence at the company's premises were quite consistent with the company remaining in legal possession and rateable occupation; and

(e) accordingly, the rating authority had failed to discharge the onus which had shifted to them and therefore the receivers were not the rateable occupiers.

---

[22] *Rees v Boston BC* [2002] 1 W.L.R. 1304 (CA), 1321B–D in respect of the liability of a receiver.

See also *Australian Mutual Provident Society v Geo. Myers & Co Ltd* (1931) 47 C.L.R. 65 (High Court of Australia), 82, per Dixon J.

[23] In *Re Marriage, Neave & Co* [1896] 2 Ch. 663 (CA).

[24] *Ratford and Hayward v Northavon DC* [1987] Q.B. 357 (CA).

[25] *Ratford and Hayward v Northavon DC* [1987] Q.B. 357 (CA), 378–379.

Slade L.J. concluded[26] as follows:

> "Save for those cases such as *Richards v Overseers of Kidderminster* [1896] 2 Ch. 212, where the terms of the receiver's appointment have effected or required dispossession of the company, I think that no case has been cited to us in which a receiver has ever been held to be in rateable occupation of occupied premises. The reason, I infer, is not far to seek. Any occupation of the relevant premises enjoyed by a receiver will normally be enjoyed by him solely in his capacity as agent for some other party. Though it is possible for him to take independent possession of the premises as principal, such cases, I suspect, may be comparatively rare."

(c) Liability of receivers for occupied property rates: post-liquidation

19–007 An administrative receiver of a company is deemed to be the company's agent unless and until the company goes into liquidation.[27] On liquidation, therefore, the receiver's agency for the company determines, as does his right and power to create liabilities on the part of the company. As noted above, a critical factor in the Court of Appeal's reasoning in Ratford was that the receiver occupied the property as agent of the company. Once that agency determines on liquidation it might accordingly be thought that the main obstacle in the way of imposing liability on the receiver, who continues beneficial occupation after liquidation, would be removed.

This argument was considered and rejected by the Court of Appeal in *Rees v Boston Borough Council*.[28] The facts of the case were that administrative receivers of a company had been appointed pursuant to a debenture which provided for the receivers to be deemed to be the company's agents. The receivers carried on the company's business at its own premises, making site visits about once a week. Subsequently the company was placed in creditors' voluntary liquidation and the receivers' agency terminated. The receivers continued to run the company exactly as they had done before. Seven months after going into liquidation all the assets of the company were sold. The council, the rating authority for the area, made demand on the receivers for payment of non-domestic rates for the seven-month period between commencement of liquidation and the sale of the company's assets. On the receivers' application for directions as to their liability for rates, the judge found that they were not liable on the ground that although they were in rateable occupation post-liquidation they were occupying on behalf of either the company or the liquidator. The council appealed.

The Court of Appeal rejected the council's proposition that the cesser of the receivers' agency status somehow operated of itself to produce a change in rateable occupation. The Court of Appeal held that: (i) the actions of a receiver

---

[26] *Ratford and Hayward v Northavon DC* [1987] Q.B. 357 (CA), 378–379.
[27] Insolvency Act 1986, s.44(1)(a).
[28] *Rees v Boston BC* [2002] 1 W.L.R. 1304 (CA).

and manager in managing a company's business did not, without more, amount to rateable occupation of that company's premises by him, since for rating purposes any occupation enjoyed by the receiver and manager as agent of that company was occupation by the company; and (ii) post-liquidation there was no change of rateable occupation, and at all material times the company had remained in rateable occupation of the premises. It did not follow from the termination of the receivers' agency that the receivers had "dispossessed" the company and themselves become the rateable occupiers.

3. UNOCCUPIED PROPERTY RATES

Rates may be levied in respect of unoccupied properties. Where this is done, the special feature is that the rate is levied on the "owner" of the property.[29] The term "owner" is defined as meaning "the person entitled to possession".[30]

19–008

(a) Liability of an administrator for unoccupied property rates

Since an administrator is ordinarily entitled to possession of the company's unoccupied premises purely as a result of his agency,[31] his entitlement to possession is to be attributed to the company, with the result that the administrator is not personally liable for rates.[32] It is the company and not the administrator who is to be regarded as being entitled to possession, since the administrator's right can only subsist qua agent of the company.

19–009

(b) Liability of receivers for unoccupied property rates: pre-liquidation

The potential liability upon a receiver in respect of rates, where the company over whose assets he is appointed receiver is the owner of unoccupied property, was considered in detail by Arden J. in *Brown v City of London*.[33] Receivers, who were appointed by the debenture holder in November 1993, secured the relevant properties, oversaw repairs required by former tenants, employed various professional advisers in connection with the properties, and agreed to sell the properties. The properties were sold in March 1995 by the debenture holder pursuant to powers in the debenture. The local authority sought recovery of unoccupied property rates for the period between November 1993 and March 1995, either through imposing personal liability on the

19–010

---

[29] Local Government Finance Act 1988, s.45(1)(b).

[30] Local Government Finance Act 1988, s.65.

[31] See para.69 of Sch.B1 of the Insolvency Act 1986 (as inserted by s.248(2) of the Enterprise Act 2002 with effect from September 15, 2003 pursuant to SI 2003/2093). The position was the same under s.14(5) of the Insolvency Act 1986 as originally enacted.

[32] The principle is the same as regards receivers. See above, and see also *Brown v City of London* [1996] 1 W.L.R. 1070, also reported sub nom. *Re Sobam BV* [1996] 1 B.C.L.C. 446.

[33] *Brown v City of London Corp* [1996] 1 W.L.R. 1070, also reported as *Re Sobam BV* [1996] 1 B.C.L.C. 446.

receivers, or through a direction of the court that the receivers pay the rates out of the assets of the company.

Arden J. rejected the local authority's claim. In order to impose personal liability on the receivers, the local authority needed to establish that the receivers were "the owner" of the property, i.e. the persons entitled to possession of the property. The Judge held that the entitlement of an agent to possession must be attributed to his principal. Accordingly, since the receivers were appointed on terms that they were agents of the company, the receivers were not "entitled to possession" of the property and were accordingly not liable themselves to pay the rates.

The Judge considered that the earlier case of *Banister v Islington LBC*,[34] in which the Divisional Court had imposed personal liability in respect of unoccupied property rates on a receiver appointed out of court as agent of the company, was to be regarded, because of its special facts, as an exception to the general principle to be derived from *Ratford*. In the *Banister* case the receiver had originally been in possession of the property for the purpose of managing the business, and had not disputed that as such he had been in rateable occupation. The Divisional Court held that upon voluntarily giving up possession the receiver remained the person entitled to possession.

19–011   In view of the *Ratford* decision, it is unlikely that the special facts which occurred in *Banister* would occur again: a receiver such as that in the *Banister* case will almost certainly not be found to have been in rateable occupation on similar facts. In the absence of such a finding it will be the company that will have remained in rateable occupation so that when the company ceases occupation it will be the company and not the receiver that remains entitled to possession. In the event that there is a risk of liability on facts similar to *Banister*, it is considered that this liability could be avoided by the debenture holder releasing the unoccupied properties from his charge.

In rejecting the local authority's claim in *Brown v City of London*, Arden J. also rejected the following three additional arguments: (i) that the receivers should be directed to pay the rates as an expense of the receivership; (ii) that the receivers were required to pay the rates by reason of the incorporation into the debenture of s.109(8) of the Law of Property Act 1925[35]; and (iii) that the receivers should be directed to pay the rates because otherwise they might incur liability for fraudulent trading.

In rejecting the argument that the receivers should be required to pay the rates as an expense of the receivership,[36] Arden J. applied In *Re Atlantic Computer Systems Plc*,[37] in which the Court of Appeal held that the liability for rent under an existing lease would not be held to be payable as an expense of the receivership,[38] and held that there was no distinction to be drawn between an ongoing liability for rates and an ongoing liability for rent.

---

[34] *Banister v Islington LBC* (1972) 71 L.G.R. 239.
[35] This sub-section provides for the receiver to apply monies received by him in discharge of rents, taxes, rates and outgoings whatever affecting the mortgaged property.
[36] *Brown v City of London Corp* [1996] 1 W.L.R. 1070, 1085–1086.
[37] *Re Atlantic Computer Systems Plc* [1992] Ch. 505 (CA).
[38] *Re Atlantic Computer Systems Plc* [1992] Ch. 505 (CA), 524.

In support of the argument based on s.109(8) of the Law of Property Act **19–012** 1925, the local authority had relied upon the Court of Appeal decision in *Sargent v Customs & Excise Commissioners*[39] to the effect that a receiver, as the holder of a discretion, could not exercise that discretion against paying VAT collected from tenants to the VAT authorities. Arden J. distinguished the *Sargent* decision on the grounds that, whereas it might be said that a tenant paying VAT to the receiver did so in the expectation that it would be paid on to the VAT authorities, the receivers in the *Sobam* case had not received any funds from third parties.[40] Moreover, it was not possible to quantify, even in approximate terms, the value of the benefit which the companies and the debenture-holders received from the council in respect of the rates payable by the companies.[41]

Finally, the contention that the receivers might be found liable for fraudulent trading was rejected on the basis that the receivers' decision to postpone the sale of the properties was done in performance of their duties to the bank, that the council's claim was an unsecured one to which only assets of the company not required to pay the bank were applicable, that the receivers' decision did not deprive the council of any of its rights to have recourse against those assets, and that it did not prejudice the council.[42]

(c) Liability of receivers for unoccupied property rates: post-liquidation

The legislation relating to post-liquidation liability for unoccupied property **19–013** rates is as follows. First, the Local Government Finance Act 1988, s.45(1), provides:

"A person (the ratepayer) shall as regards a hereditament be subject to a non-domestic rate in respect of a chargeable financial year if the following conditions are fulfilled in respect of any day in the year—(a) on the day none of the hereditament is occupied, (b) on the day the ratepayer is the owner of the whole of the hereditament, (c) the hereditament is shown for the day in a local non-domestic rating list in force for the year, and (d) on the day the hereditament falls within a class prescribed by the Secretary of State by regulations".

Secondly, the Non-Domestic Rating (Unoccupied Property) (England) Regulations 2008,[43] reg.3, provides: "The class of non-domestic hereditaments prescribed for the purposes of section 45(1) of the Act consists of all relevant non-domestic hereditaments other than those described in regulation 4." Regulation 4(k) refers to any hereditament whose owner is a company which is being wound up.

---

[39] *Sargent v Customs & Excise Commissioners* [1995] 1 W.L.R. 821 (CA).
[40] See also *Re Grey Marlin Ltd* [2000] 1 W.L.R. 370, 375.
[41] *Brown v City of London Corp* [1996] 1 W.L.R. 1070, 1084.
[42] *Brown v City of London Corp* [1996] 1 W.L.R. 1070, 1086–1088.
[43] SI 2008/386.

As a result of these provisions, a company which is the "owner" of an unoccupied property (i.e. the person entitled to possession of that property[44]) will not be liable for rates in respect of that property for any period after the commencement of the company's winding-up.

19–014   In the period prior to the commencement of the winding-up, a receiver who acts solely as the agent of a company is treated as being entitled to possession of the company's unoccupied premises purely as a result of his agency. For this reason, the receiver's entitlement to possession is attributed to the company.[45] It is therefore the company which is liable to pay rates. The receiver, who is not the "owner" of the premises, is not so liable. In such a case, the commencement of the company's winding-up will not affect the receiver's position: he will continue to have no liability to pay rates in respect of the unoccupied property. The only change produced by the commencement of the company's winding-up will be that the company will cease to be liable. As a result, neither the receiver nor the company will have any liability to pay rates in respect of the unoccupied property after the commencement of the winding-up.

The position will be different where the receiver has become entitled to possession of the unoccupied premises for reasons outside the scope of his agency.[46] In such a case, the receiver will continue after the commencement of the company's winding-up to be liable for rates in respect of the unoccupied property. Any liability which the company may have had as a joint owner of the property will cease with the commencement of the winding-up,[47] but this will not affect the receiver's position.

The potential liability of a debenture-holder after the commencement of the liquidation is a question which has never been decided by the courts.[48]

4.   DISTRESS ON GOODS OF THE COMPANY

19–015   A local authority's common law right to distrain is preserved (but made subject to pre-conditions) by the Non-Domestic Rating (Collection and Enforcement) (Local Lists) Regulations 1989,[49] reg.14, which provides: "Where a liability order has been made, the authority which applied for the order may levy the appropriate amount by distress and sale of the goods of the debtor against whom the order was made". The better interpretation of reg.14 is that the common law remedy is retained, but made subject to the pre-conditions contained in the regulations, including the requirement to obtain a liability order under reg.12.

---

[44] Local Government Finance Act 1988, s.65.

[45] See above for a discussion of this principle, which was laid down in *Brown v City of London* [1996] 1 W.L.R. 1070, also reported sub nom. *Re Sobam BV* [1996] 1 B.C.L.C. 446.

[46] See, e.g. *Banister v Islington LBC* (1972) 71 L.G.R. 239, although as a result of Arden J.'s decision in *Brown v City of London Corp* [1996] 1 W.L.R. 1070 such a case is likely to be very rare.

[47] For situations involving joint ownership, see the Local Government Finance Act 1988, s.50, and the Non-Domestic Rating (Collection and Enforcement) (Miscellaneous Provisions) Regulations 1990 (SI 1990/145).

[48] This point was referred to, but not decided, in both *Brown* and in the earlier decision of *Re Leigh Estates (UK) Ltd* [1994] B.C.C. 292.

[49] SI 1989/1058.

(a)   Distress in administration

The availability of a moratorium in order to protect an insolvent company is **19–016** central to the concept of administration.[50] The statutory moratorium provisions expressly prohibit the commencement or continuation of distress against the company or the property of the company, except with the consent of the administrator or the permission of the court.[51]

If the administrator does not consent to distress, the local authority may apply to the court for permission to distrain. The onus of making out such a case for permission will be on the local authority.[52] The court will be required to carry out a balancing exercise between the interests of the local authority and the interests of creditors as a whole.[53]

In light of the fact that the company in administration is liable to pay rates falling due during the period of administration in full as an expense of the administration, the circumstances in which a local authority would need to distrain for rent against a company in administration are severely reduced. The possibility remains that a local authority might seek to distrain in respect of unpaid rates for the period prior to the commencement of the administration. In that case, however, it is unlikely that leave would be given to distrain, particularly where distress would involve the seizure of goods which are necessary or at least reasonably required for the continuation of the company's business by the administrator. Another situation in which a local authority might seek leave to distrain is where it unclear whether or when the administrator may have sufficient liquid funds to pay the rates as an expense of the administration.[54] But here too it seems unlikely that leave would readily be given.

Where the court is called upon to carry out the balancing exercise in the **19–017** context of an application for distress by a local authority in relation to rates, the court will have regard to the financial position of the company, its ability to pay rates, the administrator's proposals, the period for which the administration of the company has been in place and is expected to remain in place, the effect on the administration if leave is given and the effect on the local authority if leave

---

[50] See *Report of the Review Committee on Insolvency Law and Practice* (1982) (Cmnd 8558) (the *Cork Report*); *Bristol Airport Plc v Powdrill* [1990] Ch. 744 (CA); *Re Atlantic Computer Systems Plc* [1992] Ch. 505 (CA). The availability of the moratorium under the Insolvency Act 1986 as originally enacted was governed by ss.9, 10 and 11. The availability of the moratorium is now governed by s.8 of the Insolvency Act 1986 (as inserted by s.248(1) of the Enterprise Act 2002 with effect from September 15, 2003 pursuant to SI 2003/2093) and paras 10 to 39 inclusive of Sch.B1 of the Insolvency Act 1986 (as inserted by s.248(2) of the Enterprise Act 2002 with effect from September 15, 2003 pursuant to SI 2003/2093). This topic is covered in more detail in Ch.9 of this work.

[51] See paras 43(6) and 44 of Sch.B1 of the Insolvency Act 1986 (as inserted by s.248 of the Enterprise Act 2002 with effect from September 15, 2003 pursuant to SI 2003/2093). This was formerly governed by ss.10(1)(c) and 11(3)(d) and 248 of the Insolvency Act 1986 as originally enacted.

[52] *Re Atlantic Computer Systems Plc* [1992] Ch. 505 (CA).

[53] *Royal Trust Bank v Buchler* [1989] B.C.L.C. 130.

[54] In *Goldacre (Offices) Ltd v Nortel Networks UK Ltd (In Administration)* [2010] Ch. 455, [28], H.H.J. Purle QC noted that the treatment of rent as an expense under the Lundy Granite principle is not necessarily determinative of the point of time at which the rent should be paid.

is refused, the end sought to be achieved by the administrators, the prospects of that result being achieved and the history of the administration to date.[55]

(b) Distress in receivership

19–018   In a receivership, the property in the possession of a company will only be vulnerable to distress if it may properly be described as "the goods of the debtor" within reg.14 of the Non-Domestic Rating (Collection and Enforcement) (Local Lists) Regulations 1989.[56]

It is well established that property subject to a crystallised floating charge does not belong to a debtor company. *Re ELS Ltd, Ramsbottom v Luton Borough Council*,[57] is authority for the proposition that property subject to a crystallised floating charge cannot be described as "goods of the debtor" and is therefore not amenable to distress. The position ought therefore to be simple. The only difficulty lies in the Court of Appeal decision in *Re Marriage, Neave & Co*,[58] in which the Court of Appeal reached the opposite conclusion.

In *Re Marriage, Neave & Co* the right to distrain for rates was the same as that now provided by reg.14 of the Non-Domestic Rating (Collection and Enforcement) (Local Lists) Regulations 1989, i.e. it depended upon whether such goods were "goods of the debtor". Lindley L.J. pointed out that the rates in question could "only be distrained for upon the goods of the person assessed".[59]

19–019   The point argued and dealt with in the judgments was whether the debenture deed in that case transferred the goods in question to the trustees so as to make them no longer the property of the company. Unfortunately, the terms of the relevant deeds are not fully set out in the report but there appears to have been:

(a)   a demise to trustees by a trust deed[60]; and

(b)   a debenture with conveyance of property of the company generally, with the express exception of chattels which could be charged without the registration of a bill of sale, the security to constitute a floating charge.[61]

Some further clues to the wording can be gained from the facts relating to the same company and the same documents set out in *Paterson v Gas Light and Coke Co*.[62]

Counsel for the churchwardens and overseers submitted in opening in *Re Marriage, Neave & Co* that the goods were not covered by the debenture trust deed and therefore belonged to the company.[63] They also contended: "A

---

[55] *Re Atlantic Computer Systems Plc* [1992] Ch. 505 (CA).
[56] SI 1989/1058.
[57] *Re ELS Ltd, Ramsbottom v Luton BC* [1995] Ch. 11. This case is considered at para.19–022, below.
[58] *Re Marriage, Neave & Co* [1896] 2 Ch. 663 (CA).
[59] *Re Marriage, Neave & Co* [1896] 2 Ch. 663 (CA), 672.
[60] *Re Marriage, Neave & Co* [1896] 2 Ch. 663 (CA), 664.
[61] *Re Marriage, Neave & Co* [1896] 2 Ch. 663 (CA), 664.
[62] *Paterson v Gas Light and Coke Co* [1896] 2 Ch. 476 (CA), 476–477.
[63] *Re Marriage, Neave & Co* [1896] 2 Ch. 663 (CA), 668.

debenture charging the goods of the company is merely an equitable charge by way of a floating security, the goods remaining the property of the company subject to that charge".[64]

Counsel for the debenture-holders submitted that the goods were "assigned to the trustees of the debenture deed" and were therefore were not the goods of the company.[65] They submitted: "the effect of the debentures themselves is that the goods belong to the debenture-holders subject only to the company's equity of redemption".[66]

19–020

There is no record of any argument to the effect that, whilst goods subject to a floating charge remained the goods of the company prior to crystallisation, they ceased to be goods of the company after crystallisation. Nor do the judgments deal with this point.

Lindley L.J. held that the debenture deed did include the chattels but only had the effect of creating "an equitable charge" on the goods. The goods therefore belonged to the company subject to such a charge.[67]

Lopes L.J. agreed and stated that the goods were excepted from the trust deed, could not therefore be said to belong to the debenture holders and belonged to the company subject to the equitable charge.[68]

Rigby L.J. distinguished the judgment of North J. in *Richards v Overseas of Kidderminster*[69] (where it had been held that distress for rates was not available) on the grounds that in that case "there was an actual assignment of the goods to other persons, and that assignment was relied upon".[70]

19–021

None of the judgments refers to the fact that the proposed distress would have taken place after the crystallisation of the floating charge resulting from both liquidation and receivership affecting the company.[71] None of the judgments considers the point that such crystallisation resulted in a completed assignment of the chattels in favour of the debenture-holders.[72]

Accordingly, what *Re Marriage, Neave & Co* actually deals with and decides in terms of arguments put forward and considered is that the creation of a floating charge over assets of a company does not make them cease to be the goods of the company for the purposes of distress for rates. The facts

---

[64] *Re Marriage, Neave & Co* [1896] 2 Ch. 663 (CA), 668.
[65] *Re Marriage, Neave & Co* [1896] 2 Ch. 663 (CA), 669–670.
[66] *Re Marriage, Neave & Co* [1896] 2 Ch. 663 (CA), 670.
[67] *Re Marriage, Neave & Co* [1896] 2 Ch. 663 (CA), 673.
[68] *Re Marriage, Neave & Co* [1896] 2 Ch. 663 (CA), 675.
[69] *Richards v Overseas of Kidderminster* [1896] 2 Ch. 212.
[70] *Re Marriage, Neave & Co* [1896] 2 Ch. 663 (CA), 678.
[71] *Re Marriage, Neave & Co* [1896] 2 Ch. 663 (CA), 665.
[72] *George Barker v Eynon* [1974] 1 W.L.R. 462 (CA), 467, per Edmund Davies L.J., citing *Biggerstaff v Rowatt's Wharf Ltd* [1896] 2 Ch. 93 (CA); *NW Robbie & Co Ltd v Witney Warehouse Ltd* [1963] 1 W.L.R. 1324 (CA). Both Lindley and Lopes L.JJ. gave judgments both in *Re Marriage, Neave & Co* (July 28 and 30, 1896) and *Biggerstaff* (April 14 and 15, 1896). In *Biggerstaff* it was held that a debtor of the company in receivership could set off a cross-claim despite notice of a floating charge covering the debt due to the company. Lindley L.J. and Lopes L.J. based their decisions on the fact that the company could carry on its business as if the debenture did not exist (at 101 and 103). Only Kay L.J. pointed out that the assignment created by the floating charge did not become complete until the receiver was appointed. *Biggerstaff* was not cited in *Re Marriage, Neave & Co*.

themselves deal with a post-crystallisation situation, but such a situation and its legal effects are not considered.

In *Re Roundwood Colliery*[73] the Court of Appeal held, in the context of a contractual right to distrain (given to a landlord) in respect of goods belonging to the company but off the demised premises, that goods over which a floating charge had not crystallised when distress was put in still belonged to the company and were available for distress. This was not affected by crystallisation taking place after distress was put in but before it was enforced. On the other hand, it seems clear from *Re Roundwood Colliery* that, had crystallisation occurred prior to distress being put in, "as between the landlord and the debenture-holders, these goods had become the property of the latter before the landlord seized them".[74]

19–022   It is not absolutely clear why the crystallisation point had not occurred to Lindley L.J. when in the previous year he gave his judgment in *Re Marriage, Neave & Co*. The explanation may be that the arguments of counsel in *Re Roundwood Colliery* in the Court of Appeal in 1897 (although not at first instance in 1896) appear to have referred to the significance of crystallisation on the appointment of a receiver.[75] The arguments also refer to *Re Marriage, Neave & Co*, but the case is not picked up in the judgments. The different approaches to crystallisation in the two cases may therefore simply be the result of the point being argued in *Re Roundwood Colliery* but not in *Re Marriage, Neave & Co*.[76]

In coming to their conclusion in *Re Marriage, Neave & Co*, two members of the Court of Appeal were influenced by the consideration that distress was the only remedy for recovering rates, since the bringing of an action to recover rates was then impossible.[77] Rates can now be recovered by action.[78] At a time when rates could not be sued for but when they were still preferential, and it was thought that a local authority had a prima facie right to distrain for rates despite the crystallisation of a floating charge over the relevant goods, the receiver was able to obtain an injunction to prevent distress on the basis that rates were preferential and that any such distress might give the local authority an unfair preference over the other preferential creditors.[79] As a result of their preferential status, local authorities in practice tended to agree to rely on their

---

[73] *Re Roundwood Colliery* [1897] 1 Ch. 373 (CA).

[74] *Re Roundwood Colliery* [1897] 1 Ch. 373 (CA), 393, per Lindley L.J.

[75] *Re Roundwood Colliery* [1897] 1 Ch. 373 (CA), 387–388.

[76] The approach in *Re Roundwood Colliery* has been followed in New Zealand in *Metropolitan Life v Essere Print Ltd* (1990) N.Z.C.L.C. 66,775, 66,779, per Jeffries J., a case concerning a New Zealand statute dealing with distress for rent. *Re Marriage, Neave & Co* was not cited. Jeffries J's decision was affirmed by the New Zealand Court of Appeal ([1991] 3 N.Z.L.R. 170) without *Re Roundwood Colliery* being mentioned in the judgments.

[77] *Re Marriage, Neave & Co* [1896] 2 Ch. 663 (CA), 674, per Lindley L.J. and 676, per Lopes L.J.

[78] Non-Domestic Rating (Collection and Enforcement) (Local Lists) Regulation 1989 (SI 1989/1058), reg.20.

[79] *Taggs Island Casino Hotel v Richmond BC* [1967] R.A. 70. Failure to give effect to preferential creditors' rights gave rise to a cause of action against the receiver: *Westminster City Council v Treby* [1936] 2 All E.R. 21; *Woods v Winskill* [1913] 2 Ch. 303; *Westminster v Haste* [1950] Ch. 442.

preferential status and did not attempt to distrain in respect of pre-receivership liabilities for rates.[80] There was therefore no need to apply for an injunction to restrain distress. Under the Insolvency Act 1986, rates are no longer preferential,[81] so that it is not clear whether, if distress were in principle to be available, a receiver can any longer apply to restrain distress. It certainly seems arguable that a receiver should be able to protect the preferential creditors to whom he owes statutory duties from loss of priority to a claim for rates, which the legislature has demoted to having an unsecured non-preferential status. Even if the local authority were to be held to have priority over the debenture-holder, the legislature appears to have demoted the local authority below the remaining preferential creditors, who should therefore in principle have priority over rates.

The authorities and arguments referred to above were considered by Ferris J. in *Re ELS Ltd, Ramsbottom v Luton BC*.[82] He held that:

(a) *Re Marriage, Neave & Co* applied "only to a mere charge which does not operate by way of assignment and which ... confers no power, without the assistance of the court, to appoint a receiver, take possession or sell";

(b) If *Re Marriage, Neave & Co* could not be confined in this way, the later Court of Appeal decisions in *Biggerstaff v Rowatt's Wharf*,[83] *Re Roundwood Colliery*[84] and *Robbie v Witney Warehouse*[85] were inconsistent with it and he was entitled to follow them in preference to *Re Marriage, Neave & Co*.

Ferris J. therefore held that the local authorities in that case could not distrain **19–023** in respect of assets over which a floating charge had crystallised by means of the appointment of receivers. The alternative argument based on the priority rights of preferential creditors[86] was left open.

The right of distress (were it applicable) could only be exercised in respect of the goods of the company on the rated property. Once the receiver has sold the goods, any right to distrain would be lost and there is no right to the proceeds.[87] If tenants of the company's property pay the receiver rents inclusive of rates, the amount of the rates so paid is not recoverable by the rating authority from the receiver.[88]

[80] Samwell, *Corporate Receiverships*, 2nd edn (1988, ICAEW), p.81.
[81] Insolvency Act 1986, s.175 and Sch.6.
[82] *Re ELS Ltd, Ramsbottom v Luton BC* [1995] Ch. 11.
[83] *Biggerstaff v Rowatt's Wharf* [1896] 2 Ch. 93 (CA) (in fact a slightly earlier case: see above, fn.72).
[84] *Re Roundwood Colliery* [1897] 1 Ch. 373 (CA).
[85] *NW Robbie & Co Ltd v Witney Warehouse Co Ltd* [1963] 1 W.L.R. 1324 (CA).
[86] See above, para.19–021.
[87] *Re British Fullers Earth Co Ltd* (1901) 17 T.L.R. 232.
[88] *Re Mayfair and General Property Trust Ltd* [1945] 2 All E.R. 523; *Liverpool Corp v Hope* [1938] 1 K.B. 751 (CA).

5.   PAYMENT OUT OF ASSETS

(a)   Payment out of assets by an administrator

19–024   In administrations pursuant to the Insolvency Act 1986 as originally enacted, the administrator had the power to pay rates as an expense of the administration in an appropriate case,[89] but the rating authority had no right to demand payment of rates, and there was no room for what the Court of Appeal referred to as the hard-and-fast liquidation expenses principle.[90]

The statutory position has now changed. The provisions relating to administration expenses[91] are very similar to those relating to liquidation expenses.[92] The principles governing the payment of liquidation expenses were considered by the House of Lords in *Re Toshoku Finance UK Plc*,[93] in which Lord Hoffmann said that rates incurred after the liquidation date were payable as an expense of the liquidation.[94] He concluded: "The rates would have been an obligation incurred after the liquidation which (unlike rent) was not provable and was therefore payable in full".[95]

In *Exeter CC v Bairstow*[96] David Richards J. held that the approach to r.4.218 of the Insolvency Rules 1986 taken by the House of Lords in *Toshoku Finance* applied equally to r.2.67(1) of the Insolvency Rules 1986. He considered that it was inconceivable that parliament had intended r.2.67(1) to be interpreted differently to essentially the same provisions in r.4.218. Accordingly, he held that occupied property rates were necessary disbursements within r.2.67(1)(f) of the Insolvency Rules and para.99(3) of Sch.B1 to the Insolvency Act 1986 and thus payable as an expense in an administration.[97]

He also decided, obiter, that there was no distinction between occupied and unoccupied property rates in this regard so that the latter were also payable as an expense in an administration. The law has since been amended, however, so that unoccupied property rates are no longer payable where the owner of the relevant property is a company in administration.[98] This mirrors the position where a company goes into liquidation.[99]

---

[89] para.13 of Sch.1 of the Insolvency Act 1986 as originally enacted. See the discussion in *Re Atlantic Computer Systems Plc* [1992] Ch. 505 (CA), 529C–F, per Nicholls L.J.

[90] *Re Atlantic Computer Systems Plc* [1992] Ch. 505 (CA), 527E–528H.

[91] Insolvency Rules 1986, r.2.67(1).

[92] Insolvency Rules 1986, r.4.218.

[93] *Re Toshoku Finance UK Plc (In Liquidation)* [2001] 1 W.L.R. 671 (HL).

[94] *Re Toshoku Finance UK Plc (In Liquidation)* [2001] 1 W.L.R. 671 (HL), 680C–681C. See also *Re National Arms & Ammunition Co* (1885) 28 Ch. D. 474 (CA) and *Re Blazer Fire Lighter Ltd* [1895] 1 Ch. 402.

[95] *Re Toshoku Finance UK Plc (In Liquidation)* [2001] 1 W.L.R. 671 (HL), 681C. See also 682H–683D, in which he overruled the decision of Sir Donald Nicholls V.C. in *Re Kentish Homes Ltd* [1993] B.C.C. 212.

[96] *Exeter City Council v Bairstow* [2007] 4 All E.R. 437.

[97] See Ch.4, above for a fuller discussion of the *Exeter City Council v Bairstow* decision and its impact on administration expenses more generally.

[98] The Non-Domestic Rating (Unoccupied Property) (England) Regulations 2008 (SI 2008/386), regs 3, 4(1). For the equivalent provision in respect of Wales, see SI 2008/2499 and for Scotland see SSI 2008/83, reg. 2.

[99] See above, at para.19–013.

(b) Payment out of assets by a receiver

Section 109(8) of the Law of Property Act 1925, which is frequently incorpo- **19–025**
rated into or repeated in debentures with certain extensions and modifications,
provides, inter alia, for the payment of rates out of monies received by the
receiver. This does not give the local authority any right to enforce payment.[100]
The rationale appears to be that the local authority is not one of the class for
whose benefit the statutory duty was created.

Where the provisions merely apply as a matter of contract, the local authority
has no contractual relationship with the receiver, or for that matter with the
debenture-holder or the company. In relation to contracts entered into after
May 11, 2000, however, the question arises whether the terms of the contract
provide the local authority with a remedy pursuant to the Contracts (Rights of
Third Parties) Act 1999. The answer is probably in the negative for it is to be
inferred that there is no intention to confer a benefit on the local authority. No
doubt in many, indeed most, cases the application of the Act will be excluded
by the express terms of the debenture.

The receiver may, however, be liable to the company as mortgagor if the
company suffers loss from a failure to pay rates.[101]

6. EXCLUSION FROM POSSESSION

Where a company in administration or receivership is the subject of a "sit-in" **19–026**
or "work-in" by the workforce, the company may cease to be the rateable occupier and there may come a point where the workforce becomes such instead. In
Re Briant Colour Printing Co Ltd[102] a voluntary liquidator dismissed all the
employees, who promptly occupied the company's factory as part of a "work-
in" and excluded the liquidator from the premises. Although the company
(acting by the liquidator) took possession proceedings and obtained an appropriate order, it never became necessary to enforce it because a purchaser was
found who was acceptable to the workforce. The local authority sought a
declaration that the rates during the relevant period should be paid as an
expense of the winding-up. The Court of Appeal upheld Slade J.'s judgment
that the company was not in rateable occupation whilst the liquidator was
excluded and expressed the view that, if the company was not in rateable occupation, the workforce was. In this context, it should be remembered that a
person can be in rateable occupation without the consent of the owner of the
property.[103]

---

[100] *Liverpool Corp v Hope* [1938] 1 K.B. 751 (CA); see also *Re John Willment (Ashford) Ltd*
[1980] 1 W.L.R. 73.

[101] *Visbord v Federal Taxation Commissioner* (1943) 68 C.L.R. 354, 385–386.

[102] *Re Briant Colour Printing Co Ltd* [1977] 1 W.L.R. 942 (CA).

[103] *Assessment Committee of Holywell Union v Halkyn Drainage Co* [1895] A.C. 117 (HL), 125,
per Lord Herschell. See also *Westminster City Council v Tomlin* [1989] 1 W.L.R. 1287 (CA).

Chapter 20

Trusts

1. Trusts

20–001   Property held on trust by the company will not normally fall under any of the debenture-holder's charges. Nor will it form part of the property of a company under the control of administrators. Whilst this principle may be relatively easy to apply in the case of an express trust,[1] difficult situations can arise where the terms of the trust are unclear, or where persons who might otherwise be ordinary unsecured creditors claim priority by virtue of an entitlement under a resulting, constructive or implied trust. For a valid trust to be created, the three certainties, namely of intention (i.e. certainty of words), subject matter (i.e. the trust property) and objects (i.e. the beneficiaries), must all be present.

20–002   Certainty of intention is established objectively: the subjective intention of the settlor is irrelevant.[2] Certainty of intention can be inferred from the conduct of the settlor, such as payment of monies into a separate bank account, and hence the expression "certainty of words" can be too restrictive.[3] Certainty of intention refers to the intention of the settlor alone: it is not necessary that the beneficiaries should even be aware of the trust.[4] A trust does not fail for want of certainty merely because its subject matter is at present uncertain, if the terms of the trust are sufficient to identify its subject matter in the future.[5]

---

[1] But see, e.g. the difficulties encountered in *Re ILG Travel Ltd (In Administration)* [1996] B.C.C. 21 and cf. the approach of the Court of Appeal of New South Wales in *Stephens Travel Service v Qantas Airways* (1998) 13 N.S.W.L.R. 331.

[2] *Twinsectra v Yardley* [2002] 2 A.C. 164 (HL), [71] per Lord Millett; and see *Mills v Sportsdirect.com Retail Ltd (formerly Sports World International Ltd)* [2010] 2 B.C.L.C. 143, [55], where the Judge specifically ignored the evidence of the settlor's subjective intention; *Re Lehman Brothers International (Europe)* [2010] EWHC 2914 (Ch), [225(v)] and [225(vi)], and [239], pointing out that the words used by the parties may be persuasive, but they are not conclusive. The decision is under appeal. In *Re Chelsea Cloisters Ltd* (1980) 41 P. & C.R. 98 (CA), the Court of Appeal appears, however, to have taken into account the subjective intentions of the settler: see para.20–005, below.

[3] *Mills v Sportsdirect.com Retail Ltd* (formerly Sports World International Ltd) [2010] 2 B.C.L.C. 143 supra note 2, per Lewison J. [52]–[54].

[4] *Re BA Peters Plc* (In Administration) [2010] 1 B.C.L.C. 110, [18] (Nicholas Strauss QC); and [2010] 1 B.C.L.C. 142 (CA), [9] per Lord Neuberger, approving the following passage from the first instance judgment: "Where parties have agreed that money will be paid into a separate account and will be held on trust, a trust is created. Even where the parties have not expressly agreed that money should be held on trust, a trust is created if the settlor pays money into a separate account for the benefit of specific third parties: see *Re Lewis's of Leicester Ltd* [1995] B.C.C. 514."

[5] *Re Lehman Brothers International (Europe) (In Administration)* [2010] EWHC 2914 (Ch), [225 (iv)] and [235]. The decision is under appeal.

In *Re Kayford*,[6] is an example of an express trust, inferred in part from the conduct of the settlor. The company, being on the verge of liquidation, sought and obtained advice on how to safeguard customers who sent deposits with orders. A separate account was used for new deposits and the company's bank was told of the arrangement. Megarry J. held that the intention to create a trust was clear even though the word "trust" was not used and the subject matter and beneficiaries were sufficiently certain.[7] The subject matter being personalty, no writing was needed. Payment into a separate bank account was indicative of, but not essential to, the creation of a trust.[8]   **20–003**

One can contrast with this the case of *Re London Wine Company (Shippers) Ltd.*[9] The company sold wine for investment, and often merely "kept" wine for the client without any particular bottles being appropriated to any particular contract of sale. The buyer was sent a certificate purporting to signify his beneficial ownership of the wine purchased by him. Certain buyers suggested after the appointment of the receiver that, even if title to the wine had failed to pass under the usual rules relating to sale of goods, the company held the wine on trust for them. Oliver J. held that the trust failed for uncertainty of subject matter, since the wine which would have been beneficially owned had not been   **20–004**

---

[6] *Re Kayford (In Liquidation)* [1975] 1 W.L.R. 279.

[7] It seems that Megarry J. envisaged that each beneficiary of the trust fund (i.e. customer) had a distinct beneficial interest in the trust fund; see the discussion in *Hunter v Moss* [1993] 1 W.L.R. 934, 943B–945F (Colin Rimer QC).

[8] cf. *Re English and American Insurance Co Ltd* [1994] 1 B.C.L.C. 649 (where an insurance company agreed to hold all monies relating to a particular class of its business in a segregated account, and was found to hold the account on trust for the assureds); *Re Lewis's of Leicester Ltd* [1995] B.C.C. 514 (where trusts were held to be established in favour of concessionaires of a department store); *Re Holiday Promotions (Europe) Ltd* [1996] B.C.C. 671 (where the alleged trust funds were deposits in respect of holidays, but where there was no segregated account and no sufficient indication of any intention to create a trust); *OT Computers Ltd (In Administration) v First National Tricity Finance Ltd* [2004] Ch. 317 (CA) (two trust funds set up in favour of customers of the company and suppliers); *Re Pinnacle Entertainment Ltd* and *Re Windsong Ltd* Unreported October 27, 2010. In the *OT* case, the fund in favour of customers satisfied the three certainties, notwithstanding practical difficulties in determining the entitlement of the customers between themselves; there was, however, no valid trust of the fund in favour of suppliers because it was inherently uncertain which suppliers ("for supply of urgent goods") were intended to benefit. The valid trust was, it appears, a trust for the benefit of the entire class of customers who made payments to the company, whether or not the company then paid an equivalent sum into the trust account, and hence their beneficial entitlement in the trust fund abated ratably in the event of a shortfall: compare *Brazzill v Willoughby* [2010] 2 B.C.L.C. 259 (CA) (Kayford-type trust account set up by an insolvent bank on the terms of a supervisory notice issued by the FSA held to be a trust for the entire class of depositors, whether or not any sum equivalent to their deposits were paid into the account, rather than a "client account" type trust, where the beneficiaries consist only of those whose monies are actually paid into the trust account), Under regulations applicable to insurance brokers, premiums were to be held in an "insurance broking account", or IBA. Monies held in an IBA account were not, without more, held by the broker on trust: *Re Multi-Guarantee Co Ltd* Unreported July 15, 1987; followed in *Mann v Coutts & Co* [2004] 1 All E.R. (Comm.) 1, cf. *Re Telesure Ltd* [1997] B.C.C. 580 which concerned an application for a Berkeley Applegate Order (see paras 20–023 to 20–031, below) in respect of whether monies in an IBA account were held on trust for insurers. It appears that the insurers contended that there had been specific agreements to hold the funds on trust (see at 581C), hence the insurers' case rested on more than the mere fact that the funds were paid into an IBA account. In *Re Branston & Gothard Ltd* [1999] 1 All E.R. (Comm) 289, monies held by a stockbroker in a "client money requirement" account were held to be trust monies.

[9] *Re London Wine Company (Shippers) Ltd* [1986] P.C.C. 121.

segregated and could not be identified. The argument that the company held a specified proportion of the wine on trust, so that the buyer became an equitable tenant in common of the entire stock of wine, was also rejected.[10]

20–005 *Re Kayford* was considered by the Court of Appeal in *Re Chelsea Cloisters Ltd*.[11] In that case an insolvency accountant supervising the affairs of a company in serious financial trouble placed deposits from tenants into a separate account. The intention to create a separate fund apart from the company's property available to its creditors generally was held to be sufficient to create a trust. In *Re Farepak Foods and Gifts Ltd*[12] the company had similarly attempted to create a trust of certain proceeds received into its accounts after the date on which the company had decided to cease trading. The company traded as a form of savings company. Customers would typically pay relatively small sums periodically, which could then be exchanged for hamper vouchers or similar items come Christmas. Crucially, the monies were collected, in the first instance, by a number of agents: the agents were not obliged to keep the monies collected separate from other, or their own, monies: and those agents then periodically paid the monies which they had collected on to the company. Since the agents were agents of the company (and not of the customers), as and when the customers paid the monies to the agents, the customers became creditors of the company. Therefore, the attempt by the company to create a trust of monies received into the company's accounts after it had decided to cease trading failed, since the effect was to prefer the claims of those creditors over others. Although the conclusions reached were merely provisional, they were confirmed when the issues came before the court once more for final determination.[13]

20–006 It is fundamental to the existence of a trust that the trustee is bound to keep the trust property separate from his own and apply it exclusively for the benefit of the beneficiary: hence, any right on the part of the alleged trustee to mix the alleged trust monies with his own and use them for his own cash flow would be inconsistent with the existence of a trust.[14] Hence, in cases where the alleged

---

[10] Similar issues arose against a similar factual background in *Re Stapylton Fletcher Ltd (In Administrative Receivership)* [1994] 1 W.L.R. 1181, which also concerned the purchase and storage of wine. However, on the facts of Stapylton, when a customer contracted to purchase wine, that wine was taken from the company's general trading stock, moved to an adjacent storage unit, and stored with wine of the same character and vintage which had already been bought by other customers. Judge Paul Baker QC held that this segregation from the general stocks of the company was the crucial distinction from the *London Wine Shippers* case, as it meant that the wine was ascertained for the purposes of s.16 of the Sale of Goods Act 1979. The fact that the bottles were then mixed with other wine of the same character and vintage, and thus could not be identified as belonging to any particular customer, meant that the customer became a tenant in common of the whole bulk of the wine of that character and vintage, along with the other customers who had bought such wine.

[11] *Re Chelsea Cloisters (In Liqidation)* (1980) 41 P. & C.R. 98 (CA).

[12] *Re Farepak Foods and Gifts Ltd* [2008] B.C.C. 22.

[13] *Re Farepak Foods and Gifts Ltd (In Liquidation)* [2010] B.C.C. 735. The existence of certain limited trust claims was conceded by those representing the unsecured creditors: but only where the company had received payments from customers after the date on which the company had ceased trading.

[14] *Paragon Finance plc v Thakrar & Co (a firm)* [1999] 1 All E.R. 400 (CA), 416, per Millett L.J.; cf. *Ayerst v C&K (Construction) Ltd* [1976] A.C. 167 (HL), 180 per Lord Diplock, stating that the "essential characteristic" which distinguishes trust from other property is that trust property

trust property is money, an obligation, or absence of any obligation, to pay the alleged trust monies into a segregated account is significant. It has been said that the requirement to keep monies separate is normally an indicator that they are impressed with a trust, and that the absence of such a requirement, if there are no other indicators of a trust, normally negatives it: the fact that a transaction contemplates the mingling of funds is, therefore, not necessarily fatal to a trust.[15] Nonetheless, in *Re Lehman Brothers International (Europe)*[16] the Court of Appeal held that a statutory trust was capable of applying to client monies before those monies had been segregated; the fact that the money was not to be used for the firm's own purposes was the essential requirement for a trust.[17] In *Re Lehman Brothers International (Europe); Pearson v Lehman Brothers Finance SA*[18], Briggs J. commented that broad and general statements about the "core characteristics" of a trust needed to be addressed with some caution, since a consensual disapplication of some fiduciary obligation generally regarded as a basic feature of a trust may not necessarily prevent a trust arising. The true principle, it was said, is that while there are no hard and fast rules whereby the consensual disapplication of some basic trustee duty precludes the recognition of a trustee beneficiary relationship between the parties, nonetheless the greater the extent to which those duties are disapplied, the harder it will be for the court to conclude that the parties objectively intended to create such a relationship.

Both the *Kayford* and *London Wine* decisions were considered in relation to certainty of subject matter in *Hunter v Moss*.[19] The *London Wine* approach to certainty was held to apply only to tangibles and not to intangibles, on the grounds that tangible assets, even where they appear to be part of a homogeneous mass, are physically separate and therefore distinguishable from others in the same mass.[20] Furthermore, certain items in such a mass may have distinguishing characteristics, e.g. wine that has gone bad through faulty storage. By contrast, intangibles such as shares are not distinguishable from each other and need not be separately identified in any way. There is therefore sufficient certainty of subject matter where a trust is declared as to a particular percentage of the shares in a company where the trustee has more than enough shares to form the subject matter of the trust, even if the shares subject to the trust are not separately identified.

20–007

"... could not be used or disposed of by the legal owner for his own benefit, bust must be used or disposed of for the benefit of other persons".

[15] *R. v Clowes* [1994] 2 All E.R. 316 (CA), 325, per Watkins L.J.; and compare *Re Kayford* [1975] 1 W.L.R. 279 at fn.6.

[16] *Re Lehman Brothers International (Europe) (In Administration)* [2011] 2 B.C.L.C. 184 (CA).

[17] *Re Lehman Brothers International (Europe) (In Administration)* [2011] 2 B.C.L.C. 184 (CA), [85], per Arden L.J.

[18] *Re Lehman Brothers International (Europe) (In Administration); Pearson v Lehman Brothers Finance SA* [2010] EWHC 2914 (Ch), [255]–[260]. The decision is under appeal.

[19] *Hunter v Moss* [1993] 1 W.L.R. 934; affirmed by the Court of Appeal, [1994] 1 W.L.R. 452 (CA) with abbreviated reasons on the point in question. As far as one can tell from the reports, the facts did not involve insolvency.

[20] At 940.

TRUSTS

20–008   Whether the decision in *Hunter v Moss* is good law is not entirely clear, given in particular the decision of the Privy Council in *Re Goldcorp Exchange Ltd*.[21] A company in receivership had dealt in gold and other precious metals, and agreed to sell unascertained bullion to its customers for future delivery. Each customer received an invoice or certificate signifying his ownership. The company did not, in fact, keep sufficient bullion to satisfy all of its customers' contracts, and there was no appropriation of any of the bullion to any of those contracts. The company got into financial difficulties, and receivers were appointed. The judgment of the Board was delivered by Lord Mustill, who explained why a contract for the sale of unascertained goods could pass no title to any such goods. A buyer could not acquire title to goods unless and until it is known to what goods that title relates. Notwithstanding that both parties might agree and intend that property to goods shall pass, from "the very nature of things" property cannot pass until the goods are ascertained.[22] This reasoning was held to apply equally to an argument that a title in equity could be created by the sale.[23] Hence, the reasoning in the *London Wine Shippers* case was expressly applied and approved by the Privy Council.[24]

20–009   There is little doubt that the reasoning of the Board in *Goldcorp* sits uneasily with the decision in *Hunter v Moss*. Lord Mustill explains that neither legal nor equitable title can pass until it is clear to which title, hence which goods, the transaction is supposed to relate. That same reasoning would also dictate that no effective declaration of trust was made in *Hunter v Moss*, as the parties in *Hunter v Moss* could not possibly know to which of the shares the trust related. The fact that all the shares were the same could not affect the logic of the reasoning adopted in *Goldcorp*.

20–010   The apparent tension between the two decisions was considered by Neuberger J. in *Re Harvard Securities Ltd*; sub nom. *Holland v Newbury*.[25] That case also concerned title in shares which had not been appropriated to any contract of sale. After a thorough review of the relevant authorities and texts, Neuberger J. concluded that *Hunter v Moss* was binding on him, and that, whilst "not particularly convinced by the distinction",[26] the reasoning in *Hunter v Moss* applied to shares and other intangibles, whilst the reasoning in *Goldcorp* applied to chattels. It appears that, unless and until the issue is raised before the House of Lords, this distinction represents the law.[27]

---

[21] *Re Goldcorp Exchange Ltd (In Receivership)* [1995] 1 A.C. 74 (PC).

[22] *Re Goldcorp Exchange Ltd (In Receivership)* [1995] 1 A.C. 74 (PC), 89E-90G—see now Sale of Goods Act 1979, s.20A, inserted by the Sale of Goods (Amendment) Act 1995.

[23] *Re Goldcorp Exchange Ltd (In Receivership)* [1995] 1 A.C. 74 (PC), 90G.

[24] *Re Goldcorp Exchange Ltd (In Receivership)* [1995] 1 A.C. 74 (PC), 100A. On this basis, there is not always a trust where specific performance of a contract for the sale or supply of a commodity is available, for specific performance may be available in respect of goods which are neither specific nor ascertained if there are no alternative sources of supply: see *Chitty on Contracts*, 30th edn (London: Sweet & Maxwell, 2008), Vol.1, para.28.017–28.018.

[25] *Re Harvard Securities Ltd (In Liquidation)*; sub nom. *Holland v Newbury* [1998] B.C.C. 567.

[26] *Re Harvard Securities Ltd (In Liquidation)*; sub nom. *Holland v Newbury* [1998] B.C.C. 567, 577.

[27] See *Re CA Pacific Finance Ltd (In Liquidation)* [2000] 1 B.C.L.C. 494 (CFI (HK)), 509 and *Re Harvard Securities Ltd (In Liquidation)* [1998] B.C.C. 567, 575 where reliance is placed on the distinction and it is pointed out that leave to appeal was refused in *Hunter v Moss* after the report

Hunter v Moss was considered and distinguished, without adverse comment, **20–011** by the Court of Appeal in *Re Lehman Brothers International (Europe)*,[28] where certain clients of the firm contended that a trust arose in respect of obligations owed by the firm to those clients, but prior to any appropriation of funds in respect of such obligations. The court held that no trust could exist without property to which the trust could attach, thus distinguishing *Hunter v Moss*, where the shareholding was in existence and since the shares were fungible the trust property could be identified.[29] In *Re Lehman Brothers International (Europe); Pearson v Lehman Brothers Finance SA*,[30] *Hunter v Moss* was accepted as authority for the proposition that a trust of part of a fungible mass without the appropriation of any specific part of it for the beneficiary does not fail for uncertainty of subject matter, provided that the mass is sufficiently identified and provided also that the beneficiary's proportionate share of it is not itself uncertain. Counsel described the principle embodied in *Hunter* as the basis upon which securities are intermediated in the modern world. Briggs J. stated that the difficulty in applying *Hunter v Moss* to any case not on almost identical facts lies in the absence of any clearly expressed rationale as to how such a trust works in practice: the judge preferred the view that such a trust works by creating a beneficial co-ownership share in the identified fund, rather than the conceptually much more difficult notion of seeking to identify a particular part of the fund which the beneficiary owns outright.

The circumstances in which a company in receivership which had acted as a **20–012** mercantile agent might hold the proceeds of book debts on trust for its principal were discussed by the Court of Appeal in *Triffitt Nurseries (A Firm) v Salads Ltd*.[31] The claimants were the producers of salad vegetables which were sold to supermarkets and wholesale markets by the company in receivership prior to the receivers being appointed. The claimants accepted that prior to the receivership the proceeds of the debts paid by the markets for the vegetables were owned by the company, since the company had the right to mix the

---

of the Privy Council decision in *Goldcorp*. In *White v Shortall* [2006] NSCW 1379, the Judge (Campbell J.) was not bound to follow *Hunter v Moss*, and his judgment, therefore, includes a lengthy analysis of the academic criticism, both favourable and unfavourable, accorded to that decision, as well as relevant case law. Campbell J. concluded from his own analysis of the legal principles that there was no reason why a trust of a certain number of shares in a larger mass should be invalid. The Judge also commented, at [245]–[247], that there could be a valid trust over part of a debt: compare *Goode Legal Problems of Credit and Security*, 4th edn (London: Sweet & Maxwell, 2008), para.2–06, and the discussion in *Hunter v Moss* [1993] 1 W.L.R. 934 at first instance before Colin Rimer QC, as to whether it is possible to declare a trust of part of a bank account balance prior to segregation or appropriation of the sum concerned. An ingenious justification for the decision in *Hunter v Moss* is suggested by Professor Roy Goode in *Legal Problems of Credit and Security*, 4th edn (London: Sweet & Maxwell, 2008), paras 2–06 and 6–09. He there suggests that shares of the same issue by a company are not fungibles, but merely fractions of a single asset (the asset being the entire share capital of the issuing company); which asset is held in common by the shareholders. There is, therefore, no more difficulty in creating a trust of, say, 50 unidentified shares out of 100, than creating a trust of a one-quarter interest in a racehorse.

[28] *Re Lehman Brothers International (Europe) (In Administration)* [2011] 2 B.C.L.C. 184 (CA).
[29] *Re Lehman Brothers International (Europe)(In Administration)* [2011] 2 B.C.L.C. 184, per Arden L.J. [171]; Neuberger L.J. [235].
[30] *Re Lehman Brothers International (Europe) (In Administration); Pearson v Lehman Brothers Finance SA* [2010] EWHC 2914 (Ch), [225(iii)] and [227]–[235]. The decision is under appeal.
[31] *Triffitt Nurseries v Salads Ltd* [2000] 1 All E.R. (Comm) 737 (CA).

proceeds of the book debts with its own monies, and to take its commission out of those proceeds. The claimants argued that upon the appointment of receivers and the cessation of the company's business, the proceeds of debts still outstanding at that time and collected by the receivers were subject to a trust in their favour, and that at the date of the receivership the claimants had been entitled to demand payment direct from the markets. The arguments were rejected by the Court of Appeal, on the basis that the company's title to the book debts was not somehow limited or defeasible, but absolute, and that the appointment of receivers and the cessation of business did not alter that fact. The only way in which the claimants might have succeeded in claiming the proceeds from the receivers was if the receivers had been guilty of sharp practice in obtaining payment, which was not suggested. A claim to the proceeds would also have succeeded if the receivers had, after their appointment, accepted further consignments and sold further produce (whenever consigned)—in which case the receivers might be deemed personally to have adopted the contracts.

20–013   In *Associated Alloys Pty Ltd v A.C.N. 001 452 106 Pty Ltd*[32] the majority of the High Court of Australia recognised the effectiveness of an express trust of the proceeds of sale of goods supplied under a retention of title clause. The trust applied to the proceeds of sale of all products which were made using steel supplied by the sellers, the beneficial interest of the sellers being stated to be equal to the amount owing from the buyers to the sellers at the time of receipt of the proceeds. It was held that the absence of any express requirement on the buyer to keep the proceeds separate from his own assets did not affect the existence of the trust, since the trust itself was express and hence the obligation to keep the proceeds separate existed by necessary implication in any event.[33] The High Court of Australia was prepared to imply a term that the debt owing from the buyer to the seller at the time of receipt of the proceeds was discharged pro tanto on receipt by the buyer of the proceeds, so that no equity of redemption vested in the buyer.[34] The case is discussed further in Ch.3.

20–014   A form of trust which can arise in insolvency situations with some frequency is the so-called "*Quistclose* trust", named after the decision of the House of Lords in *Barclays Bank Ltd v Quistclose Investments Ltd*.[35] Where a loan to a borrower is made exclusively for a specific purpose, and the borrower is not free to apply the money for any other purpose, the borrower has fiduciary obligations in respect of the monies lent, which the court will enforce. Frequently, the cases concern a loan by the lender to the borrower to enable the borrower to pay his creditors, or some of them, but the principle is not limited to such cases.

---

[32] *Associated Alloys Pty Ltd v A.C.N. 001 452 106 Pty Ltd* (2000) 171 A.L.R. 568 (High Court of Australia).
[33] See further *Stephens Travel Service International Pty Ltd v Qantas Airways* (1988) 13 N.S.W.L.R. 331 (NSWCA); *Walker v Corboy* (1990) 19 N.S.W.L.R. 382 (NSWCA); and cf. *Re ILG Travel Ltd (In Administration)* [1996] B.C.C. 21.
[34] See also *Re SSSL Realisations (2002) Ltd* [2005] 1 B.C.L.C. 1, [49]–[54].
[35] *Barclays Bank Ltd v Quistclose Investments Ltd* [1970] A.C. 567 (HL). For commentary on the implications of these trusts for bankers, see further paras 24–023 to 24–024, below.

The *Quistclose* case was followed in *Re Northern Developments (Holdings)*   **20–015**
Ltd,[36] where a group of lenders paid a large sum into an account in the name of
the company to be paid to the creditors of a subsidiary, which was in financial
trouble. The subsidiary went into receivership when just over half the fund
remained in being. It was held, following the *Quistclose* case,[37] that there was
a "purpose trust"[38] affecting the monies enforceable by the lenders and by the
creditors of the subsidiary.

A further "*Quistclose*" situation occurred in *Carreras Rothmans Ltd v
Freeman Mathews Treasure Ltd*[39] where monies were paid into a special
account by the principal to enable its advertising agent, then in financial difficulties, to pay sums owed by the agent to certain creditors. The agent went into
liquidation. It was held, following the *Quistclose* and *Northern Developments*
decisions, that the monies were subject to a trust and that:

"... the principle in all these cases is that equity fastens on the conscience
of the person who receives from another property transferred for a specific
purpose only and not therefore for the recipient's own purposes, so that

[36] Unreported October 6, 1978 per Megarry V.C.

[37] *Barclays Bank Ltd v Quistclose Investments Ltd* [1970] A.C. 567 (HL).

[38] A purpose trust is a trust where the trust property is earmarked for use for a particular purpose,
and is not available to be used for any other purpose. "Instances in the books are legion": per
Dillon L.J. in *Re EVTR* [1987] B.C.L.C. 646 (CA), [651c], a case where a special purpose loan led
to a constructive trust in favour of the lender. See also *Re Goldcorp Exchange Ltd (In Receivership)*
[1995] 1 A.C. 74 (PC) especially at 140–135. For recent examples in which express purpose trusts
been found not to have been created see *Re Holiday Promotions (Europe)* [1996] B.C.C. 671; *Re
Challoner Club Ltd (In Liquidation)*, *Times*, November 4, 1997. *Box v Barclays Bank Plc* [1998]
Lloyd's Rep Bank 185; *Re Griffin Trading Co* [2000] B.P.I.R. 256 and *Re Farepak Food and Gifts
Ltd (In Administration)* [2008] B.C.C. 22; and [2010] B.C.C. 735. The Court of Appeal in
Twinsectra Ltd v Yardley [1999] Lloyd's Rep. Bank 438 (CA) in applying *Quistclose* suggested
that in principle the degree of certainty with regard to the objects of a *Quistclose* type trust "need
be no more than is necessary to enable the restriction on the recipient's use of the money to be
identified and enforced," per Clarke L.J. at [76] of the judgment. In the House of Lords reported at
[2002] 2 A.C. 164 (HL), 184 Lord Millett said it was "well established that a loan to a borrower
for a specific purpose where the borrower is not free to apply the moneys for any other purpose
gives rise to fiduciary obligations on the part of the borrower which a court of equity will enforce".
He added that although in earlier cases the purpose was to enable the borrower to pay his creditors
or some of them "the principle is not limited to such cases" (see [68]), and at [74] added
that the question in every case was whether the parties intended the money to be at the free disposal
of the recipient and such freedom was necessarily excluded by an agreement that the money
remains the property of the lender unless and until applied in accordance with his directions and
insofar as not so applied it must be returned to him. See also *Barnabas Hurst-Bannister v New Cap
Reinsurance Corp Ltd* [2000] Lloyd's Rep. I.R. 166. cf. *OT Computers Ltd (In Administration) v
First National Trinity Finance Limited* [2007] W.T.L.R. 165, and *Re Margaretta Ltd (In
Liquidation)* [2005] B.P.I.R. 834, [16]. In *Kingate Global Fund Ltd v Knightsbridge (USD) Fund
Ltd* [2009] SC (Bda) 39 Civ (CA (Bermuda)), concluded that subscription monies paid by intending
subscribers in a Madoff feeder fund were held on a "*Quistclose*" trust for the benefit of the
intending subscribers pending the issue and allotment of shares. The Bermudan Court of Appeal
held that there was no principle or rule of law deriving from *Moseley v Cressey's Co* (1865) L.R.
1 Eq. 405, whereby monies paid to a company for the purchase of shares in the company were
presumed to form part of the assets of the company prior to issue and allotment, absent some
extraordinary special term (such as the term in *Re Nanwa Gold Mines* [1955] 1 W.L.R. 1080,
where the prospectus stated that application monies would be held in a separate account pending
issue).

[39] *Carreras Rothmans Ltd v Freeman Mathews Treasure Ltd (In Liquidation)* [1985] Ch. 207,
per Peter Gibson J.

such person will not be permitted to treat the property as his own and to use it for other than the stated purpose."[40]

20–016   For some time after the decision in *Quistclose*, there was debate as to the nature of the *Quistclose* trust, and in particular who owned the beneficial interest in the loaned monies. The debate has now been resolved by the decision of the House of Lords in *Twinsectra Ltd v Yardley*.[41] If A lends money to B, such monies to be used solely for a specific purpose and no other, then during the period that B holds the money prior to fulfilling the purpose, the monies are held on resulting trust for A, but subject to a power (or, indeed, duty) in B to apply the monies for the stated purpose. If the monies are paid by B for the stated purpose, title to the monies vests, of course, in the payees, and A has merely a contractual right in debt to repayment of the loan. If for some reason the purpose cannot be carried out (typically, because B becomes insolvent) then the monies remain held on trust for A, who is entitled to the return of the monies in specie as beneficiary by revoking the power or mandate to B to apply the monies for the stated purpose.

20–017   Where a lender advances monies to a company in financial difficulties for the payment of creditors or, as in *Quistclose* itself, to pay declared but unpaid dividends, then if the borrower enters formal insolvency proceedings, the purpose behind the loan can, in a sense, still be achieved: as the monies belong to the lender and not the insolvent company, no preference would result if the creditors were paid notwithstanding insolvency. But typically the lender will have some motive beyond ensuring payment to creditors as such–normally, the survival of the company. If the lender's object in giving the power or mandate is frustrated, as often by formal insolvency, the lender is entitled to revoke the mandate and demand return of the money. Insolvency will not always frustrate the lenders' object. In *Re Margaretta Ltd*,[42] a company sold a property and the VAT element of the price was paid into a separate account pending determination of what VAT, if any, was payable. The subsequent insolvency of the company prior to payment did not frustrate the object of the payment, and hence payment was directed to be paid to Customs and Excise. It was there noted that, although normally the beneficial interest under a *Quistclose* trust will remain, at all times prior to payment, in the lender, there may be circumstances where the third party intended to benefit from the trust might acquire a beneficial interest, where the obvious intention of the transaction would be frustrated if the lender retained a power of revocation, or where the intended recipient gets to know of the existence of the trust, in which case he might acquire a beneficial interest by virtue of an estoppel, or perfection of an assignment.[43]

20–018   In *Du Preez Ltd v Kaupthing Singer & Friedlander (Isle of Man) Ltd*,[44] a disappointed depositor of an insolvent bank contended that it was entitled to

---

[40] At 222B.
[41] *Twinsectra Ltd v Yardley* [2002] 2 A.C. 164 (HL), especially per Lord Millet at [68]–[103].
[42] *Re Margaretta Ltd* [2005] B.C.C. 506.
[43] *Re Margaretta Ltd* [2005] B.C.C. 506, [24].
[44] *Du Preez Ltd v Kaupthing Singer & Friedlander (Isle of Man) Ltd (In Liquidation)* (2010) 12 I.T.E.L.R. 943.

priority over the other unsecured creditors of the bank by virtue of an alleged "*Quistclose*" trust. The depositor held a credit balance with the bank, and shortly before provisional liquidators were appointed, gave instructions that a substantial part of that credit balance should be transferred to a third party's account at an unrelated (and solvent) bank. At the time that provisional liquidators were appointed, the bank had made the requisite debit entry on the account balance in anticipation of the transfer being effected, but the transfer was never completed. The bank's liquidator's contended that the depositor should prove for the account balance (including the sum intended to be transferred) as an ordinary unsecured creditor. The depositor contended that he was the beneficiary of a "*Quistclose*" trust, and hence entitled to payment in full of the sum he had sought to transfer. The sole basis for alleging the existence of a trust was the instruction to transfer (whereby, the depositor contended, the bank was instructed to use the money in the account for the sole purpose of making the transfer to the third party) and the provisional debiting of the account. The claim was dismissed. The Staff of Government Division (the Isle of Man equivalent of the Court of Appeal) held that it was an essential element of any "*Quistclose*" trust that the exclusive purpose for which monies are to be used by the trustee/recipient be communicated before or at the same time as the transfer of the money to that trustee/recipient. On normal banking law principles, money paid to a bank by a depositor is owned by the bank, and the relationship between the bank and its customer is merely that of debtor and creditor. Given that the depositor paid no new money to the bank at the time that it gave the bank instructions to transfer the money, but merely requested the transfer of part of its pre-existing credit balance, there could be no question of any "*Quistclose*" trust arising.[45] A further argument, based on the decision in *Re Kayford*, that the bank had declared itself a trustee of the "monies" to be transferred also failed. A bank might, in theory, declare itself a trustee of part of its own assets for the benefit of a customer (as indeed was the case on the facts of *Brazzill v Willoughby* [2010] 2 B.C.L.C. 259). However, the mere acceptance of the transfer instruction and provisional debiting of the customer's account did not amount to a declaration of trust; and in any event, the depositor's account balance was a debt owing from the bank to the customer, and a trust could not be declared over the bank's own liability.

In *Cooper v PRG Powerhouse Ltd*[46] an ex-employee of a company made a **20–019** payment to the company on the understanding that the company would pay an equivalent sum as the final instalment owing to a finance company in respect of a car driven by him. The ex-employee was aware that his payment to the company would be credited to the company's payroll account and mixed with funds of the company. The payment was not made subject to any express direc-

---

[45] In the course of its judgment, at [49], the Staff of Government Division commented that if the depositor had paid monies to the bank on the express basis that such sum was to be paid forthwith to the account of a third party at a third party bank, a "*Quistclose*" trust would have arisen. Given the fundamental principle that the relationship of a customer who pays money to his bank is ordinarily merely that of debtor and creditor, it is considered that the circumstances in which a "*Quistclose*" trust could arise in such a scenario will be highly unusual.

[46] *Cooper v PRG Powerhouse Ltd* [2008] 2 All E.R. (Comm) 964.

tion that his payment was to be used only for the purposes of paying off the instalment. The company entered administration before the company had made payment to the finance company. The court concluded that the ex-employee's payment to the company was held by the company subject to a "*Quistclose*" trust, and since the purpose had failed, the ex-employee was entitled to payment in full. On the facts, it is difficult to discern the basis on which the court concluded that the monies paid by the ex-employee were to be used exclusively for the purpose of payment to the finance company, and hence why the court concluded that the monies were held on trust.

20–020   Of course, a *Quistclose* trust might, in appropriate circumstances, come into existence after formal insolvency proceedings as well as before. In *Re Niagara Mechanical Services International Ltd (in Administration)*[47] monies paid to administrators of a company for the specific purpose of paying a sub-contractor were held on a *Quistclose* trust, and the lender was thus entitled to their return in specie when the administrators did not use the monies for that purpose.

20–021   The fact of the insolvency of the recipient of monies at the time of payment by a third party might in itself ground a claim that the monies are held by the insolvent recipient on trust either for the ultimate intended beneficiary or for the payer. In *Re Japan Leasing (Europe) Plc*,[48] instalments for the purchase of an aircraft were paid to a company in administration as representative of a number of vendors. The court held that the monies were held on constructive trust for the vendors, as it would be unconscionable for the administrators to seek to retain the monies.[49]

20–022   The *Niagara* and *Japan Leasing* cases each concerned companies in administration. In principle there is no reason to believe that the result would have differed had the companies been in administrative receivership, or any other form of insolvency proceeding.[50] It is notable, however, that in *Japan Leasing*

---

[47] *Re Niagara Mechanical Services International Ltd (in Administration)* [2001] B.C.C. 393.
[48] *Re Japan Leasing (Europe) Plc* [1999] B.P.I.R. 911.
[49] The reasoning is essentially the same as that of Bingham J. (as he then was) in *Neste Oy v Lloyds Bank Plc* [1983] 2 Lloyd's Rep. 658, where it was held that a payment made by a shipowner to his broker at a time when the broker had already resolved to cease trading (and hence there was no prospect of the monies being used to pay various third parties intended to be paid with the monies advanced) was held on constructive trust for the shipowner. The decision in *Neste Oy* has been the subject of some criticism, though in *Re Farepak Foods and Gifts Ltd (In Administration)* [2008] B.C.C. 22, Mann J. said that the decision was "clear enough and can be reconciled with principle" on the basis that the trust was based not solely on the pricking of conscience of the recipient company, but also on the payment having been made (to the knowledge of the recipient company) under a mistake. Nonetheless, Mann J. could not hold that the monies in that case received into the company's accounts after the company had decided to cease trading were held on trust. First, difficulties arose by reason of the clearing cycle for payments: a payment actually received by the company after the decision to cease trading might nonetheless have been paid in (in the sense of the relevant payment mechanism activated) before the company had decided to cease trading, in which case the payment was not made under any mistake. Secondly, the payments into the company's accounts were not made by the company's customers, but by agents of the company who received the monies from the customers. Thus, the relevant date of receipt by the company (and hence the relevant date for determining whether the mistake was operative) was the date of receipt by the agents. See the further consideration given to this issue by Warren J. when the issues came before the court for final determination, at [2010] B.C.C. 735.
[50] In *Neste Oy*, the company had resolved to cease trading and was about to invite the appointment of receivers.

the alternative grounds for the decision were: (i) that payment to the vendors should in any event be made as an expense of the administration,[51] on the basis that other parties' property was being retained and used for the benefit of the administrator; and (ii) on the basis of *Ex p. James*. Both these grounds depended on the fact that administrators are officers of the court.[52] In the *Niagara* case, an alternative argument advanced by the lender on the basis of *Ex p. James* was similarly founded on the status of the administrators as officers of the court.[53] No similar argument could be addressed if the company were in administrative receivership (or voluntary liquidation) as such receivers, and voluntary liquidators, are not officers of the court.[54]

2. BERKELEY APPLEGATE ORDERS

Assets of an insolvent company which are held on trust do not form part of the property of the company in respect of which an insolvency practitioner is otherwise appointed as administrator or liquidator. At first sight, therefore, an office-holder appointed in respect of a company which is the legal owner of trust assets should not attempt to administer or realise those trust assets, and normally his involvement with such assets will be limited, at most, to accounting for them to the beneficial owners. Hence, if, after taking advice, the insolvency practitioner is sure as to which assets are held on trust, and which are not, it may be that he will be able to proceed simply by managing and realising the non-trust assets in the usual way. Alternatively, and again if the existence of a trust of certain assets is clear, the insolvency practitioner, or the beneficiaries of the trust, may apply to court for the appointment of a receiver to manage and realise the trust assets for the benefit of the beneficiaries.[55]   **20–023**

But the affairs of the company may be significantly more complex and the routes described above impossible or inappropriate. It may be unclear whether there is indeed a trust in respect of certain assets (or proportions of assets) or not, and hence whether those assets can be claimed by third party beneficiaries, or whether they should be managed and realised by the office-holder for the benefit of the company and its creditors; and, if assets are held on trust, the identity of the beneficial owners, and their interests in the various trust assets, may be unclear.[56] The resolution of these various difficulties may well involve   **20–024**

---

[51] But see Ch.4, above on administration expenses.

[52] See at *Re Japan Leasing (Europe) Plc* [1999] B.P.I.R. 911, 923G–925F.

[53] See *Re Niagara Mechanical Services International Ltd (in Administration)* [2001] B.C.C. 393, [35].

[54] *Ex p. James* was also sought to be prayed in aid in *Re Farepak Foods and Gifts Ltd (In Administration)* [2008] B.C.C. 22. The principle in that case did not, the Judge held, allow the court to reach a decision which might be seen as fair on a palm tree justice basis, but overrode the legal interests of the company and other creditors.

[55] See *Re Berkeley Applegate (Investment Consultants) Ltd (No.1)* [1989] Ch. 32, 41 B–C. The application would be made under the Supreme Court Act 1981, s.37 and CPR Pt 69. It appears that the court further has jurisdiction to appoint a new or substitute trustee under the Trustee Act 1925, s.41.

[56] In *Berkeley Applegate Investment Consultants) Ltd (No.1)* [1989] Ch. 32, 41B–D, the judge commented that the appointment of a receiver would have presented certain difficulties in that case because, first, until the liquidator had carried out a good deal of work the necessary basis of fact

the office-holder in carrying out detailed factual investigations. It may further involve him in seeking advice, and the directions of the court, on any of the various issues described above.[57]

20–025 In such circumstances, an issue arises as to the funding of any investigations which the insolvency practitioner carries out. Prima facie, the remuneration and expenses of an insolvency practitioner cannot be paid out of assets subject to a trust, as those assets belong to the third party beneficiaries, and not the company. But the court has jurisdiction, in the circumstances set out below, to award an office-holder an allowance in respect of his remuneration and expenses chargeable against trust assets.

20–026 The leading case is *Re Berkeley Applegate (Investment Consultants) Ltd.*[58] The case concerned an investment company, whose business was to accept funds from third party investors for investment, by way of mortgage advances, in property. The company was placed in creditors' voluntary liquidation. As at the commencement of the liquidation, the company held cash at various bank accounts, designated as client accounts. It further held numerous mortgages, taken as security for monies lent by the company to finance the acquisition of various properties. The liquidator carried out a very considerable amount of work, namely a preliminary investigation of the company's affairs prior to his appointment, and, following his appointment, answering enquiries from investors and borrowers, ascertaining the non-trust assets of the company, managing investments, and some further work in relation to pure liquidation matters. The liquidator applied to the court for directions, seeking the court's determination as to whether the various mortgages and cash at bank were held on trust, and if so, for whom. The liquidator further applied for an order that he was entitled to be paid his proper expenses and remuneration out of the trust assets in the event that the non-trust assets of the company were insufficient.

---

for such an appointment (that is to say, the existence of trust assets) had not been established, and secondly, each mortgage was held on a distinct trust for a distinct investor or group of investors. Given that a liquidator or administrator will, in any event, need to satisfy himself as to which assets are trust assets, and which not, in many cases the appointment of a receiver or trustee to investigate such issues would lead to a duplication of costs. In Australia, it has been held that unless there is some conflict of interest, a liquidator, rather than court-appointed receiver, should identify trust and non-trust assets as part of his task of doing all things necessary for the winding-up of the company: *Australian Securities and Investments Commission v Rowena Nominees Pty Ltd* (2003) 45 A.C.S.R. 424.

[57] A problem which sometimes arises where the court's directions are sought on the existence of a trust is that the cost of obtaining such directions may severely deplete the putative trust assets, thus defeating the object. The problem may be acute if representative creditors are appointed to argue for or against the existence of a trust, and their costs indemnified out of the trust assets. Thus in *Re Equilift Ltd (Iin Liquidation)* [2010] B.C.C. 860, H.H. Judge Purle QC took the pragmatic approach of directing the liquidators to seek leading counsel's advice as to the existence of trust claims. The opinion of counsel advised that the trust claims were unlikely to succeed. Hence the liquidators were further directed to write to potential trust claimants, informing them of counsel's conclusions; stating that they could challenge counsel's conclusion, but would run the risk of an adverse costs order if they unsuccessfully averred that a trust existed; and authorising the liquidators to distribute the assets in accordance with counsel's opinion in the event that his conclusions were not challenged. In so distributing the assets, the liquidators would have the protection of the court's powers under s.61 of the Trustee Act 1925 if it later turned out that any of the assets were, in fact, held on trust. Compare the similarly pragmatic approach of Warren J. in *Re Farepak Foods and Gifts Ltd (In Liquidation)* [2010] B.C.C. 735.

[58] *Re Berkeley Applegate (Investment Consultants) Ltd (No.1)* [1989] Ch. 32.

The court held that the various mortgages and cash at bank were held on **20–027** trust.[59] The court further held that the liquidator was, in principle, entitled to payment of his proper remuneration and expenses out of the trust assets. The basis of the jurisdiction was a general principle that, where a person seeks to enforce a claim to an equitable interest in property, the court has a discretion to require as a condition of giving effect to that equitable interest that an allowance be made for costs incurred and for skill and labour expended in connection with the administration of the property.[60] The discretion is to be sparingly exercised, but factors that will operate in favour of its being exercised include the fact that, if the work had not been done by the person to whom the allowance is sought to be made, it would have had to be done either by the person entitled to the equitable interest or by a receiver appointed by the court whose fees would have been borne by the trust property.[61] The jurisdiction of the court to award such an allowance existed notwithstanding that the contracts pursuant to which the third parties had invested their monies provided that they should bear none of the expense of managing the investments, though this was a factor to be taken into account in the exercise of the court's discretion.[62] The court ordered enquiries as to: (i) the quantum of the liquidator's remuneration and costs to which he should be entitled; and (ii) how the remuneration and costs should be borne as between the various trust and non-trust assets of the company.[63]

On the first enquiry, the court determined that the liquidator was entitled to **20–028** remuneration and costs which far exceeded the non-trust assets of the company.[64] On the second enquiry, the court held that only the costs of the

---

[59] That part of the decision is reported at (1988) 4 B.C.C. 274.

[60] *Re Berkeley Applegate (Investment Consultants) Ltd (No.1)* [1989] Ch. 32, 50H. The *Berkeley Applegate* principle, where it applies, permits the office-holder to claim an allowance from the trust assets, and is not in the nature of a personal claim against the beneficiary: *Green v Bramston* [2011] B.P.I.R. 44, [42]. In that case, the contention that a trustee in bankruptcy's claim to an allowance under the *Berkeley Applegate* principle as against assets held beneficially for a company in liquidation was provable in the liquidation was rejected; an allowance under the *Berkeley Applegate* principle resulted in "… a proprietary interest in priority to that of the beneficiary …", according to the Judge.

[61] *Re Berkeley Applegate (Investment Consultants) Ltd (No.1)* [1989] Ch. 32, 50H–51B. The principle was, the deputy judge held, part of a seamless whole of equitable principles, which included the jurisdiction to award expenditure on the preservation of trust property as "salvage". A similar principle appears to lie behind the decision in the House of Lords in *Buchler v Talbot* [2004] 2 A.C. 298 (HL) that where a liquidator realises property subject to a floating charge, the costs of realisation are deductible from the proceeds of the property: see at [19] (per Lord Nicholls) and [62]–[63] (per Lord Millett); see also *Re Movitex Ltd* [1990] B.C.C. 491. The principle may not apply where the work carried out and for which an allowance is sought is not work necessary to establish beneficial ownership of assets between the putative beneficiaries inter se, but work carried out so as to establish a claim by the person carrying out the work to the assets themselves: *Green v Bramston* [2011] B.P.I.R. 44. In that case, a trustee in bankruptcy sought an allowance for work carried out in establishing the beneficial ownership of certain properties to which the trustee laid claim on behalf of the estate. No allowance was made for this work, since the work was adverse to the interests of the true beneficiaries.

[62] *Re Berkeley Applegate (Investment Consultants) Ltd (No.1)* [1989] Ch. 32, 52G–53B.

[63] See *Re Berkeley Applegate (Investment Consultants) Ltd (No.3)* (1989) 5 B.C.C. 803, 804D.

[64] *Re Berkeley Applegate (Investment Consultants) Ltd (No.3)* (1989) 5 B.C.C. 803, 804G–H. For a discussion of the inquiries, see *Green v Bramston* [2011] B.P.I.R. 44.

liquidator incurred in respect of the liquidation of the non-trust assets, thus the company's own assets, could be paid out of those assets, and that the remuneration and costs incurred by the liquidator in administering the trusts as de facto trustee could not be so charged.[65] The court further held that, as between the two categories of beneficiaries, the remuneration and costs should, albeit in a rough and ready manner, be apportioned according to whether the remuneration and costs had been incurred in respect of one set of trust assets, or the other.[66]

20–029   Whilst the decision as to the allocation of the remuneration and expenses in *Berkeley Applegate* was based on the interpretation of the statute dealing specifically with a liquidator's remuneration,[67] the principle is applicable more broadly. Although, the entitlement of an administrator to remuneration, whilst broadly stated in the Insolvency Rules,[68] is limited to property of the company (including property subject to a floating charge), and hence would not include property held on trust for third parties,[69] it appears equitable that, where costs have been incurred in respect of the administration and realisation of certain assets, those assets should bear those costs. The principle is not confined to assets held on trust, but can apply wherever the court considers it appropriate that those seeking to exercise equitable rights over property should be required to recompense those who have spent time and money in realising the fund or identifying the

---

[65] *Re Berkeley Applegate Investment Consultants Ltd (No.3)* (1989) 5 B.C.C. 803, 805D–H. The court rejected the argument that, since each investor was contractually entitled to have the trust administered for free, the entirety of the remuneration and expenses incurred in administering the trusts should be borne by the non-trust assets. The investors were, however, entitled to prove in the liquidation to the extent that their assets had been depleted by bearing such remuneration and expenses. The distinction drawn by Peter Gibson J. between the costs of winding-up and the costs of administration has been criticised in Australia, where it is pointed out that the task of a liquidator in a winding up will necessarily involve identifying which assets are trust assets, and accounting to the beneficiaries for property held on bare trust: *Re GB Nathan & Co Pty Ltd* (1991–1992) 5 A.C.S.R. 673.

[66] *Re Berkeley Applegate (Investment Consultants) Ltd (No.3)* (1989) 5 B.C.C. 803, 806A–807B; see also *Re Eastern Capital Futures Ltd (In Liquidation)* (1989) 5 B.C.C. 223, where the liquidator of a broker in commodity futures, which held client funds and contracts on trust for the clients, was permitted to take his remuneration from trust assets as if they were company assets. The liquidator's remuneration was in that case calculated on the realisation scale under the Insolvency Regulations 1986 (SI 1986/1944), and subject to any contrary agreement of the liquidator and creditors' committee, to be paid proportionately out of the two funds. The contention that the remuneration must always be so calculated was rejected, rightly it is submitted, in *Green (Tranckle's Trustee) v Bramston (Kingshouse Developments Ltd's Liquidator)* [2011] B.P.I.R. 44, [38], where the allowance was based on a reasonable charge for the work carried out, together with all reasonable expenditure.

[67] i.e. in a creditors' voluntary liquidation, Insolvency Act 1986, s.115. See also *Re Mineral Resources Ltd* [1999] B.C.C. 422, 437D–438B.

[68] Insolvency Rules 1986, r.2.106(1).

[69] Insolvency Act 1986, Sch.B1, para.99. To the same effect on the original provisions of the Insolvency Act 1986 applicable to administrators, see *Tom Wise Ltd v Fillimore* [1999] B.C.C. 129, where remuneration for work carried out on the company's affairs, which also benefited the beneficiaries, was not permitted to be charged against the trust assets. In *Polly Peck International Plc (In Administration) v Henry* [1999] 1 B.C.L.C. 407, administrators sought a direction that a new trustee be appointed to the company's pension scheme, and that that trustee be entitled to charge for his services from the pension trust assets, notwithstanding that the pension trust deeds made no provision for the remuneration of trustees. The application was refused, as the administrators themselves were competent to administer the trusts, and the cost of so doing should be borne by the company.

entitlements to it. Thus in *Re Sports Betting Media Ltd*,[70] replacement administrators who had carried out work in identifying the entitlements of expense creditors under the statutory charge under para.99(4) of Sch.B1 of the Insolvency Act 1986 were held entitled to remuneration for their work, notwithstanding the absence of any express right to pay remuneration from the charged assets under the 1986 Act or Rules. In *Townsend v Biscoe*,[71] administrators obtained an order under para.71 of Sch.B1 entitling them to sell property subject to a legal charge as if it were not subject to security, on condition that the "net proceeds" of disposal of the property be paid to the charge holder. The charge holder contended that only estate agents' and solicitors' fees for the actual sale of the property should be deducted from the proceeds accounted for to the charge holder. The court, relying in part on the *Berkeley Applegate* principle, held that all proper costs, charges and expenses incurred in the preservation and realisation of the property, including (it seems) some element of the administrators' remuneration, were properly deductible from the proceeds of sale.

Whilst in *Berkeley Applegate* itself the liquidator's application was not made before considerable costs had been incurred, it is plainly sensible for an insolvency practitioner faced with a situation where work needs to be carried out on assets which are, or may be, held on trust to apply to the court for a direction that he is entitled to charge for future work out of those assets.[72] Otherwise, the practitioner runs the risk of the being out of pocket if the court refuses to exercise its discretion in his favour.[73] **20–030**

If assets are held by a company on trust, or arguably on trust, for third parties, the office-holder might be faced with litigation brought by the claimant beneficiaries, or may initiate such litigation himself. In such a situation, the courts will not generally order that the office-holder's costs and expenses of defending or pursuing such litigation be paid out of the disputed assets in advance of judgment in the litigation, at least if the litigation is hostile.[74] Whilst **20–031**

---

[70] *Re Sports Betting Media Ltd (In Administration)* [2008] B.C.C. 177; see also *Re Trident Fashions Plc* Unreported October 12, 2005, where a pre-emptive order was made in similar circumstances.

[71] Unreported August 10, 2010.

[72] See the closing comments of Edward Nugee QC in *Re Berkeley Applegate (Investment Consultants) Ltd (No.3)* [1989] Ch. 32, 53E. An anticipatory order was made in *Re Telesure Ltd* [1997] B.C.C. 580. Where such an order is made, determination of the quantum of the remuneration, and as to which fund will bear the costs, is typically left for determination at a later date: see the form of order made by the registrar in *Re Telesure Ltd* [1997] B.C.C. 580, 581D–G, subject to comments of Jacob J. thereon at 581H–582B.

[73] Indeed, the failure to apply at an early stage might prejudice the position of the practitioner on the application when eventually made: *Tom Wise Ltd v Fillimore* [1999] B.C.C. 129, 134E–G. A pre-emptive order was also made in favour of the liquidator in *Re Trident Fashions Plc* Unreported October 12, 2005, in respect of his investigations as to the entitlement of expense creditors in preceding administrations of the company to property subject to the statutory charge arising under the Insolvency Act 1986, Sch.B1, para.99(4). The liquidator was further authorised to employ the former administrators to assist in such investigation.

[74] *Re Telesure Ltd* [1997] B.C.C. 580, where the order made by the registrar was limited on appeal so as not to cover the liquidator's costs of hostile litigation against the claimant beneficiaries. Compare *Re Local London Residential Ltd* [2004] 2 B.C.L.C. 72, where Evans-Lombe J. allowed limited access to the proceeds of sale of property claimed beneficially by third parties to allow the liquidator, inter alia, to defend the litigation pursued by those third parties; cf. *Alsop Wilkinson v Neary* [1996] 1 W.L.R. 1220.

the court has jurisdiction to make such a pre-emptive order for costs, it is a different jurisdiction from that exercised in respect of *Berkeley Applegate* orders, and is more sparingly exercised.[75]

20–032   No reported case raises the issue whether a *Berkeley Applegate* order could be made in favour of administrative receivers. A debenture charging the undertaking of the company will not ordinarily cover trust assets. The source of the jurisdiction exercised in *Berkeley Applegate* appears to extend only to trustees or fiduciaries[76]: and whilst an administrative receiver clearly owes fiduciary duties to his appointor, it is doubtful whether such duties are owed to the company or its other creditors generally, even when the receiver acts as agent of the company prior to liquidation. Notwithstanding the status of administrative receiver as "office-holder" under the 1986 Act,[77] and his undoubted duties to unsecured creditors, his primary duty is to his appointor. But it may be that in an appropriate case, where the court can be satisfied that work carried out in respect of trust assets is necessary or beneficial to the beneficiaries, and does not simply form part of work which necessarily falls to the receiver in seeking to realise assets for the benefit of the debenture-holder, an order for payment out of trust assets might be made.

---

[75] In the first instance, the court will need to be satisfied that the office-holder has not been able to raise a fighting fund from creditors. If so satisfied, the factors which the court may take into account are: (i) the merits of the claim; (ii) the likely order for costs at trial; (iii) the justice of the case; and (iv) special factors: see *Re Biddencare Ltd* [1994] 2 B.C.L.C. 160.

[76] See the discussion in *Berkeley Applegate* [1989] Ch. 32, 52B–F, where the deputy judge rejected the argument that the jurisdiction did not exist because a liquidator was a mere fiduciary, and not a trustee. One may query whether the apposite analysis does not relate to the status of the company itself, rather than the office-holder.

[77] See above, Ch.8.

Chapter 21
Retention of Title

"Unsecured creditors rank after ... holders of floating charges and they receive **21–001** a raw deal".[1] An unpaid supplier of goods in an administration or receivership is a mere unsecured creditor for the price and the administrator or receiver can make use of the goods for the benefit of the administration or receivership without paying him. The supplier in turn will often strive to gain priority by means of provisions in the contract of supply which attempt to retain his title to the goods or may insist that he be given a charge in respect of the goods supplied. Section 19(1) of the Sale of Goods Act 1979 expressly acknowledges the possibility of a retention of title condition by providing:

> "Where there is a contract for the sale of specific goods or where goods are subsequently appropriated to the contract, the seller may, by the terms of the contract or appropriation, reserve the right of disposal of the goods until certain conditions are fulfilled; and in such a case, notwithstanding the delivery of the goods to the buyer, or to a carrier or other bailee or custodier for the purpose of transmission to the buyer, the property in the goods does not pass to the buyer until the conditions imposed by the seller are fulfilled."[2]

It has long been recognised that the owner of goods can lease them to a **21–002** company and yet retain legal title so as to gain priority over other creditors. In *McEntire v Crossley Bros Ltd*,[3] the suppliers hired a machine to an individual on the basis that once a number of instalments were paid, title would pass. Meanwhile a plate was to remain affixed to the machine stating that the suppliers were the owners. The House of Lords held that the agreement did not constitute an unregistered charge and title did not pass to the individual's assignee in bankruptcy.

Alternatively, the supplier can attempt to retain the equitable or beneficial **21–003** interest in the goods by means of a trust which would make the company a bare trustee of the property. In that case the trusteeship will be recognised and enforced as long as the property or its proceeds are traceable and unless and

---

[1] per Templeman L.J. in *Borden (UK) Ltd v Scottish Timber Products Ltd* [1981] Ch. 25 (CA).
[2] Where title to goods is successfully retained, and goods are re-possessed by the original vendor pursuant to contractual rights and credit notes are issued in respect of such goods then for VAT purposes amending entries ought to be made for the relevant VAT accounts for the prescribed accounting period within which the original supply fell. Where receivers are appointed this has the effect that the VAT accounting period automatically ends the day before receivership (replacing the normal quarterly VAT period), and a new VAT quarter commences on the day of appointment. See *Brunel Motor Co Ltd v Revenue and Customs Commissioners* [2009] S.T.C. 1146, [2] and [38].
[3] *McEntire v Crossley Bros Ltd* [1895] A.C. 457 (HL).

until the property has been disposed of or charged to a purchaser in good faith for value without notice of the trust.[4] Such an attempt was made in *Re Bond Worth Ltd*[5] where the sellers attempted to retain "equitable and beneficial ownership" of the goods supplied until paid for or resold, but the buyer's complete freedom to deal with the goods in the ordinary course of business was held to be inconsistent with the notion of a trust creating an absolute rather than a security interest and on its true construction the contract was found to create a registrable floating charge.[6]

21–004   As a further alternative the supplier may require the company to grant a charge over the property supplied and/or other assets of the company. In this event the charge will usually only be effective against another creditor or an administrator or the liquidator of the company if registered.[7]

These situations and devices are considered further below.

1.   RETENTION OF LEGAL TITLE

21–005   The most frequent retention of title provision arising in the course of supply of goods on credit provides for the supplier to retain title until payment or other performance of some other obligation by the buyer.[8]

21–006   Whether the supplier retains his legal title under the arrangement with the company depends not only on the language and form but also on the substance of the transaction. The parties' intentions and the label they have placed upon the transaction are a guide, but the real question in each case is the true nature of the substantive rights of the parties. If the substantive rights or their exercise are inconsistent with retention, then there will be no retention of title.[9]

21–007   In *Re Peachdart*[10] the seller supplied leather to the company to be made into handbags. The conditions of sale reserved title to the leather until payment was received in full. The seller argued as part of his case that throughout the process of manufacture the company remained a bailee of the goods. This contention was rejected by Vinelott J.:

---

[4] The receiver who has disposed of the property without notice of the trust is subject to no personal liability: see *Competitive Insurance Company v Davies Investments Ltd* [1975] 1 W.L.R. 1240.

[5] *Re Bond Worth Ltd* [1980] Ch. 228.

[6] This result may be contrasted with the successful attempt to create a trust over goods supplied and their proceeds in the Australian case of *Associated Alloys Pty Ltd v ACN 001 452 106 Pty Ltd* [2000] 202 C.L.R. 588 (High Court of Australia). As discussed below, it is doubtful whether an English court would take the same approach to the issue of the creation of a trust as the majority in the High Court of Australia. The judgment of Kirby J., who dissented on the issue of the creation of a trust, contains a brief but useful summary of the state of the law relating to retention of title clauses in England, Scotland, Ireland, New Zealand, Australia, Canada and the United States.

[7] Companies Act 2006, s.874, and see above, Ch.3.

[8] See generally on ROT clauses *Benjamin's Sale of Goods*, 8th edn (London: Sweet & Maxwell, 2010), para.5–131 ff. See also *Chitty on Contracts*, 30th edn (London: Sweet & Maxwell, 2008), Vol.2, para.43–202 ff.

[9] *Welsh Development Agency v Export Finance Co Ltd* [1992] B.C.C. 270 (CA); *Orion Finance v Crown Financial Management* [1996] B.C.C. 621 (CA), 625–627 per Millett L.J.; and see above, para.3–014. Note *ICS Ltd v West Bromwich B.S.* [1998] 1 W.L.R. 896 (HL), 912F to 913F per Lord Hoffmann.

[10] *Re Peachdart* [1984] Ch. 131.

"It seems to me that the parties must have the intention that at least after a piece of leather had been appropriated to be manufactured into a handbag and work had started on it (when the leather would cease to have any significant value as raw material) the leather would cease to be the exclusive property of [the sellers] … and that [the sellers] would thereafter have a charge on handbags in the course of manufacture and on the distinctive products which would come into existence at the end of the process of manufacture (the value of which would be derived for the most part from [the company's] reputation and skill in design and the skill in his workforce) … that I accept does some violence to the language."[11]

In *Chaigley Farms Ltd v Crawford Kaye & Grayshire Ltd*,[12] the retention of   **21–008**
title clause extended to "livestock" but the object of the contract was the supply of animals for slaughter. The buyer was held to have the authority to slaughter and thereby acquire title to the various parts of the animal.[13] Such authority continued despite the receivership until specifically revoked. Thus, the retention of title may be defeasible if the company is given power to deal with or change the identity of the goods.

2. RETENTION OF BENEFICIAL OWNERSHIP

As with the retention of legal title, the substantive rights of the parties will   **21–009**
decide whether the beneficial ownership is retained. For there to be an effective retention of beneficial ownership there must be a duty imposed to segregate the goods and proceeds and keep them distinct. The court must also be satisfied that the true relationship between the parties is a fiduciary one, rather than merely that of debtor and creditor.

One of the earliest authorities in this area was the *Romalpa* case,[14] where   **21–010**
the relevant clause provided for retention of title until payment of everything due from the company to the seller. The company was obliged (inter alia) to store the goods in such a way as to identify them as the property of the seller. Although there was no provision for keeping the proceeds of resale separate, the Court of Appeal held that the proceeds could be traced by the sellers on the grounds that the various provisions of the retention of title clause replaced the normal debtor/creditor relationship of seller and buyer with a fiduciary relationship. The decision is open to question and the case has frequently been distinguished[15]; it may well have been the concession by the receiver that the company had been a bailee of the goods which was crucial in leading to this

---

[11] *Re Peachdart* [1984] Ch. 131, 142.
[12] *Chaigley Farms Ltd v Crawford Kaye & Grayshire Ltd (t/a Leylands)* [1996] B.C.C. 957.
[13] That result is queried below.
[14] *Aluminium Industrie Vaassen B.V. v Romalpa Aluminium Ltd* [1976] 1 W.L.R. 676 (CA).
[15] See below, para.21–013. In *Specialist Plant Services v Braithwaite* (1987) 3 B.C.C. 119 (CA) the opposite result to that in the *Romalpa* case was achieved by the Court of Appeal despite the use of similar wording in the clause. It is considered that the *Romalpa* case could now be regarded as wrongly decided.

result.[16] Four more recent authorities illustrate with greater clarity the proposition stated at the beginning of this section.

21–011   In *Re Andrabell Ltd*[17] the seller supplied travel bags to the company and reserved title until payment in full. All the bags were sold by the company in the ordinary course of business and the proceeds of sale were paid into the company's ordinary current account. The lack of any obligation to store the goods separately and the lack of any obligation to keep the proceeds of sale separate were important factors in the decision that there was no fiduciary relationship and that the seller had no interest in the proceeds of sale.

21–012   In *Re Shulman Enterprises*[18] the company was a freight forwarder with agency contracts in the IATA common form with various carriers. This form of contract provided that monies received by the company in respect of freight as agent for the carrier belonged to the carrier. The company had also granted a security interest over all its assets to its bankers. The company filed for bankruptcy under Chapter 11 of the US Bankruptcy Code and a dispute arose whether receivables for freight belonged to the carriers or the bank. The United States Court of Appeals for the Second Circuit held that the court was not bound by the terminology of the IATA agreement:

> "where the public interests or the rights of third parties are involved, the relationship between contracting parties must be determined by its real character rather than by the form and colour that the parties have given it."

The absence of any provision requiring the company to segregate receipts of freight from its own monies was an important factor in leading the court to hold that, despite the language used, the relationship was simply that of debtor and creditor, and that the bankers, and not the carriers, were accordingly entitled to the receivables.[19]

21–013   In *E. Pfeiffer Weinkellerei-Weineinkauf GmbH & Co v Arbuthnot Factors Ltd*[20] the claimant, Pfeiffer, supplied wine to *Springfield Wine Importers Ltd*, on terms that Springfield could sell on in business operations carried on in due order, and: "all claims that he gets from the sale or due to another legal reason regarding our goods, with all rights including his profit amounting to his obligations towards us, will be passed on to us".[21] Springfield sub-sold the wine to sub-purchasers on credit terms and then entered into a factoring agreement with Arbuthnot Factors Ltd in relation to the money owed by the sub-purchasers. Pfeiffer argued that the relationship between itself and Springfield was a fiduciary one, and that accordingly it was entitled to the proceeds of the sub-sales as beneficial owner. *Arbuthnot Factors Ltd* argued that any beneficial interest

---

[16] *Re Bond Worth* [1980] Ch. 228, 662.

[17] *Re Andrabell* [1984] 3 All E.R. 407.

[18] *Re Shulman Enterprises*, 744 F. 2d 393 (1983).

[19] Note also *Re Lewis's of Leicester Ltd* [1995] B.C.C. 514 (whether trust created over payments received from concessionaries) and *Re Pinnacle Entertainment Ltd (In Administration)* October 27, 2010 held that a trust was created over monies set aside to pay suppliers who supplied in the twilight period of two weeks up to the appointment of administrators, and see para.20-003, above.

[20] *E. Pfeiffer Weinkellerei-Weineinkauf GmbH & Co v Arbuthnot Factors Ltd* [1988] 1 W.L.R. 150.

[21] See at 610, and see below, para.21-061, for the full clause.

which Pfeiffer had in the proceeds was in the nature of a charge which was void for non-registration. Phillips J. distinguished the *Romalpa* decision and held that the provisions of the retention of title clause were inconsistent with a fiduciary relationship, and that the true relationship between Pfeiffer and Springfield was that of debtor and creditor with Pfeiffer having an interest by way of security in respect of the debts created by the sub-sales. Such a registrable charge was void as against Springfield's creditors for non-registration.[22]

In *Compaq Computer Ltd v Abercorn Group Ltd*[23] Compaq Computer Ltd **21–014** had supplied computer products to Abercorn Group Ltd under a dealership agreement which reserved title until payment of the price of those products and any other sums owing by Abercorn Group Ltd to Compaq Computer Ltd. Abercorn Group Ltd sub-sold these goods, and assigned the proceeds of such sub-sales under an invoice discounting agreement to the second defendant, Kellock. Compaq Computer Ltd argued that Abercorn Group Ltd held the goods as bailee and agent by virtue of the dealership agreement, that Abercorn Group Ltd were under a fiduciary duty to account for these proceeds to Compaq Computer Ltd, and that accordingly Compaq Computer Ltd were entitled to the proceeds of sale. The defendants argued that such rights as were created over the proceeds of sale were a charge on book debts or a floating charge on Abercorn Group Ltd's undertaking or property which was accordingly void for non-registration. Mummery J. held that the true relationship between Compaq Computer Ltd and Abercorn Group Ltd was not a fiduciary relationship.[24]

3. CREATION OF CHARGE

"Any contract which, by way of security for the payment of a debt, confers **21–015** an interest in property defeasible or destructible upon payment of such debt, or appropriates such property for the discharge of the debt, must necessarily be regarded as creating a mortgage or charge".[25]

"I can see nothing in principle to prevent a vendor and a purchaser of specific ascertained chattels from expressly agreeing that the vendor shall have a mortgage or charge over such chattels to secure the payment of the unpaid purchase price, in addition to or in substitution for any lien which might be conferred on him by the Sale of Goods Act".[26]

Where the legal property in the goods remains in or is passed back to the seller a charge will be a legal charge. If, however, the legal property has passed to the company and remains with it, the charge will be equitable.[27]

---

[22] See per Phillips J. at 615–616.

[23] *Compaq Computer Ltd v Abercorn Group Ltd* (t/a Osiris) [1991] B.C.C. 484.

[24] See per Mummery J. at 495; see below, para.21–065.

[25] per Slade J. in *Re Bond Worth* [1980] Ch. 228, 248.

[26] *Re Bond Worth* [1980] Ch. 228, 249.

[27] See para.3–003 above, and the dicta of Atkin L.J. in *National Provincial and Union Bank v Charnley* [1924] 1 K.B. 431 (CA), 449; *Swiss Bank Corp v Lloyds Bank Ltd* [1982] A.C. 584 (HL), 594; and *Re Charge Card Services Ltd* [1987] Ch. 150, 176.

21–016   Where a seller takes a charge from the company over goods sold to it or over the proceeds of resale of such goods, the charge will usually fall within a class requiring registration under s.860 of the Companies Act 2006.[28] A charge over the goods themselves, under which the company remains in possession of the goods, will probably come within the category of charges which if executed by an individual would be registrable as a bill of sale.[29] A charge over future proceeds of sale will be registrable as a charge on book debts and/or as a floating charge.[30]

21–017   If such a charge requires registration but is not registered, the company itself remains bound by the charge[31] but the charge is void as against a liquidator, administrator or creditor of the company.[32]

4. LOSS OF TITLE

21–018   Even where title is successfully retained as against a company, including its administrator or receiver, title may still be lost to third parties under certain rules of law applying in favour of purchasers in good faith in the interests of commerce. The most frequently encountered of such rules are encapsulated in ss.21 and 25 of the Sale of Goods Act 1979. In the case of each section, for the retained title of the seller to be lost to a third party purchaser, there must have been a sub-sale which purportedly passed title in the property from the original buyer to the third party purchaser.[33] It is not enough if there is merely an agreement to sell, and in this respect it should be noted that a sub-sale which is itself governed by a retention of title clause is merely an agreement to sell and not a sale.[34] Title can also be lost when goods supplied are incorporated into the goods of another or made into new goods during a manufacturing process. These possibilities are examined below.

(a) Buyer in possession

21–019   Section 25 of the Sale of Goods Act 1979 provides:

---

[28] *Tatung v Galex Telesure Ltd* (1989) 5 B.C.C. 325. The reasoning of the decision was approved in *Re Weldtech Equipment Ltd* [1991] B.C.C. 16.

[29] Companies Act 2006, s.860(7)(b).

[30] Companies Act 2006, s.860(7)(f) or (g); *Re Armagh Shoes* [1984] B.C.L.C. 405 (Northern Ireland, per Hutton J.); *Re Bond Worth* [1980] Ch. 228; *Re Brightlife Ltd* [1987] Ch. 200; *Royal Trust Bank v National Westminster Bank* [1996] B.C.C. 613, 618, 619, per Millett L.J. cf. *Re Spectrum Plus Ltd (In Liquidation)* [2005] 2 A.C. 680 (HL), where the debenture was expressed to grant the bank a fixed charge over book debts, but where the House of Lords decided that on its proper construction the debenture created a floating charge instead (which did not have priority over the claims of preferential creditors).

[31] At least whilst it is a going concern: see *Re Monolithic Building Co* [1915] 1 Ch. 643 (CA). See also *Mace Builders (Glasgow) Ltd v Lunn* [1986] Ch 459.

[32] Companies Act 2006, s.874.

[33] See *Shaw v Commissioner of Police* [1987] 1 W.L.R. 1332 (CA), especially at 1337 per Lloyd L.J.

[34] *Re Highway Foods International Ltd* [1995] B.C.C. 271; *P4 Ltd v Integrated Solutions Plc* [2006] B.L.R. 150.

"Where a person having bought or agreed to buy goods obtains, with the consent of the seller, possession of the goods or the documents of title to the goods, the delivery or transfer by that person, or by a mercantile agent acting for him, of the goods or documents of title, under any sale, pledge, or other disposition thereof, to any person receiving the same in good faith and without notice of any lien or other right of the original seller in respect of the goods, has the same effect as if the person making the delivery or transfer were a mercantile agent in possession of the goods or documents of title with the consent of the owner."

In *Archivent Sales & Developments Ltd v Strathclyde*[35] the sellers agreed to **21–020** sell goods to the company for incorporation into a building upon which the company was working as a contractor. The sellers retained title to the goods. The goods were delivered to site and were included in an interim certificate, which was paid by the employers. The company never paid the sellers and went into receivership. The sellers sued the employers, claiming title to the goods. The sellers argued that the employers were not protected by the predecessor to s.25 of the Sale of Goods Act 1979 because the buyer company had never been in possession of the goods, since they passed directly into the control of the employers and because there was no delivery by the company to the employer. The Scottish Court of Session held that the employer's control did not preclude possession on the part of the company. Moreover, delivery to the employer by the company was established by evidence that the goods had been measured by the employer's surveyor and not rejected. Accordingly, the seller had lost title to the goods and title had been acquired by the employer.

In *Four Point Garage Ltd v Carter*[36] a customer agreed to buy a particular **21–021** make and model of car from a dealer company. The dealer bought such a car from another dealer and arranged delivery direct to the customer. The other dealer retained title to the car. The customer's dealer went into liquidation having failed to pay for the car. Simon Brown J. held, inter alia, that title passed to the customer under s.25 of the Sale of Goods Act 1979 since no distinction could be drawn between, on the one hand, a delivery to a buyer who then delivers to a sub-buyer and, on the other hand, a direct delivery by a seller to a sub-buyer. The direct delivery constituted constructive delivery to the buyer and constructive delivery by the buyer to the sub-buyer.

(b) Apparent authority

Section 21 of the Sale of Goods Act 1979 provides in so far as material, that: **21–022**

"where goods are sold by a person who is not their owner, and who does not sell them under the authority or with the consent of the owner, the buyer acquires no better title to the goods than the seller had, unless the

---

[35] *Archivent Sales & Developments Ltd v Strathclyde* (1985) 27 B.L.R. 98 (Court of Session, Outer House).
[36] *Four Point Garage Ltd v Carter* [1985] 3 All E.R. 12.

owner of the goods is by his conduct precluded from denying the seller's authority to sell."

In many cases, retention of title provisions expressly or impliedly authorise a resale and therefore the sale takes place with the authority or consent of the owner.[37] Where, however, resale is not permitted or is only permitted in circumstances not observed by the company, the question arises whether the seller is estopped by his conduct from claiming title as against the third party purchaser. The answer depends on whether the seller has "invested the person dealing with them with the indicia of property"[38] so as to estop the seller from asserting his claim to title.

(c) Accessio and specificatio

21–023   A seller who has successfully reserved title can nevertheless lose it in certain circumstances where the goods are incorporated into the goods of another or made into a new object altogether.

21–024   In order to clarify this subject it is useful to look briefly to a system of law which has developed detailed principles, i.e. Roman law. The basic concepts are: (a) accessio, the incorporation of an accessory belonging to A into a principal object belonging to B, whereby the accessory adheres to the principal, e.g. a handle to a cup; and (b) specificatio, the creation of a new product by A from the materials of B or of B and C, e.g. where grapes and sugar are made into wine.

21–025   The first question in either Roman or English law appears to be whether there is any effective contractual provision governing the ownership of the accessory or the new product as the case may be. Thus, Robert Goff L.J. in the *Clough Mill* case[39] stated that it was open to the parties to a sale contract to agree that a new product would belong to the seller.[40] Subject to established rules relating to charges, penalties, forfeiture, etc, there appears to be no reason why the parties cannot freely contract as to ownership in such cases. Such a contract will require careful drafting. In *Specialist Plant Services Ltd v Braithwaite Ltd*[41] goods were supplied to the defendant on terms that:

> "[if] the said goods and materials or any part thereof supplied hereunder in any way whatsoever become a constituent of another article or other articles the Company shall be given the ownership of this (these) new article(s) as surety for the full payment of what the customer owes the Company. To this end the Company and the customer now agree that

---

[37] For implied authorisation, see *Aluminium Industrie Vaassen BV v Romalpa Aluminium Ltd* [1976] 1 W.L.R. 676 (CA), 689; *Re Bond Worth* [1980] Ch. 228, 246; and *Four Point Garage v Carter* [1985] 3 All E.R. 12, 16, per Simon Brown J.

[38] per Lord Halsbury in *Henderson v Williams* [1895] 1 Q.B. 521 (CA), 525.

[39] *Clough Mill v Martin* [1985] 1 W.L.R. 111 (CA).

[40] At 119H.

[41] *Specialist Plant Services Ltd v Braithwaite Ltd* (1987) 3 B.C.C. 119 (CA).

the ownership of the article(s) in question, whether finished or not, are to
be transferred to the Company".[42]

The company applied for an injunction to prevent the receiver from selling **21–026**
machines into which had been incorporated parts which it had supplied. The
Court of Appeal held that the retention of title clause created a charge by way
of security over the machines which was void for non-registration, and
accordingly there was no basis for the granting of the injunction.[43]

In the absence of agreement, the Roman law rules were in summary as **21–027**
follows: if the goods of A and B were mixed so that they were readily sepa-
rable, no change of ownership took place,[44] unless the goods of A. could be
seen as an accessory of the goods of B (e.g. a handle and pan where the handle
is attached by a screw). In that case the identity of the accessory merged with
that of the principal and A lost his ownership. There were rules providing
compensation for A.[45] Where A's materials were used to make a new object,
one view was that the new object belonged to the owner of the materials.
Another view held that it belonged to the maker. Justinian effected a compromise solution whereby the new object belonged to its maker if not reducible
to its original form but otherwise remained in the ownership of the owner of
the materials.[46]

In English law, by contrast, the fact that A's goods have become accessory to **21–028**
B's is immaterial if separation can take place without damage to the principal
item: A retains his ownership.[47] If separation would involve such damage, A's
ownership is lost by accession.[48] In the case of the creation of a new object, the
Borden case[49] shows that where the new object is not reducible to its original
form, the supplier of the material loses his ownership and prima facie the
buyer/maker acquires title. This suggests that in this respect English law
follows the Justinianic compromise. Where the skill and labour expended on
the materials becomes a major component of value, English law will tend to
imply an intention for title to vest in the maker.[50]

In *Chaigley Farms Ltd v Crawford Kaye & Grayshire Ltd*,[51] it was held that **21–029**
title was lost to animals upon slaughter, apparently (or at least partly) because
the meat, having been separated from the hide, bone, blood, etc. was a new
object. It is respectfully doubted whether meat is a new object. The actual

---

[42] *Specialist Plant Services Ltd v Braithwaite Ltd* (1987) 3 B.C.C. 119 (CA), 120.
[43] See per Balcombe L.J. at 123.
[44] This was "confusio": see the discussion in *Foskett v McKeown* [2001] 1 A.C. 102 (HL), per
Lord Hoffmann, 115F–G, per Lord Hope (dissenting), 121A–E, per Lord Millett, 141.
[45] See Buckland, *Textbook of Roman Law*, 3rd edn (Cambridge University Press, 1963),
pp.210–211.
[46] Buckland, *Textbook of Roman Law*, 3rd edn (Cambridge University Press, 1963), p.215.
[47] *Hendy Lennox (Industrial Engines) v Grahame Puttick* [1984] 1 W.L.R. 485. The summary
of what this case decides in *Chaigley Farms Ltd v Crawford, Kaye & Grayshire Ltd (t/a Leylands)*
[1996] B.C.C. 957, 961D appears to confuse the English and Roman law tests.
[48] *Appleby v Myers* (1867) L.R. 2 C.P. 651, 659–660, per Blackburn J.
[49] *Borden (UK) Ltd v Scottish Timber Products Ltd* [1981] Ch. 25 (CA).
[50] *Re Peachdart Ltd* [1984] Ch. 131.
[51] *Chaigley Farms Ltd v Crawford Kaye & Grayshire Ltd (t/a Leylands)* [1996] B.C.C. 957.

result in the case could perhaps be justified on the basis that the intention of the parties on the facts of that case was limited to the seller retaining title in "livestock", which term in the context did not include slaughtered animals or the parts into which such animals were to be divided, such as hide, bones, blood, meat, etc.[52]

21–030   If a party wrongfully mixes goods belonging to another with his own goods of substantially the same nature and quality (e.g. oil), and they cannot be separated for practical purposes, the mixture is held in common by both parties such that the innocent party is entitled to receive from the mixture a quantity equal to that of his goods which went into the mixture.[53] If there is doubt as to either the quantity or quality of the mixture, the matter should be resolved in the innocent party's favour and he is entitled to claim damages from the wrongdoer for losses suffered, in respect of quality or otherwise, as a result of the admixture.[54]

21–031   Where materials are incorporated into real property so as to become part of the real property, title passes by operation of law to the owner of the land irrespective of any retention of title clause.[55] This outcome is dependent upon fulfillment of the necessary criteria for transformation of a chattel into a fixture. Whether an item remains a chattel or becomes part of the land depends on the degree and purpose of the annexation, with emphasis on the purpose.[56] If the attachment is temporary, in order that the item can be used for its own sake, it will remain a chattel.[57] But if the attachment is permanent and for the better enjoyment of the land, it will be a fixture.[58] If a piece of machinery has become part of the land, then the same applies to its component parts, even if they are individually capable of removal.[59] Similarly, a lift or an escalator is likely to be

---

[52] See *Chaigley Farms Ltd v Crawford Kaye & Grayshire Ltd (t/a Leylands)* [1996] B.C.C. 957, 963.

[53] cf. *Re CKE Engineering Ltd (In Administration)* [2007] B.C.C. 975, where the court considered the ownership of zinc which had been mixed and melted in a galvanising tank, and held that in determining the proprietary interests in the zinc, it was an established principle that where the chattels of two persons were intermixed by agreement so that the several portions could no longer be distinguished, the proprietors had an interest in common in proportion to their respective shares, and if there was a diversity in quality in the intermixed substances the whole should be divided and the greater allowance made to the owner whose substance was better or finer than that of the other. See also *Mercer v Craven Grain Storage Ltd* [1994] C.L.C. 328 (HL) where it was held that grain suppliers who held their grain at a depot continued to own the grain despite lawful mixing of the grain and despite each owner's grain being indistinguishable from the grain of others.

[54] *Indian Oil Corporation Ltd v Greenstone Shipping SA (Panama) (The Ypatianna)* [1988] Q.B. 345, per Staughton J. See also *Mercer v Craven Grain Storage Ltd* [1994] C.L.C. 328 (HL), 329E–G (storers of grain were not entitled to question the title of depositors of the grain because the storers were only bailees). See also the discussion in *Foskett v McKeown* [2001] 1 A.C. 102 (HL), 141, per Lord Millett.

[55] See further below, Ch.25, at para.25–025 et seq.

[56] *Holland v Hodgson* (1872) L.R. 7 C.P. 328, cited with approval in *Elitestone Ltd v Morris* [1997] 1 W.L.R. 687 (HL) which distinguished between a chattel, a fixture and an object which becomes part of the land. *Berkeley v Poulett* [1977] 1 E.G.L.R. 86 (CA).

[57] e.g. *Blower and Sedens v Workers' Compensation Board* (1983) 50 A.R. 66, affirmed 68 A.R. 156 (Alberta CA) (two-ton crane sitting on track bolted to floor remained a chattel).

[58] e.g. *Belgrave Nominees Pty Ltd v Barling-Scott Airconditiong (Aust.) Pty Ltd* [1984] V.R. 947 (Sup Court of Victoria) (air-conditioning plant installed on the roof of a building was a fixture).

[59] *Sheffield and South Yorkshire Permanent Benefit Society v Harrison* (1884–85) L.R. 15 Q.B.D. 358 (CA).

a fixture even if intended to be replaced during the life of the building. The attachment is not temporary in that they are designed to remain in situ until replaced, and their purpose is for the benefit of the building rather than the enjoyment of the equipment in itself.

(i) Tenant's fixtures

Where the annexation is by a tenant for the purpose of his trade, the items in question remain the property of the tenant if capable of removal "without losing their essential character"[60] or their "essential utility or value"[61] or without causing "irreparable damage"[62] to the freehold.[63] At the end of the tenancy, the tenant is entitled as against the landlord to sever and remove such items, restoring them to the character of chattels.[64] It does not matter whether the chattels originally affixed belonged to the tenant or were hired to him by a third party.[65] **21–032**

(ii) Mortgagees

Once a chattel has become a fixture, it will vest in a mortgagee of the land, whether the annexation occurs before or after the mortgage,[66] and the mortgagor loses any right to remove it.[67] Incorporation will normally override any retention of title clause in the supplier's terms and conditions.[68] If the items were supplied on terms that the supplier could enter and repossess them, e.g. if instalments under a hire-purchase agreement were not paid, the supplier would have an equitable interest in the nature of a right of entry which would bind and have priority over the rights of any subsequent mortgagee apart from a legal mortgagee without notice of the supplier's right.[69] The rights of a prior mortgagee would not be affected unless he had granted an implied licence to the mortgagor to enter into such a contract and consented to allow the supplier to **21–033**

---

[60] *Young v Dalgety Plc* [1987] 1 E.G.L.R. 116 (CA), 119.

[61] *Webb v Frank Bevis* [1940] 1 All E.R. 247.

[62] *Young v Dalgety Plc* [1987] 1 E.G.L.R. 116 (CA); *Spyer v Phillipson* [1931] 2 Ch. 183 (CA), 209–210.

[63] *New Zealand Government Property Corporation v H.M. & S. Ltd* [1982] Q.B. 1145 (CA).

[64] *Bain v Brand* (1876) L.R. 1 App. Cas. 762 (HL), 772; *Hobson v Gorringe* [1897] 1 Ch. 182 (CA), 192; *New Zealand Government Property Corporation v H.M. & S. Ltd* [1982] Q.B. 1145 (CA).

[65] See the vases referred to in the previous note and *Re Galway Concrete Ltd* [1983] I.L.R.M. 402. A contract to sell the right to enter and remove tenants' fixtures did not require to be evidenced in writing under s.4 of the Statute of Frauds (see *Hallen v Runder* (1834) 1 C.M. & R. 266; *Lee v Gaskell* (1876) L.R. 1 Q.B.D. 700) and accordingly does not fall within the requirement of s.2 of the Law of Property (Miscellaneous Provisions) Act 1989 that a contract for the sale of interests in land should be in writing.

[66] *Reynolds v Ashby & Son* [1904] A.C. 466 (HL), 473 per Lord Lindley.

[67] *Gough v Wood* [1894] 1 Q.B. 713 (CA), 718 per Lindley L.J

[68] *Re Yorkshire Joinery Co Ltd* (1967) 111 S.J. 701.

[69] *Re Morrison, Jones & Taylor Ltd* [1914] 1 Ch. 50 (CA), 58. It is suggested that an alternative (and preferable) analysis would be that the hirer had a legal interest, namely a "licence couple with an interest": cf. *Hounslow LBC v Twickenham Garden Development Ltd* [1971] Ch. 233, 254, and *Megarry and Wade: The Law of Real Property*, 7th edn (London: Sweet & Maxwell, 2008), para.34–005 ff.

sever and remove its chattels at any time before, but not after, the mortgagee
entered into possession.[70]

5.   INCORPORATION OF THE RETENTION OF TITLE CLAUSE INTO THE CONTRACT

21–034   In order to discover whether title has been retained, one must first determine
whether the retention of title clause has been incorporated in the contract
between the seller and the company.

21–035   The clearest case of incorporation arises where the company has by some duly
authorised agent signed a contractual document incorporating a retention of title
clause into the relevant contract or contracts of sale. The signature will be effective even if the document is not read and even if it is in "regrettably small print".[71]
A misrepresentation, however, about the effect of the clause will prevent it being
incorporated, even by means of a signed document.[72] Lack of authority on the
part of the signatory may also be a defence, subject to the question of implied or
ostensible authority. The signatory will be held to be impliedly authorised to sign
the document if it is of a kind which is within the usual scope of a person in his
position with the company.[73] He will be held to have ostensible authority if he
was held out by the company as having authority to sign documents of that
kind.[74] Other contractual defences also apply and thus the receiver will want to
ascertain the circumstances in which any such document was executed.

21–036   In the absence of any signed document the seller must prove that the
company was aware or ought to have been aware of the retention of title
clause.[75] Another way of putting this is that the seller must have given reasonable notice of the clause.[76] The notice will prima facie not be sufficient if it is
contained in a non-contractual document[77] or in a post-contractual document.[78]
Thus, one might have thought that retention of title clauses contained in such
post-contractual documents as invoices and delivery notes will be ineffective.
However, the seller may have an argument based on a "course of dealing". This
appears to mean that if there has been a course of transactions where post-
contractual notice of the clause has been given, the company may be bound
even though its agent or officer has not read the clause.[79] The rationale appears

---

[70] *Gough v Wood* [1894] 1 Q.B. 713 (CA), 720; *Ellis v Glover & Hobson Ltd* [1908] 1 K.B. 388
(CA), 397.
[71] *L'Estrange v F Graucob* [1934] 2 K.B. 394.
[72] *Curtis v Chemical Cleaning Co* [1951] 1 K.B. 805 (CA).
[73] *Hely-Hutchinson v Brayhead* [1968] 1 Q.B. 549 (CA).
[74] *Freeman & Lockyer v Buckhurst Park Properties* [1964] 2 Q.B. 480 (CA), 503, per Diplock
L.J.; and see the very clear exposition in *British Bank of the Middle East v Sun Life Assurance Co
of Canada (UK) Ltd* [1983] 2 Lloyd's Rep. 9 (HL).
[75] per Scrutton L.J. in *L'Estrange v F Graucob* [1934] 2 K.B. 394, 403.
[76] *Parker v SE. Ry.* (1877) L.R. 2 C.P.D. 416 (CA).
[77] *Chapelton v Barry UDC* [1940] 1 K.B. 532 (CA); *McCutcheon v David MacBrayne Ltd*
[1964] 1 W.L.R. 125 (HL); *Burnett v Westminster Bank* [1966] 1 Q.B. 742.
[78] *Olley v Marlborough Court* [1949] 1 K.B. 532 (CA); *Chapelton v Barry UDC* [1940] 1 K.B.
532 (CA).
[79] *Spurling v Bradshaw* [1956] 1 W.L.R. 461 (CA); *Snow v Woodcroft* [1985] B.C.L.C. 54; cf.
British Crane Hire v Ipswich Plant Hire [1975] Q.B. 303 (CA).

to be that the post-contractual notice is reasonable notice for the purposes of incorporation in future contracts.

There may be a difference in the degree of notice required to incorporate a   **21–037** clause that might be regarded as an "unusual" type of retention of title clause as opposed to a "usual" one.[80] An allegation by a receiver that a clause is an "unusual" one and therefore needs some special degree of notice to be incorporated may require to be proved by evidence. In the *Robert Horne* case[81] the "unusual" nature of the clause was conceded. In the *John Snow* case[82] Boreham J. decided the clause was "not so unusual" in the absence of evidence to show that it was unusual.

There may also be an incorporation problem where the seller and the   **21–038** company have used different forms with inconsistent terms. A provision in one set of terms stating that it overrides any terms put forward by the other party does not decide this conflict.[83] The correct analysis appears to be the traditional one of offer and acceptance.[84] Where the offer incorporates one set of terms and the acceptance incorporates an inconsistent set of terms, the acceptance amounts to a counter-offer.[85] The question then is whether the counter-offer is accepted, otherwise there is no consensus at all.[86]

6.   EFFECT OF DIFFERENT TYPES OF RETENTION OF TITLE CLAUSE

(a)   Introduction

"There has been a spate of decisions in recent years concerning these   **21–039** so-called Romalpa cases. But it is of great importance to bear in mind that these cases have been concerned with different clauses, very often in materially different terms."[87]

The types of retention of title clause commonly in use divide up between the "simple" type of clause where only title to the goods sold is attempted to be retained and the "complex" type of clause which attempts to create rights over proceeds of resale or hire. "Simple" and "complex" clauses are often combined in a series of clauses or sub-clauses. A distinction may also have to be drawn between "fixed" retentions, where title is retained only until the particular goods in question are paid for, and "floating" retentions, which provide for title

---

[80] *Robert Horne Paper Co Ltd v Rioprint Ltd* Unreported November 10, 1978; *John Snow & Co v Woodcroft* [1985] B.C.L.C. 54.

[81] *Robert Horne Paper Co Ltd v Rioprint Ltd* Unreported November 10, 1978.

[82] *John Snow & Co v Woodcroft* [1985] B.C.L.C. 54.

[83] *Butler Machine Tool Co v Ex-Cell-o-Corp* [1979] 1 W.L.R. 401 (CA), 402.

[84] *Butler Machine Tool Co v Ex-Cell-o-Corp* [1979] 1 W.L.R. 401 (CA) per Lawton and Bridge L.JJ.

[85] *Butler Machine Tool Co v Ex-Cell-o-Corp* [1979] 1 W.L.R. 401 (CA) per Lawton and Bridge L.JJ.

[86] *Butler Machine Tool Co v Ex-Cell-o-Corp* [1979] 1 W.L.R. 401 (CA) per Lawton and Bridge L.JJ.

[87] *Clough Mill v Martin* [1985] 1 W.L.R. 111 (CA), per Goff L.J.

to remain in the seller until, e.g. all sums due from the buyer company to the seller have been discharged.

(b) Simple retention of title

21–040 Section 2 of the Sale of Goods Act 1979 defines a contract for the sale of goods as one "by which the seller transfers or agrees to transfer the property in goods to the buyer". Section 16 provides that in the case of a sale of unascertained goods no property in the goods is transferred unless and until the goods are ascertained. Section 17 provides that in the case of specific or ascertained goods property passes when the parties intend. Such intention is to be ascertained by looking to the terms of the contract, the parties' conduct and the circumstances of the case.

21–041 Section 18 of the Sale of Goods Act 1979 sets out detailed rules for ascertaining the presumed intention of the parties in relation to the passing of property if a different intention does not appear from the agreement. Generally speaking, in such cases property passes upon delivery.

21–042 Where goods have not been paid for, the seller has certain limited statutory rights, e.g. a lien whilst he remains in possession, and a right of stoppage in transit.[88] Once the seller has parted with possession and the property in the goods, he normally has no satisfactory statutory remedy if the buyer becomes insolvent and defaults, even if the buyer still has possession of the goods.

21–043 Where the buyer goes into administration or receivership, goods supplied by an unpaid seller in which the property has passed to the buyer are caught by the usual floating charge on stock, etc. In order to avoid this, a seller can attempt to insert into the contract of sale a clause whereby property in goods sold is not to pass unless and until it has been paid for. If effectively incorporated into the contract, there is no doubt that such a clause will be valid and effective to preserve the seller's rights to the goods against a debenture-holder.[89]

(c) Floating retention

21–044 The simple retention of title clause referred to above suffers from certain drawbacks. Often it is not easy to identify whether the particular goods held by a buyer going into administration or receivership have been paid for. It may well happen that the goods still held by the buyer have been paid for but the buyer owes money to the seller for goods which have been resold. A common solution is to provide that property in goods is not to pass until all goods supplied have been paid for. In that case, as long as there remains a sum due to the seller, any goods supplied by the seller and held by the buyer when it goes into administration or receivership will be covered by the retention of title clause.

21–045 Whilst under the Sale of Goods Act 1979 the parties to a contract are free to decide when property passes, the creation of such a floating retention might at

---

[88] See Sale of Goods Act 1979, Pt V.
[89] *Clough Mill v Martin* [1985] 1 W.L.R. 111 (CA).

first sight appear to offend against the statutory principle that notice should be given of floating charges by registration.[90] However, see para.23-049 below.

In the *Romalpa* case,[91] the contract provided that property was only to pass **21-046** once the buyer had paid all that was due to the seller. At first instance, the seller's right to recover goods held by the buyer's receiver was "admitted".[92] It was also admitted that the retention of title clause had made the buyer a bailee for the seller in respect of the goods.[93] In these circumstances, it could hardly have been argued that the floating retention amounted to a floating charge.[94]

In *Snow v Woodcroft*,[95] the contract again provided for property to pass only **21-047** when the buyer had met all indebtedness to the seller. The concessions made in the *Romalpa* case were not repeated. Nevertheless, Boreham J. cited the *Romalpa* case as authority for the validity of a clause providing for retention of title "until the buyer has discharged the whole of his indebtedness to the seller".[96]

It can be argued from the first instance decision in Romalpa[97] and from the **21-048** Court of Appeal's decision in *Clough Mill v Martin*[98] that floating retention cannot fall within s.860 of the Companies Act 2006 because any charge would not be "created by" the buyer company. But such an argument assumes the very thing to be proved, i.e. it assumes that as a matter of construction of the contract the clause can and does operate as a valid and effective floating retention of title as opposed to a transfer of title subject to a floating charge.[99] Although the Court of Appeal decision in *Clough Mill v Martin*[100] dealt with a simple form of clause, the dicta in the case tended to suggest that a floating retention would not be construed to be a floating charge. Thus, for example, Goff L.J. specifically considered the application of the retention of title clause in that case to situations where the seller claimed title to partly-paid goods and, whilst accepting that the effect of the retention of title clause was very similar to that of a charge, he held that the clause did not create a charge.[101]

In *Armour v Thyssen Edelstahlwerke AG*[102] a German company, Thyssen **21-049** Edelstahlwerke AG, supplied steel strips to Carron Company Ltd, a Scottish company, on terms that "all goods delivered by us remain our property (goods remaining in our ownership) until all debts owed to us including any balances

---

[90] See Companies Act 2006, ss.860.

[91] *Aluminium Industrie Vaassen B.V. v Romalpa Aluminium Ltd* [1976] 1 W.L.R. 676 (CA).

[92] *Aluminium Industrie Vaassen B.V. v Romalpa Aluminium Ltd* [1976] 1 W.L.R. 676 (CA), 780D–780E.

[93] *Aluminium Industrie Vaassen B.V. v Romalpa Aluminium Ltd* [1976] 1 W.L.R. 676 (CA), 680H.

[94] See per Goff L.J. in *Clough Mill v Martin* [1985] 1 W.L.R. 111 (CA), 114H.

[95] *Snow v Woodcroft* [1985] B.C.L.C. 54.

[96] *Snow v Woodcroft* [1985] B.C.L.C. 54, 62F–62G.

[97] *Aluminium Industrie Vaassen B.V. v Romalpa Aluminium Ltd* [1976] 1 W.L.R. 676 (CA), per Mocatta J.

[98] *Clough Mill v Martin* [1985] 1 W.L.R. 111 (CA), 119D, 121, 122–124, 125.

[99] cf. the converse point made by Oliver L.J. in *Clough Mill v Martin* [1985] 1 W.L.R. 111 (CA), 123.

[100] *Clough Mill v Martin* [1985] 1 W.L.R. 111 (CA).

[101] *Clough Mill v Martin* [1985] 1 W.L.R. 111 (CA), 120–121. See also William Goodhart QC's note on *Clough Mill* (1986) 49 M.L.R. 96.

[102] *Armour v Thyssen Edelstahlwerke AG* [1991] 2 A.C. 339 (HL).

existing at relevant times … are settled."[103] Receivers were appointed to Carron Company Ltd. The Scottish Outer House and, on appeal, the Inner House of the Court of Session held that the clause constituted an attempt, ineffective under the law of Scotland, to create a right of security over corporeal moveables without transfer of possession and that title to the steel strip had passed to Carron Company Ltd on delivery and thus formed part of the general assets of the company available to creditors. The House of Lords, after citing ss.17 and 19 of the Sale of Goods Act 1979, held that the parties in the contract of sale clearly expressed their intention that the property in the steel strips should not pass to Carron Company Ltd until all debts due by it to *Thyssen Edelstahlwerke AG* had been paid, and Lord Keith could see no grounds for refusing to give effect to that intention.[104] He commented:

"I am, however, unable to regard a provision reserving title to the seller until payment of all debts due to him by the buyer as amounting to the creation by the buyer of a right of security in favour of the seller. Such a provision does in a sense give the seller security for the unpaid debts of the buyer. But it does so by way of a legitimate retention of title, not by virtue of any right over his own property conferred by the buyer."[105]

It therefore appears now to be settled at the highest level that a "floating retention" does not of itself constitute a floating or indeed any other charge.

21–050   If goods are sold subject to a retention of title clause[106] and the purchaser then on-sells and delivers the goods to a sub-purchaser also subject to a retention of title clause, then the original seller will retain title to the goods in the hands of the sub-purchaser unless and until the sub-purchaser pays the purchaser the price of the goods.[107]

(d) Claims to proceeds of sale

21–051   In practice, where the proceeds of resale have been received prior to administration or receivership, they will often have disappeared into an overdrawn bank account. On the other hand, claims to tracing may arise where the proceeds of resale have not yet been received or where they have been kept in a traceable form.

21–052   Where the retention of title clause makes no express provision with regard to the proceeds of resale but simply reserves title to the goods, the first question that arises is whether the buyer had any right of resale prior to going into administration or receivership. In the *Romalpa* case,[108] the Court of Appeal mentioned with apparent approval the agreement between the parties that a

---

[103] *Armour v Thyssen Edelstahlwerke AG* [1991] 2 A.C. 339 (HL), 926c.
[104] See per Lord Keith at 928f.
[105] See per Lord Keith at 929a.
[106] cf. para.21–070 below.
[107] *Re Highway Foods International* [1995] B.C.C. 271.
[108] *Aluminium Industrie Vaassen B.V. v Romalpa Aluminium Ltd* [1976] 1 W.L.R. 676 (CA).

term was to be implied permitting resale whilst the price of the goods remained unpaid.[109] The argument turned upon whether the term to be implied was a right to resell on the buyer's own account or on behalf of the seller. The Court of Appeal found that the normal creditor/debtor relationship had been replaced as a result of the special provisions in the contract in that case by a fiduciary relationship, which meant that resales were made on behalf of the seller. This suggests that in the case of a simple retention provision the ordinary debtor/creditor relationship would persist and an implied term would, in so far as it permitted resale, permit it on the buyer's own account, so that the proceeds became the property of the buyer. This was precisely the effect of the decision in *Re Andrabell Ltd*[110] In that case, there was a simple form of clause and credit was given for a fixed period rather than terminating with resale. This suggested that the proceeds of sale could be dealt with as the buyer thought fit and negatived any fiduciary relationship. In the absence of such a relationship the seller had no interest in the proceeds of sale. It was also held that, in the case of a clause setting out detailed provisions for payment, a term imposing an obligation to account would not be implied since it was not necessary to give business efficacy to the agreement.

A similar position arises in the case of goods supplied for incorporation into   **21–053**
some larger product or for manufacture into a new product. In *Hendy Lennox Industrial Engines Ltd v Grahame Puttick Ltd*[111] a clause in a sale of engines to be incorporated into generating sets which simply reserved title and permitted retaking in the event of default was held not to give rise to a fiduciary relationship in relation to the proceeds of resale. In *Borden (UK) Ltd v Scottish Timber*[112] a simple retention of title clause relating to the sale of resin to be made into chipboard was held not to give rise to a fiduciary relationship and the buyers were held entitled to use the goods for manufacture in such a way that the manufactured products became the property of the buyer. It was further held that a tracing right extending to the manufactured products would constitute a floating charge. In an administration or in a liquidation such a floating charge would be void unless registered.[113]

The greatest difficulty arises where express provision is made in a complex   **21–054**
form of clause in relation to proceeds of resales. We have already seen that in the *Romalpa* case[114] the clause was held to give rise to a fiduciary relationship and it was held that the proceeds of resale could be traced. The question arises whether a clause simply following the *Romalpa* model would today be effective.

In the *Borden* case,[115] Bridge L.J. described that type of clause as "presum-   **21–055**
ably effective". Other subsequent judicial pronouncements on the decision in

---

[109] At 684C, 693B–693C, 693H; see also *Four Point Garage Ltd v Carter* [1985] 3 All E.R. 12.
[110] *Re Andrabell Ltd* [1984] 3 All E.R. 407, per Peter Gibson J.
[111] *Hendy Lennox (Industrial Engines) Ltd v Grahame Puttick Ltd* [1984] 1 W.L.R. 485, per Staughton J.
[112] *Borden (UK) Ltd v Scottish Timber Products Ltd* [1981] Ch. 25 (CA).
[113] Companies Act 2006, ss.860, 874.
[114] *Aluminium Industrie Vaassen B.V. v Romalpa Aluminium Ltd* [1976] 1 W.L.R. 676 (CA).
[115] *Borden (UK) Ltd v Scottish Timber Products Ltd* [1981] Ch. 25 (CA).

the *Romalpa* case suggest that it might not today be decided in the same way. In the *Bond Worth* case,[116] Slade J. regarded as "a concession of crucial importance" the admission that the retention of title clause had made the buyers bailees of the goods. In the *Borden* case,[117] Bridge L.J. regarded the "bailee" concession as a clearly distinguishing feature in the *Romalpa* case. Templeman L.J. in the *Borden* case[118] cited a comment by Roskill L.J. in the *Romalpa* case where, in refusing leave to appeal, he stated that the *Romalpa* decision "could not govern any other case". In *Clough Mill v Martin*[119] Goff L.J. considered that the decision in the *Romalpa* case was based on the concession that title to the goods remained with the sellers and that the buyers became bailees of the foil on delivery to them.

21–056   In *Specialist Plant Services v Braithwaite*[120] the Court of Appeal actually reached the opposite conclusion to that held in the *Romalpa* case on similar wording, but without explaining how that could be reconciled with *Romalpa*.

21–057   The *Romalpa* case has been distinguished in English cases dealing with complex clauses in a manufacturing situation. In *Re Peachdart Ltd*[121] leather was supplied for making into handbags. There was a clause in many ways similar to the one in the *Romalpa* case. The effective dispute concerned the proceeds of sale of completed and uncompleted handbags. Vinelott J. considered it a "vital difference" that the *Romalpa* case concerned the proceeds of sale of unmanufactured goods. In the case in question he found that the parties could not have intended, even assuming that the buyer became a bailee on delivery, that the buyers would remain bailees throughout the manufacturing process so that the sellers whilst unpaid could enter the buyer's premises and remove partly or completely manufactured handbags and that on a sale of a handbag the buyer would be obliged to pay the proceeds into a separate account not to be used in the course of trade. The seller also had a factual problem in that the sale records of the buyer relating to the handbags did not identify the supplier of the leather, so that the sellers could not connect any finished product to its unpaid raw materials. Thus although the clause expressly provided for a fiduciary relationship and for tracing, Vinelott J. found that the parties must have intended that at the latest when manufacturing work began on a piece of leather it would cease to be the seller's property and the seller would have a charge on handbags in the course of manufacture which would in due course shift to the proceeds of sale. This was despite an express provision that property in the leather would "remain" with the seller. In coming to this conclusion Vinelott J. appeared to be influenced by the fact that once manufacture began the leather ceased to have any significant value as raw material and the value in the finished product would derive mostly from the buyer's skill and

---

[116] *Bond Worth* [1980] Ch. 228.
[117] *Borden (UK) Ltd v Scottish Timber Products Ltd* [1981] Ch. 25 (CA).
[118] *Borden (UK) Ltd v Scottish Timber Products Ltd* [1981] Ch. 25 (CA).
[119] *Clough Mill v Martin* [1985] 1 W.L.R. 111 (CA).
[120] *Specialist Plant Services v Braithwaite* (1987) 3 B.C.C. 119 (CA).
[121] *Re Peachdart Ltd* [1984] Ch. 131, per Vinelott J.

reputation. The sellers conceded in that case that a charge such as was found by Vinelott J. was void for non-registration.[122]

In *Clough Mill v Martin*[123] the Court of Appeal was, in a case involving a **21–058** complex clause, only faced with a claim to the goods themselves. The goods had not been manufactured and a claim of this type had been conceded in *Re Peachdart Ltd*. After finding that the simple retention of title part of the clause did not amount to a registrable charge, the Court of Appeal went on to consider the situation where manufacture had taken place. The goods supplied consisted of yarn and the buyer was a manufacturer of fabrics. The fourth part of the clause provided that if any of the goods were "incorporated in or used as material for other goods ... the property in the whole of such goods shall be and remain with the seller". Goff L.J. considered the position where, after default in payment, the seller had terminated the contract of sale and resold the manufactured product over which he claimed title. He found it impossible to believe that the parties intended the seller to have the windfall of the value of the new product without having to account to the buyer for any surplus over the sum due to the seller. To avoid this there had to be a trust or a charge. An intention to create a trust was discounted on the grounds that sellers must know that other sellers reserve title and "the prospect of two lots of material, supplied by different sellers, each subject to a *Romalpa* clause which vests in the seller the legal title in a product manufactured from both lots of material, is not at all sensible".[124] Accordingly, Goff L.J. considered that this part of the clause created a charge, although he recognised that he was doing "violence to the language" of the relevant part of the clause. Oliver L.J. felt that it was not necessary to decide the point but was inclined to agree with Goff L.J.[125]

Sir John Donaldson M.R. considered, first, that where, despite incorpora- **21–059** tion, etc, the goods remained separate and identifiable, the attempt in the clause to acquire title to other goods which had never belonged to the seller created a charge by the buyer in relation to those goods. Where the goods ceased to be identifiable and the new product belonged to the buyer, the clause would again create a charge.

With regard to the incidental question to whom such a new product belonged, **21–060** the Court of Appeal expressed no concluded view, but again the dicta are of interest. In the *Hendy Lennox* case[126] the goods had simply been incorporated in a way in which they remained easily removable without damaging the larger entity. There was no new product and title had not passed as a result of the incorporation. In the *Borden* case the goods had undergone an irreversible

---

[122] See also *Modelboard Ltd v Outer Box Ltd* [1992] B.C.C. 945, per Michael Hart QC (held title to cardboard passed once processed such that the vendor's interest was by way of charge); see *Ian Chisholm Textiles Ltd v Griffiths* [1994] B.C.C. 96 per David Neuberger QC (held title to cloth passed once it was combined to any significant extent with goods owned by another such that the vendor's interest was by way of charge); see *Chaigley Farms Ltd v Crawford, Kaye & Grayshire Ltd* [1996] B.C.C. 957, per Garland J. (held title to livestock passed once the livestock was slaughtered).
[123] *Clough Mill v Martin* [1985] 1 W.L.R. 111 (CA).
[124] *Clough Mill v Martin* [1985] 1 W.L.R. 111 (CA), 120E–120F.
[125] *Clough Mill v Martin* [1985] 1 W.L.R. 111 (CA), 124H.
[126] *Hendy Lennox* [1984] 1 W.L.R. 485.

process of manufacture and a new product was created. It was there held that tracing could not extend to the new product. The sellers had lost their owner-ship of the resin supplied by them and any interest in the new chipboard product would have been by way of charge. The chipboard itself belonged to the buyer/manufacturer. In the *Clough Mill* case,[127] Goff L.J. was of the view that it was open to the parties to agree that the new product would belong to the seller. Oliver L.J. reserved his view but seemed inclined to agree with Goff L.J. on this point. Sir John Donaldson M.R. expressed no view on the ownership of new products point. The importance of the question of ownership in this context is that if the new product belongs to the buyer, the seller's rights will not have been "retained" but must necessarily have been created by the buyer company and accordingly may constitute a registrable charge; but if the seller obtained an original title under the terms of the sale agreement, the question of the creation of a charge by the company will only arise in the windfall situation considered by Goff and Oliver L.JJ.

21–061   Neither the *Peachdart*[128] nor the *Clough Mill*[129] decision dealt with the ordi-nary resale situation where a complex form of clause is employed. Cases since *Peachdart* and *Clough Mill* show a strong inclination by the English courts to distinguish *Romalpa* in resale and analogous situations where a complex form of clause has been used. In *E. Pfeiffer Weinkellerei-Weineinkauf GmbH & Co v Arbuthnot Factors Ltd*[130] the relevant clause stated:

> "The buyer is only allowed to dispose of the goods or to sell them in busi-ness operations carried out in due order and as long as there is no delay in payment. All claims that he gets from the sale or due to another legal reason regarding our goods, with all rights including his profit amounting to his obligations towards us, will be passed on to us. On demand the buyer is obliged to notify the assignment of the claim, to give us in writing all necessary information concerning the assertion of our claims, and to deliver up all necessary documents."[131]

21–062   Phillips J. distinguished the case from *Romalpa* by reference to the proceeds of sale provisions.[132] He noted that Springfield Wine Importers Ltd's claims were only passed on up to the amount of its outstanding obligations to Pfeiffer, which was inconsistent with the proposition that the beneficial interest in all proceeds was to be vested in Pfeiffer.[133] Secondly, he stated that "the language used is essentially that of assignment or cession by Springfield of rights owned by Springfield", and thus he held that the clause constituted an agreement whereby Springfield assigned to Pfeiffer future choses in action

---

[127] *Clough Mill v Martin* [1985] 1 W.L.R. 111 (CA).
[128] *Re Peachdart Ltd* [1984] Ch. 131.
[129] *Clough Mill v Martin* [1985] 1 W.L.R. 111 (CA).
[130] *E. Pfeiffer Weinkellerei-Weineinkauf GmbH & Co v Arbuthnot Factors Ltd* [1988] 1 W.L.R. 150; for the facts see above, para.21–013.
[131] See at 610.
[132] See per Phillips J. at 615, 1st column.
[133] See at 615, 2nd column.

which were owned by Springfield, namely, future debts owed by sub-purchasers. Thus, what was created was a charge by way of security over property of Springfield.[134]

In *Tatung (UK) Ltd v Galex Telesure Ltd*,[135] a supplier of electrical goods **21–063** supplied equipment to three companies which went into receivership. The supplier argued they were entitled to the proceeds of sale or hire of such goods. With regard to proceeds, there were two relevant clauses. The first provided that:

"The buyer shall be at liberty to sell the goods in the ordinary course of business in the name of the buyer and as principal and not as agent for the company notwithstanding the fact that title to the goods has not then passed to the buyer but the benefit of any such contract of sale and the proceeds of any such sale shall belong to the company absolutely."[136]

The second provided that:

"the buyer shall have the power to resell or otherwise deal with the goods in the ordinary course of business in the name of the buyer on condition: ... (b) that the proceeds of resale or other dealing shall in any period preceding payment of the full price as aforesaid be held by the buyer in a separate account as trustee thereof for the company."[137]

Despite the "trustee" wording in the second formula, Phillips J. rejected the **21–064** submission that the defendant companies were fiduciaries of the goods prior to disposal and thus also rejected the submission that the claimants derived an absolute equitable interest in the proceeds of the goods after their disposal. He noted that the claimant's interest in the proceeds of sale and hire were defeasible upon payment of the debts owed to the claimants, and he held that accordingly they were interests by way of security rather than an absolute interest. He went on to state that this conclusion entirely accorded with the requirements of business efficacy having regard to the basic relationship between the claimants and defendants of vendors and purchasers.[138]

In *Compaq Computer Ltd v Abercorn Group Ltd*[139] the relevant clause **21–065** stated:

"In so far as the dealer may sell or otherwise dispose of the Compaq products or receive any moneys from any third party in respect of the Compaq products, he shall strictly account to Compaq for the full proceeds thereof (or such moneys as the dealer shall receive) as the seller's bailee

---

[134] See at 616.

[135] *Tatung (UK) Ltd v Galex Telesure Ltd* (1989) 5 B.C.C. 325. The reasoning of the decision was approved in *Re Weldtech Equipment Ltd* [1991] B.C.C. 16.

[136] See at 328.

[137] See at 328

[138] See at 333h.

[139] *Compaq Computer Ltd v Abercorn Group Ltd* [1991] B.C.C. 484. For the facts see above, para.21–014.

or agent and shall keep a separate account of all such proceeds or moneys for such purpose."[140]

Mummery J. noted that the beneficial interest of the seller in the debts was determinable on the payment of the debts, and consequently the rights and obligations of the parties were in reality and in substance characteristic of those of the parties to a charge and not of those in a trustee/beneficiary or other fiduciary relationship.[141]

21–066   A strikingly different approach to the subject has been taken in dicta of the High Court of Australia in *Associated Alloys Pty Ltd v ACN*.[142]

In that case, steel was supplied to be manufactured into various steel products. The retention of title clause provided for retention of title to the goods, for their custody by the buyer as "fiduciary agent and bailee" and:

> "In the event that the [buyer] uses the goods/products in some manufacturing ... process ..., then the buyer shall hold such part of the proceeds of such manufacturing ... as relates to the goods/ products in trust for the [seller]. Such part shall be deemed to equal in dollar terms the amount owing by the [buyer] to the [seller] at the time of the receipt of such proceeds."

It is important to note that the seller's claim failed and was bound to fail at every level, because the seller failed to prove the receipt of relevant "proceeds" by the buyer. Nevertheless, the case is interesting because of its discussion of and very divergent views expressed about attempts to create a trust over proceeds of manufactured products using goods to which title had been retained.

21–067   The decision of the New South Wales Court of Appeal and the forceful dissent of Kirby J. in the High Court of Australia followed the approach of the English cases discussed above and considered that there was a registrable charge on book debts.

21–068   The majority of the High Court, however, distinguished the English cases on the following grounds:

> (1) The true construction of the wording in this case was that the trust was over only the "proceeds" and not the debts from which those proceeds resulted. In coming to this conclusion, the majority recognised that it followed from their approach that the buyer could completely nullify the effect of the provision by dealing with the debts in such a way that no relevant proceeds would arise.[143]

---

[140] See at 491d.

[141] See at 495g.

[142] *Associated Alloys Pty Ltd v ACN* [2000] 202 C.L.R. 588.

[143] At 576. See, in England a similar approach by Lloyd J. in *Re SSSL Realisations* (2002) Ltd [2005] 1 B.C.L.C. 1, affirmed sub. nom. *Squires v AIG Europe* [2006] Ch. 610 (CA) and para.3–030, above.

(2) The trust did not require an express segregation provision, since the obligation to segregate followed from the trust.[144]

(3) The provision did not create a "windfall" problem.[145]

(4) The trust was not defeasible upon payment of the debt,[146] because a term was to be implied to the effect that the constitution of a trust over proceeds to that extent discharged the debt.[147] It is respectfully doubted whether the English courts, on the basis of the authorities discussed above, would have taken the same view. It is suggested that the more likely intention of the parties was that the proprietary trust rights would co-exist with the debt until discharge of the debt, providing security for it. Suppose for example that the proceeds held on trust were quite properly placed into a segregated account at X bank, but the bank went into liquidation, whilst the buyer remained solvent. On the view of the majority, the seller could only claim (via the trust) in the bank's insolvency. It is difficult to believe that the parties really intended to deprive the seller of his usual right to enforce the debt. The commercial sense of the transaction was that the trust of the proceeds would provide "security" for the debt.

(e) Post-administration/receivership transactions

Where retention of title rights are void on the grounds of being an unregistered but registrable charge, they can be challenged by the administrator.[148] A receiver (whether acting as agent of the company or as principal) will stand in the shoes of the company and exercise its rights and thus in theory should be in no better or worse position than the company itself. In practice, however, where any rights claimed by the seller would be void as against the debenture-holder who appointed the receiver on the grounds of constituting an unregistered but registrable charge, the receiver will be able to take advantage of such invalidity. (Strictly speaking, the appointor should be joined in any proceedings to take the registration point.[149] But in practice costs can be saved by agreeing to waive this technical requirement).[150]   **21–069**

In cases where the sale contract has not been terminated and where there is an express or implied right of resale,[151] unless that right has been effectively   **21–070**

---

[144] At 579.

[145] cf. the discussion of the *Clough Mill* decision: *Clough Mill v Martin* [1985] 1 W.L.R. 111 (CA), above.

[146] In which case it would have amounted to a trust by way of charge: see the English cases discussed above.

[147] At 582–583.

[148] *Smith v Bridgend CBC* [2002] 1 A.C. 336 (HL), 337C–337D: the words in s.395 Companies Act 1985 "void against … the administrator" bore the connotations "void against the company in administration".

[149] See *Independent Automatic Sales Ltd v Knowles and Foster* [1962] 1 W.L.R. 974.

[150] As occurred in *Re Peachdart Ltd* [1984] Ch. 131, per Vinelott J.

[151] See also ss.21(1) and 25 Sale of Goods Act 1979. See also *Fashoff (UK) Ltd v Linton* [2008] B.C.C. 542 (application by original vendor to re-possess goods dismissed because of the delay of the original vendor in bringing the application, in circumstances where goods had been sold by the

terminated, an administrator or a receiver may cause the company to resell the goods.[152] In such a case the administrator or receiver will hold the proceeds subject to any effective trust imposed by the sale contract which would have bound the company on any such sale by the company, but if no trust is imposed or no registered charge created over the proceeds binding on the appointing debenture-holder[153], the proceeds will form part of the administration or receivership realisations. If the contract is terminated and the seller intervenes to prevent resales, it will probably be implicit in any arrangement (whether sanctioned by the court or otherwise) which enables the administrator or receiver to continue resales that the entitlement to the proceeds of resales will be determined on the basis of entitlement to the goods themselves prior to resale.[154]

21–071 An administrator is obliged to perform his functions with the objectives specified in Sch.B1, para.3(1) to the Insolvency Act 1986 (i.e. rescuing the company as a going concern, or achieving a better result for the company's creditors as a whole than would be likely if the company were wound up or realising property in order to make a distribution to one or more secured or preferential creditors).

21–072 To achieve one or other of the purposes the administrator may well want to procure the company to sell goods in the possession of the company, but which are not owned by the company. Paragraph 111(1) of Sch.B1 to the Insolvency Act 1986 defines a "hire purchase agreement" as including "a conditional sale agreement, a chattel leasing agreement and a retention of the title agreement".

21–073 Paragraph 72(1) of Sch.B1 to the Insolvency Act 1986 provides that the court may by order enable the administrator of a company to dispose of goods which are in the possession of the company under a hire purchase agreement as if all the rights of the owner under the agreement were vested in the company. By para.72(2) an order under sub-para.(1) may be made only on the application of the administrator and where the court thinks that the disposal of the goods would be likely to promote the purpose of administration in respect of the company.

21–074 Paragraph 72(3) provides that an order under para.72 is subject to the condition that there be applied towards discharging the sums payable under the hire

---

administrator of a company to a third party subject to conditions that they were to be retained by the third party for a specified time during which claims could be made, and that property in the goods would not pass until that time had elapsed).

[152] *Chaigley Farms Ltd v Crawford, Kaye & Grayshire Ltd* [1996] B.C.C. 957. *Sandhu v Jet Star Retail Ltd* [2011] EWCA Civ 459 (administrator permitted to procure the company to re-sell goods in circumstances where the original vendor had failed to terminate the contractual licence to re-sell). See also *Fairfax Gerrard Holdings Ltd v Capital Bank Plc* [2008] 1 All E.R. (Comm) 632 (CA). The original seller will retain the claim for the price against the company, which would ordinarily be a provable debt (r.13.12(1) and (3) of the Insolvency Rules 1986).

[153] See s.860 Companies Act 2006.

[154] As a matter of practice, often an undertaking will be given to pay the value of the goods or return the goods, in the event that the original seller can prove a valid retention of title claim: *Lipe Ltd v Leyland DAF Ltd* [1993] B.C.C. 385 (CA). See also *Hendy Lennox v Grahame Puttick Ltd* [1984] 1 W.L.R. 485, 497A–497B. In *Hachette UK Ltd v Borders (UK) Ltd* [2009] EWHC 3487 (Ch) the court directed the administrators to provide information to the claimants about sales of book titles which may have been supplied by the claimants in order to allow the claimants to assess their rights, and formulate claims in conversion which may have been available to them against the administrators. See also below on Sch.B1, para.72 Insolvency Act 1986.

purchase agreement the net proceeds of disposal of the goods and any additional money required to be added to the net proceeds so as to produce the amount determined by the court as the net amount which would be raised on a sale of the goods at market value.[155]

Where a supplier claiming under a retention of title clause has refused to agree to resales by the receiver and has commenced proceedings which threaten to prejudice the receivership by holding up the use or resale of goods supplied, the receiver may be able to obtain relief by invoking the court's power in certain circumstances to order a sale of goods to which title is in dispute.[156] In practice a receiver will be likely to offer an undertaking to a retention of title claimant (to pay the value of the goods in the event of the claimant proving his claim) in order to prevent the claimant from successfully applying for an injunction restraining sale.[157]   **21–075**

7. THE EC REGULATION ON INSOLVENCY PROCEEDINGS 2000

The EC Regulation on Insolvency Proceedings 2000 includes within its scope administrations (including appointments made by filing prescribed documents with the court), but does not include receiverships.[158]   **21–076**

The EC Regulation makes express provision for retention of title claims by art.7, which provides: **21–077**

"1. The opening of insolvency proceedings against the purchaser of an asset shall not affect the seller's rights based on a reservation of title where at the time of the opening of proceedings the asset is situated within the territory of a Member State other than the State of opening of proceedings.

2. The opening of insolvency proceedings against the seller of an asset, after delivery of the asset, shall not constitute grounds for rescinding or terminating the sale and shall not prevent the purchaser from acquiring title where at the time of the opening of proceedings the asset sold is situated within the territory of a Member State other than the State of the opening of proceedings.

3. Paragraphs 1 and 2 shall not preclude actions for voidness, voidability or unenforceability as referred to in Article 4(2)(m)."[159]

---

[155] cf. *Stanley Holmes & Sons Ltd v Davenham Trust Plc* [2007] B.C.C. 485 (CA), held that a judge ought to come to a judicial conclusion about the market value as a matter of fact (rather than splitting the difference between two expert valuations to give a mid-point figure).

[156] CPR r.25.1(1)(c)(v), which permits a party to proceedings to apply for the sale of chattels in question in the proceedings which are of a perishable nature or "which for any other good reason it is desirable to sell quickly".

[157] *Lipe Ltd v Leyland DAF Ltd* [1993] B.C.C. 385 (CA).

[158] art.1(1) and Annex A of the EC Regulation on Insolvency Proceedings 2000. For a commentary and annotated guide on the provisions of the regulation see Moss, Fletcher and Isaacs, *The EC Regulation on Insolvency Proceedings,* 2nd edn (Oxford: Oxford University Press, 2009).

[159] art.4(2)(m) states "The law of the State of the opening of proceedings shall determine the conditions for the opening of those proceedings, their conduct and their closure. It shall determine in particular: ... (m) the rules relating to the voidness, voidability or unenforceability of legal acts detrimental to all other creditors".

8.   INSOLVENCY ACT 1986

21–078   Section 43 of the Insolvency Act 1986 authorises an administrative receiver to apply to the court to enable him to sell property over which he is a receiver or manager free of any prior "security". The property in question must, in the context,[160] be property of the company charged to the debenture-holder, which in turn prevents this section applying to property the subject of an effective retention of title clause. A contrary argument could perhaps be based on the definition of "security",[161] which, if read literally, seems wide enough to cover a valid retention of title clause. It is considered that since s.43 extends only to property beneficially owned by the company, an administrative receiver could not apply under this section to sell goods to which title had been validly retained. This view is perhaps supported by the distinction drawn in the equivalent provision applying to administrators[162] between, on the one hand, "property of the company subject to a security" and, on the other, goods in the possession of the company but subject to security rights involving retention of ownership, including hire-purchase agreements, chattel leases and retention of title clauses. If this view is correct, administrative receivers remain vulnerable to pressure where goods the subject of an undoubtedly valid retention of title clause need to be sold as part of the business or other property of the company charged to the debenture-holder.

---

[160] See Insolvency Act 1986, s.43(7).
[161] Insolvency Act 1986, s.248(b).
[162] Insolvency Act 1986, para.5 (formerly s.15) 71 and 72.

Chapter 22

Set-off

1. INTRODUCTION

Set-off is a huge and complex subject. In the words of one reviewer of a leading **22–001** text on set-off, it "is a body of law that offers fearsome technicality but few issues that really stir the blood[1]". It would take a very weighty tome indeed to cover such fearsome technicality in detail.[2] Instead, this chapter focuses on the key issues that arise when a company acting by its receivers or administrators, or a creditor of such a company, seeks to set off against a debt that it owes to its counterparty a cross-claim owing by that counterparty. In order to do so, however, it is necessary to consider (briefly) what is meant (and not meant) by set-off in this chapter, the different types of set-off that arise and some of the fundamental principles that determine whether or not set-off is available. These matters are considered in the first part of this chapter.

When a company goes into administration and the administrator gives notice of his intention to make a distribution to creditors, a statutory set-off rule comes into play under the insolvency legislation which is similar to the rules that apply in the case of bankruptcy[3] or liquidation[4]; the administration set-off rule is (most likely) mandatory, operates automatically and cannot be excluded by the agreement of the parties.[5] This rule, and the impact of administration on set-off rights more generally, are considered in Pt 2 of this chapter. There is no such statutory set-off rule under the insolvency legislation which comes into play when a receiver is appointed over the assets of a company (although the liquidation set-off rule will apply if the company is concurrently in liquidation). The grant of security, or the appointment of a receiver, may, however, have an impact on the availability of other forms of set-off rights and this is considered in Pt 3 below. Finally, Pt 4 of this chapter considers the international dimension and, in particular, the impact of art.6 of the EC Insolvency Regulation on rights of set-off generally and insolvency set-off in particular.

---

[1] Blom, (1989) *5 Banking and Finance Law Review* 246 on S.R. Derham, *The Law of Set-off*, 2nd edn.

[2] Two principal works on set-off under English law are Philip Wood, *English and International Set-off* (London: Sweet & Maxwell, 1989) which is over 1,200 pages and S.R. Derham, *The Law of Set-off*, 3rd edn (Oxford: Oxford University Press, 2003) which is over 900 pages. See also Shelagh McCracken, *A Banker's Remedy of Set-off*, 2nd edn (London: Bloomsbury Professional, 1998).

[3] Insolvency Act 1986, s.323.

[4] Insolvency Rules 1986, r.2.85.

[5] By analogy with *National Westminster Bank Ltd v Halesowen Presswork and Assemblies Ltd* [1972] A.C. 785 (HL) which considered the liquidation set-off rule, r.4.90 of the Insolvency Rules 1986. See further analysis in Pt 2 of this chapter.

(a)   Meaning and importance of set-off

22–002   It is difficult to give a comprehensive definition of set-off which embraces the many different legal forms that are covered by this expression. In general, however, set-off arises where one party (A) has a claim against another party (B) in circumstances where B has a cross-claim against A; in such circumstances, B may be able to "set off" the amount of the cross-claim against what B owes to A so that B is only liable to pay the balance, if any, to A. For example, if A has supplied goods to B and B is under an obligation to pay £1,000 in respect of the purchase price but, under the same or a separate contract, B has a liquidated damages claim of £300 against A for (say) late delivery of the goods, B may be able to set off against its obligation to pay £1,000 its cross-claim of £300 so that it is only obliged to pay to A the balance of £700. An example in a lending scenario might be where a borrower owes £1 million to its bank lender but has a deposit account with the same bank with a credit balance of £50,000. If the borrower goes into liquidation, the bank may be able to set off the credit balance of the deposit account against what is owed by the borrower so that the bank only has to prove for the balance of £950,000 in the borrower's liquidation.

Outside of an insolvency scenario, there are various different types of set-off, each of which is discussed briefly below. A question arises as to whether the different types of set-off affect the substantive rights of the parties against each other (so as to reduce or extinguish the claim or result in a merger of the claim and the cross-claim) or whether the set-off merely operates at a procedural level (at least until both causes of action have been merged in a single judgment by the court). In other words, is the set-off a substantive defence to payment (which can be exercised by the party asserting the set-off as a self-help remedy outside of any legal proceedings) or a mere cross-claim which can only be asserted in any legal proceedings? The answer to this question depends on the type of set-off being asserted. Independent or legal set-off is a matter of procedure and cash-flow[6] but does not affect the parties' substantive rights. As a matter of procedure, it enables a defendant to require its cross-claim (even if based upon a wholly different subject matter) to be tried together with the claimant's claim instead of having to be the subject of a separate action. As a matter of cash-flow, it relieves a debtor from having to find the cash to satisfy a judgment in favour of the claimant before the defendant's cross-claim has been determined. Independent set-off does not operate so as to reduce or discharge the claim except in any legal proceedings in which the set-off is asserted. On the other hand, transaction or equitable set-off operates as a substantive defence so that the party invoking the set-off is treated as only being liable for the balance of the claim (as reduced by the amount of the cross-claim).

22–003   Insolvency set-off[7] is not merely procedural and does affect the substantive rights of the parties by enabling the creditor to use its indebtedness to the

---

[6] *Stein v Blake (No.1)* [1996] A.C. 243 (HL), 251, per Lord Hoffmann.
[7] Throughout this chapter, this is the expression which is used to refer to the set-off rights that arise under the insolvency legislation in a bankruptcy, liquidation or administration.

insolvent debtor as a form of security. A right of set-off can be vital in such a scenario. In the examples given above, if B (the recipient of the goods) were insolvent but set-off were not available, the supplier, A, would have to pay the liquidated damages claim of £300 in full to B's insolvent estate but would only be likely to receive a dividend (along with B's other creditors) for its debt claim of £1,000. Likewise, in the second example, the bank would have to repay the deposit to the borrower and then rank with the borrower's other creditors for the full amount of its loan.

In such an insolvency scenario, English law generally favours a right of set-off (provided certain conditions are satisfied as discussed below). There are various policy arguments in favour of this approach including that it would be unjust for a creditor to be obliged to perform its obligation in full but to get only partial performance of its claim against an insolvent debtor,[8] that set-off reduces the potential "domino" effect which the insolvency of a market participant could have on the market, that set-off reduces exposures and therefore the cost of credit and regulatory capital requirements, and that set-off lowers administrative costs by reducing the potential multiplicity of payments or actions. Not all jurisdictions share this view of insolvency set-off and the opposing policy is that set-off is a major violation of the pari passu principle because a creditor with a set-off gets paid in full to the extent of the cross-claim.[9]

A right of set-off may also be of particular importance in the scenarios set out below.

(i) Winding-up petition

If the company has an arguable defence of set-off to the full amount claimed **22–004** by the petitioner, the presentation and advertisement of a winding-up petition should be restrained.[10] The existence of a mere cross-claim, though substantially overlapping the petitioner's debt, is not a ground for restraining the petition, but is relevant only to the exercise of discretion by the court in deciding whether to make the order for winding-up at the substantive hearing of the petition.[11]

(ii) Exercise of rights and remedies

A cross-claim qualifying as a set-off (but no other cross-claim) is a defence not **22–005** merely to the claim to payment but also to a claim to invoke rights or remedies available upon non-payment, e.g. forfeiture of a lease for non-payment of rent,[12]

---

[8] In *Forster v Wilson* (1843) 12 M. & W. 191, 204, Park B. said that the purpose of insolvency set-off was "to do substantial justice between the parties".

[9] See Philip Wood, *English and International Set-off* (London: Sweet & Maxwell, 1989) (at fn.2), paras 21–51 to 24–120, for a comparative law analysis of which jurisdictions allow and do not allow insolvency set-off.

[10] *McDonald's Restaurants Ltd v Urbandivide Co* [1994] 1 B.C.L.C. 306.

[11] See *Re A Company (No.0012209 of 1991)* [1992] 1 W.L.R. 351 and see below, at para.22–068.

[12] *British Anzani (Felixstowe) Ltd v International Marine Management (UK) Ltd* [1980] Q.B. 137. See also *Liverpool Properties v Old Bridge* (1985) 276 E.G. 1352 (CA).

distress by a landlord,[13] withdrawal of a vessel for non-payment of hire,[14] or forfeiture of interest under a joint venture,[15] or available upon default, e.g. under a mortgage which restricts the mortgagee's right to take possession or appoint a receiver on the happening of a default.[16]

In drafting debentures, secured creditors may well wish to incorporate provisions designed to exclude set-off and to provide for conclusive certificates in respect of the indebtedness to limit the scope for challenges by the mortgagor to actual or proposed appointments of receivers on grounds related to the existence or amount of the debt.

(b) Set-off distinguished from netting, counterclaim, flawed assets and security

(i) Netting

22–006 The expressions "set-off" and "netting" are often used interchangeably and "netting" can have different meanings in different jurisdictions. In the financial markets, the term "netting" tends to be used for an agreement whereby the claims and cross-claims of the various participants are cancelled and replaced with a single "net" payment. For example, the termination payment under an ISDA Master Agreement works in this way. Netting is defined in the Financial Markets and Insolvency (Settlement Finality) Regulations 1999[17] as:

> "the conversion into one net claim or obligation of different claims or obligations between participants resulting from the issue and receipt of transfer orders between them, whether on a bilateral or multilateral basis and whether through the interposition of a clearing house, central counterparty or settlement agent or otherwise."

---

[13] *Eller v Grovecrest* [1995] Q.B. 272 (CA)—the dictum to the contrary in *Connaught Ltd v Indoor Leisure* [1994] 1 W.L.R. 501, 511, per Neill L.J., was not cited in *Eller*.

[14] *Federal Commerce & Navigation Co Ltd v Molena Alpha Inc* [1978] Q.B. 927 (CA), 974. In *BICC v Burndy Corp* [1985] Ch. 232 (CA), Dillon L.J. (with whom Ackner L.J. concurred) held that, in the case of an agreement by a co-owner to transfer his half interest in certain patents to his co-owner on default of payment of sums due under the agreement, it was a defence to a claim to specific performance of the obligation to transfer alleged to have been triggered by such default that there was a legal set-off of sums due under an unconnected contract. Kerr L.J. dissented on this question, holding that (at any rate if no claim to a legal set-off had previously been notified) only an equitable set-off would be sufficient for this purpose, i.e. a claim which impeached the claimant's title to specific performance.

[15] Per Dillon L.J. in *BICC Plc v Burndy Corp* [1985] Ch. 232 (CA), 247.

[16] *Ashley Guarantee Plc (formerly Gulf Guarantee Bank)v Zacaria* [1993] 1 W.L.R. 62 (CA), cited with approval in *TSB Bank Plc v Platts* [1998] 2 B.C.L.C. 1, 10. In the *Ashley Guarantee* case, Nourse L.J. at p.6–68 on the basis of Slade L.J.'s judgment in *National Westminster Bank v Skelton* [1993] 1 W.L.R. 72 (CA) considered that:
(i) in the absence of any contractual or statutory constraint, the mortgagee's right to possession is not defeated by a cross-claim even if liquidated, admitted and in excess of the mortgage arrears or a right to unliquidated damages giving rise to a right of set-off;
(ii) a right to liquidated damages giving rise to a right of set-off may defeat the right to possession if equal to the arrears.

[17] SI 1999/2979, reg.2(1). These regulations have been amended on a number of occasions, most recently by SI 2011/245, but none of the amendments changes the definition of netting referred to above.

The different types of netting arrangement, and the impact of an insolvency of one of the participants, are considered further below.[18]

(ii) Counterclaim

A right of set-off should be distinguished from a defendant's right to counter-claim which arises under the Civil Procedure Rules r.20.4. Set-off operates by way of a defence to the claimant's claim (so that there is only one judgment or claim for the balance). Counterclaim, on the other hand, is a procedural device whereby the court may consider independent cross-claims in the same proceedings; the claim and the counterclaim are treated as independent claims for all purposes except execution.[19] There are important distinctions between set-off and counterclaim in an application for summary judgment; only if the cross-claim of the defendant qualifies as set-off will the cross-claim stand as a defence.

22–007

(iii) Flawed assets

Rather than the parties relying on set-off, a contract can be drafted so that the payment obligation of a particular party (A) is conditional or contingent upon a particular event occurring (such as the payment of a separate debt by the counterparty, B, or even by a third party). The contractual provision may constitute a contingency or "flaw" on the prospective payment obligation of A so that B has no entitlement to payment if the condition is not satisfied. Looking at it from B's perspective, the condition acts as a "flaw" in B's contractual right to payment. This is not a set-off because, until the event has happened, the debtor has no liability against which it can set off its cross-claim.

22–008

Both the Court of Appeal and the House of Lords have given strong endorsements (albeit on an obiter basis) of the concept of a "flawed asset" in *Re Bank of Credit and Commerce International SA (No.8)*[20] which arose out of the collapse of Bank of Credit and Commerce International. The liquidators of BCCI sought directions from the English court in circumstances where BCCI had lent money to a principal debtor and received a deposit from a third party surety on terms that the deposit was charged to BCCI to secure repayment of the loan. The terms of the letter of charge expressly prohibited the depositor from dealing with the deposit or withdrawing it while the principal debt remained unpaid and gave the bank the power to set off the amount of the deposit against the principal debt. The case was principally about insolvency set-off and the legal nature of a "charge-back" but, having considered these issues, Rose L.J. in the Court of Appeal gave some support for the flawed asset analysis when he said:

---

[18] See Pt 1(c)(iii) below in relation to contractual set-off and part 1(c)(vi) below in relation to insolvency set-off.

[19] Under the Civil Procedure Rules, the counterclaim is designated as a "Part 20 claim", illustrating that it is separate from the claimant's claim.

[20] *Re Bank of Credit and Commerce International SA (No.8)* [1996] Ch. 245 (CA); [1998] A.C. 214 (HL). This decision is also referred to as *Morris v Agrichemicals Ltd.*

"These provisions fetter the depositor's use of the deposit while the principal debt remains unpaid. In his hands the deposit–his chose in action–is a flawed asset. If he becomes insolvent, the asset forms part of the insolvent estate, but it remains a flawed asset subject to the same contractual restrictions as before."[21]

22–009 On appeal to the House of Lords, Lord Hoffmann referred back to this part of Rose L.J.'s judgment and said:

"The Court of Appeal said that the bank could obtain effective security in other ways . . . If the deposit was made by a third party, it could enter into contractual arrangements such as the limitation on the right to withdraw the deposit in this case, thereby making the deposit a 'flawed asset.' All this is true. It may well be that security provided in these ways will in most cases be just as good as that provided by a proprietary interest."[22]

In *BCCI (No 8)*, the "flaw" (or limitation on the right to withdraw the deposit) was by reference to the obligations of a third party to repay a loan. What if, instead, the contract provides that a party (A) will only become obliged to make a particular payment if the counterparty (B) is not subject to any insolvency proceedings on the date that the payment would otherwise fall due? In other words, what if B's right to payment is conditional upon its not being subject to any insolvency proceedings on the due date?[23]

This type of arrangement was recently considered by the Supreme Court in the context of a structured finance transaction involving one of the US Lehman Brothers entities, Lehman Brothers Special Financing Inc (LBSF)[24]. At the request of the rating agencies, the security trust deed contained a provision whereby LBSF, as swap counterparty, was to be paid out of the proceeds of enforcement of the security in priority to noteholders unless an event of default occurred under the swap agreement in which case the noteholders were to be paid in priority to LBSF. The events of default included the bankruptcy of LBSF (or of the holding company, Lehman Brothers Holding Inc, as guarantor) and failure to pay. The provisions of the security trust deed could be seen as a "flawed asset" as LBSF's right to be paid in priority to noteholders was conditional upon no event of default having occurred under the swap agreement. The

---

[21] At 262–263.

[22] At 576.

[23] This form of wording is sometimes used in a derivatives context in relation to "self-referenced credit linked notes".

[24] *Belmont Park Investments PTY Ltd (Respondent) v BNY Corporate Trustee Services Ltd and Lehman Brothers Special Financing Inc (Appellants)* [2011] 3 W.L.R. 521 (SC). This was previously referred to as the *Perpetual* case (as the Perpetual notes contained very similar provisions) but the Perpetual noteholders settled with LBSF prior to the Supreme Court hearing. See also *Lomas v JFB Firth Rixson Inc* [2011] 2 B.C.L.C. 120 (which is subject to an appeal) concerning s.2(a)(iii) of the ISDA Master Agreement, a flawed asset provision whereby the defaulting party's right to payment is conditional upon no event of default having occurred or being outstanding in relation to it. For a narrow view regarding flawed asset provisions triggered by insolvency, see Sarah Worthington, "Insolvency Deprivation, Public Policy and Priority Flip Clauses" (2010) 7(1) Int. C.R. 28.

clause was referred to in the judgment as the "flip clause" (because the priority of the parties "flipped" in certain prescribed circumstances)[25].

The question for the English court[26] was whether, if LBSF had been subject to English insolvency proceedings rather than bankruptcy proceedings under Ch.11 of the US Bankruptcy Code, the provisions of the security trust deed would infringe the English law "anti-deprivation principle" whereby "there cannot be a valid contract that a man's property shall remain his until his bankruptcy, and on the happening of that event shall go over to someone else and be taken away from his creditors".[27]

In a unanimous decision, the court held that there was no infringement of the rule, although the reasoning of their Lordships was very different from those of the courts below. The key factor now appears to be whether the transaction in question is a bona fide one, with no deliberate intention to evade insolvency law. In this regard, the court indicated that a commercially sensible transaction entered into in good faith should not be held to infringe the anti-deprivation rule. The court held that, although turning on fine verbal distinctions (that have been described as "little short of disgraceful to our jurisprudence"), the distinction between a conditional interest that can be determined on bankruptcy and an absolute interest that can subsequently be defeated by bankruptcy was well-established and could only be dislodged by legislation. However, the court noted that categorising the asset as a "flawed asset" (or the right to payment as a conditional one) should not be considered to be determinative in itself of the question of whether the contractual provisions will be held to be effective. In particular, if the flawed asset or conditional interest is drafted so that it determines or changes on bankruptcy, the anti-deprivation principle is capable of applying and the provision will only be effective on one of the other grounds dealt with in the judgment (such as the good faith test).

Although the judgment is helpful in that it did give effect to the commercial intentions of the parties, it remains to be seen how easy the "commercially sensible transaction" test is to apply in practice when structuring or opining on these types of transaction.

---

[25] This description is inaccurate, however, as it suggests that LBSF had a vested interest in the security of which it was deprived, by virtue of the "flip", upon the occurrence of an event of default; it would have been preferable if the clause could have been referred to as a conditional payment clause.

[26] The litigation also raises some interesting conflict of law questions as the same provisions were also considered by Judge Peck of the US Bankruptcy Court in *Lehman Brothers Special Financing Inc v BNY Corporate Trustee Services Limited* Case No.09–01242 (Bankr. S.D.N.Y.) (JMP). Judge Peck held that the flip clause was an invalid ipso facto provision under the US Bankruptcy Code. Leave to appeal the decision to the US District Court was granted but the Perpetual noteholders settled before the appeal could be held. Judge Peck's decision did not extend to the Belmont noteholders but it is still open to LBSF to go back to Judge Peck in this regard. Interestingly, to date, neither the English nor the US Bankruptcy Court has been asked to determine which law prevails (i.e. English law as the governing law of the agreements and the *lex situs* of the secured assets or US bankruptcy law as the law governing the bankruptcy proceedings of LBSF).

[27] *Ex p Jay; In re Harrison* (1880) L.R. 14 Ch. D 19 (CA), 26 by Cotton L.J.

(iv)   Security and charge-backs

22–010   Although set-off has a security function, the creation or existence of a right of set-off does not mean that a security interest has been created by any party to the set-off agreement. Hence, the creation of a right of set-off does not (of itself) confer on the creditor a security interest in the debtor's cross-claim. In principle, under English law, a clear expression of intention would be needed in order to create a charge[28] and mutual set-off arrangements would not usually meet that test (although this would depend on the language used). This means that the set-off agreement would generally fall outside the provisions of the Companies Act 2006 that require the registration of certain types of charge by companies registered in, or having an established place of business in, England and Wales.[29]

The distinction between set-off and security has, to a certain extent, been blurred by the decision in *Re Bank of Credit and Commerce International SA (No.8)* in which the House of Lords held that there is no conceptual reason why a bank should not be able to take a charge over its own customer's credit balance. If the customer has been required by the bank to maintain a deposit with the bank by way of "cash cover" for a particular facility, and the customer is not able to withdraw the deposit until the facility has been repaid, it may be possible to argue that the agreement results in the creation of a charge in favour of the bank over the deposit. This will always depend on the facts of the particular case and the wording of the relevant agreements.[30]

In some cases, a party may seek to protect its position by the use (in the same agreement) of flawed asset wording, set-off language and the taking of security. This is sometimes referred to as the "triple cocktail" (or "triple-decker" for the less alcoholically minded). For example, in the context of a deposit held by a bank by way of cash cover for particular obligations, the agreement may provide that the bank has no obligation to repay the deposit unless or until the obligations have been satisfied (the flawed asset wording) but, to the extent that the bank is obliged to repay the deposit, the bank will have the right to set-off against the obligations the amount of the deposit (the set-off wording) and, as a final layer of protection in case neither the flawed asset wording nor the set off is effective, the bank will take a charge over the deposit (a charge-back).

(c)   Forms of set-off

22–011   Before considering set-off in the context of an administration or receivership, it is necessary to consider the different forms of set-off at a general level. This is because, during an administration, the non-insolvency set-off rules will be relevant unless and until the administrator gives notice of his intention to make

---

[28] *Swiss Bank Corp v Lloyds Bank Ltd* [1982] A.C. 584 (HL), 595.
[29] Companies Act 2006, ss.860–877.
[30] See the discussion in Derham, *The Law of Set-off*, 3rd edn (Oxford: Oxford University Press, 2003) (fn.2 above), paras 16.78 to 16.91.

distributions to creditors. In a receivership, there is no insolvency set-off rule that comes into play (unless the company is concurrently in liquidation) and so, again, the non-insolvency set-off rules will apply (subject to the impact that the grant of the security, or the appointment of the receiver, has upon those set-off rules).

There are various ways in which the different types of set-off can be subdivided and unfortunately different terms are sometimes used to refer to the same concepts. The labels traditionally used by the courts are unhelpful and so this chapter adopts the five main types of set-off referred to by Mr Wood.[31] In the case of all of these types of set-off other than contractual set-off, both the claim and the cross-claim must be monetary claims or claims which can be converted into monetary claims (rather than property claims or performance obligations) and there must be "mutuality" between the parties (see Pt 1(c) (vi)(3) below).

(i) Independent set-off

This type of set-off is sometimes referred to as statutory set-off (as it originates **22–012** from the former Statutes of Set-off dating from the early eighteenth century) and sometimes as legal set-off (to distinguish it from equitable set-off as discussed below). It occurs where the claim and the cross-claim do not arise out of the same transaction but are independent of each other.

In order for this form of set-off to be available:

(a) both the claim and the cross-claim must be liquidated or ascertainable with certainty;

(b) the set-off must generally be raised in the context of judicial proceedings (rather than being exercised as a self-help remedy)[32] as it is purely a procedural defence which does not operate to reduce or extinguish the claimant's claim (until the point that judgment is given for the balance). The tender by the debtor of the creditor's primary claim less the amount of the cross-claim will not generally be valid tender of payment; and

(c) in general, the cross-claim must be due and payable before the claimant commences its action in order for the defendant to plead the cross-claim by way of set-off (although this does not apply in relation to a counterclaim).

(ii) Transaction set-off

This type of set-off is sometimes referred to as equitable set-off as it was **22–013** developed by the courts of equity to allow a wider right of set-off than would

---

[31] In Wood, *English and International Set-off* (London: Sweet & Maxwell, 1989) (see fn.2).

[32] There are exceptions to this general rule as discussed by Wood, *English and International Set-off* (London: Sweet & Maxwell, 1989) (see fn.2), paras 2.46–2.67.

have been available at law.[33] It arises where the claim and the cross-claim arise out of the same transaction or such closely connected transactions that it would be inequitable for one claim to be enforced without the cross-claim being taken into account.[34] Unlike independent set-off, it can be exercised as a self-help remedy so that the debtor can deduct what it is owed from the amount it owes (outside of any judicial proceedings) and only pay the balance. This will be good legal tender of the creditor's claim. Furthermore, neither the claim nor the cross-claim needs to be liquidated. If the debtor's cross-claim is unliquidated and the debtor quantifies its loss by reasonable assessment made in good faith and deducts the sum so quantified, the debtor may not be in default even if its assessment turns out to be wrong.[35]

Examples of closely connected transactions include the price for goods and a damages cross-claim for defects[36]; charterhire and a cross-claim for unseaworthiness of the vessel[37]; rent and a cross-claim for repairs[38]; salary and a cross-claim for defective work[39]; the price for building works and a cross-claim for defects in the work[40]; and the price of equipment under a supply contract and damages for repudiation of a separate installation contract where (on the facts) the two contracts had become inseparable.[41] A bank deposit and obligations owed under a bank loan or mortgage loan may also be closely connected if the customer is required to make the deposit under the terms of the loan. Not all claims and cross-claims arising out of the same transaction are eligible for set-off.

(iii)   Contractual set-off and exclusions of set-off

22–014   Contractual set-off is a right of set-off created by contract where such right may not otherwise exist. Very slight evidence is usually sufficient to establish a contractual set-off right.[42] The contract may give the parties the right or option to set off or the set-off may be mandatory so as to produce a net balance. Outside of an insolvency of either of the parties, general principles of freedom of contract apply and the contractual rights will be effective even if a right of

---

[33] This label is confusing, however, as the courts of equity also applied the Statutes of Set-off by analogy where all the conditions for statutory set-off were present except that one of the cross-claims was equitable. Furthermore, a form of transaction set-off was developed by the common law courts as "abatement" in circumstances where either the claim or the cross-claim was unliquidated. For these (and other) reasons, the terms "independent" and "transaction" set-off are used in this chapter rather than "legal" and "equitable" set-off.

[34] Per Lord Denning M.R. in *Federal Commerce and Navigation Ltd v Molena Alpha Inc* [1978] Q.B. 927 (CA), 975; *TSB Bank Plc v Platts* [1998] 2 B.C.L.C. 1 (CA), 10, CA: see also *British Anzani (Felixstowe) Ltd v International Marine Management (UK) Ltd* [1980] Q.B. 137 and *Melville v Grapelodge* (1980) 39 P. & C.R. 179.

[35] Per Lord Denning in *The Nanfri* [1978] Lloyd's Rep. 132 (CA), 140.

[36] This is acknowledged by statute in s.53(1)(a) of the Sale of Goods Act 1979.

[37] *The Nanfri* [1978] Q.B. 927 (CA).

[38] *British Anzani (Felixstow) Ltd v International Marine Management (UK) Ltd* [1980] Q.B. 137.

[39] *The Phoenix* (1832) 2 Hagg 420; *Sim v Rotherham MB C* [1987] Ch. 216.

[40] *Young v Kitchen* (1878) L.R. 3 Ex. D. 127.

[41] *Geldof Metaalconstructie NV v Simon Carves Limited* [2010] 4 All E.R. 847 (CA).

[42] *Wallis v Bastard* (1853) 4 De G.M. & G. 251.

independent or transaction set-off would not have been available (for example because the claims are unliquidated, contingent, expressed in different currencies, non-monetary claims or where is no mutuality between the parties), provided that the clause is not construed as creating a security interest which is void for lack of registration.[43] Once the insolvency set-off rules come into play, however, any contractual provisions which are inconsistent with the insolvency set-off rules will no longer be effective.

Contractual set-off is mainly used to establish:

(a) a self-help set-off in circumstances where the claim and the cross-claim are not sufficiently connected so as to qualify for transaction set-off;

(b) a set-off where one of the claims has not matured;

(c) a set-off of independent claims where one (or both) is unliquidated—in which case the contract may contain provisions regarding how the claim is to be quantified for set-off purposes;

(d) a set-off of multicurrency claims–again, the contract is likely to provide for how the claims are to be converted into the same currency for set-off purposes;

(e) the "set-off" of a liability to deliver property against a monetary claim (by converting the obligation to deliver property into an obligation to pay a prescribed amount); and

(f) the set-off of non-mutual claims.[44]

One example of a contractual arrangement which may involve set-off is a netting agreement. There are various different types of netting arrangement, sometimes referred to as "close-out netting", "novation netting" and "settlement netting".[45] Close-out netting is a process intended to reduce exposures on "open" (i.e. executory or unperformed) contracts if one party should become insolvent or a like event occurs before the settlement date. The agreement typically provides that, on an event of default in relation to one party, the other party can terminate all outstanding contracts between the parties, calculate the losses and gains on each contract and then set them off so that only a balance is owing.[46] Novation netting (or contract consolidation) is a process whereby the parties agree that all contracts between them shall be consolidated into a single contract as soon as each new contract is entered into. Each new contract

---

[43] *Re Tudor Glass Holdings Ltd* (1984) 1 B.C.C. 98982.

[44] See Pt 1(c)(vi)(3) below regarding mutuality in this regard.

[45] See *Commissioners for HMRC v Enron Europe Ltd* [2006] B.C.C. 953 for a good description of the different types of netting arrangements.

[46] If the claims on either side are not monetary claims (but include, e.g. an obligation to deliver assets), there may be a mechanism for accelerating or rescinding the contracts and replacing the delivery obligation with a monetary one. This is because, with the exception of contractual set-off, generally only monetary claims can be set off pursuant to the different types of set-off referred to in this chapter.

is amalgamated with any existing contract. Settlement or payment netting is an agreement to net payments or deliveries of the same currency or asset which fall due on the same date. It applies only to amounts or deliveries due on the same date and only if the payments are in the same currency or are the same asset.

22–015   The main objectives of netting arrangements are to reduce costs and administrative burdens (by decreasing the paper flow and number of individual transactions), to minimise the risks associated with a participant becoming insolvent (because the losses to other participants will be reduced if all the insolvent counterparty's open contracts can be cancelled and any losses or gains replaced with a single net balance) and thus to reduce the risks of systemic failure. In some jurisdictions (including the UK), a netting arrangement may be contrary to the insolvency set-off rules if done on a multiparty basis. This is considered in Pt 1(c)(vi)(4) below.

In light of the importance of close-out netting and set-off to the financial markets, certain contractual set-off and netting arrangements are protected from the risk of counterparty insolvency by specialist legislation including the Settlement Finality Directive[47] (which protects designated settlement systems), art.7 of the Financial Collateral Directive[48] (which protects a close-out netting provision in a financial collateral arrangement, as defined in the Directive), art.6 of the European Regulation on Insolvency Proceedings[49] and arts 23 and 25 of the Credit Institutions Winding Up Directive[50] (as discussed in Pt 4 below).

In some cases, rather than wishing to expand the rights of set-off by contract, the parties may wish to exclude rights of set-off. Such rights can be excluded by agreement[51] but clear and unambiguous words must be used.[52] For example, an agreement to pay "without deduction and abatement" will not necessarily exclude set-off rights.[53] A clause precluding set-off may be construed strictly.[54] It may also require justification as being reasonable under s.13(1)(b) of the

---

[47] Directive 98/26/EC of the European Parliament and of the Council on settlement finality in payment and securities settlement systems as implemented in the UK by the Financial Markets and Insolvency (Settlement Finality) Regulations 1999 (SI 1999/2979). The UK implementing regulations have been amended various times including, most recently, by SI 2011/245.

[48] European Parliament and Council Directive 2002/47/EC on financial collateral arrangements as implemented in the UK by the Financial Collateral Arrangement (No.2) Regulations 2003 (SI 2003/3226). The UK implementing regulations have been amended by SI 2009/2462, SI 2010/2993 and most recently by SI 2011/245.

[49] Council Regulation (EC) No.1346/2000 on insolvency proceedings [2000] OJ L160/1.

[50] Directive 2001/24/EC on the Reorganisation and Winding up of Credit Institutions, implemented in the UK through the Credit Institutions (Reorganisation and Winding Up) Regulations 2004 (SI 2004/1045).

[51] *John Dee Group Ltd v WMH (21) Ltd* [1998] B.C.C. 972 (CA); *Coca Cola v Finsat International Ltd* [1998] Q.B. 43 (CA); *BICC Plc v Burndy Corp* [1985] Ch. 232 (CA), 248; *Continental Illinois v Papanicolaou* [1986] 2 Lloyd's Rep. 441 (CA); *Hong Kong and Shanghai Banking Corporation v Kloeckner & Co AG* [1990] 2 Q.B. 514; *Re Kaupthing Singer and Friedlander Ltd (In Administration), Newcastle Building Society v Mills* [2009] 2 Lloyd's Rep. 154.

[52] *Esso Petroleum v Milton* [1997] 1 W.L.R. 938 (CA).

[53] *Edlington Properties Ltd v JH Fenner & Co Ltd* [2006] 1 W.L.R. 1583 (CA).

[54] *Re Richbell Strategic Holdings Ltd* [1997] 2 B.C.L.C. 429.

Unfair Contract Terms Act 1977[55] but the exception from this requirement of clauses in "any contract so far as it relates to the creation or transfer of an interest in land"[56] extends to such clauses in a charge of land.[57] A contractual exclusion of set-off will not be effective to prevent set-off rights arising under the insolvency set-off rules when the requisite conditions are met (see below).

(iv) Current account set-off

This form of set-off is sometimes called combination and is the right given to a bank operating different accounts for the same customer to combine them and treat them as one, setting off any debit balance on one account against a credit balance on the other. The right will arise provided that there is no express or implied agreement to keep the accounts separate.[58] It is available as a self-help remedy, operating as a substantive right so that the different accounts are consolidated and the customer's position is reduced to a single net debt or credit balance. The right is sometimes exercisable without any demand being made in relation to the overdrawn account   **22–016**

(v) Retainer or fund set-off

Retainer or fund set-off applies to funds, such as trust funds, which are not   **22–017**
legal entities. Where a person is liable to contribute money to the fund, and is entitled to a share of that fund as beneficiary or creditor, then in certain cases the administrator of the fund may retain the contributor's share to cover the unpaid contribution, whether or not the contribution is unliquidated. This is sometimes referred to as the rule in *Cherry v Boultbee*[59] after the leading case in this area.

Where the contributor's share is a pro rata participation in the fund, the contributor's share is generally calculated by ascertaining what it would have been if the contributor had paid its contribution to the fund and then deducting its contribution from that notional share.

The Court of Appeal had previously considered the rule in *Cherry v Boultbee* in the context of a deed of indemnity.[60] The facts of the case are complex but,

---

[55] *Stewart Gill Ltd v Horatio Myer & Co Ltd* [1992] Q.B. 600 (CA); *Skipskredittforeningen v Emperor Navigation SA* [1998] 1 Lloyd's Rep. 66; *Esso Petroleum v Milton* [1997] 1 W.L.R. 938 (CA). In *Governor & Company of the Bank of Scotland v Singh* Unreported June 17, 2005, it was held that a "no set-off" clause was subject to the test of reasonableness in the Unfair Contract Terms Act 1977 but, as the defendant had received legal advice in respect of the agreement in which the clause appeared, the clause was not unfair. The Unfair Contract Terms in Consumer Contracts Regulations 1999 did not apply to the guarantee (given by the director of a company to a bank) in which the "no set-off" clause appeared as the director did not have a trade, business or profession as a guarantor and so was not a "supplier" for the purposes of the Regulations.

[56] s.1(2) and Sch.1.

[57] Consider *Electricity Supply Nominees Ltd v IAF Group Ltd* [1993] 1 W.L.R. 1059 (lease).

[58] In *Re European Bank, Agra Bank Claim* (1872) L.R. 8 Ch. App. 41 (CA); *Garnett v M'Kewan* (1872) L.R. 8 Ex. 10.

[59] *Cherry v Boultbee* (1839) My. & C. 442.

[60] *Squires v AIG Europe (UK) Ltd* [2006] Ch. 610 (CA).

put simply, the surety (Stations) had a right of indemnity against the principal debtor (its parent, Group) but also owed Group monies in respect of an inter-company loan. Both companies were in liquidation. If Group had been able to prove for the amount of the inter-company loan,[61] Stations would not have been able to set off its indemnity claim against Group's proof of debt because of the rule against double proof.[62] The liquidators of Stations argued that, notwithstanding the lack of set-off, the rule in *Cherry v Boultbee* applied so that Group had to bring into account in the liquidation of Stations–not by way of set-off, but as a contribution to the whole of the distributable fund–the value of Stations' indemnity claim.

22–018   The Court of Appeal held:

(a) when considering the distribution of a fund in equity, a person cannot share in a fund in relation to which he or she is also a debtor without first contributing to the whole by paying his or her debt;

(b) this general rule is applicable not only where a principal debtor is indebted to the fund but also where the fund has a right to be indemnified by the principal debtor against a liability which the fund might be required to meet in the future as surety for a debt owed by the principal debtor to a principal creditor. It is not necessary that the liability to the principal creditor has been satisfied out of the fund; it is enough that it might have to be satisfied in the future;

(c) this general rule (when applied to a case where the fund has a right to be indemnified by the principal debtor) is not displaced by the bankruptcy or liquidation of the principal debtor. There is no inconsistency with the rule against double proof, which would prevent the fund from proving in the bankruptcy or liquidation of the principal debtor in competition with the principal creditor.

However, in a recent Supreme Court decision,[63] it was held that the rule against double proof does have primacy over the rule in *Cherry v Boultbee*. Hence although the latter rule may be said to fill the gap left by the disapplication of set-off, it does not work in opposition to set-off and the rule against double proof will prevail.

Therefore, in an insolvency context, the rule in *Cherry v Boultbee* will no longer have application in the distribution of a fund (such as the assets in an insolvent estate) where mutual set-off is prevented by the rule against double-proof.

---

[61] On the facts, Group was prevented from proving for this debt by a widely drafted non-competition clause in favour of a creditor, AIG.

[62] In *Re Oriental Commercial Bank* (1871–72) L.R. 7 Ch. App. 99 (CA), 103–104; In *Re Polly Peck Plc* [1996] 2 All E.R. 433, 442.

[63] *Re Kaupthing Singer and Friedlander Ltd (In Administration)* [2011] UKSC 48.

(vi)   Insolvency set-off

This is the right of set-off which arises under the insolvency legislation. It has   **22–019**
been suggested that this is the most important form of set-off because it has a
security function and it is only on insolvency that the "security" really matters.[64]

Prior to the changes that were made to the insolvency legislation following
the coming into force of the corporate insolvency provisions of Enterprise Act
2002, insolvency set-off only arose in the case of a bankruptcy of an individual
(s.323 of the Insolvency Act 1986) or the liquidation of a company (r.4.90 of
the Insolvency Rules 1986); no insolvency set-off rule applied where an
administrator had been appointed.[65] For the reasons given in Pt 2 below,
however, the Insolvency (Amendment) Rules 2003[66] which came into force on
September 15, 2003 introduced a new insolvency set-off rule (r.2.85 of the
Insolvency Rules 1986) that applies in an administration if the administrator
gives notice under r.2.95 that he proposes to make a distribution to creditors.
The wording of r.2.85 closely corresponds to the wording of r.4.90 (subject to
some important differences discussed in Pt 2 below) and hence it is worth
considering some basic principles which relate to all forms of insolvency
set-off before turning to the detail of r.2.85.

(1)   Mandatory nature of insolvency set-off.   Where the claim and the cross-   **22–020**
claim are mutual (see below) and the other requirements for insolvency set-off
are met, insolvency set-off is mandatory under English law.[67] In other words,
any agreement not to set-off is ineffective if the creditor has the right to prove
and the right of set-off would otherwise have been available under the relevant
insolvency set-off rule. Furthermore, the court does not have any discretion to
disapply the insolvency set-off rules.[68] Although there is not yet any authority
on this point in relation to r.2.85, in view of the similarity between the terms
and effect of r.4.90 and r.2.85, it would be safe to assume that administration
set-off is equally mandatory once the administrator has given notice of his
intention to make distributions to creditors.

The set-off is self-executing and operates automatically from the date on
which the rule requires the account to be taken[69] (i.e. the commencement of the
bankruptcy in the case of s.323, the date the company goes into liquidation in
the case of r.4.90 and the date of the notice of distribution to creditors in the
case of r.2.85). There is no need for the creditor to prove for the claim in order

---

[64] Wood, *English and International Set-off* (London: Sweet & Maxwell, 1989) (see fn.2),
para.1–29.

[65] *Re Isovel Contracts Ltd* [2001] All E.R. (D) 440 (Nov), [33]: "rule 4.90 is clearly limited to
companies in liquidation. Had Parliament wished to apply it to companies in administration, it
could have done so. It did not . . . there is no ground in law or in justice for extending the principle
of insolvency set-off beyond the circumstances to which Parliament has said it shall apply, namely
liquidations."

[66] SI 2003/1730.

[67] *National Westminster Bank Ltd v Halesowen Presswork & Assemblies Ltd* [1972] A.C. 785
(HL).

[68] *Re Bank of Credit & Commerce International SA (No.11)* [1997] Ch. 213.

[69] *Stein v Blake (No.1)* [1996] A.C. 243 (HL), 254, per Lord Hoffmann.

to be able to exercise the right of set-off and there is no prescribed procedure for claiming the set-off (which operates automatically).[70] This means that, if the creditor assigns its claim to a third party after the date on which the account is to be taken, it will only be assigning the net balance after the set-off.[71]

Although the account between the insolvent company and the creditor is considered to be taken as at the relevant date specified in the set-off provision, in practice the account cannot be taken until a later date (as it will take a period of time for the insolvency officeholder to investigate the position in relation to claims owing to and from the insolvent company). The insolvency officeholder is able to take into account events that happen after the relevant date (such as the crystallisation of a contingent claim or an unliquidated claim becoming liquidated) when taking the account for set-off purposes.[72] This is sometimes referred to as the "hindsight principle".[73]

22–021 *(2) Due and contingent claims.*   All three insolvency set-off rules state that the mutual claims to be set off must be "due". The House of Lords has confirmed that the word "due" means "owing" or "outstanding" rather than "accrued due and payable".[74]

The position in relation to contingent claims (such as a claim under a guarantee of a loan where no demand has been made on the loan or where no default has yet occurred in respect of the loan) and future claims (such as a claim to pay money on a date which is not yet due) owing by or to the insolvent company has recently been clarified and affected by The Insolvency (Amendment) Rules 2005.[75] Prior to these changes, the position appeared to be that a contingent debt owed by the company in liquidation (and, by analogy, the company in administration) was capable of valuation pursuant to r.4.86 (or, by analogy, r.2.81) of the Insolvency Rules 1986 and so was required to be included in the account for set-off purposes. As there was no similar mechanism for valuing a contingent claim owed to the insolvent company, such a claim was not available for set-off.[76] If the contingency occurred during the course of the winding up, the quantified claim could be set-off but not otherwise. This meant that, in practice, if the contingency occurred after the dissolution of the insolvent company to whom the debt was owed, the company would need to be restored to the register in order for the liquidator to distribute

---

[70] *Stein v Blake (No.1)* [1996] A.C. 243 (HL), 252; *Re Daintrey Ex p. Mant* [1900] 1 Q.B. 546 (CA).

[71] *Enterprise Managed Services Ltd v Tony McFadden Utilities Ltd* [2011] 1 B.C.L.C. 414.

[72] See r.4.86 and r.2.81 of the Insolvency Rules 1986.

[73] See, e.g. *Sovereign Life Assurance Co v Dodd* [1892] 2 Q.B. 573 (CA).

[74] *Stein v Blake (No.1)* [1996] A.C. 243 (HL).

[75] SI 2005/527 which came into force on April 1, 2005.

[76] See, e.g. *Stein v Blake (No.1)* [1996] A.C. 243 (HL). Although there were unhelpful decisions to the contrary (including *In re a Debtor* [1956] 1 W.L.R. 1226 (CA), Lord Hoffmann dispelled these doubts in *Secretary of State for Trade and Industry v Frid* [2004] 2 A.C. 506 (HL) when he stated: "it is not, however, necessary for the purposes of rule 4.90(2) [now r.4.90(3)] that the debt should have been due and payable before the [date of resolution for winding up]. It is sufficient that there should have been an obligation arising out of the terms of the contract or statute by which a debt sounding in money would become payable upon the occurrence of some future event or events."

the receipt to the creditors; at that point, the creditor owing the (now crystallised) claim would be able to set off that claim against any amounts still due to it from the insolvent company.[77] The principle behind this rule was that it would be unfair for a solvent party who owes a contingent claim to be compelled to discharge that contingent liability through a mandatory set-off when (depending on the subsequent events) that claim might never crystallise.

The changes to r.2.85 and r.4.90 which took effect on April 1, 2005 reflect a **22–022** different policy. Contingent and future debts owing to and by the insolvent company are now to be set off provided they arise out of obligations incurred prior to the relevant "cut-off" date (referred to below). Rule 2.85(4) and r.4.90(4) now specifically provide that a sum shall be regarded as being "due" to or from the insolvent company for the purposes of set-off whether: (a) it is payable at present or in the future; (b) the obligation by virtue of which it is payable is certain or contingent; or (c) its amount is fixed or liquidated, or is capable of being ascertained by fixed rules or as a matter of opinion.

Contingent debts are to be estimated in accordance with rr.2.81 and 4.86 (as appropriate) and future debts are to be valued in accordance with r.2.105, rule 4.94 and rule 11.13 (debts payable at a future time).[78] The formula for the discounting of future debts has also been changed by The Insolvency (Amendment) Rules 2005 in response to defects in the original drafting noted by Lord Millett in the House of Lords' decision in *Re Park Air Services Ltd.*[79]

By way of contrast, if the balance of the claim, after set-off, is a sum owing to the insolvent company and all or part of that balance results from a contingent or prospective debt owed by the solvent counterparty, then the balance (or such part of it as results from the contingent or prospective debt) only becomes payable by the counterparty when the debt actually becomes due and payable. In other words, the set-off provisions do not accelerate the payment of contingent or future debts payable by a solvent counterparty otherwise than for the purposes of set-off.

Although not expressly stated in the revised insolvency set-off rules, it is **22–023** thought that the normal rules allowing an "appeal" against the admission or rejection of a proof in whole or in part would be available to any creditor wishing to challenge the valuation (for set-off purposes) by the liquidator or administrator of any incoming contingent claim. It is not clear what would happen if, having valued the incoming contingent claim for set-off purposes, the circumstances changed (so that, for example, the contingent claim crystallised at more than its valuation or it became apparent that the contingent claim could never, in fact, arise). If the liquidator or administrator still had assets available for distribution, an adjustment could be made in subsequent distributions to take into account the change of circumstances. It appears unlikely that there could be any claw-back of distributions already made if there were no such available assets.

---

[77] *MS Fashions Ltd v BCCI SA (No.2)* [1993] B.C.C. 70.

[78] See *Re Kaupthing, Singer and Friedlander Ltd (In Administration)* [2010] Bus. L.R. 1500 (CA) referred to below for a more detailed discussion of the valuation rules that apply in the context of r.2.85.

[79] *Re Park Air Services Plc* [2000] 2 A.C. 172 (HL).

22–024   *(3) Mutuality*. All three insolvency set-off rules require there to be "mutual dealings" between the insolvent person or company, and any creditor proving or claiming to prove for its debt, in order for the set-off rule to apply. This is based on the principle that one person's claim should not be used to pay another person's debt. In order for the claims to be mutual, each party must be personally liable on the claim it owes and beneficially entitled to the cross-claim it is owed.[80] The claim and the cross-claim must be owed between the same persons (i.e. the same legal persons) in the same right (i.e. not in a representative capacity).

So, for example, a trustee cannot set off against a personal liability which it owes to a creditor a cross-claim held by it for the benefit of the trust fund. Likewise, a bank may not set off a loan owed by a parent company against the bank's liability to repay a deposit to a subsidiary of that parent.[81]

An initial or apparent mutuality may be destroyed by the intervention of a third party. For example, if a borrower owes money to its bank and has placed a deposit with that bank, there would appear to be mutuality between the bank's claim for the repayment of the loan and the borrower's claim for the repayment of the deposit. Mutuality may have been destroyed, however, if the borrower has assigned the benefit of its right to the return of the deposit to a third party. The principal situations identified by Mr Wood[82] as giving rise to a destruction of mutuality are assignments, charges (or other forms of security), judicial enforcement orders (such as garnishee orders),[83] agency relationships, joint debtor or creditor relationships and trusts. The grant of security, and the impact that this has on the different types of set-off rights, will be particularly relevant in the context of a receivership and so this is considered further in Pt 3 below.

22–025   Where a creditor desires to protect itself against the loss of a set-off caused by an assignment, charge or declaration of trust, it can include contractual

---

[80] See Wood, *English and International Set-off* (London: Sweet & Maxwell, 1989) (above, fn.2), at para.14–29: "Mutuality sees through to the real beneficial ownership, regardless of who is the legal, nominal, titular or procedural holder of the claim or procedurally the appropriate plaintiff. It is the beneficial owner's property which is not to be appropriated to pay another's debt. If the owner is insolvent, his estate would be deprived of an asset which rightfully should be available for his general creditors."

[81] See, however, (by analogy) *Michael Simpson and Peter Normal Spratt (as Joint Liquidators and Deemed Official Receivers of Kaupthing Singer and Friedlander (Isle of Man) Ltd and Kaupthing Singer and Friedlander (Isle of Man) Ltd (In Liquidation) v Light House Living Ltd and Elle Macpherson* CHP 2010/11 (High Court Isle of Man) regarding the insolvency set-off provisions under the law of the Isle of Man (which are in a similar form to the English insolvency set-off provisions). On the basis that the insolvency set-off provisions were based on equitable principles, allowing the court to do substantial justice between the parties to mutual dealings upon the insolvency of either of them, the court allowed a set-off between a deposit held by the bank for Elle Macpherson against a mortgage debt legally owed to the bank by an SPV company, LHLL, that had been set up by Elle Macpherson to preserve her anonymity on the basis that the deposit and the debt were "mutual in substance". The court endorsed the concept of a party (in this case Ms Macpherson) being "beneficially liable" for a particular obligation. The facts of the case were unusual and it is not thought that this decision would give rise to any general departure from the strict requirements for mutuality.

[82] Wood, *English and International Set-off* (London: Sweet & Maxwell, 1989) (see fn.2), Chs 16–21.

[83] The existence of a company voluntary arrangement does not negate mutuality: *Penwith DC v VP Developments Ltd* [2005] B.C.L.C. 607.

prohibitions against such activities. In *Linden Gardens Trust Ltd v Lenesta Sludge Ltd*[84] it was held that a contractual prohibition against assignment would be effective to exclude an assignee's rights against the original contracting party even though the assignment would be effective as between the assignor and the assignee. Lightman J. held, in *Don King Productions Inc v Warren (No.1)*,[85] that a clause prohibiting an assignment "preserves the parties' rights of set-off against each other and saves them having any concern whether there has or has not been, or preserving any record of, any assignment of the benefit of the contract by the other party."[86]

(4) Multiparty netting arrangements. The insolvency set-off rules require **22–026** mutual dealings between two parties. An arrangement which purports to allow set-off or netting between more than two parties will therefore be inconsistent with the insolvency set-off rules.

In *British Eagle & International Airlines Ltd v Air France* [1975] 1 W.L.R. 758, the House of Lords considered a multiparty netting arrangement that provided for the liabilities between airlines participating in a clearing arrangement to be transferred to a clearing-house and netted out on a multilateral basis so that only the balance would be paid. One of the airlines participating in the arrangements went into liquidation. The House of Lords held that any netting out which had taken place before a member's winding up was binding on the liquidator but the clearing arrangement could not operate after the commencement of the winding up of the member because this would be contrary to the pari passu principle. This is because the multiparty netting arrangement would have the effect that an asset of the member airline (namely its claim against another member) would not be available to the general body of creditors of the member but instead would be distributed exclusively among the clearing house members. The court ruled that the airline company's liquidator could recover sums payable to it by other members of the clearing-house which were not netted prior to the winding-up petition. Similarly, the other members of the clearing-house were entitled to prove in the liquidation for the sums payable to them.

The basis for the court's decision, which was supported by a 3–2 majority of the House of Lords, was that the clearing house arrangement purported to achieve by contract a multilateral netting arrangement which went beyond what would have been possible under the mandatory set-off provisions. The effect of such an arrangement may, however, turn on its drafting. If the netting arrangement is drafted so that no amount is due to or from the various parties other than the single (net) payment provided for in the agreement, there will

---

[84] *Linden Gardens Trust Ltd v Lenesta Sludge Ltd* [1994] 1 A.C. 85 (HL).
[85] *Don King Productions Inc v Warren (No.1)* [2000] Ch. 291 (CA).
[86] In the *Don King* case, a trust over the rights in question was upheld, notwithstanding the prohibition on assignment, on the basis that the trust did not effect the position as between the original contracting parties. Lightman J. was not asked to consider whether the trust would destroy mutuality for insolvency set-off purposes and, if so, whether the court had any discretion to disapply this effect of the trust in view of the prohibition on assignment (notwithstanding the comments made in *Re Bank of Credit & Commerce International SA (No.11)* [1997] Ch. 213 regarding the mandatory nature of the insolvency set-off rules).

be no "asset" (i.e. any incoming claim) of which the insolvent debtor is being divested.[87] This area is complex and the outcome may depend on the language used.[88]

22–027   In the event of an insolvency of a party to a netting arrangement, a number of questions arise as set out below:

    (a) Could the netting arrangement be set aside as being in breach of the pari passu principle, the insolvency set-off rules or any other principles of the relevant insolvency law (as was the case in *British Eagle* as discussed above)?

    (b) Could the provisions which determine how the single (net) payment is to be determined be challenged (for example as a penalty if the clause is not a genuine pre-estimate of loss or because any contractual provisions for the conversion of foreign currency claims are inconsistent with the insolvency rules in this regard[89])?

    (c) Will any contractual rescission or acceleration clauses be effective in the insolvency of the counterparty? While there is nothing to prevent a contractual termination or acceleration as a matter of English insolvency law, many other jurisdictions have provisions (sometimes referred to as ipso facto provisions) which prevent anyone other than the insolvency office-holder from terminating open contracts.

    (d) Could the insolvency office-holder "cherry-pick" the contracts which are the subject to the netting arrangement by insisting on performance of the profitable ones and rescinding or disclaiming the unprofitable ones?

    (e) Could any of the contracts (or the netting agreement itself) be set aside in an insolvency (for example, as a transaction at an undervalue under s.238 of the Insolvency Act 1986)? This may be unlikely if the contracts have been entered into on arm's length terms and for the benefit of both (or all) of the parties although this will clearly depend on the "claw-back" provisions of the relevant insolvency law.

22–028   *(5) Provable debts.* In order to be able to exercise a right of insolvency set-off, the creditor must be entitled to prove its debt in the bankruptcy, liquidation or administration (even though, as stated above, the creditor is not actually required to prove its debt). Generally all liabilities are provable whether they are present or future, liquidated or unliquidated, actual or contingent. There are

---

[87] Indeed, this is how the courts below and two of the judges in the House of Lords interpreted the arrangements in *British Eagle*. Furthermore, when considering the redrafted IATA rules, the High Court of Australia held that there was no debt due to the member airlines, and therefore no property passing into the estate, so that there could be no question of a contract purporting to remove property from the estate: *IATA v Ansett* [2008] B.P.I.R. 57.

[88] See, e.g. S.R. Derham, *The Law of Set-off*, 3rd edn (Oxford: Oxford University Press, 2003) (fn.2), paras 16.28–16.42.

[89] See rr.4.91 and 2.86 of the Insolvency Rules 1986 but note also regs 12 and 14 of the Financial Collateral Arrangements (No.2) Regulations 2003 (SI 2003/3226).

certain debts, however, which are not provable (including the following) and, in all of these circumstances, a right of set-off would not be available:

(a) debts excluded from proof by the rule against double proof (which prevents two creditors from proving against the insolvent company for what is substantially the same debt). This rule most commonly arises in the case of a guarantee where the guarantor cannot prove against the principal debtor (in respect of its right of indemnity under the guarantee) in competition with the principal creditor[90];

(b) debts where the creditor has agreed not to prove (for example, until certain senior debts have been paid in full)[91];

(c) certain unenforceable debts, such as time-barred claims,[92] foreign revenue claims[93] and penal demands;

(d) post-insolvency rent and other periodical payments[94];

(e) post-insolvency interest[95]; and

(f) claims arising after the "cut-off" date referred to in r.13.12 (being the date of liquidation or administration as the case may be). This temporal restriction on what constitutes a provable debt was discussed in the recent case of *Re Nortel GmbH*[96] regarding the ranking of certain pension liabilities arising from a "financial support direction" that might be issued by The Pensions Regulator following the commencement of the administration. As the liabilities only came into existence following the exercise of a discretion by The Pensions Regulator *after* the commencement of the administration, it was held that the liabilities could not be provable debts and, as Briggs J. did not want the liabilities to fall into a "black hole" (and be irrecoverable), it was held that the liabilities must be expenses of the administration. Following

[90] *Re Oriental Commercial Bank* (1871) L.R. 7 Ch. App. 99 (CA).

[91] *Squires v AIG Europe (UK) Ltd* [2006] Ch. 610 (CA). Such an agreement not to prove would preclude a right of insolvency set-off. See Wood, *English and International Set-off* (London: Sweet & Maxwell, 1989) (fn.2), para.7–51.

[92] *Pott v Clegg* (1847) 16 M. & W. 321.

[93] Unless these are revenue claims arising within the European Union (which may now be enforceable under the provisions of Council Regulation (EC) No.1346/2000 on insolvency proceedings [2000] OJ L160/1)—see Ch.31, below.

[94] r.4.92 and r.2.87 of the Insolvency Rules 1986 provide that, in the case of rent and other payments of a periodical nature, the creditor may only prove for unpaid amounts up to the date of the liquidation or administration and so only such amounts are available for set-off. Any amounts which fall due after the date of liquidation or administration may, depending on whether the property is being used for the benefit of the insolvent estate, be payable as an expense (see Pt 2(f) below).

[95] Likewise r.4.93 and r.2.88 of the Insolvency Rules 1986 provide that a creditor can only prove for interest up to the date on which the company went into liquidation or administration; interest for periods after this date is not provable (unless there is a surplus remaining after paying all provable debts). Therefore the creditor can only set off its claim for interest up to the date of the liquidation or administration.

[96] *Re Nortel GmbH* [2011] B.C.C. 277. This decision is subject to appeal. See also Ch.4, above regarding administration expenses and STOP PRESS, after the preface to this work, on the Court of Appeal decision in *Nortel*.

this decision, there have been suggestions that r.13.12 should be amended so as to ensure that liabilities of this type are treated as provable debts.[97] The "cut-off" date is referred to below in the context of the insolvency set-off rules.

22–029 *(6) Cut-off date and prohibition on build-up of set-offs.* Claims owing to or from the insolvent company are not eligible for insolvency set-off if they were incurred after a certain date, and claims owing by the insolvent company are not eligible for insolvency set-off if they were acquired by the creditor after a certain date. This date is referred to in this chapter as the "cut-off date". The basic policy behind this concept is to prevent the creation of claims, or the trafficking in claims, after the solvent party has notice of the insolvency of the counterparty. The main object of the rule is to prevent creditors from improving their set-off position where an insolvency is imminent.[98] The following example illustrates how two parties could improve their respective positions by the trafficking in claims, to the detriment of the other creditors of the insolvent company, if this was not prevented by the cut-off date:

A owes B a debt of 100. A becomes insolvent and B realises that it is likely to receive a dividend of about 10 so that B's claim is only worth 10 to it. A third company, C, owes A a debt of 50. In the liquidation of A, C would have to pay this debt in full. If, however, C were to purchase B's debt, C would be able to set off the full amount of what it owes to A and will not have to pay this in A's liquidation. If C pays more than 10 for B's debt (but less than 50), both C and B will have benefited. The other unsecured creditors of A will, however, have been prejudiced as A will not receive an asset (i.e. the right to be repaid 50 by C).

As a consequence of the insolvency set-off rules, however, C would only be able to acquire B's debt (for set-off purposes) prior to the cut-off date; if C were to acquire the debt after this date, it would not be available for set-off.

22–030 Not all of the events that give rise to the cut-off depend upon notice to, or the actual knowledge of, the solvent party and so, in some instances, a claim incurred or acquired after the cut-off date will not be available for set-off even where the creditor has no knowledge of the debtor's financial difficulties. The events that do not depend upon notice or knowledge are things that (in theory at any rate) the solvent party could have discovered by carrying out the necessary searches.[99]

---

[97] Such changes (albeit in different forms) have been proposed by the Insolvency Lawyers Association and the City of London Law Society Insolvency Subcommittee in response to requests by The Insolvency Service for proposed solutions to the issues caused by the *Nortel* decision.

[98] This policy objective does not explain why debts incurred by the insolvent company, rather than the solvent counterparty, after the cut-off date are excluded from the insolvency set-off provisions.

[99] Such as a telephone search of the Central Index of Winding Up Petitions or a search of the Companies Registry. These searches are frequently inconclusive and there is currently no central index of administration applications or documents filed with the court to commence an administration.

The cut-off date in an administration is referred to in detail in Pt 2(c) below. In a liquidation, the cut-off date is (broadly) the first to occur of:

(a) the time when the creditor had notice of a meeting of creditors under s.98 of the Insolvency Act 1986 or a petition for the winding up of the company;

(b) in circumstances where the liquidation was immediately preceded by an administration, the time when the creditor had notice that an administration application was pending or that a notice of intention to appoint an administrator had been given;

(c) regardless of notice, the time the company goes into liquidation or, if the liquidation is immediately preceded by an administration, the commencement of the administration.[100]

As a matter of English law, the cut-off date is a relatively short period prior to the commencement of the liquidation or administration and there is nothing to prevent the acquisition of claims for set-off purposes prior to this date. If the insolvent company is not a party to the assignment, but there is merely a bilateral transaction between the seller and the purchaser of the debt (i.e. B and C in the example given above), the acquisition could not be challenged, in the insolvent company's liquidation or administration, as a transaction at an under-value or a preference under ss.239 and 238 of the Insolvency Act 1986. In an old bankruptcy case,[101] the court declined to allow a set-off where the party acquiring the debt had notice of a stoppage of payments by the insolvent debtor even though this was before the cut-off date (at that time, an "act of bank-ruptcy") in the bankruptcy set-off rule. This case has been used to argue that, if the party acquiring the debt does so in contemplation of the insolvency of the debtor, the debt may not be available for insolvency set-off purposes even if the cut-off date has not occurred. The report is not very satisfactory but it appears that the actual grounds for the decision were that, in order for the transfer to be effective, some act was necessary by the insolvent counterparty and this was a preference and therefore disallowed. If, however, the assign-ment is simply a matter between the assignor and the assignee (and the insol-vent debtor takes no part in these arrangements), there could clearly be no preference argument (as the insolvent debtor would not do anything or suffer anything to be done). Furthermore, following the changes that were made to r.4.90 and r.2.85 of the Insolvency Rules 1986 by the Insolvency (Amendment) Rules 2005, the rules should be considered to be comprehensive and only mutual dealings disallowed under the provisions in r.2.85 or r.4.90 should not to be considered in the set-off account.

(7) Property claims and foreign currency claims. Finally, to be available **22–031** for insolvency set-off, the claim must be a monetary claim (arising out of a

[100] Insolvency Rules 1986, r.4.90(2).
[101] *Watts v Christie* (1849) 11 Beav. 546. See also *Re Eros Films Ltd* [1963] Ch. 565.

debtor-creditor relationship) rather than a property claim (such as a proprietary right for the delivery of money or other property).

If the claim owing by the insolvent company is denominated in a foreign currency then, regardless of what exchange rates are specified in the agreement, for insolvency set-off purposes, the claim must be converted into sterling at the official exchange rate (which is stated to be the middle exchange rate on the London Foreign Exchange Market at the close of business, as published for the date in question[102]) prevailing on the date when the company went into liquidation or administration (as the case may be).[103]

An exception to this is provided by reg.14 of the Financial Collateral Arrangements (No.2) Regulations 2003.[104] Where a party to a financial collateral arrangement, or a party to a close-out netting provision in a financial collateral arrangement, goes into liquidation or administration, r.4.91 and 2.86 are disapplied in favour of the contractual provisions unless the arrangement provides for an unreasonable exchange rate. It is thought that this provision applies only for the purposes of protecting and giving effect to the contractual terms of any close-out netting provision and does not go wider than this and allow a creditor to prove an unsecured net claim (i.e. after operation of close-out netting or, in relation to a security financial collateral arrangement, after appropriation of available security) in the contractual currency (rather than in sterling).[105]

2. Set-off in Administration

22–032 Prior to the changes that were made by the corporate insolvency provisions of the Enterprise Act 2002, there was no general power for an administrator to make distributions to creditors and so no need, in an administration, for an insolvency set-off rule (which is an essential part of the machinery of proving a debt). On September 15, 2003, a number of important changes were made to the administration regime including the introduction of a new power, exercisable by the administrator with the leave of the court, to make distributions to unsecured creditors.[106] This meant that various rules (similar to the rules that apply in a liquidation) had to be introduced into Pt 2 of the Insolvency Rules 1986 to allow creditors to prove their debts in the administration in circumstances where the administrator obtains the leave of the court to make distributions. The new rules include set-off provisions pursuant to r.2.85 of the Insolvency Rules 1986.

Following the introduction of the new r.2.85, the Insolvency Service announced that it was intending to consult a number of leading academics and

---

[102] In fact, there is no such published rate and so, in an unreported decision in *Kaupthing Singer and Friedlander Ltd (in administration)* Unreported June 16, 2009, the court held that the administrators should use the spot exchange rate published by the Bank of England for the date in question.

[103] r.4.91 and r.2.86 of the Insolvency Rules 1986.

[104] SI 2003/3226.

[105] This would be in keeping with recitals 5 and 7 of the Financial Collateral Directive 2002/47/ EC as well as the decision in *In Re Lines Bros Ltd (In Liquidation)* [1983] Ch. 1 (CA).

[106] para.65(3) of Sch.B1 to the Insolvency Act 1986.

specialists regarding r.2.85 and r.4.90. Following this consultation, both r.2.85 and r.4.90 were amended[107] to "harmonise the effect of set off in liquidation and administration respectively and to provide greater detail and clarity regarding the meaning of the set-off rules."[108]

The wording of r.2.85 (as amended) follows very closely the wording of r.4.90 and so it is likely that the case law regarding liquidation set-off (including its mandatory and automatic effect) will apply equally to administration set-off. Hence the principles set out in Pt 1(c)(vi) above (including those in relation to contingent and future claims) will apply in relation to administration set-off, just as they apply to liquidation set-off. There is a key difference, however, between the two insolvency set-off rules. In a liquidation, r.4.90 will automatically come into play as soon as the company goes into liquidation whereas an account only needs to be taken for the purposes of r.2.85 if the administrator gives notice (pursuant to r.2.95) that he proposes to make a distribution to creditors (the meaning of this expression is considered below). Until this point in time, a creditor will only be able to exercise a right of set-off if another form of set-off (as set out in Pt 1(c)(i)–(v) above is available. It will not usually be known, at the date on which the company goes into administration, whether the administrator will be making distributions to creditors (and so whether r.2.85 will come into play). This is considered further below.

Part 2 of this chapter therefore considers: **22–033**

(a) the impact of the administration moratorium, and any company voluntary arrangement or scheme of arrangement which may be proposed by the administrator, on the other forms of set-off which may be available to a creditor prior to the coming into effect of r.2.85;

(b) the difference between the "cut-off date" (i.e. the date intended to prevent the build-up of insolvency set-off rights) and the "set-off date" (i.e. the date on which the account is taken for set-off purposes) in r.2.85 and the practical consequences of this distinction for creditors;

(c) when r.2.85 comes into play and what is meant by a "distribution" for these purposes;

(d) the interaction between r.2.85 and the expense doctrine and whether it is problematic for creditors that post-administration claims cannot be included in the account for the purposes of r.2.85;

(e) the detailed consideration of r.2.85 in the administration of *Kaupthing, Singer and Friedlander Ltd*; and

(f) possible proposals for reform of r.2.85.

---

[107] By The Insolvency (Amendment) Rules 2005 (SI 2005/527), which came into force on April 1, 2005.
[108] Stephen Leinster, former Director of Policy, Technical, Legislative and Professional Regulation at the Insolvency Service.

(a)   Wording of administration set-off rule

22–034   Rule 2.85 (as amended) provides as follows:

Rule 2.85 Mutual credits and set-off

(1) This rule applies where the administrator, being authorised to make the distribution in question, has, pursuant to rule 2.95 given notice that he proposes to make it.

(2) In this rule "mutual dealings" means mutual credits, mutual debts or other mutual dealings between the company and any creditor of the company proving or claiming to prove for a debt in the administration but does not include any of the following:

    (a) any debt arising out of an obligation incurred after the company entered administration;

    (b) any debt arising out of an obligation incurred at a time when the creditor had notice that:

        (i) an application for an administration order was pending; or

        (ii) any person had given notice of intention to appoint an administrator;

    (c) any debt arising out of an obligation where:

        (i) the administration was immediately preceded by a winding up; and

        (ii) at the time the obligation was incurred the creditor had notice that a meeting of creditors had been summoned under section 98 or a petition for the winding up of the company was pending;

    (d) any debt arising out of an obligation incurred during a winding up which immediately preceded the administration; or

    (e) any debt which has been acquired by a creditor by assignment or otherwise, pursuant to an agreement between the creditor and any other party where that agreement was entered into:

        (i) after the company entered administration;

        (ii) at a time when the creditor had notice that an application for an administration order was pending;

        (iii) at a time when the creditor had notice that any person had given notice of intention to appoint an administrator;

        (iv) where the administration was immediately preceded by a winding up, at a time when the creditor had notice that a meeting of creditors had been summoned under section 98 or that a winding up petition was pending; or

        (v) during a winding up which immediately preceded the administration.

(3) An account shall be taken as at the date of the notice referred to in paragraph (1) of what is due from each party to the other in respect of

the mutual dealings and the sums due from one party shall be set off against the sums due from the other.

(4) A sum shall be regarded as being due to or from the company for the purposes of paragraph (3) whether:

    (a) it is payable at present or in the future;

    (b) the obligation by virtue of which it is payable is certain or contingent; or

    (c) its amount is fixed or liquidated, or is capable of being ascertained by fixed rules or as a matter of opinion.

(5) Rule 2.81 shall apply for the purposes of this Rule to any obligation to or from the company which, by reason of its being subject to any contingency or for any other reason, does not bear a certain value.

(6) Rules 2.86 to 2.88 shall apply for the purposes of this Rule in relation to any sums due to the company which:

    (a) are payable in a currency other than sterling;

    (b) are of a periodical nature; or

    (c) bear interest.

(7) Rule 2.105 shall apply for the purposes of this Rule to any sum due to or from the company which is payable in the future.

(8) Only the balance (if any) of the account owed to the creditor is provable in the administration. Alternatively the balance (if any) owed to the company shall be paid to the administrator as part of the assets except where all or part of the balance results from a contingent or prospective debt owed by the creditor and in such a case the balance (or that part of it which results from the contingent or prospective debt) shall be paid if and when that debt becomes due and payable.

(9) In this rule "obligation" means an obligation however arising, whether by virtue of an agreement, rule of law or otherwise.

(b) Impact of moratorium on contractual and other forms of set-off

As referred to above, until the administrator gives notice (pursuant to r.2.95) of **22–035** his intention to make a distribution to creditors, r.2.85 will not come into play. A creditor may, however, have a right of set-off pursuant to one of the other forms of set-off referred to in Pt 1(c)(i)–(v) above. For example, the creditor may have a contractual right of set-off, a right to combine accounts (if the creditor is a bank) or an independent or transaction set-off. The question therefore arises as to whether the creditor can exercise that (non-insolvency) right of set-off following the commencement of an administration of the counterparty notwithstanding the moratorium on creditor action that arises pursuant to paras 43 and 44 of Sch.B1 to the Insolvency Act 1986.

The impact of the moratorium on set-off rights will depend upon the nature of the set-off right being exercised. The moratorium should not prevent the exercise of a self-help remedy (such as a contractual right of set-off, a transaction set-off or the right to combine accounts). In *Electro Magnetic(s) Ltd v Development Bank of Singapore Ltd*,[109] the Court of Appeal in Singapore was asked to consider the impact on the respondent bank's contractual set-off rights and right to combine accounts of certain provisions of the Singapore Companies Act 1990 which arose in the judicial management of the appellant company. The provisions are very similar to para.43 of Sch.B1 to the Insolvency Act 1986 and include a moratorium on any steps taken to enforce any charge or security over the company's property and on the commencement or continuation of any other proceedings or other legal process against the company and its property. The court held that:

(a)   a right of set-off is not a security within the meaning of the relevant sections. "A security over a property consists of some real or proprietary interest, legal or equitable, in the property as distinguished from a personal right or claim thereon. A right of set-off is a personal right; it is a right given by contract or by law to set one claim against the other and arrive at a balance." The respondents, therefore, merely had a contractual and personal right to set off the credit balance of the appellants in one account against their debit balance in another or to combine the two and net the balance; and

(b)   the exercise of a self-help right of set-off did not constitute the commencement or continuation of other proceedings. "[T]he word 'proceedings' connotes a process initiated whether in court or by way of arbitration or a step in such process. An exercise of a right of set-off is an extra-legal step and is not such a process or a step in such process."

22–036   If the set-off can only be exercised through legal proceedings (as is generally the case with independent set-off), the consent of the administrator or the leave of the court will be required, pursuant to para.43(6) of Sch.B1 to the Insolvency Act 1986, to commence or continue any proceedings in order to allow the company in administration to raise an independent set-off, or possibly even for the creditor to raise the set-off by way of a defence in any proceedings brought by the company in administration.[110]

---

[109]   *Electro Magnetic(s) Ltd v Development Bank of Singapore Ltd* [1994] 1 S.L.R. 734.
[110]   See *Stehar Knitting Mills Pty Ltd v Southern Textile Converters Pty Ltd* [1980] 2 N.S.W.L.R. 514, although this case concerned a scheme of arrangement which prevented the commencement or continuation of any action, proceedings, suit or arbitration rather than the application of the moratorium in an administration. For the contrary view, see *Peat v Jones* (1881) L.R. 8 Q.B.D. 147 (CA) and *Mersey Steel & Iron Co v Naylor, Benson & Co* (1882) L.R. 9 Q.B.D. 648 where set-off in the context of actions by an insolvency representative against a creditor of the insolvent was held not to be a "proceeding" for the purposes of the insolvency stay of proceedings. The difference can be explained on the basis that, in *Peat v Jones* and *Mersey Steel & Iron Co*, the relevant insolvency set-off rule would have provided for a right of set-off if the defendant had proved for its cross-claim rather than raising it by way of defence. As r.2.85 does not come into play until the notice of distribution, the leave of the court or the consent of the administrator may be required (by

(c) Impact of scheme of arrangement or voluntary arrangement

Notwithstanding the changes to the purpose of administration in para.3(1) of **22–037** Sch.B1 to the Insolvency Act 1986, an administrator may still put together proposals for a company voluntary arrangement under s.1 of the Insolvency Act 1986 or a scheme of arrangement under ss.895 to 901 of the Companies Act 2006 (for example as a means of rescuing the company). So long as the arrangement is approved by the requisite majorities of members and creditors (and, in the case of a scheme of arrangement, is sanctioned by the court), it may have the effect of postponing the maturity of a creditor's claim, or reducing the amount of such claim, notwithstanding the fact that the creditor in question did not vote in favour of the proposals. Either of these events could have an impact on the creditor's right of set-off. Until the arrangement is approved and the postponement or discharge becomes binding, the creditor will be able to exercise its set-off right (subject to the comments made above regarding the impact of the moratorium).

It is theoretically possible that a voluntary arrangement or scheme of arrangement could be approved or sanctioned without the creditor in question receiving notice of the proposals (and so being given the opportunity to exercise its set-off right prior to the arrangement becoming binding on creditors). In practice, however, it is unlikely that the administrator would be unaware of any significant creditor and the administrator would be under an obligation to notify all creditors of whom he is aware of the proposals for the scheme or voluntary arrangement.

Furthermore, the creditor may be able to apply to court on the grounds of unfair prejudice (in the case of voluntary arrangement[111]) or on the basis that the classes of creditors have not been properly constituted or that the scheme is unfair (in the case of a scheme of arrangement) if the creditor is put at a special disadvantage (for example because the set-off provisions in the proposed arrangement are substantially different from the provisions that would have applied under the liquidation or administration set-off rules[112]).

(d) The cut-off and set-off dates

(i) Differences between liquidation and administration set-off rules

Once the administrator gives notice (under r.2.95) that he proposes to make **22–038** a distribution to creditors, r.2.85 comes into play and will supersede any

---

analogy with *Stehar Knitting Mills Pty Ltd*) to assert a set-off by way of a defence in any legal proceedings commenced by the administrator on behalf of the company prior to any notice of distribution being given.

[111] Insolvency Act 1986, s.6. For successful application under s.6 in a different context, see *Prudential Assurance Co Ltd v PRG Powerhouse Ltd* [2007] B.C.C. 500.

[112] See *Re Telewest Communications Plc (No.2)* [2005] B.C.C. 36, however, where the court sanctioned a scheme of arrangement notwithstanding the fact that the provisions for valuing foreign currency claims were different to the ones that would have applied in a liquidation under r.4.91 of the Insolvency Rules 1986.

contractual rights of set-off which are inconsistent with the provisions of
r.2.85. In order to appreciate fully the key difference between r.4.90 and r.2.85
of the Insolvency Rules 1986, it is important to distinguish between two
concepts, referred to in this chapter as the "cut-off date" and the "set-off date".

(1) The "cut-off date" is referred to in Pt 1(c)(vi)(6) above and is the date
    after which claims incurred or acquired by the solvent counterparty,
    or incurred by the insolvency company, can no longer be included in
    the account for set-off purposes. In the case of r.2.85, the cut-off date
    depends on whether there has been a liquidation immediately prior to
    the administration:

    (a) administration with no preceding liquidation: the cut-off date is
        the earlier of:
        (i) the date the company entered into administration; and
        (ii) the date on which the creditor had notice of an administra-
             tion application or that a person had given notice of intention
             to appoint an administrator; and
    (b) administration with immediately preceding liquidation: the cut-off
        date is the earlier of:
        (i) the date of commencement of the liquidation; and
        (ii) the date on which the creditor had notice that a meeting of
             creditors had been summoned under s.98 of the Insolvency
             Act 1986 or that a petition for the winding up of the company
             was pending.[113]

(2) The "set-off date" is the date on which the account of what is due
    from each party to the other in respect of the mutual dealings is to be
    taken and the sums due from one party are to be set off against the
    sums due from the other. In the case of most liquidations, the set-off
    date (i.e. the date the company goes into liquidation) is likely to occur
    shortly after the earliest cut-off date (i.e. the date of notice of a
    winding up petition[114]). In the case of an administration, the set-off
    date is the date on which (having obtained the leave of the court to do
    so under para.65(3) of Sch.B1 to the Insolvency Act 1986) the admin-
    istrator gives notice (under r.2.95) that he is proposing to make a
    distribution to creditors. This date could occur some months after the
    commencement of the administration; indeed, in the administration
    of Lehman Brothers International (Europe), the administrators gave
    notice under r.2.95 (and therefore the set-off date occurred) some
    15 months after the commencement of the administration. The
    problem for creditors is that, if the administrator does give the r.2.95
    notice (thus triggering the set-off date for the purposes of the admin-
    istration set-off rule), any claims that were incurred or acquired after

---

[113] Insolvency Rules 1986, r.2.85(2).
[114] The period could be longer if, following the presentation of the winding up petition, a
provisional liquidator is appointed.

the (much earlier) cut-off date will not be included in the account for set-off purposes. The implications of this for creditors are considered further below.

(ii) Reasons for, and consequences of, difference between set-off and cut-off dates

So why is there such a difference between the set-off date and the cut-off date **22–039** in an administration? When the concept of a mandatory and self-executing administration set-off rule was first raised in the consultation regarding the Enterprise Act 2002, some concern was expressed at the idea that such a rule might apply from the commencement of the administration. This would have had the effect of freezing positions (for example under running accounts or hedging agreements) and could have prevented the administrator from being able to continue to trade. This was hardly in keeping with the emphasis on rescue in respect of the new administration provisions. It was agreed that the administration set-off rule was only necessary once the administrator had concluded that a rescue of the company was not possible and that the administration should be used, instead, to make distributions to creditors (i.e. a liquidating administration). This is why r.2.85 does not apply automatically from the moment of administration (as r.4.90 does in a liquidation). The rule only applies if and when the administrator gives notice under r.2.95 that he proposes to make a distribution (the meaning of which is considered below). Up to that point, the usual contractual, transaction or independent set-off rights will continue to apply.

The account for set-off purposes is therefore taken at the date the administrator gives notice of the distribution (i.e. the "set-off date" is the date of notice of the distribution); it is not backdated to the date of administration. This is important if there has been post-administration trading which has resulted in changes in positions. For the purposes of r.2.85, the "cut-off" date (preventing the build-up of set-off rights) is backdated once the administrator decides that he is going to make a distribution. As referred to above, the cut-off date will be the date of administration, the earlier date of notice of an administration application or notice of an intention to appoint an administrator or the earlier date of a subsequent winding-up which immediately precedes the date of administration and so there could be a substantial period between the cut-off date and the set-off date (i.e. the date of notice of the distribution).

There are two limbs to the cut-off date: **22–040**

(a) new debts arising out of obligations which were incurred (either by the company in administration or the creditor) after the cut-off date will not be available for set-off under r.2.85. The meaning of this expression in the context of contingent and future claims is considered in Pt 1(c)(vi)(2) above. This limb of the cut-off rule works both ways and prevents the build-up of set-off rights for r.2.85 purposes in relation to sums due both from and to the company (rather than just sums due from the company which was the language used in r.4.90

prior to the recent amendments[115]). The Australian set-off provisions[116] include sums due from and to the company and this
approach may have been adopted in respect of r.2.85 to encourage
post-administration debtors who have no contractual or other rights
of set-off to pay up rather than waiting to see whether they will
acquire a right of set-off under r.2.85; and

(b) debts which were acquired by a creditor (by assignment or otherwise)
     pursuant to an agreement entered into after the cut-off date will not
     be available for set-off under r.2.85. The amendments to r.2.85 have
     clarified that it is the date of the agreement that is important for these
     purposes, rather than the date on which the claim was acquired
     pursuant to the agreement, and this should address the concerns about
     claims which are compulsorily reacquired by the creditor after the
     cut-off date but pursuant to an agreement entered into prior to
     the cut-off date (for example, under a repurchase agreement or on the
     redemption of security).[117]

(iii)   Practical implications for creditors

22–041   In practice (and subject to the litigation risk referred to below), this means
that, post administration but prior to a r.2.95 notice, creditors can continue to
exercise "non-insolvency" set-off rights (such as contractual, transaction or
independent set-off rights) even if the claims have arisen post administration
but creditors cannot build up claims for the purposes of exercising a right of
set-off under r.2.85 in the future (for example, if no other right of set-off is
available to them). Furthermore, if the non-insolvency set-off right is inconsistent with the provisions of r.2.85 (as discussed below), the creditor will need
to exercise that non-insolvency set-off right prior to notice being given under
r.2.95; if it fails to do so, the non-insolvency set-off right will be lost once the
insolvency set-off rule comes into play (the "use it or lose it" approach). In
other words, in an administration, there may (subject to the comments made
below) be a "set-off window" in which creditors can exercise contractual rights
of set-off (for example) which are wider than the set-off available under r.2.85.
Unfortunately it may not always be clear from the outset whether a distribution
to creditors might ultimately be made: even if the administrator states in his
proposals that he is seeking to rescue the company or to sell the business as a
going concern, the circumstances might subsequently change and the administration may become a liquidating one. The prudent advice to a creditor must
therefore be to exercise any non-insolvency set-off right (rather than to risk
losing it) even though such advice is unlikely to assist with the rescue or
continued trading of the company in administration.

---

[115] The Insolvency (Amendment) Rules 2005 (SI 2005/527). Rule 4.90 was changed so that
there is now no discrepancy between the two rules in this regard.

[116] Bankruptcy Act 1966, s.86(2) and Corporations Act 2001, s.553C(2).

[117] See Wood, *English and International Set-off* (London: Sweet & Maxwell, 1989) (fn.2
above), para.7.244 and following.

It is understood that, in the administration of Lehman Brothers International (Europe) (LBIE), a number of creditors exercised (or purported to exercise) contractual rights of set-off during the "set-off window" referred to above (i.e. prior to the administrators giving the r.2.95 notice). In some cases, the contractual set-off rights were very broad and, on their terms, allowed a creditor to set off cross-affiliate claims or claims that may have been acquired from a third party since the date of administration. While the effect of r.2.85 is that a creditor will not be able to exercise such a wide contractual set-off right following the giving of the r.2.95 notice (as the insolvency set-off rule will override any contractual provisions which are inconsistent with the requirements for mutuality in r.2.85), there is nothing in the express terms of r.2.85 (or elsewhere in the insolvency legislation) which would appear to prevent this. The counter-argument is that the exercise of non-mutual contractual set-offs during the set-off window is contrary to public policy but such public policy arguments should not be extended arbitrarily when they would interfere with the fundamental principle of freedom of contract.[118] For the reasons given in Pt 1(c)(vi)(6) above, it would appear that only mutual dealings disallowed under the provisions of r.2.85 (or r.4.90) should be excluded on public policy grounds. It is understood that the LBIE administrators may be seeking to bring a test case regarding contractual set-offs exercised during the set-off window.[119]

A concern has also been raised regarding r.2.85 in respect of creditors who also owe pre-administration debts. Because the Crown is treated as a single entity for set-off purposes, this is likely to be particularly relevant in the case of the different Crown departments. For example, the Crown (by its department HM Customs and Revenue) may be a debtor in respect of its obligation to make a VAT rebate but also a creditor (through its department the Redundancy Payments Office) in respect of its right of indemnity for redundancy payments made by it in respect of the company's employees. As a practical matter, if there is no other right of set-off available, could the party concerned simply refuse to pay its pre-administration debt in order to "wait and see" if it will acquire a right of set-off under r.2.85 (if the administration becomes a liquidating one)? It seems unlikely that this will cause problems in practice for two reasons. First, unless and until a right of set-off arises under r.2.85, the party will have no grounds on which to refuse to pay the pre-administration debt and so payment could be enforced (in the usual way) by the administrator. Secondly, similar issues arose prior to the introduction of the administration set-off rule (as such a party could have refused to pay its debts in the administration process in case there were a subsequent liquidation in which the party would acquire a right of set-off pursuant to r.4.90). This did not, in practice, prevent pre-administration debtors from paying their debts.

A further issue arises in that, as a result of the cut-off date, post-administration liabilities will not be available for set-off under r.2.85. Whether this is a problem

---

[118] *Printing and Numerical Registering Co v Sampson* (1875) L.R. 19 Eq. 462, 465.

[119] The Financial Markets Law Committee wrote to the Insolvency Service on November 9, 2010 seeking clarification of the rights of set-off that could be exercised during the "set-off window" but no response has been received to date.

in practice will depend upon whether such post-administration liabilities are payable as an expense of the administration (so that the creditor does not need the security function that a right of set-off would give because it is able to rely on the priority given to administration expenses). This is considered further in Pt 2(f) below.

(e) Meaning of distribution

22–042 The administration set-off rule comes into play when the administrator, being authorised to make the distribution in question, has pursuant to r.2.95 given notice that he proposes to make it. "Distribution" is not defined in either r.2.85 or r.2.95 and this gives rise to the question of what "distribution" means for these purposes.

The expression "distribution" is used in a number of places in Sch.B1 to the Insolvency Act 1986. For example, the third objective in para.3(1) of Sch.B1 is to realise property in order to make a "distribution" to one or more secured or preferential creditors. Paragraph 65(3) also refers (impliedly) to distributions to secured and preferential creditors when providing that a distribution may not be made to a creditor who is neither secured nor preferential unless the court gives permission. The expression is also referred to in the heading of Ch.10 of the Insolvency Rules 1986 which applies when the administrator makes, or proposes to make, a distribution to any class of creditors (r.2.68). Secured creditors are not expressly excluded from the expression "creditors" for the purposes of r.2.68. Hence the question arises as to whether a "distribution" (for the purposes of r.2.85) is limited to a distribution to unsecured (including preferential) creditors or whether it could include any payments made to secured creditors.

It seems clear that a payment made to a fixed charge creditor pursuant to the condition of a court order under para.71(3) of Sch.B1 would not constitute a "distribution" to that secured creditor. Furthermore, if the secured creditor is able to obtain the leave of the court (under para.43(2) of Sch.B1) to enforce its security outside of the administration process, any recoveries will not be "distributions" for the purposes of the administration provisions. What is more problematic, however, is the categorisation of payments made to the floating charge-holder in respect of floating charge assets realised by the administrator (after the necessary deductions have been made for the administration expenses, the preferential creditors and the s.176A prescribed part). Will the secured creditor will have to go through the proving process is order to recover the floating charge element of its security and, if so, is this to be treated as a "distribution" for the purposes of Ch.10 of the Insolvency Rules 1986[120] including

---

[120] Not only would this have an impact on whether r.2.85 comes into play but it would also affect payments of interest to the secured creditor (as r.2.88 provides that, unless there are surplus assets, interest is only provable up to the date of the administration or earlier liquidation whereas a secured credit agreement will usually give the secured creditor the right to default interest until payment) and the conversion of foreign currency claims (as r.2.86 provides that any foreign currency claim will be converted into sterling at the official exchange rate (defined as the middle exchange rate on the London Foreign Exchange Market at the close of business) prevailing on the date when the company entered administration (or liquidation if earlier) whereas a secured credit agreement will usually contain its own provisions for the exchange of foreign currency claims).

r.2.85? This requirement would seem inconsistent with the provisions of r.2.83(1) (whereby a secured creditor is entitled to prove for the balance of its claim, after deducting the amount that has been realised in respect of its security) and rr.2.90–2.94 (whereby a secured creditor can disclose its security in its proof of debt, put a value on this security and prove for the balance, allowing the administrator to redeem the security at the value put upon it in the creditor's proof); these provisions appear to envisage that, to the extent that the claim is secured, it will not be part of the proof of debt process.

Furthermore, in the notice that is to be given pursuant to r.2.95, the adminis-   **22–043**
trator is required to state whether the distribution in question is to preferential creditors or preferential creditors and unsecured creditors (r.2.95(2)(b)); the rule makes no reference to secured creditors.

For these reasons, it would appear safe to assume that r.2.85 (and the other provisions of Ch.10 of the Insolvency Rules 1986) only come into play if the administrator proposes to make a distribution to unsecured (including preferential) creditors or secured creditors in respect of any unsecured element of their claims; the non-insolvency set-off rules will continue to apply if the administrator makes any payments to secured (including floating charge) creditors.

(f)   Administration expenses and interplay with rule 2.85

As stated above, debts arising out of an obligation incurred (by the company   **22–044**
or the creditor) after the cut-off date are not available for set-off under r.2.85. This could include any liabilities incurred by the administrator, on behalf of the company, after the commencement of the administration. Unless and until the r.2.95 notice is given, the creditor may have other set-off rights (such as a contractual right of set-off) which will entitle it to set off the post-administration liability against any cross-claim owed by it to the company in administration. On the giving of such notice, the contractual right of set-off would be lost as it is inconsistent with the provisions of r.2.85. The question therefore arises as to what protection such a creditor would have in respect of the post-administration liabilities of the company if a r.2.95 notice were to be given. In other words, why should a creditor hoping to rely on a right of set-off as part of its credit protection continue to trade with the company after the commencement of the administration?

In most cases, if the administrator causes the company to incur new liabilities post-administration, these liabilities will be payable as an expense of the administration[121]; such expenses are payable in priority to pre-administration unsecured claims and claims secured by a floating charge.[122] There are various

---

There were no suggestions, during the consultations and debates regarding the Enterprise Act 2002 that the new provisions were intended to have such a significant impact on secured claims and it therefore seems inconceivable that this is the effect of the provisions.

[121] See Ch.4, above. A number of recent cases, including *Exeter City Council v Bairstow* [2007] 4 All E.R. 437, *Goldacre (Offices) Ltd v Nortel Networks UK Ltd (In Administration)* [2010] Ch. 455 and *Re Nortel GmbH* [2011] B.C.C. 277 have suggested that: (a) the concept of an administration expense is very uncertain at present; and (b) the expense liabilities could be very extensive. See, on the Court of Appeal decision in *Nortel*, STOP PRESS, after the preface to this work.

[122] para.99 of Sch.B1 to the Insolvency Act 1986.

reasons why this may not be as attractive to the creditor as having a right of set-off:

(a) first, the expression "administration expense" is not defined in the insolvency legislation and, following the introduction of r.2.67 of the Insolvency Rules 1986, there is some uncertainty as to whether there is now a definitive code of what does (and does not) constitute an expense[123] or whether the flexible approach adopted by Nicholls L.J. in *Atlantic Computer Systems Plc*[124] continues to apply. In view of this uncertainty, any party entering into a contract with a company acting by its administrator should ensure that the contract makes it clear that any liabilities arising under the contract are payable as an expense of the administration;

(b) secondly, the administration may turn out to be an insolvent one (meaning that there are insufficient unsecured or floating charge assets to pay all of the expenses of the administration in full). In such a case, and absent a court order under r.2.67(3) altering the order of priority of the expense liabilities, the administrator will be required to pay the expenses in the order of priority set out in r.2.67. If there are insufficient assets to pay in full the sub-category of expenses which includes the creditor's claim, the creditor may only receive a pro rata share of the assets.[125] If, on the other hand, the creditor were able to exercise a right of set-off, and the amount it owed the company was greater than the amount that it was owed, it would be able to set off the full amount of the liability owed to it (rather than receiving a partial payment in this regard);

(c) the creditor may prefer, for its own reasons, to rely on a right of set-off rather than receiving a payment as an expense of the administration. Take the example of a number of derivative transactions (some pre- and some post-administration) entered into under a single ISDA Master Agreement. The counterparty may wish to be able to set off credit and debit balances in respect of all outstanding transactions under the Master Agreement (rather than being required to treat pre- and post-administration liabilities separately).

(g)   Detailed consideration of rule 2.85 by court

22–045   The High Court decision in *Re Kaupthing, Singer and Friedlander Ltd (In Administration)*[126] sought to clarify a number of highly technical points arising

---

[123] By analogy with r.4.218(1) which applies in a liquidation and the House of Lords' decision in *Re Toshoku Finance UK Plc (In Liquidation)* [2002] 1 W.L.R. 671 (HL). This was the approach taken in the cases cited in fn.120 above.

[124] *Atlantic Computer Systems Plc* [1998] 1 W.L.R. 422 (CA).

[125] If there are sufficient assets to make a partial payment in respect of this sub-category of expense, but not to pay these expenses in full, the administrator will be required to pay the expenses within the sub-category pro rata and on a pari passu basis.

[126] *Re Kaupthing, Singer and Friedlander Ltd (In Administration)* [2010] 1 B.C.L.C. 222.

out of the application of r.2.85. In particular, the court looked at how the discounting mechanism (applicable to debts payable in the future) is to be applied when debts are set off, how debts in a foreign currency are to be valued for set-off purposes, how interest-bearing debts are treated for set-off purposes and the application of set-off to debts which are both interest-bearing and future debts. One point (in relation to the set-off of future debts) has been clarified by the Court of Appeal[127] but the rest of the High Court's decision remains. Given the importance of this decision regarding the construction of r.2.85, it is analysed in some detail below.

The case concerned the administration of Kaupthing, Singer and Freidlander Limited (KSF), the UK regulated subsidiary of the Icelandic bank. KSF entered into administration on October 8, 2008. Its creditors included various trade and other creditors, the Financial Services Compensation Scheme and some 3000 depositors (whose deposits were not transferred to ING). Some of the creditors also had borrowings from KSF (many not repayable until a date in the future), giving rise to the application of r.2.85. On May 20, 2009, the administrators gave notice of their intention to make a distribution to creditors (having obtained permission from the court to do so) and, as part of the process, sought clarification from the court on four particular issues arising out of the application of r.2.85.

(i) Meaning of "future debts" for the purposes of the discounting mechanism

The first issue concerned the application of the discounting mechanism in **22–046** respect of future debts (contained in r.2.105) in the context of set-off. The discounting mechanism is a formula applied to a debt payable in the future to discount the debt to its present day value (that is, to take account of the fact that the debt, or a dividend thereon, is to be paid early). Set-off applies to future debts just as it does to present debts[128] and the discounting mechanism is stated to apply when setting off future debts[129].

As referred to above, the account to be taken, for set-off purposes, of what is due to each party is calculated as at the date the administrator gives notice of his intention to make a distribution (the "set-off date"). However, the discounting mechanism (framed in the context of a proof of debt) is stated to apply to debts "of which payment is not due at the date of the declaration of the dividend".

Ordinarily (when there is no set-off), the discounting mechanism works fine; if the debt is still future at the date the distribution is made, it will simply be discounted to take account of the fact that it is being paid early. But how does this work in the context of administration set off where the set off date is the date of the r.2.95 notice but the discounting is to apply if the debt is not due at the date of the declaration of the dividend? Does the discounting mechanism apply to all debts which are future at the set-off date or does it apply only to debts which are still future at the date the distribution is made?

---

[127] *Re Kaupthing, Singer and Friedlander Ltd (In Administration)* [2011] B.C.C. 555 (CA).
[128] r.2.85(4)(a).
[129] r.2.85(7).

The High Court held that the discounting mechanism applies only to debts which are still future at the date the distribution is made. Although the account of what is due is taken at the set-off date, the "hindsight principle" (referred to by Lord Hoffman in *Stein v Blake*[130]) enables events which have occurred since then (e.g. where a debt has since become due and payable) to be brought into account. Debts which cease to be future debts between the r.2.95 notice and the distribution itself are to be set off at their full value (i.e. with no discounting). In effect, this will mean revising the set-off account (i.e. without the discount) in respect of debts which have ceased to be future since the set-off date each and every time a dividend is made.[131]

(ii)   Quantification of foreign debts

22–047   The second issue concerned the rules for quantifying the amount to be set off and, in particular, the date for converting foreign debts into sterling for set-off purposes.

Rule 2.85(6) provides that the rules on the quantification of claims for proof purposes[132] are to apply when calculating administration set-off but refer only to the application of those rules in relation to sums *due to* the company (in this case, borrowings from KSF). No reference is made to sums due *by* the company (e.g. US dollar deposits held by KSF). The question arose as to how such debts (due by the company) should be quantified for set-off purposes: on what date (and accordingly at what rate) should such claims be converted into GBP?

The High Court held that, despite the wording in r.2.85(6), the rules on quantification (and, notably, conversion into sterling) applied equally to sums due by the company and sums due to the company. This was on the basis that: a creditor proving against a company in administration is required to convert any foreign currency debt into sterling at the official exchange rate on the date of administration; r.2.86 (a proof of debt rule) does not refer to debts due to the company (as the company does not prove for debts owing to it); the purpose of r.2.85(6) is to subject the company to the same quantification rules, when applying administration set-off, as apply to a creditor. There is no need to refer in r.2.85(6) to the quantification rules applying to debts due by the company (for which a creditor must prove) as creditors are subject to these rules anyway. Absent the application of these rules to sums *due to* the company, the company would be able to value debts due to it for set-off purposes at any advantageous date it chose.

(iii)   Treatment of interest on debts due to the company

22–048   The third issue concerned the treatment, for set-off purposes, of interest payable on debts due to KSF (e.g. depositors who also had borrowings with KSF) and

---

[130] *Stein v Blake (No.1)* [1996] A.C. 243 (HL).

[131] Note that the discounting mechanism is determined by reference to the commencement of the administration (and not the date of the declaration of the dividend).

[132] Namely r.2.86 (debts payable in a foreign currency), r.2.87 (payments of a periodical nature) and r.2.88 (interest-bearing debts).

in particular whether interest accruing on such debts after the date of administration should be brought into the set-off calculation.

Rule 2.88 provides that pre-administration interest[133] on debts owing to creditors is provable in the administration but post-administration interest is not. Post-administration interest can only be claimed if there is a surplus (i.e. after the debts, including pre-administration interest, of all unsecured creditors have been paid in full). Post-administration interest is effectively subordinated.

Rule 2.85(6) extends the application of this rule (for the purposes of administration set-off) to debts due *to* the company. The administrators sought to argue that this did not make sense because: (i) there is no restriction on the administrator claiming post-administration interest on debts due to the company; and (ii) it is a nonsense to talk about post-administration interest being paid, on a subordinated basis, from a "surplus" existing in the assets of a debtor. Accordingly, the administrators argued that post-administration interest on debts due to KSF should be included in the set-off calculation in the same way as the KSF administrators would have been entitled to claim the full amount of the debt due to KSF (including post-administration interest) had there been no set-off.

The High Court held that post-administration interest should be ignored for **22–049** the purposes of set-off in respect of both debts due *to* and *by* the company. As a result of the set-off, there will be a balance owing one way or the other. If the balance is due *by* the company (i.e. in respect of a claim for which the creditor has proved), then the creditor will be entitled to receive, pari passu with other unsecured creditors, a dividend on the amount of the balance and will only receive payment in respect of subordinated post-administration interest in the event of a surplus (i.e. on the same basis as any other unsecured creditor who does not have the benefit of set-off).

Where, however, the balance is a sum due *to* the company, the administrator is entitled to pursue the debtor (in this case, borrowers) for the balance plus all post-administration interest. This is because r.2.88 applies only to debts for which a creditor is proving and there is no equivalent prohibition on a company in administration claiming and recovering post-administration interest due to it except in the context of set-off. In other words, r.2.85(6) applies r.2.88 but only for the purposes of set-off. Once set-off has been applied and the balance ascertained, r.2.85(8) states that any balance owed to the company shall be paid to the administrator as part of the assets of the company.

Moreover, interest payable on the balance due to the company is calculated as from the date of the administration (and not the set-off date). This is because r.2.85(6) only requires post-administration interest to be disregarded for the purposes of set-off; it does not purport to alter the underlying liability for interest. Credit will need to be given for any interest paid since the date of the administration on so much of the debt as has been extinguished by the set-off process.

---

[133] That is, interest accrued prior to commencement of the administration.

Whilst the above analysis seems straightforward in theory, the difficulty with it in practice (as argued by KSF creditors) is that it will not always be self-evident which debts due to the company have been set off (in whole or in part) and which debts remain to be paid (as represented by the balance). If, for example, a borrower has several loans with differing interest terms, how do the administrators determine which have been satisfied by set-off and which continue as part of the balance? Should the set-off always be applied on a pro rata basis?[134]

(iv) Treatment of interest-bearing debts which are also future debts

22–050 The final issue concerned the treatment of interest-bearing debts which are also future debts.

The discounting of future debts uses a formula whereby "X" (the value of the admitted proof) is reduced by an amount representing the early payment period; that period is calculated by reference to the commencement of the administration (and not, as noted above, the date of actual payment or r.2.95 notice, even though payment may be some considerable time after the administration commenced). The requirement to discount is subject to the debt still being future at the date the distribution is actually made. Because the formula operates by reference to the admitted proof as a whole, the discounting applies also to that part of the proof that represents pre-administration interest. As noted above, post-administration interest may not form part of a proof.

Where set-off applies, the court was asked to determine how "X" is to be determined where a debt is both future and interest-bearing. In particular, how do the provisions regarding interest and the discounting of future debts interrelate? Does "X" include or exclude interest up to the scheduled future repayment date?

In the High Court, the administrators argued that, in respect of future debts due *to* the company, the company should be allowed to set off not only the principal due at the set-off date but also interest calculated up to the scheduled repayment date. On appeal, the administrators raised a new argument that, because there is no acceleration of the debtor's liability by virtue of the set-off, a future debt due to the company should be discounted only to the extent necessary to achieve the set-off, so that the balance (due but not yet payable) is the non-discounted balance.

22–051 The High Court held that "X" did not include post-administration interest. In respect of debts owing to and by the company, interest arising after the administration and before the date of the distribution is left out of the account. By excluding interest from the set-off calculation, the otherwise impossible task of ascertaining what the interest rate will be (where the rate of interest is a floating rate linked to LIBOR) for the remaining term of the loan, is avoided.

Overturning the High Court's decision, the Court of Appeal held that future debts due to the company are to be discounted, but only to the extent necessary

---

[134] This would be consistent with the analysis in *Re Unit 2 Windows Ltd* [1985] 1 W.L.R. 1383.

to achieve the set-off (i.e. the Court of Appeal accepted the new argument raised by the administrators on appeal). Consequently, if, after the set-off, the balance is owed to the depositor, it will receive a dividend on the balance to which the discounting formula will apply. However, if the balance is in favour of the company, the company may not demand immediate payment and the balance (which will not have been discounted) will remain outstanding until the contractual maturity date, bearing contractual interest.

The Court of Appeal gave a worked example (taken from the administrators' skeleton) as to how this would work in practice where a customer has deposited £100 repayable on July 31, 2010 and has borrowed £1,000 repayable on July 31, 2018:

(i) the £100 deposit due to the customer repayable July 31, 2010 would be discounted back to May 20, 2009[135] (the date the administrators gave the r.2.95 notice) to £94.34;

(ii) that part of the £1,000 loan due to KSF repayable July 31, 2018 which is required to produce a figure of £94.34 when discounted back to May 20, 2009,[136] is £147.75;

(iii) the £94.34 (which represents the present value of the £100 deposit) and £94.34 (which represents the present value of £147.75 of the loan) are then set off against each other, so as to extinguish both;

(iv) the remainder of the loan of £852.25 (i.e. £1,000 less £147.75), which is not required for the purposes of set-off, remains due and payable by the customer on July 31, 2018 in accordance with r.2.85(8).

(h) Proposals for reform of rule 2.85

Some of the issues considered in this chapter regarding the administration **22–052** set-off rule were raised by the Financial Markets Law Committee (the FMLC) in November 2007 in a paper entitled "Legal assessment of r.2.85 of the Insolvency Rules 1986 and its interplay with other insolvency provisions in respect of post-administration liabilities owed to counterparties" (the Issue 108 paper). At the request of the Insolvency Service, the FMLC has now prepared an Addendum to the Issue 108 paper which, amongst other things, suggests proposed amendments to r.2.85 in order to push forward the cut-off date so that this would coincide with the set-off date (as those expressions are referred to above).[137] It is not yet known whether the Insolvency Service will pursue these suggested amendments.

---

[135] The period from May 20, 2009 to 1 July 31, 2010 is 1 year, 2 months, 10 days producing a figure for "n" of 1.1944.

[136] The period from May 20, 2009 to July 31, 2018 is 9 years, 2 months, 10 days producing a figure for "n" of 9.1944.

[137] Both the Issue 108 paper and the Addendum are available on the FMLC's website *http://www.fmlc.org*.

3. SET-OFF IN RECEIVERSHIP

22–053 There is no insolvency set-off rule which comes into play when a receiver is appointed over the assets of a company (unless the company is also in liquidation in which case r.4.90 will apply). The giving of notice of the grant of security, or the appointment of the receiver, may, however, have an impact upon the availability to creditors of other forms of set-off rights. In this respect, there is a significant difference between a mortgage, assignment or fixed charge on the one hand and an uncrystallised floating charge on the other hand (as discussed below); in the case of a floating charge, it will be the appointment of the receiver (which has the effect of crystallising the floating charge), rather than the giving of notice of the charge, which has the impact upon the availability of the set-off rights.

In relation to the rights of set-off that are available to the company in receivership, the company acting by its receiver is entitled to the same rights of set-off as would have been available if no security had been created. In this respect, the grant of the security has a one-sided impact on the availability of set-off between the secured creditor (on the one hand) and the company's unsecured creditors (on the other).

Part 3 of this chapter therefore considers:

(a) the effect of notice of a mortgage, assignment or fixed charge on the debtor's set-off rights and what "notice" means for these purposes;

(b) if the security is floating, the effect this has on set-off rights (both prior to and following crystallisation, including by the appointment of a receiver); and

(c) the set-off position in relation to new contracts entered into by the receiver on behalf of the company.

(a) Effect of notice of creation of security interests

22–054 Except in the case of a court-appointed receiver, a receiver will be appointed pursuant to security granted by the company to the holder of the security. The security may take the form of a legal or equitable mortgage, a legal or equitable assignment by way of security, a fixed or floating charge, a pledge or a lien. In each case, and with the exception of floating charge security, the giving of notice of the creation of such security will have an impact on the mutuality between a claim owed by the company granting the security to a third party and a claim owed by that third party to the company. This is because the benefit of the latter claim has been mortgaged, assigned, charged, pledged or liened to the holder of the security and so no longer "belongs" to the company. For the purposes of Pt 3 of this chapter, the third party wishing to exercise the right of set-off is referred to as the "counterparty",[138] the company in receivership is

---

[138] This term is used to avoid using the labels "debtor" or "creditor" which may be confusing. The counterparty is a "debtor" in respect of the amount owed to the company. Where the amount owed by the company to the counterparty exceeds the amount of the cross-claim owed by the counterparty to the company, the counterparty will actually be (overall) a creditor of the company.

referred to as the "company" and the mortgagee, assignee, chargee, pledgee or holder of the lien is referred to as the "secured creditor".

It is considered that there is no difference, for set-off mutuality purposes, between the effect of a legal and equitable mortgage, a legal or equitable assignment by way of security, a fixed charge, a pledge or a lien[139] and hence the expression "security interests" used below is intended to cover all forms of security other than a floating charge. A floating charge has a different effect on set-off mutuality because, prior to crystallisation, such a charge does not constitute a specific assignment of any particular asset of the company and therefore does not destroy the mutuality between the claims owing to and from the company or the counterparty.

If the counterparty receives notice (as discussed below) of any security **22–055** interest (other than a floating charge), and the claim owed by the counterparty to the company is included in that security, the only cross-claims which the counterparty will be able to set off following that notice will be:

(a) cross-claims (whenever arising and even if this is after the notice of the creation of the security interest) which are sufficiently connected with the claim owed by the counterparty so as to give rise to a transaction set-off. In other words, the secured creditor takes subject to equitable rights of set-off arising under agreements that were in existence at the time the counterparty was given notice of the security interest; it is the date of the agreements rather than the date on which the cross-claim accrues that is important for these purposes.[140] This will include any of the cross-claims referred to in Pt 1(c)(ii) above. There is no universal rule, however, that all cross-claims arising out of the same contract as the assigned claim will be available for transaction set-off[141]; if transaction set-off is not available, it will only be possible to set off the cross-claim if it "accrues due" prior to the notice (see para.(iii) below);

(b) contractual rights of set-off where the contract of set-off was entered into prior to the notice of the security interest, the claim owing by the counterparty was incurred before such notice and the cross-claim owing by the company was incurred or acquired before such notice;

---

[139] See Wood, *English and International Set-off* (London: Sweet & Maxwell, 1989) (fn.2 above), paras 16–186 to 16–224.

[140] *Newfoundland Government v Newfoundland Railway Co* (1888) L.R. 13 App. Cas. 199 (PC), explained by Lord Simon in *The Aries* [1977] 1 W.L.R. 185 (HL), 193: "You cannot equitably take the benefit of an assignment without also assuming its burdens; both flow out of and are inseparably connected with the same transaction". There is an apparent exception to this principle. A tenant who has a claim against its lessor cannot set off that claim against a claim by a purchaser or mortgagee of the lessor's estate in respect of liabilities under the lease accruing after the sale or mortgage e.g. rent) unless the tenant's claim constitutes an interest in land. A mere claim for damages, e.g. for breach of contract, cannot affect the purchaser or mortgagee, whether or not it had notice (*Reeves v Pope* [1914] 2 K.B. 291 (CA) and *Edlington Properties Ltd v JH Fenner & Co Ltd* [2006] 1 W.L.R. 1583 (CA)).

[141] *Newfoundland Government v Newfoundland Railway Co* (1888) L.R. 13 App. Cas. 199 (PC); *Business Computers Ltd v Anglo-African Leasing Ltd* [1977] 2 All E.R. 741, 748.

(c) unrelated or unconnected cross-claims against the company which qualify for independent set-off and which have "accrued due" before the counterparty received notice of the security (the meaning of this phrase is discussed further below);

(d) cross-claims which give rise to substantive defences and rights of abatement open to the counterparty against the company, whether or not existing at the time the counterparty received notice of the security interest. This is an application of the principle that *nemo dat quod non habet*: the company cannot transfer by way of security greater rights than it itself possesses; and

(e) (possibly) insolvency set-off rights where the security has been created in breach of a negative pledge or restriction on the creation of security (as discussed below).

(i) Meaning of "accrued due"

22–056 If there is an actual debt due from the company to the counterparty at the time the counterparty receives notice of the creation of the security interest, and that debt is not in any respect contingent, it will be deemed to have "accrued due" even if it is not payable until some date after the notice is received. Where transaction set-off does not apply, such a debt will be available for set-off by the counterparty following the notice so long as it falls due for payment before the date on which the counterparty is required to pay its debt. In other words, the obligation must be a present debt, even if it is payable in the future (*debitum in praesenti, solvendum in futuro*) rather than, for example, a purely contingent liability.

It can sometimes be difficult to establish what this actually means in relation to debts that arise out of agreements or arrangements entered into prior to the date of notice, but which do not fall due for payment until after the date of notice. Case law has established that the following are debts which have "accrued due" for these purposes:

(a) the price for goods delivered prior to the date of notice where the price fell due for payment prior to such notice[142];

(b) a liquidated claim for partial failure of consideration (in respect of goods paid for but not delivered) which arose prior to the relevant date[143];

(c) a call on shares made prior to the date of notice but which was payable after the date of notice[144];

---

[142] *Moore v Jervis* (1845) 2 Coll. 60.

[143] *Biggerstaff v Rowatt's Wharf Ltd* [1896] 2 Ch. 93 (CA). In this case, the relevant date was the date of appointment of receivers which crystallised the floating charge rather than the date of notice of the creation of the security interest.

[144] *Christie v Taunton, Delmard Lane & Co* [1893] 2 Ch. 175, cf. *Woodhams v Anglo-Australian & Universal Family Life Assurance Co* (1861) 3 Giff. 238 where the call for shares was made after the notice of the security and where the set-off was not allowed. This was also the case in *Christie v Taunton* in respect of calls made after the winding up.

(d) a liability which is treated in law as dating back to an event which took place prior to the relevant date[145]; and

(e) a claim in respect of an overdrawn account, even where no demand for repayment has been made in respect of the overdraft prior to the relevant date.[146] It seems likely that the overdraft is only available for set-off up to the amount of the debit balance as at the relevant date the notice was received (as the claim in respect of any further amounts would not have accrued due prior to this date) but this is not considered in any of the cases referred to in fn.143.

The following cross-claims, on the other hand, have been held to have "accrued due" after the date of notice and so were not available for set-off (in circumstances where transaction set-off was not available): **22–057**

(a) rent due and payable after notice although incurred under a lease entered into prior to the notice[147]; and

(b) a debt which was still contingent at the time of notice[148];

(c) a liquidated damages claim arising on the termination of a hire purchase agreement which took place following the relevant date,[149] notwithstanding the fact that the counterparty had the right to terminate the hire purchase agreement, but had failed to do so, prior to the relevant date.[150]

---

[145] In *Handley Page Ltd v Customs and Excise Commissioners* [1970] 2 Lloyd's Rep. 459, it was agreed between Handley Page Ltd and Rockwell Ltd that Handley Page should accept two six-month bills of exchange drawn by Rockwell who would then pay an import deposit to Customs under Handley Page's name and that Handley Page would receive repayments of the deposit. Rockwell discounted the bills and paid the deposit. Before the bills became due, Handley Page went into receivership and subsequently dishonoured the bills on presentation. Rockwell paid the bills, recovered the deposit from Customs and sought to set off the amount of the bills against its debt to the company and against its liability to account to the company for the deposit. Set-off was allowed on the basis that: (a) the debts were part of the same contract, or at any rate closely connected; and (b) Rockwell's liability on the bills dated back to the date they were discounted, i.e. before the receiver was appointed.

[146] *Jeffreys v Agra & Masterman's Bank* (1866) L.R. 2 Eq. 674; *Roxburge v Cox* (1881) L.R. 17 Ch. D. 520 (CA) and *Marathon Electrical Manufacturing Corp v Mashreqbank PSC* [1997] 2 B.C.L.C. 460. In the last case, the assigned claim was the proceeds of a letter of credit which were payable after the date of the assignment. Although the court agreed with the general principle that effective notice of assignment can only be given in respect of an existing debt, the court held that this could include debts payable in the future under an agreement existing at the time of the assignment.

[147] *Watson v Mid Wales Railway Co* (1866–67) L.R. 2 C.P. 593.

[148] In *Re Pinto Leite* [1929] 1 Ch. 221.

[149] Which, in this case, was the date of the appointment of the receivers rather than the date of notice of the creation of the security because the security in question was a floating charge and the appointment of the receivers completed the assignment of the claim owing by the counterparty (see below).

[150] *Business Computers Ltd v Anglo-African Leasing Ltd* [1977] 1 W.L.R. 578.

What if the cross-claim comprises the counterparty's right to the return of a deposit[151] held by a bank in circumstances where the bank has assigned to a third party the benefit of a loan owed to it by the counterparty (assuming that the deposit is not sufficiently connected with the loan for transaction set-off to apply)? Although the assignment would usually be in respect of the counterparty's rights in respect of the deposit (rather than of the bank's rights in respect of the loan), the situation posited above could arise in the context of a securitisation by the bank of a loan portfolio. There is no authority directly on this point[152] and there are arguments for and against the view that the claim in respect of the deposit would have "accrued due" at the time that notice of the assignment was given by the bank. In *N Joachimson (A Firm) v Swiss Bank Corp (Costs)*,[153] it was held that, for the purposes of the limitation periods, a debt comprising a current account with a bank did not become due and payable until a demand had been made on the bank by the customer. This term was implied into the agreement between the customer and the bank in respect of the current account. On the basis of *Joachimson*, it appears likely that, in the case of a deposit account, a demand must have been given prior to the date of notice for the deposit to be available for independent set-off.

(ii) Meaning of "notice"

22–058 On the basis that certain cross-claims which accrue due after notice of the creation of the security interest are excluded from set-off, the question arises as to what amounts to notice. Although there is little case law on this subject, it would appear that the notice does not need to be formal or in writing and that any circumstances which bring it to the mind of the counterparty that a debt it owes the company may be the subject of security would be sufficient notice for these purposes.

It is suggested, however, that the notice must be actual notice and must be expressed in plain and unambiguous terms.[154] It is doubtful whether constructive notice by registration of the charge under s.860 of the Companies Act 2006 would be effective notice for set-off purposes. The argument in favour of

---

[151] A distinction should be made between a demand deposit (which is only repayable in the event of a demand being made by the customer) and a time deposit (which falls due for payment on a particular date and is not subject to any contingency). A time deposit is likely to be treated as a present debt, payable in the future. If, however, the deposit is only repayable in certain circumstances (e.g. on payment to the bank by a third party in the case of a security deposit) and that event has not occurred prior to the date of notice, the better view is the obligation to repay the deposit will not have "accrued due" prior to the date of notice and, should the event occur after the date of notice, the obligation will not be available for set-off. Furthermore, if, after the date of notice, a borrower withdraws the deposit and makes a new deposit, the new deposit will not "accrue due" prior to the notice and so will not be available to set off.

[152] Although *Cavendish v Geaves* (1857) 24 Beav. 163 involved a current account in respect of which a demand had not been made at the time of notice of assignment, the facts of this case are complex as there had been two assignments and notice of one had not been given prior to the bankruptcy of the bank holding the account.

[153] *N Joachimson (A Firm) v Swiss Bank Corp (Costs)* [1921] 3 K.B. 110 (CA).

[154] *James Talcott v John Lewis* [1940] 3 All E.R. 592 and see *Halsbury's Laws of England*, 4th edn, Vol.6, para.48. See also *By Appointment (Sales) Ltd v Harrods* Unreported December 1, 1977 (CA); *Cowan de Groot v Eagle Trust* [1992] 4 All E.R. 700.

treating registration as notice in this context rests on the view that registration constitutes notice of a charge, even if not notice of its terms.[155] Professor Goode[156] has suggested a qualification to this view. His qualification is that notice of a charge is given by registration "only to those who could reasonably be expected to search", and this would "normally exclude a buyer in the ordinary course of business".

A counter-argument to treating registration as notice for set-off purposes is that there is no express statutory requirement when registering a charge to state whether the charge is fixed or floating. As discussed below, notice of a floating charge will not prevent further independent set-off rights from accruing. Until recently, registration would not necessarily disclose on a search whether the assignment was complete or not.[157] Current practice appears to be to require an applicant for registration to disclose whether a charge is fixed or floating and this is now noted on the register.

A counterparty ought not, therefore, to be fixed with notice simply by reason **22–059** of the registration of the charge. But if the counterparty has in fact done a search, and it is clear from the search that there is a fixed charge on its debt, this must be notice sufficient to complete the title of the secured creditor and to crystallise the rights as between counterparty and the secured creditor, since notice to the counterparty does not have to come from the company granting the security or the secured creditor.[158]

Registration of a fixed charge on book debts at the Companies Registry may constitute the giving of notice to the Crown (of which the Companies Registry is an emanation) preventing any other Crown Department, such as HM Revenue and Customs, from setting off subsequent liabilities of the company against prior debts to the company.

(b)   Effect of floating charges

Notice of the existence of a floating charge does not affect the counterparty's **22–060** right to set off cross-claims which accrue due after the date of such notice.[159] This is because a floating charge gives no property rights over any particular asset until crystallisation and is not to be treated as a complete assignment until such time. A counterparty who continues to deal with the company after receiving notice of the creation of a floating charge will therefore be entitled to set off cross-claims which accrue due following the counterparty's notice of the creation of the floating charge.

---

[155] *Wilson v Kellund* [1910] 2 Ch. 306, 313; *Siebe Gorman v Barclays Bank* [1979] 2 Lloyd's Rep. 142 where it was held that registration of the charge did not amount to notice of a special provision restricting dealing with the property charged. *Siebe Gorman* was not overturned by *Re Spectrum Plus Ltd (In Liquidation)* [2005] 2 A.C. 680 (HL) on this particular point.

[156] Goode, *Legal Problems of Credit and Security*, 3rd edn (London: Sweet & Maxwell, 2003), p.83.

[157] For the effect of registration of a floating charge, see *Biggerstaff v Rowatt's Wharf* [1896] 2 Ch. 93 (CA).

[158] *Lloyd v Banks* (1867–68) L.R. 3 Ch. App. 488 and see *Halsbury's Laws of England*, 4th edn (London: LexisNexis Butterworths, 1991), Vol.6.

[159] *Biggerstaff v Rowatt's Wharf Ltd* [1896] 2 Ch. 93 (CA).

When the charge is enforced (e.g. by the appointment of a receiver), the charge will crystallise and will be treated as a fixed assignment of all debts comprised within the charge by the chargor to the chargee. In *George Barker (Transport) Ltd v Eynon*,[160] Davies L.J. stated that:

> "A floating charge is ambulatory and hovers over the property until some event occurs which causes it to settle and crystallise into a specific charge ... one of the events which causes crystallisation is the appointment of a receiver ... one consequence of the receiver's appointment by the debenture holders was that the incomplete assignment constituted by the [floating charge] became converted into a completed equitable assignment to them of the assets charged ..."

22–061 In the case of a floating charge, the relevant date by which cross-claims must have accrued due to be available for independent set-off is therefore the date of notice of the crystallisation of the floating charge. In many cases, this will be the date on which the counterparty receives notice that a receiver has been appointed and, generally speaking, a counterparty will be able to set off any cross-claims which have accrued due prior to this date. The counterparty will only be able to set off any cross-claims arising after the date it receives notice of the receivers' appointment if the cross-claim qualifies for transaction set-off.

(c) Receivership contracts

22–062 Where a cross-claim is due to the counterparty prior to the date on which a receiver is appointed and the receiver (after his appointment) causes the company to enter into a new contract with the counterparty, it is unclear whether the counterparty can set off its cross-claim against any claim which might subsequently arise against it under the new contract.

In the New Zealand case of *Rendell v Doors & Doors Ltd (In Liquidation)*,[161] the company owed a counterparty a liquidated cross-claim prior to the appointment of the receiver. The receiver as agent of the company sold further doors to the counterparty which was liable to pay the price for the doors. The claim against the counterparty was immediately and automatically assigned to the secured creditor and the company went into liquidation. It was held that there was no mutuality for set-off purposes as the assigned claim owed for the doors was subject to the security in favour of the secured creditor.

The decision in *Rother Iron Works Ltd v Canterbury Precision Engineers*[162] supports a different view. In this case, the counterparty was owed monies in respect of goods sold and delivered prior to the receivership. The receiver delivered further goods to the counterparty after his appointment (although under the existing contract rather than a new one entered into by the receiver) and was met with a claim to set off which was allowed by the Court of Appeal on the basis

---

[160] *George Barker (Transport) Ltd v Eynon* [1974] 1 All E.R. 900 (CA), 905.
[161] *Rendell v Doors & Doors Ltd* (In Liquidation) [1975] 2 N.Z.L.R. 191.
[162] *Rother Iron Works Ltd v Canterbury Precision Engineers Ltd* [1974] Q.B. 1 (CA).

that the cross-claim had accrued due prior to the appointment of the receiver. The court held that the claim which became subject to the debenture charge was not the total amount of the post-receivership claim against the counterparty but rather the net amount (having deducted the amount of the cross-claim).

In the *Rother Iron Works* case, the receiver could, it is thought, have insisted on payment in full at the time of delivery or else have repudiated the sale contract and refused to deliver unless a new contract was made, expressly excluding rights of set-off. The case thus reveals a trap for unwary receivers.

(d) Crown debts

In a receivership, it is quite common for different emanations of the Crown to **22–063** be debtors and creditors of the company in receivership. The Crown will be treated as one indivisible entity for these purposes even if acting through different government departments.[163]

Generally speaking, set-off may be pleaded both by and against the Crown by virtue of the Crown Proceedings Act 1947. In any proceedings brought by the Crown, the defendant would need the leave of the court in order to plead set-off against a claim for taxes, duties or penalties.[164] Furthermore, a set-off may not be pleaded by the Crown (in any proceedings against the Crown) or by any person (in any proceedings brought by the Crown) without the permission of the court:

(a) if the Crown is sued or sues in the name of a government department and the subject matter of the set-off does not relate to that department; or

(b) if the Crown is sued or sues in the name of the Attorney General.[165]

These provisions do not apply in the case of insolvency set-off (which takes effect automatically and does not depend on a proceeding) and it has been held that an insolvency set-off could occur in relation to obligations to pay tax to, and the right to a tax refund from, the relevant revenue authorities.[166]

The Crown's right of set-off may be affected by its receipt of notice of the creation of security or the appointment of a receiver. In most cases, the type of set-off which is most likely to be relevant here is independent set-off (as it is unlikely that the Crown's claim and cross-claim will be sufficiently connected to qualify for transaction set-off). In accordance with the rules discussed above, the Crown would not be able to set off against any obligation to pay a tax refund (for example) a cross-claim against the company which arose after the Crown received the relevant notice.[167]

---

[163] *Secretary of State for Trade and Industry v Frid* [2004] 2 A.C. 506 (HL).
[164] Crown Proceedings Act 1947, s.35(2)(g); CPR 66.4.
[165] Crown Proceedings Act 1947, s.35(2)(g); CPR 66.4.
[166] *Re DH Curtis (Builders) Ltd* [1978] Ch. 162.
[167] See above in relation to the impact of registration of security under s.860 of the Companies Act 2006 and whether this constitutes notice to the Crown.

(e)   Pro rata sharing clause

22–064   In a syndicated loan agreement, there may well be a "pro rata sharing clause" to the effect that, if any one bank in the syndicate receives a payment (including by way of set-off), part of this payment will be redistributed to the other syndicate members in accordance with their pro rata exposures in respect of the loan. This could therefore be relevant in a receivership context where a receiver is appointed pursuant to the security granted in respect of a syndicated loan. There are various ways in which the redistribution may be treated under the pro rata sharing clause; for example, the clause may provide that, to the extent of the redistribution, the lender which recovered the payment is subrogated to the rights of the other lenders against the borrower.[168] This is intended to protect the other syndicate members where one lender is the account bank (for example) and so has a right of set-off in this capacity.

The pro rata sharing clause can cause difficulties if the lender with the right of set-off has multiple exposures to the borrower. For example, the company may owe the lender amounts in respect of a syndicated loan containing a pro rata sharing clause but also under separate agreements (such as in respect of bonds issued by the company) without such provisions. If the lender is holding a deposit for the company, the lender may wish to set off the amount of deposit against the company's obligations in respect of the agreements without the pro rata sharing clause so that the lender is not required to redistribute to any other party any part of the payment received by way of set-off. The question arises as to whether the lender is still able to do this following an administration or liquidation of the borrower in circumstances where r.2.85 and r.4.90 come into play.

Assuming that none of the obligations of the borrower are secured, it would appear that, following the coming into play of r.2.85 and r.4.90, the lender cannot choose to set off the borrower's obligations under agreements other than the syndicated loan in priority to the borrower's obligations under the syndicated loan. The relevant insolvency set-off rule will instead operate pro rata across all of the borrower's obligations. There are no cases directly on point but there are cases which could be applied by way of analogy where a creditor has multiple claims against a debtor and one of these claims is preferential (i.e. the debtor would have to pay the creditor in priority to other creditors) and the other is not. In these circumstances, if the creditor has a right of set off in respect of a cross-claim which it owes to the debtor, the creditor would clearly prefer to argue that the set-off was applied first against the non-preferential claim so that the creditor can retain its priority status in respect of its preferential claim.

22–065   In *Re EJ Morel (1934) Ltd*,[169] Buckley J. held that the set-off should be first applied against the preferential claim as, if the creditor received full payment (by way of the set-off), it was "reasonable" that the payment should be treated

---

[168] Some clauses include an exception to the pro rata sharing provisions whereby a lender need not make any redistributions of the amounts it recovers by way of set-off if it would not, after the redistribution, have a valid claim against the insolvent company.

[169] *Re EJ Morel (1934) Ltd* [1962] Ch. 21.

as being in respect of the debt which would rank first in priority. In the subsequent case of *Re Unit 2 Windows Ltd*,[170] this reasoning was rejected. Walton J. pointed out that "reasonableness" often depends on the point of view of the person considering it. He considered that the right approach was to apply the set-off pro rata across the two claims. This has now been followed in Australia and it is generally considered to be the right approach[171].

In a receivership context, clearly at least one of the borrower's obligations will be secured. The pro rata approach in *Re Unit 2 Windows* does not apply if the creditor has multiple claims and one of these is secured and one is unsecured. The cases establish that the creditor is entitled to rely on its security in respect of the secured debt and not to have the secured claim dealt with in the liquidation (or, by analogy, administration) so that the set-off would only apply in respect of the unsecured debt. If, however, the secured creditor chooses to surrender the security and to prove for the underlying debt as an unsecured claim, it would appear (by analogy with *Re Unit 2 Windows*) that the set-off would apply pro rata to the two claims (although there is no authority dealing with the position in relation to two ordinary, non-preferential claims). If the secured creditor were to value its security and to prove for the difference between the value of the security and the underlying debt (i.e. the shortfall), again, it would appear that the set-off would be applied pro rata.

The impact of this can be seen by considering the following example. If the lender owed 50 to the borrower in respect of a deposit but was owed 50 in respect of unsecured bonds and 50 under an unsecured syndicated credit agreement, it would appear (by analogy with *Re Unit 2 Windows*) that, if the borrower were to go into liquidation, the set-off of 50 would be applied *pro rata* to the lender's claims under its bonds and the credit agreement so that 25 of the amount owing to the lender under the credit agreement would be discharged by the set-off. This would bring into play the pro rata sharing provisions and the lender would have to redistribute part of the 25 to the other syndicate members. If in the liquidation the borrower is only able to make a distribution of, say, 20 per cent in relation to its unsecured debts, the lender will not recover the full amount of what it has redistributed through its subrogation rights in respect of the other lenders' claims against the borrower.

If the syndicated loan agreement contains a pro rata sharing clause, it would be prudent for a bank lender to seek legal advice regarding the impact of the clause before purporting to exercise any right of set-off in respect of any monies of the borrower which that lender may be holding.

(f) Practical lessons

It is important to bear in mind that a receiver appointed otherwise than by **22–066** the court may generally cause the company to repudiate its contracts. Upon

---

[170] *Re Unit 2 Windows Ltd* [1985] 1 W.L.R. 1383.
[171] A different approach was taken in *Turner v Inland Revenue Commissioners* [1993] B.C.C. 299 (Court of Session, Outer House) but this was a Scottish bankruptcy case where the laws are different to those in England.

appointment, a receiver should therefore take a close look at existing contracts, including any potential set-offs, and wherever possible repudiate burdensome contracts or set-off arrangements. Where the company has yet to perform works or deliver goods to a debtor of the company under a pre-receivership contract, the receiver should contact the creditor and agree to exclude any set-off before causing the company to perform. The exclusion should, if possible, be under seal to prevent any arguments about consideration although an express or implied agreement not to repudiate the contract should suffice as consideration for the agreement to exclude set-off.

Some very complicated problems can arise where a debenture-holder puts companies in a group into receivership and a surplus arises on a group level. The companies will generally have given cross-guarantees of each other's indebtedness to the debenture-holder. Often all or some of them will have gone into liquidation before the receivership is completed.

Once the existence of a surplus from the receiverships becomes obvious, the receiver, who is bound by the equities belonging to the companies,[172] has the duty of working out rights of marshalling between the companies and of ensuring that the correct sums are paid to the correct companies. In *Re St Clair Sampson Ltd*,[173] seven companies in a group executed cross-guarantees to a bank, and each company charged its assets as security to the bank. A receiver was appointed over the assets of each company and sufficient proceeds were realised to repay the bank, leaving a surplus across the group of £195,000. The liquidator of St Clair Sampson, which had paid substantially more than its due proportion of the total indebtedness of the group to the bank, claimed that the surplus remaining in the hands of the receiver should be distributed by calcu-lating what each company would have paid if it had (so far as its assets were sufficient) discharged its own indebtedness to the bank and an equal share of the deficiency attributable to the indebtedness to the bank of those companies which were unable to discharge that indebtedness in full. Two of the other companies in the group were owed substantial sums by St Clair Sampson on trading account. Their joint liquidators admitted that St Clair Sampson had claims for contribution against those companies, but claimed that, by virtue of the proviso to s.5 of the Mercantile Law Amendment Act 1856,[174] these claims for contribution were secured claims only to the extent of any amount by which the contribution claim against each company exceeded the intercompany indebtedness due from St Clair Sampson to that company. The Court of Appeal held that the intercompany indebtedness was not to be set off against the contri-bution claims in this way.

22–067   There are two important features of the decision for present purposes. First, a receiver holding a surplus must ensure that it is paid to the correct party. If there is doubt and no agreement between the parties potentially affected, the receiver will need to seek directions from the court. Secondly, s.5 of the

---

[172] *Freevale v Metrostore* [1984] Ch. 199; *Telemetrix Plc v Modern Engineers* (1985) 1 B.C.C. 99417.
[173] *Brown v Cork* [1985] B.C.L.C. 363 (CA).
[174] See *Rowlatt on Principal and Surety*, 5th edn (London: Sweet & Maxwell, 1999), p.274.

Mercantile Law Amendment Act 1856 operates by way of subrogation to the creditor's rights and entitles the creditor's full claim to be used to obtain payment. This does not permit a cross-claim available against the surety entitled to contribution to be raised by way of set-off. The reference in the proviso to "the just proportion to which . . . [an underpaying co-surety] . . . shall be justly liable" is a reference to the amount which is recoverable from the underpaying co-surety pursuant to s.5, not to that amount adjusted so as to allow for other indebtedness between the parties.

Counsel for the liquidators of St Clair Sampson also sought to argue (and the Court of Appeal appeared to accept) that where, at the commencement of the relevant winding up, the principal creditor had not been paid in full, the relevant insolvency set-off rule prevented any set-off.[175] It is not clear, however, why insolvency set-off was relevant to a subrogated secured claim which stands outside a liquidation. In any event, following the changes that were made to r.4.90 and r.12.85 to clarify that claims that are still contingent at the relevant date can still be included in the account for insolvency set-off purposes, this argument would not now be available.

4.   INTERNATIONAL AND EUROPEAN DEVELOPMENTS

In the event of a failure of a global entity (i.e. one with assets, creditors or business activities in more than one jurisdiction), questions may arise as to which insolvency set-off rules should apply. This is particularly relevant given the differences in approach to set-off of different jurisdictions (see para.22–003, above). This issue arose in the liquidation of The Bank of Credit and Commerce International S.A. (BCCI),[176] a Luxembourg incorporated bank which was placed into concurrent liquidation proceedings in Luxembourg, England and the Cayman Islands. Under Luxembourg insolvency law, set-off is prohibited except in very narrow circumstances. Under English insolvency law, however, set-off is permitted so long as the requirements referred to in this chapter are satisfied. Hence the question of which insolvency set-off provisions should prevail was a crucial one.

BCCI's liquidators in Luxembourg, England and the Cayman Islands agreed that the liquidation should be a joint enterprise with BCCI's creditors (wherever situated) receiving the same level of dividend. Hence the English liquidators wished to release funds from the realisation of the English assets to the Luxembourg liquidators for a distribution amongst the creditors in accordance with Luxembourg law. They applied to the English court for directions as to whether, before releasing those funds, they should retain sufficient funds to satisfy counterparties entitled to take advantage of any set-off available to them under r.4.90.

Although the English court recognised that the Luxembourg liquidation was the principal liquidation (having been commenced in the place of incorporation), with the winding up of BCCI in England being an "ancillary"

22–068

---

[175] *Re A Debtor (No.66 of 1955)* [1956] 1 W.L.R. 1226 (CA).
[176] In *Re Bank of Credit and Commerce International S.A. (No.10)* [1997] Ch. 213.

liquidation, it held that this did not relieve the court of its obligation to apply English law (including English insolvency law) to the resolution of any issue in the winding up brought before it. Accordingly, the court directed the English liquidators to retain sufficient funds for the dividends that net creditors, entitled to take advantage of the insolvency set-off rules, would receive in the English liquidation (no provision was required to be made for net debtors as there would be no credit for which they could prove).

The English law in relation to set-off must also be viewed in light of developments in European law and, in particular, art.6 of the EC Insolvency Regulation[177] and arts 23 and 25 of the Credit Institutions Winding Up Directive.[178]

The starting position under the EC Insolvency Regulation is that the insolvency law of the Member State in which "main" or "secondary" insolvency proceedings are commenced will determine the rules regarding the conditions under which set-offs may be invoked (art.4(2)(d) of the EC Insolvency Regulation). The position is similar under the Credit Institutions Winding Up Directive where the insolvency laws of the "home Member State" will, in the first instance, determine the insolvency set-off rules (arts 3 and 10). As an exception to this general rule, art.6 of the EC Insolvency Regulation provides that "the opening of insolvency proceedings shall not affect the right of creditors to demand the set-off of their claims against the claims of the [insolvent] debtor, where such a set-off is permitted by the law applicable to the insolvent debtor's claim" and art.23 of the Credit Institutions Winding Up Directive provides that "the adoption of reorganisation measures or the opening of winding-up proceedings shall not affect the right of creditors to demand the set-off of their claims against the claims of the credit institution, where such a set-off is permitted by the law applicable to the credit institution's claim". Article 25 of the Credit Institutions Winding Up Directive also provides that "netting agreements shall be governed solely by the law of the contract which governs such agreements". There is no similar protection for netting agreements in the EC Insolvency Regulation.

To give an example of how this would work under the EC Insolvency Regulation, if a company is subject to main insolvency proceedings in France but the insolvent company's cross-claim arises under an agreement governed by English law, any inability of a creditor to set off the cross-claim as a matter of French insolvency law would not prevent the creditor from setting off the cross-claim if such a right of set-off was permitted by English law (as the law governing the agreement under which the cross-claim arises). It is the law governing the insolvent debtor's cross-claim, and not the law governing any set-off agreement, that is relevant in this respect.

Article 6 of the EC Insolvency Regulation does not prevent any actions for voidness, voidability and unenforceability (as referred to in art.4(2)(m) of the EC Insolvency Regulation) in respect of the agreement under which the claim

---

[177] Council Regulation (EC) No.1346/2000 on insolvency proceedings [2000] OJ L160/1.

[178] Directive 2001/24/EC, implemented in the UK through the Credit Institutions (Reorganisation and Winding Up) Regulations 2004 (SI 2004/1045).

or cross-claim, or the right of set-off, arises. The same applies in relation to art.23 of the Credit Institutions Winding Up Directive.

Both art.6 of the EC Insolvency Regulation and art.25 of the Credit **22–069** Institutions Winding Up Directive give rise to a number of questions which have not yet been addressed by the English court or the European Court of Justice. These are considered below in the context of art.6 although similar issues would arise in relation to art.25.

(a) Does the law applicable to the insolvent debtor's claim need to be a law of a Member State? Arguments against this view include the fact that art.13 of the EC Insolvency Regulation (for example) expressly states that the applicable law must be the law of a Member State and, if this had been the intention in respect of art.6, similar wording could have been included in art.6. Also, if set-off is to provide a "guarantee function" as the *Virgos-Schmit Report*[179] suggests, then why should this be limited to contracts governed by the law of a Member State? There are arguments to the contrary. Paragraph 93 of the *Virgos Schmit Report* notes that, apart from arts 6 and 14, the other exceptions are in favour of the law of another Member State and arts 6 and 14 must "by systemic arguments" be interpreted in the same way.

(b) Once the law applicable to the insolvent debtor's claim has been determined, which set-off provisions of this law are to apply? For example, if the debtor has the right to repayment in respect of a bank deposit and the deposit agreement is governed by English law, would it be the English insolvency set-off rules, the English contractual set-off rules or the English set-off rules in relation to the combination of accounts that would apply (each of which may give a different answer as to whether there is a right of set-off)? Does the answer to this question depend on whether there is actually (or could be) an insolvency proceeding in England? It seems logical to look at the facts of the situation and only to consider insolvency set-off if insolvency proceedings in respect of the debtor have actually been commenced in England[180] but para.109 of the *Virgos-Schmit Report* suggests that the conditions for insolvency set-off are applicable, regardless of whether there are, or could be, any insolvency proceedings in the jurisdiction of the applicable law.[181]

(c) Does the right of set-off, or the debtor's cross-claim, need to arise prior to the opening of insolvency proceedings? Although there is nothing in art.6 to this effect, the *Virgos-Schmit Report* states (para.110) that art.6 only applies to rights of set-off arising in respect

---

[179] See Ch.31, below.

[180] This would avoid any difficulties in the assumptions that would otherwise need to be made regarding the timing and type of any theoretical insolvency proceedings in England in order to determine whether the conditions for exercising a right of insolvency set-off were satisfied.

[181] In the context of EEA credit institutions, there could be no insolvency proceedings in England if the "home Member State" was elsewhere in the EEA.

of mutual claims incurred prior to the opening of insolvency proceedings. This would appear to indicate that the relevant contract(s) under which the claims arise must have been entered into prior to the opening of proceedings (rather than that the claims must both have crystallised, and the right of set-off arisen, prior to this date).

(d) How does art.6(1) relate to art.6(2)? As stated above, art.6 does not prevent actions under the insolvency avoidance provisions of the Member State in which insolvency proceedings are opened. But what if those insolvency laws prohibit set-off because it is held that this is an improper preference of a particular creditor and so contrary to the avoidance provisions? If art.6(2) were to be construed in this way, then art.6(1) would not serve any guarantee function. It seems more likely that art.6(2) is to be construed as meaning that the relevant insolvency officeholder in the main or secondary insolvency proceedings can challenge the entering into of the transaction which gives rise to the right of set-off, and not the exercise of the set-off right itself.

(e) Does Article 6 only apply to set-off or would it extend to close-out netting?[182] Netting can properly be characterised as a purely contractual method of arriving at a net liability which might otherwise have been arrived at through the set-off of gross liabilities whereas a set-off is the extinguishment of a debt by way of payment affected through a right of set-off. On its terms, it would appear that art.6 only applies to set-off in a strict sense so that other related questions (such as whether contacts can be terminated or "closed out" and claims accelerated) are to be determined by the Member State in which insolvency proceedings are commenced. This distinction between set-off and netting would, however, exclude, from the effect of art.6, many of the standard close-out mechanisms in market standard master agreements (such as the ISDA Master Agreement).

(f) On a similar but related point, which law determines the claims that are eligible for set-off and how such claims are to be quantified (e.g. do the claims have to be liquidated, matured or payable by a particular date and how are foreign currency claims, contingent claims, future claims or unquantified claims to be valued for set-off purposes)? Is this to be construed as part of the set-off or is set-off (for art.6 purposes) to be given the very narrow meaning of the extinguishment of a debt by payment affected through a right of set-off once the claim and the cross-claim have been quantified by other means or rules? It would make commercial sense to give art.6 a wide interpretation and to say that these matters fall within a right of set-off; this seems to be supported by para.109 of *Virgos-Schmit*

---

[182] The fact that there is a separate protection for netting agreements under the Credit Institutions Winding Up Directive seems particularly curious in this respect as it is not only credit institutions that enter into such agreements.

which states that, if the *lex concursus* does not allow for set off because the claims are not liquidated etc, art.6 constitutes an exception to the general application of that law in this respect.

(g) What is the effect of art.20 of the EC Insolvency Regulation which requires a creditor who has obtained through any means total or partial satisfaction of its claim post insolvency proceedings to return what he has obtained to the liquidator? There are exceptions for arts 5 and 7 but not for art.6. Is this merely an oversight?

Until there have been any decisions regarding the meaning of art.6, it is difficult to give any definitive answers to these questions.

Chapter 23

Liens

1. INTRODUCTION

23–001 If a company is in administration or receivership and part of its property is subject to a lien in favour of a creditor, the administrator or receiver may wish to know whether he can take possession of the property, notwithstanding the lien (particularly if the property is valuable or is needed for the purposes of running the business of the company). Conversely, the holder of the lien will be at an advantage over unsecured creditors if it can retain possession of the property until the money owing to it is repaid as this will give it a bargaining position. This chapter considers the impact of an administration or receivership on the lien-holder's rights in respect of the property which is the subject of the lien and whether the administrator or receiver will be entitled to delivery up of the property, notwithstanding the lien.

(a) Meaning of lien

23–002 A lien is a particular type of security interest which (with the exception of an equitable lien) depends upon possession although the addition of a power of sale will not necessarily convert the lien into an equitable charge.[1] There are five different types of lien, only the first of which is consensual, the other four arising by operation of law:

> (a) a *contractual lien* (which, as its name implies, arises out of a contractual relationship between the parties) differs from a pledge as the goods are not deposited for the purpose of security but rather for some other purpose (such as the repair, transport or warehousing of the goods)[2];
>
> (b) a *common law or possessory lien* is a right conferred by law to detain goods until money owed to the holder of the goods has been paid. Examples include the lien of a mechanic over a car left with him,[3] the lien of a bank over securities or instruments deposited with it for collection[4] or the lien of a broker or custodian over securities belonging to the client but held by the broker or custodian. This type of lien can also exist over intangible property (such as a chose in

---

[1] *Re Hamlet International Plc (In Administration)* [2000] B.C.C. 602 (CA).
[2] *Re Cosslett (Contractors) Ltd* [1997] B.C.C. 724 (CA), 733.
[3] *Albermarle Supply Co Ltd v Hind & Co* [1928] 1 K.B. 307 (CA).
[4] *Sewell v Burdick (The Zoe)* (1884) L.R. 10 App. Cas. 74 (HL).

action); for example, an auctioneer may have a lien (in respect of the auctioneer's charges) over the price payable by the buyer to the seller;

(c) an *equitable lien* is a form of equitable charge which arises by opera-tion of equity from the relationship between the parties. It exists inde-pendently of possession but cannot be enforced against a purchaser for value of a legal estate without notice of it.[5] An example would be the lien of the vendor of land to secure the purchase price, enforce-able by means of an order for sale;

(d) a *maritime lien* is a claim given by law over a ship and its cargo to secure debts in relation to matters such as salvage and seamen's wages[6]; and

(e) a *statutory lien* (as its name implies) arises out of statute. Examples include the statutory charge which arises under s.41(1) of the Sale of Goods Act 1979 and which entitles the unpaid seller to retain the goods in order to secure the price and the right of an airport to detain an aircraft for unpaid airport charges under s.88 of the Civil Aviation Act 1982.

A common example of a possessory lien is a solicitor's lien (for unpaid costs) on any property being held or recoverable by the solicitor on behalf of the client. This could include tangible property (such as the books and records of the client company) or intangible property (such as the client's right to payment in respect of a judgment obtained by the client against a defendant). The solic-itor can enforce such lien pursuant to the procedure set out in s.73(1) of the Solicitors Act 1974. The lien is not restricted to funds received before insol-vency proceedings in relation to the client are commenced provided that the lien was in existence prior to that date[7]. The impact of an administration or receivership on this type of lien is considered below.

(b) Registration

Pursuant to s.860(1) of the Companies Act 2006, certain charges created by a company are required to be registered. The two conditions for triggering this section are that: **23–003**

(a) the interest brought into existence is not a mere possessory lien (which is not registrable) but a charge[8]; and

---

[5] See *Snell's Equity*, 31st edn (London: Sweet & Maxwell, 2005).
[6] *The Halycon Isle* [1981] A.C. 221 (PC), referred to in *Oceanconnect UK Ltd v Angara Maritime Ltd* [2011] 1 All E.R. (Comm) 193 (CA).
[7] *Hammonds v Thomas Muckle & Sons Ltd* [2006] B.P.I.R. 704.
[8] *Re Wallis and Simmonds (Buildings) Ltd* [1974] 1 W.L.R. 391, considering the provisions of s.95 of the Companies Act 1948. See also *Re Welsh Irish Ferries Ltd (The Ugland Trailer)* [1986] Ch. 471.

(b)   the interest is created by the company whether expressly or impliedly and does not arise by operation of law.[9]

Hence a lien falling within any of the categories referred to above will not require registration under s.860 unless it is characterised as a charge rather than a lien.

(c)   Priorities

23–004   A lien will not have priority over a prior registered fixed charge or a prior registered crystallised floating charge save with the express or implied consent of the debenture-holder.[10] A lien will, however, have priority over a prior uncrystallised floating charge unless the charge contains a prohibition on the creation of such liens and the grantee of the lien has actual knowledge of such prohibition.[11] This is because the floating charge is an incomplete equitable assignment which permits the creation of such liens in the ordinary course of business.[12] In a case where there is such a prohibition and knowledge of the prohibition, a lien created by the company can only enjoy priority with the express or implied consent of the debenture-holder.[13] Constructive knowledge of the prohibition is insufficient to postpone the lien to the floating charge. Knowledge of the floating charge does not constitute knowledge of any prohibition contained therein, for the floating nature of the charge implies authority to carry on the company's ordinary course of business.[14] Actual knowledge of a prohibition on the creation of charges or liens will not operate to postpone a lien arising by operation of law, for such a lien is not created by the company.[15]

2.   LIENS AND ADMINISTRATIONS

23–005   The appointment of an administrator will have three principal effects on the holder of any lien over the company's property, each of which is considered further below:

(a)   under s.246 of the Insolvency Act 1986, a lien over the books, papers or other records of the company will be unenforceable to the extent that its enforcement would deny possession of such books, papers or other records to the administrator (but with an exception for documents which give title to property);

---

[9] *Brunton v Electrical Engineering Corp* [1892] 1 Ch. 434 (solicitor's lien); *London & Cheshire Insurance Co v Laplagrene Property Co* [1971] Ch. 499 (unpaid vendor's lien) considering the provisions of s.95 of the Companies Act 1948.
[10] *Brown v Associated British Motors Ltd* [1932] N.Z.L.R. 655.
[11] *Re British Tea Table Co (1897) Ltd* (1909) 101 L.T. 707; *George Barker (Transport) Ltd v Eynon* [1974] 1 W.L.R. 462 (CA); *Parsons v Sovereign Bank of Canada* [1913] A.C. 160 (PC).
[12] *Business Computers Ltd v Anglo-African Leasing Co Ltd* [1977] 1 W.L.R. 578.
[13] *Williams v Allsup* (1861) 10 C.B.N.S. 417; *Tappenden (t/a English & American Autos) v Artus* [1964] 2 Q.B. 185 (CA).
[14] *Brunton v Electrical Engineering Corp* [1892] 1 Ch. 434 (solicitor's lien for fees incurred after commencement of receivership).
[15] *Brunton v Electrical Engineering Corp* [1892] 1 Ch. 434.

(b) under s.236 of the Insolvency Act 1986, an administrator can apply to the court for an order that certain persons produce any books, papers or other records in their possession or under their control relating to the company or its promotion, formation, business, dealings, affairs or property; and

(c) where the lien is over property that does not fall within the category of books, papers or other records of the company, the lien will remain valid but the lien-holder will be unable to take any steps to enforce the lien without the consent of the administrator or the permission of the court by virtue of para.43 of Sch.B1 to the Insolvency Act 1986.

(a) Unenforceability of lien over books, papers and records of the company

Section 246 of the Insolvency Act 1986 applies where a company enters administration, goes into liquidation or a provisional liquidator is appointed. It does not apply where a receiver is appointed (although a receiver may be able to obtain the company's books, papers and records under s.236 of the Insolvency Act 1986 as considered below). The section ensures that an administrator (as well as a liquidator or provisional liquidator) is not prevented from taking possession of the company's books, papers and other records on the grounds that a lien is claimed over them (for example by a solicitor or accountant in respect of unpaid fees). The lien will be rendered unenforceable to the extent required to enable the relevant office-holder to obtain possession of the books, papers or other records.

There is an exception in s.246(3) for documents which give title to property and which are held as such. In *Osborne Clarke v Carter Commercial Developments*,[16] Osborne Clarke sought the leave of the court (under what was then s.11(3)(c) of the Insolvency Act 1986[17]) to enforce its lien over its client company's title deeds to a commercial property following the administration of the client company. Osborne Clarke was owed approximately £450,000 in respect of unpaid fees and had been holding the title deeds at the time at which the administration application was made although no reference was made to this fact in the administration application. Mr Justice Jacob held that the lien was not unenforceable under s.246 as the title deeds fell within the exception in s.246(3) and he gave leave to Osborne Clarke to retain the deeds notwithstanding the fact that the question of the workability of the administration (given the lien) had not been addressed in the application for administration.

The effect of s.246 on the holder of any lien is limited to a lien over the books, papers and records of the company in administration. In relation to liens over other categories of goods, the lien will remain valid but the lien-holder

23–006

---

[16] *Osborne Clarke v Carter Commercial Developments* [2002] All E.R. (D) 13 (Feb). See also *Re SEIL Trade Finance Ltd* [1992] B.C.C. 538.

[17] The impact of this section and para.43 of Sch.B1 to the Insolvency Act 1986 is considered below.

will require the consent of the administrator, or the permission of the court, in order to enforce the lien (as discussed below).

(b) Inquiry into the company's dealings

23–007 Section 236 of the Insolvency Act 1986 governs inquiries into the company's dealings and the powers of the court to request the provision of certain information. The court may, on the application of the administrator (as well as an administrative receiver, liquidator or provisional liquidator), summon certain persons to produce any books, papers or other records in their possession or under their control relating to the company or its promotion, formation, business, dealings, affairs or property. Such persons can be any officer of the company, any persons known or suspected to have in their possession any property of the company or supposed to be indebted to the company or any person whom the court thinks capable of giving information concerning the promotion, formation, business, dealings, affairs or property of the company.[18]

Where the administrator is able to assert the company's proprietary right to a document under s.246 of the Insolvency Act 1986, there will be no need for the administrator to obtain an order for its production under s.236. An order under s.236 may, however, be required where the exception to s.246 applies (i.e. in the case of a document which gives title to property and which is held as such). Furthermore, s.246 does not apply in the case of an administrative receivership (as referred to below).

A solicitor is not entitled to refuse to produce any of the documents referred to in s.236 on the grounds of a lien on such documents in respect of professional services rendered prior to the relevant insolvency proceedings. This has been explained on the following bases:

(a) the court summons is merely for inspection of the documents rather than delivery up (which would destroy the lien)[19]; and

(b) section 236 confers third party status on the relevant office-holder so that the office-holder is not, when seeking the order, acting solely as the company's agent; a solicitor's lien only entitles the holder to retain documents as against the client and not third parties.[20]

(c) Moratorium on security enforcement

23–008 A lien which is not caught by s.246 of the Insolvency Act 1986 will remain valid but, in the case of administration, no steps may be taken to enforce the

---

[18] In relation whether s.236 can be used to compel a statutory body (such as the Serious Fraud Office) to produce documents relating to an insolvent company that have been obtained under compulsory powers, see *Morris v Director of the Serious Fraud Office* [1993] Ch. 372, as cited in the recent case of *Standard Life Assurance v Topland Col Ltd* [2011] 1 W.L.R. 2162.

[19] *Re Tolemand and England Ex p. Bramble* (1879–80) L.R. 13 Ch. D 885 regarding s.96 of the Bankruptcy Act 1869, a statutory predecessor to s.236 of the Insolvency Act 1986.

[20] *Re Aveling Barford Ltd* [1989] 1 W.L.R. 360, citing *In re Hawkes, Ackerman v Lockhart* [1898] 2 Ch. 1 (CA).

lien without the consent of the administrator or the permission of the court.[21] The moratorium does not prevent the creation or perfection of security and so, if the creditor comes into possession of the relevant asset after the commencement of the administration, a lien may still come into existence.[22] The questions arise, however, as to what is meant by the expression "steps taken to enforce" in the context of a possessory lien and when the permission of the court is required in this context.

These questions were considered by the Court of Appeal in *Bristol Airport Plc v Powdrill*.[23] Following the making of an administration order in respect of Paramount Airways Ltd, Bristol airport sought ex parte leave to exercise its statutory right under s.88 of the Civil Aviation Act 1982 to detain two aircraft for unpaid airport charges. The aircraft had landed at Bristol airport following the commencement of the administration. Without obtaining the leave of the court, Birmingham airport prevented an aircraft from leaving the airport (by parking a lorry loaded with concrete in front of it) and served the captain of the aircraft with a "lien notice". Later that day, Birmingham airport obtained ex parte leave to detain the aircraft until an inter partes hearing.

The Court of Appeal considered that the statutory right of detention under s.88 of the Civil Aviation Act 1982 was very similar to a common law or possessory lien as it was a right of retention of chattels enjoyed by a creditor against the payment of its charges for services rendered in relation to those chattels. Even if this statutory right was not strictly to be regarded as a lien, it would certainly fall within the description of "other security" in s.248 of the Insolvency Act 1986. Hence the decision in *Powdrill* should apply by analogy to contractual and common law liens.

23–009

Counsel for the airports argued that the overt act necessary to constitute the exercise of the statutory right of detention (i.e. the blocking of the aircraft or the service of a notice of lien) was not a step taken to enforce the security but rather a step taken to create or perfect the security (which is not prohibited by the moratorium). Sir Nicolas Browne-Wilkinson V.C. held that the word "enforce", when used in s.11(3) in relation to a lien,[24] prima facie includes the assertion by the lien-holder of its right to retain the property that is the subject of the lien. The coming into possession of the relevant asset would not, of itself, be a step taken to enforce the security but a refusal to hand over the asset to the administrators, following a request for delivery up, would be. He was "not persuaded that, just because the overt act of detention created or perfected the security, it was not also the taking of a step to enforce that security. There is no legal reason why the same act should not have the dual effect as being both the perfection of the security and a step taken to enforce it".[25]

---

[21] para.43(2) of Sch.B1 to the Insolvency Act 1986, replacing s.11(3)(c).

[22] *Re London Flight Centre (Stansted) Ltd* [2002] All E.R. (D) 52. This was confirmed, in relation to funds coming into the hands of a solicitor after the date of administration and thus being caught by the solicitor's lien, in *Hammonds v Thomas Muckle & Sons Ltd* [2006] B.P.I.R. 704.

[23] *Bristol Airport Plc v Powdrill* [1990] Ch. 744 (CA).

[24] And so, by analogy, when used in para.43(2) of Sch.B1.

[25] *Bristol Airport Plc v Powdrill* [1990] Ch. 744 (CA), 764.

Counsel for the airports also submitted that, by being forced to give up possession of the aircraft to the administrators, the airports would lose their security (and that this would always be the case in relation to a possessory lien). Although this practical consideration was acknowledged by the court, Sir Nicolas Browne-Wilkinson V.C. pointed out that, if the court was satisfied that the administrator needed possession of the asset for the purposes of the administration, the court could, in the exercise of its discretion, impose terms whereby the lien over the asset was retained, notwithstanding the loss of possession, or providing some other suitable security for the lien-holder. Furthermore, Sir Nicolas Browne-Wilkinson V.C. considered that the airport would run no risk of being in contempt of court if it detained the aircraft while it made every effort to obtain the leave of the court under s.11(3)(c).

23–010   The refusal to hand over the asset which is the subject of the lien will be a step taken to enforce security (for the purposes of s.11(3)(c) and para.43(2) of Sch.B1) even if it is not the administrator, but rather another authorised agent of the company, who makes the request for delivery up of the asset. In *Re London Flight Centre (Stansted) Ltd*,[26] the applicant company entered into a contract with the respondent for the maintenance of the applicant's aircraft. The contract included a contractual lien in favour of the respondent over all goods in the respondent's possession for all sums owed to it at any time by the applicant. The applicant granted security over the aircraft to a third party and, when the applicant got into financial difficulties, the secured creditor appointed receivers over the aircraft. The applicant subsequently went into administration but the administrators allowed the receivers to remain in office. The receivers leased the aircraft to another company. The respondent provided maintenance under a contract (containing a similar lien) and, on the expiry of the lease, obtained possession of the aircraft from the lessee.

The applicant's administrator proposed a voluntary arrangement which was approved by the unsecured creditors and supported by the secured creditor. The arrangement provided that the applicant should recommence business with the use of the aircraft. The receivers pursued an action for delivery up against the respondent so that they could obtain possession of the aircraft and hand it over to the administrator under the terms of the voluntary arrangement. The court rejected the respondent's argument that it had not yet taken any steps to enforce the lien because the receivers, and not the administrator, had asked it to deliver up possession of the aircraft, on the basis that the respondent knew that the receivers and the administrator were united in their approach in relation to the possession of the aircraft.

23–011   If the lien-holder seeks the leave of the court in order to retain the goods in question, the court is likely to consider the guidelines set out in *Re Atlantic Computer Systems Plc*,[27] when determining whether or not to grant such leave. In both the *Powdrill* case and *London Flight Centre*, the lien-holder was refused the permission of the court to enforce its lien (by retaining the relevant

---

[26] *Re London Flight Centre (Stansted) Ltd* [2002] All E.R. (D) 52.
[27] *Re Atlantic Computer Systems Plc* [1992] Ch. 505 (CA), as applied in the recent decision in *Rubin v Cobalt Pictures Limited* [2011] B.P.I.R. 334.

asset). This was partly because the asset in question (i.e. the aircraft) was needed by the administrators in order to carry out the business of the company. A further significant factor in both cases was that the asset had come into the possession of the creditor after the commencement of the administration so that, at the date on which the administrators were appointed, the creditor was merely an unsecured creditor. This can be contrasted with the position of the solicitors in *Osborne Clarke v Carter Commercial Developments Ltd*[28] where the title deeds were in the possession of the solicitors when the administrators were appointed; in this case, the solicitors were given leave to enforce the lien.

3.   LIENS AND RECEIVERSHIPS

Where a receiver is appointed in respect of a company, neither s.246 of the **23–012** Insolvency Act 1986 nor the moratorium under para.43 of Sch.B1 will come into play and any lien created by the company, or arising by operation of law, will not be affected by these provisions. If, however, the receiver is an administrative receiver, the receiver will have the right to apply to court under s.236 of the Insolvency Act 1986 (as referred to above) and any person holding any books, records or other papers of the company will not be able to refuse to produce them on the basis of any lien over those documents.[29] This section is therefore particularly important in the context of an administrative receivership as the receiver will not be able to assert the company's proprietary right to a document which is the subject of a lien under s.246 of the Insolvency Act 1986.

Outside of the context of s.236, the question of whether or not a lien is enforceable against the receivers of a company will depend on whether the lien, or the security pursuant to which the receiver is appointed, has priority. As referred to above, if the lien comes into existence prior to the crystallisation of a floating charge, it will have priority and, even if the lien-holder is aware of a prohibition preventing the company from creating any mortgage or charge in priority to the floating charge, this will not prevent the lien from having priority if it arises by operation of law.[30]

It is more problematic, however, when the assets over which the lien is asserted come into the possession of the creditor after the appointment of the receivers (and so following the crystallisation of the floating charge). This was considered in the case of *George Barker (Transport) Ltd v Eynon*.[31] The relevant events were as follows:

> (a) *prior to the appointment of the receiver*: a contract for the transport of goods was made between the carrier and the company; the contract

---

[28] *Osborne Clarke v Carter Commercial Developments Ltd* [2002] All E.R. (D) 13 (Feb). See also *Euro Commercial Leasing Ltd v Cartwright & Land* [1995] B.C.C. 830.

[29] *Re Aveling Barford Ltd* [1989] 1 W.L.R. 360.

[30] *Brunton v Electrical Engineering Corp* [1892] 1 Ch. 434.

[31] *George Barker (Transport) Ltd v Eynon* [1974] 1 W.L.R. 462 (CA), followed in *Re ELS (formerly English Lifestyle)* [1995] Ch. 11.

provided for a contractual lien over the goods to secure all sums due to the carrier; the company owed money to the carrier in respect of goods transported prior to the receivership; and the company ordered the carriage of a particular consignment of meat; and

(b) *following notice of the appointment of the receiver*: the carriers collected the meat but retained it at their depot against payment of the costs due to them both prior to and following the appointment of the receiver.

23–013 The court allowed the carriers to set up a lien against the receiver in respect of the sums due both prior to and following the receiver's appointment on the basis that the carriers' rights in respect of the lien had not arisen or come into existence when they took possession of the meat (i.e. after the appointment of the receiver) but rather (as contractual rights) at the time when the contract for the transport of the meat was made (i.e. prior to the receiver's appointment). It was immaterial that the rights had not become exercisable until after that date.

As a practical point, Stamp L.J. commented that the receiver, acting as agent for the company, could have repudiated the contract, leaving the carriers with a claim in damages. If the receiver had repudiated the contract while the goods were still in the possession of the company, and had refused the carriers the opportunity of performing their obligations under the contract, the carriers would not have been able to obtain the possession which enabled them to exercise their lien.[32] On the evidence, the court did not consider that the receiver had attempted to repudiate the contract in this case until after the carriers had obtained possession of the goods.

Edmund Davies L.J. pointed out, however, that an earlier attempt by the receiver to repudiate the contract may not have assisted in this case because, even if the receiver had sought to repudiate the contract prior to the date on which the carriers obtained possession of the goods, the carriers could legitimately refuse to accept the repudiation and could instead insist on fulfilling their part of the contract.[33] Unless the receiver is in a position to retain the relevant goods, a repudiation of the contract by the receiver may not assist.

23–014 As a further practical point, if the asset in question is a wasting asset, there may be no time for the receiver to negotiate a new agreement (with either the existing carrier or a new entity) excluding any lien in respect of pre-receivership debts and the receiver may have little choice but to allow the existing carrier to perform the existing contract. In the *George Barker* case (where the asset in question was cartons of meat), the receiver needed to come to an arrangement in relation to the transport of the meat as a matter of urgency. An oral agreement

---

[32] *George Barker (Transport) Ltd v Eynon* [1974] 1 W.L.R. 462 (CA), 471.

[33] *George Barker (Transport) Ltd v Eynon* [1974] 1 W.L.R. 462 (CA), 470. See also *Avery v Bowden* (1855) 119 E.R. 647; *Denmark Productions Ltd v Boscobel Productions Ltd* [1968] 3 All E.R. 513 (CA), 527. Blanchard, *The Law of Company Receiverships in Australia and New Zealand* (Wellington, N.Z.: Butterworths, 1982), para.904 points out that, unless the receiver can physically prevent the carriage, the carrier might refuse to accept the repudiation and try to insist on performance without an order for specific performance (citing *White & Carter (Councils) Ltd v McGregor* [1962] A.C. 413 (HL)).

was therefore reached that the carriers would transport the meat without prejudice to any general lien they might have on the goods, the receiver would pay the carriers' charges for such transport and if the carriers could subsequently establish that they were entitled to refuse to deliver the cartons of meat pursuant to their general lien, the receiver would pay the sum owed to them by the company. For the reasons given above, the court subsequently held that the general lien was effective and had priority over the security pursuant to which the receiver had been appointed.

Chapter 24

Bankers*

24–001 Administrators and receivers will come across bankers in several contexts. Where the office-holder is a receiver who is appointed by the company's banker, he will usually be expected to open an account with the appointing bank and relatively few problems arise. This chapter is principally concerned with administrators or with receivers who are not bank appointees. Following their appointment, an office-holder will invariably wish to take control of the company's bank accounts for the purposes of the receivership or administration. However, the company's existing relationships with its bankers can pose special problems of set-off and priority. This chapter considers how a receiver and administrator may deal with bank accounts following their appointment, and the rights that may be exercised by a banker over those accounts.

1. ACTIONS BY THE OFFICE-HOLDER

(a) Dealings with the company's account

24–002 Both administrators and receivers should immediately upon appointment give notice of their appointment to the company's bankers. In the case of an administrator, this will revoke the authority of the directors to deal with any monies otherwise standing to the credit of the company.[1] Provided that the company's monies at its bankers (more accurately, the banker's debt to the company) are within the charges in respect of which the receiver is appointed, the same is true in the case of a receiver. The bank, upon receiving such notice, will no longer be able to rely upon the usual company mandate entitling one or more directors or officers to control the account and will have to accept the sole control of the office-holder. Likewise, in the absence of an agreement with the office-holder, any cheques or bills of exchange drawn prior to the office-holder's appointment but presented or payment instructions received after notice of the appointment must be dishonoured or refused. It follows that generally all company bank accounts will be immediately frozen upon receipt of notice of the office-holder's appointment.

24–003 The office-holder will need to carefully consider whether to continue the company's previous banking relationships, and he may decide to keep some

---

* This chapter is based on the work of David Marks QC of the fourth edition.
[1] See generally Insolvency Act 1986, Sch.B1, para.64 which provides that the directors may not exercise management powers so as to interfere with the exercise of the administrator's powers without the consent of the administrator. In rare cases, the office-holder may consent to directors continuing to exercise their powers post-appointment where it is necessary for the continued trading of the business.

pre-appointment accounts open. This could be for a variety of reasons. There may be a substantial number of debtor receipts due to be paid to the company by way of direct debits or standing orders, and it would be difficult in practice for collection of those receipts to be moved to a new account. A company may use merchant facilities provided by their bankers to accept customer payments by credit or debit, and electronic systems such as "Autopay" or "Bacs" for the payment of salaries and other multiple payments. The office-holder clearly may benefit from the adoption and continued use of such facilities, for example, in the case of a retail company with many trading outlets. Finally, it will not always be possible to identify who are creditors of the company immediately following the office-holder's appointment and the office-holder will wish to avoid opening accounts with new banks who may be creditors of the company. For these reasons, the office-holder may prefer to reach an agreement with the company's existing bankers as to the operation of the company's pre-appointment accounts.[2] In doing so, he will seek to enter into an agreement with the bank to ensure that there is no combination or set-off between pre and post appointment receipts. However, if it can do so under the terms of the company's facilities, the bank may prefer to terminate the banking relationship—particularly if the existing accounts include both debit and credit balances which are subject to an agreement to keep the accounts separate (as to which see below).

(b) Opening new accounts by office-holder

In addition to any pre-appointment accounts which are retained, an adminis- **24–004** trator or receiver will commonly also wish to open new accounts for receipts and payments post appointment. Where a receiver is appointed by a clearing bank, the bank can be expected to require that the receiver's account or accounts be opened at one of its branches which will normally be at the branch where the company's own account or accounts were maintained. If the office-holder is a receiver not appointed by a clearing bank or is an administrator then, in the absence of other considerations, he will have discretion as to which bank or banks he will choose at which to open his accounts. Clearly he will be likely to select one where there is no question of any pre-appointment debt being owed by the company. Where an office-holder proposes to open an account with a bank that is owed money by the company, he must consider carefully the possi-bility of the bank seeking to exercise rights of set-off against his future credit balances. In the case of a receiver, a creditor bank will have notice of the appointor's security and of the crystallisation of any floating charges on notice of the appointment of a receiver. It follows that the creditor bank will not be able to set-off the company's pre-existing overdrawn account with it against any credits paid into the receivership account, assuming of course that such

---

[2] Conversely, in present times when the security of large clearing banks has been called into question, an office-holder will consider the credit risk associated with the company's existing bankers, and in the case of significant cash reserves, take steps to minimise such risk through a spread of investments.

credits consist of monies falling within the appointor's security. However, an administrator, whose position in this respect is necessarily different, should invariably obtain the specific agreement of the bank to exclude set-off before proceeding and a cautious receiver will, despite his appointor's security, follow the same course.

24–005 To minimise delay following their appointment, many accounting firms have agreed protocols for the opening of new accounts with the clearing banks in the United Kingdom. The protocols set out the procedure agreed between the clearing bank and the accounting firm in the event that a member of the firm requires a bank account following an insolvency appointment. The protocol will generally set out the type of account to be opened and the terms that will apply. Importantly, the Know Your Customer (KYC) requirements for the insolvency practitioners named in the protocol will have been satisfied in advance, considerably quickening the process for opening an account. The office-holder will be a signatory on each new account which is to be opened. However, office-holders in practice often act by members of the staff of the firms of accountants to which they belong. As such, there will be a pre-agreed list with the clearing bank of members of the officeholder's staff who are authorised to operate the mandate on the account. In the absence of an agreed protocol, the bank's requirements for opening new accounts will need to be satisfied which may delay matters. Increasingly, English-appointed office-holders have to deal with company accounts that are located overseas which can introduce further complexity and delay to the process.

24–006 Where new accounts are opened, the office-holder may wish to instruct the company's pre-appointment bankers to transfer any credit balances (if any remain after combination of accounts) to the new account or accounts. The bank holding the credit balance will want to see evidence of the office-holder's appointment and may well seek to satisfy itself as far as practicable that the appointment has been validly made. If such checks are not made and it subsequently turns out that the appointment was invalid, unless there is any estoppel binding the company, a bank that parts with the company's money will (it seems) be acting in breach of mandate. On the other hand, there may not be any loss: either the company is likely to be able to recover its monies from the office-holder or, in so far as the office-holder has paid off the company's liabilities, the bank may be afforded equitable relief.[3] The special statutory protection afforded to persons dealing with an office-holder[4] extends only to acts beyond the office-holder's powers and not to a situation where he is invalidly appointed and has no power at all.[5]

(c) Accounts in the company's name

24–007 A receiver will, until winding-up, normally act as agent for the company under the terms of the debenture or charge. An administrative receiver is deemed to

---

[3] *B Liggett (Liverpool) v Barclays Bank Ltd* [1928] 1 K.B. 48.
[4] Insolvency Act 1986, ss.42(3) and 232 and Sch.B1, para.59(3).
[5] See further, *OBG Ltd v Allan* [2008] 1 A.C. 1 (HL), [89]–[92] per Lord Hoffmann.

be the agent of the company unless and until there is a winding-up[6] and an administrator also performs his functions in an agency capacity.[7] When an office-holder opens an account he should do so ideally in the name of the company but make his position as agent clear. The account would in such a situation be entitled "Account of X Ltd, A.B. [Office-Holder]".[8]

(d) Accounts in the office-holder's name

The alternative, and exceptional, course is for the office-holder to open an account in his own name, but making the special position of the account clear, e.g. by entitling it "X, [Office-holder] of Y Ltd". In this case a receiver's[9] account can be taken into overdraft after winding-up.[10]

24–008

(e) Segregation of funds

Statement of Insolvency Practice 11 (E&W) lays down guidelines for the handling of funds by insolvency office-holders. Funds and assets belonging to the company must be maintained separately from those of the office-holder or his firm. In addition, an office-holder should take steps to ensure that funds are held in a bank account or accounts which meet the following criteria[11]:

24–009

- All money standing to the credit of the account(s) is held by the office-holder as case money and the bank is not entitled to combine the account with any other account (including any global, omnibus, master, hub, nominee, sub accounts or similar) or exercise any right to set-off or counterclaim against money in that account in respect of any money owed to it on any other account (including any global, omnibus, master, hub, nominee, sub accounts or similar) of the office-holder or his firm;

- Interest payable on the money in the account(s) must be credited to that account(s);

- The bank must describe the account(s) in its records to make it clear that the money in the account does not belong to the office-holder or his firm;

- No individual case funds/account(s) can be set-off against any overdrawn case funds/accounts.

---

[6] Insolvency Act 1986, s.44(1)(a).

[7] Sch.B1, para.69

[8] If an office-holder signs cheques drawn in the company's name, it seems that the cheque will be that of the company and not the office-holder: see *Bondina v Rollaway Shower Blinds* [1986] 1 W.L.R. 517 (CA), a case where a director signed a cheque under the company name and was held to have signed the company's cheque (rather than his own) on the grounds that his signature adopted the wording on the cheque relating to the company. See also *Jenice Ltd v Dan* [1994] B.C.C. 43.

[9] This does not apply to administrators because administration and liquidation are mutually exclusive procedures.

[10] A receiver who after his signature on a contractual document merely adds the words "Receiver for X Ltd" is to be treated as contracting personally: *Kettle v Dunster* (1926) 43 T.L.R. 770.

[11] Statement of Insolvency Practice 11 (E&W), para.2.2.

It will be the responsibility of the office-holder to put the bank on notice of the nature of the accounts and to ensure any accounts meet the above criteria, for otherwise it seems a banker is entitled to treat monies passing through the account as the customer's own.[12]

24–010   In the instances where an office-holder receives a cheque payable to the office-holder or his firm which cannot be endorsed to the insolvent estate, he may clear such cheques through his own account or that of his firm.[13] However, such accounts should be operated on a trust basis and maintained separately from the firm's office accounts, and any funds should be transferred into the accounts for the administration or receivership as soon as possible.

24–011   If there are secured creditors, any new accounts which are opened should include separate fixed and floating charge realisations accounts, reflecting the interest of preferential creditors in the latter, but not in the former. Sometimes certain items of expenditure which are necessarily incurred for the benefit of fixed charge realisations may (for convenience) be paid from the floating charge account. In such cases payments will be duly reallocated to the latter account.

24–012   There should be a separate account or sets of accounts for each company's banking arrangements where an office-holder is appointed in respect of a group of companies. In addition, office-holders should record all transactions during the period of their stewardship of the company's affairs.[14] Office-holders are required to ensure that records are maintained to identify the funds (including any interest earned thereon) and other assets of each case for which they have responsibility as insolvency office-holder.

2.   RIGHTS OF BANKER

(a)   Banker's right to combine accounts

24–013   Under its pre-existing relationship with the company, a bank is likely to have a power to combine different accounts of the company, either by reason of an express provision in a debenture or in terms governing the account, or under the general law.[15] It has been held that where a customer has more than one account with its bank, one in credit and another in debit, the banker is entitled to combine the accounts to produce a single net balance, unless he has made

---

[12] *Thomson v Clydesdale Bank Ltd* [1893] A.C. 282 (HL). Also see *Clark v Ulster Bank Ltd* [1950] N.I. 132.

[13] Statement of Insolvency Practice 11 (E&W), para.2.3.

[14] The need to maintain suitable records reflects the provisions of the Insolvency Rules 1986, rr.2.47 and 3.32 regarding the office-holder's abstract of receipts and payments.

[15] The right to combine has sometimes been inaccurately referred to as the operation of "the banker's lien" which is a separate right: Lord Denning M.R. and Buckley L.J. (dissenting) in *Halesowen Presswork v National Westminster Bank* [1971] 1 Q.B. 1 (CA) and Lord Cross (dissenting) on appeal; *National Westminster Bank v Halesowen Presswork* [1972] A.C. 785 (HL), 814. For a discussion of the rights to combine which are beyond the scope of this chapter, see Derham, *The Law of Set-off*, 4th edn (Oxford: Oxford University Press, 2010), pp.675–739 and Hapgood, *Paget's Law of Banking*, 13th edn (Butterworths, 2007), pp.713–723. Also, see Wood, *English and International Set-off* (London: Sweet & Maxwell, 1989), p.91.

some express or implied agreement to keep them separate.[16] In an insolvency scenario, this right to combine accounts will place the bank in a privileged position in comparison with the company's other creditors. Combination requires the debts to be presently due and payable and the bank will not be entitled to retain sums to meet contingent or unmatured liabilities of the customer, in the absence of a contractual right.[17] However, it makes no difference that the accounts are maintained at different branches of the bank, and is sometimes exercisable without prior notice to the customer.[18] The right will generally be evidenced by the bank making book-keeping entries of debiting one account and crediting another, although it has been suggested that a prompt assertion of rights by the bank would be sufficient.[19]

An agreement to keep accounts separate may be made expressly or may be implied, although the mere opening of separate accounts will not create such an agreement.[20] For instance, there will usually be held to be an implied agreement that the bank will not combine accounts where one account is a loan account and the other is a current account.[21] For otherwise, as explained by Scrutton L.J. in *Bradford Old Bank v Sutcliffe*,[22] no customer could safely draw on his current account if he had a loan account greater than the credit balance on his current account.[23]   **24–014**

It is a question of construction as to when an agreement to keep accounts separate comes to an end. In the *Halesowen* case[24] the House of Lords held that whilst it was competent for the parties to determine the duration of their agreement, the courts would readily infer that it was only intended to continue in force during the active life of the company or whilst it continues as a going concern. Accordingly, such agreements must come to an end on the   **24–015**

---

[16] *Garnett v M'Kewan* (1872) L.R. 8 Ex. 10, approved by the Privy Council in *Prince v Oriental Bank Corp* (1878) L.R. 3 App. Cas. 325 (PC); *Halesowen Presswork v National Westminster Bank* [1971] 1 Q.B. 1 (CA), 34.

[17] *Jeffryes v Agra and Masterman's Bank* (1866) L.R. 2 Eq 674, 680. In contrast, it is common to include an express right in a debenture for a bank to retain sums in a suspense account with which to meet future liabilities of the borrower.

[18] *Garnett v M'Kewan* (1872) L.R. 8 Ex. 10.

[19] *Halesowen Presswork v National Westminster Bank* [1971] 1 Q.B. 1 (CA), 19. See also the detailed discussion by Rory Derham in *The Law of Set-off* (Oxford University Press, 2010), p.676 that the nature of the right is a matter of accounting, rather than set-off and as such, a specific act of combination should not be required.

[20] *National Westminster Bank Ltd v Halesowen Presswork and Assemblies Ltd* [1971] 1 Q.B. 1 (CA), 35. Also see comments of Roskill J. at first instance in *National Westminster Bank Ltd v Halesowen Presswork and Assemblies Ltd* [1971] 1 Q.B. 1 (CA), 21 where he said that "The critical question must always be 'What was the contract?' and not whether a particular account or accounts bear one title rather than another."

[21] *Bradford Old Bank v Sutcliffe* [1918] 2 K.B. 833 (CA); *Re EJ Morel (1934) Ltd* [1962] Ch. 21; *National Westminster Bank Ltd v Halesowen Presswork and Assemblies Ltd* [1972] A.C. 785 (HL).

[22] *Bradford Old Bank Ltd v Sutcliffe* [1918] 2 K.B. 833 (CA).

[23] *Bradford Old Bank Ltd v Sutcliffe* [1918] 2 K.B. 833 (CA), 847. Also see comments of Pickford L.J. at 839. The comments of Scrutton L.J. were cited with approval by Lord Cross in the House of Lords in *National Westminster Bank Ltd v Halesowen Presswork and Assemblies Ltd* [1972] A.C. 785 (HL), 809.

[24] *National Westminster Bank Ltd v Halesowen Presswork and Assemblies Ltd* [1972] A.C. 785 (HL).

liquidation of the company, at which point the bank would be entitled to combine accounts.[25]

24-016   Notice of the appointment of a receiver or administrator to one of its customers or that such an appointment is pending, may cause a bank to consider whether to combine accounts. Where the bank in question is the appointor and the office-holder is its receiver, few problems will arise in practice because the bank and the receiver will terminate the company's previous banking relationship and will combine accounts. The situation is likely to be different where the bank is not the receiver's appointor or the office-holder is an administrator.

24-017   If there has been pre-appointment agreement between the company and its banker to keep certain accounts separate, it will be necessary to determine whether such an agreement survives the appointment of the office-holder. There are some important distinctions between those of receivership and administration on the one hand and winding-up on the other to consider in this context. First, a receivership or an administration does not necessarily mean the end of the company as a going concern. Therefore, there may have to be a close examination of the facts in each case to see whether the banking relationship has ceased or whether the company has ceased to be a going concern in order to determine whether any agreement to keep accounts separate has come to an end. In the case of administration, but not receivership, the set-off rule applicable in administrations (r.2.85 of the Insolvency Rules 1986) may apply.[26] The rule applies if the administrator gives notice under r.2.95 that he proposes to make a distribution to creditors, and, whilst there is no authority as yet on the point, it is thought that the rule is mandatory once the notice of intention by the administrator is given.[27] Finally, where there is a fixed charge on bank accounts or on book debts, the bank may be unable to assert any right of combination because it is on notice of the existence of the charge. It is therefore common at the time such security is granted for a chargee to request the account bank to acknowledge that it has notice of the security, to avoid any issues of set-off or combination.

24-018   An example of an agreement to keep accounts separate which survived the appointment of a receiver and entitled the receiver to claim a credit balance is *Direct Acceptance Corp v Bank of New South Wales*.[28] The company, which was controlled by the debenture-holder's nominees, agreed with the company's bankers that the existing overdraft would be frozen and a new account opened as part of an informal receivership. The possibility of a receiver being appointed was mentioned. It was expressly agreed that there would be no set-off between the old and new accounts. Nevertheless, when the company went into receivership, the bank claimed the right to combine accounts and take the credit on the new account towards the liability of the old account. The bank argued for an implied term that the accounts would be kept separate only whilst the new account remained a current account, and suggested that on the

---

[25] *National Westminster Bank Ltd v Halesowen Presswork and Assemblies Ltd* [1972] A.C. 785 (HL), per Viscount Dilhorne at 805–806, per Lord Cross at 811, per Lord Kilbrandon at 820.
[26] See above, Ch.22, para.22–032. No such rule applies in the case of receivership: see above, Ch.22, para.22–053.
[27] See above, Ch.22, para.22–020.
[28] *Direct Acceptance Corp v Bank of New South Wales* (1968) 88 W.N. (Pt 1) (NSW) 498.

appointment of the receiver, operations on the new account "would, if not necessarily, at any rate in practice, cease".[29] On the rather special facts of that case, Macfarlan J. refused to imply any such term. Further, he held that whilst "there may be many considerations of practice" why the operation of the account should not continue after receivership, there was no rule of law preventing the operation of the new account after the appointment of a receiver.[30] The receiver was entitled to claim the credit balance on the new account.

(b)   Combination of accounts and preferential debts

In *Re E.J. Morel*[31] the company originally had one current account, which was substantially overdrawn. To reduce the company's liabilities, it was arranged that its overdrawn current account (No.1 account) was frozen. A new current account (No.2 account) was opened and a wages account (No.3 account) was also opened. The bank as a lender for the payment of wages was a preferential creditor to the extent that the sums in respect of wages paid by it, if left unpaid, would have been preferential debts in a receivership or winding-up.[32] Wages were drawn monthly and whenever a debit to the wages account was more than four months old (after which it would cease to be preferential) the amount of the debit was transferred from the No.2 account to the wages account. The No.2 account was to be kept in credit to a sufficient extent always to cover the debit on No.3 account, with the intention that the whole of the debit balance on the No.3 account was preferential at all times. When the company was wound-up its balances were as follows:

- No.1 account: £1,839 DR.

- No.2 account: £1,544.12s.4d. CR.

- No.3 account: £1,623.11s.11d. DR.

In order to maximise its preferential claim, the bank claimed to set-off the credit on the No.2 account against the debit of the No.1 account rather than against the No.3 account. The liquidator claimed that the No.2 account had to be set-off against the No.3 account. Buckley J. held that the No.1 account could not be combined with the No.2 account. As the No.1 account had been frozen and was no longer capable of being operated in the ordinary way as a current account, it had assumed the character of a loan account.[33] The result was that the usual term implied by the court in the case of loan accounts and current accounts applied so that the banker was not free to combine the accounts of different character. Furthermore, the judge considered that the arrangements meant that the No.2 and No.3 accounts were interdependent and in substance

24–019

---

[29] *Direct Acceptance Corp v Bank of New South Wales* (1968) 88 W.N. (Pt 1) (NSW) 49, 503.
[30] *Direct Acceptance Corp v Bank of New South Wales* (1968) 88 W.N. (Pt 1) (NSW) 49, 504.
[31] *Re EJ Morel* [1962] Ch. 21.
[32] See now Insolvency Act 1986, ss.175 and 386, and Sch.6, para.11.
[33] *Re EJ Morel* [1962] Ch. 21, 31.

one account, so that in effect only minimal sums were advanced by the bank towards wages to the extent that the debit on the wages account exceeded the credit on the No.2 account on winding-up.

24–020 In reaching his decision in *Re E.J. Morel*, Buckley J. was concerned with the construction of the accounts, rather than the application of set-off under the insolvency legislation. However, he also considered the position as if insolvency set-off applied to all three accounts as separate accounts, and held the No.2 account should be first set-off against the No.3 account so as to reduce the preferential claim as far as possible.[34] This dictum was disapproved by Walton J. in *Re Unit 2 Windows Ltd*[35] in a case involving set-off against the preferential claims of the Crown. He held that, where set-off was available against both a preferential and non-preferential debt, the set-off should apply rateably over the two debts. Walton J. based this conclusion on the true construction of the statutory provisions applicable in a bankruptcy and liquidation and by analogy, his reasoning would also apply to r.2.85 of the Insolvency Rules 1986 that applies in the case of administration.

24–021 In the case of receivership, it has already been noted that the existence of security may prevent a banker from exercising rights of combination. In the case of floating charge security, such rights will be restricted once the bank has notice of crystallisation of the debenture by the appointment of a receiver.[36] The question arises whether the bank is restricted in the exercise of its right of combination prior to this time. In *Re EJ Morel*,[37] Buckley J. suggested that a banker was entitled to combine accounts as it saw fit, which is consistent with the principles of the common law appropriation.[38]

(c) Combination of accounts and deposits for special purposes

24–022 Where prior to administration or receivership the company makes a deposit of separately identifiable monies with bankers for a special purpose of which they have notice at the time of deposit,[39] and this earmarking is effective to create a trust of the monies, the bank will not be able to combine or set-off the accounts so as to take the benefit of such credits against any overdrawn balances.[40] The appointment of an administrator or receiver will not effect a change in the beneficial ownership of monies collected in by the company in respect of which a special purpose arrangement exists.

---

[34] *Re EJ Morel* [1962] Ch. 21, 34. Also see above, Ch.22, para.22-065 for a fuller discussion in the context of set-off under the insolvency provisions.

[35] *Re Unit 2 Windows Ltd (In Liquidation)* [1985] 1 W.L.R. 1383. cf. the position in Scotland, where there exists a law of compensation or retention: see *Turner v Inland Revenue Commissioners* [1993] B.C.C 299 (Court of Session, Outer House).

[36] *Business Computers Ltd v Anglo-African Leasing Co Ltd* [1977] 1 W.L.R. 578.

[37] *Re EJ Morel* [1962] Ch. 21, 31; *Barclays Bank Ltd v TOSG Trust Fund Ltd* [1984] B.C.L.C. 1, 22.

[38] Derham, *The Law of Set-off*, 4th edn (Oxford: Oxford University Press, 2010), p.688–689.

[39] *Union Bank of Australia v Murray-Aynsley* [1898] A.C. 693 (PC).

[40] *Barclays Bank Ltd v Quistclose Investments Ltd* [1970] A.C. 567 (HL). As to these trusts generally, see Ch.20. See also Swadling (Ed.), *The Quistclose Trust: Critical Essays* (Oxford: Hart Publishing, 2004).

For this principle to apply it is not necessary that the bank should have **24–023** express notice of a trust as long as it has notice of the relevant facts creating the trust. Thus, in *Barclays Bank Ltd v Quistclose Investments Ltd*[41] a lender placed monies in a special bank account to be used only for the payment of dividends by a company in financial trouble. The company went into liquidation and the dividend was not paid. It was held that the monies in the account were held on trust for the lender. Lord Wilberforce explained in the leading speech:

> "That arrangements of this character for the payment of a person's credi-
> tors by a third person, give rise to a relationship of a fiduciary character or
> trust, in favour, as a primary trust, of the creditors, and secondarily, if the
> primary trust fails, of the third person, has been recognised in a series of
> cases over some 150 years."[42]

And later, he said:

> "When the purpose has been carried out (i.e. the debt paid) the lender has
> his remedy against the borrower in debt: if the primary purpose cannot be
> carried out, the question arises if a secondary purpose (i.e. repayment to
> the lender) has been agreed, expressly or by implication: if it has, the
> remedies of equity may be invoked to give effect to it, if it has not (and
> the money is intended to fall within the general fund of the debtor's assets)
> then there is the appropriate remedy for recovery of a loan."[43]

In the case of *Quistclose*, the court found there was a sufficient intention by the parties to create a secondary trust in favour of the lender when the primary purpose of paying a dividend failed. It followed that the monies could not be set-off by the bank against any debit balances of the company.

A bank may even be bound by such a trust where it does not know all the **24–024** facts but is put on inquiry. In *Neste Oy v Lloyd's Bank*,[44] the bank had a right of set-off applying to accounts of different companies in a group, including a company referred to as "PSL". The plaintiff, a shipowner, regularly made payments into PSL's account to enable PSL, as the plaintiff's agent, to discharge debts incurred by the plaintiff's vessels. PSL did not have to keep such sums separate and Bingham J. declined to hold that such payments were generally held on trust. However, in relation to the final payment made by the plaintiff, at a time when the debts covered by the payment had not been discharged by

---

[41] *Barclays Bank Ltd v Quistclose Investments Ltd* [1970] A.C. 567 (HL). Also see *WP Greenhalgh & Sons v Union Bank of Manchester* [1924] 2 K.B. 153.

[42] *Barclays Bank Ltd v Quistclose Investments Ltd* [1970] A.C. 567 (HL), 580.

[43] *Barclays Bank Ltd v Quistclose Investments Ltd* [1970] A.C. 567 (HL), 581–582. In *Twinsectra Ltd v Yardley* [2002] 2 A.C. 164 (HL), 187, Lord Millett rejected the approach of there being two successive trusts and preferred the view that the beneficial interest in the funds remained throughout in the lender. See further M. Smolyansky, "Reining in the Quistclose Trust: a Response to Twinsectra v Yardley" (2010) 16(7) T & T 558, 558–568 and Lord Millett, "The Quistclose Trust: A reply" (2010) 17(1) T & T 7, 7–16.

[44] *Neste Oy v Lloyd's Bank* [1983] 2 Lloyd's Rep. 658. See further, *Dubey v Revenue and Customs Commissioners* [2008] B.C.C. 22.

PSL and PSL knew that it was ceasing trade and would not give value for the payment, Bingham J. held that sum was held on constructive trust for the plaintiff. Whilst the bank did not know all the facts at the time it received this sum, it had been put on inquiry by being told that PSL was to cease trading and to invite the bank to appoint a receiver. An inquiry at that stage would have elicited the facts giving rise to the constructive trust. As a result, the bank was not entitled to set-off this final sum. Bingham J. added: "By the time the set-off was effected the bank was even more clearly on notice".[45] Although this is true, it is suggested that notice at any time after the payment was irrelevant, since a payment without constructive notice would have given the bank a vested right to combine accounts.[46] It is also doubtful that the plaintiff should have been promoted effectively to the status of a secured creditor in respect of the final payment, instead of being left to his right of proof.[47] There are many cases of equal hardship to makers of deposits and prepayments where the device of a constructive trust has not been imported to cure the absence of an express or implied trust.[48]

(d) Banker's lien

24–025 In addition to the right to combine accounts, a banker will enjoy a common law lien over all securities deposited with them as bankers by the customer for any debt owing by the customer, unless there is an express or implied agreement to the contrary.[49] The lien applies to all bills of exchange and cheques received by the banker for its customer, and other "paper securities"[50] but may not extend to property deposited with the bank for safe custody.[51] It is thought that a banker enjoys a power to sell the property that is the subject of the lien.[52] For a discussion on the impact of an administration or receivership on a lien-holder's rights, see Ch.23, above.

3. BORROWING POWERS AND PERSONAL LIABILITY

24–026 In every case a proposed lending bank will have to scrutinise carefully the borrowing powers of the office-holder. By Sch.1, para.3 to the Insolvency Act 1986 the powers of an administrator include the power to raise or borrow money and grant security in respect of any such sums over the company's

[45] *Neste Oy v Lloyd's Bank* [1983] 2 Lloyd's Rep. 658, 667.
[46] See *Clark v Ulster Bank Ltd* [1950] N.I. 132, where it was held that, upon receiving notice that the customer's No.2 account was a trust account, the bank was entitled to combine it with the No.1 account as at the date of receiving such notice.
[47] However, in *Kingscroft Insurance Co v Weavers* [1993] 1 Lloyd's Rep. 187, *Neste Oy* was referred to with approval but was held not to apply to the facts of that case, which concerned bank deposits created by an underwriting agent in the names of certain of its principals, who subsequently went into provisional liquidation.
[48] See Ch.20, above.
[49] *Brandao v Barnett* (1846) 12 Cl. & Fin. 787 (HL).
[50] *Davis v Bowsher* (1794) 5 Term. Rep. 488; *Wylde v Radford* (1863) 33 L.J. Ch. 51.
[51] *Brandao v Barnett* (1846) 12 Cl. & Fin. 787 (HL) (exchequer bills).
[52] See Hapgood, *Paget's Law of Banking*, 13th edn (London: Lexis Nexis, 2007), para.29.3 at p.706; *Banks and Remedies*, edited by Blair, 2nd edn (Informa, 1999), p.53.

property. Any borrowings would reflect the particular needs of the administrator and of the administration as a whole. The Act does not provide for any personal liability on the part of an administrator. Instead, advances made to a company in administration will be secured by the statutory charge provided for in Sch.B1, para.99(4) and rank ahead of the administrator's own remuneration and expenses.[53] The administrator will wish to avoid personal liability for the borrowings wherever possible, and may require any facility to be expressly limited in recourse to the company's assets in the administrator's possession.

In the case of an administrative receiver the same power to borrow is deemed **24–027** to be provided except in so far as they are inconsistent with any provisions of the debenture.[54] In the case of other receivers, there will generally be an express power to borrow in the debenture. Alternatively, if the receiver is an agent of the company and he has an express power to carry on the company's business, there may be an implied power to borrow, on the basis that a trading company will be held to have an implied power to borrow for the purposes of its business.[55]

As to security, the debenture may well authorise the receiver to give security **24–028** and to give it ahead of the appointor's charges. In the case of administrative receivers, there is a deemed power to give security in the absence of a contrary provision in the debenture[56] but (it seems) no deemed power to give such security with priority over the appointor.[57] In the case of other receivers, a power to carry on business may imply a power to give security for borrowings.[58] However, a power to give such security priority over the debenture-holder is only likely to be implied where the receiver is the agent of the debenture-holder.[59]

Any advances to a company in receivership, but not in liquidation, will **24–029** generally involve the receiver in causing the company to make a post-receivership contract. Unless personal liability is excluded (and the receiver in practice is reluctant to accept such liability), a receiver will be personally liable to repay any such advances.[60]

In *Hill Samuel & Co Ltd v Laing*[61] the Outer House of the Court of Session **24–030** held that a receiver who had opened an account at his appointing bank in his own name could be liable[62] for the sums due on the account, applying the principles embodied in the Scottish equivalent to s.44(1)(b) of the Insolvency

---

[53] See generally Ch.27, below.

[54] Insolvency Act 1986, s.42 and Sch.1, para.3.

[55] *General Auction Estate Co v Smith* [1891] 3 Ch. 432.

[56] Insolvency Act 1986, s.42, Sch.1, para.3.

[57] See below, Ch.28.

[58] *General Auction Estate Co v Smith* [1891] 3 Ch. 432; *Re Patent File Co* (1870) L.R. 6 Ch. App. 83 (CA), 86, 88.

[59] See *Robinson Printing Co Ltd v Chic Ltd* [1905] 2 Ch. 123.

[60] Insolvency Act 1986, s.37 and also in the case of administrative receivers, pursuant to the Insolvency Act 1986, s.44(1)(b).

[61] *Hill Samuel & Co Ltd v Laing* (1988) 4 B.C.C. 9 (Court of Session, Outer House).

[62] The court held that there had to be an inquiry into the nature of the arrangement. The receiver alleged that there was an implied term in the banking contract to the effect that any advances were made at the bank's own risk.

Act 1986.[63] The court held that the standard wording in a debenture stipulating that the receiver was to be the agent of the company and that the company should "alone be personally liable" for the acts and defaults of a receiver only applied as between the appointing bank and the company and did not exempt the receiver from liability under the statutory provision. Moreover, the court held that the equivalent of s.44(1)(b) applied to contracts between the receiver and the appointing bank and rejected the argument that it applied only as between the receiver and third parties.

24–031   The power of a receiver to borrow as agent of the company must terminate on liquidation, for thereafter the receiver cannot create fresh debts or liabilities of the company.[64] Thus, once the company has gone into liquidation, all loans must be to the receiver personally or his appointor.[65] The determination of the receiver's agency for the company on liquidation will not otherwise affect the receiver's power to deal with any monies standing to the credit of bank accounts. In principle, if an account maintained in the company's account goes into overdraft after liquidation, it should be redesignated the receiver's personal account, but in practice this does not always happen.

---

[63] Formerly Companies (Floating Charges and Receivers) (Scotland) Act 1972, s.17(2). Now see Insolvency Act 1986, s.57(2). Both sections provide for personal liability in respect of any contract entered into by a receiver "except in so far as the contract otherwise provides". cf. *Re Boynton Ltd* [1910] 1 Ch. 519, where a court-appointed receiver borrowed money from a bank without any express exclusion of personal liability. (Court-appointed receivers are personally liable on contracts entered into by them unless liability is excluded.) It was held that the fact that the receiver was an officer of the court administering assets under its control was a factor pointing to an implied exclusion of personal liability.

[64] See above, Ch.7.

[65] *Robinson Printing Co Ltd v Chic Ltd* [1905] 2 Ch. 123.

Chapter 25

Construction Contracts

1. FEATURES OF CONSTRUCTION CONTRACTS

It has been estimated that the construction industry gives rise to between 15 **25–001**
and 20 per cent of all insolvencies.[1] A construction contract imposes complex
performance obligations on both parties, and can be hard to fit within the law
of security, assignment or novation, which arose in the context of dealings in
debts. It is becoming more common to incorporate a trust to protect payments.
This practice causes difficulty where the terms of the contract conflict with the
law of trusts. Case law emanating from the industry illustrates the conflict
between freedom of contract and the pari passu rule, identifies contractual and
procedural rights functioning as security, and describes the nature of property
subject to a contingency. This chapter considers a few of the areas of particular
concern to administrators appointed to construction companies.[2]

Construction contracts have certain special characteristics:

(a) the industry uses many different standard forms which are often
     revised by the drafting bodies and amended by the parties,[3] and
     which tend to be lengthy and difficult to construe[4];

(b) most of the work is carried out by sub-contractors resulting in chains
     of contracts under which one contract may incorporate the terms of
     others higher up the chain;

(c) responsibility for decisions often rests with the architect or the engi-
     neer who, although appointed as the agent of the employer, owes an
     independent duty to both employer and contractor to act fairly[5];

(d) the employer is given considerable "security" for performance: all
     payment obligations are qualified in one way or another[6] and there is

---

[1] Lowe and Moroke, "Insolvency in the UK construction sector", ARCOM 2010 Conference,
http://www.arcom.ac.uk.

[2] See generally, Davis, *Construction Insolvency: Security, Risk and Renewal in Construction
Contracts*, 4th edn (London: Sweet & Maxwell, 2011).

[3] The principal standard forms in use in the United Kingdom are JCT 2005 for building work
and NEC3 for engineering work. Internationally the FIDIC Red Book is widely used. Each body
has produced variants of these forms, including subcontracts.

[4] See generally Furst and Ramsey, *Keating on Building Contracts*, 8th edn (London: Sweet &
Maxwell, with supplement, 2008).

[5] *Sutcliffe v Thackrah* [1974] A.C. 727 (HL).

[6] Payment to the contractor normally depends on the issue of certificates; interim payments are
on account of the contract sum and are subject to adjustment later; retention is conditional on the
works being completed; payment is subject to suspension on a termination; or to direct payments
being made to sub-contractors or suppliers; or to set-off or abatement generally.

extensive use of bonds and guarantees. By contrast, the contractor is afforded minimal "security" for payment[7];

(e) plant and materials which are fixed to the land as part of the permanent works lose the quality of a chattel and become part of the land whether or not they have been paid for[8]; and

(f) aspects of construction contracts relating to payment, set-off and adjudication of disputes are now governed by statute.[9] Most disputes are now decided by adjudicators, the majority of whom do not have a legal background.

2. TERMINATION CLAUSES

25–002 One of the main reasons why a contractor might contemplate administration is that the procedure facilitates the orderly completion[10] or restructuring[11] of ongoing contracts. The difficulty is that the standard forms provide reciprocal rights of termination in the event of the administration of either party.[12]

Insolvency is not necessarily a breach of contract.[13] It is therefore important to check in each case whether the contract includes administration as a termination event,[14] and that any notice procedure has been correctly followed. In one case,[15] a contractor gave a notice of termination without specifying which of the various grounds in the subcontract it was relying on. The termination clause included both "insolvency" and administration as termination events, but an administrator was only appointed the day after the notice was served. The subcontractor argued that the termination was wrongful and amounted to a repudiation. To protect its position, the contractor served a second notice, expressly relying on the administrator's appointment. Jackson J. found at [37] that the first notice was unclear and the subcontract remained on foot until it was validly terminated by the second notice.

---

[7] "Security" for contractors is found in a minority of cases and is usually limited to a trust of part of the contract sum or a payment guarantee.

[8] *Sims v London Necropolis Co* (1885) 1 T.L.R. 584.

[9] Housing Grants, Construction and Regeneration Act 1996, considered below.

[10] e.g. *Re Harris Simons Construction Ltd* [1989] 1 W.L.R. 368; *Re Redman Construction Ltd* [2004] EWHC 3468 (Ch).

[11] *Corbett v Nysir UK Ltd* [2008] EWHC 2670 (Ch).

[12] Such rights are not challenged in practice, and their validity may have been affirmed by the decision of the Supreme Court on the anti-deprivation rule in *Belmont Park Investments Pty Ltd and others v BNY Corporate Trustee Services Ltd* [2011] 3 W.L.R. 521 (SC). See above, para.22–009.

[13] *Re Agra Bank Ex p. Tondeur* (1867–68) L.R. 5 Eq. 160. Under a JCT form, following an insolvency termination, a breach will normally occur only on the failure to pay a sum due after the works have been completed and the final account determined: *Perar BV v General Surety & Guarantee Co Ltd* (1994) 66 B.L.R. 72 (CA), 85.

[14] The current edition of NEC3 includes the making of an administration order only. In the case of a pay when paid clause in a subcontract, this was held not to include an administration out of court, as the provision was construed strictly as an exemption clause: *William Hare Ltd v Shepherd Construction Ltd* [2010] B.L.R. 358 (CA).

[15] *RWE-Industrie-Loesungen GmbH v Thyssen Schachtbau GmbH* [2006] EWHC 2111 (TCC).

Some sub-contracts provide for automatic termination in the event of a **25–003** termination under the main contract in order to enable the contractor to deny the sub-contractor further access to the site without being in repudiatory breach.

The standard forms do not expressly exclude the common law, which applies **25–004** in addition to the express termination clause.[16] In *LMK v Aegon Insurance*[17] the court was asked to assume that a works contractor was already in repudiatory breach before administrative receivers were appointed to it. The management contractor relied on a termination clause entitling it to terminate "the works" for insolvency before realising that the contract was defective in that it did not entitle the contractor to recover its losses caused by the termination. It was held that, on a true construction of the works contract, the reliance on the termination clause did not prevent the contractor from accepting a repudiation at common law later and claiming damages to the full extent of its losses. Conversely, there is authority that where a termination event is also a repudiatory breach, the innocent party could accept the other's repudiation, and as an alternative, exercise its contractual right to termination.[18]

It may be commercially necessary for an administrator to terminate a construction contract. In *BLV Realty v Batten*[19] administrators appointed by the court over an insolvent employer terminated an agreement with a construction manager for irremediable breaches. The manager issued an application under para.74 of Sch.B1 to the Insolvency Act 1986 for an order that either they withdraw the notice of termination and pay its pre-administration invoices or be replaced by new administrators. Rejecting the application, Norris J. held that the manager had not shown that the termination was wrongful. Nor would a wrongful termination necessarily have been a breach of duty by the administrators. He held at [20]: "It may be in the interests of the creditors as a whole that one particular contract with one particular creditor is terminated (even wrongfully)." He added at [22]: "Unequal or differential treatment is not necessarily unfair treatment." The manager's complaint was not that its interests as a creditor were being harmed but its interest as a contractor because other contractors were being kept on while it was not. The judge also noted that the

---

[16] In *Perar BV v General Surety & Guarantee Co Ltd* (1994) 66 B.L.R. 71 (CA), the contract (in JCT 81 form) expressly preserved the common law in the context of the power to terminate, but not in the sub-clause conferring post-termination rights. The Court of Appeal considered that the parties must have intended to exclude the common law as far as the post-termination rights were concerned and that the sub-clause constituted a complete code. This aspect of the decision is questionable since it appears close to the "argument from redundancy" criticised by Lord Hoffmann in *Beaufort Developments (NI) Ltd v Gilbert-Ash (NI) Ltd* [1999] 1 A.C. 266 (HL), 273. Clause 8.3.1 of JCT 05 preserves common law rights in respect of the whole termination clause, which can no longer therefore be described as a "complete code".

[17] *Laing Management Ltd (formerly Laing Contracting Ltd) v Aegon Insurance Co (UK) Ltd* (1997) 86 B.L.R. 70, Judge Humphrey Lloyd QC. See also *Stocznia Gdanska SA v Latvian Shipping Co (Repudiation)* [2002] 2 All E.R. (Comm) 768 (CA); *Dalkia Utilities Services Plc v Celtech International Ltd* [2006] 1 Lloyd's Rep. 599.

[18] *Shell Egypt West Manzala GmbH v Dana Gas Egypt Ltd (formerly Centurian Petroleum Corp)* [2010] EWHC 465 (Comm), [34], per Tomlinson J. In that case, however, the notice was construed as an unequivocal election to terminate under the contract.

[19] *BLV Realty v Batten* [2010] B.P.I.R. 277.

order sought was tantamount to specific performance in circumstances where the employer was totally reliant on third party funding.[20]

On a large project, a contractor enters into a direct agreement with the funder whereby it agrees to give notice before terminating the building contract to enable the funder if it so desires to step in and assume the employer's responsibilities, usually by substituting a new entity. In *The Royal Bank of Scotland v Chandra*[21] a bank agreed to a direct agreement under which it was *obliged* to step in. This was required as security for payment by the contractor (Costain) as the employer was a special purpose vehicle and the directors had no previous experience of property development. When the works were close to practical completion, the bank appointed administrative receivers to the employer. Offers to Costain to continue with the company in receivership without step-in or to nominate the existing company as the employer under a step-in guaranteed by the bank were both rejected. Completion was procured by the receivers forming a new special purpose vehicle whose liabilities to Costain were guaranteed by the bank. The employer in receivership was its sole shareholder and director and the new SPV acted as the employer's agent in completing the work. The bank provided additional funding to the employer to settle Costain's claims and to finance the cost to complete.

In a claim by the bank to enforce personal guarantees given by the directors, it was held by David Richards J. that the effect of the step-in was to terminate the employer's involvement with the contract: all existing and future obligations were assumed by the bank or its nominee as if it had been an original party to the contract. It followed that the employer and its guarantors were not liable under JCT 98 or the direct agreement in respect of the completion of the development ([53]–[55]). (The bank had argued that Costain's original contract continued in parallel with a new contract with the substituted entity.) However, the bank was entitled to recover the additional costs of completion from one of the guarantors as "expenses incurred ... in connection with the Property" under its fixed and floating charge (at [60]). Alternatively, the bank could have recovered in restitution, or by analogy with the right of recoupment from the proceeds of sale of a mortgagee in possession, or in subrogation at least as far as pre-receivership liabilities were concerned (at [62]–[65]).

25–005   As well as conferring the power to terminate, express clauses also give the employer access to a bundle of rights which are intended to facilitate the completion of the works. These rights include:

(a) to terminate the contractor's licence and repossess the site;

(b) to engage another contractor to complete the work;

(c) to suspend all further payment to the contractor until after the completion of the works;

---

[20] The court did not refer to other cases, such as *Astor Chemical Ltd v Synthetic Technology Ltd* [1990] B.C.C. 97, which indicate that an administrator lacks the power to repudiate contracts.
[21] *The Royal Bank of Scotland Plc v Chandra* [2010] 1 Lloyd's Rep. 677.

Trading Tanker v Flota Petrolena Ecuatoriana (The Scaptrade)[36] and subsequent cases it has been emphasised that the jurisdiction only extends to contracts which involve the forfeiture of proprietary or possessory rights.[37]

It is an unresolved question whether relief from forfeiture would be available **25–010** in relation to an ordinary building contract. Relief from forfeiture was granted in the unusual case of *Underground (Civil Engineering) Ltd v Croydon LBC*[38] where the employer terminated the contractor's employment and re-entered the site when only three weeks' work remained outstanding, but only on the ground that the contractor was to become entitled to a 127-year lease of the property within one month after practical completion. It was stated, obiter, that relief would not have been available in the case of an ordinary building contract in view of the absence of any proprietary or possessory right which might justify the court's intervention.[39] Although an ordinary building contract will contain terms giving the contractor the right to "possession" of the site and a right not to be hindered or prevented in the carrying out of the building works on the site, it would no doubt be argued that unlike the indefinite possessory rights conferred on a hirer under a hire-purchase agreement or on a lessee under a finance lease, which rights are the main purpose of the contract and qualify and limit the owner's general right to the property in question, the rights conferred on a contractor under a building contract are strictly limited and designed simply to enable the contractor to carry out the main purpose of the contract, which is the supply by him to the employer of building services.

5. SUSPENSION OF PAYMENT

Suspension of payment on termination freezes the contractor's receivables **25–011** pending the completion of the works and the final account. By postponing collection of book debts, suspension ensures that property will be available against which the employer can recover any additional costs and associated losses by way of set-off. Most forms include an automatic suspension of

---

available in relation to four finance leases of video-editing equipment, but not granted due to the equipment having been sold to a third party prior to the date of the hearing. The court ordered payment to the lessee from an escrow account representing the proceeds of sale of the equipment).

[36] *Scandinavian Trading Tanker v Flota Petrolena Ecuatoriana (The Scaptrade)* [1983] 2 A.C. 694 (HL) (relief not available in relation to a hiring under a time charter of a ship which gave no interest in or right of possession to the vessel but which was simply a contract for services to be rendered to the charterer by the shipowner through the shipowner's employees, namely the master and crew).

[37] See, e.g. *Sport International Bussum v Inter-Footwear* [1984] 1 W.L.R. 776 (HL) (relief not available in relation to a purely contractual licence to use trade marks and names). cf. *On Demand Information Plc v Michael Gerson (Finance) Plc* [2001] 1 W.L.R. 155 (CA), 171, in which Robert Walker L.J. stated: "Contractual rights which entitle the hirer to indefinite possession of chattels so long as hire payments are duly made, and which qualify and limit the owner's general property in the chattels, cannot aptly be described as purely contractual rights". This dictum was approved by the House of Lords although the decision of the Court of Appeal was reversed on other grounds: [2003] 1 A.C. 368 (HL), 29.

[38] *Underground (Civil Engineering) Ltd v Croydon LBC* [1990] E.G.C.S. 48. By analogy, relief may be available where the contractor also has an interest in the development project.

[39] See also *Westminster Properties Pty Ltd v Comco Constructions Pty Ltd* (1991) 5 W.A.R. 191 (CA of Western Australia) (no relief for the employer against termination by the contractor).

payment: sums due cease to be due[40] or provisions requiring further payment cease to apply.[41]

In *Melville Dundas Ltd (In Receivership) v George Wimpey UK Ltd*[42] a contractor went into administrative receivership before completing the works. The contract was governed by the Housing Grants, Construction and Regeneration Act 1996[43] which provides by s.111 that the withholding of a sum due is conditional on service of a notice before the final date for payment. The House of Lords held, by a majority of 3:2, that a notice was not required under JCT 98 where the receivers were appointed after the final date for payment had passed. The security function of suspension of payment was recognised by Lord Hoffmann at [13]:

> "Mr Howie said that to allow the employer *any* security in the form of an
> unpaid instalment would be to allow him to profit from his own wrong.
> But the security arises, not from the terms of the contract but from the law
> of bankruptcy set-off."

In principle the same ought to apply to a termination on the appointment of administrators.

25–012   A current area of controversy is whether the suspension should apply where the sum is due pursuant to an adjudicator's decision. In a non-insolvency case,[44] the Court of Appeal stated that the policy of the 1996 Act, which was to protect the contractor's cash flow, should prevail over the employer's security under the suspension of payment clause. In *Straw Realisations (No.1) Ltd v Shaftsbury House (Developments) Ltd*,[45] that approach was applied to an insolvency termination. In that case, the building contract also provided that an adjudicator's decision would be final unless notice were given within three months of intention to challenge it. No such notice had been given. The finality of the adjudication decision backing up the debt was sufficient, in the judge's view, to distinguish the case from *Melville Dundas v George Wimpey*. He also considered himself bound to follow *Fersons v Levolux*. Since then, the effect of the decision in *Melville Dundas* has been enshrined in statute.[46]

The efficacy of adjudication rests on the parties' agreement to implement adjudicators' decisions pending a final hearing of the dispute in court or by

---

[40] GC/Works/1 (1998), cl.57(1)(a).

[41] Under cl.27.6.4.1 of JCT 98, the suspension does not apply to sums due for 28 days or more before termination which the employer has "unreasonably not discharged". Under cl.8.5.3.1 of JCT 05 the suspension takes effect on the occurrence of a terminable insolvency event whether or not a notice of termination has been given.

[42] *Melville Dundas Ltd (In Receivership) v George Wimpey UK Ltd* [2007] 1 W.L.R. 1136 (HL).

[43] See para.25–058 below.

[44] *Levolux A.T. Ltd v Ferson Contractors Ltd* [2003] 1 All E.R. (Comm) 385 (CA). On the facts of this case suspension of payment was not available to the contractor in any event as it was implicit in the adjudicator's decision that the termination was wrongful. The court proceeded on the assumption that the termination had been lawful.

[45] *Straw Realisations (No.1) Ltd v Shaftsbury House (Developments) Ltd* [2011] B.L.R. 47.

[46] Housing Grants, Construction and Regeneration Act 1996, s.111(10), substituted by s.144 of the Local Democracy, Economic Development and Construction Act 2009.

arbitration.[47] There is a conflict therefore between the employer's duty to pay under the decision and its right to withhold payment under the termination clause. It is submitted that the ratio of *Melville Dundas* was that, where termination is by reason of insolvency, the suspension of payment is intended to facilitate insolvency set-off. The security of which Lord Hoffmann spoke lies in being able to treat the termination clause as a self-contained accounting process which applies insolvency set-off for the purposes of the contract. On this view, it would be immaterial whether the contractor has a simple debt or a debt whose payment has been ordered by an adjudicator or even a debt which is finally binding on the employer, as all would be subject to set-off under rr.2.85 or 4.90 of the Insolvency Rules 1986.[48] *Melville Dundas* concerned an administrative receivership, which does not in itself concern insolvency set-off; a fortiori, the reasoning of the decision would apply to administration, which can.

6. NOVATION

The law of novation developed in the context of the transfer of debt obligations.[49] It can be difficult to apply to the bilateral performance obligations created by construction contracts.[50] It is used by administrators as the means of transferring contracts as part of a business sale. Under a novation, the original contract between A and B is terminated, and a new contract is created between A and C on the same or varied terms[51], including any implied terms.[52] B, the insolvent company, drops out of the picture.   **25–013**

At common law, a novation discharges the original contract by releasing the parties from further performance, while preserving accrued causes of action. In practice, it is common to vary the common law position by providing that the novation takes effect as if the purchaser had been a party from the inception of the works, thereby accepting liability for any breaches extant at the date of novation. The insolvent company is then released from its contingent liability. Whether a novation achieves this result is a question of construction.[53]

As well as obtaining consideration from the purchaser in return for the right to approach employers to novate contracts, which may take the form of

---

[47] *Jim Ennis Construction v Premier Asphalt Ltd* (2009) 125 Con. L.R. 141.

[48] See, generally, Ch.22, above.

[49] *Rouse v Bradford Banking* [1894] 2 Ch. 32 (CA).

[50] See JCT Practice Note 24, and its Scottish counterpart, the SBCC Insolvency Practice Guide for precedent novations of construction contracts.

[51] *Scarfe v Jardine* (1882) L.R. 7 App. Cas. 345 (HL); *Tito v Waddell (No.2)* [1977] Ch. 106, 287; *Chatsworth Investments v Cussins (Contractors)* [1969] 1 W.L.R. 1 (CA); *Westminster City Council v Reema Construction Ltd (No.2)* (1990) 24 Con. L.R. 26; *Linden Gardens Trust Ltd v Lenesta Sludge Disposals Ltd* [1994] 1 A.C. 85 (HL).

[52] *Bernhard's Rugby Landscapes Ltd v Stockley Park Consortium Ltd* (1997) 82 B.L.R. 39.

[53] *W & J Leigh v CBI Nederland* Unreported June 20, 1985; *Yarm Road v Costain* Unreported July 30, 2001; *Tesco Stores v Costain Construction* [2003] EWHC 1487 (TCC); *Enterprise Managed Services v Tony McFadden* [2011] 1 B.C.L.C. 414. cf. *Blyth & Blyth v Carillion Construction* (2001) 79 Con. L.R. 142; *CMA CGM SA v Hyundai MIPO Dockyard Co Ltd* [2009] 1 All E.R. (Comm) 568.

an upfront fee plus a percentage of the value of contracts novated, the administrator hopes to recover property given as security for the contractor's counter-indemnity to surety companies for bonding the contracts, often in the form of cash deposits. The intention is that the purchaser will procure its own bonds, making it possible for the company's bonds to be cancelled.

Other issues of concern for administrators include the question whether a novation constitutes a relevant transfer under the TUPE Regulations,[54] and whether a novation by the directors before the commencement of the administration could be voidable as a transaction at an undervalue.[55]

It is now common for direct agreements to provide for the mandatory novation of a construction contract to the funder's nominee in the event of the employer's insolvency.[56] Although mandatory novation has been upheld by the court in the context of the substitution of a new party to an inter-bank agreement,[57] where the terms remained the same, the position may be different where the terms have to be renegotiated. With a construction contract, the position of the independent certifier also has to be taken into account: it may be necessary to novate his appointment.

7. ASSIGNMENT

25–014   Unlike a novation, an assignment only transfers the benefit rather than the burden of the contract.[58] Thus, an employer who assigns the benefit of a contract to a funder retains the burden of funding retention on request from the contractor.[59] The application of this principle to construction contracts is not straightforward. If an employer assigns, its assignee becomes entitled to the benefit of the contractor's performance, i.e. the building work. But it does not follow that the assignee can exercise all of the employer's rights, such as the power to order variations. In *L/M International Construction v The Circle Ltd Partnership*[60], Staughton L.J. remarked:

> "When the benefit of a contract is assigned, the character of the obligation is not changed. Before the assignment, the [construction] managers were, in some respects, obliged to act on the instructions or directions of the [employer]. The assignment could not change that and render them subject to the orders of [the assignee banks]. A new agreement would be needed to achieve that."

[54] See below, para.25–035 and, generally, Ch.16, above.
[55] *Buildspeed Construction v Theme* [2000] 4 S.L.R. 776.
[56] See above, para.25–004.
[57] *Habibsons Bank Ltd v Standard Chartered Bank (Hong Kong) Ltd* [2011] 2 W.L.R. 1165 (CA).
[58] *Nokes v Doncaster Amalgamated Collieries Ltd* [1940] A.C. 1014 (HL).
[59] *JF Finnegan Ltd v Ford Sellar Morris Developments Ltd (No.2)* (1991) 27 Con. L.R. 41.
[60] *L/M International Construction Inc v The Circle Ltd Partnership* (1995) 49 Con. L.R. 12 (CA), 22. See also *Don King (Productions) Inc v Warren* [2000] Ch. 291, 321, per Lightman J.; affirmed [2000] Ch. 327 (CA).

If a contractor assigns, its assignee becomes primarily entitled to all the **25–015**
contractor's rights to payment. Where a contract is subject to adjudication, it
appears that the assignee can adjudicate against the debtor to enforce payment.[61]
In such a case, if it is later found that a payment was made to the assignee
pursuant to an adjudicator's decision which was wrong, the duty to repay
would lie with the assignor, as part of the burden.[62] Where the benefit and
burden are separated by an assignment, there is a risk that the contractor would
be bound to continue working even after a wrongful refusal to pay by the
debtor. Although there is no English authority on the point, it appears that the
contractor would not be able to invoke a contractual right to terminate for non-
payment, as the right to payment had become vested in the assignee.

Many examples of assignment problems in connection with construction **25–016**
contracts could be given. It is against this background that the standard forms,
with the notable exception of NEC3, all include express terms barring assignment of the whole or part[63] of the benefit of the contract without the other
party's consent. Such terms are enforced by the court, and are likely to be
binding on an administrator.[64] An assignment of the benefit of a contract which
contains a bar on assignment confers no rights in the assignee against the
debtor;[65] but the assignor will be under a duty to apply the benefit on behalf of
the assignee.[66] In the absence of consent, a bar on assignment can only be
overcome by a transfer under a statutory power.[67]

At first sight, a bar on assignment also prevents a charge being taken over
the contract.[68] There are many statements in the cases to the effect that a charge
over a chose in action takes effect as an assignment by way of security.[69]
However, there are also statements to the contrary.[70] If a charge can validly be
taken, and a receiver is appointed, a possible analysis is that it is open to the
receiver to exercise the charge holder's rights under the security to take
proceedings in the company's name, but not to assert the rights of an assignee,
e.g. to demand payment or performance in its own right.[71]

---

[61] In *Enterprise Managed Services Ltd v Tony McFadden Utilities Ltd* [2010] B.L.R. 89, [49],
Coulson J. stated that "as a matter of law, an assignment of a right to adjudicate can be legitimate,
although such a right needs to be attached to the underlying contract."

[62] By analogy with *Pan Ocean Shipping Co Ltd v Creditcorp Ltd (The Trident Beauty)* [1994] 1
W.L.R. 161 (HL).

[63] *Yeandle v Wynn Realisations Ltd* (1995) 47 Con. L.R. 1 (CA); *Floods of Queensferry Ltd v
Shand Construction Ltd (No.1)* [1997] C.L.C. 588 (CA); *Herkules Piling Ltd v Tilbury Construction*
[1992] 61 B.L.R. 107.

[64] Compare the liquidation cases of *Ruttle Plant Hire Ltd v Secretary of State for Environment
Food and Rural Affairs* [2008] 2 All E.R. (Comm) 264; *Ruttle Plant Hire Ltd v Secretary of State
for Environment Food and Rural Affairs (No.2)* [2009] 1 All E.R. 448.

[65] *Helstan Securities Ltd v Hertfordshire County Council* [1978] 3 All E.R. 262; *Linden Gardens
Trust Ltd v Lenesta Sludge Disposal Ltd* [1994] 1 A.C. 85 (HL).

[66] *Linden Gardens Trust Ltd v Lenesta Sludge Disposal Ltd* [1994] 1 A.C. 85 (HL), 108.

[67] e.g. *Co-Operative Group v Stansell* [2006] 1 W.L.R. 1704 (CA); *Re Metronet Rail* [2008] 2
All E.R. 75.

[68] The point was conceded by Counsel in *Re Turner Corp* (1995) 17 A.C.S.R. 761.

[69] e.g. *Colonial Mutual v ANZ Bank* [1995] 1 W.L.R. 1140 (PC), 1144; *Business Computers Ltd
v Anglo-African Leasing Ltd* [1977] 1 W.L.R. 578.

[70] *Re Charge Card Services (No.2)* [1987] Ch. 150, 176; *Re Bond Worth* [1980] Ch. 228, 250.

[71] cf. *Foamcrete (UK) Ltd v Thrust Engineering* [2002] B.C.C. 221 (CA), although the decision
is doubtful.

8. DIRECT PAYMENT

25–017 Most of the work on a construction project is sub-contracted. Payment is channelled through the contractor who is beneficially entitled (in the absence of a trust) to all sums payable under interim certificates, even if the contract obliges it to "pay over" sums identified by the certificate to particular sub-contractors.[72] It is in the employer's interest that the sub-contractors are paid since otherwise they may suspend work causing delay and disruption to the project. Historically the standard forms have recognised the employer's interest by allowing it to pay the sub-contractors direct, and to be discharged from liability to the contractor to that extent, in two situations:

(a) where the architect certifies that the contractor has failed to prove payment of previous sums.[73] This power is available from the inception of the contract but is normally limited to payment to nominated sub-contractors[74];

(b) where the contractor's employment has been terminated.[75] This power can be exercised in favour of any supplier or sub-contractor and is not subject to any prior architect's certificate.

25–018 In either case, the effect is to convert a duty to pay the contractor into a power to pay the contractor's creditors on that project and to set off the amount of such payments against the contractor's receivables. Direct payment clauses are therefore strictly construed.[76] The payment is usually made by the employer in its own right but under one form it is made as agent for the contractor,[77] and under another, pursuant to a deemed assignment by the contractor to the sub-contractor.[78] The discharge may be achieved by a right of deduction or set-off,[79] by automatic reduction,[80] by treating the payment as part of the cost of completing the works,[81] as discharging the debt owed by the employer,[82] or by imposing on the contractor a duty to repay.[83] The efficacy of these differing approaches will depend on the proper construction of each clause.

---

[72] *Veitchi Co v Crowley Russell & Co Ltd* [1972] S.C. 225 (Court of Session, Outer House).

[73] JCT 98, cl.35; Egglestone, *The ICE Conditions of Contract*, 7th edn (London: Blackwells, 2001), cl.59(7); *FIDIC Works of Civil Engineering Construction Subcontract*, 1st edn (FIDIC, 1999), cl.5.4. This power has been omitted from JCT 2005.

[74] GC/Works/1 (1998), cl.48(4) applies to any sub-contractor or supplier but only allows the employer to withhold payment to the contractor until the proof has been provided.

[75] JCT 98, cl.27; GC Works/1 (1998), cl.57. There is no power to pay direct on termination under JCT 2005, or the ICE, NEC3 or FIDIC forms.

[76] *JA Milestone & Sons Ltd v Yates Castle Brewery Ltd* [1938] 2 All E.R. 439.

[77] SIA (Singapore Institute of Architects), 5th edn (1997), cl.32.

[78] *HM Attorney General v McMillan & Lockwood Ltd* [1991] 1 N.Z.L.R. 53 CA (NZ).

[79] e.g. JCT 98, cl.27.

[80] e.g. JCT 98, cl.35.

[81] SIA (Singapore Institute of Architects), 5th edn (1997), cl.32.

[82] *AN Bail Co v Gingras* [1982] 2 S.C.R. 475 (Sup Court of Canada).

[83] FIDIC, Test edn, (1998), cl.5.4.

Direct payment clauses potentially conflict with the policy underlying bank- **25–019**
ruptcy, administration and winding up. In *Re Wilkinson Ex p. Fowler*[84] direct
payments were made to suppliers after the contractor went bankrupt pursuant
to a clause which applied if the engineer considered that the contractor had
unreasonably delayed payment. Bigham J. held that the payments and the
consequential deductions from sums otherwise due to the bankrupt were
validly made. But the trustee had conceded that the clause was an authority
given by the contractor which was not revoked on his bankruptcy, and relevant
authority against the employer's case[85] was not cited to the court. Nevertheless,
Re Wilkinson was followed in *Re Tout and Finch*[86] in which Wynn-Parry J.
approved payments to nominated sub-contractors pursuant to a direct payment
clause which took effect on the winding-up of the contractor. In that case, the
subcontractors were entitled to payment in any event as equitable assignees of
the contractor's right to retention under the main contract. In neither of these
cases was the pari passu rule raised in argument. The reasoning in these cases
has been adopted in Australia[87] and the Republic of Ireland.[88]

In the *British Eagle*[89] case, contractual provisions resulting in a distribution **25–020**
of the company's property in a manner contrary to the pari passu rule[90]
were invalidated. Neither *Re Wilkinson* nor *Re Tout and Finch* were cited
in argument in *British Eagle* and the House of Lords held that an authority
given by the airlines to IATA analogous to that given by the contractor in *Re
Wilkinson* was revoked on winding up. In a recent case, it was suggested that
the deciding factor is whether the property in question "is a chose in action
representing the quid pro quo for something already done.[91] For these reasons,
it is submitted that *Re Wilkinson* and *Re Tout and Finch* (as far as it concerns
the direct payment clause) should no longer be followed, as has been held in
Canada,[92] Singapore,[93] New Zealand,[94] Northern Ireland[95] and Hong Kong.[96]
It should be noted that the scope of the anti-deprivation rule has recently been
considered by the Supreme Court in *Belmont Park Investments Pty Ltd and*

---

[84] *Re Wilkinson Ex p. Fowler* [1905] 2 K.B. 713.
[85] *Re Holt Ex p. Gray* (1888) 15 L.J.Q.B. 5.
[86] *Re Tout and Finch* [1954] 1 W.L.R. 178.
[87] *Re C.G. Monkhouse Properties Ltd* (1968) S.R. (N.S.W.) 429 (Sup Court of NSW); *Gericevich Contracting Pty Ltd v Sabemo (W.A.) Pty Ltd* [1984] 9 A.C.L.R. 452 (Sup Court of Western Australia).
[88] *Glow Heating Ltd v Eastern Health Board* (1992) 8 Const. L.J. 56 (High Court of Ireland).
[89] *British Eagle International Air Lines Ltd v Compagnie Nationale Air France* [1975] 1 W.L.R. 758 (HL).
[90] Contained in the Companies Act 1948, s.302, the Companies Act 1985, s.597, and now in the Insolvency Act 1986, s.107.
[91] *Lomas v JFB Firth Rixson Inc* [2010] EWHC 3372 (Ch), [108] per Briggs J.
[92] *AN Bail Co v Gingras* [1982] 2 S.C.R. 475, Sup Court of Canada (*British Eagle* not cited).
[93] *Joo Yee Construction Pte Ltd v Diethelm Industries Pte Ltd* [1990] 2 M.L.J. 66 (High Court of Singapore).
[94] *HM Attorney General v McMillan & Lockwood Ltd* [1991] 1 N.Z.L.R. 53 (NZCA).
[95] *B. Mullan & Sons (Contractors) Ltd v Ross* (1996) 54 Con. L.R. 161, (CA of Northern Ireland).
[96] *Golden Sand Marble Factory Ltd v Easy Success Enterprises Ltd* [1999] 2 H.K.C. 356 (High Court of Hong Kong).

others v BNY Corporate Trustee Services Ltd[97] that rule having been concisely
stated as follows:

> "Once the Insolvency Act regime has come into effect a contractual provi-
> sion which seeks to remove property out of the estate and to vest it in a
> third party cannot override the provisions of the Act."[98]

25–021 The anti-deprivation rule has been applied to administration.[99] Although there
are no direct payment clauses in the current editions of the JCT and NEC3
forms, they are often found in bespoke contracts, and, increasingly, in ad hoc
arrangements put in place during the contract. The case law reviewed above
therefore remains of relevance.

An arrangement for direct payment can be made collateral to a main or sub-
contract, either at the inception or at some later stage of the work In a Scottish
case,[100] a steelwork sub-contractor recovered payment from the employer in
full after the contractor entered compulsory liquidation. The sub-contractor
considered the contractor to be a bad credit risk and refused to enter into a sub-
contract with him unless the employer made direct payments. The arrangement
was oral, and subject to the contractor's waiver of rights under the main
contract, which was later forthcoming. The sub-contract then entered into did
not supersede or affect the employer's obligation, which the court construed as
an independent payment undertaking, a primary obligation which survived the
liquidation, to pay all sums due or to become due under the sub-contract on
receipt of the sub-contractor's VAT invoice.

25–022 An assurance of direct payment can take effect as a collateral contract, a
letter of comfort, or a guarantee. In one case,[101] a sub-contractor was threatening to terminate for non-payment unless the employer agreed to make direct
payment. The employer orally agreed that, if it could not persuade the contractor
to pay, it would pay the sub-contractor direct out of money withheld from sums
due to the contractor, by "redirecting" the money. The court construed this
arrangement as a secondary obligation, a suretyship guarantee, which was
unenforceable because it was not evidenced in writing.

25–023 There appears to be no authority on the effect of receivership or administration on direct payment clauses. If the contractor's debts were subject to a
floating charge, it may be argued that the clause should be invalidated on the
ground that it deprives preferential creditors of their statutory priority under

---

[97] *Belmont Park Investments Pty Ltd and others v BNY Corporate Trustee Services Ltd* [2011]
3 W.L.R. 521 (SC).

[98] *Perpetual Trustee Co Ltd v BNY Corporate Trustee Services Ltd* [2010] Ch. 347 (CA), [163]
per Patten L.J.

[99] *Mayhew v King* [2011] EWCA Civ 328.

[100] *Brican Fabrications Ltd v Merchant City Development Ltd* [2003] B.L.R. 512 (Court of
Session, Inner House, Extra Division).

[101] *Actionstrength Ltd v International Glass Engineering* [2003] 2 A.C. 541 (HL). cf. *Braspetro
Oil Services Co v FPSO Construction Inc* [2007] 2 All E.R. (Comm) 924. Cresswell J. (direct
payments to sub-contractors by the end-user on an energy project pursuant to side letters ancillary
to a supervision agreement); *PC Partitions v Canary Wharf Contractors* [2004] EWHC 1766
(TCC); *International Finance Corporation v DSNL Offshore* [2007] 2 All E.R. (Comm) 305.

s.40 of the Insolvency Act 1986.[102] Against this, the employer might argue that the rights of preferential creditors can only attach to the proceeds of debts collected by the receiver after taking account of equities of third parties, and that its right of recourse following direct payment is such an equity,[103] alternatively that it was an inherent flaw in the charged property.

The effect of administration on the validity of direct payments will depend on the wider question of the consequences of administration on set-off generally[104] and the scope of the anti-deprivation rule.[105]   **25–024**

9. RETENTION OF TITLE

In addition to the retention of title problems encountered in other industries,[106] administrators appointed to contractors will need to consider: (1) whether items have become part of the land; (2) whether property has passed pursuant to another contract in the chain; and (3) the potential effect of s.25 of the Sale of Goods Act 1979 in the special context of a construction project.   **25–025**

(a) Chattel or fixture

Construction work involves the annexation to land of different kinds of chattel: building materials, more significant items of plant or machinery or complex structures fabricated off-site. Whether these items remain chattels or become part of the land depends on the degree and purpose of the annexation,[107] with the emphasis on the purpose, as is explained above at para.21–031.[108]   **25–026**

(b) Precautions for contractors

A contractor should consider the means available to protect his right of entry and removal as against any pre-existing and later created mortgages. As regards the former, he should investigate whether any such mortgages exist and, if they do, obtain the agreement of such mortgagees to the priority of his right of removal over their rights. As regards the latter, he should protect his equitable interest (in case of registered land) by registration of a notice. In unregistered land, a right of entry is protected by the doctrine of notice.[109]   **25–027**

---

[102] Such an argument would only be possible if the receivership commenced before September 15, 2003: Enterprise Act 2002, s.251.

[103] *Business Computers Ltd v Anglo-African Leasing Ltd* [1977] 1 W.L.R. 578. See above, Ch.22.

[104] See above, Chs 6 and 22.

[105] See above, para.25–020.

[106] See above, Ch.21.

[107] *Holland v Hodgson* (1872) L.R. 7 C.P. 328, cited with approval in *Elitestone Ltd v Morris* [1997] 1 W.L.R. 687 (HL) which distinguished between a chattel, a fixture and an object which becomes part of the land.

[108] *Berkley v Poulett* (1976) 241 E.G. 911 (CA). In this connection, it is worth contrasting two Australian cases on the status of steam and gas co-generation facilities: *Origin Energy v Commissioner of State Revenue* [2007] WASAT 302 (fixture); *Commissioner of State Revenue v Uniqema* [2004] VSCA 82 (Victoria CA) (not a fixture). In *Dalkia Utilities v Celtech* [2006] 1 Lloyd's Rep. 599 a power plant was held to be a tenant's fixture.

[109] *Shiloh Spinners v Harding* [1973] A.C. 691 (HL).

(c)   Passing of title up the chain

25–028 The general rule is that title to materials supplied under a building contract will pass to the landowner on incorporation.[110] Where the contract provides for payment under interim certificates, there is authority that title to unfixed materials will pass to the employer on the issue of the relevant certificate.[111] It is thought more likely that title to unfixed materials will be held to pass to the employer on payment only if the main contract clearly evinces such an intention.[112] This is the assumption behind the interlocking provisions of the standard forms of main and sub-contract under which title passes to the employer on payment of the contractor[113] and the sub-contractor agrees not to deny that the employer has become the owner of its materials in that event even if the sub-contractor has not been paid for them.[114]

(d)   Section 25 of the Sale of Goods Act 1979

25–029 Under this section (discussed above at para.21–018), a person who has bought or agreed to buy goods and who obtains possession of them with the seller's consent can transfer title by delivering or transferring the goods under a sale, pledge or other disposition to any third person who receives the goods in good faith and without notice of any right of the original seller in respect of them. Section 25 has been invoked in the construction industry in cases of contractor insolvency. If the employer can show that it had paid for unfixed goods before the insolvency which had been supplied to the contractor under a contract for the sale of goods and that it had no notice of any retention of title clause, it can rely on the section as a defence to a claim by the unpaid supplier.[115] If materials are supplied under a sub-contract for goods and services, however, the employer has no defence.[116] Receivers appointed to the contractor may be able to prevent the owner repossessing his goods by offering a personal undertaking that, should the claim prove to be valid, they would either return the goods or pay their invoice values.[117]

---

[110] *Tripp v Armitage* (1839) 4 M. & W. 687, 698.

[111] *Banbury Railway Co v Daniel* (1884) 54 L.J. Ch. 265.

[112] *Egan v State Transport Authority* (1982) 31 S.A.S.R. 481, 537, 542 (Sup Court of South Australia), not following *Banbury Railway Co v Daniel* (1884) 54 L.J. Ch. 265.

[113] See, e.g. JCT 2005, cl.2.24.

[114] See, e.g. JCT Standard Building Sub-Contact, cl.2.15.2.

[115] *Archivent Sales & Developments Ltd v Strathclyde Regional Council* (1984) 27 B.L.R. 98 (Court of Session, Outer House). The case proceeded on the assumption that payment under cl.14 of JCT 63 was a "disposition" under s.25. See also *Four Point Garage Ltd v Carter* [1985] 3 All E.R. 12; *W Hanson (Harrow) Ltd v Rapid Civil Engineering Ltd* (1987) 38 B.L.R. 106; *P4 Ltd v Unite Integrated Solution Plc* [2006] B.L.R. 150.

[116] *Dawber Williamson Roofing Ltd v Humberside CC* (1979) 14 B.L.R. 70 (a case on the Sale of Goods Act 1893, s.25); *Sauter Automation Ltd v Goodman (Mechanical Services) Ltd* (1986) 34 B.L.R. 81.

[117] *Lipe Ltd v Leyland DAF Ltd* [1993] B.C.C. 385 (CA), discussed in Ch.21 above at para.21–075; see also *Mayflower Foods Ltd v Barnard Brothers Ltd* (1997) 14(1) B.L.M. 1.

10.   PLANT AND EQUIPMENT

On the contractor's insolvency, it may be important for the employer to be able   **25–030**
to use the contractor's plant and equipment for the completion contract,
especially if it was manufactured specifically for the project. To this end, the
employer often reserves various rights which can take effect from the execution of the contract, the delivery of the plant to site or the termination of the
contractor's employment.

The employer may reserve a right to seize, use and/or sell the plant on termi-   **25–031**
nation. It may be argued that such rights constitute registrable security. For
example, in *Smith v Bridgend CBC*,[118] it was held that a power of sale in the
ICE (5th edn) termination clause was a floating charge over plant and equipment which was not binding on an administrator of the contractor for want of
registration under s.395 of the Companies Act 1985. The powers to take possession of and use the plant in order to complete the works were not, however, in
the nature of a charge and remained binding. The employer transferred the plant
to the completion contractor who later sold it. The employer was held liable for
damages in conversion to the contractor in administration. As its rights were
limited to the use rather than the sale of the plant, the employer was not entitled
to an equitable set-off of its costs of completing the works against its liability
for conversion damages. The problem of non-registration could have been
avoided by providing for a transfer of ownership on delivery to site,[119] in which
case the contract would not have been capable of registration as an instrument
which if executed by an individual would be registrable as a bill of sale.[120]

11.   COPYRIGHT

Copyright subsists in plans, drawings, computer software and a building   **25–032**
itself,[121] but not in architectural ideas or design concepts. In the industry it is
asserted by architects and engineers, design and build contractors and specialist
sub-contractors. A client who commissions design work becomes the owner
of the work on payment but is not entitled to copy it without the designer's
consent. Thus an administrator appointed over an employer who wishes to sell
a partly-completed site together with the right to use a designer's plans and
drawings without further payment will need to check the terms governing
copyright in them.

Some standard forms of appointment contain a bar on the assignment of a
licence to use drawings without the designer's consent.[122] In general such

---

[118] *Smith v Bridgend CBC* [2002] 1 A.C. 336 (HL). See also *Young v Matthew Hall Mechanical & Electrical Engineers Pty Ltd* (1988) 13 A.C.L.R. 399 (Sup Court of Western Australia).
[119] *Bennett & White (Calgary) Ltd v Municipal District of Sugar City (No.5)* [1951] A.C. 786 (PC).
[120] *Reeves v Barlow* (1883–1884) L.R 12 Q.B.D. 436 (CA).
[121] Copyright Designs and Patents Act 1988, ss.1, 3 and 4; *Meikle v Maufe* [1941] 3 All E.R. 144.
[122] The RIBA Form of Archtect's Appointment (2010 edn) provides that consent to assignment shall not be unreasonably withheld or delayed. The designer grants an express licence to the client but is given the power to suspend it for non-payment. It is submitted that the right to suspend the licence would be an equity binding any assignee of the appointment.

clauses are upheld by the court and it will be necessary to discuss with the designer the terms on which it is prepared to give its consent.[123] Where the appointment contains an express licence with no restriction on assignment, it may not necessarily entitle the assignee to use the drawings to complete the project. In *Thurgood v Coyle*[124] the employer under a JCT form was granted an irrevocable royalty free licence to use the drawings to complete the "works" which were defined as works "to be designed and constructed by the contract [sic] under the contract." The licence did not, therefore, extend to a completion contract entered into by the purchaser with a different contractor. However, the consultants had entered into warranties with the employer whereby they granted similar licences for all purposes relating to the "project" which was defined simply by reference to the design and construction of works at the property. Those licences included the right to grant sub-licences and were transferable without the consultants' consent. Lewison J. held that the licences in the warranties were "free-standing" rights and were not subject to the same limitation as the licence granted by the JCT form. He therefore held that administrators appointed to the employer were entitled to transfer the licences as part of a sale of the site and that the purchaser could use them for the purpose of completing the development.

In the absence of an express licence, a licence to copy is usually implied, limited to the purpose for which the work was originally procured.[125] To what extent can the designer use its copyright as leverage to obtain payment of its unsecured debt? In an Australian case, an architect sued a mortgagee who had gone into possession on the winding-up of the employer. The court held that the employer's implied licence had passed to the mortgagee and was irrevocable, having been granted in return for the right to recover the debt by the ordinary litigation process. Copyright could not be used to "render valueless what might be an enormous past investment in the building".[126] Similarly, in *Hunter v Fitzroy Robinson & Partners*,[127] Oliver J. refused an application by an architect to prevent another firm using his designs after the employer went into receivership. The receivers had purported to assign the copyright licence to the purchaser on the sale of the building.

25-033   In *Cowlishaw v O&D Building Contractors Ltd*[128] administrators attempted to use s.236 of the Insolvency Act 1986 to force a contractor to provide copies of various classes of document, including drawings and specifications, ostensibly to help them decide whether to sell an incomplete development or build out. The contractor relied on its copyright and denied that the developer was entitled in the absence of payment to a licence to use them. The judge held that he had jurisdiction to make the order sought but refused to exercise his

---

[123] *Mateffy Perl Nagy Pty Ltd v Devefi Pty Ltd* [1992] I.P.R. 505 (Fed Court of Australia).

[124] *Thurgood v Coyle* [2007] EWHC 2696 (Ch).

[125] *Blair v Osborne and Tomkins* [1971] 2 Q.B. 78 (CA); *Stovin-Bradford v Volpoint Properties Ltd* [1971] Ch. 1007 (CA); *Ray v Classic FM Plc* [1998] F.S.R. 622, 640–644; *Meridian International Services v Richardson* [2008] All E.R. (D) 17 (Jun) (CA) (ultimate employer had no implied licence to source code).

[126] *Ng v Clyde Securities Ltd* [1976] 1 N.S.W.L.R. 443 (High Court of NSW), 446, per Wootten J.

[127] *Hunter v Fitzroy Robinson & Partners* (1977) 10 B.L.R. 84.

[128] *Cowlishaw v O&D Building Contractors Ltd* [2009] N.P.C. 112.

discretion in the administrators' favour. He did not see how they could make use of the drawings without breaching the contractor's copyright. He was impressed by the contractor's objection that the administrators were unjustly trying to take the benefit of its work without paying for it. The contractor had suspended its employment under the contract for non-payment before the commencement of the administration. Judge David Cooke stated at [36]: "The benefits will accrue, in the first instance at least, to the secured creditor which declined to fund the continuation of the project prior to administration." In the end, the only category ordered concerned warranties and guarantees to the extent they were already in force and capable of benefiting the employer and its successors in title.

12. EMPLOYEES

Whether a person is an employee is an important question for many reasons.[129] **25–034** There is no single test for people working in the construction industry and much depends on the facts.[130] For example, in *Ferguson v John Dawson & Partners (Contractors) Ltd*[131] the claimant was taken on by the defendant's site agent, who informed him that "there were no cards, we were purely working as a lump labour force".[132] The case concerned a claim for damages for breach of statutory duty in respect of injuries sustained at work. One of the questions that arose was whether the claimant was an employee since such a duty was owed to an employee but not to a self-employed person. The Court of Appeal noted that working on the "lump" meant that deductions would not be made for tax or national insurance; it was a device which was convenient for both parties, "but which in reality did not affect the relationship of the parties or the perform-ance of the substance of the contract between them".[133] The claimant's situa-tion could be summed up by saying that he did as he was told and was paid an hourly wage for so doing, thus making him an employee.[134]

The Transfer of Undertakings (Protection of Employment) Regulations **25–035** 2006[135] may apply where a purchaser novates contracts previously carried on by an insolvent contractor. In *Rolfe v Amey Construction Ltd*[136] administrative receivers appointed to Farr Plc sold to Amey the right to seek novations of 37 of Farr's ongoing contracts. A few employers refused to co-operate with Amey

---

[129] e.g. when considering preferential debts falling within Category 5 of Sch.6 to the Insolvency Act 1986, the TUPE Regulations and the Construction Industry Tax Deduction Scheme.

[130] See Ryley and Goodwyn, *Employment Law for the Construction Industry*, 2nd edn (London: Thomas Telford Publishing, 2008).

[131] *Ferguson v John Dawson & Partners (Contractors) Ltd* [1976] 1 W.L.R. 1213 (CA).

[132] *Ferguson v John Dawson & Partners (Contractors) Ltd* [1976] 1 W.L.R. 1213 (CA), 1217.

[133] *Ferguson v John Dawson & Partners (Contractors) Ltd* [1976] 1 W.L.R. 1213 (CA), 1219, per Megaw L.J.

[134] See also *Lee Ting Sang v Chung Chi-Keung* [1990] 2 A.C. 374 (PC); *Lane v Shire Roofing Co (Oxford) Ltd* [1995] I.R.L.R. 493 (CA); *Bolwell v Redcliffe Homes Ltd* [1999] P.I.Q.R. P243 (CA); *Costain Building & Engineering Ltd v Smith* [2000] I.C.R. 215 (EAT); *Byrne Brothers (Formwork) Ltd v Baird* [2002] I.R.L.R. 496; *Castle Construction (Chesterfield) Ltd v Revenue and Customs Commisioners* [2009] S.T.C. (S.C.D.) 97.

[135] See above, Ch.16.

[136] *Rolfe v Amey Construction Ltd* Unreported November 13, 1992.

who eventually obtained novations of 33 contracts. Some of Farr's employees were not taken on by Amey and applied to the Secretary of State for Employment for redundancy payments, but they were refused on the ground that there had been a relevant transfer under the Regulations under which Amey had assumed liability for the employees who had been made redundant. On Amey refusing to meet the payments, the employees applied to an industrial tribunal which upheld their claim. Amey's acquisition amounted to a relevant transfer of Farr's construction business since:

(a) part of the consideration paid by Amey was for goodwill which was defined as including all intellectual property rights relating to the novated contracts;

(b) Amey had obtained almost all of Farr's ongoing contracts, and would have novated more of them had the employers agreed;

(c) disruption was kept to a minimum through Amey paying key subcontractors direct;

(d) before entering into the agreement with the receivers, Amey had offered employment to key site and head office staff;

(e) Amey took over part of Farr's premises and some plant and equipment and site accommodation under a separate agreement.

25–036 Under the Construction Industry Scheme,[137] a contractor is obliged to make a deduction on account of tax at the rate of 20 or 30 per cent from any payment made to a subcontractor (other than for materials supplied) unless the subcontractor is registered with HMRC to receive payments gross. Registration not only confers a significant cash flow benefit, it is often a condition of admission to tender lists. It may be cancelled if the subcontractor is late in paying tax in the absence of "reasonable excuse", which has been construed as including events such as sudden loss of market or withdrawal of credit as experienced during the recent recession.[138]

13. CONSTRUCTION BONDS AND GUARANTEES

25–037 Construction contracts are often supported by surety bonds and demand guarantees.[139] The issuers of such documents can play an important role in the restructuring of a contractor. In particular administrators are keen to obtain the release of any property provided to bondsmen as security for the company's

---

[137] Finance Act 2004, ss.57–77, and Income Tax (Construction Industry Scheme) Regulations 2005 (SI 2005/2045), both as amended.
[138] *Mutch v Revenue and Customs Commissioners* [2010] S.T.I. 233; *Connaught Contracts v Revenue and Customs Commissioners* [2011] S.T.I. 140.
[139] Moss and Marks, *Rowlatt on Principal and Surety*, 5th edn (London: Sweet & Maxwell, 1999), Ch.17.

counter-indemnity. They may also wish to recover the excess of the proceeds of a bond call over and above the beneficiary's actual loss.[140]

(a) Surety bonds

The issuer of a surety bond agrees to pay the employer a fixed amount on condition that if the contractor performs the construction contract the promise to pay is void and the issuer is released from the bond. As the bond is conditioned on the contractor's performance it takes effect as a guarantee.[141] Difficulties arise in practice if the bond also includes wording entitling the employer to payment on demand,[142] or requires notice of potential claims to be given within a short period after the relevant breach[143] or that proceedings be issued within a short time after completion,[144] or when the expiry of the bond is made contingent on the issue of a certificate under the contract.[145] Unless it expressly provides otherwise, a guarantor is not bound by the decision of an adjudicator[146] or an arbitrator[147] made against the principal debtor under the contract.

25–038

(b) Demand guarantees

A demand guarantee is a primary obligation[148] and is usually issued in the form of a bank undertaking to pay up to a fixed sum on receipt of a demand accompanied by such documents as may be specified in the guarantee.[149] The draftsman sometimes uses language more appropriate to a secondary obligation, resulting in a difficult issue of construction.[150] But the most common issue with a demand guarantee remains that of "unfair calling".

25–039

---

[140] See *Spiersbridge Property Developments v Muir Construction* [2008] S.C.L.R. 362 (Court of Session, Outer House).

[141] *Trafalgar House Construction (Regions) Ltd v General Surety & Guarantee Co Ltd* [1996] A.C. 199 (HL).

[142] *Harmon Contract (UK) Ltd v Cigna Insurance Co of Europe SA NV* Unreported April 16, 1992; *TBV Power Ltd v Elm Energy and Recycling (UK) Ltd* Unreported November 21, 1995.

[143] *Oval (717) Ltd v Aegon Insurance Co (UK) Ltd* (1997) 85 B.L.R. 97.

[144] *Clydebank v Fidelity & Deposit Company of Maryland*, 1916 S.C. (H.L.) 69 (HL); *De Vere Hotels Ltd v Aegon Insurance Co (UK) Ltd* [1998] C.I.L.L. 1346.

[145] *OTV Birwelco Ltd v Technical & General Guarantee Co Ltd* [2002] 4 All E.R. 668; *Alston Combined Cycles Ltd v Henry Boot Construction Plc* [2002] 1 A.C. 321 (HL).

[146] *Beck Interiors v Russo* [2010] B.L.R. 37.

[147] *Re Kitchen* (1881) L.R. 17 Ch. D. 668 (CA); *Sabah Shipyard v Pakistan* [2008] 1 Lloyd's Rep. 210.

[148] Even so, it may be necessary to make extensive reference to the underlying contract to ascertain the purpose of the guarantee: *TTI Team Telecom International Ltd v Hutchison 3G UK Ltd* [2003] 1 All E.R. (Comm.) 914.

[149] The JCT has agreed forms of demand bond for use with JCT 98 and JCT 05 with the British Bankers Association securing the earning of an advance payment, the delivery of off-site materials and the repayment of retention. See also *Uniform Rules for Demand Guarantees* (ICC Publication No.758, 2010).

[150] See, e.g. *Esal (Commodities) Ltd v Oriental Credit Ltd and Wells Fargo Bank NA* [1985] 2 Lloyd's Rep. 546 (CA); *Caja de Ahorros del Mediterraneo v Gold Coast Ltd* [2002] 1 All E.R. (Comm) 142 (CA).

(c) Unfair calling

25-040 If the employer's demand only has to be accompanied by a statement that the contractor is in breach of contract, there is a risk it will be based on a false statement, especially if the bank has agreed to accept such a statement as conclusive.[151] The court considers that the contractor takes the risk of the bond being called in that situation and will not grant an injunction restraining the bank from paying in the absence of clear and manifest fraud by the employer of which the bank has notice.[152] This is known as "the fraud exception" as it displaces the ordinary criteria for an interlocutory injunction and is based on the policy of not undermining international trade by interfering with unconditional or documentary banking obligations.[153] The contractor's remedy is to bring proceedings against the employer under the contract[154] but until the works have been completed and the final account agreed[155] it may not be clear whether there is a cause of action. In the meantime, the contractor suffers loss of cash flow (as the bank will have recovered its payment to the employer from the contractor under its counter-indemnity) and assumes the risk of the employer's insolvency before repayment. Nevertheless, the court is willing to intervene to prevent injustice in appropriate cases:

(a) If the bond requires service of a prior notice on the contractor which has not in fact been served, a statement that the notice was properly served may be treated as fraudulent and an injunction granted against the bank under the fraud exception[156];

(b) Where the evidence of fraud is powerful but not quite sufficient the court may order summary judgment against the bank but grant a stay of execution to allow the contractor to litigate the underlying dispute[157];

(c) If the bond gives rise to serious questions of construction as to its obligation and a wrongful call could harm the contractor's commercial

---

[151] *Bache & Co (London) Ltd v Banque Vernes et Commerciale de Paris SA* [1973] 2 Lloyd's Rep. 437 (CA); *Carey Value Added v Grupo Urvasco* [2011] 2 All E.R. (Comm) 140.

[152] *Edward Owen Engineering Ltd v Barclays Bank International Ltd* [1978] Q.B. 159 (CA).

[153] The policy only applies where the bond is issued by a bank. In other cases there is a presumption against the construction of the document as a demand guarantee: *Marubeni Hong Kong & South China Ltd v Mongolia* [2005] 1 W.L.R. 2497 (CA).

[154] See, e.g. *ENS Ltd v Derwent Cogeneration Ltd* (1998) 62 Con. L.R. 141.

[155] *Cargill International SA v Bangladesh Sugar and Food Industries Corp* [1996] 4 All E.R. 563, affirmed [1998] 1 W.L.R. 461 (CA) suggests that a term may normally be implied that the bond proceeds will be brought into account at the final account stage. See also *Tradigrain v State Trading Corp of India* [2006] 1 All E.R. (Comm) 197.

[156] *Kvaerner John Brown Ltd v Midland Bank Plc* [1998] C.L.C. 446, Cresswell J.; cf. *Permasteelisa Japan v Bouyguestroi* [2007] EWHC 3508 (QB); *Enka Insaat v Banco Popolare dell'Alto Adige* [2009] C.I.L.L. 2777.

[157] *Balfour Beatty Civil Engineering v Technical and General Guarantee Co Ltd* (1999) 68 Con. L.R. 180 (CA); see also *Solo Industries UK Ltd v Canara Bank* [2001] 1 W.L.R. 1800 (CA) (summary judgment against bank refused).

reputation or its future bonding capacity, an injunction may be granted[158];

(d) An injunction may also be granted in cases where there is a genuine issue to be tried as to whether the bond has expired according to its terms[159] or that, by certifying under the bond, the engineer was threatening to interfere with the underlying contract.[160]

14. RETENTION TRUSTS[161]

Retention is a conditional debt defeasible by set-off. It is conditional on the issue of certificates of practical completion (when half is released) and of making good defects (when the balance becomes due); it is defeasible by rights of recourse conferred by the contract or available at common law. Retention is withheld under both main and sub-contracts and has traditionally been regarded as security for performance.[162] The conditional nature of retention means that payment may be deferred for a long time. The JCT forms provide the contractor with security for payment of retention in the form of a contractual trust. There are four particular areas to consider: constitution, sub-trusts, recourse and registrability.

25–041

(a) Constitution

Clause 4.18 of JCT 2005 provides that:

25–042

"1. the Employer's interest in the Retention is fiduciary as trustee for the Contractor (but without obligation to invest);
...
3. The Employer shall ... if the Contractor so requests, at the date of payment under each Interim Certificate place the Retention in a separate bank account–".

Construed together, the two parts of this clause impose a duty on the employer to create a trust on request. Once a request has been made, the court will grant specific performance by a mandatory injunction ordering the employer to pay an amount equivalent to the retention into a designated trust account.[163] The same applies if the express duty to fund the retention contained in clause 4.18.3 is deleted but clause 4.18.1 remains.[164]

---

[158] *Simon Carves Ltd v Ensus UK Ltd* [2011] B.L.R. 340; *Hawker Siddeley Power Engineering Ltd v Peterborough Power Ltd* Unreported May 9, 1994.
[159] *Gibraltar Homes Ltd v Agroman (Gibraltar) Ltd* Unreported No.15 of 1996, Gibraltar CA; *Lorne Stewart Plc v Hermes Kreditversicherungs AG* Unreported October 22, 2001.
[160] *Press Construction Ltd v Penspen Ltd and Barclays Bank Plc* Unreported April 16, 1996.
[161] Moss, "Retention Trusts" (1992) 5 Insolv. Int. 25.
[162] *Calvert v London Dock* (1838) 2 Keen's Rep. 638.
[163] *Rayack Construction Ltd v Lampeter Meat Co Ltd* (1979) 12 B.L.R. 30.
[164] *Wates Construction (London) Ltd v Franthom Property Ltd* (1991) 53 B.L.R. 23 (CA).

25–043   The account represents the identifiable property necessary to constitute the trust. If administrative receivers[165] or a liquidator[166] were appointed in relation to the employer before this could be done, specific performance would not be granted and the contractor would be an ordinary unsecured creditor in respect of its retention. The position on the appointment of administrators is at yet untested.

If the administrator is appointed by the holder of a qualifying floating charge or the administrator has given notice of intention to make a distribution under r.2.85 of the Insolvency Rules 1986, the situation would be very similar to administrative receivership and liquidation respectively, and specific performance would be inappropriate. In other cases, the contractor would have to obtain permission from the court to issue proceedings under para.43 of Sch.B1 to the Insolvency Act 1986.[167] In the absence of special facts, the court is not normally prepared to give permission where the relief sought would elevate a contractual right into a proprietary interest. In practice, applications are only likely to be entertained where the contractor seeks a declaration that an arrangement which was in existence before the commencement of the administration gave rise to an interest in the company's property which should be protected by a trust. In addition, by analogy with an application for a final charging order, the court may enquire into the solvency of the employer in administration before making its decision.[168]

25–044   A request can be made at any time during the contract[169] but not, it seems, after termination of the contractor's employment.[170] Interlocutory injunctions have been granted on the eve of the employer's formal insolvency[171] but doubt has been cast on this practice by Scott L.J.:

> "It is at this point that I should mention the doubts I feel regarding the specific enforceability of an obligation to set aside a retention fund. In a case where the employer is insolvent when the application for a mandatory order is made, the mandatory order would, assuming it were complied with, give preference to the contractor as against other unsecured creditors. I do not see any reason why the court should do such a thing …"[172]

---

[165] *MacJordan Construction Ltd v Brookmount Erostin Ltd* [1992] B.C.L.C. 350 (CA).

[166] *Re Jartay Developments Ltd* (1982) 22 B.L.R. 134.

[167] See above, Ch.9.

[168] *Monte Developments Ltd (in administration) v Court Management Consultants Ltd* [2011] 1 W.L.R. 1579. See also *Harms Offshore v Bloom* [2010] Ch. 187 (CA), [24].

[169] *JF Finnegan Ltd v Ford Sellar Morris Developments Ltd (No.1)* (1991) 53 B.L.R. 38; *Bodill & Sons (Contractors) Ltd v Mattu* [2007] C.I.L.L. 2553 (after completion of a substantial part if not the whole of the works).

[170] *Balfour Beatty Ltd v Britannia Life Ltd* [1997] S.L.T. 10 (Court of Session, Outer House).

[171] *JF Finnegan Ltd v Ford Sellar Morris Developments Ltd (No.2)* (1991) 27 Con. L.R. 41; cf. *GPT Realisations Ltd (In Liquidation) v Panatown Ltd* (1992) 61 B.L.R. 88, in which an injunction sought by administrative receivers appointed to a contractor was refused in part on grounds of lateness.

[172] *MacJordan Construction Ltd v Brookmount Erostin Ltd* [1992] B.C.L.C. 350 (CA), 359.

This dictum of Scott L.J. appears to be in conflict with generally applicable **25–045** insolvency principles as set out in *Roberts Petroleum v Bernard Kenny Ltd.*[173] That case concerned the discretion of the court to make absolute a charging order nisi so as to create security in favour of a judgment creditor of an insolvent debtor. In dealing with the race between the judgment creditor for security and the shareholders acting to protect the general body of creditors, Lord Brightman stated:

> "... Roberts applied to the District Registrar for a charging order in the hope of obtaining an advantage over other unsecured creditors; ... the shareholders of Kenny, on professional advice, put the company into voluntary liquidation at short notice in the hope of depriving Roberts of that advantage. Neither step nor counter step casts any discredit on those involved. There is nothing in the nature of sharp practice on either side, nor has this been suggested in your Lordships' House. A person who has the misfortune to have given credit to a company which runs into financial difficulties has every right to seek to secure himself. And such company or its other creditors have every right to hasten liquidation in order to thwart such a purpose".[174]

If the approach put forward by Lord Brightman is the correct one, then it would **25–046** seem to be perfectly acceptable for a contractor or sub-contractor to apply for a mandatory order to set up a trust retention fund notwithstanding the obvious insolvency of the employer. It is equally open to a debenture-holder to appoint an administrator or a receiver to protect his security or for shareholders, as in *Roberts Petroleum v Bernard Kenny Ltd*, or the company or a creditor to seek to protect the general body of creditors by causing the company to go into liquidation or administration. None of these approaches is discreditable. It would not seem to be right for the court to refuse relief merely because the employer or contractor against whom proceedings are brought is insolvent when other concerned parties have adequate remedies.

(b) Sub-contract trusts

The trust wording has been construed as an equitable assignment to the sub- **25–047** contractor of the contractor's proportion of the retention withheld under the main contract.[175] The cases have concerned applications in the winding up of the contractor for directions whether the employer could set off against the subcontractors' retention,[176] or the liquidator should account to them on receipt of payment from the employer[177] or, it seems, for retention already collected by him.[178]

---

[173] *Roberts Petroleum Ltd v Bernard Kenny Ltd (In Liquidation)* [1983] 2 A.C. 192 (HL).
[174] *Roberts Petroleum Ltd v Bernard Kenny Ltd (In Liquidation)* [1983] 2 A.C. 192 (HL), 206.
[175] *Re Tout and Finch Ltd* [1954] 1 W.L.R. 178.
[176] *Re Arthur Sanders Ltd* (1981) 17 B.L.R. 125.
[177] *Re Tout and Finch Ltd* [1954] 1 W.L.R. 178.
[178] *Harry Bibby & Co Ltd v Neill Construction Ltd* [1973] E.G.D. 52 (CA).

(c) Rights of recourse

25-048 Clause 4.13.2 of JCT 2005 provides:

> "Notwithstanding his fiduciary interest in the Retention ... the Employer is entitled to exercise any rights under this Contract of withholding or deduction from sums due or to become due to the Contractor against any amount due under an Interim Certificate ..."

This provision reflects the function of retention as a security for performance and enables the employer to make withdrawals from the trust account without being in breach of trust provided the withdrawal is permitted by the contract, e.g. the requirements of the Housing Grants, Construction and Regeneration Act 1996 have been observed.[179] If a right of set-off exceeding the retention arose before the contractor's request that it be funded, the court would not grant an injunction.[180] In this connection, the employer has been described as an active, self-interested trustee[181] rather than a beneficiary of the trust.[182]

25-049 There is a tension between the right of retention as performance security and the retention trust as payment security. At first sight the employer is entitled to recourse against the whole retention, including that attributable to work carried out by sub-contractors, even if the sub-contractors are not in breach. Although hard on the sub-contractors, this is the logical outcome of privity of contract. The imposition of a trust as security for payment ought not to affect the overriding purpose of retention as security for performance. However, the court has overridden the employer's rights of recourse by allowing sub-contractors to recover retention in this situation. In *Re Arthur Sanders* Nourse J. stated that:

> "... the position as between employer, contractor and subcontractor under the present RIBA Conditions [JCT 63] and the FASS Sub-contract [the Green Form] is that the employer holds a due proportion of the retentions on trust for the contractor as trustee for the Sub-contractor".[183]

25-050 Nourse J. concluded at [140] that the sub-contractor's proportion of retention could never be a "sum due" to the contractor since it could only be received by the contractor as trustee. His analysis was approved by the Court of Appeal in *P.C. Harrington Contractors Ltd v Co Partnership Developments Ltd*[184] which concerned the JCT management contract. In that case, a retention trust had been set up before administrative receivers were appointed to the management contractor. The architect certified that the cost to complete the works exceeded

---

[179] See para.25–058, below.
[180] *Henry Boot Building Ltd v The Croydon Hotel & Leisure Co Ltd* (1985) 36 B.L.R. 41 (CA).
[181] Hayton, "The Significance of Equity in Construction Contracts" [1994] 1 *Construction Law Yearbook* 19.
[182] *Wates Construction (London) Ltd v Franthom Property Ltd* (1991) 53 B.L.R. 23 (CA).
[183] *Re Arthur Sanders Ltd* (1981) 17 B.L.R. 125, 138.
[184] *PC Harrington Contractors Ltd v Co Partnership Developments Ltd* (1998) 88 B.L.R. 44 (CA).

the balance of the retention account which was withdrawn by the employer. A works contractor successfully claimed its proportion of retention direct from the employer on the ground, among other things, that the employer's right of recourse extended only to retention withheld against the management contractor's fee.

It is submitted that the analysis of Nourse J. in *Re Arthur Sanders* and of the Court of Appeal in *Harrington v Co Partnership* fails to take adequate cognisance of the employer's right of recourse.[185] In *Saipem SpA v Rafidain Bank*[186] it was suggested that a construction trust be construed in two stages: first, as a matter of contract as if there were no trust, and only then to see whether the imposition of a trust made a difference. It is possible that, had the Court of Appeal in *Harrington v Co Partnership* adopted this approach, it might have concluded that the employer's right of recourse was an inherent limitation in the chose in action forming the subject matter of the trust.[187]   **25–051**

A further issue concerns the effect of termination of the contractor's employment on the trust. The Scottish case of *Balfour Beatty v Britannia Life*[188] concerned facts almost identical to those in *Harrington v Co Partnership* with the exception that the trust account had not been set up before administrative receivers were appointed to the contractor. The Court of Session took a different view on the construction of the management and works contracts, and, in particular, held that the payment regime in the termination clause superseded the other provisions in the contract.   **25–052**

"At best the rights of management contractors against employers remain contingent until the final payment provisions of the contract come into effect. A trust of a contingent sum cannot survive an event that evacuates the contingency, or leaves it incapable of fulfilment. The net effect is that upon determination of the contract any trust which did subsist in favour of the works contractors terminates and is of no continuing substance … in that event the protection of the employer's interests is paramount."[189]

The contingency was the certificate of making good defects which had not been issued before the termination.[190] Alternatively, the court might have held that the termination clause was one of the terms of the trust. Until the works could be completed and the final account of the completion contractor agreed,   **25–053**

---

[185] The reasoning in *Re Arthur Sanders* was not followed for this reason in *Hsin Chong Construction Co Ltd v Yaton Realty Co Ltd* (1986) 40 B.L.R. 119 (High Court of Hong Kong), or in *Balfour Beatty Ltd v Britannia Life Ltd* [1997] S.L.T. 10 (Court of Session, Outer House).

[186] *Saipem SpA v Rafidain Bank* [1994] C.L.C. 253 (CA).

[187] cf. *KBH Construction Pty Ltd v Lidco Aluminium Products Pty Ltd* (1991) 7 B.C.L. 183 (Sup Court of NSW) ("one of the terms of the trust qualifying the builder's obligations as trustee and limiting the sub-contractor's beneficial entitlement", per Giles J. at 191).

[188] *Balfour Beatty v Britannia Life* [1997] S.L.T. 10 (Court of Session, Outer House).

[189] *Balfour Beatty v Britannia Life* [1997] S.L.T. 10 (Court of Session, Outer House), per Lord Penrose.

[190] The same situation as in *Harrington*, but in that case the Court of Appeal appears to have waived the conditionality of retention on the ground that the trust gave the works contractor a vested interest in the fund, and restricted the effect of the termination clause to retention withheld against the contractor's fee.

it would not be known whether the employer was net debtor or creditor of the contractor, and the trust should therefore continue as protection for the contractor and the works contractors in the meantime. The position is different where the project has been satisfactorily completed and neither employer nor contractor claims any right of recourse against retention. In that case, the contractor becomes a bare trustee and the sub-contractors have a direct right against the employer.[191] Similarly, a contractor might have a right against a funder if the terms as to retention in the finance agreement and the main contract were back to back.[192]

(d) Registrability

25–054 Retention as such is simply a deduction sanctioned by the contract. Although it operates as an informal security, it is not a mortgage or charge over the property of the debtor in the contractual relationship and therefore there is no registration requirement under s.860 of the Companies Act 2006. The JCT forms are silent as to the purpose of the retention trust, although clearly it functions as security for payment. Industry practice is not to treat the trust as registrable even if could be described as a charge. There is no English authority on the point.[193] However, in a case concerning a retention trust set up under an Australian standard form,[194] the court assumed without argument that the account took effect as a charge but concluded that it was not a charge over a book debt, relying on English authorities,[195] and was not registrable.

15. CONSTRUCTION TRUSTS AND ESCROWS

25–055 The trust is also used to protect interim payments against the risk of employer insolvency. In *Lovell Construction Ltd v Independent Estates Plc*,[196] the main contract was in the JCT 1980 form but the parties had a side agreement whereby the employer agreed a schedule of monthly payments on account of the contract sum. The employer agreed to deposit in a trust account one month in advance the amount specified in the schedule in respect of the following month's work. The agreement stated that it was to facilitate payment under the contract and nominated the parties' solicitors as trustees of the account, the terms of the trust being that payment should be made on presentation of the architect's certificates issued under the contract. Fixed charge receivers were appointed to

[191] *Saunders v Vautier* (1841) 4 Beav. 115. This appears to be the basis of the cases considered at para.25–050, above.
[192] Hayton, "The Significance of Equity in Construction Contracts" [1994] 1 *Construction Law Yearbook* 19, 21. Such a claim failed in *Re Jartay Developments Ltd* (1982) 22 B.L.R. 134 because the terms were different, but the facts were unusual.
[193] In *Lovell Construction Ltd v Independent Estates Plc* [1994] 1 B.C.L.C. 31, it was left undecided whether, had the trust of the contract sum been a charge, it would have been registrable as a charge over a book debt. An argument that it was an unregistered floating charge was abandoned as the employer could not use the account in the ordinary course of business: see *Wates Construction (London) Ltd v Franthom Property Ltd* (1991) 53 B.L.R. 23 (CA).
[194] *Re Old Inns Ltd* (1994) 13 A.C.S.R. 141 (Sup Court of NSW).
[195] *Re Brightlife Ltd* [1987] Ch. 200, and subsequent cases discussed in Ch.3 above.
[196] *Lovell Construction Ltd v Independent Estates Plc* [1994] 1 B.C.L.C. 31.

the development and the employer went into liquidation. The liquidator argued that the side letter was a charge over book debts, which was not binding on him for want of registration under s.395 of the Companies Act 1985. The court rejected the claim, holding that the machinery laid down by the agreement was the means of payment rather than security for payment, and therefore no charge was created.[197]

Many problems with trust and escrow accounts[198] concern the conditions for payment out, e.g. on an insolvency termination if the architect ceases to act[199] or where international sanctions or a change in local law prevent the issue of the necessary certificate[200] or where an administrator or a receiver decides to "mothball" the project.[201] In addition, the terms of the escrow may permit payment of interim certificates but not damages or sums due on a termination.[202] In an Australian case, a trust to pay sub-contractors was held to have been terminated when the employer and the contractor varied the main contract by deleting the terms under which the trust had been set up.[203]   **25–056**

The Office of Government Commerce is actively promoting the use of "project bank accounts" on high value public works contracts[204] and both the JCT and NEC have issued optional clauses for use with their forms. As with the retention trust, the employer is a trustee of the account; and like the "Lovell" trust, it is intended to facilitate payment rather than stand as security for payment; but there are significant differences from both of these devices. The account is funded by the employer monthly in arrears, in accordance with a schedule agreed with the contractor, which identifies the interest in the account attributable to the contractor and each of the relevant subcontractors and suppliers named as beneficiaries. It is the schedule which identifies the trust property.[205] The intention is that the bank mandate will authorise the bank to distribute the fund automatically on receipt of the schedule signed by both trustees. The bank is not concerned with certificates issued under the contract. There appears to be no right of recourse in either trustee against the fund, and it seems that any abatement and set-off will occur before the agreement of the schedule. The arrangement could be characterised as a direct payment trust.   **25–057**

---

[197] Compare *Gray v G-T-P Group* [2011] 1 B.C.L.C. 313 in which a declaration of trust over an escrow account was held to be an unregistered floating charge.

[198] See *Re Namco UK Ltd* [2003] 2 B.C.L.C. 78; *Integrated Building Services v Pihl Ltd* [2010] B.L.R. 622.

[199] *Lovell Construction Ltd v Independent Estates Plc* [1994] 1 B.C.L.C. 31.

[200] *Saipem SpA v Rafidain Bank* [1994] C.L.C. 253 (CA), followed by David Richards J. in *Saipem SpA v Rafidain Bank (In Provisional Liquidation)* [2007] EWHC 3119 (Ch), which concerned another contract on the same project.

[201] Hayton, "The Significance of Equity in Construction Contracts" [1994] 1 *Construction Law Yearbook* 19, 29.

[202] *Bouygues v Shanghai Links* [1998] 2 H.K.L.R.D. 479 (High Court of Hong Kong).

[203] *Stork Electrical Pty Ltd v Leighton Contractors Pty Ltd* [2001] A.C.L. Rep 430 Qld (Queensland CA); Quick and Davis, "The Construction Trust—an Empty Remedy?" [2002] I.C.L.R. 474.

[204] See *http://www.cabinetoffice.gov.uk/content/office-government-commerce-ogc* for the OGC precedent trust deed.

[205] Compare *Re Lehman Brothers International (Europe) (In Administration)* [2009] EWHC 2545 (Ch), [56].

There is as yet no case law on the project bank account. It is evidently important to integrate the various documents required: the construction contract, the trust deed, subcontract forms, and the bank mandate. Depending on the facts, administrators may seek to claim the monies standing to the credit of the account by challenging its trust status or argue that it takes effect as an unregistered charge, a preference, or as a direct payment agreement infringing the anti-deprivation rule.[206]

Finally, a trust may arise to protect a payment made for a specific purpose in accordance with *Barclays Bank Ltd v Quistclose Investments Ltd*.[207] In one case, a contractor took out a loan to pay an arbitrator's fees to enable him to take up the award. On his bankruptcy, it was held that the loan had been made for a specific purpose and was repayable out of the proceeds of the award ahead of other creditors.[208] In another, a payment to administrators appointed to a contractor to enable them to pay a subcontractor so that it returned to site and commissioned its work was treated by them as a general payment on account of sums due. It was held that the money was subject to a *Quistclose* trust and that the administrators were under an equitable obligation to pay an equivalent sum back to the employer.[209]

16. THE HOUSING GRANTS, CONSTRUCTION AND REGENERATION ACT 1996

25–058 A "construction contract" which falls within the definition in the Housing Grants, Construction and Regeneration Act 1996[210] has to contain specific terms as to adjudication, payment and set-off. In default, the terms of the Scheme for Construction Contracts[211] will be implied.[212] Certain agreements for the development and financing of projects, as well as bonds and guarantees, are excluded from the Act.[213] The standard forms include their own adjudication procedure. Bespoke forms often incorporate one of the available sets of adjudication rules. The main features of statutory adjudication are:

(a) either party has the right to refer a dispute to adjudication at any time[214];

---

[206] See above, para.25–002.

[207] *Barclays Bank Ltd v Quistclose Investments Ltd* [1970] A.C. 567 (HL), discussed in Ch.20.

[208] *Re McKeown* [1974] N.I.L.R. 226 (High Court of Northern Ireland).

[209] *Re Niagara Mechanical Services International Ltd (In Administration)* [2001] B.C.C. 393.

[210] Housing Grants, Construction and Regeneration Act 1996, ss.104–107. The definition is complex but will probably include most commercial construction contracts. Contracts which are oral for supply only, or for residential occupiers are excluded. The Act has been amended inter alia by Pt 8 of the Local Democracy, Economic Development and Construction Act 2009.

[211] The Scheme for Construction Contracts (England and Wales) Regulations 1998 (SI 1998/649).

[212] Housing Grants, Construction and Regeneration Act 1996, s.114.

[213] The Construction Contracts (England and Wales) Exclusion Order 1998 (SI 1998/648).

[214] Housing Grants, Construction and Regeneration Act 1996, s.108; *Connex South Eastern Ltd v M.J. Building Services Group Plc* [2005] 1 W.L.R. 3323 (CA).

(b) the adjudicator has to reach a decision within 28 days, which can be extended by 14 days with the consent of the referring party or longer if both parties agree[215];

(c) the adjudicator's decision is binding until the dispute is finally determined by litigation or arbitration[216] and in the meantime the parties agree to carry it out[217];

(d) the parties are jointly and severally liable for the adjudicator's fees and expenses[218] but it appears that an adjudicator has no power to make an order for costs, and therefore security for costs, without the parties' agreement.[219]

Adjudication is a "proceeding" for the purposes of para.43 of Sch.B1 to the **25–059** Insolvency Act 1986 and cannot be brought against a company in administration without the consent of the administrator or permission of the court.[220]

If permission is not forthcoming, account can only be taken of the employer's cross-claims if they are eligible for set-off or otherwise amount to a defence in an adjudication brought by the administrator. In the light of these factors, administrators have used the adjudication procedure to pursue claims and recover book debts. A recent case has established, however, that, even if an adjudicator's decision in favour of a company in administration is enforced by summary judgment, execution of the judgment will be stayed, even where the contract provides that the decision be final.[221] A stay is also likely to be ordered where the claimant is in administrative receivership.[222] If the claimant is subject to a company voluntary arrangement, the court will take account of the circumstances leading to the agreement of the CVA, as well as the claimant's current trading position. A relevant factor is whether non-payment of the debt in question significantly contributed to the claimant's financial difficulty.[223] If the claimant is in liquidation, the court's policy is to refuse summary judgment[224] on the basis that adjudication is not the proper forum to deal with

---

[215] Housing Grants, Construction and Regeneration Act 1996, s.108(2); Scheme for Construction Contracts, para.19(1).

[216] Housing Grants, Construction and Regeneration Act 1996, s.108(3).

[217] *Jim Ennis Construction v Premier Asphalt* (2009) 125 Con. L.R. 141.

[218] Scheme for Construction Contracts, para.25.

[219] *Northern Developments (Cumbria) Ltd v J & J Nichol* [2000] B.L.R. 158, 167; *Yuanda (UK) Co Ltd v WW Gear Construction* [2011] 1 All E.R. (Comm) 550.

[220] *A. Straume (UK) Ltd v Bradlor Developments Ltd* [2000] B.C.C. 333; *Joinery Plus Ltd v Laing Ltd* [2003] B.L.R. 184; *Canary Riverside Development (Private) Ltd v Timtec International Ltd* (2003) 19 Const. L.J. 283 (leave refused in all three cases).

[221] *Straw Realisations(No.1) Ltd v Shaftsbury House Developments Ltd* [2011] B.L.R. 47.

[222] *Rainford House Ltd (In Administrative Receivership) v Cadogan Ltd* [2001] B.L.R. 416; *Baldwins Industrial Services Plc v Barr Ltd* [2003] B.L.R. 176.

[223] *Mead General Building v Dartmoor Properties* [2009] B.C.C. 510 (stay refused); *Pilon v Breyer Group Plc* [2010] B.L.R. 452 (stay would have been ordered, had summary judgment not been refused).

[224] *Bouygues UK Ltd v Dahl-Jensen UK Ltd* [2000] B.L.R. 522 (CA); *Harwood Construction v Lantrode Ltd* Unreported November 24, 2000 (stay pending the hearing of a winding-up petition against the claimant).

liquidation set-off.[225] In rare cases, the court has been prepared to grant a stay on the ground of the claimant's informal insolvency.[226]

25–060   The use of "pay when paid" clauses is now restricted by statute to cases where the non-payment is due to specific insolvency events affecting the paying party, including administration, the appointment of an administrative receiver or a receiver or manager of its property, and a winding-up order or resolution.[227]

25–061   Set-off and abatement in connection with construction contracts are also regulated by the Act which overlays certain procedural conditions to the valid exercise of contractual and common law rights, e.g. service of a "withholding notice" specifying the nature and amount of the cross-claim within a strict time period before the debt becomes due and payable.[228] Non-compliance results in the loss of such rights against the payment concerned but not against future sums provided the conditions are satisfied in relation to them.

Set-off is not generally permitted against a payment ordered by an adjudicator.[229]

17. ARBITRATION

25–062   Under the Arbitration Act 1996, proceedings issued in court under a contract containing an arbitration clause are now subject to a mandatory stay for arbitration.[230] An administrative receiver will have the power, unless specifically excluded in the debenture under which he is appointed, to "refer to arbitration any question affecting the company".[231] An administrator has the same power.[232] In the short term having to go to arbitration may be an immediate disadvantage to a receiver or administrator of the contractor because invariably as claimant he will have to make an initial payment on account to the arbitrator and in addition will have to bear half of the interim accounts that the arbitrator submits. Arbitrators may ask for a substantial payment on account of fees to be incurred at the hearing and will not release their awards until all their fees have been discharged.[233] Such arbitrations may tend to involve receivers in a greater drain on financial resources than may occur in a case brought to court.

---

[225] *Enterprise Managed Services v Tony McFadden Utilities Ltd* [2011] 1 B.C.L.C. 414.

[226] e.g. *Camden LBC v Makers* (2009) 124 Con. L.R. 32 (claimant had ceased trading, had lost the support of its parent, and was balance sheet insolvent).

[227] Housing Grants, Construction and Regeneration Act 1996, s.113; *Aqua Design & Play International Ltd (t/a Aqua Design) (In Liquidation) v Kier Regional Ltd (t/a French Kier Anglia)* [2003] B.L.R. 111 (CA); *Hills Electrical & Mechanical Plc v Dawn Construction Ltd*, 2004 S.L.T. 477 (Court of Session, Outer House); *William Hare Ltd v Shepherd Construction Ltd* [2010] B.L.R. 358 (CA).

[228] Housing Grants, Construction and Regeneration Act 1996, ss.110–111. *Rupert Morgan Building Services (LLC) Ltd v Jervis* [2004] 1 W.L.R. 1867 (CA).

[229] *Interserve Industrial Services Ltd v Cleveland Bridge UK Ltd* [2006] EWHC 741 (TCC); *William Verry Ltd v Camden LBC* [2006] EWHC 761 (TCC).

[230] Arbitration Act 1996, s.9.

[231] Insolvency Act 1986, s.42, and Sch.1, para.6.

[232] Insolvency Act 1986, Sch.1, para.6.

[233] This is also a feature of adjudication practice: *Faithful and Gould Ltd v Archal Ltd* Unreported June 1, 2001.

18.   PAYMENT IN COURT

It sometimes happens that a receiver finds on his appointment over the prop-   **25–063**
erty of a contractor that one asset of the company is a sum paid into court as an
offer of settlement. Such a payment cannot be taken out without the court's
permission.[234] The question then arises as to whether the court will give leave
for that sum to be recovered by the receiver acting in the name of the contractor.
In the Court of Appeal case of *Peal Furniture Ltd v Adrian Share (Interiors)
Ltd*[235] leave to withdraw the money in court was given to the receiver. A differently constituted Court of Appeal in a liquidation case, *WA Sherratt Ltd v John
Bromley (Church Stretton) Ltd*[236] subsequently held that the *Peal Furniture*
case was decided per incuriam. The Court of Appeal in *Sherratt* held that a
payment into court fell within a line of bankruptcy cases which decided that
the other parties to the litigation became a potentially secured creditor to the
extent of the payment in.[237] In so far as the opposing party recovered judgment
he would be a secured creditor in a supervening bankruptcy up to the amount
in court. In the *Sherratt* case the Court of Appeal thus held that, in view of the
fact that a payment constituted a potential security, the subsequent winding-up
was not a sufficient reason to allow a liquidator of the company to withdraw
the sums in court.

By inference, the appointment of a receiver would not be a sufficient reason   **25–064**
to give leave to withdraw such sums since the payment into court will constitute a potential security ranking ahead of the debenture-holder's charge.[238] An
order for payment to one of the parties' solicitors to be held by them "to the
order of the court" confers the same level of protection as a payment into
court,[239] although a payment into a solicitors' joint escrow account by one
party in order to discharge a freezing order obtained by the other "pending
further order of the court" will not constitute a charge over the account.[240] A
solicitor's undertaking given against the background of a freezing order has
been held not to constitute a trust affording priority to a creditor in the administration of the solicitor's client.[241]

---

[234] CPR Part 36.6(5) replacing RSC Ord.22, without, it seems, affecting the relevance of the
cases discussed below.
[235] *Peal Furniture Co Ltd v Adrian Share (Interiors) Ltd* [1977] 1 W.L.R. 464 (CA).
[236] *WA Sherratt Ltd v John Bromley (Church Stretton) Ltd* [1985] Q.B. 1038 (CA).
[237] *Re Gordon* [1897] 2 Q.B. 516; *Re Ford* [1900] 2 Q.B. 211; *Dessau v Rowley* [1916] W.N.
238; *Re A Debtor* (1932) 101 L.J. Ch. 372.
[238] *Toprak Enerji Sanayi AS v Sale Tilney Technology Plc* [1994] 3 All E.R. 483, 503, per Judge
Diamond QC.
[239] *Re Mordant (A Bankrupt)* [1996] 1 F.L.R. 334; see also *Choski Tube Co Ltd v Corrotherm
Industries Ltd* Unreported June 24, 1998 (CA).
[240] *Flightline Ltd v Edwards* [2003] 1 W.L.R. 1200 (CA); *Technocrats International v Fredic
Ltd* [2005] 1 B.C.L.C. 467; *Kastner v Jason* [2005] 1 Lloyd's Rep. 397 (CA).
[241] *Tradegro (UK) Ltd v Wigmore Street Investments Ltd* [2011] EWCA Civ 268.

Chapter 26

Environmental Law

1. Introduction

26–001 This chapter addresses environmental law issues as may be relevant to the rights, duties, acts or omissions of and on the part of Administrators and Receivers. Reference should be made to specialist works concerning more detailed aspects of environmental law as well as relevant causes of action applicable to persons other than Administrators and Receivers.[1]

Reference should also be made to relevant specialist works on the effects of environmental law on other insolvency practitioners such as liquidators.[2]

The incidents of environmental law on the operations of administrators and receivers are a matter of, still, relatively recent interest. For many years third parties with an interest in assets under the control of administrators or receivers did not focus on environmental law because environmental concerns were regarded as peripheral. It was thought that such concerns with respect to the operations of administrators and receivers were a matter for the official environmental regulatory authorities and that the latter would not be likely to take action because, of a view that the involvement of administrators or receivers meant that it was unlikely that there would be funds available to address environmental issues

26–002 Such considerations continue, but are changing for a number of reasons.

First, the environmental regulators are subject to ever greater public and legal pressure to address environmental pollution and to control incidents so that doing nothing is not an option for them.

Secondly, there is an increased understanding that environmental law is a source of individual and third party rights.[3] Thirdly, there is a growing understanding that European Union (EU) law can have a direct impact on the operations of administrators and receivers as persons in control of activities that may

---

[1] See, e.g. *Clerk & Lindsell on Torts*, 20th edn (London: Sweet & Maxwell, 2010).

[2] See, e.g. *Totty & Moss on Insolvency* (looseleaf), Sweet & Maxwell, Ch.H1.

[3] See, e.g. the following detailed reports: *Access to Justice in Environmental Matters and the Role of NGOs, Empirical Findings and Legal Appraisal* (Eds: De Sadeleer, Roller and Dross, Europa Publishing, 2005); the *Environmental Justice Report* and the various sources cited on access to court on environmental matters; R. Macrory and M. Woods, *Modernising Environmental Justice: Regulation and the Role of an Environmental Tribunal* (2003). UCL—*http://www.ucl. ac.uk/law/environment/tribunals/*. By "third party rights" here is meant rights for individuals or interest groups to protect non-personal or non–proprietary interests, such as protection of the environment.

adversely impact on the environment.[4] In part, this growing awareness is influenced or affected by the privatisation of key activities potentially impacting on the environment such as those of the former public utilities. There is also a growing awareness amongst environmental regulators and third parties that rights or obligations arising under EU law can be applied directly to a variety of persons including insolvency practitioners such as administrators and receivers,[5] that inconsistent national law and practices must be disapplied[6] and that under EU law protections and immunities available to administrators and/or receivers under national law regarding their activities as administrators and/or receivers might not be able to be relied upon, with direct recourse to EU law supplying a suitable remedy against them.[7] Fourthly, there is a growing realisation that environmental permits or licences may have a positive economic value for a company, and that they should be managed appropriately.[8] It is not necessarily the case that all such and related assets need be disposed of as quickly as possible.

The matters set out below are intended to raise awareness of the current and potential effects of environmental regulatory regimes on the operations of administrators and receivers. In addition, they are intended as an additional consideration to assist in the decision of which is the most appropriate insolvency regime for a given company the activities of which may impact on the environment and which takes into account what best protects the value of the assets of the company. This Chapter may also assist in deciding in respect of what property it is desirable to appoint a receiver—see further, above at, Ch.7.

2. OVERVIEW OF ENVIRONMENTAL CONTROL REGIMES

(a) Domestic Law

Few activities of industrial companies are not affected by some form of **26–003** state environmental control. Usually this is through the requirement that their activities are unlawful without or must be carried out in accordance with an

---

[4] See, by way of example, the (ultimately unsuccessful) attempts by the Environment Agency to attach primary responsibility for environmental control on liquidators and/or funds in the liquidation in *Re Celtic Extraction Ltd (In Liquidation); Re Bluestone Chemicals Ltd (In Liquidation)* [2001] Ch. 475 (CA) (cf. the comments of the Court of Appeal in *Re Rhondda Waste Disposal Ltd* [2001] Ch. 57, [19] as to possibilities of bringing criminal proceedings against administrators as those in control of polluting incidents); and to access monies under a trust deed, intended to be available for environmental clean-up, in *Environment Agency v Hillridge Ltd* [2004] 2 B.C.L.C. 358.

[5] See the sources cited at fnn.7–8, and below at paras 26–017 to 26–022 indicating rights for individuals provided by EU environmental directives.

[6] For a comprehensive review of the relevant case law at Community level on this obligation to disapply inconsistent national rules see the leading case of *Kobler v Austria* (C-224/01) [2004] Q.B. 848 (ECJ).

[7] See below at paras 26–019 to 26–021, and see, by way of illustration, *R. v Secretary of State for Transport Ex p. Factortame* [1991] 1 A.C. 603 (HL) requiring an interim injunction against the Crown (overturning the previous Crown immunity, and allowing for the first time disapplication of an Act of Parliament pending a ruling from the ECJ).

[8] See *Re Celtic Extraction Ltd (In Liquidation); Re Bluestone Chemicals Ltd (In Liquidation)* [2001] Ch. 475 (CA).

environmental permit. Within domestic legislation,[9] the most obvious examples are those that apply to emissions to air or discharges to water or to land; and other controls on waste handling, transfer, recovery and disposal.[10] In addition, there are statutory controls over land contaminated in the past,[11] the impounding or abstracting of water,[12] the control of major accident hazards arising involving dangerous substances,[13] or the use of hazardous substances,[14] or radioactive substances,[15] and statutory nuisance.[16]

Such control systems regulate not only the direct impact on the environment in terms of emissions to air, discharges to water or impact on land but also set operating conditions in terms of what techniques are permitted and in what manner the activities are to be operated.[17]

It is to be noted that environmental regulatory regimes such as the Environmental Permitting (England and Wales) Regulations 2010 ("the Environmental Permitting Regulations") usually now regulate in a comprehensive and integrated manner in a single permit actual or potential adverse impacts on the environment as a whole.[18] The range of activities subject to the stringent Environmental Permitting Regulations include energy industries, combustion, gasification, liquefaction and refining, the production and processing of metals, mineral industries, chemical industries, waste management, paper and pulp manufacture, coating activities, manufacture of dyestuffs, timber activities and even intensive farming.[19]

26–004 In respect of each of these pieces of legislation provision is made for criminal offences for breach of either: (i) the relevant environmental permit/licence[20] usually on a strict liability basis[21]; or (ii) breach of legislative provisions themselves.[22] These offences are often characterised by liability terminology such

---

[9] Though itself mostly derived from EU directives.

[10] All under the Environmental Permitting (England and Wales) Regulations 2010 (SI 2010/675) ("the Environmental Permitting Regulations"), reg.12.

[11] Such as the Environmental Protection Act 1990 (EPA), Pt IIA, and see further, below, at paras 26–034 to 26–046.

[12] See the Water Resources Act 1991, Pt II, Ch.11 and the Water Resources (Abstraction and Impounding) Regulations 2006 (SI 2006/641).

[13] See the Control of Major Accident Hazard Regulations 1999 (SI 1999/743).

[14] See the Planning (Hazardous Substances) Act 1990, and the Planning (Hazardous Substances) Regulations 1992 (SI 1992/656).

[15] Also, as from April 6, 2010, regulated under the Environmental Permitting Regulations 2010.

[16] See the Environmental Protection Act 1990, Pt III.

[17] See fn.10.

[18] See also *United Utilities Plc v Environment Agency* [2006] Env. L.R. 42, where the Court of Appeal decision illustrates the tendency towards supporting the application of regulatory systems of an increasingly stringent and integrated nature rather than those that might apply but which are less comprehensive or strict in environmental protection terms. The statements in the Court of Appeal are unaffected by the decision in the House of Lords at [2007] 1 W.L.R. 2707.

[19] See Sch.1 thereto.

[20] See, e.g. for activities within Sch.1 to the Environmental Permitting Regulations, reg.38(2).

[21] See, e.g. as regards water pollution contrary to the former Water Resources Act 1991, s.85 (as to which see now the Environmental Permitting Regulations 2010, regs 12 and 38); *Empress Car Co (Abertillery) Ltd v National Rivers Authority* [1999] 2 A.C. 22 (HL); and *Express Ltd v Environment Agency* [2005] 1 W.L.R. 223. This case law is currently considered to hold good on this point in relation to the Environmental Permitting Regulations.

[22] See, e.g. with water pollution incidents and for waste management licences, the Environmental Permitting Regulations, regs 12 and 38.

as "causing"[23] or "knowingly causing"[24] the incident in question or "knowingly permitting"[25] the incident in question. Criminal liability may be "direct" in the sense that the liability attaches to the person for example "causing", or "indirect" in the sense of the standard provision for attribution of criminal liability to directors, shadow directors and so forth.[26] Increasingly, with criminal liability will attach obligations for clean up or remediation of the environment adversely affected by the criminal act in question.[27]

Civil liability arises in the environmental context under causes of action such as negligence,[28] nuisance,[29] *Rylands v Fletcher*,[30] trespass,[31] breach of statutory duty,[32] or other torts such as the tort of waste.[33]

(b) EU Law

EU law is the source of most national environmental regulatory provisions, so   **26–005**
recourse to the underlying EU directives will be made by those aiming to rely
on them against receivers or administrators where the national regulatory
regime does not fully implement the requirements of the directives.

The operation of EU law here is examined in some detail below. However, it is useful at this stage to consider what provision has been made as regards potential liabilities of administrators and receivers in the context of environmental liability, whether arising at the instance of the official regulators and/or third parties. The key issue is the meaning of the term "operator".

Under Council Directive 2008/1/EC[34] concerning integrated pollution prevention and control (the IPPC Directive) provision is made for imposing obligations for compliance with the substantive provisions of the IPPC Directive on the "operator". "Operator" is defined as "any natural or legal, private or public person who operates or controls the installation or, where this is provided for in national legislation, to whom decisive economic power over the technical functioning of the installation has been delegated".[35] The Environmental Permitting Regulations, reg.7 provides for "operator" to be the person who will have control over a future operating regulated facility or who

---

[23] See, e.g. the Environmental Permitting Regulations 2010, regs 12 and 38 on polluting controlled waters.

[24] See, e.g. the Environmental Permitting Regulations 2010, reg.12(1)(a), with reg.38(1)(b).

[25] See, e.g. the Environmental Permitting Regulations 2010, reg.12(1), with reg.38(1)(b); and the Salmon and Freshwater Fisheries Act 1975, s.4(1).

[26] See, e.g. Environmental Protection Act 1990, s.157(1) and s.158; the Water Resources Act 1991, s.217; and the Environmental Permitting Regulations 2010, reg.41.

[27] See the Environmental Protection Act 1990, ss.79A et seq for contaminated land; the Environmental Protection Act 1990, s.81 as regards statutory nuisances; and the Environmental Permitting Regulations 2010, reg.44 in respect of breaches of reg.38(1), (2) or (3).

[28] See below, paras 26–029 to 26–030.

[29] See below, paras 26–029 to 26–030.

[30] See below, paras 26–029 to 26–030.

[31] See below, paras 26–029 to 26–030.

[32] See below, paras 26–031 to 26–033.

[33] *Mancetter Developments v Garmanson* [1986] Q.B. 1212 (CA).

[34] [2008] OJ L24/4.

[35] art.2(12).

does have control or, after the facility ceases to operate, who is the holder of the permit. As appears more fully below, these terms may be considered as so "providing for" in respect of those to whom has been delegated such decisive economic power under the EU directives.

26–006 The EU formulation for "operator" indicated above is found in other EU environmental legislation such as the Incineration of Waste Directive 2000/76/EC,[36] art.3(11); Directive 1999/13/EC on the imitation of emissions of volatile organic compounds,[37] art.2(6); and with slight variations as in Directive 96/82/EC on the Control of major accident hazards,[38] art.2(3); and the Landfill Directive 1999/31/EC,[39] art.2(1).

Furthermore, under EC Directive 2004/35/EC[40] on environmental liability with regard to the prevention and remedying of environmental damage, provision is made for non-criminal liability for clean-up of the environment, including at the suit of environmental interest groups.[41] The primary obligation is imposed on "operators", meaning: "any natural or legal, private or public person who operates or controls the occupational activity or, where this is provided for in national legislation, to whom decisive economic power over the technical functioning of such an activity has been delegated, including the holder of the permit or authorisation for such an activity or the person registering or notifying such an activity." This key definition should apply under the national implementing legislation (as to which see below) and has the potential to attach to administrators and receivers.

3. OVERVIEW OF THE REGULATORY AND ENFORCEMENT AUTHORITY FOR ENGLAND

26–007 The primary authority for regulating and enforcing the environmental regimes discussed in this Chapter is the Environment Agency (the Agency).[42] The Agency is an independent body corporate.[43] Its pollution control powers are: "exercisable for the purpose of preventing or minimising, or remedying or mitigating the effects of, pollution of the environment".[44] The Agency has the power to institute criminal proceedings in England and Wales.[45]

---

[36] [2000] OJ L332/91.
[37] [1999] OJ L85/1.
[38] [1997] OJ L10/13.
[39] [1999] OJ L182/1.
[40] [2004] OJ L143/56.
[41] See below at paras 26–047 to 26–050.
[42] Provision has been made for the exercise of functions of the Agency in Wales through the National Assembly for Wales (Transfer of Functions) Order 1999 (SI 1999/672) art.2, Sch.1; while separate provision is made also for a separate agency in Scotland—the Scottish Environmental Protection Agency (SEPA), and for Northern Ireland—the Environment and Heritage Service (the EHS).
[43] Environment Act 1995 s.1(1) and s.1(5).
[44] Environment Act 1995, s.5(1).
[45] Environment Act 1995, s.37(1), but note the transfer of functions under the Environment Act 1995, s.1 to the National Assembly for Wales, by the National Assembly for Wales (Transfer of Functions) Order 1999 (SI 1999/672), art.2, Sch.1.

Under the Environment Act, an "enforcing authority"[46] can give a suitable person written authority[47] to exercise wide-ranging powers for purposes such as: to determine whether a relevant pollution control enactment is being, or has been, complied with[48]; and to exercise or perform a pollution control function.[49]

The powers which may be so exercised include: a power of entry (which, in   **26–008** an emergency, includes entry by force)[50]; powers to investigate,[51] including taking samples,[52] measurements and photographs[53]; and the power to require any person whom the Agency has reasonable cause to believe can give any relevant information to answer any questions it thinks fit to ask and to sign a declaration of truth of the answers.[54] Failure to comply with a due requirement is a criminal offence.[55]

4. OVERVIEW OF THE POSITION OF ADMINISTRATORS AND RECEIVERS IN RELATION TO COMPANY ASSETS AS REGARDS ENVIRONMENTAL CONSIDERATIONS

As appears further below the main concerns here for administrators and   **26–009** receivers relate to the degree of control and/or management exercised or exercisable over assets and/or operations with actual or potential adverse impact on the environment. As far as potential criminal liability is concerned, it is necessary in each case to examine in detail the scope of the authority to act, manage or direct acts or activities or avoid default that is conferred on an administrator or receiver[56] and/or what they have assumed specifically to do.[57]

Such issues of control and management are to be considered from two perspectives: (i) national law; and (ii) EU law. As discussed below (at para.26–023 (et seq.), a number of core issues arise for consideration under EU law on whether it is national law that alone determines whether there is relevant control or management of relevant assets for the purpose of EU law (that is, is there in effect a renvoi to national law here—as in the case with the Landfill Directive in para.26–006 above) or whether the definitions that apply are autonomous

---

[46] e.g. the Secretary of State, the Agency, SEPA, or a local enforcing authority (effectively, a local authority in its environmental protection capacity), see the Environment Act 1995, s.108(15).

[47] Environment Act 1995, s.108(1).

[48] Environment Act 1995, s.108(1)(a).

[49] Environment Act 1995, s.108(1)(b).

[50] Environment Act 1995, s.108(4)(a).

[51] Environment Act 1995, s.108(4)(c).

[52] Environment Act 1995, s.108(4)(f).

[53] Environment Act 1995, s.108(4)(e).

[54] Environment Act 1995, s.108(4)(j).

[55] Environment Act 1995, s.110(1), (2)(a), etc: the obstruction offence can be tried on indictment, with a maximum penalty of two years' imprisonment (the Environment Act 1995, s.110(4)(a)(ii)).

[56] See, by way of example as regards a charge of breach of the then Water Resources Act 1991, s.85(1) (causing entry into controlled waters of polluting matter) (see now the Environmental Permitting Regulations, regs 12 and 38) *Environment Agency v Biffa Waste Services Ltd* [2006] 3 All E.R. (D) 355 (Mar).

[57] cf. the Insolvency Act 1986, Sch.B1, para.100(2) as to specific allocation of functions where more than one person is appointed as administrator.

EU definitions with their own independent scope of application and to which any national law is subject.[58] As further discussed below, these considerations may involve fundamental questions as to the applicability in the context of EU law of domestic protection/immunities from suit for administrators and receivers in relation to their status as "agents" for the company and/or under statute (see para.26–023, below).

(a) Domestic Law[59]

(i) Powers to manage

26–010   In terms of the objectives of their appointment, an administrator appointed under Pt II and Sch.B1 of the Insolvency Act 1986 is not in the same position as an administrative receiver operating pursuant to the provisions of Pt III of the Act. The latter was primarily appointed to realise the company's assets for the benefit of the secured creditor whereas the former was appointed to manage the affairs of the company.[60] Although administration is intended to be "only an interim and temporary regime"[61] and is "not to remain in force for a long time",[62] it is "designed to revive, and to seek the continued life of the company if at all possible".[63]

Generally a receiver will be granted powers under the debenture to manage the company's property, including with a view to carrying on the business and selling it as a going concern.

Such powers generally enable the management of the company's property to be taken out of the hands of the directors and entrusted to the person chosen or so appointed.[64] It has been said that "[t]he receiver replaces the board as the person having the authority to exercise the company's powers",[65] and also that the appointment puts the powers of the directors to control the business of the company in abeyance during the period of receivership.[66] This situation may be material for understanding how the position of a receiver or administrator would be considered under EU law as to "operating" or "controlling" plant, installations or occupational activities, and/or whether they are therefore the person in national law to whom "decisive economic power" has been delegated, as to which see further below.

26–011   Although, therefore, the appointment of an administrator or receiver does not of itself terminate the office of director,[67] such loss of control may entail

---

[58] See, for an example of the application of both concepts under a single EU legal act, *Re Eurofood IFSC Ltd* (C-341/04) [2006] Ch. 508 (ECJ) on Regulation (EC) No.1346/2000 on insolvency proceedings [2000] OJ L160/1. See Ch.31.

[59] See Ch.8 for a more detailed discussion on "Taking Control" and the incidents attaching to the positions of administrators and receivers.

[60] *Astor Chemical Ltd v Synthetic Technology Ltd* [1990] B.C.C. 97.

[61] *Re Atlantic Computer Systems Plc* [1992] Ch. 505 (CA), 528, per Nicholls L.J.

[62] *Re Arrows* [1992] B.C.C. 131, 135.

[63] *Re MTI Trading Systems Ltd* [1998] B.C.C. 400 (CA), 402 per Saville L.J.

[64] See *Re Joshua Shaw & Sons* (1989) 5 B.C.C. 188, 190.

[65] See *Village Cay Marina Ltd v Acland* [1998] 2 B.C.L.C. 327 (PC), 333, per Lord Hoffmann.

[66] *Moss Steamship Company Ltd v Whinney* [1912] A.C. 254 (HL), 263 per Lord Atkinson.

[67] See also *Re Barton Manufacturing Co Ltd* [1998] B.C.C. 827, 828.

the conclusion that the directors themselves are unlikely to be able to act to safeguard the interests of creditors. It may be that such a situation as regards the directors means that they are unable to act to safeguard, protect or act in relation to interests of other third parties and/or the environment. The implication that arises in such circumstances is that it is the receiver or administrator who is in such a position.

(ii)   Tortious liability—general

As set out further in Chs 13 and 14 above, receivers and administrators may be   **26–012** personally liable if they have committed a tort, or assumed a personal responsibility for the acts constituting the tort, or where they ordered or procured the commission of the tort by the company. So, for example, liability for the tort of waste may arise if that resulted from an act carried out on the instructions of the receiver or administrator.[68]

5. ENVIRONMENTAL ASSETS AND LIABILITIES

The history of industrial development in the United Kingdom has left a legacy   **26–013** of contamination.[69] Concerns over contamination are likely to arise when administrators and receivers are required to deal with land and buildings that were used for industrial operations, particularly in the nineteenth century and down to the post-Second World War period (when environmental protection controls were minimal to non-existent). It was only with the passing of the Environmental Protection Act 1990 (EPA), with the introduction of a regime aimed at integrated permitting for the potentially most polluting processes, and the conversion of waste disposal licences to waste management licences with attendant higher standards for regulating waste management, that rigorous controls over industrial processes were uniformly imposed on industrial sites and activities.

As a result, when, for example, acting as receiver or administrator over land and other assets of a company active in or on a site of former industrial manufacture care is required to be taken so that a proper appraisal of likely adverse effects from past activities and those continuing is carried out. Moreover, when an industrial site is operational, in order to protect administrators and receivers from possible direct personal liability, it may be that even standard acts of administrators and receivers, such as discharging employee contracts, are not to be effected in such a manner that no practical controls over any continuing adverse impact on the environment are provided for, or that adverse effects on

---

[68] cf. *Mancetter Developments v Garmanson* [1986] Q.B. 1212 (CA).

[69] See also the discussion in *Circular Facilities (London) Ltd v Sevenoaks District Council* [2005] Env. L.R. 35; and *R. (on the application of National Grid Gas Plc (previously Transco Plc)) v Environment Agency* [2006] 1 W.L.R. 3041, reversed as to the determination of liability of *Transco Plc* by the House of Lords at [2007] 1 W.L.R. 1780; and the Defra 2010 Consultation Paper referred to at fn.161 below.

the environment are caused.[70] Many industrial activities operate subject to
trade effluent consents providing for discharges to public sewers issued by
sewerage undertakers under the Water Industry Act 1991, Pt IV, Ch.III, or
under discharge consents for discharges to controlled waters issued by the
Agency under the Environmental Permitting Regulations. If a receiver or
administrator fails to take adequate steps to prevent breach of the consent
conditions, he may make himself liable for "causing" or for "knowingly
permitting" an offence contrary to the Environmental Permitting Regulations
2010, regs 12 and 38.

26–014   Moreover, much of industrial land may well have been contaminated
such that the state of the land itself poses an actual or potential present or
future risk of adversely affecting other land and/or controlled waters. The
Contaminated Land Regime introduced in the EPA, Pt IIA is outlined
below, with reference to its specific provision for protection of insolvency
practitioners.

As indicated above, most activities likely to have an adverse impact on the
environment are now subject to some form of environmental regulatory
control. One key issue for administrators and receivers is whether an environmental permit is required for the activities in question and has been obtained.
For example, if the company is producing and handling waste itself on its own
site, does it have an Environmental Permit under the Environmental Permitting
Regulations? If the company operates a "water-hungry" activity, such as a
golf-course or food or beverages production, and has its own source of water,
has an abstraction licence been obtained and if so, is it being complied with? In
any such case, if the answer is "no", not only might the asset have potentially
a lower value but whatever activities are ongoing could well be illegal or be
being conducted illegally.

26–015   Such environmental permits are transferable in that the person identifiable
as "operator" of the permit may alter[71] and are, in principle, as between transferor and transferee transferable for valuable consideration,[72] although now
most if not all such transfers are subject to the approval of the environmental
regulator. Provision is also made for environmental permits to be varied,[73]

---

[70] cf. *Environment Agency v Biffa Waste Services Ltd* [2006] 3 All E.R. (D) 355 (Mar), where
the Divisional Court indicated that close attention needed to be paid to exactly what responsibility
was accepted or assumed by, in that case, a contractor, and for that purpose suggested that the
courts should look to documents of appointment in considering liability for "causing" or "knowingly permitting" pollution of controlled waters.

[71] See generally as regards Environmental Permits, the Environmental Permitting Regulations,
reg.21, with Sch.5, Pt 1; and the Water Resources Act, s.59 as regards abstraction and impounding
licences.

[72] See, acknowledging this in the case of waste management licences under the Environmental
Protection Act—*Re Celtic Extraction Ltd (In Liquidation); Re Bluestone Chemicals Ltd (In
Liquidation)* [2001] Ch. 475 (CA), but the principle should apply to all types of environmental
permits.

[73] See, generally, the Environmental Permitting Regulations 2010, reg.20; and for abstraction
and impounding licences—Water Resources Act, s.59 (and see also the Water Resources
(Abstraction and Impounding) Regulations 2006 (SI 2006/641)).

suspended,[74] revoked[75] and surrendered[76]—all situations that may affect the value of the permits themselves and likewise of the assets or business in relation to which they apply. Furthermore, generally, the fact that a particular commercial operation cannot lawfully continue without (i) the permit and (ii) compliance with its terms means that consideration must be given to retention of the permit and ongoing compliance with the permit conditions in order to realise a sale as a going concern and/or to avoid civil and/or criminal liabilities arising for the receiver or administrator.

Environmental permits may therefore have a positive value. It may also be noted specifically with regard to abstraction licences that they have value also in that the rights granted thereunder may be transferred as to part only, with an apportionment being made as between "rights" entitlement holders.[77] Environment permits are often (especially in relation to activities subject to the Environmental Permitting Regulations) expensive to obtain,[78] so that surrendering a permit where that is an option may reduce the attractiveness of the assets where the assets cannot be operated commercially without a new permit being obtained.

Contrariwise, it may also be that the permit conditions have been breached **26–016** in the past and/or that there are ongoing unlawful activities being carried out in breach of permit conditions. Even where permit conditions are not being breached, a permit condition requiring remediation of the land after operations at the site have concluded[79] may mean that the asset is onerous property. All may reduce the value of the assets available overall.

6. EUROPEAN UNION ENVIRONMENTAL LAW

(a) EU law—general relevance and potential application to the operations of administrators and receivers

This section sets out general considerations of EU law the purpose of which is **26–017** to provide the framework for the review that follows and then to address specific issues under EU environmental law of particular interest or concern for administrators and receivers.

---

[74] See, generally, the Environmental Permitting Regulations 2010, reg.37.

[75] See, generally, the Environmental Permitting Regulations 2010, reg.22.

[76] See, generally, the Environmental Permitting Regulations 2010, regs 24–25.

[77] See Water Resources Act 1991, s.59D. See also the Environment Agency's website on "Accessing Water Resources" for indications of how the Agency will operate this scheme of apportionment as authorised regulator—*http://www.environment-agency.gov.uk/static/documents/Business/wrt_leaflet_1875063.pdf.*

[78] To obtain an Environmental Permit for the operation of a new or extended part of a landfill an operator may well expect to pay upwards of some £150,000 for investigations and external expert input.

[79] As has been the case as a standard provision for what were formerly PPC Permits or Landfill Permits—but this stricture may have been alleviated with regard to such permits and licences as Environmental Permits under the Environmental Permitting Regulations, reg.25, and Sch.5, Pt 1, para.14.

Much of environmental law in the United Kingdom is now driven by or required pursuant to EU law, principally through EU directives. Directives may be a direct source of rights and obligations that may be applied by or against administrators and receivers in the event of their non-implementation in full or at all in the United Kingdom. This may be particularly pertinent where the insolvency practitioner is a court-appointed practitioner or otherwise an officer of the court as such a person may be considered to be an element of the state, likewise for persons such as special administrators appointed in respect of operators like the water or sewerage undertakers,[80] and administrative receivers of entities such as companies wholly-owned by elements of the state such as local authorities.

National legislation implementing those directives must be construed so as to achieve the end intended, such intention to be deduced from the spirit and wording of the directives. Therefore, definitions in national legislation of persons such as "operators" of plant and installations as well as "holder" or "producer" must be construed and applied in accordance with EU law.

26–018 Article 288 of the Treaty on the Functioning of the European Union (TFEU) requires the United Kingdom to transpose EU directives into national law by way of legally binding provisions which safeguard the rights and obligations imposed by the directives. In implementing a directive, as transposed into national law, the United Kingdom must respect and act compatibly with general principles of EU law. These principles[81] include the principle of effectiveness,[82] of legal certainty,[83] and of proportionality.[84] In addition, where one is dealing with environmental directives, implementation of such directives must respect the principles of the European Union's Environmental Policy in arts 191–193 TFEU, such as the principle that pollution be rectified as a priority at source, that the polluter pays, and the principle that any burdens (including as to costs or expenditure) lawfully able to be imposed under a directive are in any event only those that are necessary.

In the absence of specific national legislation compatible with the principle of legal certainty under EU law[85] and/or statutory authority compatible with EU law, the competent authorities in the United Kingdom lack legal authority to impose obligations asserted to be necessary to implement a directive. This applies especially where breach of such a condition entails criminal liability.[86]

---

[80] See the Water Industry Act 1991 (WIA), ss.24 et seq, and see Ch.8 above more generally on supplies by utilities.

[81] See further here the specialist work, T. Tridimas, *General Principles of EU Law*, 2nd edn (Oxford: Oxford University Press, 2006).

[82] It is a well-established general principle of EU law that EU legislation must be construed and applied so as to ensure the "useful effect" (*effet utile*) of the EU provision in question—see by way of an early example in relation to directives *Grad v Finanzamt Traunstein* (9/70) [1970] E.C.R. 825.

[83] *Commission v Italy* (300/81) [1983] E.C.R. 449, [10].

[84] *R. v Secretary of State for the Environment, Transport and the Regions Ex p. Standley* [1999] Q.B. 1279, [43ff] et seq.

[85] See *Commission v Italy* (300/81) [1983] E.C.R. 449, [10]; and *Commission v Austria* (C-194/01) [2004] E.C.R. I-4579, [39].

[86] See *Criminal Proceedings against Arcaro* (C-168/95) [1996] E.C.R. I-4705, [33]–[38].

A directive may not of itself impose obligations on a private person and may **26–019** not therefore be relied on as such against him.[87] Member States are not able to take advantage of their own wrong in not having transposed a directive in order to try to apply the non-transposed directive in whole or in part against an individual.[88] Similarly a non-transposed directive cannot be used to aggravate or determine a criminal liability.[89] On the other hand, individuals[90] may rely on EU case law to the effect that the provisions of a directive may be taken into account by national courts to review whether the national authority has kept within the limits of discretion left to it by the directive.[91]

However, where provisions of a non-implemented directive meet the requirements for "direct effect" (effectively, that the provision is precise and unconditional, the latter meaning that no further measures are required at EU or national level to crystallise the legal right or obligation in question)[92] such provisions may be applied against or relied on against all elements of the state by an individual, regardless of the capacity in which that element of the state is acting.[93]

In the context especially of privatisation of former state entities such as **26–020** water authorities (now water and/or sewerage undertakers),[94] gas suppliers,[95] electricity providers,[96] and services such as waste disposal,[97] where those entities satisfy the test in *Foster v British Gas Plc*[98]—a body whatever its legal form, which has been made responsible, pursuant to a measure adopted by the State, for providing a public service under the control of the State, and has for that purpose special powers beyond those which result from the normal rules

---

[87] See, among others, *Collino v Telecom Italia SpA* (C-343/98) [2001] All E.R. (EC) 405, [20]; but see *R. (on the application of Wells) v Secretary of State for Transport, Local Government and the Regions* (C-201/02) [2005] All E.R. (EC) 323, [54]–[61] whereby directives may be prayed in aid by a person to their benefit even though its application in that context requires a burden being placed on another where that other is seeking a permission, such as a planning consent, requiring the agreement of a public body thereto and which agreement is conditioned by an EU directive.

[88] See by way of illustration and useful summary, *Gemeente Emmen* (C-468/93) [1996] All E.R. (EC) 372 (ECJ), as per the Advocate General's Opinion, paras 28–34; and *Arcaro* (C-168/95) [1996] E.C.R. I-4705, above fn.86, [33]–[38].

[89] See also *Collino v Telecom Italia SpA* (C-343/98) [2001] All E.R. (EC) 405, [20], above, fn.87; *Niselli* (C-457/02) [2004] E.C.R. I-10853, [20]; and *Mulliez* (C-23/03, C-52/03, C-133/03, C-337/03 and C-473/03) [2006] E.C.R. I-3923, [35].

[90] The word "individual" here includes corporate entities.

[91] See *Luxembourg v Linster* (C-287/98) [2000] E.C.R. I-6917, [28]–[39].

[92] See, e.g. *Becker v Finanzamt Münster-Innenstadt* (8/81) [1982] E.C.R. 53, [25]; *Van Duyn v Home Office* (41/74) [1974] E.C.R. 1337, 1356; and *Pubblico Ministero v Ratti* (148/78) [1979] E.C.R. 1629, 1651.

[93] *Marshall v Southampton and South West Hampshire AHA (No.1)* (C-152/84) [1986] Q.B. 401, [49]; and *Foster v British Gas Plc* (C-188/89) [1991] 1 Q.B. 405 (ECJ).

[94] See the Water Act 1989, the Water Resources Act 1991 and the Water Industry Act 1991.

[95] See the Gas Act 1986.

[96] (including nuclear electricity power generators)—see the Electricity Act 1989.

[97] See the previously applicable provisions in the Environmental Protection Act 1990, s.32 and Sch.10. However, note that from October 18, 2005, this section and Schedule ceased to have effect—see the Clean Neighbourhoods and Environmental Act 2005, ss.47, 107 and Sch.5, Pt 4. It is unclear what, if any, effect this may have on the status otherwise of existing wholly-owned Local Authority Waste Disposal Companies (LAWDCs).

[98] *Foster v British Gas Plc* (C-188/89) [1991] 1 Q.B. 405.

applicable in relations between individuals[99]—then the operations of such privatised entities, in relation to the services they supply within the application of the test, also come within the direct application of non-implemented (elements of) directives.

In the case of privatised water utilities, the courts here have already held that direct reliance may be placed by an individual on non-implemented directives.[100] An ECJ Advocate General has held that the provision of utilities operations by municipal undertakings under the control of municipalities comes within this extensive application of non-implemented directives.[101]

It is suggested that where, under the Environmental Protection Act 1990, Pt II, s.32 a Local Authority Waste Disposal Company (LAWDC) was created, and that body remains under the control of the local authority, the LAWDC remains an element of the state for these purposes. This is a matter of practical importance for administrators and receivers as it has been held that LAWDCs may be put into administration.[102]

26–021 It is considered that court-appointed insolvency practitioners are likely to be considered as elements of the state, and hence bodies against whom non-implemented directives may be applied directly. In any event, it is suggested that if not, the statutory position of the latter is such that they may well otherwise satisfy the Foster test anyway[103] (see further above—para.26–020). It is possible that the insolvency practitioners defined in the Insolvency Act 1986, Sch.B1 as "officers of the court" are likewise liable to be considered as elements of the state for this purpose.

The ECJ has held in the *Marleasing* case[104] that where a Member State has failed to transpose a directive, all elements of the state come under an obligation to interpret "as far as possible" national law in the area in question so as to seek to give effect to the spirit and wording of the directive. If court-appointed insolvency practitioners are elements of the state for this purpose, they will be obliged to respect this obligation directly. The same will apply if administrators appointed under the Insolvency Act 1986, s.8 and Sch.B1 are all "officers of the court" to the same effect. In any event, the relevant national provisions would be subject to the *Marleasing* principles should the relevant issue go to court.

Marleasing is concerned with a case where: (i) a Member State has failed to transpose in whole or in part a directive and; (ii) that failure is to the possible detriment of an individual. The interpretation obligation applies only so as to protect the rights of individuals.[105] It does not operate so as to enable elements

---

[99] *Foster v British Gas Plc* (C-188/89) [1991] 1 Q.B. 405 (ECJ), [19]–[20].

[100] *Griffin v South West Water Services Ltd* [1995] I.R.L.R. 15; and *Bowden v South West Water Services Ltd* [1999] 3 C.M.L.R. 180 (CA).

[101] *Kampelmann v Landsschaftsband Westfalen-Lippe* (C-235–C-258/96) [1997] E.C.R. I-6907, 6918 per Advocate-General Jacobs.

[102] *Environment Agency v Clark (administrator)* [2001] Ch. 57 (CA).

[103] See also the Court of Appeal, taking a wide approach to state entities for this purpose, *NUT v St Mary's Church of England School* [1997] 3 C.M.L.R. 630 (CA), 635, per Schiemann L.J., as he then was.

[104] *Marleasing* (C-106/89) [1990] E.C.R. I-4135.

[105] *Arcaro* (C-168/95) [1996] E.C.R. I-4705, [33]–[38], above, fn.86.

of the state, including the courts, to apply non-transposed parts of a directive against an individual[106] so as to increase the burdens on an individual.[107]

(i) Creation of rights and obligations for individuals under EU Law

There are various instances where the ECJ has held that EU environmental **26–022** directives are intended to give rise to rights and obligations for individuals which individuals may enforce directly or indirectly—directly, in the sense of reliance on the concept of "direct effect" against the (elements of the) State, or by way of the *Marleasing* interpretative rule; and indirectly, where individuals can rely on the directive to require or resist acts of elements of the state in violation of the terms of a directive's requirements imposed on the State.[108]

Such situations have arisen, for example, in relation to the Groundwater Directive 80/68/EEC[109] in a case against Germany[110]; in the case of the Environmental Impact Assessment Directive 85/337/EEC[111]; the Wild Birds Directive 79/409/EEC[112]; Air Quality Directive 80/779/EEC[113]; the Nitrates Directive 91/676/EEC[114]; the Dangerous Substances Directive 76/464/EEC[115]; the Waste Framework Directive 75/442/EEC.[116]

(b) Specific considerations

(i) "Operator"

To identify whether the term "operator" in an EU directive might apply to **26–023** administrators or receivers it is necessary to consider the context of the instrument in question and the terminology used. As indicated above, the terminology varies between directives.

The core question is whether EU terms such as "operator" are solely an EU law term, in which case national definitions are not decisive but an autonomous EU meaning will apply. Whether the term is defined by EU law and/or national law depends on whether there is: (i) an express reference to national law—such as in the Landfill Directive 99/31/EC—"the natural or legal person

---

[106] See *Arcaro* (C-168/95) [1996] E.C.R. I-4705, [33]–[38], above, fn.86.

[107] This may be relevant, e.g. to situations within the Environmental Liability Directive 2004/35/EC (as to which see below), which has been transposed by the United Kingdom after a delay of nearly two years.

[108] *Aannamaersbedrijf PK Kraaijveld BV ea v Gedeputeerde Staten van Zuid-Holland* (C-72/95) [1996] E.C.R. I-5403, 5403.

[109] [1980] OJ L20/43. With Directive 2006/118/EC [2006] OJ L372/19.

[110] *Commission v Germany* (131/88) [1991] E.C.R. I-825, [7].

[111] [1985] OJ L175/40, but since significantly amended: consolidated text is at *http://eur-lex.europa.eu/LexUriServ/LexUriServ.do?uri=CONSLEG:1985L0337:20090625:EN:PDF.*

[112] [1979] OJ L103/1. And see *R. v Secretary of State Ex p. RSPB* (C-44/95) [1997] Q.B. 206.

[113] [1980] OJ L229/30. And see *Commission v Germany* (361/88) [1991] E.C.R. I-2567.

[114] [1991] OJ L375/1. And see *Ex p. Standley* (C-293/97) [1999] Q.B. 1279 (ECJ).

[115] [1976] OJ L129/23 (since repealed by Directive 2006/11/EC [2006] OJ L64/52. And see *Commission v Ireland* (C-282/02) [2005] E.C.R. I-4653 (ECJ).

[116] [1975] OJ L194/39, since repealed. See now Directive 2008/98/EC [2008] OJ L312/2; and see *Commission v Greece* (C-387/97) [2000] E.C.R. I-5047.

responsible for a landfill in accordance with the internal legislation of the
Member State where the landfill is located" (art.2(1)); (ii) necessarily a reference to the status of such a person in national law because there is no need for
an autonomous EU definition—cf. the *Eurofood IFSC* case[117]; (iii) the term is
necessarily or by implication an autonomous EU law one[118]; and/or (iv) the
reference to national law requires that the national law comprises sufficient
content so as to meet the intended EU objective in relation to the terminology
used and ensure the "result to be achieved". It is considered that, at least as
regards use of the term "operator" in the IPPC Directive, and the Environmental
Liability Directive, at least possibility (iii) or (iv) should apply.

It is a fundamental point in EU law that the obligation as to implementation of
a directive is as to the "result to be achieved"[119] and always to ensure the effectiveness of the directive in any event. Hence, using the Landfill Directive definition as illustration, is the reference to "the person responsible" one that remains,
in the case of a company holding an environmental permit for a landfill, a reference to the company notwithstanding that an administrator has been appointed,
or is that a reference to the administrator per se? It is suggested that such terminology in EU law is a reference to the person who is in a position to and who
takes or is deemed to have taken "responsibility" for the landfill. That question
is likely to be fundamentally one of fact applying domestic law but aiming to
ensure that the essence of the required "responsibility" provided for under the
directive is met, with its resolution in any given case ultimately turning on the
extent to which the administrator or receiver has displaced/replaced the directors
and their ability to take decisions as regards the running of the landfill (including
by reference to the availability of funds to this end) for the purposes of meeting
the obligations intended to be imposed by the Landfill Directive on "operators".
That could mean that an administrator or receiver is the "person responsible",
and the fact that under English law they may be regarded/deemed as agent of the
company may not suffice to protect against a direct personal responsibility.

26–024   The Environmental Permitting Regulations, reg.7 suggests that the words
"has control" includes at least "operates" for the purposes of the environmental
directives indicated above. Were it otherwise the United Kingdom would be
taken to have breached its obligations to implement the directive, and it is to be
assumed that the United Kingdom acts so as to ensure compliance with its EU
obligations. However, the terminology of "has control" suggests a broader,
functional objective, especially when contrasted/compared with the term
"operates" in the IPPC Directive. Bearing in mind the need for national implementing legislation to be construed as far as possible so as to give effect to the

---

[117] *Re Eurofood IFSC* (C-341/04) [2006] Ch. 508 (ECJ), and above, para.26–009.
[118] See *Re Eurofood IFSC Ltd* (C-341/04) [2006] Ch. 508 (ECJ). According to settled case-law,
the terms used in a provision of EU law which makes no express reference to the law of the
Member States for the purpose of determining its meaning and scope are normally to be given
throughout the EU an autonomous and uniform interpretation which must take into account the
context of the provision and the purpose of the legislation in question—see, to this effect, *Ekro*
(327/82) [1984] E.C.R. 107, [11]; *Luxembourg v Linster* (C-287/98) [2000] E.C.R. I-6917, [43];
and *R. (on the application of Wells) v Secretary of State for Transport, Local Government and the
Regions* (C-201/02) [2004] E.C.R. I-723, [37].
[119] *Commission v UK* (C-337/89) [1992] E.C.R. I-6103, [24].

spirit and wording of a directive—see the interpretative obligation under Marleasing—and the need for directives to ensure their effet utile—it is likely that it is the wider meaning that should be that applied by the national courts.[120]

Those considerations suggest that it may well be that an administrator or receiver is a person who "has control" for these purposes. That, in turn, may well suggest that the protection offered by their position as "agent" may not suffice to deflect otherwise personal liability onto the company. That position may attain all the more strongly if it can be said that the correct analysis of the status as "agent" of receivers is "simply in order to free the debenture-holders who appointed him from responsibility for his acts".[121] Attaching personal liability in circumstances described above need not interfere with that established purpose, and may be said to promote achievement of the goal of effective environmental protection intended under the EU environmental directives[122] (and national implementing law). However, this analysis raises the further question as to its effect on the validity of the status of an administrative receiver as agent where that status is "deemed" by statute.[123]

In the context of the definition of "operator", the scope of the words—"or, where this is provided for in national legislation, to whom decisive economic power over the technical functioning of the installation has been delegated" is unclear. It is not obvious that this attribution of responsibility must be one of a choice expressed as such in national legislation, rather than be one arising from the situation obtaining in national law. For example, does it necessarily cover administrators in the light of case law suggesting that, whilst an administrator may seek guidance of the court in the light of a substantial change in the circumstances which led to the making of the administration order, he should not seek the court's guidance on making "commercial decisions"?[124]   **26–025**

A major concern as to the possible extensive meaning of "operator" for these purposes may arise in such cases. It may be that an administrator or receiver has a right to be indemnified in relation to any such liabilities arising, in particular where they are to be quantified in monetary terms. However, if personal liability attaches due to EU law, will that indemnity extend to cover such liabilities? Moreover, if a liability attaches under EU law where such a liability would not apply otherwise under domestic law, and the indemnity applies, might this operate to reduce the monies available for distribution and grant a priority over (other) creditors?   **26–026**

[120] See also above, at para.26–021.
[121] *Lawson v Hosemaster* [1965] 1 W.L.R. 1399, 1410 per Cross J. reversed on appeal [1966] 1 W.L.R. 1300 (CA). This point may apply with greater vigour if it is accepted in England and Wales that a statement that a company should "alone be personally liable" for the acts and defaults of a receiver is one that applies as between the debenture-holder and the company, so as not to exempt a liability, there, under statute—see *Hill Samuel & Co Ltd v Laing* (1988) 4 B.C.C. 9 (Court of Session, Outer House), and see above, Ch.13. See, too, the points made with reference to fn.118.
[122] See, e.g. *ARCO Chemie Nederland* (C-418/97 and C-419/97) [2002] Q.B. 646, [36]–[40].
[123] See the Insolvency Act 1986, s.44(1)(a), and more generally s.8, Sch.B1, para.69.
[124] See *Re CE King* [2000] 2 B.C.L.C. 297, per Neuberger J. The same questions arise in relation to the Environmental Liability Directive (as to which see below).

(ii) "Holder" and "producer"

26–027 These concepts apply in relation to the revised Waste Framework Directive 2008/98/EEC,[125] and as regards the management of "waste". Under the directive, "holder" means "the producer of waste or the natural or legal person who is in possession of it". "Producer" means "anyone whose activities produce waste ("the original producer") and/or anyone who carries out pre-processing, mixing or other operations resulting in a change in the nature or composition of the waste".

"Producer" might have been thought only to include those with an active involvement in production (and the associated activities mentioned). However, in 2004 the ECJ ruled that where conduct leading to waste being discarded "can be attributed to the conduct" of an undertaking that undertaking may be considered to be the "holder", and with it, the "producer" of the waste.[126] The case concerned inter alia whether a petroleum company supplying petrol to a service station with which it had a contractual management arrangement with an individual might be a holder or producer of waste comprising soil contaminated by hydrocarbons from leaking petrol storage tanks at the service station. The ECJ considered that the directive required the term "holder" to be broadly defined, and that "the activities of the undertaker [petroleum company]" could be considered to have produced waste if the state of the tanks and the leak of the hydrocarbons could "be attributed to a disregard of contractual obligations" by the petroleum company or "to any actions which could render [it] liable".

26–028 Where administrators or receivers take over the operation of contracts, this case suggests that a liability may attach to them for their disregard of the contractual obligations. Again, this comes back to the extent of control accepted/assumed by an administrator or receiver in the circumstances of the case.

The ECJ also seemed to consider that the term "possession" was to be construed widely and not confined to physical possession or the right to call for immediate physical possession.[127]

7. LIABILITY REGIMES

(a) Civil and administrative[128] liability regimes for environmental torts common law liability

26–029 It is a fundamental principle of the common law that a damaged party can claim redress if his private interests have been harmed by the act or omissions

---

[125] See fn.116.
[126] *Re Van de Walle, Texaco Belgium SA* (C-1/03) [2005] All E.R. (EC) 1139, [57]–[61].
[127] *Re Van de Walle, Texaco Belgium SA* (C-1/03) [2005] All E.R. (EC) 1139, [55].
[128] By "administrative" here is intended the regime providing for acts from public bodies imposing obligations on third parties which do not equate with civil regime controls such as injunctions or with criminal law convictions and court-sanctioned penalties or orders. Such administrative controls include abatement notices under the Environmental Protection Act 1990, s.80; or enforcement notices under the Environmental Permitting Regulations, reg.36 in the case of Environmental Permits.

of another. Such liability can arise at common law including under the following headings:

(a) Private nuisance: this arises where an activity, generally on the defendant's land, represents an unlawful interference with the claimant's land including use or enjoyment of his land. The defendant is usually the person who caused the nuisance, but an occupier can be liable for continuing or adopting a nuisance, if he knows or ought to know of the nuisance, and is in a position where it would be possible for him to prevent it.[129]

(b) Public nuisance: this arises where the defendant's nuisance affects the public. It is primarily a crime,[130] which is prosecuted by the Attorney General or local authority,[131] but it can also found an action in tort by a private citizen who has suffered particular damage.[132]

(c) *Rylands v Fletcher*[133]: this principle provides for strict liability for damage caused by the escape of hazardous substances held on the defendant's land.[134]

As a matter of domestic law, absent EU law considerations, as regards tort liability (not for these purposes including trespass)[135] it seems generally accepted that acts of an administrator or receiver in the guise as "agent" and for the purposes of carrying out the function of agent will not per se attract a personal liability.[136] For tortious liability to attach the administrator or receiver must have ordered or procured the commission of the tortious acts by the company.[137]

As a result, it is a question of fact and degree whether, in the context of individual torts, in particular those which might be characterised as "environmental torts", the acts or omissions attributable to an administrator or receiver constitute the tort.

26–030

---

[129] *Sedleigh-Denfield v O'Callaghan* [1940] A.C. 880 (HL).

[130] Although, it was long accepted that public nuisance was appropriately a strict liability crime: see *Sherras v De Rutzen* [1895] 1 Q.B. 918; in *R v Rimmington, R v Goldstein* [2006] 1 A.C. 459, the House of Lords considered the requirement for mens rea to be established by the prosecution.

[131] e.g. *Att Gen v PYA Quarries Ltd (No.1)* [1957] 2 Q.B. 169 (CA).

[132] e.g. *Halsey v Esso Petroleum Co Ltd* [1961] 1 W.L.R. 683; and *Tate & Lyle Industries v Greater London Council* [1983] 2 A.C. 509 (HL).

[133] *Rylands v Fletcher* (1868) L.R. 3 H.L. 330 (HL).

[134] There had been discussion whether this tort should be subsumed fully within nuisance, but this assimilation was rejected by the House of Lords in *Transco Plc v Stockport MBC* [2004] 2 A.C. 1 (HL).

[135] Trespass appears generally to be treated differently—see further at Chs 12 and 13.

[136] *Mancetter Developments v Garmanson* [1986] Q.B. 1212 (CA); *Williams v Natural Life Ltd* [1998] 1 W.L.R. 830 (HL).

[137] *Mancetter Developments v Garmanson* [1986] Q.B. 1212 (CA). cf. the interesting discussion by Briggs J. on the application of this case to nuisance, suggesting a possible lesser risk of liability for administrators, in his interlocutory Judgment in *John Smith & Company (Edinburgh) Ltd v Richard John Hill* [2010] 2 B.C.L.C. 556, [36]–[37] by reference to *MCA Records Inc v Charly Records Ltd (No.5)* [2002] B.C.C. 650 (CA).

Nuisance is a tort to land[138] and an interference with rights over land[139] arising from a non-reasonable use of land. Private nuisance may be one or other of three types: (1) nuisance by encroachment on a neighbour's land; (2) nuisance by direct physical injury to a neighbour's land; and (3) nuisance by interference with a neighbour's quiet enjoyment of his land. It has been described as "protean".[140]

Liability in nuisance generally arises as a result of actions by and attributable to those making use of "their" land.[141] Persons liable in nuisance include the actual creator whether or not in occupation of the land from where the nuisance emanates,[142] and a wrongdoer may create the nuisance also by servants, agents or otherwise.[143] Furthermore, as indicated above, an occupier of land "continues" a nuisance if, with knowledge or presumed knowledge of its existence, he fails to take the reasonable means to bring it to an end with ample time to do so, and he "adopts" it if he makes any use of the ... artificial contrivance which constitutes the nuisance.[144]

It is suggested that the real issues therefore are those of "possession" and/or "control". It is suggested that it is possible, given the potentially wide scope of the powers over and in relation to a company's assets that an administrator or receiver may have, for a liability in nuisance to attach to their acts or omissions so as to render them personally liable to third parties. The same approach should apply to the cause of action under *Rylands v Fletcher*.[145]

(i) Breach of statutory duty

26–031 Some statutes expressly provide for responsibility of administrators and/or receivers. For example, the Mines and Quarries Act 1954, which addresses potential environmental issues in the sense of adverse impact on human health, and indirect effect for the environment from ill-protected mines and quarries, by s.181 provides:

"where the business of a person who, by virtue of the foregoing provisions of this section is, for the purposes of this Act, to be taken to be

---

[138] *Hunter v Canary Wharf Ltd* [1997] A.C. 655 (HL), 695A–B, per Lord Lloyd.

[139] *Hunter v Canary Wharf Ltd* [1997] A.C. 655 (HL), 688E, per Lord Goff.

[140] *Hunter v Canary Wharf Ltd* [1997] A.C. 655 (HL), 723, per Lord Hope, echoing *Sedleigh-Denfield v O'Callaghan* [1940] A.C. 880 (HL). See also *Arscott v Coal Authority* [2005] Env. L.R. 6 (CA), per Laws L.J.

[141] In *Crown River Cruises Ltd v Kimbolton Fireworks Ltd* [1996] 2 Lloyd's Rep. 533, liability attached to owners of a ship stationed temporarily in the Thames, but which was the source of the nuisance in question.

[142] *Hall v Beckenham* [1949] 1 K.B. 716.

[143] *Page Motors v Epsom & Ewell BC* (1981) 125 S.J. 590 (CA); and *Winch v Mid Bedfordshire DC* [2002] All E.R. (D) 380 (Jul).

[144] *Sedleigh-Denfield v O'Callaghan* [1940] A.C. 880 (HL); and *Green v Lord Somerleyton* [2004] 1 P. & C.R. 33 (CA).

[145] "an extension of the law of nuisance"—*Cambridge Water Co v Eastern Counties Leather Plc* [1994] 2 A.C. 264 (HL), although *Rylands v Fletcher* is not to be completely assimilated to nuisance—*Transco Plc v Stockport MBC* [2004] 2 A.C. 1 (HL). Note the general defence in *Rylands v Fletcher* is now "ordinary user"—*Transco Plc v Stockport MBC* [2004] 2 A.C. 1 (HL).

owner of a mine … is carried on by a liquidator, receiver or manager, or by some other person authorised to carry it on by an order of the court of competent jurisdiction, the liquidator, receiver, manager or other person shall be taken for the purposes of this Act to be an additional owner of the mine or quarry."

In the absence of specific mention of administrators or receivers, the position seems to be that where statutory duties are imposed on a person of a given description, for example as broker of waste,[146] and the administrator or receiver "assumes" that role, then liability for breach of the duty may attach personally.[147] However, whether the role has been assumed is one of fact but conclusions as a matter of law, it appears, are those of policy as regards the statutory duty in question.[148] It is therefore important to bear in mind the strong supervisory control that the courts have identified for themselves in assuring stringent protection of the environment, and ensuring that, where possible, there should be someone with responsibility to avoid the damage to the environment or to take responsibility for that damage arising.[149]

For an example, perhaps by way of analogy, in *Lord Advocate v Aero Technologies Ltd*[150] a receiver was appointed by a debenture holder over a factory manufacturing explosives. The Factories Act 1875 imposed a duty on the "occupier" to act with "due precaution" to secure the factory and prevent accidents. When the Health and Safety Executive (HSE) was informed by the receivers that they intended to leave the premises without steps being taken to secure the factory, the HSE sought an interlocutory injunction. The receivers claimed they were mere agents of the company. The Scottish Outer House rejected the claim by the receivers, stating[151] that it was necessary to look at the reality of the situation in determining who the occupier was. The provisions of s.2 of the Explosives Act 1875 were there "in the interests of public safety and should not … be elided on some highly technical ground." Having regard to the fact that they were acting as managers for the company they were for practical purposes in occupation of the premises in order that they carry out their task. Therefore, the court held, the requirement to comply with the statutory duty was a management function and accordingly the court could see no reason

26–032

---

[146] Further to the Environmental Protection Act 1990, s.34(1) on the "duty of care" as regards waste.

[147] cf. *Meigh v Wickenden* [1942] 2 K.B. 160 under the Factories Act 1937.

[148] cf. the statements made in *Lord Advocate v Aero Technologies Ltd (In Receivership)*, 1991 S.L.T. 134 (Court of Session, Outer House); and *Southern Water Authority v Nature Conservancy Council* [1992] 1 W.L.R. 775 (HL), 781 per Lord Mustill.

[149] cf. *National Rivers Authority v Alfred McAlpine Homes (East) Ltd* [1994] 4 All E.R. 286, per Morland J; and *Empress Car Co (Abertillery) Ltd v National Rivers Authority* [1999] 2 A.C. 22 (HL).

[150] *Lord Advocate v Aero Technologies Ltd (In Receivership)*, 1991 S.L.T. 134 (Court of Session, Outer House). It may be said that this case is an example of an injunction being sought in the context of protecting against commission of a criminal liability, although it may also be pointed out that the purpose of the HSE is not simply to prosecute but rather to ensure compliance, where necessary, ahead of time, with health and safety at work. See for further discussion on this and like cases, Jarvis and Fordham, *Lender Liability, Environmental Risk and Debt* (Cameron May, 1993), p.137 et seq.

[151] per Lord Sutherland, at 136.

in principle why the receivers should not be occupiers for the purposes of the statute.

This suggests that the courts will, not surprisingly, consider each statute in its own context and with a view to its particular purpose. The importance of environmental protection is also an obvious "public interest" similar in status and gravity to protection of human health and safety. This can be seen from as far back as 1972 where the offence of pollution of controlled waters contrary to the then Rivers (Prevention of Pollution) Act 1951 s.2(1)[152] was said in *Alphacell Ltd v Woodward*[153] to be one of those "... acts which in the public interest are prohibited under a penalty".[154] This applies equally, if not more so, for the reasons set out above, with respect to legislation intended to implement or give effect to EU environmental directives.[155]

26–033   A "contrast" with this latter case, but exemplifying the importance of the particular facts in their particular statutory context, may be seen in *Midland Bank Ltd v Conway Corp.*[156] In that case the bank had received rent cheques from a tenant to his landlady, which the bank credited to the landlady's account. The local authority sought to impose an abatement notice under the Public Health Act 1936 in respect of the property which had fallen into disrepair and served it on the bank as "owner". Section 343 of the Act defined "owner" as the person for the time being receiving the rackrent of the premises ... whether on his own account or as agent or trustee for any other person". The local magistrates made the bank subject to a nuisance order as the bank had not complied with the abatement notice. On a case stated the bank was successful, the court holding that the bank had merely acted as a "conduit pipe". The court did, however, suggest that there might be "special circumstances" in another situation that could have brought the bank "into such a special relationship with the freeholder as to constitute them her agents for the purposes of this section." In this context, the court said that application to the bank of the term "owner" was artificial here as it had "nothing to do with whether the person served is capable of abating the nuisance or has the authority to abate the nuisance".

The case suggests that the status of agent would not have prevented service of the abatement notice. In fact, the Divisional Court has subsequently held that where a person receiving rent is a "true managing agent", he may be a person on whom an abatement notice may properly be served under the

---

[152] See, now, more comprehensively, the Water Resources Act 1991, s.85.

[153] *Alphacell Ltd v Woodward* [1972] A.C. 824 (HL).

[154] *Alphacell Ltd v Woodward* [1972] A.C. 824 (HL), 832, per Viscount Dilhorne, citing *Sweet v Parsley* [1970] A.C. 132 (HL), 149. It was also said in that case that such offences were "not criminal in any real sense". It is suggested that it would not now be considered that pollution of controlled waters was "not criminal in any real sense"—cf. for views tending now to the contrary, *National Rivers Authority v Alfred McAlpine Homes (East) Ltd* [1994] 4 All E.R. 286, per Morland J. and *Empress Car Co (Abertillery) Ltd v National Rivers Authority* [1999] 2 A.C. 22 (HL), 32 per Lord Hoffmann.

[155] Given, particularly, the intent to provide for rights for and protection of individuals, and see, by way of example, *Commission v Italy* (262/85) [1987] E.C.R. 3073, [9]; *ARCO Chemie Nederland* (C-418/97 and C-419/97) [2000] E.C.R. I-4475, [36]–[40]; and *Commission v Germany* (C-98/03) [2006] E.C.R. I-53.

[156] *Midland Bank Ltd v Conway Corp* [1965] 1 W.L.R. 1165.

Environmental Protection Act 1990, s.80.[157] The Environmental Protection Act 1990, s.81A(9) provides: "in this section—'owner', in relation to any premises, means a person (other than a mortgagee not in possession) who, whether in his own right or as trustee for any other person, is entitled to receive the rack rent of the premises or, where the premises are not let at a rack rent, would be so entitled if they were so let …" It would then be for the agent to have recourse, if available, to the defence of "reasonable excuse" for not having complied. The court was referred to the *Conway* case, and discussed it, but must have considered that a "true" managing agent did have the capabilities and authority the absence of which had led the court in *Conway* to reject application of the section to the bank.

(ii)   The Contaminated Land Regime[158]

The Environment Act 1995 (the EA) amended the Environmental Protection   **26–034** Act 1990 to introduce a new regime to deal with contaminated land.[159] This is an area of environmental liability most likely to arise for administrators and receivers under domestic law.[160] Whilst this has been and currently is likely to be of particular concern to them where dealing with land previously within the ownership or control of predecessors of privatised industries or utilities, proposed changes by Defra in December 2010 to the statutory and other guid-ance[161] which drives this regime may well mean that fewer sites are designated "contaminated land"—see further below.[162]

Contaminated land is presently defined as land which appears to the local authority for the relevant district to be: in such a condition, by reason of substances in, on or under the land, that (a) significant harm is being caused or there is a significant possibility of such harm being caused; or (b) pollution of

---

[157] *Camden LBC v Gunby* [2000] 1 W.L.R. 465.

[158] Reference may still usefully be made to more detailed works such as Tromans and Turrall-Clarke, *Contaminated Land: The New Regime* (London: Sweet & Maxwell, 2000), although this latter work may need to be reviewed in light of any amendments by Defra to the contaminated land regime, likely to take place in 2011.

[159] The provisions are contained in/provided for by the Environmental Act 1995, s.57, which was brought into force by the Environment Act 1995 (Commencement No.16 and Saving Provision) (England) Order 2000 (SI 2000/340).

[160] Defra estimates as drawn from its 2010 December Consultation Document on reform of the guidance on the regime put an average cost of some £250k per hectare.

[161] The Defra Consultation Document is at *http://www.defra.gov.uk/corporate/consult/contami-nated-land/101215-contaminated-land-condoc.pdf.*

[162] Depending, however, most probably, on the terminology of the statutory provisions regarding the transfer of liabilities to the privatised entities—see *R (on the application of National Grid Plc (formely Transo Plc) v Environment Agency* [2007] 1 W.L.R. 1780. The House of Lords reversed the decision of Forbes J. at [2006] 1 W.L.R. 3041 and held that the Contaminated Land Regime did not operate (at least as regards the transfer of liabilities regarding the national gas provider priva-tised by the Gas Act 1986) to create a deemed retrospective liability. The reach of the House's ruling is likely to be elaborated in subsequent case law as the House did not exclude all liability of a successor under the Contaminated Land Regime regarding other schemes for the transfer of liabilities.

controlled waters[163] is being, or is likely to be, caused.[164] [165] The Secretary of State is empowered to issue guidance on how the local authorities are to exercise their discretion,[166] and questions of what harm or possibility of harm is significant, or when pollution of controlled waters is being or is likely to be, caused, must be determined in accordance with such guidance.[167]

"Harm" is defined as "harm to the health of living organisms or other interference with ecological systems of which living organisms form part and in the case of man, harm to his property.[168]

The Secretary of State has set the threshold of harm at what some have regarded as a pragmatic level, and provided for different degrees of importance to be assigned to different descriptions of living organisms or ecological systems, different places, descriptions of harm to health or property, or other interference.[169] There have been criticisms that the guidance is either too imprecise or misunderstood in application such that more sites than necessary have been designated and/or overly costly remediation has been required from persons who should not have had to pay or to pay as much (see the Defra Consultation Document, at, for example, paras 51–53).

What follows is a brief overview of the current regime, but changes may be adopted in the course of 2011 that reflect the options for change expressed by Defra in its December 2010 Consultation Document.[170]

(iii)   Identification of contaminated land

26–035   Local authorities are under a duty to cause their areas to be inspected from time to time, for the purpose of identifying any contaminated land, and of enabling them to decide whether any such land requires to be designated as a special site.[171] Defra Guidance instructs how such investigations are to be carried out.[172]

---

[163] Note that, in relation to England and Wales, the term "controlled waters" has the same meaning as in Pt III of the Water Resources Act 1991 except that "ground waters" does not include waters contained in underground strata but above the saturation zone", the latter an amendment introduced by the Water Act 2003, s.86.

[164] The Environmental Protection Act 1990, s.78A(2). Note that from a day to be appointed, this sub-paragraph will read "significant pollution of controlled waters is being caused or there is a significant possibility of such pollution being caused."—see the Water Act 2003, s.86, with s.105(3) and (6).

[165] The Defra Consultation Document proposes to activate the amendment noted in the previous footnote. This could materially reduce the number of sites to be designated and to reduce the scope and extent of any required remediation for any such "contaminated land".

[166] See the Environmental Protection Act 1990, ss.78A(2), (5), 78YA, inserted by the Environment Act 1995, s.57.

[167] The present Guidance is in Circular 01/2006, at *http://www.defra.gov.uk/environment/ quality/land/contaminated/documents/circular01–2006.pdf.*

[168] The Environmental Protection Act 1990, s.78A(4).

[169] See the Environmental Protection Act 1990, s.78A(6) and Circular 01/2006.

[170] The Consultation Document is at *http://www.defra.gov.uk/corporate/consult/contaminated-land/101215-contaminated-land-condoc.pdf.* The Consultation closed in March 2011.

[171] The Environmental Protection Act 1990, s.78B(1).

[172] Contaminated Land Inspection Strategies May 2001 at *http://www.defra.govuk/environment/ land/contaminated/pdf/la-inspect.pdf.*

When a local authority identifies contaminated land, it must notify the Agency, the owner of the land, anyone who appears to be in occupation of the land, and anyone who might have to bear the burden of a clean-up operation (as an "appropriate person").[173] The local authority must then decide whether to designate the land as a "special site", after having consulted the Agency.[174]

The criteria for deciding which land is to be designated a special site in set **26–036** out in the Contaminated Land (England) Regulations 2006 (SI 2006/1380).[175] Regulation 2 sets out the relevant criteria, and includes: the fact that land is in such a state that it affects controlled waters used or intended to be for the supply of drinking water, is affected by waste acid tars, is land subject to regulation under the Environmental Permitting Regulations, or is land within a nuclear site or is land used by the Ministry of Defence.

Special sites are to be dealt with by the Agency itself, while non-special site contaminated land will be dealt with by the local authority (in either case, referred to as "the enforcing authority" in this context). When a local authority decides contaminated land in its area is to be designated a special site, it must notify the Agency, the owner of the land,[176] anyone who appears to be an occupier of the land, and anyone who might have to bear the burden of a clean-up operation.[177]

(iv) The remediation notice

Once a local authority has identified land as contaminated,[178] or the land is **26–037** designated a special site,[179] the enforcing authority must serve a remediation notice (or more than one) on each "appropriate person", specifying what that person is to do and how long he has in which to do it,[180] including the proportion they bear as to any remediation costs.[181] The remediation required must be "reasonable", having regard to: "(a) the cost which is likely to be involved; and (b) the seriousness of the harm, or pollution of controlled waters, in question".[182]

(v) The "appropriate person"

Under the statutory scheme, the appropriate person to carry out whatever **26–038** remedial work the enforcing authority considers reasonable (and so to be the

---

[173] Environmental Protection Act 1990, s.78B(3).

[174] Environmental Protection Act 1990, s.78C(1). Secondary legislation adopted pursuant to Pt IIA provides for inter alia when sites are to be regarded as "special sites" for these purposes—see the Contaminated Land (England) Regulations 2006 (SI 2006/1380); and see, too, s.78C(3).

[175] Further to the Environmental Protection Act 1990, s.78C(8), (9), (10) which provided for regard to be had in particular, to the twin tests that: (a) serious harm would or might be caused; or (b) serious pollution of controlled waters would be, or would be likely to be, caused, by reason of substances in, on or under the land.

[176] See below at para.26–038.

[177] Environmental Protection Act 1990, s.78C(1)(b), (2).

[178] Environmental Protection Act 1990, s.78E(1)(b).

[179] Environmental Protection Act 1990, s.78E(1)(a).

[180] Environmental Protection Act 1990, s.78E(1).

[181] Environmental Protection Act 1990, s.78E(3).

[182] Environmental Protection Act 1990, s.78E(4).

recipient of a remediation notice) is in the first instance, the person(s) who caused or knowingly permitted the contaminating substance(s) to be in, on or under the land[183]; or (if no such person can be found), the owner or occupier for the time being of the land in question.[184]

In this context, "owner" in relation to land in England and Wales[185] means:

"a person (other than a mortgagee not in possession) who, whether in his own right or as trustee for any other person, is entitled to receive the rack rent of the land, or, where the land is not let at a rack rent, would be so entitled if it were so let."[186]

(vi)   Timing of a remediation notice

26–039 Where it appears to the enforcing authority that there is imminent danger of serious harm, or of serious pollution of controlled waters, the authority can serve a remediation notice immediately,[187] otherwise, a three-month waiting period applies,[188] during which the enforcing authority must aim to consult any intended recipient of a remediation notice, and the owner and any occupier of the land, as to what is to be done by way of remediation.[189]

(vii)   Appeal against a remediation notice

26–040 A recipient of a remediation notice has 21 days in which to appeal. Appeal is to the Secretary of State.[190]

(viii)   Penalties for non-compliance

26–041 Failure to comply with any of the requirements of a remediation notice without reasonable excuse is an offence.[191] In general, the punishment is a fine not exceeding level 5 on the standard scale and a further daily fine of one-tenth of the level 5 amount.[192] If the contaminated land in question is "industrial trade

---

[183] Environmental Protection Act 1990, s.78F(2). Note that this includes a person who caused or knowingly permitted a substance to be on, in or under the land which has produced a contaminating substance by chemical reaction or biological process: the Environmental Protection Act, s.78F(9). cf. *R. (on the application of National Grid Plc (formely Transco Plc) v Environment Agency* [2007] 1 W.L.R. 1780, where the House of Lords held that liability under the Contaminated Land Regime did not extend to the transfer of liabilities of the national gas provider privatised by the Gas Act 1986.

[184] Environmental Protection Act 1990, s.78F(4), (5).

[185] There is a different definition for Scotland—EPA, s.78A(9).

[186] Environmental Protection Act 1990, s.78A(9).

[187] Environmental Protection Act 1990, s.78H(4).

[188] Environmental Protection Act 1990, s.78H(3) (specifying different notices to trigger the three-month period in different circumstances).

[189] Environmental Protection Act 1990, s.78H(1). This would provide the opportunity, in a non-urgent case, for an insolvency practitioner to disclaim contaminated land as onerous property.

[190] Environmental Protection Act 1990, s.78L(1)(b), and reg.8 of the Contaminated Land (England) Regulations 2006.

[191] Environmental Protection Act 1990, s.78M(1).

[192] Environmental Protection Act 1990, s.78M(3).

or business premises"[193] the punishment is a fine of up to £20,000 together with a daily fine of £2,000.[194]

If the enforcing authority is of the opinion that proceedings for an offence against a person who has failed to comply with the requirements of a remediation notice would be an ineffectual remedy, it may take High Court proceedings to secure compliance with the remediation notice.[195]

(ix) Remedial action by the enforcing authority

The enforcing authority has power to take remedial action itself in certain **26–042** circumstances, for example if: it considers it necessary for the purpose of preventing the occurrence of any serious harm, or serious pollution of controlled waters, of which there is imminent danger[196]; or the recipient of a remediation notice has failed to comply.[197] In such circumstances, the enforcing authority is entitled to recover costs of the remedial works from the appropriate person(s) by way of a charging notice.[198]

(x) The charging notice

The charging notice applies where the enforcing authority decides to recover **26–043** costs of remedial works from a person who is the owner of the land and who caused or knowingly permitted the contamination.[199]

The charging notice carries interest from the date of service until the whole amount is paid[200]; and the costs and accrued interest are a charge on the premises which consist of or include the contaminated land in question.[201]

Anyone served with either a charging notice or a copy of such a notice has 21 days from the date of service to appeal against the notice.[202]

To enforce its charge, an enforcing authority is given all the powers and **26–044** remedies of a mortgagee by deed under the Law of Property Act 1925,[203] including powers of sale and lease, of accepting surrenders of leases, and of appointing a receiver.

---

[193] Defined in Environmental Protection Act 1990, s.78M(6) as "premises used for any industrial, trade or business purposes or premises not so used on which matter is burnt in connection with any industrial, trade or business process, and premises are used for industrial purposes where they are used for the purposes of any treatment or process as well as where they are used for the purpose of manufacturing".
[194] Environmental Protection Act 1990, s.78M(4); the Secretary of State is empowered to substitute a higher figure (s.78M(4)).
[195] Environmental Protection Act 1990, s.78M(5).
[196] Environmental Protection Act 1990, s.78N(3)(a).
[197] Environmental Protection Act 1990, s.78N(3)(c).
[198] Environmental Protection Act 1990, s.78P(1).
[199] Environmental Protection Act 1990, s.78P(3).
[200] Environmental Protection Act 1990, s.78P(4)(a).
[201] Environmental Protection Act 1990, s.78P(4)(b).
[202] Environmental Protection Act 1990, s.78P(8).
[203] Environmental Protection Act 1990, s.78P(11).

(xi)   Protection for insolvency practitioners, etc

26–045   Some statutory limitation on the personal liability of insolvency practitioners and official receivers has been introduced where the liability arises in connection with contaminated land. Although this will probably be the most common source of environmental liabilities in the context of insolvency, it is important to remember that in respect of other forms of liability, practitioners remain at risk.

For the purposes of Pt IIA of Environmental Protection Act 1990, the following categories of persons are given protection[204]:

(a)   a person acting as an insolvency practitioner, within the meaning of s.388 of the Insolvency Act 1986[205];

(b)   the official receiver acting in a capacity which would fall within s.388 of the Insolvency Act 1986[206];

(c)   the official receiver acting as receiver or manager[207];

(d)   a special manager of a company in liquidation under s.177 of the Insolvency Act 1986, or of a bankrupt's estate or business (or that of a debtor where the official receiver has been appointed as interim receiver) under s.370 of the Insolvency Act 1986[208];

(e)   the accountant in bankruptcy (in Scottish bankruptcy procedures)[209];

(f)   a person acting as receiver or receiver and manager either under any enactment[210] or appointed by court order or any other instrument.[211]

Section 78X(3) of Environmental Protection Act 1990 provides that when acting in the above capacities (defined as acting in a relevant capacity), a person:

"(a) shall not thereby be personally liable, under this Part, to bear the whole or any part of the cost of doing any thing by way of remediation, unless that thing is to any extent referable to substances whose presence in, on or under the contaminated land in question is a result of any act done or omission made by him which it was unreasonable for a person acting in that capacity to do or make; and

---

[204] Environmental Protection Act 1990, s.78X(3), (4).
[205] Environmental Protection Act 1990, s.78X(4)(a).
[206] Environmental Protection Act 1990, s.78X(4)(b); by s.388(5) of the Insolvency Act 1986, the definition of "act as insolvency practitioner" normally excludes official receivers.
[207] Environmental Protection Act 1990, s.78X(4)(c).
[208] Environmental Protection Act 1990, s.78X(4)(d).
[209] Environmental Protection Act 1990, s.78X(4)(e).
[210] As, e.g. one appointed under Environmental Protection Act 1990, s.78P(11): see above.
[211] Environmental Protection Act 1990, s.78X(4)(f).

(b) shall not thereby be guilty of an offence under or by virtue of section 78M above unless the requirement which has not been complied with is a requirement to do some particular thing for which he is personally liable to bear the whole or any part of the cost".

An insolvency practitioner (or the official receiver in an equivalent capacity) will not normally incur any personal liability for clean-up costs merely as "owner" or "occupier" of contaminated land. Even if acts or omissions by an insolvency practitioner result in pollution, the practitioner may still escape liability by showing that those acts or omissions were reasonable in the context. Case law will determine what steps are or are not reasonable. Practitioners will wish to err on the side of caution, but it appears that, where such a course is available, the mere act of disclaiming contaminated land would not generally be considered unreasonable.[212] The protection of insolvency practitioners under the Contaminated Land Regime in domestic law may not be so extensive under the regime required further to the Environmental Liability Directive. **26-046**

(xii)   The Environmental Liability Directive

The Directive (2004/35/EC)[213] was due to have been transposed into national law by 30 April 2007. It has been implemented by the Environmental Damage (Prevention and Remediation) Regulations 2009 (the ED Regulations),[214] which came into force with effect from March 1, 2009. They are thus late, and the United Kingdom is in breach of its obligations under the Directive.[215] **26-047**

The ED Regulations are aimed at the prevention and remedying of environmental damage—specifically, damage to habitats and species protected by EU law, damage to water resources, and land contamination which presents a threat to human health. It applies only to damage from incidents occurring after it comes into force (thus applying to incidents prior to the Regulations in 2009).[216] The Regulations, which do not cover "traditional damage" (that is, economic loss, personal injury and property damage), have the following characteristics: they are based on the polluter pays principle[217]; polluters should meet their liability by remediating the damaged environment directly, or by **26-048**

---

[212] cf. *Environment Agency v Hillridge Ltd* [2004] 2 B.C.L.C. 358, where disclaimer of a waste management licence implied necessarily disclaimer of a trust fund set up to provide monies for remediation of the land in question. The waste management licence, and with it, the trust fund went to the Crown as bona vacantia notwithstanding that the Environment Agency was a co-signatory to the trust fund deed.

[213] [2004] OJ L143/56.

[214] SI 2009/153 as regards England and SI 2009/995 as regards Wales. Non-statutory guidance on application of these Regulations is at *http://www.defra.gov.uk/environment/policy/liability/pdf/indepth-guide-regs09.pdf.*

[215] This Chapter does not address the potential problems that may arise from this delay in transposition.

[216] The temporal effects of the Directive are explained in *Raffinerie Mediterranee (ERG) SpA v Ministero dello Sviluppo Economico* (C-378/08) [2010] 3 C.M.L.R. 9.

[217] There is a helpful explanation of the scope and operation of the "polluter pays" concept in the Directive in *Raffinerie Mediterranee (ERG) SpA v Ministero dello Sviluppo Economico* (C-378/08) [2010] 3 C.M.L.R. 9.

taking measures to prevent imminent damage, or by reimbursing competent authorities who, in default, remediate the damage or take action to prevent damage; the competent authorities are responsible for enforcing the regime in the public interest, or by taking action to remediate or prevent damage and recover the costs from the operator; strict liability applies in respect of damage to land, water and biodiversity from activities regulated by specified EU legislation identified in Sch.2; fault-based liability applies otherwise in respect of biodiversity damage; defences apply for damage caused by an act of armed conflict, natural phenomenon, or from compliance with a permit, and emissions which at the time they were authorised were not considered to be harmful according to the best available scientific and technical knowledge.

Where an operator is not liable, the United Kingdom has subsidiary responsibility for remedying that damage. Individuals and others who may be directly affected by actual or possible damage, and qualified entities (non-Governmental Organisations) may request action by a competent authority, and seek judicial review of the authority's action or inaction.

26-049   The definition of "operator" in the Directive is: "any natural or legal, private or public person who operates or controls the occupational activity or, where this is provided for in national legislation, to whom decisive economic power over the technical functioning of such an activity has been delegated, including the holder of the permit or authorisation for such an activity or the person registering or notifying such an activity." That in the ED Regulations (reg.2) is the "person who operates or controls such an activity, including the holder of a permit or authorisation relating to that activity, or the person registering or notifying such an activity". It is suggested, however, that it cannot be ruled out that this directive may be held to apply to administrators and receivers.

26-050   The Regulations are aimed at remediation of environmental damage which is concrete and quantifiable and provides that a causal link should be established between the damage and the identified polluter(s). It does not apply to cases of personal injury, to damage to private property or to economic loss but does not affect rights as regards these types of liability. In addition, an operator should not be required to bear the costs of preventive or remedial actions taken pursuant to the ED Regulations in situations where the damage in question or imminent threat thereof is the result of certain events beyond the operator's control.

The option in the Environmental Liability Directive to allow that operators who are not at fault or negligent shall not bear the cost of remedial measures in situations where the damage in question is the result of emissions or events explicitly authorised or where the potential for damage could not have been known when the event or emission took place[218] has been adopted in the ED Regulations.[219]

---

[218] Preamble, para.20, and art.8(4). Note that this may well be less strict that the position under the existing Contaminated Land Regime–cf. *R. (on the application of National Grid Plc (formerly Transco Plc) v Environment Agency* [2007] 1 W.L.R. 1780 (HL).
[219] reg.19(3)(d).

(b) Criminal liability

It seems clear that administrators and receivers may be criminally liable under **26–051** environmental legislation. Liability attaches to persons having particular status, such as as "owner" or "occupier" and/or by virtue of their ability to direct or control operations and/or by virtue of their involvement in relation to the same.

The most important of such terminology are: "owner", "occupier", "causing", "knowingly permit", "person responsible", "consent or connivance", and "director, manager, secretary or other similar officer of the body corporate or a person who was purporting to act in such capacity".

Sometimes there is a definition of the particular term in the body of a particular statute, which at least serves as a starting point to understand what the scope of the term is. Where the statute is silent or incomplete, it is necessary to look at how the courts have approached such terms in the context of similar statutes, or on previous versions of current legislation. There have been some cases involving the liability of receivers. Moreover, previous cases may offer only partial guidance; it should be noted that the House of Lords has said that such words will "draw their meaning entirely from the purpose for which and the context in which they are used".[220]

(i) "Owner"

Under the waste management environmental permits and statutory nuisance **26–052** schemes, it is the "owner" who becomes liable (for example, to a fine for breach of an abatement notice in respect of a statutory nuisance (without reasonable excuse),[221] or to pay clean-up costs in respect of such a statutory nuisance[222]).

Other statutes have included, within the definition of "owner", for example, those in receipt of rents,[223] receivers,[224] and a person entitled to possession.[225]

In *Solomons v R Gertzenstein Ltd*,[226] the Court of Appeal considered whether a (LPA) receiver was the "owner" and therefore liable for breach of statutory duty arising out of a fire in a house in Soho used by various businesses. It was held that the receiver was the "owner" under s.33(1) of the London Building Acts (Amendment) Act 1939 but was not the "owner" under s.5 of the London Building Act 1930. As a matter of statutory construction, it was the latter definition which was applicable, and so determinative of the issue.

---

[220] *Southern Water Authority v Nature Conservancy Council* [1992] 1 W.L.R. 775 (HL), 781 per Lord Mustill.

[221] See the Environmental Protection Act 1990, s.80.

[222] See the Environmental Protection Act 1990, s.81: note that in this case, the phrase is "any person who is for the time being the owner thereof".

[223] e.g. London Building Acts (Amendment) Act 1939; and the Public Health Act 1936.

[224] e.g. Mines and Quarries Act 1954.

[225] e.g. General Rating Act 1967, s.17B; note that in *Westminster City Council v Haymarket Publishing Ltd* [1981] 1 W.L.R. 677, the Court of Appeal held this did not include a mortgagee not in possession.

[226] *Solomons v R Gertzenstein Ltd* [1954] 2 Q.B. 243 (CA).

It should be noted that even where there are defined terms in the various environmental statutes, they are not necessarily consistent. The Environmental Protection Act 1990, as originally drafted, had no definition of "owner". That has now been amended for the purposes of Pt IIA, which deals with contaminated land (but not for any other purpose). The Environmental Protection Act 1990 definition of "owner" becomes: "a person (other than a mortgagee not in possession) who, whether in his own right or as trustee for any other person, is entitled to receive the rack rent of the land, or, where the land is not let at a rack rent, would be so entitled if it were so let".[227] Under the Control of Pollution Act 1974 (COPA), the definition of "owner" does not exclude a mortgagee not in possession: "the person for the time being receiving the rack rent of the premises in connection with which the word is used, whether on his own account or as agent or trustee for another person, or who would so receive the rack rent if the premises were let at a rack rent".[228] The Water Resources Act (WRA) uses the same definition of "owner",[229] but excludes a mortgagee not in possession from the effects of certain provisions.[230]

(ii)   "Occupier"

26–053 It is the "occupier" who receives a waste removal notice under the Environmental Protection Act 1990, s.59; unless he complies, or has a reasonable excuse, or can convince a court that he did not deposit, knowingly cause or knowingly permit the waste, he becomes criminally liable and also liable for clean-up costs. Similarly, an "occupier" is liable for emergency clean-up costs incurred by the waste regulation authority. "Occupier" is also used in the Public Health Act and the COPA, but neither the EPA nor these other statutes incorporate a definition.

The courts have taken two broad approaches in considering who is an "occupier":

(a)   The "control" test: the House of Lords in *Wheat v Lacon*[231] decided for Occupiers Liability Act purposes that a brewery was the occupier of a pub where the claimant's husband had died in a fall through its servant-manager. Lord Denning said[232]: "wherever a person has a sufficient degree of control over premises that he ought to realise that any failure on his part to use care may result in injury ... he is an 'occupier'".

(b)   The "comprehensive and stable relationship" test: the House of Lords in *Southern Water Authority v Nature Conservancy Council*,[233] considered the phrase "owner or occupier" in an environmental protection context; a water authority who came onto a Site of Special

---

[227] Environmental Protection Act 1990, s.78A(9).
[228] COPA, s.105(1).
[229] Water Resources Act, s.221.
[230] i.e. those in Pt II, Ch.II and Sch.2.
[231] *Wheat v E Lacon & Co Ltd* [1966] A.C. 552 (HL).
[232] *Wheat v E Lacon & Co Ltd* [1996] A.C. 552 (HL), 578.
[233] *Southern Water Authority v Nature Conservancy Council* [1992] 1 W.L.R. 775 (HL).

Scientific Interest solely to carry out work there was held not to have been an "occupier" under s.28(5) of the Wildlife and Countryside Act 1981. Lord Mustill said[234]:

"the occupier is someone who, although lacking the title of an owner, nevertheless stands in such a comprehensive and stable relationship with the land as to be, in company with the actual owner, someone to whom the mechanisms [of the statute] can sensibly be made to apply".

Other examples are: **26–054**

(a) In *Meigh v Wickenden*,[235] the receiver and manager appointed by a debenture holder were held liable for a breach of the Factories Act 1937, where there had been a failure to provide a strong guard for the cutter of a milling machine, and an employee had been injured. The finding of the justices was upheld on appeal. This was so notwithstanding that the debenture had provided that the receiver was deemed to be the agent of the company.

(b) In *Lord Advocate v Aero Technologies Ltd (in receivership)*,[236] it was held by the Scottish Outer House that receivers appointed pursuant to a debenture were for practical purposes in occupation of a factory where certain dangerous explosives were stored; the receivers had intended to leave the factory without making it safe, and Lord Sutherland granted an injunction to prevent them doing so.[237]

It appears likely that, in general, as indicated above, a receiver will be an "occupier" of a factory for environmental liability purposes, and the same would appear to be true of an administrator.

(iii) "Causing"

Causation arises in both the common law and the statutory context. For **26–055** example, one who "causes or knowingly permits" pollution of controlled waters is guilty of an offence,[238] and liable to pay clean-up costs.[239] The phrase has been discussed by the House of Lords in various cases, and has to some extent arguably been materially altered in substance from what was connoted

---

[234] *Southern Water Authority v Nature Conservancy Council* [1992] 1 W.L.R. 775 (HL), 782.

[235] *Meigh v Wickenden* [1942] 2 K.B. 160.

[236] *Lord Advocate v Aero Technologies Ltd (In Receivership)*, 1991 S.L.T. 134 (Court of Session, Outer House).

[237] Note that Lord Sutherland considered the case of *Ratford and Hayward v Northavon DC* [1987] Q.B. 357 (CA), in which receivers were held not to be occupiers in the sense of attracting liability for unpaid rates; he preferred to look at "the reality of the situation". He was prepared to consider the company and the receivers as joint occupiers.

[238] The Environmental Permitting Regulations 2010, reg. 12(1)(b).

[239] The Environmental Permitting Regulations 2010, reg. 44.

in certain phrases in the earlier case of *Alphacell Ltd v Woodward*.[240] In that case it was said that "causing" contemplates some active operation[241] or positive act.[242] ("Knowingly permits", on the other hand, can involve a failure to prevent, accompanied by the requisite knowledge.) The House of Lords rejected any requirement for fault, or for knowledge, where "causes" was concerned: liability here is strict.

26-056   In *Empress Car Co (Abertilley) Ltd v National Rivers Authority*[243] the House of Lords essentially said that causation was a matter of common sense and the correct question was whether the defendant caused the acts constituting the offence in question, including within this common sense approach cases where merely having a system of pipes in place provided the occasion for the factual scenario of pollution to arise and so, for commission of the offence to occur. It is unclear, but is to be doubted, whether, as suggested in *Alphacell Ltd v Woodward*, it is necessary for criminal liability to arise to have an "active operation" or "positive act" other than in the widest sense.

As indicated above, the process involved here should require an investigation into who had the occasion or duty to act and did not.[244] It is unclear currently how far this attribution of liability will stretch to cases where it might be said there was no culpability on the part of a defendant.[245]

(iv)   "Knowingly permits"

26-057   This is the statutory partner of "causing" or "knowingly causing". In general, the courts understand "to permit" as: "to give leave for an act which without that leave could not legally be done, or to abstain from taking reasonable steps to prevent the act where it is within a man's power to prevent it"[246], but cases have emphasised one or other limb of the definition.

In *Ashcroft v Cambro Waste Products*,[247] the Divisional Court found that the defendant company was guilty of "knowingly permitting" deposit of waste other than in accordance with the conditions of a licence,[248] where the company knew of the act constituting the pollution; it was not necessary for the company to have any further knowledge, for example, of the terms of the licence.[249] This

---

[240] *Alphacell Ltd v Woodward* [1972] A.C. 824 (HL).

[241] *Alphacell Ltd v Woodward* [1972] A.C. 824 (HL), 834 per Lord Wilberforce.

[242] *Alphacell Ltd v Woodward* [1972] A.C. 824 (HL), 846 per Lord Cross.

[243] *Empress Car Co (Abertilley) Ltd v National Rivers Authority* [1999] 2 A.C. 22 (HL); and see also *Express Ltd v Environment Agency* [2005] 1 W.L.R. 223.

[244] *Environment Agency v Biffa Waste Services Ltd* [2006] 3 All E.R. (D) 355 (Mar).

[245] Note that it is arguable that although there is no mens rea required for such offences, as they are strict liability offences, it is still necessary to establish some blameworthiness, otherwise the ECHR protection of the presumption of innocence may be infringed—cf. *R. v G* [2006] 1 W.L.R. 2052 (CA). It is unclear likewise whether criminal liability without culpability is acceptable under EU law: in accordance with the "principle of culpability" penalties which are applied without regard to culpability of the accused are contrary to EU law—see the case law cited in the Advocate General's opinion in *Othmar Michaeler* (C-55/07), [57].

[246] *Berton v Alliance Economic Investment Co Ltd* [1922] 1 K.B. 742 (CA), 759, per Atkin L.J.

[247] *Ashcroft v Cambro Waste Products* [1981] 1 W.L.R. 1349.

[248] In a prosecution under the Control of Pollution Act 1974, s.3.

[249] See also, under the then Environmental Protection Act 1990, s.33(1)(a) *Shanks & McEwan (Teeside) Ltd v Environment Agency* [1999] Q.B. 333.

was significant because the director, who was the "controlling mind" of the company, had not in fact known of the terms of the licence; the foreman, who had known, was not part of the "controlling mind". Conversely, in *Westminster City Council v Croyalgrange*[250] the House of Lords took a more lenient approach to an allegation that the defendant had knowingly permitted use of premises as a sex establishment, where the director of the defendant gave evidence that it had honestly believed that a licence application was pending. Lord Bridge said that the use of the word "knowingly" in the relevant section made it impossible to find a Parliamentary intention to create a strict-liability offence.[251]

(v) "Person responsible"

Under the Environmental Protection Act 1990, s.80, an abatement notice can **26–058** be served on the "person responsible". This term is defined in s.79(7) as "the person to whose act, default or sufferance the nuisance is attributable",[252] but it should be noted that more than one person may in fact be responsible.[253]

(vi) "Consent or connivance"

A director, manager, secretary or other similar officer of the body corporate or **26–059** a person who was purporting to act in such capacity may be personally liable in respect of an offence by a body corporate, if the offence was committed with the consent or the connivance of the person or the offence is attributable to the neglect of that person.[254] An insolvency practitioner acting in respect of a company can be regarded as a "similar officer" to a director or manager.[255] However, it is suggested that liability probably only arises where it can be shown that he was a decision-maker having both the power and responsibility to decide corporate strategy policy and strategy.[256] This could, as suggested above, include an administrator or receiver.

[250] *Westminster City Council v Croyalgrange* [1986] 1 W.L.R. 674 (HL).
[251] *Westminster City Council v Croyalgrange* [1986] 1 W.L.R. 674 (HL), 682, and see also *Latif v Middlesborough Council* [1997] EWHC Admin 315.
[252] See *Camden LBC v Gunby* [2000] 1 W.L.R. 465; and contrast with *Midland Bank Ltd v Conway Corp* [1965] 1 W.L.R. 1165.
[253] See Environmental Protection Act 1990, s.81(1).
[254] See the Environmental Permitting Regulations, reg.41.
[255] cf. *Environment Agency v Kevin Barry Stout (Liquidator of Mineral Resources Ltd)* [1999] 1 All E.R 746.
[256] *R. v Boal* [1992] Q.B. 591 (CA); and *Woodhouse v Walsall MBC* [1994] 1 B.C.L.C. 435.

Chapter 27

Distribution and Vacation of Office by Administrators

1. INTRODUCTION

27–001 This chapter deals with changes of administrators and ending administrations. It also deals with distribution powers, which fall to be considered before closing a case, and the discharge of former administrators from liability.

The principal legislative provisions of Sch.B1 to the Insolvency Act 1986 are as follows:

- Distribution (para.65);

- Ending administration (paras 76 to 86); and

- Replacing administrators (paras 87 to 99).

The legislative phraseology in this area is a little confusing and paragraph headings in Sch.B1 use different phrases to those deployed in the paragraphs themselves.[1] An understanding of the various procedures now available for the termination of administration and the removal from office of administrators can be hampered by the multiplicity of labels used to describe them. For the purposes of this chapter, "removal" means the removal of the administrator from office, including where he vacates office if he ceases to be qualified to act as an insolvency practitioner, "resignation" denotes an administrator resigning his office, "termination" means the company ceases to be in administration and "discharge" means the administrator being discharged from liability following ceasing to be an administrator.

2. REMOVAL

(a) Removal of administrator by court

27–002 The court is empowered to remove an administrator even if the administrator was appointed out of court.[2] However, a company does not cease to be in administration merely because an administrator vacates office (by reason of resignation, death or otherwise) or is removed from office.[3] The power of removal is

---

[1] e.g. "substitution" in paras 96 and 97, which relate to replacement of an administrator.
[2] para.88.
[3] para.1(2)(d). The applicant should normally take steps to ensure that a replacement can take office as soon as the order takes effect.

free-standing and very wide[4] although in *Sisu Capital Fund Ltd v Tucker*, Warren J. held that it would not be easy to think of any circumstance in which the court would remove an administrator under para.88 without due cause being shown.[5] By analogy with liquidation cases, it would be for the applicant to show "cause" as to why the administrator should be removed from office and this would be measured by reference to the real, substantial, honest, interests of the administration, and the purpose for which the administrator is appointed.[6] The court will carry out a balancing exercise when considering such an application and one factor the court will have regard to will be the wishes of the majority of creditors[7]. The court will expect the administrator to be efficient, vigorous and unbiased in his conduct of the administration and should have no hesitation in removing him if satisfied that he has failed to live up to those standards, unless it can be said with reasonable confidence that he will live up to those standards in the future. But the court should have in mind whether his removal will encourage similar applications by disgruntled creditors in other cases without proper cause and there would likely be cost implications of orders for removal.[8] In relation to disgruntled creditors, *BLV Realty Organization Ltd v Batten*[9] established that the duty of administrators to perform their functions in the interests of creditors as a whole did not mean that the obligation had to be performed in an identical way in relation to each creditor. The application for the removal of the joint administrators failed in this instance as unequal treatment of creditors did not amount to unfair treatment where there were sound commercial reasons for differential treatment. The required threshold to justify the removal of an administrator required perversity or bad faith in the exercise of commercial judgement by the administrator. It may also be right to remove an administrator where the circumstances are such that, through no fault of his own, he is perceived to be biased in favour of one or more of the creditors, or indeed, where the circumstances are such that it is not longer practicable for him to carry

---

[4] *Re St Georges Property Services (London) Ltd (In Administration)*, CA NB; sub nom. *Finnerty v Clark* [2011] N.P.C. 90 (CA).

[5] *Sisu Capital Fund Ltd v Tucker* [2006] 1 All E.R. 167 (the judgment mistakenly refers to liquidation). See *Re Portsmouth City Football Club (In Administration)* [2011] B.C.C. 149. However, with regard to unfair prejudice to the interests of landlords as creditors, see *Mourant & Co Trustees Ltd v Sixty UK Ltd (In Administration)* [2010] B.C.C. 882 and *Prudential Assurance Co Ltd v PRG Powerhouse Ltd* [2007] B.C.C. 500. See also *Re Edennote Ltd* [1996] B.C.C. 718 (CA), where, Nourse L.J. held that the difference in language between ss.172(2) and 108(?) was immaterial and therefore despite s.108(2) having the express inclusion of "on cause shown", the provisions of s.172(2) would in many, if not all, circumstances require "cause" to be shown. For the test of reasonableness, see *Abbey Forwarding Ltd v Hone* [2010] B.P.I.R. 1053.

[6] *Re Adam Eyton Ltd Ex p. Charlesworth* (1887) L.R. 36 Ch. D. 229 (CA), 306, per Bowen L.J. See also *Re Buildlead Ltd (In Liquidation)* [2005] B.C.C. 138. For what amounts to reasonableness, see *Re St Georges Property Services (London) Ltd (In Administration)* [2011] B.C.C. 64.

[7] *Clydesdale Financial Services Ltd v Smailes* [2009] B.C.C. 810

[8] *Sisu Capital Fund Ltd v Tucker* [2006] 1 All E.R. 167, [85], per Warren J. See also *AMP Enterprises Ltd v Hoffman* [2002] B.C.C. 996; *Re Keypak Homecare Ltd* (1987) 3 B.C.C. 558 and *Re CE King Ltd* [2000] 2 B.C.L.C. 297.

[9] *BLV Realty Organization Ltd v Batten* [2010] B.P.I.R. 277.

out his functions, irrespective of hisconduct.[10] Most applications for removal will involve a degree of criticism and the court must think carefully before acceding to claims that an administrator could have done better or done things earlier. Proportionality, and perhaps a greater regard to the future than the past,[11] as well as consideration of the impact on the administrator's professional standing and reputation[12] are all matters which the court should take into account. The key requirement is good cause. Allegations of misfeasance or incompetence need not be shown, if there is a case that may best be addressed after a replacement administrator has investigated all the circumstances.[13] An application for an order challenging the administrator's conduct under para.74 may be made in addition, or in the alternative, to para.88 as a means of seeking the removal of the administrator, as in *Sisu Capital*.[14]

Applications may be brought under para.88 in circumstances where an administrator moves firm or has been expelled from his firm. In such instances the court must consider the circumstances and whether the interests of creditors are best served by acceding to an application for removal.[15]

An application made pursuant to para.88 must state the grounds for the request and be served on the administrator, the applicant for the administration order, the person who appointed the administrator, the creditors' committee (if there is one), any joint administrators, the company and all its creditors.[16] If an

---

[10] *Re Gordon & Breach Science Publishers Ltd* [1995] B.C.C. 261, *Re A&C Supplies Ltd* [1998] B.C.C. 708, *Re Polly Peck International Plc* (Unreported), *Re Corbenstoke Ltd (No.2)* (1989) 5 B.C.C. 767 and *Deloitte & Touche AG v Johnson* [1999] 1 W.L.R. 1605 (PC). For an analysis of the case law on conflicts of interest see *Sisu Capital Fund Ltd v Tucker* [2006] 1 All E.R. 167, per Warren J. at [91] to [133]. The appointment of a conflicts administrator (that is, an independent insolvency practitioner whose role is to resolve upon a particular course of action in circumstances where it is not possible for the administrator to do so without compromising his duty to act in the best interest of his client or clients) as an alternative to the removal from office of an administrator would likely be considered appropriate were it to be in the best interests of the estate to address the conflict, or perceived conflict, in this way.

[11] *AMP Enterprises Ltd v Hoffman* [2003] 1 B.C.L.C. 319, [39], per Neuberger J. (see also Hansard (HL), October 21, 2002, at col 1108) and *Re Sisu Capital Fund Ltd v Tucker* [2006] B.P.I.R. 154, [86], per Warren J. See also, *Re Adbury Estates Ltd* [2003] B.C.C. 696. For proportionality, see *Re St Georges Property Services (London) Ltd (In Administration)* [2011] B.C.C. 64.

[12] *Re Edennote Ltd* [1996] 2 B.C.L.C. 389 (CA), 398F, per Nourse L.J.

[13] *Shepheard v Lamey* [2001] B.P.I.R. 939, *Re Buildlead Ltd (In Liquidation)* [2005] B.C.C. 138 and *Clydesdale Financial Services Ltd v Smailes* [2009] B.C.C. 810. In *Sisu Capital Fund Ltd v Tucker* [2006] 1 All E.R. 167, Warren J. held that in light of his conclusions on unfair prejudice and the application under s.6 that no question of removing the officeholders arose under para.74 and/or 88 or ss.108 and 171. He did, however, hold that to the extent that any claims were not released by the company voluntary arrangements that the applicants could bring an application under the misfeasance provisions set out in para.75. At [89] he had held that "if there is a possibility of misfeasance proceedings against a liquidator he should ordinarily be removed". The statements can be reconciled on the basis that good cause had to be shown and that a possibility that misfeasance proceeding may be brought is a relevant but not necessarily a determinative factor. The courts have generally declined to intervene without "good cause"; see *Re Portsmouth City Football Club (In Administration)* [2011] B.C.C. 149 and *Re York Gas Ltd (In Creditors' Voluntary Liquidation)* [2011] B.C.C. 447.

[14] *Sisu Capital Fund Ltd v Tucker* [2006] 1 All E.R. 167. See para.74(4)(d) which gives the court power on an application to challenge the administrator's conduct to provide for the appointment of an administrator to cease to have effect.

[15] *Re Sankey Furniture Ltd Ex p. Harding* [1995] 2 B.C.L.C. 594; *Re A&C Supplies Ltd* [1998] B.C.C. 708; *Re Equity Nominees Ltd* [2000] B.C.C. 84; *Cork v Rolph* (2001) 98 (7) L.S.G. 40; and *Saville v Gerrard and Pick* [2005] B.C.C. 433.

[16] r.2.122(1) and (2) but the co urt has power to dispense with any failure to serve the application on all creditors see *Clydesdale Financial Services Ltd v Smailes* [2009] B.C.C. 810.

order is made removing the administrator, the court shall give a copy of the order to the applicant who, as soon as reasonably practicable, must send a copy to the administrator and the applicant must, also within five business days of the order being made, send a copy of the order to all those to whom the initial application was sent.[17] A copy of the order must also be sent to the Registrar of Companies.[18]

Despite comparisons between cases involving the removal of a liquidator **27–003** and the court's treatment in *Sisu Capital* of an application to remove an administrator, it is noteworthy that the Rules are different. Rules 4.119 and 4.110, which relate to liquidations, have several important features which have not found their way into the corresponding provisions pertaining to an application under para.88. In the case of the removal of a liquidator by the court, the court has express powers under the Rules to dismiss an application without a hearing, to require the applicant to make a deposit or give security for the liquidator's costs and, subject to any contrary order of the court, the costs of the application are not payable out of the assets.[19] These provisions serve to filter out at an early stage those applications which the court does not regard as making out a prima facie case. It is regrettable that such provisions do not apply to an application under para.88.

The persons who can make a para.88 application are not limited by statute, but it is unlikely that anyone who does not have a direct interest in the removal will be allowed to make an application. Therefore a debtor of a company or a contributory, having no financial interest in the outcome of the administration, is unlikely to have standing to remove an administrator.[20] The court's jurisdiction in those cases under para.88 which involve the removal of the administrator is broad and would include a Member State liquidator as well as former partners of the administrator in circumstances where the administrator had retired or been expelled from the partnership.[21]

(b) Substitution of administrator by creditors' meeting

Where an administrator has been appointed by a company or its directors out **27–004** of court, under para.22, and there is no holder of a qualifying floating charge in respect of the company's property, a creditors' meeting may replace the administrator.[22] This provision is a power of substitution to replace an administrator who is in office. If there is a vacancy, the company or its directors have

---

[17] r.2.122(3) and r.2.122(4).

[18] r.2.122(5) and r.2.133(5), which obliges the administrator to give notice to, or provide a copy of the order to any member State liquidator.

[19] rr.4.119(2), (3) and (5) and 4.120(2), (3) and (5) and *Re Buildlead Ltd* [2003] 4 All E.R. 864. The best interests of the liquidation are foremost in deciding whether to remove a liquidator; see *Managa Properties Ltd v Brittain* [2009] 1 B.C.L.C. 689. Costs on an indemnity basis may be awarded against an administrator who unreasonably refuses an application for his removal, see *Shepheard v Lamey* [2001] B.P.I.R. 939 and *Coyne v DRC Distribution Ltd* [2008] B.C.C. 612 (CA).

[20] *Deloitte & Touche AG v Johnson* [1999] 1 W.L.R. 1605 (PC) and *Re Corbenstoke Ltd (No.2)* (1989) 5 B.C.C. 767 respectively. See also *Walker Morris (a firm) v Khalastchi* [2001] 1 B.C.L.C. 1.

[21] See *Re A&C Supplies Ltd* [1998] B.C.C. 708.

[22] paras 97(1) and (2). See also r.2.48(9).

the power to appoint a replacement under paras 93 and 94. This power is conferred on a creditors' meeting rather than any creditors' committee. The creditors' meeting may only act in replacing the administrator if the new administrator's consent to act is presented to the meeting before the replacement is made.[23] The court has an express power under r.4.115, on the application of any creditor to regulate meetings to be held or proposed to be summoned for the purpose of removing a liquidator and the court is empowered to give directions as to the mode of summoning it, the sending out and return of forms of proxy, the conduct of the meeting and any other matters which appear to the court to require regulation or control. No similar power is provided for in the case of a meeting convened under para.97, which appears to be an oversight. The procedure under para.97 enables the creditors to overturn any out of court administrator's appointment made by the company or the directors, which is unacceptable to creditors, without the cost of an application to court. The replacement appointment must be notified and advertised and all statements, consents etc as are required for the original administrator shall also be required in the case of a replacement. Further, all forms and notices must clearly identify that the administrator is a replacement administrator.[24] The replacement appointment is also required to send notice of his appointment to the Registrar of Companies.[25]

(c) Substitution of administrator by a prior qualifying floating charge-holder

27–005 A floating charge holder may apply to the court for substitution of an administrator appointed pursuant to para.14 where he is the holder of a prior floating charge.[26] For these purposes, one floating charge is prior to another if it was created first or it is to be treated as having priority in accordance with an agreement to which the holder of each floating charge was party.[27] No guidance is given as to the circumstances in which the court may exercise its discretion on such an application, and consideration is likely to be given to the powers conferred by para.15 on the holder of a prior floating charge enabling him to make his own appointment before the administrator's appointment. Further, the court will likely have regard to the power available to such floating charge holders under para.103 to apply for, or sanction the application for the appointment of, an additional administrator and, in particular, whether this alternative is more appropriate. It would therefore seem that the applicant must show "cause" justifying the administrator's removal from office, and the court will require evidence as to why the applicant did not make the appointment at the

---

[23] para.97(3).

[24] r.2.126.

[25] r.2.128.

[26] para.96 (rr.2.126 and 2.129 apply).

[27] para.96(3). The drafting of para.96(3) is far from clear (see Sims and Briggs, "Enterprise Act 2002—Corporate Wrinkles", (2004) 17 Insolv. Int. 49) and does not address the situation where different floating charge assets have different priorities as between the holders of floating charges, as to which, see Ch.3.

outset, and why the appropriate course is not to appoint an additional administrator, at the behest of the applicant, under para.103. On a strict reading of the
provisions, the applicant need not show that the floating charge is enforceable
because para.16 does not apply, since the appointment is not made under
para.14 but unenforceability would be a factor crucial to the court's decision
whether to accede to any such application.

3. AUTOMATIC VACATION OF OFFICE

An administrator vacates offices if he ceases to be qualified to act as an insol- **27–006**
vency practitioner in relation to the company.[28] Such vacation takes effect
automatically without any further requirement.[29] Notwithstanding the former
administrator is under an obligation to give notice of his vacation of office to
the Registrar of Companies[30] and to the court and other interested parties, as
applicable, in the circumstances set out in Sch.B1, para.89(2). He is also under
an obligation as soon as reasonably practicable to deliver up to the person
succeeding him as administrator the assets (after deduction of any expenses
properly incurred and distributions made by him) and further deliver up to that
person the administration records and the company's books, papers and other
records (this being the case also where the administrators ceases to be in office
as a consequence of removal and resignation).[31] The company remains in
administration even though the administrator has vacated office.[32]

Where the administrator dies, it is the duty of his personal representatives to
give notice of the fact to the court, specifying the date of death. This does not
apply if notice has been given by a partner in the firm of the deceased administrator who is qualified to act as an insolvency practitioner or is a member of
any body recognised by the Secretary of State for the authorisation of insolvency practitioners, or by others who produce to the court the relevant death
certificate or a copy of it. Where a person gives notice to the court he shall also
give notice to the Registrar of Companies.[33]

4. RESIGNATION OF ADMINISTRATOR

An administrator may resign only in prescribed circumstances, as set out in the **27–007**
Rules.[34] Those grounds are ill health, his intention to cease to be in practice as
an insolvency practitioner, or the existence of some conflict of interest or
change of personal circumstances, which precludes or makes impracticable the
further discharge by him of the duties of administrator.[35] Further, the administrator may, with permission of the court, give notice of his resignation on other

---

[28] para.89(1). See s.390 for the qualification requirement to act as an insolvency practitioner.
[29] *Re AJ Adams (Builders) Ltd* [1991] B.C.C. 62 and *Donaldson v O'Sullivan* [2009] 1 W.L.R.
924 (CA).
[30] r.2.123.
[31] r.2.129.
[32] para.1(2)(d).
[33] r.1.124.
[34] para.87(1) and rule 2.119.
[35] r.2.119(1).

grounds.[36] The administrator shall, in all cases, give at least seven days' notice
of his intention to resign, or to apply for the court's permission to do so, to any
continuing administrator, and any creditors' committee, but if these is no such
administrator nor creditors' committee, to the company and its creditors.[37] He
shall also give notice to any Member State liquidator.[38] Where the administrator was appointed by the holder of a qualifying floating charge under
para.14, the notice of intention to resign shall also be sent to his appointor and
to the holder of any prior qualifying floating charge.[39] Where the administrator
was appointed by the company or the directors of the company under para.22,
a copy of the notice of intention to resign shall also be sent to the appointor and
all holders of a qualifying floating charge.[40] Notice of the resignation itself
needs be filed with the court, with a copy sent to the Registrar of Companies,[41]
and, not more than five business days after it has been filed with the court, to
all those to whom notice of intention to resign was sent.[42] Some guidance as to
the kind of personal circumstances which may render the carrying on of the
administrator's duties "impracticable" was given in *Re Alt Landscapes Ltd*.[43]
Here an application was made to remove and replace two insolvency practitioners who were the office-holders in various bankruptcies, voluntary arrangements and liquidations, following of the closure of the local office of an
accountancy firm. It was held that "impracticable" connoted something not far
short of impossibility, so that the undesirability or inexpediency of a particular
course on the present facts did not entitle the applicants to resign: they must be
instead be removed by order.[44] As where an administrator automatically
vacates office, the resignation of the administrator does not result in the
company ceasing to be in administration.[45]

5.   FILLING A VACANCY IN THE OFFICE OF ADMINISTRATOR

27–008   Where an administrator dies, resigns, is removed from office under para.88 or
vacates offices because he ceases to be qualified, there are procedures set out
in paras 91 to 95 for the vacancy to be filled. In each case, they apply both if
the office of administrator has become vacant and where more than one person
was acted jointly or concurrently as the administrator. The procedure varies
depending upon the mode of appointment of the outgoing administrator. Where

[36] r.2.119(2).
[37] r.2.120(1).
[38] r.2.120(2).
[39] r.2.120(3). The drafting is rather curious in terms of requiring notice to be given to: (1) all
holders of prior qualifying floating charges; and (2) to the person who appointed the administrator
under para.14; and (3) for a copy of the notice also to be sent to the holder of the floating charge
by virtue of which the appointment was made since (2) and (3) would usually be the same party.
[40] r.2.120(4).
[41] r.2.121(2).
[42] rr.2.121(2)(3) and (4).
[43] *Re Alt Landscapes Ltd* [1999] B.P.I.R. 459.
[44] cf. *Re Sankey Furniture Ltd Ex p. Harding* [1995] 2 B.C.L.C. 594. The qualification relates
both to his qualification generally and to his qualification in relation to the company and the appropriate security, see s.390(3).
[45] para.1(2)(d).

the court made the appointment, only the court may replace the administrator and the application to appoint the replacement ought to be made by the creditors' committee (if there is one) or any co-administrators, although it can be made by the company, its directors or any of the creditors if the creditors' committee or a remaining co-administrator are not "taking reasonable steps" to appoint a replacement.[46] Once appointed, the procedure used on appointment of the original administrator must be adhered to (i.e. interested parties notified, advertisements placed and the Registrar of Companies informed).[47] If the original appointment was made out of court by the floating charge holder or the company or its directors, such parties may appoint a replacement.[48] If the company or its directors are appointing a replacement they must first receive consent from any holder of a qualifying floating charge, and if not received, permission is needed from the court.[49] In circumstances where a court application is required, the provisions of r.2.125 shall apply.[50]

6. ADDITIONAL ADMINISTRATORS

The Act gives an express statutory power to appoint an additional administrator, provided the current administrators consent to it.[51] This is a useful procedure where, for example, a "conflicts" administrator is required or where it is felt that, for whatever reason, additional administrators are needed.[52] Where the company entered administration by administration order, an application must be made by the court or by one of the persons who did apply or could have applied for that order, or on the application of the person or persons acting as administrator of the company.[53] Where the original administrator was appointed by the holder of a qualifying floating charge under para.14, an

27–009

---

[46] para.91(1) and (2). It is not considered possible for the outgoing administrator (albeit he could do so under para.63) or the outgoing administrator's firm to make the application because neither is a party entitled to do so under para.91(1), see *Re Equity Nominees Ltd* [2000] B.C.C. 84 (but elsewhere the court has not sought to draw distinctions between the outgoing administrator's firm and his co-appointee, see *Re A&C Supplies Ltd* [1998] B.C.C. 708, despite this approach sitting uneasily with the provisions).

[47] r.2.126 and rule 2.128.

[48] para.93 and 94.

[49] paras 93(2) and 94(2).

[50] r.2.125(1) requires that where an application is made to court under paras 91(1) or 95, the application shall be accompanied by a written statement in Form 2.2B by the person proposed to be the replacement administrator. Rule 2.125(2) requires the application, where the original administrator was appointed under an administration order, a copy of the application shall be served, in addition to those persons listed in para.12(2) and r.2.6(3) on the person who made the application. Where the application to court is made under para.95, the application shall be accompanied by an affidavit setting out the applicant's belief as to the matters set out in that paragraph. Provisions as to service, the hearing and notification of the order as set out in rr.2.8, 2.9, 2.10, 2.12, 2.14(1) and (2) shall apply.

[51] para.103(1) and (6). Despite the lack of such similar express power under the old regime, the courts were able to surmount this omission *Clements v Udal* [2001] B.C.C. 658, *Cyma Petroleum Ltd v Cyma Holdings Ltd* Unreported December 22, 2000.

[52] The court may give supplementary directions delineating different areas of responsibility to be performed by one or more of the administrators, see *Polly Peck International Plc* Unreported October 25, 1990. *Re Ionica Plc* Unreported October 29, 1998 per Rattee J., and *Re TXU UK Ltd* Unreported March 11, 2004 per Rimer J. See also para.100(2).

[53] para.103(2).

additional appointment can only be made by the holder of that charge or by the court on the application of the person or persons acting as administrator of the company.[54] Where the original administrator was appointed by the company or its directors under para.22(1) or (2), an additional appointment must be made either by the court, on the application of the person or persons acting as the administrator of the company, or by the company and each person who is the holder of a qualifying floating charge, or failing such consent being provided, with the permission of the court.[55]

7. DISTRIBUTIONS

(a) General

27–010   Prior to ending administration, an administrator will need to consider whether to make distributions to creditors. An administrator has an express statutory power to make distributions, which represents a significant departure from the pre-Enterprise Act position.[56] The general power of an administrator to make a distribution to the creditor of a company is contained in Sch.B1, para.65(1), and the same rules that apply in a winding-up as regards preferential creditors also apply in respect of such a distribution.[57]

It is also permissible for an administrator to make a payment otherwise than in accordance with para.65 and his default power to make payments which are necessary or incidental to the performance of his functions[58] if he thinks so acting is likely to assist achievement of the purpose of administration.[59]

It is within the jurisdiction of the court to allow an English administrator of a foreign registered company to make such departures from the English distribution and priority rules, and to apply instead local rules of distribution, where he thinks this is likely to assist achievement of the purpose of the administration[60] but there is no need for the court to agree with this subjective judgment on the part of the administrator.[61] On an application for directions by an administrator, the court may sanction such a distribution in circumstances where the available alternatives would involve unnecessary delay and expense, and the administrator's proposals have received the support of either the creditors' committee or, if no such committee exists, the main creditors of the company likely to be affected by the making of the proposed payments.[62]

---

[54] para.103(3).
[55] para.103(4) and (5). Rules 2.127 and 2.128 apply in terms of notification and advertisement of the additional administrator's appointment.
[56] Under the old law, the jurisdiction to distribute in an administration was notoriously restrictive, its ambit defined by case law.
[57] para.65(2) and s.175.
[58] Sch.1, para.13.
[59] para.66.
[60] *Re Collins & Aikman Europe SA* [2006] B.C.C. 861 per Lindsay J and *Re Nortel Networks* [2010] B.C.C. 21. See also *Re MG Rover Espana SA* [2006] B.C.C. 599. Such decisions avoid the need for separate secondary proceedings under the EC Insolvency Regulation (1346/2000). See *Re Alitalia Linee Aeree Italiane SpA* [2011] 1 W.L.R. 2049.
[61] *Re Collins & Aikman Europe SA* [2006] B.C.C. 861, [31].
[62] *Re Collins & Aikman Europe SA* [2006] B.C.C. 861, [45]–[48].

For all these purposes a debt of a company is any debt or liability to which the company is subject at the date it goes into administration or to which it later becomes subject by reason of any obligation incurred before that date.[63] A liability is a liability to pay money or money's worth, including any liability under an enactment, any liability for breach of trust, any liability in contract, tort or bailment, and any liability arising out of an obligation to make restitution.[64] It is material for these purposes whether any such debt or liability is present or future, certain or contingent, fixed or liquidated or capable of being ascertained by fixed rules or as a matter of opinion.[65] Any tortious liabilities of the company are provable in its administration if either the cause of action has accrued at the date on which the company goes into administration or all the elements necessary to establish the cause of action exist at such date except for actionable damage.[66]

(b) Paragraph 65

(i) Leave of the court

Paragraph 65 of Sch.B1 gives the administrator the power to make a distribution to any of the company's creditors, a discretion which is subject to obtaining the court's permission in the case of a creditor which is neither secured nor preferential.[67] The legislation does not lay down the criteria the court has to apply in deciding whether to give its permission. Nevertheless, in *Re GHE Realisations Ltd*,[68] Rimer J. stated that consideration of each of the following factors is material to the question of whether the court will give its permission, albeit not necessarily determinative of the matter[69]:

27–011

    (i) that the administrator has sufficient funds to make the proposed distribution;

    (ii) that he does not propose an exit from administration into a voluntary liquidation under para.83;

    (iii) that his statement of proposals, as approved by the creditors, included a proposal to make the relevant distribution; and

---

[63] r.13.12(1) and (5).

[64] rr.13.12 (4) and (5). For the purposes of rr.13.12(1)(b) and (3) "debt" includes an order for costs (*Tottenham Hotspur Plc v Edennote Plc* [1994] B.C.C. 681).

[65] rr.13.12(3) and (5).

[66] rr.13.12(2) and (5). The inclusion of future tort claimants in the definition of "debt" was effected by the Insolvency (Amendment) Rules 2006 (SI 2006/1272), following the decision of David Richards J. in *Re T&N Ltd* [2006] 1 W.L.R. 1728. See also *Re Beloit Walmsley Ltd* [2009] 1 B.C.L.C. 584.

[67] paras 65(1) and 65(3). The better view is that the court's jurisdiction to give permission under para.65(3) is free-standing and is not limited, for example, by considerations of whether the court could properly make a direction under para.68(2) in terms of the permission sought. See also *Re HPJ UK Ltd (In Administration)* [2007] B.C.C. 284.

[68] *Re GHE Realisations Ltd* [2006] 1 W.L.R. 287.

[69] *Re GHE Realisations Ltd* [2006] 1 W.L.R. 287, [7] and [8].

(iv) that the payment of the proposed distribution was consistent with the functions and duties of the administrator and any of his actual or intended proposals.

The most obvious instance in which the court's permission will be sought will be in circumstances where the administrator proposes to make a distribution to unsecured creditors following a realisation of the company's assets by using administration as a surrogate mechanism for the distribution rules applicable in a liquidation, thereby rendering entry into liquidation unnecessary. There are obvious costs benefits to avoiding entry into liquidation by these means, which favours such a distribution.[70]

It is suggested that, in determining whether to permit such a distribution in administration, as opposed to moving to liquidation for the purposes of distribution of any surplus funds, the court will conduct a balancing exercise to weigh the relative benefits of the different procedures. The critical consideration in such cases is likely to be which of the procedure produces the greater good for the body of the company's unsecured creditors.

(ii)   Notice

27-012   The administrator is obliged to give notice to the company's creditors of his intention to declare and distribute a dividend in accordance with r.2.95.[71] Rule 2.95(1) provides that the administrator must give the creditors 28 days' notice of any proposed distribution.[72] The administrator is obliged to send his notice to all creditors whose addresses are known to him and any member state liquidator appointed in relation to the company,[73] stating whether the distribution is to preferential creditors or preferential creditors and unsecured creditors, as well as the value of any prescribed part distribution proposed to be made for the benefit of unsecured creditors, where appropriate.[74] Rule 2.95(3) further provides that he must not declare a dividend unless he has by public advertisement invited creditors to prove their debts.[75] Any notice given pursuant to r.2.95(1) and public advertisement made pursuant to r.2.95(3) must state that the administrator intends to make a distribution within the period of two months from the last date for proving, specifying whether the dividend is interim or final, and specifying a final date not less than 21 days from the date of the notice by which all creditors must lodge their proofs.[76]

---

[70] Note, however, the recent decisions in *Re Lune Metal Products Ltd (In Administration)* [2007] B.C.C. 217 (CA) and *Re Leyland Printing Co Ltd (In Administration)* [2011] B.C.C. 358.
[71] r.2.68(2). Whilst the rules in r.2.96 et seq have no equivalent under the old administration regime, they are based on the liquidation equivalents in rule 11.1 et seq.
[72] r.2.95(1).
[73] r.2.95(2)(a).
[74] rr.2.95(2)(b) and (c).
[75] r.2.95(3). This is subject to the exception that, as regards an intended dividend to preferential creditors, the administrator need only give notice to the creditors whose debts he has reason to believe are preferential, and public advertisement is necessary only if the administrator thinks fit (r.2.95(5)).
[76] r.2.95(4).

(iii)   Proving

Any person claiming to be a creditor of the company must submit his claim in   **27–013**
writing to the administrator in order to prove for his debt in the administration.[77] Although the proof submitted does not need to be in a particular form, it
must be made out by, or under the direction of, the creditor concerned, be
signed by him or a person authorised on his behalf[78] and contain the information listed in r.2.72(3)(b). This includes the creditor's name and address, the
total amount of his claim on the date the company entered administration,[79]
whether the claim includes outstanding uncapitalised interest or VAT, the
extent to which the debt is preferential, particulars of how and when the debt
was incurred, particulars of any security held, details of any reservations of
title in respect of the underlying goods and, if relevant, the particulars of any
person other than the creditor signing the proof.[80] The proof must specify any
supporting documents by reference to which the debt can be substantiated and,
whilst it is not essential that such documents are submitted along with the
proof, this is subject to the administrator's power to call for production of such
documents where he thinks it necessary.[81]

The following rules apply in relation to quantifying a claim:

(i)   There must be deducted from the claim all trade and other
discounts which would have been available to the company but for
its administration except any discount for immediate, early or cash
settlement.[82]

(ii)   If a debt was incurred or is payable in a foreign currency, the amount of
such debt shall be converted into sterling at the official exchange rate
prevailing on the date when the company entered administration.[83]

(iii)   In relation to rent and other periodic payments, creditors may prove
for any amounts due and unpaid up to the date when the company
entered administration,[84] as well as, in the case of payments which
were accruing due, an amount proportional to that which would have
fallen due at that date if the debt were accruing from day to day.[85]

(iv)   Where a debt proved in the administration bears interest, that interest
is provable as part of the debt except in so far as it is payable in

---

[77] r.2.72(1). Note the change in terminology from the previous administration regime, under
which a creditor seeking to recover his debt in whole or part "lodged a claim" rather than "proved
for a debt" (r.2.72(2)).

[78] r.2.72(3)(a).

[79] This must be net of any payments subsequently received and also take account of any adjustment by way of set-off in accordance with r.2.85 (r.2.72(3)(b)(ii)).

[80] r.2.72(3).

[81] rr.2.72 (4) and (5). The rules are, however, different in relation to proofs in respect of negotiable instruments such as cheques (see r.2.82).

[82] r.2.84.

[83] r.2.86(1). See also r.2.86(2). cf. r.4.91 in relation to liquidation.

[84] r.2.87(1).

[85] r.2.87(2).

respect of any period after the company entered administration.[86] If the debt is due by virtue of a written instrument, interest may be claimed from when the debt was payable until the company's entry into administration.[87] In respect of any other debt, interest may be claimed from the date of any written demand for payment until the company's entry into administration (provided notice was given that interest would be payable from the date of demand to the date of payment).[88] In either of the foregoing cases, the rate of interest to be claimed is the rate specified in s.17 of the Judgments Act 1838 on the date when the company entered administration.[89] Further, any surplus remaining after payment of the debts proved must first be applied in paying interest which has accrued on those debts since the company entered administration[90] at the Judgments Act rate or, if greater, the rate applicable to the debt apart from the administration.[91]

(v)   A creditor may prove for a debt which was payable at a time after the date when the company entered administration, subject to an adjustment in accordance with r.2.105 where payment is made before time.[92]

Following submission of his proof of debt, a creditor may withdraw it or vary it as to the amount claimed only with the agreement of the administrator.[93] Unless the court orders otherwise, every creditor bears the cost of proving his own debt[94] and the costs incurred by the administrator in estimating any debt the value of which is uncertain are payable as an expense of the administration.[95]

The administrator is obliged to allow inspection of all proofs lodged with him at all reasonable times on any business day by any creditor who has submitted a proof of debt which has not been rejected or by any contributory of the company.[96]

Any proof of debt submitted in administration may be admitted for dividend either for the whole or part of the amount claimed by the particular creditor.[97] If, however, the administrator wholly or partially rejects a proof, he is obliged to send to the creditor concerned, as soon as is reasonably practicable, a written statement of his reasons for doing so.[98] If a creditor is dissatisfied with the

---

[86] r.2.88(1).
[87] r.2.88(3).
[88] rr.2.88(4) and (5).
[89] r.2.88(6).
[90] r.2.88(7).
[91] r.2.88(9).
[92] r.2.89. Note that r.2.105(2) now takes into account distributions previously made to a creditor, so that the reduction applies to the amount remaining outstanding in respect of the admitted proof (as opposed to the full amount). The amendment was made by the Insolvency (Amendment) Rules 2005 (SI 2005/527) following Lord Millett's comments in *Re Park Air Services Plc* [2000] 2 A.C. 172 (HL), [88].
[93] r.2.79.
[94] r.2.74(a).
[95] rr.2.74(b) and r.2.81(1).
[96] r.2.75.
[97] r.2.77(1).
[98] r.2.77(2).

administrator's decision with respect to his proof, he may apply to the court for the decision to be reversed or varied, provided he does so within 21 days of his receipt of the administrator's statement.[99] Further, any other creditor may make an application to court for the reversal or variation of the administrator's admission or rejection of any claim in whole or in part, provided he does so within 21 days of becoming aware of the administrator's decision.[100]

Unless the court orders otherwise, the administrator is not personally liable for the costs incurred by any creditor in an application for the reversal or variation of the administrator's decision in respect of a particular proof of debt.[101] It is also worth mentioning that the court may expunge entirely or reduce the amount claimed in a proof on an application by either the administrator or, where the administrator declines to interfere in the matter, by a creditor.[102]

The administrator is obliged to estimate the value of any debt where its value is uncertain, subject to his power to revise such estimate in the light of any change in circumstance or information becoming available to him, and to inform the creditor concerned of his estimate and any subsequent revision of it.[103] The amount provable in the administration in such a case is the value of the estimate for the time being.[104]

(iv) Set-off

Rule 2.85 of the Rules is the insolvency set-off provision applicable in admin- **27–014** istration and is dealt with in Ch.22 of this work.

(v) Secured creditors

Although r.2.68(1) of the Rules provides that Ch.10 of the Rules applies where **27–015** the administrator makes, or proposes to make, a distribution to any class of creditors, the better view is that this reference to "distributions" refers only to payments made by the administrator out of the assets of the company, rather than in respect of realisations of secured assets.[105] The Act itself makes no such distinction, and the term "distribution" is used to refer to payments made by the administrator to unsecured and preferential creditors, as well as to secured creditors out of the proceeds of realisations of charged assets.[106] Nevertheless, it seems clear that a secured creditor does not have to prove for a distribution to the extent of the value of his security. The rules relating to disposals of

---

[99] r.2.78(1).

[100] r.2.78(2). As to the procedure for the filing and, where relevant, return of a proof on an application for the reversal or variation of the administrator's decision in respect of the same, see rr.2.78(3) to (5).

[101] r.2.78(6).

[102] r.2.80(1). Notice of any such application must be sent to the creditor whose proof is disputed and, in the case of an application by another creditor, to the administrator (r.2.80(2)).

[103] r.2.81(1).

[104] r.2.81(2).

[105] This is subject, of course, to the application of the Rules to the making of distributions from realisations of assets subject to a floating charge to preferential creditors (s.175 and para.65(2)) and unsecured creditors by virtue of the prescribed part provisions (s.176A), as the case may be.

[106] para.65(3).

property subject to fixed or floating charge security affirm the view that application of the proceeds of such realisations fall outside the distribution procedures set down in the Rules. Where the secured creditor obtains the consent of the administrator or permission of the court to enforce security over the company's property,[107] notwithstanding the operation of the statutory moratorium on legal process applicable in administration, it is suggested that a payment of the proceeds of such realisation to the secured creditor would not amount to a distribution within the meaning of the regime set out in the Rules for distributions. Similarly, on application by the administrator, the court may order the administrator freely to dispose of property subject to a fixed charge where it thinks this is likely to promote the purposes of the administration, provided the net proceeds of such disposal as applied towards discharging the sums secured[108] and there would be no obvious purpose in applying the distribution rules.

A secured creditor may however prove for a distribution following realisation of his security in respect of any balance of the debt due to him over and above the amount realised[109] or he may wish to prove in anticipation of a shortfall. Such a secured creditor must include in his proof particulars of his security, the date on which it was given and the value which he puts on it.[110] He should also include in his proof details of any documents by reference to which the debt can be substantiated, and, whilst it is not essential that any such documents be submitted with the proof in the first instance, the administrator has the power to call for production to him of such documents.[111] If a secured creditor omits to disclose his security in his proof of debt, he is bound to surrender his security for the general benefit of creditors, unless the court orders otherwise on application by him, on the grounds that the omission was inadvertent or the result of an honest mistake.[112]

The administrator may at any time give 28 days' notice to a secured creditor that he proposes to redeem the security at the value put on it in the creditor's proof,[113] whereupon the creditor has 21 days (or such longer period as the administrator may allow) in which, if he so wishes, to exercise his right to revalue his security.[114] A secured creditor may at any time alter the value put upon his security in his proof of debt with the permission of the administrator or the leave of the court.[115] However, he may revalue only with the permission of the court where he is the applicant for an administration order or the appointor of the administrator and has in the application or notice of appoint-

---

[107] para.43(2).

[108] paras 71(1), 71(2) and 71(3).

[109] r.2.83(1). In addition, r.2.83(2) provides that should a secured creditor voluntarily surrender his security for the general benefit of creditors, he may prove for the whole of his debt as if he were unsecured.

[110] r.2.72(3)(vii).

[111] rr.2.72(4) and (5).

[112] r.2.91(1). Where the court grants relief under this Rule, it may require the creditor's proof to be amended on such terms as it considers just (r.2.91(2)).

[113] r.2.92(1). Where the administrator redeems the security in this way, the cost of transferring it is payable out of the assets of the company (r.2.92(3)).

[114] r.2.92(2).

[115] r.2.90(1).

ment put a value on his security, or, alternatively, he has voted in respect of any unsecured balance of the debt owed to him.[116]

If the administrator is dissatisfied with the value which a secured creditor puts on his security (whether in his proof or by way of revaluation as described above), he may require any property comprised in the security to be offered for sale,[117] the terms of such sale being as agreed or as the court may direct.[118] If it is decided that the sale should be by auction, the administrator may appear and bid on behalf of the company and the creditor may appear and bid on his own behalf.[119]

It is also worth mentioning that where a secured creditor who has valued his security subsequently realises it, whether or not he is directed to do so by the administrator, the net amount thereby realised is substituted for his previous valuation and is in all respects treated as an amended valuation made by him.[120]

(vi)   Declaring and paying a dividend

Where the administrator intends a distribution to be a sole and final dividend, **27–016** he is obliged, after the date specified in his notice under rr.2.95(1) as the date up to which proofs may be lodged, to defray:

(i)   any outstanding expenses of a liquidation or provisional liquidation that immediately preceded the administration;

(ii)   any items payable in accordance with the provisions of Sch.B1, para.99[121];

(iii)   any amounts which would be payable out of the company's property in accordance with the provisions of Sch.B1, para.99, if he were to cease to be the administrator of the company[122]; and

to declare and distribute the dividend without regard to the claim of any person in respect of a debt not already proved.

The administrator is also obliged, within seven days of the date specified in his r.2.95(1) notice, and unless he has already dealt with them, to admit, reject or make such provisions as he thinks fit in respect of proofs submitted to him.[123]

Within the period of two months from the last date for proving, the administrator must declare the dividend to the relevant class or classes of creditors to

---

[116] r.2.90(2).
[117] r.2.93(1).
[118] r.2.93(2).
[119] r.2.93(2).
[120] r.2.94.
[121] See, however, *Re Huddersfield Fine Worsteds Ltd/Globe Worsted Company Ltd* and *Re Ferrotech Ltd/Re Granville Technology Group Ltd* [2005] 4 All E.R. 886 (CA) and *Re Leeds United Association Football Club Ltd* [2008] B.C.C. 11. See further Ch.4.
[122] r.2.68(3).
[123] r.2.96(1).

which he gave notice pursuant to r.2.95(1).[124] This obligation does not normally lie where there is a pending application to the court to reverse or vary the administrator's decision on a proof, or to expunge a proof or reduce the amount claimed.[125] The administrator is not obliged to deal with proofs lodged after the last date for proving, but he may do so if he thinks fit.[126] Where the administrator declares a dividend he is obliged to give notice of such declaration to all creditors who have proved their debts and, if relevant, any member state liquidator appointed in relation to the company.[127] The dividend may be distributed simultaneously with the notice of declaration.[128]

Provided he has the permission of the creditors or the creditors' committee, as appropriate, the administrator may divide any unsold assets amongst the company's creditors according to the estimated value, by way of distribution in specie, where they cannot be readily or advantageously sold.[129]

(vii)   Ranking of creditors

27–017   An administrator is bound to make payments to preferential creditors in priority to all other debts, with only the expenses of the administration being paid in precedence to them.[130] As in a winding-up, preferential debts in an administration rank equally among themselves and must be paid in full, unless the assets of the company are insufficient to meet them, in which case they abate in equal proportions.[131] The categories of preferential creditors are limited to contributions to occupational pension schemes, remuneration of employees and levies on coal and steel production.[132] In an administration, the date that determines the existence and the amount of a preferential debt is the date on which the company enters administration.[133] For a discussion of the position in relation to a company which is being wound-up, see para.28–048, below.

The prescribed part provisions which allow for a share of the company's assets to be made available for the benefit of unsecured creditors are applicable in administration as they are in receivership.[134] These are dealt with below, at para.28–053 et seq.[135]

Non-preferential debts rank equally between themselves and insofar as the assets are insufficient to allow payment in full, they abate in equal proportions

---

[124] rr.2.97(1) and 2.95(4)(a).
[125] r.2.97(2).
[126] r.2.96(2).
[127] r.2.98(1). The particulars to be contained in the declaration notice are listed at r.2.98(2).
[128] r.2.99(1).
[129] r.2.71.
[130] para.65(2) and s.175(1). See further Ch.4.
[131] para.65(2) and s.175(2)(a).
[132] para.65(2), s.386(1) and paras 8–15A of Sch.6.
[133] ss.387(1) and 387(3A). cf. the position in receivership (see para.28–047).
[134] s.176A(1).
[135] For an example of the disapplication of the prescribed part provisions by way of a court order under s.176A(5), see Re Hydroserve Ltd [2007] All E.R. (D) 184 and Re International Sections Ltd (In Liquidation) [2009] B.C.C. 574.

between themselves.[136] The case of *Re Courts Plc (In Liquidation)*[137] reiterated this point as the High Court confirmed that an order for the disapplication of the requirement to make a prescribed part of a company's assets available for unsecured creditors must apply equally to all creditors. In this instance, there was no jurisdiction for a partial disapplication in line with the principle of pari passu distribution in the treatment of unsecured creditors.

(viii)   Dissolution

Once a distribution has been made pursuant to para.65(3) and the administrator   **27–018** thinks the company has no further funds to distribute to its creditors, he is then normally under a duty to send a notice to this effect to the registrar of companies[138] and the company is deemed to be dissolved three months after the administrator's registration of such a notice.[139] This is subject to the administrator's ability under para.84(2) to apply to the court to disapply para.84(1) in the event that an exit route other than dissolution is appropriate. The administrator's appointment ceases to have effect on the registration of the notice.[140] There is no need for a court-appointed administrator sending a notice pursuant to para.84(1) to make a separate application to terminate his appointment or to discharge the administration order.[141]

8.   ENDING ADMINISTRATION—TERMINATION

(a)   Automatic end of administration

Schedule B1, para.76 of Insolvency Act 1986 provides for the appointment of an   **27–019** administrator to cease to have effect at the end of the period of one year beginning with the date on which it takes effect.[142] This automatic end to the appointment of an administrator applies however the administrator was appointed and, by virtue of Sch.B1, para.1(2)(c) of Insolvency Act 1986, the company ceases to be in administration as a consequence of such automatic cessation. The provision is a harsh one, caused not so much by the period in question but by its automatic effect: there is no ability to extend this term either by order of the

---

[136] r.2.69.

[137] *Re Courts Plc (In Liquidation)* [2009] 1 W.L.R. 1499.

[138] *Re GHE Realisations* [2005] EWHC 2400 (Ch), [24], per Rimer J. (giving the example of the administrator forming the view that there should instead be a winding-up by the court as possibly being an exceptional case in which a disapplication of para.84(1) might be appropriate). The relevant time for the purposes of para.84(1) is the time at which the administrator forms a view as to the company having no further property for distribution to its creditors, which need not be at the outset and may even be the case following a sale of the company's assets. cf. *Re Ballast Plc* [2005] 1 W.L.R. 1928.

[139] paras 84(2) and 84(6). The administrator must, as soon as is reasonably practicable, file a copy of the notice with the court and send a copy of the notice to each creditor of whose claim and address he is aware: para.84(5).

[140] para.84(4).

[141] *Re Ballast Plc* [2005] 1 W.L.R. 1928.

[142] As to when an administration takes effect, see Ch.5.

court[143] or with the consent of creditors[144] after its expiry.[145] Experience from other pieces of legislation which have provisions which expire by effluxion of time, shows that there is a real risk that a number of former administrators will be caught off guard by this provision, which leads one to consider what remedies may be available to affected parties as a consequence.

Schedule B1, para.98(1), provides that where a person ceases to be the administrator of a company, including where he is removed from office under Sch.B1, para.76, he is discharged from liability in respect of any "action" of his as administrator. Paragraph 98(2) provides that the discharge under para.98(1) only takes effect in the case of an administrator appointed under para.14 or 22 at a time appointed by resolution of the creditors' committee or, if there is no committee, by resolution of the creditors or in any case at a time specified by the court. Therefore the administrator who finds himself out of office and out of time to seek an extension as a result of para.76 will find that no discharge is forthcoming under para.98(1) until a determination is made under para.98(2).

27–020   What would be the liability of the former administrator in the above circumstances? Like directors, administrators owe their duties to the company[146] for which they act and therefore an individual unsecured creditor would not have a freestanding right to pursue a claim. Therefore, a claim for breach of duty in failing to seek an extension would appear to be a claim, which could potentially be brought under Sch.B1, para.75 (but not Sch.B1, para.74 since this requires that the company is in administration at the time of its making),[147] by any of the parties set out in para.75(2), including a creditor or contributory of the company, provided that this is being done in furtherance of the class remedy rights, conferred by this paragraph, and not motivated by a grievance peculiar to any such party which does not affect the company at large. There is a difficulty reconciling such an action (which would require an allegation of breach of duty resulting in the general body of creditors suffering some form of loss), with the duty of the administrator under Sch.B1, para.4 to perform his functions as quickly and efficiently as is reasonably practicable It is thought that it is perfectly possible for an administrator to be in breach of duty in failing to seek an extension under para.76, notwithstanding the overriding duty conferred by para.4 and that such duties are not mutually exclusive. Parliament conferred the mechanisms under para.76 to extend the administrator's term of office and thereby recognised that in certain instances it will take more than one year to conclude the administration and therefore the administrator may be duty bound to seek such an extension. The former administrator who carries on acting having failed to note that his appointment has automatically ended by virtue of

---

[143] para.77(1)(b).

[144] para.78(4)(c).

[145] The company or its directors could not simply re-appoint the administrator under Sch.B1, para.22 since they may only make such an appointment if the company has not in the previous 12 months been in administration as a result of either a direct appointment by the company or its directors or an application by them (Sch.B1 para.23). Any such re-appointment would, in those circumstances, need to be done by the holder of a qualifying floating charge or by the court.

[146] See *Charalambous v B&C Associates* [2009] 43 E.G. 105 (C.S.) and *Hague v Nam Tai Electronics* [2008] B.C.C. 295 (PC).

[147] *Kyrris v Oldham* [2004] B.C.C. 111 (CA), para.75(2)(c).

para.76, may be liable to the company in tort for damages for his actions in interfering with the possession of the company or interfering with its property and potentially to third parties for breach of warranty of authority and interference with contracts. It would appear that in those circumstances, Sch.B1, para.21 (where the appointment is discovered to be invalid rather than where the appointment is valid but expires under para.76) and para.104 (where the act of an administrator is valid in spite of a defect in his appointment or qualification[148]) would not assist the unwitting former administrator.

(b) Court application for extension of administrator's term of office

Under Sch.B1, para.76(2), the court may on the application of an administrator **27–021** extend the administrator's term of office by court order for a specified period. The application needs to be made by the administrator, rather than any other interested party, and the requirement is that the court order is made prior to the expiry of the administrator's term of office[149] so that merely issuing the application prior to that date will not suffice. In *Re E-Squared Ltd* and *Re Sussex Pharmaceutical Ltd*,[150] David Richards J. held that para.83 requires an administrator to be in office when he sends a notice to the Registrar of Companies to convert an administration into a creditors' voluntary liquidation. However, there is no requirement in para.83 that an administrator must still be in that office when the notice is actually registered by the registrar of companies. Such cases turn on the proper construction of para.83(6) and do not detract from the clear words of para.77(1)(b), which expressly requires the order—not the application—to be made before the expiry of the administrator's term of office. That said, in *Re TT Industries Ltd*,[151] H.H.J. Norris, sitting as a deputy judge of the High Court in Birmingham, held that an extension of the administration could be ordered notwithstanding the lapse of the administrator's appointment, where an application for extension had already been made and there were grounds to indicate that the delay was at least in part due to the way the application had been handled by the court staff.[152] There is a rising concern among registrars at Companies Court that applications to extend administrations are needlessly being made very close to the automatic expiry date, usually a day or two before. The court's expectations for receiving such an application have recently been revised from four weeks to at least six weeks before the administration is due to expire. The rationale for this is to allow the court time to consider whether the application should be considered on paper or at a hearing. Only "unusual reasons" can warrant a late application but as there is little further clarification on what constitutes an "unusual reason", this carve-out must be treated with caution by administrators. Moreover, non-compliance

---

[148] para.104 is consistent with the provisions of s.232 Insolvency Act 1986 insofar as it only validates defects relating to the procedure for appointment.

[149] para.77(1)(b).

[150] *Re Sussex Pharmaceutical Ltd* [2006] 1 W.L.R. 3414.

[151] *Re TT Industries Ltd* [2006] B.C.C. 372.

[152] Sealy and Milman, *Annotated Guide to the Insolvency Legislation 2010*, Vol. 1, p.584.

with the new six week deadline will result in a court order excluding the administrator's costs of the application from being paid as an expense of the administration. Failure to make applications to extend administrations in good time prior to the automatic expiry date are to be avoided and would result in lost sanctions against administrators should they fail to do so.

An application to court for an extension of the administration must be accompanied by a progress report for the period since either the last progress report (if any) or the date the company entered administration.[153] If the court grants an extension (which it may do in respect of an administrator whose term of office has already been extended by order or by consent[154]), then the administrator shall as soon as is reasonably practicable notify the Registrar of Companies[155] of the relevant order. Schedule B1 provides no express guidance as to the criteria the court has to apply in considering whether such an extension should be granted. In the unreported case of *Re Trident Fashions Plc*,[156] it was held that the test the court should apply on such an application should be similar to that applied on the making of an administration order on the application to court,[157] that is whether the extension of the administration is reasonably likely to achieve the purpose of the administration. The court also took account of the fact that it was considered unlikely that creditors would suffer prejudice as a result of the extension and also that a number of interested parties had consented to the extension. Accordingly, notwithstanding the obligation on the part of the administrator to perform his functions as quickly and efficiently as is reasonably practicable, it is expected that where there are good reasons justifying such an extension and the benefits outweigh any potential prejudice to an affected party taking account of possible limitation issues,[158] the court in its discretion will grant the extension. The evidence in support of such an application can be commensurate with the level of information now required in support of an application to the court for an administration order.

(c) Consent procedure for extension of administrator's term of office

27–022   An alternative to seeking an extension from the court is to obtain the creditors' consent[159] (in writing or signified at a creditors' meeting[160]) to an extension. By this method the term of the administration can be extended for a period not exceeding six months, provided that consent is received from:

[153] r.2.112(1) Insolvency Rules 1986.
[154] para.77(1)(a).
[155] paras 77(2).
[156] See P. Ridgeway and R. Beckwith, "Administrations: One Year On" (2005) 18 Insolv. Int. 27.
[157] Sch.B1, para.11(b).
[158] See *Re Cosslett (Contractors) Ltd* [2004] EWHC 658 (Ch) and *Re Maxwell Fleet and Facilities Management Ltd* [2000] 1 All E.R. 464, albeit that the distinction between liquidation and administration on limitation would seem harder to sustain under the new administration regime.
[159] para.76(2)(b).
[160] para.78(3).

(a) each secured creditor[161]; and

(b) the unsecured creditors entitled to at least 50 per cent of the company's unsecured debts (which proportion need not include any unsecured creditor who fails to respond to a request for consent)[162] but where the statement of proposals states that the administrator thinks that the company has insufficient property to enable a distribution to be made to unsecured creditors other than by virtue of s.176A(2)(a), the consent need only be given by each of the secured creditors and the preferential creditors whose debts amount to more than 50 per cent of the preferential debts of the company, disregarding debts of any creditor who fails to respond to a request for consent.[163]

The request for consent must come with a progress report.[164] The administration may only be extended once by consent.[165] Further, extension by consent is not available if any extension has already been granted by the court,[166] nor if the term of the administration has already expired.[167] Since the consent procedure cannot be used if an extension has already been granted by the court, it is likely that the administrator will first seek the consent of creditors, with any further extensions being sought from the court. There may be appropriate instances (for example, where there may be uncertainty as to which creditors are required to consent), where an application to court to extend the administrator's tenure of office will be made without having first sought the consent of the creditors. Further, the court may make an order in circumstances where the consent of creditors has not been forthcoming (albeit that any active opposition to the extension of the administrator's appointment, would, no-doubt, be taken into account by any court in determining whether to exercise its discretion to grant any such order). Once an administrator's term is extended by consent, he

27–023

---

[161] A recurring potential difficulty with the new regime relates to the requirement for consent from each secured creditor of the company. The definition of a "secured creditor" under s.248(1)(a) is such that consents may be required from secured creditors who have little, if any, interest in the administration process including secured creditors with security over cash or shares and rights under the Financial Collateral Arrangements (No.2) Regulations 2003. This could lead, either through apathy or a particular bargaining position being taken, to secured creditors frustrating the administrator's intentions. When the question was being considered during the course of the Enterprise Bill's progress through the House of Lords, the fact that it may not be timely or practical to obtain the consent of everyone was recognised, (with either a 75 per cent majority in number or value test being considered). However, the amendment was withdrawn, with Lord McIntosh of Haringey, noting that the administrator would have, in any event, the right to apply for an extension from the court as an alternative and also "more importantly, in reality the administrator must elicit the support of the secured creditors ... to avoid them enforcing their security immediately at the end of an administration moratorium thus probably destroying the possibility of a rescue." Hansard (HL) October 21, 2002, Column 1123.

[162] para.78(1).
[163] para.78(2).
[164] r.2.112(2).
[165] para.78(4).
[166] para.78(4).
[167] para.78(4).

must notify the Registrar of Companies and notice must also be filed with the court.[168]

Within five business days of automatic termination, the administrator must file in court a notice of automatic termination in the prescribed form together with a final progress report.[169] A copy of the notice and report must be sent as soon as possible to the Registrar of Companies and all persons who received a copy of the proposals.[170] The final progress report must be in the form specified in r.2.47 Insolvency Rules 1986 and include a summary of the administrator's proposals, any major amendments to, or deviations from, those proposals, the steps taken during the administration and the outcome of the administration.[171] The reference to an obligation on the part of an administrator to give notice and file a final progress report (failing which he is liable to a fine[172]) may seem in conflict with the fact that the administrator's appointment has already ceased to have effect by virtue of Sch.B1, para.76 and, without the provisions of Sch.B1, para.98, the administrator being discharged from liability following the administrator giving notice and filing the final progress report. Accordingly, one would expect the time specified by the court, the creditors' committee or the resolution of the creditors to have regard to these requirements for the purposes of determining under para.98 at what time the discharge takes effect. Notwithstanding this possible conflict, the former administrator has the authority and the obligation to perform those roles provided for by the Act and Rules in circumstances in which it is expressly acknowledged that they will occur after the cessation of the administrator's appointment.

(d) Court ending administration on application of administrator

27–024   The administrator may, under Sch.B1, para.79(1), make an application to the court for his appointment to cease to have effect from a specified time.[173] Paragraph 79(2) provides that the administrator shall[174] make such an application if he thinks that the purpose of the administration cannot be achieved or if he thinks that the company should not have entered administration (for example, where it is found to be solvent) or a creditors' meeting requires him to make such an application.[175] In any of these scenarios, there is a right or

---

[168] para.78(5)—see also r.2.133(5), which provides that where the administrator is obliged to give notice to, or provide a copy of a document (including an order of the court) to, the court, the Registrar of Companies or the official receiver, the administrator shall give notice or provides copies, as the case may be, to any member state liquidator appointed in relation to the company.

[169] r.2.111.

[170] r.2.111 and r.13.13(1) for the meaning of the expression "business day".

[171] r.2.110.

[172] r.2.111(3).

[173] para.79(1).

[174] In *Re Transbus International Ltd* [2004] 1 W.L.R. 2654, held that the word "shall" for the purposes of para.68(2) was mandatory and required the administrator to act in accordance with the directions of the court, "if the court gives them". The reference to "shall" is to be contrasted with the word "may" in para.83(3) as to which see *Re Ballast Plc (In Administration)* [2005] 1 W.L.R. 1928.

[175] para.79(2).

obligation to make the application irrespective of the method by which the company entered into administration. Further, under Sch.B1, para.79(3), the administrator of a company shall make an application if the administration is pursuant to an administration order and the administrator thinks (following a rational thought process)[176] that the purpose of the administration has been successfully achieved in relation to the company.[177] Accordingly, para.79 has three limbs: a discretionary right on the part of the administrator to apply to end the administration, an obligation to do so in certain circumstances (which, presumably, will invariably occur where there has been a failure of the administration process) and an obligation to do so, if the purpose of administration has been successfully achieved in those cases where the court has made an administration order. The court, on an application under para.79, may adjourn the hearing conditionally or unconditionally, dismiss the application, make an interim order or make any order it thinks appropriate (whether in addition to, in consequence of, or instead of, the order applied for).[178] As a procedure it has been described as leaving the company "in limbo" once the administration has ended,[179] with, as a practical consequence, either control being returned to its directors or (where this is not appropriate) the administrator petitioning for the compulsory winding up of the company.[180] This description is arguably an over simplification since there will be instances where, following an application under para.79, it is appropriate for the company to be restored to the control of its directors, where arrangements for its dissolution or liquidation can be put in place outside the procedures under paras 83 and 84 or where a company voluntary arrangement or scheme of arrangement under s.425 of the Companies Act 1985 has been approved. Indeed, none of the procedures outlined in paras 76 to 81 provide for the termination of the administrator's appointment to be followed by any other insolvency regime; accordingly, in each case it will be for the administrator to judge what procedure, if any, should govern the company's immediate future after the end of his term of office.

In the case of *Re Ballast Plc*[181] the court was asked to determine, in the case of three companies in administration, whether an administrator appointed by the court who thought that the purpose of the administrations had been successfully achieved was obliged pursuant to para.79(3) to make such applications for his appointments to cease to have effect where it was intended that two of

27-025

---

[176] For a discussion on the meaning of the word "thinks" where used in the Insolvency Act 1986 see Marion Simmons QC, "Enterprise Act and Plain English" (2004) 17 Insolv. Int. 76. See also *Unidare Plc v Cohen* [2006] Ch. 489.

[177] para.79(3).

[178] para.79(4).

[179] The power to make an application under para.79(1) is not confined to the circumstances in para.79(2) or (3) which oblige the administrator to make the application, see *Re TM Kingdom Ltd (In Administration)* [2007] B.C.C. 480. *Re GHE Realisations Ltd (formerly Gatehouse Estates Ltd)* [2006] 1 W.L.R. 287, [22], and Dear IP, Issue 22—March 2005.

[180] As Millett J. observed in *Re Barrow Borough Transport Ltd* [1989] B.C.L.C. 653, 658: "... the court will not discharge the administration order where the company is insolvent unless proper proposals are put forward to achieve the realisation of the company's assets and their distribution amongst the creditors, and that requires a liquidation." The decision was approved by the Court of Appeal in *Oakley Smith v Greenberg* [2004] B.C.C. 81 (CA).

[181] *Re Ballast Plc (In Administration)* [2005] 1 W.L.R. 1928.

the companies would move from administration to creditors' voluntary liquidation pursuant to para.83 and the remaining company from administration to dissolution pursuant to para.84. Blackburne J. held that applications under para.(3) would be unnecessary, with the procedure under para.79 being a distinct and separate exit-route from the procedures under paras 83 and 84, and it being open to the administrators to have recourse to these without first applying for any order under para.79. This decision was followed by Rimer J. in *Re GHE Realisations Ltd* where, after noting that any application under para.79 could fit in with the automatic provisions to the like effect in para.84(4), he also held that para.84 is by itself able to bring the administrator's appointment to an end and no application under para.79(3) was or is necessary.[182] This represents a common sense approach by the courts in circumstances where an administrator has acted responsibly in seeking a direction from the court and where there was a stated intention to use either the procedure under paras 83 or 84. However, those paras do not obviate the requirement for an administrator to make an application under para.79 should circumstances so dictate and the administrators cannot invoke the procedures under paras 83 or 84.

(e)   Termination of administration where objective achieved

27–026   If an administrator appointed out of court under either para.14 or 22 thinks that the purpose of the administration (being one of the three objectives set out in Sch.B1, para.3(1)) has been sufficiently[183] achieved in relation to the company he may file a notice in the prescribed form with the court and with the Registrar of Companies, whereupon the administrator's appointment shall cease to have effect[184] but an administrator appointed by way of administration order from the court cannot terminate the administration under this provision. The procedure does not compel the administrator to end the administration in this manner if the purpose of the administration has been sufficiently achieved. Nor should it be used if to do so would result in the company being left in a state of limbo as described in para.27–024, above. It might be the case that the administrator is still able to make an application to court under para.79 if further relief is needed as part of the termination process (e.g. the making of a winding-up order). However, the difficulty this presents is that, in order to invoke this jurisdiction, it would seem that the administrator needs to come within one or other of the situations set out in para.79[185] and the only one which is not

---

[182] *Re GHE Realisations Ltd* [2006] 1 W.L.R. 287, at [25]. The decision has also been followed in *Re Preston & Duckworth Ltd (In Liquidation)* [2006] B.C.C. 133; *Re Graham* Unreported March 26, 2007; *Re T M Kingdom Ltd* [2007] B.C.C. 480.

[183] In terms of the standard of what represents "sufficient" achievement, it is submitted that this represents an objective test having regard to whether a reasonable insolvency practitioner would think that the purpose of the administration had been sufficiently achieved.

[184] paras 80(2) and (3) (albeit that r.2.113(3) provides that time of the court's endorsement of the notice shall be the date and time from which the appointment shall cease to have effect, which para.80(3) stipulates the time as being when the notice is filed with the court and the Registrar of Companies. Unlike para.80(3), there is no requirement for the appointment to cease to have effect on registration of a notice by the Registrar of Companies.

[185] See para.27–024, above.

inconsistent with para.80 and the sufficient achievement of the purpose of the administration by an administrator appointed out of court is para.79(1), which entitles any administrator to apply to court, at any time for the appointment to cease to have effect from a specified time. The court's power under para.79(4) to make any order it thinks appropriate has to be made on an application to end the administrator's appointment. Therefore, if the appointment is brought to an end under the procedure set out in para.80 there can be no application under para.79. Further, in circumstances where an application is brought under para.79(1) this would render the procedure set out in para.80 nugatory as a means of bringing to an end the administrator's appointment. Accordingly where an administrator appointed out of court intends to place the company into compulsory liquidation, the correct course is to make an application to end the administration under para.79(1) and then, in conjunction with such an application, issue a winding-up petition under s.124 Insolvency Act 1986 (which then requires the administrator to notify creditors whether he intends to seek appointment as liquidator under r.2.114(4) Insolvency Rules 1986).

Under r.2.33(6) of the Insolvency Rules 1968, where the administrator **27–027** intends to apply to the court or file a notice under para.80(2) for the administration to cease at a time before he has sent a statement of his proposals to creditors in accordance with para.49, he shall, at least 10 days before he makes such an application (or files such a notice), send to all creditors of the company (so far as he is aware of their addresses) a report containing the information required by r.2.33 para.(2)(a)–(p). The fact that the Rules expressly acknowledge such a situation is consistent with the case of *Re Charnley Davies Business Services Ltd*[186] where the court discharged administration orders without any creditors' meeting being summoned under the provisions then in effect under s.23 Insolvency Act 1986. Under para.80(4), where the administrator files a notice, together with a final progress report, he shall send to every creditor of the company of whose claim and address he is aware, within five business days, a copy of the notice and accompanying report. In the alternative, he shall publish such notice in the prescribed manner[187] and undertake to provide a copy of the notice of end of administration (presumably on request and accompanied by the final progress report) to any creditor of the company. The administrator has also to send, as soon as reasonably practicable, and within five business days, a copy of the notice to all those persons who were notified of his appointment and to the company (the publication of notice only being an alternative in the case of creditors).

(f) Court ending administration on application of creditor

On the application of a creditor, the court may order that the appointment of the **27–028** administrator cease to have effect at a specified time.[188] An application under

---

[186] *Re Charnley Davies Business Services Ltd* (1987) 3 B.C.C. 408.
[187] para.80(4), 80(5), rr.2.110(1), 2.113(5) and 2.113(6).
[188] para.81(1).

this procedure must allege an improper motive, either: (a) in the case of an administrator appointed by an administration order, on the part of the applicant for the order; or (b) in any other case on the part of the person who appointed the administrator.[189] On an application under this procedure, the court may adjourn the hearing, dismiss the application, make an interim order or make any order it thinks appropriate.[190] Service of the application shall be effected not less than five business days before the date fixed for the hearing. The administrator, applicant or appointor, or holder of the floating charge by virtue of which the appointment was made is entitled to appear at the hearing.[191] A copy of the application shall be served on the administrator and the person who either made the application for the administration order or made the appointment.[192] There is no statutory guidance on what amounts to improper motivation for these purposes although it would seem that one need only show that (on a subjective basis) the appointment was underpinned by an improper motive. However, an improper motive should be distinguished from a motive which has an incidental or private benefit for the appointor, neither of which renders an otherwise good faith and proper motive improper.[193]

For a useful and full exposition of the construction of "proper motive", see *Kerr & Hunter on Receivers and Administrators*, 19th edn (London: Sweet & Maxwell, 2009), Ch.17.

---

[189] para.81(2).

[190] para.81(3). Only para.81(2) requires the application to allege an improper motive there is no requirement for the court to establish such a motive before making any order under para.81(3) (although one would expect that the court would need to be satisfied of this before providing for the appointment of the administrator to cease to have effect or granting any form of substantive relief). However, this area demonstrates particular lack of foresight on the part of the draftsmen in leaving the court with no guidance on how it should exercise its wide discretion under para.81(3) and on whether the establishment of an improper motive is a prerequisite to any substantive order or indeed whether it needs to be satisfied of the basis of the improper motive as alleged or whether any other improper motive determined by the court will suffice. Indeed, there may be situations, where an improper motive (which need not be the only motive) on the part of the applicant is established but that there are good reasons why the company should remain in administration. In that instance, the court may dismiss the application leaving the applicant with a finding of improper motive but without the cessation of the administration.

[191] r.2.115(2)—presumably the court would not regard r.2.115(2) as precluding others from attending and appearing on such an application (see r.7.53(1). See also *Re Dianoor Jewels Ltd* [2001] 1 B.C.L.C. 450 and *Re Bydand Ltd* [1997] B.C.C. 915 where the court refused to rescind a winding-up order made on the petition of a district council based on the company's inability to pay debts following liability orders for unpaid non-domestic rates. The petition was in the wrong sum because some of the liability orders were disputed but there was an undisputed element of debt exceeding the statutory minimum. The fact that the district council's principal (a county council) had pending proceedings against the company did not attribute to the district council some sufficiently improper motive to justify rescission. See also *Dennis Rye Ltd v Bolsover DC* [2009] 4 All E.R. 1140 (CA).

[192] r.2.115(2).

[193] It may seem that the "improper motive" test is a charter for any disaffected party to impugn the administrator's appointment but one would hope and expect that the courts would take a robust view and confine this remedy to those situations where there is clear impropriety on the part of the appointor. In particular, it is submitted that it should be confined to cases of abuse of the administration procedure rather than used as a means of trying to frustrate those cases where the purpose of administration is reasonably likely to be achieved. *Re Dianoor Jewels Ltd* [2001] 1 B.C.L.C. 450; and see also *Cornhill Insurance Plc v Cornhill Financial Services Ltd* [1992] B.C.C. 818 (CA).

9. TERMINATION FOLLOWED BY LIQUIDATION

(a) Introduction

It is incumbent on the administrator to arrange for the continuing management **27–029** of the company and its affairs upon the termination of an administration.[194] In this regard, the administrator's proposals are required to include provision for how the administration is to end.[195] If the company has been returned to solvency it might be appropriate for control to be restored to the directors.[196] It may also be sufficient for the administration to be terminated without further order or relief[197] where the company has entered a voluntary arrangement[198] with its creditors or a scheme of arrangement[199] is sanctioned by the court. Where, however, the company has not been returned to solvency it will be necessary for an administrator where an administration order was made on a petition presented prior to September 15, 2003[200] to take steps to place the company into liquidation and for administration orders or applications made on or after September 15, 2003 and out-of-court appointments made on or after the same date)[201] the administrator remains under an obligation to place the company into liquidation or, in the circumstances outlined below, to have the company dissolved.[202]

(b) Compulsory liquidation

An administrator has power to petition for the winding-up of the company.[203] **27–030** The petition must comply with r.4.7(7), in particular: (i) it should be expressed to be the petition of the company acting by its administrator; (ii) it should state the name of the administrator, the date the company entered administration and the court case number; and (iii) to the extent applicable under the new regime, the petition must also include an application under para.79(2) of Sch.B1 seeking an order that the appointment of the administrator shall cease

---

[194] See, for instance *Re Barrow Borough Transport Ltd* [1990] Ch. 227 for discussion of an administrator's duty under the old regime. For discussion on the termination of an administration see Ch.12 below.

[195] See the Insolvency Rules 1986, r.2.33(2)(m).

[196] It is not essential for the company's long-term solvency to be assured, provided the proposed business plan stands a fair chance of success and is in the best interests of the company and its creditors generally: *Re Olympia & York Canary Wharf Holdings* [1993] B.C.C. 866.

[197] Under the new regime, this may be achieved by implementing the notice procedure at para.80.

[198] See the Insolvency Act 1986, s.1.

[199] See the Companies Act 1985, s.425.

[200] See the Enterprise Act 2002 (Commencement No.4 and Transitional Provisions and Savings) Order 2003 (SI 2003/2093).

[201] See the Enterprise Act 2002 (Commencement No.4 and Transitional Provisions and Savings) Order 2003 (SI 2003/2093).

[202] See *Re Barrow Borough Transport Lt*d above at 234e–f; *Oakley Smith v Greenberg* [2004] B.C.C. 81 (CA).

[203] For the new regime see Insolvency Act 1986, Sch.B1, para.60 and Sch.1, para.21. For the old regime, see Insolvency Act 1986, s.14(1)(b) and Sch.1, para.21.

to have effect. For the circumstances in which an application under para.79 ought to be made under the new regime, see paras 27–024 and 28–024, above. Under the old regime the petition was required to include an application under s.18 of the Insolvency Act 1986 seeking the discharge of the administration order and such relief as the court thinks fit.[204]

27–031   The petition should be presented to the court which has jurisdiction for the administration.[205] This will clearly be the court that made an administration order in respect of a court appointment and, presumably, will be the court where notice was filed in respect of an out-of-court appointment. The petition will be treated, for procedural purposes, in the same way as a petition by the contributories of the company.[206] As a result, the petition should not be advertised except at the direction of the court.[207]

27–032   Upon making a winding-up order the court has power to appoint the administrator as the liquidator of the company.[208] This will often be desirable as the administrator should be familiar with the company and its affairs. It should be noted, however, that the court does not have power to appoint any other individual as liquidator besides the outgoing administrator.[209]

27–033   Where an administrator seeks to be made liquidator he must notify all creditors of the company in accordance with r.4.7(10) and file a report at court not less than two days before the return date setting out all responses which must include any objections. It will not ordinarily be appropriate for the court to make the appointment where the actions of the administrator are or appear likely to be subject to legitimate complaint.[210]

(c)   Voluntary liquidation

27–034   There can be significant cost advantages to winding up the affairs of a company in creditors' voluntary liquidation in contrast to compulsory liquidation. Prior to April 1, 2004 these advantages arose from the obligation on a liquidator to pay all sums received in the course of the liquidation into the Insolvency Services Account (ISA) due to the higher charges and stricter time limits that applied in compulsory liquidation.[211] As from April 1, 2004 the liquidator of a voluntary liquidation is no longer required to pay receipts into the ISA at all,[212] which has further increased the attractiveness of this procedure.

---

[204] r.4.7(7)(c).
[205] r.4.7(8).
[206] r.4.7(9) with the effect that Ch.4 of the Rules applies, i.e. rr.4.22–4.24. This is not strictly adhered to in practice since, unlike a contributories' petition, the administrator's petition will be heard in open court as opposed to being listed for a directions hearing in chambers.
[207] r.4.23(1)(c).
[208] s.140(1).
[209] *Re Exchange Travel (Holdings) Ltd (No.2)* [1992] B.C.C. 954.
[210] *Re Exchange Travel (Holdings) Ltd (No.2)* [1992] B.C.C. 954. See *Re Charnley Davies Business Services Ltd* (1987) 3 B.C.C. 408 for a case in which the outgoing administrator was appointed despite facing criticism.
[211] See the Insolvency Proceedings (Fees) Order 2004 (SI 2004/593) and formerly the Insolvency Fees Order 1986 (SI 1986/2030) (as amended).
[212] See the Insolvency (Amendment) Regulations 2004 (SI 2004/472).

Paragraph 83 of Sch.B1 provides an out-of-court procedure which permits **27–035** an administrator to place a company into creditors' voluntary liquidation where the administrator thinks that: (i) the total amount which each secured creditor of the company is likely to receive has been paid to or set aside for him[213]; and (ii) a distribution will be made to unsecured creditors, if there are any.[214]

In *Unidare Plc v Cohen*[215] the court held that an administrator will not **27–036** satisfy the requirement that he "thinks" the conditions have been satisfied unless the decision has been reached through a rational thought process, but the court refused to allow the decision to be challenged by reference to an objective standard. It will, on this basis, be difficult to question an administrator's decision that the conditions have been satisfied.

An administrator who is seeking to implement the procedure set out at **27–037** para.83 of Sch.B1 must: (i) send a notice to the registrar of companies stating that para.83 applies[216]; (ii) file a copy of the notice with the court[217]; (iii) send a copy of the notice to each creditor of whose claim and address he is aware[218] and to all those who received notice of the administrator's appointment.[219] The Registrar of Companies is required to register the notice upon receipt[220] following which the appointment of the administrator shall cease to have effect[221] and the company shall be wound up as if a resolution for winding up under s.84 of the Act were passed on the day on which the notice is registered.[222] The out-of-court procedure under para.83 applies whether or not the administrator is appointed by an order of the court and there is no need for a separate application under para.79 of Sch.B1.[223]

---

[213] para.83(1)(a).

[214] para.83(1)(b). For the requirements in Scotland, see para.83(2). In so far as the old regime still applies there are two obstacles to a company entering creditors' voluntary liquidation. First, it is not possible to pass a winding-up resolution while the company is in administration (s.11(3)(a)). This can be overcome by the court making an order for the discharge of the administration that is conditional on the passing of a winding-up resolution or making an order for discharge that is not drawn up by the court until the resolution has been received. The second difficulty arises from the provisions that determine the "relevant date" (s.387(3)(a) and (c)) for the purpose of identifying preferential creditors. Where a company that is in administration enters compulsory liquidation the relevant date will be the date on which the company entered administration, in contrast to creditors' voluntary liquidation where it will be the date on which the resolution was passed. This difference has the potential to exclude a significant number of creditors from receiving payment on a preferential basis. Following a period of uncertainty, it is now well established that the court has power to remove the distinction between compulsory and voluntary liquidation by ordering the liquidator to pay preferential creditors on the same basis as would apply in a compulsory liquidation or, alternatively, to establish a trust for the benefit of those creditors which will be binding upon future liquidators. See *Re Mark One (Oxford St) plc* [1999] 1 W.L.R. 1445, departing from *Re Powerstore (Trading) Ltd*, above; see also *Re Wolsey Theatre Co Ltd* [2001] B.C.C. 486; *Re UCT (UK) Ltd* above, and *Re Oakhouse Property Holdings Ltd* [2003] B.P.I.R. 469. For a different approach see *Re Phillip Alexander Securities & Futures Ltd* [1999] 1 B.C.L.C. 124.

[215] *Unidare Plc v Cohen* [2006] Ch. 489.

[216] para.83(3). The notice should be sent on Form 2.34B, see r.2.117(1).

[217] para.83(5)(a).

[218] para.83(5)(b). See r.2.117(2).

[219] r.2.117A(1).

[220] para.83(4).

[221] para.83(6)(a).

[222] para.83(6)(b).

[223] *Re Ballast Plc (In Administration)* [2005] 1 W.L.R. 1928.

27–038   Since there will be no formal resolution for the winding-up of the company the ordinary procedures that apply upon entering voluntary liquidation are modified or removed, including the requirement to hold a s.98 meeting.[224] The liquidator will be the outgoing administrator unless there is an alternative nomination by the creditors in the prescribed form.[225] It is not possible for a company to enter members' voluntary liquidation under para.83, since this exit route is excluded.[226]

27–039   Where the para.83 procedure is implemented the "relevant date" for the purpose of determining preferential creditors will be the same as for compulsory liquidation, i.e. the date on which the company entered administration.[227] This is due to the introduction of s.387(3)(ba) of the Act, which makes it unnecessary to obtain an order of the court in order to avoid the potential injustice to preferential creditors which could arise under the old regime.

27–040   As an alternative, a company in administration can enter creditors' voluntary liquidation where this forms part of the administrator's original or revised proposals.[228] The proposals must include the details of the proposed liquidator and also state that the creditors are free to nominate a different person to act as liquidator.[229] The creditors are then at liberty to change the identity of the proposed liquidator by modifying the proposals.[230] The appointment of the liquidator will take effect from the date on which the proposals are approved by the creditors, whether in the original or modified form.[231]

27–041   Where, however, the administrator does not make a proposal that the company enter creditors' voluntary liquidation and the requirements of para.83 are not satisfied, the company will only be able to enter creditors' voluntary liquidation further to an application to court for a conditional order in the same way that was developed under the old regime, as outlined at paras 27–008 and 27–009 above.

(d)   Miscellaneous; EC Regulation

27–042   Where an administrator is appointed in territorial proceedings prior to the opening of main proceedings in another Member State, the liquidator of the main proceedings is entitled to apply to have the administration converted to winding-up proceedings where this is "in the interests of the creditors in the main proceedings".[232]

---

[224] para.83(8).

[225] para.83(7). See rr.2.45(2)(g) and 2.117(3).

[226] para.83(8)(c), which excludes the operation of s.89 of the Act.

[227] The "onset of insolvency" would also be the same date for compulsory liquidation as voluntary liquidation, see s.240(d). See fn.214 above.

[228] r.2.33(2)(m).

[229] para.83(7)(a).

[230] r.2.45(2)(g).

[231] r.2.117A(2).

[232] EC Regulation on Insolvency Proceedings 2000 (implemented by SI 2002/1037 and SI 2002/1240), art.37.

The mandatory language of art.37 of the EC Regulation appears to require **27–043**
the court with jurisdiction over the administration[233] to order the conversion
into liquidation without the ability to exercise any discretion, but this is
presumably subject to the court being satisfied that the conversion would be in
the interests of the creditors in the main proceedings. This interpretation, which
gives the court at least a limited discretion, is consistent with the wording of
the rules which set out the procedure for making the application.[234]

Whatever the correct interpretation of the court's duty to make an order for **27–044**
conversion, it is clear that the court is permitted to convert the administration
into either compulsory or voluntary liquidation.[235] Where an order is made
for conversion into voluntary liquidation the company shall be wound up
as if a resolution were passed in accordance with s.84 of the Act on the day
on which the order is made.[236] Upon making an order for conversion the
court can provide for such consequential relief as it considers necessary or
desirable.[237]

In terms of procedure, the liquidator's application for conversion must be **27–045**
commenced by originating application. The application must confirm that: (i)
the main proceedings have been opened in relation to the company in a Member
State other than the United Kingdom; (ii) the deponent's belief that conversion
into a winding-up would prove to be in the interests of the creditors in the main
proceedings; (iii) the deponent's belief whether the company should enter
voluntary or compulsory winding-up; and (iv) all such matters that may assist
the court in deciding whether to make such an order and the need or desirability for any particular consequential relief,[238] which should include the basis
of the deponent's belief in relation to the matters set out above.

10.   TERMINATION FOLLOWED BY A DISSOLUTION

An administrator is under a duty to file a notice[239] with the Registrar of **27–046**
Companies where he thinks that the company has no property which might
permit a distribution to its creditors.[240] When deciding whether to file the relevant notice the administrator need only be concerned with the existing position
of the company,[241] such that it does not matter whether the company previously
held assets which were or could have been distributed for the benefit of its

---

[233] As before, this presumably refers to the court that made the administration order in respect
of a court appointment, and the court where notice was filed in respect of an out-of-court
appointment.
[234] See for instance r.2.132(1) which states the court can make "such order as it thinks fit" and,
more pertinently, r.2.131(1)(d)(i).
[235] r.2.132(3).
[236] r.2.132(3).
[237] r.2.132(2).
[238] r.2.131(1).
[239] The notice should be on Form 2.35B, see the Insolvency Rules 1986, r.2.118(1).
[240] para.84(1).
[241] *Re GHE Realisations Ltd (formerly Gatehouse Estates Ltd)* [2006] 1 W.L.R. 287; and *Re
Preston & Duckworth Ltd (In Liquidation)* Lawtel, October 7, 2005.

creditors.[242] The Registrar of Companies is required to register the notice[243] and the company is deemed to be dissolved three months thereafter.[244]

The administrator's duty to file the notice can be disapplied by the court following an application by the administrator.[245] This may be appropriate where, for instance, the administrator considers that the affairs of the company require further investigation. Where, however, administrator makes no such application and files the relevant notice, the administrator must as soon as reasonably practicable: (i) file a copy of the notice with the court[246]; and (ii) send a copy of the notice to each of the creditors of whose claim and address he is aware[247] and to all those who received notice of the administrator's appointment.[248] If the administrator fails without reasonable excuse to send notice under (i) and (ii) he will be guilty of an offence.[249]

The three-month period can be extended, suspended or disapplied by the court on the application of the administrator or another interested person.[250] In such an event the administrator is under a duty to inform the Registrar of Companies as soon as reasonably practicable.[251]

27–047   There is no specific provision to enable the court to restore the administration in the event that further assets are discovered (following dissolution of the company). If this situation were to arise the appropriate action would be for the former administrator or other interested party to make an application to court for the restoration of the company to the register of companies.[252] Presently, such an application to the court for restoration could be necessary for the purposes of seeking rights under the Third Parties (Rights Against Insurers) Act 1930. The administrator's decision to move from administration to

---

[242] In *Re GHE Realisations Ltd (formerly Gatehouse Estates Ltd)* [2006] 1 W.L.R. 287, Rimer J. refused to follow the obiter comments of Blackburne J. to the contrary in *Re Ballast Plc (In Administration)* [2005] 1 W.L.R. 1928; see also *Re Preston & Duckworth Ltd (In Liquidation)* [2006] B.C.C. 133; and Dear IP, No.22, March 2005.

[243] para.84(3). Note that this is a requirement that the notice be registered, not merely served, as to which on October 21, 2002 (Hansard, October 21, 2002, column 1125), Lord McIntosh of Haringey said, "The [Enterprise] Bill includes various references to the administrator filing documents with the Registrar of Companies, but in technical terms this means the document arriving in whatever state it may be in at Companies House. In other words, Companies House considers that it has been filed when it arrives in the post room. In most instances in the Bill this is acceptable since nothing substantive flows from the filing. However, there are two important occasions on which an action or change in circumstance is instigated on a document being accepted by the Registrar of Companies. It then becomes particularly important that the terminology used in the Bill is precise, to mean that the substantive effect is from when the document is put on the register, not merely when it has arrived at Companies House. The two occasions are those dealt with in the two paragraphs affected by these amendments, which deal with the end of the administration, when the company is either to move into creditors' voluntary liquidation, in order that the administrator can make distributions to creditors, or, in those cases where nothing is left to distribute, is to be dissolved." See also Dear IP, Issue 22, March 2005, p.6.10.

[244] para.84(6).
[245] para.84(2).
[246] para.84(5)(a).
[247] para.84(5)(b).
[248] r.2.118(2).
[249] para.84(9).
[250] para.84(7).
[251] para.84(8). The administrator should use Form 2.36B, see r.2.118(4).
[252] Companies Act 1985, s.651.

dissolution, as opposed to liquidation, could directly disadvantage a creditor with rights under the Third Parties (Rights Against Insurers) Act 1930 since this may necessitate their making an application for restoration in order to establish liability[253] against the assured. Reform of the 1930 Act, in the form of the Third Parties (Rights Against Insurers) Act 2010, is likely to come into force.[254] The proposed change in the law would remove the harsh requirement to have the dissolved insured company restored to the register in order to establish liability. The new Act allows direct proceedings against the insurer to be directly taken, creditors with such third party rights would be at an advantage compared to the position under the 1930 Act. In the interim, in circumstances where the administrator is aware of the potential for creditors to bring claims under the Act, and the additional cost, delay and expense that may be incurred as a consequence of an application for restoration having to be made, it may be that it would be more appropriate for the company to move from administration to liquidation. As to the Pensions Act 2004 provisions for the assumption by the Pension Protection Fund Board of responsibility for failed pension schemes following an insolvency event,[255] and the events triggering notification obligations to the Board, see Ch.17, above.

11. OTHER METHODS OF TERMINATION

The court has power to provide for the appointment of the administrator to cease to have effect where the administrator has reported to the court that the initial creditors' meeting has failed to approve administrator's proposals or revisions to those proposals.[256] Further, under s.5(3), where a decision approving a company voluntary arrangement has been made, the court can provide for the appointment of the administrator to cease to have effect[257] and on an application under para.74, the court may provide for the appointment of an administrator to cease to have effect.[258] Challenging the administrator's

27–048

---

[253] *Bradley v Eagle Star Insurance Co Ltd* [1989] A.C. 957 (HL).

[254] Third Parties (Rights Against Insurers) Act gained royal assent on March 26, 2010 but the Secretary of State for Justice announced on June 2, 2010 that no commencement date will be declared until there has been a full review of all inherited Labour legislation by the Department for Business, Innovation and Skills.

[255] s.121(3) of the Pensions Act 2004, see Dear IP, Issue 23, June 2005.

[256] para.55(2)(a). As to whether para.55(2)(e) would enable the court to replace the administrator rather than end the administration under para.55(2)(a) in circumstances where the court concluded that the proposals were likely to be approved if an alternate administrator appointed, would seem to be a possibility.

[257] para.5(3)(a). Albeit that a proposal for a company voluntary arrangement (or compromise or arrangement under s.425 of the Companies Act 1985) is likely to lead to the purpose of administration being sufficiently achieved and therefore the procedures in either paras 79 or 80 being most appropriate. See also Dear IP, Enterprise Act (Corporate Insolvency Provisions) Special Edition 2003, p.1.18. The court shall not make an order under s.5(3)(a) at any time before the end of the period of 28 days after the later of the chairman's reports has been made to the court under s.4(b), nor while a hearing or an appeal from a ruling under s.6 is pending (s.5(4)). One would expect the court on an application under para.79 to have regard to the same challenge periods to the company voluntary arrangement and that also an administrator should not seek to terminate the administration under para.79, where, at that time, the court would not do so under s.5(3), because of s.5(4). Nor should it be a means to circumvent the requirements under rr.2.113 or 2.114.

[258] para.74(4)(e).

conduct under para.74, could lead to the administrator's removal, but not the cessation of administration. The court has the ability to make any order it thinks appropriate[259] and it does not seem that para.88 should apply to the exclusion of para.74.[260] The court has jurisdiction, on an application for directions under para.63, to direct that the administrator's appointment should cease to have effect. Further, the court may also provide that the appointment of an administrator may cease to have effect where it makes a winding-up order pursuant to a petition presented by the Secretary of State, if it is satisfied that it is in the public interest to do so, or by the Financial Services Authority where the company has been carrying on a regulated authority without being so authorised under the Financial Services and Markets Act 2000, and it is insolvent or the court is of the opinion that it is just and equitable that it should be wound up.[261]

Pursuant to art.37 of the EC Regulation a liquidator in main proceedings can apply to the court for the administration to be converted into a winding up.

12.   RESCISSION BY COURT OF ADMINISTRATION ORDER

27-049   It was held in *Re Sharps of Truro Ltd*[262] that the principle of disclosure applicable to without notice applications applied with even more force to an administration petition because the legislation made no provision for a dissenting creditor to apply to set aside an administration order. In *Cornhill Insurance Plc v Cornhill Financial Services Ltd*[263] stated that the power conferred by r.7.47 of the Insolvency Rules 1986 to review, rescind or vary orders made in the exercise of insolvency jurisdiction by which an administration order had been granted was applicable.[264] Whilst there is overlap between this power and that granted to a creditor seeking an order to terminate pursuant to para.81, this power, although, seemingly unlimited, is nevertheless a true appeal procedure. Rule 7.47 represents a means by which a challenge can be made to the grant of an administration order. However, it is submitted that such procedure is now unlikely to be used in preference to para.81 although, unlike para.81, it does allow any aggrieved party (with a tangible interest in the company), not just a creditor, to make an application.[265] Examples include a contributory or where a Member State liquidator alleges want of jurisdiction to open "main insolvency proceedings", within the meaning given to such term by the EC Regulation.[266] Further, in the cases of paras 74 and 81, by analogy with the

---

[259] para.74(3)(e).
[260] *Re Sisu Capital Fund Ltd v Tucker* [2006] 1 All E.R. 167, albeit that the procedures for replacement under paras 91 to 95 are limited to where the administrator is removed from office under para.88.
[261] para.82; s.124A (1); s.367 Financial Services and Markets Act 2000.
[262] *Re Sharps of Truro Ltd* [1990] B.C.C. 94.
[263] *Cornhill Insurance Plc v Cornhill Financial Services Ltd* [1992] B.C.C. 818 (CA).
[264] See also *Re Tasbian Ltd (No.2)* [1990] B.C.C. 322 (CA). Note, however, that r.7.47 provides no applicability as a basis of challenging an out-of-court appointment since it represents the power of the court to review, rescind or vary its own order.
[265] *Re Cornhill Insurance Plc v Cornhill Financial Services* [1992] B.C.C. 818 (CA) cf. *Re Chelmsford City Football Club (1980) Ltd* [1991] B.C.C. 133.
[266] rr.2.133(2) and (3) deem the Member State liquidator to be a creditor for the purposes of the

case law under s.27, it would seem that these remedies are not intended to enable a creditor to challenge the administration order itself.[267]

Subject to the qualifications set out below, the power to rescind an administration order is likely to succeed if, when making the administration order, the court was not aware of the relevant factual background or was mistaken as to material facts. Even if there has been a failure of disclosure on the part of the applicant, if the administration order is seen as being in the best interests of the company and creditors, it is unlikely to be rescinded[268] and is unlikely to be appropriate after the administration has been in force for a significant period. Rule 7.47 is, in fact, broken down into two constituent (albeit interdependent) parts: r.7.47(1) conferring the power on the court to review, rescind or vary any order and r.7.47(2) conferring a right of appeal with the latter being a true appeal (the former should not be used as a means of circumventing the latter because of this), where it is therefore necessary to show that the original order was based on an error of law or wrongful exercise of discretion.[269] Notwithstanding that the jurisdiction under r.7.47(1) is very wide, it is clear that such power is one that the court will exercise sparingly, and only in exceptional circumstances.[270] Nor would it be an appropriate course to rescind the order in circumstances where the order could be reviewed or varied, directions given or redress provided for under para.74.

The effect of rescission of an administration order is an area largely unexplored in case law. Rescission would render the order a nullity, but the administrator should no doubt comply with the requirements of r.2.116, by notifying the Registrar of Companies, attaching a copy of the court order and a copy of his final progress report. As to the administrator's remuneration and expenses, subject to any order to the contrary made by the court on rescission of the administration order, para.99(1) has applicability howsoever a person ceases to be an administrator, including where the administrator's appointment "ceases to have effect". But what of the appointment which is deemed never to have had effect or be valid from the outset? Paragraph 104 would not support a claim by a person for remuneration where there was an irregularity in his

27–050

rules referred to in r.2.133(3). However, r.2.133(3) provides that rr.2.133(2) and (3) are without prejudice to the generality of the right to participate referred to in para.3 of art.32 of the EC Regulation such that a liquidator in main or secondary proceedings is empowered to participate in other proceedings on the same basis as a creditor and therefore would be entitled to proceed under para.81. However, disputes as to where the debtor's centre of main interest is based may not equate to there being an improper motive of the applicant for the purposes of para.81(2). See also *Re Dianoor Jewels Ltd* [2001] 1 B.C.L.C. 450.

[267] *Cornhill Insurance Plc v Cornhill Financial Services* [1992] B.C.C. 818 (CA), 827 and Dillon J. at 858 in the Court of Appeal.

[268] *Re MTI Trading Systems Ltd (In Administration)* [1998] B.C.C. 400.

[269] *Re Probe Data Systems Ltd (No.3)* [1991] B.C.C. 428, *Re Tasbian Ltd (No.3)* [1991] B.C.C. 435 and *Re Industrial & Commercial Securities Plc* (1989) 5 B.C.C. 320. The court may, however, rescind a winding-up order made by the registrar despite there not be grounds for an appeal from his decision, *Re Dollar Land (Feltham) Ltd* [1995] B.C.C. 740. However, see also *Re Metrocab Ltd* [2010] 2 B.C.L.C. 603.

[270] See *Fitch v Official Receiver* [1996] 1 W.L.R. 242 (CA), which concerns the corresponding provision in personal insolvency under s.375. See also *Scottish & Newcastle Ltd v Raguz* [2010] B.P.I.R. 945.

appointment[271] and para.21 affords an indemnity only in the case of the appointment by a qualifying floating charge-holder under para.14. Further, para.104 is directed at an administrator's action where there are defects in form or procedure in the administrator's appointment or qualification and does not validate acts done by an administrator appointed by an order which is subsequently rescinded.

13.   VACATION OF OFFICE: DISCHARGE OF LIABILITY

27–051   Where a person ceases to be the administrator of a company (whether because he vacates office by reason of resignation, death or otherwise, because he is removed from office or because his appointment ceases to have effect), the outgoing administrator is discharged from liability in respect of any action of his as administrator.[272]

The discharge takes effect:

(a)   in the case of an administrator who has died, on the filing with the court of notice of his death[273];

(b)   in the case of an administrator appointed under para.14 or 22, at a time appointed by resolution of the creditors' committee or, if these is no committee, by resolution of the creditors[274]; or

(c)   in any case, at a time specified by the court.[275]

For the purposes of the application under (b) above, an administrator will be discharged if a resolution is passed by each secured creditor subsequent to a statement by the administrator that the company has insufficient property to make a distribution to unsecured creditors other than by s.176A(2)(a).[276] Where there is insufficient property to make a distribution to preferential creditors, the resolution will need passing by the preferential creditors whose debts amount to 50 per cent of the preferential debts (but ignoring the debts of creditors who fail to respond to an invitation to give or withhold approval).[277]

27–052   Discharge applies to liability accrued before the discharge takes effect[278] and a discharged administrator will not be beyond the court's powers pursuant to para.75. An application under para.75 may be made in respect of an admin-

---

[271] *Re Allison, Johnson & Foster Ltd Ex p. Birkenshaw* [1904] 2 K.B. 327.

[272] para.98(1).

[273] para.98(2)(a).

[274] para.98(2)(b).

[275] para.98(2)(c). Paragraph 98(2)(c) enables the court, in any case, to specify the time from which the discharge takes effect. This would enable a former administrator to seek discharge where the creditors' committee or creditors or unable or unwilling to do so. As to whether the court can specify a time different from one set by paras 98(a) or (b) is not immediately apparent. It would seem that, unlikely s.20(1)(b), the draftsman may have intended this, for example, in circumstances where discharge was opposed.

[276] For a case disapplying that section, *Re Hydroserve Ltd* [2003] All E.R. (D) 184. However, see cautionary note in *Re International Sections Ltd (In Liquidation)* [2009] B.C.C. 574.

[277] para.98(3).

[278] para.98(4)(a).

istrator who has been discharged under para.98 only with permission of the court.[279]

It is unlikely that an administrator will be discharged from liability immediately upon the discharge of the administration order, but rather, there will likely be a postponement to allow any investigations into the administration to be conducted or claims against him to be determined.[280] In any event, a discharge is unlikely to be forthcoming until some time after he sends out his final progress report.[281] A court is likely to have jurisdiction to set aside an order for discharge from liability provided that the application is brought by a person with appropriate locus standi who advances a strong case that the administration was conducted fraudulently or that the original discharge was obtained by fraud, but not on any basis that there was or might have been an irregularity during the conduct of the administration or inaccurate statement in the application for discharge.

Where a person ceases to be the administrator of a company (whether because he vacates office by reason of resignation, death or otherwise, because he is removed from office or because his appointment ceases to have effect), his remuneration, any expenses and sums payable in respect of a debt or liability arising out of a contract entered into by him, or his predecessor, are charged on and payable out of property of which he had custody or control immediately before cessation, in priority to any security which is a floating charge on its creation.[282] See Ch.4, above, for consideration in detail of these provisions.

---

[279] para.75(6).

[280] *Re Charnley Davies Business Services Ltd* (1987) 3 B.C.C. 408; *Barclays Mercantile v Sibec Developments Ltd* [1992] 1 W.L.R. 1253; *Re Sheridan Securities Ltd* (1988) 4 B.C.C. 200; and *Re Exchange Travel (Holdings) Ltd* [1992] B.C.C. 954.

[281] r.2.47.

[282] *Re Newscreen Media Group Plc (In Liquidation)* [2009] 2 B.C.L.C. 353

Chapter 28

Distribution and Vacation of Office by Receivers

1. REMOVAL

(a) Removal by debenture-holder

28–001 A receiver appointed by a debenture-holder (other than an administra tive receiver) can be removed by his appointor unless there is a stipulation to the contrary in the debenture or in his appointment. Notice of removal is only effective on receipt by the receiver.[1]

28–002 An administrative receiver can only be removed by a court order made under s.45 of the Insolvency Act 1986. This reflects the enhanced status of qualified administrative receivers[2] and is designed to prevent attempts to interfere with their performance of their statutory duties.[3]

(b) Removal by the court

28–003 The Insolvency Act 1986 gives no guidance to a court acting on an application for removal of an administrative receiver under s.45. It is, however, likely that the court would apply the same case-law principles that continue to be applicable to the removal of other receivers under the court's inherent jurisdiction. These principles indicate that the application to remove a receiver may be made by a person with a sufficient interest to make it.[4] This includes the company, another debenture-holder, the receiver himself[5] or his appointor.[6] An application can also be made by a partner in the receiver's firm, where that firm

---

[1] *Windsor Refrigerator Co Ltd v Branch Nominees Ltd* [1961] Ch. 375 (CA), 398, per Donovan L.J. For general information on the question of removal, see S.A. Frieze, "Removing An Office Holder" (1997) (6) Insolv. Int. 43.

[2] See above, Ch.1.

[3] For such an attempt, see *IRC v Goldblatt* [1972] Ch. 498 where the particular stratagem proved unsuccessful.

[4] See *Deloitte & Touche A.G. v Johnson* [1999] 1 W.L.R. 1605 (PC) for principles governing the removal of liquidators under Cayman law, s.106 of the Companies Law (1995 rev.). The Privy Council held that as well as standing in a technical sense, an applicant normally needed to have a real interest in the matter. Thus, where removal was sought on the basis of a conflict of interest, a creditor may well have a real interest, but a potential debtor will not. A creditor for a very small sum who will not be materially affected may have technical standing but no real interest: see *Walker Morris v Khalastchi* [2001] 1 B.C.L.C. 1.

[5] An application by an administrative receiver is rarely likely to be justified in view of the statutory right to resign: see below.

[6] *Strong v Carlyle Press* [1893] 1 Ch. 268 (CA).

has day-to-day conduct of the receivership.[7] The applicant must show sufficient cause for removal. The court will not lightly intervene.[8]

In the ordinary case, the debenture-holder will be left to appoint a **28–004**
replacement,[9] but in an appropriate case the court may be persuaded to replace
the administrative receiver with a receiver appointed by the court.[10] Where an
administrative receiver is removed by the court, he must comply with the
notice requirements under the Insolvency Act 1986 and the Companies Act
2006.

(c) Displacement

Where a receiver is appointed in respect of a second or subsequent charge, this **28–005**
does not prevent prior chargees from making their own appointments. For the
sake of convenience the prior chargee might appoint the same person. If he
appoints someone else, that receiver will take precedence. Where the displaced
receiver under the second or subsequent charge has been appointed by the
court, a receiver appointed by the prior chargee will need to seek the leave of
the court to get possession of the charged assets, unless the order making the
appointment states that the order is made "without prejudice to the rights of
prior encumbrancers".[11]

(d) Ceasing to be qualified

An administrative receiver automatically vacates office if he ceases to be quali- **28–006**
fied to act as an insolvency practitioner in relation to the company in
question.[12]

Under rule 3.35 of the Insolvency Rules 1986, the receiver must give the
same notices as if he had resigned and r.3.33 were relevant.[13]

(e) The making of an administration order

The court has no discretion to make an administration order where administra- **28–007**
tive receivers have been appointed over a company unless the person who
appointed the administrative receivers consents to the making of an administration order or the court thinks that the charge would be liable to be set aside
as a transaction at an undervalue or preference or to be avoidable as a floating

---

[7] *Donaldson v O'Sullivan* [2009] 1 W.L.R. 924 (CA); *Re A & C Supplies Ltd* [1998] B.C.C.
708; *Re Equity Nominees Ltd* [2000] B.C.C. 84; *Clements v Udal* [2001] B.C.C. 658.
[8] *Re Neon Signs (Australasia) Ltd* [1965] V.R. 125.
[9] The court has no power to appoint a replacement administrative receiver: see *Re A&C
Supplies* [1998] B.C.C. 708, 713.
[10] See below, Ch.29.
[11] *Re Metropolitan Amalgamated Estates* [1912] 2 Ch. 497; *Underhay v Read* (1887) L.R. 20
Q.B.D. 209 (CA). See below, Ch.29.
[12] Insolvency Act 1986, s.45(2).
[13] r.3.33 is considered below at para.28–009.

charge pursuant to s.245 of the Insolvency Act 1986.[14] Where an administration order is made, an administrative receiver must vacate office.[15] The
administrative receiver is not obliged to give notice to the company.[16]
An administrative receiver who vacates office on an administrator being
appointed is relieved of any duty which he might have to pay preferential
creditors.[17]

(f) Death

28–008 When an administrative receiver dies, his appointor must give notice to the
Registrar of Companies, to the company (or any liquidator of the company)
and to any creditors' committee. This notice must be given as soon as the
appointor becomes aware of the death of the administrative receiver.[18]

2. RESIGNATION

28–009 Non-administrative receivers are unable to resign unless this is specifically
provided for in the debenture, or in the appointment, or unless the debenture-
holder consents. Administrative receivers are permitted to resign "by giving
notice . . . in the prescribed manner to such persons as may be prescribed" by
rules made pursuant to s.45(1) of the Insolvency Act 1986. The relevant rule is
r.3.33 of the Insolvency Rules 1986. Where he resigns, the administrative
receiver must give at least seven days' notice to his appointor, the company and
any creditors' committee. Where the company is in liquidation, the notice
should be given to the liquidator. The notice must state the date on which the
resignation is to take effect. Notice must also be given to the Registrar of
Companies.

28–010 It is difficult to see why the position of all receivers was not equated by the
Insolvency Act. The position of non-administrative receivers remains a peculiar one. Whilst unable to resign, they are unlikely to be compelled by a court
to carry out any duties involving personal discretion or judgment, for this
would be analogous to ordering specific performance of a contract for personal
services.[19] The court is likely, despite any objection by the appointor, on application by the receiver to order his removal (if appropriate) on terms that the
receiver meets out of his own pocket any additional costs and expenses and
any losses occasioned to the appointor. In any ordinary case such compensation should be an adequate remedy for the appointor. The court may order the
receiver to comply with statutory provisions requiring the filing of documents

---

[14] Insolvency Act 1986 Sch.B1, para.39. *Re Chesterton International Ltd* [2005] B.P.I.R. 1103.
[15] Insolvency Act 1986 Sch.B1, para.41(1).
[16] Insolvency Act 1986 Sch.B1 para.41. Insolvency Rules 1986, r.3.35 as amended by the
Insolvency (Amendment) Rules 1986 (SI 1986/1919), Insolvency Act 1986, para.41(3).
[17] Insolvency Act 1986, Sch.B1, para.41(3)(b). It is unclear whether any distributions already
made to preferential creditors on account will stand. It would seem likely that they will stand,
although there is no authority on this point.
[18] Insolvency Rules 1986, r.3.34.
[19] See *Hill v CA Parsons & Co* [1972] Ch. 305 (CA).

or similar non-discretionary tasks, exercising a jurisdiction in this respect analogous to that exercised over liquidators.

3.   INDEMNITY AND CHARGES

When removed from office, a non-administrative receiver can retain sums   **28–011**
payable to preferential creditors for the purpose of discharging his personal
liability to pay such preferential creditors.[20] Since those sums are payable out
of assets coming into his hands[21] it seems to follow that a non-administrative
receiver who vacates his position is entitled to retain and realise assets subject
to a floating charge in order to pay preferential creditors. In the usual case
where a non-administrative receiver is made agent of the company in respect
of the period until any liquidation, he can claim an implied right of indemnity
against the receivership assets for his costs, expenses, remuneration and all
sums for which he is personally liable.[22] There is also a specific statutory
indemnity out of the assets where he becomes personally liable on a post-
receivership contract made by him.[23]

Under the Insolvency Act 1986, all administrative receivers (in respect of   **28–012**
the period prior to any liquidation) are deemed to be agents of the company and
have a specific statutory indemnity with regard to personal liability incurred
upon post-receivership contracts and any contract of employment they have
"adopted".[24] As agents they also have an implied right of indemnity out of the
assets in respect of their costs, expenses, remuneration and any other sums for
which they are personally liable, such as an undertaking to pay any sums due
to a retention of title claimant.[25] Neither indemnity extends to losses or liabilities incurred in consequence of his own negligence or default.[26]

In the absence of an express agreement governing the remuneration of an   **28–013**
administrative receiver, a receiver is entitled to receive a reasonable sum
pursuant to s.15 of the Sale of Goods and Services Act 1979. What is reasonable is dictated by the market rate for such services.[27]

The 1986 Act further provides that where at any time an administrative   **28–014**
receiver, receiver or manager vacates office:

---

[20] *IRC v Goldblatt* [1972] Ch. 498.
[21] Insolvency Act 1986, s.40.
[22] See *Hill v Venning* [1972] 4 A.C.L.R. 555.
[23] Insolvency Act 1986, s.37(1).
[24] Insolvency Act 1986, s.44(1)(b). On the meaning of "adoption" in relation to s.44(1)(b), see above, Ch.16.
[25] *Lipe Ltd v Leyland DAF* [1993] B.C.C. 385 (CA). Retention of title claims generally are dealt with above in Ch.21. *Lipe v Leyland DAF* [1993] B.C.C. 385 (CA) does not apply in a case brought under Regulation (EC) No.44/2001 on Enforcement of Judgments in Civil Matters ([2001] OJ L12/1) where the interim relief sought in this country mirrors relief sought in a Member State which seeks to attack sales effected by a company prior to the appointment of administrative receivers as well as those effected after their appointment (*UCA France Champignon v FF Ltd (In Receivership)* [2003] B.P.I.R. 299).
[26] *R.A. Price v Henderson* [1989] N.Z.L.R. 257 (NZCA), 262.
[27] *Munns v Perkins* [2002] B.P.I.R. 120.

(a) his remuneration and any expenses properly incurred by him; and

(b) any indemnity to which he is entitled out of the assets of the company,

shall be charged on and paid out of any property of the company which is in his custody or under his control at that time in priority to any security held by the person by or on whose behalf he was appointed.[28]

28–015   The practical problem no doubt sought to be resolved by the creation of a charge is that a receiver's lien for his remuneration, etc. is ordinarily lost if the receiver hands over monies or other assets in his hands immediately upon vacating office. The new provision appears to provide a secured right of payment out of the assets in respect of remuneration, expenses and rights of indemnity without any need to retain the assets to ensure payment. In practice, it is questionable whether the charge created by this provision will ever persuade a receiver who vacates office to part with assets over which he has a lien in situations where he would not already have been willing to hand them over in return for an appropriate undertaking. The reason is that the charge created by this provision would seem to be unprotected as against bona fide purchasers without notice of the charged assets.

4. DUTY TO CEASE ACTING

28–016   A validly appointed receiver is entitled to remain in place so long as there remains a contingent liability secured by the debentures.[29] However, once a receiver has in his hands sufficient monies to discharge all the debts of the company which he is bound to discharge, all possible claims which could be made against him and in respect of which he is entitled to an indemnity, his own remuneration, and all monies secured by the charges under which he was appointed, it will be his duty to cease acting,[30] in the absence of any provision to the contrary in the charge under which he has been appointed. Receivers who pay off their debenture-holders, thereby ceasing to be receivers, and who

---

[28] Insolvency Act 1986, ss.45(3) (administrative receivers) and s.37(4) (other receivers and managers). Where an administrative receiver vacates office on the making of an administration order, his remuneration is charged on and paid out of any property of the company which was in his custody or under his control immediately before he vacated office (Insolvency Act 1986, Sch.B1, para.41(3)(a)). "Remuneration" includes expenses properly incurred and an indemnity to which the administrative receiver is entitled out of the assets of the company (Insolvency Act 1986, Sch.B1, para.41(4)(a)). The charge imposed takes priority over security held by the person to whom or on whose behalf the administrative receiver was appointed (Insolvency Act 1986, Sch.B1, para.41(4)(b)). The provision for payment is subject to the general moratorium provided by Sch.B1, para.43 (Insolvency Act 1986, Sch.B1, para.41(4)(c)).
[29] *OBG Ltd v Allan* [2001] B.P.I.R. 111, appealed on other grounds [2008] 1 A.C. 1 (HL).
[30] *Rottenberg v Monjack* [1992] B.C.C. 688; Kerr, *The Law and Practice as to Receivers*, 17th edn (London: Sweet & Maxwell, 1989), p.437. Kerr suggests that the receiver's duty is to cease acting "forthwith", but presumably this means "with all due expedition", and not literally forthwith. The receiver will have tasks to perform, e.g. making distributions and closing bank accounts before he can be expected to file notice of ceasing to act. See also in relation to the duty to accept redemption, *Downsview Nominees Ltd v First City Corp Ltd* [1993] 2 W.L.R. 86 (PC) discussed in Ch.13, above.

do not reserve further funds for costs cannot continue to act as receivers in order to raise further funds to pay themselves.[31] The duty to cease acting does not come into force so long as there remains a contingent liability secured by the debenture.[32]

Whilst the duty can easily be stated in principle, it can cause great difficulty   **28–017** in practice. This is particularly so where the company is not in liquidation and yet is insolvent. The dilemma in such cases has been illustrated by a receiver recalling[33] the detailed background of the case of *Re GL Saunders Ltd*.[34] In that case the receiver was appointed over fixed and floating charge assets. There was a large claim by preferential creditors in the receivership, far larger than the extent of the floating charge realisations available to them. Within a few months enough had been realised from fixed charge realisations to repay the debenture-holder, but the company was not yet in liquidation. By this time "the receivership had reached a stage where the receiver could have concluded his work and handed the assets back to the company". The receiver does not explain whether by this stage he had also realised all the floating charge assets, as appears to be required by what is now s.40 of the Insolvency Act 1986. The receiver appeared to regard the existence of the duty to make such realisations as being in doubt. In the event, the receiver baulked at the prospect of handing the insolvent company's assets to the directors and adopted the "common practice" of leaving a small amount of the debenture-holder's debt unpaid. The receiver preferred this as "the correct moral and ethical approach". Whilst that may well be so, this approach cannot absolve a receiver of his legal duty to terminate the receivership and hand the assets back to the company, whether or not there is a liquidator.

One possible answer to the dilemma for an administrative receiver may lie   **28–018** in the express power to present a winding-up petition conferred on him by the Insolvency Act 1986[35] in the absence of any provision to the contrary in the debenture. The objection might be raised that the administrative receiver has no locus standi to present such a petition where it is not necessary to protect the assets subject to the debenture-holder's charge.[36] Where the company is clearly insolvent and no voluntary arrangement with creditors is in force, it is suggested that the court may accept that it is proper for an administrative receiver to look

---

[31] *Rottenberg v Monjack* [1992] B.C.C. 688.

[32] See *Re Rudd & Son Ltd* (1986) 2 B.C.C. 98955 (CA); *Law Debenture Trust Corporation Plc v Concord Trust* [2007] All E.R. (D) 149 (Jun) and cf. *Banner Lane Realisations Ltd v Berisford* [1997] 1 B.C.L.C. 380 (CA) where future debts secured by a debenture included contingent debts. In accordance with the same principle, a guarantor who pays a sum demanded by the secured creditor as being payable at the date of demand has no right to subrogation to the security if the creditor or the receiver incurs further liabilities secured by the charge between the dates of demand and payment: *Austin v Royal* (1998–1999) 47 N.S.W.L.R. 27 (NSWC).

[33] Hatton and Cooke, "Fixed Charge Surplus. The Argument is Over" [1985] 1 IL & P 137.

[34] *Re GL Saunders Ltd (In Liquidation)* [1986] 1 W.L.R. 215.

[35] s.42 and para.21 of Sch.1: see above, para.15–002.

[36] Prior to the Insolvency Act 1985, in order to petition, a receiver needed to show some benefit to the charged assets: see *Re Emmadart Ltd* [1979] Ch. 540.

to the interest of the general body of unsecured creditors. This is particularly so when it is considered that an administrative receiver shares with liquidators and administrators the special status of "office-holder".[37]

28–019   The receiver cannot put the company into voluntary liquidation, as he has no power to convene a meeting of the company in order to pass a winding-up resolution.[38]

28–020   Where the receiver remains in office when the company is placed in liquidation, he may wish to postpone the dissolution of the company when liquidation has been concluded. If he has sufficient reason for delaying dissolution, he can make an application to the court to defer dissolution.[39]

28–021   Where the administrative receiver vacates office at the end of his receivership, he must give notice to any liquidator who has been appointed, as well as to members of any creditors' committee in the receivership.[40] All receivers must give notice to the Registrar of Companies of ceasing to act, and that fact is to be noted on the Register of Charges.[41] Section 45(4) of the Insolvency Act 1986 imposes an additional requirement on an administrative receiver to give notice to the Registrar of Companies. This can be done by endorsement on the notice given under the Companies Act 2006.[42]

5. DISTRIBUTION OF REALISATIONS

28–022   The specific provisions of each charge or debenture must be considered, but generally the debenture will adopt, often with modifications, the scheme of ss.109(8) and 109(6) of the Law of Property Act 1925. The order of payment set out below is one which reflects common provisions in debentures. The receiver owes a duty both to the company[43] and to the debenture-holder[44] to make payments in the order stipulated, and the company and debenture-holder may at any time agree to a variation in the order,[45] but no duty is owed to third parties to make payment to them in accordance with a stipulated or varied order for payment.[46]

---

[37] See above, Ch.8.

[38] *Valorem Ltd v Rilett* [2004] 1 All E.R. 894 (CA).

[39] Under the Insolvency Act 1986, s.201 (voluntary liquidation) or s.205 (compulsory liquidation).

[40] Insolvency Rules, r.3.35(1).

[41] Companies Act 2006, s.871(2).

[42] Insolvency Rules, r.3.35(2).

[43] *Yourell v Hibernian Bank Ltd* [1918] A.C. 372 (HL), 387; *Visbord v FCT* (1943) 68 C.L.R. 354; *Re Kentish Homes Ltd* [1993] B.C.C. 212, 219G–221E (overruled on other grounds in *Re Toshoku Finance UK Plc* [2002] 1 W.L.R. 671 (HL)).

[44] *Leicester Permanent Building Society v Butt* [1943] Ch. 308.

[45] *Yourell v Hibernian Bank Ltd* [1918] A.C. 372 (HL).

[46] *Leicester Permanent Building Society v Butt* [1943] Ch. 308; *Yourell v Hibernian Bank Ltd* [1918] A.C. 372 (HL); *Liverpool Corp v Hope* [1938] 1 K.B. 751 (CA) (no duty to rating authority to pay rates); and see the VAT cases dealt with in Ch.19, above.

(a) Fixed charge realisations[47]

(i) Costs of realisation

Were the Law of Property Act 1925, s.109(8) to be followed unvaried in the charge or debenture, the receiver's costs charges and expenses would be subsumed, together with his remuneration, under the lower heading of receiver's "commission". However, it is commonly provided that the receiver should have his costs, charges and expenses separately.[48] It is obviously beneficial for the debenture-holder and receiver alike to provide that this sum should be paid as a first charge on realisations.   **28–023**

In the case of a winding-up, a creditor can in some circumstances apply to the court for an order for the payment of a sum as part of the "costs of the winding-up". A notable example occurs in the case of an application by a landlord for the payment of rent as part of the costs of the winding-up where the liquidator has retained possession of leased premises for the benefit of the winding-up.[49] However, the concept "costs of the receivership" cannot be used by a creditor to found any analogous application in the case of a receiver appointed out of court.[50]   **28–024**

The receiver may discharge or agree with a creditor to discharge as part of the costs of the receivership a debt and liability of the company incurred prior to (as well as after) the commencement of the receivership if its discharge is required in the interests of the receivership, e.g. in order to preserve valuable goodwill and secure continued supplies.[51] But the receiver cannot properly discharge any such liability and afford the creditor such a preference over all other creditors (secured and unsecured) unless this course is commercially justified. A "moral" claim to such priority does not afford a basis of itself to such payment, though the receiver may take into account the consequence to the receivership of a failure to satisfy such a claim.[52]   **28–025**

---

[47] This heading deals with assets caught by a charge which was always a fixed charge and not with assets subject to a crystallised floating charge: those assets are dealt with under the heading of "floating charge realisations".

[48] See *Marshall v Cottingham* [1982] Ch. 82. See, for an analysis of the circumstances in which receivers can recover costs and expenses, *Vedalease Ltd v Averti Developments Ltd* [2007] 2 E.G.L.R. 125.

[49] e.g. *Re ABC Coupler Engineering (No.3)* [1970] 1 W.L.R. 702. There is a discussion of cases and the underlying principles in *Re Atlantic Computer Systems Plc* [1992] Ch. 505 (CA), a case concerning administration orders. For the position in relation to liquidation expenses, see *Re Toshoku Finance UK Plc* [2002] 1 W.L.R. 671 (HL).

[50] *Nicoll v Cutts* (1985) 1 B.C.C. 99427 (CA); *Re Atlantic Computer Systems Plc* [1992] Ch. 505 (CA). As to expenses generally, see Ch.4 above. (The actual decision in *Nicoll v Cutts* relating to employment contracts (as opposed to the general receivership principle) was in part reversed by statute: see the detailed discussion in Ch.16, above.)

[51] *Nicoll v Cutts* (1985) 1 B.C.C. 99427 (CA), 99430; *Leyland DAF Ltd v Automotive Products Plc* [1993] B.C.C. 389 (CA).

[52] A fiduciary cannot be charitable or satisfy merely moral claims at the expense of the beneficiaries unless either duly authorised or such action is justified in the interests of the beneficiaries. cf. *Buttle v Saunders* [1950] 2 All E.R. 193.

(ii) "all rents, taxes, rates and outgoings whatever affecting the mortgaged property"[53]

28–026 The receiver has a discretion as between himself and the debenture-holder,[54] but generally speaking is under no obligation[55] to creditors, to make these payments or to agree with a creditor to do so. Obviously the receiver will wish to make payments where he has incurred personal liability.[56] He will also wish to make payments where the only liability is that of the company alone, but where the creditor will otherwise withhold services or supplies or where otherwise there will be jeopardy to the company's goodwill required for the continuation of the company's business or its beneficial realisation.[57] Three limitations on the free exercise of this discretion do exist:

(a) Circumstances may arise where the receiver can only properly exercise his discretion in favour of payment. In *Re John Willment (Ashford) Ltd*[58] the receiver had caused the company to trade and receive VAT payments in respect of supplies subject to VAT. The question put to Brightman J. was whether the receiver could use the sums of VAT received by the company to repay the debenture-holder, despite the company's obligation to pay a like sum of VAT to the Customs and Excise. Brightman J. took a dim view of this suggestion. He held that causing the company not to pay would constitute causing the company to commit a criminal offence, and in the circumstances the discretion could only properly be exercised in favour of making the payment.[59]

---

[53] Law of Property Act 1925, s.109(8)(i). A court-appointed receiver, is, like an out of court receiver acting in an agency capacity, not assessable to capital gains tax in respect of her realisations (*Commissioner of the Inland Revenue v Piacentini* [2003] Q.B. 1497).

[54] *Re John Willment (Ashford) Ltd* [1980] 1 W.L.R. 73, 77 and see above, Ch.19.

[55] *Liverpool Corp v Hope* [1938] 1 K.B. 751 (CA). Creditors who have no right themselves to compel payment cannot achieve their goal indirectly via a liquidator's right to enforce payment on behalf of the company as mortgagor: *Re Kentish Homes Ltd* [1993] B.C.C. 212, 221F–222B. Overruled on other grounds in *Re Toshoku Finance UK Plc (In Liquidation)* [2002] 1 W.L.R. 671 (HL).

[56] See above, Ch.13. In such a case, the creditor of the receiver is entitled by way of subrogation to the receiver's right of indemnity out of the receivership assets: *Re British Power Traction Ltd* [1910] 2 Ch. 470. Under s.44(1) of the Insolvency Act 1986, where a company in administrative receivership goes into liquidation and the company continues to conduct business from its premises which business is run by the administrative receivers, the administrative receivers are not personally liable for payment of non-domestic rates in respect of the premises from the commencement of the liquidation. This remains the case notwithstanding the fact that the administrative receivers' status as agents of the company ceased at that time; s.44(1) of the Insolvency Act 1986. *Ratford v Northavon DC* [1987] 357. Administrative receivers appointed under a valid debenture over a company's undertaking are not in rateable occupation of the company's premises either before or after the company goes into liquidation (*Re Beck Foods Ltd*; sub nom. *Boston BC v Rees* (Pill and Jonathan Parker L.JJ.) [2002] 1 W.L.R. 1304 (CA)).

[57] For statutory restrictions on the withholding of supplies see above, Chs 8 and 13. For a case on withholding supplies by a receiver see *Re Transtec Automotive (Campsie) Ltd* [2001] B.C.C. 403.

[58] *Re John Willment (Ashford) Ltd* [1980] 1 W.L.R. 73: and see also *Sargent v Customs and Excise Commissioners* [1995] 1 W.L.R. 821 (CA); *Re Grey Marlin Ltd* [2000] 1 W.L.R. 370.

[59] A non-payment of VAT is no longer a criminal offence and the current position in relation to VAT is discussed in detail in Ch.13 above.

The *Willment* case was distinguished by Vinelott J. in *Re Liverpool Commercial Vehicles Ltd*,[60] where VAT had been received in the form of a credit arising out of the repossession of goods by a supplier and no actual monies had been paid to the receivers. The receivers were not obliged to pay to the Customs and Excise a sum equal to that credited.

(b) Since any payment operates to "prefer" the payee to the debenture-holder, subsequent chargees and other creditors, the receiver must first satisfy himself that the making of the payment is in the interest of the receivership and not merely that the making of the payment is just.

(c) The receiver must consider whether non-payment of the sums author-ised to be paid under this heading might cause loss to the company as mortgagor or the debenture-holder. For the company or debenture-holder may be able to claim that the receiver owes them a duty to make payment[61] and may be able to claim damages from the receiver, if non-payment leads to loss. Unless there is a surplus for the mort-gagor, it is unlikely that it would be able to show any loss.[62] In the case of the debenture-holder, non-payment is usually to his benefit. There is also a theoretical possibility of the mortgagor obtaining an injunction to compel payment, but it is difficult to see in what circum-stances it would be right to grant such an injunction.[63]

(iii) The receiver's remuneration included in the heading of the "commission" under the Law of Property Act 1925, s.109(8)(iii) or an equivalent provision in the debenture

Under the Law of Property Act 1925, s.109(6) unless varied, the receiver's "commission" includes the receiver's remuneration, costs, charges and expenses. The amount actually payable is that specified in the receiver's appointment up to a rate of five per cent of all money received but if none is specified, the maximum rate of five per cent prevails. Frequently the debenture varies s.109 by providing that the remuneration is to be such reasonable remu-neration as is agreed between the receiver and debenture-holder.[64] This type of clause gives more flexibility, since it is often difficult to predict how much work the receivership will require. Whilst the five per cent rate may be reason-able in the case of receivers of income, for whom s.109(6) was originally

28–027

[60] *Re Liverpool Commercial Vehicles Ltd* (1984) 1 B.C.C. 99237, 99241.
[61] *Visbord v FCT* [1943] 68 C.L.R. 354.
[62] See, e.g. *Re Kentish Homes Ltd* [1993] B.C.C. 212, 221C (overruled on other grounds in *Toshoku Finance* [2002] 1 W.L.R. 671 (HL)). Unless and until there is such a surplus, it may also be the case, depending on the terms of the debenture, that the right to receive damages is charged to the debenture holder.
[63] See *Re John Willment (Ashford) Ltd* [1980] 1 W.L.R. 73.
[64] If the debenture does not expressly limit the remuneration that can be agreed to a reasonable sum, such a limitation, it is suggested, can readily be implied.

meant, it can produce odd results in the case of receipt of realisations. While there may be an easy realisation of several million pounds, it may require lengthy and difficult legal proceedings to make a relatively small recovery. It might be fairer to provide for the easy, lucrative work to be charged on a time basis and the difficult unrewarding work to be charged on the Official Receiver's scale in liquidations. A proper alternative in a very substantial case would be to agree a time basis throughout. Such variations can be found in practice.

28–028   Whatever basis underlies the remuneration which is claimed, receivers appointed by the court should bear in mind their duties as fiduciaries to justify the fees which they incur in protecting, getting in and realising the assets of the estate.[65]

(iv)   Interest due to the debenture-holder under the Law of Property Act 1925, s.109(8)(iv) or a similar provision in the debenture

28–029   This is a straightforward head of payment.

(v)   The capital due to the debenture-holder under the Law of Property Act 1925, s.109(8)(v) or a similar provision in the debenture

28–030   Again, this is a straightforward calculation.

(vi)   Residue

28–031   Any "residue" goes to the company, being the person "who is otherwise entitled to the mortgaged property" under the proviso to the Law of Property Act 1925, s.109(8) or a similar provision in the debenture, assuming that there are no subsequent chargees. It makes no difference from a legal point of view whether the company is in liquidation or not.

28–032   Sometimes it will be clear at a relatively early stage in the receivership that there will be funds available after paying the charge-holder in full. In such a case, the administrative receiver and the charge-holder may be prepared to transfer surplus funds to the liquidator, or to release certain assets from the charge in order for the liquidator to be able to deal with those assets. Liquidators are often asked to undertake to return funds or assets to the administrative receiver if the receiver is subsequently notified of preferential claims or claims against him as receiver, of which he was not previously aware. Such an undertaking is usually limited to the funds or assets transferred to the liquidator

---

[65] See *Mirror Group Newspapers Plc v Maxwell* [1998] B.C.C. 324; [1999] B.C.C. 684. See also Mr Justice Lightman, "Officeholders Charges—Cost Control and Transparency" (1998) 11 Insolv. Int. 1. As a practical matter, it should be noted that the assessment of the remuneration of a court-appointed receiver, pursuant to Ord.30, r.3(2)(b) of the Rules of the Supreme Court, does not involve the assessment of costs in the Chancery Division. As a result no fee is payable under item 29(d) of the Schedule to the Supreme Court Fees Order (*Mirror Group Newspapers Plc v Maxwell*, *Times*, May 22, 2000).

by the administrative receiver which remain in the hands of the liquidator. A liquidator may, in these circumstances, be prepared to agree to give the administrative receiver prior notice of any proposed distribution to creditors. Undertakings of this type should only be sought and given where the administrative receiver has not yet discharged all his own obligations. Where he has done so, he has a duty to vacate office. It would therefore not be appropriate for him to seek an indemnity or undertaking from the liquidator before transferring any surplus assets or funds to him.

Where a receiver is appointed under fixed and floating charges and the debenture-holder has been paid in full, there may be a surplus of fixed charge realisations. This surplus should be paid to the company, though preferential creditors may be unsatisfied, unless the terms of the fixed charge provide otherwise. The receiver may wish to satisfy the claims of preferential creditors who will not otherwise be met from floating charge realisations, but it has been established by case law that the fixed charge surplus should normally be paid to the company and not to the preferential creditors.   **28–033**

In *Re Lewis Merthyr Consolidated Collieries*[66] the Court of Appeal held that the priority given to preferential creditors in respect of realisations of assets subject to a floating charge[67] applied only to assets caught by the floating charge, even where the receiver was also appointed under a fixed charge.   **28–034**

In *Re GL Saunders Ltd*[68] the receiver had been appointed under fixed and floating charges. There were huge debts to preferential creditors which more than exhausted the floating charge realisations. On the other hand the fixed charge realisations were sufficient to pay the debenture-holder in full and leave a large surplus. By the time the receiver issued his summons for directions the company was in liquidation. The question posed by the receiver was whether he should pay the surplus of fixed charge realisations to the liquidator or to the preferential creditors. There were important differences in the consequences of each course. A direct payment to preferential creditors would have left the liquidator without any monies to pay his costs of the winding-up or his remuneration. Moreover, because the liquidation had begun well after the commencement of the receivership, the amounts treated as preferential in the liquidation were different (and in fact much less) than the sums which would be treated as preferential in the receivership. These consequences were however, regarded as irrelevant to the legal result, which was that, following the *Lewis Merthyr* case,[69] the surplus on fixed charged realisations had to be paid to the liquidator and not to the preferential creditors. On the basis of: (a) the wording of the particular debenture; and (b) the effective discharge of the debenture (since the debenture-holder had been paid in full), a surplus of fixed charged realisations did not fall within the floating charge so as to bring the preferential creditors' rights into play.   **28–035**

---

[66] *Re Lewis Merthyr Consolidated Collieries (No.1)* [1929] 1 Ch. 498 (CA).
[67] Now in the Insolvency Act 1986, s.40.
[68] *Re GL Saunders Ltd (In Liquidation)* [1986] 1 W.L.R. 215.
[69] *Re Lewis Merthyr Consolidated Collieries (No.1)* [1929] 1 Ch. 498 (CA).

(b)   Floating charge realisations (including crystallised floating charges)

28–036   The usual order of payments out of sums realised from assets subject to a charge which as created was a floating charge is similar to that referred to in respect of fixed charge realisations, save for:

(i)   the special priority of preferential creditors; and

(ii) the prescribed part to be retained for unsecured creditors.[70]

(i)   Preferential creditors

28–037   *Rights to priority.*   Section 40(1) of the Insolvency Act 1986 provides that, where the receiver is appointed on behalf of the holders of any debentures of the company[71] secured by "a charge which, as created, was a floating charge" and the company is not at the time of appointment[72] being wound-up, preferential creditors are to be paid in priority to the debenture-holders out of assets coming into the hands of the receiver. Preferential creditors have priority over the holders of all floating charges, not just those pursuant to which a receiver had been appointed.[73] It was held by the Court of Appeal in the *Lewis Merthyr* case[74] that the reference to assets coming into the hands of the receiver only applied to assets subject to a floating charge and not assets subject to a fixed charge.[75] In *Re GL Saunders Ltd*,[76] it was held that the fixed charge surplus arising after the debenture-holder had been paid in full did not fall within the floating charge.

28–038   Before the Insolvency Act 1986 the rights of preferential creditors could be defeated by a crystallisation of the floating charge prior to the appointment of a receiver, so that the charge was no longer a floating charge by the material date.[77] The effectiveness of a provision in a debenture whereby the debenture-holder could crystallise the floating charge prior to the appointment of a

---

[70] Insolvency Act 1986, s.176A; Insolvency 1986, r.3.39.

[71] The word "company" as used in s.40 does not include an entity incorporated under the Industrial and Provident Societies Acts: *Re Devon and Somerset Farmers Ltd* [1994] Ch. 57, as approved and followed in *Re Dairy Farmers of Britain Ltd* [2010] Ch. 63. cf. the approach to the meaning of "company" in the context of administrative receivership in *Re International Bulk Commodities Ltd* 1993] Ch. 77 and see the discussion in relation to foreign incorporated companies in Ch.30.

[72] For the policy reasons underlying the different treatment of fixed and floating charges in this context, see *Re Portbase Clothing Ltd* [1993] Ch. 388.

[73] *Re H&K (Medway) Ltd* [1997] 1 W.L.R. 1422. See also Insolvency Act 1986, s.40(2); Companies Act 2006, s.754.

[74] *Re Lewis Merthyr Consolidated Collieries (No.1)* [1929] 1 Ch. 498 (CA).

[75] See also *Re Portbase Clothing Ltd* [1993] Ch. 388, 20E–F; cf. *Re MC Bacon Ltd (No.2)* [1990] 3 W.L.R. 646.

[76] *Re GL Saunders Ltd (In Liquidation)* [1986] 1 W.L.R. 215. See para.28–035, above.

[77] *Stein v Saywell* (1969) 121 C.L.R. 529 (although this case has been reversed by statute in most states of its native Australia) and see *Re Christonette International Ltd* [1982] 1 W.L.R. 1245; *Re Woodroffes (Musical Instruments) Ltd* [1986] Ch. 366; *Re Brightlife Ltd* [1987] Ch. 200.

receiver by giving notice to the company was accepted by Nourse J. in *Re Woodroffes (Musical Instruments) Ltd*.[78] In that case he also accepted the argument that a cesser of business crystallised a floating charge over the company's assets.[79] Subsequently, Hoffmann J. held in *Re Brightlife Ltd*[80] that crystallisation by notice prior to winding up defeated the rights of preferential creditors.

The effect of the Insolvency Act 1986 was to ensure that crystallisation of a floating charge at any time between its creation and the appointment of a receiver or a liquidation[81] no longer defeated the special rights of preferential creditors.[82]   **28–039**

If a receiver ignores the preferential creditors' rights to payment out of assets in his hands, he is personally liable to pay damages for breach of statutory duty in the sums he should have paid to them.[83] The courts do not take kindly to attempts to evade liability to pay preferential creditors. Thus, where debenture-holders removed the receiver and obtained payment of floating charge realisations without the deduction of sums due to preferential creditors, both the receiver and the debenture-holder were held liable to the preferential creditors.[84] It is unclear whether notice of the claims made by the preferential creditors is a prerequisite to a debenture-holder's liabilities. In *IRC v Goldblatt*.[85] Goff J. held that a debenture-holder would hold monies on constructive trust for a preferential creditor where the monies were received with notice of a statutory duty under which they should have been paid in settlement of a prior claim. The obligation continues even if the debenture-holder has been repaid[86] or if the company goes into liquidation during the course of the receivership.[87] Whether notice is in fact necessary for such a claim has been questioned on the basis that such a claim would be for restitutionary damages arising on breach of statutory duty.[88]   **28–040**

As a result of s.45 of the Insolvency Act 1986 a debenture holder can no longer remove an administrative receiver directly, but the latter has a right to resign. If he does so, he must be sure to discharge any sums payable to preferential creditors before handing any assets or any sum to any subsequent receiver or to the debenture-holder, if the risk of personal liability to the preferential creditor is to be obviated.   **28–041**

Where a receiver resigns and is replaced by a second receiver, the first must pay or provide for the preferential debts of which he had notice, before   **28–042**

---

[78] *Re Woodroffes (Musical Instruments) Ltd* [1986] Ch. 366.
[79] See also *William Gaskell Group Ltd v Highley* [1993] B.C.C. 200, 208.
[80] *Re Brightlife Ltd* [1987] Ch. 200.
[81] Now Insolvency Act 1986, s.40(1) (receiver); s.175(2)(b) and s.251 (liquidation).
[82] See *Re Portbase Clothing Ltd* [1993] Ch. 388; *Mond v Hammond Suddards (No.2)* [2000] Ch. 40 (CA).
[83] *Woods v Winskill* [1913] 2 Ch. 303; *Westminster City Council v Treby* [1936] 2 All E.R. 21; *Westminster Corp v Haste* [1950] Ch. 442; *IRC v Goldblatt* [1972] Ch. 498.
[84] *IRC v Goldblatt* [1972] Ch. 498.
[85] *IRC v Goldblatt* [1972] Ch. 498.
[86] *Re Pearl Maintenance Services Ltd* [1995] B.C.C. 657.
[87] *Re Eisc Teo Ltd* [1991] I.L.R.M. 760.
[88] See the discussion by Professor Goode in (1981) *Journal of Business Law* 476, and *Totty and Moss on Insolvency*, [H2.11].

accounting to the second receiver.[89] In practice, however, the second receiver or the first receiver's appointor will usually grant the first receiver an indemnity.

(ii)   Categories of preferential claims[90]

28–043   Many of the categories of preferential debts, including debts due to the Inland Revenue, Customs and Excise and Social Security Contributions were removed by s.251 of the Enterprise Act 2002, s.386 of the Insolvency Act 1986 and Sch.6 to the Insolvency Act 1986. The surviving categories are as follows.

28–044   *Pension contributions.* Pension contributions to occupational pension schemes and state scheme premiums under Sch.3 to the Social Security Pensions Act 1975.

28–045   *Remuneration of employees.*

    (a)   Sums due to employees or former employees by way of remuneration in respect of the whole or part of a four-month period before the relevant date up to a limit to be set by the Secretary of State. This category includes remuneration ordered under a protective award.[91]

    (b)   Accrued holiday remuneration in respect of any period prior to the relevant date due to a person dismissed before, on or after the relevant date.

    (c)   Sums advanced and applied for the payment of debts which would otherwise have been preferential under (a) or (b).

28–046   *Levies on coal and steel production.*   Sums due at the relevant date in respect of certain ECSC levies and in respect of certain surcharges.

28–047   *The relevant date.*   As a result of s.40 of the Insolvency Act 1986, where a receiver is appointed on behalf of holders of debentures secured by a charge which "as created" was a floating charge, and if at the date of such appointment there has been no resolution to wind up the company and no winding-up order has been made,[92] the "relevant date" for preferential payments, which have to be paid prior to the debenture-holder's claims, is the date of appointment of a receiver under the relevant floating charge.[93] In practice the floating charge will often cover all or substantially the whole of the company's assets and the receiver will be an administrative receiver, but the preferential creditor's priority and the "relevant date" apply irrespective of this.

---

[89] *IRC v Goldblatt* [1972] Ch. 498, 505C, per Goff J.
[90] Insolvency Act 1986, s.175 and Sch.6.
[91] See above, Ch.16.
[92] "In the course of being wound up" in the section does not apply merely where a petition has been presented: *Re Christonette International Ltd* [1982] 1 W.L.R. 1245 and cf. Insolvency Act 1986, s.247(2).
[93] Insolvency Act 1986, s.387(4).

Where a winding-up resolution has been passed or a winding-up order made **28–048** prior to the appointment of a receiver, the following rules apply[94]:

(a) Where a winding-up order followed "immediately" upon the discharge of an administration order, the "relevant date" is that of the making of the administration order.

(b) (with effect from May 31, 2002) where the winding-up is by the court and the winding-up order was made following conversion of administration into winding up, by virtue of art.37 of the EC Regulation, the "relevant date" is the date on which the company entered administration.

(c) (with effect from May 31, 2002) where the company is deemed to have passed a resolution for voluntary winding up by virtue of an order following conversion of administration into winding up under art.37 of the EC Regulation, the "relevant date" is the date on which the company entered administration.

(d) Where the company is being wound up following administration pursuant to para.83 of Sch.B1 to the Insolvency Act 1986, the "relevant date" is the date on which the company entered administration.

(e) Where a company is in administration and no other provision applies, the "relevant date" is the date on which the company entered administration.

(f) In other cases, where there is a resolution to wind up the company, that is the "relevant date"; where there is no such resolution, it is the date of the winding-up order or the date of any earlier appointment of a provisional liquidator.

Where a winding-up follows a receivership, the preferential creditors may well **28–049** be different for the purposes of the winding-up and the receivership because of the different relevant dates in each case.[95]

(iii) Set-off against preferential claims

Frequently a creditor who has both preferential and non-preferential claims **28–050** against a company also owes it money. One situation where this occurs is where the company has money at its bankers and those bankers have advanced monies both for non-preferential purposes and also for wages or a wages account.[96]

---

[94] Insolvency Act 1986, s.387.
[95] This was assumed in *Re GL Saunders Ltd (In Liquidation)* [1986] 1 W.L.R. 215.
[96] As in *Re EJ Morel (1954) Ltd* [1962] Ch. 21.

28–051   The problem of set-off which arises was stated by Walton J. in the winding-up case of *Re Unit 2 Windows Ltd*[97]:

> "If . . . there is a creditor who, but for a set-off of £Z, would have claims against the company of £X which would be preferential, and £Y which would be non-preferential, then, on the assumption that Z is less than X + Y, how . . . are the two claims of the creditor, the preferential and the non-preferential to be calculated?"

Three possible solutions are mentioned by Walton J.:

(a)   £Z could first be set off against the non-preferential claim of £Y and any balance against the preferential claim of £X. This solution would benefit the preferential creditor concerned;

(b)   £Z could be spread rateably as between £X and £Y;

(c)   £Z could first be set off against preferential claims. This would favour other preferential creditors (if there are insufficient funds to pay them in full) and/or the debenture-holder.

Walton J. opted for solution (b) on the construction of the special statutory provisions applicable to set-offs in winding up. These do not apply in receivership[98] and therefore *Re Unit 2 Windows Ltd* is not directly applicable. However, in construing the statutory provisions Walton J. opted for a result which he considered to be "the only logical and sensible solution".[99] On that basis, this solution should apply to receivership situations in the absence of a contrary agreement.

(iv)   Remuneration and preferential creditors

28–052   Generally speaking, debentures provide for payment of remuneration out of charged assets without distinguishing between assets subject to fixed and floating charges. This raises the question whether a receiver could properly favour the debenture-holder by taking his remuneration out of the floating charge assets. It is considered that remuneration should be taken rateably from each class of asset, but the point is not free from doubt.[100] A further question is whether the receiver and the debenture-holder can by agreement prejudice the

---

[97] *Re Unit 2 Windows Ltd* [1985] 1 W.L.R. 1383, 1385. cf. the position in Scotland: *Turner, Petitioner* [1993] B.C.C. 299 (Court of Session, Outer House).
[98] *Business Computers Ltd v Anglo African Leasing Ltd* [1977] 1 W.L.R. 578. Nor do they apply in Scotland: see *Turner, Petitioner* [1993] B.C.C. 299 (Court of Session, Outer House).
[99] *Re Unit 2 Windows Ltd* [1985] 1 W.L.R. 1383, 1388H.
[100] The solution suggested appears to be fair and just. cf. the solution adopted by Walton J. to the set-off problem discussed above. Another possible analogy would be to regard the receiver as a first chargee (for his remuneration) over two assets (the fixed and floating charge assets) and the debenture-holder and preferential creditors as second chargees in each case: see *Flint v Howard* [1893] 2 Ch. 54 (CA), 72 following *Barnes v Racster* 62 E.R. 944.

preferential creditors in this way. The courts would presumably see such an agreement as a breach of the receiver's duty to pay preferential creditors and thus void.[101] Likewise, a provision in a debenture providing for remuneration to be paid, e.g. only out of assets subject to a floating charge, may be void as contravening the policy of the statutory provisions. On the other hand it may be that different rates of remuneration can be provided for fixed and floating charge realisations either in the debenture or, if the debenture permits, by agreement, if and in so far as these different rates genuinely attempt to reflect lesser or greater difficulties or likely difficulties in the realisations concerned.

(v) Share of assets for unsecured creditors[102]

The receiver is required to make a prescribed part of the company's net property available for the satisfaction of unsecured debts and is not permitted to distribute that part to the proprietor of a floating charge except in so far as it exceeds the amount required for the satisfaction of unsecured debts.[103] The company's "net property" is defined as the amount of its property which would, but for the provisions of s.176A of the Insolvency Act 1986, be available for the satisfaction of claims of holders of debentures secured by, or holders of, any floating charge created by the company.[104]   **28–053**

The prescribed part is calculated as follows: **28–054**

(a) Where the net property is less than £10,000, as 50 per cent of that property.

(b) Where the net property is at least £10,000, as 50 per cent of the first £10,000, together with 20 per cent of the property which exceeds £10,000, to a maximum of £600,000.[105]

The costs associated with the prescribed part are to be paid out of that part.[106]

Within three months (or such longer period as the court may allow) of the date of his appointment, the receiver is required[107] to send to creditors (details of whose names and addresses are available to him), notice of his appointment and a report which is to include[108]:   **28–055**

---

[101] *IRC v Goldblatt* [1972] Ch. 498.
[102] Insolvency Act 1986, s.176A(2). Introduced by the Enterprise Act 2002, s.252 with effect from September 15, 2003. This section applies to all receiverships where there is a floating charge, including administrative receiverships and court-appointed receiverships. It does not apply to fixed charge receiverships where there is no floating charge.
[103] Insolvency Act 1986, s.176A(2).
[104] Insolvency Act 1986, s.176A(6).
[105] Insolvency Act 1986 (Prescribed Part) Order 2003 (SI 2003/2097).
[106] Insolvency Rules 1986, r.12.2(2).
[107] Insolvency Rules 1986, r.3.39. Rule 3.39(1) excepts the administrative receiver from the specific reporting obligation, but that obligation is already imposed by the Insolvency Act 1986, s.48.
[108] Insolvency Rules 1986, r.3.39(2).

    (a) to the best of the receiver's knowledge and belief:

        (i) an estimate of the value of the prescribed part (whether or not he proposes to make an application to the court for non-payment of the prescribed part);

        (ii) an estimate of the value of the company's net property;

    (b) whether, and if so why, he proposes to make an application to the court for non-payment of the prescribed part); and

    (c) whether he proposes to present a petition for the winding-up of the company.

28–056 The estimate prepared by the receiver is not required to include any information, the disclosure of which could seriously prejudice the commercial interests of the company. If such information is excluded from the calculation, the estimate is to be accompanied by a statement of that effect.[109]

28–057 Where the receiver thinks that it is impracticable to send the required report or where full details of the unsecured creditors of the company are not available to him, he may (instead of sending a report) publish a notice to the same effect in such newspaper as he thinks most appropriate for ensuring that it comes to the notice of the company's unsecured creditors.[110]

28–058 Where the obligation to make the required report exists[111]:

    (a) the receiver may present a petition for the winding-up of the company if the company is unable to pay its debts[112];

    (b) where a liquidator or administrator has been appointed to the company, the receiver must deliver up the sums representing the prescribed part to him;

    (c) in any other case, the receiver shall apply to the court for directions as to the manner in which he is to discharge his duties in relation to the retention of the prescribed part, and he is required to act in accordance with such directions as the court gives.

28–059 The requirement to make a retention of the prescribed part does not apply to a company if the company's net property is less than the prescribed minimum, and the receiver thinks that the cost of making a distribution to unsecured creditors would be disproportionate to the benefits.[113] The requirement also does not apply to a company if the court makes an order on an application by the receiver that he be excused from making the distribution, on the ground that

---

[109] Insolvency Rules 1986, r.3.39(3).
[110] Insolvency Rules 1986, r.3.39(4).
[111] Insolvency Rules 1986, r.3.40.
[112] As defined by s.122(1)(f).
[113] Insolvency Act 1986, s.176A(3).

the cost of making a distribution to unsecured creditors would be dispropor-tionate to the benefits.[114]

The provisions relating to the prescribed part only apply to floating charges **28–060** which were created on or after September 13, 2003.[115]

(vi) Costs and expenses of winding up

One issue which used to be relevant to the distribution of floating charge assets **28–061** was the priority to be accorded to the costs and expenses of winding up (as discussed in Ch.4).

The question whether a liquidator should be able to treat costs incurred by **28–062** him in unsuccessful litigation against a receiver as expenses of the winding up gave rise to a number of recent decisions (*Re MC Bacon Ltd*[116]; *Re Exchange Travel (Holdings) Ltd (No.3); Katz v McNally*[117]; *Mond v Hammond Suddards*[118]; and *Lewis v Inland Revenue Commissioners*[119]). The question has now been settled by an amendment to r.4.218(1)(a) of the Insolvency Rules 1986[120] which makes it clear that the expenses of liquidation include expenses or costs relating to the conduct of any legal proceedings which a liquidator has power to bring or defend whether in his own name or in the name of the company. This question is at present of limited interest in the context of a receivership as the decision of the House of Lords in *Re Leyland DAF*; sub nom. *Buchler v Talbot*[121] has made it clear that the expenses of a liquidation cannot be paid out of the assets subject to a crystallised floating charge. The House of Lords pointed out that there are two distinct funds, which have not been pooled, which belong to different parties, which are actually or poten-tially administered by different office-holders, and which are subject to different statutory regimes. Each fund must bear its own costs of administra-tion, and neither is required to bear the costs of administering the other. In particular, the assets comprised in the crystallised floating charge are not

---

[114] Insolvency Act 1986, s.176A(5). Insolvency Rules 1986, r.7.3A and 7.3B govern the making of such applications. Where the court makes an order under this section, it shall as soon as reason-ably practicable send two sealed copies of the order to the applicant and a sealed copy to any other insolvency practitioner who holds office in relation to the company. The receiver is required to send a sealed copy of the order to the company. The receiver is also required to give notice to each creditor (including by newspaper) of whose claim and address he is aware, unless the court directs otherwise. The receiver is also required to give notice to the Registrar of Companies. (Insolvency Rules 1986, r.12.22). The provision has now been judicially considered in a number of cases: *Re Hydroserve Ltd* [2008] B.C.C. 175; *Re International Sections Ltd* [2009] B.C.C. 574; *Ames Bernard Stephen and David John Hill, Joint Administrators Of QMD Hotels Ltd*, 2011 G.W.D. 1–42 (Court of Session, Outer House). The court will not disapply s.176A(2) simply because the dividend would be small.

[115] Insolvency Act 1986, s.176A(9).

[116] *Re MC Bacon Ltd* [1991] Ch. 127.

[117] *Re Exchange Travel (Holdings) Ltd (No.3)*; sub nom. *Katz v McNally* [1997] B.C.C. 784 (CA).

[118] *Mond v Hammond Suddards* (No.2) [2000] Ch. 40 (CA).

[119] *Lewis v Inland Revenue Commissioners* [2001] 3 All E.R. 499 (CA).

[120] Brought in by the Insolvency (Amendment) (No.2) Rules 2002 (SI 2002/2712).

[121] *Re Leyland DAF*; sub nom. *Buchler v Talbot* [2004] 2 A.C. 298 (HL).

DISTRIBUTION AND VACATION OF OFFICE BY RECEIVERS

required to bear the costs and expenses of the winding up. The decision of the court in *Re Barleycorn Enterprises Ltd* [1970] Ch. 465 was overturned.[122]

28–063   In addition, a liquidator has no cause of action to recover, from a debenture-holder, monies paid by administrative receivers to the debenture-holder in respect of floating charge realisations, which should have been paid to preferential creditors. Only the preferential creditors have a right to recover these monies from the debenture-holder.[123]

(c)   Where the debenture-holder is missing

28–064   Generally speaking debenture-holders are banks or other lending institutions. In a number of cases, however, they are private appointors. Where such private appointors are humans, they may disappear (as humans sometimes do). This leaves the receiver with the problem that he has monies which ought to be paid to the missing debenture-holder. He can await the appearance of the debenture-holder, but the more practical alternative may be to pay any monies into court under s.63 of the Trustee Act 1925.[124] Although as between the mortgagor and mortgagee monies in a receiver's hands are regarded as belonging to the mortgagor until actual payment to the mortgagee (and accordingly the mortgagor is at risk if they are lost or misappropriated by the receiver[125]) nonetheless as between receiver and the mortgagee the receiver holds any monies as trustee for the debenture-holder (and then as to any surplus as trustee for the mortgagor).[126]

(d)   Duties on redemption

28–065   The receiver and mortgagee are duty bound on redemption to return the charged assets to the company or other person with a prior right to the equity of redemption (e.g. a second mortgagee).[127] Where an administrative receiver ceases to act, the administrative receiver must hand to the company (or its liquidator) all the records in his possession which belong to the company.

28–066   In relation to documents, three different categories may exist:

> (a)   documents generated pursuant to the duty to manage the business and sell assets—these must be delivered up to the person entitled to the return of the assets;

---

[122] *Leyland DAF* was reversed by s.176ZA Insolvency Act 1986. See paras 4–010 to 4–012, above.

[123] *Re BHT (UK) Ltd* [2004] B.C.C. 301.

[124] For the procedure, see CPR, 37PD.9.

[125] *White v Metcalf* [1903] 2 Ch. 567, 571.

[126] *Bacal Contracting Ltd v Modern Engineering (Bristol) Ltd* [1980] 2 All E.R. 655, 659g–h. The essentials of any trusteeship are clearly satisfied: (1) the receiver owes fiduciary duties; and (2) he is under a duty to keep the debenture-holder's monies separate from his own *(Henry v Hammond* [1913] 2 K.B. 515). See also *Smiths Ltd v Middleton* [1979] 3 All E.R. 842. In *Visbord v FCT* (1943) 68 C.L.R. 354 (High Court of Australia), Starke J. referred to the receiver's duty to pay the surplus to the mortgagee as a mandate and "not . . . a trust" (at 376) whereas Williams J. referred to the receiver as holding realisations "in a fiduciary capacity on behalf of the mortgagee and the mortgagor . . ." (at 387).

[127] *Downsview v First City Corp* [1993] A.C. 295 (PC).

(b) documents generated for the purpose of providing advice or information about the receivership to the mortgagee—these belong to the mortgagee;

(c) documents generated for the purpose of enabling the receiver to discharge his professional duties (save for those which fall within (a) or (b) above) belong to the receiver.[128]

The receiver has a duty to maintain sufficient accounting information to enable the directors to discharge their statutory duties to publish accounts.[129] Regulation 10A of the Insolvency Regulations 1986 requires a receiver to keep records for six years or to hand them to a successor as "the responsible insolvency practitioner". An abstract of receipts and payments must be filed within two months of ceasing to act, unless the court extends this time limit.[130]

---

[128] *Gomba Holdings v Minories Finance* (1987) 3 B.C.C. 643, affirmed [1988] 1 W.L.R. 1231 (CA).
[129] *Smiths Ltd v Middleton* [1979] 3 All E.R. 842.
[130] Insolvency Rules 1986, r.3.32.

Chapter 29

Receivers Appointed by the Court

1. INTRODUCTION

29–001 Under a succession of statutes since 1873, culminating in the Supreme Court Act 1981,[1] the High Court has had jurisdiction to appoint a receiver at any stage in proceedings in all cases in which it appears to the court to be just and convenient to do so.[2] The jurisdiction is discretionary and accordingly as a matter of principle ought not to be fettered by rules.[3]

There are, however, a very limited number of rules of law and an abundance of rules of practice to which the court will have regard in deciding any application for the appointment of a receiver. The distinction between these rules is that rules of law bind in every case and are (unless later held to be wrongly stated or reversed by statute) immutable. On the other hand, rules of practice are merely guidelines of varying weight (often merely expressions of common sense) which may give way in the particular circumstances of a particular case and which are subject to evolution and review in changing times and social conditions.[4] The risk of confusion of rules of practice and rules of law must constantly be guarded against.[5]

The principal rule of law in this area is that the jurisdiction to appoint a receiver, like the jurisdiction to grant an injunction, can only be exercised in aid of some legal or equitable right.[6] This right usually, although not invariably, is constituted by a cause of action[7]. As limited exceptions to this rule, an injunction may be granted in aid of other orders, to prevent dissipation of assets

---

[1] s.37(1). An arbitration agreement may confer on the arbitrator a power to appoint a receiver, but such a provision is rarely found. The alternative is for the court to appoint a receiver in aid of the arbitration proceedings under s.44(2)(e) of the Arbitration Act 1996: see Mustill and Boyd, *Commercial Arbitration*, 2nd edn (London: Butterworths, 1989), p.331 (as updated in the 2001 Companion).

[2] For an application for the appointment of a receiver of a company which was rejected as unjust and inconvenient, see *Williams & Humbert Ltd v W&H Trade Marks (Jersey)* [1986] A.C. 368 (HL), 429–430.

[3] *Kirklees Metropolitan BC v Wickes Building Supplies* [1993] A.C. 227, 265.

[4] *Italmare Shipping Co v Ocean Tanker Co Inc (The Rio Sun)* [1982] 1 W.L.R. 158 (CA). See also *Fourie v Le Roux* [2007] 1 W.L.R. 320 (HL).

[5] For an elaboration of the distinction, see the 3rd edition of this book, para.30–003.

[6] *Siskina v Distos Compania* [1979] A.C. 210 (HL); *ED&F Man (Sugar) v Evaland Shipping* [1989] 2 Lloyd's Rep. 192; *Mercedes Benz AG v Leiduck* [1996] A.C. 284 (PC); *Morris v Murjani* [1996] 1 W.L.R. 848 (CA). In Australia, see *Bond Brewing Holdings Ltd v National Australia Bank Ltd* (1990) 1 A.C.S.R. 445 (Full Court of the Supreme Court of Victoria). The appointment of a receiver may be made by an interim order or on final judgment or as a form of execution.

[7] *Channel Tunnel Group v Balfour Beatty Ltd* [1993] A.C. 334 (HL), 362B–D, applied in *Mercantile Group (Europe) AG v Aiyela* [1994] Q.B. 366 (CA).

and to prevent the defendant acting in an unconscionable manner. In accordance with this rule, the court cannot at the instance of a secured creditor appoint a receiver and manager of the security and other property with a view to the combined and advantageous sale of the charged and uncharged property together, since the creditor has no interest in or right in respect of the uncharged property.[8] There is a further rule of law that where Parliament has conferred on a particular body powers and duties in relation to the management of a business or undertaking and in so doing has shown an intention that no other body shall execute those powers or undertake those duties, the court cannot by the appointment of a receiver or manager vest those powers or duties in anyone else.[9] Subject only to these limitations, the court has an unlimited power to appoint a receiver if it is just and convenient to do so.[10]

The rules of practice relating to the appointment of a receiver are essentially the same as those governing the grant of an injunction. Thus a receiver will not be appointed unless the appointment secures some legitimate advantage for the applicant. No appointment will be made if, for example, the property is valueless or incapable of beneficial realisation.[11] **29–002**

The court will not, save in extraordinary circumstances, appoint a receiver on an application without notice[12] but it will not shrink from doing so where it is appropriate.[13] Where the appointment of a receiver is sought as an interim or protective measure, a cross-undertaking in damages will ordinarily be required of the applicant in favour of the other party to the litigation, whether the order

---

[8] *Britannia Building Society v Crammer* [1997] B.P.I.R. 596.

[9] *Rio Properties Inc v Gibson Dunn & Crutcher* [2004] 1 W.L.R. 2702 (CA), 2715. See also *Maclaine Watson & Co Ltd v International Tin Council* [1988] Ch. 1, 17C (approved [1989] Ch. 253 (CA), 271), where Millett J. declined to appoint a receiver to an organisation established by treaty between sovereign states on the ground that the right invoked was not justiciable in the English court.

[10] *Derby v Weldon (No.3)* [1990] Ch. 65 (CA), 76–77, per Lord Donaldson M.R., citing Jessel M.R. to like effect in *Beddow v Beddow* (1878) L.R. 9 Ch. D. 89, 93. See also *Parker v Camden London BC* [1986] Ch. 162 (CA), 173, 176; *Bourne v Colodense* [1985] I.C.R. 291 (CA); *Maclaine Watson & Co Ltd v International Tin Council* [1988] Ch. 1, 17C (approved [1989] Ch. 253 (CA), 271). There is no longer any basis for refusing to appoint a receiver by way of equitable execution simply because such an appointment would not have been made by the Court of Chancery prior to 1873: see *Soinco v Novokuznetsk Aluminium Plant* [1998] Q.B. 406 and *Masri v Consolidated Contractors International Co SAL* [2009] Q.B. 450 (CA), [184].

[11] *J Walls v Legge* [1923] 2 K.B. 240 (CA). Since the appointment of a receiver is a costly procedure, in exercising its discretion whether to grant equitable execution the court must carefully consider the cost-effectiveness of the proposed appointment; indeed, CPR PD 69 para.5, specifically provides that where a judgment creditor applies for the appointment of a receiver as a method of enforcing a judgment, "in considering whether to make the appointment the court will have regard to—(1) the amount claimed by the judgment creditor; (2) the amount likely to be obtained by the receiver; and (3) the probable costs of his appointment." The same consideration should be relevant to a proposed appointment pre-judgment: see *Beach Petroleum NL v Johnson* (1992) 9 A.C.S.R. 404 (Federal Court of Australia).

[12] *Re Connolly Bros Ltd (No.1)* [1911] 1 Ch. 731 (CA), 742; *National Australia Bank v Bond Brewing* [1991] 1 V.L.R. 386 ("only the most pressing need can warrant such an invasion without notice"). For an example of such an appointment, see *Clarke v Heathfield* [1985] I.C.R. 203 (CA).

[13] *Don King Productions v Warren* [2000] B.C.C. 263.

is made with or without notice.[14] The same may not be true where the receiver is appointed by way of equitable execution.[15]

2. TYPES OF COURT RECEIVERSHIP

29-003 The court may appoint several different types of receivers in respect of a company. It may appoint a receiver and manager of a company's business and undertaking. In this case the powers of the directors to conduct its business and dispose of its assets are in abeyance for the duration of the receivership.[16]

The court may also appoint a receiver or receiver and manager of the company itself in cases where the company is incapable of managing its own affairs by reason of the absence of a properly constituted board or deadlock on the board of directors.[17] The same approach may also be adopted where there is dissension on the board following misconduct or an irretrievable breakdown between the shareholders in a "quasi-partnership" and a petition has been presented for the winding up of the company or under Companies Act 2006, s.994 claiming that the affairs of the company have been or are being conducted in a manner which is unfairly prejudicial to the interests of the members or some of them.[18] The appointment will, however, only be made as a temporary measure pending the resolution of the difficulties which prevent the board from exercising control of the company's affairs or which make it inappropriate that they should do so.[19] Thus in the case of litigation relating to a "quasi-partnership" company, a receiver and manager may be appointed pending the dismissal of the petition, the making of a winding up order, or the making of an

---

[14] *National Australia Bank Ltd v Bond Brewing Holdings Ltd* (1990) 1 A.C.S.R. 722 (High Court of Australia). Note that a cross-undertaking will not extend to losses suffered by third parties: *Smithkline Beecham Plc v Apotex Europe Ltd* [2007] Ch. 71 (CA).

[15] *Allied Irish Bank v Ashford Hotels Ltd* [1998] B.C.C. 440 (CA), 446–447. If a receiver is appointed under the provisions of the Criminal Justice Act 1988, the usual cross-undertaking is not required to be given: *Hughes v Customs & Excise Commissioner* [2003] 1 W.L.R. 177 (CA). No remedy is available other than under the cross-undertaking in damages if it turns out that the appointment should not have been made: *Pollnow v Garden Mews-St Leonard Pty Ltd* (1985) 9 A.C.L.R. 82; *Capewell v Customs and Excise Commissioners* [2007] 1 W.L.R. 386 (HL). However, s.89 of the Criminal Justice Act 1988 empowers the High Court to award compensation in limited circumstances on the application of "a person who held property which was realisable property".

[16] *Moss Steamship Company Co Ltd v Whinney* [1912] A.C. 254 (HL), 263.

[17] See *Stanfield v Gibbon* [1925] W.N. 11 and *Te Runanganui o Ngati Kahunguku Inc v Scott* [1995] 1 N.Z.L.R. 250 (NZ). For an interesting case in which the court appointed its own receivers in order to overcome the practical difficulties created by the appointments out of court by different lenders of two receivers over the same property with equal priority, see *Bass Breweries v Delaney* [1994] B.C.C. 851.

[18] *Wilton Davies v Kirk* [1997] B.C.C. 770; *Re Worldhams Park Golf Course Ltd* [1998] 1 B.C.L.C. 554. See also *Duffy v Super Centre Development Corp* [1967] 1 N.S.W.R. 382 and *Wayland v Nidamon Pty* (1986) 11 A.C.L.R. 209; and compare *Verhelst v Going Places Travel Centre Pty* (1980) A.C.L.C. 34, 138.

[19] See *Stanfield v Gibbon* [1925] W.N. 11. Such a receiver is entitled to make all reasonable requests for information from any party to the dispute to enable him to carry on the business, and those requests should be complied with: *Parsons v Mather & Platt* [1977] 1 W.L.R. 855.

order under Companies Act 2006, s. 996 regulating the management of the company or directing one party to sell his shares to the other.[20]

The court may also appoint a receiver or a receiver and manager of a company or specified assets at the instance of a person who claims that he owns assets which have been improperly transferred to the company,[21] or at the instance of a shareholder[22] or creditor[23] if assets are in jeopardy because of the risk of misappropriation or dissipation by those in control of its affairs[24] or because of breach or evasion of a freezing injunction.[25] Since the appointment of a receiver displaces the defendant as the person in control of his assets and is therefore an invasive remedy, the court will need to be satisfied that sufficient protection against dissipation cannot be given to the applicant by the grant of an injunction or other less invasive measures.[26] The court is most unlikely to appoint a receiver simply to provide a regime for the proper administration of the affairs of a company in financial difficulties where the

---

[20] See *Re A Company (No.000596 of 1986)* [1987] B.C.L.C. 133. The appointment may extend to the company's wholly owned subsidiaries: *Wilton Davis v Kirk* [1997] B.C.C. 770. The slur and adverse effect on the assets and business of the company caused by those in the outside world failing to distinguish between receivers appointed on grounds of insolvency and receivers appointed in the context of a s.994 petition will weigh with the court, as well as its expense: see *Jaber v Science & Information Technology Ltd* [1992] B.C.L.C. 764 and *Re Mountforest Ltd* [1993] B.C.C. 565. The court has jurisdiction under Companies Act 2006, s.996 to direct that the party whose conduct occasioned the appointment should bear the receiver's costs and expenses: *Re Worldhams Golf Course* [1998] 1 B.C.L.C. 554.

[21] *Bank of Credit and Commerce International (In Liquidation) SA v BRS Kumar Brothers Ltd* [1994] 1 B.C.L.C. 211.

[22] e.g. on the presentation of a petition to wind up or under s.994 or on the institution of a derivative claim.

[23] Including a claimant in an action against the company.

[24] See *Krishna v Chandra* [1928] A.I.R. 49, 50, per Lord Sumner. The purpose of a freezing injunction—and, it is suggested, the appointment of a receiver at the behest of a claimant—is not to rewrite the established principles of insolvency law by giving the claimant some form of security which he does not enjoy, or indirectly to achieve a similar result by interfering with the payment of other debts by a company in the ordinary course of business: see *The Angel Bell* [1981] Q.B. 65 and *K/S A/S Admiral Shipping v Portlink Ferries* [1984] 2 Lloyd's Rep. 166 (CA). See also *Normid Housing Association v Ralph & Mansell* [1989] 1 Lloyd's Rep. 265 (CA), 275. For examples of the appointment of receivers to ensure that disputed property was properly managed pending trial, see *Hart v Emelkirk* [1983] 1 W.L.R. 1289 and *Daiches v Bluelake Investments* (1986) 51 P. & C.R. 51.

[25] *International Credit and Investment Co (Overseas) Ltd v Adham* [1998] B.C.C. 134. In *Wallace Kevin James v Merrill Lynch International Bank Ltd* [1998] 1 S.L.R. 785, two (subsequently remedied) breaches of a freezing injunction were held not to justify "the extreme remedy of a receivership order". The applicant for a receiver "must make out a clear case not only that the protection of the interests of people to whom the company may be or become liable require protection, but also that a lesser remedy which does not involve removing the administration of the company from the directors would fit the circumstances of the case": *Beach Petroleum NL v Johnson* (1992) 9 A.C.S.R. 404. To avoid the irrevocable damage which the appointment may cause the court may impose a protective regime under the supervision of an independent accountant: *Don King Productions v Warren (No.3)* [2000] B.C.C. 263.

[26] *JSC BTA Bank v Ablyazov* [2010] EWHC 1779 (Comm). In *National Australia Bank Ltd v Bond Brewing Holdings Ltd* (1990) 1 A.C.S.R. 445 the Supreme Court of Victoria held that whilst there was no principle that a court could only be appointed at the behest of someone asserting a proprietary interest in the property concerned, the applicant nevertheless had to show both that he was seeking to protect some legal or equitable right and that no other adequate remedy was available to protect that right. In this latter respect the law in Australia may be more restrictive than the approach in England as set out in *Derby v Weldon (Nos 3 and 4)* [1990] Ch. 65 (CA). See also *Global Funds Management (NSW) Ltd v Burns Philp Trustee Co* (1990) 3 A.C.S.R. 183.

company objects to the appointment.[27] The overriding issue in all cases will be whether the appointment is the appropriate remedy in the particular circumstances of the case, having regard in particular to the damage which may be occasioned by the appointment to the defendant and third parties.[28]

The appointment by the court of a receiver of a company will not necessarily preclude the directors exercising their power to obtain without the approval of the receiver or the court legal advice and representation on behalf of the company relating to the receivership, though it may preclude exercise of the power to do so in relation to strategic planning or corporate restructuring.[29]

29–004 The court may appoint a receiver by way of equitable execution over any asset of the company, including future debts[30] and causes of action of the company against the company's directors for breach of duty.[31] The original basis for such appointment was to act as a substitute where execution at law would be ineffective to enable a judgment creditor to obtain payment of his judgment debt,[32] but the appointment may now be made whenever it is just and convenient to do so.[33]

The effect of such an appointment may be both negative and positive. Negatively, the appointment operates as an injunction restraining the company from dealing with the asset in question. Positively, the order may authorise the receiver to realise or otherwise bring to account the asset in question, and (in the case of a cause of action) to sue in the name of the company. The order will operate to create a charge in favour of the judgment creditor if, but only if, the receiver is directed by the order to hold the asset for or to pay its proceeds or other realisation to the judgment creditor.[34] The effect of the appointment may be nullified by the making of a winding up order or the appointment of a provisional liquidator prior to completion of the execution.[35]

The court may appoint a receiver ad litem of a company in receivership for the limited purpose of determining whether the company has a cause of action

---

[27] In *National Australia Bank Ltd v Bond Brewing Holdings Ltd* (1990) 1 A.C.S.R. 445, the Supreme Court of Victoria held that where a company resisted the appointment, a receiver would not be appointed simply in order to provide a regime for the administration of a financially embarrassed company. Refusing an application for special leave to appeal, the High Court of Australia ((1990) 1 A.C.S.R. 722) was willing to assume that circumstances could exist in which a receiver could be appointed in respect of a company not expressly alleged to be insolvent at the instance of an unsecured creditor, but upheld the decision of the Supreme Court of Victoria on the facts.

[28] *Derby v Weldon (No.3)* [1990] Ch. 65 (CA), 77B–E.

[29] *Corp of Peterborough v Kawartha* (2010) Carswell Ont. 7995.

[30] *Soinco SACI v Novokuznetsk Aluminium Plant* [1998] Q.B. 406; *Masri v Consolidated Contractors International Co SAL (No.2)* [2009] Q.B. 450 (CA), [184].

[31] See *Levermore v Levermore* [1979] 1 W.L.R. 1277 (Fam Div).

[32] See, e.g. *Re Shephard* (1890) L.R. 43 Ch. D. 131 (CA).

[33] *Soinco SACI v Novokuznetsk Aluminium Plant* [1998] Q.B. 406; *Masri v Consolidated Contractors International Co SAL* [2009] Q.B. 450 (CA), [184]. For a criticism of Colman J.'s decision in *Soinco* that the court has jurisdiction to appoint a receiver by way of equitable execution to receive future debts as well as debts due or accrued due, see Andrew Pena, "A New Remedy: High Court Appoints Receiver by Way of Equitable Execution Over Future Debts" (1997) 17(1) *Litigation* 20, 20–24 .

[34] *Re Potts Ex p. Taylor* [1893] 1 Q.B. 648 (CA); *Re Pearce* [1919] 1 K.B. 354 (CA), *Flightline v Edwards* [2003] 1 W.L.R. 1200 (CA).

[35] *Croshaw v Lyndhurst Ship Co* [1897] 2 Ch. 154, 162–163.

against the debenture-holder and/or the receiver and if appropriate to prosecute such actions.[36]

The court may, on the application of a secured creditor, appoint a receiver **29–005** and manager of the company's undertaking to protect the interests of the creditor.[37] The court has jurisdiction to make such an appointment irrespective of whether the secured creditor has himself power to make such an appointment out of court,[38] but it is rare for such a secured creditor to want an appointment by the court. As a practical matter, the only occasion when it is likely that a secured creditor will apply for such an order will be when the debenture does not in the particular circumstances authorise such an appointment out of court, or where his entitlement to make the appointment is disputed or open to question.[39] In such a case, the court has jurisdiction to make an appointment.[40]

In the exercise of this jurisdiction, the court will in the ordinary case respect the right of the company to carry on its business without interference by the creditor until the occurrence of an event which under the terms of the debenture gives the creditor a right to intervene. But notwithstanding the absence of a provision to this effect in the debenture, the court may, in the exercise of its discretion, make such appointment if:

(a) the security is in jeopardy[41];

(b) the company is in default of payment of either principal or interest[42]; or

(c) the company ceases to be a going concern.[43]

The ground of "jeopardy" should not be given a narrow meaning, and the filing of a creditor's winding up petition has been held to justify the appointment of

---

[36] *Swisstex Finance Pty Ltd v Lamb* (1985) 10 A.C.L.R. 135.

[37] The order for the appointment of a receiver may be made on the application of a subsequent incumbrancer if the prior incumbrancer has neither taken possession nor appointed a receiver: *Re Metropolitan Amalgamated Estates* [1912] 2 Ch. 497. The appointment by the court of a receiver at the instigation of a creditor other than the debenture-holder will not automatically crystallise a floating charge unless the debenture specifically so provides: consider *Bayhold Financial Corp Ltd v Clarkson Co Ltd* (1991) 10 C.B.R. (3d) 159 (Supreme Court of Nova Scotia, Appellate Division).

[38] *Britannia Building Society v Crammer* [1997] B.P.I.R. 596, citing *Tillett v Nixon* (1884) L.R. 25 Ch. D. 238.

[39] See also the unusual facts of *Bass Breweries v Delaney* [1994] B.C.C. 851, where one of two rival secured creditors sought the appointment of court receivers to act independently in circumstances in which two rival debenture-holders with equal priority had both appointed receivers pursuant to the powers in their charges.

[40] *McMahon v North Kent Ironworks Co* [1891] 2 Ch. 148. Though the circumstances for such an order must be rare, the court may appoint a receiver notwithstanding that the debenture-holder has already done so: *Re Slogger Automatic Feeder Co Ltd* [1915] 1 Ch. 478, and see para.29–013.

[41] *Re Victoria Steamboats* [1897] 1 Ch. 158; *Re New York Taxi Cab Co Ltd* [1913] 1 Ch. 1; *Re Tilt Cove Copper Co Ltd* [1913] 2 Ch. 588. In the absence of a provision entitling him to do so, a debenture-holder has no right to appoint a receiver on the ground that his security is in jeopardy: he has merely an "equity" to apply to the court for such an appointment on this ground: *Cryne v Barclays Bank* [1987] B.C.L.C. 548 (CA).

[42] *Re Crompton & Co Ltd* [1914] 1 Ch. 954.

[43] *Hubbuck v Helms* (1887) 56 L.T. 232; *Hodson v Tea Co* [1880] L.R. 14 Ch. D. 859.

a receiver by the court.[44] But a mere lack of present assets equal to the debenture-holder's eventual debt is not sufficient if the company is not in financial difficulties and there is no evidence: (a) that the charged assets are at risk of being seized; or (b) that the company will be unable to pay the sums due to the debenture-holder at the end of the day.[45]

29–006   The appointment may be limited to the assets in jeopardy, and not extend to assets free from risk because, for example, they are the subject of a fixed charge.[46] The court may also appoint a receiver and manager of a company's undertaking on the application of the creditor or the company in a case where the validity of the creditor's debenture or appointment of a receiver is in dispute.

The court will only appoint a receiver and manager of a business if the charge includes the goodwill of the business or the preservation of the security requires that the business is continued. The appointment will only be made so as to give an opportunity for a beneficial realisation of the security by a sale of the business as a going concern or pending resolution of a dispute as to the entitlement to the business.[47] The business may be carried on in England or abroad.[48]

In a case where a beneficial realisation requires the sale, or inclusion in a sale, of an asset, and there is a dispute between the debenture-holder and company as to whether the asset is charged or whether the debenture is valid, notwithstanding that the company objects to the sale the court may order such sale, making in the order appropriate provision for safeguarding the proceeds (or any part thereof) to await the resolution of the dispute.[49] An application for such an order may be made by a court-appointed receiver or by a receiver appointed out of court. The order may include any appropriate consequential order for vacating entries (e.g. estate contracts or cautions) at the Land Charges Registry and the Land Registry.[50] If the company owns an asset which is not charged, though the beneficial realisation of its charged asset requires that this asset is also included in the sale, the court cannot order a sale of the uncharged asset against the wishes of the company. If the company persists in its objection to the inclusion of the asset in the sale, the receiver can only seek to put the company into liquidation and hope for greater co-operation in the sale from the liquidator than he has received from the directors.

---

[44] *Re Victoria Steamboats* [1897] 1 Ch. 158.

[45] *Re New York Taxi Cab Co Ltd* [1913] 1 Ch. 1, as explained in *Re Tilt Cove Copper Co Ltd* [1913] 2 Ch. 588. The *Tilt Cove* case itself concerned a proposal to give all of the company's assets to the shareholders, and a receiver was appointed at the behest of the debenture holders.

[46] *Grigson v Taplin* (1915) 112 L.T. 985.

[47] *Halsbury's Laws of England*, 4th edn (London: LexisNexis Butterworths, 1991), Reissue Vol.39(2), paras 482–483. The court may authorise the manager to borrow money on security having priority to any existing debenture if the money is required to preserve the assets and goodwill, though even in this case the security will be postponed to the receiver's right to an indemnity unless contrary provision is made: *Greenwood v Algeciras Railway* [1894] 2 Ch. 205.

[48] *Re Huinac Copper Mines Ltd* [1910] W.N. 218.

[49] CPR r.25.1(1)(c)(v). See also Insolvency Act 1986, ss.114(3)(c) and 166(3)(b), and *Arab Bank Plc v Mercantile Holdings Ltd* [1994] Ch. 71.

[50] *Hornsea Potteries v Destian* Unreported May 11, 1984 (CA).

Instead of applying for the appointment of a receiver by the court, any cred- **29–007**
itor (secured or otherwise) may pursue the alternative remedy of presenting a
winding-up petition and applying immediately thereafter for the appointment
of a provisional liquidator.[51] A creditor has the right by such means to protect
the company's assets so that they are available for equal distribution amongst
all the creditors.[52] The availability of this alternative remedy may be relevant
on an application for the appointment of a receiver and manager, for it may
afford a more convenient and satisfactory method of realising the company's
assets and protecting its creditors.

3.   PROCEDURE ON APPLICATION FOR APPOINTMENT

The procedure for applying for the appointment of a receiver is set out in CPR **29–008**
Pt 69. Under CPR r.69.2(1) the court may appoint a receiver before proceedings have commenced,[53] during proceedings, or after judgment has been given.
The appointee must be independent of the parties and impartial.[54] The Practice
Direction to CPR Pt 69 sets out the evidence and other information which
should accompany an application.[55] The court will ordinarily appoint the
nominee of a mortgagee if the nominee is qualified and otherwise unobjection-
able. As a matter of law, the appointee does not have to be qualified to act as an
insolvency practitioner in relation to the company, for the provisions of
Insolvency Act 1986, Pt XIII do not apply to any receiver of a company other
than an administrative receiver, and a receiver appointed by the court is not an
administrative receiver.[56] But no doubt in practice the courts will require that
its appointees and officers have identical qualifications. The court has a discretion whether to order that the receiver provides security.[57] If the order does

---

[51] See para.2–045, above. This remedy was successfully invoked by the debenture-holder in
Gamelstaden Plc v Brackland Magazines Ltd [1993] B.C.C. 194, when precluded by an injunction
granted without notice from enforcing its security.

[52] *Re Dry Docks Corporation of London* (1888) L.R. 39 Ch. D. 306 (CA), 314.

[53] Note, however, that the court will normally only consider making an order before proceedings
have started if notice of the application has been served: CPR PD 69, para.2.1. See also CPR
r.25.2(2) for obtaining an order before proceedings have started.

[54] In the matter of *Angel's Castle Pre-School Pty Ltd (In Liquidation)* [2010] FCA 786 (Federal
Court of Australia).

[55] CPR PD 69, paras 3 and 4.

[56] See para.29–009(g) below.

[57] CPR r.69.5 and CPR PD 69, para.7. The security shall be by an extension of the bond provided
under the Insolvency Practitioner Regulations 1990 (if he is a licensed insolvency practitioner) or
by guarantee unless the court otherwise directs: (CPR PD 69, para.7). Since a court-appointed
receiver is personally liable for his acts or omissions he is almost invariably required to furnish
security as a term of his appointment. Whilst the court has power to dispense with security in
certain cases, it will rarely do so, especially in the case of a company receivership, and will generally only do so where: (i) the amount involved in the action is small; (ii) the applicant is made
answerable for the acts or defaults of the receiver; (iii) the receiver is appointed without remuneration; or (iv) the scope and purpose of the receivership are so limited that the court waives security:
see J. O'Donovan, *Company Receivers and Administrators*, 2nd edn (Sydney: LBC, 1992). CPR
PD 69, para.4.1(4) specifically provides that "if the applicant is asking the court to allow the
receiver to act—(a) without giving security; or (b) before he has given security or satisfied the
court that he has security in place, [he is required to] explain the reasons why that is necessary".

require security the appointment will be conditional and ineffective until the receiver provides the requisite security, unless the court gives liberty to act forthwith. This it may do if the applicant is willing and able to give an undertaking to be responsible for the receiver's acts and defaults.

4. CHOICE BETWEEN APPOINTMENT IN AND OUT OF COURT

(a) Disadvantages

29–009 The appointment of a receiver or receiver and manager by the court has substantial disadvantages for the mortgagee.

(a) There is first of all the expense and trouble of the application to the court and any delay which may occur until the order is made (ordinarily after a hearing on notice) and drawn up, and any security required by the order is provided by the receiver.

(b) The selection of the receiver or receiver and manager is in the hands of the court which may have regard to the wishes of the company. In practice, the court gives effect to any proper choice of the mortgagee, but the appointee must be seen to be independent,[58] in stark contrast with an appointee under a debenture.

(c) Unlike the appointee out of court,[59] a court-appointed receiver or receiver and manager is no-one's agent and certainly not an agent of the company.[60] It has traditionally[61] been thought that the appointment of a receiver and manager by the court operates to terminate the employment of the company's employees.[62] Hence, if their employment is continued it is under a new contract with the receiver. The termination of the employees' contracts of employment with the company gives rise to rights to damages against the company.[63] The need to avoid this result may be a legitimate ground upon which the company may seek to oppose the appointment of the receiver. The appointment does not affect the directors' tenure of office or right to remuneration.[64]

---

[58] *In the matter of Angel's Castle Pre-School Pty Ltd (In Liquidation)* [2010] F.C.A. 786 (Federal Court of Australia); *Halsbury's Laws of England*, 4th edn (London: LexisNexis Butterworths, 1991), Vol. 39(2), para.845–851. The position may be different in the case of a receiver appointed by way of equitable execution: *Fuggle v Bland* (1882–83) L.R. 11 Q.B.D; 711; *Cummins v Perkins* [1899] 1 Ch. 16 (CA).

[59] *Griffiths v Secretary of State for Social Services* [1974] Q.B. 468, 485–486.

[60] *Channel Airways v Manchester City Council* [1974] 1 Lloyd's Rep. 456.

[61] For an alternative view that the appointment of a receiver by the court need not invariably result in the termination of employment contracts, see J. O'Donovan, *Company Receivers and Administrators*, 2nd edn (Sydney: LBC, 1992), citing *International Harvester Export v International Harvester Australia* (1982) 7 A.C.L.R. 391 and *Sipad Holding DDPO v Popovic* (1996) 12 A.C.L.C. 307, 309.

[62] See, e.g. *Reid v Explosives Co Ltd* (1887) L.R. 19 Q.B.D. 264 (CA), and see para.16–003, above.

[63] *Measures Bros Ltd v Measures* [1910] 2 Ch. 248 (CA); *Re Mack Trucks (Britain) Ltd* [1967] 1 W.L.R. 780.

[64] *Re South Western of Venezuela (Barquisimeto) Railway Co* [1902] 1 Ch. 701.

(d) The court-appointed receiver is personally liable under contracts entered into by him, though he expressly contracts as receiver and manager.[65] He is, however, entitled to an indemnity out of the assets of the company to the extent that they are sufficient.[66]

(e) The court-appointed receiver has to go through the procedures (and incur the costs) of applications to the court for authority if any proposed action lies outside the ambit of any existing order[67] and in any event in respect of submitting his accounts, fixing his remuneration[68] and obtaining his discharge.

(f) The court-appointed receiver is considered to be appointed for the benefit, not of the debenture-holder alone, but of all persons interested in the assets of the company. Accordingly, unlike the receiver appointed out of court who acts for the primary benefit of the debenture-holder who appointed him, the court appointed receiver is under a duty to hold the scales evenly between the company and the debenture-holder. Thus Buckley L.J. said in *Re Newdigate Colliery Ltd*[69]:

> "It has been truly said that in the case of a legal mortgage the legal mortgagee can take possession if he chooses of the mortgaged property, and being in possession can say 'I have nothing to do with the mortgagor's contracts. I shall deal with this property as seems to me most to my advantage . . .' This appellant is not in that position. He is an equitable mortgagee who has obtained an order of the court under which its officer takes possession of assets in which the mortgagee and mortgagor are both interested, with the duty and responsibility of dealing with them fairly in the interest of both parties."

Accordingly, the court-appointed receiver has a continuing duty to preserve the goodwill of the company's business for the benefit of all persons interested, and (though he is not personally bound by or liable under existing contracts)[70] he should not disregard existing

---

[65] *Re Burt, Boulton and Hayward v Bull* [1895] 1 Q.B. 276 (CA). He does not incur personal liability if he merely causes the company to carry out contracts already made prior to his appointment: *Parsons v Sovereign Bank of Canada* [1913] A.C. 160 (PC).

[66] *Boehm v Goodall* [1911] 1 Ch. 155; *Capewell v Customs and Excise Commissioners* [2007] 1 W.L.R. 386 (HL).

[67] If the receiver enters into a contract which is conditional upon obtaining the approval of the court, the court will require to be satisfied before it gives such approval that the entry into the contract is in the interests of the company and its creditors, not as at the date of the contract, but as at the date that approval is given: *Yap Yoke Luan v Ong Wee Tok* [1984] 1 M.L.J. 23.

[68] His remuneration must be fixed by the court before he is entitled to appropriate to his own use funds of the receivership: *Cape v Redarb Pty Ltd* (1992) 10 A.C.L.C. 333 (Federal Court of Australia).

[69] *Re Newdigate Colliery Ltd* [1912] 1 Ch. 468 (CA), 477–478. His role has been described as that of a caretaker: *Paterson v Gaslight & Coke Co* [1896] 2 Ch. 476 (CA).

[70] e.g. to pay interest payable during the receivership on mortgages made prior to the receivership order: see *Bayhold Financial Corp Ltd v Clarkson Co Ltd* (1991) 10 C.B.R. (3d) 159 (Supreme Court of Nova Scotia, Appellate Division).

contracts and cease carrying on the business merely because this course would accelerate repayment to the debenture-holder.[71] The receiver appointed out of court is under no such continuing duty.[72] The duty does not extend to requiring him to carry out a contract if to do so would necessitate borrowing money ranking in priority to the debenture and the contract would prove unprofitable.[73]

(g) The court-appointed receiver is neither an administrative receiver nor an office-holder for the purposes of Insolvency Act 1986, for the definition requires that the appointment be made by or on behalf of the debenture-holder.[74] Most significantly, the court-appointed receiver is not vested with the rights and privileges conferred on office-holders by Insolvency Act 1986, ss.233–237 and 246(1), and in particular the various powers of investigation and the right to continued supplies from utilities.[75]

(h) In a case where the company denies the existence of the debt or the existence or validity of the security, the court may order that the receiver release to the company sufficient funds to challenge the right of the claimant to the order.[76]

(b) Advantages

29–010 The appointment by the court has, potentially, certain advantages over the appointment out of court:

(a) Where the validity of the debenture or right to appoint a receiver is disputed, the court may appoint a receiver and authorise him to enter

---

[71] *Parsons v Sovereign Bank of Canada* [1913] A.C. 160 (PC). He may close the company's business without the prior approval of the court if the business has no, or ceases to have any, goodwill: *Bayhold Financial Corp Ltd v Clarkson Co Ltd* (1991) 10 C.B.R. (3d) 159 (Supreme Court of Nova Scotia, Appellate Division).

[72] He may, however, be expected to wish to preserve goodwill by completing rather than repudiating contracts: *Ashby Warner v Simmons* [1936] 2 All E.R. 697 (CA), 709.

[73] *Re Thames Ironworks* (1902) 106 L.T. 674.

[74] Insolvency Act 1986, ss.29(2)(a) and 251; see *Re A&C Supplies Ltd* [1998] B.C.C. 708. The contrary is argued by I. Fletcher in *The Law of Insolvency*, 4th edn (London: Sweet & Maxwell, 2009), 14–026, *Totty & Moss on Insolvency*, para.D1–25, and R. Schumacher, "Court-appointed administrative receivers?" (1993) 9 I.L. & P. 43. The critical part of the definition of "administrative receiver" in s.29(2)(a) is that the appointment is made by or on behalf of (and not merely at the instance of) the debenture holder. Insolvency Act 1986, s.32 does not afford any contra-indication: it merely provides that an application to the court may be made on behalf of debenture holders to appoint a receiver of a company which is being wound up. Nor does this section create difficulties for employees under ss.127(1)(c) and 106(5)(c) of the Employment Protection (Consolidation) Act 1978: the appointment of a receiver by a debenture holder gives rise to a presumption of insolvency, but the appointment of a receiver by the court does not, for the appointment may be made for reasons unconnected with insolvency. The position is different under Scots Law: see Insolvency Act 1986, ss.51 and 251.

[75] See also Ch.8.

[76] See *Royal Bank of Canada v West-Can Resource* (1990) 3 C.B.R. (3d) 55 and *Royal Bank of Canada v Tower Aircraft* (1991) 3 C.B.R. (3d) 60.

into transactions (such as sales) binding on the mortgagee and the company irrespective of the outcome of the dispute.[77]

(b) The court-appointed receiver may be authorised by the court to borrow money on security having priority to any existing debenture if the money is required to preserve the assets and goodwill (though the security will be postponed to the receiver's right to an indemnity unless contrary provision is made).[78]

(c) Foreign courts may on occasion (but not invariably) be more ready to recognise and give effect to the status and power of the court-appointed receiver on grounds of comity.[79]

5.   THE RECEIVER AS AN OFFICER OF THE COURT

The court-appointed receiver, unlike the receiver appointed out of court, is an **29–011** officer of the court. As such an officer he may apply to the court for guidance on matters of law and the propriety or reasonableness of exercise of a discretion or power, but not as to its wisdom.[80] His status has a number of consequences for third parties. Thus, in the case of a court-appointed receiver (but not a receiver appointed out of court):

(a) a landlord cannot distrain[81] and the receiver cannot be sued[82] without the permission of the court.[83] The rightfulness of a claim by or against the receiver will be determined on an application to the court in the proceedings in which the receiver is appointed.[84] Since the receiver should not be subjected to vexatious or harassing claims, permission will not be granted to proceed with an action against a receiver unless the applicant satisfies the court that his claim is a genuine one, in the sense that the allegations which he seeks to make are such as to call for an answer from the receiver[85];

---

[77] See above. Likewise, the court may appoint a receiver to resolve conflicts between mortgagees whose charges rank equally: see *Bass Breweries Ltd v Delaney* [1994] B.C.C. 851.

[78] *Greenwood v Algeciras Railways* [1894] 2 Ch. 205 (CA). If he borrows in excess of any limit set, he may be denied an indemnity out of the assets of the company: *Bayhold Financial Corp Ltd v Clarkson Co Ltd* (1991) 10 C.B.R. (3d) 159 (Supreme Court of Nova Scotia, Appellate Division).

[79] cf. para.30 016, below. See also Dicey, Morris and Collins, *The Conflict of Laws*, 14th edn (London: Sweet & Maxwell, 2006, with 4th Cumulative Supplement, 2011), paras 30–127 to 30–129.

[80] *Maricente v Baptiste* [2000] 48 N.S.W.L.R. 724.

[81] *Sutton v Rees* (1869) 9 Jur N.S. 456.

[82] *LP Arthur (Insurance) Ltd v Sisson* [1966] 1 W.L.R. 1384. See also *Re Magic Aust Pty Ltd* (1992) 10 A.C.L.C. 929 (court-appointed liquidator).

[83] *Hand v Blow* [1901] 2 Ch. 721 (CA), 735; *Re Maidstone Palace of Varieties Ltd* [1909] 2 Ch. 283.

[84] *Inland Revenue Commissioners v Hoogstraten* [1985] Q.B. 1077 (CA), 1093.

[85] *McGowan v Chadwick and Grant* [2003] B.P.I.R. 647 (CA), [78], per Jonathan Parker L.J.

(b) a payment by the receiver in the course of his duties will not in general be open to challenge on a subsequent liquidation as a preference, since it is to be treated as a payment authorised by the court[86];

(c) the receiver as an officer of the court is subject to the obligation, not merely to act lawfully, but also in accordance with principles of justice and honest dealing.[87] This obligation extends to payment of the costs of proceedings which he has brought or defended on behalf of the company[88];

(d) it is further arguable that, in his capacity as an officer of the court, some of the functions performed by the receiver ought properly to be characterised as of a "public nature", thus rendering the receiver subject to the strictures of the Human Rights Act 1998.[89]

29–012 The status of the court-appointed receiver as an officer of the court has consequences in the field of contempt. Interference with the performance of his duty or his possession of property may constitute a contempt of court.[90]

Receivers appointed out of court are not similarly protected.[91] Likewise, breach of duty by the court-appointed receiver may constitute a contempt.[92] A third party with a claim against the property over which the receiver has been appointed should apply to the court for leave to enforce his rights. The court will then adjudicate upon the rival claims, seeking to do justice between those interested.[93]

---

[86] *International Harvester Export Co v International Harvester Australia Co* [1983] V.R. 539, 549. While Insolvency Act 1986, s.239(7) precludes the argument that a payment could not be preferential simply because it had been authorised by the court, a liquidator would in general find it difficult to satisfy the s.239(5) requirement that a payment made by a court-appointed receiver had been made because the company was influenced by a desire to prefer. And where the payment is to a debenture-holder and is consistent with the terms of the debenture, then for the purposes of s.239(4)(b) the position of the debenture-holder would not usually have been improved compared with the position in which it would otherwise have been in the event of an insolvent liquidation.

[87] *Re Tyler Ex p. Official Receiver* [1907] 1 K.B. 865 (CA); *Condon Ex p. James* (1874) L.R. 9 Ch. App. 609 (CA). For a recent consideration of the principle, see *Young v ACN* (2005) 218 A.L.R. 449. For the analogous position of the administrator as an officer of the court, see para.12–006, above.

[88] *Re London Metallurgical Co* [1895] 1 Ch. 758; *Re Wenborn & Co* [1905] 1 Ch. 413; *Re MT Realisation* [2004] 1 W.L.R. 1678.

[89] See by analogy the discussion of the possible applicability of the Human Rights Act 1998 to administrators, at paras 12–066 to 12–067, above.

[90] See, e.g. *Re Mead Ex p. Cochrane* (1875) L.R. 20 Eq. 282 (ousting from possession); and *Searle v Choat* (1884) L.R. 25 Ch. D. 723 (CA) (suing receiver). Until a receiver has taken steps to obtain control of assets situated abroad in accordance with local law, it may not be a contempt for a creditor who is not a party to the litigation in which the receiver was appointed to attempt to seize those assets first: see *Re Maudslay, Sons and Field* [1900] 1 Ch. 602. For a study of a court-appointed receiver's status in the context of the N.U.M. strike, see G. Lightman, "A Trade Union in Chains" (1987) C.L.P. 25.

[91] See *Re Hill's Waterfall Estate and Gold Mining Co* [1896] 1 Ch. 947, 954; *Re Magic Aust Pty Ltd* (1992) 10 A.C.L.C. 929 ("improper pressure").

[92] *Re Gent* (1889) L.R. 40 Ch. D. 190.

[93] See, e.g. *Randfield v Randfield* (1860) 1 Drew. & Sm. 310; *Re Maidstone Palace of Varieties Ltd* [1909] 2 Ch. 283; and *LP Arthur (Insurance) Ltd v Sisson* [1966] 1 W.L.R. 1384.

6. INTER-RELATIONSHIP OF APPOINTMENTS BY COURT AND OUT OF COURT

The court may make an appointment of a receiver during a subsisting receiver- **29–013**
ship out of court.[94] The effect of such an order is to displace the debenture-
holder's receiver[95] and terminate his authority to act as agent of the company.[96]
If an appointment is made by the court on the application of a second or subsequent mortgagee, the prior mortgagee may subsequently appoint a receiver, but
such receiver cannot exercise his powers as such without the prior leave of the
court[97] unless the court order making the appointment states that the order is
made "without prejudice to the rights of prior incumbrancers".[98]

7. POWERS, DUTIES AND LIABILITIES

In general, the powers of a receiver appointed by the court are governed by **29–014**
the terms of the order appointing him. The receiver appointed by way of
equitable execution will generally have very limited powers of management
(if any), whereas other court-appointed receivers and managers, such as
those appointed pending resolution of litigation to determine who should
manage the company, may have far-reaching powers of management. If the
receiver enters into transactions which are beyond his powers, a third party
without notice that the receiver was acting beyond his powers may enforce the
transaction.[99]

In general, a receiver appointed by the court ought not to bring proceedings
in the action in which he was appointed, but should adopt a neutral position.[100]
The receiver does not acquire title to the company's property and cannot in his
own name sue upon causes of action vested in the company.[101] The receiver has
no right, without the leave of the court, to bring proceedings in the name of the
company.[102] If he wishes to institute proceedings to recover or protect property
over which he is appointed, the receiver should generally seek the assistance of
a party to the action who should make such an application, with the receiver
having power to do so in default or in cases of urgency.[103]

---

[94] *Re Slogger Automatic Feeder Co Ltd* [1915] 1 Ch. 478.
[95] *Re Maskelyne British Typewriters* [1898] 1 Ch. 133 (CA).
[96] *Hand v Blow* [1901] 2 Ch. 721 (CA), 732.
[97] *Re Metropolitan Amalgamated Estates* [1912] 2 Ch. 497.
[98] *Underhay v Read* (1887) L.R. 20 Q.B.D. 209 (CA).
[99] *Moss Steamship Co Ltd v Whinney* [1912] A.C. 254 (HL); and see I. Fletcher, *The Law of Insolvency*, 4th edn (London: Sweet & Maxwell, 2009), para.14–016.
[100] *Comyn v Smith* (1823) 1 Hog. 81.
[101] *ASIC v Takaran (No.2)* (2003) 194 A.L.R. 743.
[102] *Viola v Anglo-American Cold Storage Co* [1912] 2 Ch. 305; *Re Scottish Properties Ltd* (1977) 2 A.C.L.R. 264.
[103] *Parker v Dunn* (1845) 8 Beav. 498; *Re Sacker* (1888) L.R. 22 Q.B.D. 179 (CA).

29–015   A receiver appointed by the court is under the same fiduciary duties[104] and duties of care[105] as the receiver appointed out of court. So, for example, a court-appointed receiver must act in good faith and must not compete with the company or seek to profit from his position.[106] If he wishes to purchase, whether himself or through a company, any of the property over which he is appointed, he can only do so with the leave of the court.[107] The court-appointed receiver must take reasonable care to obtain the best price reasonably obtainable for any property which he sells.[108] A court-appointed receiver is to be treated in the same way as an out-of-court receiver would have been for the purposes of income tax or capital gains tax liability arising from dealings with the assets subject to the receivership.[109] Since an out-of-court receiver is an agent of the company and has no liability for gains made in disposing of assets in receivership, a court-appointed receiver is similarly free from liability, and an indemnity for tax liability is therefore usually unnecessary.[110]

As an officer of the court the receiver appointed by the court has one important privilege in relation to his conduct of the receivership. The court has power, on his release or discharge, to protect the receiver from liability for acts done in the course of his duties, but will only do so after investigation or making provision for the investigation of claims of which the court has notice.

8.   DISCHARGE

29–016   The court may discharge the receiver if it is just to do so, e.g. if the original appointment should never have been made or if default, misconduct or other ground for unfitness is shown, e.g. the existence of a material conflict of interest which cannot properly be resolved in some other way. If the company goes into liquidation, the court may direct that the liquidator replace the receiver if the assets of the company are at least sufficient to pay the secured creditors and no conflict of interest is likely to arise between the secured and

---

[104] *Re Magadi Soda Company Ltd* (1925) 41 T.L.R. 297; *Mirror Group Newspapers Plc v Maxwell* [1998] B.C.C. 324, 333 (a fiduciary duty to protect, get in, realise and ultimately pass on to others assets and property).

[105] *Inland Revenue Commissioners v Hoogstraten* [1985] Q.B. 1077 (CA). In *Clarke v Heathfield* [1985] I.C.R. 203 (CA), Dillon L.J. said: "The question of indemnity to sequestrators appointed by the court was considered by this court in the case of *IRC v Hoogstraten*: the position of a court appointed receiver cannot be significantly different". The receiver is not immune from suit by the person on whose application he was appointed: *LP Arthur (Insurance) Ltd v Sisson* [1966] 1 W.L.R. 1384. See also *Procopi v Maschakis* (1969) 211 E.G. 31 (receiver is not invariably bound to accept offer of highest bidder, e.g. if tardy and vacillating). If a receiver is discharged by a consent order, the parties may agree to excuse the receiver from all liability arising from his performance even if such claims are unknown at the time of the release: *Weston v Dayman* [2008] 1 B.C.L.C. 250 (CA).

[106] *Re Gent* (1892) 40 W.R. 267; *Re Newdigate Colliery Ltd* [1912] 1 Ch. 468 (CA); and *Duffy v Super Centre Development Ltd* [1967] 1 N.S.W.R. 382.

[107] *Re Magadi Soda Co Ltd* (1925) 41 T.L.R. 297; *Nugent v Nugent* [1908] 1 Ch. 546 (CA).

[108] *Telsen Electric v JJ Eastick* [1936] 3 All E.R. 266; *AIDC v Co-operative Farmers* (1978) 2 A.C.L.R. 543; *Cape v Redbarb (No.2)* (1992) 10 A.C.L.C. 1272, 1282.

[109] See ss.75–77 of the Taxes Management Act 1970.

[110] *Inland Revenue Commissioners v Piacentini* [2003] Q.B. 1497.

other creditors.[111] Such a replacement cannot be made by the court in case of a receiver appointed out of court.[112]

9. REMUNERATION, LIEN AND INDEMNITY

A receiver appointed by the court has an entitlement to an indemnity out of, **29-017** and a lien over, the assets in respect of which he is appointed for costs and expenses reasonably incurred and his remuneration, irrespective of whether the order for his appointment was rightly made[113] or the receivership proved beneficial. Even if the receiver carries on his receivership unnecessarily and should have agreed that his receivership should have been discharged at a time before a court application is made to terminate his receivership, the assets bear those costs and expenses reasonably incurred by him in respect of his role as receiver[114], including those costs and expenses incurred after his discharge.[115] He is under a duty to keep a close control on fees incurred for professional services and to satisfy himself that all costs incurred are reasonable and proportionate in all the circumstances.[116] The remuneration must be authorised by the court, which may direct that such remuneration shall be fixed by reference to such scales or rates of professional charges as it thinks fit, or that it shall be assessed on the standard basis by a costs judge or a district judge.[117] The receiver must justify the reasonableness and prudence of the tasks undertaken for which remuneration is sought, in the same way as he must justify the reasonableness and prudence of incurring disbursements for which he seeks allowance and reimbursement.[118]

The receiver may insist, as a condition of accepting appointment, that the person seeking his appointment or someone else be personally responsible for his remuneration and indemnify him. In default of some such agreement, the

---

[111] *Strong v Carlyle Press* [1893] 1 Ch. 268 (CA).
[112] *Re Joshua Stubbs Ltd* [1891] 1 Ch. 475 (CA).
[113] *Capewell v Customs and Excise Commissioners* [2007] 1 W.L.R. 386 (HL).
[114] *Sinclair v Glatt* [2009] 1 W.L.R. 1845 (CA), [1].
[115] *Glatt v Sinclair* [2011] Lloyd's Rep. F.C. 143, where Kenneth Parker J. granted the former receiver permission to recover from the receivership assets his costs of an unsuccessful application for permission to bring an action against him as receiver, notwithstanding that he had already been discharged as receiver, stating, at [9]: "The issue is one of principle, and in my view the answer in the present context should not depend upon the fortuitous contingency of when an applicant launches his claim against the receiver and when he seeks permission from the Court".
[116] Consider *Capewell v Customs and Excise Commissioners* [2005] 1 All E.R. 900 (CA) (guidelines for receivers appointed under Pt VI of the Criminal Justice Act 1988). In the absence of any special statutory rules, receivers appointed under the Criminal Justice Act 1988 are to be treated in law in the same way as a "common law" receiver appointed under order of the court: *Capewell v Customs & Excise Commissioners* [2005] B.P.I.R. 1266 (CA).
[117] CPR r.69.7 and CPR PD 69, para.9; and see *Hughes v Customs & Excise Commissioner* [2003] 1 W.L.R. 177 (CA), 197 (Arden L.J.). The continuation of the receivership cannot be challenged on grounds of excessive costs; such allegations should be dealt with through the mechanism of CPR Part 69.7: *Capewell v Revenue and Customs Commissioners* [2007] 1 W.L.R. 386 (HL).
[118] *Mirror Group Newspapers Plc v Maxwell (No.1)* [1998] 1 B.C.L.C. 638 (the taxation is reported [1999] B.C.C. 684); *Brook v Reed* [2011] 3 All E.R. 743 (CA). See, too, Mr Justice Lightman, "Office Holders' Charges: Cost Control and Transparency" (1998) 11 Insolv. Int. 1.

receiver can only look to the assets the subject of the receivership.[119] He has a lien over all the assets over which he is appointed: the lien is not limited to those over which he has assumed control and it survives his discharge, for the lien is independent of possession or a continuing right to possession.[120] The effect of his lien is that the receiver may be entitled to recover his costs and expenses from innocent third parties who have the misfortune to have their assets tied up in some way with the defendant.[121] Given the potential injustice of the operation of this principle, it is possible that in an appropriate case art.1 of the First Protocol of the European Convention for the Protection of Human Rights and Fundamental Freedoms could limit the costs and expenses recoverable from an innocent third party.[122] The court cannot order that a party shall be liable for part of a receiver's remuneration in substitution for recovery from the assets in the receivership, even if the receivership wrongly continued for longer than it ought to have done.[123]

10.   RECEIVERSHIP AND FOREIGN INSOLVENCY PROCEEDINGS

29–018   A receiver will not be appointed by way of equitable execution of a foreign judgment unless an English judgment has been obtained or the foreign judgment has been registered under CPR Pt 74.[124]

The willingness of the courts to assist and co-operate in the case of foreign liquidations, administrations and receiverships is considered in Ch.30. It is sufficient to say that the assistance may include the appointment of a receiver of the company in question or of some or all of its assets.

---

[119] *Alliance & Leicester Building Society v Edgeshop Ltd (No.2)* [1995] 2 B.C.L.C. 506 (CA), 507G.

[120] *Mellor v Mellor* [1992] 1 W.L.R. 517.

[121] *Sinclair v Glatt* [2009] 1 W.L.R. 1845 (CA), [39] (Elias L.J.).

[122] *Sinclair v Glatt* [2009] 1 W.L.R. 1845 (CA), [42] (Elias L.J., obiter).

[123] *Capewell v Customs and Excise Commissioners* [2007] 1 W.L.R. 386 (HL). The remuneration and costs may fall within the ambit of the cross-undertaking in damages given by the party on whose application the receiver is appointed.

[124] *Perry v Zissis* [1977] 1 Lloyd's Rep. 607 (CA).

Chapter 30

Conflict of Laws

This chapter identifies and discusses various problems that may arise in rela- **30–001** tion to receivership or administration in situations involving a foreign element.[1] Very broadly speaking, a relevant foreign element may be involved where a company is incorporated outside the United Kingdom or where a company incorporated in the United Kingdom is possessed of assets situated outside the United Kingdom, though these situations should not be regarded as exhaustive of those which may arise. It is important to note that these conflict of laws rules may be displaced by mandatory EU or EEA conflicts rules in cases affected by the European Insolvency Regulation and by Directives concerning the insolvency of insurers and financial institutions.[2]

1. VALIDITY OF FLOATING CHARGE

A floating charge has both a contractual and proprietary character. It originates in **30–002** a contract entered into between the company and the ultimate debenture-holder but on crystallisation of the charge there is an immediate creation of a fixed charge over the assets of the company with the consequence that unsecured creditors are unable to enforce any rights against the property covered by the charge. As a matter of English law, the charge may extend to movable property (tangible or intangible) and immovable property, whether situated in England or abroad.

(a) Capacity

The initial question which may arise is whether a company has capacity to **30–003** create a charge of this nature. In the context of a situation with a foreign element present, this involves the further question of what law will govern the company's capacity to create the charge. There is no direct English authority on this question, but it has been persuasively argued that the proper approach is to

---

[1] For general discussion see Dicey, Morris and Collins, *The Conflict of Laws*, 14th edn (London: Sweet & Maxwell, 2006, with cumulative supplements), pp.1345–1491; Fletcher, *Insolvency in Private International Law*, 2nd edn (Oxford: Oxford University Press, 2005); Smart, *Cross-Border Insolvency*, 2nd edn (London: Sweet & Maxwell, 1998); Anton, *Private International Law*, 2nd edn (Oxford: Oxford University Press, 1991), pp.716–722; Gough, *Company Charges*, 3rd edn (London: Lexis Nexis Butterworths, 2007), Ch.23; Collins (1978) 27 I.C.L.Q. 691 reprinted in *Essays in International Litigation and the Conflict of Laws* (1994), p.433.

[2] On the European Regulation on Insolvency Proceedings, see Ch.31, below and also Moss, Fletcher and Isaacs, *The EC Regulation on Insolvency Proceedings: A Commentary and Annotated Guide*, 2nd edn (Oxford: Oxford University Press, 2009). On the EU Directives on insurers and financial institutions see Moss and Wessels, *EU Banking and Insurance Insolvency* (Oxford: Oxford University Press, 2006).

consider whether the company has power to grant a mortgage over its assets under the law of the place of its incorporation,[3] the latter law generally being the law which determines the capacity of a company.[4] In other words, it matters not that the company has no capacity under the law of the place of its incorporation to create a floating charge as such: it is enough that the company has, under the law of its place of incorporation, the capacity to give a mortgage over its assets.[5]

(b) Authority of corporate representatives

30–004 Whether directors or others purporting to represent the company have authority to execute a charge will be determined by the law of the place of incorporation since it is that law which determines who are the company's officials authorised to act on its behalf.[6]

(c) Governing law

30–005 Assuming the company has capacity, and those executing the charge have the necessary authority, according to the foregoing principles, it may then be necessary to determine the law which governs the contractual aspects of the charge. Although the proprietary effects of the charge may ultimately depend on the *lex situs* of any assets alleged to fall within its terms, the contractual aspects of the charge are governed by the law applicable to the contract, in this case a contract of mortgage.[7] Accordingly, where the parties have, as is common, chosen a law to govern the contract, that choice of law will normally

---

[3] Collins (1978) 27 I.C.L.Q. 691, 695–699.

[4] See Dicey, Morris and Collins, *The Conflict of Laws*, 14th edn (London: Sweet & Maxwell, 2006), pp.1345–1347. This rule is unaffected by the implementation of the Rome Convention on the Law Applicable to Contractual Obligations [1980] O.J. L266/1 in the Contracts (Applicable Law) Act 1990, and subsequently by the entry into force of the Rome I Regulation (Regulation (EC) No.593/2008 [2008] OJ L177/6), since questions concerning the legal capacity of a company are excluded from the scope of the uniform rules contained in the Convention and in the Regulation respectively: see (for the Rome Convention) the Contracts (Applicable Law) Act 1990, Sch.I, art.1(2)(e), and art.1(2)(f) of the Rome I Regulation (which replaces the Convention in relation to contracts concluded as from December 17, 2009): [2008] OJ L 177/6.

[5] See *Re International Bulk Commodities Ltd* [1993] Ch. 77. cf. *Carse v Coppen* 1951 S.C. 233 (Court of Session, Inner House, 1 Div), decided when floating charges were not recognised under Scots law. Such recognition was first permitted in the Companies (Floating Charges and Receivers) (Scotland) Act 1972. See now Bankruptcy and Diligence (Scotland) Act 2007, ss.38–47, and Insolvency Act 1986, ss.50–71. The development of the floating charge as a form of security known to Scots law is summarised by Lord Hope of Craighead in *Re Spectrum Plus Ltd (In Liquidation)* [2005] 2 A.C. 680 (HL), 49–51.

[6] *Banco de Bilbao v Sancha and Rey* [1938] 2 K.B. 176 (CA); *Carl Zeiss Stiftung v Rayner & Keeler Ltd* [1967] 1 A.C. 853 (HL) 919, 939, 972. See also *Bank of Ethiopia v National Bank of Egypt and Liguori* [1937] Ch. 513; *Damon Compania Naviera SA v Hapag-Lloyd International SA (The Blankenstein)* [1985] 1 W.L.R. 435 (CA). The law of the place of incorporation also determines whether directors have been validly appointed: *Sierra Leone Telecommunications Co Ltd v Barclays Bank Plc* [1998] 2 All E.R. 820. And see Foreign Companies (Execution of Documents) Regulations 1994, below, para.30–007. The question of whether an organ may bind a company or body corporate or unincorporate to a third party is excluded from the scope of the Rome I Regulation, art.1(1)(g)—and from the scope of the Rome Convention by art.1(2)(f), and see Collins (1978) 27 I.C.L.Q. 691.

[7] *Re Anchor Line (Henderson Bros) Ltd* [1937] Ch. 483.

be treated as effective by an English court.[8] In the absence of such a choice of law, the contract will be governed by the law of the country identified according to the provisions contained in art.4 of the Rome I Regulation.[9] Applying the latter principle, where an English company creates a charge over all of its undertaking and assets in the English form, the applicable law is almost certain to be English law.[10] The law applicable to the charge will determine (capacity apart) the validity and effect of the charge in its contractual respects and will also govern matters of construction.[11] The importance of distinguishing between the contractual and proprietary effects of a charge may be seen in the principle that if the contract creating the mortgage (charge) is subject to English law, an English court may enforce it in personam even if the charge is not recognised as effective by the *lex situs*.[12]

(d)   Role of English law

Where a contract allegedly creating a charge is governed by a foreign appli- **30–006**
cable law, it will, nonetheless, for the purposes of English proceedings, be for
English law to determine whether a charge[13] requiring registration[14] in England

---

[8] This was true under common law choice of law rules, which applied to contracts entered into on or before April 1, 1991: see, e.g. *Vita Food Products Inc v Unus Shipping Co Ltd (In Liquidation)* [1939] A.C. 277 (PC); Dicey and Morris, *The Conflict of Laws*, 11th edn (London: Sweet & Maxwell, 1987), pp.1115–1182. It is equally true under the Rome Convention which applies to contracts entered into between April 1, 1991 and December 17, 2007 (see art.3(1)), and under the Rome I Regulation which applies top contracts entered into after December 17, 2007 (see art.3(1) together with art.28). See Dicey, Morris and Collins, *The Conflict of Laws*, 14th edn (London: Sweet & Maxwell, 2006), pp.1560–1580. If the submission in the text is correct and a floating charge is a species of mortgage, then the rules of the Regulation (and formerly those of the Convention) should apply to determine the applicable law. It is possible, however, that a floating charge may be construed as a "question governed by the law of companies" and thus excluded from the Regulation by virtue of art.1(2)(f), and from the Convention by virtue of its art.1(2)(e). If this construction is eventually adopted, there is not likely to be any practical difference since the common law, the Rome I Regulation and the Rome Convention are very similar in relation to the power to choose the governing law.

[9] art.4 of the Rome I Regulation contains a series of rules for determining the law governing a contract in the absence of an effective choice by the parties under art.3. Although the exact conclusion to be reached will depend on the circumstances, and on the nature of the contract that is concluded, the provisions of art.4(3) and (4) maintain the possibility that the contract will be governed by the law of the country with which it is most closely connected. A different formulation is contained in art.4(1) of the Rome Convention, whereby rebuttable presumptions are utilised to ascertain what the most closely connected law will be: see art.4(2) and (3) of the Convention: see Dicey, Morris and Collins, pp.1580–1589. If applicable (see above, fn.8), the Rome Convention will determine the law governing contracts entered into between April 1, 1991 and December 17, 2007. The common law rules were very similar in effect: see Dicey and Morris, *The Conflict of Laws*, 11th edn (London: Sweet & Maxwell, 1987), pp.1190–1197.

[10] *Re Anchor Line (Henderson Bros) Ltd* [1937] Ch. 483.

[11] *Re Anchor Line (Henderson Bros) Ltd* [1937] Ch. 483. See Rome I Regulation, art.12(1). For the Rome Convention (see Collins (1978) 27 I.C.L.Q. 691), if applicable, see art.10(1) of the Convention, subject to Contracts (Applicable Law) Act 1990, s.2(2).

[12] *British South Africa Co v De Beers Consolidated Gold Mines Ltd* [1910] 2 Ch. 502 (CA); *Re Smith* [1916] 2 Ch. 206; *Re Anchor Line (Henderson Bros) Ltd* [1937] Ch. 483.

[13] *Re Interview Ltd* [1975] I.R. 382, 395–396; *Kruppstahl AG v Quittmann Products Ltd* [1982] I.L.R.M. 551, 560. As to whether the charge will extend to property located abroad, see below, paras 30-027 to 30-021.

[14] *Re Weldtech Equipment Ltd* [1991] B.C.C. 16; *Re Interview Ltd* [1975] I.R. 382; *Kruppstahl AG v Quittmann Products Ltd* [1982] I.L.R.M. 551.

has in fact been created though it will be necessary for the court to look to the terms of the contract and their effect under the foreign governing law to ascertain whether the elements which constitute a charge in English law are in fact present.[15] Accordingly a contract governed by a foreign law may, for the purpose of English proceedings, give rise to a charge even if the contract would not have that effect under the foreign law, for example because that law did not recognise such a form of security.[16]

(e) Formalities

30–007 The Companies Act 2006 contains provisions concerning the manner in which documents are to be executed by a company incorporated in Great Britain,[17] which provisions have been applied, with necessary adaptations and modifications, to companies incorporated outside Great Britain.[18] As adapted and modified, s.43 of the 2006 Act establishes that a company incorporated outside Great Britain may make a contract[19] in any manner permitted by the laws of the territory in which it is incorporated[20] or, where a contract is made on behalf of such a company, it may be so made by any person who, in accordance with the law of the territory in which the company is incorporated, is acting under the authority (express or implied) of that company.[21] As adapted and modified, s.44 of the 2006 Act enables a document to be executed in any manner permitted by the laws of the territory in which the company is incorporated.[22] A document which is signed by a person or persons who, in accordance with the laws of the territory in which the company is incorporated, is or are acting under the authority (express or implied) of the company and which is expressed (in whatever form of words) to be executed by the company, has the same effect, in relation to that company, as it would have in relation to a company incorporated in England if executed under the common seal of a company so incorporated.[23] In favour of a purchaser (which includes a mortgagee) a document shall be deemed to be duly executed by a company incorporated outside Great Britain if it purports to be signed by a person or persons who, in accordance with the laws of the territory in which the company is incorporated, is or are

---

[15] *Re Weldtech Equipment Ltd* [1991] B.C.C. 16. cf. *Hammer and Sohne v HWT Realisations Ltd* 1985 S.L.T. (Sh. Ct.) 21 (Sh Ct); *Kruppstahl AG v Quittmann Products Ltd* [1982] I.L.R.M. 551, 559.

[16] See *Benjamin's Sale of Goods*, 8th edn (London: Sweet & Maxwell, 2010), para.26–157; Gough, *Company Charges*, 2nd edn (London: Butterworths, 1996), pp.634–635.

[17] Companies Act 2006, ss.43–47 and 51, and for Scotland, s.48. See above, Ch.3.

[18] Overseas Companies (Execution of Documents and Registration of Charges) Regulations 2009 (SI 2009/1917). See *Azov Shipping Co v Baltic Shipping Co (No.3)* [1999] 2 All E.R. (Comm) 453. For Scotland, see Companies Act 2006, s.48,

[19] The same considerations apply to the execution of a debenture: see Ch.3 above, and Foreign Companies (Execution of Documents and Registration of Charges) Regulations 2009 (SI 2009/1917), reg.4.

[20] Foreign Companies (Execution of Documents and Registration of Charges) Regulations 2009 (SI 2009/1917), reg.4.

[21] Foreign Companies (Execution of Documents and Registration of Charges) Regulations 2009 (SI 2009/1917), reg.4.

[22] Companies Act 2006, s.44(1), as adapted and modified by reg.4.

[23] Companies Act 2006, s.44(2), as adapted and modified by reg.4.

acting under the authority (express or implied) of that company.[24] As a consequence of these provisions a debenture may be regarded as duly executed by a foreign company if the execution conforms to the requirements of the law of the country in which the company is incorporated.

2. EXTRATERRITORIAL APPLICATION OF INSOLVENCY ACT 1986

The receivership or administration of a company in England will be conducted in accordance with English law and particularly the provisions of the Insolvency Act 1986.[25] Difficulties may arise in determining the territorial reach of relevant provisions of the Act where the receiver or administrator seeks to exercise powers under the Act against persons resident abroad or where there are creditors abroad or the company has assets which are situated abroad. Ultimately, of course, the territorial reach of any particular provision depends on the intention of Parliament but, as is so often the case, the intention of Parliament is seldom explicit so that it is necessary to interpret the relevant provisions.

30–008

Section 238 of the Insolvency Act 1986 enables an administrator[26] to apply for an order setting aside a transaction entered into by the company with "any person" at an undervalue.[27] In *Re Paramount Airways Ltd (No.2)*[28] it was held that the section applies, in relation to the administration of an English company, to any person whether that person is resident in England or not. In principle, therefore, there would seem to be no territorial limitation on the operation of this provision. In practice, however, there are two ways in which this wide jurisdiction may be limited. First, s.238(3) provides that where such an application is made, the court shall make such order as it thinks fit for the purpose of restoring the position to what it would have been if the company had not entered into the transaction: this discretion is sufficiently wide to enable the

---

[24] Companies Act 2006, s.44(3), as adapted and modified by reg.4.
[25] See *Re Bank of Credit and Commerce International SA (No.10)* [1997] Ch. 213, holding that the English court has no power to disapply the English rule on set-off in liquidation (Insolvency Rules, 1986, r.4.90) or any other substantive rule forming part of the statutory insolvency scheme contained in the Insolvency Act 1986 and the Insolvency Rules 1986. That principle was applied at first instance in *Re HIH Casualty & General Insurance Ltd* [2006] 2 All E.R. 671, 91–94 (David Richards J.), which concerned concurrent liquidations in England and Australia. It is not thought that the decision of the Court of Appeal in the latter case ([2007] 1 All E.R. 177), in which *Re BCCI (No.10)* was distinguished in cases where a request had been made under s.426 of the Insolvency Act 1986, casts doubt on this principle. The final appellate hearing of the *HIH* case before the House of Lords has seemingly left the matter open to question: [2008] 1 W.L.R. 852 (HL), Two of their Lordships (Lords Hoffmann and Walker) declared that in cases where concurrent liquidations were taking place there was authority to the effect that the English court is not obliged to apply all elements of the statutory insolvency scheme, whereas two other members of the Appellate Committee (Lords Scott and Neuberger) were of the opinion that no such power existed at common law. However, all five members of the Committee were in agreement that such power exists where s.426 of the Act of 1986 is applicable. The approach of Lords Hoffmann and Walker was followed by the Court of Appeal in *Rubin v Eurofinance SA* [2011] Ch. 133 (CA) (appeal to the Supreme Court pending). See also *New Cap Reinsurance Corp Ltd (In Liquidation) v Grant* [2011] EWHC 677 (Ch) (upheld on other grounds by the Court of Appeal: [2011] EWCA Civ 971).
[26] Or a liquidator, but not a receiver: Insolvency Act 1986, s.238(1).
[27] See above, Ch.15.
[28] *Re Paramount Airways Ltd (No.2)* [1993] Ch. 223 (CA).

court to make no order at all in an appropriate case. Where a foreign element is involved, the court has to be satisfied that the party against whom the order is to be made is sufficiently connected with England for it to be just and proper to make the order.

Whether such a connection is established will depend on all the circumstances of the case. Regard will be had to the residence and place of business of the party concerned, that party's connection with the company, the purpose of the transaction which is being attacked, the nature and locality of the property involved, the circumstances in which the party became involved in the transaction or received a benefit from it or acquired the property in question, whether the party acted in good faith, and whether under any relevant foreign law the party acquired a title free of any other claims to it. These factors will have to be balanced in the light of the facts of the case. But overall the court will seek to ensure that it does not act oppressively or vexatiously in operating the very wide jurisdiction it possesses.

30–009   A second limitation may also be imposed at an earlier stage in the inquiry, for proceedings under s.238 may not be brought against a person outside the English jurisdiction unless the court grants permission for the proceedings to be served on that person abroad pursuant to Pt 6 of the Civil Procedure Rules 1998, with such modifications as the court may direct.[29] In deciding whether it is a suitable case for permission to be granted, the court will have special regard to the strength or weakness of the plaintiff's claim that the defendant has an appropriate connection with the English jurisdiction as described above.[30]

It would seem that the above principles established in relation to s.238 of the 1986 Act apply with equal force in cases where it is alleged that a company has given a preference to any person in contravention of s.239[31] of the 1986 Act.[32] It would equally seem to apply both to orders in relation to extortionate credit transactions entered into by any person with the company which fall foul of s.244 of the Insolvency Act 1986 and also to the provisions concerning the avoidance of certain floating charges contained in s.245.[33] It has, additionally, been held that the powers of the court to set aside a transaction defrauding creditors at the suit of a victim of the transaction,[34] extend to a foreign company and exist in respect of a transaction governed by foreign law, even a transaction relating to foreign land.[35] In such a case it may be enough that the defendant is subject to the jurisdiction of the English court without it being necessary for any further connection with England to exist.[36]

---

[29] Insolvency Rules 1986, r.12A.20, inserted by the Insolvency (Amendment) Rules 2010 (SI 2010/686) with effect from April 6, 2010.

[30] *Re Paramount Airways Ltd (No.2)* [1993] Ch. 223 (CA), 240–241.

[31] An application may be made by a liquidator or administrator but not by an administrative receiver: ss.238(1), 239(1).

[32] *Re Paramount Airways Ltd (No.2)* [1993] Ch. 223 (CA), 233, 236–238.

[33] Again applications may be made under these sections by an administrator or liquidator but not by an administrative receiver: ss.238(1), 244(1), 245(1).

[34] Insolvency Act 1986, ss.423–425. An application may also be made by a liquidator or administrator but not by an administrative receiver: Insolvency Act 1986, s.424(1)(a).

[35] *Jyske Bank (Gibraltar) Ltd v Spjeldnaes (No.2)* [2000] B.C.C. 16.

[36] *Jyske Bank (Gibraltar) Ltd v Spjeldnaes (No.2)* [2000] B.C.C. 16. And see *Re Howard Holdings Inc* [1998] B.C.C. 549 (application of Insolvency Act 1986, s.214 in liquidation of

In *Re Seagull Manufacturing Co Ltd*[37] it was held that the court had jurisdiction under s.133 of the Insolvency Act 1986 to order the public examination of a director of an English company in compulsory liquidation regarding the promotion, formation or management of the company or as to the conduct of its business or affairs, or his conduct or dealings in relation to the company, irrespective of the nationality of the director or whether he is resident or present in England. This jurisdiction was said to extend to any person within the class of persons referred to in the section,[38] although the court has a discretion as to the manner and place of such service which can extend to ordering service out of the jurisdiction.[39]

It may well be that a similar approach to that taken in *Re Seagull* **30–010** *Manufacturing Co Ltd* will be applied with regard to the powers which an administrative receiver or administrator under s.234 of the Insolvency Act 1986 has in relation to obtaining possession of the company's property, books, papers or records. Likewise, a similar approach may also be taken to s.235 of the Insolvency Act 1986, which deals with the duty of officers and certain other persons connected with the company to co-operate with, amongst others, an administrative receiver or administrator.

Section 236 of the Insolvency Act 1986 empowers the court, on an application by, inter alia, an administrative receiver or administrator to order the examination on oath of an officer of the company, a person known or suspected to have in his possession any property of the company or supposed to be indebted to the company or a person thought to be capable of giving information concerning the promotion, formation, business dealings, affairs or property of the company.[40] The section also permits the making of an order requiring such persons to produce any books, papers or other records in his possession or under his control which relate to the company.[41] As to the former power, it has been held that the jurisdiction exists to enable the court to summon a person subject to the section irrespective of whether the relevant person is resident in the jurisdiction or has been personally served in the jurisdiction.[42] As to the

---

foreign company); *Re Seagull Manufacturing Co Ltd (In Liquidation) (No.2)* [1994] Ch. 91 (application of Company Directors' Disqualification Act 1986 to director irrespective of whether director a British subject or resident in England).

[37] *Re Seagull Manufacturing Co Ltd (No.1)* [1993] Ch. 345 (CA), distinguishing *Re Tucker) (A Bankrupt) Ex p. Tucker* [1990] Ch. 148 (CA).

[38] See s.133(1).

[39] Insolvency Rules 1986, r.12A.20. And see *Re Busytoday Ltd* [1992] 1 W.L.R. 683.

[40] s.236(2).

[41] s.236(3).

[42] *McIsaac and Wilson, Petitioners* [1994] B.C.C. 410 (Court of Session, Outer House). In the 2nd edition of this work, paras 32–032 to 32–037, attention was drawn to the difficulty in reaching this conclusion presented by *Re Tucker (A Bankrupt) Ex p. Tucker* [1990] Ch. 148 (CA), concerned with the interpretation of s.25 of the Bankruptcy Act 1914. *McIsaac and Wilson, Petitioners* suggests that these difficulties will be ignored, that the *Tucker* case will be regarded as limited to the interpretation of the legislative provision involved in that case, and that the modern trend of decisions indicates an intention to give s.236 of the 1986 Act extraterritorial effect: see *Re Seagull Manufacturing Co Ltd (In Liquidation)* [1993] Ch. 345 (CA); *Re Paramount Airways Ltd* [1993] Ch. 223 (CA); *Re Mid East Trading Ltd* [1998] 1 All E.R. 577 (CA). In *McIsaac, Petitioners* it was said, however, that, where necessary, it might be possible to enforce orders made under s.236(2) against persons outside the jurisdiction in the country where they were resident, pursuant to Insolvency Act 1986, s.426 (see below, paras 30–032 to 30–038). This is clearly incorrect. Section 426 deals with the obligations of a UK court to render assistance to a foreign court which is

latter power, it has been held that the court may make an order requiring production of documents which are located abroad.[43] The making of such an order (as making an order for examination)[44] lies within the discretion of the court.[45] To obtain, for example, an order for production of documents it will be necessary for the office-holder to demonstrate that he reasonably requires to see the documents[46] in order to carry out his statutory functions and that production of them does not impose an unnecessary or unreasonable burden on the person required to produce them.[47]

Where the powers referred to above are applied as against persons outside the jurisdiction of the English court, it will be necessary to obtain the permission of the court for service in the relevant country.[48] Where an order is made under s.236 of the 1986 Act against a person who is present in England, the court may restrain that person from leaving the jurisdiction or require that he give security as a condition of leaving the country.[49]

30–011   When a company is in administration, and between the presentation of an administration application and the making of the order, there are statutory restrictions on proceedings and on enforcement of security by creditors.[50] Where a company has assets abroad or creditors abroad, the question arises as to whether these prohibitions are limited to activities in the United Kingdom or whether they extend worldwide.

A similar question has been raised by the provisions of s.130(2) of the Insolvency Act 1986 which prohibits the commencement of proceedings against a company without the leave of the court after a winding-up order has been made or a provisional liquidator has been appointed. In *Re Vocalion (Foreign) Ltd*,[51] it was held that the application of the predecessor of this section as a matter of construction should be limited to proceedings in the United Kingdom.

---

designated by the Secretary of State for that purpose. The section has no concern with the obligation of a foreign court to render assistance to a UK court. Further, in that case the relevant documents were situated in New York and the court was clearly wrong in assuming that the United States was a relevant country for the purposes of Insolvency Act 1986, s.426(11) since it has not been designated as such by the Secretary of State: see Smart (1996) 41 J. Law Soc. Scotland 141.

[43] *Re Mid East Trading Ltd* [1998] 1 All E.R. 577 (CA).

[44] *McIsaac and Wilson, Petitioners* [1994] B.C.C. 410 (Court of Session, Outer House). See also *Re Seagull Manufacturing Co Ltd (In Liquidation)* [1993] Ch. 345 (CA); *Re Paramount Airways Ltd* [1993] Ch. 223 (CA).

[45] *Re Mid East Trading Ltd* [1998] 1 All E.R. 577 (CA). See above, Ch.8.

[46] The documents must be documents which relate to the company in respect of which the application is made: *Re Mid East Trading Ltd* [1998] 1 All E.R. 577 (CA), 585–590.

[47] See *British and Commonwealth Holdings Plc (Joint Administrators) v Spicer & Oppenheimer* [1993] A.C. 426 (HL); *Re Bank of Credit and Commerce International SA (No.12)* [1997] B.C.C. 561. The court may take account of the risk that the relevant person might be exposed to liability under the law of the country where the documents are situated: *Re Mid-East Trading Ltd* [1998] 1 All E.R. 577 (CA), 590–593; see *Mackinnon v Donaldson, Lufkin & Jenrette Securities Corp* [1986] Ch. 482. See above, Ch.8.

[48] Insolvency Rules 1986, r.12.12. See *Re Seagull Manufacturing Co Ltd (In Liquidation)* [1994] Ch. 91; *Re Paramount Airways* [1993] Ch. 223 (CA).

[49] *Re Oriental Credit Ltd* [1988] Ch. 204; *Re Bank of Credit and Commerce International SA (No.7)* [1994] 1 B.C.L.C. 455. See also *Morris v Murjani* [1996] 1 W.L.R. 848 (CA). Such an order may also be made in respect of applications under the Insolvency Act 1986, ss.133, 238–239, 244–245, 423–425.

[50] Insolvency Act 1986, Sch.B1, paras 42–44; and see above, Ch.9.

[51] *Re Vocalion (Foreign) Ltd* [1932] 2 Ch. 196; and see *Re Dynamics Corporation of America* [1976] 1 W.L.R. 757.

More recently, the Court of Appeal has cited that case with approval in relation to s.130(2), although there was no argument to the contrary.[52] On the other hand, in Scotland it has been held that the section applies to proceedings in foreign courts and that an injunction will be granted enforcing the prohibition against anyone within the jurisdiction.[53] The significance of this divergence in the context of a winding-up is reduced by the recognition and assertion of an equitable jurisdiction by the English courts to restrain persons subject to the jurisdiction from commencing or continuing proceedings calculated to defeat the right on the winding-up of all unsecured creditors[54] (who are in the nature of cestuis que trust with beneficial interests extending to all the company's property under the statutory scheme)[55] to the administration and distribution of the company's assets on the basis of equality and payment pari passu.[56]

In previous editions of this work it was suggested that the approach of giving the company administration statutory stay provisions of the Insolvency Act 1986 extra-territorial effect is preferable.[57] In particular, it was argued, there would appear to be no scope for exercise of the equitable jurisdiction since there is, in the case of an administration, no vested right on the part of unsecured creditors.[58] Administration is a collective procedure in the interests of all creditors, and one of its purposes may be a "more advantageous realisation of the company's assets than would be effected on a winding up",[59] but no trust arises and the company does not cease to be beneficial owner of its assets, nor do the creditors acquire any beneficial interests therein. It was noted that the alternative construction to the effect that the company administration statutory stay has no extra-territorial effect must be conducive to an unseemly scramble by creditors for foreign assets, a course which (if generally available) must undermine the efficacy of the legislation as a means of giving a breathing space to companies. However, the Court of Appeal in *Harms Offshore AHT Taurus GmbH & Co KG v Bloom*[60] decided that the statutory moratorium in administration under para.43(6) of Sch.B1 to the Insolvency Act 1986 has no extraterritorial reach but is limited to legal process within the jurisdiction. But the Court of Appeal also affirmed that there is a wider duty, as is also true of liqui-

---

[52] *Re Mitchell v Carter, Buckingham International Plc (In Liquidation) (No.1)* [1997] B.C.C. 71.

[53] See *California Redwood Co Ltd v Walker* (1886) 13 R. 816 and *Redwood Co Ltd v Merchant Banking Co of London* (1886) 13 R. 1202.

[54] Secured creditors will readily be given leave to commence proceedings against the company. To the extent that they rest on their security, they are outside the statutory scheme and in any proceedings against the company they are enforcing rights, not against the company, but to their own property: per Brightman L.J. in *Re Aro Co Ltd* [1980] Ch. 196 (CA), 203.

[55] *R. v Registrar of Companies Ex p. Central Bank of India* [1986] Q.B. 1114 (CA), 1162 per Dillon L.J.; *Victoria Housing Estates Ltd v Ashpurton Estates Ltd* [1983] Ch. 110 (CA), 23, per Lord Brightman.

[56] *Re Vocalion (Foreign) Ltd* [1932] 2 Ch. 196, *Re Mitchell v Carter, Buckingham International Plc (In Liquidation) (No.1)* [1997] B.C.C. 71; *Re Mitchell v Carter, Buckingham International Plc (No.2)* [1998] B.C.C. 943 (CA) and see *Re Calgary & Edmonton Land Co (In Liquidation)* [1975] 1 W.L.R 355 and consider *British Airways v Laker Airways* [1985] A.C. 58 (HL).

[57] See, e.g. the fourth edition of this work (2007), Ch.32 at para.32–011.

[58] Note that there might be an argument in the case of an administration which is bound to result in a liquidation, that unsecured creditors have sufficient in the way of prospective rights to enable an injunction to be granted to prevent proceedings abroad.

[59] Insolvency Act 1986, s.8(3)(d).

[60] *Harms Offshore AHT Taurus GmbH & Co KG v Bloom* [2010] Ch. 187 (CA).

dations, to protect the assets of the company in administration both within and outside the jurisdiction, and that the court should exercise its powers to enable the administrators to exercise their statutory functions. This may include, in appropriate cases, the granting of anti-suit injunctions to prevent creditors from taking advantage of foreign attachments.[61]

30–012   It is of course true that it might be unfair for English creditors who are subject to the jurisdiction of the court to be restrained from exercising rights abroad when foreign creditors not subject to such jurisdiction are not so restrained. Such potential unfairness can be remedied by the power of the court (and, in certain situations, the administrator) to grant permission to proceed.

If the statutory stay imposed by the Insolvency Act 1986 amounted to a moratorium[62] on debts and liabilities, on established principles of conflict of laws, it could only be expected to be given effect to abroad where English or Scots law is the law applicable to the transaction giving rise to the liability.[63] That is because a moratorium, properly so-called, discharges or modifies the relevant obligation and only the law applicable to the obligation is regarded in the conflict of laws as being able to discharge or modify the obligation. But as has been seen in Ch.9, paras 42–44 of Sch.B1 to the Insolvency Act 1986 do not discharge or modify obligations but only restrain remedies for their enforcement. Such a stay of remedies, given that it does not discriminate against foreign creditors, may be enforced by foreign courts even where the liability whose enforcement is stayed is governed by a foreign law. A foreign court may also be expected to recognise the administrator as the governing body of the company entitled to act on its behalf, since this is a matter for the law of the place of incorporation.[64]

Moreover, the English court may grant an injunction against a creditor who is subject to the jurisdiction of the court to prevent him from commencing or continuing proceedings or doing any act outside the United Kingdom prohibited by the Act.[65] Further, under the so-called doctrine of *hotchpot*, if the creditor subject to the jurisdiction obtains satisfaction by means forbidden by the law, he may be required to disgorge his receipts to the administrator.[66] Under the same equitable doctrine, any creditor not subject to the jurisdiction who has obtained satisfaction abroad in this way may expect to be required, as a condition of being heard in the administration proceedings or obtaining any benefit under any scheme or of obtaining any acceptance of his proof in a subsequent liquidation, to pay over all sums so received.[67]

---

[61] *Harms Offshore AHT Taurus GmbH & Co KG v Bloom* [2010] Ch. 187 (CA), [21]–[27].

[62] For the use of the term "moratorium" in this context, see above, Ch.9.

[63] *National Bank of Greece and Athens SA v Metliss* [1958] A.C. 509 (HL); *Adams v National Bank of Greece SA* [1961] A.C. 255 (HL). See also *New Zealand Loan and Mercantile Agency v Morrison* [1898] A.C. 349 (PC) (Companies Act Scheme).

[64] *Carl Zeiss Stiftung v Rayner and Keeler Ltd* [1967] 1 A.C. 853 (HL), 919, 972, 588.

[65] cf. *Re Central Sugar Factories of Brazil* [1894] 1 Ch. 369; *Re Vocalion (Foreign) Ltd* [1932] 2 Ch. 196. And see *Mitchell v Carter* [1997] B.C.C. 71 (and [1997] B.C.C. 907 (CA)); *Mitchell v Buckingham International Plc (No.2)* [1998] B.C.C. 943 (CA). See below, paras 32–031 et seq.

[66] *Re Oriental Island Steam Co* (1874) L.R. 9 Ch. App. 557 (CA); *Mitchell v Carter* [1997] B.C.C. 907 (CA), 912–913, per Millett L.J.

[67] *Re Oriental Island Steam Co* (1874) L.R. 9 Ch. App. 557 (CA); *Mitchell v Carter* [1997] B.C.C. 907 (CA), 912–913, per Millett L.J.

3.   RECOGNITION OF RECEIVERS: INTRA-UNITED KINGDOM

(a) Provisions

The law relating to the recognition in England of receivers appointed under the   **30–013**
law of another part of the United Kingdom is governed by explicit statutory
provisions. Thus, a receiver appointed under the law of Scotland or Northern
Ireland in respect of the property of a corporation having created a charge
which, as created, was a floating charge, may exercise his powers in England.[68]
The recognition of these receivers' powers is, however, subject to the qualification that their exercise should not be inconsistent with English law.[69]
Accordingly, although a Scottish receiver should be entitled, prima facie, to
exercise the same powers over English assets as he possesses in relation to
Scottish assets, English law will remain in ultimate control. A charge created
by a Scottish company over property located in England does not require registration in England,[70] though the charge must be registered in Scotland to the
extent that such registration is required by ss.878 to 892 of the Companies Act
2006.[71] Those provisions form part, not only of the law of Scotland, but also
the law of England and Wales, so that an unregistered charge granted by a
Scottish company over assets located in England may be unenforceable for
non-registration in an English court.[72]

The sections enabling the power of a receiver appointed under the law of
Scotland or Northern Ireland to be recognised in England also have the wider
effect of establishing the mutual recognition of receivers appointed under the
law of England, Scotland and Northern Ireland as the case may be. Accordingly,
an English receiver may exercise his powers in Scotland though the exercise
of such powers must be consistent with Scots law.[73] Any charge created by an
English company over property located in Scotland does not require registration in Scotland,[74] but such a charge must be registered in England in the
usual way.[75]

Section 426 of the Insolvency Act 1986, which applies to England and
Wales, Scotland and Northern Ireland, provides for mutual judicial assistance
between courts within the various parts of the United Kingdom and for such
assistance between those courts and the courts of any relevant country or

---

[68] For receivers appointed under the law of Scotland, see Insolvency Act 1986, s.72; for
receivers appointed under the law of Northern Ireland, see Administration of Justice Act 1977, s.7.
[69] The qualification is established in each of the above sections.
[70] Companies Act 2006, Pt 25, Ch.2 (ss.878–892).
[71] See also Bankruptcy and Diligence (Scotland) Act 2007 (asp 3), Pt 2 (not yet in force).
[72] *Arthur D Little Ltd (In Administration) v Ableco Finance LLC* [2003] Ch. 217, 22–24.
[73] In *Gordon Anderson (Plant) Ltd v Campsie Construction Ltd and Anglo-Scottish Plant Ltd*
1977 S.L.T. 7 (Court of Session, Inner House, 1 Div), a majority of the Court of Session held that
the then equivalent to s.72 of the Insolvency Act 1986 (Companies (Floating Charges and
Receivers) (Scotland) Act 1972, s.15(4), repealed by Administration of Justice Act 1977, s.7) had
the effect of giving an English receiver the same security over Scottish assets that a Scottish
receiver would obtain. See too, *Norfolk House Plc (in receivership) v Repsol Petroleum Ltd* 1992
S.L.T. 235 (Court of Session, Outer House).
[74] Companies Act 2006, Part 25, Chap.1 (ss.860–877).
[75] Companies Act 2006, Part 25, Chap.1 (ss.860–877).

territory.[76] Such assistance may be provided in relation to insolvency law, the definition of which extends to the provisions of the Insolvency Act 1986 which deal with English and Scottish administrations and receiverships and also to the corresponding provisions of the relevant Northern Irish legislation.[77] The nature of the assistance to be provided lies within the discretion of the court whose assistance is requested,[78] but it would seem that this provision may have the effect of increasing the mutual recognition of administrators' and receivers' powers within the United Kingdom. Tending in the same direction is the requirement in the Insolvency Act 1986 which imposes a mutual obligation on United Kingdom courts to recognise each other's orders made in the exercise of jurisdiction in relation to insolvency law,[79] the definition of which includes the law concerning administrators and receivers.[80] Such recognition could thus extend to administrators and receivers appointed by the courts of the various parts of the United Kingdom. The mutual duty of recognition, in this context, is subject to the important qualification that a court is not bound to recognise the order of a court in another part of the United Kingdom to the extent that such order affects property situated within the jurisdiction of the court which is asked to recognise it.[81]

4.   RECOGNITION OF RECEIVERS: FOREIGN APPOINTMENT

(a)   Out of court

30–014   The position of a foreign receiver appointed otherwise than by court order and the extent to which such a receiver's powers will be recognised in England has never been directly considered in a reported English decision. In *Cretanor Maritime Co Ltd v Irish Marine Management Ltd*[82] a company incorporated in the Republic of Ireland created a floating charge over its assets in favour of a bank. The company had assets in England but had been restrained, by means of a freezing injunction, from dealing with them. Subsequently the charge crystallised and a receiver was appointed who sought to have the injunction discharged. It was held that the receiver, as agent of the company according to Irish law, was bound by the injunction in the same way as the company would have been

---

[76] Insolvency Act 1986, s.426(4). As to the meaning of "relevant country or territory", see below, para.30–033.

[77] Insolvency Act 1986, s.426(4), (10)(a), (b), and (c). For the Northern Irish legislation see Companies (Northern Ireland) Order 1986 (SI 1986/1032 (N.I.6)) and Insolvency (Northern Ireland) Order 1989 (SI 1989/2405 (N.I.19)). The English court may also exercise its own general powers, beyond those of "insolvency law" as defined in s.426(10), in providing assistance in particular cases: *Hughes v Hannover* [1997] B.C.C. 921 (CA). See below, para.30–035.

[78] Insolvency Act 1986, s.426(5). A request is authority for the court to which the request is made to apply its own law of receivership or the comparable corresponding law of the requesting court: Insolvency Act 1986, s.426(5). In exercising its discretion under s.426(5) the court shall have regard, in particular, to its rules of private international law. See below, para.30–036.

[79] Insolvency Act 1986, s.426(1) and (2).

[80] Insolvency Act 1986, s.426(1), (2), (10)(a), (b) and (c).

[81] Insolvency Act 1986, s.426(1) and (2).

[82] *Cretanor Maritime Co Ltd v Irish Marine Management Ltd (The Cretan Harmony)* [1978] 1 W.L.R. 966 (CA).

had no receiver been appointed. It may be deduced, by implication, from this result that, had no injunction been granted, the receiver could have exercised in England whatever rights were available to him under Irish law. Accordingly, it is submitted that where a receiver is appointed under a law other than the law of a part of the United Kingdom in respect of the property of a corporation and in consequence of the corporation having created a charge (which as created was a floating charge), he may exercise his powers in England if the exercise of those powers is authorised by the law of the country in which the company is incorporated.[83] This view accords with principle. A receiver appointed pursuant to a charge normally acts, prior to liquidation, as agent of the corporation which created the charge. On general principle, the law of the place of incorporation determines who is entitled to act on behalf of the corporation.[84] After liquidation a receiver is no longer agent but retains his power to act in the corporation's name to dispose of the corporation's assets. It is suggested even in this case that it is the law of the place of incorporation which determines who has the power to act in the name of the corporation to dispose of its assets.

If the foregoing submissions are accepted, then a receiver's authority will be recognised in England to the extent that his powers are consistent with English law.[85] It follows from this that where his authority is so recognised, then priority as between him and any other claimants will be governed by English law,[86] despite the fact that English creditors might be prejudiced in the sense that, were the receiver's authority not recognised, those creditors would have prior claims.[87]

The foregoing submissions assume, of course, that the charge has been validly created and that it extends to the property being claimed by the receiver in accordance with the principles discussed earlier in this chapter.[88]

The obligation to register charges[89] extends to charges on property in England **30–015** which are created and to charges on property in England which is acquired by a company incorporated outside Great Britain which has an established place of business in England.[90] For the English registration provisions to apply, the company must have an established place of business in England at the time of

---

[83] Dicey, Morris and Collins, *The Conflict of Laws,* 14th, edn (London: Sweet & Maxwell, 2006), r.167 and pp.1397–1407. See also *Re CA Kennedy Co Ltd and Stibbe-Monk Ltd* (1976) 74 D.L.R. (3d) 87; Collins (1978) 27 I.C.L.Q. 611, 707–710 reprinted in *Essays in International Litigation and the Conflict of Laws* (1994), p.433. The same principle governs recognition of the powers of a liquidator appointed under foreign law. See Dicey, Morris and Collins, *The Conflict of Laws*, 14th edn (London: Sweet & Maxwell, 2006), r.166 and pp.1385–1397. As to appointments of office-holders analogous to administrators, see *Felixstowe Dock and Railway Co v US Lines Inc* [1989] 2 W.L.R. 109 and below, paras 30–023 to 30–026.

[84] *Banco de Bilbao v Sancha and Rey* [1938] 2 K.B. 176 (CA).

[85] cf. Administration of Justice Act 1977, s.7; Insolvency Act 1986, s.72; above, para.30–013. See also *Re B* [1990–91] C.I.L.R. (Notes) 7 (Grand Court, Cayman Islands).

[86] *Re CA Kennedy Co Ltd and Stibbe-Monk Ltd* (1976) 74 D.L.R. (3d) 87, 92–93; see also *Re McKenzie Grant & Co* (1899) 1 W.A.L.R. 116; Picarda, *Law Relating to Receivers Managers and Administrators*, 4th edn (London: Butterworths, 2006), pp.731–732.

[87] See *Re CA Kennedy Co Ltd and Stibbe-Monk Ltd* (1976) 74 D.L.R. (3d) 87, 95–96.

[88] See above, paras 30–002 to 30–007.

[89] See Companies Act 2006, Pt 25, Ch.1. For further discussion, see above, Ch.3.

[90] Overseas Companies (Execution of Documents and Registration of Charges) Regulations 2009 (SI 2009/1917), Schedule, maintaining in force with respect to charges created before October 1, 2009 the effects of Companies Act 1985, s.409 (repealed).

the creation of the charge,[91] but charges created prior to the establishment of a place of business in England do not require registration.[92] The registration provisions contained in Pt 25, Ch.1 of the Companies Act 2006 apply whether or not the company has registered in accordance with the requirements of Pt 34 of that Act.[93]

A foreign receiver appointed out of court may be in a position to invoke the provisions of the Insolvency Act 1986 which enable the English court, on the request of a court in any relevant country or territory, to provide assistance in matters relating to the receivership. This power is discussed separately below.[94]

5. RECOGNITION OF RECEIVERS: APPOINTMENT BY FOREIGN COURT[95]

30–016   The circumstances in which a receiver appointed by a foreign court may secure recognition of his powers in relation to English assets in England has not been authoritatively settled in the reported cases.[96] However, it is clear that the principles are different to those which apply to determine the recognition of a receiver pursuant to a private appointment under foreign law.[97] This difference arises because, in principle, when recognition of a receiver appointed by a foreign court is involved, the English court must satisfy itself that the foreign court was jurisdictionally competent to make the appointment according to the relevant principles of English private international law. Consequently, it becomes necessary to determine when English law will regard a foreign court as possessing such competence.[98] Where such competence is established and there are no applicable general principles of conflict of laws precluding recognition, comity requires recognition to be afforded.[99] In the case of a private appointment, the validity of the appointment must be strictly proved and comity has no place.[100]

[91] Re Oriel Ltd (In Liquidation) [1986] 1 W.L.R. 180 (CA).

[92] Re Oriel Ltd (In Liquidation) [1986] 1 W.L.R. 180 (CA).

[93] Slavenburg's Bank NV v Intercontinental Natural Resources Ltd [1980] 1 W.L.R. 1076. See above, Ch.3.

[94] See below, paras 30–032 to 30–038. Other less formal methods of assistance may also be available.

[95] See also Ch.31.

[96] See Houlditch v Marquis of Donegal (1834) 8 Bli. N.S. 301; Re Maudslay, Sons and Field [1900] 1 Ch. 602; Macaulay v Guaranty Trust Co of New York (1927) 44 T.L.R. 99; Re Kooperman [1928] W.N. 101; Schemmer v Property Resources Ltd [1975] Ch. 273; Perry v Zissis [1977] 1 Lloyd's Rep. 607 (CA); Derby & Co v Weldon (No.6) [1990] 1 W.L.R. 1139 (CA); International Credit and Investment Co (Overseas) Ltd v Adham (Jurisdiction) [1994] 1 B.C.L.C. 66, affirmed [1999] I.L.Pr. 302 (CA); Larkins v National Union of Mineworkers [1985] I.R. 671; Thorne Ernst and Whinney Inc v Sulpetro Ltd (1987) 47 D.L.R. (4th) 315; Canadian Imperial Bank of Commerce v Idanell Korner Ranch Ltd [1990] 6 W.W.R. 612; Re Young [1955] St.R.Qd. 254; White v Verkouille [1990] 2 Qd.R. 191; Canadian Arab Financial Corp v Player [1984] C.I.L.R. 63 (Cayman Islands CA).

[97] See Re B [1990–91] C.I.L.R. (Notes) 7 (Grand Court, Cayman Islands).

[98] For discussion see Dicey, Morris and Collins, The Conflict of Laws, 14th edn (London: Sweet & Maxwell, 2006), pp.1400–1402.

[99] Canadian Arab Financial Corporation v Player [1984] C.I.L.R. 63 (Cayman Islands CA).

[100] Re Anchor Line (Henderson Bros) Ltd [1937] Ch. 483. See also Gwembe Valley Development Co Ltd.(In Receivership) v Koshy [2000] B.C.C. 1127.

As a general principle, the foreign court will be regarded as jurisdictionally competent if there is a "sufficient connection between the company in respect of which the receiver is appointed ('the defendant') and the jurisdiction in which the foreign receiver was appointed to justify recognition of the foreign court's order".[101] While this much may be accepted, it is not possible to state with complete certainty the circumstances in which such sufficient connection may exist.[102] At the outset, recognition will be accorded to an appointment made by a court in the country in which the company is incorporated.[103]

Secondly, it is likely that an appointment will be recognised if the defendant submitted to the jurisdiction of the court which appointed the receiver,[104] though in this context submission by a subsidiary of the defendant is likely to be regarded as insufficient to justify recognition.[105] It is also possible that the English court will recognise the order of a foreign court if the appointment is made by a court of a country other than that in which the company is incorporated, if the appointment is recognised by the courts of the country in which the company is incorporated.[106]

A sufficient connection, for these purposes, ought to include factual connection between the company and the relevant jurisdiction where the appointment is made. Accordingly it is, in principle, possible to support the view that an appointment made by a court in a country where the central management and control of the company is exercised should be entitled to recognition.[107] The claim to recognition on this ground will, perhaps, be stronger if there is no, or little, likelihood of any intervention by the courts of the place of incorporation.[108] A strong factual link justifying recognition may also be thought to exist where the appointment is made by a court in a country where the company carries on business.[109]

30–017

---

[101] *Schemmer v Property Resources Ltd* [1975] Ch.273, 287: see too, *International Credit and Investment Co (Overseas) Ltd v Adham (Jurisdiction)* [1994] 1 B.C.L.C. 66, 70–71, affirmed [1999] I.L.Pr. 302 (CA); *White v Verkouille* [1990] 2 Qd.R. 191.

[102] See the cautious and tentative exposition by Goulding J. in *Schemmer v Property Resources Ltd* [1975] Ch. 273.

[103] *International Credit and Investment Co (Overseas) Ltd v Adham (Jurisdiction)* [1994] 1 B.C.L.C. 66, affirmed [1999] I.L.Pr. 302 (CA), explicitly recognising an appointment made by the courts of the country in which the company was incorporated; *Schemmer v Property Resources Ltd* [1975] Ch. 273. And see *North Australian Terrritory Co Ltd v Goldsborough Mort & Co Ltd* (1889) 61 L.T. 716; *Macaulay v Guaranty Trust Co of New York* (1927) 44 T.L.R. 99; *Larkins v National Union of Mineworkers* [1985] I.R. 671, 689–693. The conclusion is reinforced by the analogy with the recognition of the authority of a liquidator appointed under the law of the place of incorporation; see Dicey, Morris and Collins, *The Conflict of Laws*, 14th edn (London: Sweet & Maxwell, 2006), r.166 and pp.1385–1389.

[104] *Schemmer v Property Resources Ltd* [1975] Ch. 273; *International Credit and Investment Co (Overseas) Ltd v Adham (Jurisdiction)* [1994] 1 B.C.L.C. 66, 70–71; *White v Verkouille* [1990] 2 Qd.R. 191. And see *Thorne Ernst & Whinney Inc v Sulpetro Ltd* (1987) 47 D.L.R. (4th) 315; *Canadian Imperial Bank of Commerce v Idanell Korner Ranch Ltd* (1990) 6 W.W.R. 610.

[105] *Schemmer v Property Resources Ltd* [1975] Ch. 273.

[106] *Schemmer v Property Resources Ltd* [1975] Ch. 273, 287. See also Smart, *Cross-Border Insolvency*, 2nd edn (London: Butterworths, 1998), p.167; *Macaulay v Guaranty Trust Co of New York* (1927) 44 T.L.R. 99.

[107] *Schemmer v Property Resources Ltd* [1975] Ch. 273.

[108] See Dicey, Morris and Collins, *The Conflict of Laws*, 14th edn (London: Sweet & Maxwell, 2006), pp.1386–1387, 1400–1402; *Re Azoff-Don Commercial Bank* [1954] Ch. 315.

[109] *Schemmer v Property Resources Ltd* [1975] Ch. 273.

The strength of this link may be particularly compelling if that is the only country where business is carried on.

It seems to be established, on the other hand, that "reciprocity" by itself will not be regarded as a ground of recognition, i.e. that it will be insufficient to justify recognition merely to show that the appointment made by the foreign court was made in circumstances where, mutatis mutandis, an English court would have had jurisdiction to appoint a receiver.[110]

Assuming that an English court regards the appointment as made in circumstances where the foreign court possesses the necessary jurisdictional competence, the appointment may nevertheless fail to gain recognition if it does not accord with what one might refer to as general principles of the conflict of laws. Thus, for example, in *Schemmer v Property Resources Ltd*[111], a receiver had been appointed in the United States, pursuant to the Securities Exchange Act 1934, to take possession of certain assets of a Bahamian company which were situated, amongst other places in England. It was held that the American statute was a penal law unenforceable in the English courts, so that any appointment made pursuant to it could not be recognised because it stemmed from a law bearing this penal character.[112]

30–018   The principle in the *Schemmer* case has been followed and extended in *Hong Kong in NanusAsia Co Inc v Standard Chartered Bank*,[113] where it was held that a receiver appointed by the United States Court in an insider trading case would not be recognised. The receiver had been careful to seek only disgorgement of profits in the interests of the victims and had not sought to enforce any penal relief available under United States law. Even without the penal element, recognition was denied on the basis that the receiver was appointed under public law provisions. The issue arose in the context of a trial of the issue whether the bank holding the ill-gotten proceeds had a defence to a claim by the wrongdoer's company to payment over of the monies. The bank was held entitled to hold on to these funds on the grounds that they might be held on constructive trust for the victims. This was held not to be an indirect enforcement of US public law.

In *Larkins v National Union of Mineworkers*,[114] the English court had appointed sequestrators over the property of the National Union of Mineworkers in relation to the union's failure to comply with the orders of the court during the

---

[110] *Schemmer v Property Resources Ltd* [1975] Ch. 273; *Derby & Co Ltd v Weldon (No.6)* [1990] 1 W.L.R. 1139 (CA), 1150. See also *Re Trepca Mines Ltd* [1960] 1 W.L.R. 1273 (CA); *Société Co-operative Sidmetal v Titan International Ltd* [1966] 1 Q.B. 828; *Felixstowe Dock and Railway Co v US Lines Inc* [1989] Q.B. 360, 374–375.

[111] *Schemmer v Property Resources Ltd* [1975] Ch. 273.

[112] See, generally, Dicey, Morris and Collins, *The Conflict of Laws*, 14th edn (London: Sweet & Maxwell, 2006), pp.104 et seq.

[113] *Hong Kong in NanusAsia Co Inc v Standard Chartered Bank* [1988] H.K.C. 377. See also *Stutts v Premier Benefit Trust* [1992–1993] C.I.L.R. 605 (Cayman) which follows and applies *NanusAsia* and *Schemmer*. The Cayman court refused to recognise a United States SEC Receiver. In *Philadelphia Alternative Asset Fund Ltd* (February 22, 2006 Cayman Grand Court) an attempt by a United States CFTC Receiver to block the making of a winding-up order was rejected and recognition refused. The case-law mentioned here was cited to the court but is not mentioned in the judgment.

[114] *Larkins v National Union of Mineworkers* [1985] I.R. 671.

miners' strike in 1984. The sequestration order empowered the sequestrators to take proceedings in the Republic of Ireland to recover union funds on deposit there with a bank. Subsequently, the English court appointed, on an interlocutory basis, a receiver of the union who was given authority to bring proceedings in any jurisdiction to recover assets of the union. The Irish High Court held that the claim by the sequestrators could not be maintained since sequestration was a penal process in which it was sought to establish the authority of the court by punishing recalcitrant litigants for contempt. As far as the claim by the receiver was concerned, the Irish court made no order since the appointment was of an interlocutory character. The court did seem prepared to recognise that a claim by a receiver not appointed on an interlocutory basis could, in principle, be maintained since there were independent grounds for the appointment and the receivership was not an indirect method of enforcing the sequestration such that it amounted to an indirect method of enforcing a foreign penal law.[115]

Where the foreign receiver gains recognition, he may be permitted to sue for the recovery of the assets in his own name.[116] Here the receiver's power receives direct recognition, though, as an alternative, the English court may create an English receivership to act as auxiliary to the principal receivership.[117] Whichever solution is adopted, the receiver may collect English property and give a good discharge for it.[118] In an appropriate case, the foreign appointee may be required to give security for costs.

A receiver appointed by a foreign court may be able to take advantage of the provisions of the Insolvency Act 1986 which relate to judicial assistance. This matter is discussed below

6.   ADMINISTRATIVE RECEIVERS

In the present context, the question for consideration is whether the status of administrative receiver is confined to a person appointed in relation to a company registered under the Companies Act 2006 or whether it also exists in relation to a person appointed as a receiver or manager of a foreign (unregistered) company. In *Re International Bulk Commodities Ltd*,[119] it was held that a receiver appointed in relation to a foreign company can be an administrative receiver for the purposes of the 1986 Act and is therefore able to exercise the powers under that Act which are available to such a person. By virtue of s.251   **30–019**

---

[115] This could be questionable if the receiver was under an obligation to account for any sums to the sequestrators, a point not decided in the case.

[116] See *Macaulay v Guaranty Trust Co of New York* (1927) 44 T.L.R. 99.

[117] *Schemmer v Property Resources Ltd* [1975] Ch. 273; *Re Kooperman* [1928] W.N. 101; 72 Sol.Jo. 400; *Re Young* [1955] St R. Qd. 254.

[118] *Schemmer v Property Resources Ltd* [1975] Ch. 273; see also *Lepage v San Paulo Copper Estates Ltd FS* [1917] W.N. 216.

[119] *Re International Bulk Commodities Ltd* [1993] Ch. 77. The correctness of this decision was doubted in *Re Devon and Somerset Farmers Ltd* [1994] Ch. 57, but it was ultimately distinguished on the basis that it was a decision which was authority on the powers of receivers of foreign companies appointed under debentures so that, in consequence, it did not extend to an English unregistered company. For discussion, see Dicey, Morris and Collins, *The Conflict of Laws*, 14th edn (London: Sweet & Maxwell, 2006), pp.1404–1405; Smart, *Cross-Border Insolvency*, 2nd edn (London: Butterworths, 1998), pp.130–136; Moss (1993) 6 Insolv. Int. 19; (1994) 7 Insolv. Int. 33.

of the Insolvency Act 1986, the relevant definition of a company, for these purposes, was to be found (at that date) in s.735 of the Companies Act 1985 (corresponding for this purpose to ss.1 and 1171 of the Companies Act 2006) so that unless the contrary intention appeared, "company" meant a company registered under the Companies Act 1985. Mummery J. held, however, that a contrary intention could be deduced from the construction of the provisions of the Insolvency Act 1986 relating to administrative receivers and from the Act as a whole: Parliament intended that "company" should not be confined to one registered under the 1985 Act but should include any company liable to be wound up under the provisions of Pt V of the Insolvency Act 1986.[120] Since a foreign company could be wound up under these provisions, a receiver of it could be an administrative receiver. The debenture in that case was secured by a floating charge in the English form.[121] This leaves open the effect of an appointment made under a debenture governed by a foreign law. It is suggested, however, that if:

(a)   such an appointment creates a floating charge recognised by English law; and

(b)   a receiver is appointed whose appointment is recognised by English law; and

(c)   the receiver meets the relevant English statutory criteria,

the receiver will be regarded as an administrative receiver. It is probable that a foreign appointee's powers would be limited to those which are not inconsistent with English law.[122] More general limitations may be placed on the appointee's powers by general principles of the conflict of laws, e.g. a foreign appointee may be precluded from exercising powers in England which are conferred by a foreign law if these powers are penal in the English sense.[123]

30–020   No reason of principle seems to prevent the provisions concerning mutual recognition as between England and Scotland in s.72 of the Insolvency Act 1986 being extended to administrative receivers despite the fact that they are not explicitly mentioned in that section.[124] This conclusion seems to follow because a receiver for the purposes of s.72 includes a manager and a receiver and manager[125] and an administrative receiver, as far as the English provisions of the 1986 Act are concerned, must initially be one of these in addition to satisfying the other criteria established by the Act,[126] and, in relation to the Scottish provisions, an administrative receiver must initially be a receiver who also satisfies

---

[120] As to the winding up of foreign companies, see *Stocznia Gdanska v Latreefers (No.2)* [2001] B.C.C. 174 (CA).

[121] *Re International Bulk Commodities Ltd* [1993] Ch. 77, 86.

[122] cf. Insolvency Act 1986, s.72(1).

[123] cf. *Schemmer v Property Resources Ltd* [1975] Ch. 273, above, para.30–017; Insolvency Act 1986, ss.28, 50.

[124] cf. Insolvency Act 1986, ss.37(1), 38(1) which explicitly exclude administrative receivers.

[125] Insolvency Act 1986, s.72(2).

[126] Insolvency Act 1986, s.29(2).

the additional requirements of the Act.[127] If this submission is accepted, the administrative receiver can only exercise his powers in the other jurisdiction to the extent that those powers are not inconsistent with the law applicable there.[128]

7. ADMINISTRATION

An important feature of the Insolvency Act 1986 was the creation of the office of administrator.[129] At least three questions may arise in the context of private international law. The first is whether an English court has power to make an administration trading order in respect of a foreign company. Related to this, following the reforms made to the administration procedure by the Enterprise Act 2002, is the question whether a foreign company can be placed in administration by the out of court appointment of an administrator made by the company or its directors, or by the holder of a qualifying floating charge. The third question is the extent to which officers analogous to administrators, appointed under a foreign law, are entitled to have their status recognised in England and to exercise in England either the powers conferred upon them by the relevant foreign law or those available to an administrator in England. Recognition at common law is dealt with in s.(b) below; the English court's powers under s.426 are discussed in s.9 below; the effects of the European Insolvency Regulation on matters of jurisdiction and recognition are discussed in Ch.31; while the UNCITRAL Model Law is discussed in Ch.32.

30–021

(a) Powers of English court

(i) Under the European Insolvency Regulation

Under art.3 of the European Insolvency Regulation the English court may appoint an administrator in respect of a foreign company that has either its centre of main interests or (if its centre of main interests is in another EU Member State, apart from Denmark) an establishment in England.[130] Similarly, in a case to which the European Insolvency Regulation is applicable any power to appoint an administrator directly which would be exercisable by the company or its directors, or by the holder of a qualifying floating charge, in respect of a company formed and registered under the current or former companies legislation in force in England may equally be exercised in relation to a foreign-formed company

30–022

---

[127] Insolvency Act 1986, ss.51, 251.

[128] Insolvency Act 1986, s.72(1).

[129] Whether a person has authority to apply for an administration order, or to appoint an administrator directly, in respect of an English company may depend on a foreign law, e.g. where the English company is owned by a foreign company and an officer of the foreign company acting on the latter's behalf seeks to procure an administration order, or to appoint an administrator, in the name of the English company, the officer's authority so to act may depend on the law of the country in which the foreign company is incorporated. But whether that person has locus standi so to apply depends upon Insolvency Act 1986, Sch.B1, para.12 or para.22 (as the case may be): see *Re MTI Trading Systems Ltd (In Administration)* [1997] B.C.C. 703.

[130] See, e.g. *Re Collins & Aikman Corp Group (Application for Administration Orders)* [2006] B.C.C. 606.

which has its centre of main interests in this country. Such power of appointment may also be exercised in relation to a foreign company which has its centre of main interests in another EU Member State (other than Denmark) provided that the company has an establishment in this country. The European Insolvency Regulation is dealt with in Ch.31.

(ii)   Cases not within the scope of the European Insolvency Regulation

More difficult is the question whether, in a case not governed by the European Insolvency Regulation, the English court has power, absent a letter of request under s.426, to make an administration order against a foreign company in other circumstances. The scope of the jurisdiction exercisable by the courts of this country was amended by statutory instrument with effect from April 13, 2005.[131]

30–023 *Before April 13, 2005.* In at least two judgments at first instance decided between 1986 and 2002 it had been assumed that an English court had no power to make an administration order in respect of a foreign company[132] and one of these decisions had been referred to, in that respect, without approval, disapproval, discussion or hearing argument on the point, by the Court of Appeal in a case in which the point was not in issue.[133] A more cautious and open view on the question had also been expressed at first instance in a case in which the point did not expressly arise for decision.[134] In view of this inconclusive state of authority, it seemed appropriate to treat the question as an arguable one and to consider the question on the merits.[135]

In *Re Dallhold Estates (UK) Pty Ltd*,[136] it was held that an English court could, on the request of a court of a designated country, make an administration order in relation to a foreign company pursuant to s.426 of the Insolvency Act 1986, but it was said also, in that case, that the court did not have original jurisdiction to make such an order. The reason was that s.8 of the Insolvency Act 1986 as originally enacted enabled the court to make an administration order in respect of a "company" which was defined for those purposes by s.735 of the Companies Act 1985 (then in force)[137] as a company formed and registered under that Act or any of its predecessors.

---

[131] Insolvency Act 1986 (Amendment) Regulations 2005 (SI 2005/879).

[132] *Felixstowe Dock and Railway Co v US Lines Inc* 1989] Q.B. 360; *Re Dallhold Estates (UK) Pty Ltd* [1992] B.C.C. 394.

[133] *Hughes v Hannover* [1997] B.C.C. 921 (CA), 933, referring to *Re Dallhold Estates (UK) Pty Ltd* [1992] B.C.C. 394.

[134] *Re International Bulk Commodities Ltd* [1993] Ch. 77.

[135] See also Gabriel Moss QC, "Administration Orders for Foreign Companies" (1993) 6 Insolv. Int. 19; (1994) 7 Insolv. Int. 33; Dicey, Morris and Collins, *The Conflict of Laws*, 14th edn (London: Sweet & Maxwell, 2006), pp.1158–1159; Smart, *Cross-Border Insolvency*, 2nd edn (London: Butterworths, 1998), pp.130–136.

[136] *Re Dallhold Estates (UK) Pty Ltd* [1992] B.C.C. 394.

[137] s.735(1)(a) and (b) applied to the Insolvency Act 1986 by the Insolvency Act 1986, s.251. The corresponding provisions of the Companies Act 2006, now in force, are ss.1 and 1171.

It was seen in the context of discussion of administrative receivers[138] that it had been emphasised in *Re International Bulk Commodities Ltd*[139] that the definitions in the former s.735 of the Companies Act 1985 (currently contained in ss.1 and 1171 of the Companies Act 2006) apply unless the contrary intention appears. And there it was held that a receiver appointed in respect of a foreign company could be an administrative receiver since the provisions of the Insolvency Act 1986, which deal with the latter, could be construed as yielding such a contrary intention. Could a similar argument be mounted in relation to the making of an administration order?

Supporting a negative conclusion would be an argument to the effect that, since an administrator is solely a creature of English legislation, the administration procedure should apply only to companies created by that country's legislation. Here there is a contrast with the position of an administrative receiver since the latter's status originates in a contract and the English legislation merely ascribes particular powers to him.[140] It was, however, difficult to accept this argument with complete confidence because it tended to bypass the proper question which should be posed. That question was whether or not Parliament intended the power to appoint an administrator to exist in respect of foreign companies and the answer to that question must be deduced from the proper construction of the relevant statutory provisions.[141]

If one considers the statutory purpose for which an administration order may be made, it might be thought that an intention to extend such an order to foreign companies was indicated. An administrator has to perform his functions with the object of rescuing the company as a going concern, achieving a better result for creditors than is likely on a winding up, or realising property in order to make a distribution to secured or preferential creditors.[142] If the English court were to be presented with a problem concerning a company incorporated in Liberia which, while it had a sufficient connection to England to allow the making of a winding up order,[143] had neither a centre of main interests nor an establishment in England, and the survival of the company could be secured by the making of an administration order, why should such an order not have been capable of being made? The English court would have had jurisdiction to wind up the company, at least if there were creditors here who would receive a benefit if the company was wound up. Since a purpose of administration is to achieve a better result for creditors than on a winding-up, it was hard to see what reason of policy there might be for denying jurisdiction to make the administration order. The opposite conclusion would mean that the company might be killed but not cured, a proposition that does not accord with common sense.

The foregoing conclusion was perhaps reinforced when one considered that, according to *Re Dallhold Estates (UK) Pty Ltd*,[144] the English court has

[138] See above, paras 30–019 to 30–020.
[139] *Re International Bulk Commodities Ltd* [1993] Ch. 77.
[140] *Re International Bulk Commodities Ltd* [1993] Ch. 77, 85–86.
[141] *Re International Bulk Commodities Ltd* [1993] Ch. 77, 84–85.
[142] Insolvency Act 1986, Sch.B1, para.3(1); see above, Ch.6.
[143] See *Stocznia Gdanska SA v Latreefers Inc (No.2)* [2001] B.C.C. 174 (CA).
[144] *Re Dallhold Estates (UK) Pty Ltd* [1992] B.C.C. 394.

"indirect" jurisdiction under s.426 of the Insolvency Act 1986 to make the order on a request by a court of a designated country.[145] While one could accept that a court can do indirectly that which it has power to do directly, the proposition that the court may do indirectly what it cannot do directly is much more difficult to support even when, as in this case, that conclusion was expressed as the proper interpretation of relevant provisions of an English statute.[146]

If the above views were accepted, prior to April 2005 it was possible to argue (though admittedly, in the light of the authorities, with some hesitation) that the definition of company in s.735 of the Companies Act 1985 (then in force) did not apply since the original provisions of the Insolvency Act 1986 which related to administration orders revealed a contrary intention, viz that such orders might be made in respect of a foreign unregistered company. Whether such an order would be made would depend on whether it was appropriate in the circumstances of the particular case.[147] The state of uncertainty remained, however until Sch.B1 to the Insolvency Act 1986 was amended in the manner described next below.

30–024   *Since April 13, 2005.*   As a result of an amendment to Sch.B1 to the Insolvency Act 1986, company administrations are now expressly restricted to: (a) a company registered under the Companies Act 2006 in England and Wales or in Scotland; (b) a company incorporated in an EEA State other than the UK; and (c) a company incorporated outside the EEA but having its centre of main interests in a Member State of the European Union (except Denmark).[148]

This amendment retains the cross-reference to art.3 of the European Insolvency Regulation and it also allows administration orders for EEA registered companies, but otherwise leaves foreign registered companies outside the scope of the administration procedure. This is an illogical and retrograde step wholly out of keeping with the spirit of the rescue culture. There is no policy reason why a foreign company with a sufficient connection with the UK should not be capable of benefiting from administration proceedings under the English legislation. No doubt there will be scope for such a company to move its centre of main interests to a location within the EU (excluding Denmark) before applying.

---

[145] Insolvency Act 1986, s.426(5), (11).

[146] Insolvency Act 1986, s.426(5), (11).

[147] See above, Ch.6.

[148] Insolvency Act 1986, Sch.B1, paras 111(1A), 111(1B), inserted by the Insolvency Act 1986 (Amendment) Regulations 2005 (SI 2005/879), regs 2(1), 4(a), as from 13 April, 2005, thereby reversing the effect of the ruling in *Re The Salvage Association* [2004] 1 W.L.R. 174. By reg.2(3) an "EEA State" means a state that is a contracting party to the Agreement on the European Economic Area signed at Oporto on May 2, 1992. The EEA Agreement has the effect of liberalising trade between the states belonging to the EU and those belonging to the European Free Trade Association (EFTA). The latter group currently consists of Iceland, Liechtenstein and Norway. Note that in consequence of the provision in para.111(1A)(b) of Sch.B1 administration is available in the case of a company incorporated in Denmark (an EEA state), although that country is not participating in the EU Insolvency Regulation and is expressly excluded from the scope of para.111(1A)(c) (which is based on the location of the COMI).

(b)   Recognition of Foreign Appointment

Procedures of the same general nature as the administration procedure exist in   **30–025**
the insolvency laws of other countries. Particularly well-known in this respect
is the procedure established by Ch.11 of the United States Bankruptcy Code.[149]
The English court may be willing to recognise office-holders appointed under
Ch.11 under common law principles, and on that basis to give them the active
assistance of the English court so long as there is no prejudice to any creditor
in England and no provision of the Insolvency Act that would be infringed. In
the *Navigator Holdings* case,[150] a judgment of the Privy Council on appeal
from the Isle of Man, Lord Hoffmann said (at [22]):

> "At common law, their Lordships think it is doubtful whether assistance
> could take the form of applying provisions of the foreign insolvency law
> which form no part of the domestic system. But the domestic court must
> at least be able to provide assistance by doing whatever it could have done
> in the case of a domestic insolvency. The purpose of recognition is to
> enable the foreign office holder or the creditors to avoid having to start
> parallel insolvency proceedings and to give them the remedies to which
> they would have been entitled if the equivalent proceedings had taken
> place in the domestic forum."

Applying that principle, the Privy Council held that the Manx Court had power
to give effect to a provision of a Ch.11 plan transferring shares in a Manx
company to its creditors because there was jurisdiction to sanction a scheme of
arrangement having the same effect under the Companies Act in the Isle of
Man. The Privy Council's clear statement as to the nature and extent of the
common law powers inherent in recognition of foreign office-holders, and its
willingness to recognise a US rescue procedure in relation a Manx company,
may provide impetus to the further development of this jurisdiction in circumstances where s.426 and the UNCITRAL Model Law are inapplicable.[151] The
precise nature and circumstances in which relief may be obtained develops on
a case-by-case basis, but some guidance may be obtained from cases on
winding up. By analogy with winding up, an English court might regard the
courts of the place of incorporation[152] as having principal control but neverthe-

---

[149] Ch.11 procedure is described in *Cambridge Gas Transport Corp v Official Committee of
Unsecured Creditors of Navigator Holdings Plc* [2007] 1 A.C. 508 (PC); *Felixstowe Dock and
Railway Co v US Lines Inc* [1989] Q.B. 360, 366–370; Boshkoff in Fletcher (ed.), *Cross-Border
Insolvency: Comparative Dimensions* (UKNCCL, 1990), pp.60–64.

[150] *Cambridge Gas Transport Corp v Official Committee of Unsecured Creditors of Navigator
Holdings Plc* [2007] 1 A.C. 508 (PC).

[151] *Cambridge Gas Transport Corp v Official Committee of Unsecured Creditors of Navigator
Holdings Plc* [2007] 1 A.C. 508 (PC). See too *Banque Indosuez SA v Ferromet Resources Inc*
[1993] B.C.L.C. 112. See also *Re Phoenix Kapitaldienst GmbH* [2008] B.P.I.R. 1082.

[152] It can be noted that, in his judgment in *Re HIH Casualty & General Insurance Ltd*, decided
sub nom. *McGrath v Riddell* [2008] 1 W.L.R. 852 (HL), [31], Lord Hoffmann suggested that the
established test at English law for determining the seat of the principal liquidation of a company,
namely the company's domicile based upon its place of incorporation, might not necessarily be the
most suitable one to employ under modern conditions, and that the "centre of main interests"

less conduct an ancillary winding-up of the company in relation to its English assets in accordance with English law, while at the same time working in harmony with the foreign court at the place of incorporation. A case for recognition may be made if the procedure is instigated in a country where the company's central management and control is exercised, particularly if the company is incorporated elsewhere for reasons of legal or commercial convenience[153] and there is no likelihood of any action being taken, in relation to the company, in the country where it is incorporated.[154] Lastly, the case for recognition is relatively strong where the company itself petitions for an order analogous to an administration order in a country other than that in which it is incorporated since in such a case it can clearly be said that the company has submitted to the jurisdiction of the courts of that country.[155]

30–026   It is unlikely, however, that the English court will assist a foreign court using its common law powers if the assistance would interfere with the rights of creditors proving in England under the Insolvency Act. Where s.426 of the Insolvency Act is inapplicable, the power of the English court to interfere with a creditor's rights to a distribution in accordance with the statutory scheme is limited.[156] Similarly, the English court may also intervene to prevent a turnover of assets to be distributed in accordance with a foreign insolvency regime, even absent a formal insolvency in England. In *Felixstowe Dock and Railway Co v US Lines Inc*,[157] a US corporation carrying on business worldwide, and which was registered in England under the Companies Act 1985,[158] was undergoing reorganisation in the United States pursuant to Ch.11. In the United States, Ch.11 proceedings involve an automatic stay restraining all persons, including

---

concept, as used by the EU Insolvency Regulation, "may be more appropriate". See also Lord Hoffmann's earlier obiter dictum in delivering the judgment of the Privy Council in *Cambridge Gas* [2007] 1 A.C. 508 (PC), [19]: "It may be that the criteria for recognition should be wider, but that question does not arise in this case."

[153] cf. *Re A Company (No.00359 of 1987)* [1988] Ch. 210.

[154] See *Re Vocalion (Foreign) Ltd* [1932] 2 Ch. 196; *Re Azoff-Don Commercial Bank* [1954] Ch. 315; *Stocznia Gdanska SA v Latreefers Inc (No.2)* [2001] B.C.C. 174 (CA).

[155] Smart, *Cross-Border Insolvency*, 2nd edn (1998), pp.177–178. See also *Re International Power Industries Inc* [1985] B.C.L.C. 128; *Barclays Bank Plc v Homan* [1992] B.C.C. 757 (CA).

[156] See *Re Bank of Credit and Commerce International SA (No.10)* [1997] Ch. 213, applied at first instance in *Re HIH Casualty & General Insurance Ltd* [2006] 2 All E.R. 671. As indicated above in para.30–008, it is not thought that the decision of the Court of Appeal in the latter case ([2007] 1 All E.R. 177), in which *Re BCCI (No.10)* was distinguished where a request had been made under s.426 of the Insolvency Act 1986, casts doubt on this principle, though the position may be different if remission would bring countervailing benefits. Unfortunately, the divided opinions of the House of Lords delivered in the final appeal of the *HIH* case have seemingly left the matter in a state of uncertainty (see fn.25 above). See, however, *Re SwissAir Schweizerische Luftverkehr-AG* [2010] B.C.C. 667, which concluded that nothing in the ruling of the House of Lords in the *HIH* case would prevent the granting of common law assistance where there is no material difference in creditors' priority under the foreign law as compared to English insolvency law.

[157] *Felixstowe Dock and Railway Co v United States Lines Inc* [1989] Q.B. 360. For comment on this case see Ziegel in Lian et al. (eds.), *Current Developments in International Banking and Corporate Financial Operations* (Singapore: Butterworth & Co (Asia), 1989), p.313; Westbrook in Clarke (ed.), *Current Issues in Insolvency Law* (1991), p.27; Morse in Rajak (ed.), *Insolvency Law: Theory and Practice* (1993), pp.217–220; Dicey, Morris and Collins, *The Conflict of Laws*, 14th edn (London: Sweet & Maxwell, 2006), pp.1387–1389; Smart, *Cross-Border Insolvency*, 2nd edn (London: Butterworths, 1998), pp.177–178; Fletcher, *Insolvency in Private International Law*, 2nd edn (Oxford: Oxford University Press, 2005), paras 3.115–3.117.

[158] s.691.

those located outside the United States, from commencing or continuing proceedings against the corporation. The claimants, two English companies and a Dutch company, reacted to this by seeking and obtaining, in England, freezing injunctions against the company to prevent it removing its assets from the jurisdiction. The US corporation applied to have the injunction set aside so as to permit the English assets to be transferred to the United States and administered as part of the Ch.11 scheme. This application was refused.

According to Hirst J., "the court would in principle always wish to co-operate in every proper way with an order like the present [United States] one made by a court in a friendly jurisdiction".[159] He was urged to accept a proposition to the effect that since an English court possessed jurisdiction over an English company in similar circumstances, it should concede to the American court a jurisdiction which it claimed for itself—the so-called principle of comity or reciprocity. Hirst J. was not, however, prepared to discharge the injunction by reference to this principle. Discharge of the injunction would, in his view, have caused substantial prejudice to the claimants: the re-organisation of the company envisaged in the Ch.11 proceedings involved its discontinuing activities in the European market and in such circumstances, had the assets been repatriated to the United States, the claimants could have derived no real benefit since the assets would have been used to keep the company alive and as a going concern to pursue activities in the United States only. Hirst J. further doubted whether, in a converse set of circumstances, a United States court would have released assets situated in the United States with a view to their being repatriated to England for utilisation in an English administration procedure. It appears that the critical point which led Hirst J. to maintain the injunction was what he regarded as the discriminatory nature of the Ch.11 proceedings in that case, i.e. the benefiting of American creditors at the expense of European creditors.

8. ENGLISH RECEIVERS AND ADMINISTRATORS ACTING ABROAD

A receiver or an administrator, whether holding office by virtue of a direct **30–027** appointment or by way of appointment by the court, may seek to exercise his powers in a jurisdiction outside the United Kingdom. This section attempts to identify the difficulties which such appointees may face, largely by way of reference to receivers,[160] though some difficulties of the same or similar nature will also be faced by administrators.

In principle, a receiver appointed under English law in relation to the property of an English company which is situated in a foreign country and in consequence of the company having created a charge which, as created, is a floating

---

[159] *Felixstowe Dock and Railway Co v United States Lines Inc* [1989] Q.B. 360, 376. See also *Barclays Bank Plc v Homan* [1992] B.C.C. 757 (CA); *Hughes v Hannover* [1997] B.C.C. 921 (CA), 940.

[160] Dicey, Morris and Collins, *The Conflict of Laws*, 14th edn (London: Sweet & Maxwell, 2006), pp.1402–1404; Picarda, *Law Relating to Receivers Managers and Administrators*, 4th edn (London: Butterworths, 2006), pp.727–729, 733–735, and 742–743; Collins (1978) 27 I.C.L.Q. 691, 700–701, reprinted in *Essays in International Litigation and the Conflict of Laws* (1994), p.433.

charge will be free to exercise his powers in the foreign country only to the extent that the foreign country recognises the charge as valid and effective and regards the receiver as having the power so to act.[161]

Initially, a distinction must be drawn between the question whether, as a matter of English law, the charge extends to property abroad and the very different question whether the charge will be recognised in the foreign jurisdiction.[162] As to the first question, it is not in doubt that an English floating charge usually covers the assets of a company both present and future, irrespective of where the assets are located, so that the charge will extend to foreign assets. Thus, in *British South Africa Co v De Beers Consolidated Mines Ltd*,[163] it was held that an English debenture which purported to create a charge over all the property and assets of an English company operated in relation to the company's land abroad as an agreement to charge the land and thus was a valid equitable security in the eyes of English law. In *Re Anchor Line (Henderson Brothers) Ltd*[164] an English shipping company owned property located in Scotland. It executed a floating charge in Scotland over all of its undertaking, property and assets in favour of a Scottish bank, which charge was registered in England. At the time, floating charges were unknown to Scots law, which would give no effect to them.[165] When the company went into liquidation and its assets were sold off, the question arose whether, in the distribution of the proceeds, effect should be given to the floating charge to the extent that the proceeds of sale represented Scottish property. The question was answered in the affirmative and in consequence those proceeds were payable to the chargeholder. In effect, therefore, in consequence of the charge being governed by English law the English court may enforce it in personam even if it is not a valid and effective charge by the *lex situs*.[166]

30–028   Whatever the effect of the charge may be as a matter of English law, the charge may nonetheless not be recognised as valid and effective by the *lex situs* of the assets against which the receiver wishes to enforce it. The foreign jurisdiction may take exception to the charge on a number of grounds.

First, a receiver may be denied capacity to sue in the foreign jurisdiction either because his status is not recognised as such, or because his status, as a matter of English law, is different to that which he would possess under the law of the foreign country. Thus American courts have often said that, although it is incumbent on them as a matter of comity to enforce valid foreign voluntary

---

[161] Insolvency Act 1986, ss.72(1), 426(2).

[162] See Companies Act 2006, s.866(2) which envisages that in the case of charges registered in the United Kingdom "further proceedings may be necessary to make the charge valid or effectual according to the law of the country in which the property is situated". On the recognition of English floating charges in France, see Dahan, 1996 *Clunet* 381.

[163] *British South Africa Co v De Beers Consolidated Mines Ltd* [1910] 1 Ch. 354, affirmed [1910] 2 Ch. 502 (CA); reversed on other grounds [1912] A.C. 52 (HL).

[164] *Re Anchor Line (Henderson Brothers) Ltd* [1937] Ch. 483.

[165] Recognition was permitted by Companies (Floating Charges and Receivers) (Scotland) Act 1972. See now Bankruptcy and Diligence (Scotland) Act 2007, ss.38–47; Insolvency Act 1986, ss.50–71.

[166] See also *Re Commonwealth Agricultural Services Engineers Ltd* [1928] S.A.S.R. 343; Collins (1978) 27 I.C.L.Q. 691, 700–701, reprinted in *Essays in International Litigation and the Conflict of Laws* (1994), p.433.

assignments, such comity does not extend to enforcement when such enforcement prejudices US creditors.[167] Here there is a tendency in the American courts to confuse the English notion of a receiver with the notion of a court-appointed receiver in bankruptcy proceedings, which works to the disadvantage of receivers who seek to operate in the United States.[168] A less parochial attitude may operate in other foreign jurisdictions. Thus, in *Re CA Kennedy Co Ltd and Stibbe-Monk Ltd*,[169] an Ontario court was faced with competing claims to a debt owed to a company which had given a floating charge over its assets to an English bank. The debt was claimed by a judgment creditor under a Quebec judgment debt and by the receiver appointed by the bank. The court held that the priority of these competing claims had to be determined by the *lex situs* of the debt (asset) which was the law of Ontario. Expressly rejecting the somewhat hostile American attitude, the court accorded recognition to the appointment of the English receiver. Such recognition accords with the proper analysis of the receiver's status in English law. If, for conflict of laws purposes, a receiver could be viewed as an officer of the company, as a matter of principle, his powers and capacity to act should depend on the law of the place of incorporation.[170] It is arguable that, for conflict of laws' purposes, the receiver is an officer of the company although the Court of Appeal in England has held that under English domestic law he is not.[171] Moreover, a receiver, at least prior to liquidation, is an agent of the company[172] and his agency should be recognised, e.g. by analogy to the general recognition of a liquidator's agency.

A second and fatal difficulty is where the charge is repugnant to the law of the place where the assets of the company, claimed by the receiver, are situated. Thus, in *Carse v Coppen*,[173] it was conceded by the parties and accepted by the court that, since floating charges were at that time repugnant to Scots law, a Scottish court could not regard an English floating charge created by a Scottish company as affecting Scottish property. Indeed a majority of the Court of Session went further and held that the company could not create a valid charge over its English property either.

A third problem presents itself where the charge is ineffective because of a **30–029** failure to comply with mandatory requirements of the *lex situs*, particularly a

---

[167] See the discussion of these cases in *Re CA Kennedy Co Ltd and Stibbe-Monk Ltd* (1976) 74 D.L.R. (3d) 87, 95–96. See also Restatement, Second, *The Conflict of Laws*, s.406, comment (a); Collins, (1978) 27 I.C.L.Q. 691, 708–710, reprinted in *Essays in International Litigation and the Conflict of Laws* (1994), p.433, suggesting that a more liberal attitude is displayed by an American court in *Clarkson Co Ltd and Rapid Data Corporation v Rockwell International*, Supp. 792 (1977). cf. *Larkins v National Union of Mineworkers* [1985] I.R. 670, 683–684; *Derby & Co Ltd v Weldon (Nos 3 and 4)* [1990] Ch. 65 (CA), 84–86, 94, 96; *Derby & Co Ltd v Weldon* (No.6) [1990] 1 W.L.R. 1139, 1150 (CA).

[168] Collins, (1978) 27 I.C.L.Q. 691, 708–709, p.1.

[169] *Re CA Kennedy Co. Ltd and Stibbe-Monk Ltd* (1976) 74 D.L.R. (3d) 67.

[170] See Dicey, Morris and Collins, *The Conflict of Laws*, 14th edn (London, Sweet & Maxwell, 2006), pp.1399–1404.

[171] See Collins, (1978) 27 I.C.L.Q. 691, 707. The English Court of Appeal decision referred to is *Re B Johnson & Co (Builders) Ltd* [1955] Ch. 634 (CA).

[172] See above, Ch.15. After liquidation, a receiver no longer has his agency, but retains his power to dispose of its property.

[173] *Carse v Coppen* 1951 S.C. 233 (Court of Session, Inner House, 1 Div).

registration requirement. Prudence demands that where charges are created over the foreign property of a company, such charges should be registered in the country or countries where the property is situated if this is required by the law of that foreign country,[174] a course which is particularly difficult if the property has moved from one country to another in the time between the creation of the charge and the attempt to enforce it in a different foreign country. In *Luckins v Highway Motel (Caernarvon) Pty Ltd*,[175] a company incorporated in Victoria, which carried on the business of coach tour operator, conducted tours which passed through Western Australia where debts were incurred by the company for, amongst other things, food and accommodation. The company had created a floating charge over all its asset wherever situated, the charge being registered in Victoria but not in Western Australia. Subsequently the charge crystallised and a receiver was appointed in Victoria. A Western Australian creditor obtained a judgment against the company in Western Australia and sought to execute that judgment through seizure of a bus belonging to the company which was then situated in Western Australia. The receiver claimed that the bus was subject to the receivership. The High Court of Australia held that, if the charge was validly created over the bus by the law of the State where it was situated at the time of such creation, the charge was in principle capable of being recognised in Western Australia.[176] But such recognition was subject to compliance with the mandatory requirements of Western Australian law. By incurring various debts in Western Australia, the company could be held to be doing business there. This being the case, there was an obligation to register the charge in accordance with Western Australian legislation. It is, of course, implicit in this conclusion that, were there no obligation to register the charge in that State, the charge would have been valid and effective over property situated there at the time when it was sought to enforce the charge.

Where the charge does not gain recognition in the foreign country where the assets are situated, a further consequence is that the English court will not, at the instance of the debenture-holders, restrain a creditor from bringing proceedings to recover a debt in a foreign country out of assets which are situated there. This much appears from *Liverpool Marine Credit Co v Hunter*[177] where it was held that mortgagees of a ship were not entitled in English proceedings to prevent an English unsecured creditor of the owner of the ship from arresting the ship in New Orleans since the mortgage would not be recognised under the law of Louisiana. This decision was applied in *Re Maudslay, Sons & Field*,[178] where an English company created a charge over its assets which included a sum of money owed to it by a French company. A receiver was appointed by debenture-holders. An English creditor of the company sought to attach the debt owed by the French company in France, the response to which was an action in England by the debenture-holders to restrain the creditor from so

---

[174] See Companies Act 2006, s.866(2) referred to in para.30–027, above.
[175] *Luckins v Highway Motel (Caernarvon) Pty Ltd* (1975) 133 C.L.R. 164.
[176] *Luckins v Highway Motel (Caernarvon) Pty Ltd* (1975) 133 C.L.R. 164, 174–175.
[177] *Liverpool Marine Credit Co v Hunter* (1867–68) L.R.3 Ch. App. 479 (CA).
[178] *Re Maudslay, Sons & Field* [1900] 1 Ch. 602.

proceeding. According to French law, the debt could only be charged effectively as against the French company if the charge was registered in France and notice of it was given to the French company. No such registration or notice was effected. The court refused to make an order in favour of the debenture-holders. The fact that the receiver was appointed could not affect the position which would normally prevail and in which the creditor would be free to pursue a claim in France since, in the absence of registration and notice required by French law, the receiver had not perfected his title to the assets according to French law.

Where a creditor has obtained an English judgment against the company **30–030** prior to the appointment of a receiver, if the charge subsequently crystallises and a receiver is appointed, the judgment will be unenforceable against the company in England.[179] In such circumstances the creditor may seek to enforce the judgment in a foreign country where the company has assets. The courts of that country may be prepared to recognise the judgment and enforce it despite the existence of the English charge, either because that country does not recognise floating charges as such, or, if it does recognise them, because the charge has not been registered as required by that country's law.[180]

Lastly, in the case of a receiver appointed by the court, a foreign jurisdiction may decline to recognise a receiver's appointment because it is interlocutory[181] or more generally because the appointment is made pursuant to a rule of English law which is regarded by the foreign court as being penal in nature.[182]

An English receiver or administrator may seek to take legal action abroad **30–031** with a view to giving greater effect to the receivership or administration of the company. In *Barclays Bank Plc v Homan*,[183] an English registered company, Maxwell Communications Corporation Plc, was subject to an administration order in England. The company had repaid to Barclays Bank, shortly before the administration order was made, the sum of US $30 million to pay off the overdraft on its account with the Holborn branch of Barclays. The money was initially paid into Barclay's New York branch using funds raised from the sale of a US subsidiary, and then paid to the Holborn branch. This payment constituted a potentially voidable preference under s.239(4) of the Insolvency Act 1986, since it put the bank into a better position than it would otherwise have been in the event of the company being liquidated. According to s.239(5) of the 1986 Act, a court is not to make an order for the repayment unless the debtor company was influenced by a desire to put the creditor in a better position. The bank took the view that it might be able to rely on this defence.

---

[179] *Norton v Yates* [1906] 1 K.B. 112; *Davey & Co v Williamson & Sons* [1898] 2 Q.B. 194; and see above, para.14–006.

[180] See the decision of the French Cour de Cassation of October 19, 1977 in (1978) Rev Crit. DIP. 617. See also, Dahan, 1996 *Clunet* 381. cf. *Mitchell v Carter* [1997] B.C.C. 71; *Mitchell v Buckingham International Plc (No.2)* [1998] B.C.C. 943 (CA).

[181] *Larkins v National Union of Mineworkers* [1985] I.R. 671. See above, para.30–018.

[182] *Larkins v National Union of Mineworkers* [1985] I.R. 671 cf. *Schemmer v Property Resources Ltd* [1975] Ch. 273, above, paras 30–017 to 30–018.

[183] *Barclays Bank Plc v Homan* [1992] B.C.C. 757 (CA). See also *Re Bank of Credit and Commerce International SA (No.9)* [1994] 1 W.L.R. 708 (CA).

The administrators brought proceedings against the bank in the United States (where there were also proceedings under Ch.11 of the United States Bankruptcy Code and where the principal assets of the company were situated) with a view to recovering the US $30 million. Section 547 of the United States Bankruptcy Code has much the same effect as s.239 of the English Insolvency Act 1986 as regards the definition of a preference but does not contain a provision equivalent to s.239(5) of the 1986 Act. Accordingly, in US proceedings, the intention of the debtor company in making the payment would be irrelevant. The bank therefore sought, in these English proceedings, to restrain the administrators from making this claim in the United States.

The Court of Appeal held that the principles to be applied in determining whether an injunction should be granted were those generally applicable to determining the issue of whether a plaintiff should be prevented, by order, from proceeding in a foreign jurisdiction. According to these principles,[184] if the only issue was whether an English or a foreign court was the most appropriate forum for the action, the foreign court should decide it on the principle of forum non conveniens and the English court should not interfere. But if the English court concluded that pursuit of the action in the foreign court would be vexatious and oppressive and that England was the natural forum, it could properly grant an injunction restraining the claimant from pursuing the foreign proceedings. Whether the action abroad was vexatious or oppressive depended on the possible injustice to the defendant if the injunction was not granted and the possible injustice to the claimant if it was: in determining the outcome, the English court had to balance these factors.

The bank had argued that it would be at a disadvantage in the United States because of the absence of a provision equivalent to s.239(5) of the Insolvency Act 1986 in s.547 of the United States Bankruptcy Code, and that this rendered proceedings in the United States vexatious or oppressive. This contention was rejected. The disadvantage to the bank had to be balanced against the advantage to the English administrator in proceeding in the United States on behalf of all the company's creditors. Although United States law was different from English law, there was nothing inherently oppressive about the difference, particularly in light of the fact that United States law might be more favourable to the bank in other respects. Accordingly, the administrators were free to pursue the claim in the United States.[185]

Were a receiver to seek to bring proceedings abroad with a view to obtaining an advantage under a foreign law, the same principles would presumably apply.

---

[184] Established in *SNI Aerospatiale v Lee Kui Jak* [1987] A.C. 871 (PC). And see *Airbus Industrie GIE v Patel* [1999] 1 A.C. 119 (HL).

[185] Other factors relevant to the exercise of the court's discretion were that an injunction might have been wholly ineffective because the examiner on behalf of M.C.C. could have been authorised by the US court to bring the preference claim and that the forum non conveniens point could have been raised by the bank in the US Bankruptcy Court proceedings. In fact the US declined to apply US law.

9. JUDICIAL ASSISTANCE

Reference has already been made to the duty of mutual assistance which exists **30–032** between courts within the United Kingdom in matters of insolvency law, the definition of which includes the law relating to administrative receivers and administrators.[186] The relevant section of the Insolvency Act 1986, namely s.426, goes beyond the intra-United Kingdom dimension and provides a powerful and flexible means by which the English court has power to assist the courts of a limited number of foreign jurisdictions.[187]

The key provisions of s.426 as applied to international cases are subss.(4) and (5):

"(4) The courts having jurisdiction in relation to insolvency law in any part of the United Kingdom shall assist the courts having the corresponding jurisdiction in any other part of the United Kingdom or any relevant country or territory.

(5) For the purposes of subs.(4) a request made to a court in any part of the United Kingdom or in a relevant country or territory is authority for the court to which the request is made to apply, in relation to any matters specified in the request, the insolvency law which is applicable by either court in relation to comparable matters falling within its jurisdiction.

In exercising its discretion under this subsection a court shall have regard, in particular, to the rules of private international law."

A number of comments must be made on the scope of these subsections.

(a) Territorial scope

Although on its face s.426(4) seems to establish an obligation to provide rele- **30–033** vant assistance, in international cases (as opposed to intra-United Kingdom cases) the obligation only extends to a "relevant country or territory". Relevant country or territory means, for these purposes, any of the Channel Islands,[188] the Isle of Man and any country or territory designated for the purpose of the subsection by the Secretary of State. Orders have been made designating

---

[186] Insolvency Act 1986, s.426(1), (4), (5) and (10).

[187] For general discussion, see Dicey, Morris and Collins, *The Conflict of Laws*, 14th edn (London: Sweet & Maxwell, 2006), pp.1389–1397; Fletcher, *The Law of Insolvency*, 4th edn (2009), paras 31–006 to 31–015; Fletcher, *Insolvency in Private International Law*, 2nd edn (Oxford: Oxford University Press, 2005), Ch.4, paras 4.04 to 4.26; Smart, *Cross-Border Insolvency*, 2nd edn (London: Butterworths, 1998), Ch.15; Woloniecki (1986) 35 I.C.L.Q. 644; Polonsky (1996) 113 S.A.L.J. 109.

[188] The relevant provisions of s.426 may be extended to any of the Channel Islands thus enabling courts in any jurisdiction to which the section is extended to provide assistance to English courts in matters of receivership, administration or liquidation: Insolvency Act 1986, s.442; see SI 1989/2409 extending s.426(4), (5), (10) and (11) of the 1986 Act, with modifications, to Guernsey: see *Re Seagull Manufacturing Co Ltd* [1993] Ch. 345 (CA). As to Jersey, see Dessain (1998) 11 Insolv. Int. 25.

various countries.[189] The provisions, in terms, impose an obligation on English courts to provide assistance to any relevant country or territory and do not require proof of any reciprocity. It would be in accordance with the policy of the legislation that in deciding whether to designate any particular country or territory, the Secretary of State should have regard to the probability of the English courts obtaining assistance from the courts of that country or territory in comparable matters.[190]

(b) Duty to assist arises between courts

30-034 The duty of assistance under s.426 arises only as between courts. Accordingly, before the English court can act it must have received a request from a relevant foreign court so to act,[191] so that a foreign receiver or administrator (or liquidator for that matter) cannot approach the English court directly. It seems likely that any foreign court in which insolvency proceedings have been commenced (provided it is in a designated country or territory) may request assistance though the English court may, in its discretion, decline the assistance requested if the foreign country is not recognised by the English court as possessing, say, the authority to appoint a receiver or an administrator.

(c) Meaning of "insolvency law"

30-035 Section 426(5) provides that a request from a foreign court is authority for the English court to apply, in relation to the "matters specified in the request",[192] either English insolvency law or the insolvency law of the requesting court in relation to comparable matters.[193] For these purposes, "insolvency law" means, in relation to England and Wales, provision made by or under the Insolvency

---

[189] SI 1986/2123 designates Anguilla, Australia, The Bahamas, Bermuda, Botswana, Canada, Cayman Islands, Falkland Islands, Gibraltar, Hong Kong, Ireland, Montserrat, New Zealand, St Helena, Turks and Caicos Islands, Tuvalu and the Virgin Islands. SI 1996/253 designates Malaysia and South Africa. SI 1998/2766 designates Brunei-Darussallam.

[190] See *Hughes v Hannover* [1997] B.C.C. 921 (CA), 932–933; *England v Smith*; sub nom. *Re Southern Equities Corp Ltd* [2001] Ch. 419 (CA).

[191] It must be emphasised that s.426 only extends to incoming request for assistance. It does not enable an English court to request assistance from a court in a relevant country or territory: cf. *McIsaac, Petitioners* [1994] B.C.C. 410. On the seeking of such assistance by English courts, see now art.1(2)(b) and (c) of Sch.1 to the Cross-Border Insolvency Regulations 2006 (SI 2006/1030), enacting for Great Britain the UNCITRAL Model Law on Cross-Border Insolvency. The 2006 Regulations are dealt with in Ch.31, below. Other more generally applicable co-operative procedures may become relevant in insolvency cases; see, e.g. Evidence (Proceedings in other Jurisdictions) Act 1975; *Re International Power Industries NV* [1985] B.C.L.C. 128.

[192] A letter of request in entirely general terms will be ineffective to trigger the jurisdiction of the English court under s.426: *Fourie v Le Roux* [2007] 1 W.L.R. 320 (H), 57–60 (per Blackburne J.). There was no appeal on this point: see *Fourie v Le Roux* [2007] 1 W.L.R. 320 (HL).

[193] *Re Dallhold Estates (UK) Pty Ltd* [1992] B.C.C. 394; *Re Bank of Credit and Commerce International SA (No.9)* [1994] 3 All E.R. 764, reversed in part, but not on this point, [1994] 1 W.L.R. 708 (CA); *Re Focus Insurance Co Ltd* [1996] B.C.C. 659; *Re Business City Express Ltd* [1997] B.C.C. 826; *Hughes v Hannover* [1997] B.C.C. 921 (CA); *Re JN Taylor Finance Pty Ltd* [1999] B.C.C. 197; *England v Smith, Re Southern Equities Corp Ltd* [2001] Ch. 419 (CA). A foreign law may be applied even though it would necessarily disapply a provision of English law: *Re HIH Casualty & General Insurance Ltd* [2008] 1 W.L.R. 852 (HL).

Act 1986 as well as certain provisions of the Company Directors Disqualification Act 1986.[194] The expression thus includes the English law relating to administrative receivership and administration.[195] In relation to any relevant country or territory the expression means so much of the law of that country or territory as corresponds to the provisions referred to above.[196] In *Hughes v Hannover Ruckversicherungs AG*[197] it was held by the Court of Appeal that for the purposes of s.426(5) the above definitions of insolvency law were exhaustive.[198] The court indicated that s.426(4) which refers to "courts having *jurisdiction in relation to insolvency law in any part of the United Kingdom*"[199] only served, in its use of the expression "insolvency law", to identify the court on which the obligation to provide assistance was imposed.[200] It did not indicate that the English court could only apply insolvency law as defined for the purposes of s.426(5).[201] As s.426(5) added to rather than restricted the power to assist under s.426(4), the latter section enabled the English court when requested for assistance to exercise its own general jurisdiction and powers, whilst s.426(5) enabled the court to apply the insolvency law of England and Wales as defined in the Insolvency Act 1986, or so much of the law of a relevant country or territory as corresponds to it.

The reference to "insolvency law" is apt to include both substantive and procedural insolvency law.[202] When, however, an English court is requested to provide assistance in the form of application of relevant principles of foreign insolvency law, issues may arise as to when a rule of foreign insolvency law "corresponds" to a relevant provision of English insolvency law. First, it has been held by the Court of Appeal that in discharging the obligation to provide assistance to a foreign liquidator engaged in the gathering of information, the court should apply any principles, practices or discretions that the court requesting the assistance would apply in exercising its powers under the foreign law.[203]

In such circumstances, application of the law of the requesting court should not be circumscribed by limitations to be found in the corresponding provisions

---

[194] Insolvency Act 1986, s.426(10)(a).

[195] *Re Dallhold Estates (UK) Pty Ltd* [1992] B.C.C. 394.

[196] Insolvency Act 1986, s.426(10)(d).

[197] *Hughes v Hannover* [1997] B.C.C. 921 (CA).

[198] *Hughes v Hannover* [1997] B.C.C. 921 (CA), 937. Thus liquidators could not obtain an order to restrain proceedings against the company under Insolvency Act 1986, s.130(2), since that section may not be used to restrain foreign proceedings and the same territorial limitation was imposed under Bermudan law, the law of the requesting court: *Hughes v Hannover* [1997] B.C.C. 921 (CA), 941: see *Re Vocalion (Foreign) Ltd* [1932] 2 Ch. 196.

[199] Emphasis added.

[200] *Hughes v Hannover* [1997] B.C.C. 921 (CA), 937.

[201] *Hughes v Hannover* [1997] B.C.C. 921 (CA), 937–938.

[202] *Re Bank of Credit and Commerce International SA (No.9)* [1994] 3 All E.R. 764, reversed in part, but not on this point, [1994] 1 W.L.R. 708 (CA).

[203] *Re Southern Equities Corp Ltd, England v Smith* [2001] Ch. 419 (CA), disapproving *Re JN Taylor Finance Pty Ltd* [1999] B.C.C. 197. cf. *Re HIH Casualty & General Insurance Ltd* [2007] 1 All E.R. 177 (CA), where the English court, exercising its discretion on the basis of the information placed before it at that stage, refused to remit assets to Australia for distribution in accordance with Australian insolvency law. On appeal to the House of Lords, their Lordships were unanimously of the view that s.426 supplied authority for the exercise of the discretion to remit the assets to Australia: [2008] 1 W.L.R. 852 (HL).

of the insolvency law of England,[204] unless some principle of English public policy would be infringed were the foreign law to be applied according to its terms. Secondly, foreign insolvency law need not be identical to English insolvency law to correspond to it and indeed, it may be possible for an English court to exercise powers under foreign insolvency law which are not available to the court under English law. Thus, in *Re Business City Express Ltd*[205] a request for assistance was received from an Irish court in which the English court was asked to make a scheme of arrangement, entered into in Ireland after a company had gone into examinership there, binding upon English creditors. There was no provision of English law by which this could be done. The court applied Irish law to the creditors without discussing the question of whether Irish law corresponded to any provision made by or under the Insolvency Act 1986. Nonetheless, it seems appropriate in the light of the policy behind s.426[206] to give the expression "corresponds" a broad interpretation. In the particular context of *Re Business City Express Ltd*, it can be readily said that examinership in Irish law corresponds to English administration and that the appointment of an administrator may, but will not necessarily, lead to the approval of a creditor's voluntary arrangement or the sanctioning of a scheme of arrangement. This should surely be enough to enable it to be said that Irish Law "corresponds" to English law. As explained below, it is, however, open to the court in any particular case to determine whether it is appropriate, in the light of the matters specified in the request, for the court to exercise its discretion to provide the assistance requested under the relevant foreign law.

(d) Nature of the duty to assist

30–036 Section 426(4) requires, in terms, that the English court "shall assist" the foreign court which issues the request for assistance. Despite the apparently mandatory tone of this language, the court is not bound to accede to the assistance requested.[207] The correct approach is to consider whether the requested assistance can properly be granted,[208] so that the appropriate assistance (including whether to apply English law or that of the requesting court) is

---

[204] *Re Southern Equities Corp Ltd* [2001] Ch. 419 (CA). It was held that an English court should accede to a request from the Supreme Court of South Australia see king examination of a person allegedly concerned with the affairs of a company under Australia Corporations Law, s.596B notwithstanding the fact that such an order would not be made under the corresponding (but different) provision of Insolvency Act 1986, s.236 because the order would be regarded as oppressive. Contrast *Re JN Taylor Finance Pty Ltd* [1999] B.C.C. 197 where such an order under the same section of the Australian Law was denied because it would not have been granted under s.236.

[205] *Re Business City Express Ltd* [1997] B.C.C. 826.

[206] *Re Southern Equities Corp Ltd* [2001] Ch. 419 (CA).

[207] *Re Dallhold Estates (UK) Pty Ltd* [1992] B.C.C. 394; *Re Bank of Credit and Commerce International SA (No.9)* [1994] 3 All E.R. 764, reversed in part, but not on this point, [1994] 1 W.L.R. 708 (CA); *Re Focus Insurance Co Ltd* [1996] B.C.C. 659; *Re Business City Express Ltd* [1997] B.C.C. 826; *Hughes v Hannover* [1997] B.C.C. 921 (CA); *Re Southern Equities Corp Ltd, England v Smith* [2001] Ch. 419 (CA); *Re HIH Casualty & General Insurance Ltd* [2007] 1 All E.R. 177 (CA), 200, [52].

[208] *Hughes v Hannover* [1997] B.C.C. 921 (CA); *Re Southern Equities Corp Ltd, England v Smith* [2001] Ch. 419 (CA).

ultimately a matter for the discretion of the court. Section 426(5) and the case law provides guidance as to how the discretion should be exercised. First, the court should comply with the request if it may properly do so. Secondly, this will involve a consideration of all the circumstances including, for example, whether the relief sought will prejudice the creditors or any class of them and whether there would be other advantages sufficient to counteract such prejudice.[209] The circumstances which are of particular relevance are likely to vary depending upon the relief sought. Thirdly, the court is required, by the second sentence of s.426(5) to have regard in particular to the rules of private international law. However, while this provision may be important in circumstances where there is an obviously relevant principle of private international law,[210] it has been stigmatized as obscure and ill-thought out[211] and may often have no effect on the exercise of the English court's discretion. Fourthly, where the English court has to decide whether to apply English insolvency law or that of the requesting court pursuant to s.426(5), the starting point will be the policy and principles of English law.[212] It is for the party seeking to justify a departure from English law, whether by reference to private international law or otherwise. Fifthly, the English court is therefore unlikely to assist if acting pursuant to the request would infringe English public policy, though the English court should be particularly careful before concluding that the law of a relevant country or territory bore this stigma.

(e) Particular examples

The English court has applied many different provisions of English law at the **30–037** request of a foreign court. It has made an administration order over a foreign company.[213] It has applied Pt I of the Insolvency Act (dealing with company voluntary arrangements) to a foreign company.[214] It has applied the provisions of the Insolvency Act 1986 concerning transactions at an undervalue[215] when

---

[209] *Re HIH Casualty & General Insurance Ltd* [2007] 1 All E.R. 177 (CA), 200, [52]. The degree of connection to England of the person in respect of whom the requesting court invites the English court to give assistance is a consideration which is material to the exercise of the English court's discretion: *Fourie v Le Roux* [2007] 1 W.L.R. 320 (HL).

[210] e.g. if a request for assistance were to be received from a foreign court and the effect of acceding to the request would be to enforce that country's penal or revenue laws in England, the English court might refuse to accede to the request having regard to the well-established rule of private international law that an English court will not enforce a foreign penal or revenue law. See *Al Sabah v Grupo Torras* [2005] 2 A.C. 333 (PC), 355, [47]. In relation to the exclusionary rule concerning foreign revenue laws, however, the terms of enactment of the UNCITRAL Model Law on Cross-Border Insolvency within the United Kingdom have removed that ground of exclusion from having any application in relation to creditors' rights of participation in British insolvency proceedings: see art.13 of Sch.1 to the Cross-Border Insolvency Regulations 2006 (SI 2006/1030), discussed in Ch.31, below.

[211] *Re HIH Casualty & General Insurance Ltd* [2007] 1 All E.R. 177 (CA), 200, [52], adopting the observation of Lawrence Collins J. in *Re Television Trade Rentals Ltd* [2002] B.C.C. 807, [17].

[212] *Re HIH Casualty & General Insurance Ltd* [2007] 1 All E.R. 177 (CA), [70].

[213] *Re Dallhold Estates (UK) Pty Ltd* [1992] B.C.C. 394.

[214] *Re Television Trade Rentals Ltd* [2002] B.C.C. 807.

[215] *Re Bank of Credit and Commerce International SA (No.9)*, [1994] 3 All E.R. 764 reversed, but not on this point, [1994] 1 W.L.R. 708 (CA).

requested so to act by a foreign court.[216] The English court has held that the provisions of the Insolvency Act 1986 concerned with fraudulent and wrongful trading[217] may be applied under s.426.[218] A request pursuant to s.426 may persuade the court to order examination of an officer of a company under s.236 of the 1986 Act[219] and, where appropriate, the court may also order production of documents.[220] The English court also has the opportunity, in consequence of a request from a court in a designated country or territory, to apply its general powers, e.g. to grant an injunction.[221]

The English court has also applied provisions of the law of the requesting court. In *Smith v England*, the Court of Appeal made an order requiring examination of a person pursuant to s.596B of the Australian Corporations Law, even though such an order would not have been made under the corresponding (but different) provisions of s.236 of the Insolvency Act 1986.[222] In addition, s.426 has been used to allow a South African liquidator to bring proceedings in England under the South African provisions similar to ss.213 and 423 of the Insolvency Act.[223] Section 426 has also been applied to render a foreign scheme of arrangement binding on English creditors because it would have this binding character under foreign law despite the fact that the scheme could not be made binding under English law.[224]

In *Re HIH Casualty & General Insurance Ltd*[225] the House of Lords, reversing the decisions reached by the courts below, held that there was authority under s.426 for the English court to respond to a request by the Supreme Court of New South Wales that English provisional liquidators of Australian insurance companies should remit assets that they had collected to Australia for distribution in accordance with Australian insolvency law, where the effect of such a distribution would have been to prejudice all creditors of save for the Australian insurance creditors. The case is of importance in demonstrating that, while under s.426 the English court may be able to assist a foreign court in the collection of the assets of, an insolvent company, and also to remit such assets as are found in England even where such assistance will interfere with the rights of creditors to participate in the distribution of the insolvent estate, there remains an unresolved divergence of opinion among the judiciary sitting at the highest appellate level regarding the extent to which the English court can exercise such power at common law in cases where s.426 cannot

---

[216] Insolvency Act 1986, s.238. No doubt other provisions of the 1986 Act which are concerned with the adjustment of prior transactions will also be applied in appropriate cases: Insolvency Act 1986, ss.239–246, 423–424. See *Jyske Bank (Gibraltar) Ltd v Spjeldnaes* [2000] B.C.C. 16.

[217] Insolvency Act 1986, ss.212–214.

[218] *Re Bank of Credit and Commerce SA (No.9)* [1994] 1 W.L.R. 708 (CA).

[219] See *Re JN Taylor Finance Pty Ltd* [1999] B.C.C. 197; *Re Southern Equities Corp Ltd, England v Smith* [2001] Ch. 419 (CA).

[220] See *Bell Group Finance Pty Ltd v Bell Group (UK) Holdings Ltd* [1996] B.C.C. 505. See also *Re Mid East Trading Ltd* [1998] 1 All E.R. 577 (CA).

[221] Insolvency Act 1986, s.426(4); *Hughes v Hannover* [1997] B.C.C. 921 (CA).

[222] *Smith v England* [2001] Ch. 419 (CA), applied in *Duke Group Ltd v Carver* [2001] B.P.I.R. 459.

[223] *Fourie v Le Roux* [2007] 1 W.L.R. 320 (CA).

[224] *Re Business City Express Ltd* [1997] B.C.C. 826.

[225] *Re HIH Casualty & General Insurance Ltd* [2007] 1 All E.R. 177 (CA) dismissing an appeal from the decision of David Richards J. [2006] 2 All E.R. 671.

apply.[226] It may be asserted with confidence however that, in the absence of any factor within the foreign insolvency law representing a marked divergence from the accepted standards embodied in the English law and its statutory principles, there is nothing in the *HIH* decision of the House of Lords to suggest that the English court is precluded from exercising its common law power to remit assets for administration or distribution under a foreign insolvency proceeding which is taking place in a country whose jurisdiction over the matter is recognised according to English law.[227] A subsequent example of the successful use of s.426 has been in the direct enforcement of an Australian judgment arising from a preference avoidance action brought by the Australian liquidator.[228]

(f) Informal co-operation

The formal procedures available under s.426 of the Insolvency Act 1986 do not **30–038** preclude voluntary co-operation between officers appointed under the laws of different countries where a company may be undergoing re-organisation or liquidation. Indeed such co-operation may be of great practical value in "global" insolvencies.[229]

---

[226] *Re HIH Casualty & General Insurance Ltd* [2008] 1 W.L.R. 852 (HL). Two of their Lordships (Lord Hoffmann, with whom Lord Walker agreed) declared that in cases where concurrent liquidations were taking place there was long-settled authority to the effect that the English court has power to disapply elements of the statutory insolvency scheme, whereas two other members of the Appellate Committee (Lords Scott and Neuberger) were of the opinion that no such power existed at common law. However, all five members of the Committee were in agreement that such power exists where s.426 of the Act of 1986 is applicable.

[227] *Re SwissAir Schweizerische Luftverkehr-AG* [2010] B.C.C. 667.

[228] *New Cap Reinsurance Corp Ltd (In Liquidation) v Grant* [2011] EWCA Civ 971 (CA).

[229] See *Re Bank of Credit and Commerce International SA (No.2)* [1992] B.C.L.C. 579 (CA); *Re Bank of Credit and Commerce International SA (No.3)* [1993] B.C.L.C. 106; *Re Bank of Credit and Commerce International SA (No.10)* [1997] Ch. 213; *Re Maxwell Communications Corporation Plc* [1993] 1 W.L.R. 1402; *Barclays Bank Plc v Homan* [1992] B.C.C. 757 (CA); *Re Maxwell Communications Corporation Plc*, 93 F. 2d 1036 (1996); Fletcher [1997] J.B.L. 471.

Chapter 31

The EC Regulation on Insolvency Proceedings

1. Introduction: Nature and Purpose OF THE REGULATION

31–001 In Pt I of this chapter the European Union Regulation on Insolvency Proceedings will be considered, with particular regard to the impact on receiverships and administrations in which there is an international dimension.[1] The Regulation was adopted by the Council of the European Union pursuant to powers contained in the Treaty Establishing the European Community. It is accordingly referred to in this chapter as the "EC Regulation". For those already familiar with the principal characteristics of a cross-border insolvency, and the typical problems confronting the insolvency practitioner, the European Union (formerly known as the European Community)[2] introduces a special range of issues and complexities. The fundamental principles of the Union, based upon the concept of a unified internal market, may be brought into play in various ways during the course of an international insolvency. Typical problems include: the incompatibility of different national systems of insolvency law; legal and procedural obstacles to recognition of the office-holder's standing to represent the collectivised interests in the insolvent estate and to assert claims to the debtor's foreign assets; and the numerous possibilities for exploitative behaviour by creditors and debtors alike. Into this latter category fall such practices as the ring-fencing of assets for the exclusive advantage of a restricted sub-group of creditors linked to a specific country; the utilisation of so-called "bankruptcy havens" for the purpose of defeating attempts to gather and administer property on a collective basis; and the potential for creditors to experience discriminatory treatment in consequence of their location in different jurisdictions. These, and related issues, are the subject of a copious doctrinal literature reflecting a wide diversity of

---

[1] Council Regulation (EC) No.1346/2000 on insolvency proceedings [2000] OJ L160/1 is reproduced below in Appendix 3.

[2] In this chapter, the abbreviations "EU" and "EC" are employed, together with the convenient form of reference to "the Union", etc. The term "liquidator" is used throughout this chapter in the special sense employed by the EC Regulation itself, namely "any person or body whose function is to administer or liquidate assets of which the debtor has been divested or to supervise the administration of his affairs" (art.2(b)). Annex C to the Regulation lists, for each participating Member State, the office holders to which this definition applies. For the United Kingdom the list is as follows: "Liquidator; Supervisor of a Voluntary Arrangement; Administrator; Official Receiver; Trustee; Provisional Liquidator; Judicial Factor." The most recent versions of Annexes A, B and C were generated by an amending Regulation of June 9, 2011: Council Implementing Regulation (EU) No.583/2011, [2011] OJ L160/52.

approaches.[3] Although a consideration of the doctrinal aspects of the subject lies outside the scope of this chapter, it should be noted that these have had an important influence on the evolving saga of the EU insolvency project, and that the provisions of the Regulation are in many cases the outcome of a delicate process of achieving a consensus among negotiators from the then 15 Member States which, between them, represented most of the possible schools of thought about insolvency law and policy in both its domestic and international aspects.

The doctrinal disagreements referred to above extend to such fundamental   **31–002** questions as the very admissibility of the principle of parallel—or concurrent—insolvency proceedings in relation to the same debtor. Problems of fair treatment of parties in interest, especially in relation to expectations reasonably formed in a pre-insolvency context, are encountered irrespective of the approach favoured—whether unitary or pluralist. If the attempt is made to subject all parties to the insolvency system of a single state, this can result in the defeat of expectations for parties whose dealings with the debtor were based on alternative assumptions as to governing law. On the other hand, if it is conceded that multiple insolvency proceedings may take place to reflect the debtor's significant connections with different legal systems, there are associated problems of how to ensure fairness in the treatment of different groups of creditors with a view to minimising any arbitrary discrimination between them. This can entail a recourse to what are, in essence, basic equitable principles including the so-called "hotchpot" principle and the rule against double proof by a creditor in respect of what is in reality one and the same claim.[4]

The need to address such problems was foreseen by the authors of the original Treaty of Rome,[5] and special provision was made in art.220 requiring the Member States to conclude conventions on a number of matters, including:

"–the simplification of formalities governing the reciprocal recognition and enforcement of judgments of courts and of arbitration awards."

The obligation imposed by art.220(4) was interpreted as a command to address all categories of civil and commercial legal business, including insolvency matters. By a further leap of vision, proper regulation of the processes of recognition and enforcement was deemed to necessitate the imposition of a mandatory framework of rules to control the exercise of jurisdiction by courts throughout the Member States. This resulted in the development of the "direct" or "double" convention as the instrument of choice. Non-insolvency matters

[3] See, e.g. I.F. Fletcher, *Insolvency in Private International Law*, 2nd edn (Oxford University Press, 2005), Ch.1.

[4] On the hotchpot rule, see Fletcher, *Insolvency in Private International Law*, 2nd edn (Oxford University Press, 2005), paras 2.97 to 2.101; Look Chan Ho, "On *Pari Passu*, Equality and Hotchpot in Cross-Border Insolvency" [2003] L.M.C.L.Q. 95. With regard to the rule against double proof see *Re Polly Peck* [1996] 2 All E.R. 433, 441f–443d; *Squires (Liquidators of SSSL Realisations (2002) Ltd) v AIG Europe (UK) Ltd* [2006] Ch. 610 (CA); and *Re Kaupthing Singer and Friedlander Limited (in administration)* [2011] UKSC 48.

[5] Treaty establishing the European Economic Community, signed in Rome on March 25, 1957. This entered into force on January 1, 1958 and is still in force, though much amended, as part of the complex series of treaties which currently link 27 European states as members of the EU.

were resolved separately, and relatively quickly, by the Brussels Convention of September 27, 1968.[6] In contrast, separate and protracted efforts continued until as late as May 1996 in the ultimately unsuccessful attempt to establish an EU Bankruptcy Convention to which all of the then 15 Member States would become contracting parties.[7] The work may be broadly divided between Phase I (to 1980); and Phase II (April 1990–May 1996). As a bridging event between these two phases, we may note the significance of the Council of Europe Convention on Certain International Aspects of Bankruptcy (The Istanbul Convention of June 5, 1990, which is not yet in force.)[8]

31–003   The second phase of the EU project came tantalisingly close to success, but was prevented from attaining the required unanimity of signatures due to the last-minute disengagement of the United Kingdom, for reasons of international politics that were unrelated to the subject matter of the Convention itself. Fortunately, after a further hiatus of three years, the fruits of so many years' collective labour were salvaged thanks to a fresh initiative by the German and Finnish republics, which successively held the presidency of the EU Council of Ministers during 1999. In its revived form, the project was submitted to the Council as a proposed regulation. This type of legislative act is significant in that a regulation has the force of directly applicable law in every Member State according to the terms of art.249 (previously numbered as art.189) of the EC Treaty in its amended form. This eleventh-hour conversion into a standard mode of EU legislative instrument has the further advantage of eliminating the lengthy delay that would have been anticipated before entry into force as a convention could have occurred, pending completion of the separate domestic procedures for ratification by each of the Member States.

The Regulation on Insolvency Proceedings was adopted by the Council on May 29, 2000.[9] To allow time for any consequential internal adjustments in the insolvency systems of the Member States a two-year postponement of its entry into force was effected by art.47 of the Regulation. On the day thus appointed, May 31, 2002, the Regulation entered into force without any national legislative measures being taken by the Member States, and its provisions take precedence over any inconsistent provisions of their existing domestic laws.[10] On May 1, 2004, 10 new Member States joined the European Union, thereby

[6] Convention on Jurisdiction and the Recognition and Enforcement of Judgments in Civil and Commercial Matters, September 27, 1968. The Brussels Convention has now been replaced by Council Regulation 44/2001/EC, [2001] OJ L12/1 ("the Brussels I Regulation") which took effect from March 1, 2002.

[7] For a more detailed account of the history of the EU Bankruptcy Convention project, see Fletcher, *Insolvency in Private International Law*, 2nd edn (Oxford University Press, 2005), Ch.7, paras 7–01 to 7–28.

[8] E.T.S., No.136. Text published (in English and French) in Fletcher, *Insolvency in Private International Law*, 2nd edn (Oxford University Press, 2005), at Appendix III, with commentary on the Convention Ch.6.

[9] Council Regulation (EC) No.1346/2000, [2000] OJ L160/1.

[10] One technical matter to be noted is that, because the EC Regulation is based on arts 61(c) and 67(1) of the EC Treaty (as amended by the Treaty of Amsterdam), its provisions do not have effect in Denmark, which secured an exemption from measures adopted on that basis. It was expected that a parallel arrangement—possibly in the form of a Convention concluded between Denmark and the other member states—would be devised in order that a unitary approach to insolvency matters could be secured across the EU as a whole. However, to date no steps have been taken to accomplish such an accommodation.

increasing the total membership to 25. Under the terms of the Treaty and Act of Accession, signed in Athens on April 16, 2003, the newly joining Member States became fully subject to all existing provisions of Community legislation, including the EC Regulation on Insolvency Proceedings. Special provisions were included in the Act of Accession to amend the Regulation so that its Annexes A, B, and C contain references to the relevant types of insolvency and winding-up proceedings, and to the relevant types of office holder under those proceedings, for each of the states in question.

On January 1, 2007 a further increase in the membership of the EU occurred with the accession of Bulgaria and Romania. This brought the total membership to 27 states, of which 26 are participating in the Insolvency Regulation. An amending regulation was adopted on November 20, 2006 to extend the Regulation to the latest two Member States.[11] Annexes A, B and C of the EC Regulation have been amended from time to time to accommodate changes to the insolvency laws of several states. Conveniently, the amending regulation embodies the consolidated texts of all three Annexes to the EC Regulation in their current form.[12]

In the remainder of this Part of the chapter, the provisions of the Regulation on Insolvency Proceedings will be examined and their effects explained.[13]

2. SCOPE AND IMPACT OF THE REGULATION ON INSOLVENCY PROCEEDINGS

(a) Outline

The Regulation imposes direct control over the exercise of jurisdiction to open insolvency proceedings in any of the Member States. It also regulates, by **31–004**

---

[11] Council Regulation (EC) No.1791/2006, [2006] OJ L363/1.

[12] Regulation (EU) No.583/2011, [2011] OJ L160/1. (The versions of Annexes A, B and C to Regulation No.1346/2000, which are reproduced in Appendix 3 below, are as enacted by Regulation (EU) No.583/2011).

[13] There is currently no officially published version issued by the EU itself of the final text of the proposed Convention on Insolvency Proceedings (the "Convention"), on which the text of the Regulation is closely modelled. An authentic version in English of the text as opened for signature between November 23, 1995 and May 23, 1996 was placed in the public domain as part of the internal processes of scrutiny and consultation within the UK. The text is contained in a Consultative Document published in February 1996 by the Insolvency Service of the Department of Trade and Industry (UK). The same text was also included (as Appendix 3, containing some minor textual inaccuracies) in the *7th Report of the House of Lords Select Committee on the European Communities*, published on March 26, 1996 (HL Paper 59, available from HMSO). The Consultative Document also contains (as Annex B) the original version of the *Explanatory Report on the Convention*, drafted in far from perfect English. A greatly improved, revised version of the Report by Professor M. Virgos and Mr E. Schmit, (hereafter referred to as the "*Virgos-Schmit Report*") was produced as EU Council Document 6500/96, DRS 8 (CFC), Brussels, May 3, 1996, with restricted circulation. This document serves as a valuable aid to interpretation. It must be emphasised that the document carries no official status and that there are presently no indications as to the possibility of an amended version being published. However, the English courts appear to have accepted that it may be useful to have regard to it (see for example *Syska v Vivendi Universal* [2009] 2 All E.R. (Comm) 891 (CA), [20]; *Re Stanford International Bank (In Receivership)* [2011] Ch. 33 (CA), [36]). The full text of the English version of the *Virgos-Schmit Report* is included in Moss, Fletcher and Isaacs, *The EC Regulation on Insolvency Proceedings, A Commentary and Annotated Guide*, 2nd edn (Oxford University Press, 2009), at Appendix 2, and in I. F. Fletcher, *Insolvency in Private International Law*, 2nd edn (Oxford University Press, 2005) at Appendix VII. See also M. Virgos and F. Garcimartin, *The European Insolvency Regulation: Law and Practice* (Kluwer, 2004).

means of uniform rules for choice of law, the law applicable to such proceedings and to matters closely affected by a party's insolvency (third parties' rights in rem; set-off; reservation of title; contracts relating to immovable property; payment systems and financial markets; contracts of employment; registrable rights in immovable property, ships or aircraft; patents and trade marks; the validity of transactions pre- and post-commencement of insolvency proceedings that have detrimental consequences for the general body of creditors; and the effects of insolvency proceedings on pending lawsuits that involve rights or assets of the debtor). All these matters are the subject of provisions in Ch.I (arts 1–15).[14] It next deals with the recognition in the other Member States of insolvency proceedings opened in any of them whose courts have jurisdiction pursuant to art.3. This includes the vital questions of the effects of recognition, the powers of the office-holder (referred to throughout as "the liquidator"), and the formalities required to establish the liquidator's status for the purpose of acting abroad. These matters fall within Ch.II (arts 16–26). Next, the possibility of opening secondary insolvency proceedings at the behest of various interested parties is the subject of provisions in Ch.III (arts 27–38). There are useful, if limited, provisions in Ch.IV (arts 39–42), concerning the rights of all creditors to receive information from the liquidator and to lodge claims in the insolvency proceedings. Lastly, Ch.V (arts 43–47) contains transitional and final provisions dealing with entry into force, review and amendment of the Regulation, as well as its relationship to specific conventions dealing with insolvency matters to which certain of the Member States are or may become parties (see art.44).

Two further aspects of the Regulation should be noted. First, its substantive provisions are preceded by no less than 33 paragraphs of preliminary recitals or Preambles. While such formal recitals are a standard feature of EC/EU legislation, supplying the legal basis for the measure in question as well as giving an indication of the underlying motivations for its enactment, the number and prolixity of the Preambles to the EC Regulation are exceptional. Their purpose is doubtless to furnish some compensation for the lack of any official *travaux préparatoires* to serve as an aid to interpretation of the Regulation.[15] When courts encounter a need to interpret and apply the Regulation their attention can be drawn to the Preambles, which provide some guidance on the meaning and approach to be preferred.[16] Secondly, the Regulation is supplemented by three Annexes—A, B and C—which list, with respect to each Member State concerned, the names of the insolvency proceedings under the national system of insolvency law which come within the scope of the Regulation (Annexes A and B), and the official titles of the office holders in those proceedings (Annex C). These lists can be (and have already been) amended from time to time using the procedure established by art.45.

---

[14] The choice of law rules of the Regulation are discussed in detail in below, paras 31–026 to 31–045.

[15] See above, fn.13, with reference the *Explanatory Report* previously produced in relation to the text when it was in the form of a Convention.

[16] "[A] 'teleological' approach is to be adopted when construing the [EC] Regulation": *Re Alitalia Linee Aeree Italiane* [2011] 1 W.L.R. 2049, [26], per Newey J.

(b) Subject matter

The types of proceedings covered and categories of debtor to which the **31–005** Regulation applies are as specified in art.1(1), which provides that it shall apply to: "collective insolvency proceedings which entail the partial or total divestment of a debtor and the appointment of a liquidator". A most important series of excepted cases is created by art.1(2), which states that the Regulation shall not apply to "insolvency proceedings concerning insurance undertakings, credit institutions, investment undertakings which provide services involving the holding of funds or securities for third parties, or to collective investment undertakings".[17] These exclusions in relation to entities operating within the financial services sector come as a result of separate EU initiatives to introduce harmonisation in this sector by means of Directives which include standardised provisions governing the insolvency of such enterprises. The relevant initiatives are Council Directive 2001/17/EC on the Reorganisation and Winding Up of Insurance Undertakings[18] and Directive of the European Parliament and of the Council 2001/24/EC on the Reorganisation and Winding Up of Credit Institutions.[19]

Leaving aside proceedings concerning debtors within art.1(2), the scope of art.1(1) should be identical to the scope of the exception in art.1(2)(b) of Council Regulation (EC) 44/2001 on jurisdiction and the recognition and enforcement of judgments in civil and commercial matters (Judgments Regulation).[20] This is because these two Community instruments "were intended to dovetail almost completely with each other" and they were drafted "[t]o avoid, as far as possible, leaving lacunae between the scope of the two [regulations]".[21] "[T]he [EC] Regulation . . . and the . . . Judgments Regulation are intended to provide mutually exclusive codes in relation to jurisdiction: the former is confined to insolvency and analogous proceedings, whereas the latter applies to other civil and commercial proceedings (save for those specifically excluded, such as, for example, arbitration)."[22]

Nevertheless, the operation in practice of the demarcation between the EC Regulation and the Judgments Regulation has not been straightforward. Recent case-law suggests the following propositions.

---

[17] "[T]he exception in Art.1(2) does not relate to investment undertakings generally, nor to investment undertakings providing any services to third parties but only to those investment undertakings which provide services to third parties of the relevant description, namely 'services involving the holding of funds or securities for third parties'": *Byers v Yacht Bull Corporation* [2010] B.C.C. 368, [37], per Sir Andrew Morritt, C.

[18] Reorganisation and Winding Up of Insurance Undertakings and Directive of the European Parliament [2001] OJ L110/28.

[19] Reorganisation and Winding Up of Credit Institutions [2001] OJ L125/15.

[20] art.1(2)(b) of the Judgments Regulation provides that it shall not apply to "bankruptcy, proceedings relating to the winding-up of insolvent companies or other legal persons, judicial arrangements, compositions and analogous proceedings".

[21] *Schlosser Report on the Brussels Convention* [1979] OJ C59/91, [53].

[22] *Gibraltar Residential Properties v Gibralcon 2004 SA* [2011] B.L.R. 126, [37]. See also Look Chan Ho, "Interfacing the Insolvency Regulation with the Judgments Regulation: *Oakley v Ultra Vehicle Design*" (2005) 2 *International Corporate Rescue* 196, 199.

First, a civil action in the context of an insolvency to set aside a transaction falls within the EC Regulation (i.e. within the exclusion in art.1(2)(b) of the Judgments Regulation) if it derives directly from the insolvency proceedings and is closely connected to them. This requirement of close connection is likely to be satisfied if the action may only be brought by a liquidator and is intended to increase the insolvent debtor's assets.[23]

Secondly, an action to recover assets which is not based on the law of the insolvency proceedings and requires neither the opening of such proceedings nor the involvement of a liquidator falls outside the EC Regulation. An example is an action brought by a seller against an insolvent purchaser based on a reservation of title clause. The mere fact that the liquidator is a party to the proceedings is not sufficient to classify them as proceedings deriving directly from the insolvency and being closely linked to proceedings for realising assets.[24]

Thirdly, "the fact that a defendant in commercial proceedings is the subject of insolvency proceedings in another Member State is not of itself a ground for depriving the . . . Judgments Regulation of application".[25]

Fourthly, where the principal claim is the declaration as to beneficial ownership arising under the general law, the existence of dependent or alternative claims under insolvency law would not change the nature of the principal claim.[26]

Fifthly, a dispute falls within the EC Regulation (i.e. within the exclusion in art.1(2)(b) of the Judgments Regulation) if it concerns solely the ownership of assets transferred in insolvency proceedings by the liquidator pursuant to statutory provisions which derogate from the general rules of private law and provide that, in the case of insolvency, debtors lose the right freely to dispose of their assets and the liquidator has to administer the assets in insolvency on behalf of the creditors, including effecting any necessary transfers.[27]

Sixthly, the determination of a winding-up petition founded upon disputed debts falls within the EC Regulation, even where the dispute is subject to pending proceedings in another Member State's court.[28]

Seventhly, a scheme of arrangement under Pt 26 of the Companies Act 2006 in respect of a solvent company falls within the Judgments Regulation.[29]

Article 2 of the Regulation contains eight paragraphs, lettered (a) to (h), which supply the definitions of a number of key concepts and terms that are used. The list is by no means exhaustive, however, and it is certain that many crucial matters will require judicial interpretation with the guidance, ultimately, of the European Court of Justice. Of the definitions which are supplied, mention should be made of that in para.(a), which states that "Insolvency proceedings" means the collective proceedings referred to in art.1(1), as listed

---

[23] *Seagon v Deko Marty Belgium NV* (C-339/07) [2009] 1 W.L.R. 2168 (ECJ).
[24] *German Graphics Graphische Maschinen v Schee* (C-292/08) [2009] E.C.R. I-8421.
[25] *Gibraltar Residential Properties v Gibralcon 2004* [2011] B.L.R. 126, [28].
[26] *Byers v Yacht Bull Corporation* [2010] B.C.C. 368.
[27] *SCT Industri AB v Alpenblume AB* (C-111/08) [2009] E.C.R. I-5655.
[28] *Citigate Dewe Rogerson v Artaban Public Affairs* [2011] 1 B.C.L.C. 625.
[29] *Re Rodenstock GmbH* [2011] Bus. L.R. 1245. See also Look Chan Ho, "Making and Enforcing International Schemes of Arrangement" [2011] J.I.B.L.R. 434.

in Annex A to the Regulation. As already mentioned, Annex A provides, for each Member State in turn, a list of the proceedings found within the law of that country which are considered to fall within the letter and spirit of art.1(1), and thus qualify for inclusion. The proceedings are listed in the language of the country to whose system they pertain. For the United Kingdom, these are:

- winding-up by or subject to the supervision of the court;

- creditors' voluntary winding-up (with confirmation by the court);

- administration, including appointments made by filing prescribed documents with the court;

- voluntary arrangements under insolvency legislation (which would cover both the Insolvency Act 1986 or the Insolvent Partnerships Order 1994); and

- bankruptcy or sequestration.

Following the belated inclusion of the office of provisional liquidator in the **31–006** latest iteration of Annex C, it can be stated that the appointment of a provisional liquidator by a court in the United Kingdom, made in the context of a pending petition for the winding up of an insolvent company, by an order which dispossesses the debtor, constitutes a decision opening insolvency proceedings for the purposes of art.16 of the Regulation. This can give rise to an obligation for the courts of other Member States to recognise the proceedings as the "main" proceedings with respect to the company in question. This conclusion follows from the decision of the European Court of Justice in *Re Eurofood IFSC Ltd*.[30]

It is notable that all the UK insolvency procedures listed above involve a role for the court either at their inception or in their confirmation at an early stage, or at least they allow the court's jurisdiction to be invoked by an interested party to ensure that the proceedings are properly conducted. The inclusion of creditors' voluntary liquidation, which is in practice the most frequently used type of liquidation procedure for insolvent companies, was only made possible through the insertion of the proviso that there be confirmation by the court. New insolvency rules, Insolvency Rules 7.62 and 7.63, were inserted (by Insolvency (Amendment) Rules 2002, SI 2002/1307) into the Insolvency Rules 1986 to provide a mechanism whereby a voluntary liquidator may apply to the court for an order confirming the voluntary liquidation for these purposes.

---

[30] *Re Eurofood IFSC Ltd* (C-341/04) [2006] Ch. 508 (ECJ), [45]–[58]. The opinion of A.G. Jacobs, delivered on September 27, 2006, reached the same conclusion using different reasoning: see [47] to [88] inclusive of the Opinion together with [152(1)], reported at [2006] Ch. 508 (ECJ). (Note: the entry for Ireland in Annex C to the Regulation, listing the types of liquidators referred to in art.2(b), includes "Provisional Liquidator"). For a criticism of the ECJ's decision on this point, see Moss, "Asking the Right Questions? Highs and Lows of the European Court of Justice (ECJ) Judgment in *Eurofood*" (2006) 19 Insolv. Int. 97, 99–101.

The repeated references in arts 1 and 2 to the "collective" nature of the proceedings to which the Regulation is applicable suggests one powerful reason why administrative receivership and other types of receivership (even where the court is involved in the process of appointment) have been omitted from the list of proceedings in Annex A relating to the UK. This is also the case with the Republic of Ireland, whose insolvency law still closely resembles that of the UK. Although receivership—especially that arising from the existence of a floating charge—plays an important role in the practical operation of the insolvency laws of both the UK and Ireland, the procedure is essentially a remedy designed to advance the interest of one particular type of secured creditor, with whom resides the sole initiative as to its utilisation. Hence it cannot readily be reconciled with the "collectivity" concept that infuses the Regulation. A further aspect of administrative receivership previously considered to militate against its inclusion within the scope of the Regulation is that it commences through a direct act of appointment by the creditor without recourse to a court. However, with the modification of the procedure for administration under the reforms imported by Pt 10 of the Enterprise Act 2002, a company can now enter administration through an out of court appointment as an alternative to the seeking of an administration order. The modification to the third indent of the UK listing in Annex A to the Regulation, quoted in para.32–005, reflects that change to the administration procedure, and thereby removes one former basis of objection to the inclusion of administrative receivership. Nevertheless, the fact that administrative receivership is essentially an individual, rather than a collective, process suffices to perpetuate its omission from the list of insolvency proceedings in Annex A, so that the Regulation is not applicable to administrative receivership under any circumstances.

31–007   As a consequence of this exclusion, the non-availability to an administrative receiver of the recognition and assistance provided under the EU Regulation to office-holders in other types of insolvency proceedings may affect the choice of procedure to be embarked upon whenever consideration is being given to the optimum way in which to attempt to rescue an ailing UK or Irish company which has significant assets and interests in other EU countries. Although receivership can, in appropriate circumstances and in the right hands, be a very swift and effective vehicle for achieving a business rescue, a receiver can encounter severe difficulties in a case where it is necessary to enlist the co-operation of foreign courts.[31] Therefore it may prove to be tactically advantageous to opt for one of the forms of rescue procedure, such as administration or a voluntary arrangement, that attract the automatic benefits imparted by the Regulation.

A further important technical term is defined by art.2(c), which states that "winding-up proceedings" means "insolvency proceedings within the meaning of point (a) involving realising the assets of the debtor, including where the proceedings have been closed by a composition or other measure terminating the insolvency, or closed by reason of the insufficiency of the assets". Proceedings which come within this definition are listed in Annex B. For the UK, they are:

---

[31] See Ch.30, above.

- winding-up by or subject to the supervision of the court;

- winding up through administration, including appointments made by filing prescribed documents with the court;

- creditors' voluntary winding up (with confirmation by the court); and

- bankruptcy or sequestration.

The above is a shorter list than that contained in Annex A to indicate those proceedings which qualify as "insolvency proceedings". Inevitably, this means that a more restricted range of options is available wherever the Regulation requires that proceedings shall be "winding up proceedings"—as in the case of arts 3(3), 16(2) and 27, relating to the opening of secondary proceedings.[32] The original wholesale omission of administrations and the continued omission of voluntary arrangements from the scope of the secondary bankruptcy process may prove detrimental to the attainment of some types of rescue strategy for businesses with cross-border operations. The scope of operation of the concept of "winding up proceedings" has already been broadened by the addition of winding up through administration introduced by Council Regulation 603/2005/EC. **31–008**

(c)   Time of entry into force: non-retrospective effect

By art.47 the Regulation entered into force on May 31, 2002. Article 43 declares that it shall apply only to insolvency proceedings opened after its entry into force, and further states that "Acts *done by a debtor* before the entry into force of this Regulation shall continue to be governed by the law which was applicable to them at the time they were done" (emphasis added).[33] There is a potential for confusion and uncertainty here regarding which previous events qualify as "acts done by the debtor". The *Virgos-Schmit Report*, originally prepared in relation to the proposed EC Convention, went some way towards assisting in the task of determining issues of validity in transitional cases by stating that "the determination of the acts done by the debtor and the time at which they are done are governed by the applicable law".[34] The basic intention behind the rule is to ensure that relations to which the debtor is party remain subject to the law which governed the debtor's acts at the time of acting.[35] **31–009**

---

[32] e.g. the restricted range of procedures permitted in such circumstances may preclude the most commercially appropriate course from being followed where the debtor's business is not viable in the place of its centre of main interests, but has a viable branch in another State. See P. Omar, "Jurisdiction in the European Insolvency Convention" (1999) 10 I.C.C.L.R. 225. See below, para.31–023, for Secondary Insolvency Proceedings.

[33] e.g. *SCT Industri AB (In Liquidation) v Alpenblume AB* (C-111/08) [2009] E.C.R. I–5655, [18] of the judgment of the court.

[34] *Virgos-Schmit Report*, above, fn.13, at para.306.

[35] *Virgos-Schmit Report*, above, fn.13, at para.306. See also paras 303–305 of the *Report*.

(d)   International jurisdiction

31–010   The Regulation is so designed as to establish a hierarchical scheme of primary and subsidiary jurisdictional competence in relation to a debtor meeting the specific qualifying criterion, namely that the centre of the debtor's main interests is situated within the territory of a Member State. In the case of such a debtor, the opening of main insolvency proceedings is precluded save in those Member States on whose courts the Regulation confers jurisdiction, regardless of whether the debtor might elsewhere fulfil any locally-evolved rules for taking jurisdiction. It must be emphasised that there is no attempt to regulate or interfere with the taking of jurisdiction under national laws in respect of any debtor whose centre of main interests lies outside the EU. In such cases alternative grounds for exercising jurisdiction (such as a "doing of business" or a "presence of assets" test) can still be used in any EU State where the locally prescribed test for "minimum contacts" happens to be met, but with the important proviso that such proceedings will not qualify for recognition or enforcement in other Member States by virtue of the Regulation (although they may be recognised on a case-by-case basis according to the rules of private international law of each State separately). It is suggested, with respect, that this is a welcome contrast to the treatment of civil and commercial judgments under the Brussels I Regulation of December 22, 2000, which has hostile propensities for defendants domiciled outside the EU because of the effect of its art.4, which enables long-arm jurisdiction to be taken against them in one EU State with the further consequence that any resulting judgment is automatically enforceable in all the others.[36]

Although the Regulation makes repeated reference to "courts", it should be noted that its provisions are not exclusively confined to cases where proceedings are commenced or conducted in the formal context of a court. Preamble (10) specifically calls attention to the fact that insolvency proceedings do not necessarily involve the intervention of a judicial authority, and states that: "The expression *court* in this Regulation should be given a broad meaning and include a person or body empowered by national law to open insolvency proceedings".

(i)   Primary competence—main proceedings

31–011   Article 3(1) provides that the courts of the Member State within the territory of which the centre of the debtor's main interests is situated shall have jurisdiction to open insolvency proceedings. It is significant that there is no comprehensive definition of "centre of main interests" (COMI), but there is one especially important presumption supplied by art.3(1) itself:

---

[36] For trenchant criticism of this and other xenophobic properties of the original Brussels Convention of 1968, see K. Nadelmann, 67 Colum. L.Rev 995 (1967); 5 CML Rev409 (1966–67); 82 Harv L.Rev 1282 (1968). See also I.F. Fletcher, *Conflict of Laws and European Community Law* (Oxford University Press, 1982), Ch.4, pp.117–120. The effects produced by art.4 of the 1968 Convention are perpetuated by the provisions of art.4 of the Brussels I Regulation (Council Regulation (EC) No.44/2001, [2001] OJ L12/1).

"In the case of a company or legal person, the place of the registered office shall be presumed to be the centre of its main interests *in the absence of proof to the contrary*" (emphasis added).

The presumption supplied under art.3(1) is thus a rebuttable one,[37] and moreover is confined to the case where the debtor is a company or legal person. Nevertheless, it offers a useful point of departure for those wishing to locate the correct forum for commencement of insolvency proceedings involving a company, and it will be incumbent upon those who seek to have the proceedings dismissed for want of jurisdiction to sustain the burden of proving that the company's centre of main interests is in another Member State. Significantly the Regulation is silent as to the nature of the requisite "proof" that must be furnished in order to rebut the presumption established by art.3(1). Nor does it contain any provision for resolving the contrasting possibilities of either a "positive" conflict of jurisdiction between the courts of two Contracting States, each of which concludes on the evidence before it that the debtor's COMI lies within its territory; or a "negative" conflict, where the converse arises. An example of the way in which such conflicts could occur in practice is provided by the case of *BCCI SA*, where the bank's state of incorporation was Luxembourg, but the English courts quite reasonably concluded that its main operational base was in England.[38] One could imagine that, were a similar case to arise under the Regulation, courts in both Luxembourg and the UK could readily persuade themselves that the COMI of BCCI was located within their jurisdiction for the purposes of art.3(1). In practice, much would depend on the timing of the first approach to the one court rather than the other, and the extent to which the court first seized took care to perform the task of determining the location of the debtor's centre of main interests in a spirit of fidelity to the principle of mutual trust that is meant to infuse the working of this Regulation. There is also a risk of different evidence being submitted to the different courts and the risk of different findings of fact by the respective courts.[39]

An additional indication of the intended meaning of the expression "centre **31–012** of main interests" has been supplied by Recital (13) to the Regulation, which declares:

---

[37] In *Interedil Srl v Fallimento Interedil Srl* (C-396/09) (ECJ) (October 20, 2011) the Italian court made a reference to the ECJ for a preliminary ruling on the question: "Is the concept of COMI in Art.3(1) of the EC regulation to be interpreted in accordance with Community law or national law and, if the former, how is that term to be defined?" The ECJ, at [41] to [59] of the judgment, affirmed that "centre of main interests" is to be given an autonomous and uniform interpretation under EU law. The court gave guidance on the relevant criteria for determining the debtor's COMI.

[38] *Re BCCI SA (No.11)* [1997] Ch. 213. This case is further discussed in para.31–034, below.

[39] Recital (22) to the Regulation declares that: "Recognition of judgments delivered by the courts of the Member States should be based on the principle of mutual trust; to that end, grounds for non-recognition should be reduced to the minimum necessary".

"The 'centre of main interests' should correspond to the place where the debtor conducts the administration of his interests on a regular basis and is therefore ascertainable by third parties".

Transparency and objective ascertainability are therefore given special emphasis in the required approach to interpretation, as is the indication that regard should be paid to the position of third parties and the reasonable expectations formed in the course of their dealings with the debtor.

31–013   *The developing case law on jurisdiction to open proceedings.*   Since May 2006 all questions concerning jurisdiction to open insolvency proceedings based on the whereabouts of the debtor's COMI must be approached in the light of the decision of the European Court of Justice in *Re Eurofood IFSC.*[40]

31–014   *The ECJ and the Eurofood case.*   The salient facts of the case were as follows. Eurofood IFSC Ltd (the company) was incorporated and registered in Ireland. It is a wholly owned subsidiary of Parmalat Spa, a company incorporated in Italy which is the parent of the Parmalat corporate group. Eurofood's principal objective was the provision of financing facilities for companies in the Parmalat group. The company's registered office is at the International Financial Services Centre, Dublin (IFSC), and it is thereby eligible to enjoy a low tax liability by virtue of carrying on activity for the provision of internationally traded financial services to be provided only to non-resident persons or bodies. The company had no employees and its administration was provided under contract in Dublin by the Bank of America. The Irish and Italian directors of the company met in Dublin (either in person or by telephone conference). The company only ever entered into three transactions, two of which were guaranteed by the parent, Parmalat. The third transaction was a "swap" agreement with Bank of America. Eurofood's creditors under the first two transactions are owed in excess of US $122 million, which the company has no means to pay. In late 2003 Parmalat Spa was found to be in deep financial crisis, which led to the insolvency of many of its key companies. On December 23, 2003 the Italian Parliament passed into law decree No.347 providing for the extraordinary administration of companies with more than 1,000 employees and debts of no less than €1 billion. On December 24, Parmalat Spa was admitted to extraordinary administration proceedings by ministerial decision, and an extraordinary administrator appointed. On December 27 a court in Parma confirmed that Parmalat was insolvent and placed it in extraordinary administration. On January 27, 2004, Bank of America presented to the Irish High Court a petition for the winding up of Eurofood, alleging that the company was insolvent and claiming a debt due to it in excess of US $3.5 million. On the same date Bank of America also applied ex parte for the appointment of a provisional liquidator. Also on that same day the Irish court appointed a provisional liquidator to Eurofood with powers to take possession of all its assets, to manage its affairs, to open a bank account in its name and to retain the services of a solicitor. The order of

---

[40] *Re Eurofood IFSC Ltd* (C-341/04) [2006] Ch. 508 (ECJ).

appointment made no explicit pronouncement regarding the COMI of Eurofood, nor did it make a finding of insolvency at that stage. On February 9, 2004 the Italian Ministry admitted Eurofood, as a group company, to the extraordinary administration of Parmalat, and the next day the Parma court made an order acknowledging the filing of a petition to declare the insolvency of Eurofood and setting February 17 as the date for hearing that petition. The provisional liqui-dator appointed by the Irish court was only informed of the Italian hearing on February 13 and, although legally represented before the Parma court at the hearing, subsequently complained of a failure on the part of the extraordinary administrator to provide him with essential documents filed with the court for the purpose of preparing an effective submission of his case. On February 20, the Parma court gave judgment opening insolvency proceedings concerning Eurofood, declaring it to be insolvent, determining that its COMI was in Italy and appointing the extraordinary administrator of Parmalat as extraordinary administrator also of Eurofood. At a subsequent hearing in the Irish court on March 2 to 4, 2004 of the petition of Bank of America for the winding up of Eurofood, the Irish court ruled that insolvency proceedings had been opened in Ireland at the date of presentation of the petition; that Eurofood's COMI was in Ireland and therefore the proceedings opened as of January 27, 2004 were main insolvency proceedings within the meaning of the EC Regulation; that the purported opening of main proceedings by the Parma court was in contraven-tion of the applicable requirements of the EC Regulation and could not alter the fact that insolvency proceedings were already extant in Ireland; and that the failure of the Italian extraordinary administrator to put Eurofood's creditors on notice of the hearing before the Parma court, and further failure to furnish the provisional liquidator with relevant documentation prior to the hearing, had amounted to a lack of due process such as to warrant the Irish court refusing to give recognition to the decision of the Parma court under art.26 of the Regulation. The Irish court concluded by finding that Eurofood was grossly insolvent, and it made a winding up order in respect of Eurofood whereby the provisional liquidator was appointed as liquidator of the company. That judgment of the Irish High Court was challenged on appeal before the Irish Supreme Court at the instance of the Italian extraordinary administrator. The appellate court referred five questions to the ECJ for preliminary ruling in relation to the inter-pretation of Regulation 1346/2000. On September 27, 2005 Advocate-General Jacobs delivered his Opinion in which the rulings by the Irish High Court in its order of March 23, 2004 were essentially endorsed in the proposed answers to all five questions. In its judgment of May 2, 2006 the ECJ, while expressing its decision in terms which differ from those of the Advocate-General in several respects, delivered responses to four of the five questions which were also capable of sustaining the position that the Irish proceedings should prevail. The ECJ on this occasion elected not to address the second of the five questions referred to it, concerning the time of opening of proceedings, on the ground that the matter was already resolved by the answer given to the first question, whereby the appointment of a provisional liquidator was declared to be capable of amounting to the opening of insolvency proceedings within the meaning of the Regulation as applicable to Irish insolvency procedures.

31–015   One of the questions referred to the ECJ by the Irish Supreme Court concerned the determining factor to be applied for the purpose of identifying the COMI of a subsidiary company, where it and its parent have their respective registered offices in two different Member States. Although the Opinion of the Advocate-General, delivered on September 27, 2005,[41] offers some support for the application of the "head office function" test as a means of determining whether a company's COMI is somewhere other than the State where that company's registered office is located, he did not consider that the mere fact that a parent company is in a position to control its subsidiary's policy determines the latter's COMI within the meaning of the Regulation.[42] The mere fact that one company was in a position to control the policy of another did not, in the Advocate-General's estimation, demonstrate that it did in fact control that policy. Moreover, in order to meet the additional requirement expressed in Recital (13) to the Regulation (quoted in para.31–012 above) that the place from which the debtor conducts the administration of its interests must be "ascertainable by third parties", the functional realities must be readily ascertainable by third parties if the presumption within art.3(1), based on the purely formal criterion of the location of the registered office, is to be displaced. The ECJ in its Judgment of May 2, 2006 echoed and indeed amplified those views. Having affirmed that the concept of the "centre of main interests" is peculiar to the Regulation and that it has an autonomous meaning which must be interpreted in a uniform way, the court declared that the centre of main interests "must be identified by reference to criteria which are both objective and ascertainable by third parties."[43] Thus it followed, in the judgment of the court, that the "simple presumption" laid down by the Regulation in favour of the registered office of the company "can be rebutted only if factors which are both objective and ascertainable by third parties enable it to be established that an actual situation exists which is different from that which locating it at that registered office is deemed to reflect."[44] While the court suggested, by way of illustration, that an overriding of the presumption contained in art.3(1) could be achieved in the case of a "letterbox" company not carrying on business in the territory of the Member State in which its registered office is situated, it went on to assert that where a company carries on its business in the territory of the Member State where its registered office is situated "the mere fact that its economic choices are or can be controlled by a parent company in another Member State is not enough to rebut the presumption laid down by the Regulation."[45] The court did not, however, provide an indication of what additional evidence of the actual exercise of control by parent over subsidiary would be either necessary or sufficient to overcome the presumption as to the

---

[41] The Opinion of Advocate-General Jacobs is reported at *Re Eurofood IFSC Ltd* (C-341/04) [2005] B.C.C. 1021.

[42] See [110]–[126] of the opinion of the Advocate-General.

[43] See [26]–[37] of the judgment, especially at [30]–[34]; *Re Eurofood IFSC Ltd* (C-341/04) [2006] B.C.C. 397, 405–406.

[44] See [34] of the judgment.

[45] See [35]–[37] of the judgment (where the same propositions are stated twice in close succession).

location of the COMI of the subsidiary. It is suggested, on the basis of such statements as are included in the judgment of the court, that the presumption that COMI is in the place of the registered office is a strong one, whose rebuttal requires strict proof of the fact that the company has regularly and consistently conducted its head office functions at a different location to the place of the registered office, and that it has done so in a manner which provides transparent and unequivocal evidence, that is ascertainable by third parties, to indicate that the COMI has moved elsewhere.

In *Re Stanford International Bank*[46] the Court of Appeal followed *Eurofood*   **31–016** to establish the following propositions regarding COMI:

"(1)   [E]ach company or individual has its own COMI ... [I]t is not possible to have a COMI of some loose aggregation of companies and individuals ...

(2)   [T]he [COMI] presumption 'can be rebutted only [by] factors which are both objective and ascertainable'. That this test is not the same as the head office functions test adopted by Lewison J in *Re Lennox Holdings Ltd* and Lawrence Collins J in *Re Collins & Aikman Corp Group* [2006] BCC 606 para 16 is plain ...

(3)   Thus it is conclusively established that the factors relevant to a rebuttal of the presumption must be both objective and ascertainable by third parties. Lewison J. confined factors ascertainable by third parties to matters already in the public domain and what a typical third party would learn as a result of dealing with the company and excluded those which might be ascertained on enquiry. The good sense of this conclusion is demonstrated by the cases in English domestic law relating to constructive notice and its various degrees ... To extend ascertainability to factors, not already in the public domain or apparent to a typical third party doing business with the company, which might be discovered on enquiry would introduce into this area of the law a most undesirable element of uncertainty.

(4)   Whether or not factors, not already in the public domain or so apparent, ascertainable on reasonable enquiry are relevant to a rebuttal of the presumption that cannot extend the range of ascertainable factors to the fraudulent Ponzi scheme. That, inevitably, is neither a matter of general knowledge nor ascertainable on reasonable enquiry. It was suggested that after the fraudulent scheme had been uncovered the facts as to its previous existence had become public knowledge and should be relevant to the rebuttal of the presumption. No doubt the COMI of a company may change as the situation of its registered office may change, but it can only do so

---

[46] *Re Stanford International Bank Ltd (In Receivership)* [2011] Ch. 33 (CA).

by reference to main interests which it still has and facts within the public domain or so apparent at the time of their occurrence."47

The *Stanford* interpretation of the *Eurofood* COMI test is now generally assumed to be settled law.[48]

31–017   It is accepted that just as the COMI presumption may be rebutted, the COMI location may be moved.[49] Frequently a debtor's COMI is moved from its country of incorporation to another jurisdiction for the purpose of effecting a restructuring under the insolvency laws of the new jurisdiction.

Before we consider case-law on COMI migration, it is first necessary to consider how the COMI presumption may be rebutted. The ECJ in *Eurofood* said that the COMI presumption "can be rebutted only if factors which are both objective and ascertainable by third parties enable it to be established that an actual situation exists which is different from that which locating it at that registered office is deemed to reflect. That could be so in particular in the case of a 'letterbox' company not carrying out any business in the territory of the member state in which its registered office is situated".[50] An example of a "letterbox" company is found in *Re Kaupthing Capital Partners II Master LP Inc*.[51] There the court determined London to be the COMI of a limited partnership established in Guernsey, having concluded from the evidence that Master's head office functions were in fact conducted in London by the operator and by investment and other managers, and that it would have been apparent to third parties doing business with Master that this was the case. Hence the court was satisfied that the presumption that Master's COMI was in Guernsey had been rebutted by objective and ascertainable factors, as stipulated in the *Stanford* decision, so that the English court had jurisdiction under the EC Regulation.[52]

Another example of a successful rebuttal of the COMI presumption is *Re European Directories (DH6) BV*,[53] in which a Dutch-formed company designated its branch office in Chiswick as the designated Head Office of the company. Furthermore the company, which did not have a business address in The Netherlands, wrote to its creditors and counterparties to notify them that the Chiswick address was the new address for correspondence. Among other factors linking the company to its English adoptive COMI, its website listed the Chiswick office as the company's address and stated that the company's operational

---

[47] *Re Stanford International Bank Ltd (In Receivership)* [2011] Ch. 33 (CA), [56]. Note that although *Stanford* concerned the interpretation of COMI under the Cross-Border Insolvency Regulations 2006, it is also an authority on the meaning of COMI under the EC Regulation because the Court of Appeal held that the *Eurofood* COMI test applied equally to the Cross-Border Insolvency Regulations 2006. The Court of Appeal decision on this point has been the subject of a measure of academic criticism, see Look Chan Ho, "Misunderstanding the Model Law: *Re Stanford International Bank*" (2011) 26:7 J.I.B.F.L. 395.
[48] *Re Kaupthing Capital Partners II Master LP Inc* [2011] B.C.C. 338, [13].
[49] *Re Hellas Telecommunications (Luxembourg) II SCA* [2010] B.C.C. 295, [3]; *Re European Directories (DH6) BV* [2011] B.P.I.R. 408, [38]. See also fn.37 regarding *Interedil Srl v Fallimento Interedil Srl* (C-396/09) (ECJ) (October 20, 2011).
[50] *Re Eurofood IFSC* (C-341/04) [2006] Ch. 508, [34]–[35].
[51] *Re Kaupthing Capital Partners II Master LP Inc* [2011] B.C.C. 338, [13].
[52] *Re Kaupthing Capital Partners II Master LP Inc* [2011] B.C.C. 338, [2], [4], [14], [17]–[19], [26] and [27].
[53] *Re European Directories (DH6) BV* [2011] B.P.I.R. 408.

headquarters was in London. There was further evidence to show the company had a bank account in London, the sole signatory to which was the chief financial officer based at the Chiswick office, and that creditors communicated with the company and its advisors in London. The court held that the company had discharged the onus which rested upon it to demonstrate that the presumption that the COMI is the place of its registered office had indeed been rebutted.[54]

Unsurprisingly, some debtors have manufactured factors used to rebut the COMI presumption in order to move the COMI location. For instance, in *Re Hellas Telecommunications (Luxembourg) II SCA*,[55] the court accepted that the COMI of a Luxembourg entity had moved from Luxembourg to England. The court held thus:

"[I]t is said that the company's COMI was changed from Luxembourg to England in the middle of August this year. I have to consider the position as at today's date. That is to say some three months on. The objective and ascertainable facts on which the company relies in support of its contention that it has shifted its COMI are that its head office and principal operating address is now in London, albeit that the premises it occupies are relatively modest since the company is no more than a financing and shareholding vehicle. The company's creditors were notified of its change of address around that time and an announcement was made by way of a press release that its activities were shifting to England. It has opened a bank account in London and all payments are made into and from that bank account although there still remains a bank account in Luxembourg to deal with minor miscellaneous payments. It has registered under the Companies Act in this country, although its registered office remains in Luxembourg and it may remain liable to pay tax in Luxembourg too.

The purpose of the COMI is to enable creditors in particular to know where the company is and where it may deal with the company. Therefore, it seems to me that one of the most important features of the evidence, which is the feature I mention next, is that all negotiations between the company and its creditors have taken place in London.

On that evidence I am satisfied that the company has moved its COMI from Luxembourg to England . . ."[56]

As was explained above at para.31–003, fn.10, Denmark did not participate in the **31–018** adoption the Regulation despite its being a full member of the European Union. Recital (33) to the Regulation carefully states that Denmark "is therefore not bound by it nor subject to its application" That provides the basis for concluding that the Regulation has no application in a case where the COMI of the debtor is located in Denmark: the courts of the other 26 Member States are then free to deploy their domestic rules of jurisdiction, just as in those cases where the

---

[54] *Re European Directories (DH6) BV* [2011] B.P.I.R. 408, [43]–[44], per H.H.J. Raynor QC.
[55] *Re Hellas Telecommunications (Luxembourg) II SCA* [2010] B.C.C. 295.
[56] *Re Hellas Telecommunications (Luxembourg) II SCA* [2010] B.C.C. 295, [4]–[6], per Lewison J.

COMI is found to be in some non-Member State. This argument found favour with the English court in *Re Arena Corporation Ltd*[57] in which the debtor, a company formed under the laws of the Isle of Man, was held to have its COMI in Denmark. By virtue of its having some assets in England, the company also had 'sufficient connection' with the UK to allow the English court to exercise a winding up jurisdiction under s.221 of the Insolvency Act 1986.

Further examples of the English courts' approach to the test to be applied when considering the location of a company's COMI are found in the *Daisytek*[58], *Crisscross*[59], and *Collins & Aikman*[60] cases[61] in which a functional ("head office functions" or "command and control") test for locating the COMI was applied. A notable feature of each of those two cases was that they arose in the context of insolvency affecting a group of companies which happened to have been formed and registered under the laws of different States, but which upon a functional analysis could be shown to be administered in a systematic manner from a single geographical location. One weakness of the Regulation is that it makes no provision for the insolvency of corporate groups. This inevitably prevents the Regulation from providing an effective response to some of the commercial issues which typically present themselves in the context of international insolvency, where it is often the case that a business venture is conducted by means of a network of corporate entities, which may have been formed under the law of one country or (more usually) under the laws of two or more. It is often the case that it would be advantageous if the affairs of an insolvent group could be administered under a single insolvency regime, through some species of procedural (if not substantive) consolidation of proceedings. In the *Daisytek, Crisscross,* and *Collins & Aikman* cases, the English court was able to achieve a de facto administrative consolidation of the conduct of the parallel insolvency proceedings concerning the members of the group by first ruling upon its competence to exercise jurisdiction over each of the individual members of the group, and then appointing the same insolvency practitioner to be the office holder in each of the respective proceedings. Nevertheless, it must be acknowledged that each of the proceedings was legally distinct from the others, so that it would be necessary for the office holder to maintain scrupulous attention to the specific interests of the distinct sets of creditors and other interested parties. Moreover, all three cases were decided prior to the ECJ ruling in the *Eurofood* case, and the respective judicial conclusions as to the location of the COMI of the companies in question must nowadays be approached with caution.

31–019   A debtor's centre of main interests is to be determined at the time the court is required to decide whether to open insolvency proceedings. In cases where insolvency proceedings are opened by the presentation of a petition, that time

---

[57] *Re Arena Corporation Ltd* [2004] B.P.I.R. 415 (CA).
[58] *Re Daisytek-ISA Ltd* [2003] B.C.C. 562.
[59] *Re Crisscross Telecommunications Group* Unreported May 20, 2003.
[60] *Re Collins & Aikman Corp Group* [2006] B.C.C. 606.
[61] Some of these cases are described in detail in I.F. Fletcher, *Insolvency in Private International Law*, 2nd edn (Oxford University Press, 2005), paras 7.67–7.74.

will normally be the hearing of the petition.[62] However, the ECJ has ruled that the court of the Member State within the territory of which the centre of the debtor's main interests is situated at the time when the debtor lodges the request to open insolvency proceedings retains jurisdiction to open those proceedings if the debtor moves the centre of his main interests to the territory of another Member State after lodging the request, but before the proceedings are opened.[63] It should therefore follow that, where involuntary proceedings are commenced by the act of a creditor presenting a petition for the opening of insolvency proceedings to the court of the Member State in which, according to the evidence current as at that point in time, the centre of the debtor's main interests is situated, that court should also retain jurisdiction to open the proceedings requested even if the debtor moves the centre of his main interests before the time when the court can hear and determine the creditor's application.[64]

The relevant principle is that of *perpetuatio fori*[65] whereby once proceedings are taken with jurisdictions, that jurisdiction cannot be lost. The policy behind the application of the principle here is to deter forum-shopping.[66]

It should also be noted that r.1.3(2)(q) of the Insolvency Rules 1986 (as amended) requires the directors' proposal for a CVA to state whether the EC Regulation will apply, and if so, whether the proceedings will be main proceedings, secondary proceedings or territorial proceedings. Further, r.1.24(2)(ca) requires that the report of the chairman of the meetings of the company and of the creditors to consider approving a CVA must state whether, in the opinion of the supervisor: (i) the EC Regulation applies to the voluntary arrangement; and (ii) if so, whether the proceedings are main proceedings, secondary proceedings or territorial proceedings. It is suggested that neither of the two forms of declaration made under r.1.3(2)(q) or r.1.24(2)(ca) (as the case may be) should be equated with a formal judicial pronouncement as to the location of the COMI of the company in question. Thus it would be open to a person with the requisite standing to challenge a voluntary arrangement approved by meetings of the company and its creditors by making an application to the court under s.6(1) of, or para.38(1) of Sch.1A to, the Insolvency Act 1986 on the ground that the location of the company's COMI was wrongly identified by those responsible for confirming that this vital jurisdictional test was met, and that this constitutes a "material irregularity at or in relation to either of the meetings", as specified in s.6(1)(b) of, and in para.38(1)(b) of Sch.1A to, the Insolvency Act 1986.

---

[62] *Shierson v Vlieland-Boddy* [2005] 1 W.L.R. 3966 (CA). However, this decision must be read in the light of the ruling of the ECJ in *Re Staubitz-Schreiber* (C-1/04) [2006] B.C.C. 639, See also *Interedil Srl v Fallimento Interedil Srl* (C-396/09) (ECJ) (October 20, 2011).

[63] *Re Staubitz-Schreiber* (C-1/04) [2006] B.C.C. 639.

[64] It may also be submitted that where the court is required to determine the debtor's centre of main interests in the context of an application for permission to serve the petition out of the jurisdiction, the time for the determination would be at the hearing of that application.

[65] Virgos and Garcimartin, *The European Insolvency Regulation* (Kluwer, 2004), para.68.

[66] Virgos and Garcimartin, *The European Insolvency Regulation* (Kluwer, 2004), para.68.

(ii)   Subsidiary competence—secondary proceedings

31–020   Article 3(2) states that, where the centre of the debtor's main interests is situated within the territory of a Member State, the courts of another Member State have a jurisdiction to open insolvency proceedings only if the debtor possesses *an establishment* in the territory of that other Member State. Most importantly, art.3(2) further provides that the effects of such proceedings are restricted to the local assets of the debtor. Moreover, where insolvency proceedings have already been opened at the forum of primary competence, any proceedings opened elsewhere on the basis of an establishment can only be secondary proceedings (as defined in Ch.III). Also, territorial proceedings based on the existence of an establishment can only be opened prior to main insolvency proceedings under art.3(1) in circumstances where special preconditions within art.3(4) are met.

The meaning to be ascribed to the term "establishment" is thus of crucial importance in controlling the exercise of jurisdiction to open territorial proceedings—and especially those which are to be classed as "secondary proceedings"—with respect to a debtor whose centre of main interests lies in a different Member State. "Establishment" is defined in art.2(h) as: "any place of operations where the debtor carries out a non-transitory economic activity with human means and goods"[67] The mere presence of assets, such as a bank account or even immovable property (of itself and without more) does not constitute an "establishment" for the purposes of the Regulation and hence does not enable local territorial proceedings to be opened. Some insight into the intentions underlying the formulation of the concept of establishment was provided by the *Virgos-Schmit Report* to the proposed EC Convention from which the present text was derived. In that document the term is described as a place of operations through which the debtor carries out "economic activities on the market (i.e. externally), whether the said activities are commercial, industrial or professional", to which is added the further comment that "A purely occasional place of operations cannot be classified as 'an establishment'. A certain stability is required . . . The decisive factor is how the activity appears externally, and not the intention of the debtor."[68] To this one might observe that the

---

[67] cf. the somewhat altered form of words used in the equivalent definition in art.2(f) of the UNCITRAL Model Law, discussed below, para.32–008. It should be noted that the English term "goods", which appears in the English version of both texts, is potentially misleading as an intended synonym for the French legal term "biens" (which can refer to intangible, as well as tangible, property). It is submitted that the judicial approach to interpretation of the crucial term "establishment" should seek to arrive at an autonomous meaning that will allow uniformity of effect to be achieved between the different legal traditions. In *Telia AB v Hilcourt (Docklands) Ltd* [2003] B.C.C. 856, the court rejected the submission that the business premises of a subsidiary company could rank as an "establishment" of the parent for the purposes of art.3(2) of the Regulation. Although no supporting reason is offered in the judgment of the court, this ruling seems to have been based on the premise that the separate corporate identity of the subsidiary must be respected. Hence, of itself and without more, the conduct of an economic activity in England by the subsidiary did not, in law, constitute the simultaneous conduct of an economic activity by the parent company at that same location.

[68] *Virgos-Schmit Report* (see above, fn.13), para.71. See also *Interedil Srl v Fallimento Interedil Srl* (C-396/09) (ECJ) (October 20, 2011).

novel concept of "establishment", even with the help of the definition and explanatory comments provided (or perhaps even, because of these), will in some cases prove to be elusive and controversial. It seems inescapable that the European Court of Justice will at some stage—and perhaps on several occasions—be required to provide interpretative guidance on this matter. It is suggested that the essential question that the judge of fact must seek to answer is whether the debtor maintains a "place of business" within the jurisdiction in which the opening of secondary—or territorial—proceedings is sought by a suitably qualified party.

Although there has not been much English case-law on the meaning of establishment, there are many persuasive authorities under Ch.15 of the US Bankruptcy Code establishing the following[69]:

"Unlike with the determination of COMI, chapter 15 provides no evidentiary presumption in connection with the determination of whether a debtor has an establishment in a particular jurisdiction. The petitioner has the burden of proof on whether a debtor has an establishment in the country of the foreign proceeding."[70]

"The existence of an 'establishment' is essentially a factual question, with no presumption in its favor."[71]

"The mere presence of assets in a given location does not, by itself, constitute a place of operation."[72]

"Auditing activities and preparation of incorporation papers performed by a third party do not in plain language terms constitute 'operations' or 'economic activity' by the [debtor]."[73]

"[I]n order to have a 'place of operations' . . . [the debtor] must have had 'a place from which economic activities are exercised on the market (i.e. externally), whether the said activities are commercial, industrial or professional' at the time [of] the petition for recognition."[74]

"In the context of corporate debtors, there must be a place of business for there to be an establishment."[75]

---

[69] For in-depth discussion of the Ch.15 cases, see Look Chan Ho, *Cross-Border Insolvency: A Commentary on the UNCITRAL Model Law*, 3rd edn (Globe Publishing, 2011) (forthcoming).

[70] *In Re British American Insurance Company Ltd* 425 BR 884, 915 (Bankr SD Fla 2010).

[71] *In Re Bear Stearns High-Grade Structured Credit Strategies Master Fund, Ltd*, 389 BR 325, 338 (SDNY 2008).

[72] *Lavie v Ran (In re Ran)* 607 F3d 1017, 1027 (5th Cir Tex 2010). However, the absence of assets might suggest the absence of establishment. *Re Bear Stearns High-Grade Structured Credit Strategies Master Fund, Ltd* 389 BR 325, 339 (SDNY 2008) ("In general, section 1521(c) of the Bankruptcy Code limits the scope of relief available in a nonmain proceeding to relief related to assets located in the nonmain jurisdiction or closely connected thereto, while a plenary bankruptcy proceeding where the [debtors] are located would control the [debtors'] principal assets. The fact that the [debtors] had no assets in the Cayman Islands at the time of filing supports the conclusion that nonmain recognition would be inappropriate.").

[73] *Re Bear Stearns High-Grade Structured Credit Strategies Master Fund, Ltd* 389 BR 325, 339 (SDNY 2008).

[74] *Lavie v Ran (In re Ran)* 607 F3d 1017, 1027 (5th Cir Tex 2010).

[75] *Lavie v Ran (In re Ran)* 607 F3d 1017, 1027 (5th Cir Tex 2010). *Re Bear Stearns High-Grade Structured Credit Strategies Master Fund, Ltd* 374 BR 122, 131 (Bankr SDNY 2007) ("there must be . . . a local place of business.").

"To have an establishment in a country, the debtor must conduct business in that country. The location should constitute a 'seat for local business activity' for the debtor . . . The terms 'operations' and 'economic activity' require showing of a local effect on the marketplace, more than mere incorporation and record-keeping and more than just the maintenance of property."[76]

"Equating a corporation's principal place of business to an individual debtor's primary or habitual residence, a place of business could conceivably align with the debtor having a secondary residence or possibly a place of employment in the country where the receiver claims that he has an establishment."[77]

"[A]n individual's bankruptcy proceeding pending in another country and related debts alone are [not] sufficient to constitute an establishment under Chapter 15 . . . [R]ecognition based on the existence of the bankruptcy proceeding and debts alone poses problems. First, a bankruptcy proceeding is by definition a transitory action, but recognition as a nonmain proceeding requires that the debtor carry out nontransitory activity in a location . . . To permit a transitory action, i.e., the existence of [foreign] bankruptcy proceeding and corresponding debts alone to constitute the basis for finding nontransitory economic activity, would be inappropriate because it would go against the plain meaning of the statute. Second, if [the debtor's] bankruptcy proceeding and associated debts, alone, could suffice to demonstrate an establishment, this would render the framework of Chapter 15 meaningless. There would be no reason to define establishment as engaging in a nontransitory economic activity. The petition for recognition would simply require evidence of the existence of the foreign proceeding. But the statute requires more than that – it requires evidence of a foreign proceeding and that the proceeding meet the definition of foreign nonmain proceeding."[78]

(e) Recognition of insolvency proceedings

31–021 The basic principle of recognition is supplied by art.16(1), whereby any judgment opening insolvency proceedings handed down by a court of a Member State which has jurisdiction pursuant to art.3 shall be recognised in all

---

[76] *Re British American Insurance Company Ltd* 425 BR 884, 915 (Bankr SD Fla 2010).

[77] *Lavie v Ran (In re Ran)* 607 F3d 1017, 1027 (5th Cir Tex 2010).

[78] *Lavie v Ran (In re Ran)* 607 F3d 1017, 1026, 1028 (5th Cir Tex 2010); *Re British American Insurance Company Ltd*, 425 BR 884 (Bankr SD Fla 2010). It is interesting to note that while finding an establishment based solely on the existence of an insolvency proceeding is problematic, "[t]here may be instances where a foreign representative remains in place for an extended period, and relocates all of the primary business activities of the debtor to his location (or brings business to a halt), thereby causing creditors and other parties to look to the judicial manager as the location of a debtor's business. This could lead to the conclusion that the center of its main interest has become lodged with the foreign representative" (*In Re British American Insurance Co Ltd* 425 BR 884, 914 (Bankr SD Fla 2010)); see also *Re British American Isle of Venice (BVI), Ltd* 441 BR 713 (Bankr SD Fla 2010).

other Member States *from the time that it becomes effective in the State of the opening of proceedings*. Two further, vital principles are established under the next two articles. Article 17(1) provides that the judgment opening main proceedings under art.3(1) shall, *with no further formalities*, produce the same effects in any other Member State as under the law of the State of opening of proceedings, except where the Regulation provides otherwise and as long as no secondary proceedings are opened in the other Member State under art.3(2)[79];

> "[I]t follows from Article 16(1) of the Regulation, read in conjunction with Article 17(1), that the judgment opening insolvency proceedings in a Member State is to be recognised in all the other Member States from the time that it becomes effective in the State of the opening of proceedings and that it is, with no further formalities, to produce the same effects in any other Member State as under the law of the State of the opening of proceedings. In accordance with Article 25 of the Regulation, recognition of all judgments other than that relating to the opening of insolvency proceedings also occurs automatically."[80]

Article 18(1) provides that the liquidator appointed by a court which has jurisdiction under art.3(1);

> "may exercise *all the powers conferred on him by the law of the State of opening of proceedings in another Member State*, as long as no secondary proceedings have been opened there nor any preservation measure to the contrary has been taken there pursuant to a request for opening of secondary proceedings in that State" (emphasis added).[81]

Article 18(3) further states that the liquidator may, in particular, remove the debtor's assets from the territory of the Member State in which they are situated, (subject to arts 5 and 7),[82] but in exercising his powers he must comply with the law of the Member State within whose territory he intends to take action.

A further advantage for the office-holder is conferred by art.19, whereby   **31–022**
the liquidator's appointment shall be evidenced by a certified copy of the original decision appointing him or any other certificate issued by the court which has jurisdiction. Although a translation into the official language, or one of the official languages, of the Member State in which he intends to act may be required, no further legalisation or other similar formality shall be required—a provision which obviates the need for obtaining an *exequatur*[83] as a precondi-

---

[79] "[O]nly the opening of secondary insolvency proceedings is capable of restricting the universal effect of the main insolvency proceedings": *MG Probud Gdynia* (C-444/07) [2010] B.C.C. 453 (ECJ), [24].

[80] *MG Probud Gdynia* (C-444/07) [2010] B.C.C. 453 (ECJ), [26].

[81] *MG Probud Gdynia* (C-444/07) [2010] B.C.C. 453 (ECJ), [23].

[82] arts 5 and 7 are discussed in paras 31–030 and 31–035 below.

[83] The term "exequatur"—also known as an "executive judgment", denotes a formal judgment authorising the execution of a foreign judgment where validity has been recognised through a special legal procedure in the recognising State. Such procedures can effectively amount to a

tion to the taking of essential action in certain civil law countries. This provision has great practical significance, both in terms of the acceleration of the liquidator's ability to take timely and effective steps in relation to foreign assets (where they are located in other Member States), and in the potential savings in costs in comparison to those which have hitherto had to be incurred in order to obtain a judicial order of enforcement from a foreign court (especially where local creditors resist the application).

The judgment of the European Court of Justice in *Re Eurofood IFSC Ltd*[84] has provided guidance regarding the recognition of the opening of insolvency proceedings. Among the questions the Irish Supreme Court referred to the ECJ was one asking whether the jurisdiction assumed by the court of a Member State to open main insolvency proceedings may be reviewed by a court of another Member State in which recognition has been applied for. In answering this question in the negative, and thereby endorsing the view taken by Advocate-General Jacobs in his opinion delivered earlier in the proceedings, the ECJ emphasised that the rule of recognition laid down by art.16(1) is based on the principle of mutual trust, and that this principle requires that where main insolvency proceedings are opened in one Member State, the courts in another Member State must recognise those proceedings without being able to review the jurisdiction of the opening State.[85] The correct procedure, in a case where a party in interest wishes to question the correctness of the basis on which jurisdiction has been exercised by the court in which insolvency proceedings have been opened, is to invoke whatever rights of appeal or other recourse (such as an application to set aside) are available under the law of the Member State where the proceedings were opened. The ECJ, in answer to a further question submitted by the referring court in the *Eurofood* case, dealt with an exception to the general rule of automatic and unquestioning recognition under the Regulation. Article 26 of the Regulation, properly interpreted, does permit a court in one Member State to refuse to recognise proceedings opened in another Member State on the grounds of public policy, such as where the decision to open the proceedings was taken in flagrant breach of the fundamental right to be heard, which a person concerned by such proceedings enjoys.[86] Such grounds must reach the required community standard and not merely any lower national standard, so that for example recognition cannot be denied for a failure to give an adequate oral hearing required by domestic law if overall the procedure was fair and did enable the relevant party to put his case adequately.[87]

---

retrial of the case, and may include the possibility of revising both the factual and legal determinations of the original judgment, and even the adjustment of the amount of the award. Inevitably such procedures add to the costs of recognition and enforcement of foreign judgments, and can give rise to substantial delay.

[84] *Re Eurofood IFSC* (C-341/04) [2006] Ch. 508, and see para.31-017, above.

[85] See the judgment of the ECJ, May 2, 2006, at paras 38–44. See also the Opinion of the Advocate-General (above, fn.30) at paras 96–105, and *MG Probud Gdynia* (C-444/07) [2010] B.C.C. 453 (ECJ), [27]–[29].

[86] *Re Eurofood IFSC Ltd* (C-341/04) [2006] Ch. 508 (ECJ), [60]–[68]; *MG Probud Gdynia* (C-444/07) [2010] B.C.C. 453 (ECJ), [34].

[87] *Re Eurofood IFSC Ltd* (C-341/04) [2006] Ch. 508 (ECJ), [68].

(f)   Secondary insolvency proceedings

Chapter III of the Regulation enables secondary proceedings to be opened, **31–023** where jurisdiction arises from the existence of an establishment of the debtor in the Member State in question, purely by virtue of the opening of main proceedings elsewhere under art.3(1). There is thus no need for independent satisfaction of the local law's test for determining the debtor's insolvency. The mere fact (if such be the case) that the debtor's local establishment is trading normally and does not meet any applicable test under local insolvency laws that would enable insolvency proceedings to be opened, is for this purpose not relevant.

Secondary proceedings can only be winding-up proceedings of the types listed in Annex B for each Member State. This may generate obstacles to the effective implementation of main proceedings which are aimed at rescue and rehabilitation, rather than liquidation of the debtor's business.[88] It may be noted that art.33 enables the liquidator in the main proceedings to obtain a stay of the secondary proceedings by application to the court which opened them, but there are unclear limitations to the obligation of the court to grant the stay, which can in any event only be obtained for periods of three months at a time (albeit such orders granting stay are renewable). Using art.33 "would . . . halt the realisation of assets located in the State of the secondary proceedings. But it would not prevent the continuation of winding-up proceedings in the Member States in which each of the Companies is incorporated . . . and the effect of the commencement and continuation of such proceedings is likely to be to cause the relevant Company to cease to trade save for the purposes of winding up".[89]

One way of controlling the opening of secondary proceedings would be for the court opening main insolvency proceedings to issue a letter of request to the courts of other Member States asking those courts to put in place arrangements under which the insolvency officeholders of the main proceedings will be given notice of any request or application for the opening of secondary insolvency proceedings. The letter will also request the foreign courts to permit the insolvency officeholders of the main proceedings to make submissions on any such applications in respect of the potential damage which secondary proceedings might have on the interests of the estate and the creditors of the relevant debtor.[90]

Further, in order to undermine the economic incentive to commence secondary proceedings elsewhere subsequent to English main proceedings, the English court may permit English officeholders to treat local creditors in accordance with local insolvency priority.[91]

According to both art.3(2) and art.27, secondary proceedings are confined in **31 024** their effect to assets of the debtor situated within the territory of the Member State in which they are opened. They are, however, governed by the law of the

---

[88] However, sometimes secondary proceedings are necessary in order to resolve matters for the benefit of the creditors as a whole, e.g. *Re Nortel Networks SA (No.2)* [2010] B.C.C. 21.

[89] *Re Nortel Networks SA* [2009] B.C.C. 343, [13] (Patten J.).

[90] *Re Nortel Networks SA* [2009] B.C.C. 343.

[91] e.g. *Re MG Rover Espana SA* [2006] B.C.C. 599; *Re MG Rover Belux* [2007] B.C.C. 446; *Re Collins & Aikman Europe* [2006] B.C.C. 861.

Member State in which they are opened (art.28), which reveals their primary value, namely to enable local expectations with regard to such matters as priority of entitlement to dividend to be met, to the extent that the locally situated assets are sufficient for this purpose, or to ensure that a locally perfected security interest retains full validity and priority as conferred under the local law. Notably, art.29 permits the opening of secondary proceedings to take place on the request of either the liquidator in the main proceedings or any other person or authority empowered to request the opening of insolvency proceedings under the law of the State in which their opening is requested.

It is obvious that situations will occur in which the question of the *situs* of assets at a particular moment in time will be crucial to the outcome of competing claims arising under rival proceedings (primary or secondary), or under the operation of the special choice of law rules in arts 4–15 inclusive.[92] Some definitional rules are supplied by art.2(g) to determine the meaning of *situs* with respect to certain types of asset, but it should be noted that many types of intangible, movable property are not covered by this provision.[93]

31–025   Other important principles regarding the administration of assets under the system of primary and secondary proceedings are established by art.32, and also by art.20. Any creditor may lodge his claim in the main proceedings and in any secondary proceedings, and the liquidators in the respective sets of proceedings are to lodge in the other proceedings claims which have already been lodged in the proceedings for which they were appointed. This reaffirms the principle of collective treatment of all creditors' claims in the insolvency of the same debtor, but may engender considerable administrative complexity in cross-accounting and record keeping. The proposition that no creditor should gain an advantage over others of co-ordinate rank, either by means of any private acts of diligence or through participation in extraterritorial insolvency proceedings, is respected and applied by art.20. This provision effectively embodies the *hotchpot* rule whereby such recoveries must be accounted for to the liquidator in any proceedings in which the creditor seeks to participate, and the creditor can only begin to share in distributions when creditors of the same ranking or category have obtained an equivalent dividend.

If, by some chance, the liquidation of assets in the secondary proceedings results in the full satisfaction of all claims allowable under those proceedings, art.35 specifies that any surplus assets remaining are to be transferred to the liquidator in the main proceedings. In practice, no doubt, the limited pool of assets comprising the available estate in the secondary proceeding will in most cases be exhausted when payment has been made to those creditors whose

---

[92] The Regulation does not make provision to indicate what should happen where assets are wrongfully removed from a particular jurisdiction before the relevant time. It must be presumed that the liquidator will bring proceedings in the State in which they are subsequently located to bring about the repatriation of the assets to the State in which his appointment took place.

[93] Commentators have discussed this at some length, e.g. Moss, Fletcher and Isaacs: *The EC Regulation on Insolvency Proceedings, A Commentary and Annotated Guide*, 2nd edn (Oxford University Press, 2009), pp.137–139; Philip Smart, "Rights In rem, Article 5 and the EC Insolvency Regulation: An English Perspective" (2006) 15 *International Insolvency Review* 17, 27–29; Miguel Virgos and Francisco Garcimartín, *The European Insolvency Regulation: Law and Practice* (Kluwer Law International, 2004), pp.163–168.

claims enjoy preferential status according to local insolvency law. Where the process of distribution reaches the level of the non-preferential claims, it should be a matter for the primary and secondary liquidators to resolve between themselves the most efficient way in which to administer the distributional process. Thus, loss of value might be avoided if the balance of funds available in the secondary estate were used to meet claims of local, non-preferential creditors by payments to them matching the proportion of dividend which the primary liquidator is able to pay to creditors of the same degree whose claims are channelled via the main administration. Of course both liquidators must act with vigilance to ensure that no creditor is able to violate the principle against double recovery, as might happen if the same claim were processed separately in the two administrations.

(g)   Uniform rules on conflict of laws

One of the principal features of the Regulation is the creation of certain uniform conflict-of-law rules for insolvency proceedings to which the Regulation applies.[94] The Regulation establishes a general rule which, subject to defined exceptions, allocates matters to the law of the State in which proceedings have been opened.[95] Consequently, the Regulation's general choice-of-law rule is one of the means by which main insolvency proceedings are given universal, EU wide effect—the law of the State of opening of proceedings applies and is to be given effect across the whole of the EU.   **31–026**

The law of the State of opening of proceedings does not apply for all purposes. This limitation is necessary because, in the words of Recital (24) to the Regulation, "automatic recognition of insolvency proceedings to which the law of the opening State normally applies may interfere with the rules under which transactions are carried out in other Member States. To protect legitimate expectations and the certainty of transactions in Member States other than that in which proceedings are opened, provisions should be made for a number of exceptions to the general rule".[96] By allocating particular issues to a state other than that of the state of opening, these exceptions establish limits on the extraterritorial effect of the law of the State of the opening of main proceedings and therefore enshrine a number of significant policy decisions regarding the balance to be maintained between the law of the forum and other potentially relevant and competing jurisdictions.[97]

---

[94] Note that one of the objectives set out in the mandate given to the Working Group, established in 1989 by the EEC Council of Ministers to draft the Convention, was to "harmonise certain conflict rules that bear on the administration of bankruptcies . . ." M. Balz, "The European Union Convention on Insolvency Proceedings" (1996) 70 Am. Bankr. L.J. 485, 495.

[95] art.4.

[96] See also Recitals (25)–(28) which provide explanations of the need, and justifications, for the exceptional treatment given by the Regulation to rights in rem, set-off, payment systems and financial markets and employees' claims.

[97] "The purpose of these rules is to delineate the issues which are properly governed by insolvency law from those that should be treated as non-bankruptcy issues because non-bankruptcy policies should prevail, and then to determine the law applicable to such insolvency law situations", Balz, "The European Union Convention on Insolvency Proceedings" (1996) 70 Am. Bankr. L.J. 485, 506.

The general rule is set out in art.4. This provides that, save as otherwise provided in the Regulation, the law applicable to insolvency proceedings and their effects shall be that of the Member State within the territory of which such proceedings are opened (the "State of the opening of proceedings").

31–027   Article 4 stipulates that the law of the State of the opening of proceedings is to determine the conditions for the opening of those proceedings, their conduct and their closure and in particular:

(a) against which debtors insolvency proceedings may be brought on account of their capacity;

(b) the assets which form part of the estate and the treatment of assets acquired by or devolving on the debtor after the opening of the insolvency proceedings;

(c) the respective powers of the debtor and the liquidator;

(d) the conditions under which set-offs may be invoked;

(e) the effects of insolvency proceedings on current contracts to which the debtor is party;

(f) the effects of the insolvency proceedings on proceedings brought by individual creditors, with the exception of lawsuits pending;

(g) the claims which are to be lodged against the debtor's estate and the treatment of claims arising after the opening of insolvency proceedings;

(h) the rules governing the lodging, verification and admission of claims;

(i) the rules governing the distribution of proceeds from the realisation of assets, the ranking of claims and the rights of creditors who have obtained partial satisfaction after the opening of insolvency proceedings by virtue of a right in rem or through a set-off;

(j) the conditions for and the effects of closure of insolvency proceedings, in particular by composition;

(k) creditors' rights after the closure of insolvency proceedings;

(l) who is to bear the costs and expenses incurred in the insolvency proceedings;

(m) the rules relating to the voidness, voidability or unenforceability of legal acts detrimental to all the creditors.

Thus, the general rule allocates to the state of the opening of proceedings issues relating to the "conditions for the opening of the proceedings, their conduct and their closure" and then provides a more detailed list of issues which "in particular" are governed by such law. This is intended to be a non-exhaustive list of matters which relate to the opening, conduct and closure of proceedings.[98] In this way, the law of the State of the opening of proceedings determines the procedural and substantive effects of the insolvency proceedings. The substantive effects referred to are those typical of insolvency law, i.e. effects which are necessary for the insolvency proceeding to fulfil its aims.[99]

The ambit of art.4 therefore appears to be wide ranging. Because the **31–028** Regulation applies to and focuses on collective insolvency proceedings which entail the partial or total divestment of a debtor and the appointment of a liquidator,[100] the model used for the purposes of art.4 is that of a liquidation or bankruptcy and the activities and matters identified in art.4 are those which typically occur or arise in a liquidation or bankruptcy (i.e. the rights of creditors to participate in the insolvency, the effect of the insolvency on the rights of creditors to bring proceedings against the assets of the company and the powers and rights of the insolvency officeholder).

Included in the list are "creditors' rights after the closure of insolvency proceedings" and this presumably includes the effect of a discharge in bankruptcy proceedings. It also appears to include the effect of a variation or discharge of indebtedness arising under a voluntary arrangement.[101] Voluntary arrangements can be used in a wide variety of circumstances; at one end of the spectrum are cases in which there is a realisation of assets and distribution of the proceeds to creditors in full and final settlement of creditors' claims (i.e. a quasi-liquidation) whilst at the other end of the spectrum are cases which involve a debt restructuring in which the debtor's liabilities are rescheduled or restructured (with a consequential discharge or variation of the debtor's liabilities perhaps in consideration for the issue of new debt and without the realisation of assets or the payment of a cash dividend to creditors). Article 4 appears to apply to both types of case with the result that the validity of the variation or discharge of indebtedness is governed by the law of the State of the opening of proceedings. In the context of a voluntary arrangement in the UK, the rule that the discharge or variation of liabilities made and arising under it is effective in relation to all obligations of the debtor, no matter what the governing law of the debt in question, does not represent a change in the law since, as a matter of English law, a voluntary arrangement (by analogy with the law relating to the discharge of indebtedness in an English bankruptcy and a scheme of arrangement[102] would be effective as against all creditors bound by the voluntary arrangement wherever domiciled and whatever the law governing the debt in question. To the extent that a main proceeding commenced in a state other than

---

[98] *MG Probud Gdynia* (C-444/07) [2010] B.C.C. 453 (ECJ), [25].

[99] See, in relation to the equivalent provisions of the Convention (to the extent that it can be treated as having a bearing on the interpretation of the Regulation) the *Virgos-Schmit Report*, above, fn.13, para.90.

[100] See art.1(1).

[101] See Annex A which refers, in the section covering the UK, to "voluntary arrangements under insolvency legislation".

[102] See, Dicey, Morris and Collins, *The Conflict of Laws*, 14th edn (London: Sweet & Maxwell, 2006), r.194 and in relation to schemes of arrangement, *New Zealand Loan & Mercantile Agency Company v Morrison* [1898] A.C. 349 (PC). See also Dicey, Morris, and Collins, *The Conflict of Laws*, 14th edn (London: Sweet & Maxwell, 2006), p.1512, fn.83. See generally Dicker and Segal, "Cross Border Insolvencies and Rescues: The English Perspective" (1999) 8 Int. Insolv Rev 127.

the UK makes provision for the variation or discharge of the obligations of the debtor, then the English courts will have to recognise and give effect to the discharge under the law of that State even in cases where the obligation discharged or varied is governed by English law. This would seem to overturn the traditional English rule that only a variation or discharge under English law is effective to discharge obligations governed by English law.[103]

31–029   The application of national insolvency law by the courts in the State of the opening of proceedings, and the automatic extension of its effects to all Member States, may interfere with the rules under which transactions are carried out in these States. Therefore, to protect legitimate expectations and the certainty of transactions in States other than the one in which proceedings are opened, the Regulation provides for a number of exceptions to the general rule.[104]

These exceptions (contained in arts 5–15 of the Regulation) can be divided into two categories:

(a) the Regulation excludes certain rights over assets located abroad from the effects of the insolvency proceedings[105]; and

(b) the Regulation ensures that certain effects of the insolvency proceedings are governed not by the law of the State of the opening of proceedings but by the law of another State.[106]

It should be noted that these provisions, when referring to the jurisdiction that displaces the State of the opening as the governing law, generally make express reference to the law of another Member State. This form of words clearly has the effect of restricting the benefit of the exception to those cases where the applicable law of the right or transaction in question happens to be that of another EU Member State (other than Denmark). In certain cases, however, namely those falling under arts 6 or 14, no limiting words have been employed in drafting the relevant provisions to confine their effects in that way. Accordingly, on a literal construction of those two articles the jurisdiction to which the Regulation will allocate a particular issue could be a State outside the EU. An argument has been advanced to suggest that the literal meaning of arts 6 and 14 should be disregarded, on the basis that the Regulation is limited

---

[103] Dicey, Morris and Collins, *The Conflict of Laws*, 14th edn (London: Sweet & Maxwell, 2006), r. 200. Note that the construction argued for above seems to be supported by the views of the Chairman of the EEC Working Group which was responsible for drafting the Convention: "[I]t has long been argued by some that the law governing the debtor's obligations (lex contractus) should be applied to the issue of discharge, at least cumulatively, i.e., in addition to the law of the opening State. Article 4 now clarifies that only the law of the opening State will govern." Balz, "The European Union Convention on Insolvency Proceedings" (1996) 70 Am. Bankr. L.J. 485, 508. Note also that the traditional English rule may no longer be valid even as a matter of common law: Look Chan Ho, "Recognising Foreign Insolvency Discharge and Stare Decisis" [2011] J.I.B.L.R. 266; Look Chan Ho, "Applying Foreign Law—Realising the Model Law's Potential" [2010] J.I.B.L.R. 552.
[104] arts 5–15.
[105] arts 5, 7, 8, 11 and 14.
[106] arts 6, 9, 10, 12, 13–15.

to the intra-Community effect of insolvency proceedings.[107] If this approach were to be accepted, it would be left to Member States in these cases to decide what choice-of-law rules to apply. It is submitted, with respect, that the commercial expectations of parties are best protected, within the spirit proclaimed by Recital (24) of the Regulation, by giving the provisions of arts 6 and 14 a literal construction so that the law of any State identified by the relevant Article should apply whether or not the State is a Member of the EU. Ultimately, no doubt, the matter will have to come before the ECJ for an interpretative ruling.

(i)   Rights of secured creditors (rights in rem)

Article 5(1) states as follows: **31–030**

"The opening of insolvency proceedings shall not affect the rights *in rem* of creditors or third parties in respect of tangible or intangible, movable or immovable assets (both specific assets and collections of indefinite assets as a whole which change from time to time) belonging to the debtor which are situated within the territory of another Member State at the time of the opening of proceedings."[108]

In order to come within art.5 (and therefore avoid the law of the State of the opening of proceedings affecting the right in rem in question) it is necessary to establish: (1) the existence of rights in rem in favour of creditors or other third parties; and (2) the fact that the assets in question are situated within the territory of another Member State at the time of the opening of proceedings.

Article 5 does not provide a definition of rights in rem but states that rights in rem shall "in particular mean":

(a) the right to dispose of assets or have them disposed of and to obtain satisfaction from the proceeds of or income from those assets, in particular by virtue of a lien or a mortgage;

(b) the exclusive right to have a claim met, in particular a right guaranteed by a lien in respect of the claim or by assignment of the claim by way of a guarantee;

(c) the right to demand the assets from, and/or to require restitution by, anyone having possession or use of them contrary to the wishes of the party so entitled;

(d) a right in rem to the beneficial use of assets.

---

[107] M. Virgos and F. Garcimartin, *The European Insolvency Regulation: Law and Practice* (Kluwer Law International, 2004), at points 27 and 245.

[108] See also Recital (25) to the Regulation which explains the reasons for the exceptional treatment for rights in rem and that "the basis, validity and extent of . . . a right in rem should . . . normally be determined according to the *lex situs* and not be affected by the opening of insolvency proceedings".

31–031 The absence of a definition appears to be deliberate and to leave the question of what constitutes a right in rem to the law of the State where the assets in question are located. This was certainly the case in relation to the Convention— para.100 of the *Virgos-Schmit Report* noted that:

> "the Convention does not intend to impose its own definition of a right *in rem* running the risk of describing as rights *in rem* legal positions which the law of the State where the assets are located does not consider to be rights *in rem* or of not encompassing rights *in rem* which do not fulfil the conditions of that definition . . . For this reason the characterisation of a right *in rem* must be sought in the national law which, according to the normal pre-insolvency conflict of law rules, governs rights *in rem* (in general the *lex rei sitae* at the relevant time)".

Recital (25) to the Regulation suggests that it is intended that this approach should apply to the Regulation also. Recital (25) explains that the "basis, validity and content of . . . a right *in rem* should . . . normally be determined according to the *lex situs*". Whether this approach is the correct one in the context of the Regulation, and the meaning to be given to and status of the art.5(2) examples of rights in rem, must await a ruling in due course by the ECJ.

In many cases the issue whether a particular right constitutes a right in rem will, as a matter of English law, be uncontroversial. There will be cases where it will become necessary carefully to examine the ambit of the reference to "rights in rem" to see whether particular types of right or remedy under English law can be said to be rights in rem for this purpose.[109] Considerable concern had been expressed in this context as to whether the floating charge would satisfy the requirements of a right in rem. The uncertainties have been removed by the inclusion in the Regulation of the words "(both specific assets and collections of indefinite assets as a whole which change from time to time)", which words were not incorporated into the Convention but were added to ensure that the floating charge was adequately covered.

31–032 The question also arises as to whether art.5 applies only to rights in rem in existence at the date of the commencement of the relevant insolvency proceedings or to rights in rem created thereafter. The *Virgos-Schmit Report* in relation to the Convention suggested that if a right in rem is created after the commencement of insolvency proceedings it is not covered or protected by art.5.[110]

It should also be noted that rights in rem are not immune from the effect of proceedings to which the Regulation relates. If the law of the State where the assets are located imposes a stay on the enforcement of security following the commencement of a local insolvency proceeding, the liquidator in the main

---

[109] Consider, for instance, restitutionary proprietary remedies and rights under a constructive trust. See the distinction made between rights in rem and rights ad rem in R. Goode, "Property and Unjust Enrichment" in Andrew Burrows (ed.), *Essays on the Law of Restitution* (1991), pp.215, 217 and see, generally, W. Swadling's chapter, "Property" in Birks and Rose (eds), *Lessons of the Swaps Litigation* (2000).

[110] *Virgos-Schmit Report*, (above, fn.13), para.103.

proceeding or any other person empowered to do so may request secondary insolvency proceedings to be opened in that State if the debtor has an establishment there.[111] The secondary proceedings are conducted according to local law and affect the rights of secured creditors with assets in that jurisdiction in the same way as in purely domestic proceedings.

Note that art.5 does not prevent actions for voidness, voidability or unenforcability based on the *lex concursus* (see art.4(2)(m)). So even where a third party has a right in rem in respect of an asset situated in another Member State the rights of such third party may be challenged under, and vulnerable to attack pursuant to, the claw back laws of the relevant insolvency proceeding. But the third party may still rely on the protection given by art.13 where the relevant detrimental act can be treated as being subject to the law of a Member State other than that of the state of the opening and that law does not allow any challenge in the relevant case.

(ii) Set-off

Under the general rule applicable by virtue of art.4, insolvency set-off is   **31–033** .subject to the law of the state of the opening of the insolvency proceedings. If insolvency proceedings are opened, it therefore falls to the law of the state of the opening of proceedings to govern the availability of set off and the conditions under which set-off can be exercised against a claim of the debtor.

Article 6 of the Regulation provides additional protection for certain rights of set-off. It states that: "The opening of insolvency proceedings shall not affect the right of creditors to demand the set-off of their claims against the claims of the debtor, where such a set-off is permitted by the law applicable to the insolvent debtor's claim". Accordingly, rights of set off permitted by and arising in accordance with the law applicable to the insolvent debtor's claim are protected and cannot be diminished or otherwise affected by reason of the commencement of main proceedings—art.6 therefore provides a safe harbour for such rights of set-off. The reference to the "law applicable to the insolvent debtor's claim" needs to be considered in light of the nature of the debtor's claim. In the case of a contractual cross claim by the debtor (against the creditor's claim), presumably the proper law of that cross claim is the applicable law.[112] Such an approach has the considerable merits of simplicity and

---

[111] See arts 3(2) and 29. Note that the Working Group established to draft the Convention debated at length whether security holders with foreign situated collateral should be subjected to the insolvency law of the State in which the collateral is located, at least in cases where the law of the opening State provides for some effect of insolvency on the rights of secured creditors. But such an approach was thought to be too complex. See Balz, "The European Union Convention on Insolvency Proceedings" (1996) 70 Am. Bankr. L.J. 485, 509.

[112] This seems to be the case irrespective of the nature of the set off relied on by the creditor because art.6 is directed to the law applicable to the claim and not the law applicable to or governing the availability of the asserted right of set-off. In England, where a person seeks to establish a set-off in a cross-border context, it is necessary to consider the nature of the right of set-off relied upon in order to establish the applicable choice of law rule and therefore the law governing the availability of a set-off. See, e.g. *Meyer v Dresser* (1864) 16 C.B.N.S 646, 665, 666; *Maspons y Hermano v Mildred Goyeneche & Co* (1881–82) L.R. 9 Q.B.D. 530 (CA); Rory Derham, *Derham on the Law of Set-Off*, 4th edn (Oxford University Press, 2010), para.2.55, and

predictability—creditors will be able, at least in straightforward situations which do not involve an insolvent debtor which has a multiplicity of claims, to establish easily the law governing the availability of set-off in the event of their counterparty's insolvency and to draft documentation to ensure that set-off will be available under that law.[113]

The position is far from clear where the insolvent debtor's claim is non-contractual, e.g. a claim in tort; what then is the law applicable to the insolvent debtor's claim (presumably it is necessary to apply the relevant choice of law rules such as that applied in England pursuant to Regulation (EC) No.864/2007 of the European Parliament and of the Council of July 11, 2007 on the law applicable to non-contractual obligations) and whose choice of law rules decide the applicable law in a case involving a foreign element?

31–034   It is interesting to compare the approach laid down by the Regulation with the current position under English law which can be illustrated with reference to a case in which the English court considered the position of a Luxembourg bank which was simultaneously subject to insolvency proceedings in Luxembourg and a winding-up in England.[114] Because the bank was incorporated in Luxembourg, the winding-up in England was to be treated as ancillary to the Luxembourg proceedings[115]; a question arose as to what law should govern rights of set-off in the English proceedings. This was a particularly serious practical problem because rights of set-off are very limited under Luxembourg law. The English court held that the English rules applied so that insolvency set-off was available and, indeed, was mandatory and self-executing.[116] If the Regulation had been in effect, the result would have been the same. English law, as the law of the state of the opening of proceedings— whether the proceedings were main or territorial proceedings—would govern the availability of set-off rights although any rights of set off permitted by the law applicable to BCCI's claim against the creditor would have been protected and unaffected by the winding up (so that the creditor could rely on such rights if it chose to do so). It is worth noting that, if the bank did not have an establishment in England, it could not under the Regulation be wound up in England

---

Wood, *English and International Set-Off*, para.23–026. The nature and type of set-off seem to be irrelevant for the purpose of art.6 which simply focusses on the cross-claim ("the insolvent debtor's claim") which forms the basis of the creditor's set-off and the law relating to it, rather than the type of set-off relied upon and the law applicable to the question of whether set-off is available.

[113] See Recital (26) to the Regulation.

[114] See *Re Bank of Credit & Commerce International SA (No.11)* [1997] Ch. 213. While insolvency proceedings in respect of a credit institution are not subject to the Regulation they are subject to the Credit Institutions (Reorganisation and Winding up) Regulations 2004 which contain in art.28 a safe harbour for set-offs equivalent to the protection provided by art.6 of the Regulation. In any event, the principles enunciated by the court in *Re BCCI (No.11)* are not limited to insolvency proceedings in respect of credit institutions. The House of Lords has subsequently considered the nature and scope of English liquidations of foreign companies subject to insolvency proceedings abroad (see *Re HIH Casualty and General Insurance* [2008] 1 W.L.R. 852 (HL)).

[115] See *Re Bank of Credit & Commerce International SA (No.11)* [1997] Ch. 213, 238–246. The proceeding was limited to assets in the UK, although the English court questioned the jurisdictional basis for ancillary liquidations. Interestingly, since it was arguable that management of the Bank was conducted in and from London, (see p.224), under the Regulation the English proceeding might have been the main proceeding.

[116] See *Re Bank of Credit & Commerce International SA (No.11)* [1997] Ch. 213, 246–248.

and creditors would therefore have lost their English rights of set-off and would be limited to their rights under Luxembourg law, subject, of course, to the operation of art.6. If BCCI's claims were governed by English law then rights of set-off permitted under English law would be protected; but it is open to question whether this is a reference to liquidation set-off under English law or to pre-insolvency set-off under English law. It is suggested that it is more appropriate consider liquidation set-off on the basis of the debtor's deemed liquidation in England. This seems to be consistent with the *Virgos-Schmit Report* which says this:

> "If the 'lex concursus' allows for set-off, no problem will arise and Article 4 should be applied in order to claim the set-off as provided for by the law. On the other hand, if the 'lex concursus' does not allow for set-off (e.g. since it requires both claims to be liquidated, matured and payable prior to a certain date), then Article 6 constitutes an exception to the general application of that law in this respect, by permitting the set-off according to the conditions established for *insolvency set-off* by the law applicable to the insolvent debtor's claim . . ."[117]

(iii) Reservation of title

Under art.7, where a buyer becomes insolvent, the insolvency proceedings will not affect the rights of a seller based on a reservation of title clause if at the time of the opening of the insolvency proceedings, the asset claimed is situated within the territory of a Member State other than the State in which the proceedings are opened.[118] Thus the fact of a debtor company's going into administration in main proceedings in England will not give rise to a stay on the seller's right to repossess goods in the company's possession[119] where those goods are located in another Member State at the time of the buyer's entry into administration.   **31–035**

However, where the seller becomes insolvent after delivery of an asset to a buyer, the seller will not have grounds to rescind or terminate the sale.[120] The buyer, therefore, will not be prevented from acquiring title where at the time of the opening of proceedings the purchased asset is located within the territory of a Member State other than the State of the opening of proceedings.

Where the asset is located in the same Member State as that in which insolvency proceedings in respect of a purchaser are opened (at the time of opening of these proceedings), an action by the seller against the purchaser based on a reservation of title clause is subject to the jurisdictional rules of the Judgments Regulation.[121]

---

[117] *Virgos-Schmit Report*, above, fn.13, para.109 (emphasis added).
[118] See art.7(1). This provision presumably does not prevent the English law provisions making a charge over goods (arising out of a purported reservation of title clause) void for non registration following the liquidation of the buyer merely because the goods were located in another Member State when the winding up order is made.
[119] Insolvency Act 1986, Sch.B1, para.43(3).
[120] See art.7(2).
[121] *German Graphics Graphische Maschinen v Schee* (C-292/08) [2009] E.C.R. I-8421.

(iv)   Contracts relating to immovable property

31–036   Article 8 stipulates that: "The effects of insolvency proceedings on a contract conferring the right to acquire or make use of immovable property shall be governed solely by the law of the Member State within the territory of which the immovable property is situated".

(v)   Payment systems and financial markets

31–037   Article 9 states: "[T]he rights and obligations of parties to a payment or settlement system or to a financial market shall be governed solely by the law of the Member State applicable to that system or market". The intention of art.9 is for the effects of an insolvency proceeding in another Member State on transactions subject to a payment or settlement system or financial market to be the same as those arising in proceedings under national law.[122] This approach is designed to preserve the integrity of settlement systems and financial markets and to prevent damaging market disruptions following an insolvency of a market participant. This means that the impact of Pt VII of the Companies Act 1989 on the operation of UK settlement systems and markets will not be affected by an insolvency proceeding in another Member State.[123]

(vi)   Contracts of employment

31–038   Article 10 provides: "The effects of insolvency proceedings on employment contracts and relationships shall be governed solely by the law of the Member State applicable to the contract of employment".[124]

(vii)   Rights subject to registration

31–039   Article 11 provides: "The effects of insolvency proceedings on the rights of the debtor in immovable property, a ship or an aircraft subject to registration in a public register shall be determined by the law of the Member State under the authority of which the register is kept".

(viii)   Community patents and trade marks

31–040   Article 12 states: "For the purposes of this Regulation a Community patent, a Community trade mark or any other similar right established by Community law may be included only in the proceedings referred to in art.3(1) [main proceedings]."

---

[122] See generally Recital (27) to the Regulation.
[123] See also The Financial Markets and Insolvency (Settlement Finality) Regulations 1999 which implement Directive 98/26/EC on settlement finality in payment and securities settlement systems and which modify the law of insolvency in various respects.
[124] See Recital (28) to the Regulation which explains the purpose of art.10.

(ix) Detrimental acts protected from avoidance

Article 13 states: **31–041**

"Article 4(2)(m) shall not apply where the person who benefited from a legal act detrimental to all the creditors provides proof that:

- the said act is subject to the law of a Member State other than that of the State of the opening of proceedings; and
- that law does not allow any means of challenging that act in the relevant case."

As with the exercise of rights of set-off, the Regulation provides a two-tiered approach for dealing with the law governing the avoidance of pre-insolvency transactions. In general, the law of the Member State where the proceedings are opened governs, subject to the availability of a safe harbour protection.

The basic rule of the Regulation is that under art.4, the law of the State of the opening of proceedings governs any possible voidness, voidability, or unenforceability of acts that may be detrimental to all the creditors' interests. This same law determines the conditions to be met, the manner in which the nullity and voidability function, and the legal consequences of nullity and voidability. Article 13 provides an exception to the law of the State of opening of proceedings. The defence must be pursued by, and the burden of proof is on, the party who relies on it. The aim of art.13 is to uphold the legitimate expectations of creditors or third parties regarding the validity of an act or transaction undertaken in accordance with the normally applicable national law.[125]

In order for the defence to be available it is necessary for the party relying on it first to establish that the impugned act or transaction is "subject to"[126] the law of a Member State other than the State where the proceedings are opened. Second, the party must establish that the law of that other State does not allow a challenge by "any means" and "in the relevant case". "Any means" appears to connote that the act or transaction in question cannot be challenged using either rules which are applicable on an insolvency or other general rules of the applicable national law.[127] "In the relevant case" means that the act or transaction should not be capable of being challenged in the actual circumstances of the case.

The approach adopted by the Regulation for these purposes can be compared   **31–042** with the previously developed approach of the English court to the question of what law governs the application of avoidance provisions in cases with a foreign element. An illustration of the English approach can be found in *Re Paramount Airways Ltd (No.2)*.[128] In that case, administrators made a claim for repayment of sums paid by an insolvent English company from its English

---

[125] See *Virgos-Schmit Report*, above, fn.13, para.138.
[126] Query the meaning of "subject to" here? In the case of a contract presumably it means the governing law of the contract.
[127] See *Virgos-Schmit Report*, above, fn.13, para.137.
[128] *Re Paramount Airways Ltd (No.2)* [1993] Ch. 223 (CA).

bank account to Hambros Bank, Jersey (Hambros Jersey); the sum was to be credited to an account in the name of a Jersey company administration agent. The payment was made on the instructions of a person who was both a director and chairman of the English company. The money was ultimately paid to an account in Hambros Jersey; the account was held by a Panamanian company allegedly owned and controlled by that person.[129] The payment received by the Panamanian company was used to reduce its overdraft with Hambros Jersey. The administrators of the English company alleged that the payments to the Panamanian company were transactions at an undervalue[130] made at a time when the English company was insolvent.[131] The claim against Hambros Jersey was based on the fact that it received a benefit from the repayment of the overdraft of the Panamanian company other than in good faith, for value, and without notice of the relevant circumstances. The question was whether an order could be made against a defendant (i.e. Hambros Jersey) out of the jurisdiction (Jersey).

The Court of Appeal held that the statutory avoidance provisions[132] allow a claim to be made against "any person". As a matter of jurisdiction, such provisions were not subject to any territorial limitation, but, even where the court had jurisdiction to set aside a transaction, it retained a discretion under the applicable statutory provisions as to the order it would make. Where a foreign element was involved, the English court would have to be satisfied, with respect to the relief sought against him, that the defendant was sufficiently connected with England for the order to be just and proper. When considering "sufficient connection" the court would regard a number of factors, including:

"residence and place of business of the defendant, his connection with the insolvent, the nature and purpose of the transaction being impugned, the nature and locality of the property involved, the circumstances in which the defendant became involved in the transaction or received a benefit from it or acquired the property in question, whether the defendant acted in good faith, *whether under any relevant foreign law the defendant acquired an unimpeachable title free from any claims even if the insolvent had been adjudged bankrupt or wound up locally.* The importance to be attached to these factors will vary from case to case."[133]

31-043 If the administration proceedings in this case had been subject to the Regulation (as the main proceedings) then pursuant to the basic rule under art.4, English law (as the law of the Member State where the proceedings had been opened) would initially have applied to determine the validity and avoidability of the challenged transactions. It is unclear whether the English court will still be able or prepared to apply the sufficient connection test. It is arguable that art.4 provides the court with jurisdiction and a direction to apply English law as the

[129] *Re Paramount Airways Ltd (No.2)* [1993] Ch. 223 (CA).
[130] Insolvency Act, 1986, s.238.
[131] *Re Paramount Airways Ltd (No.2)* [1993] Ch. 223 (CA), 231.
[132] Insolvency Act, 1986, s.423.
[133] *Re Paramount Airways Ltd (No.2)* [1993] Ch. 223 (CA), 240 (emphasis added).

lex concursus subject only to the availability of the art.13 defence.[134] Then in order for the court to establish the availability of the art.13 defence, it would have been necessary for the English court to determine first, what was the relevant "detrimental act" for the purposes of art.13 and secondly, the law that the act was "subject to". In the context of the facts of the *Paramount Airways* case, it can be seen that the selection of the relevant "detrimental act" and the law to which it was subject would not necessarily be straightforward.[135] The question also arises as to whether, where the parties to a payment are in a contractual relationship and the payment is made pursuant to the contract, the governing law of the contract will be the law to which the payment, as the relevant detrimental act (assuming that the contract itself is not challenged), is subject.

(x) Protection of third-party purchasers

Article 14 of the Regulation concerns acts of disposal that take place after the opening of the insolvency proceedings. Protection is provided to purchasers who acquire an asset for consideration (i.e. not gratuitously). The assets protected are immovable assets; ships or aircraft subject to registration in a public register; and "securities whose existence pre-supposes registration in a register laid down by law".

    31–044

    The validity of disposal is to be governed by the law of the State where the immovable asset is situated or under the authority of which the register is kept. Once again, this provision is designed to ensure the integrity of transactions by providing the same level of protection for bona fide purchasers for value in proceedings in another Member State as would arise in domestic proceedings.

(xi) Effect on lawsuits pending

Under art.15, "the effects of insolvency proceedings on a lawsuit pending concerning an asset or a right of which the debtor has been divested are to be governed solely by the law of the Member State in which that law suit is pending". The effect of the commencement of the relevant insolvency proceedings on enforcement action begun by individual creditors (prior to the opening of the proceedings) is governed by the law of the State of the opening[136] so that the collective insolvency proceedings may stay or prevent any individual enforcement action brought by creditors against the debtor's assets.

    31–045

---

[134] The alternative view is that since art.4 only directs that English law be applied, the ordinary discretion under English law not to apply English law avoidance rules in the absence of a sufficient connection continues to be available.

[135] Presumably the "act" in that case was the initial transfer by the company to the account of the administration agent on terms that authorised the subsequent transfer to the Panamanian company.

[136] art.4(2)(f). Note that this states that the law of the State in which proceedings are opened governs the effects of insolvency proceedings on proceedings brought by individual creditors with the exception of law suits pending.

The reference to "lawsuit pending" includes pending references to arbitration. Accordingly, the Court of Appeal has affirmed that even where under the *lex concursus* the effect of the opening of insolvency proceedings is to invalidate an arbitration clause and to require any pending arbitration proceedings to be continued, art.15 operated so as to apply English law to determine the effect of the insolvency proceedings on a pending arbitration in London. Since there was no provision of English law which prevented the arbitration from continuing, the arbitration was allowed to proceed.[137]

Article 15 refers to a "lawsuit pending concerning an asset or right of which the debtor has been divested". What does this mean? It has been held at first instance in England, following a decision of an appellate court in Austria and having regard to the other language versions of art.15, that since the purpose of the article is to deal with claims against, or relating to, such of the estate of the debtor as is affected by the insolvency the "divestment" in question is that which takes place by reason of the insolvency proceedings. The expression is not intended to refer to the type of action that is brought by the creditor.[138]

(h)   Creditors' right to lodge claims

31–046   Chapter IV of the Regulation (arts 39–42) contains a limited, but useful, set of provisions aimed at improving the position of creditors in an international insolvency case. When creditors are obliged to participate in foreign-based proceedings, disadvantages can be experienced either as a consequence of explicit provisions of the local law (direct discrimination), or as a product of more subtle—even logistical and informational—factors (indirect discrimination). Both kinds of discrimination receive some corrective attention.

Very significantly, art.39 declares:

"Any creditor who has his habitual residence, domicile or registered office in a Member State other than the State of the opening of proceedings, *including the tax authorities and social security authorities of Member States*, shall have the right to lodge claims in the insolvency proceedings in writing" (emphasis added).

In terms of the traditional principles embodied in the law of the UK, for example, this overrides, for the benefit of the tax and social security authorities of other EU Member States, the effect of the rule in *India v Taylor*.[139] The wording of this provision makes it clear that the benefits hereby conferred under the Regulation are reserved for the exclusive advantage of EU-based creditors. The treatment of creditors from outside the frontiers of the Union is unregulated, and so falls to be governed by the laws and practices of the State of opening of the proceedings in question.

---

[137] *Syska v Vivendi Universal* [2009] 2 All E.R. (Comm) 891 (CA).
[138] *Syska v Vivendi Universal* [2009] 1 All E.R. (Comm) 244.
[139] *India v Taylor* [1955] A.C. 491 (HL).

There are further provisions in arts 40–42 whereby the liquidator is under a duty immediately to inform all known creditors who have their habitual residence, domicile or registered office in the other Member States. This must be done as soon as insolvency proceedings are opened. The notification is to bear the heading "Invitation to lodge a claim. Time limits to be observed" in all the official languages of the institutions of the EU (arts 40, 42(1)), but the notice itself need only be in the official language, or one of the official languages, of the State of the opening of proceedings. Conversely, creditors are permitted to lodge their claim in the official language of the Member State of their habitual residence, domicile or registered office, but may be required (at the liquidator's discretion) to provide a translation into an official language of the State of the opening of proceedings (art.42(2)). **31–047**

It will be observed that the qualifying criteria for eligibility to benefit from the provisions of Ch.IV in favour of creditors from other Member States are based upon the "functional" factors of habitual residence, domicile, or the location of the registered office (in the case of a company). It is noteworthy that there is no reference in the provisions of Ch.IV to the factor of nationality. It is therefore of no consequence whether a creditor (or a debtor) is a national of any of the Member States, for the purposes of the Regulation's operation, nor with regard to the enjoyment of any rights or privileges arising thereunder. Equally of significance is the corollary to this, namely that it is not a matter of relevance, for the purpose of determining standing to invoke or take benefit from provisions of the Regulation, that the party in question happens to be a citizen of a State that is not a member of the EU What matters is simply whether that party currently has the requisite "functional" connection with one of the Member States, by meeting one (at least) of the three stated criteria.

(i) Interpretation by the Court of Justice

Under the successive iterations of the Treaty establishing the European Community the European Court of Justice has had jurisdiction to give preliminary rulings concerning the validity and interpretation of acts of the institutions of the Community. Between 1999 and 2009, that jurisdiction was exercised pursuant to art.234 (formerly numbered as 177) of the EC Treaty as revised by the Treaty of Amsterdam.[140] In principle therefore the Regulation on Insolvency Proceedings, as an act of the Council entering into force on May 31, 2002, fell within the scope of art.234. However, as a measure adopted pursuant to the powers conferred under Title IV of the EC Treaty (and in particular, based on arts 61(c) and 67(1)), the jurisdiction of the ECJ to deliver interpretative rulings at the request of a national court was subject to special conditions and restrictions imposed by art.68 (formerly art.73p). Article 68(1), while in force, allowed such a reference to be made only where a question on the interpretation of the Regulation was raised in a case pending before a court or tribunal of **31–048**

---

[140] The EC Treaty was considerably amended by the Treaty of Amsterdam of 1997, which entered into force for the United Kingdom on May 1, 1999. Article 12 of the Amsterdam Treaty effected a wholesale renumbering of the articles of the EC Treaty, as indicated in the text.

a Member State against whose decisions there is no judicial remedy under national law. Thus, only an appellate court of last resort (according to the nature and status of the proceedings in question) was eligible to seize the Court of Justice of such a request. The terms of art.68(1) had the effect of making it obligatory for a national court of final resort to request a ruling if it considered that a decision on the question of interpretation was necessary to enable it to give judgment.

31–049   The provisions of art.68(1) were particularly ill-suited to the resolution of interpretative problems under the Insolvency Regulation. The inevitable delay, and added cost, of pursuing an appeal to the highest level within the national legal system would in most cases furnish a severe constraint upon utilisation of the facility to seek a ruling from the ECJ in cases where, by definition, insolvency is a factor. This undoubtedly retarded the process of obtaining clarification on a number of matters of considerable practical importance in the years immediately after the Regulation entered into force. It must be acknowledged however that the fact that access to the ECJ was thus restricted had a possible element of merit in as much as it deprived parties of a possible tactical weapon during the course of insolvency-related litigation in which the time element is especially critical, so that the ability to seek to persuade a court of first instance to refer a question to the ECJ could be potentially damaging to the collective interest of those involved. Nevertheless, on balance the interests of justice are better served by arrangements which permit a relatively speedy clarification of points on which the law is uncertain, and any avoidance of unnecessary costs incurred through purely formal references to domestic courts of intermediate appellate jurisdiction is greatly to be desired. It is therefore a very welcome development that as a consequence of the entry into force of the Lisbon Treaty on December 1, 2009 the former art.68 lapsed and the limitation laid down in that provision on the right to refer a question to the ECJ for a preliminary ruling disappeared. Therefore, since December 1, 2009 courts and tribunals within the Member States against whose decisions there is a judicial remedy under domestic law are nevertheless eligible to refer questions to the ECJ where acts adopted under Title IV of the EC Treaty are concerned.[141] The jurisdiction of the ECJ to give preliminary rulings is currently governed by art.267 of the Treaty on the Functioning of the European Union (TFEU) which replaced the former art.234 from December 1, 2009.[142]

(j)   Final observations

31–050   The EC Regulation and its implications must be carefully considered by all parties who engage in commercial dealings with a counterparty having substantial links (amounting at least to the maintenance of a place of business) within any State which is a member of the European Union. The possibility

---

[141] *Interedil Srl v Fallimento Interedil Srl* (C-396/09) (ECJ) October 20, 2011 (as yet unreported), at paras [18]–[21] of the judgment, citing the earlier decision of the court in *Werynski* (C-238/09) [2011] E.C.R I-0000 (as yet unreported), at [28] and [29].

[142] For the Consolidated Text of the TFEU as established by the Lisbon Treaty, see O.J. C.83/47, 30.3.2010.

that either primary or secondary insolvency proceedings (or in certain circumstances, proceedings of both kinds) may be opened in relation to the counterparty in one or more of the Member States must be taken into account when assessing the risks arising from any transaction, particularly where it is intended to give rise to a credit-based relationship extending over a considerable period of time. In any debtor-creditor relationship which has cross-border aspects, it is vital for the creditor to be able to anticipate in which jurisdiction the debtor may be amenable to undergo insolvency proceedings, and also to know what assets would then be comprised in those proceedings and what law or laws would be applied to determine the rights and interests of the various parties affected. Therefore, it may be prudent to engineer the agreement in such a way that it is incumbent upon the EU-based party to make full and proper disclosure of material facts bearing upon that party's amenability to the insolvency jurisdiction of courts that are subject to the EC Regulation. A further disclosure requirement may need to be incorporated to cover the contingency that developments in the debtor's modus operandi subsequent to the commencement of the agreement may have the effect that they alter or extend the jurisdictional "catchment" that obtained at the time the agreement was concluded. Indeed, lenders may deem it advisable to make provision for it to be a default event on the part of the debtor to do anything which could bring about a change in its jurisdictional circumstances without giving the creditor advance notification (and obtaining authorisation to proceed).

Similar considerations apply to any act of the debtor that produces a change in the location of key assets—especially those affected by real security—where this could materially alter the potential outcome for a party in interest by bringing into play any provision of the Regulation that could trigger the application of a different system of law from the one which hitherto may have been reasonably anticipated by that party.[143]

---

[143] There are instructive examples in the *Maxwell* Saga of multiple, successive pledges, etc. of the same asset in favour of parties in divers jurisdictions, resulting in horrendous complexities for the lawyers and accountants to wrangle over, with an enormous net loss of value to the creditors involved in the battle. Such practices are by no means unique to the *Maxwell* case, although the scale of the misappropriations in that case was exceptional.

Chapter 32

The UNCITRAL Model Law

32–001 In May 1997 the United Nations Commission on International Trade Law (UNCITRAL) adopted a Model Law on Cross-Border Insolvency (the Model Law).[1] Subsequently, a Guide to Enactment of the Model Law on Cross-Border Insolvency was issued by UNCITRAL as an authoritative resource for use by States which wish to enact the Model Law, or are considering whether to do so. Both the Model Law itself and the Guide to Enactment are available on the UNCITRAL website.[2] The Guide to Enactment will also serve as an aid to interpretation of the Model Law's provisions as and when enacted.[3] Provision was included in the Insolvency Act 2000 for the Model Law to be given effect in the United Kingdom by regulations made by statutory instrument.[4] The enabling provision allows for implementation with or without modification, and it further allows for amendment of any provision of s.426 of the Insolvency Act 1986. Enacting provisions were brought into force in Great Britain on April 4, 2006 (The Cross-Border Insolvency Regulations 2006 (SI 2006/1030)) and in Northern Ireland on April 12, 2007 (The Cross-Border Insolvency Regulations (Northern Ireland) 2007 (SRNI 2007/115)). From the latter date, therefore, the Model Law has been in force throughout the United Kingdom.

The following summary explains the scope of the Model Law, and its potential impact on cross-border cases of receiverships and administrations.

1. STRUCTURE

32–002 The Model Law consists of 32 articles, each of which is drafted as a "model provision" suitable for enactment into the existing laws of any State minded to do so. A State which takes the step of enacting any of the Model Law's provisions (not necessarily all, or any prescribed proportion of them) is referred to as an "Enacting State". An Enacting State is thus left free to enact as much, or as little, of the Model Law as it is prepared to accept at any given time, and is also left to decide on the appropriate form and means of transposing those provisions into its domestic law. As enacted in this way, the provisions become enforceable exclusively within the Enacting State: in contrast to the EU

---

[1] UNCITRAL 30th Session, May 12–30, 1997: Records of the General Assembly of the United Nations, 52nd Session, Supplement No.17 (A152/17), Pt II, paras 12–225. The text of the Model Law as adopted is included in that document at Annex I (pp.68–78).
[2] *http://www.uncitral.org/uncitral/en/uncitral_texts/insolvency/1997Model.html.*
[3] UN General Assembly, Document AICN.9/442 (December 19, 1997). The Guide To Enactment is reproduced in Appendix 4 below.
[4] Insolvency Act 2000, s.14. (See below, at para.32–018).

Regulation on Insolvency Proceedings, no rules of direct jurisdiction are involved, and there are no rules of choice of law. The grounds on which jurisdiction is exercisable are important because the nature of the recognition to be accorded to a foreign proceeding, and hence the quality of assistance and relief that the foreign representative may request, are determined by the circumstances under which jurisdiction was exercised in the commencement of the original proceedings.

The key principle of the Model Law is that it is not predicated upon reciprocity between States. Once a State has enacted any of the Model Law's provisions, these are available to be invoked in any case to which, objectively speaking, they are applicable. There is no condition or requirement to the effect that the foreign representative must have been appointed under the law of a State which is itself an Enacting State. There may be scope for this factor to be taken into account by the court of an Enacting State when exercising any discretion it may have regarding the provision of relief and assistance to a foreign representative.

2. SCOPE OF APPLICATION OF THE MODEL LAW

Reference is made throughout the Model Law to "foreign proceeding", a term **32–003** which is defined by art.2(a) as:

> "a collective judicial or administrative proceeding in a foreign State, including an interim proceeding, pursuant to a law relating to insolvency in which proceeding the assets and affairs of the debtor are subject to control or supervision by a foreign court for the purpose of reorganisation or liquidation."

This definition clearly precludes the application of the Model Law's provisions to cases of administrative receivership as constituted under Pt III of the Insolvency Act 1986, or the equivalents under Scottish law or under the laws of other common law countries which have adopted floating charge receivership. Conversely, an administration proceeding under Pt II of the Insolvency Act 1986 qualifies as a "foreign proceeding", since administrations are "collective" in character and are also "judicial" in the sense that they are subject to the control or supervision of the court even in those cases where an out-of-court appointment takes place. Arguably, voluntary arrangements under Pt I or Pt VIII of the Insolvency Act 1986 should qualify, since they also are collective and the court has a close involvement even though the procedures are not initiated by a court order.[5]

---

[5] The expressions "foreign proceeding" and "foreign representative" derive from language and definitions contained in the US Bankruptcy Code, notably s.101(23) and (24) and s.304. Section 304 was repealed in October 2005 following the introduction of a new Ch.15 into the Bankruptcy Code. Chapter 15 incorporates the Model Law into the US Bankruptcy Code, with some modifications. It should be noted, e.g. that the definition of "foreign proceeding" in the Model Law is slightly different from the definition in s.101(23) prior to its amendment in 2005 and that the 2005 amendments are slightly different from the definitions in the Model Law. While s.304 has been

Article 1(2) allows every Enacting State the option of excluding the Model Law from having application to designated categories of proceeding that are subject to a special insolvency regime under the laws of that State. Typically, this option will be exercised in relation to banks and insurance companies, but other species of debtor may be exempted, as the Enacting State sees fit. This could include non-traders in the case of those States (such as Mexico) which restrict the application of insolvency law to debtors engaged in trade or commerce. In the case of the United States the Model Law has been excluded from applying to "consumer debtors", as defined by s.109(e) of the Bankruptcy Code, who are citizens or permanent residents of the United States.

32–004   The Model Law (or such parts of it as an Enacting State decides to adopt) is enacted into domestic law like any other statute, and the courts of that State are thus required to give effect to it in the orthodox manner. In contrast to the international obligations imposed on States which become parties to a treaty or convention, there is no active requirement that a State must take any special step to notify other States, or even to notify UNCITRAL itself, of its enactment of the Model Law's provisions. In principle, a State could elect to take no action at all with regard to those parts of its existing law which it considers are already in conformity with those provisions. In the case of the United Kingdom, while it is arguable that many of the Model Law's provisions in terms of access, recognition and assistance are currently met under the existing rules of common law (as opposed to the more restricted application of the provisions of s.426 of the Insolvency Act 1986), there were important reasons in favour of its being implemented as a clearly identifiable part of our legislation in the manner facilitated by the Insolvency Act 2000. This has ensured that the United Kingdom's position as an Enacting State is plainly demonstrable and can be widely publicised. It will also make the law's provisions internationally accessible without the need to study the case precedents, many of which date from the eighteenth and nineteenth centuries. That said, as is plain from the judgments in cases such as *Cambridge Gas Transport Corporation v The Official Committee of Unsecured Creditors of Navigator Holdings Plc*[6], *Re HIH Casualty and General Insurance Ltd*[7] *and Rubin v Eurofinance SA*[8], the common law still has an important (and developing) role to play in cross-border insolvency.

(a)   Access and recognition under the terms of the Model Law

32–005   A primary benefit for the practitioner is that the Model Law creates a right of immediate and direct access to the courts of the Enacting State to put the case

---

repealed and replaced by Ch.15, access to the jurisprudence which developed under s.304 is preserved in the context of the new s.1507 (dealing with availability of additional assistance following the grant of recognition).

[6] *Cambridge Gas Transport Corporation v Official Committee of Unsecured Creditors of Navigator Holdings Plc* [2007] 1 A.C. 508 (PC).

[7] *Re HIH Casualty and General Insurance Ltd* [2008] 1 W.L.R. 852 (HL).

[8] *Rubin v Eurofinance SA* [2011] Ch.133 (CA). An appeal from the decision of the Court of Appeal is due to be heard by the Supreme Court in March 2012.

for recognition and to apply for relief and assistance in timely fashion. This can include the obtaining of interim relief pending the formal grant of recognition. This can be especially valuable given the well-known fact that in cross-border insolvency speed and timing are of the essence. Article 9 is therefore of fundamental importance:

"A foreign representative is entitled to apply directly to a court in this State."

Especially noteworthy is the absence of any precondition to this right of access, such as any requirement that the foreign proceeding must first have been accorded formal recognition before the right of access can be exercised (which would give rise to circularity problems). But, in practical terms, standing to invoke the right accorded by art.9 is dependent upon the ability to establish "foreign representative" status, as defined by art.2(d):

" 'Foreign representative' means a person or body, including one appointed on an interim basis, authorised in a foreign proceeding to administer the reorganisation or the liquidation of the debtor's assets or affairs or to act as a representative of the foreign proceeding".

This definition in turn leads back to the key concept of "foreign proceeding", **32–006** defined in art.2(a).[9] Furthermore, common sense dictates that the foreign representative will wish to avoid the wastage of costs (and any potential liability) that would ensue from an attempt to invoke legal process within the Enacting State in a case where it ultimately transpires that the foreign proceeding does not meet the criteria for recognition under the Model Law. It is essential to be sure of one's ground—but the vital principle is that rapid steps can be taken to protect the debtor's assets from local acts of individual enforcement without the customary hiatus that ensues from the need to obtain an order of recognition and execution (known in civil law countries as an exequatur) from the local court before anything can be done under the law of that State.

Special mention should also be made of the "procedural safe conduct" afforded to practitioners by art.10. This is a vital protection for an office holder appointed in one jurisdiction who needs to take action in another State, for example to seek a protective remedy to prevent individual creditors from seizing assets of the company. The risk for the office holder is that under the procedural laws of some States such a step may render the office holder, and through him the assets of the company over which he holds appointment, amenable to the jurisdiction of the other State in respect of separate claims against the company or its officers. Article 10 of the Model Law seeks to counter this peril by establishing the concept of limited jurisdiction where the foreign representative appears for the sole purpose of making an application to a court in an Enacting State pursuant to the Model Law. Such an application does not subject the applicant or the foreign assets and affairs of the debtor to

[9] See above, para.32–003, and remarks in above, fn.5.

the jurisdiction of the courts of that State for any purpose other than the application. Once that defined threshold has been passed however, the foreign representative may be subject to conditions imposed by the court (using art.22(2)), as well as being obliged to respect the general requirements of the local law.

Article 11 confers on the foreign representative the further right to apply to commence a proceeding under the local insolvency law of the Enacting State if the conditions for commencing such a proceeding are otherwise met. This may prove to be a valuable weapon in the practitioner's armoury, because it will "collectivise" all matters affecting the debtor's estate in the Enacting State in question, and should put a halt to local action by individual creditors directed against particular assets. Once again, the absence of any precondition referring to recognition of the foreign proceeding is noteworthy.

It should be noted that a foreign representative will be recognised as such not only for the purpose of the formal insolvency proceedings in which they are appointed but also, as part and parcel of those proceedings, for the purpose of adversarial proceedings in which they pursue claims for the benefit of the insolvent estate[10].

32–007   The practical advantages of the separation of the right of direct access from the actual process of obtaining recognition of the foreign proceeding have already been considered. Nevertheless it is axiomatic that the material benefits to be made available under the Model Law are ultimately dependent upon the foreign proceeding meeting the criteria for international recognition that have been implanted in its provisions. These are contained in arts 15–17. Two categories of recognition are available: the foreign proceeding may qualify as a "main" or as a "non-main" proceeding, according to the circumstances under which it has been opened under the law of the foreign state. The defining characteristics of the two categories are indicated by the terms of the two definitions provided in art.2(b) and (c) respectively:

> "(b) 'foreign main proceeding' means a foreign proceeding taking place in the State where the debtor has the centre of its main interests;
> (c) 'foreign non-main proceeding' means a foreign proceeding, other than a foreign main proceeding, taking place in a State where the debtor has an establishment within the meaning of subparagraph (f) of this article."

Two further concepts thus require to be defined: centre of main interests (COMI), and establishment.

The COMI is not defined in the Model Law, although the same expression is used in the Istanbul Convention and also in the EC Regulation.[11] Article 16(3) supplies a rebuttable presumption that the debtor's registered office, or habitual residence in the case of an individual, is presumed to be the COMI. It is to be assumed that courts will regard it as incumbent upon any party who contends

---

[10] *Rubin v Eurofinance SA* [2011] 2 W.L.R. 121 (CA), [24]–[25] and [60]–[61] per Ward L.J.
[11] See above, paras 31–011 to 31–019.

that the debtor's COMI is in a different State from that indicated by applying the presumption to prove that this is the case. Logically, there should be only one place which constitutes "the" centre of the debtor's main interests: use of the definite article in the texts of both art.2(b) and art.16(3) presupposes that it is possible to identify its whereabouts. Experience in the operation of the EU Regulation on Insolvency Proceedings suggests that this may not always be so: even with the assistance of the presumption, courts in different States may reach different conclusions about the "true" location of the debtor's COMI.

The leading case in England and Wales as to the proper approach to locating a debtor's COMI for the purposes of The Cross-Border Insolvency Regulations 2006 is *Re Stanford International Bank Ltd.*[12] In that case, which involved cross-applications for recognition made by the Antiguan liquidators and the US Receiver, the Court of Appeal determined that the COMI test under the Model Law was the same test as that which applies for the purposes of the EU Regulation on Insolvency Proceedings. The Court of Appeal explained that the COMI test was first adopted in the European Convention on Insolvency Proceedings. In that context it was plain from the *Virgos-Schmit Report* (para.75) that the appropriate test depended on ascertainability by those who dealt with the debtor so that they should know which law would govern the debtor's insolvency. Recital 13 of the EU Regulation was intended to reflect that rationale. The derivation of COMI in the Model Law and the various guides to its interpretation in that context show that it was intended that it should bear at least a similar meaning. Nothing in the respective contexts of the EU Regulation and the Model Law requires different meanings to be given to the phrase COMI.

The Court of Appeal also made clear that: (1) Each company or individual has its own COMI—it is not possible to have a COMI of some loose aggregation of companies and individuals; (2) the presumption contained in art.16(3) can be rebutted only by factors which are both objective and ascertainable. This test is not the same as the head office functions test; (3) so long as the head office functions of a company are ascertainable by third parties, it will be important in identifying the company's COMI to identify where those functions are carried out; (4) to extend ascertainability to factors, not already in the public domain or apparent to a typical third party doing business with the company, which might be discovered on enquiry would introduce into this area of the law a most undesirable element of uncertainty.[13]

The term *establishment* is defined in para.(f) of art.2 as follows: 32–008

"any place of operations where the debtor carries out a non-transitory economic activity with human means and goods or services."

---

[12] *Re Stanford International Bank Ltd (In Receivership)* [2011] Ch. 33 (CA). For commentary on the COMI test post-*Stanford*, see Professor Bob Wessels, "COMI: past, present and future" [2011] (2011) 24(2) Insolv. Int. 17, 17–23.

[13] *Re Stanford International Bank Ltd (In Receivership)* [2011] Ch. 33 (CA), [56] per Sir Andrew Morritt, Chancellor.

This definition has been adapted from one already included in the EU Regulation (as art.2(h)), with the addition of the final two words ("or services").[14] It is apparent that the intention is to exclude the possibility that the mere presence of assets belonging to the debtor can be regarded as furnishing a basis for exercising insolvency jurisdiction that will enjoy international recognition. The compound set of criteria, to the effect that there must be "a place of operations" at which the debtor carries out a "non-transitory economic activity" whereby "human means" are combined with either "goods" or "services" ensures that the passive presence of assets, without more, cannot be classified as an establishment. Nor can a purely temporary or occasional place of operations fulfil the terms of the definition in art.2(f): what is required, effectively, is that the debtor shall be shown to maintain a "place of business" within the jurisdiction in question.

Under art.15(1), the foreign representative applies to the court of the Enacting State for recognition of the foreign proceeding in which he or she has been appointed. Article 15(2)–(4) specifies the documentation required in support of the application and art.16 sets out the presumptions concerning recognition. The grounds for recognition are specified in art.17(1). It should be noted that art.6 furnishes as a ground for refusal of recognition, or of other assistance, that to grant it would be manifestly contrary to the public policy of the Enacting State. In performing their task of balancing the request for recognition and assistance with concerns to uphold the basic values of domestic public policy, courts should pay regard to the general admonition in art.8 that in the interpretation of the Model Law "regard is to be had to its international origin and to the need to promote uniformity in its application and the observance of good faith". This provision has been designed for the purpose of promoting international co-operation and is aimed at nurturing a respect for comity between courts in cross-border insolvency proceedings.

32–009   The two alternative categories of recognition for the purposes of unlocking the benefits of assistance according to the terms of the Model Law—namely as a foreign main, or as a foreign non-main, proceeding—are confirmed by art.17(2). Article 17(4) (reinforced by the notification requirements in art.18) allows the court of the Enacting State to terminate or modify recognition in the light of altered circumstances or further information coming to the notice of the court. Article 17(3) places emphasis on speed of determination.

(i)   Interim relief pending recognition

32–010   Article 19 provides for discretionary relief under the law of the Enacting State from the time of the filing of the application for recognition until the application is determined. This is a matter for the discretion of the court concerned: a non-exhaustive list of examples of such relief is provided by art.19(a)–(c) (with cross-reference to art.21(1)).

---

[14] See above, para.31–020.

(b) Consequences of recognition under the Model Law: relief and assistance

Article 20 applies only to cases where a foreign proceeding is recognised as a   **32–011**
main proceeding. The effects under art.20 are automatic and are not dependent
on the exercise of any judicial discretion. They are:

(a) a stay on the commencement or continuation of individual actions
     or proceedings concerning the debtor's assets, rights, obligations or
     liabilities (but see art.20(3));

(b) a stay on any type of execution against the debtor's assets; and

(c) a suspension of the debtor's right to transfer, encumber or otherwise
     dispose of any assets.

Under art.20(2) the Enacting State is allowed to superimpose any exceptions to
the automatic stay which are found elsewhere in its domestic insolvency law,
so that they also apply in relation to a foreign main proceeding. For example,
in respect of the right of a secured creditor to enforce security subsisting over
the property of the debtor, or the power of the court to grant specific relief from
the effects of the stay upon application by a creditor (e.g. permission granted
by the court under paras 44 and 43(2) of Sch.B1 to the Insolvency Act 1986 to
allow a secured creditor to enforce security following the issue of an application for an administration order (or following the giving of notice of intention
to appoint an administrator under paras 15(1) or 27(1)) or during the period
when such an order is in force) can be accommodated. By art.31, recognition
of a foreign proceeding as a main proceeding gives rise to a rebuttable presumption of the debtor's insolvency for the purpose of commencing an insolvency
proceeding under the law of the Enacting State.

Article 21 applies to all cases where a foreign proceeding is recognised,   **32–012**
whether as a main or as a non-main proceeding. It confers a general discretionary power upon the court of the Enacting State to grant "any appropriate
relief", including those specified in art.21(a)–(g) inclusive.[15] The forms of
relief described in art.21(a)–(c) overlap those of art.20(1) which will take
effect automatically in the case of a foreign main proceeding: they are available on a discretionary basis in the case of a non-main proceeding. The forms
of relief in art.21(d)–(g) are discretionary in all cases. Article 21(2) offers the
further prospect of application by the foreign representative for the making of
an order by the court of the Enacting State for the turnover of assets to him.
The court's power is discretionary, and it must also be satisfied that the
interests of creditors in the Enacting State itself are "adequately protected".
The meaning of the latter expression, which is seemingly derived from the law
and practice under the Bankruptcy Code of the United States,[16] is given no

---

[15] art.21 is reproduced in Appendix 4 below.
[16] See K.D. Yamamoto (2004) 13 Int. Insolv Rev 87–114.

formal definition for the purposes of the Model Law, and will therefore require judicial elucidation when it is tested in proceedings before national courts.

By art.(2), the court may attach conditions to any relief granted under arts 19 or 21.

Under art.23, recognition of a foreign proceeding enables the foreign representative to initiate the types of actions which are available under the law of the Enacting State to enable the office holder in insolvency proceedings to avoid acts detrimental to the interests of creditors generally. In the case of a foreign non-main proceeding, art.23(3) requires that the court must be satisfied that the action relates to assets which, under the law of the Enacting State, should be administered in the foreign non-main proceeding.

32–013   By art.24, upon recognition of a foreign proceeding the foreign representative acquires standing to intervene in any proceedings in the Enacting State in which the debtor is a party. Article 12 (which logically belongs in Ch.II of the Model Law with other provisions dealing with the consequences of recognition) allows the foreign representative to participate in a proceeding regarding the debtor under the insolvency laws of the Enacting State. According to the Guide to Enactment, the right of "participation" is a limited one, merely enabling the foreign representative to make petitions, requests or submissions.

(c)   Cross-border co-operation between courts and office holders—co-ordination of concurrent proceedings

32–014   Chapter IV of the Model Law (arts 25, 26 and 27) implants provisions in the law of the Enacting State to enable the courts of that State to co-operate with foreign courts and foreign representatives. In practice, the essential channels of communication will be established and sustained through the principle of allowing direct communication between the courts of the respective States and between the courts of the Enacting State and any foreign representative, including by telephone.[17] Although these precepts will be familiar to judges operating within the Anglo-American common law tradition, where the doctrine of comity has long been used as a basis for international co-operation and assistance, concrete statutory confirmation of the doctrine's obligatory character, and clarification of its contents, are welcome developments. This is even more true for those jurisdictions in which there is a less developed tradition of judicial activism in international matters and in particular for those in which the courts have an ingrained disposition (and in many instances are actually subject to a constitutional duty) not to purport to exercise any power that is not explicitly sanctioned by a legislative provision of some kind.

---

[17] A precedent for an English court to engage in such court-to-court communication was established in the case of *Re Cenargo International Plc (No.862 of 2003)* Unreported April 14, 2003, but noted in (2003) 16 Insolv. Int. 47, 47–48. In a specially convened conference call, in which the legal representatives of all the parties were able to participate, Lightman J. in London and Judge Drain of the US Bankruptcy Court for the Southern District of New York engaged in a discussion to explore how their two courts could work in harmony in relation to the simultaneous proceedings being conducted in their respective jurisdictions in relation to the same company. A full transcript of the discussion was made, but has not been published. See also S. Shandro and R. Tett, INSOL World 2003 (Fourth Quarter), 33–35.

Chapter V (arts 28–32 inclusive) complements the provisions on co-opera-tion by means of specific directives as to the procedures to be followed in cases where there are concurrent proceedings under the laws of different States, in the interests of securing the optimum co-ordination between them. Article 32 is worthy of note: it embodies the celebrated principle of hotchpot, long a familiar feature of English case law concerned with the equalisation of distri-bution among creditors in multi-jurisdiction insolvency. The essence of this rule is that a creditor who has already received partial satisfaction of his unse-cured balance of claim against the debtor by participating in a process of distri-bution taking place in another jurisdiction is not allowed to participate in any other such process without fully accounting for what has already been received in respect of the claim for which proof is lodged. Then, after due allowance has been made for those amounts, the creditor is not entitled to be paid any share of the current distribution so long as the payment to the other creditors whose claims are ranked in the same class is proportionately less than the payment the creditor has already received.

(d) Creditors' rights of access and participation

Although the Model Law is mainly concerned with the foreign representatives' rights of access to courts,[18] Ch.II (arts 9–14) also contains some provisions which confer rights of access upon foreign creditors. Article 13 implants into the law of the Enacting State the principle that foreign creditors are to have the same rights as local creditors regarding the commencement of, and participa-tion in, an insolvency proceeding. This broad proposition is qualified by the important provision in art.13(2), that this does not affect the ranking of claims in an insolvency proceeding under local law. This leaves open the possibility that an Enacting State may maintain in force any provisions of its laws whereby claims of foreign creditors are allocated a lower ranking than those of local creditors (as is the case under the laws of a number of Latin American states). Article 13(2) contains a proviso, amounting to a "safety net", which states that claims of foreign creditors shall not be ranked lower than the class of general, non-preferential claims according to local law. This proviso carries a further sub-proviso that allows a foreign claim to be relegated below the class of ordi-nary claims if its characteristics correspond to those of a special category of postponed claims under the local law e.g. in the UK, debts due from a company to a person held responsible for wrongful or fraudulent trading: Insolvency Act 1986, s.215(4)).

32–015

The position of foreign revenue claims and of other claims of foreign public authorities is one of the most controversial aspects of international insolvency law. Outside the sphere of application of the art.39 of the EU Regulation on Insolvency Proceedings (as explained above at para.31–046) the English law rule—that such claims are excluded from any distributional process in this country as a matter of public policy—had otherwise remained intact.[19] On the

---

[18] See above, para.32–005.
[19] *India v Taylor* [1955] A.C. 491 (HL).

face of it art.13 of the Model Law (taken in isolation) necessitates a change to this rule, by requiring foreign fiscal and public claims to be accorded at least the same treatment as ordinary, unsecured debts. In an Enacting State which chooses to regard such a change of practice with regard to foreign revenue claims as deeply offensive to its sense of public policy, the status quo may perhaps be maintained using the "public policy exception" in art.6. However, as is explained below, the United Kingdom has opted to embrace the change and thereby maintain uniformity as between cases governed by the EU Regulation and those coming within the scope of the Model Law.[20]

Rights of foreign creditors to receive adequate notification of the successive stages of proceedings, in step with the issuance of notification to local creditors, are governed by art.14. The principle of equality of treatment is to apply, which means that creditors' rights in actual cases will vary with the provisions of the local law of the State in which the proceedings take place. A certain minimum assurance is generated by art.14(2), which requires foreign creditors to be notified individually, unless the court considers that under the circumstances some other form of notification would be more appropriate (i.e. the mere fact that notification of local creditors can be validly effected by means of public advertisement alone does not enable a similar practice to be followed in relation to foreign creditors, unless the court actively decides that this would be more appropriate). Article 14(3) deals with time limits applicable to foreign creditors in filing their claims. The logistical problems of compliance with foreign procedural requirements, within time limits that may be strictly circumscribed, are notorious. No specific time limits are laid down: what is required is that the period allowed be "reasonable". Clearly this is a matter over which there may be considerable disagreement, and no international uniformity of the lengths of such periods seems likely to emerge. The best that can be hoped for is a clear indication of the applicable period in any given case, and a timely communication of the relevant information to the creditors concerned.

(e)   Enactment of the Model Law

(i)   Current situation

32–016   Whether to enact the Model Law, either in full or partially, is a decision to be taken by each State according to its national policy regarding international insolvency matters and its view of the priority to be accorded to their resolution. In the case of an international treaty or convention, which requires a specified number of ratifications in order to enter into force, States which have participated in the process of negotiating the text may feel a sense of moral obligation not to inconvenience their negotiating partners by neglecting to take the steps necessary to enable their own ratification to take place. The Model Law generates no such sense of urgency for any individual State, even one

---

[20] As explained below at para.32–028, the UK enactment of the Model Law has brought about the abrogation, at any rate in relation to insolvency matters, of the rule in *India v Taylor* [1955] A.C. 491 (HL).

which was actively involved in its development, since such delay does not impede other States from proceeding to give it effect within their own domestic law. It was therefore predictable that the global process of enactment of the Model Law would be somewhat haphazard, and that the rate of progress might not be as rapid as some of the law's proponents had hoped. The ultimate success of a purely voluntary instrument such as the Model Law depends upon it attracting the endorsement of a critical mass of States which wield significant economic and commercial influence in global terms, so that their example in standard-setting encourages other States to follow suit. Despite a somewhat hesitant start to this process, recent indications suggest that the desired momentum in terms of uptake among the major trading nations of the world is beginning to materialise.

According to the UNCITRAL website,[21] legislation based on the Model Law has been adopted in Eritrea (1998), Japan (2000), Mexico (2000), South Africa (2000), Montenegro (2002), Poland (2003), Romania (2003), the British Virgin Islands (2003), Serbia (2004), the United States of America (2005), Colombia (2006), New Zealand (2006), Great Britain (2006), Republic of Korea (2006), Northern Ireland (2007), Slovenia (2007), Australia (2008), Canada (2009), Mauritius (2009) and Greece (2010).

(ii)   Enactment of the Model Law in the United States of America

In the United States, which had played a prominent part in the development of the Model Law under the auspices of UNCITRAL, legislative measures to enact the Model Law were tabled before Congress as early as April 1998. However, that initiative along with a series of successors fell victim to the hazards of the domestic political process and it was not until 2005 that bankruptcy reform legislation containing a Chapter enacting the Model Law was passed and signed into law.[22] The relevant provisions took effect from October 17, 2005 as a new Ch.15 of the US Bankruptcy Code and simultaneously replaced the pre-existing law on ancillary proceedings under s.304 (repealed) of the Bankruptcy Code, while aspiring to assimilate and preserve the best features of the former provision.   **32–017**

(iii)   Enactment of the Model Law in the United Kingdom

The United Kingdom is a full member of UNCITRAL and was an active participant in the process which resulted in the adoption of the Model Law. Indeed, the presence on the Working Group of official representatives of the United Kingdom who had previously been engaged in negotiating the text of the EU Regulation on Insolvency Law was one of the factors which helped to ensure continuity and compatibility between the two near-contemporary   **32–018**

---

[21] http://www.uncitral.org/uncitral/en/uncitral_texts/insolvency/1997Model_status.html.
[22] Enactment of the Model Law in the United States was effected by the Bankruptcy Abuse Prevention and Consumer Protection Act 2005 (Public Law 109–108), Title VIII, whose provisions are reproduced in Appendix 5 below.

international projects. Section 14(1) of the Insolvency Act 2000 serves as an enabling provision to confer upon the Secretary of State for Trade and Industry (as the relevant governmental department was then known) the power to make regulations for the purpose of giving effect to the UNCITRAL Model Law. The terms of s.14(1) confer a considerable element of discretion on the Secretary of State as to the manner and degree of enactment. Moreover care was taken to enable the process of enactment to be combined with a wider appraisal of the international context in which United Kingdom insolvency law is increasingly required to operate, including the implications for the working of s.426 of the Insolvency Act 1986 (co-operation between courts). Accordingly, s.14(2) provides that the regulations may: (a) apply any provision of insolvency law in relation to foreign proceedings (whether begun before or after the regulations come into force); (b) modify the application of insolvency law (whether in relation to foreign proceedings or otherwise); (c) amend any provision of s.426 of the Insolvency Act 1986; and (d) apply or, as the case may be, modify the application of insolvency law in relation to the Crown. In preparing for enactment of the Model Law, the Insolvency Service organised a consultative exercise during 2005 on the basis of draft Cross-Border Insolvency Regulations circulated together with a questionnaire. A "Summary of Responses and Government Reply" was issued in March 2006.[23] The Regulations as finally enacted incorporate a number of significant changes made as a result of the consultative process.

(iv)   The Cross-Border Insolvency Regulations 2006

32–019   The UNCITRAL Model Law was given the force of law in Great Britain by the Cross-Border Insolvency Regulations 2006 (the 2006 Regulations), which entered into force on April 4, 2006.[24] The fact that these Regulations are confined in their territorial effect to England, Wales and Scotland should be noted. The Model Law was made applicable in Northern Ireland by means of Statutory Rules, the Cross-Border Insolvency Regulations (Northern Ireland) 2007 (SRNI 2007/115), which came into force as of April 12, 2007. The latter Regulations contain a number of specific provisions which are necessitated by the separate character of some of the legislation and legal institutions of Northern Ireland. It is essential to refer to the 2007 Regulations in any matter relating to the operation of the Model Law within Northern Ireland.

    The 2006 Regulations consist of six component parts: the enacting provisions themselves (regs 1–8 inclusive), together with five Schedules. Schedule 1 contains the text of the Model Law in the form in which it has the force of law in Great Britain; Schs 2 and 3 respectively make provision about procedural matters in England and Wales and in Scotland; Sch.4 makes

---

[23] The Consultation Paper issued on August 22, 2005, and also the Summary of Responses and Government Reply, can be viewed on the Insolvency Service website: *http://www.insolvency.gov.uk/insolvencyprofessionandlegislation/*.

[24] SI 2006/1030. The Regulations are reproduced in Appendix 4 below.

provision for the delivery of notices to the registrar of companies; and Sch.5 sets out the forms that are to be used for applications and orders made pursuant to the Regulations. In the following account of the provisions of the 2006 Regulations, the operation of the Model Law in Great Britain (England and Wales and Scotland) is described in paras 32–020 to 32–032, below. Unless the contrary is indicated, references to numbered "articles" of the Model Law are references to the version of the text which is enacted in Sch.1 to the 2006 Regulations. The chief points of divergence between the 2006 Regulations and those of 2007, which are in force for Northern Ireland, are noted in para.32–033, below.

(v) Scope and interpretation

The basic policy towards enactment of the Model Law was to keep as closely **32–020** as possible to the original UNCITRAL text. However, as noted above at para.32–002, the Model Law itself allows enacting States considerable freedom in shaping the relevant legislation so as to make it compatible with the structure and content of their domestic laws. This includes an unrestricted freedom to exclude proceedings concerning certain types of entities, such as banks or insurance companies or other financial institutions, that are subject to special insolvency regimes and which the State wishes to exclude from the operation of the Model Law. Article 1(2), as enacted for Great Britain, contains a list of 13 categories of corporate entities which are excluded from the scope of the Model Law. This is an important provision as it not only determines *in limine* whether a foreign representative will be eligible to seek recognition and relief in Great Britain, but it also determines whether an office holder appointed in insolvency proceedings opened in any part of Great Britain will be subject to the provisions of the Model Law in the course of carrying out his duties. In each instance, the matter to be established is whether the debtor company in respect of which the proceedings are taking place falls within any of the excluded categories. Accordingly, art.1(2), together with the further provisions of paras (3) to (7) inclusive, are an essential point of first reference for any party considering whether to undertake any action in Great Britain based upon the Model Law, because the outcome of that inquiry may be to reveal that the Model Law cannot furnish any assistance in the instant case.[25]

Article 2 contains an extensive list of definitions of terms. These include such novel, but necessary, expressions as "British insolvency law" and "British insolvency officeholder" (art.2(a) and (b)), and also the provision in para.(q) that "references to the law of Great Britain include a reference to the law of either part of Great Britain (including its rules of private international law)". The concluding words within brackets indicate that the courts of this country are required to have regard to the potential impact of the rules of

---

[25] There is a possibility that the list of excluded proceedings in art.1(2) may be amended at some future date so that, for example, credit institutions and insurance companies may be included within the scope of the Model Law. Paragraph7.20 of the Explanatory Memorandum to the Regulations indicates that this matter remains under consideration.

private international law when responding to applications for recognition and assistance. This will be especially important in the context of foreign non-main proceedings when dealing with such questions as whether a particular asset should be administered in the foreign proceeding, for example when there is an application for turnover of assets to the foreign representative (art.21(2), (3)). More generally, a reference to private international law may be warranted in cases where a foreign representative seeks to invoke a remedy under British insolvency law for the purpose of impeaching a transaction previously entered into by the debtor (art.23(5)).[26]

The definition of "establishment" in art.2(e) merits comment. Paragraph (e) declares that an establishment means "any place of operations where the debtor carries out a non-transitory economic activity with human means and assets or services". There is a crucial change of wording by comparison to the definition of the same term in the official English version of the original text of the Model Law (there contained in art.2(f)), and also in the equivalent definition contained in the English text of the EU Regulation (there contained in its art.2(h)). Both of the latter texts employ the term "goods" when seeking to express one of the essential characteristics of an establishment. This is an infelicitous choice of wording because if read literally it would exclude intangible assets, and also immovables, whereas the term "biens", which is employed in the French versions of the texts of the Model Law and of the EC Regulation, can apply to both tangible and intangible assets of all kinds. The discreet adjustment of the text of the definition is therefore to be welcomed. Apart from the amendment to the wording of the definition of "establishment", the definitions of the other four terms which play key roles in the operation of the Model Law—"foreign proceeding", "foreign main proceeding", "foreign non-main proceeding" and "foreign representative" are identical in their drafting to the definitions contained in art.2 of the original text of the Model Law.[27]

(vi)   Interpretation

32–021   As aids to interpretation of any provision of the Model Law as set out in Sch.1 to the 2006 Regulations, reg.2(2) states that the following documents may be considered: (a) the UNCITRAL Model Law itself; (b) any documents of UNCITRAL and its working group relating to the preparation of the Model Law; and (c) the Guide to Enactment of the Model Law prepared by UNCITRAL

---

[26] For judicial consideration of the meaning and significance of the statutory reference to "the rules of private international law" as used in s.426(5) of the Insolvency Act 1986, see *Re Television Trade Rentals Ltd* [2002] B.C.C. 807, [16]–[18], per Lawrence Collins J; *Re HIH Casualty and General Insurance Ltd* [2007] 1 All E.R. 177 (CA), [55], per Morritt, V.C. and [71], per Carnwath L.J. In his judgment delivered during the final appeal in the *HIH* case Lord Neuberger, referring to s.426(4) and (5), alluded to "the slightly mystifying reference therein to 'the rules of private international law'": *McGrath v Riddell* [[2008] 1 W.L.R. 852 (HL), [81]. Article 21 of the Model Law is discussed below at para.32–026; art.23 at para.32–029.

[27] See art.2(g)–(j) for the four definitions referred to. The order of listing of definitions in art.2 as enacted by the 2006 Regulations differs from the order used in the original text of the Model Law. Therefore the paragraphs containing the respective definitions bear different letters to those of their counterparts in the original text of art.2.

in May 1997.[28] The authorisation of these specific aids to interpretation is without prejudice to any general practice of the courts with regard to interpretation, and it should also be borne in mind that art.8 of the Model Law itself declares that:

> "In the interpretation of this Law, regard is to be had to its international origin and to the need to promote uniformity in its application and the observance of good faith."

With art.8 in mind, it is expected that courts in Great Britain will be alert to the need to maintain consistency, so far as can be achieved, between the interpretation of provisions and expressions contained in the Model Law and the associated provisions found within the EU Regulation (for example with regard to such terms as "centre of main interests" and "establishment").This appears to have been the case in *Re Stanford International Bank Ltd*[29] where the approach to identifying the debtor's COMI was guided by the ECJ's decision in *Re Eurofood IFSC Ltd*[30] notwithstanding the tension between that approach and the approach contained in certain of the US cases on the meaning of COMI in the context of Ch.15, which cases were dealt with somewhat perfunctorily by the Court of Appeal[31].

(vii) Interaction with other established bases of recognition and assistance

The Model Law is intended to provide a set of minimum standards for interna-   **32–022**
tional co-operation in insolvency matters. It does not preclude an enacting State from maintaining other, more extensive rules and practices applicable to international insolvency cases. Such rules may be generated under domestic law as part of that State's general approach to international insolvency matters, or may have more restricted application within a grouping of foreign states with which special arrangements are in place. In the case of Great Britain, three additional bases of co-operation can be identified, all of which remain in operation alongside the new regime contained in the Model Law. These are:

    (a) the principles developed at common law for the recognition of foreign insolvency proceedings and their effects, and for granting assistance to foreign office holders[32];

---

[28] UNCITRAL Document A/CN.9/442, published by the United Nations (ISBN 92–1-133608–2), mentioned above in para.32–001.

[29] *Re Stanford International Bank Ltd (In Receivership)* [2011] Ch. 33 (CA) (see above, para.32–007).

[30] *Re Eurofood IFSC Ltd* (C-341/04) [2006] Ch. 508 (ECJ).

[31] See the Chancellor's judgment at [55].

[32] See above, Ch.30. The common law principles for granting recognition and assistance, applicable respectively to the insolvency of individuals and that of companies, are also described in *Dicey, Morris and Collins on the Conflict of Laws*, 14th edn (London: Sweet & Maxwell, 2006), Chs 30 and 31 and in I.F. Fletcher, *Insolvency in Private International Law*, 2nd edn (Oxford University Press, 2005), Chs 2 and 3 (see also the relevant parts of the latest supplements to each of those works).

(b) the comprehensive regime governing insolvency proceedings which are subject to the EU Regulation on Insolvency Proceedings where the location of the debtor's COMI is within the territory of one of the 26 EU Member States to which the Regulation is applicable[33]; and

(c) the special statutory procedure under s.426 of the Insolvency Act 1986 which authorises international judicial co-operation between courts in the United Kingdom and courts in a designated list of foreign countries or territories.[34]

In relation to the third of the above bases of co-operation it may be noted that although express authorisation was included in s.14(2)(c) of the Insolvency Act 2000 to amend any provision of s.426 of the Act of 1986, that option was not exercised. This policy decision has ensured that applicants have a wide range of options available to them. Although it may appear that the resulting profusion of bases for seeking recognition and assistance may amount to a confusing embarrassment of riches, it is thought that it is preferable to preserve the fruits of those arrangements which have evolved between this country and a number of foreign jurisdictions with which there is a tradition of enhanced co-operation. However, it is necessary to understand the respective character-istics of the different forms of assistance that are now available, in order to make an informed choice of the optimum vehicle for use in any given case. By identifying the appropriate avenue of approach it should be possible to maximise the effectiveness of the assistance obtainable from British courts. For example, a foreign proceeding that has been commenced using a "presence of assets" or "sufficient connection" basis of jurisdiction in circumstances where the debtor has neither its COMI, nor even an establishment, in the State in question, would not be eligible for recognition under the Model Law and thus could not obtain assistance from a British court on that basis. However, if the foreign proceeding has been commenced in a jurisdiction which qualifies as a "relevant country or territory" for the purposes of s.426 of the Insolvency Act 1986, the assistance of a court in any part of the United Kingdom could be sought using the procedure under that section, and could potentially be more extensive in scope than the assistance obtainable under the provisions of the Model Law.[35] On the other hand, if the foreign insolvency proceeding has been opened in a jurisdiction to which the benefits of s.426 of the Insolvency Act

---

[33] See above, Ch.31. For detailed accounts of the EU/EC Regulation and its effects, see I.F. Fletcher, *Insolvency in Private International Law*, 2nd edn (Oxford University Press, 2005), Ch.7; G. Moss, I.F. Fletcher and S. Isaacs (eds), *The EC Regulation on Insolvency Proceedings, A Commentary and Annotated Guide*, 2nd edn (Oxford University Press, 2009).

[34] For an account of the operation of s.426 of the Insolvency Act 1986, see I.F. Fletcher, *Insolvency in Private International Law*, 2nd edn (Oxford University Press, 2005), Ch.4, paras 4.04–4.26.

[35] Assistance under s.426(5) can include the application of "the insolvency law which is applicable by either court in relation to comparable matters". However, the UK court retains the discretion to determine the nature of the assistance actually to be given in response to the request. In the example given in the text, the UK court's freedom to assist would be restricted if, e.g. the COMI of the debtor were shown to be located in an EU Member State (other than Denmark).

1986 have not been extended, the principles of recognition and assistance at common law may offer some prospect of discretionary assistance from the English court, even if the foreign proceeding does not meet the criteria allowing it to be classified as either a "foreign main proceeding" or as a "foreign non-main proceeding" under the Model Law.[36] This is also the case where, for example, the foreign proceeding is of a type which is excluded from the scope of the Model Law, either because it does not conform to the definition of "foreign proceeding" in art.2(i), or because the debtor happens to belong to one of the categories of excluded entity listed in art.1(2).[37] For example, a foreign proceeding involving the appointment of a receiver (whether by the court or under an out-of-court mode of appointment) would not be classifiable as a "foreign proceeding" within the meaning of art.2(i) of the Model Law, but might be eligible for recognition at common law.[38] In the example just given it may also be possible (depending on the identity of the foreign jurisdiction concerned) for the foreign court to request the assistance of the English court under s.426 of the Insolvency Act 1986.

(viii) Special rules for resolving conflicts between bases of recognition

In the light of what is stated above, the courts in this country may encounter the need to examine four separate bodies of legal rules pertaining to the recognition of a foreign insolvency proceeding and to the grant of relief and other assistance. Hence there is a potential for some element of conflict or inconsistency to be discovered between the separate sources of law which are potentially applicable. Article 3 of the Model Law as enacted in Great Britain provides that to the extent that the Model Law conflicts with an obligation of the UK under the EU/EC Insolvency Regulation the requirements of the Regulation shall prevail. Although no other direction is given to the courts on the approach to be taken in cases where the Model Law and the EU Regulation are found to be simultaneously engaged, it is assumed that the judiciary will use their best endeavours to arrive at a sensible and workable accommodation as and when the need arises. Regulation 3(2) of the Cross-Border Insolvency Regulations 2006 complements the provision in art.3 by declaring that in the case of any conflict between any provision of British insolvency law or of Pt 3 of the Insolvency Act 1986 and the 2006 Regulations, the latter shall prevail. Thus in a case where provisions are found to be in conflict with each other, the

32–023

---

[36] For an example of the kind of flexible response of which the common law is capable in the present day, see *Cambridge Gas Transport Corporation v The Official Committee of Unsecured Creditors of Navigator Holdings Plc* [2007] 1 A.C. 508 (PC).

[37] For the definition of "foreign proceeding" under the Model Law, see above, para.32–003. The list of excluded entities contained in art.1(2), as enacted for Great Britain, is referred to in para.32–020, above.

[38] See, e.g. *Macaulay v Guaranty Trust of New York* (1927) 44 T.L.R. 99; *Schemmer v Property Resources Ltd* [1975] Ch. 273; *Re CA Kennedy & Co Ltd and Stibbe-Monk Ltd* (1977) 74 D.L.R. (3d) 87; and *Re Stanford International Bank Ltd* [2011] Ch. 33 (CA), [16]–[29]. See also the discussion in Ch.31 above, at paras 31–016 to 31–017.

Model Law prevails over British insolvency law, but the EU Regulation prevails over both.

(ix)   Recognition of a foreign proceeding and "relief"

32–024   To unlock the benefits of the Model Law a foreign representative must first obtain recognition of the proceeding under which his or her appointment was made. Application for recognition is made to the appropriate court in accordance with the terms of art.15. Article 4 specifies the competent court for the purposes of the recognition of foreign proceedings and co-operation with foreign courts: in England and Wales these functions are to be performed by the Chancery Division of the High Court, and in Scotland by the Court of Session. Article 17(3) declares that an application for recognition of a foreign proceeding "shall be decided upon at the earliest possible time". The crucial determination to be made by the court is whether the foreign proceeding comes within the scope of the Model Law as defined by art.1, and if so whether it is eligible for recognition as a "foreign main proceeding" or as a "foreign non-main proceeding" as defined by art.2(g) and (h) of the Model Law in force for Great Britain, corresponding to art.2(b) and (c) of the original text of the Model Law as described above.[39] Among the consequences which follow upon such recognition are various species of "relief" which provide protection for the debtor and its assets and interests against most forms of actions, proceedings or executions by creditors (Arts 20, 21).

(x)   Automatic stay: Article 20

32–025   Where a foreign proceeding is recognised as a "foreign main proceeding", art.20 triggers what is in effect an "automatic stay" protecting the debtor's assets, rights, obligations and liabilities. Application can be made to the court by the foreign representative or by a person affected by the stay to seek its lifting or suspension, in whole or in part (art.20(6)). The court is also empowered to modify or terminate the stay of its own motion. It is also provided by art.20(5) that the stay does not affect the right to request or otherwise initiate the commencement of a proceeding under British insolvency law (for example, the taking of steps to place a company in either compulsory or voluntary liquidation, or to put it into administration), or the right to file claims in such a proceeding. Notably, art.20(2) delineates the extent of the automatic stay so that it is expressed to be co-extensive with that which would arise if, in the case of an individual, the debtor had been adjudged bankrupt (or undergone sequestration of his estate under Scottish law), or in the case of a debtor other than an individual had been the subject of a winding-up order. It is also expressly provided that the exceptions to the stay, and the nature of the court's discretion to grant release from its effects, are to be identical to those which would apply under the law of Great Britain in a comparable case. Thus, for example, the court may apply the principles developed under s.127 of the Insolvency Act

---

[39] See above, para.32–007.

1986 in relation to the validation of post-commencement dispositions of property of the company where the property in question is or was situate in this country. The effects of the automatic stay are further curtailed by art.20(3) which states that the stay and suspension does not affect a number of specified rights, including the right to take any steps to enforce security over the debtor's property, or to take any steps to repossess goods in the debtor's possession under a hire purchase agreement (as defined in art.2(k)),[40] or the right of a creditor to set off its claim against a claim of the debtor, if such rights would have been exercisable in the event of the debtor's bankruptcy, sequestration or winding up (as the case may be). The stay is also declared not to affect any right exercisable under a financial market contract in connection with the provisions of UK legislation which are excluded from the scope of the Model Law by the provisions of art.1(4).

In *Cosco Bulk Carrier Co Ltd v Armada Shipping SA*,[41] Briggs J. sought to "identify what are the legal principles applicable to the exercise of discretion in relation to applications for, or to discharge, a stay under the Model Law".[42] Briggs J. stated that art.20(2) was expressed to prevail over arts 20(1) and (3) and clearly identified the British insolvency code as the primary source of an understanding as to the effect of recognition of a foreign main proceeding both in terms of its immediate effect and in terms of the court's powers in relation to the automatic stay prescribed by art.20(1).[43] He added that the only provision of the Model Law framed in a way which might be thought to override art.20(2) is art.22(1), which requires the court to be satisfied that the interests of creditors, including secured creditors, and other interested persons, including if appropriate the debtor, are adequately protected but that the principles upon which the court acts under s.130(2) of the Insolvency Act 1986 (compulsory liquidation) (and presumably under para.43 of Sch.B1 to the Insolvency Act 1986 (administrations)) are such as fully to implement that objective.[44]

(xi) Discretionary relief: Article 21

Article 21 sets out a number of forms of relief that may be granted by the court **32–026** at the request of the foreign representative upon recognition of a foreign proceeding, whether as main or non-main. Several of these replicate the terms of the automatic stay that results from recognition of a foreign main proceeding, so that the same forms of relief can be granted at the discretion of the court in the case of a foreign non-main proceeding. However other species of relief available under art.21 are additional to those arising under art.20.

These include the power of the court under para. (d) to order examination of witnesses or the taking of evidence or the delivery of information concerning the debtor's assets, affairs, rights, obligations or liabilities. Article 21(1)(d)

---

[40] art.2(k) states that "hire purchase agreement" includes a conditional sale agreement, a chattel leasing agreement, and a reservation of title agreement.
[41] *Cosco Bulk Carrier Co Ltd v Armada Shipping SA* [2011] 2 All E.R. (Comm) 481.
[42] At [38] and following.
[43] At [45].
[44] At [46]–[49].

was considered by the court in *Picard v FIM Advisers LLP* in the context of the Madoff affair.[45] The court held, at [23], that art.21(1)(d) has both a jurisdictional and a discretionary component. The court must be satisfied that the information sought concerns the debtor's assets, affairs, rights, obligations or liabilities. If it is so satisfied then it has a discretion to order the delivery of that information. In exercising that discretion it must have regard to all relevant circumstances and ensure that the interests of the person against whom the order is sought are adequately protected. It was common ground in that case that it is appropriate for the court to have regard to the principles upon which the court will exercise its powers under s.236 and s.366 of the Insolvency Act 1986.

A further power is conferred by para.(e) enabling the court to entrust the administration or realisation of all or part of the debtor's assets located in Great Britain to the foreign representative or to another person designated by the court. This power with respect to the management of assets is carried still further by the terms of art.21(2), which authorises the court to entrust the distribution of all or part of the debtor's assets located in Great Britain to the foreign representative or another designated person. (This is the power which was driving the competing office-holders in making their respective recognition applications in *Stanford*.) A turnover order of this kind may be made upon recognition of the foreign proceeding as either a main or a non-main proceeding, but in each case the exercise of the court's discretion is subject to the proviso that the court must be satisfied that the interests of creditors in Great Britain are adequately protected.

The principle of "adequate protection", which has been a long-established aspect of US law on so-called "ancillary proceedings" in international insolvency cases, is given further substance by art.22, including the express assertion that the "interests of creditors" include those of any secured creditors or parties to hire-purchase agreements, and that the court must also be satisfied that the interests of "other interested persons, including if appropriate the debtor" are adequately protected. To reinforce the scope for the court to assure the requisite level of protection, art.22(2) empowers the court to subject any relief granted in the exercise of its discretionary powers under arts 19 or 21 to conditions, including the provision of security or caution by the foreign representative. It should be emphasised that the imposition of a requirement that the foreign representative should furnish security is not an automatic or mandatory aspect of the granting of relief, and the onus is therefore on any interested party to bring any legitimate concerns about the adequacy of protection of creditors' interests to the attention of the court.

The Model Law contemplates that, in a situation where there are competing requests, remittal of the assets will be to the place where the foreign main proceeding is taking place.[46] An important, and as yet unanswered, question is

---

[45] *Picard v FIM Advisers LLP* [2011] 1 B.C.L.C. 129.
[46] *Re Swissair Schweizerische Luftverkehr-Aktiengesellschaft* [2010] B.C.C 667, [15], per David Richards J.

whether the discretionary relief which can be granted under art.21 includes the application of foreign law.[47]

(xii) Discretion to extend the automatic stay

It was noted above that the extent of the automatic stay resulting from recogni- **32–027** tion of a main proceeding is equated to that which arises under British insolvency law in the case of bankruptcy or liquidation proceedings. The nature of that statutory moratorium is different from, and in several respects less extensive than, the moratorium which is imposed under Sch.B1 to the Insolvency Act 1986 in the case of company administration. Article 21(1)(g) gives the court a discretion to grant "any additional relief that may be available to a British insolvency officeholder under the law of Great Britain including any relief provided under para.43 of Sch.B1". This provision enables the court, if persuaded that it is appropriate to do so, to over-ride the rights which would otherwise be exercisable by secured creditors and other types of creditor through the combined effects of art.20(2) and (3) (described above), so that they are exercisable only with the consent of the officeholder or, alternatively, with the consent of the court itself. The imposition of such additional restrictions upon the exercise of creditors' rights could be a key contribution to an attempt to rescue or restructure a corporate debtor having interests and assets in a plurality of jurisdictions. The potential value of this provision is therefore considerable and a recent example of its use and operation arose in *D/S Norden A/S v Samsun Logix Corp*.[48] In that case, a secured creditor applied for an order enabling it to enforce its security in circumstances where the court had made an order that no step may be taken to enforce any security over the debtor company's property (the debtor company being subject to a Korean receivership which had been recognised under the 2006 Regulations[49]) except with the consent of its receiver or the permission of the court. The stay had been ordered pursuant to art.21(1)(g). The application was, in the circumstances of the case, dismissed and the stay continued but conditional upon the debtor company and its receiver undertaking not to argue that the secured creditor was bound by any future decision of the Korean court to invalidate its security as a result of it participating in the Korean proceedings by which the receiver was challenging the security.[50]

(xiii) Foreign penal or revenue claims

Article 13(1) proclaims the general right of foreign creditors to participate in a **32–028** proceeding under British insolvency law on equal terms with creditors in Great

---

[47] The debate falls outside the scope of this book. However, the arguments are canvassed in an article by Look Chan Ho, "Applying Foreign Law—Realising the Model law's Potential" [2010] J.I.B.L.R. 552–567. See also *Rubin v Eurofinance SA* [2011] Ch. 133 (CA) from which an appeal to the Supreme Court is expected to be heard in March 2012.

[48] *D/S Norden A/S v Samsun Logix Corp* [2009] B.P.I.R. 1367.

[49] *Samsun Logix Corp v DEF* [2009] B.P.I.R. 1502.

[50] For further commentary, see: Look Chan Ho, "Smoothing cross-border insolvency by synchronising the UNCITRAL Model Law: in re Samsun Logix Corporation" [2009] J.I.B.F.L. (July / August) 395.

Britain. This principle is supplemented by the provision in art.13(2) which
declares that this rule does not affect the ranking of claims under British insolvency law, except that a claim of a foreign creditor shall not be given a lower
priority than that of general unsecured claims solely because the holder of the
claim is a foreign creditor. These propositions would not necessarily bring
about the admission to proof of claims characterised as penal or revenue claims
submitted by or on behalf of a foreign state or public authority, because of a
long established exclusionary rule of public policy whereby such claims are
denied enforcement in Great Britain.[51] That exclusionary rule is now partially
over-ridden in the case of proceedings under British insolvency law by art.13(3)
which declares that "[A] claim may not be challenged solely on the grounds
that it is a claim by a foreign tax or social security authority . . ." However the
provision goes on to state that a claim may be challenged: (a) on the ground
that it is in whole or in part a penalty; or (b) on any other ground that a claim
might be rejected in a proceeding under British insolvency law. Thus the
exclusionary rule with respect to foreign penal claims remains intact, and care
has been taken to ensure that the liberalisation of the treatment of foreign
revenue or social security claims does not exempt such claims from having to
meet the general criteria applied under our insolvency law to determine the
admissibility of claims to proof.

(xiv) Transaction avoidance: Article 23

32–029 The provisions within the nine paragraphs of art.23, which bears the heading
"Actions to avoid acts detrimental to creditors", are of considerable importance. The main thrust of art.23 is to confer on the foreign representative
standing to make an application to the court under a number of specified
sections of the Insolvency Act 1986 (or under the Bankruptcy (Scotland) Act
1985) to bring about the impeachment of transactions entered into by the
debtor to the detriment of creditors. The following remedies are thereby made
available: the avoidance of transactions at an undervalue; preferences (or, in
Scotland, gratuitous alienations or unfair preferences); extortionate credit
transactions; floating charges to secure past indebtedness; the recovery of
excessive pension contributions made by individual debtors; and the avoidance
of transactions defrauding creditors.[52] By art.23(2) the listed provisions of
British insolvency legislation are made applicable whether or not the debtor
has been adjudged bankrupt (or undergone Scottish sequestration) or, in the
case of a company, is being wound up or is in administration. However, the
provisions in question apply with the modifications set out in para.(3), which
supplies a specially modified test for establishing whether a time is to be
regarded as a "relevant time" in relation to each of the avoidance provisions in

---

[51] *India v Taylor* [1955] A.C. 491 (HL). See I.F. Fletcher, *Insolvency in Private International Law*, 2nd edn (Oxford University Press, 2005), para.2.94.
[52] The statutory provisions listed in art.23(1) under which the foreign representative may seek the avoidance of prior transactions are: ss.238, 239, 242, 243, 244, 245, 339, 340, 342A, 343, and 423 of the Insolvency Act 1986, and ss.34, 35, 36, 36A, and 61 of the Bankruptcy (Scotland) Act 1985.

which this criterion has a crucial role. In each case, the criterion to be applied is that of "the date of the opening of the relevant insolvency proceedings". The means of determining the date of the opening of the foreign proceeding is prescribed by para.(4), which declares that this "shall be determined in accordance with the law of the State in which the foreign proceeding is taking place, including any rule by virtue of which the foreign proceeding is deemed to have opened at an earlier time".

The drafting of the test for determining the date from which the hardening off periods are to be calculated for impeachment purposes reflects a concern to escape from the uncertainties which have emerged in the context of analogous provisions in the EU Regulation on Insolvency Proceedings. The latter defines the expression "the time of the opening of proceedings" as "the time at which the judgment opening proceedings becomes effective, whether it is a final judgment or not". This begs the question whether any domestic rule concerning the relation back of the effects of such a judgment is to be assimilated into the process of fixing the time at which the judgment "becomes effective", a question which was still awaiting a ruling from the ECJ when the Cross-Border Insolvency Regulations 2006 entered into force.[53] By enacting the Model Law in terms which unequivocally assimilate the impact of the foreign State's relation back rule, the Regulations have simplified the task of calculating the running of time in order to determine whether a given transaction may be impeachable using the provisions found in British insolvency law. It will be for the foreign representative to adduce expert evidence to satisfy the British court as to the effective date of commencement of the foreign insolvency proceedings for the purpose of attacking any particular transaction. A further matter to bear in mind is that the requirement under art.2(q) (already referred to in para.32–020, above) whereby the rules of private international law are to be included for the purpose of applying the law of Great Britain ensures that a court of this country can counteract "forum-shopping" tactics on the part of the foreign representative if it concludes that under applicable rules of conflict of laws it is not the appropriate forum in which the transaction in question should be impeached. Such questions of principle are especially likely to arise in the context of a foreign non-main proceeding, and it is significant that art.23(5) specifies that in such cases the court must be satisfied that the art.23 application relates to assets that, under the law of Great Britain, should be administered in the foreign non-main proceeding.[54]

---

[53] See *Re Eurofood IFSC Ltd* (C-341/04) [2006] Ch. 508 (ECJ). In his Opinion delivered on September 27, 2005, A-G Jacobs proposed that an affirmative answer should be given to the question whether the time of the opening of insolvency proceedings should be interpreted as including the effect of any deemed relation back under the law of the state of opening: see [89]–[95], reported at [2006] Ch. 508 (ECJ). In the judgment of the ECJ, delivered on May 2, 2006, the court refrained from deciding the point: see [59] of the judgment of the court, also reported at [2006] Ch. 508 (ECJ). The *Eurofood* case is discussed in detail at para.31–014 et seq., above.

[54] See also art.23(7) enabling the court to give directions to ensure that the interests of creditors in Great Britain are adequately protected.

(xv)   Non-retrospective application of Article 23

32–030   An important restriction is imposed by art.23(9) to limit the temporal application of art.23(1). The clawback remedies which fall within the scope of art.23 do not apply to any acts or transactions made or entered into before April 4, 2006 (the date on which the Regulations entered into force). The rationale behind this rule of non-retrospective application is that at the time such pre-April 2006 transactions were entered into they could only have been attacked, using the remedies provided under British insolvency law, in the context of insolvency proceedings opened in this country (or, in cases where s.426 of the Insolvency Act 1986 could be invoked, if the court in its discretion so ordered). Therefore, if a case arises in which potentially impeachable transactions are found to have taken place before April 4, 2006, the appropriate course is to seek to open a proceeding under British insolvency law and for the officeholder to invoke the appropriate remedies to seek the avoidance of the transactions in question. The possibility to pursue this course is preserved by the combined effects of art.20(5) and art.23(8). A concurrent proceeding of this kind will be subject to the requirements of Ch.IV of the Model Law with respect to cooperation between courts, and between the British insolvency officeholder and foreign courts or foreign representatives. Although the commencing of an insolvency proceeding in this country may be facilitated, in the case where the foreign proceeding is recognised as a main proceeding, by the presumption of insolvency imposed by art.31, this may be tempered in some cases by the effects of the EU Regulation on Insolvency Proceedings. If the COMI of the debtor happens to be located in one of the participating Member States of the EU, the over-arching prescriptions of the jurisdictional regime embodied in the Regulation will preclude the opening of an insolvency proceeding in Great Britain or Northern Ireland unless the debtor has an establishment some part of the United Kingdom. It should also be noted that if concurrent proceedings are opened in this way, the British officeholder's capability to attack any antecedent transactions will have to be established using the date of opening of the English (or Scottish) proceedings as point of reference from which to ascertain whether the transaction took place at a "relevant time". This may have the consequence in some cases that the "hardening off" period of the transaction in question will have expired before the requisite steps take place to initiate the proceeding under British insolvency law, even though the period had not expired at the time of the opening of the foreign insolvency proceeding.

(xvi)   Co-operation with foreign courts and foreign representatives

32–031   Chapter IV of the Model Law consists of just three articles, numbered 25 to 27, which delineate a framework for cooperation in international insolvency matters. Some nuances of drafting may be noted whereby the text of these provisions as enacted for Great Britain differs from the original UNCITRAL version of the Model Law. Thus, in art.25(1), cooperation between a court of Great Britain and foreign courts or foreign representatives is placed on a discretionary basis by the use of the permissive words "may cooperate", where the UNCITRAL text renders this a matter of obligation by the use of the word "shall". Article 25(2) replicates faithfully the equivalent provision of the original UNCITRAL text, and provides that:

"The court is entitled to communicate directly with, or to request information or assistance directly from, foreign courts or foreign representatives."

This is a significant provision because it supplies legislative authority for the practice already embarked upon as a judicial innovation in such cases as *Cenargo* (referred to above at para.32–014), whereby direct court-to-court communication may be undertaken, with the agreement of the parties, by means of a live telephone conference.

In art.26, the obligation of a British insolvency officeholder to cooperate "to the maximum extent possible" with foreign courts or foreign representatives is expressed in mandatory terms by the use of the word "shall", echoing in this respect the UNCITRAL original. However, the British version dilutes the force of that obligation by inserting the qualifying phrase "to the extent consistent with his other duties under the law of Great Britain". These additional words were inserted as a consequence of responses to the consultative exercise conducted while the Regulations were in draft form, and are intended to enable the British officeholder to adjust the nature and quality of his cooperation in the event of any perceived conflict of interest between his own position and that of the foreign representative. In appropriate cases this dispensation may allow the British officeholder to reduce the extent of cooperation without the necessity to seek directions from the court, which might otherwise be a prudent means of safeguarding his own legal position in the event of subsequent challenge.

(xvii)   Commencement of a concurrent proceeding

Article 28 imposes a control upon the effects of any concurrent proceeding   **32–032** commenced under British insolvency law after recognition of a foreign main proceeding in relation to the same debtor. The British proceeding is rendered "territorial" in scope, by confining its effects to assets of that debtor which are located in Great Britain and, to the extent necessary to implement cooperation and coordination under arts 25–27 inclusive, to other assets of the debtor that, under the law of Great Britain, should be administered in that proceeding. This provision has the welcome consequence that it replicates the approach of the EU Regulation in terms of the distinction made between "main" and "territorial" (including "secondary") proceedings. However, the Model Law differs from the EU Regulation in that art.28 does not restrict the jurisdiction to open such territorial proceedings to cases where the debtor has an establishment in the State in question: the original UNCITRAL text imposes the less exacting criterion that the debtor must have assets in the State in question. The version of art.28 which has been enacted for Great Britain is even more liberally drafted, to reflect the tradition that has evolved in recent years, particularly in relation to the winding up of foreign companies, whereby jurisdiction may be exercised, even in the absence of assets, provided the debtor has "sufficient connection" with this country. That practice is allowed to continue thanks to the omission of the words "may be commenced only if the debtor has assets in this State". In the absence of the precondition which the missing phrase would have imposed jurisdiction to open proceedings is exercisable, both with regard to individuals and companies, in accordance with well established criteria concerning the nexus that is required to exist between the debtor and this country according to our legislation and case law. The fact that such proceedings, when opened in the circumstances specified in art.28, will be deprived of the universal effect which our law would previously have claimed for them is, as it happens, a timely answer to the complaint uttered by Sir Richard Scott V.C. in the *Cosmos* case, to the effect that: "It is . . . somewhat of a weakness in our own winding-up law that it is not possible to have a winding up of a foreign company limited to its activities and assets in this jurisdiction."[55]

(xviii) The Cross-Border Insolvency (Northern Ireland) Regulations 2007

32–033   As explained above at para.32–019, the effects of The Cross-Border Insolvency Regulations 2006 were confined to England and Wales and Scotland, thereby leaving the position of Northern Ireland to be covered by means of a separate instrument at a later date. That lacuna was rectified by The Cross-Border Insolvency Regulations (Northern Ireland) 2007 (SRNI 2007/115), which came into force as of April 12, 2007. Since that date the UNCITRAL Model Law has had effect throughout the United Kingdom. It is important to note, however, that there are some differences between the versions of the two enactments which apply in different parts of the United Kingdom, and this fact must be borne in mind by anyone who contemplates making use of any provisions of the Model Law in Northern Ireland, as opposed to within England, Wales or Scotland. It is advisable to scrutinise the relevant text with some care, in case the variation in the drafting (and in certain instances in the substance also) happen to have a material bearing upon the matter which is to be the subject of the application.

The Regulations enacted for Northern Ireland (the 2007 Regulations) consist of just seven numbered regulations, together with four schedules. Schedule 1 contains the text of the Model Law as in force in Northern Ireland. Comparison of the text of Sch.1 with the equivalent Schedule in the 2006 Regulations in force in Great Britain reveals some divergences, which may lay traps for the unwary. Of particular practical significance is the fact that, as between the two wings of the United Kingdom, the list of excluded companies and other entities to which the Model law does not apply are not fully identical. The exclusionary provisions of art.1(2) of Sch.1 to the 2006 Regulations are more numerous than those in the

---

[55] *Banco Nacional de Cuba v Cosmos Trading Corp* [2000] B.C.C. 910 (CA), 915.

corresponding art.1(2) contained in the 2007 Regulations, so that it is essential to refer to the version of art.1 that is in force within the relevant part of the United Kingdom when checking whether the proceeding in question relates to a company or person to which the Model Law does or does not apply.

More variations emerge when the two sets of "definitions" provided in art.2 are compared with each other. In most cases, although the definitions themselves are identically worded (or are identical in substance even if they contain references that are specific to the law and institutions of the relevant part of the United Kingdom) they bear different numbering, which may occasion some confusion unless care is taken to identify the proper version to which reference is being made. Thus the definition of "foreign main proceeding" is supplied in art.2(g) in the 2006 Regulations, but in art.2(f) in the 2007 version applicable to Northern Ireland, while the definition of "establishment" appears in art.2(e) in the 2006 text, but in art.2(c) in the 2007 version. In the two examples just given the actual substance of the definitions is identical, but this is not fully the case with the respective definitions of "British insolvency law" as supplied by art.2(a) in the 2006 Regulations, and the corresponding definition of "Northern Ireland insolvency law" given in art.2(k) in the 2007 Regulations. This is because, in addition to the inevitable particularisation of the geographical references and associated insolvency legislation which specifically apply to the separate parts of the United Kingdom, there is a curious omission from the text of art.2 of Sch.1 to the 2007 Regulations in that there is no counterpart to the supplementary provision contained in art.2(q) of the version enacted for Great Britain. As discussed in para.32–020 above, the latter provides that "references to the law of Great Britain include a reference to the law of either part of Great Britain (including its rules of private international law)". The absence of an equivalent prompting to the court in Northern Ireland to be alert to the potential for choice of law issues to arise in the context of cross-border insolvency cases is somewhat puzzling. In this context it can also be mentioned that there is no counterpart in the 2007 Regulations to reg.7 of the 2007 Regulations for Great Britain, whereby explicit provision is made concerning co-operation between courts in either part of Great Britain exercising jurisdiction in relation to cross-border insolvency. Some additional, bridging provision seems to be required to cement the alliance between the courts in Northern Ireland and those of mainland Britain.

One potential consequence resulting from the fact that the 2006 Regulations and the 2007 Regulations were enacted some twelve months apart arises in relation to the transaction avoidance rules enacted in both versions of art.23 of the Model Law in force in the various parts of the United Kingdom (see para.32–029 above). Article 23(9) (in both versions) restricts the application of that article to transactions entered into after the date on which the Model Law enters into force in that part of the United Kingdom. Since the Model Law entered into force in Great Britain slightly more than one year before it came into force in Northern Ireland, some transactions which were entered into between April 4, 2006 and April 12, 2007 will be impeachable using art.23 in Great Britain but not in Northern Ireland. The significance of this discrepancy will progressively disappear with the passage of time.

Subject to what is said above, the remaining provisions of the version of the Model Law contained in Sch.1 to the 2007 Regulations differ from the equivalent text of the 2006 Regulations merely in respect of the drafting transpositions needed to adapt the text so that it makes specific reference to "Northern Ireland" in place of "Great Britain" (or any part thereof), and to the appropriate legislative provisions that are in force there. In substance, and with the exception of certain cases involving applications under art.23, the Model Law should operate in all parts of the United Kingdom in a standardised manner, mutatis mutandis. When participating in a proceeding before a court in Northern Ireland practitioners will need to refer to the detailed provisions in Schs 2–4 inclusive of the 2007 Regulations. These (like their counterparts in the 2006 Regulations) contain specific provisions to regulate matters of procedure (Sch.2), and notices to be delivered to the Registrar of Companies (Sch.3), and they also provide templates of the relevant forms for use in Northern Ireland (Sch.4).

(xix) Practical considerations when making use of the Model Law

32–034   Since the benefits of the Model Law are in principle to be made available by the enacting State without regard to questions of reciprocity, the potential opportunities for office holders appointed under the insolvency law of any part of the United Kingdom should be borne in mind whenever assets of the debtor company are known to be located in any foreign country which has already taken the step of enacting the Model Law. This in turn may in some cases influence the choice of procedure, particularly where it is possible to opt for either administration or administrative receivership. The fact that an administrator has the status of "foreign representative" for the purposes of the Model Law, whereas an administrative receiver does not, could enable an office holder of the former kind to take more effective, and timely, action in other relevant jurisdictions to conserve the assets than could be achieved by an administrative receiver. Moreover, it should be noted that in certain respects the EU Regulation and the UNCITRAL Model Law are capable of complementing and reinforcing each other, so that an administrator should be able to enjoy significant scope for action across 26 of the 27 EU Member States, in addition to being able to claim recognition and access to the courts of all countries throughout the world where the Model Law has been incorporated into the national law.

One final note of caution must be registered. The numerous points of divergence, as noted above, between the original text of the UNCITRAL Model Law and the versions which have been enacted in Great Britain and in Northern Ireland should serve as a reminder that other States which enact the Model Law have had similar opportunities to introduce variations in the wording of the text to suit local requirements. The authentic text of the relevant enacting measures should always be carefully studied. By the same token, it is imperative that anyone who contemplates making use of the Model Law within the United Kingdom should closely scrutinise the actual provisions of The Cross-Border Insolvency Regulations 2006 or The Cross-Border

Insolvency (Northern Ireland) Regulations 2007, as appropriate. It would be inadvisable for them to assume that the substance of the Model Law as it applies within the relevant part of the United Kingdom is in every material respect identical either to that of the original UNCITRAL text itself, or to the terms in which it has been enacted in any other State with which the user may be familiar.

APPENDIX 1—STATUTES

Law of Property Act 1925

(15 & 16 GEO. 5, C. 20)

Powers incident to estate or interest of mortgagee

A1–001   **101.**—(1) A mortgagee, where the mortgage is made by deed, shall, by virtue of this Act, have the following powers, to the like extent as if they had been in terms conferred by the mortgage deed, but not further (namely):

(i)   A power, when the mortgage money has become due, to sell, or to concur with any other person in selling, the mortgaged property, or any part thereof, either subject to prior charges or not, and either together or in lots, by public auction or by private contract, subject to such conditions respecting title, or evidence of title, or other matter, as the mortgagee thinks fit, with power to vary any contract for sale, and to buy in at an auction, or to rescind any contract for sale, and to re-sell, without being answerable for any loss occasioned thereby; and

(ii)   A power, at any time after the date of the mortgage deed, to insure and keep insured against loss or damage by fire any building, or any effects or property of an insurable nature, whether affixed to the freehold or not, being or forming part of the property which or an estate or interest wherein is mortgaged, and the premiums paid for any such insurance shall be a charge on the mortgaged property or estate or interest, in addition to the mortgage money, and with the same priority, and with interest at the same rate, as the mortgage money; and

(iii)   A power, when the mortgage money has become due, to appoint a receiver of the income of the mortgaged property, or any part thereof; or, if the mortgaged property consists of an interest in income, or of a rent-charge or an annual or other periodical sum, a receiver of that property or any part thereof: and

(iv)   A power, while the mortgagee is in possession, to cut and sell timber and other trees ripe for cutting, and not planted or left standing for shelter or ornament, or to contract for any such cutting and sale, to be completed within any time not exceeding twelve months from the making of the contract.

(1A) Subsection (1)(i) is subject to section 21 of the Commonhold and Leasehold Reform Act 2002 (no disposition of part-units)

(2) Where the mortgage deed is executed after the thirty-first day of December, nineteen hundred and eleven, the power of sale aforesaid includes the following powers as incident thereto (namely):

(i)   A power to impose or reserve or make binding, as far as the law permits, by covenant, condition, or otherwise, on the unsold part of the mortgaged property or any part thereof, or on the purchaser and any property sold, any restriction or reservation with respect to building on or other user of land, or with respect to mines and minerals, or for the purpose of the more beneficial working thereof, or with respect to any other thing:

(ii)   A power to sell the mortgaged property, or any part thereof, or all or any mines and minerals apart from the surface:

(a)   With or without a grant or reservation of rights of way, rights of water, easements, rights, and privileges for or connected with building or other purposes in relation to the property remaining in mortgage or any part thereof, or to any property sold: and

(b) With or without an exception or reservation of all or any of the mines and minerals in or under the mortgaged property, and with or without a grant or reservation of powers of working, wayleaves, or rights of way, rights of water and drainage and other powers, easements, rights, and privileges for or connected with mining purposes in relation to the property remaining unsold or any part thereof, or to any property sold: and

(c) With or without covenants by the purchaser to expend money on the land sold.

(3) The provisions of this Act relating to the foregoing powers, comprised either in this section, or in any other section regulating the exercise of those powers, may be varied or extended by the mortgage deed, and, as so varied or extended, shall, as far as may be, operate in the like manner and with all the like incidents, effects, and consequences, as if such variations or extensions were contained in this Act.

(4) This section applies only if and as far as a contrary intention is not expressed in the mortgage deed, and has effect subject to the terms of the mortgage deed and to the provisions therein contained.

(5) Save as otherwise provided, this section applies where the mortgage deed is executed after the thirty-first day of December, eighteen hundred and eighty-one.

(6) The power of sale conferred by this section includes such power of selling the estate in fee simple or any leasehold reversion as is conferred by the provisions of this Act relating to the realisation of mortgages.

Appointment, powers, remuneration and duties of receiver

109.—(1) A mortgagee entitled to appoint a receiver under the power in that behalf **A1–002** conferred by this Act shall not appoint a receiver until he has become entitled to exercise the power of sale conferred by this Act, but may then, by writing under his hand, appoint such person as he thinks fit to be receiver.

(2) A receiver appointed under the powers conferred by this Act, or any enactment replaced by this Act, shall be deemed to be the agent of the mortgagor; and the mortgagor shall be solely responsible for the receiver's acts or defaults unless the mortgage deed otherwise provides.

(3) The receiver shall have power to demand and recover all the income of which he is appointed receiver, by action, distress, or otherwise, in the name either of the mortgagor or of the mortgagee, to the full extent of the estate or interest which t he mortgagor could dispose of, and to give effectual receipts accordingly for the same, and to exercise any powers which may have been delegated to him by the mortgagee pursuant to this Act.

(4) A person paying money to the receiver shall not be concerned to inquire whether any case has happened to authorise the receiver to act

(5) The receiver may be removed, and a new receiver may be appointed, from time to time by the mortgagee by writing under his hand.

(6) The receiver shall be entitled to retain out of any money received by him, for his remuneration, and in satisfaction of all costs, charges, and expenses incurred by him as receiver, a commission at such rate, not exceeding five per centum on the gross amount of all money received, as is specified in his appointment, and if no rate is so specified, then at the rate of five per centum on that gross amount, or at such other rate as the court thinks fit to allow, on application made by him for that purpose.

(7) The receiver shall, if so directed in writing by the mortgagee, insure to the extent, if any, to which the mortgagee might have insured and keep insured against loss or damage by fire, out of the money received by him, any building, effects, or property comprised in the mortgage, whether affixed to the freehold or not, being of an insurable nature.

(8) Subject to the provisions of this Act as to the application of insurance money, the receiver shall apply all money received by him as follows, namely:

(i) In discharge of all rents, taxes, rates, and outgoings whatever affecting the mortgaged property; and

(ii) In keeping down all annual sums or other payments, and the interest on all principal sums, having priority to the mortgage in right whereof he is receiver: and

(iii) In payment of his commission, and of the premiums on fire, life, or other insurances, if any, properly payable under the mortgage deed or under this Act, and the cost of executing necessary or proper repairs directed in writing by the mortgagee; and

(iv) In payment of the interest accruing due in respect of any principal money due under the mortgage; and

(v) In or towards discharge of the principal money is so directed in writing by the mortgagee;

and shall pay the residue, if any, of the money received by him to the person who, but for the possession of the receiver, would have been entitled to receive the income of which he is appointed receiver, or who is otherwise entitled to the mortgaged property.

Unfair Contract Terms Act 1977

(c. 50)

PART I

AMENDMENT OF LAW FOR ENGLAND AND WALES AND NORTHERN IRELAND

Introductory

Scope of Part I

1.—(1) For the purposes of this Part of this Act, "negligence" means the breach— **A1–003**

(a) of any obligation, arising from the express or implied terms of a contract, to take reasonable care to exercise reasonable skill in the performance of the contract:

(b) of any common law duty to take reasonable care or exercise reasonable skill (but not any stricter duty);

(c) of the common duty of care imposed by the Occupiers' Liability Act 1957 or the Occupiers Liability Act (Northern Ireland) 1958:

but liability of an occupier of premises for breach of an obligation or duty towards a person obtaining access to the premises for recreational or educational purposes, being liability for loss or damage suffered by reason of the dangerous state of the premises, is not a business liability of the occupier unless granting that person such access for the purposes concerned falls within the business purposes of the occupier.

(2) This Part of this Act is subject to Part III: and in relation to contracts, the operation of sections 2 to 4 and 7 is subject to the exceptions made by Schedule 1.

(3) In the case of both contract and tort, sections 2 to 7 apply (except where the contrary is stated in section 6(4)) only to business liability, that is liability for breach of obligations or duties arising—

(a) from things done or to be done by a person in the course of a business (whether his own business or another's); or

(b) from the occupation of premises used for business purposes of the occupier:

and references to liability are to be read accordingly but liability of an occupier of premises for breach of an obligation or duty towards a person obtaining access to the premises for recreational or educational purposes, being liability for loss or damage suffered by reason of the dangerous state of the premises, is not a business liability of the occupier unless granting that person such access for the purposes concerned falls within the business purposes of the occupier.

(4) In relation to any breach of duty or obligation, it is immaterial for any purpose of this Part of this Act whether the breach was inadvertent or intentional, or whether liability for it arises directly or vicariously.

Avoidance of liability for negligence, breach of contract, etc

Negligence liability

2.—(1) A person cannot by reference to any contract term or to a notice given to **A1–004** persons generally or to particular persons exclude or restrict his liability for death or personal injury resulting from negligence.

(2) In the case of other loss or damage, a person cannot so exclude or restrict his liability for negligence except in so far as the term or notice satisfies the requirement of reasonableness.

(3) Where a contract term or notice purports to exclude or restrict liability for negligence a person's agreement to or awareness of it is not of itself to be taken as indicating his voluntary acceptance of any risk.

Liability arising in contract

A1–005   **3.**—(1) This section applies as between contracting parties where one of them deals as consumer or on the other's written standard terms of business.

(2) As against that party, the other cannot by reference to any contract term—

    (a) when himself in breach of contract, exclude or restrict any liability of his in respect of the breach; or

    (b) claim to be entitled—

        (i) to render a contractual performance substantially different from that which was reasonably expected of him, or

        (ii) in respect of the whole or any part of his contractual obligation, to render no performance at all.

except in so far as (in any of the cases mentioned above in this subsection) the contract term satisfies the requirement of reasonableness.

* * * * *

Evasion by means of secondary contract

A1–006   **10.**—A person is not bound by any contract term prejudicing or taking away rights of his which arise under, or in connection with the performance of another contract, so far as those rights extend to the enforcement of another's liability which this Part of this Act prevents that other from excluding or restricting.

Explanatory provisions

The "reasonableness" test

A1–007   **11.**—(1) In relation to a contract term, the requirement of reasonableness for the purposes of this Part of this Act, section 3 of the Misrepresentation Act 1967 and section 3 of the Misrepresentation Act (Northern Ireland) 1967 is that the term shall have been a fair and reasonable one to be included having regard to the circumstances which were, or ought reasonably to have been, known to or in the contemplation of the parties when the contract was made.

(2) In determining for the purposes of section 6 or 7 above whether a contract term satisfies the requirement of reasonableness, regard shall be had in particular to the matters specified in Schedule 2 to this Act; but this subsection does not prevent the court or arbitrator from holding, in accordance with any rule of law, that a term which purports to exclude or restrict any relevant liability is not a term of the contract.

(3) In relation to a notice (not being a notice having contractual effect), the requirement of reasonableness under this Act is that it should be fair and reasonable to allow reliance on it, having regard to all the circumstances obtaining when the liability arose or (but for the notice) would have arisen.

(4) Where by reference to a contract term or notice a person seeks to restrict liability to a specified sum of money, and the question arises (under this or any other Act) whether the term or notice satisfies the requirement of reasonable ness, regard shall be had in particular (but without prejudice to subsection (2) above in the case of contract terms) to—

    (a) the resources which he could expect to be available to him for the purpose of meeting the liability should it arise; and

    (b) how far it was open to him to cover himself by insurance.

(5) It is for those claiming that a contract term or notice satisfies the requirement of reasonableness to show that it does.

* * * * *

Varieties of exemption clause

13.—(1) To the extent that this Part of this Act prevents the exclusion or restriction   **A1–008** of any liability it also prevents—

    (a) making the liability or its enforcement subject to restrictive or onerous conditions;

    (b) excluding or restricting any right or remedy in respect of the liability, or subjecting a person to any prejudice in consequence of his pursuing any such right or remedy;

    (c) excluding or restricting rules of evidence or procedure:

and (to that extent) sections 2 and 5 to 7 also prevent excluding or restricting liability by reference to terms and notices which exclude or restrict the relevant obligations or duty.

(2) But an agreement in writing to submit present or future differences to arbitration is not to be treated under this Part of this Act as excluding or restricting any liability.

Interpretation of Part I

14.—In this Part of this Act—   **A1–009**

  "business" includes a profession and the activities of any government department or local or public authority;

  "goods" has the same meaning as in [the Sale of Goods Act 1979];

  "hire-purchase agreement" has the same meaning as in the Consumer Credit Act 1974;

  "negligence" has the meaning given by section 1(1);

  "notice" includes an announcement, whether or not in writing, and any other communication or pretended communication; and

  "personal injury" includes any disease and any impairment of physical or mental condition.

* * * * *

Section 1(2)   SCHEDULE 1

SCOPE OF SECTIONS 2 TO 4 AND 7

A1–010   1. Sections 2 to 4 of this Act do not extend to—

    (a) any contract of insurance (including a contract to pay an annuity on human life):

    (b) any contract so far as it relates to the creation or transfer of an interest in land, or to the termination of such an interest, whether by extinction, merger, surrender, forfeiture or otherwise;

    (c) any contract so far as it relates to the creation or transfer of a right or interest in any patent, trade mark, copyright or design right, registered design, technical or commercial information or other intellectual property, or relates to the termination of any such right or interest:

    (d) any contract so far as it relates—

        (i) to the formation or dissolution of a company (which means any body corporate or unincorporated association and includes a partnership), or

        (ii) to its constitution or the rights or obligations of its corporators or members;

    (e) any contract so far as it relates to the creation or transfer of securities or of any right or interest in securities.

2. Section 2(1) extends to—

    (a) any contract of marine salvage or towage;

    (b) any charterparty of a ship or hovercraft; and

    (c) any contract for the carriage of goods by ship or hovercraft;

but subject to this sections 2 to 4 and 7 do not extend to any such contract except in favour of a person dealing as consumer.

3. Where goods are carried by ship or hovercraft in pursuance of a contract which either—

    (a) specifies that as the means of carriage over part of the journey to be covered, or

    (b) makes no provision as to the means of carriage and does not exclude that means.

then sections 2(2), 3 and 4 do not, except in favour of a person dealing as consumer, extend to the contract as it operates for and in relation to the carriage of the goods by that means.

4. Section 2(1) and (2) do not extend to a contract of employment, except in favour of the employee.

5. Section 2(1) does not affect the validity of any discharge and indemnity given by a person, on or in connection with an award to him of compensation for pneumoconiosis attributable to employment in the coal industry, in respect of any further claim arising from his contracting that disease.

Sections 11(2), 24(2)   SCHEDULE 2

"GUIDELINES" FOR APPLICATION OF REASONABLENESS TEST

A1–011   The matters to which regard is to be had in particular for the purposes of sections 6(3), 7(3) and (4), 20 and 21 are any of the following which appear to be relevant—

    (a) the strength of the bargaining positions of the parties relative to each other, taking into account (among other things) alternative means by which the customer's requirements could have been met:

(b)   whether the customer received an inducement to agree to the term, or in accepting it had an opportunity of entering into a similar contract with other persons, but without having to accept a similar term:

(c)   whether the customer knew or ought reasonably to have known of the existence and extent of the term (having regard, among other things, to any custom of the trade and any previous course of dealing between the parties):

(d)   where the term excludes or restricts any relevant liability if some condition is not complied with, whether it was reasonable at the time of the contract to expect that compliance with that condition would be practicable:

(e)   whether the goods were manufactured, processed or adapted to the special order of the customer.

Employment Protection (Consolidation) Act 1978

(c. 44)

PART VII

INSOLVENCY OF EMPLOYER

Priority of certain debts on insolvency

A1–012   **121.** [Repealed by the Insolvency Act 1985 (c. 65). Sch.1(1) and the Bankruptcy (Scotland) Act 1985 (c. 66) s.75(2).]

Employee's rights on insolvency of employer

A1–013   **122.**—[Repealed by the Employment Rights Act 1996 (c.18). Sch.3–see below, para.A1-031.]

Payment of unpaid contributions to occupational pension scheme

A1–014   **123.**—[Repealed by the Pension Schemes Act 1993 (c.48)–see below, para.A1-041.]

Complaint to industrial tribunal

A1–015   **124.**—[Repealed by the Employment Rights Act 1966 (c.18)–see below, para.A1-037.]

Transfer to Secretary of State of rights and remedies

A1–016   **125.**—[Repealed by the Employment Rights Act 1966 (c.18)–see below, para.A1-038.]

Power of Secretary of State to obtain information in connection with application

A1–017   **126.**—[Repealed by the Employment Rights Act 1966 (c.18)–see below, para.A1-039]

Interpretation of ss. 122 to 126

A1–018   **127.**—[Repealed by the Employment Rights Act 1966 (c.18)–see below, para.A1-032]

Charging Orders Act 1979

(c. 53)

Charging orders

Charging orders

1.—(1) Where, under a judgment or order of the High Court or a county court, a **A1–019** person (the "debtor") is required to pay a sum of money to another person (the "creditor") then, for the purpose of enforcing that judgment or order, the appropriate court may make an order in accordance with the provisions of this Act imposing on any such property of the debtor as may be specified in the order a charge for securing the payment of any money due or to become due under the judgment or order.

(2) The appropriate court is—

    (a) in a case where the property to be charged is a fund in court, the court in which that fund is lodged;

    (b) in a case where paragraph *(a)* above does not apply and the order to be enforced is a maintenance order of the High Court, the High Court or a county court;

    (c) in a case where neither paragraph *(a)* nor paragraph *(b)* above applies and the judgment or order to be enforced is a judgment or order of the High Court for a sum exceeding £2,000; the High Court or a county court; and

    (d) in any other case, a county court.

In this section "county court limit" means the county court limit for the time being specified in an Order in Council under section 145 of the County Courts Act 1984, as the county court limit for the purposes of this section and "maintenance order" has the same meaning as in section 2*(a)* of the Attachment of Earnings Act 1971.

(3) An order under subsection (1) above is referred to in this Act as a "charging order".

(4) Where a person applies to the High Court for a charging order to enforce more than one judgment or order, that court shall be the appropriate court in relation to the application if it would be the appropriate court, apart from this subsection, on an application relating to one or more of the judgments or orders concerned.

(5) In deciding whether to make a charging order the court shall consider all the circumstances of the case and, in particular, any evidence before it as to—

    (a) the personal circumstances of the debtor, and

    (b) whether any other creditor of the debtor would be likely to be unduly prejudiced by the making of the order.

Properly which may be charged

2.—(1) Subject to subsection (3) below, a charge may be imposed by a charging **A1–020** order only on—

    (a) any interest held by the debtor beneficially—

        (i) in any asset of a kind mentioned in subsection (2) below, or

        (ii) under any trust: or

    (b) any interest held by a person as trustee of a trust ("the trust"), if the interest is in such an asset or is an interest under another trust and—

        (i) the judgment or order in respect of which a charge is to be imposed was made against that person as trustee of the trust, or

    (ii) the whole beneficial interest under the trust is held by the debtor unencumbered and for his own benefit, or

    (iii) in a case where there are two or more debtors All of whom are liable to the creditor for the same debt, they together hold the whole beneficial interest under the trust unencumbered and for their own benefit.

(2) The assets referred to in subsection (1) above are—

    (a) land,

    (b) securities of any of the following kinds—

        (i) government stock,

        (ii) stock of any body (other than a building society) incorporated within England and Wales,

        (iii) stock of any body incorporated outside England and Wales or of any state or territory outside the United Kingdom, being stock registered in a register kept at any place within England and Wales,

        (iv) units of any unit trust in respect of which a register of the unit holders is kept at any place within England and Wales, or

    (c) funds in court.

(3) In any case where a charge is imposed by a charging order on any interest in an asset of a kind mentioned in paragraph *(b)* or *(c)* of subsection (2) above, the court making the order may provide for the charge to extend to any interest or dividend payable in respect of the asset.

Provisions supplementing sections 1 and 2

A1–021   **3.**—(1) A charging order may be made either absolutely or subject to conditions as to notifying the debtor or as to the time when the charge is to become enforceable, or as to other matters.

(2) The Land Charges Act 1972 and the Land Registration Act 1925 shall apply in relation to charging orders as they apply in relation to other orders or writs issued or made for the purpose of enforcing judgments.

(3) In section 49 of the Land Registration Act 1925 (protection of certain interests by notice) there is inserted at the end of subsection (1) the following paragraph—

"*(g)* charging orders (within the meaning of the Charging Orders Act 1979) which in the case of unregistered land may be protected by registration under the land Charges Act 1972 and which notwithstanding section 59 of this Act, it may be deemed expedient to protect by notice instead of by caution."

(4) Subject to the provisions of this Act, a charge imposed by a charging order shall have the like effect and shall be enforceable in the same courts and in the same manner as an equitable charge created by the debtor by writing under his hand.

(5) The court by which a charging order was made may at any time, on the application of the debtor or of any person interested in any property to which the order relates, make an order discharging or varying the charging order.

(6) Where a charging order has been protected by an entry registered under the Land Charges Act 1972 or the Land Registration Act 1925, an order under subsection (5) above discharging the charging order may direct that the entry be cancelled.

(7) The Lord Chancellor may by order made by statutory instrument amend section 2(2) of this Act by adding to, or removing from, the kinds of asset for the time being referred to there, any asset of a kind which in his opinion ought to be so added or removed.

(8) Any order under subsection (7) above shall be subject to annulment in pursuance of a resolution of either House of Parliament.

Completion of execution

4.—[Repealed by the Insolvency Act 1985 (c.65), s.235, Sched. 10. Pt. II.]   A1–022

Companies Act 1985

(c. 6)

PART I

FORMATION AND REGISTRATION OF COMPANIES; JURIDICAL STATUS AND MEMBERSHIP

* * * * *

CHAPTER III

A COMPANY'S CAPACITY; FORMALITIES OF CARRYING ON BUSINESS

A company's capacity not limited by its memorandum [s.39, CA 2006]

A1–023   35.—(1) The validity of an act done by a company shall not be called into question on the ground of lack of capacity by reason of anything in the company's memorandum.

(2) A member of a company may bring proceedings to restrain the doing of an act which but for subsection (1) would be beyond the company's capacity; but no such proceedings shall lie in respect of an act to be done in fulfilment of a legal obligation arising from a previous act of the company.

(3) It remains the duty of the directors to observe any limitations on their powers flowing from the company's memorandum; and action by the directors which but for subsection (1) would be beyond the company's capacity may only be ratified by the company by special resolution.

A resolution ratifying such action shall not affect any liability incurred by the directors or any other person: relief from any such liability must be agreed to separately by special resolution.

(4) The operation of this section is restricted by section 30B(1) of the Charities Act 1960 and section 112(3) of the Companies Act 1989 in relation to companies which are charities: and section 322A below (invalidity of certain transactions to which directors or their associates are parties) has effect notwithstanding this section.

Power of directors to bind the company [s.40, CA 2006]

A1–024   35A.—(1) In favour of a person dealing with a company in good faith, the power of the board of directors to bind the company, or authorise others to do so, shall be deemed to be free of any limitation under the company's constitution.

(2) For this purpose—

  (a)   a person "deals with" a company if he is a party to any transaction or other act to which the company is a party;

  (b)   a person shall not be regarded as acting in bad faith by reason only of his knowing that an act is beyond the powers of the directors under the company's constitution: and

  (c)   a person shall be presumed to have acted in good faith unless the contrary is proved.

(3) The references above to limitations on the directors' powers under the company's constitution include limitations deriving—

  (a)   from a resolution of the company in general meeting or a meeting of any class of shareholders, or

  (b)   from any agreement between the members of the company or of any class of shareholders.

(4) Subsection (1) does not affect any right of a member of the company to bring proceedings to restrain the doing of an act which is beyond the powers of the directors: but no such proceedings shall lie in respect of an act to be done in fulfilment of a legal obligation arising from a previous act of the company.

(5) Nor does that subsection affect any liability incurred by the directors, or any other person, by reason of the directors' exceeding their powers.

(6) The operation of this section is restricted by section 30B(l) of the Charities Act 1960 and section 112(3) of the Companies Act 1989 in relation to companies which are charities; and section 322A below (invalidity of certain transactions to which directors or their associates are parties) has effect notwithstanding this section.

No duty to enquire as to capacity of company or authority of directors [s.40(2)(b)(i), CA 2006]

35B.—A party to a transaction with a company is not bound to enquire as to whether it is permitted by the company's memorandum or as to any limitation on the powers of the board of directors to bind the company or authorise others to do so.   A1–025

* * * * *

PART XII

REGISTRATION OF CHARGES

CHAPTER 1

REGISTRATION OF CHARGES (ENGLAND AND WALES)

Certain charges void if not registered [ss.860(1), 861(5), 870(1), 874(1), (2), (3), CA 2006]

395.—(1) Subject to the provisions of this Chapter, a charge created by a company   A1–026
registered in England and Wales and being a charge to which this section applies is, so far as any security on the company's property or undertaking is conferred by the charge, void against the liquidator [or administrator] and any creditor of the company, unless the prescribed particulars of the charge together with the instrument (if any) by which the charge is created or evidenced, are delivered to or received by the registrar of companies for registration in the manner required by this Chapter within 21 days after the date of the charge's creation.

(2) Subsection (1) is without prejudice to any contract or obligation for repayment of the money secured by the charge; and when a charge becomes void under this section, the money secured by it immediately becomes payable.

Charges which have to be registered [ss.860(7), 861(1), (2), (3), (4), (5), CA 2006]

396.—(1) Section 395 applies to the following charges—   A1–027

- (a) a charge for the purpose of securing any issue of debentures,
- (b) a charge on uncalled share capital of the company,
- (c) a charge created or evidenced by an instrument which, if executed by an individual, would require registration as a bill of sale,
- (d) a charge on land (wherever situated) or any interest in it, but not including a charge for any rent or other periodical sum issuing out of the land.
- (e) a charge on book debts of the company,
- (f) a floating charge on the company's undertaking or property,
- (g) a charge on calls made but not paid,

(h)   a charge on a ship or aircraft, or any share in a ship,

(i)   a charge on goodwill, on a patent or a licence under a patent, on a trademark or on a copyright or a licence under a copyright.

(2) Where a negotiable instrument has been given to secure the payment of any book debts of a company, the deposit of the instrument for the purpose of securing an advance to the company is not, for purposes of section 395, to be treated as a charge on those book debts.

(3) The holding of debentures entitling the holder to a charge on land is not for purposes of this section deemed to be an interest in land.

(4) In this Chapter, "charge" includes mortgage.

* * * * *

PART XXVI

INTERPRETATION

* * * * *

"Company," etc. [s.1(1), CA 2006]

A1–028   **735.**—(1) In this Act—

(a)   "company" means a company formed and registered under this Act. or an existing company.

(4) The definitions in this section apply unless the contrary intention appears.

"Director" and "shadow director" [ss.250, 251, CA 2006]

* * * * *

741.—(1) In this Act. "director" includes any person occupying the position of director, by whatever name called.

(2) In relation to a company, "shadow director" means a person in accordance with whose directions or instructions the directors of the company are accustomed to act.

However, a person is not deemed a shadow director by reason only that the directors act on advice given by him in a professional capacity.

(3) For the purposes of the following provisions of this Act, namely—

section 309 (directors' duty to have regard to interests of employees),
section 319 (directors' long-term contracts of employment),
sections 320 and 322 (substantial property transactions involving directors),
[section 322B (contracts with sole members who are director), and]
sections 330 to 346 (general restrictions on power of companies to make loans, etc. to directors and others connected with them).

(being provisions under which shadow directors are treated as directors), a body corporate is not to be treated as a shadow director of any of its subsidiary companies by reason only that the directors of the subsidiary are accustomed to act in accordance with its directions or instructions.

Law of Property (Miscellaneous Provisions) Act 1989

(c. 34)

Deeds and their execution

1.1. (1) Any rule of law which—

A1–029

- *(a)* restricts the substances on which a deed may be written;
- *(b)* requires a seal for the valid execution of an instrument as a deed by an individual; or
- *(c)* requires authority by one person to another to deliver an instrument as a deed on his behalf to be given by deed.

is abolished.

(2) An instrument shall not be a deed unless—

- *(a)* it makes it clear on its face that it is intended to be a deed by the person making it or, as the case may be, by the parties to it (whether by describing itself as a deed or expressing itself to be executed or signed as a deed or otherwise), and
- *(b)* it is validly executed as a deed by that person or, as the case may be, one or more of those parties.

(3) An instrument is validly executed as a deed by an individual if, and only if—

- *(a)* it is signed—
  - (i) by him in the presence of a witness who attests the signature; or
  - (ii) at his direction and in his presence and the presence of two witnesses who each attest the signature; and
- *(b)* it is delivered as a deed by him or a person authorised to do so on his behalf.

(4) In subsections (2) and (3) above "sign", in relation to an instrument, includes making one's mark on the instrument and "signature" is to be construed accordingly.

(5) Where a solicitor or licensed conveyancer, or an agent or employee of a solicitor or licensed conveyancer, in the course of or in connection with a transaction involving the disposition or creation of an interest in land, purports to deliver an instrument as a deed on behalf of a party to the instrument, it shall be conclusively presumed in favour of a purchaser that he is authorised so to deliver the instrument.

(6) In subsection (5) above—

"disposition" and "purchaser" have the same meanings as in the Law of Property Act 1925;

"duly certificated notary public" has the same meaning as it has in the Solicitors Act 1974, by virtue of section 87 of that Act; and

"interest in land" means any estate, interest or charge in or over land or in or over the proceeds of sale of land.

(7) Where an instrument under seal that constitutes a deed is required for the purposes of an Act passed before this section comes into force, this section shall have effect as to signing, sealing or delivery of an instrument by an individual in place of any provision of that Act is to signing, sealing or delivery.

(8) The enactments mentioned in Schedule 1 to this Act (which in consequence of this section require amendments other than those provided by subsection (7) above) shall have effect with the amendments specified in that Schedule.

(9) Nothing in subsection (1)(b), (2), (3), (7) or (8) above applies in relation to deeds required or authorised to be made under—

(a)   the seal of the county palatine of Lancaster:
(b)   the seal of the Duchy of Lancaster: or
(c)   the seal of the Duchy of Cornwall.

(10) The references in this section to the execution of a deed by an individual do not include execution by a corporation sole and the reference in subsection (7) above to signing, sealing, or delivery by an individual does not include signing, sealing or delivery by such a corporation.

(11) Nothing in this section applies in relation to instruments delivered as deeds before this section comes into force.

* * * * *

A1–030   **Section 4**   SCHEDULE 2

REPEALS

Chapter	Short title	Extent of repeal
15 & 16 Geo. 5 c. 20	The Law of Property Act 1925	Section 40. Section 73. In section 74(3), the words "and in the case of a deed by affixing his own seal."
1971 c. 27	The Powers of Attorney Act 1971	Section 1(2). In section 7, subsection (1), the words "and seal" and in subsection (2), the words "or (4)".

Employment Rights Act 1996

(c. 18)

PART XII

Employee's rights and insolvency of employer

182 If, on an application made to him in writing by an employee, the Secretary of **A1–031**
State is satisfied that—

(a) the employee's employer has become insolvent,
(b) the employee's employment has been terminated, and
(c) on the appropriate date the employee was entitled to a fee paid the whole or part of any debt to which this Part applies,

the Secretary of State shall, subject to section 186, pay the employee out of the National Insurance Fund the amount to which, in the opinion of the Secretary of State, the employee is entitled in respect of the debt.

Insolvency

183—(1) An employer has become insolvent for the purposes of this Part— **A1–032**

(a) where the employer is an individual, if (but only if) subsection (2) is satisfied, [. . .]
(b) where the employer is a company, if (but only if) subsection (3) is satisfied, and
(c) where the employer is a limited liability partnership, if (but only if) subsection (4) is satisfied.

(2) This subsection is satisfied in the case of an employer who is an individual—

(a) in England and Wales if—

(i) he has been adjudged bankrupt or has made a composition or arrangement with his creditors, or
(ii) he has died and his estate falls to be administered in accordance with an order under section 421 of the Insolvency Act 1986, and

(b) in Scotland if—

(i) sequestration of his estate has been awarded or he has executed a trust deed for his creditors or has entered into a composition contract, or
(ii) he has died and a judicial factor appointed under section 11A of the Judicial Factors (Scotland) Act 1889 is required by that section to divide his insolvent estate among his creditors.

(3) This subsection is satisfied in the case of an employer which is a company—

(a) if a winding up order . . . has been made, or a resolution for voluntary winding up has been passed, with respect to the company,
(aa) if the company is in administration for the purposes of the Insolvency Act 1986.
(b) if a receiver or (in England and Wales only) a manager of the company's undertaking has been duly appointed, or (in England and Wales only) possession has been taken, by or on behalf of the holders of any debentures secured by a floating charge, of any property of the company comprised in or subject to the charge, or
(c) if a voluntary arrangement proposed in the case of the company for the purposes of Part I of the Insolvency Act 1986 has been approved under that Part of that Act.

(4) This subsection is satisfied in the case of an employer which is a limited liability partnership—

    (a) if a winding-up order, an administration order or a determination for a voluntary winding-up has been made with respect to the limited liability partnership.

    (b) if a receiver or (in England and Wales only) a manager of the undertaking of the limited liability partnership has been duly appointed, or (in England and Wales only) possession has been taken, by or on behalf of the holders of any debentures secured by a floating charge, of any property of the limited liability partnership comprised in or subject to the charge, or

    (c) if a voluntary arrangement proposed in the case of the limited liability partnership for the purposes of Part I of the Insolvency Act 1986 has been approved under that Part of that Act.

Debts to which Part applies

A1–033   **184**—(1) This Part applies to the following debts—

    (a) any arrears of pay in respect of one or more (but not more than eight) weeks,

    (b) any amount which the employer is liable to pay the employee for the period of notice required by section 86(1) or (2) or for any failure of the employer to give the period of notice required by section 86(1),

    (c) any holiday pay—

        (i) in respect of a period or periods of holiday not exceeding six weeks in all, and

        (ii) to which the employee became entitled during the twelve months ending with the appropriate date,

    (d) any basic award of compensation for unfair dismissal [or so much of an award under a designated dismissal procedures agreement as does not exceed any basic award of compensation for unfair dismissal to which the employee would be entitled but for the agreement], and

    (e) any reasonable sum by way of reimbursement of the whole or part of any fee or premium paid by an apprentice or articled clerk.

(2) For the purposes of subsection (1)(a) the following amounts shall be treated as arrears of pay—

    (a) a guarantee payment,

    (b) any payment for time off under Part VI of this Act or section 169 of the Trade Union and Labour Relations (Consolidation) Act 1992 (payment for time off for carrying out trade union duties etc),

    (c) remuneration on suspension on medical grounds under section 64 of this Act and remuneration on suspension on maternity grounds under section 68 of this Act, and

    (d) remuneration under a protective award under section 189 of the Trade Union and Labour Relations (Consolidation) Act 1992.

(3) In subsection (1)(c) "holiday pay", in relation to an employee, means—

    (a) pay in respect of a holiday actually taken by the employee, or

    (b) any accrued holiday pay which, under the employee's contract of employment, would in the ordinary course have become payable to him in respect of the period of a holiday if his employment with the employer had continued until he became entitled to a holiday.

(4) A sum shall be taken to be reasonable for the purposes of subsection (1)(e) in a case where a trustee in bankruptcy, or (in Scotland) a permanent or interim trustee

(within the meaning of the Bankruptcy (Scotland) Act 1985), or liquidator has been or is required to be appointed—

   (a)   as respects England and Wales, if it is admitted to be reasonable by the trustee in bankruptcy or liquidator under section 348 of the Insolvency Act 1986 (effect of bankruptcy on apprenticeships etc), whether as originally enacted or as applied to the winding up of a company by rules under section 411 of that Act, and
   (b)   as respects Scotland, if it is accepted by the permanent or interim trustee or liquidator for the purposes of the sequestration or winding up.

The appropriate date

185. In this Part "the appropriate date"—   **A1–034**

   (a)   in relation to arrears of pay (not being remuneration under a protective award made under section 189 of the Trade Union and Labour Relations (Consolidation) Act 1992) and to holiday pay, means the date on which the employer became insolvent,
   (b)   in relation to a basic award of compensation for unfair dismissal and to remuneration under a protective award so made, means whichever is the latest of—

        (i)   the date on which the employer became insolvent,
        (ii) the date of the termination of the employee's employment, and
        (iii) the date on which the award was made, and

   (c)   in relation to any other debt to which this Part applies, means whichever is the later of—

        (i)   the date on which the employer became insolvent, and
        (ii) the date of the termination of the employee's employment.

Limit on amount payable under section 182

186.—(1) The total amount payable to an employee in respect of any debt to which   **A1–035**
this Part applies, where the amount of the debt is referable to a period of time, shall not exceed—

   (a)   £280 in respect of any one week, or
   (b)   in respect of a shorter period, an amount bearing the same proportion to £280 as that shorter period bears to a week.

   (2) [. . .]

Role of relevant officer

187.—(1) Where a relevant officer has been, or is required to be, appointed in   **A1–036**
connection with an employer's insolvency, the Secretary of State shall not make a payment under section 182 in respect of a debt until he has received a statement from the relevant officer of the amount of that debt which appears to have been owed to the employee on the appropriate date and to remain unpaid.

   (2) If the Secretary of State is satisfied that he does not require a statement under subsection (1) in order to determine the amount of a debt which was owed to the employee on the appropriate date and remains unpaid, he may make a payment under section 182 in respect of the debt without having received such a statement.

   (3) A relevant officer shall, on request by the Secretary of State, provide him with a statement for the purposes of subsection (1) as soon as is reasonably practicable.

   (4) The following are relevant officers for the purposes of this section—

(a)   a trustee in bankruptcy or a permanent or interim trustee (within the meaning of the Bankruptcy (Scotland) Act 1985),

(b)   a liquidator,

(c)   an administrator,

(d)   a receiver or manager,

(e)   a trustee under a composition or arrangement between the employer and his creditors, and

(f)   a trustee under a trust deed for his creditors executed by the employer.

(5) In subsection (4)(e) "trustee" includes the supervisor of a voluntary arrangement proposed for the purposes of and approved under, Part I or VIII of the Insolvency Act 1986.

Complaints to industrial tribunals

A1–037   **188.**—(1) A person who has applied for a payment under section 182 may present a complaint to an industrial tribunal—

(a)   that the Secretary of State has failed to make any such payment, or

(b)   that any such payment made by him is less than the amount which should have been paid.

(2) An industrial tribunal shall not consider a complaint under subsection (1) unless it is presented—

(a)   before the end of the period of three months beginning with the date on which the decision of the Secretary of State on the application was communicated to the applicant, or

(b)   within such further period as the tribunal considers reasonable in a case where it is not reasonably practicable for the complaint to be presented before the end of that period of three months.

(3) Where an industrial tribunal finds that the Secretary of State ought to make a payment under section 182, the tribunal shall—

(a)   make a declaration to that effect, and

(b)   declare the amount of any such payment which it finds the Secretary of State ought to make.

Transfer to Secretary of State of rights and remedies

A1–038   **189**—(1) Where, in pursuance of section 182, the Secretary of State makes a payment to an employee in respect of a debt to which this Part applies—

(a)   on the making of the payment any rights and remedies of the employee in respect of the debt (or if the Secretary of State has paid only part of it, in respect of that part) become rights and remedies of the Secretary of State, and

(b)   any decision of an industrial tribunal requiring an employer to pay that debt to the employee has the effect that the debt (or the part of it which the Secretary of State has paid) is to be paid to the Secretary of State.

(2) Where a debt (or any part of a debt) in respect of which the Secretary of State has made a payment in pursuance of section 182 constitutes—

(a)   a preferential debt within the meaning of the Insolvency Act 1986 for the purposes of any provision of that Act (including any such provision as applied by any order made under that Act) or any provision of the Companies Act 1985, or

(b)   a preferred debt within the meaning of the Bankruptcy (Scotland) Act 1985 for the purposes of any provision of that Act (including any such provision as applied by section 11A of the Judicial Factors (Scotland) Act 1889), the rights which become rights of the Secretary of State in accordance with subsection (1) include any right arising under any such provision by reason of the status of the debt (or that part of it) as a preferential or preferred debt.

(3) In computing for the purposes of any provision mentioned in subsection (2)(a) or (b) the aggregate amount payable in priority to other creditors of the employer in respect of—

    (a)   any claim of the Secretary of State to be paid in priority to other creditors of the employer by virtue of subsection (2), and

    (b)   any claim by the employee to be so paid made in his own right,

any claim of the Secretary of State to be so paid by virtue of subsection (2) shall be treated as if it were a claim of the employee.

(4) [. . .]

(5) Any sum recovered by the Secretary of State in exercising any right, or pursuing any remedy, which is his by virtue of this section shall be paid into the National Insurance Fund.

Power to obtain information

190—(1) Where an application is made to the Secretary of State under section 182 in respect of a debt owed by an employer, the Secretary of State may require— **A1–039**

    (a)   the employer to provide him with such information as he may reasonably require for the purpose of determining whether the application is well-founded, and

    (b)   any person having the custody or control of any relevant records or other documents to produce for examination on behalf of the Secretary of State any such document in that person's custody or under his control which is of such a description as the Secretary of State may require.

(2) Any such requirement—

    (a)   shall be made by notice in writing given to the person on whom the requirement is imposed, and

    (b)   may be varied or revoked by a subsequent notice so given.

(3) If a person refuses or wilfully neglects to furnish any information or produce any document which he has been required to furnish or produce by a notice under this section he is guilty of an offence and liable on summary conviction to a fine not exceeding level 3 on the standard scale.

(4) If a person, in purporting to comply with a requirement of a notice under this section, knowingly or recklessly makes any false statement he is guilty of an offence and liable on summary conviction to a fine not exceeding level 5 on the standard scale.

(5) Where an offence under this section committed by a body corporate is proved—

    (a)   to have been committed with the consent or connivance of, or

    (b)   to be attributable to any neglect on the part of,

any director, manager, secretary or other similar officer of the body corporate, or any person who was purporting to act in any such capacity, he (as well as the body corporate) is guilty of the offence and liable to be proceeded against and punished accordingly.

(6) Where the affairs of a body corporate are managed by its members, subsection (5) applies in relation to the acts and defaults of a member in connection with his functions of management as if he were a director of the body corporate.

Pension Schemes Act 1993

(c. 48)

PART VII

CHAPTER II

Interpretation of Chapter II

A1–040   **123.**—(1) For the purposes of this Chapter, an employer shall be taken to be insolvent if, but only if, in England and Wales—

(a) he has been adjudged bankrupt or has made a composition or arrangement with his creditors;

(b) he has died and his estate falls to be administered in accordance with an order under section 421 of the Insolvency Act 1986; or

(c) where the employer is a company—

(i) a winding-up order or an administration order is made or a resolution for voluntary winding up is passed with respect to it.

(ii) a receiver or manager of its undertaking is duly appointed.

(iii) possession is taken, by or on behalf of the holders of any debentures secured by a floating charge, of any property of the company comprised in or subject to the charge, or

(iv) a voluntary arrangement proposed for the purpose of Part I of the Insolvency Act 1986 is approved under that Part.

(2) For the purposes of this Chapter, an employer shall be taken to be insolvent if, but only if, in Scotland—

(a) sequestration of his estate is awarded or he executes a trust deed for his creditors or enters into a composition contract;

(b) he has died and a judicial factor appointed under section 11A of the Judicial Factors (Scotland) Act 1889 is required by that section to divide his insolvent estate among his creditors; or

(c) where the employer is a company—

(i) a winding-up order or an administration order is made or a resolution for voluntary winding up is passed with respect to it,

(ii) a receiver of its undertaking is duly appointed, or

(iii) a voluntary arrangement proposed for the purpose of Part I of the Insolvency Act 1986 is approved under that Part.

(3) In this Chapter—

"contract of employment", "employee", "employer" and "employment" and other expressions which are defined in the Employment Rights Act 1996 have the same meaning as in that Act; "holiday pay" means—

(a) pay in respect of holiday actually taken; or

(b) any accrued holiday pay which under the employees contract of employment would in the ordinary course have become payable to him in respect of the period of a holiday if his employment with the employer had continued until he became entitled to a holiday;

"occupational pension scheme" means any scheme or arrangement which provides or is capable of providing, in relation to employees in any description of employment, benefits, in the form of pensions or otherwise, payable to or in respect of any such employees on the termination of their employment or on their death or retirement.

(4) For the purposes of this Chapter, the definition of personal "pension scheme" in section 1 has effect with the substitution for the words "employed earners" of the word "employees".

(5) Any reference in this Chapter to the resources of a scheme is a reference to the funds out of which the benefits provided by the scheme are from time to time payable.

Duty of Secretary of State to pay unpaid contributions to schemes

124.—(1) If, on an application made to him in writing by the persons competent to act in respect of an occupational pension scheme or a personal pension scheme, the Secretary of State is satisfied— **A1–041**

    (a)   that an employer has become insolvent; and

    (b)   that at the time he did so there remained unpaid relevant contributions falling to be paid by him to the scheme,

then, subject to the provisions of this section and section 125, the Secretary of State shall pay into the resources of the scheme the sum which in his opinion is payable in respect of the unpaid relevant contributions.

(2) In this section and section 125 "relevant contributions" means contributions falling to be paid by an employer to an occupational pension scheme or a personal pension scheme, either on his own account or on behalf of an employee, and for the purposes of this section a contribution shall not be treated as falling to be paid on behalf of an employee unless a sum equal to that amount has been deducted from the pay of the employee by way of a contribution from him.

(3) Subject to subsection (3A), the sum payable under this section in respect of unpaid contributions of an employer on his own account to an occupational pension scheme or a personal pension scheme shall be the least of the following amounts—

    (a)   the balance of relevant contributions remaining unpaid on the date when he became insolvent and payable by the employer on his own account to the scheme in respect of the 12 months immediately preceding that date;

    (b)   the amount certified by an actuary to be necessary for the purpose of meeting the liability of the scheme on dissolution to pay the benefits provided by the scheme to or in respect of the employees of the employer;

    (c)   an amount equal to 10 per cent, of the total amount of remuneration paid or payable to those employees in respect of the 12 months immediately preceding the date on which the employer became insolvent.

(3A) Where the scheme in question is a money purchase scheme, the sum payable under this section by virtue of subsection (3) shall be the lesser of the amounts mentioned in paragraph (a) and (c) of that subsection.

(4) For the purposes of subsection (3)(c). "remuneration" includes holiday pay, statutory sick pay, statutory maternity pay under Part V of the Social Security Act 1986 or Part XII of the Social Security Contributions and Benefits Act 1992, and any payment such as is referred to in section 184(2) of the Employment Rights Act 1996.

(5) Any sum payable under this section in respect of unpaid contributions on behalf of an employee shall not exceed the amount deducted from the pay of the employee in respect of the employees contributions to the scheme during the 12 months immediately preceding the date on which the employer became insolvent.

Certification of amounts payable under section 124 by insolvency officers

125.—(1) This section applies where one of the officers mentioned in subsection (2) ("the relevant officer") has been or is required to be appointed in connection with an employer's insolvency. **A1–042**

(2) The officers referred to in subsection (1) are—

    (a)   a trustee in bankruptcy;

    (b)   a liquidator;

(c)   an administrator;

(d)   a receiver or manager; or

(e)   a trustee under a composition or arrangement between the employer and his creditors or under a trust deed for his creditors executed by the employer;

and in this subsection "trustee", in relation to a composition or arrangement, includes the supervisor of a voluntary arrangement proposed for the purposes of and approved under Part I or VIII of the Insolvency Act 1986.

(3) Subject to subsection (5), where this section applies the Secretary of State shall not make any payment under section 124 in respect of unpaid relevant contributions until he has received a statement from the relevant officer of the amount of relevant contributions which appear to have been unpaid on the date on which the employer became insolvent and to remain unpaid; and the relevant officer shall on request by the Secretary of State provide him as soon as reasonably practicable with such a statement.

(4) Subject to subsection (5), an amount shall be taken to be payable, paid or deducted as mentioned in subsection (3)(a) or (c) or (5) of section 124 only if it is so certified by the relevant officer.

(5) If the Secretary of State is satisfied—

(a)   that he does not require a statement under subsection (3) in order to determine the amount of relevant contributions that was unpaid on the date on which the employer became insolvent and remains unpaid, or

(b)   that he does not require a certificate under subsection (4) in order to determine the amounts payable, paid or deducted as mentioned in subsection (3) (a) or (c) or (5) of section 124.

he may make a payment under that section in respect of the contributions in question without having received such a statement or, as the case may be, such a certificate.

Complaint to industrial tribunal

A1–043   126.—(1) Any persons who are competent to act in respect of an occupational pension scheme or a personal pension scheme and who have applied for a payment to be made under section 124 into the resources of the scheme may present a complaint to an employment tribunal, that—

(a)   the Secretary of State has failed to make any such payment; or

(b)   any such payment made by him is less than the amount which should have been paid.

(2) Such a complaint must be presented within the period of three months beginning with the date on which the decision of the Secretary of State on that application was communicated to the persons presenting it or, if that is not reasonably practicable, within such further period as is reasonable.

(3) Where an employment tribunal finds that the Secretary of State ought to make a payment under section 124, it shall make a declaration to that effect and shall also declare the amount of any such payment which it finds that the Secretary of State ought to make.

Transfer to Secretary of State of rights and remedies

A1–044   127.—(1) Where in pursuance of section 124 the Secretary of State makes a payment into the resources of an occupational pension scheme or a personal pension scheme in respect of any contributions to the scheme, any rights and remedies in respect of those contributions belonging to the persons competent to act in respect of the scheme shall, on the making of the payment, become rights and remedies of the Secretary of State.

(2) Where the Secretary of State makes any such payment as is mentioned in subsection (1) and the sum (or any part of the sum) falling to be paid by the employer on account of the contributions in respect of which the payment is made constitutes—

(a) a preferential debt within the meaning of the Insolvency Act 1986 for the purposes of any provision of that Act (including any such provision as applied by an order made under that Act) or any provision of the Companies Act 1985, or

(b) a preferred debt within the meaning of the Bankruptcy (Scotland) Act 1985 for the purposes of any provision of that Act (including any such provision as applied by section 11A of the Judicial Factors (Scotland) Act 1889),

then, without prejudice to the generality of subsection (1), there shall be included among the rights and remedies which become rights and remedies of the Secretary of State in accordance with that subsection any right arising under any such provision by reason of the status of that sum (or that part of it) as a preferential or preferred debt.

(3) In computing for the purposes of any provision referred to in subsection (2)(a) or (b) the aggregate amount payable in priority to other creditors of the employer in respect of—

(a) any claim of the Secretary of State to be so paid by virtue of subsection (2), and

(b) any claim by the persons competent to act in respect of the scheme,

any claim falling within paragraph (a) shall be treated as if it were a claim of those persons; but the Secretary of State shall be entitled, as against those persons, to be so paid in respect of any such claim of his (up to the full amount of the claim) before any payment is made to them in respect of any claim falling within paragraph (b).

APPENDIX 2—STATUTORY INSTRUMENTS

The Civil Procedure Rules 1998

(SI 1998/3132)

PART 25

INTERIM REMEDIES

Orders for interim remedies

A1–001   **25.1**—(1) The court may grant the following interim remedies—

    (*a*)   an interim injunction;

    (*b*)   an interim declaration;

    (*c*)   an order—

        (i) for the detention, custody or preservation of relevant property;

        (ii) for the inspection of relevant property;

        (iii) for the taking of a sample of relevant property;

        (iv) for the carrying out of an experiment on or with relevant property;

        (v) for the sale of relevant property which is of a perishable nature or which for any other good reason it is desirable to sell quickly; and

        (iv) for the payment of income from relevant property until a claim is decided;

    (*d*)   an order authorising a person to enter any land or building in the possession of a party to the proceedings for the purposes of carrying out an order under sub-paragraph (c);

    (*e*)   an order under section 4 of the Torts (Interference with Goods) Act 1977 to deliver up goods;

    (*f*)   an order (referred to as a "freezing injunction")—

        (i) restraining a party from removing from the jurisdiction assets located there; or

        (ii) restraining a party from dealing with any assets whether located within the jurisdiction or not;

    (*g*)   an order directing a party to provide information about the location of relevant property or assets or to provide information about relevant property or assets which are or may be the subject of an application for a freezing injunction;

    (*h*)   an order (referred to as a "search order") under section 7 of the Civil Procedure Act 1997 (order requiring a party to admit another party to premises for the purpose of preserving evidence etc.);

    (*i*)   an order under section 33 of the Supreme Court Act 1981 or section 52 of the County Courts Act 1984 (order for disclosure of documents or inspection of property before a claim has been made);

    (*j*)   an order under section 34 of the Supreme Court Act 1981 or section 53 of the County Courts Act 1984 (order in certain proceedings for disclosure of documents or inspection of property against a non-party);

    (*k*)   an order (referred to as an order for interim payment) under rule 25.6 for payment by a defendant on account of any damages, debt or other sum (except costs) which the court may hold the defendant liable to pay;

(*l*)   an order for a specified fund to be paid into court or otherwise secured, where there is a dispute over a party's right to the fund;

(*m*)   an order permitting a party seeking to recover personal property to pay money into court pending the outcome of the proceedings and directing that, if he does so, the property shall be given up to him; and

(*n*)   an order directing a party to prepare and file accounts relating to the dispute. (Rule 34.2 provides for the court to issue a witness summons requiring a witness to produce documents to the court at the hearing or on such date as the court may direct)

(2) In paragraph (1)(c) and (g), "relevant property" means property (including land) which is the subject of a claim or as to which any question may arise on a claim.

(3) The fact that a particular kind of interim remedy is not listed in paragraph (1) does not affect any power that the court may have to grant that remedy.

(4) The court may grant an interim remedy whether or not there has been a claim for a final remedy of that kind.

* * * * *

PART 40

JUDGMENTS, ORDERS, SALE OF LAND, ETC

II. Sale of land etc. and Conveyancing Counsel

Scope of this Section

40.15—(1) This Section—   A2–002

(a)   deals with the court's power to order the sale, mortgage, partition or exchange of land; and

(b)   contains provisions about conveyancing counsel.

(Section 131 of the Supreme Court Act 1981 provides for the appointment of the conveyancing counsel of the Supreme Court.)

(2) In this Section "land" includes any interest in, or right over, land.

Power to order sale etc.

40.16 In any proceedings relating to land, the court may order the land, or part of it,   A2–003
to be—

(a)   sold;

(b)   mortgaged;

(c)   exchanged; or

(d)   partitioned.

Power to order delivery up of possession etc.

40.17 Where the court has made an order under rule 40.16, it may order any party to   A2–004
deliver up to the purchaser or any other person—

(a)   possession of the land;

(b)   receipt of rents or profits relating to it; or

(c)   both.

Reference to conveyancing counsel

40.18—(1) The court may direct conveyancing counsel to investigate and prepare a   A2–005
report on the title of any land or to draft any document.

(2) The court may take the report on title into account when it decides the issue in question.

(Provisions dealing with the fees payable to conveyancing counsel are set out in the practice direction relating to Part 44).

Party may object to report

A2–006   **40.19**—(1) Any party to the proceedings may object to the report on title prepared by conveyancing counsel.

(2) Where there is an objection, the issue will be referred to a judge for determination.

(Part 23 contains general rules about making an application.)

* * * * *

SCHEDULE 1

RSC ORDER 30

RECEIVERS

Order to apply to High Court and County Court

A2–007   **A1.** This order applies to proceedings both in the High Court and the county court.

Application for receiver and injunction

A2–008   **1.**—(1) An application for the appointment of a receiver made in existing proceedings must be made in accordance with CPR Part 23 and the practice direction supplementing that Part.

(2) An application for an injunction ancillary or incidental to an order appointing a receiver may be joined with the application for such order.

(3) The relevant practice direction will apply to an application for the immediate grant of such an injunction.

Giving of security by receiver

A2–009   **2.**—(1) A judgment or order directing the appointment of a receiver may include such directions as the court thinks fit as to the giving of security by the person appointed.

(2) Where by virtue of any judgment or order appointing a person named therein to be receiver a person is required to give security in accordance with this rule he must give security approved by the court duly to account for what he receives as receiver and to deal with it as the court directs.

(3) Unless the court otherwise directs, the security shall be by guarantee.

(4) The guarantee must be filed in the office or registry of the court in which the claim is proceeding and it shall be kept as of record until duly vacated.

Remuneration of receiver

A2–010   **3.**—(1) A person appointed receiver shall be allowed such proper remuneration, if any, as may be authorised by the court.

(2) The court may direct that such remuneration shall be—

    (*a*)   fixed by reference to such scales or rates of professional charges as it thinks fit; or

    (*b*)   assessed by a costs judge or a district judge.

(3) Where remuneration is assessed by a costs judge or district judge following a direction under paragraph 2(b). CPR rules 44.4(1) and (2) and 44.5(1) will apply

as though the remuneration were costs directed to be assessed on the standard basis.

(4) An appeal shall lie from the assessment in accordance with section 8 of CPR Part 47 (CPR rules 47.21 to 47.27).

Service of order and notice

4. A copy of the judgment or order appointing a receiver shall be served by the party **A2–011** having conduct of the proceedings on the receiver and all other parties to the proceedings in which the receiver has been appointed.

Receiver's accounts

5.—(1) A receiver shall submit such accounts to such parties at such intervals or on **A2–012** such dates as the court may direct.

(2) Any party to whom a receiver is required to submit accounts may, on giving reasonable notice to the receiver, inspect, either personally or by an agent, the books and other papers relating to such accounts.

(3) Any party who is dissatisfied with the accounts of the receiver may give notice specifying the item or items to which objection is taken and requiring the receiver within not less than 14 days to file his accounts with the court and a copy of such notice shall be filed in the office or registry of the court dealing with the proceedings.

(4) Following an examination by or on behalf of the court of an item or items in an account to which objection is taken the result of such examination must be certified by a Master, the Admiralty Registrar, a district judge of the Family Division or a district judge, as the case may be, and an order may thereupon be made as to the incidence of any costs or expenses incurred.

Payment into court by receiver

6. The court may fix the amounts and frequency of payments into court to be made **A2–013** by a receiver.

Default by receiver

7.—(1) Where a receiver fails to attend for the examination of any account of his, or **A2–014** fails to submit any account, provide access to any books or papers or do any other thing which he is required to submit, provide or do, he and any or all of the parties to the cause or matter in which he was appointed may be required to attend the court to show cause for the failure, and the court may give such directions as it thinks proper including, if necessary, directions for the discharge of the receiver and the appointment of another and the payment of costs.

(2) Without prejudice to paragraph (1) where a receiver fails to attend for the examination of any account of his or fails to submit any account or fails to pay into court on the date fixed by the court any sum required to be so paid, the court may disallow any remuneration claimed by the receiver and may, where he has failed to pay any such sum into court, charge him with interest at the rate currently payable in respect of judgment debts in the High Court on that sum while in his possession as receiver.

Directions to receivers

8. A receiver may at any time request the court to give him directions and such **A2–015** request shall state in writing the matters with regard to which directions are required.

RSC ORDER 51

RECEIVERS: EQUITABLE EXECUTION

Appointment of receiver by way of equitable execution

1. Where an application is made for the appointment of a receiver by way of equi- **A2–016** table execution, the court in determining whether it is just or convenient that the appointment should be made shall have regard to the amount claimed by the judgment creditor, to the amount likely to be obtained by the receiver and to the probable costs of his appointment and may direct an inquiry on any of these matters or any other matter before making the appointment.

Masters etc. may appoint receiver

A2–017   **2.** A Master and the Admiralty Registrar and a district judge of the Family Division shall have power to make an order for the appointment of a receiver by way of equitable execution and to grant an injunction if, and only so far as, the injunction is ancillary or incidental to such an order.

Application of rules as to appointment of receiver, etc.

A2–018   **3.** An application for the appointment of a receiver by way of equitable execution may be made in accordance with Order 30, rule 1 and rules 2 to 6 of that order shall apply in relation to a receiver appointed by way of equitable execution as they apply in relation to a receiver appointed for any other purpose.

The Transfer of Undertakings (Protection of Employment) Regulations 2006

(SI 2006/246)

The Secretary of State makes the following Regulations in exercise of the powers conferred upon him by section 2(2) of the European Communities Act 1972 (being a Minister designated for the purposes of that section in relation to rights and obligations relating to employers and employees on the transfer or merger of undertakings, businesses or parts of businesses and section 38 of the Employment Relations Act 1999.

Citation, commencement and extent

1.—(1) These Regulations may be cited as the Transfer of Undertakings (Protection **A2–019** of Employment) Regulations 2006.

(2) These Regulations shall come into force on 6 April 2006.

(3) These Regulations shall extend to Northern Ireland, except where otherwise provided.

Interpretation

2.—(1) In these Regulations—   **A2–020**

"assigned" means assigned other than on a temporary basis;

"collective agreement", "collective bargaining" and "trade union" have the same meanings respectively as in the 1992 Act;

"contract of employment" means any agreement between an employee and his employer determining the terms and conditions of his employment;

references to "contractor" in regulation 3 shall include a sub-contractor;

"employee" means any individual who works for another person whether under a contract of service or apprenticeship or otherwise but does not include anyone who provides services under a contract for services and references to a person's employer shall be construed accordingly;

"insolvency practitioner" has the meaning given to the expression by Part XIII of the Insolvency Act 1986;

references to "organised grouping of employees" shall include a single employee;

"recognised" has the meaning given to the expression by section 178(3) of the 1992 Act;

"relevant transfer" means a transfer or a service provision change to which these Regulations apply in accordance with regulation 3 and "transferor" and "transferee" shall be construed accordingly and in the case of a service provision change falling within regulation 3(1)(b), "the transferor" means the person who carried out the activities prior to the service provision change and "the transferee" means the person who carries out the activities as a result of the service provision change;

"the 1992 Act" means the Trade Union and Labour Relations (Consolidation) Act 1992;

"the 1996 Act" means the Employment Rights Act 1996;

"the 1996 Tribunals Act" means the Employment Tribunals Act 1996;

"the 1981 Regulations" means the Transfer of Undertakings (Protection of Employment) Regulations 1981.

(2) For the purposes of these Regulations the representative of a trade union recognised by an employer is an official or other person authorised to carry on collective bargaining with that employer by that trade union.

(3) In the application of these Regulations to Northern Ireland the Regulations shall have effect as set out in Schedule 1.

A relevant transfer

A2–021   3.—(1) These Regulations apply to—

(a) a transfer of an undertaking, business or part of an undertaking or business situated immediately before the transfer in the United Kingdom to another person where there is a transfer of an economic entity which retains its identity;

(b) a service provision change, that is a situation in which—

(i) activities cease to be earned out by a person ("a client") on his own behalf and are carried out instead by another person on the client's behalf ("a contractor");

(ii) activities cease to be carried out by a contractor on a client's behalf (whether or not those activities had previously been carried out by the client on his own behalf) and are carried out instead by another person ("a subsequent contractor") on the client's behalf; or

(iii) activities cease to be carried out by a contractor or a subsequent contractor on a client's behalf (whether or not those activities had previously been earned out by the client on his own behalf) and are carried out instead by the client on his own behalf,

and in which the conditions set out in paragraph (3) are satisfied.

(2) In this regulation "economic entity" means an organised grouping of resources which has the objective of pursuing an economic activity, whether or not that activity is central or ancillary.

(3) The conditions referred to in paragraph (1)(b) are that—

(a) immediately before the service provision change—

(i) there is an organised grouping of employees situated in Great Britain which has as its principal purpose the carrying out of the activities concerned on behalf of the client;

(ii) the client intends that the activities will, following the service provision change, be carried out by the transferee other than in connection with a single specific event or task of short-term duration; and

(b) the activities concerned do not consist wholly or mainly of the supply of goods for the client's use.

(4) Subject to paragraph (1), these Regulations apply to—

(a) public and private undertakings engaged in economic activities whether or not they are operating for gain;

(b) a transfer or service provision change howsoever effected notwithstanding—

(i) that the transfer of an undertaking, business or part of an undertaking or business is governed or effected by the law of a country or territory outside the United Kingdom or that the service provision change is governed or effected by the law of a country or territory outside Great Britain;

(ii) that the employment of persons employed in the undertaking, business or part transferred or, in the case of a service provision change, persons employed in the organised grouping of employees, is governed by any such law;

(c) a transfer of an undertaking, business or part of an undertaking or business (which may also be a service provision change) where persons employed in the undertaking, business or part transferred ordinarily work outside the United Kingdom.

(5) An administrative reorganisation of public administrative authorities or the transfer of administrative functions between public administrative authorities is not a relevant transfer.

(6) A relevant transfer—

(a) may be effected by a series of two or more transactions; and

(b) may take place whether or not any property is transferred to the transferee by the transferor.

(7) Where, in consequence (whether directly or indirectly) of the transfer of an undertaking, business or part of an undertaking or business which was situated immediately before the transfer in the United Kingdom, a ship within the meaning of the Merchant Shipping Act 1995 registered in the United Kingdom ceases to be so registered, these Regulations shall not affect the right conferred by section 29 of that Act (right of seamen to be discharged when ship ceases to be registered in the United Kingdom) on a seaman employed in the ship.

Effect of relevant transfer on contracts of employment

4.—(1) Except where objection is made under paragraph (7), a relevant transfer shall not operate so as to terminate the contract of employment of any person employed by the transferor and assigned to the organised grouping of resources or employees that is subject to the relevant transfer, which would otherwise be terminated by the transfer, but any such contract shall have effect after the transfer as if originally made between the person so employed and the transferee. **A2–022**

(2) Without prejudice to paragraph (1), but subject to paragraph (6), and regulations 8 and 15(9), on the completion of a relevant transfer—

(a) all the transferor's rights, powers, duties and liabilities under or in connection with any such contract shall be transferred by virtue of this regulation to the transferee; and

(b) any act or omission before the transfer is completed, of or in relation to the transferor in respect of that contract or a person assigned to that organised grouping of resources or employees, shall be deemed to have been an act or omission of or in relation to the transferee.

(3) Any reference in paragraph (1) to a person employed by the transferor and assigned to the organised grouping of resources or employees that is subject to a relevant transfer, is a reference to a person so employed immediately before the transfer, or who would have been so employed if he had not been dismissed in the circumstances described in regulation 7(1), including, where the transfer is effected by a series of two or more transactions, a person so employed and assigned or who would have been so employed and assigned immediately before any of those transactions.

(4) Subject to regulation 9, in respect of a contract of employment that is, or will be, transferred by paragraph (1), any purported variation of the contract shall be void if the sole or principal reason for the variation is—

(a) the transfer itself; or

(b) a reason connected with the transfer that is not an economic, technical or organizational reason entailing changes in the workforce.

(5) Paragraph (4) shall not prevent the employer and his employee, whose contract of employment is, or will be, transferred by paragraph (1), from agreeing a variation of that contract if the sole or principal reason for the variation is—

(a) a reason connected with the transfer that is an economic, technical or organizational reason entailing changes in the workforce; or

(b) a reason unconnected with the transfer.

(6) Paragraph (2) shall not transfer or otherwise affect the liability of any person to be prosecuted for, convicted of and sentenced for any offence.

(7) Paragraphs (1) and (2) shall not operate to transfer the contract of employment and the rights, powers, duties and liabilities under or in connection with it of an employee who informs the transferor or the transferee that he objects to becoming employed by the transferee.

(8) Subject to paragraphs (9) and (11), where an employee so objects, the relevant transfer shall operate so as to terminate his contract of employment with the transferor but he shall not be treated, for any purpose, as having been dismissed by the transferor.

(9) Subject to regulation 9, where a relevant transfer involves or would involve a substantial change in working conditions to the material detriment of a person whose contract of employment is or would be transferred under paragraph (1), such an employee may treat the contract of employment as having been terminated, and the employee shall be treated for any purpose as having been dismissed by the employer.

(10) No damages shall be payable by an employer as a result of a dismissal falling within paragraph (9) in respect of any failure by the employer to pay wages to an employee in respect of a notice period which the employee has failed to work.

(11) Paragraphs (1), (7), (8) and (9) are without prejudice to any right of an employee arising apart from these Regulations to terminate his contract of employment without notice in acceptance of a repudiatory breach of contract by his employer.

Effect of relevant transfer on collective agreements

A2–023   5. Where at the time of a relevant transfer there exists a collective agreement made by or on behalf of the transferor with a trade union recognised by the transferor in respect of any employee whose contract of employment is preserved by regulation 4(1) above, then—

(a) without prejudice to sections 179 and 180 of the 1992 Act (collective agreements presumed to be unenforceable in specified circumstances) that agreement, in its application in relation to the employee, shall, after the transfer, have effect as if made by or on behalf of the transferee with that trade union, and accordingly anything done under or in connection with it, in its application in relation to the employee, by or in relation to the transferor before the transfer, shall, after the transfer, be deemed to have been done by or in relation to the transferee; and

(b) any order made in respect of that agreement, in its application in relation to the employee, shall after the transfer, have effect as if the transferee were a party to the agreement.

Effect of relevant transfer on trade union recognition

A2–024   6.—(1) This regulation applies where after a relevant transfer the transferred organised grouping of resources or employees maintains an identity distinct from the remainder of the transferee's undertaking.

(2) Where before such a transfer an independent trade union is recognised to any extent by the transferor in respect of employees of any description who in consequence of the transfer become employees of the transferee, then, after the transfer—

(a) the trade union shall be deemed to have been recognised by the transferee to the same extent in respect of employees of that description so employed; and

(b) any agreement for recognition may be varied or rescinded accordingly.

Dismissal of employee because of relevant transfer

A2–025   7.—(1) Where either before or after a relevant transfer, any employee of the transferor or transferee is dismissed, that employee shall be treated for the purposes of Part X of the 1996 Act (unfair dismissal) as unfairly dismissed if the sole or principal reason for his dismissal is—

(a) the transfer itself; or

(b) a reason connected with the transfer that is not an economic, technical or organizational reason entailing changes in the workforce.

(2) This paragraph applies where the sole or principal reason for the dismissal is a reason connected with the transfer that is an economic, technical or organisational reason entailing changes in the workforce of either the transferor or the transferee before or after a relevant transfer.

(3) Where paragraph (2) applies—

(a) paragraph (1) shall not apply;

(b) without prejudice to the application of section 98(4) of the 1996 Act (test of fair dismissal), the dismissal shall, for the purposes of sections 98(1) and 135 of that Act (reason for dismissal), be regarded as having been for redundancy where section 98(2)(c) of that Act applies, or otherwise for a substantial reason of a kind such as to justify the dismissal of an employee holding the position which that employee held.

(4) The provisions of this regulation apply irrespective of whether the employee in question is assigned to the organised grouping of resources or employees that is, or will be, transferred.

(5) Paragraph (1) shall not apply in relation to the dismissal of any employee which was required by reason of the application of section 5 of the Aliens Restriction (Amendment) Act 1919 to his employment.

(6) Paragraph (1) shall not apply in relation to a dismissal of an employee if the application of section 94 of the 1996 Act to the dismissal of the employee is excluded by or under any provision of the 1996 Act, the 1996 Tribunals Act or the 1992 Act.

Insolvency

8.—(1) If at the time of a relevant transfer the transferor is subject to relevant insol-   **A2–026**
vency proceedings paragraphs (2) to (6) apply.

(2) In this regulation "relevant employee" means an employee of the transferor—

(a) whose contract of employment transfers to the transferee by virtue of the operation of these Regulations; or

(b) whose employment with the transferor is terminated before the time of the relevant transfer in the circumstances described in regulation 7(1).

(3) The relevant statutory scheme specified in paragraph (4)(b) (including that sub-paragraph as applied by paragraph 5 of Schedule 1) shall apply in the case of a relevant employee irrespective of the fact that the qualifying requirement that the employee's employment has been terminated is not met and for those purposes the date of the transfer shall be treated as the date of the termination and the transferor shall be treated as the employer.

(4) In this regulation the "relevant statutory schemes" are—

(a) Chapter VI of Part XI of the 1996 Act;

(b) Part XII of the 1996 Act.

(5) Regulation 4 shall not operate to transfer liability for the sums payable to the relevant employee under the relevant statutory schemes.

(6) In this regulation "relevant insolvency proceedings" means insolvency proceedings which have been opened in relation to the transferor not with a view to the liquidation of the assets of the transferor and which are under the supervision of an insolvency practitioner.

(7) Regulations 4 and 7 do not apply to any relevant transfer where the transferor is the subject of bankruptcy proceedings or any analogous insolvency proceedings which have been instituted with a view to the liquidation of the assets of the transferor and are under the supervision of an insolvency practitioner.

Variations of contract where transferors are subject to relevant insolvency proceedings

A2–027   9.—(1) If at the time of a relevant transfer the transferor is subject to relevant insolvency proceedings these Regulations shall not prevent the transferor or transferee (or an insolvency practitioner) and appropriate representatives of assigned employees agreeing to permitted variations.

(2) For the purposes of this regulation "appropriate representatives" are—

(a) if the employees are of a description in respect of which an independent trade union is recognised by their employer, representatives of the trade union; or

(b) in any other case, whichever of the following employee representatives the employer chooses—

(i) employee representatives appointed or elected by the assigned employees (whether they make the appointment or election alone or with others) otherwise than for the purposes of this regulation, who (having regard to the purposes for, and the method by which they were appointed or elected) have authority from those employees to agree permitted variations to contracts of employment on their behalf;

(ii) employee representatives elected by assigned employees (whether they make the appointment or election alone or with others) for these particular purposes, in an election satisfying requirements identical to those contained in regulation 14 except those in regulation 14(1)(d).

(3) An individual may be an appropriate representative for the purposes of both this regulation and regulation 13 provided that where the representative is not a trade union representative he is either elected by or has authority from assigned employees (within the meaning of this regulation) and affected employees (as described in regulation 13(1)).

(4) In section 168 of the 1992 Act (time off for carrying out trade union duties) in subsection (1), after paragraph (c) there is inserted—

", or

(d) negotiations with a view to entering into an agreement under regulation 9 of the Transfer of Undertakings (Protection of Employment) Regulations 2006 that applies to employees of the employer, or

(e) the performance on behalf of employees of the employer of functions related to or connected with the making of an agreement under that regulation.".

(5) Where assigned employees are represented by non-trade union representatives—

(a) the agreement recording a permitted variation must be in writing and signed by each of the representatives who have made it or, where that is not reasonably practicable, by a duly authorised agent of that representative; and

(b) the employer must, before the agreement is made available for signature, provide all employees to whom it is intended to apply on the date on which it is to come into effect with copies of the text of the agreement and such guidance as those employees might reasonably require in order to understand it fully.

(6) A permitted variation shall take effect as a term or condition of the assigned employee's contract of employment in place, where relevant, of any term or condition which it varies.

(7) In this regulation—

"assigned employees" means those employees assigned to the organised grouping of resources or employees that is the subject of a relevant transfer;

"permitted variation" is a variation to the contract of employment of an assigned employee where—

(a) the sole or principal reason for it is the transfer itself or a reason connected with the transfer that is not an economic, technical or organisational reason entailing changes in the workforce; and

(b) it is designed to safeguard employment opportunities by ensuring the survival of the undertaking, business or part of the undertaking or business that is the subject of the relevant transfer;

"relevant insolvency proceedings" has the meaning given to the expression by regulation 8(6).

Pensions

10.—(1) Regulations 4 and 5 shall not apply—

    A2–028

(a) to so much of a contract of employment or collective agreement as relates to an occupational pension scheme within the meaning of the Pension Schemes Act 1993; or

(b) to any rights, powers, duties or liabilities under or in connection with any such contract or subsisting by virtue of any such agreement and relating to such a scheme or otherwise arising in connection with that person's employment and relating to such a scheme.

(2) For the purposes of paragraphs (1) and (3), any provisions of an occupational pension scheme which do not relate to benefits for old age, invalidity or survivors shall not be treated as being part of the scheme.

(3) An employee whose contract of employment is transferred in the circumstances described in regulation 4(1) shall not be entitled to bring a claim against the transferor for—

(a) breach of contract; or

(b) constructive unfair dismissal under section 95(1)(c) of the 1996 Act,

arising out of a loss or reduction in his rights under an occupational pension scheme in consequence of the transfer, save insofar as the alleged breach of contract or dismissal (as the case may be) occurred prior to the date on which these Regulations took effect.

Notification of Employee Liability Information

11.—(1) The transferor shall notify to the transferee the employee liability information of any person employed by him who is assigned to the organised grouping of resources or employees that is the subject of a relevant transfer—

    A2–029

(a) in writing; or

(b) by making it available to him in a readily accessible form.

(2) In this regulation and in regulation 12 "employee liability information" means—

(a) the identity and age of the employee;

(b) those particulars of employment that an employer is obliged to give to an employee pursuant to section 1 of the 1996 Act;

(c) information of any—

    (i) disciplinary procedure taken against an employee;

    (ii) grievance procedure taken by an employee,

within the previous two years, in circumstances where the Employment Act 2002 (Dispute Resolution) Regulations 2004 apply;

(d) information of any court or tribunal case, claim or action—

(i)   brought by an employee against the transferor, within the previous two years;

(ii) that the transferor has reasonable grounds to believe that an employee may bring against the transferee, arising out of the employee's employment with the transferor; and

(e) information of any collective agreement which will have effect after the transfer, in its application in relation to the employee, pursuant to regulation 5(a).

(3) Employee liability information shall contain information as at a specified date not more than fourteen days before the date on which the information is notified to the transferee.

(4) The duty to provide employee liability information in paragraph (1) shall include a duty to provide employee liability information of any person who would have been employed by the transferor and assigned to the organised grouping of resources or employees that is the subject of a relevant transfer immediately before the transfer if he had not been dismissed in the circumstances described in regulation 7(1), including, where the transfer is effected by a series of two or more transactions, a person so employed and assigned or who would have been so employed and assigned immediately before any of those transactions.

(5) Following notification of the employee liability information in accordance with this regulation, the transferor shall notify the transferee in writing of any change in the employee liability information.

(6) A notification under this regulation shall be given not less than fourteen days before the relevant transfer or, if special circumstances make this not reasonably practicable, as soon as reasonably practicable thereafter.

(7) A notification under this regulation may be given

(a)   in more than one instalment;

(b)   indirectly, through a third party.

Remedy for failure to notify employee liability information

A2–030   **12.**—(1) On or after a relevant transfer, the transferee may present a complaint to an employment tribunal that the transferor has failed to comply with any provision of regulation 11.

(2) An employment tribunal shall not consider a complaint under this regulation unless it is presented—

(a)   before the end of the period of three months beginning with the date of the relevant transfer;

(b)   within such further period as the tribunal considers reasonable in a case where it is satisfied that it was not reasonably practicable for the complaint to be presented before the end of that period of three months.

(3) Where an employment tribunal finds a complaint under paragraph (1) well-founded, the tribunal—

(a)   shall make a declaration to that effect; and

(b)   may make an award of compensation to be paid by the transferor to the transferee.

(4) The amount of the compensation shall be such as the tribunal considers just and equitable in all the circumstances, subject to paragraph (5), having particular regard to—

(a)   any loss sustained by the transferee which is attributable to the matters complained of; and

(b)   the terms of any contract between the transferor and the transferee relating to the transfer under which the transferor may be liable to pay any sum to the transferee in respect of a failure to notify the transferee of employee liability information.

(5) Subject to paragraph (6), the amount of compensation awarded under paragraph (3) shall be not less than £500 per employee in respect of whom the transferor has failed to comply with a provision of regulation 11, unless the tribunal considers it just and equitable, in all the circumstances, to award a lesser sum.

(6) In ascertaining the loss referred to in paragraph (4)(a) the tribunal shall apply the same rule concerning the duty of a person to mitigate his loss as applies to any damages recoverable under the common law of England and Wales, Northern Ireland or Scotland, as applicable.

(7) Section 18 of the 1996 Tribunals Act (conciliation) shall apply to the right conferred by this regulation and to proceedings under this regulation as it applies to the rights conferred by that Act and the employment tribunal proceedings mentioned in that Act.

Duty to inform and consult representatives

13.—(1) In this regulation and regulations 14 and 15 references to affected employees, **A2–031** in relation to a relevant transfer, are to any employees of the transferor or the transferee (whether or not assigned to the organised grouping of resources or employees that is the subject of a relevant transfer) who may be affected by the transfer or may be affected by measures taken in connection with it, and references to the employer shall be construed accordingly.

(2) Long enough before a relevant transfer to enable the employer of any affected employees to consult the appropriate representatives of any affected employees, the employer shall inform those representatives of—

(a) the fact that the transfer is to take place, the date or proposed date of the transfer and the reasons for it;

(b) the legal, economic and social implications of the transfer for any affected employees;

(c) the measures which he envisages he will, in connection with the transfer, take in relation to any affected employees or, if he envisages that no measures will be so taken, that fact; and

(d) if the employer is the transferor, the measures, in connection with the transfer, which he envisages the transferee will take in relation to any affected employees who will become employees of the transferee after the transfer by virtue of regulation 4 or, if he envisages that no measures will be so taken, that fact.

(3) For the purposes of this regulation the appropriate representatives of any affected employees are—

(a) if the employees are of a description in respect of which an independent trade union is recognised by their employer, representatives of the trade union; or

(b) in any other case, whichever of the following employee representatives the employer chooses—

(i) employee representatives appointed or elected by the affected employees otherwise than for the purposes of this regulation, who (having regard to the purposes for, and the method by which they were appointed or elected) have authority from those employees to receive information and to be consulted about the transfer on their behalf;

(ii) employee representatives elected by any affected employees, for the purposes of this regulation, in an election satisfying the requirements of regulation 14(1).

(4) The transferee shall give the transferor such information at such a time as will enable the transferor to perform the duty imposed on him by virtue of paragraph (2)(d).

(5) The information which is to be given to the appropriate representatives shall be given to each of them by being delivered to them, or sent by post to an address notified by them to the employer, or (in the case of representatives of a trade union) sent by post to the trade union at the address of its head or main office.

(6) An employer of an affected employee who envisages that he will take measures in relation to an affected employee, in connection with the relevant transfer, shall consult the appropriate representatives of that employee with a view to seeking their agreement to the intended measures.

(7) In the course of those consultations the employer shall—

    (a)   consider any representations made by the appropriate representatives; and
    (b)   reply to those representations and, if he rejects any of those representations, state his reasons.

(8) The employer shall allow the appropriate representatives access to any affected employees and shall afford to those representatives such accommodation and other facilities as may be appropriate.

(9) If in any case there are special circumstances which render it not reasonably practicable for an employer to perform a duty imposed on him by any of paragraphs (2) to (7), he shall take all such steps towards performing that duty as are reasonably practicable in the circumstances.

(10) Where—

    (a)   the employer has invited any of the affected employee to elect employee representatives: and
    (b)   the invitation was issued long enough before the time when the employer is required to give information under paragraph (2) to allow them to elect representatives by that time,

the employer shall be treated as complying with the requirements of this regulation in relation to those employees if he complies with those requirements as soon as is reasonably practicable after the election of the representatives.

(11) If, after the employer has invited any affected employees to elect representatives, they fail to do so within a reasonable time, he shall give to any affected employees the information set out in paragraph (2).

(12) The duties imposed on an employer by this regulation shall apply irrespective of whether the decision resulting in the relevant transfer is taken by the employer or a person controlling the employer.

Election of employee representatives

A2–032   **14.**—(1) The requirements for the election of employee representatives under regulation 13(3) are that—

    (a)   the employer shall make such arrangements as are reasonably practicable to ensure that the election is fair;
    (b)   the employer shall determine the number of representatives to be elected so that there are sufficient representatives to represent the interests of all affected employees having regard to the number and classes of those employees;
    (c)   the employer shall determine whether the affected employees should be represented either by representatives of all the affected employees or by representatives of particular classes of those employees;
    (d)   before the election the employer shall determine the term of office as employee representatives so that it is of sufficient length to enable information to be given and consultations under regulation 13 to be completed;

(e)   the candidates for election as employee representatives are affected employees on the date of the election;

(f)   no affected employee is unreasonably excluded from standing for election;

(g)   all affected employees on the date of the election are entitled to vote for employee representatives;

(h)   the employees entitled to vote may vote for as many candidates as there are representatives to be elected to represent them or, if there are to be representatives for particular classes of employees, may vote for as many candidates as there are representatives to be elected to represent their particular class of employee;

(i)   the election is conducted so as to secure that

   (i)   so far as is reasonably practicable, those voting do so in secret; and

   (ii)   the votes given at the election are accurately counted.

(2) Where, after an election of employee representatives satisfying the requirements of paragraph (1) has been held, one of those elected ceases to act as an employee representative and as a result any affected employees are no longer represented, those employees shall elect another representative by an election satisfying the requirements of paragraph (1)(a), (e), (f) and (i).

Failure to inform or consult

15.—(1) Where an employer has failed to comply with a requirement of regulation 13 or regulation 14, a complaint may be presented to an employment tribunal on that ground—   **A2–033**

(a)   in the case of a failure relating to the election of employee representatives, by any of his employees who are affected employees;

(b)   in the case of any other failure relating to employee representatives, by any of the employee representatives to whom the failure related;

(c)   in the case of failure relating to representatives of a trade union, by the trade union; and

(d)   in any other case, by any of his employees who are affected employees.

(2) If on a complaint under paragraph (1) a question arises whether or not it was reasonably practicable for an employer to perform a particular duty or as to what steps he took towards performing it, it shall be for him to show—

(a)   that there were special circumstances which rendered it not reasonably practicable for him to perform the duty; and

(b)   that he took all such steps towards its performance as were reasonably practicable in those circumstances.

(3) If on a complaint under paragraph (1) a question arises as to whether or not an employee representative was an appropriate representative for the purposes of regulation 13, it shall be for the employer to show that the employee representative had the necessary authority to represent the affected employees.

(4) On a complaint under paragraph (1)(a) it shall be for the employer to show that the requirements in regulation 14 have been satisfied.

(5) On a complaint against a transferor that he had failed to perform the duty imposed upon him by virtue of regulation 13(2)(d) or, so far as relating thereto, regulation 13(9), he may not show that it was not reasonably practicable for him to perform the duty in question for the reason that the transferee had failed to give him the requisite information at the requisite time in accordance with regulation 13(4) unless he gives the transferee notice of his intention to show that fact; and the giving of the notice shall make the transferee a party to the proceedings.

(6) In relation to any complaint under paragraph (1), a failure on the part of a person controlling (directly or indirectly) the employer to provide information to the employer

shall not constitute special circumstances rendering it not reasonably practicable for the employer to comply with such a requirement.

(7) Where the tribunal finds a complaint against a transferee under paragraph (1) well-founded it shall make a declaration to that effect and may order the transferee to pay appropriate compensation to such descriptions of affected employees as may be specified in the award.

(8) Where the tribunal finds a complaint against a transferor under paragraph (1) well-founded it shall make a declaration to that effect and may—

    (a) order the transferor, subject to paragraph (9), to pay appropriate compensation to such descriptions of affected employees as may be specified in the award; or

    (b) if the complaint is that the transferor did not perform the duty mentioned in paragraph (5) and the transferor (after giving due notice) shows the facts so mentioned, order the transferee to pay appropriate compensation to such descriptions of affected employees as may be specified in the award.

(9) The transferee shall be jointly and severally liable with the transferor in respect of compensation payable under sub-paragraph (8)(a) or paragraph (11).

(10) An employee may present a complaint to an employment tribunal on the ground that he is an employee of a description to which an order under paragraph (7) or (8) relates and that—

    (a) in respect of an order under paragraph (7), the transferee has failed, wholly or in part, to pay him compensation in pursuance of the order;

    (b) in respect of an order under paragraph (8), the transferor or transferee, as applicable, has failed, wholly or in part, to pay him compensation in pursuance of the order.

(11) Where the tribunal finds a complaint under paragraph (10) well-founded it shall order the transferor or transferee as applicable to pay the complainant the amount of compensation which it finds is due to him.

(12) An employment tribunal shall not consider a complaint under paragraph (1) or (10) unless it is presented to the tribunal before the end of the period of three months beginning with—

    (a) in respect of a complaint under paragraph (1), the date on which the relevant transfer is completed; or

    (b) in respect of a complaint under paragraph (10), the date of the tribunal's order under paragraph (7) or (8),

or within such further period as the tribunal considers reasonable in a case where it is satisfied that it was not reasonably practicable for the complaint to be presented before the end of the period of three months.

Failure to inform or consult: supplemental

A2–034   **16.**—(1) Section 205(1) of the 1996 Act (complaint to be sole remedy for breach of relevant rights) and section 18 of the 1996 Tribunals Act (conciliation) shall apply to the rights conferred by regulation 15 and to proceedings under this regulation as they apply to the rights conferred by those Acts and the employment tribunal proceedings mentioned in those Acts.

(2) An appeal shall lie and shall lie only to the Employment Appeal Tribunal on a question of law arising from any decision of, or arising in any proceedings before, an employment tribunal under or by virtue of these Regulations; and section 11(1) of the Tribunals and Inquiries Act 1992 (appeals from certain tribunals to the High Court) shall not apply in relation to any such proceedings.

(3) "Appropriate compensation" in regulation 15 means such sum not exceeding thirteen weeks' pay for the employee in question as the tribunal considers just and equitable having regard to the seriousness of the failure of the employer to comply with his duty.

(4) Sections 220 to 228 of the 1996 Act shall apply for calculating the amount of a week's pay for any employee for the purposes of paragraph (3) and, for the purposes of that calculation, the calculation date shall be—

    (a) in the case of an employee who is dismissed by reason of redundancy (within the meaning of sections 139 and 155 of the 1996 Act) the date which is the calculation date for the purposes of any entitlement of his to a redundancy payment (within the meaning of those sections) or which would be that calculation date if he were so entitled;

    (b) in the case of an employee who is dismissed for any other reason, the effective date of termination (within the meaning of sections 95(1) and (2) and 97 of the 1996 Act) of his contract of employment;

    (c) in any other case, the date of the relevant transfer.

Employers' Liability Compulsory Insurance

17.—(1) Paragraph (2) applies where—   A2–035

    (a) by virtue of section 3(1)(a) or (b) of the Employers' Liability (Compulsory Insurance) Act 1969 ("the 1969 Act"), the transferor is not required by that Act to effect any insurance; or

    (b) by virtue of section 3(1)(c) of the 1969 Act, the transferor is exempted from the requirement of that Act to effect insurance.

(2) Where this paragraph applies, on completion of a relevant transfer the transferor and the transferee shall be jointly and severally liable in respect of any liability referred to in section 1(1) of the 1969 Act, in so far as such liability relates to the employee's employment with the transferor.

Restriction on contracting out

18. Section 203 of the 1996 Act (restrictions on contracting out) shall apply in rela- A2–036
tion to these Regulations as if they were contained in that Act, save for that section shall not apply in so far as these Regulations provide for an agreement (whether a contract of employment or not) to exclude or limit the operation of these Regulations.

Amendment to the 1996 Act

19. In section 104 of the 1996 Act (assertion of statutory right) in subsection (4)— A2–037

    (a) the word "and" at the end of paragraph (c) is omitted; and
    (b) after paragraph (d), there is inserted—

", and

    (e) the rights conferred by the Transfer of Undertakings (Protection of Employment) Regulations 2006.".

Repeals, revocations and amendments

20.—(1) Subject to regulation 21, the 1981 Regulations are revoked.   A2–038
(2) Section 33 of, and paragraph 4 of Schedule 9 to, the Trade Union Reform and Employment Rights Act 1993 are repealed
(3) Schedule 2 (consequential amendments) shall have effect.

Transitional provisions and savings

21.—(1) These Regulations shall apply in relation to—   A2–039

    (a) a relevant transfer that takes place on or after 6 April 2006;
    (b) a transfer or service provision change, not falling within sub-paragraph (a), that takes place on or after 6 April 2006 and is regarded by virtue of any enactment as a relevant transfer.

(2) The 1981 Regulations shall continue to apply in relation to—

(a) a relevant transfer (within the meaning of the 1981 Regulations) that took place before 6 April 2006;

(b) a transfer, not falling within sub-paragraph (a), that took place before 6 April 2006 and is regarded by virtue of any enactment as a relevant transfer (within the meaning of the 1981 Regulations).

(3) In respect of a relevant transfer that takes place on or after 6 April 2006, any action taken by a transferor or transferee to discharge a duty that applied to them under regulation 10 or 10A of the 1981 Regulations shall be deemed to satisfy the corresponding obligation imposed by regulations 13 and 14 of these Regulations, insofar as that action would have discharged those obligations had the action taken place on or after 6 April 2006.

(4) The duty on a transferor to provide a transferee with employee liability information shall not apply in the case of a relevant transfer that takes place on or before 19 April 2006.

(5) Regulations 13, 14, 15 and 16 shall not apply in the case of a service provision change that is not also a transfer of an undertaking, business or part of an undertaking or business that takes place on or before 4 May 2006.

(6) The repeal of paragraph 4 of Schedule 9 to the Trade Union Reform and Employment Rights Act 1993 does not affect the continued operation of that paragraph so far as it remains capable of having effect.

SCHEDULE 1 — Regulation 2 **A2–040**

APPLICATION OF THE REGULATIONS TO NORTHERN IRELAND

1. These Regulations shall apply to Northern Ireland, subject to the modifications in this Schedule.

2. Sub-paragraph (1)(b) of regulation 3 and any other provision of these Regulations insofar as it relates to that sub-paragraph shall not apply to Northern Ireland.

3. Any reference in these Regulations—

(a) to an employment tribunal shall be construed as a reference to an Industrial Tribunal; and

(b) to the Employment Appeal Tribunal shall be construed as a reference to the Court of Appeal.

4. For the words from "Paragraph (1)" to "the 1992 Act" in regulation 7(6) there is substituted—

"Paragraph (1) shall not apply in relation to a dismissal of an employee if the application of Article 126 of the Employment Rights (Northern Ireland) Order 1996 to the dismissal of the employee is excluded by or under any provision of that Order, the Industrial Tribunals (Northern Ireland) Order 1996 or the 1992 Act insofar as it extends to Northern Ireland, the Industrial Relations (Northern Ireland) Order 1992 or the Trade Union and Labour Relations (Northern Ireland) Order 1995".

5. For the words from "In this Regulation" to "Part XII of the 1996 Act" in regulation 8(4) there is substituted—

"In this Regulation the "relevant statutory schemes" are—

(a) Chapter VI of Part XII of the Employment Rights (Northern Ireland) Order 1996 ("the 1996 Order");

(b) Part XIV of the 1996 Order".

6. For paragraph (4) of regulation 9 there is substituted—

"In article 92 of the 1996 Order (time off for carrying out trade union duties) in paragraph (1), for the full stop at the end of sub-subparagraph (c) there is inserted—

"(d) negotiations with a view to entering into an agreement under regulation 9 of the Transfer of Undertakings (Protection of Employment) Regulations 2006 that applies to employees of the employer, or

(e) the performance on behalf of employees of the employer of functions related to or connected with the making of an agreement under that regulation.".".

7. For the words from "Paragraph (2)" to "the employee's employment with the transferor" in regulation 17 there is substituted—

"Paragraph (2) applies where—

(a) by virtue of article 7(a), 7(aa) or 7(b) of the Employers' Liability (Defective Equipment and Compulsory Insurance) (Northern Ireland) Order 1972 ("the 1972 Order"), the transferor is not required by that Order to effect any insurance; or

(b) by virtue of article 7(c) of the 1972 Order, the transferor is exempted from the requirement of that Order to effect insurance.

(2) Where this paragraph applies, on completion of a relevant transfer the transferor and the transferee shall be jointly and severally liable in respect of any liability referred to in article 5(1) of the 1972 Order, in so far as such liability relates to the employee's employment with the transferor".

8. In regulation 2 for "the 1992 Act" there is substituted "the Industrial Relations (Northern Ireland) Order 1992" and for "Part XIII of the Insolvency Act 1986" there is substituted "Part XII of the Insolvency (NI) Order 1989".

9. In regulation 5 for "sections 179 and 180 of the 1992 Act" there is substituted "Article 26 of the Industrial Relations (NI) Order 1992 No.807 (NI 5)".

10.—(1) In regulation 10 for "the Pensions Schemes Act 1993" there is substituted "the Social Security Pensions (Northern Ireland) Order 1975".

(2) In regulation 11 for "the Employment Act 2002 (Dispute Resolution) Regulations 2004" there is substituted "the Employment (Northern Ireland) Order 2003 (Dispute Resolution) Regulations (NI) 2004".

(3) In regulation 12 for "Section 18 of the 1996 Tribunals Act" there is substituted "Article 20 of the Industrial Tribunals (NI) Order 1996 No. 1921 (NI 18)".

(4) In regulation 16—

    (a) for "Section 18 of the 1996 Tribunals Act" there is substituted "Article 20 of the Industrial Tribunals (NI) Order 1996 No. 1921 (NI 18)"; and

    (b) for any reference to "those Acts" there is substituted a reference to "those Orders".

11. For a reference to a provision of the 1996 Act in column one of Table 1 there is substituted the corresponding reference to the Employment Rights (Northern Ireland) Order 1996 in column two of Table 1—

Table 1

Column 1	Column 2
Provision of the Employment Rights Act 1996	**Equivalent Provision in the Employment Rights (Northern Ireland) Order 1996**
Part X	Part XI
Section 98(4)	Article 130(4)
Section 98(1)	Article 130(1)
Section 135	[Article 170]1
Section 98(2)(c)	Article 130(2)(c)
Section 95(1)(c)	Article 127(1)(c)
Section 1	Article 33
Section 205(1)	[Article 247(1)]2
Sections 220–228	Articles 16–24
Section 139	Article 174
Section 155	Article 190
Section 95(1)	Article 127(1)
Section 95(2)	Article 127(2)
Section 97	Article 129
Section 203	Article 245
Section 104	Article 135

12. Any expression used in this Schedule which is defined in the Interpretation Act (Northern Ireland) 1954 shall have the meaning assigned by that Act.

SCHEDULE 2   Regulation 20   **A2–041**

CONSEQUENTIAL AMENDMENTS

References to the 1981 Regulations

1. In the following provisions, for "Transfer of Undertakings (Protection of Employment) Regulations 1981" or "Transfer of Undertakings (Protection of Employment) Regulations 1981 (S.I. 1981/1794)" there is substituted "Transfer of Undertakings (Protection of Employment) Regulations 2006"—

(a)   section 2(2) of the Property Services Agency and Crown Suppliers Act 1990;
(b)   paragraph 8 of Schedule 1 to the New Roads and Street Works Act 1991;
(c)   paragraph 5 of Schedule 1 to the Ports Act 1991;
(d)   section 9(1) of the Export and Investment Guarantees Act 1991;
(e)   section 168(1)(c) of the Trade Union and Labour Relations (Consolidation) Act 1992;
(f)   paragraph 8 of Schedule 2 to the Roads (Northern Ireland) Order 1993;
(g)   paragraph 6 of Schedule 1 to the Ports (Northern Ireland) Order 1994;
(h)   section 129(1)(b) of the Education Act 2002;
(i)   section 102(8) of the Local Government Act 2003;
(j)   sections 3(6)(a) and 32(6)(b) of, and paragraph 12(1) of Schedule 3 to, the Horserace Betting and Olympic Lottery Act 2004;
(k)   section 90(4) of the Clean Neighbourhoods and Environment Act 2005;
(l)   section 39(5) of the Equality Act 2006.

Industrial Training Act 1982

2.—(1) Section 3B of the Industrial Training Act 1982 (transfer of staff employed by industrial training boards) is amended as follows.

(2) In subsection (2), for "Transfer of Undertakings (Protection of Employment) Regulations 1981" there is substituted "Transfer of Undertakings (Protection of Employment) Regulations 2006".

(3) In subsection (3)(a), for "within the meaning of those Regulations" there is substituted "to which those Regulations apply".

Ordnance Factories and Military Services Act 1984

3.—(1) Paragraph 2 of Schedule 2 to the Ordnance Factories and Military Services Act 1984 (application of 1981 Regulations to ordnance factories transfer schemes) is amended as follows.

(2) In sub-paragraph (1), for the words from "for" to the end there is substituted "for a transfer that is a relevant transfer for the purposes of the 2006 regulations".

(3) In sub-paragraphs (2) and (6), for "1981 regulations", in both places where it occurs, there is substituted "2006 regulations".

(4) In sub-paragraph (3) for the words from "the 1981 regulations" to the end there is substituted "the 2006 regulations as if, immediately before the appointed day, they were employed in the entity subject to the transfer".

(5) In sub-paragraph (4)(b)—

(a)   for "with the undertaking or part" there is substituted "with the entity subject to the transfer", and
(b)   for the words from "the 1981 regulations" to "or part" there is substituted "the 2006 regulations as if he were employed in the entity subject to the transfer".

(6) In sub-paragraph (7), for the definition of "the 1981 regulations" there is substituted—

" "the 2006 regulations" means the Transfer of Undertakings (Protection of Employment) Regulations 2006."

Dockyard Services Act 1986

4.—(1) Section 1 of the Dockyard Services Act 1986 (transfer of persons engaged in dockyard services) is amended as follows.

(2) In subsection (4)—

    (a) for the words from the beginning to "Regulations 1981" there is substituted "The Transfer of Undertakings (Protection of Employment) Regulations 2006",

    (b) for the words from "an undertaking" to "those Regulations" there is substituted "an undertaking to whose transfer those Regulations apply", and

    (c) for the words from "a part" to "a business" there is substituted "a part of that undertaking to whose transfer those Regulations apply".

(3) In subsection (5)—

    (a) for the words from the beginning to "Regulations 1981" there is substituted "The Transfer of Undertakings (Protection of Employment) Regulations 2006",

    (b) for "regulation 10", in both places where it occurs, there is substituted "regulation 13", and

    (c) for "regulation 11" there is substituted "regulations 15 and 16".

Dartford-Thurrock Crossing Act 1988

5.—(1) Schedule 5 to the Dartford-Thurrock Crossing Act 1988 (transfers of staff) is amended as follows.

(2) In paragraphs 3(1) and 4, for "the Employment Transfer Regulations", in both places where it occurs, there is substituted "the Transfer of Undertakings (Protection of Employment) Regulations 2006".

(3) In paragraph 4, for "Regulation 7" there is substituted "Regulation 10".

(4) In paragraph 6—

    (a) in sub-paragraph (2), for "this Schedule", in both places where it occurs, there is substituted "Part 1 of this Schedule", and

    (b) after that sub-paragraph there is inserted—

"(3) Expressions used in Part 2 of this Schedule to which a meaning is given by the Transfer of Undertakings (Protection of Employment) Regulations 2006 have the same meaning in Part 2 of this Schedule."

Atomic Weapons Establishment Act 1991

6.—(1) Section 2 of the Atomic Weapons Establishment Act 1991 (provisions applying to the transfer of certain employees) is amended as follows.

(2) In subsection (1)—

    (a) for the words from the beginning to "Regulations 1981" there is substituted "The Transfer of Undertakings (Protection of Employment) Regulations 2006", and

    (b) for the words from "an undertaking" to "those Regulations" there is substituted "an undertaking to whose transfer those Regulations apply".

(3) In subsection (2), for the words from "a part" to "a business" there is substituted "a part of that undertaking to whose transfer those Regulations apply".

Railways Act 1993

7. In section 151 of the Railways Act 1993 (general interpretation), in subsection (6), for the words from "the Transfer" to the end there is substituted "the Transfer of Undertakings (Protection of Employment) Regulations 2006, in their application in relation to a relevant transfer within the meaning of those regulations".

Employment Tribunals Act 1996

8. In section 4 of the Employment Tribunals Act 1996 (composition of a tribunal), in subsection (3)(ca), for the words from "regulation 11(5)" to "Regulations 1981" there is substituted "regulation 15(10) of the Transfer of Undertakings (Protection of Employment) Regulations 2006".

Industrial Tribunals (Northern Ireland) Order 1996

9. In Article 6 of the Industrial Tribunals (Northern Ireland) Order 1996 (composition of a tribunal), in paragraph (3)(ab), for the words from "regulation 11(5)" to "Regulations 1981" there is substituted "regulation 15(10) of the Transfer of Undertakings (Protection of Employment) Regulations 2006".

Employment Rights Act 1996

10. In each of the following provisions of the Employment Rights Act 1996, for the words from "Regulations 10" to "Regulations 1981" there is substituted "regulations 9, 13 and 15 of the Transfer of Undertakings (Protection of Employment) Regulations 2006"—

    (a)   section 47(1)(a) and (1A);
    (b)   section 61(1)(a);
    (c)   section 103(1)(a) and (2).

Employment Rights (Northern Ireland) Order 1996

11. In each of the following provisions of the Employment Rights (Northern Ireland) Order 1996 for the words from "Regulations 10" to "Regulations 1981" there is substituted "regulations 9, 13 and 15 of the Transfer of Undertakings (Protection of Employment) Regulations 2006"—

    (a)   Article 70(1)(a)and (1A);
    (b)   Article 89(1)(a);
    (c)   Article 134(1)(a) and (2).

Income Tax (Earnings and Pensions) Act 2003

12.—(1) The Income Tax (Earnings and Pensions) Act 2003 is amended as follows.

(2) In section 498 (no charge on shares ceasing to be subject to share incentive plan in certain circumstances), in subsection (2)(c), for the words from "a transfer" to the end there is substituted "a relevant transfer within the meaning of the Transfer of Undertakings (Protection of Employment) Regulations 2006".

(3) In Schedule 2 (approved share incentive plans), in paragraph 32(2)(c), for the words from "a transfer" to the end there is substituted "a relevant transfer within the meaning of the Transfer of Undertakings (Protection of Employment) Regulations 2006".

Pensions Act 2004

13.—(1) Section 257 of the Pensions Act 2004 (conditions for pension protection) is amended as follows.

(2) In subsection (1), for paragraph (a) there is substituted—

"(a) there is a relevant transfer within the meaning of the TUPE regulations,".

(3) Subsection (6) is omitted.

(4) In subsection (8), in the definition of the "TUPE Regulations", for the words from "Transfer" to the end there is substituted "Transfer of Undertakings (Protection of Employment) Regulations 2006".

Energy Act 2004

14.—(1) Paragraph 10 of Schedule 5 to the Energy Act 2004 (supplementary provisions about nuclear transfer schemes) is amended as follows.

(2) In sub-paragraphs (1), (2) and (3), in each place where it occurs, for "1981 regulations" there is substituted "2006 regulations".

(3) In sub-paragraph (1)—

(a) after "an undertaking", in both places where it occurs, there is inserted "or business", and

(b) for "that undertaking or part" there is substituted "that undertaking or business or that part of an undertaking or business".

(4) After sub-paragraph (1), there is inserted—

"(1A) The 2006 regulations apply to a service provision change—

(a) in accordance with a nuclear transfer scheme, or

(b) in accordance with a modification agreement,
as if (in so far as that would not otherwise be the case) the references in those regulations to the transferor were references to the person by whom the activities affected by the service provision change were carried out immediately before the coming into force of the service provision change."

(5) In sub-paragraph (2), after "a transfer" there is inserted "(or service provision change)".

(6) In sub-paragraph (3), after "transfer", in both places where it occurs, there is inserted "(or service provision change)".

(7) In sub-paragraph (4), for the definition of "undertaking" there is substituted—

"references to a service provision change are references to a service provision change falling within regulation 3(1)(b) of the 2006 regulations."

The Cross-Border Insolvency Regulations 2006

(SI 2006/1030)

These Regulations are made in exercise of the powers conferred by section 14 of the Insolvency Act 2000.

In accordance with section 14(6) of that Act, the Lord Chancellor and the Scottish Ministers have agreed to the making of these Regulations.

A draft of these Regulations has been laid before Parliament in accordance with section 14(5) of that Act and approved by a resolution of each House of Parliament.

Accordingly, the Secretary of State makes the following Regulations:

Citation, commencement and interpretation

1.—(1) These Regulations may be cited as the Cross-Border Insolvency Regulations 2006 and shall come into force on the day after the day on which they are made.   **A2–042**

(2) In these Regulations "the UNCITRAL Model Law" means the Model Law on cross-border insolvency as adopted by the United Nations Commission on International Trade Law on 30th May 1997.

UNCITRAL Model Law to have force of law

2.—(1) The UNCITRAL Model Law shall have the force of law in Great Britain in   **A2–043**
the form set out in Schedule 1 to these Regulations (which contains the UNCITRAL Model Law with certain modifications to adapt it for application in Great Britain).

(2) Without prejudice to any practice of the courts as to the matters which may be considered apart from this paragraph, the following documents may be considered in ascertaining the meaning or effect of any provision of the UNCITRAL Model Law as set out in Schedule 1 to these Regulations—

(a)   the UNCITRAL Model Law;
(b)   any documents of the United Nations Commission on International Trade Law and its working group relating to the preparation of the UNCITRAL Model Law; and
(c)   the Guide to Enactment of the UNCITRAL Model Law (UNCITRAL document A/CN.9/442) prepared at the request of the United Nations Commission on International Trade Law made in May 1997.

Modification of British insolvency law

3.—(1) British insolvency law (as defined in article 2 of the UNCITRAL Model Law   **A2–044**
as set out in Schedule 1 to these Regulations) and Part 3 of the Insolvency Act 1986 shall apply with such modifications as the context requires for the purpose of giving effect to the provisions of these Regulations.

(2) In the case of any conflict between any provision of British insolvency law or of Part 3 of the Insolvency Act 1986 and the provisions of these Regulations, the latter shall prevail.

Procedural matters in England and Wales

4. Schedule 2 to these Regulations (which makes provision about procedural matters   **A2–045**
in England and Wales in connection with the application of the UNCITRAL Model Law as set out in Schedule 1 to these Regulations) shall have effect.

Procedural matters in Scotland

5. Schedule 3 to these Regulations (which makes provision about procedural matters   **A2–046**
in Scotland in connection with the application of the UNCITRAL Model Law as set out in Schedule 1 to these Regulations) shall have effect.

Notices delivered to the registrar of companies

A2–047   **6.** Schedule 4 to these Regulations (which makes provision about notices delivered to the registrar of companies under these Regulations) shall have effect.

Co-operation between courts exercising jurisdiction in relation to cross-border insolvency

A2–048   **7.**—(1) An order made by a court in either part of Great Britain in the exercise of jurisdiction in relation to the subject matter of these Regulations shall be enforced in the other part of Great Britain as if it were made by a court exercising the corresponding jurisdiction in that other part.

(2) However, nothing in paragraph (1) requires a court in either part of Great Britain to enforce, in relation to property situated in that part, any order made by a court in the other part of Great Britain.

(3) The courts having jurisdiction in relation to the subject matter of these Regulations in either part of Great Britain shall assist the courts having the corresponding jurisdiction in the other part of Great Britain.

Disapplication of section 388 of the Insolvency Act 1986

A2–049   **8.** Nothing in section 388 of the Insolvency Act 1986 applies to anything done by a foreign representative—

    (a)   under or by virtue of these Regulations;

    (b)   in relation to relief granted or cooperation or coordination provided under these Regulations.

A2–050   SCHEDULE 1

UNCITRAL MODEL LAW ON CROSS-BORDER INSOLVENCY

Regulation 2(1)

CHAPTER I

GENERAL PROVISIONS

Article 1. Scope of Application

1. This Law applies where—

    (a)   assistance is sought in Great Britain by a foreign court or a foreign representative in connection with a foreign proceeding; or

    (b)   assistance is sought in a foreign State in connection with a proceeding under British insolvency law; or

    (c)   a foreign proceeding and a proceeding under British insolvency law in respect of the same debtor are taking place concurrently; or

    (d)   creditors or other interested persons in a foreign State have an interest in requesting the commencement of, or participating in, a proceeding under British insolvency law.

2. This Law does not apply to a proceeding concerning—

    (a)   a company holding an appointment under Chapter 1 of Part 2 of the Water Industry Act 1991 (water and sewage undertakers) or a qualifying licensed water supplier within the meaning of section 23(6) of that Act (meaning and effect of special administration order);

    (b)   Scottish Water established under section 20 of the Water Industry (Scotland) Act 2002 (Scottish Water);

    (c)   a protected railway company within the meaning of section 59 of the Railways Act 1993 (railway administration order) (including that section as it has effect by virtue of section 19 of the Channel Tunnel Rail Link Act 1996 (administration));

(d) a licence company within the meaning of section 26 of the Transport Act 2000 (air traffic services);

(e) a public private partnership company within the meaning of section 210 of the Greater London Authority Act 1999 (public-private partnership agreement);

(f) a protected energy company within the meaning of section 154(5) of the Energy Act 2004 (energy administration orders);

(g) a building society within the meaning of section 119 of the Building Societies Act 1986 (interpretation);

(h) a UK credit institution or an EEA credit institution or any branch of either such institution as those expressions are defined by regulation 2 of the Credit Institutions (Reorganisation and Winding Up) Regulations 2004 (interpretation);

(i) a third country credit institution within the meaning of regulation 36 of the Credit Institutions (Reorganisation and Winding Up) Regulations 2004 (interpretation of this Part);

(j) a person who has permission under or by virtue of Parts 4 or 19 of the Financial Services and Markets Act 2000 to effect or carry out contracts of insurance;

(k) an EEA insurer within the meaning of regulation 2 of the Insurers (Reorganisation and Winding Up) Regulations 2004 (interpretation);

(l) a person (other than one included in paragraph 2(j)) pursuing the activity of reinsurance who has received authorisation for that activity from a competent authority within an EEA State; or

(m) any of the Concessionaires within the meaning of section 1 of the Channel Tunnel Act 1987.

3. In paragraph 2 of this article—

(a) in sub-paragraph (j) the reference to "contracts of insurance" must be construed in accordance with—

    (i) section 22 of the Financial Services and Markets Act 2000 (classes of regulated activity and categories of investment);

    (ii) any relevant order under that section; and

    (iii) Schedule 2 to that Act (regulated activities);

(b) in sub-paragraph (l) "EEA State" means a State, other than the United Kingdom, which is a contracting party to the agreement on the European Economic Area signed at Oporto on 2 May 1992.

4. The court shall not grant any relief, or modify any relief already granted, or provide any cooperation or coordination, under or by virtue of any of the provisions of this Law if and to the extent that such relief or modified relief or cooperation or coordination would—

(a) be prohibited under or by virtue of—

    (i) Part 7 of the Companies Act 1989;

    (ii) Part 3 of the Financial Markets and Insolvency (Settlement Finality) Regulations 1999; or

    (iii) Part 3 of the Financial Collateral Arrangements (No. 2) Regulations 2003;

in the case of a proceeding under British insolvency law; or

(b) interfere with or be inconsistent with any rights of a collateral taker under Part 4 of the Financial Collateral Arrangements (No. 2) Regulations 2003 which could be exercised in the case of such a proceeding.

5. Where a foreign proceeding regarding a debtor who is an insured in accordance with the provisions of the Third Parties (Rights against Insurers) Act 1930 is recognised under this Law, any stay and suspension referred to in article 20(1) and any relief granted by the court under article 19 or 21 shall not apply to or affect—

    (a)   any transfer of rights of the debtor under that Act; or

    (b)   any claim, action, cause or proceeding by a third party against an insurer under or in respect of rights of the debtor transferred under that Act.

6. Any suspension under this Law of the right to transfer, encumber or otherwise dispose of any of the debtor's assets—

    (a)   is subject to section 26 of the Land Registration Act 2002 where owner's powers are exercised in relation to a registered estate or registered charge;

    (b)   is subject to section 52 of the Land Registration Act 2002, where the powers referred to in that section are exercised by the proprietor of a registered charge; and

    (c)   in any other case, shall not bind a purchaser of a legal estate in good faith for money or money's worth unless the purchaser has express notice of the suspension.

7. In paragraph 6—

    (a)   "owner's powers" means the powers described in section 23 of the Land Registration Act 2002 and "registered charge" and "registered estate" have the same meaning as in section 132(1) of that Act; and

    (b)   "legal estate" and "purchaser" have the same meaning as in section 17 of the Land Charges Act 1972.

Article 2. Definitions

For the purposes of this Law—

    (a)   "British insolvency law" means—

        (i)   in relation to England and Wales, provision extending to England and Wales and made by or under the Insolvency Act 1986 (with the exception of Part 3 of that Act) or by or under that Act as extended or applied by or under any other enactment (excluding these Regulations); and

        (ii)   in relation to Scotland, provision extending to Scotland and made by or under the Insolvency Act 1986 (with the exception of Part 3 of that Act), the Bankruptcy (Scotland) Act 1985 or by or under those Acts as extended or applied by or under any other enactment (excluding these Regulations);

    (b)   "British insolvency office-holder" means—

        (i)   the official receiver within the meaning of section 399 of the Insolvency Act 1986 when acting as liquidator, provisional liquidator, trustee, interim receiver or nominee or supervisor of a voluntary arrangement;

        (ii)   a person acting as an insolvency practitioner within the meaning of section 388(c) of that Act but shall not include a person acting as an administrative receiver; and

        (iii)   the Accountant in Bankruptcy within the meaning of section 1 of the Bankruptcy (Scotland) Act 1985 when acting as interim or permanent trustee;

    (c)   "the court" except as otherwise provided in articles 14(4) and 23(6)(b), means in relation to any matter the court which in accordance with the provisions of article 4 of this Law has jurisdiction in relation to that matter;

(d) "the EC Insolvency Regulation" means Council Regulation (EC) No. 1346/2000 of 29 May 2000 on Insolvency Proceedings;

(e) "establishment" means any place of operations where the debtor carries out a non-transitory economic activity with human means and assets or services;

(f) "foreign court" means a judicial or other authority competent to control or supervise a foreign proceeding;

(g) "foreign main proceeding" means a foreign proceeding taking place in the State where the debtor has the centre of its main interests;

(h) "foreign non-main proceeding" means a foreign proceeding, other than a foreign main proceeding, taking place in a State where the debtor has an establishment within the meaning of sub-paragraph (e) of this article;

(i) "foreign proceeding" means a collective judicial or administrative proceeding in a foreign State, including an interim proceeding, pursuant to a law relating to insolvency in which proceeding the assets and affairs of the debtor are subject to control or supervision by a foreign court, for the purpose of reorganisation or liquidation;

(j) "foreign representative" means a person or body, including one appointed on an interim basis, authorised in a foreign proceeding to administer the reorganisation or the liquidation of the debtor's assets or affairs or to act as a representative of the foreign proceeding;

(k) "hire-purchase agreement" includes a conditional sale agreement, a chattel leasing agreement and a retention of title agreement;

(l) "section 426 request" means a request for assistance in accordance with section 426 of the Insolvency Act 1986 made to a court in any part of the United Kingdom;

(m) "secured creditor" in relation to a debtor, means a creditor of the debtor who holds in respect of his debt a security over property of the debtor;

(n) "security" means—

    (i) in relation to England and Wales, any mortgage, charge, lien or other security; and

    (ii) in relation to Scotland, any security (whether heritable or moveable), any floating charge and any right of lien or preference and any right of retention (other than a right of compensation or set off);

(o) in the application of Articles 20 and 23 to Scotland, "an individual" means any debtor within the meaning of the Bankruptcy (Scotland) Act 1985;

(p) in the application of this Law to Scotland, references howsoever expressed to—

    (i) "filing" an application or claim are to be construed as references to lodging an application or submitting a claim respectively;

    (ii) "relief" and "standing" are to be construed as references to "remedy" and "title and interest" respectively; and

    (iii) "stay" is to be construed as references to restraint, except in relation to continuation of actions or proceedings when they shall be construed as a reference to sist; and

(q) references to the law of Great Britain include a reference to the law of either part of Great Britain (including its rules of private international law).

Article 3. International obligations of Great Britain under the EC Insolvency Regulation

To the extent that this Law conflicts with an obligation of the United Kingdom under the EC Insolvency Regulation, the requirements of the EC Insolvency Regulation prevail.

Article 4. Competent court

1. The functions referred to in this Law relating to recognition of foreign proceedings and cooperation with foreign courts shall be performed by the High Court and assigned to the Chancery Division, as regards England and Wales and the Court of Session as regards Scotland.

2. Subject to paragraph 1 of this article, the court in either part of Great Britain shall have jurisdiction in relation to the functions referred to in that paragraph if—

    (a) the debtor has—

          (i) a place of business; or

          (ii) in the case of an individual, a place of residence; or

          (iii) assets,

        situated in that part of Great Britain; or

    (b) the court in that part of Great Britain considers for any other reason that it is the appropriate forum to consider the question or provide the assistance requested.

3. In considering whether it is the appropriate forum to hear an application for recognition of a foreign proceeding in relation to a debtor, the court shall take into account the location of any court in which a proceeding under British insolvency law is taking place in relation to the debtor and the likely location of any future proceedings under British insolvency law in relation to the debtor.

Article 5. Authorisation of British insolvency office-holders to act in a foreign State

A British insolvency office-holder is authorised to act in a foreign State on behalf of a proceeding under British insolvency law, as permitted by the applicable foreign law.

Article 6. Public policy exception

Nothing in this Law prevents the court from refusing to take an action governed by this Law if the action would be manifestly contrary to the public policy of Great Britain or any part of it.

Article 7. Additional assistance under other laws

Nothing in this Law limits the power of a court or a British insolvency office-holder to provide additional assistance to a foreign representative under other laws of Great Britain.

Article 8. Interpretation

In the interpretation of this Law, regard is to be had to its international origin and to the need to promote uniformity in its application and the observance of good faith.

CHAPTER II

ACCESS OF FOREIGN REPRESENTATIVES AND CREDITORS TO COURTS IN GREAT BRITAIN

Article 9. Right of direct access

A foreign representative is entitled to apply directly to a court in Great Britain.

Article 10. Limited jurisdiction

The sole fact that an application pursuant to this Law is made to a court in Great Britain by a foreign representative does not subject the foreign representative or the foreign assets and affairs of the debtor to the jurisdiction of the courts of Great Britain or any part of it for any purpose other than the application.

Article 11. Application by a foreign representative to commence a proceeding under British insolvency law

A foreign representative appointed in a foreign main proceeding or foreign non-main proceeding is entitled to apply to commence a proceeding under British insolvency law if the conditions for commencing such a proceeding are otherwise met.

Article 12. Participation of a foreign representative in a proceeding under British insolvency law

Upon recognition of a foreign proceeding, the foreign representative is entitled to participate in a proceeding regarding the debtor under British insolvency law.

Article 13. Access of foreign creditors to a proceeding under British insolvency law

1. Subject to paragraph 2 of this article, foreign creditors have the same rights regarding the commencement of, and participation in, a proceeding under British insolvency law as creditors in Great Britain.

2. Paragraph 1 of this article does not affect the ranking of claims in a proceeding under British insolvency law, except that the claim of a foreign creditor shall not be given a lower priority than that of general unsecured claims solely because the holder of such a claim is a foreign creditor.

3. A claim may not be challenged solely on the grounds that it is a claim by a foreign tax or social security authority but such a claim may be challenged—

  (a)   on the ground that it is in whole or in part a penalty, or
  (b)   on any other ground that a claim might be rejected in a proceeding under British insolvency law.

Article 14. Notification to foreign creditors of a proceeding under British insolvency law

1. Whenever under British insolvency law notification is to be given to creditors in Great Britain, such notification shall also be given to the known creditors that do not have addresses in Great Britain. The court may order that appropriate steps be taken with a view to notifying any creditor whose address is not yet known.

2. Such notification shall be made to the foreign creditors individually, unless—

  (a)   the court considers that under the circumstances some other form of notification would be more appropriate; or
  (b)   the notification to creditors in Great Britain is to be by advertisement only, in which case the notification to the known foreign creditors may be by advertisement in such foreign newspapers as the British insolvency office-holder considers most appropriate for ensuring that the content of the notification comes to the notice of the known foreign creditors.

3. When notification of a right to file a claim is to be given to foreign creditors, the notification shall—

  (a)   indicate a reasonable time period for filing claims and specify the place for their filing;
  (b)   indicate whether secured creditors need to file their secured claims; and
  (c)   contain any other information required to be included in such a notification to creditors pursuant to the law of Great Britain and the orders of the court.

4. In this article "the court" means the court which has jurisdiction in relation to the particular proceeding under British insolvency law under which notification is to be given to creditors.

CHAPTER III

RECOGNITION OF A FOREIGN PROCEEDING AND RELIEF

Article 15. Application for recognition of a foreign proceeding

1. A foreign representative may apply to the court for recognition of the foreign proceeding in which the foreign representative has been appointed.

2. An application for recognition shall be accompanied by—

    (a) a certified copy of the decision commencing the foreign proceeding and appointing the foreign representative; or

    (b) a certificate from the foreign court affirming the existence of the foreign proceeding and of the appointment of the foreign representative; or

    (c) in the absence of evidence referred to in sub-paragraphs (a) and (b), any other evidence acceptable to the court of the existence of the foreign proceeding and of the appointment of the foreign representative.

3. An application for recognition shall also be accompanied by a statement identifying all foreign proceedings, proceedings under British insolvency law and section 426 requests in respect of the debtor that are known to the foreign representative.

4. The foreign representative shall provide the court with a translation into English of documents supplied in support of the application for recognition.

Article 16. Presumptions concerning recognition

1. If the decision or certificate referred to in paragraph 2 of article 15 indicates that the foreign proceeding is a proceeding within the meaning of sub-paragraph (i) of article 2 and that the foreign representative is a person or body within the meaning of sub-paragraph (j) of article 2, the court is entitled to so presume.

2. The court is entitled to presume that documents submitted in support of the application for recognition are authentic, whether or not they have been legalised.

3. In the absence of proof to the contrary, the debtor's registered office, or habitual residence in the case of an individual, is presumed to be the centre of the debtor's main interests.

Article 17. Decision to recognise a foreign proceeding

1. Subject to article 6, a foreign proceeding shall be recognised if—

    (a) it is a foreign proceeding within the meaning of sub-paragraph (i) of article 2;

    (b) the foreign representative applying for recognition is a person or body within the meaning of sub-paragraph (j) of article 2;

    (c) the application meets the requirements of paragraphs 2 and 3 of article 15; and

    (d) the application has been submitted to the court referred to in article 4.

2. The foreign proceeding shall be recognized—

    (a) as a foreign main proceeding if it is taking place in the State where the debtor has the centre of its main interests; or

    (b) as a foreign non-main proceeding if the debtor has an establishment within the meaning of subparagraph (e) of article 2 in the foreign State.

3. An application for recognition of a foreign proceeding shall be decided upon at the earliest possible time.

4. The provisions of articles 15 to 16, this article and article 18 do not prevent modification or termination of recognition if it is shown that the grounds for granting it were fully or partially lacking or have fully or partially ceased to exist and in such a case, the court may, on the application of the foreign representative or a person affected by recognition, or of its own motion, modify or terminate recognition, either altogether or for a limited time, on such terms and conditions as the court thinks fit.

Article 18. Subsequent information

From the time of filing the application for recognition of the foreign proceeding, the foreign representative shall inform the court promptly of—

(a) any substantial change in the status of the recognised foreign proceeding or the status of the foreign representative's appointment; and

(b) any other foreign proceeding, proceeding under British insolvency law or section 426 request regarding the same debtor that becomes known to the foreign representative.

Article 19. Relief that may be granted upon application for recognition of a foreign proceeding

1. From the time of filing an application for recognition until the application is decided upon, the court may, at the request of the foreign representative, where relief is urgently needed to protect the assets of the debtor or the interests of the creditors, grant relief of a provisional nature, including—

(a) staying execution against the debtor's assets;

(b) entrusting the administration or realisation of all or part of the debtor's assets located in Great Britain to the foreign representative or another person designated by the court, in order to protect and preserve the value of assets that, by their nature or because of other circumstances, are perishable, susceptible to devaluation or otherwise in jeopardy; and

(c) any relief mentioned in paragraph 1 (c), (d) or (g) of article 21.

2. Unless extended under paragraph 1(f) of article 21, the relief granted under this article terminates when the application for recognition is decided upon.

3. The court may refuse to grant relief under this article if such relief would interfere with the administration of a foreign main proceeding.

Article 20. Effects of recognition of a foreign main proceeding

1. Upon recognition of a foreign proceeding that is a foreign main proceeding, subject to paragraph 2 of this article—

(a) commencement or continuation of individual actions or individual proceedings concerning the debtor's assets, rights, obligations or liabilities is stayed;

(b) execution against the debtor's assets is stayed; and

(c) the right to transfer, encumber or otherwise dispose of any assets of the debtor is suspended.

2. The stay and suspension referred to in paragraph 1 of this article shall be—

(a) the same in scope and effect as if the debtor, in the case of an individual, had been adjudged bankrupt under the Insolvency Act 1986 or had his estate sequestrated under the Bankruptcy (Scotland) Act 1985, or, in the case of a debtor other than an individual, had been made the subject of a winding-up order under the Insolvency Act 1986; and

(b) subject to the same powers of the court and the same prohibitions, limitations, exceptions and conditions as would apply under the law of Great Britain in such a case,

and the provisions of paragraph 1 of this article shall be interpreted accordingly.

3. Without prejudice to paragraph 2 of this article, the stay and suspension referred to in paragraph 1 of this article, in particular, does not affect any right—

(a) to take any steps to enforce security over the debtor's property;

(b) to take any steps to repossess goods in the debtor's possession under a hire-purchase agreement;

(c) exercisable under or by virtue of or in connection with the provisions referred to in article 1(4); or

(d) of a creditor to set off its claim against a claim of the debtor,

being a right which would have been exercisable if the debtor, in the case of an individual, had been adjudged bankrupt under the Insolvency Act 1986 or had his estate sequestrated under the Bankruptcy (Scotland) Act 1985, or, in the case of a debtor other than an individual, had been made the subject of a winding-up order under the Insolvency Act 1986.

4. Paragraph 1(a) of this article does not affect the right to—

(a) commence individual actions or proceedings to the extent necessary to preserve a claim against the debtor; or

(b) commence or continue any criminal proceedings or any action or proceedings by a person or body having regulatory, supervisory or investigative functions of a public nature, being an action or proceedings brought in the exercise of those functions.

5. Paragraph 1 of this article does not affect the right to request or otherwise initiate the commencement of a proceeding under British insolvency law or the right to file claims in such a proceeding.

6. In addition to and without prejudice to any powers of the court under or by virtue of paragraph 2 of this article, the court may, on the application of the foreign representative or a person affected by the stay and suspension referred to in paragraph 1 of this article, or of its own motion, modify or terminate such stay and suspension or any part of it, either altogether or for a limited time, on such terms and conditions as the court thinks fit.

Article 21. Relief that may be granted upon recognition of a foreign proceeding

1. Upon recognition of a foreign proceeding, whether main or non-main, where necessary to protect the assets of the debtor or the interests of the creditors, the court may, at the request of the foreign representative, grant any appropriate relief, including—

(a) staying the commencement or continuation of individual actions or individual proceedings concerning the debtor's assets, rights, obligations or liabilities, to the extent they have not been stayed under paragraph 1(a) of article 20;

(b) staying execution against the debtor's assets to the extent it has not been stayed under paragraph 1(b) of article 20;

(c) suspending the right to transfer, encumber or otherwise dispose of any assets of the debtor to the extent this right has not been suspended under paragraph 1(c) of article 20;

(d) providing for the examination of witnesses, the taking of evidence or the delivery of information concerning the debtor's assets, affairs, rights, obligations or liabilities;

(e) entrusting the administration or realisation of all or part of the debtor's assets located in Great Britain to the foreign representative or another person designated by the court;

(f) extending relief granted under paragraph 1 of article 19; and

(g) granting any additional relief that may be available to a British insolvency office-holder under the law of Great Britain, including any relief provided under paragraph 43 of Schedule B1 to the Insolvency Act 1986.

2. Upon recognition of a foreign proceeding, whether main or non-main, the court may, at the request of the foreign representative, entrust the distribution of all or part of the debtor's assets located in Great Britain to the foreign representative or another person designated by the court, provided that the court is satisfied that the interests of creditors in Great Britain are adequately protected.

3. In granting relief under this article to a representative of a foreign non-main proceeding, the court must be satisfied that the relief relates to assets that, under the law of Great Britain, should be administered in the foreign non-main proceeding or concerns information required in that proceeding.

4. No stay under paragraph 1(a) of this article shall affect the right to commence or continue any criminal proceedings or any action or proceedings by a person or body having regulatory, supervisory or investigative functions of a public nature, being an action or proceedings brought in the exercise of those functions.

Article 22. Protection of creditors and other interested persons

1. In granting or denying relief under article 19 or 21, or in modifying or terminating relief under paragraph 3 of this article or paragraph 6 of article 20, the court must be satisfied that the interests of the creditors (including any secured creditors or parties to hire-purchase agreements) and other interested persons, including if appropriate the debtor, are adequately protected.

2. The court may subject relief granted under article 19 or 21 to conditions it considers appropriate, including the provision by the foreign representative of security or caution for the proper performance of his functions.

3. The court may, at the request of the foreign representative or a person affected by relief granted under article 19 or 21, or of its own motion, modify or terminate such relief.

Article 23. Actions to avoid acts detrimental to creditors

1. Subject to paragraphs 6 and 9 of this article, upon recognition of a foreign proceeding, the foreign representative has standing to make an application to the court for an order under or in connection with sections 238, 239, 242, 243, 244, 245, 339, 340, 342A, 343, and 423 of the Insolvency Act 1986 and sections 34, 35, 36, 36A and 61 of the Bankruptcy (Scotland) Act 1985.

2. Where the foreign representative makes such an application ("an article 23 application"), the sections referred to in paragraph 1 of this article and sections 240, 241, 341, 342, 342B to 342F, 424 and 425 of the Insolvency Act 1986 and sections 36B and 36C of the Bankruptcy (Scotland) Act 1985 shall apply—

    (a) whether or not the debtor, in the case of an individual, has been adjudged bankrupt or had his estate sequestrated, or, in the case of a debtor other than an individual, is being wound up or is in administration, under British insolvency law; and

    (b) with the modifications set out in paragraph 3 of this article.

3. The modifications referred to in paragraph 2 of this article are as follows—

    (a) for the purposes of sections 241(2A)(a) and 342(2A)(a) of the Insolvency Act 1986, a person has notice of the relevant proceedings if he has notice of the opening of the relevant foreign proceeding;

    (b) for the purposes of sections 240(1) and 245(3) of that Act, the onset of insolvency shall be the date of the opening of the relevant foreign proceeding;

    (c) the periods referred to in sections 244(2), 341(1)(a) to (c) and 343(2) of that Act shall be periods ending with the date of the opening of the relevant foreign proceeding;

    (d) for the purposes of sections 242(3)(a), (3)(b) and 243(1) of that Act, the date on which the winding up of the company commences or it enters administration shall be the date of the opening of the relevant foreign proceeding; and

    (e) for the purposes of sections 34(3)(a), (3)(b), 35(1)(c), 36(1)(a) and (1)(b) and 61(2) of the Bankruptcy (Scotland) Act 1985, the date of sequestration or granting of the trust deed shall be the date of the opening of the relevant foreign proceeding.

4. For the purposes of paragraph 3 of this article, the date of the opening of the foreign proceeding shall be determined in accordance with the law of the State in which the foreign proceeding is taking place, including any rule of law by virtue of which the foreign proceeding is deemed to have opened at an earlier time.

5. When the foreign proceeding is a foreign non-main proceeding, the court must be satisfied that the article 23 application relates to assets that, under the law of Great Britain, should be administered in the foreign non-main proceeding.

6. At any time when a proceeding under British insolvency law is taking place regarding the debtor—

    (a) the foreign representative shall not make an article 23 application except with the permission of—

        (i) in the case of a proceeding under British insolvency law taking place in England and Wales, the High Court; or

        (ii) in the case of a proceeding under British insolvency law taking place in Scotland, the Court of Session; and

    (b) references to "the court" in paragraphs 1, 5 and 7 of this article are references to the court in which that proceeding is taking place.

7. On making an order on an article 23 application, the court may give such directions regarding the distribution of any proceeds of the claim by the foreign representative, as it thinks fit to ensure that the interests of creditors in Great Britain are adequately protected.

8. Nothing in this article affects the right of a British insolvency office-holder to make an application under or in connection with any of the provisions referred to in paragraph 1 of this article.

9. Nothing in paragraph 1 of this article shall apply in respect of any preference given, floating charge created, alienation, assignment or relevant contributions (within the meaning of section 342A(5) of the Insolvency Act 1986) made or other transaction entered into before the date on which this Law comes into force.

Article 24. Intervention by a foreign representative in proceedings in Great Britain

Upon recognition of a foreign proceeding, the foreign representative may, provided the requirements of the law of Great Britain are met, intervene in any proceedings in which the debtor is a party.

CHAPTER IV

COOPERATION WITH FOREIGN COURTS AND FOREIGN REPRESENTATIVES

Article 25. Cooperation and direct communication between a court of Great Britain and foreign courts or foreign representatives

1. In matters referred to in paragraph 1 of article 1, the court may cooperate to the maximum extent possible with foreign courts or foreign representatives, either directly or through a British insolvency office-holder.

2. The court is entitled to communicate directly with, or to request information or assistance directly from, foreign courts or foreign representatives.

Article 26. Cooperation and direct communication between the British insolvency office-holder and foreign courts or foreign representatives

1. In matters referred to in paragraph 1 of article 1, a British insolvency office-holder shall to the extent consistent with his other duties under the law of Great Britain, in the exercise of his functions and subject to the supervision of the court, cooperate to the maximum extent possible with foreign courts or foreign representatives.

2. The British insolvency office-holder is entitled, in the exercise of his functions and subject to the supervision of the court, to communicate directly with foreign courts or foreign representatives.

Article 27. Forms of cooperation

Cooperation referred to in articles 25 and 26 may be implemented by any appropriate means, including—

(a) appointment of a person to act at the direction of the court;
(b) communication of information by any means considered appropriate by the court;
(c) coordination of the administration and supervision of the debtor's assets and affairs;
(d) approval or implementation by courts of agreements concerning the coordination of proceedings;
(e) coordination of concurrent proceedings regarding the same debtor.

CHAPTER V

CONCURRENT PROCEEDINGS

Article 28. Commencement of a proceeding under British insolvency law after recognition of a foreign main proceeding

After recognition of a foreign main proceeding, the effects of a proceeding under British insolvency law in relation to the same debtor shall, insofar as the assets of that debtor are concerned, be restricted to assets that are located in Great Britain and, to the extent necessary to implement cooperation and coordination under articles 25, 26 and 27, to other assets of the debtor that, under the law of Great Britain, should be administered in that proceeding.

Article 29. Coordination of a proceeding under British insolvency law and a foreign proceeding

Where a foreign proceeding and a proceeding under British insolvency law are taking place concurrently regarding the same debtor, the court may seek cooperation and coordination under articles 25, 26 and 27, and the following shall apply—

(a) when the proceeding in Great Britain is taking place at the time the application for recognition of the foreign proceeding is filed—

(i) any relief granted under article 19 or 21 must be consistent with the proceeding in Great Britain; and
(ii) if the foreign proceeding is recognised in Great Britain as a foreign main proceeding, article 20 does not apply;

(b) when the proceeding in Great Britain commences after the filing of the application for recognition of the foreign proceeding—

(i) any relief in effect under article 19 or 21 shall be reviewed by the court and shall be modified or terminated if inconsistent with the proceeding in Great Britain;
(ii) if the foreign proceeding is a foreign main proceeding, the stay and suspension referred to in paragraph 1 of article 20 shall be modified or terminated pursuant to paragraph 6 of article 20, if inconsistent with the proceeding in Great Britain; and
(iii) any proceedings brought by the foreign representative by virtue of paragraph 1 of article 23 before the proceeding in Great Britain

commenced shall be reviewed by the court and the court may give
such directions as it thinks fit regarding the continuance of those
proceedings; and

(c) in granting, extending or modifying relief granted to a representative of a
foreign non-main proceeding, the court must be satisfied that the relief
relates to assets that, under the law of Great Britain, should be administered
in the foreign non-main proceeding or concerns information required in that
proceeding.

Article 30. Coordination of more than one foreign proceeding

In matters referred to in paragraph 1 of article 1, in respect of more than one foreign
proceeding regarding the same debtor, the court may seek cooperation and coordination
under articles 25, 26 and 27, and the following shall apply—

(a) any relief granted under article 19 or 21 to a representative of a foreign non-
main proceeding after recognition of a foreign main proceeding must be
consistent with the foreign main proceeding;

(b) if a foreign main proceeding is recognised after the filing of an application
for recognition of a foreign non-main proceeding, any relief in effect under
article 19 or 21 shall be reviewed by the court and shall be modified or terminated if inconsistent with the foreign main proceeding; and

(c) if, after recognition of a foreign non-main proceeding, another foreign non-
main proceeding is recognised, the court shall grant, modify or terminate
relief for the purpose of facilitating coordination of the proceedings.

Article 31. Presumption of insolvency based on recognition of a foreign main proceeding

In the absence of evidence to the contrary, recognition of a foreign main proceeding is,
for the purpose of commencing a proceeding under British insolvency law, proof that
the debtor is unable to pay its debts or, in relation to Scotland, is apparently insolvent
within the meaning given to those expressions under British insolvency law.

Article 32. Rule of payment in concurrent proceedings

Without prejudice to secured claims or rights in rem, a creditor who has received part
payment in respect of its claim in a proceeding pursuant to a law relating to insolvency
in a foreign State may not receive a payment for the same claim in a proceeding under
British insolvency law regarding the same debtor, so long as the payment to the other
creditors of the same class is proportionately less than the payment the creditor has
already received.

SCHEDULE 2

PROCEDURAL MATTERS IN ENGLAND AND WALES

Regulation 4

PART 1

INTRODUCTORY PROVISIONS

Interpretation

1.—(1) In this Schedule—

"the 1986 Act" means the Insolvency Act 1986;

"article 21 relief application" means an application to the court by a foreign representative under article 21(1) or (2) of the Model Law for relief;

"business day" means any day other than a Saturday, a Sunday, Christmas Day, Good Friday or a day which is a bank holiday in England and Wales under or by virtue of the Banking and Financial Dealings Act 1971;

"CPR" means the Civil Procedure Rules 1998 and "CPR" followed by a Part or rule by number means the Part or rule with that number in those Rules;

"enforcement officer" means an individual who is authorised to act as an enforcement officer under the Courts Act 2003;

"file in court" and "file with the court" means deliver to the court for filing;

"the Gazette" means the London Gazette;

"interim relief application" means an application to the court by a foreign representative under article 19 of the Model Law for interim relief;

"main proceedings" means proceedings opened in accordance with Article 3(1) of the EC Insolvency Regulation and falling within the definition of insolvency proceedings in Article 2(a) of the EC Insolvency Regulation;

"member State liquidator" means a person falling within the definition of liquidator in Article 2(b) of the EC Insolvency Regulation appointed in proceedings to which it applies in a member State other than the United Kingdom;

"the Model Law" means the UNCITRAL Model Law as set out in Schedule 1 to these Regulations;

"modification or termination order" means an order by the court pursuant to its powers under the Model Law modifying or terminating recognition of a foreign proceeding, the stay and suspension referred to in article 20(1) or any part of it or any relief granted under article 19 or 21 of the Model Law;

"originating application" means an application to the court which is not an application in pending proceedings before the court;

"ordinary application" means any application to the court other than an originating application;

"practice direction" means a direction as to the practice and procedure of any court within the scope of the CPR;

"recognition application" means an application to the court by a foreign representative in accordance with article 15 of the Model Law for an order recognising the foreign proceeding in which he has been appointed;

"recognition order" means an order by the court recognising a proceeding the subject of a recognition application as a foreign main proceeding or foreign non-main proceeding, as appropriate;

"relevant company" means a company within the meaning of section 735(1) of the Companies Act 1985 or an unregistered company within the meaning of Part 5 of the 1986 Act which is subject to a requirement imposed by virtue of section 690A, 69(1) or 718 of the Companies Act 1985;

"review application" means an application to the court for a modification or termination order;

"the Rules" means the Insolvency Rules 1986 and "Rule" followed by a number means the rule with that number in those Rules;

"secondary proceedings" means proceedings opened in accordance with Articles 3(2) and 3(3) of the EC Insolvency Regulation and falling within the definition of winding up proceedings in Article 2(c) of the EC Insolvency Regulation;

"territorial proceedings" means proceedings opened in accordance with Articles 3(2) and 3(4) of the EC Insolvency Regulation and falling within the definition of insolvency proceedings in Article 2(a) of the EC Insolvency Regulation.

(2) Expressions defined in the Model Law have the same meaning when used in this Schedule.

(3) In proceedings under these Regulations, "Registrar" means—

    (a)   a Registrar in Bankruptcy of the High Court; and

    (b)   where the proceedings are in a district registry, the district judge.

(4) References to the "venue" for any proceedings or attendance before the court, are to the time, date and place for the proceedings or attendance.

(5) References in this Schedule to ex parte hearings shall be construed as references to hearings without notice being served on any other party, and references to applications made ex parte as references to applications made without notice being served on any other party; and other references which include the expression "ex parte" shall be similarly construed.

(6) References in this Schedule to a debtor who is of interest to the Financial Services Authority are references to a debtor who—

    (a)   is, or has been, an authorised person within the meaning of section 31 of the Financial Services and Markets Act 2000 (authorised persons);

    (b)   is, or has been, an appointed representative within the meaning of section 39 (exemption of appointed representatives) of that Act; or

    (c)   is carrying on, or has carried on, a regulated activity in contravention of the general prohibition.

(7) In sub-paragraph (6) "the general prohibition" has the meaning given by section 19 of the Financial Services and Markets Act 2000 and the reference to a "regulated activity" must be construed in accordance with—

    (a)   section 22 of that Act (classes of regulated activity and categories of investment);

    (b)   any relevant order under that section; and

    (c)   Schedule 2 to that Act (regulated activities).

(8) References in this Schedule to a numbered form are to the form that bears that number in Schedule 5.

PART 2

APPLICATIONS TO COURT FOR RECOGNITION OF FOREIGN PROCEEDINGS

Affidavit in support of recognition application

2. A recognition application shall be in Form ML 1 and shall be supported by an affidavit sworn by the foreign representative complying with paragraph 4.

Form and content of application

3. The application shall state the following matters—

    (a)   the name of the applicant and his address for service within England and Wales;

(b) the name of the debtor in respect of which the foreign proceeding is taking place;

(c) the name or names in which the debtor carries on business in the country where the foreign proceeding is taking place and in this country, if other than the name given under subparagraph (b);

(d) the principal or last known place of business of the debtor in Great Britain (if any) and, in the case of an individual, his usual or last known place of residence in Great Britain (if any);

(e) any registered number allocated to the debtor under the Companies Act 1985;

(f) brief particulars of the foreign proceeding in respect of which recognition is applied for, including the country in which it is taking place and the nature of the proceeding;

(g) that the foreign proceeding is a proceeding within the meaning of article 2(i) of the Model Law;

(h) that the applicant is a foreign representative within the meaning of article 2(j) of the Model Law;

(i) the address of the debtor's centre of main interests and, if different, the address of its registered office or habitual residence, as appropriate; and

(j) if the debtor does not have its centre of main interests in the country where the foreign proceeding is taking place, whether the debtor has an establishment within the meaning of article 2(e) of the Model Law in that country, and if so, its address.

Contents of affidavit in support

4.—(1) There shall be attached to the application an affidavit in support which shall contain or have exhibited to it—

(a) the evidence and statement required under article 15(2) and (3) respectively of the Model Law;

(b) any other evidence which in the opinion of the applicant will assist the court in deciding whether the proceeding the subject of the application is a foreign proceeding within the meaning of article 2(i) of the Model Law and whether the applicant is a foreign representative within the meaning of article 2(j) of the Model Law;

(c) evidence that the debtor has its centre of main interests or an establishment, as the case may be, within the country where the foreign proceeding is taking place; and

(d) any other matters which in the opinion of the applicant will assist the court in deciding whether to make a recognition order

(2) The affidavit shall state whether, in the opinion of the applicant, the EC Insolvency Regulation applies to any of the proceedings identified in accordance with article 15(3) of the Model Law and, if so, whether those proceedings are main proceedings, secondary proceedings or territorial proceedings.

(3) The affidavit shall also have exhibited to it the translations required under article 15(4) of the Model Law and a translation in English of any other document exhibited to the affidavit which is in a language other than English.

(4) All translations referred to in sub-paragraph (3) must be certified by the translator as a correct translation.

The hearing and powers of court

5.—(1) On hearing a recognition application the court may in addition to its powers under the Model Law to make a recognition order—

(a) dismiss the application;

(b) adjourn the hearing conditionally or unconditionally;

(c)   make any other order which the court thinks appropriate.

(2) If the court makes a recognition order, it shall be in Form ML 2.

Notification of subsequent information

6.—(1) The foreign representative shall set out any subsequent information required to be given to the court under article 18 of the Model Law in a statement which he shall attach to Form ML 3 and file with the court.

(2) The statement shall include—

(a)   details of the information required to be given under article 18 of the Model Law; and

(b)   in the case of any proceedings required to be notified to the court under that article, a statement as to whether, in the opinion of the foreign representative, any of those proceedings are main proceedings, secondary proceedings or territorial proceedings under the EC Insolvency Regulation.

(3) The foreign representative shall send a copy of the Form ML 3 and attached statement filed with the court to the following—

(a)   the debtor; and

(b)   those persons referred to in paragraph 26(3).

PART 3

APPLICATIONS FOR RELIEF UNDER THE MODEL LAW

Application for interim relief—affidavit in support

7.—(1) An interim relief application must be supported by an affidavit sworn by the foreign representative stating—

(a)   the grounds on which it is proposed that the interim relief applied for should be granted;

(b)   details of any proceeding under British insolvency law taking place in relation to the debtor;

(c)   whether, to the foreign representative's knowledge, an administrative receiver or receiver or manager of the debtor's property is acting in relation to the debtor;

(d)   an estimate of the value of the assets of the debtor in England and Wales in respect of which relief is applied for;

(e)   whether, to the best of the knowledge and belief of the foreign representative, the interests of the debtor's creditors (including any secured creditors or parties to hire-purchase agreements) and any other interested parties, including if appropriate the debtor, will be adequately protected;

(f)   whether, to the best of the foreign representative's knowledge and belief, the grant of any of the relief applied for would interfere with the administration of a foreign main proceeding; and

(g)   all other matters that in the opinion of the foreign representative will assist the court in deciding whether or not it is appropriate to grant the relief applied for.

Service of interim relief application not required

8. Unless the court otherwise directs, it shall not be necessary to serve the interim relief application on, or give notice of it to, any person.

The hearing and powers of court

9. On hearing an interim relief application the court may in addition to its powers under the Model Law to make an order granting interim relief under article 19 of the Model Law—

  (a) dismiss the application;
  (b) adjourn the hearing conditionally or unconditionally;
  (c) make any other order which the court thinks appropriate.

Application for relief under article 21 of the Model Law—affidavit in support

10. An article 21 relief application must be supported by an affidavit sworn by the foreign representative stating—

  (a) the grounds on which it is proposed that the relief applied for should be granted;
  (b) an estimate of the value of the assets of the debtor in England and Wales in respect of which relief is applied for;
  (c) in the case of an application by a foreign representative who is or believes that he is a representative of a foreign non-main proceeding, the reasons why the applicant believes that the relief relates to assets that, under the law of Great Britain, should be administered in the foreign non-main proceeding or concerns information required in that proceeding;
  (d) whether, to the best of the knowledge and belief of the foreign representative, the interests of the debtor's creditors (including any secured creditors or parties to hire-purchase agreements) and any other interested parties, including if appropriate the debtor, will be adequately protected; and
  (e) all other matters that in the opinion of the foreign representative will assist the court in deciding whether or not it is appropriate to grant the relief applied for.

The hearing and powers of court

11. On hearing an article 21 relief application the court may in addition to its powers under the Model Law to make an order granting relief under article 21 of the Model Law—

  (a) dismiss the application;
  (b) adjourn the hearing conditionally or unconditionally;
  (c) make any other order which the court thinks appropriate.

PART 4

REPLACEMENT OF FOREIGN REPRESENTATIVE

Application for confirmation of status of replacement foreign representative

12.—(1) This paragraph applies where following the making of a recognition order the foreign representative dies or for any other reason ceases to be the foreign representative in the foreign proceeding in relation to the debtor.

(2) In this paragraph "the former foreign representative" shall mean the foreign representative referred to in sub-paragraph (1).

(3) If a person has succeeded the former foreign representative or is otherwise holding office as foreign representative in the foreign proceeding in relation to the debtor, that person may apply to the court for an order confirming his status as replacement foreign representative for the purpose of proceedings under these Regulations.

Contents of application and affidavit in support

13.—(1) An application under paragraph 12(3) shall in addition to the matters required to be stated by paragraph 19(2) state the following matters—

    (a)   the name of the replacement foreign representative and his address for service within England and Wales;

    (b)   details of the circumstances in which the former foreign representative ceased to be foreign representative in the foreign proceeding in relation to the debtor (including the date on which he ceased to be the foreign representative);

    (c)   details of his own appointment as replacement foreign representative in the foreign proceeding (including the date of that appointment).

(2) The application shall be accompanied by an affidavit in support sworn by the applicant which shall contain or have attached to it—

    (a)   a certificate from the foreign court affirming—

        (i)   the cessation of the appointment of the former foreign representative as foreign representative; and

       (ii)   the appointment of the applicant as the foreign representative in the foreign proceeding; or

    (b)   in the absence of such a certificate, any other evidence acceptable to the court of the matters referred to in paragraph (a); and

    (c)   a translation in English of any document exhibited to the affidavit which is in a language other than English.

(3) All translations referred to in paragraph (c) must be certified by the translator as a correct translation.

The hearing and powers of court

14.—(1) On hearing an application under paragraph 12(3) the court may—

    (a)   make an order confirming the status of the replacement foreign representative as foreign representative for the purpose of proceedings under these Regulations;

    (b)   dismiss the application;

    (c)   adjourn the hearing conditionally or unconditionally;

    (d)   make an interim order;

    (e)   make any other order which the court thinks appropriate, including in particular an order making such provision as the court thinks fit with respect to matters arising in connection with the replacement of the foreign representative.

(2) If the court dismisses the application, it may also if it thinks fit make an order terminating recognition of the foreign proceeding and—

    (a)   such an order may include such provision as the court thinks fit with respect to matters arising in connection with the termination; and

    (b)   paragraph 15 shall not apply to such an order.

PART 5

REVIEWS OF COURT ORDERS

Reviews of court orders—where court makes order of its own motion

15.—(1) The court shall not of its own motion make a modification or termination order unless the foreign representative and the debtor have either—

    (a)   had an opportunity of being heard on the question; or

    (b)   consented in writing to such an order.

(2) Where the foreign representative or the debtor desires to be heard on the question of such an order, the court shall give all relevant parties notice of a venue at which the question will be considered and may give directions as to the issues on which it requires evidence.

(3) For the purposes of sub-paragraph (2), all relevant parties means the foreign representative, the debtor and any other person who appears to the court to have an interest justifying his being given notice of the hearing.

(4) If the court makes a modification or termination order, the order may include such provision as the court thinks fit with respect to matters arising in connection with the modification or termination.

Review application—affidavit in support

16. A review application must be supported by an affidavit sworn by the applicant stating—

    (a)   the grounds on which it is proposed that the relief applied for should be granted;

    (b)   whether, to the best of the knowledge and belief of the applicant, the interests of the debtor's creditors (including any secured creditors or parties to hire-purchase agreements) and any other interested parties, including if appropriate the debtor, will be adequately protected; and

    (c)   all other matters that in the opinion of the applicant will assist the court in deciding whether or not it is appropriate to grant the relief applied for.

Hearing of review application and powers of the court

17. On hearing a review application, the court may in addition to its powers under the Model Law to make a modification or termination order—

    (a)   dismiss the application;

    (b)   adjourn the hearing conditionally or unconditionally;

    (c)   make an interim order;

    (d)   make any other order which the court thinks appropriate, including an order making such provision as the court thinks fit with respect to matters arising in connection with the modification or termination.

PART 6

Court Procedure and Practice with Regard to Principal Applications
and Orders

Preliminary and interpretation

18.—(1) This Part applies to—

    (a)   any of the following applications made to the court under these Regulations—

        (i)   a recognition application;

        (ii)   an article 21 relief application;

        (iii)   an application under paragraph 12(3) for an order confirming the status of a replacement foreign representative;

        (iv)   a review application; and

    (b)   any of the following orders made by the court under these Regulations—

        (i)   a recognition order;

        (ii)   an order granting interim relief under article 19 of the Model Law;

        (iii)   an order granting relief under article 21 of the Model Law;

        (iv)   an order confirming the status of a replacement foreign representative; and

        (v)   a modification or termination order.

Form and contents of application

19.—(1) Subject to sub-paragraph (4) every application to which this Part applies shall be an ordinary application and shall be in Form ML 5.

(2) Each application shall be in writing and shall state—

(a) the names of the parties;

(b) the nature of the relief or order applied for or the directions sought from the court;

(c) the names and addresses of the persons (if any) on whom it is intended to serve the application;

(d) the names and addresses of all those persons on whom these Regulations require the application to be served (so far as known to the applicant); and

(e) the applicant's address for service.

(3) The application must be signed by the applicant if he is acting in person, or, when he is not so acting, by or on behalf of his solicitor.

(4) This paragraph does not apply to a recognition application.

Filing of application

20.—(1) The application (and all supporting documents) shall be filed with the court, with a sufficient number of copies for service and use as provided by paragraph 21(2).

(2) Each of the copies filed shall have applied to it the seal of the court and be issued to the applicant; and on each copy there shall be endorsed the date and time of filing.

(3) The court shall fix a venue for the hearing of the application and this also shall be endorsed on each copy of the application issued under sub-paragraph (2).

Service of the application

21.—(1) In sub-paragraph (2), references to the application are to a sealed copy of the application issued by the court together with any affidavit in support of it and any documents exhibited to the affidavit.

(2) Unless the court otherwise directs, the application shall be served on the following persons, unless they are the applicant—

(a) on the foreign representative;

(b) on the debtor;

(c) if a British insolvency office-holder is acting in relation to the debtor, on him;

(d) if any person has been appointed an administrative receiver of the debtor or, to the knowledge of the foreign representative, as a receiver or manager of the property of the debtor in England and Wales, on him;

(e) if a member State liquidator has been appointed in main proceedings in relation to the debtor, on him;

(f) if to the knowledge of the foreign representative a foreign representative has been appointed in any other foreign proceeding regarding the debtor, on him;

(g) if there is pending in England and Wales a petition for the winding up or bankruptcy of the debtor, on the petitioner;

(h) on any person who to the knowledge of the foreign representative is or may be entitled to appoint an administrator of the debtor under paragraph 14 of Schedule B1 to the 1986 Act (appointment of administrator by holder of qualifying floating charge); and

(i) if the debtor is a debtor who is of interest to the Financial Services Authority, on that Authority.

Manner in which service to be effected

22.—(1) Service of the application in accordance with paragraph 21(2) shall be effected by the applicant, or his solicitor, or by a person instructed by him or his solicitor, not less than 5 business days before the date fixed for the hearing.

(2) Service shall be effected by delivering the documents to a person's proper address or in such other manner as the court may direct.

(3) A person's proper address is any which he has previously notified as his address for service within England and Wales; but if he has not notified any such address or if for any reason service at such address is not practicable, service may be effected as follows—

    (a) (subject to sub-paragraph (4)) in the case of a company incorporated in England and Wales, by delivery to its registered office;

    (b) in the case of any other person, by delivery to his usual or last known address or principal place of business in Great Britain.

(4) If delivery to a company's registered office is not practicable, service may be effected by delivery to its last known principal place of business in Great Britain.

(5) Delivery of documents to any place or address may be made by leaving them there or sending them by first class post in accordance with the provisions of paragraphs 70 and 75(1).

Proof of service

23.—(1) Service of the application shall be verified by an affidavit of service in Form ML 6, specifying the date on which, and the manner in which, service was effected.

(2) The affidavit of service, with a sealed copy of the application exhibited to it, shall be filed with the court as soon as reasonably practicable after service, and in any event not less than 1 business day before the hearing of the application.

In case of urgency

24. Where the case is one of urgency, the court may (without prejudice to its general power to extend or abridge time limits)—

    (a) hear the application immediately, either with or without notice to, or the attendance of, other parties; or

    (b) authorise a shorter period of service than that provided for by paragraph 22(1),

and any such application may be heard on terms providing for the filing or service of documents, or the carrying out of other formalities, as the court thinks fit.

The hearing

25.—(1) At the hearing of the application, the applicant and any of the following persons (not being the applicant) may appear or be represented—

    (a) the foreign representative;

    (b) the debtor and, in the case of any debtor other than an individual, any one or more directors or other officers of the debtor, including

        (i) where applicable, any person registered under Part 23 of the Companies Act 1985 as authorised to represent the debtor in respect of its business in England and Wales;

        (ii) in the case of a debtor which is a partnership, any person who is an officer of the partnership within the meaning of article 2 of the Insolvent Partnerships Order 1994;

    (c) if a British insolvency office-holder is acting in relation to the debtor, that person;

    (d)   if any person has been appointed an administrative receiver of the debtor or as a receiver or manager of the property of the debtor in England and Wales, that person;

    (e)   if a member State liquidator has been appointed in main proceedings in relation to the debtor, that person;

    (f)   if a foreign representative has been appointed in any other foreign proceeding regarding the debtor, that person;

    (g)   any person who has presented a petition for the winding up or bankruptcy of the debtor in England and Wales;

    (h)   any person who is or may be entitled to appoint an administrator of the debtor under paragraph 14 of Schedule B1 to the 1986 Act (appointment of administrator by holder of qualifying floating charge);

    (i)   if the debtor is a debtor who is of interest to the Financial Services Authority, that Authority; and

    (j)   with the permission of the court, any other person who appears to have an interest justifying his appearance.

Notification and advertisement of order

    26.—(1) If the court makes any of the orders referred to in paragraph 18(1)(b), it shall as soon as reasonably practicable send two sealed copies of the order to the foreign representative.

    (2) The foreign representative shall send a sealed copy of the order as soon as reasonably practicable to the debtor.

    (3) The foreign representative shall, as soon as reasonably practicable after the date of the order give notice of the making of the order—

    (a)   if a British insolvency office-holder is acting in relation to the debtor, to him;

    (b)   if any person has been appointed an administrative receiver of the debtor or, to the knowledge of the foreign representative, as a receiver or manager of the property of the debtor, to him;

    (c)   if a member State liquidator has been appointed in main proceedings in relation to the debtor, to him;

    (d)   if to his knowledge a foreign representative has been appointed in any other foreign proceeding regarding the debtor, that person;

    (e)   if there is pending in England and Wales a petition for the winding up or bankruptcy of the debtor, to the petitioner;

    (f)   to any person who to his knowledge is or may be entitled to appoint an administrator of the debtor under paragraph 14 of Schedule B1 to the 1986 Act (appointment of administrator by holder of qualifying floating charge);

    (g)   if the debtor is a debtor who is of interest to the Financial Services Authority, to that Authority;

    (h)   to such other persons as the court may direct.

    (4) In the case of an order recognising a foreign proceeding in relation to the debtor as a foreign main proceeding, or an order under article 19 or 21 of the Model Law staying execution, distress or other legal process against the debtor's assets, the foreign representative shall also, as soon as reasonably practicable after the date of the order give notice of the making of the order—

    (a)   to any enforcement officer or other officer who to his knowledge is charged with an execution or other legal process against the debtor or its property; and

    (b)   to any person who to his knowledge is distraining against the debtor or its property.

    (5) In the application of sub-paragraphs (3) and (4) the references to property shall be taken as references to property situated within England and Wales.

(6) Where the debtor is a relevant company, the foreign representative shall send notice of the making of the order to the registrar of companies before the end of the period of 5 business days beginning with the date of the order. The notice to the registrar of companies shall be in Form ML 7.

(7) The foreign representative shall advertise the making of the following orders once in the Gazette and once in such newspaper as he thinks most appropriate for ensuring that the making of the order comes to the notice of the debtor's creditors—

    (a) a recognition order;

    (b) an order confirming the status of a replacement foreign representative; and

    (c) a modification or termination order which modifies or terminates recognition of a foreign proceeding,

and the advertisement shall be in Form ML 8.

Adjournment of hearing; directions

27.—(1) This paragraph applies in any case where the court exercises its power to adjourn the hearing of the application.

(2) The court may at any time give such directions as it thinks fit as to—

    (a) service or notice of the application on or to any person, whether in connection with the venue of a resumed hearing or for any other purpose;

    (b) the procedure on the application;

    (c) the manner in which any evidence is to be adduced at a resumed hearing and in particular as to—

        (i)   the taking of evidence wholly or in part by affidavit or orally;

        (ii) the cross-examination on the hearing in court or in chambers, of any deponents to affidavits;

    (d) the matters to be dealt with in evidence.

PART 7

APPLICATIONS TO THE CHIEF LAND REGISTRAR

Applications to Chief Land Registrar following court orders

28.—(1) Where the court makes any order in proceedings under these Regulations which is capable of giving rise to an application or applications under the Land Registration Act 2002, the foreign representative shall, as soon as reasonably practicable after the making of the order or at the appropriate time, make the appropriate application or applications to the Chief Land Registrar.

(2) In sub-paragraph (1) an appropriate application is—

    (a) in any case where—

        (i)   a recognition order in respect of a foreign main proceeding or an order suspending the right to transfer, encumber or otherwise dispose of any assets of the debtor is made, and

        (ii) the debtor is the registered proprietor of a registered estate or registered charge and holds it for his sole benefit,

    an application under section 43 of the Land Registration Act 2002 for a restriction of the kind referred to in sub-paragraph (3) to be entered in the relevant registered title; and

    (b) in any other case, an application under the Land Registration Act 2002 for such an entry in the register as shall be necessary to reflect the effect of the court order under these Regulations.

(3) The restriction referred to in sub-paragraph (2)(a) is a restriction to the effect that no disposition of the registered estate or registered charge (as appropriate) by the registered proprietor of that estate or charge is to be completed by registration within the meaning of section 27 of the Land Registration Act 2002 except under a further order of the court.

PART 8

MISFEASANCE

Misfeasance by foreign representative

29.—(1) The court may examine the conduct of a person who—

    (a) is or purports to be the foreign representative in relation to a debtor; or

    (b) has been or has purported to be the foreign representative in relation to a debtor.

(2) An examination under this paragraph may be held only on the application of—

    (a) a British insolvency office-holder acting in relation to the debtor;

    (b) a creditor of the debtor; or

    (c) with the permission of the court, any other person who appears to have an interest justifying an application.

(3) An application under sub-paragraph (2) must allege that the foreign representative—

    (a) has misapplied or retained money or other property of the debtor;

    (b) has become accountable for money or other property of the debtor;

    (c) has breached a fiduciary or other duty in relation to the debtor; or

    (d) has been guilty of misfeasance.

(4) On an examination under this paragraph into a person's conduct the court may order him—

    (a) to repay, restore or account for money or property;

    (b) to pay interest;

    (c) to contribute a sum to the debtor's property by way of compensation for breach of duty or misfeasance.

(5) In sub-paragraph (3) "foreign representative" includes a person who purports or has purported to be a foreign representative in relation to a debtor.

PART 9

GENERAL PROVISION AS TO COURT PROCEDURE AND PRACTICE

Principal court rules and practice to apply with modifications

30.—(1) The CPR and the practice and procedure of the High Court (including any practice direction) shall apply to proceedings under these Regulations in the High Court with such modifications as may be necessary for the purpose of giving effect to the provisions of these Regulations and in the case of any conflict between any provision of the CPR and the provisions of these Regulations, the latter shall prevail.

(2) All proceedings under these Regulations shall be allocated to the multi-track for which CPR Part 29 (the multi-track) makes provision, and accordingly those provisions of the CPR which provide for allocation questionnaires and track allocation shall not apply.

Applications other than the principal applications—preliminary

31. Paragraphs 32 to 37 of this Part apply to any application made to the court under these Regulations, except any of the applications referred to in paragraph 18(1)(a).

Form and contents of application

32.—(1) Every application shall be in the form appropriate to the application concerned. Forms ML 4 and ML 5 shall be used for an originating application and an ordinary application respectively under these Regulations.

(2) Each application shall be in writing and shall state—

    (a)   the names of the parties;

    (b)   the nature of the relief or order applied for or the directions sought from the court;

    (c)   the names and addresses of the persons (if any) on whom it is intended to serve the application or that no person is intended to be served;

    (d)   where these Regulations require that notice of the application is to be given to specified persons, the names and addresses of all those persons (so far as known to the applicant); and

    (e)   the applicant's address for service.

(3) An originating application shall set out the grounds on which the applicant claims to be entitled to the relief or order sought.

(4) The application must be signed by the applicant if he is acting in person or, when he is not so acting, by or on behalf of his solicitor.

Filing and service of application

33.—(1) The application shall be filed in court, accompanied by one copy and a number of additional copies equal to the number of persons who are to be served with the application.

(2) Subject as follows in this paragraph and in paragraph 34, or unless the court otherwise orders, upon the presentation of the documents mentioned in sub-paragraph (1), the court shall fix a venue for the application to be heard.

(3) Unless the court otherwise directs, the applicant shall serve a sealed copy of the application, endorsed with the venue of the hearing, on the respondent named in the application (or on each respondent if more than one).

(4) The court may give any of the following directions—

    (a)   that the application be served upon persons other than those specified by the relevant provision of these Regulations;

    (b)   that the giving of notice to any person may be dispensed with;

    (c)   that notice be given in some way other than that specified in sub-paragraph (3).

(5) Subject to sub-paragraph (6), the application must be served at least 10 business days before the date fixed for the hearing.

(6) Where the case is one of urgency, the court may (without prejudice to its general power to extend or abridge time limits)—

    (a)   hear the application immediately, either with or without notice to, or the attendance of, other parties; or

    (b)   authorise a shorter period of service than that provided for by sub-paragraph (5);

and any such application may be heard on terms providing for the filing or service of documents, or the carrying out of other formalities, as the court thinks fit.

Other hearings *ex parte*

34.—(1) Where the relevant provisions of these Regulations do not require service of the application on, or notice of it to be given to, any person, the court may hear the application *ex parte*.

(2) Where the application is properly made *ex parte*, the court may hear it forthwith, without fixing a venue as required by paragraph 33(2).

(3) Alternatively, the court may fix a venue for the application to be heard, in which case paragraph 33 applies (so far as relevant).

Use of affidavit evidence

35.—(1) In any proceedings evidence may be given by affidavit unless the court otherwise directs; but the court may, on the application of any party, order the attendance for cross-examination of the person making the affidavit.

(2) Where, after such an order has been made, the person in question does not attend, his affidavit shall not be used in evidence without the permission of the court.

Filing and service of affidavits

36.—(1) Unless the court otherwise allows—

    (a) if the applicant intends to rely at the first hearing on affidavit evidence, he shall file the affidavit or affidavits (if more than one) in court and serve a copy or copies on the respondent, not less than 10 business days before the date fixed for the hearing; and

    (b) where a respondent to an application intends to oppose it and to rely for that purpose on affidavit evidence, he shall file the affidavit or affidavits (if more than one) in court and serve a copy or copies on the applicant, not less than 5 business days before the date fixed for the hearing.

(2) Any affidavit may be sworn by the applicant or by the respondent or by some other person possessing direct knowledge of the subject matter of the application.

Adjournment of hearings; directions

37. The court may adjourn the hearing of an application on such terms (if any) as it thinks fit and in the case of such an adjournment paragraph 27(2) shall apply.

Transfer of proceedings within the High Court

38.—(1) The High Court may, having regard to the criteria in CPR rule 30.3(2), order proceedings in the Royal Courts of Justice or a district registry, or any part of such proceedings (such as an application made in the proceedings), to be transferred—

    (a) from the Royal Courts of Justice to a district registry; or

    (b) from a district registry to the Royal Courts of Justice or to another district registry.

(2) The High Court may order proceedings before a district registry for the detailed assessment of costs to be transferred to another district registry if it is satisfied that the proceedings could be more conveniently or fairly taken in that other district registry.

(3) An application for an order under sub-paragraph (1) or (2) must, if the claim is proceeding in a district registry, be made to that registry.

(4) A transfer of proceedings under this paragraph may be ordered—

    (a) by the court of its own motion; or

    (b) on the application of a person appearing to the court to have an interest in the proceedings.

(5) Where the court orders proceedings to be transferred, the court from which they are to be transferred must give notice of the transfer to all the parties.

(6) An order made before the transfer of the proceedings shall not be affected by the order to transfer.

Transfer of proceedings—actions to avoid acts detrimental to creditors

39.—(1) If—

(a) in accordance with article 23(6) of the Model Law, the court grants a foreign representative permission to make an application in accordance with paragraph 1 of that article; and

(b) the relevant proceedings under British insolvency law taking place regarding the debtor are taking place in the county court, the court may also order those proceedings to be transferred to the High Court.

(2) Where the court makes an order transferring proceedings under sub-paragraph (1)—

(a) it shall send sealed copies of the order to the county court from which the proceedings are to be transferred, and to the official receivers attached to that court and the High Court respectively; and

(b) the county court shall send the file of the proceedings to the High Court.

(3) Following compliance with this paragraph, if the official receiver attached to the court to which the proceedings are transferred is not already, by virtue of directions given by the Secretary of State under section 399(6)(a) of the 1986 Act, the official receiver in relation to those proceedings, he becomes, in relation to those proceedings, the official receiver in place of the official receiver attached to the other court concerned.

Shorthand writers

40.—(1) The judge may in writing nominate one or more persons to be official short-hand writers to the court.

(2) The court may, at any time in the course of proceedings under these Regulations, appoint a shorthand writer to take down the evidence of a person examined in pursuance of a court order under article 19 or 21 of the Model Law.

(3) The remuneration of a shorthand writer appointed in proceedings under these Regulations shall be paid by the party at whose instance the appointment was made or otherwise as the court may direct.

(4) Any question arising as to the rates of remuneration payable under this paragraph shall be determined by the court in its discretion.

Enforcement procedures

41. In any proceedings under these Regulations, orders of the court may be enforced in the same manner as a judgment to the same effect.

Title of proceedings

42.—(1) Every proceeding under these Regulations shall, with any necessary additions, be intituled "IN THE MATTER OF . . . (naming the debtor to which the proceedings relate) AND IN THE MATTER OF THE CROSS-BORDER INSOLVENCY REGULATIONS 2006".

(2) Sub-paragraph (1) shall not apply in respect of any form prescribed under these Regulations.

Court records

43. The court shall keep records of all proceedings under these Regulations, and shall cause to be entered in the records the taking of any step in the proceedings, and such decisions of the court in relation thereto, as the court thinks fit.

Inspection of records

44.—(1) Subject as follows, the court's records of proceedings under these Regulations shall be open to inspection by any person.

(2) If in the case of a person applying to inspect the records the Registrar is not satisfied as to the propriety of the purpose for which inspection is required, he may refuse to allow it. That person may then apply forthwith and ex parte to the judge, who may refuse the inspection or allow it on such terms as he thinks fit.

(3) The decision of the judge under sub-paragraph (2) is final.

File of court proceedings

45.—(1) In respect of all proceedings under these Regulations, the court shall open and maintain a file for each case; and (subject to directions of the Registrar) all documents relating to such proceedings shall be placed on the relevant file.

(2) No proceedings under these Regulations shall be filed in the Central Office of the High Court.

Right to inspect the file

46.—(1) In the case of any proceedings under these Regulations, the following have the right, at all reasonable times, to inspect the court's file of the proceedings—

    (a)   the Secretary of State;

    (b)   the person who is the foreign representative in relation to the proceedings;

    (c)   if a foreign representative has been appointed in any other foreign proceeding regarding the debtor to which the proceedings under these Regulations relate, that person;

    (d)   if a British insolvency office-holder is acting in relation to the debtor to which the proceedings under these Regulations relate, that person;

    (e)   any person stating himself in writing to be a creditor of the debtor to which the proceedings under these Regulations relate;

    (f)   if a member State liquidator has been appointed in relation to the debtor to which the proceedings under these Regulations relate, that person; and

    (g)   the debtor to which the proceedings under these Regulations relate, or, if that debtor is a company, corporation or partnership, every person who is, or at any time has been—

        (i)   a director or officer of the debtor;

        (ii)   a member of the debtor; or

        (iii)   where applicable, a person registered under Part 23 of the Companies Act 1985 as authorised to represent the debtor in respect of its business in England and Wales.

(2) The right of inspection conferred as above on any person may be exercised on his behalf by a person properly authorised by him.

(3) Any person may, by leave of the court, inspect the file.

(4) The right of inspection conferred by this paragraph is not exercisable in the case of documents, or parts of documents, as to which the court directs (either generally or specially) that they are not to be made open to inspection without the court's permission.

An application for a direction of the court under this sub-paragraph may be made by the foreign representative or by any party appearing to the court to have an interest.

(5) If, for the purpose of powers conferred by the 1986 Act or the Rules, the Secretary of State or the official receiver wishes to inspect the file of any proceedings under these Regulations, and requests the transmission of the file, the court shall comply with such request (unless the file is for the time being in use for the court's purposes).

(6) Paragraph 44(2) and (3) apply in respect of the court's file of any proceedings under these Regulations as they apply in respect of court records.

(7) Where these Regulations confer a right for any person to inspect documents on the court's file of proceedings, the right includes that of taking copies of those documents on payment of the fee chargeable under any order made under section 92 of the Courts Act 2003.

Copies of court orders

47.—(1) In any proceedings under these Regulations, any person who under paragraph 46 has a right to inspect documents on the court file also has the right to require the foreign representative in relation to those proceedings to furnish him with a copy of any court order in the proceedings.

(2) Sub-paragraph (1) does not apply if a copy of the court order has been served on that person or notice of the making of the order has been given to that person under other provisions of these Regulations.

Filing of Gazette notices and advertisements

48.—(1) In any court in which proceedings under these Regulations are pending, an officer of the court shall file a copy of every issue of the Gazette which contains an advertisement relating to those proceedings.

(2) Where there appears in a newspaper an advertisement relating to proceedings under these Regulations pending in any court, the person inserting the advertisement shall file a copy of it in that court.

The copy of the advertisement shall be accompanied by, or have endorsed on it, such particulars as are necessary to identify the proceedings and the date of the advertisement's appearance.

(3) An officer of any court in which proceedings under these Regulations are pending shall from time to time file a memorandum giving the dates of, and other particulars relating to, any notice published in the Gazette, and any newspaper advertisements, which relate to proceedings so pending.

The officer's memorandum is prima facie evidence that any notice or advertisement mentioned in it was duly inserted in the issue of the newspaper or the Gazette which is specified in the memorandum.

Persons incapable of managing their affairs—introductory

49.—(1) Paragraphs 50 to 52 apply where in proceedings under these Regulations it appears to the court that a person affected by the proceedings is one who is incapable of managing and administering his property and affairs either—

(a) by reason of mental disorder within the meaning of the Mental Health Act 1983; or

(b) due to physical affliction or disability.

(2) The person concerned is referred to as "the incapacitated person".

Appointment of another person to act

50.—(1) The court may appoint such person as it thinks fit to appear for, represent or act for the incapacitated person.

(2) The appointment may be made either generally or for the purpose of any particular application or proceeding, or for the exercise of particular rights or powers which the incapacitated person might have exercised but for his incapacity.

(3) The court may make the appointment either of its own motion or on application by—

(a) a person who has been appointed by a court in the United Kingdom or elsewhere to manage the affairs of, or to represent, the incapacitated person; or

(b) any relative or friend of the incapacitated person who appears to the court to be a proper person to make the application; or

(c) in any case where the incapacitated person is the debtor, the foreign representative.

(4) Application under sub-paragraph (3) may be made ex parte; but the court may require such notice of the application as it thinks necessary to be given to the person alleged to be incapacitated, or any other person, and may adjourn the hearing of the application to enable the notice to be given.

Affidavit in support of application

51. An application under paragraph 50(3) shall be supported by an affidavit of a registered medical practitioner as to the mental or physical condition of the incapacitated person.

Service of notices following appointment

52. Any notice served on, or sent to, a person appointed under paragraph 50 has the same effect as if it had been served on, or given to, the incapacitated person.

Rights of audience

53. Rights of audience in proceedings under these Regulations are the same as obtain in proceedings under British insolvency law.

Right of attendance

54.—(1) Subject as follows, in proceedings under these Regulations, any person stating himself in writing, in records kept by the court for that purpose, to be a creditor of the debtor to which the proceedings relate, is entitled at his own cost, to attend in court or in chambers at any stage of the proceedings.

(2) Attendance may be by the person himself, or his solicitor.

(3) A person so entitled may request the court in writing to give him notice of any step in the proceedings; and, subject to his paying the costs involved and keeping the court informed as to his address, the court shall comply with the request.

(4) If the court is satisfied that the exercise by a person of his rights under this paragraph has given rise to costs for the estate of the debtor which would not otherwise have been incurred and ought not, in the circumstances, to fall on that estate, it may direct that the costs be paid by the person concerned, to an amount specified.

The rights of that person under this paragraph shall be in abeyance so long as those costs are not paid.

(5) The court may appoint one or more persons to represent the creditors of the debtor to have the rights conferred by this paragraph, instead of the rights being exercised by any or all of them individually.

If two or more persons are appointed under this paragraph to represent the same interest, they must (if at all) instruct the same solicitor.

Right of attendance for member State liquidator

55. For the purposes of paragraph 54(1), a member State liquidator appointed in relation to a debtor subject to proceedings under these Regulations shall be deemed to be a creditor.

British insolvency office-holder's solicitor

56. Where in any proceedings the attendance of the British insolvency office-holder's solicitor is required, whether in court or in chambers, the British insolvency office-holder himself need not attend, unless directed by the court.

Formal defects

57. No proceedings under these Regulations shall be invalidated by any formal defect or by any irregularity, unless the court before which objection is made considers that substantial injustice has been caused by the defect or irregularity, and that the injustice cannot be remedied by any order of the court.

Restriction on concurrent proceedings and remedies

58. Where in proceedings under these Regulations the court makes an order staying any action, execution or other legal process against the property of a debtor, service of the order may be effected by sending a sealed copy of the order to whatever is the address for service of the claimant or other party having the carriage of the proceedings to be stayed.

Affidavits

59.—(1) Where in proceedings under these Regulations, an affidavit is made by any British insolvency office-holder acting in relation to the debtor, he shall state the capacity in which he makes it, the position which he holds and the address at which he works.

(2) Any officer of the court duly authorised in that behalf, may take affidavits and declarations.

(3) Subject to sub-paragraph (4), where these Regulations provide for the use of an affidavit, a witness statement verified by a statement of truth may be used as an alternative.

(4) Sub-paragraph (3) does not apply to paragraphs 4 (affidavit in support of recognition application), 7 (affidavit in support of interim relief application), 10 (affidavit in support of article 21 relief application), 13 (affidavit in support of application regarding status of replacement foreign representative) and 16 (affidavit in support of review application).

Security in court

60.—(1) Where security has to be given to the court (otherwise than in relation to costs), it may be given by guarantee, bond or the payment of money into court.

(2) A person proposing to give a bond as security shall give notice to the party in whose favour the security is required, and to the court, naming those who are to be sureties to the bond.

(3) The court shall forthwith give notice to the parties concerned of a venue for the execution of the bond and the making of any objection to the sureties.

(4) The sureties shall make an affidavit of their sufficiency (unless dispensed with by the party in whose favour the security is required) and shall, if required by the court, attend the court to be cross-examined.

Further information and disclosure

61.—(1) Any party to proceedings under these Regulations may apply to the court for an order—

  (a) that any other party—

     (i) clarify any matter which is in dispute in the proceedings; or
     (ii) give additional information in relation to any such matter, in accordance with CPR Part 18 (further information); or

  (b) to obtain disclosure from any other party in accordance with CPR Part 31 (disclosure and inspection of documents).

(2) An application under this paragraph may be made without notice being served on any other party.

Office copies of documents

62. (1) Any person who has under these Regulations the right to inspect the court file of proceedings may require the court to provide him with an office copy of any document from the file.

(2) A person's right under this paragraph may be exercised on his behalf by his solicitor.

(3) An office copy provided by the court under this paragraph shall be in such form as the Registrar thinks appropriate, and shall bear the court's seal.

"The court"

63.—(1) Anything to be done in proceedings under these Regulations by, to or before the court may be done by, to or before a judge of the High Court or a Registrar.

(2) Where these Regulations require or permit the court to perform an act of a formal or administrative character, that act may be performed by a court officer.

PART 10

COSTS AND DETAILED ASSESSMENT

Requirement to assess costs by the detailed procedure

64. In any proceedings before the court, the court may order costs to be decided by detailed assessment.

Costs of officers charged with execution of writs or other process

65.—(1) Where by virtue of article 20 of the Model Law or a court order under article 19 or 21 of the Model Law an enforcement officer, or other officer, charged with execution of the writ or other process—

(a) is required to deliver up goods or money; or
(b) has deducted costs from the proceeds of an execution or money paid to him,

the foreign representative may require in writing that the amount of the enforcement officer's or other officer's bill of costs be decided by detailed assessment.

(2) Where such a requirement is made, if the enforcement officer or other officer does not commence detailed assessment proceedings within 3 months of the requirement under sub-paragraph (1), or within such further time as the court, on application, may permit, any claim by the enforcement officer or other officer in respect of his costs is forfeited by such failure to commence proceedings.

(3) Where, in the case of a deduction of costs by the enforcement officer or other officer, any amount deducted is disallowed at the conclusion of the detailed assessment proceedings, the enforcement officer or other officer shall forthwith pay a sum equal to that disallowed to the foreign representative for the benefit of the debtor.

Final costs certificate

66.—(1) A final costs certificate of the costs officer is final and conclusive as to all matters which have not been objected to in the manner provided for under the rules of the court.

(2) Where it is proved to the satisfaction of a costs officer that a final costs certificate has been lost or destroyed, he may issue a duplicate.

PART 11

APPEALS IN PROCEEDINGS UNDER THESE REGULATIONS

Appeals from court orders

67.—(1) An appeal from a decision of a Registrar of the High Court in proceedings under these Regulations lies to a single judge of the High Court; and an appeal from a decision of that judge on such an appeal lies, with the permission of the Court of Appeal, to the Court of Appeal.

(2) An appeal from a decision of a judge of the High Court in proceedings under these Regulations which is not a decision on an appeal made to him under sub-paragraph (1) lies, with the permission of that judge or the Court of Appeal, to the Court of Appeal.

Procedure on appeals

68.—(1) Subject as follows, CPR Part 52 (appeals to the Court of Appeal) and its practice direction apply to appeals in proceedings under these Regulations.

(2) The provisions of Part 4 of the practice direction on Insolvency Proceedings supporting CPR Part 49 relating to first appeals (as defined in that Part) apply in relation to any appeal to a single judge of the High Court under paragraph 67, with any necessary modifications.

(3) In proceedings under these Regulations, the procedure under CPR Part 52 is by ordinary application and not by appeal notice.

PART 12

GENERAL

Notices

69.—(1) All notices required or authorised by or under these Regulations to be given must be in writing, unless it is otherwise provided, or the court allows the notice to be given in some other way.

(2) Where in proceedings under these Regulations a notice is required to be sent or given by any person, the sending or giving of it may be proved by means of a certificate by that person that he posted the notice, or instructed another person (naming him) to do so.

(3) A certificate under this paragraph may be endorsed on a copy or specimen of the notice to which it relates.

"Give notice" etc.

70.—(1) A reference in these Regulations to giving notice, or to delivering, sending or serving any document, means that the notice or document may be sent by post.

(2) Subject to paragraph 75, any form of post may be used.

(3) Personal service of a document is permissible in all cases.

(4) Notice of the venue fixed for an application may be given by service of the sealed copy of the application under paragraph 33(3).

Notice, etc. to solicitors

71. Where in proceedings under these Regulations a notice or other document is required or authorised to be given to a person, it may, if he has indicated that his solicitor is authorised to accept service on his behalf, be given instead to the solicitor.

Notice to joint British insolvency office-holders

72. Where two or more persons are acting jointly as the British insolvency office-holder in proceedings under British insolvency law, delivery of a document to one of them is to be treated as delivery to them all.

Forms for use in proceedings under these Regulations

73.—(1) The forms contained in Schedule 5 to these Regulations shall be used in, and in connection with, proceedings under these Regulations.

(2) The forms shall be used with such variations, if any, as the circumstances may require.

Time limits

74.—(1) The provisions of CPR Rule 2.8 (time) apply, as regards computation of time, to anything required or authorised to be done by these Regulations.

(2) The provisions of CPR rule 3.1(2)(a) (the court's general powers of management) apply so as to enable the court to extend or shorten the time for compliance with anything required or authorised to be done by these Regulations.

Service by post

75.—(1) For a document to be properly served by post, it must be contained in an envelope addressed to the person on whom service is to be effected, and pre-paid for first class post.

(2) A document to be served by post may be sent to the last known address of the person to be served.

(3) Where first class post is used, the document is treated as served on the second business day after the date of posting, unless the contrary is shown.

(4) The date of posting is presumed, unless the contrary is shown, to be the date shown in the postmark on the envelope in which the document is contained.

General provisions as to service and notice

76. Subject to paragraphs 22, 75 and 77, CPR Part 6 (service of documents) applies as regards any matter relating to the service of documents and the giving of notice in proceedings under these Regulations.

Service outside the jurisdiction

77.—(1) Sections III and IV of CPR Part 6 (service out of the jurisdiction and service of process of foreign court) do not apply in proceedings under these Regulations.

(2) Where for the purposes of proceedings under these Regulations any process or order of the court, or other document, is required to be served on a person who is not in England and Wales, the court may order service to be effected within such time, on such person, at such place and in such manner as it thinks fit, and may also require such proof of service as it thinks fit.

(3) An application under this paragraph shall be supported by an affidavit stating—

    (a) the grounds on which the application is made; and

    (b) in what place or country the person to be served is, or probably may be found.

False claim of status as creditor

78.—(1) Rule 12.18 (false claim of status as creditor, etc) shall apply with any necessary modifications in any case where a person falsely claims the status of a creditor of a debtor, with the intention of obtaining a sight of documents whether on the court's file or in the hands of the foreign representative or other person, which he has not under these Regulations any right to inspect.

(2) Rule 21.21 and Schedule 5 of the Rules shall apply to an offence under Rule 12.18 as applied by sub-paragraph (1) as they apply to an offence under Rule 12.18.

The Gazette

79.—(1) A copy of the Gazette containing any notice required by these Regulations to be gazetted is evidence of any fact stated in the notice.

(2) In the case of an order of the court notice of which is required by these Regulations to be gazetted, a copy of the Gazette containing the notice may in any proceedings be produced as conclusive evidence that the order was made on the date specified in the notice.

SCHEDULE 3   Regulation 5 **A2–052**

PROCEDURAL MATTERS IN SCOTLAND

PART 1

Interpretation

1.—(1) In this Schedule—

"the 1986 Act" means the Insolvency Act 1986;

"article 21 remedy application" means an application to the court by a foreign representative under article 21(1) or (2) of the Model Law for remedy;

"business day" means any day other than a Saturday, a Sunday, Christmas Day, Good Friday or a day which is a bank holiday in Scotland under or by virtue of the Banking and Financial Dealings Act 1971;

"the Gazette" means the Edinburgh Gazette;

"main proceedings" means proceedings opened in accordance with Article 3(1) of the EC Insolvency Regulation and falling within the definition of insolvency proceedings in Article 2(a) of the EC Insolvency Regulation;

"member State liquidator" means a person falling within the definition of liquidator in Article 2(b) of the EC Insolvency Regulation appointed in proceedings to which it applies in a member State other than the United Kingdom;

"the Model Law" means the UNCITRAL Model Law as set out in Schedule 1 to these Regulations;

"modification or termination order" means an order by the court pursuant to its powers under the Model Law modifying or terminating recognition of a foreign proceeding, the sist, restraint or suspension referred to in article 20(1) or any part of it or any remedy granted under article 19 or 21 of the Model Law;

"recognition application" means an application to the court by a foreign representative in accordance with article 15 of the Model Law for an order recognising the foreign proceeding in which he has been appointed;

"recognition order" means an order by the court recognising a proceeding the subject of a recognition application as a foreign main proceeding or foreign non-main proceeding, as appropriate;

"relevant company" means a company within the meaning of section 735(1) of the Companies Act 1985 or an unregistered company within the meaning of Part 5 of the 1986 Act which is subject to a requirement imposed by virtue of section 690A, 691(1) or 718 of the Companies Act 1985;

"review application" means an application to the court for a modification or termination order.

(2) Expressions defined in the Model Law have the same meaning when used in this Schedule.

(3) References in this Schedule to a debtor who is of interest to the Financial Services Authority are references to a debtor who—

(a) is, or has been, an authorised person within the meaning of section 31 of the Financial Services and Markets Act 2000 (authorised persons);

(b) is, or has been, an appointed representative within the meaning of section 39 (exemption of appointed representatives) of that Act; or

(c) is carrying, or has carried on, a regulated activity in contravention of the general prohibition.

(4) In sub-paragraph (3) "the general prohibition" has the meaning given by section 19 of the Financial Services and Markets Act 2000 and the reference to a "regulated activity" must be construed in accordance with—

    (a)   section 22 of that Act (classes of regulated activity and categories of investment);

    (b)   any relevant order under that section; and

    (c)   Schedule 2 to that Act (regulated activities).

(5) References in this Schedule to a numbered form are to the form that bears that number in Schedule 5.

PART 2

THE FOREIGN REPRESENTATIVE

Application for confirmation of status of replacement foreign representative

2.—(1) This paragraph applies where following the making of a recognition order the foreign representative dies or for any other reason ceases to be the foreign representative in the foreign proceedings in relation to the debtor.

(2) In this paragraph "the former foreign representative" means the foreign representative referred to in sub-paragraph (1).

(3) If a person has succeeded the former foreign representative or is otherwise holding office as foreign representative in the foreign proceeding in relation to the debtor, that person may apply to the court for an order confirming his status as replacement foreign representative for the purpose of proceedings under these Regulations.

(4) If the court dismisses an application under sub-paragraph (3) then it may also, if it thinks fit, make an order terminating recognition of the foreign proceeding and—

    (a)   such an order may include such provision as the court thinks fit with respect to matters arising in connection with the termination; and

    (b)   paragraph 5 shall not apply to such an order.

Misfeasance by a foreign representative

3.—(1) The court may examine the conduct of a person who—

    (a)   is or purports to be the foreign representative in relation to a debtor, or

    (b)   has been or has purported to be the foreign representative in relation to a debtor.

(2) An examination under this paragraph may be held only on the application of—

    (a)   a British insolvency office-holder acting in relation to the debtor,

    (b)   a creditor of the debtor, or

    (c)   with the permission of the court, any other person who appears to have an interest justifying an application.

(3) An application under sub-paragraph (2) must allege that the foreign representative—

    (a)   has misapplied or retained money or other property of the debtor,

    (b)   has become accountable for money or other property of the debtor,

    (c)   has breached a fiduciary duty or other duty in relation to the debtor, or

    (d)   has been guilty of misfeasance.

(4) On an examination under this paragraph into a person's conduct the court may order him—

    (a)   to repay, restore or account for money or property;

    (b)   to pay interest;

    (c)   to contribute a sum to the debtor's property by way of compensation for breach of duty or misfeasance.

(5) In sub-paragraph (3), "foreign representative" includes a person who purports or has purported to be a foreign representative in relation to a debtor.

PART 3

COURT PROCEDURE AND PRACTICE

Preliminary and interpretation

4.—(1) This Part applies to—

(a)   any of the following applications made to the court under these Regulations—

  (i)   a recognition application;
  (ii)   an article 21 remedy application;
  (iii)   an application under paragraph 2(3) for an order confirming the status of a replacement foreign representative;
  (iv)   a review application; and

(b)   any of the following orders made by the court under these Regulations—

  (i)   a recognition order;
  (ii)   an order granting interim remedy under article 19 of the Model Law;
  (iii)   an order granting remedy under article 21 of the Model Law;
  (iv)   an order confirming the status of a replacement foreign representative; or
  (v)   a modification or termination order.

Reviews of court orders—where court makes order of its own motion

5.—(1) The court shall not of its own motion make a modification or termination order unless the foreign representative and the debtor have either—

(a)   had an opportunity of being heard on the question, or
(b)   consented in writing to such an order.

(2) If the court makes a modification or termination order, the order may include such provision as the court thinks fit with respect to matters arising in connection with the modification or termination.

The hearing

6.—(1) At the hearing of the application, the applicant and any of the following persons (not being the applicant) may appear or be represented—

(a)   the foreign representative;
(b)   the debtor and, in the case of any debtor other than an individual, any one or more directors or other officers of the debtor, including—

  (i)   where applicable, any person registered under Part 23 of the Companies Act 1985 as authorised to represent the debtor in respect of its business in Scotland;
  (ii)   in the case of a debtor which is a partnership, any person who is a member of the partnership;

(c)   if a British insolvency office-holder is acting in relation to the debtor, that person;
(d)   if any person has been appointed an administrative receiver of the debtor or as a receiver or manager of the property of the debtor, that person;
(e)   if a member State liquidator has been appointed in main proceedings in relation to the debtor, that person;
(f)   if a foreign representative has been appointed in any other foreign proceeding regarding the debtor, that person;

    (g)   any person who has presented a petition for the winding up or sequestration of the debtor in Scotland;

    (h)   any person who is or may be entitled to appoint an administrator of the debtor under paragraph 14 of Schedule B1 to the 1986 Act (appointment of administrator by holder of qualifying floating charge);

    (i)   if the debtor is a debtor who is of interest to the Financial Services Authority, that Authority; and

    (j)   with the permission of the court, any other person who appears to have an interest justifying his appearance.

Notification and advertisement of order

7.—(1) This paragraph applies where the court makes any of the orders referred to in paragraph 4(1)(b).

(2) The foreign representative shall send a certified copy of the interlocutor as soon as reasonably practicable to the debtor.

(3) The foreign representative shall, as soon as reasonably practicable after the date of the order, give notice of the making of the order—

    (a)   if a British insolvency office-holder is acting in relation to the debtor, to him;

    (b)   if any person has been appointed an administrative receiver of the debtor or, to the knowledge of the foreign representative, as a receiver or manager of the property of the debtor, to him;

    (c)   if a member State liquidator has been appointed in main proceedings in relation to the debtor, to him;

    (d)   if to his knowledge a foreign representative has been appointed in any other foreign proceeding regarding the debtor, that person;

    (e)   if there is pending in Scotland a petition for the winding up or sequestration of the debtor, to the petitioner;

    (f)   to any person who to his knowledge is or may be entitled to appoint an administrator of the debtor under paragraph 14 of Schedule B1 to the 1986 Act (appointment of administrator by holder of qualifying floating charge);

    (g)   if the debtor is a debtor who is of interest to the Financial Services Authority, to that Authority; and

    (h)   to such persons as the court may direct.

(4) Where the debtor is a relevant company, the foreign representative shall send notice of the making of the order to the registrar of companies before the end of the period of 5 business days beginning with the date of the order. The notice to the registrar of companies shall be in Form ML 7.

(5) The foreign representative shall advertise the making of the following orders once in the Gazette and once in such newspaper as he thinks most appropriate for ensuring that the making of the order comes to the notice of the debtor's creditors—

    (a)   a recognition order,

    (b)   an order confirming the status of a replacement foreign representative, and

    (c)   a modification or termination order which modifies or terminates recognition of a foreign proceeding,

and the advertisement shall be in Form ML 8.

Registration of court order

8.—(1) Where the court makes a recognition order in respect of a foreign main proceeding or an order suspending the right to transfer, encumber or otherwise dispose of any assets of the debtor being heritable property, the clerk of the court shall send forthwith a certified copy of the order to the keeper of the register of inhibitions and adjudications for recording in that register.

(2) Recording under sub-paragraph (1) or (3) shall have the effect as from the date of the order of an inhibition and of a citation in an adjudication of the debtor's heritable estate at the instance of the foreign representative.

(3) Where the court makes a modification or termination order, the clerk of the court shall send forthwith a certified copy of the order to the keeper of the register of inhibitions and adjudications for recording in that register.

(4) The effect mentioned in sub-paragraph (2) shall expire—

(a) on the recording of a modification or termination order under sub-paragraph (3); or

(b) subject to sub-paragraph (5), if the effect has not expired by virtue of paragraph (a), at the end of the period of 3 years beginning with the date of the order.

(5) The foreign representative may, if recognition of the foreign proceeding has not been modified or terminated by the court pursuant to its powers under the Model Law, before the end of the period of 3 years mentioned in sub-paragraph (4)(b), send a memorandum in a form prescribed by the Court of Session by act of sederunt to the keeper of the register of inhibitions and adjudications for recording in that register, and such recording shall renew the effect mentioned in sub-paragraph (2); and thereafter the said effect shall continue to be preserved only if such memorandum is so recorded before the expiry of every subsequent period of 3 years.

Right to inspect court process

9.—(1) In the case of any proceedings under these Regulations, the following have the right, at all reasonable times, to inspect the court process of the proceedings—

(a) the Secretary of State;

(b) the person who is the foreign representative in relation to the proceedings;

(c) if a foreign representative has been appointed in any other foreign proceeding regarding the debtor, that person;

(d) if a British insolvency office-holder is acting in relation to the debtor, that person;

(e) any person stating himself in writing to be a creditor of the debtor to which the proceedings under these Regulations relate;

(f) if a member State liquidator has been appointed in relation to a debtor which is subject to proceedings under these Regulations, that person; and

(g) the debtor to which the proceedings under these Regulations relate, or, if that debtor is a company, corporation or partnership, every person who is, or at any time has been—

  (i) a director or officer of the debtor,

  (ii) a member of the debtor, or

  (iii) where applicable, a person registered under Part 23 of the Companies Act 1985 as authorised to represent the debtor in respect of its business in Scotland.

(2) The right of inspection conferred as above on any person may be exercised on his behalf by a person properly authorised by him.

Copies of court orders

10.—(1) In any proceedings under these Regulations, any person who under paragraph 9 has a right to inspect documents in the court process also has the right to require the foreign representative in relation to those proceedings to furnish him with a copy of any court order in the proceedings.

(2) Sub-paragraph (1) does not apply if a copy of the court order has been served on that person or notice of the making of the order has been given to that person under other provisions of these Regulations.

Transfer of proceedings—actions to avoid acts detrimental to creditors

11. If, in accordance with article 23(6) of the Model Law, the court grants a foreign representative permission to make an application in accordance with paragraph (1) of that article, it may also order the relevant proceedings under British insolvency law taking place regarding the debtor to be transferred to the Court of Session if those proceedings are taking place in Scotland and are not already in that court.

PART 3

GENERAL

Giving of notices, etc

12.—(1) All notices required or authorised by or under these Regulations to be given, sent or delivered must be in writing, unless it is otherwise provided, or the court allows the notice to be sent or given in some other way.

(2) Any reference in these Regulations to giving, sending or delivering a notice or any such document means, without prejudice to any other way and unless it is otherwise provided, that the notice or document may be sent by post, and that, subject to paragraph 13, any form of post may be used. Personal service of the notice or document is permissible in all cases.

(3) Where under these Regulations a notice or other document is required or authorised to be given, sent or delivered by a person ("the sender") to another ("the recipient"), it may be given, sent or delivered by any person duly authorised by the sender to do so to any person duly authorised by the recipient to receive or accept it.

(4) Where two or more persons are acting jointly as the British insolvency office-holder in proceedings under British insolvency law, the giving, sending or delivering of a notice or document to one of them is to be treated as the giving, sending or delivering of a notice or document to each or all.

Sending by post

13.—(1) For a document to be properly sent by post, it must be contained in an envelope addressed to the person to whom it is to be sent, and pre-paid for either first or second class post.

(2) Any document to be sent by post may be sent to the last known address of the person to whom the document is to be sent.

(3) Where first class post is used, the document is to be deemed to be received on the second business day after the date of posting, unless the contrary is shown.

(4) Where second class post is used, the document is to be deemed to be received on the fourth business day after the date of posting, unless the contrary is shown.

Certificate of giving notice, etc

14.—(1) Where in any proceedings under these Regulations a notice or document is required to be given, sent or delivered by any person, the date of giving, sending or delivery of it may be proved by means of a certificate by that person that he gave, posted or otherwise sent or delivered the notice or document on the date stated in the certificate, or that he instructed another person (naming him) to do so.

(2) A certificate under this paragraph may be endorsed on a copy of the notice to which it relates.

(3) A certificate purporting to be signed by or on behalf of the person mentioned in sub-paragraph (1) shall be deemed, unless the contrary is shown, to be sufficient evidence of the matters stated therein.

Forms for use in proceedings under these Regulations

15.—(1) Forms ML 7 and ML 8 contained in Schedule 5 to these Regulations shall be used in, and in connection with, proceedings under these Regulations.

(2) The forms shall be used with such variations, if any, as the circumstances may require.

SCHEDULE 4   Regulation 6   **A2–053**

NOTICES DELIVERED TO THE REGISTRAR OF COMPANIES

Interpretation

1.—(1) In this Schedule—

"the 1985 Act" means the Companies Act 1985;
"electronic communication" means the same as in the Electronic Communications Act 2000;
"Model Law notice" means a notice delivered to the registrar of companies under paragraph 26(6) of Schedule 2 or paragraph 7(4) of Schedule 3.

(2) Expressions defined in the Model Law or Schedule 2 or 3, as appropriate, have the same meaning when used in this Schedule.

(3) References in this Schedule to delivering a notice include sending, forwarding, producing or giving it.

Functions of the registrar of companies

2.—(1) Where a Model Law notice is delivered to the registrar of companies in respect of a relevant company, the registrar shall enter a note in the register relating to that company.

(2) The note referred to in sub-paragraph (1) shall contain the following particulars, in each case as stated in the notice delivered to the registrar—

    (a)   brief details of the court order made;
    (b)   the date of the court order; and
    (c)   the name and address for service of the person who is the foreign representative in relation to the company.

Registrar of companies to whom notices to be delivered

3.—(1) References in Schedules 2 and 3 to the registrar of companies in relation to a relevant company shall be construed in accordance with the following provisions.

(2) The notices which a relevant company is required to deliver to the registrar of companies shall be delivered—

    (a)   to the registrar for England and Wales if the company has a relevant presence in England and Wales, and
    (b)   to the registrar for Scotland if the company has a relevant presence in Scotland, and if the relevant company has a relevant presence in both parts of Great Britain, the notices shall be delivered to both registrars.

(3) For the purposes of this paragraph a "relevant presence" means—

    (a)   in the case of a company within the meaning of section 735(1) of the 1985 Act, its registered office,
    (b)   in the case of an unregistered company within the meaning of Part 5 of the 1986 Act which is subject to a requirement imposed by virtue of section 690A of the 1985 Act, a branch,

(c)   in the case of an unregistered company within the meaning of Part 5 of the 1986 Act which is subject to a requirement imposed by virtue of section 691(1) of the 1985 Act, an established place of business, and

(d)   in the case of an unregistered company within the meaning of Part 5 of the 1986 Act which is subject to a requirement imposed by virtue of section 718 of the 1985 Act, a principal place of business.

Delivery to registrar of notices

4.—(1) Electronic communications may be used for the delivery of any Model Law notice, provided that such delivery is in such form and manner as is directed by the registrar.

(2) Where the Model Law notice is required to be signed, it shall instead be authenticated in such manner as is directed by the registrar.

(3) If a Model Law notice is delivered to the registrar which does not comply with the requirements of these Regulations, he may serve on the person by whom the notice was delivered (or, if there are two or more such persons, on any of them) a notice (a non-compliance notice) indicating the respect in which the Model Law notice does not comply.

(4) Where the registrar serves a non-compliance notice, then, unless a replacement Model Law notice—

(a)   is delivered to him within 14 days after the service of the non-compliance notice, and

(b)   complies with the requirements of these Regulations or is not rejected by him for failure to comply with those requirements,

the original Model Law notice shall be deemed not to have been delivered to him.

Enforcement of foreign representative's duty to give notice to registrar

5.—(1) If a foreign representative, having made default in complying with paragraph 26(6) of Schedule 2 or paragraph 7(4) of Schedule 3 fails to make good the default within 14 days after the service of a notice on the foreign representative requiring him to do so, the court may, on an application made to it by any creditor, member, director or other officer of the debtor or by the registrar of companies, make an order directing the foreign representative to make good the default within such time as may be specified in the order.

(2) The court's order may provide that all costs of and incidental to the application shall be borne by the foreign representative.

Rectification of the register under court order

6.—(1) The registrar shall remove from the register any note, or part of a note—

(a)   that relates to or is derived from a court order that the court has declared to be invalid or ineffective, or

(b)   that the court declares to be factually inaccurate or derived from something that is factually inaccurate or forged,

and that the court directs should be removed from the register.

(2) The court order must specify what is to be removed from the register and indicate where on the register it is and the registrar shall carry out his duty under sub-paragraph (1) within a reasonable time of receipt by him of the relevant court order.

SCHEDULE 5   Schedule 2, paragraph 73   **A2–054**
                    and Schedule 3, paragraph 15

FORMS

The forms are not reproduced in this title.

The Transfer of Undertakings (Protection of Employment) (Consequential Amendments) Regulations 2006

(SI 2006/2405)

The Secretary of State makes the following Regulations in exercise of the powers conferred upon him by section 2(2) of the European Communities Act 1972 (being a Minister designated for the purposes of that section in relation to rights and obligations relating to employers and employees on the transfer or merger of undertakings, businesses or parts of businesses) and section 38 of the Employment Relations Act 1999.

A2–0

Citation, commencement and extent

1.—(1) These Regulations may be cited as the Transfer of Undertakings (Protection of Employment) Regulations 2006.

A2–0

(2) These Regulations shall come into force on 1 October 2006.

(3) These Regulations extend to Great Britain only.

Consequential Amendments

2. In regulation 20 of the Information and Consultation of Employees Regulations 2004 for "regulations 10 to 12 of the Transfer of Undertakings (Protection of Employment) Regulations 1981" in paragraph (1)(c)(ii) there shall be substituted "regulations 13 to 16 of the Transfer of Undertakings (Protection of Employment) Regulations 2006" and for "regulation 10" in paragraph (5)(b) there shall be substituted "regulation 13".

A2–0

3. In paragraph 22(5)(d) of Schedule 1 of the Employment Tribunals (Constitution and Rules of Procedure) Regulations 2004 for "regulation 11(5) of the Transfer of Undertakings (Protection of Employment) Regulations 1981" there shall be substituted "regulation 15(10) of the Transfer of Undertakings (Protection of Employment) Regulations 2006".

4. In paragraph 147(v) and (vi) of the schedule of the ACAS Arbitration Scheme (Great Britain) Order 2004 for "regulations 10 and 11 of the Transfer of Undertakings (Protection of Employment) Regulations 1981" there shall be substituted "regulations 13, 15 and 16 of the Transfer of Undertakings (Protection of Employment) Regulations 2006".

5. Regulations 3 and 4 shall not apply where the Transfer of Undertakings (Protection of Employment) Regulations 1981 continue to have application by virtue of regulation 21 of the Transfer of Undertakings (Protection of Employment) Regulations 2006.

APPENDIX 3

Council regulation (EC) No 1346/2000 of 29 May 2000 on insolvency proceedings

Including amendments made by Reg.681/2007; Council Implementing Regulation (EU) No.583/2011, of 9 June 2011, OJ L 160/52; and the Act of Accession (Athens), of 16 April 2003, OJ L 236

THE COUNCIL OF THE EUROPEAN UNION,

Having regard to the Treaty establishing the European Community, and in particular **A3–001**
Articles 61(c) and 67(1) thereof,
Having regard to the initiative of the Federal Republic of Germany and the Republic of Finland,
Having regard to the opinion of the European Parliament,
Having regard to the opinion of the Economic and Social Committee,

Whereas:

(1) The European Union has set out the aim of establishing an area of freedom, security and justice.

(2) The proper functioning of the internal market requires that cross-border insolvency proceedings should operate efficiently and effectively and this Regulation needs to be adopted in order to achieve this objective which comes within the scope of judicial cooperation in civil matters within the meaning of Article 65 of the Treaty.

(3) The activities of undertakings have more and more cross-border effects and are therefore increasingly being regulated by Community law. While the insolvency of such undertakings also affects the proper functioning of the internal market, there is a need for a Community act requiring coordination of the measures to be taken regarding an insolvent debtor's assets.

(4) It is necessary for the proper functioning of the internal market to avoid incentives for the parties to transfer assets or judicial proceedings from one Member State to another, seeking to obtain a more favourable legal position (forum shopping).

(5) These objectives cannot be achieved to a sufficient degree at national level and action at Community level is therefore justified.

(6) In accordance with the principle of proportionality this Regulation should be confined to provisions governing jurisdiction for opening insolvency proceedings and judgments which are delivered directly on the basis of the insolvency proceedings and are closely connected with such proceedings. In addition, this Regulation should contain provisions regarding the recognition of those judgments and the applicable law which also satisfy that principle.

(7) Insolvency proceedings relating to the winding-up of insolvent companies or other legal persons, judicial arrangements, compositions and analogous proceedings are excluded from the scope of the 1968 Brussels Convention on Jurisdiction and the Enforcement of Judgments in Civil and Commercial Matters, as amended by the Conventions on Accession to this Convention.

(8) In order to achieve the aim of improving the efficiency and effectiveness of insolvency proceedings having cross-border effects, it is necessary, and appropriate, that the provisions on jurisdiction, recognition and applicable law in this area should be contained in a Community law measure which is binding and directly applicable in Member States.

(9) This Regulation should apply to insolvency proceedings, whether the debtor is a natural person or a legal person, a trader or an individual. The insolvency proceedings to which this Regulation applies are listed in the Annexes. Insolvency proceedings

concerning insurance undertakings, credit institutions, investment undertakings holding funds or securities for third parties and collective investment undertakings should be excluded from the scope of this Regulation. Such undertakings should not be covered by this Regulation since they are subject to special arrangements and, to some extent, the national supervisory authorities have extremely wide-ranging powers of intervention.

(10) Insolvency proceedings do not necessarily involve the intervention of a judicial authority; the expression "court" in this Regulation should be given a broad meaning and include a person or body empowered by national law to open insolvency proceedings. In order for this Regulation to apply, proceedings (comprising acts and formalities set down in law) should not only have to comply with the provisions of this Regulation, but they should also be officially recognised and legally effective in the Member State in which the insolvency proceedings are opened and should be collective insolvency proceedings which entail the partial or total divestment of the debtor and the appointment of a liquidator.

(11) This Regulation acknowledges the fact that as a result of widely differing substantive laws it is not practical to introduce insolvency proceedings with universal scope in the entire Community. The application without exception of the law of the State of opening of proceedings would, against this background, frequently lead to difficulties. This applies, for example, to the widely differing laws on security interests to be found in the Community. Furthermore, the preferential rights enjoyed by some creditors in the insolvency proceedings are, in some cases, completely different. This Regulation should take account of this in two different ways. On the one hand, provision should be made for special rules on applicable law in the case of particularly significant rights and legal relationships (e.g. rights *in rem* and contracts of employment). On the other hand, national proceedings covering only assets situated in the State of opening should also be allowed alongside main insolvency proceedings with universal scope.

(12) This Regulation enables the main insolvency proceedings to be opened in the Member State where the debtor has the centre of his main interests. These proceedings have universal scope and aim at encompassing all the debtor's assets. To protect the diversity of interests, this Regulation permits secondary proceedings to be opened to run in parallel with the main proceedings. Secondary proceedings may be opened in the Member State where the debtor has an establishment. The effects of secondary proceedings are limited to the assets located in that State. Mandatory rules of coordination with the main proceedings satisfy the need for unity in the Community.

(13) The "centre of main interests" should correspond to the place where the debtor conducts the administration of his interests on a regular basis and is therefore ascertainable by third parties.

(14) This Regulation applies only to proceedings where the centre of the debtor's main interests is located in the Community.

(15) The rules of jurisdiction set out in this Regulation establish only international jurisdiction, that is to say, they designate the Member State the courts of which may open insolvency proceedings. Territorial jurisdiction within that Member State must be established by the national law of the Member State concerned.

(16) The court having jurisdiction to open the main insolvency proceedings should be enabled to order provisional and protective measures from the time of the request to open proceedings. Preservation measures both prior to and after the commencement of the insolvency proceedings are very important to guarantee the effectiveness of the insolvency proceedings. In that connection this Regulation should afford different possibilities. On the one hand, the court competent for the main insolvency proceedings should be able also to order provisional protective measures covering assets situated in the territory of other Member States. On the other hand, a liquidator temporarily appointed prior to the opening of the main insolvency proceedings should be able, in the Member States in which an establishment belonging to the debtor is to be found, to apply for the preservation measures which are possible under the law of those States.

(17) Prior to the opening of the main insolvency proceedings, the right to request the opening of insolvency proceedings in the Member State where the debtor has an establishment should be limited to local creditors and creditors of the local establishment or to cases where main proceedings cannot be opened under the law of the Member State where the debtor has the centre of his main interest. The reason for this restriction is that cases where territorial insolvency proceedings are requested before the main insolvency proceedings are intended to be limited to what is absolutely necessary. If the main insolvency proceedings are opened, the territorial proceedings become secondary.

(18) Following the opening of the main insolvency proceedings, the right to request the opening of insolvency proceedings in a Member State where the debtor has an establishment is not restricted by this Regulation. The liquidator in the main proceedings or any other person empowered under the national law of that Member State may request the opening of secondary insolvency proceedings.

(19) Secondary insolvency proceedings may serve different purposes, besides the protection of local interests. Cases may arise where the estate of the debtor is too complex to administer as a unit or where differences in the legal systems concerned are so great that difficulties may arise from the extension of effects deriving from the law of the State of the opening to the other States where the assets are located. For this reason the liquidator in the main proceedings may request the opening of secondary proceedings when the efficient administration of the estate so requires.

(20) Main insolvency proceedings and secondary proceedings can, however, contribute to the effective realisation of the total assets only if all the concurrent proceedings pending are coordinated. The main condition here is that the various liquidators must cooperate closely, in particular by exchanging a sufficient amount of information. In order to ensure the dominant role of the main insolvency proceedings, the liquidator in such proceedings should be given several possibilities for intervening in secondary insolvency proceedings which are pending at the same time. For example, he should be able to propose a restructuring plan or composition or apply for realisation of the assets in the secondary insolvency proceedings to be suspended.

(21) Every creditor, who has his habitual residence, domicile or registered office in the Community, should have the right to lodge his claims in each of the insolvency proceedings pending in the Community relating to the debtor's assets. This should also apply to tax authorities and social insurance institutions. However, in order to ensure equal treatment of creditors, the distribution of proceeds must be coordinated. Every creditor should be able to keep what he has received in the course of insolvency proceedings but should be entitled only to participate in the distribution of total assets in other proceedings if creditors with the same standing have obtained the same proportion of their claims.

(22) This Regulation should provide for immediate recognition of judgments concerning the opening, conduct and closure of insolvency proceedings which come within its scope and of judgments handed down in direct connection with such insolvency proceedings. Automatic recognition should therefore mean that the effects attributed to the proceedings by the law of the State in which the proceedings were opened extend to all other Member States. Recognition of judgments delivered by the courts of the Member States should be based on the principle of mutual trust. To that end, grounds for non-recognition should be reduced to the minimum necessary. This is also the basis on which any dispute should be resolved where the courts of two Member States both claim competence to open the main insolvency proceedings. The decision of the first court to open proceedings should be recognised in the other Member States without those Member States having the power to scrutinise the court's decision.

(23) This Regulation should set out, for the matters covered by it, uniform rules on conflict of laws which replace, within their scope of application, national rules of private international law. Unless otherwise stated, the law of the Member State of the opening of the proceedings should be applicable (*lex concursus*). This rule on conflict of laws should be valid both for the main proceedings and for local proceedings; the *lex concursus* determines all the effects of the insolvency proceedings, both procedural and

substantive, on the persons and legal relations concerned. It governs all the conditions for the opening, conduct and closure of the insolvency proceedings.

(24) Automatic recognition of insolvency proceedings to which the law of the opening State normally applies may interfere with the rules under which transactions are carried out in other Member States. To protect legitimate expectations and the certainty of transactions in Member States other than that in which proceedings are opened, provisions should be made for a number of exceptions to the general rule.

(25) There is a particular need for a special reference diverging from the law of the opening State in the case of rights *in rem*, since these are of considerable importance for the granting of credit. The basis, validity and extent of such a right *in rem* should therefore normally be determined according to the *lex situs* and not be affected by the opening of insolvency proceedings. The proprietor of the right *in rem* should therefore be able to continue to assert his right to segregation or separate settlement of the collateral security. Where assets are subject to rights *in rem* under the *lex situs* in one Member State but the main proceedings are being carried out in another Member State, the liquidator in the main proceedings should be able to request the opening of secondary proceedings in the jurisdiction where the rights *in rem* arise if the debtor has an establishment there. If a secondary proceeding is not opened, the surplus on sale of the asset covered by rights *in rem* must be paid to the liquidator in the main proceedings.

(26) If a set-off is not permitted under the law of the opening State, a creditor should nevertheless be entitled to the set-off if it is possible under the law applicable to the claim of the insolvent debtor. In this way, set-off will acquire a kind of guarantee function based on legal provisions on which the creditor concerned can rely at the time when the claim arises.

(27) There is also a need for special protection in the case of payment systems and financial markets. This applies for example to the position-closing agreements and netting agreements to be found in such systems as well as to the sale of securities and to the guarantees provided for such transactions as governed in particular by Directive 98/26/EC of the European Parliament and of the Council of 19 May 1998 on settlement finality in payment and securities settlement systems. For such transactions, the only law which is material should thus be that applicable to the system or market concerned. This provision is intended to prevent the possibility of mechanisms for the payment and settlement of transactions provided for in the payment and set-off systems or on the regulated financial markets of the Member States being altered in the case of insolvency of a business partner. Directive 98/26/EC contains special provisions which should take precedence over the general rules in this Regulation.

(28) In order to protect employees and jobs, the effects of insolvency proceedings on the continuation or termination of employment and on the rights and obligations of all parties to such employment must be determined by the law applicable to the agreement in accordance with the general rules on conflict of law. Any other insolvency-law questions, such as whether the employees' claims are protected by preferential rights and what status such preferential rights may have, should be determined by the law of the opening State.

(29) For business considerations, the main content of the decision opening the proceedings should be published in the other Member States at the request of the liquidator. If there is an establishment in the Member State concerned, there may be a requirement that publication is compulsory. In neither case, however, should publication be a prior condition for recognition of the foreign proceedings.

(30) It may be the case that some of the persons concerned are not in fact aware that proceedings have been opened and act in good faith in a way that conflicts with the new situation. In order to protect such persons who make a payment to the debtor because they are unaware that foreign proceedings have been opened when they should in fact have made the payment to the foreign liquidator, it should be provided that such a payment is to have a debt-discharging effect.

(31) This Regulation should include Annexes relating to the organisation of insolvency proceedings. As these Annexes relate exclusively to the legislation of Member

States, there are specific and substantiated reasons for the Council to reserve the right to amend these Annexes in order to take account of any amendments to the domestic law of the Member States.

(32) The United Kingdom and Ireland, in accordance with Article 3 of the Protocol on the position of the United Kingdom and Ireland annexed to the Treaty on European Union and the Treaty establishing the European Community, have given notice of their wish to take part in the adoption and application of this Regulation.

(33) Denmark, in accordance with Articles 1 and 2 of the Protocol on the position of Denmark annexed to the Treaty on European Union and the Treaty establishing the European Community, is not participating in the adoption of this Regulation, and is therefore not bound by it nor subject to its application,

HAS ADOPTED THIS REGULATION:

CHAPTER I

GENERAL PROVISIONS

Article 1

Scope

1. This Regulation shall apply to collective insolvency proceedings which entail the partial or total divestment of a debtor and the appointment of a liquidator.   **A3–002**

2. This Regulation shall not apply to insolvency proceedings concerning insurance undertakings, credit institutions, investment undertakings which provide services involving the holding of funds or securities for third parties, or to collective investment undertakings.

Article 2

Definitions

For the purposes of this Regulation: **A3–003**

(a) "insolvency proceedings" shall mean the collective proceedings referred to in Article 1(1). These proceedings are listed in Annex A;

(b) "liquidator" shall mean any person or body whose function is to administer or liquidate assets of which the debtor has been divested or to supervise the administration of his affairs. Those persons and bodies are listed in Annex C;

(c) "winding-up proceedings" shall mean insolvency proceedings within the meaning of point (a) involving realising the assets of the debtor, including where the proceedings have been closed by a composition or other measure terminating the insolvency, or closed by reason of the insufficiency of the assets. Those proceedings are listed in Annex B;

(d) "court" shall mean the judicial body or any other competent body of a Member State empowered to open insolvency proceedings or to take decisions in the course of such proceedings;

(e) "judgment" in relation to the opening of insolvency proceedings or the appointment of a liquidator shall include the decision of any court empowered to open such proceedings or to appoint a liquidator;

(f) "the time of the opening of proceedings" shall mean the time at which the judgment opening proceedings becomes effective, whether it is a final judgment or not;

(g) "the Member State in which assets are situated" shall mean, in the case of:

– tangible property, the Member State within the territory of which the property is situated,

> – property and rights ownership of or entitlement to which must be entered in a public register, the Member State under the authority of which the register is kept,
> – claims, the Member State within the territory of which the third party required to meet them has the centre of his main interests, as determined in Article 3(1);

(h) "establishment" shall mean any place of operations where the debtor carries out a non-transitory economic activity with human means and goods.

Article 3

International jurisdiction

A3–004 1. The courts of the Member State within the territory of which the centre of a debtor's main interests is situated shall have jurisdiction to open insolvency proceedings. In the case of a company or legal person, the place of the registered office shall be presumed to be the centre of its main interests in the absence of proof to the contrary.

2. Where the centre of a debtor's main interests is situated within the territory of a Member State, the courts of another Member State shall have jurisdiction to open insolvency proceedings against that debtor only if he possesses an establishment within the territory of that other Member State. The effects of those proceedings shall be restricted to the assets of the debtor situated in the territory of the latter Member State.

3. Where insolvency proceedings have been opened under paragraph 1, any proceedings opened subsequently under paragraph 2 shall be secondary proceedings. These latter proceedings must be winding-up proceedings.

4. Territorial insolvency proceedings referred to in paragraph 2 may be opened prior to the opening of main insolvency proceedings in accordance with paragraph 1 only:

(a) where insolvency proceedings under paragraph 1 cannot be opened because of the conditions laid down by the law of the Member State within the territory of which the centre of the debtor's main interests is situated; or

(b) where the opening of territorial insolvency proceedings is requested by a creditor who has his domicile, habitual residence or registered office in the Member State within the territory of which the establishment is situated, or whose claim arises from the operation of that establishment.

Article 4

Law applicable

A3–005 1. Save as otherwise provided in this Regulation, the law applicable to insolvency proceedings and their effects shall be that of the Member State within the territory of which such proceedings are opened, hereafter referred to as the "State of the opening of proceedings".

2. The law of the State of the opening of proceedings shall determine the conditions for the opening of those proceedings, their conduct and their closure. It shall determine in particular:

(a) against which debtors insolvency proceedings may be brought on account of their capacity;

(b) the assets which form part of the estate and the treatment of assets acquired by or devolving on the debtor after the opening of the insolvency proceedings;

(c) the respective powers of the debtor and the liquidator;

(d) the conditions under which set-offs may be invoked;

(e) the effects of insolvency proceedings on current contracts to which the debtor is party;

(f) the effects of the insolvency proceedings on proceedings brought by individual creditors, with the exception of lawsuits pending;

(g) the claims which are to be lodged against the debtor's estate and the treatment of claims arising after the opening of insolvency proceedings;

(h) the rules governing the lodging, verification and admission of claims;

(i) the rules governing the distribution of proceeds from the realisation of assets, the ranking of claims and the rights of creditors who have obtained partial satisfaction after the opening of insolvency proceedings by virtue of a right *in rem* or through a set-off;

(j) the conditions for and the effects of closure of insolvency proceedings, in particular by composition;

(k) creditors' rights after the closure of insolvency proceedings;

(l) who is to bear the costs and expenses incurred in the insolvency proceedings;

(m) the rules relating to the voidness, voidability or unenforceability of legal acts detrimental to all the creditors.

Article 5

Third parties' rights *in rem*

1. The opening of insolvency proceedings shall not affect the rights *in rem* of creditors or third parties in respect of tangible or intangible, moveable or immoveable assets—both specific assets and collections of indefinite assets as a whole which change from time to time—belonging to the debtor which are situated within the territory of another Member State at the time of the opening of proceedings. **A3–006**

2. The rights referred to in paragraph 1 shall in particular mean:

(a) the right to dispose of assets or have them disposed of and to obtain satisfaction from the proceeds of or income from those assets, in particular by virtue of a lien or a mortgage;

(b) the exclusive right to have a claim met, in particular a right guaranteed by a lien in respect of the claim or by assignment of the claim by way of a guarantee;

(c) the right to demand the assets from, and/or to require restitution by, anyone having possession or use of them contrary to the wishes of the party so entitled;

(d) a right *in rem* to the beneficial use of assets.

3. The right, recorded in a public register and enforceable against third parties, under which a right *in rem* within the meaning of paragraph 1 may be obtained, shall be considered a right *in rem*.

4. Paragraph 1 shall not preclude actions for voidness, voidability or unenforceability as referred to in Article 4(2)(m).

Article 6

Set-off

1. The opening of insolvency proceedings shall not affect the right of creditors to demand the set-off of their claims against the claims of the debtor, where such a set-off is permitted by the law applicable to the insolvent debtor's claim. **A3–007**

2. Paragraph 1 shall not preclude actions for voidness, voidability or unenforceability as referred to in Article 4(2)(m).

Article 7

Reservation of title

A3–008   1. The opening of insolvency proceedings against the purchaser of an asset shall not affect the seller's rights based on a reservation of title where at the time of the opening of proceedings the asset is situated within the territory of a Member State other than the State of opening of proceedings.

2. The opening of insolvency proceedings against the seller of an asset, after delivery of the asset, shall not constitute grounds for rescinding or terminating the sale and shall not prevent the purchaser from acquiring title where at the time of the opening of proceedings the asset sold is situated within the territory of a Member State other than the State of the opening of proceedings.

3. Paragraphs 1 and 2 shall not preclude actions for voidness, voidability or unenforceability as referred to in Article 4(2)(m).

Article 8

Contracts relating to immoveable property

A3–009   The effects of insolvency proceedings on a contract conferring the right to acquire or make use of immoveable property shall be governed solely by the law of the Member State within the territory of which the immoveable property is situated.

Article 9

Payment systems and financial markets

A3–010   1. Without prejudice to Article 5, the effects of insolvency proceedings on the rights and obligations of the parties to a payment or settlement system or to a financial market shall be governed solely by the law of the Member State applicable to that system or market.

2. Paragraph 1 shall not preclude any action for voidness, voidability or unenforceability which may be taken to set aside payments or transactions under the law applicable to the relevant payment system or financial market.

Article 10

Contracts of employment

A3–011   The effects of insolvency proceedings on employment contracts and relationships shall be governed solely by the law of the Member State applicable to the contract of employment.

Article 11

Effects on rights subject to registration

A3–012   The effects of insolvency proceedings on the rights of the debtor in immoveable property, a ship or an aircraft subject to registration in a public register shall be determined by the law of the Member State under the authority of which the register is kept.

Article 12

Community patents and trade marks

A3–013   For the purposes of this Regulation, a Community patent, a Community trade mark or any other similar right established by Community law may be included only in the proceedings referred to in Article 3(1).

Article 13

Detrimental acts

Article 4(2)(m) shall not apply where the person who benefited from an act detrimental **A3–014**
to all the creditors provides proof that:

- the said act is subject to the law of a Member State other than that of the State
 of the opening of proceedings, and
- that law does not allow any means of challenging that act in the relevant
 case.

Article 14

Protection of third-party purchasers

Where, by an act concluded after the opening of insolvency proceedings, the debtor **A3–015**
disposes, for consideration, of:

- an immoveable asset, or
- a ship or an aircraft subject to registration in a public register, or
- securities whose existence presupposes registration in a register laid down by
 law, the validity of that act shall be governed by the law of the State within
 the territory of which the immoveable asset is situated or under the authority
 of which the register is kept.

Article 15

Effects of insolvency proceedings on lawsuits pending

The effects of insolvency proceedings on a lawsuit pending concerning an asset or a **A3–016**
right of which the debtor has been divested shall be governed solely by the law of the
Member State in which that lawsuit is pending.

CHAPTER II

RECOGNITION OF INSOLVENCY PROCEEDINGS

Article 16

Principle

1. Any judgment opening insolvency proceedings handed down by a court **A3–017**
of a Member State which has jurisdiction pursuant to Article 3 shall be recognised
in all the other Member States from the time that it becomes effective in the State
of the opening of proceedings. This rule shall also apply where, on account of his
capacity, insolvency proceedings cannot be brought against the debtor in other Member
States.

2. Recognition of the proceedings referred to in Article 3(1) shall not preclude the
opening of the proceedings referred to in Article 3(2) by a court in another Member
State. The latter proceedings shall be secondary insolvency proceedings within the
meaning of Chapter III.

Article 17

Effects of recognition

1. The judgment opening the proceedings referred to in Article 3(1) shall, with no **A3–018**
further formalities, produce the same effects in any other Member State as under this
law of the State of the opening of proceedings, unless this Regulation provides

otherwise and as long as no proceedings referred to in Article 3(2) are opened in that other Member State.

2. The effects of the proceedings referred to in Article 3(2) may not be challenged in other Member States. Any restriction of the creditors' rights, in particular a stay or discharge, shall produce effects vis-à-vis assets situated within the territory of another Member State only in the case of those creditors who have given their consent.

Article 18

Powers of the liquidator

A3–019   1. The liquidator appointed by a court which has jurisdiction pursuant to Article 3(1) may exercise all the powers conferred on him by the law of the State of the opening of proceedings in another Member State, as long as no other insolvency proceedings have been opened there nor any preservation measure to the contrary has been taken there further to a request for the opening of insolvency proceedings in that State. He may in particular remove the debtor's assets from the territory of the Member State in which they are situated, subject to Articles 5 and 7.

2. The liquidator appointed by a court which has jurisdiction pursuant to Article 3(2) may in any other Member State claim through the courts or out of court that moveable property was removed from the territory of the State of the opening of proceedings to the territory of that other Member State after the opening of the insolvency proceedings. He may also bring any action to set aside which is in the interests of the creditors.

3. In exercising his powers, the liquidator shall comply with the law of the Member State within the territory of which he intends to take action, in particular with regard to procedures for the realisation of assets. Those powers may not include coercive measures or the right to rule on legal proceedings or disputes.

Article 19

Proof of the liquidator's appointment

A3–020   The liquidator's appointment shall be evidenced by a certified copy of the original decision appointing him or by any other certificate issued by the court which has jurisdiction.

A translation into the official language or one of the official languages of the Member State within the territory of which he intends to act may be required. No legalisation or other similar formality shall be required.

Article 20

Return and imputation

A3–021   1. A creditor who, after the opening of the proceedings referred to in Article 3(1) obtains by any means, in particular through enforcement, total or partial satisfaction of his claim on the assets belonging to the debtor situated within the territory of another Member State, shall return what he has obtained to the liquidator, subject to Articles 5 and 7.

2. In order to ensure equal treatment of creditors a creditor who has, in the course of insolvency proceedings, obtained a dividend on his claim shall share in distributions made in other proceedings only where creditors of the same ranking or category have, in those other proceedings, obtained an equivalent dividend.

Article 21

Publication

1. The liquidator may request that notice of the judgment opening insolvency   **A3–022**
proceedings and, where appropriate, the decision appointing him, be published in any
other Member State in accordance with the publication procedures provided for in that
State. Such publication shall also specify the liquidator appointed and whether the jurisdiction rule applied is that pursuant to Article 3(1) or Article 3(2).

2. However, any Member State within the territory of which the debtor has an establishment may require mandatory publication. In such cases, the liquidator or any
authority empowered to that effect in the Member State where the proceedings referred
to in Article 3(1) are opened shall take all necessary measures to ensure such
publication.

Article 22

Registration in a public register

1. The liquidator may request that the judgment opening the proceedings referred to in   **A3–023**
Article 3(1) be registered in the land register, the trade register and any other public
register kept in the other Member States.

2. However, any Member State may require mandatory registration. In such cases,
the liquidator or any authority empowered to that effect in the Member State where the
proceedings referred to in Article 3(1) have been opened shall take all necessary measures to ensure such registration.

Article 23

Costs

The costs of the publication and registration provided for in Articles 21 and 22 shall be   **A3–024**
regarded as costs and expenses incurred in the proceedings.

Article 24

Honouring of an obligation to a debtor

1. Where an obligation has been honoured in a Member State for the benefit of a debtor   **A3–025**
who is subject to insolvency proceedings opened in another Member State, when it
should have been honoured for the benefit of the liquidator in those proceedings, the
person honouring the obligation shall be deemed to have discharged it if he was unaware
of the opening of proceedings.

2. Where such an obligation is honoured before the publication provided for in
Article 21 has been effected, the person honouring the obligation shall be presumed, in
the absence of proof to the contrary, to have been unaware of the opening of insolvency
proceedings; where the obligation is honoured after such publication has been effected,
the person honouring the obligation shall be presumed, in the absence of proof to the
contrary, to have been aware of the opening of proceedings.

Article 25

Recognition and enforceability of other judgments

1. Judgments handed down by a court whose judgment concerning the opening of   **A3–026**
proceedings is recognised in accordance with Article 16 and which concern the course
and closure of insolvency proceedings, and compositions approved by that court shall
also be recognised with no further formalities. Such judgments shall be enforced in
accordance with Articles 31 to 51, with the exception of Article 34(2), of the Brussels

Convention on Jurisdiction and the Enforcement of Judgments in Civil and Commercial Matters, as amended by the Conventions of Accession to this Convention.

The first subparagraph shall also apply to judgments deriving directly from the insolvency proceedings and which are closely linked with them, even if they were handed down by another court.

The first subparagraph shall also apply to judgments relating to preservation measures taken after the request for the opening of insolvency proceedings.

2. The recognition and enforcement of judgments other than those referred to in paragraph 1 shall be governed by the Convention referred to in paragraph 1, provided that that Convention is applicable.

3. The Member States shall not be obliged to recognise or enforce a judgment referred to in paragraph 1 which might result in a limitation of personal freedom or postal secrecy.

Article 26

Public policy

A3–027   Any Member State may refuse to recognise insolvency proceedings opened in another Member State or to enforce a judgment handed down in the context of such proceedings where the effects of such recognition or enforcement would be manifestly contrary to that State's public policy, in particular its fundamental principles or the constitutional rights and liberties of the individual.

CHAPTER III

SECONDARY INSOLVENCY PROCEEDINGS

Article 27

Opening of proceedings

A3–028   The opening of the proceedings referred to in Article 3(1) by a court of a Member State and which is recognised in another Member State (main proceedings) shall permit the opening in that other Member State, a court of which has jurisdiction pursuant to Article 3(2), of secondary insolvency proceedings without the debtor's insolvency being examined in that other State. These latter proceedings must be among the proceedings listed in Annex B. Their effects shall be restricted to the assets of the debtor situated within the territory of that other Member State.

Article 28

Applicable law

A3–029   Save as otherwise provided in this Regulation, the law applicable to secondary proceedings shall be that of the Member State within the territory of which the secondary proceedings are opened.

Article 29

Right to request the opening of proceedings

A3–030   The opening of secondary proceedings may be requested by:

  (a) the liquidator in the main proceedings;
  (b) any other person or authority empowered to request the opening of insolvency proceedings under the law of the Member State within the territory of which the opening of secondary proceedings is requested.

Article 30

Advance payment of costs and expenses

Where the law of the Member State in which the opening of secondary proceedings is requested requires that the debtor's assets be sufficient to cover in whole or in part the costs and expenses of the proceedings, the court may, when it receives such a request, require the applicant to make an advance payment of costs or to provide appropriate security.

A3–031

Article 31

Duty to cooperate and communicate information

1. Subject to the rules restricting the communication of information, the liquidator in the main proceedings and the liquidators in the secondary proceedings shall be duty bound to communicate information to each other. They shall immediately communicate any information which may be relevant to the other proceedings, in particular the progress made in lodging and verifying claims and all measures aimed at terminating the proceedings.

2. Subject to the rules applicable to each of the proceedings, the liquidator in the main proceedings and the liquidators in the secondary proceedings shall be duty bound to cooperate with each other.

3. The liquidator in the secondary proceedings shall give the liquidator in the main proceedings an early opportunity of submitting proposals on the liquidation or use of the assets in the secondary proceedings.

A3–032

Article 32

Exercise of creditors' rights

1. Any creditor may lodge his claim in the main proceedings and in any secondary proceedings.

2. The liquidators in the main and any secondary proceedings shall lodge in other proceedings claims which have already been lodged in the proceedings for which they were appointed, provided that the interests of creditors in the latter proceedings are served thereby, subject to the right of creditors to oppose that or to withdraw the lodgement of their claims where the law applicable so provides.

3. The liquidator in the main or secondary proceedings shall be empowered to participate in other proceedings on the same basis as a creditor, in particular by attending creditors' meetings.

A3–033

Article 33

Stay of liquidation

1. The court, which opened the secondary proceedings, shall stay the process of liquidation in whole or in part on receipt of a request from the liquidator in the main proceedings, provided that in that event it may require the liquidator in the main proceedings to take any suitable measure to guarantee the interests of the creditors in the secondary proceedings and of individual classes of creditors. Such a request from the liquidator may be rejected only if it is manifestly of no interest to the creditors in the main proceedings. Such a stay of the process of liquidation may be ordered for up to three months. It may be continued or renewed for similar periods.

2. The court referred to in paragraph 1 shall terminate the stay of the process of liquidation:

    –   at the request of the liquidator in the main proceedings,
    –   of its own motion, at the request of a creditor or at the request of the liquidator in the secondary proceedings if that measure no longer appears

A3–034

justified, in particular, by the interests of creditors in the main proceedings or in the secondary proceedings.

Article 34

Measures ending secondary insolvency proceedings

A3–035   1. Where the law applicable to secondary proceedings allows for such proceedings to be closed without liquidation by a rescue plan, a composition or a comparable measure, the liquidator in the main proceedings shall be empowered to propose such a measure himself.

Closure of the secondary proceedings by a measure referred to in the first subparagraph shall not become final without the consent of the liquidator in the main proceedings; failing his agreement, however, it may become final if the financial interests of the creditors in the main proceedings are not affected by the measure proposed.

2. Any restriction of creditors' rights arising from a measure referred to in paragraph 1 which is proposed in secondary proceedings, such as a stay of payment or discharge of debt, may not have effect in respect of the debtor's assets not covered by those proceedings without the consent of all the creditors having an interest.

3. During a stay of the process of liquidation ordered pursuant to Article 33, only the liquidator in the main proceedings or the debtor, with the former's consent, may propose measures laid down in paragraph 1 of this Article in the secondary proceedings; no other proposal for such a measure shall be put to the vote or approved.

Article 35

Assets remaining in the secondary proceedings

A3–036   If by the liquidation of assets in the secondary proceedings it is possible to meet all claims allowed under those proceedings, the liquidator appointed in those proceedings shall immediately transfer any assets remaining to the liquidator in the main proceedings.

Article 36

Subsequent opening of the main proceedings

A3–037   Where the proceedings referred to in Article 3(1) are opened following the opening of the proceedings referred to in Article 3(2) in another Member State, Articles 31 to 35 shall apply to those opened first, in so far as the progress of those proceedings so permits.

Article 37

Conversion of earlier proceedings

A3–038   The liquidator in the main proceedings may request that proceedings listed in Annex A previously opened in another Member State be converted into winding-up proceedings if this proves to be in the interests of the creditors in the main proceedings.

The court with jurisdiction under Article 3(2) shall order conversion into one of the proceedings listed in Annex B.

Article 38

Preservation measures

A3–039   Where the court of a Member State which has jurisdiction pursuant to Article 3(1) appoints a temporary administrator in order to ensure the preservation of the debtor's assets, that temporary administrator shall be empowered to request any measures to secure and preserve any of the debtor's assets situated in another Member State, provided for under the law of that State, for the period between the request for the opening of insolvency proceedings and the judgment opening the proceedings.

CHAPTER IV

PROVISION OF INFORMATION FOR CREDITORS AND LODGEMENT OF THEIR CLAIMS

Article 39

Right to lodge claims

Any creditor who has his habitual residence, domicile or registered office in a Member State other than the State of the opening of proceedings, including the tax authorities and social security authorities of Member States, shall have the right to lodge claims in the insolvency proceedings in writing.

A3–040

Article 40

Duty to inform creditors

1. As soon as insolvency proceedings are opened in a Member State, the court of that State having jurisdiction or the liquidator appointed by it shall immediately inform known creditors who have their habitual residences, domiciles or registered offices in the other Member States.

A3–041

2. That information, provided by an individual notice, shall in particular include time limits, the penalties laid down in regard to those time limits, the body or authority empowered to accept the lodgement of claims and the other measures laid down. Such notice shall also indicate whether creditors whose claims are preferential or secured *in rem* need lodge their claims.

Article 41

Content of the lodgement of a claim

A creditor shall send copies of supporting documents, if any, and shall indicate the nature of the claim, the date on which it arose and its amount, as well as whether he alleges preference, security *in rem* or a reservation of title in respect of the claim and what assets are covered by the guarantee he is invoking.

A3–042

Article 42

Languages

1. The information provided for in Article 40 shall be provided in the official language or one of the official languages of the State of the opening of proceedings. For that purpose a form shall be used bearing the heading "Invitation to lodge a claim. Time limits to be observed" in all the official languages of the institutions of the European Union.

A3–043

2. Any creditor who has his habitual residence, domicile or registered office in a Member State other than the State of the opening of proceedings may lodge his claim in the official language or one of the official languages of that other State. In that event, however, the lodgement of his claim shall bear the heading "Lodgement of claim" in the official language or one of the official languages of the State of the opening of proceedings. In addition, he may be required to provide a translation into the official language or one of the official languages of the State of the opening of proceedings.

CHAPTER V

TRANSITIONAL AND FINAL PROVISIONS

Article 43

Applicability in time

A3–044   The provisions of this Regulation shall apply only to insolvency proceedings opened after its entry into force. Acts done by a debtor before the entry into force of this Regulation shall continue to be governed by the law which was applicable to them at the time they were done.

Article 44

Relationship to Conventions

A3–045   1. After its entry into force, this Regulation replaces, in respect of the matters referred to therein, in the relations between Member States, the Conventions concluded between two or more Member States, in particular:

    (a) the Convention between Belgium and France on Jurisdiction and the Validity and Enforcement of Judgments, Arbitration Awards and Authentic Instruments, signed at Paris on 8 July 1899;

    (b) the Convention between Belgium and Austria on Bankruptcy, Winding-up, Arrangements, Compositions and Suspension of Payments (with Additional Protocol of 13 June 1973), signed at Brussels on 16 July 1969;

    (c) the Convention between Belgium and the Netherlands on Territorial Jurisdiction, Bankruptcy and the Validity and Enforcement of Judgments, Arbitration Awards and Authentic Instruments, signed at Brussels on 28 March 1925;

    (d) the Treaty between Germany and Austria on Bankruptcy, Winding-up, Arrangements and Compositions, signed at Vienna on 25 May 1979;

    (e) the Convention between France and Austria on Jurisdiction, Recognition and Enforcement of Judgments on Bankruptcy, signed at Vienna on 27 February 1979;

    (f) the Convention between France and Italy on the Enforcement of Judgments in Civil and Commercial Matters, signed at Rome on 3 June 1930;

    (g) the Convention between Italy and Austria on Bankruptcy, Winding-up, Arrangements and Compositions, signed at Rome on 12 July 1977;

    (h) the Convention between the Kingdom of the Netherlands and the Federal Republic of Germany on the Mutual Recognition and Enforcement of Judgments and other Enforceable Instruments in Civil and Commercial Matters, signed at The Hague on 30 August 1962;

    (i) the Convention between the United Kingdom and the Kingdom of Belgium providing for the Reciprocal Enforcement of Judgments in Civil and Commercial Matters, with Protocol, signed at Brussels on 2 May 1934;

    (j) the Convention between Denmark, Finland, Norway, Sweden and Iceland on Bankruptcy, signed at Copenhagen on 7 November 1933;

    (k) the European Convention on Certain International Aspects of Bankruptcy, signed at Istanbul on 5 June 1990;

    (l) the Convention between the Federative People's Republic of Yugoslavia and the Kingdom of Greece on the Mutual Recognition and Enforcement of Judgments, signed at Athens on 18 June 1959;

    (m) the Agreement between the Federative People's Republic of Yugoslavia and the Republic of Austria on the Mutual Recognition and Enforcement of Arbitral Awards and Arbitral Settlements in Commercial Matters, signed at Belgrade on 18 March 1960;

(n) the Convention between the Federative People's Republic of Yugoslavia and the Republic of Italy on Mutual Judicial Cooperation in Civil and Administrative Matters, signed at Rome on 3 December 1960;

(o) the Agreement between the Socialist Federative Republic of Yugoslavia and the Kingdom of Belgium on Judicial Cooperation in Civil and Commercial Matters, signed at Belgrade on 24 September 1971;

(p) the Convention between the Governments of Yugoslavia and France on the Recognition and Enforcement of Judgments in Civil and Commercial Matters, signed at Paris on 18 May 1971;

(q) the Agreement between the Czechoslovak Socialist Republic and the Hellenic Republic on Legal Aid in Civil and Criminal Matters, signed at Athens on 22 October 1980, still in force between the Czech Republic and Greece;

(r) the Agreement between the Czechoslovak Socialist Republic and the Republic of Cyprus on Legal Aid in Civil and Criminal Matters, signed at Nicosia on 23 April 1982, still in force between the Czech Republic and Cyprus;

(s) the Treaty between the Government of the Czechoslovak Socialist Republic and the Government of the Republic of France on Legal Aid and the Recognition and Enforcement of Judgments in Civil, Family and Commercial Matters, signed at Paris on 10 May 1984, still in force between the Czech Republic and France;

(t) the Treaty between the Czechoslovak Socialist Republic and the Italian Republic on Legal Aid in Civil and Criminal Matters, signed at Prague on 6 December 1985, still in force between the Czech Republic and Italy;

(u) the Agreement between the Republic of Latvia, the Republic of Estonia and the Republic of Lithuania on Legal Assistance and Legal Relationships, signed at Tallinn on 11 November 1992;

(v) the Agreement between Estonia and Poland on Granting Legal Aid and Legal Relations on Civil, Labour and Criminal Matters, signed at Tallinn on 27 November 1998;

(w) the Agreement between the Republic of Lithuania and the Republic of Poland on Legal Assistance and Legal Relations in Civil, Family, Labour and Criminal Matters, signed in Warsaw on 26 January 1993.

2. The Conventions referred to in paragraph 1 shall continue to have effect with regard to proceedings opened before the entry into force of this Regulation.

3. This Regulation shall not apply:

(a) in any Member State, to the extent that it is irreconcilable with the obligations arising in relation to bankruptcy from a convention concluded by that State with one or more third countries before the entry into force of this Regulation;

(b) in the United Kingdom of Great Britain and Northern Ireland, to the extent that is irreconcilable with the obligations arising in relation to bankruptcy and the winding-up of insolvent companies from any arrangements with the Commonwealth existing at the time this Regulation enters into force.

Article 45

Amendment of the Annexes

The Council, acting by qualified majority on the initiative of one of its members or on a proposal from the Commission, may amend the Annexes.

A3–046

Article 46

Reports

A3–047　No later than 1 June 2012, and every five years thereafter, the Commission shall present to the European Parliament, the Council and the Economic and Social Committee a report on the application of this Regulation. The report shall be accompanied if need be by a proposal for adaptation of this Regulation.

Article 47

Entry into force

This Regulation shall enter into force on 31 May 2002.

The text of the following Annexes is as substituted by the Council Implementing Regulation (EU) No 583/2011, of 9 June 2011, OJ L 160/52

ANNEX A

A3–048　Insolvency proceedings referred to in Article 2(a)

BELGIQUE/BELGIË

- Het faillissement/La faillite,
- De gerechtelijke reorganisatie door een collectief akkoord/La réorganisation judiciaire par accord collectif,
- De gerechtelijke reorganisatie door overdracht onder gerechtelijk gezag/ La réorganisation judiciaire par transfert sous autorité de justice,
- De collectieve schuldenregeling/Le règlement collectif de dettes,
- De vrijwillige vereffening/La liquidation volontaire,
- De gerechtelijke vereffening/La liquidation judiciaire,
- De voorlopige ontneming van beheer, bepaald in artikel 8 van de faillissementswet/Le dessaisissement provisoire, visé à l'article 8 de la loi sur les faillites,

БЪЛГАРИЯ

- Производство по несъстоятелност,

ČESKÁ REPUBLIKA

- Konkurs,
- Reorganizace,
- Oddlužení,

DEUTSCHLAND

- Das Konkursverfahren,
- Das gerichtliche Vergleichsverfahren,
- Das Gesamtvollstreckungsverfahren,
- Das Insolvenzverfahren,

EESTI

- Pankrotimenetlus,

ÉIRE/IRELAND

- Compulsory winding-up by the court,
- Bankruptcy,

- The administration in bankruptcy of the estate of persons dying insolvent,
- Winding-up in bankruptcy of partnerships,
- Creditors' voluntary winding-up (with confirmation of a court),
- Arrangements under the control of the court which involve the vesting of all or part of the property of the debtor in the Official Assignee for realisation and distribution,
- Company examinership,

ΕΛΛΑΔΑ

- Η πτώχευση,
- Η ειδική εκκαθάριση,
- Η προσωρινή διαχείριση εταιρείας. Η διοίκηση και διαχείριση των πιστωτών,
- Η υπαγωγή επιχείρησης υπό επίτροπο με σκοπό τη σύναψη συμβιβασμού με τους πιστωτές,

ESPAÑA

- Concurso,

FRANCE

- Sauvegarde,
- Redressement judiciaire,
- Liquidation judiciaire,

ITALIA

- Fallimento,
- Concordato preventivo,
- Liquidazione coatta amministrativa,
- Amministrazione straordinaria,

ΚΥΠΡΟΣ

- Υποχρεωτική εκκαθάριση από το Δικαστήριο,
- Εκούσια εκκαθάριση από πιστωτές κατόπιν Δικαστικού Διατάγματος,
- Εκούσια εκκαθάριση από μέλη,
- Εκκαθάριση με την εποπτεία του Δικαστηρίου,
- Πτώχευση κατόπιν Δικαστικού Διατάγματος,
- Διαχείριση της περιουσίας προσώπων που απεβίωσαν αφερέγγυα,

LATVIJA

- Tiesiskās aizsardzības process,
- Juridiskās personas maksātnespējas process,
- Fiziskās personas maksātnespējas process,

LIETUVA

- Įmonės restruktūrizavimo byla,
- Įmonės bankroto byla,
- Įmonės bankroto procesas ne teismo tvarka,

LUXEMBOURG

- Faillite,
- Gestion contrôlée,

- Concordat préventif de faillite (par abandon d'actif),
- Régime spécial de liquidation du notariat,

MAGYARORSZÁG

- Csődeljárás,
- Felszámolási eljárás,

MALTA

- Xoljiment,
- Amministrazzjoni,
- Stralċ volontarju mill-membri jew mill-kredituri,
- Stralċ mill-Qorti,
- Falliment f'każ ta' negozjant,

NEDERLAND

- Het faillissement,
- De surséance van betaling,
- De schuldsaneringsregeling natuurlijke personen,

ÖSTERREICH

- Das Konkursverfahren (Insolvenzverfahren),
- Das Sanierungsverfahren ohne Eigenverwaltung (Insolvenzverfahren),
- Das Sanierungsverfahren mit Eigenverwaltung (Insolvenzverfahren),
- Das Schuldenregulierungsverfahren,
- Das Abschöpfungsverfahren,
- Das Ausgleichsverfahren,

POLSKA

- Postępowanie upadłościowe,
- Postępowanie układowe,
- Upadłość obejmująca likwidację,
- Upadłość z możliwością zawarcia układu,

PORTUGAL

- Processo de insolvência,
- Processo de falência,
- Processos especiais de recuperação de empresa, ou seja:
- Concordata,
- Reconstituição empresarial,
- Reestruturação financeira,
- Gestão controlada,

ROMÂNIA

- Procedura insolvenţei,
- Reorganizarea judiciară,
- Procedura falimentului,

SLOVENIJA

- Stečajni postopek,

- Skrajšani stečajni postopek,
- Postopek prisilne poravnave,
- Prisilna poravnava v stečaju,

SLOVENSKO

- Konkurzné konanie,
- Reštrukturalizačné konanie,

SUOMI/FINLAND

- Konkurssi/konkurs,
- Yrityssaneeraus/företagssanering,

SVERIGE

- Konkurs,
- Företagsrekonstruktion,

UNITED KINGDOM

- Winding-up by or subject to the supervision of the court,
- Creditors' voluntary winding-up (with confirmation by the court),
- Administration, including appointments made by filing prescribed documents with the court,
- Voluntary arrangements under insolvency legislation,
- Bankruptcy or sequestration.

ANNEX B

Winding-up proceedings referred to in Article 2(c)   **A3–049**

BELGIQUE/BELGIË

- Het faillissement/La faillite,
- De vrijwillige vereffening/La liquidation volontaire,
- De gerechtelijke vereffening/La liquidation judiciaire,
- De gerechtelijke reorganisatie door overdracht onder gerechtelijk gezag/ La réorganisation judiciaire par transfert sous autorité de justice,

БЪЛГАРИЯ

- Производство по несъстоятелност,

ČESKÁ REPUBLIKA

Konkurs,

DEUTSCHLAND

- Das Konkursverfahren,
- Das Gesamtvollstreckungsverfahren,
- Das Insolvenzverfahren,

EESTI

- Pankrotimenetlus,

ÉIRE/IRELAND

- Compulsory winding-up,
- Bankruptcy,
- The administration in bankruptcy of the estate of persons dying insolvent,
- Winding-up in bankruptcy of partnerships,
- Creditors' voluntary winding-up (with confirmation of a court),
- Arrangements under the control of the court which involve the vesting of all or part of the property of the debtor in the Official Assignee for realisation and distribution,

ΕΛΛΑΔΑ

- Η πτώχευση,
- Η ειδική εκκαθάριση,

ESPAÑA

- Concurso,

FRANCE

- Liquidation judiciaire,

ITALIA

- Fallimento,
- Concordato preventivo con cessione dei beni,
- Liquidazione coatta amministrativa,
- Amministrazione straordinaria con programma di cessione dei complessi aziendali,
- Amministrazione straordinaria con programma di ristrutturazione di cui sia parte integrante un concordato con cessione dei beni,

ΚΥΠΡΟΣ

- Υποχρεωτική εκκαθάριση από το Δικαστήριο,
- Εκκαθάριση με την εποπτεία του Δικαστηρίου,
- Εκούσια εκκαθάριση από πιστωτές (με την επικύρωση του Δικαστηρίου),
- Πτώχευση,
- Διαχείριση της περιουσίας προσώπων που απεβίωσαν αφερέγγυα,

LATVIJA

- Juridiskās personas maksātnespējas process,
- Fiziskās personas maksātnespējas process,

LIETUVA

- Įmonės bankroto byla,
- Įmonės bankroto procesas ne teismo tvarka,

LUXEMBOURG

- Faillite,
- Régime spécial de liquidation du notariat,

MAGYARORSZÁG

– Felszámolási eljárás,

MALTA

– Stralċ volontarju,
– Stralċ mill-Qorti,
– Falliment inkluż il-ħruġ ta' mandat ta' qbid mill-Kuratur f'każ ta' negozjant fallut,

NEDERLAND

– Het faillissement,
– De schuldsaneringsregeling natuurlijke personen,

ÖSTERREICH

– Das Konkursverfahren (Insolvenzverfahren),

POLSKA

– Postępowanie upadłościowe,
– Upadłość obejmująca likwidację,

PORTUGAL

– Processo de insolvência,
– Processo de falência,

ROMÂNIA

– Procedura falimentului,

SLOVENIJA

– Stečajni postopek,
– Skrajšani stečajni postopek,

SLOVENSKO

– Konkurzné konanie,

SUOMI/FINLAND

– Konkurssi/konkurs,

SVERIGE

– Konkurs,

UNITED KINGDOM

– Winding-up by or subject to the supervision of the court,
– Winding-up through administration, including appointments made by filing prescribed documents with the court,
– Creditors' voluntary winding-up (with confirmation by the court),
– Bankruptcy or sequestration.

ANNEX C

A3–050   Liquidators referred to in Article 2(b)

BELGIQUE/BELGIË

- De curator/Le curateur,
- De gedelegeerd rechter/Le juge-délégué,
- De gerechtsmandataris/Le mandataire de justice,
- De schuldbemiddelaar/Le médiateur de dettes,
- De vereffenaar/Le liquidateur,
- De voorlopige bewindvoerder/L'administrateur provisoire,

БЪЛГАРИЯ

- Назначен предварително временен синдик,
- Временен синдик,
- (Постоянен) синдик,
- Служебен синдик,

ČESKÁ REPUBLIKA

- Insolvenční správce,
- Předběžný insolvenční správce,
- Oddělený insolvenční správce,
- Zvláštní insolvenční správce,
- Zástupce insolvenčního správce,

DEUTSCHLAND

- Konkursverwalter,
- Vergleichsverwalter,
- Sachwalter (nach der Vergleichsordnung),
- Verwalter,
- Insolvenzverwalter,
- Sachwalter (nach der Insolvenzordnung),
- Treuhänder,
- Vorläufiger Insolvenzverwalter,

EESTI

- Pankrotihaldur,
- Ajutine pankrotihaldur,
- Usaldusisik,

ÉIRE/IRELAND

- Liquidator,
- Official Assignee,
- Trustee in bankruptcy,
- Provisional Liquidator,
- Examiner,

ΕΛΛΑΔΑ

- Ο σύνδικος,
- Ο προσωρινός διαχειριστής. Η διοικούσα επιτροπή των πιστωτών,

- Ο ειδικός εκκαθαριστής,
- Ο επίτροπος,

ESPAÑA

- Administradores concursales,

FRANCE

- Mandataire judiciaire,
- Liquidateur,
- Administrateur judiciaire,
- Commissaire à l'exécution du plan,

ITALIA

- Curatore,
- Commissario giudiziale,
- Commissario straordinario,
- Commissario liquidatore,
- Liquidatore giudiziale,

ΚΥΠΡΟΣ

- Εκκαθαριστής και Προσωρινός Εκκαθαριστής,
- Επίσημος Παραλήπτης,
- Διαχειριστής της Πτώχευσης,
- Εξεταστής,

LATVIJA

- Maksātnespējas procesa administrators,

LIETUVA

- Bankrutuojančių įmonių administratorius,
- Restruktūrizuojamų įmonių administratorius,

LUXEMBOURG

- Le curateur,
- Le commissaire,
- Le liquidateur,
- Le conseil de gérance de la section d'assainissement du notariat,

MAGYARORSZÁG

- Vagyonfelügyelő,
- Felszámoló,

MALTA

- Amministratur Proviżorju,
- Riċevitur Uffiċjali,
- Stralċjarju,
- Manager Speċjali,
- Kuraturi f'każ ta' proċeduri ta' falliment,

NEDERLAND

- De curator in het faillissement,
- De bewindvoerder in de surséance van betaling,
- De bewindvoerder in de schuldsaneringsregeling natuurlijke personen,

ÖSTERREICH

- Masseverwalter,
- Sanierungsverwalter,
- Ausgleichsverwalter,
- Besonderer Verwalter,
- Einstweiliger Verwalter,
- Sachwalter,
- Treuhänder,
- Insolvenzgericht,
- Konkursgericht,

POLSKA

- Syndyk,
- Nadzorca sądowy,
- Zarządca,

PORTUGAL

- Administrador da insolvência,
- Gestor judicial,
- Liquidatário judicial,
- Comissão de credores,

ROMÂNIA

- Practician în insolvenţă,
- Administrator judiciar,
- Lichidator,

SLOVENIJA

- Upravitelj prisilne poravnave,
- Stečajni upravitelj,
- Sodišče, pristojno za postopek prisilne poravnave,
- Sodišče, pristojno za stečajni postopek,

SLOVENSKO

- Predbežný správca,
- Správca,

SUOMI/FINLAND

- Pesänhoitaja/boförvaltare,
- Selvittäjä/utredare,

SVERIGE

- Förvaltare,
- Rekonstruktör,

UNITED KINGDOM

- Liquidator,
- Supervisor of a voluntary arrangement,
- Administrator,
- Official Receiver,
- Trustee,
- Provisional Liquidator,
- Judicial factor.

APPENDIX 4

UNCITRAL Model Law on Cross-Border Insolvency with Guide to Enactment

Part one

UNCITRAL MODEL LAW ON CROSS-BORDER INSOLVENCY

A4–001

Preamble

The purpose of this Law is to provide effective mechanisms for dealing with cases of cross-border insolvency so as to promote the objectives of:

(a) Cooperation between the courts and other competent authorities of this State and foreign States involved in cases of cross-border insolvency;

(b) Greater legal certainty for trade and investment;

(c) Fair and efficient administration of cross-border insolvencies that protects the interests of all creditors and other interested persons, including the debtor;

(d) Protection and maximization of the value of the debtor's assets; and

(e) Facilitation of the rescue of financially troubled businesses, thereby protecting investment and preserving employment.

Chapter I. General provisions

A4–002

Article 1. Scope of application

1. This Law applies where:

(a) Assistance is sought in this State by a foreign court or a foreign representative in connection with a foreign proceeding; or

(b) Assistance is sought in a foreign State in connection with a proceeding under [*identify laws of the enacting State relating to insolvency*]; or

(c) A foreign proceeding and a proceeding under [*identify laws of the enacting State relating to insolvency*] in respect of the same debtor are taking place concurrently; or

(d) Creditors or other interested persons in a foreign State have an interest in requesting the commencement of, or participating in, a proceeding under [*identify laws of the enacting State relating to insolvency*].

2. This Law does not apply to a proceeding concerning [*designate any types of entities, such as banks or insurance companies, that are subject to a special insolvency regime in this State and that this State wishes to exclude from this Law*].

A4–003

Article 2. Definitions

For the purposes of this Law:

(a) "Foreign proceeding" means a collective judicial or administrative proceeding in a foreign State, including an interim proceeding, pursuant to a law relating to insolvency in which proceeding the assets and affairs of the debtor are subject to control or supervision by a foreign court, for the purpose of reorganization or liquidation;

1026

(b) "Foreign main proceeding" means a foreign proceeding taking place in the State where the debtor has the centre of its main interests;

(c) "Foreign non-main proceeding" means a foreign proceeding, other than a foreign main proceeding, taking place in a State where the debtor has an establishment within the meaning of subparagraph (f) of this article;

(d) "Foreign representative" means a person or body, including one appointed on an interim basis, authorized in a foreign proceeding to administer the reorganization or the liquidation of the debtor's assets or affairs or to act as a representative of the foreign proceeding;

(e) "Foreign court" means a judicial or other authority competent to control or supervise a foreign proceeding;

(f) "Establishment" means any place of operations where the debtor carries out a nontransitory economic activity with human means and goods or services.

Article 3. International obligations of this State

A4–004

To the extent that this Law conflicts with an obligation of this State arising out of any treaty or other form of agreement to which it is a party with one or more other States, the requirements of the treaty or agreement prevail.

Article 4. [Competent court or authority]¹

A4–005

The functions referred to in this Law relating to recognition of foreign proceedings and cooperation with foreign courts shall be performed by [*specify the court, courts, authority or authorities competent to perform those functions in the enacting State*].

Article 5. Authorization of [insert the title of the person or body administering reorganization or liquidation under the law of the enacting State] to act in a foreign State

A4–006

A [*insert the title of the person or body administering a reorganization or liquidation under the law of the enacting State*] is authorized to act in a foreign State on behalf of a proceeding under [*identify laws of the enacting State relating to insolvency*], as permitted by the applicable foreign law.

Article 6. Public policy exception

A4–007

Nothing in this Law prevents the court from refusing to take an action governed by this Law if the action would be manifestly contrary to the public policy of this State.

Article 7. Additional assistance under other laws

A4–008

Nothing in this Law limits the power of a court or a [*insert the title of the person or body administering a reorganization or liquidation under the law of the enacting State*] to provide additional assistance to a foreign representative under other laws of this State.

Article 8. Interpretation

A4–009

In the interpretation of this Law, regard is to be had to its international origin and to the need to promote uniformity in its application and the observance of good faith.

---

¹ A State where certain functions relating to insolvency proceedings have been conferred upon government-appointed officials or bodies might wish to include in article 4 or elsewhere in chapter I the following provision: Nothing in this Law affects the provisions in force in this State governing the authority of [*insert the title of the government-appointed person or body*].

Chapter II. Access of foreign representatives and creditors to courts in this state

A4–010   *Article 9. Right of direct access*

A foreign representative is entitled to apply directly to a court in this State.

A4–011   *Article 10. Limited jurisdiction*

The sole fact that an application pursuant to this Law is made to a court in this State by a foreign representative does not subject the foreign representative or the foreign assets and affairs of the debtor to the jurisdiction of the courts of this State for any purpose other than the application.

A4–012   *Article 11. Application by a foreign representative to commence a proceeding under* [identify laws of the enacting State relating to insolvency]

A foreign representative is entitled to apply to commence a proceeding under [*identify laws of the enacting State relating to insolvency*] if the conditions for commencing such a proceeding are otherwise met.

A4–013   *Article 12. Participation of a foreign representative in a proceeding under* [identify laws of the enacting State relating to insolvency]

Upon recognition of a foreign proceeding, the foreign representative is entitled to participate in a proceeding regarding the debtor under [*identify laws of the enacting State relating to insolvency*].

A4–014   *Article 13. Access of foreign creditors to a proceeding under* [identify laws of the enacting State relating to insolvency]

1. Subject to paragraph 2 of this article, foreign creditors have the same rights regarding the commencement of and participation in, a proceeding under [*identify laws of the enacting State relating to insolvency*] as creditors in this State.

2. Paragraph 1 of this article does not affect the ranking of claims in a proceeding under [*identify laws of the enacting State relating to insolvency*], except that the claims of foreign creditors shall not be ranked lower than [*identify the class of general non-preference claims, while providing that a foreign claim is to be ranked lower than the general non-preference claims if an equivalent local claim (e.g. claim for a penalty or deferred-payment claim) has a rank lower than the general non-preference claims*].[2]

A4–015   *Article 14. Notification to foreign creditors of a proceeding under* [identify laws of the enacting State relating to insolvency]

1. Whenever under [*identify laws of the enacting State relating to insolvency*] notification is to be given to creditors in this State, such notification shall also be given to the known creditors that do not have addresses in this State. The court may order that

---

[2] The enacting State may wish to consider the following alternative wording to replace paragraph 2 of article 13(2): 2. Paragraph 1 of this article does not affect the ranking of claims in a proceeding under [*identify laws of the enacting State relating to insolvency*] or the exclusion of foreign tax and social security claims from such a proceeding. Nevertheless, the claims of foreign creditors other than those concerning tax and social security obligations shall not be ranked lower than [*identify the class of general non-preference claims, while providing that a foreign claim is to be ranked lower than the general non-preference claims if an equivalent local claim (e.g. claim for a penalty or deferred-payment claim) has a rank lower than the general non-preference claims*].

appropriate steps be taken with a view to notifying any creditor whose address is not yet known.

2. Such notification shall be made to the foreign creditors individually, unless the court considers that, under the circumstances, some other form of notification would be more appropriate. No letters rogatory or other, similar formality is required.

3. When a notification of commencement of a proceeding is to be given to foreign creditors, the notification shall:

(a) Indicate a reasonable time period for filing claims and specify the place for their filing;

(b) Indicate whether secured creditors need to file their secured claims; and

(c) Contain any other information required to be included in such a notification to creditors pursuant to the law of this State and the orders of the court.

Chapter III. Recognition of a foreign proceeding and relief

Article 15. Application for recognition of a foreign proceeding   **A4–016**

1. A foreign representative may apply to the court for recognition of the foreign proceeding in which the foreign representative has been appointed.

2. An application for recognition shall be accompanied by:

(a) A certified copy of the decision commencing the foreign proceeding and appointing the foreign representative; or

(b) A certificate from the foreign court affirming the existence of the foreign proceeding and of the appointment of the foreign representative; or

(c) In the absence of evidence referred to in subparagraphs *(a)* and *(b)*, any other evidence acceptable to the court of the existence of the foreign proceeding and of the appointment of the foreign representative.

3. An application for recognition shall also be accompanied by a statement identifying all foreign proceedings in respect of the debtor that are known to the foreign representative.

4. The court may require a translation of documents supplied in support of the application for recognition into an official language of this State.

Article 16. Presumptions concerning recognition   **A4–017**

1. If the decision or certificate referred to in paragraph 2 of article 15 indicates that the foreign proceeding is a proceeding within the meaning of subparagraph *(a)* of article 2 and that the foreign representative is a person or body within the meaning of subparagraph *(d)* of article 2, the court is entitled to so presume.

2. The court is entitled to presume that documents submitted in support of the application for recognition are authentic, whether or not they have been legalized.

3. In the absence of proof to the contrary, the debtor's registered office, or habitual residence in the case of an individual, is presumed to be the centre of the debtor's main interests.

Article 17. Decision to recognize a foreign proceeding   **A4–018**

1. Subject to article 6, a foreign proceeding shall be recognized if:

(a) The foreign proceeding is a proceeding within the meaning of subparagraph *(a)* of article 2;

(b) The foreign representative applying for recognition is a person or body within the meaning of subparagraph *(d)* of article 2;

(c) The application meets the requirements of paragraph 2 of article 15; and

(d) The application has been submitted to the court referred to in article 4.

2. The foreign proceeding shall be recognized:

(a) As a foreign main proceeding if it is taking place in the State where the debtor has the centre of its main interests; or

(b) As a foreign non-main proceeding if the debtor has an establishment within the meaning of subparagraph *(f)* of article 2 in the foreign State.

3. An application for recognition of a foreign proceeding shall be decided upon at the earliest possible time.

4. The provisions of articles 15, 16, 17 and 18 do not prevent modification or termination of recognition if it is shown that the grounds for granting it were fully or partially lacking or have ceased to exist.

A4–019
Article 18. Subsequent information

From the time of filing the application for recognition of the foreign proceeding, the foreign representative shall inform the court promptly of:

(a) Any substantial change in the status of the recognized foreign proceeding or the status of the foreign representative's appointment; and

(b) Any other foreign proceeding regarding the same debtor that becomes known to the foreign representative.

A4–020
Article 19. Relief that may be granted upon application for recognition of a foreign proceeding

1. From the time of filing an application for recognition until the application is decided upon, the court may, at the request of the foreign representative, where relief is urgently needed to protect the assets of the debtor or the interests of the creditors, grant relief of a provisional nature, including:

(a) Staying execution against the debtor's assets;

(b) Entrusting the administration or realization of all or part of the debtor's assets located in this State to the foreign representative or another person designated by the court, in order to protect and preserve the value of assets that, by their nature or because of other circumstances, are perishable, susceptible to devaluation or otherwise in jeopardy;

(c) Any relief mentioned in paragraph 1*(c)*, *(d)* and *(g)* of article 21.

2. [*Insert provisions (or refer to provisions in force in the enacting State) relating to notice.*]

3. Unless extended under paragraph 1*(f)* of article 21, the relief granted under this article terminates when the application for recognition is decided upon.

4. The court may refuse to grant relief under this article if such relief would interfere with the administration of a foreign main proceeding.

Article 20. Effects of recognition of a foreign main proceeding   **A4–021**

1. Upon recognition of a foreign proceeding that is a foreign main proceeding,

    (a)   Commencement or continuation of individual actions or individual proceedings concerning the debtor's assets, rights, obligations or liabilities is stayed;

    (b)   Execution against the debtor's assets is stayed; and

    (c)   The right to transfer, encumber or otherwise dispose of any assets of the debtor is suspended.

2. The scope, and the modification or termination, of the stay and suspension referred to in paragraph 1 of this article are subject to [*refer to any provisions of law of the enacting State relating to insolvency that apply to exceptions, limitations, modifications or termination in respect of the stay and suspension referred to in paragraph 1 of this article*].

3. Paragraph 1*(a)* of this article does not affect the right to commence individual actions or proceedings to the extent necessary to preserve a claim against the debtor.

4. Paragraph 1 of this article does not affect the right to request the commencement of a proceeding under [*identify laws of the enacting State relating to insolvency*] or the right to file claims in such a proceeding.

Article 21. Relief that may be granted upon recognition of a foreign proceeding   **A4–022**

1. Upon recognition of a foreign proceeding, whether main or non-main, where necessary to protect the assets of the debtor or the interests of the creditors, the court may at the request of the foreign representative, grant any appropriate relief, including:

    (a)   Staying the commencement or continuation of individual actions or individual proceedings concerning the debtor's assets, rights, obligations or liabilities, to the extent they have not been stayed under paragraph 1*(a)* of article 20;

    (b)   Staying execution against the debtor's assets to the extent it has not been stayed under paragraph 1*(b)* of article 20;

    (c)   Suspending the right to transfer, encumber or otherwise dispose of any assets of the debtor to the extent this right has not been suspended under paragraph 1*(c)* of article 20;

    (d)   Providing for the examination of witnesses, the taking of evidence or the delivery of information concerning the debtor's assets, affairs, rights, obligations or liabilities;

    (e)   Entrusting the administration or realization of all or part of the debtor's assets located in this State to the foreign representative or another person designated by the court;

    (f)   Extending relief granted under paragraph 1 of article 19;

    (g)   Granting any additional relief that may be available to [*insert the title of a person or body administering a reorganization or liquidation under the law of the enacting State*] under the laws of this State.

2. Upon recognition of a foreign proceeding, whether main or non-main, the court may, at the request of the foreign representative, entrust the distribution of all or part of the debtor's assets located in this State to the foreign representative or another person

designated by the court, provided that the court is satisfied that the interests of creditors in this State are adequately protected.

3. In granting relief under this article to a representative of a foreign non-main proceeding, the court must be satisfied that the relief relates to assets that, under the law of this State, should be administered in the foreign non-main proceeding or concerns information required in that proceeding.

A4–023   *Article 22. Protection of creditors and other interested persons*

1. In granting or denying relief under article 19 or 21, or in modifying or terminating relief under paragraph 3 of this article, the court must be satisfied that the interests of the creditors and other interested persons, including the debtor, are adequately protected.

2. The court may subject relief granted under article 19 or 21 to conditions it considers appropriate.

3. The court may, at the request of the foreign representative or a person affected by relief granted under article 19 or 21, or at its own motion, modify or terminate such relief.

A4–024   *Article 23. Actions to avoid acts detrimental to creditors*

1. Upon recognition of a foreign proceeding, the foreign representative has standing to initiate [*refer to the types of actions to avoid or otherwise render ineffective acts detrimental to creditors that are available in this State to a person or body administering a reorganization or liquidation*].

2. When the foreign proceeding is a foreign non-main proceeding, the court must be satisfied that the action relates to assets that, under the law of this State, should be administered in the foreign non-main proceeding.

A4–025   *Article 24. Intervention by a foreign representative in proceedings in this State*

Upon recognition of a foreign proceeding, the foreign representative may, provided the requirements of the law of this State are met intervene in any proceedings in which the debtor is a party.

Chapter IV. Cooperation with foreign courts and foreign representatives

A4–026   *Article 25. Cooperation and direct communication between a court of this State and foreign courts or foreign representatives*

1. In matters referred to in article 1 the court shall cooperate to the maximum extent possible with foreign courts or foreign representatives, either directly or through a [*insert the title of a person or body administering a reorganization or liquidation under the law of the enacting State*].

2. The court is entitled to communicate directly with, or to request information or assistance directly from, foreign courts or foreign representatives.

A4–027   *Article 26. Cooperation and direct communication between the* [insert the title of a person or body administering a reorganization or liquidation under the law of the enacting State] *and foreign courts or foreign representatives*

1. In matters referred to in article 1, a [*insert the title of a person or body administering a reorganization or liquidation under the law of the enacting State*] shall, in the exercise

of its functions and subject to the supervision of the court, cooperate to the maximum extent possible with foreign courts or foreign representatives.

2. The [*insert the title of a person or body administering a reorganization or liquidation under the law of the enacting State*] is entitled, in the exercise of its functions and subject to the supervision of the court, to communicate directly with foreign courts or foreign representatives.

Article 27.　Forms of cooperation

A4–028

Cooperation referred to in articles 25 and 26 may be implemented by any appropriate means, including:

(a) Appointment of a person or body to act at the direction of the court;
(b) Communication of information by any means considered appropriate by the court;
(c) Coordination of the administration and supervision of the debtor's assets and affairs;
(d) Approval or implementation by courts of agreements concerning the coordination of proceedings;
(e) Coordination of concurrent proceedings regarding the same debtor;
(f) [*The enacting State may wish to list additional forms or examples of cooperation*].

Chapter V. Concurrent proceedings

Article 28.　Commencement of a proceeding under [identify laws of the enacting State relating to insolvency] *after recognition of a foreign main proceeding*

A4–029

After recognition of a foreign main proceeding, a proceeding under [*identify laws of the enacting State relating to insolvency*] may be commenced only if the debtor has assets in this State; the effects of that proceeding shall be restricted to the assets of the debtor that are located in this State and, to the extent necessary to implement cooperation and coordination under articles 25, 26 and 27, to other assets of the debtor that, under the law of this State, should be administered in that proceeding.

Article 29.　Coordination of a proceeding under [identify laws of the enacting State relating to insolvency] *and a foreign proceeding*

A4–030

Where a foreign proceeding and a proceeding under [*identify laws of the enacting State relating to insolvency*] are taking place concurrently regarding the same debtor, the court shall seek cooperation and coordination under articles 25, 26 and 27, and the following shall apply:

(a) When the proceeding in this State is taking place at the time the application for recognition of the foreign proceeding is filed,

　(i) Any relief granted under article 19 or 21 must be consistent with the proceeding in this State; and
　(ii) If the foreign proceeding is recognized in this State as a foreign main proceeding, article 20 does not apply;

(b) When the proceeding in this State commences after recognition, or after the filing of the application for recognition, of the foreign proceeding,

　(i) Any relief in effect under article 19 or 21 shall be reviewed by the court and shall be modified or terminated if inconsistent with the proceeding in this State; and

(ii) If the foreign proceeding is a foreign main proceeding, the stay and suspension referred to in paragraph 1 of article 20 shall be modified or terminated pursuant to paragraph 2 of article 20 if inconsistent with the proceeding in this State;

(c) In granting, extending or modifying relief granted to a representative of a foreign non-main proceeding, the court must be satisfied that the relief relates to assets that, under the law of this State, should be administered in the foreign non-main proceeding or concerns information required in that proceeding.

A4–031   *Article 30. Coordination of more than one foreign proceeding*

In matters referred to in article 1. in respect of more than one foreign proceeding regarding the same debtor, the court shall seek cooperation and coordination under articles 25, 26 and 27, and the following shall apply:

(a) Any relief granted under article 19 or 21 to a representative of a foreign non-main proceeding after recognition of a foreign main proceeding must be consistent with the foreign main proceeding;

(b) If a foreign main proceeding is recognized after recognition, or after the filing of an application for recognition, of a foreign non-main proceeding, any relief in effect under article 19 or 21 shall be reviewed by the court and shall be modified or terminated if inconsistent with the foreign main proceeding;

(c) If, after recognition of a foreign non-main proceeding, another foreign non-main proceeding is recognized, the court shall grant, modify or terminate relief for the purpose of facilitating coordination of the proceedings.

A4–032   *Article 31. Presumption of insolvency based on recognition of a foreign main proceeding*

In the absence of evidence to the contrary, recognition of a foreign main proceeding is, for the purpose of commencing a proceeding under [*identify laws of the enacting State relating to insolvency*], proof that the debtor is insolvent.

A4–033   *Article 32. Rule of payment in concurrent proceedings*

Without prejudice to secured claims or rights *in rem*, a creditor who has received part payment in respect of its claim in a proceeding pursuant to a law relating to insolvency in a foreign State may not receive a payment for the same claim in a proceeding under [*identify laws of the enacting State relating to insolvency*] regarding the same debtor, so long as the payment to the other creditors of the same class is proportionately less than the payment the creditor has already received.

Part two

A4–034   **GUIDE TO ENACTMENT OF THE UNCITRAL MODEL LAW ON CROSS-BORDER INSOLVENCY**

I. PURPOSE AND ORIGIN OF THE MODEL LAW

Purpose of the Model Law

1. The UNCITRAL Model Law on Cross-Border Insolvency, adopted in 1997, is designed to assist States to equip their insolvency laws with a modern, harmonized and fair framework to address more effectively instances of cross-border insolvency. Those instances include cases where the insolvent debtor has assets in more than one State or

where some of the creditors of the debtor are not from the State where the insolvency proceeding is taking place.

2. The Model Law reflects practices in cross-border insolvency matters that are characteristic of modern, efficient insolvency systems. Thus, the States enacting the Model Law ("enacting States") would be introducing useful additions and improvements in national insolvency regimes designed to resolve problems arising in cross-border insolvency cases. Both jurisdictions that currently have to deal with numerous cases of cross-border insolvency and jurisdictions that wish to be well prepared for the increasing likelihood of cases of cross-border insolvency will find the Model Law useful.

3. The Model Law respects the differences among national procedural laws and does not attempt a substantive unification of insolvency law. It offers solutions that help in several modest but significant ways. These include the following:

(a) Providing the person administering a foreign insolvency proceeding ("foreign representative") with access to the courts of the enacting State, thereby permitting the foreign representative to seek a temporary "breathing space", and allowing the courts in the enacting State to determine what coordination among the jurisdictions or other relief is warranted for optimal disposition of the insolvency;

(b) Determining when a foreign insolvency proceeding should be accorded "recognition" and what the consequences of recognition may be;

(c) Providing a transparent regime for the right of foreign creditors to commence, or participate in, an insolvency proceeding in the enacting State;

(d) Permitting courts in the enacting State to cooperate more effectively with foreign courts and foreign representatives involved in an insolvency matter;

(e) Authorizing courts in the enacting State and persons administering insolvency proceedings in the enacting State to seek assistance abroad;

(f) Providing for court jurisdiction and establishing rules for coordination where an insolvency proceeding in the enacting State is taking place concurrently with an insolvency proceeding in a foreign State;

(g) Establishing rules for coordination of relief granted in the enacting State in favour of two or more insolvency proceedings that may take place in foreign States regarding the same debtor.

Preparatory work and adoption   **A4–035**

4. The project was initiated by the United Nations Commission on International Trade Law (UNCITRAL), in close cooperation with the International Association of Insolvency Practitioners (INSOL). The project benefited from the expert advice of INSOL during all stages of the preparatory work. In addition, assistance during the formulation of the Law, consultative assistance was provided by Committee J (Insolvency) of the Section on Business Law of the International Bar Association.

5. Prior to the decision by UNCITRAL to undertake work on cross-border insolvency, the Commission and INSOL held two international colloquiums for insolvency practitioners, judges, government officials and representatives of other interested sectors.[3]

---

[3] The first was the UNCITRAL-INSOL Colloquium on Cross-Border Insolvency, held at Vienna from 17 to 19 April 1994 (for the report on the Colloquium, see *United Nations Commission on International Trade Law Yearbook, Volume XXV:1994* (United Nations publication, Sales No. E.95.V.20), document A/CN.9/398; for the proceedings of the Colloquium, see *International Insolvency Review*, Special Conference Issue, vol. 4, 1995; and for the considerations of UNCITRAL relating to the Colloquium, see *Official Records of the General Assembly, Forty-ninth Session, Supplement No.17* (A/49/17), paras. 215–222). The second, organized to elicit the views

The suggestion arising from those colloquiums was that work by UNCITRAL should have the limited but useful goal of facilitating judicial cooperation, court access for foreign insolvency administrators and recognition of foreign insolvency proceedings.

6. When UNCITRAL decided in 1995 to develop a legal instrument relating to cross-border insolvency, it entrusted the work to the Working Group on Insolvency Law. one of the three subsidiary bodies of UNCITRAL.[4] The Working Group devoted four two-week sessions to the work on the project.[5]

7. In March 1997, another international meeting of practitioners was held to discuss the draft text as prepared by the Working Group. The participants (mostly judges, judicial administrators and government officials) generally considered that the model legislation, when enacted, would constitute a major improvement in dealing with cross-border insolvency cases.[6]

8. The final negotiations on the draft text took place during the thirtieth session of UNCITRAL, held at Vienna from 12 to 30 May 1997. UNCITRAL adopted the Model Law by consensus on 30 May 1997.[7]

In addition to the 36 State members of UNCITRAL, representatives of 40 observer States and 13 international organizations participated in the deliberations of the Commission and the Working Group.

Subsequently, the General Assembly adopted resolution 52/158 of 15 December 1997 (see annex), in which it expressed its appreciation to UNCITRAL for completing and adopting the Model Law.

---

of judges, was the UNCITRAL-INSOL Judicial Colloquium on Cross-Border Insolvency, held at Toronto from 22 to 23 March 1995 (for the report on the Judicial Colloquium, see *United Nations Commission on International Trade Law Yearbook, Volume XXVI: 1995* (United Nations publication. Sales No.E.96.V.8), document A/CN.9/413; and for the considerations of UNCITRAL relating to the Judicial Colloquium, see *Official Records of the General Assembly, Fiftieth Session, Supplement No.17* (A/50/17), paras. 382–393).

[4] *Official Records of the General Assembly, Fiftieth Session, Supplement No.17* (A/50/17), paras. 392 and 393.

[5] For the report of the Working Group on its eighteenth session, held at Vienna from 30 October to 10 November 1995, see *United Nations Commission on International Trade Law Yearbook, Volume XXVII: 1996* (United Nations publication. Sales No. E.98.V.7), document A/CN.9/419; for the report on its nineteenth session, held in New York from 1 to 12 April 1996 see *United Nations Commission on International Trade Law Yearbook, Volume XXVII: 1996* (United Nations publication. Sales No. E.98. V.7), document A/CN.9/422; and for the report on its twentieth session, held at Vienna from 7 to 18 October 1996, see *United Nations Commission on International Trade Law Year book, Volume XXVIII: 1997*, document A/CN.9/433 to be issued as a United Nations sales publication; and for the report on its twentieth session, held in New York from 20 to 31 January 1997, see *United Nations Commission on International Trade Law Yearbook, Volume XXVIII: 1997*, document A/CN.9/435, to be issued as a United Nations sales publication.

[6] The Second UNCITRAL-INSOL Multinational Judicial Colloquium on Cross-Border Insolvency was held at New Orleans from 22 to 23 March 1997 in conjunction with the 8th World Congress of INSOL held in the same city from 23 to 26 March 1997. A brief account of the Colloquium appears in the report of UNCITRAL on the work of its thirtieth session, held at Vienna from 12 to 30 May 1997 (*Official Records of the General Assembly, Fifty-second Session, Supplement No.17* FS (A/52/17), paras. 17–22).

[7] For the discussion, see the report of UNCITRAL on the work of its thirtieth session (*Official Records of the General Assembly, Fifty-second Session, Supplement No.17* (A/52/17), paras. 12–225).

II. PURPOSE OF THE GUIDE TO ENACTMENT   **A4–036**

9. UNCITRAL considered that the Model Law would be a more effective tool for legislators if it were accompanied by background and explanatory information. While such information would primarily be directed to executive branches of Governments and legislators preparing the necessary legislative revisions, it would also provide useful insight to other users of the text such as judges, practitioners and academics. Such information might also assist States in considering which, if any of the provisions should be varied in order to be adapted to the particular national circumstances.

10. The present Guide to Enactment has been prepared by the Secretariat pursuant to the request of UNCITRAL made at the close of its thirtieth session, in 1997. It is based on the deliberations and decisions of the Commission at that session.[8] when the Model Law was adopted, as well as on considerations of the Working Group on Insolvency Law which conducted the preparatory work.

III. MODEL LAW AS A VEHICLE FOR THE HARMONIZATION OF LAWS   **A4–037**

11. A model law is a legislative text that is recommended to States for incorporation into their national law. Unlike an international convention, a model law does not require the State enacting it to notify the United Nations or other States that may have also enacted it.

12. In incorporating the text of the model law into its system, a State may modify or leave out some of its provisions. In the case of a convention, the possibility of changes being made to the uniform text by the States parties (normally referred to as "reservations") is much more restricted; in particular trade law conventions usually either totally prohibit reservations or allow only specified ones. The flexibility inherent in a model law is particularly desirable in those cases when it is likely that the State would wish to make various modifications to the uniform text before it would be ready to enact it as a national law.

Some modifications may be expected in particular when the uniform text is closely related to the national court and procedural system (which is the case with the UNCITRAL Model Law on Cross-Border Insolvency). This, however, also means that the degree of and certainty about, harmonization achieved through a model law is likely to be lower than in the case of a convention. Therefore, in order to achieve a satisfactory degree of harmonization and certainty, it is recommended that States make as few changes as possible in incorporating the model law into their legal systems.

IV. MAIN FEATURES OF THE MODEL LAW   **A4–038**

Background

13. The increasing incidence of cross-border insolvencies reflects the continuing global expansion of trade and investment. However, national insolvency laws have by and large not kept pace with the trend, and they are often ill-equipped to deal with cases of a cross-border nature. This frequently results in inadequate and inharmonious legal approaches, which hamper the rescue of financially troubled businesses, are not conducive to a fair and efficient administration of cross-border insolvencies, impede the protection of the assets of the insolvent debtor against dissipation and hinder

---

[8] *Official Records of the General Assembly, Fifty-second Session, Supplement No.17* (A/52/17), para. 220.

maximization of the value of those assets. Moreover, the absence of predictability in the handling of cross-border insolvency cases impedes capital flow and is a disincentive to cross-border investment.

14. Fraud by insolvent debtors, in particular by concealing assets or transferring them to foreign jurisdictions, is an increasing problem, in terms of both its frequency and its magnitude. The modern, interconnected world makes such fraud easier to conceive and carry out. The cross-border cooperation mechanisms established by the Model Law are designed to confront such international fraud.

15. Only a limited number of countries have a legislative framework for dealing with cross-border insolvency that is well suited to the needs of international trade and investment. Various techniques and notions are employed in the absence of a specific legislative or treaty framework for dealing with cross-border insolvency. These include the following: application of the doctrine of comity by courts in common-law jurisdictions; issuance for equivalent purposes of enabling orders (*exequatur*) in civil-law jurisdictions; enforcement of foreign insolvency orders relying on legislation for enforcement of foreign judgements; and techniques such as letters rogatory for transmitting requests for judicial assistance.

16. Approaches based purely on the doctrine of comity or on *exequatur* do not provide the same degree of predictability and reliability as can be provided by specific legislation, such as the one contained in the Model Law on judicial cooperation, recognition of foreign insolvency proceedings and access for foreign representatives to courts. For example, in a given legal system general legislation on reciprocal recognition of judgements, including *exequatur*, might be confined to enforcement of specific money judgements or injunctive orders in two-party disputes, thus excluding decisions opening collective insolvency proceedings. Furthermore, recognition of foreign insolvency proceedings might not be considered as a matter of recognizing a foreign "judgement", for example, if the foreign bankruptcy order is considered to be merely a declaration of status of the debtor or if the order is considered not to be final.

17. To the extent that there is a lack of communication and coordination among courts and administrators from concerned jurisdictions, it is more likely that assets would be dissipated, fraudulently concealed, or possibly liquidated without reference to other more advantageous solutions.

As a result, not only is the ability of creditors to receive payment diminished, but so is the possibility of rescuing financially viable businesses and saving jobs. By contrast, mechanisms in national legislation for coordinated administration of cases of cross-border insolvency make it possible to adopt solutions that are sensible and in the best interest of the creditors and the debtor; the presence of such mechanisms in the law of a State is therefore perceived as advantageous for foreign investment and trade in that State.

18. The Model Law takes into account the results of other international efforts, including the Convention on Insolvency Proceedings of the European Union, the European Convention on Certain International Aspects of Bankruptcy (1990),[9] the Montevideo treaties on international commercial law (1889 and 1940), the Convention regarding Bankruptcy between Nordic States (1933) and the Convention on Private International Law (Bustamante Code) (1928).[10] Proposals from non-governmental organizations that have been taken into account include the Model International Insolvency Cooperation

---

[9] European Treaty Series, No. 136.
[10] League of Nations, *Treaty Series*, vol. LXXXVI. No. 1950.

Act and the Cross-Border Insolvency Concordat, both developed by Committee J of the Section on Business Law of the International Bar Association.

19. When the European Union Convention on Insolvency Proceedings enters into effect, it will establish a cross-border insolvency regime within the European Union for cases where the debtor has the centre of its main interests in a State member of the Union. The Convention does not deal with cross-border insolvency matters extending beyond a State member of the European Union into a non-member State.

Thus, the Model Law offers to States members of the European Union a complementary regime of considerable practical value that addresses the many cases of cross-border cooperation not covered by the Convention.

Fitting the Model Law into existing national law   A4–039

20. With its scope limited to some procedural aspects of cross-border insolvency cases, the Model Law is intended to operate as an integral part of the existing insolvency law in the enacting State. This is manifested in several ways:

(a) The amount of possibly new legal terminology added to existing law by the Model Law is limited. New legal terms are those specific to the cross-border context, such as "foreign proceeding" and "foreign representative". The terms used in the Model Law are unlikely to be in conflict with terminology in existing law. Moreover, where the expression is likely to vary from country to country, the Model Law, instead of using a particular term, indicates the meaning of the term in italics within square brackets and calls upon the drafters of the national law to use the appropriate term;

(b) The Model Law presents to enacting States the possibility of aligning the relief resulting from recognition of a foreign proceeding with the relief available in a comparable proceeding in the national law;

(c) Recognition of foreign proceedings does not prevent local creditors from initiating or maintaining collective insolvency proceedings in the enacting State (article 28);

(d) Relief available to the foreign representative is subject to the protection of local creditors and other interested persons, including the debtor, against undue prejudice: relief is also subject to compliance with the procedural requirements of the enacting State and to applicable notification requirements (article 22 and article 19, paragraph 2);

(e) The Model Law preserves the possibility of excluding or limiting any action in favour of the foreign proceeding, including recognition of the proceeding, on the basis of overriding public policy considerations, although it is expected that the public policy exception will be rarely used (article 6);

(f) The Model Law is in the flexible form of model legislation that takes into account differing approaches in national insolvency laws and the varying propensities of States to cooperate and coordinate in insolvency matters (articles 25–27).

21. The flexibility to adapt the Model Law to the legal system of the enacting State should be utilized with due consideration for the need for uniformity in its interpretation and for the benefits to the enacting State in adopting modern, generally acceptable international practices in insolvency matters.

Thus it is advisable to limit deviations from the uniform text to a minimum. One advantage of uniformity is that it will make it easier for the enacting States to obtain cooperation from other States in insolvency matters.

A4–040 Scope of application of the Model Law

22. The Model Law may be applied in a number of cross-border insolvency situations, including the following: *(a)* the case of an inward-bound request for recognition of a foreign proceeding; *(b)* an outward-bound request from a court or administrator in the enacting State for recognition of an insolvency proceeding commenced under the laws of the enacting State; *(c)* coordination of concurrent proceedings in two or more States; and *(d)* participation of foreign creditors in insolvency proceedings taking place in the enacting State (see article 1).

A4–041 Types of foreign proceedings covered

23. To fall within the scope of the Model Law a foreign insolvency proceeding needs to possess certain attributes. These include the following: basis in insolvency-related law of the originating State; involvement of creditors collectively; control or supervision of the assets and affairs of the debtor by a court or another official body; and reorganization or liquidation of the debtor as the purpose of the proceeding (see article 2, subparagraph *(a)*).

24. Within those parameters, a variety of collective proceedings would be eligible for recognition, be they compulsory or voluntary, corporate or individual, winding-up or reorganization. It also includes those in which the debtor retains some measure of control over its assets, albeit under court supervision (e.g. suspension of payments, "debtor in possession").

25. An inclusive approach is used also as regards the possible types of debtors covered by the Model Law. Nevertheless, the Model Law refers to the possibility of excluding from its scope of application certain types of entities, such as banks or insurance companies specially regulated with regard to insolvency under the laws of the enacting State (article 1, paragraph 2).

A4–042 Foreign assistance for an insolvency proceeding taking place in the enacting State

26. In addition to equipping the courts of the enacting State to deal with incoming requests for recognition, the Model Law authorizes the courts of the enacting State to seek assistance abroad on behalf of a proceeding taking place in the enacting State (article 25). Addition of the authorization for the courts of the enacting State to seek cooperation abroad may help to fill a gap in legislation in some States. Without such legislative authorization, the courts, in some legal systems, feel constrained from seeking such assistance abroad, which creates potential obstacles to a coordinated international response in case of cross-border insolvency.

27. The Model Law may similarly help an enacting State to fill a gap in its legislation as to the "outward" powers of persons appointed to administer insolvency proceedings under the local insolvency law. Article 5 authorizes those persons to seek recognition of, and assistance for, those proceedings from foreign courts.

A4–043 Foreign representative's access to courts of the enacting State

28. An important objective of the Model Law is to provide expedited and direct access for foreign representatives to the courts of the enacting State. The Model Law avoids the need to rely on cumbersome and time-consuming letters rogatory or other forms of diplomatic or consular communications that might otherwise have to be used. This facilitates a coordinated, cooperative approach to cross-border insolvency and makes fast action possible.

29. In addition to establishing the principle of direct court access for the foreign representative, the Model Law:

    (a) Establishes simplified proof requirements for seeking recognition and relief
        for foreign proceedings, which avoid time-consuming "legalization" require-
        ments involving notarial or consular procedures (article 15);

    (b) Provides that the foreign representative has procedural standing for
        commencing an insolvency proceeding in the enacting State (under the
        conditions applicable in the enacting State) and that the foreign representa-
        tive may participate in an insolvency proceeding in the enacting State
        (articles 11 and 12);

    (c) Confirms, subject to other requirements of the enacting State, access of
        foreign creditors to the courts of the enacting State for the purpose of
        commencing in the enacting State an insolvency proceeding or participating
        in such a proceeding (article 13);

    (d) Gives the foreign representative the right to intervene in proceedings
        concerning individual actions in the enacting State affecting the debtor or its
        assets (article 24);

    (e) Provides that the mere fact of a petition for recognition in the enacting State
        does not mean that the courts in that State have jurisdiction over all the assets
        and affairs of the debtor (article 10).

Recognition of foreign proceedings   **A4–044**

Decision whether to recognize a foreign proceeding

30. The Model Law establishes criteria for determining whether a foreign proceeding is
to be recognized (articles 15–17) and provides that, in appropriate cases, the court may
grant interim relief pending a decision on recognition (article 19). The decision includes
a determination whether the jurisdictional basis on which the foreign proceeding was
commenced was such that it should be recognized as a "main" or a "non-main" foreign
insolvency proceeding. Procedural matters related to notice of the filing of an application for recognition or of the decision to grant recognition are not dealt with in the
Model Law; they remain to be governed by other provisions of law of the enacting
State.

31. A foreign proceeding is deemed to be the "main" proceeding if it has been
commenced in the State where "the debtor has the centre of its main interests". This
corresponds to the formulation in article 3 of the European Union Convention on
Insolvency Proceedings, thus building on the emerging harmonization as regards the
notion of a "main" proceeding. The determination that a foreign proceeding is a "main"
proceeding may affect the nature of the relief accorded to the foreign representative.

Effects of recognition and discretionary relief available to a foreign representative   **A4–045**

32. Key elements of the relief accorded upon recognition of the representative
of a foreign "main" proceeding include a stay of actions of individual creditors against
the debtor or a stay of enforcement proceedings concerning the assets of the debtor, and
a suspension of the debtor's right to transfer or encumber its assets (article 20, paragraph 1). Such stay and suspension are "mandatory" (or "automatic") in the sense that
either they flow automatically from the recognition of a foreign main proceeding or in
the States where a court order is needed for the stay or suspension, the court is bound to
issue the appropriate order. The stay of actions or of enforcement proceedings is necessary to provide "breathing space" until appropriate measures are taken for reorganization or fair liquidation of the assets of the debtor. The suspension of transfers is
necessary because in a modern, globalized economic system it is possible for

multinational debtors to move money and property across boundaries quickly. The mandatory moratorium triggered by the recognition of the foreign main proceeding provides a rapid "freeze" essential to prevent fraud and to protect the legitimate interests of the parties involved until the court has an opportunity to notify all concerned and to assess the situation.

33. Exceptions and limitations to the scope of the stay and suspension (e.g. exceptions for secured claims, payments by the debtor made in the ordinary course of business, set-off, execution of rights *in rem*) and the possibility of modifying or terminating the stay or suspension are determined by provisions governing comparable stays and suspensions in insolvency proceedings under the laws of the enacting State (article 20, paragraph 2).

34. In addition to the mandatory stay and suspension, the Model Law authorizes the court to grant "discretionary" relief for the benefit of any foreign proceeding, whether it is a "main" proceeding or not (article 21). Such discretionary relief may consist of, for example, staying proceedings or suspending the right to encumber assets (to the extent such stay and suspension have not taken effect automatically under article 20), facilitating access to information concerning the assets of the debtor and its liabilities, appointing a person to administer all or part of those assets, and any other relief that may be available under the laws of the enacting State. Urgently needed relief may be granted already upon filing an application for recognition (article 21).

A4–046 *Protection of creditors and other interested persons*

35. The Model Law contains provisions such as the following to protect the interests of the creditors (in particular local creditors), the debtor and other affected persons; the availability of temporary relief upon application for recognition of a foreign proceeding or upon recognition is subject to the discretion of the court; it is expressly stated that in granting such relief the court must be satisfied that the interests of the creditors and other interested persons, including the debtor, are adequately protected (article 22, paragraph 1); the court may subject the relief it grants to conditions it considers appropriate; and the court may modify or terminate the relief granted, if so requested by a person affected thereby (article 22, paragraphs 2 and 3).

36. In addition to those specific provisions, the Model Law in a general way provides that the court may refuse to take an action governed by the Model Law if the action would be manifestly contrary to the public policy of the enacting State (article 6).

37. Questions of notice to interested persons, while closely related to the protection of their interests, are in general not regulated in the Model Law. Thus, such questions are governed by the procedural rules of the enacting State, some of which may be of a public-order character. For example, the law of the enacting State will determine whether any notice is to be given to the debtor or another person of an application for recognition of a foreign proceeding and the time period for giving the notice.

A4–047 **Cross-border cooperation**

38. A widespread limitation on cooperation and coordination between judges from different jurisdictions in cases of cross-border insolvency is derived from the lack of a legislative framework, or from uncertainty regarding the scope of the existing legislative authority, for pursuing cooperation with foreign courts.

39. Experience has shown that, irrespective of the discretion courts may traditionally enjoy in a State, the passage of a specific legislative framework is useful for promoting international cooperation in crossborder cases. Accordingly, the Model Law fills the

gap found in many national laws by expressly empowering courts to extend cooperation in the areas covered by the Model Law (articles 25–27).

40. For similar reasons, provisions are included authorizing cooperation between a court in the enacting State and a foreign representative and between a person administering the insolvency proceeding in the enacting State and a foreign court or a foreign representative (article 26).

41. The Model Law lists possible forms of cooperation and leaves the legislator an opportunity to list others (article 27). It is advisable to keep the list, when enacted, illustrative rather than exhaustive so as not to stymie the ability of courts to fashion remedies in keeping with specific circumstances.

Coordination of concurrent proceedings A4–048

Jurisdiction to commence a local proceeding

42. The Model Law imposes virtually no limitations on the jurisdiction of the courts in the enacting State to commence or continue insolvency proceedings. Pursuant to article 28, even after recognition of a foreign "main" proceeding, jurisdiction remains with the courts of the enacting State to institute an insolvency proceeding if the debtor has assets in the enacting State. If the enacting State would wish to restrict its jurisdiction to cases where the debtor has not only assets but an establishment in the enacting State, the adoption of such a restriction would not be contrary to the policy underlying the Model Law.

43. In addition, the Model Law deems the recognized foreign main proceeding to constitute proof that the debtor is insolvent for the purposes of commencing local proceedings (article 31). This rule would be helpful in those legal systems in which commencement of an insolvency proceeding requires proof that the debtor is in fact insolvent. Avoidance of the need for repeated proof of financial failure reduces the likelihood that a debtor may delay the commencement of the proceeding long enough to conceal or carry away assets.

Coordination of relief when proceedings take place concurrently A4–049

44. The Model Law deals with coordination between a local proceeding and a foreign proceeding concerning the same debtor (article 29) and facilitates coordination between two or more foreign proceedings concerning the same debtor (article 30). The objective of the provisions is to foster coordinated decisions that would best achieve the objectives of both proceedings (e.g. maximization of the value of the debtor's assets or the most advantageous restructuring of the enterprise). In order to achieve satisfactory coordination and to be able to adapt relief to changing circumstances, the court is in all situations covered by the Model Law, including those that limit the effects of foreign proceedings in the face of local proceedings, directed to cooperate to the maximum extent possible with foreign courts and the foreign representatives (articles 25 and 30).

45. When the local insolvency proceeding is already under way at the time that recognition of a foreign proceeding is requested, the Model Law requires that any relief granted for the benefit of the foreign proceeding must be consistent with the local proceeding. Furthermore, the existence of the local proceeding at the time the foreign main proceeding is recognized prevents the operation of article 20.

When there is no local proceeding pending, article 20 mandates the stay of individual actions or enforcement proceedings against the debtor and a suspension of the debtor's right to transfer or encumber its assets.

46. When the local proceeding begins subsequent to recognition or application for recognition of the foreign proceeding, the relief that has been granted for the benefit of the foreign proceeding must be reviewed and modified or terminated if inconsistent with the local proceeding. If the foreign proceeding is a main proceeding, the stay and a suspension, as mandated by article 20, must also be modified or terminated if inconsistent with the local proceeding.

47. When the court is faced with more than one foreign proceeding, article 30 calls for tailoring relief in such a way that will facilitate coordination of the foreign proceedings; if one of the foreign proceedings is a main proceeding, any relief must be consistent with that main proceeding.

48. Another rule designed to enhance coordination of concurrent proceedings is the one on rate of payment of creditors (article 32). It provides that a creditor, by claiming in more than one proceeding, does not receive more than the proportion of payment that is obtained by other creditors of the same class.

A4–050   **V.   ARTICLE-BY-ARTICLE REMARKS**

Title

"Model Law"

49. If the enacting State decides to incorporate the provisions of the Model Law into an existing national insolvency statute, the title of the enacted provisions would have to be adjusted accordingly, and the word "Law", which appears at various places in the title and in the text of the Model Law. would have to be replaced by the appropriate expression.

50. In enacting the Model Law, it is advisable to adhere as much as possible to the uniform text in order to make the national law as transparent as possible for foreign users of the national law (see also paragraphs 11–12 and 21 above).

A4–051   *"Insolvency"*

51. The word "insolvency", as used in the title of the Model Law, refers to various types of collective proceedings against insolvent debtors. The reason is that the Model Law (as pointed out above in paragraphs 23–24) covers proceedings concerning different types of debtors and, among those proceedings, deals with proceedings aimed at reorganizing the debtor and proceedings leading to a liquidation of the debtor as a commercial entity.

52. It should be noted that in some jurisdictions the expression "insolvency proceedings" has a narrow technical meaning in that it may refer, for example, only to collective proceedings involving a company or a similar legal person or only to collective proceedings against a natural person. No such distinction is intended to be drawn by the use of the term "insolvency" in the title of the Model Law, since the Model Law is designed to be applicable to proceedings regardless of whether they involve a natural person or a legal person as the debtor. If in the enacting State the word "insolvency" may be misunderstood as referring to one particular type of collective proceeding, another term should be used to refer to the proceedings covered by the Law.

53. However, when referring to foreign insolvency proceedings, it is desirable to utilize the wording of article 2, subparagraph *(a)*, so as not to exclude recognition of foreign proceedings that, according to article 2, subparagraph *(a)*, should be covered.

Preamble

The purpose of this Law is to provide effective mechanisms for dealing with cases of **A4–052** cross-border insolvency so as to promote the objectives of:

(a) Cooperation between the courts and other competent authorities of this State and foreign States involved in cases of cross-border insolvency;
(b) Greater legal certainty for trade and investment;
(c) Fair and efficient administration of cross-border insolvencies that protects the interests of all creditors and other interested persons, including the debtor;
(d) Protection and maximization of the value of the debtor's assets; and
(e) Facilitation of the rescue of financially troubled businesses, thereby protecting investment and preserving employment.

54. The Preamble gives a succinct statement of the basic policy objectives of the Model Law. It is not intended to create substantive rights, but rather to give a general orientation for users of the Model Law and to assist in the interpretation of the Model Law.

55. In States where it is not customary to set out preambular statements of policy in legislation, consideration might be given to including the statement of objectives either in the body of the statute or in a separate document, in order to preserve a useful tool for the interpretation of the law.

State   **A4–053**

56. The word "State", as used in the preamble and throughout the Model Law, refers to the entity that enacts the Law (the "enacting State"). The term should not be understood as referring, for example, to a state in a country with a federal system.

Discussion in UNCITRAL and in the Working Group

A/52/17, paras. 136–139.
A/CN.9/422, paras. 19–23.
A/CN.9/433. paras. 22–28.
A/CN.9/435. para. 100.

Chapter I. General provisions

Article 1. Scope of application   **A4–054**

1. This Law applies where:

(a) Assistance is sought in this State by a foreign court or a foreign representative in connection with a foreign proceeding; or
(b) Assistance is sought in a foreign State in connection with a proceeding under [*identify laws of the enacting State relating to insolvency*]; or
(c) A foreign proceeding and a proceeding under [*identify laws of the enacting State relating to insolvency*] in respect of the same debtor are taking place concurrently; or
(d) Creditors or other interested persons in a foreign State have an interest in requesting the commencement of, or participating in, a proceeding under [*identify laws of the enacting State relating to insolvency*].

2. This Law does not apply to a proceeding concerning [*designate any types of entities, such as banks or insurance companies, that are subject to a special insolvency regime in this State and that this State wishes to exclude from this Law*].

Paragraph 1

57. Article 1, paragraph 1, outlines the types of issues that may arise in cases of cross-border insolvency and for which the Model Law provides solutions: *(a)* inward-bound requests for recognition of a foreign proceeding; *(b)* outward-bound requests from a court or administrator in the enacting State for recognition of an insolvency proceeding commenced under the laws of the enacting State; *(c)* coordination of proceedings taking place concurrently in two or more States; and *(d)* participation of foreign creditors in insolvency proceedings taking place in the enacting State.

58. The words "this State" are used in the preamble and throughout the Model Law to refer to the State that is enacting the text. The national statute may use another expression that is customarily used for this purpose.

59. "Assistance" in paragraph 1, subparagraphs *(a)* and *(b)*, is meant to cover various situations, dealt with in the Model Law, in which a court or an insolvency administrator in one State may make a request directed to a court or an insolvency administrator in another State for taking a measure encompassed in the Model Law. Some of those measures the Law specifies (e.g. article 19, subparagraphs 1 *(a)* and *(b)*; article 21, subparagraphs 1 *(a)–(f)* and paragraph 2; and article 27, subparagraphs *(a)–(e)*), while other possible measures are covered by a broader formulation (such as the one in article 21, subparagraph 1*(g)*)

Paragraph 2 (Specially regulated insolvency proceedings)

60. In principle, the Model Law was formulated to apply to any proceeding that meets the requirements of article 2, subparagraph *(a)*, independently of the nature of the debtor or its particular status under national law. The only possible exceptions contemplated in the text of the Model Law itself are indicated in paragraph 2 (see, however, paragraph 66 below, for considerations regarding "consumers").

61. Banks or insurance companies are mentioned as examples of entities that the enacting State might decide to exclude from the scope of the Model Law. The reason for the exclusion would typically be that the insolvency of such entities gives rise to the particular need to protect vital interests of a large number of individuals, or that the insolvency of those entities usually requires particularly prompt and circumspect action (for instance to avoid massive withdrawals of deposits). For those reasons, the insolvency of such types of entities is in many States administered under a special regulatory regime.

62. Paragraph 2 indicates that the enacting State might decide to exclude the insolvency of entities other than banks and insurance companies; the State might do so where the policy considerations underlying the special insolvency regime for those other types of entities (e.g. public utility companies) call for special solutions in cross-border insolvency cases.

63. It is not advisable to exclude all cases of insolvency of the entities mentioned in paragraph 2. In particular, the enacting State might wish to treat, for recognition purposes, a foreign insolvency proceeding relating to a bank or an insurance company as an ordinary insolvency proceeding if the insolvency of the branch or of the assets of the foreign entity in the enacting State do not fall under the national regulatory scheme. The enacting State might also wish not to exclude the possibility of recognition of a foreign proceeding involving one of those entities if the law of the State of origin does not make that proceeding subject to special regulation.

64. In enacting paragraph 2, a State may wish to make sure that it would not inadvertently and undesirably limit the right of the insolvency administrator or court to seek assistance or recognition abroad of an insolvency proceeding conducted in the territory of the enacting State, merely because that insolvency is subject to a special regulatory regime. Moreover, even if the particular insolvency is governed by special regulation, it is advisable, before generally excluding those cases from the Model Law, to consider whether it would be useful to leave certain features of the Model Law (e.g. on cooperation and coordination and possibly on certain types of discretionary relief) applicable also to the specially regulated insolvency proceedings.

65. In any case, with a view to making the national insolvency law more transparent (for the benefit of foreign users of the law based on the Model Law), it is advisable that exclusions from the scope of the law be expressly mentioned by the enacting State in paragraph 2.

Non-traders or natural persons

66. In those jurisdictions that have not made provision for the insolvency of consumers or whose insolvency law provides special treatment for the insolvency of non-traders, the enacting State might wish to exclude from the scope of application of the Model Law those insolvencies that relate to natural persons residing in the enacting State whose debts have been incurred predominantly for personal or household purposes, rather than for commercial or business purposes, or those insolvencies that relate to non-traders. The enacting State might also wish to provide that such exclusion would not apply in cases where the total debts exceed a certain monetary ceiling.

Discussion in UNCITRAL and in the Working Group

A/52/17, paras. 141–150.
A/CN.9/422. paras. 24–33.
A/CN.9/433. paras. 29–32.
A/CN.9/435, paras. 102–106 and 179.

Article 2. Definitions   **A4–055**

For the purposes of this Law:

(a) "Foreign proceeding" means a collective judicial or administrative proceeding in a foreign State, including an interim proceeding, pursuant to a law relating to insolvency in which proceeding the assets and affairs of the debtor are subject to control or supervision by a foreign court, for the purpose of reorganization or liquidation;

(b) "Foreign main proceeding" means a foreign proceeding taking place in the State where the debtor has the centre of its main interests;

(c) "Foreign non-main proceeding" means a foreign proceeding, other than a foreign main proceeding, taking place in a State where the debtor has an establishment within the meaning of subparagraph (f) of this article;

(d) "Foreign representative" means a person or body, including one appointed on an interim basis, authorized in a foreign proceeding to administer the reorganization or the liquidation of the debtor's assets or affairs or to act as a representative of the foreign proceeding;

(e) "Foreign court" means a judicial or other authority competent to control or supervise a foreign proceeding;

(f) "Establishment" means any place of operations where the debtor carries out a non-transitory economic activity with human means and goods or services.

APPENDIX 4

Subparagraphs (a)–(d)

67. Since the Model Law will be embedded in the national insolvency law, article 2 only needs to define the terms specific to cross-border scenarios. Thus, the Model Law contains definitions of the terms "foreign proceeding" (subparagraph *(a)*) and "foreign representative" (subparagraph *(d)* but not of the person or body that may be entrusted with the administration of the assets of the debtor in an insolvency proceeding in the enacting State. To the extent that it would be useful to define in the national statute the term used for such a person or body (rather than just using the term commonly employed to refer to such persons), this may be added to the definitions in the law enacting the Model Law.

68. By specifying required characteristics of the "foreign proceeding" and "foreign representative", the definitions limit the scope of application of the Model Law. For a proceeding to be susceptible to recognition or cooperation under the Model Law and for a foreign representative to be accorded access to local courts under the Model Law, the foreign proceeding and the foreign representative must have the attributes of subparagraphs *(a)* and *(d)*.

69. The definitions in subparagraphs *(a)* and *(d)* cover also an "interim proceeding" and a representative "appointed on an interim basis". In a State where interim proceedings are either not known or do not meet the requisites of the definition the question may arise whether recognition of a foreign "interim proceeding" creates a risk of allowing potentially disruptive consequences under the Model Law that the situation does not warrant. It is advisable that, irrespective of the way interim proceedings are treated in the enacting State, the reference to "interim proceeding" in subparagraph *(a)* and to a foreign representative appointed "on an interim basis" in subparagraph *(d)* be maintained. The reason is that in the practice of many countries insolvency proceedings are often, or even usually, commenced on an "interim" or "provisional" basis. Except for being labelled as interim, those proceedings meet all the other requisites of the definition in article 2. subparagraph *(a)* Such proceedings are often conducted for weeks or months as "interim" proceedings under the administration of persons appointed on an "interim" basis, and only some time later would the court issue an order confirming the continuation of the proceedings on a non-interim basis. The objectives of the Model Law apply fully to such "interim proceedings" (provided the requisites of subparagraphs *(a)* and *(d)* are met); therefore, these proceedings should not be distinguished from other insolvency proceedings merely because they are of an interim nature. The point that an interim proceeding and the foreign representative must meet all the requirements of article 2 is emphasized in article 17, paragraph 1, according to which a foreign proceeding may only be recognized if "the foreign proceeding is a proceeding within the meaning of subparagraph *(a)* of article 2" and "the foreign representative applying for recognition is a person or body within the meaning of subparagraph *(d)* of article 2".

70. Article 18 addresses a case where, after the application for recognition or after recognition, the foreign proceeding or foreign representative, whether interim or not, ceases to meet the requirements of article 2, subparagraphs *(a)* and *(d)*, Article 18 obligates the foreign representative to inform the court promptly, after the time of filing the application for recognition of the foreign proceeding, of "any substantial change in the status of the recognized foreign proceeding or the status of the foreign representative's appointment". The purpose of the obligation is to allow the court to modify or terminate the consequences of recognition.

71. The definitions of proceedings or persons emanating from foreign jurisdictions avoid the use of expressions that may have different technical meaning in legal systems and instead describe their purpose or function. This technique is used to avoid

inadvertently narrowing the range of possible foreign proceedings that might obtain recognition and to avoid unnecessary conflict with terminology used in the laws of the enacting State. As noted in paragraph 52 above, the expression "insolvency proceedings" may have a technical meaning in some legal systems, but it is intended in subparagraph *(a)* to refer broadly to proceedings involving companies in severe financial distress.

72. The expression "centre of . . . main interests", used in subparagraph *(b)* to define a foreign main proceeding, is used also in the Convention on Insolvency Proceedings.

73. Subparagraph *(c)* requires that a "foreign non-main proceeding" take place in the State where the debtor has an "establishment". Thus, a foreign non-main proceeding susceptible to recognition under article 17, paragraph 2, may be only a proceeding commenced in a State where the debtor has an establishment in the meaning of article 2, subparagraph *(f)*. This rule does not affect the provision in article 28, namely, that an insolvency proceeding may be commenced in the enacting State if the debtor has assets there. It should be noted, however, that the effects of an insolvency proceeding commenced on the basis of the presence of assets only are normally restricted to the assets located in that State; if other assets of the debtor located abroad should, under the law of the enacting State, be administered in that insolvency proceeding (as envisaged in article 28), that cross-border issue is to be dealt with as a matter of international cooperation and coordination under articles 25–27 of the Model Law.

Subparagraph (e)

74. A foreign proceeding that meets the requisites of article 2, subparagraph *(a)*, should receive the same treatment irrespective of whether it has been commenced and supervised by a judicial body or an administrative body. Therefore, in order to obviate the need to refer to a foreign non-judicial authority whenever reference is made to a foreign court, the definition of "foreign court" in subparagraph *(e)* includes also non-judicial authorities. Subparagraph *(e)* follows a similar definition contained in article 2, subparagraph *(d)*, of the European Union Convention on Insolvency Proceedings.

Subparagraph (f)

75. The definition of the term "establishment" (subparagraph *(f)*) has been inspired by article 2, subparagraph *(h)*, of the European Union Convention on Insolvency Proceedings. The term is used in the definition of "foreign non-main proceeding" (article 2, subparagraph *(c)*) and in the context of article 17 paragraph (2), according to which, for a foreign non-main proceeding to be recognized, the debtor must have an establishment in the foreign State (see also paragraph 73 above).

Discussion in UNCITRAL and in the Working Group

A/52/17, paras. 152–158.
A/CN.9/419. paras. 95–117.
A/CN.9/422. paras. 34–65.
A/CN.9/433. paras. 33–41 and 147.
A/CN.9/435. paras. 108–113.

Article 3. International obligations of this State   **A4–056**

To the extent that this Law conflicts with an obligation of this State arising out of any treaty or other form of agreement to which it is a party with one or more other States, the requirements of the treaty or agreement prevail.

76. Article 3, expressing the principle of supremacy of international obligations of the enacting State over internal law, has been modelled on similar provisions in other model laws prepared by UNCITRAL.

77. In enacting the article, the legislator may wish to consider whether it would be desirable to take steps to avoid an unnecessarily broad interpretation of international treaties. For example, the article might result in giving precedence to international treaties that, while dealing with matters covered also by the Model Law (e.g. access to courts and cooperation between courts or administrative authorities), were aimed at the resolution of problems other than those that the Model Law focuses on. Some of those treaties, only because of their imprecise or broad formulation, may be misunderstood as dealing also with matters dealt with by the Model Law. Such a result would compromise the goal of achieving uniformity and facilitating cross-border cooperation in insolvency matters and would reduce certainty and predictability in the application of the Model Law. The enacting State might wish to provide that, in order for article 3 to displace a provision of the national law a sufficient link must exist between the international treaty concerned and the issue governed by the provision of the national law in question.

Such a condition would avoid the inadvertent and excessive restriction of the effects of the legislation implementing the Model Law. However, such a provision should not go so far as to impose a condition that the treaty concerned has to deal specifically with insolvency matters in order to satisfy that condition.

78. While in some States binding international treaties are self-executing, in other States those treaties are, with certain exceptions, not self-executing in that they require internal legislation for them to become enforceable law. With respect to the latter group of States, in view of their normal practice in dealing with international treaties and agreements, it would be inappropriate or unnecessary to include article 3 in their legislation or it might be appropriate to include it in a modified form

Discussion in UNCITRAL and in the Working Group

A/52/17, paras. 160–162.
A/CN.9/422. paras. 66–67.
A/CN.9/433. paras. 42–43.
A/CN.9/435. paras. 114–117.

A4–057   *Article 4.* [Competent court or authority]

The functions referred to in this Law relating to recognition of foreign proceedings and cooperation with foreign courts shall be performed by [*specify the court, courts, authority or authorities competent to perform those functions in the enacting State*].

79. If in the enacting State any of the functions mentioned in article 4 are performed by an authority other than a court, the State would insert in article 4 and in other appropriate places in the enacting legislation the name of the competent authority.

80. The competence for the various judicial functions dealt with in the Model Law may lie with different courts in the enacting State, and the enacting State would tailor the text of the article to its own system of court competence. The value of article 4, as enacted in a given State, would be to increase the transparency and ease of use of the insolvency legislation for the benefit of, in particular, foreign representatives and foreign courts.

81. In defining jurisdiction in matters mentioned in article 4, the implementing legislation should not unnecessarily limit the jurisdiction of other courts in the enacting State, in particular to entertain requests by foreign representatives for provisional relief.

82. In a number of States, insolvency legislation has entrusted certain tasks relating to the general supervision of the process of dealing with insolvency cases in the country to government-appointed officials who are typically civil servants or judicial officers and who carry out their functions on a permanent basis. The names under which they are known vary and include, for example, "official receiver", "official trustee" or "official assignee". The activities and the scope and nature of their duties vary from State to State. The Model Law does not restrict the authority of such officials, a point that some enacting States may wish to clarify in the law, as indicated in the footnote. However, depending on the wording that the enacting State uses in articles 25 and 26 in referring to the *title of the person or body administering a reorganization or liquidation under the law of the enacting State*", the officials may be subjected to the duty to cooperate as provided under articles 25–27.

83. In some jurisdictions, officials referred to in the preceding paragraph may also be appointed to act as administrators in individual insolvency cases. To the extent that occurs, such officials would be covered by the Model Law.

Discussion in UNCITRAL and in the Working Group

A/52/17, paras. 163–166.
A/CN.9/419. para. 69.
A/CN.9/422. paras. 68–69.
A/CN.9/433. paras. 44–45.
A/CN.9/435. paras. 118–122.

Article 5. Authorization of [insert the title of the person or body administering a reor-   **A4–058**
ganization or liquidation under the law of the enacting State] *to act in a foreign State*

A [insert the title of the person or body administering a reorganization or liquidation under the law of the enacting State] *is authorized to act in a foreign State on behalf of a proceeding under* [identify laws of the enacting State relating to insolvency], *as permitted by the applicable foreign law.*

84. The intent of article 5 is to equip administrators or other authorities appointed in insolvency proceedings commenced in the enacting State to act abroad as foreign representatives of those proceedings. The lack of such authorization in some States has proved to be an obstacle to effective international cooperation in cross-border cases. An enacting State in which administrators are already equipped to act as foreign representatives may decide to forgo inclusion of article 5, although even such a State might want to keep article 5 in order to provide clear statutory evidence of that authority.

85. Article 5 is formulated to make it clear that the scope of the power exercised abroad by the administrator would depend upon the foreign law and courts. Action that the administrator appointed in the enacting State may wish to take in a foreign country will be action of the type dealt with in the Model Law, but the authority to act in a foreign country does not depend on whether that country has enacted legislation based on the Model Law.

Discussion in UNCITRAL and in the Working Group

A/52/17, paras. 167–169.
A/CN.9/419, paras. 36–39.
A/CN.9/422, paras. 70–74.
A/CN.9/433. paras. 46–49.
A/CN.9/435. paras. 123–124.

A4–059   *Article 6. Public policy exception*

Nothing in this Law prevents the court from refusing to take an action governed by this Law if the action would be manifestly contrary to the public policy of this State.

86. As the notion of public policy is grounded in national law and may differ from State to State, no uniform definition of that notion is attempted in article 6.

87. In some States the expression "public policy" may be given a broad meaning in that it might relate in principle to any mandatory rule of national law. In many States, however, the public policy exception is construed as being restricted to fundamental principles of law, in particular constitutional guarantees: in those States, public policy would only be used to refuse the application of foreign law, or the recognition of a foreign judicial decision or arbitral award, when that would contravene those fundamental principles.

88. For the applicability of the public policy exception in the context of the Model Law it is important to note that a growing number of jurisdictions recognize a dichotomy between the notion of public policy as it applies to domestic affairs, as well as the notion of public policy as it is used in matters of international cooperation and the question of recognition of effects of foreign laws. It is especially in the latter situation that public policy is understood more restrictively than domestic public policy. This dichotomy reflects the realization that international cooperation would be unduly hampered if public policy would be understood in an extensive manner.

89. The purpose of the expression "manifestly", used also in many other international legal texts as a qualifier of the expression "public policy", is to emphasize that public policy exceptions should be interpreted restrictively and that article 6 is only intended to be invoked under exceptional circumstances concerning matters of fundamental importance for the enacting State.

Discussion in UNCITRAL and in the Working Group

A/52/17, paras. 170–173.
A/CN.9/419, para. 40.
A/CN.9/422, paras. 84–85.
A/CN.9/433. paras. 156–160.
A/CN.9/435. paras. 125–128.

A4–060   *Article 7. Additional assistance under other laws*

Nothing in this Law limits the power of a court or a [*insert the title of the person or body administering a reorganization or liquidation under the law of the enacting State*] to provide additional assistance to a foreign representative under other laws of this State.

90. The purpose of the Model Law is to increase and harmonize cross-border assistance available in the enacting State to foreign representatives. However, since the law of the enacting State may, at the time of enacting the Law, already have in place various provisions under which a foreign representative could obtain cross-border assistance and since it is not the purpose of the Law to displace those provisions to the extent that they provide assistance that is additional to or different from the type of assistance dealt with in the Model Law, the enacting State may consider whether article 7 is needed to make that point clear.

A/52/17, para. 175.

Article 8. Interpretation **A4–061**

In the interpretation of this Law, regard is to be had to its international origin and to the need to promote uniformity in its application and the observance of good faith.

91. A provision similar to the one contained in article 8 appears in a number of private-law treaties (e.g. article 7, paragraph 1, of the United Nations Convention on Contracts for the International Sale of Goods). More recently, it has been recognized that, also in a non-treaty text such as a model law, such a provision would be useful in that a State enacting a model law also has an interest in its harmonized interpretation. Article 8 has been modelled on article 3, paragraph 1, of the UNCITRAL Model Law on Electronic Commerce.

92. Harmonized interpretation of the Model Law will be facilitated by the Case Law on UNCITRAL Texts (CLOUT) information system, under which the UNCITRAL secretariat publishes abstracts of judicial decisions (and, where applicable, arbitral awards) that interpret conventions and model laws emanating from UNCITRAL. (For further information about the system, see paragraph 202 below.)

Discussion in UNCITRAL

A/52/17, para. 174.

Chapter II. Access of foreign representatives and creditors to courts in this State

Article 9. Right of direct access **A4–062**

A foreign representative is entitled to apply directly to a court in this State.

93. Article 9 is limited to expressing the principle of direct access by the foreign representative to courts of the enacting State, thus freeing the representative from having to meet formal requirements such as licences or consular action. Article 4 deals with court competence in the enacting State for providing relief to the foreign representative.

Discussion in UNCITRAL and in the Working Group

A/52/17, paras. 176–178.
A/CN.9/419, paras. 77–79 and 172–173.
A/CN.9/422, paras. 144–151.
A/CN.9/433. paras. 50–58.
A/CN.9/435, paras. 129–133.

Article 10. Limited jurisdiction **A4–063**

The sole fact that an application pursuant to this Law is made to a court in this State by a foreign representative does not subject the foreign representative or the foreign assets and affairs of the debtor to the jurisdiction of the courts of this State for any purpose other than the application.

94. Article 10 constitutes a "safe conduct" rule aimed at ensuring that the court in the enacting State would not assume jurisdiction over all the assets of the debtor on the sole

ground of the foreign representative having made an application for recognition of a foreign proceeding. The article also makes it clear that the application alone is not sufficient ground for the court of the enacting State to assert jurisdiction over the foreign representative as to matters unrelated to insolvency. The article responds to concerns of foreign representatives and creditors about exposure to all-embracing jurisdiction triggered by an application under the Model Law.

95. The limitation on jurisdiction over the foreign representative embodied in article 10 is not absolute. It is only intended to shield the foreign representative to the extent necessary to make court access a meaningful proposition. It does so by providing that an appearance in the courts of the enacting State for the purpose of requesting recognition would not expose the entire estate under the supervision of the foreign representative to the jurisdiction of those courts. Other possible grounds for jurisdiction under the laws of the enacting State over the foreign representative or the assets are not affected. For example, a tort or a misconduct committed by the foreign representative may provide grounds for jurisdiction to deal with the consequences of such an action by the foreign representative. Furthermore, the foreign representative who applies for relief in the enacting State will be subject to conditions that the court may order in connection with relief granted (article 22, paragraph 2).

96. Article 10 may appear superfluous in States where the rules on jurisdiction do not allow a court to assume jurisdiction over a person making an application to the court on the sole ground of the applicant's appearance. Enacting the article in those States would be useful, however, as it would eliminate possible concerns of foreign representatives or creditors over the possibility of jurisdiction based on the sole ground of applying to the court.

Discussion in UNCITRAL and in the Working Group

A/52/17, paras. 179–182.
A/CN.9/422, paras. 160–166.
A/CN.9/433, paras. 68–70.
A/CN.9/435. paras. 134–136.

A4–064   *Article 11. Application by a foreign representative to commence a proceeding under* [identify laws of the enacting State relating to insolvency]

A foreign representative is entitled to apply to commence a proceeding under [*identify laws of the enacting State relating to insolvency*] if the conditions for commencing such a proceeding are otherwise met.

97. Many national laws, in enumerating persons who may request the commencement of an insolvency proceeding, do not mention a representative of a foreign insolvency proceeding: under those laws, it might be doubtful whether a foreign representative might make such a request.

98. Article 11 is designed to ensure that the foreign representative (of a foreign main or non-main proceeding) has standing (or "procedural legitimation") for requesting the commencement of an insolvency proceeding. However, the article makes it clear (by the words "if the conditions for commencing such a proceeding are otherwise met") that it does not otherwise modify the conditions under which an insolvency proceeding may be commenced in the enacting State.

99. A foreign representative has this right without prior recognition of the foreign proceeding because the commencement of an insolvency proceeding might be crucial in cases of urgent need for preserving the assets of the debtor. Article 11 recognizes that

not only a representative of a foreign main proceeding but also a representative of a foreign non-main proceeding may have a legitimate interest in the commencement of an insolvency proceeding in the enacting State. Sufficient guarantees against abusive applications are provided by the requirement that the other conditions for commencing such a proceeding under the law of the enacting State have to be met.

Discussion in UNCITRAL and in the Working Group

A/52/17, paras. 183–187.
A/CN.9/422, paras. 170–177.
A/CN.9/433. paras. 71–75.
A/CN.9/435, paras. 137–146.

Article 12. Participation of a foreign representative in a proceeding under [identify laws of the enacting State relating to insolvency]   **A4–065**

Upon recognition of a foreign proceeding, the foreign representative is entitled to participate in a proceeding regarding the debtor under [*identify laws of the enacting State relating to insolvency*].

100. The purpose of article 12 is to ensure that, when an insolvency proceeding concerning a debtor is taking place in the enacting State, the foreign representative of a proceeding concerning that debtor will be given procedural standing (or "procedural legitimation") to make petitions, requests or submissions concerning issues such as protection, realization or distribution of assets of the debtor or cooperation with the foreign proceeding.

101. Article 12 is limited to giving the foreign representative standing and does not vest the foreign representative with any specific powers or rights. The article does not specify the kinds of motions that the foreign representative might make and does not affect the provisions in the insolvency law of the enacting State that govern the fate of the motions.

102. If the law of the enacting State uses a term other than "participate" to express the concept, that other term may be used in enacting the provision. It should be noted, however, that article 24 already uses the term "intervene" to refer to a case where the foreign representative takes part in an individual action by or against the debtor (as opposed to a collective insolvency proceeding).

Discussion in UNCITRAL and in the Working Group

A/52/17, paras. 188–189.
A/CN.9/422, paras. 114–115. 147 and 149.
A/CN.9/433, para. 58.
A/CN.9/435, paras. 147–150.

Article 13. Access of foreign creditors to a proceeding under [identify laws of the enacting State relating to insolvency]   **A4–066**

1. Subject to paragraph 2 of this article, foreign creditors have the same rights regarding the commencement of, and participation in, a proceeding under [*identify laws of the enacting State relating to insolvency*] as creditors in this State.

2. Paragraph 1 of this article does not affect the ranking of claims in a proceeding under [*identify laws of the enacting State relating to insolvency*], except that the claims of foreign creditors shall not be ranked lower than [*identify the class of*

general non-preference claims, while providing that a foreign claim is to be ranked lower than the general non-preference claims if an equivalent local claim (e.g. claim for a penalty or deferred-payment claim) has a rank lower than the general non-preference claims].

103. With the exception contained in paragraph 2, article 13 embodies the principle that foreign creditors, when they apply to commence an insolvency proceeding in the enacting State or file claims in such proceeding, should not be treated worse than local creditors.

104. Paragraph 2 makes it clear that the principle of non-discrimination embodied in paragraph 1 leaves intact the provisions on the ranking of claims in insolvency proceedings, including any provisions that might assign a special ranking to claims of foreign creditors. Few States currently have provisions assigning special ranking to foreign creditors. However, lest the non-discrimination principle should be emptied of its meaning by provisions giving the lowest ranking to foreign claims, paragraph 2 establishes the minimum ranking for claims of foreign creditors: the rank of general unsecured claims.

The exception to that minimum ranking is provided for the cases where the claim in question, if it were of a domestic creditor, would be ranked lower than general unsecured claims (such low-rank claims may be, for instance, those of a State authority for financial penalties or fines, claims whose payment is deferred because of a special relationship between the debtor and the creditor or claims that have been filed after the expiry of the time period for doing so). Those special claims may rank below the general unsecured claims, for reasons other than the nationality or location of the creditor, as provided in the law of the enacting State.

105. The alternative provision in the footnote (see para.A4–014) differs from the provision in the text only in that it provides wording for States that refuse to recognize foreign tax and social security claims to continue to discriminate against such claims.

Discussion in UNCITRAL and in the Working Group

A/52/17, paras. 190–192.
A/CN.9/422. paras. 179–187.
A/CN.9/433. paras. 77–85.
A/CN.9/435. paras. 151–156.

A4–067   *Article 14. Notification to foreign creditors of a proceeding under* [identify laws of the enacting State relating to insolvency]

1. Whenever under [*identify laws of the enacting State relating to insolvency*] notification is to be given to creditors in this State, such notification shall also be given to the known creditors that do not have addresses in this State. The court may order that appropriate steps be taken with a view to notifying any creditor whose address is not yet known.

2. Such notification shall be made to the foreign creditors individually, unless the court considers that, under the circumstances, some other form of notification would be more appropriate. No letters rogatory or other, similar formality is required.

3. When a notification of commencement of a proceeding is to be given to foreign creditors, the notification shall:

(a) Indicate a reasonable time period for filing claims and specify the place for their filing;

(b) Indicate whether secured creditors need to file their secured claims; and

(c) Contain any other information required to be included in such a notification to creditors pursuant to the law of this State and the orders of the court.

Paragraphs 1 and 2

106. The main purpose of notifying foreign creditors as provided in paragraph 1 is to inform them of the commencement of the insolvency proceeding and of the time-limit to file their claims. Furthermore, as a corollary to the principle of equal treatment established by article 13, article 14 requires that foreign creditors should be notified whenever notification is required for creditors in the enacting State.

107. States have different provisions or practices regarding the methods for notifying creditors; those may be, for example, publication in the official gazette or in local newspapers, individual notices, affixing notices within the court premises or a combination of such procedures. If the form of notification were to be left to national law, foreign creditors would be in a less advantageous situation than local creditors, since they typically do not have direct access to local publications. For that reason, paragraph 2 in principle requires individual notification for foreign creditors but leaves discretion to the court to decide otherwise in a particular case (e.g. if individual notice would entail excessive cost or would not seem feasible under the circumstances).

108. With regard to the form of individual notification. States may use special procedures for notifications that have to be served in a foreign jurisdiction (e.g. sending notifications through diplomatic channels). In the context of insolvency proceedings, those procedures would often be too cumbersome and time-consuming and their use would typically not provide foreign creditors timely notice concerning insolvency proceedings. It is therefore advisable for those notifications to be effected by such expeditious means that the court considers adequate. Those considerations are the reason for the provision in paragraph 2 that "no letters rogatory or other, similar formality is required".

109. Many States are party to bilateral or multilateral treaties on judicial cooperation, which often contain provisions on procedures for communicating judicial or extrajudicial documents to addressees abroad. A multilateral treaty of this kind is the Convention on the Service Abroad of Judicial and Extrajudicial Documents in Civil and Commercial Matters (1965),[11] adopted under the auspices of the Hague Conference on Private International Law. While the procedures envisaged by those treaties may constitute a simplification as compared to traditional communication via diplomatic channels, they would often be, for reasons stated in the preceding paragraph, inappropriate for cross-border insolvency cases. The question may arise whether paragraph 2, which allows the use of letters rogatory or similar formalities to be dispensed with, is compatible with those treaties. Each State would have to consider that question in the light of its treaty obligations, but generally the provision in paragraph 2 would not be in conflict with the international obligations of the enacting State because the purpose of the treaties alluded to above is typically to facilitate communication and not to preclude use of notification procedures that are even simpler than those established by the treaty: for example, article 10 of the above-mentioned Convention reads as follows:

"Provided the State of destination does not object, the present Convention shall not interfere with—

---

[11] United Nations, *Treaty Series*, vol. 658. No.9432.

(a) the freedom to send judicial documents, by postal channels, directly to persons abroad.

(b) the freedom of judicial officers, officials or other competent persons of the State of origin to effect service of judicial documents directly through the judicial officers, officials or other competent persons of the State of destination,

(c) the freedom of any person interested in a judicial proceeding to effect service of judicial documents directly through the judicial officers, officials or other competent persons of the State of destination."[12]

To the extent that there might still be a conflict between the second sentence of paragraph 2 of article 14 and a treaty, article 3 of the Model Law provides the solution.

110. While paragraph 2 mentions letters rogatory as a formality that is not required for a notification under article 14, in many States such notifications would never be transmitted in the form of a letter rogatory. A letter rogatory in those States would be used for other purposes, such as to request evidence in a foreign country or to request permission to perform some other judicial act abroad. Such use of letters rogatory is governed, for example, by the Convention on the Taking of Evidence Abroad in Civil or Commercial Matters (1970),[13] adopted under the auspices of the Hague Conference on Private International Law.

Paragraph 3

111. In some legal systems a secured creditor who files a claim in the insolvency proceeding is deemed to have waived the security or some of the privileges attached to the credit, while in other systems failure to file a claim results in a waiver of such security or privilege. Where such a situation may arise, it would be appropriate for the enacting State to include in paragraph 3, subparagraph (b), a requirement that the notification should include information regarding the effects of filing, or failing to file, secured claims.

Discussion in UNCITRAL and in the Working Group

A/52/17, paras. 193–198.
A/CN.9/419. paras. 84–87.
A/CN.9/422, paras. 188–191.
A/CN.9/433. paras. 86–98.
A/CN.9/435. paras. 157–164.

A4–068   Chapter III. Recognition of a foreign proceeding and relief

Article 15. Application for recognition of a foreign proceeding

1. A foreign representative may apply to the court for recognition of the foreign proceeding in which the foreign representative has been appointed.

2. An application for recognition shall be accompanied by:

(a) A certified copy of the decision commencing the foreign proceeding and appointing the foreign representative; or

---

[12] United Nations, *Treaty Series*, vol. 658. No.9432.
[13] United Nations, *Treaty Series*, vol. 847. No.12140.

(b)   A certificate from the foreign court affirming the existence of the foreign proceeding and of the appointment of the foreign representative; or

(c)   In the absence of evidence referred to in subparagraphs (a) and (b), any other evidence acceptable to the court of the existence of the foreign proceeding and of the appointment of the foreign representative.

3. An application for recognition shall also be accompanied by a statement identifying all foreign proceedings in respect of the debtor that are known to the foreign representative.

4. The court may require a translation of documents supplied in support of the application for recognition into an official language of this State.

Article 15 as a whole

112. Article 15 defines the core procedural requirements for an application by a foreign representative for recognition. In incorporating the provision into national law, it is desirable not to encumber the process with additional requirements beyond those referred to. With article 15, in conjunction with article 16, the Model Law provides a simple, expeditious structure to be used by a foreign representative to obtain recognition.

Article 15, paragraph 2, and article 16, paragraph 2

113. The Model Law presumes that documents submitted in support of the application for recognition need not be authenticated in any special way, in particular by legalization: according to article 16, paragraph 2, the court is entitled to presume that those documents are authentic whether or not they have been legalized. "Legalization" is a term often used for the formality by which a diplomatic or consular agent of the State in which the document is to be produced certifies the authenticity of the signature, the capacity in which the person signing the document has acted and, where appropriate, the identity of the seal or stamp on the document.

114. It follows from article 16, paragraph 2, (according to which the court "is entitled to presume" the authenticity of documents accompanying the application for recognition) that the court retains discretion to decline to rely on the presumption of authenticity or to conclude that evidence to the contrary prevails. This flexible solution takes into account the fact that the court may be able to assure itself that a particular document originates from a particular court even without it being legalized, but that in other cases the court may be unwilling to act on the basis of a foreign document that has not been legalized, particularly when documents emanate from a jurisdiction with which it is not familiar. The presumption is useful because legalization procedures may be cumbersome and time-consuming (e.g. also because in some States they involve various authorities at different levels).

115. In respect of the provision relaxing any requirement of legalization, the question may arise whether that is in conflict with the international obligations of the enacting State. Several States are parties to bilateral or multilateral treaties on mutual recognition and legalization of documents, such as the Convention Abolishing the Requirement of Legalisation for Foreign Documents (1961)[14] adopted under the auspices of the Hague Conference on Private International Law which provides specific simplified procedures for the legalization of documents originating from signatory States. In many instances, however, the treaties on legalization of documents, like letters rogatory and similar

---

[14] United Nations, *Treaty Series*, vol. 527. No.7625.

formalities, leave in effect laws and regulations that have abolished or simplified legalization procedures; therefore a conflict is unlikely to arise. For example, as stated in article 3, paragraph 2, of the above-mentioned convention[15]:

> "However, [legalisation] mentioned in the preceding paragraph cannot be required when either the laws, regulations, or practice in force in the State where the document is produced or an agreement between two or more contracting States have abolished or simplified it, or exempt the document itself from legalisation."

According to article 3 of the Model Law, if there is still a conflict between the Model Law and a treaty, the treaty will prevail.

Subparagraph 2(c)

116. In order not to prevent recognition because of non-compliance with a mere technicality (e.g. where the applicant is unable to submit documents that in all details meet the requirements of subparagraphs 2*(a)* and *(b)*), subparagraph 2*(c)* allows evidence other than that specified in subparagraphs 2*(a)* and *(b)* to be taken into account; that provision, however, does not compromise the court's power to insist on the presentation of evidence acceptable to it. It is advisable to maintain that flexibility in enacting the Model Law. Article 16, paragraph 2, which provides that the court "is entitled to presume" the authenticity of documents accompanying the application for recognition, applies also to documents submitted under subparagraph 2*(c)* (see paragraphs 114–115 above).

Paragraph 3

117. Paragraph 3 requires that an application for recognition must be accompanied by a statement identifying all foreign proceedings in respect of the debtor that are known to the foreign representative.

That information is needed by the court not so much for the decision on recognition itself but for any decision granting relief in favour of the foreign proceeding. In order to tailor such relief appropriately and make sure that the relief is consistent with any other insolvency proceeding concerning the same debtor, the court needs to be aware of all foreign proceedings concerning the debtor that may be under way in third States.

118. An express provision establishing the duty to inform is useful, firstly, because the foreign representative is likely to have more comprehensive information about the debtor's affairs in third States than the court and, secondly, because the foreign representative may be primarily concerned with obtaining relief in favour of his or her foreign proceeding and less concerned about coordination with another foreign proceeding. (The duty to inform the court about a foreign proceeding that becomes known to the foreign representative after the decision on recognition is set out in article 18; as for coordination of more than one foreign proceeding, see article 30.)

Paragraph 4

119. Paragraph 4 entitles, but does not compel, the court to require a translation of some or all documents accompanying the application for recognition. If that discretion is compatible with the procedures of the court, it is useful since it allows, when the court

---

[15] United Nations, *Treaty Series*, vol. 527. No.7625.

understands the documents, to shorten the time needed for a decision on recognition and reduces costs.

Notice

120. Different solutions exist also as to whether the court is required to issue notice of an application for recognition. In a number of jurisdictions, fundamental principles of due process, in some cases enshrined in the constitution, may be understood as requiring that a decision of the importance of the recognition of a foreign insolvency proceeding could only be made after hearing the affected parties. In other States, however, it is considered that applications for recognition of foreign proceedings require expeditious treatment (as they are often submitted in circumstances of imminent danger of dissipation or concealment of the assets) and that, because of this need for expeditiousness, the issuance of notice prior to any court decision on recognition is not required. According to that way of thinking, imposing the requirement would cause undue delay and would be inconsistent with article 17, paragraph 3, which provides that an application for recognition of a foreign proceeding should be decided upon at the earliest possible time.

121. Procedural matters related to such notice are not resolved by the Model Law and are thus governed by other provisions of law of the enacting State. The absence of an express reference to notice of the filing of an application for recognition or of the decision to grant recognition does not preclude the court from issuing such notice, where legally required, in pursuance of its own rules on civil or insolvency proceedings. By the same token, there is nothing in the Model Law that would mandate the issuance of such notice, where such requirement does not exist.

Discussion in UNCITRAL and in the Working Group

A/52/17, paras. 199–209.
A/CN.9/419. paras. 62–69 and 178–189.
A/CN.9/422. paras. 76–93 and 152–159.
A/CN.9/433, paras. 59–67 and 99–104.
A/CN.9/435. paras. 165–173.

Article 16. Presumptions concerning recognition

1. If the decision or certificate referred to in paragraph 2 of article 15 indicates that the foreign proceeding is a proceeding within the meaning of subparagraph (a) of article 2 and that the foreign representative is a person or body within the meaning of subparagraph (d) of article 2, the court is entitled to so presume.   **A4–069**

2. The court is entitled to presume that documents submitted in support of the application for recognition are authentic, whether or not they have been legalized.

3. In the absence of proof to the contrary, the debtor's registered office, or habitual residence in the case of an individual, is presumed to be the centre of the debtor's main interests.

122. Article 16 establishes presumptions that allow the court to expedite the evidentiary process; at the same time they do not prevent, in accordance with the applicable procedural law, calling for or assessing other evidence if the conclusion suggested by the presumption is called into question by the court or an interested party.

123. For comments on paragraph 2, which dispenses with the requirement of legalization, see paragraphs 113–115 above.

Discussion in UNCITRAL and in the Working Group

A/52/17, paras. 204–206.
A/CN.9/435. paras. 170–172.

Article 17. Decision to recognize a foreign proceeding

A4–070   1. Subject to article 6, a foreign proceeding shall be recognized if:

    (a)   The foreign proceeding is a proceeding within the meaning of subparagraph (a) of article 2;
    (b)   The foreign representative applying for recognition is a person or body within the meaning of subparagraph (d) of article 2;
    (c)   The application meets the requirements of paragraph 2 of article 15; and
    (d)   The application has been submitted to the court referred to in article 4.

2. The foreign proceeding shall be recognized:

    (a)   As a foreign main proceeding if it is taking place in the State where the debtor has the centre of its main interests; or
    (b)   As a foreign non-main proceeding if the debtor has an establishment within the meaning of subparagraph (f) of article 2 in the foreign State.

3. An application for recognition of a foreign proceeding shall be decided upon at the earliest possible time.

4. The provisions of articles 15, 16, 17 and 18 do not prevent modification or termination of recognition if it is shown that the grounds for granting it were fully or partially lacking or have ceased to exist.

Paragraphs 1–3

124. The purpose of article 17 is to indicate that, if recognition is not contrary to the public policy of the enacting State and if the application meets the requirements set out in the article, recognition will be granted as a matter of course.

125. Apart from the public policy exception (see article 6), the conditions for recognition do not include those that would allow the court considering the application to evaluate the merits of the foreign court's decision by which the proceeding has been commenced or the foreign representative appointed. The foreign representative's ability to obtain early recognition (and the consequential ability to invoke in particular articles 20, 21, 23 and 24) is often essential for the effective protection of the assets of the debtor from dissipation and concealment. For that reason, paragraph 3 obligates the court to decide on the application "at the earliest possible time" and the court should in practice be able to conclude the recognition process within such a short period of time.

126. Article 17 draws in paragraph 2 the basic distinction between foreign proceedings categorized as the "main" proceedings and those foreign proceedings that are not so characterized, depending upon the jurisdictional basis of the foreign proceeding (see paragraph 75 above). The relief flowing from recognition may depend upon the category into which a foreign proceeding falls. For example, recognition of a "main" proceeding triggers an automatic stay of individual creditor actions or executions concerning the assets of the debtor (article 20, subparagraphs 1*(a)* and *(b)*) and an automatic "freeze" of those assets (article 20, subparagraph 1*(c)*) subject to certain exceptions referred to in article 20, paragraph 2.

127. It is not advisable to include more than one criterion for qualifying a foreign proceeding as a main proceeding and provide that on the basis of any of those criteria a proceeding could be deemed a main proceeding. An approach involving such a "multiple criteria" would raise the risk of competing claims from foreign proceedings for recognition as the main proceeding.

128. With regard to subparagraph 2*(b)*, as noted in paragraph 73 above, the Model Law does not envisage recognition of a proceeding commenced in a foreign State in which the debtor has assets but no establishment as defined in article 2, subparagraph *(c)*.

Paragraph 4

129. A decision to recognize a foreign proceeding would normally be subject to review or rescission, as any other court decision. Paragraph 4 clarifies that the question of revisiting the decision on recognition, if grounds for granting it were fully or partially lacking or have ceased to exist, is left to the procedural law of the enacting State other than the provisions implementing the Model Law.

130. Modification or termination of the recognition decision may be a consequence of a change of circumstances after the decision on recognition, for instance, if the recognized foreign proceeding has been terminated or its nature has changed (e.g. a reorganization proceeding might be transformed into a liquidation proceeding). Also, new facts might arise that require or justify a change of the court's decision, for example, if the foreign representative disregarded the conditions under which the court granted relief.

131. A decision on recognition may also be subject to a review of whether in the decision-making process the requirements for recognition were observed. Some appeal procedures under national laws give the appeal court the authority to review the merits of the case in its entirety, including factual aspects. It would be consistent with the purpose of the Model Law and with the nature of the decision granting recognition (which is limited to verifying whether the applicant fulfilled the requirements of article 17) if an appeal of the decision would be limited to the question whether the requirements of articles 15 and 16 were observed in deciding to recognize the foreign proceeding.

Notice of decision to recognize foreign proceedings

132. As noted in paragraphs 120–121 above, procedural matters regarding requirements of notice of the decision to grant recognition are not dealt with by the Model Law and are left to other provisions of law of the enacting State.

Discussion in UNCITRAL and in the Working Group

A/52/17, paras. 29–33 and 201–202.
A/CN.9/419, paras. 62–69.
A/CN.9/422, paras. 76–93.
A/CN.9/433. paras. 99–104.
A/CN.9/435. paras. 167 and 173.

Article 18. Subsequent information   **A4–071**

From the time of filing the application for recognition of the foreign proceeding, the foreign representative shall inform the court promptly of:

   (a)   Any substantial change in the status of the recognized foreign proceeding or the status of the foreign representative's appointment; and

(b) Any other foreign proceeding regarding the same debtor that becomes known to the foreign representative.

Subparagraph (a)

133. It is possible that, after the application for recognition or after recognition, changes occur in the foreign proceeding that would have affected the decision on recognition or the relief granted on the basis of recognition. For example, the foreign proceeding may be terminated or transformed from a liquidation proceeding into a reorganization proceeding, or the terms of the appointment of the foreign representative may be modified or the appointment itself terminated. Subparagraph *(a)* takes into account the fact that technical modifications in the status of the proceedings or the terms of the appointment are frequent, but that only some of those modifications are such that they would affect the decision granting relief or the decision recognizing the proceeding; therefore, the provision only calls for information of "substantial" changes. The court would likely be particularly anxious to be kept so informed when its decision on recognition concerns a foreign "interim proceeding" or a foreign representative has been "appointed on an interim basis" (see article 2, subparagraphs *(a)* and *(d)*).

Subparagraph (b)

134. Article 15, paragraph 3, requires that an application for recognition be accompanied by a statement identifying all foreign proceedings in respect of the debtor that are known to the foreign representative.

Article 18, subparagraph *(b)*, extends that duty to the time after the application for recognition has been filed. That information will allow the court to consider whether relief already granted should be coordinated with the existence of the insolvency proceedings that have been commenced after the decision on recognition (see article 30).

Discussion in UNCITRAL

A/52/17, paras. I 13–116. 201–202 and 207.

A4–072 *Article 19. Relief that may be granted upon application for recognition of a foreign proceeding*

1. From the time of filing an application for recognition until the application is decided upon, the court may, at the request of the foreign representative, where relief is urgently needed to protect the assets of the debtor or the interests of the creditors, grant relief of a provisional nature, including:

(a) Staying execution against the debtor's assets;
(b) Entrusting the administration or realization of all or part of the debtor's assets located in this State to the foreign representative or another person designated by the court, in order to protect and preserve the value of assets that, by their nature or because of other circumstances, are perishable, susceptible to devaluation or otherwise in jeopardy;
(c) Any relief mentioned in paragraph 1 (c), (d) and (g) of article 21.

2. [*Insert provisions (or refer to provisions in force in the enacting State) relating to notice.*]

3. Unless extended under paragraph 1(f) of article 21, the relief granted under this article terminates when the application for recognition is decided upon.

4. The court may refuse to grant relief under this article if such relief would interfere with the administration of a foreign main proceeding.

Paragraph 1

135. Article 19 deals with "urgently needed" relief that may be ordered at the discretion of the court and is available as of the moment of the application for recognition (unlike relief under article 21, which is also discretionary but which is available only upon recognition).

136. Article 19 authorizes the court to grant the type of relief that is usually available only in collective insolvency proceedings (i.e. the same type of relief available under article 21), as opposed to the "individual" type of relief that may be granted before the commencement of insolvency proceedings under rules of civil procedure (i.e. measures covering specific assets identified by a creditor). However, the discretionary "collective" relief under article 19 is somewhat more narrow than the relief under article 21.

137. The reason for the availability of collective measures, albeit in a restricted form, is that relief of a collective nature may be urgently needed already before the decision on recognition in order to protect the assets of the debtor and the interests of the creditors. Exclusion of collective relief would frustrate those objectives. On the other hand, recognition has not yet been granted and, therefore, the collective relief is restricted to urgent and provisional measures. The urgency of the measures is alluded to in the opening words of paragraph 1, while subparagraph 1*(a)* restricts the stay to execution proceedings, and the measure referred to in subparagraph 1*(b)* is restricted to perishable assets and assets susceptible to devaluation or otherwise in jeopardy. Otherwise, the measures available under article 19 are essentially the same as those available under article 21.

Paragraph 2

138. Laws of many States contain requirements for notice to be given (either by the insolvency administrator upon the order of the court or by the court itself) when relief of the type mentioned in article 19 is granted. Paragraph 2 is the location where the enacting State should make appropriate provision for such notice.

Paragraph 3

139. Relief available under article 19 is provisional in that, as provided in paragraph 3, the relief terminates when the application for recognition is decided upon: however, the court is given the opportunity to extend the measure, as provided in article 21, subparagraph 1*(f)*. The court might wish to do so, for example, to avoid a hiatus between the provisional measure issued before recognition and the measure issued after recognition.

Paragraph 4

140. Article 19, paragraph 4, pursues the same objective as the one underlying article 30, subparagraph *(a)*, namely that, if there is a foreign main proceeding pending, any relief granted in favour of a foreign non-main proceeding must be consistent (or should not interfere) with the foreign main proceeding. In order to foster such coordination of pre-recognition relief with any foreign main proceeding, the foreign representative applying for recognition is required, by article 15, paragraph 3, to attach to the application for recognition a statement identifying all foreign proceedings with respect to the debtor that are known to the foreign representative.

Discussion in UNCITRAL and in the Working Group

A/52/17, paras. 34–46.
A/CN.9/419. paras. 174–177.
A/CN.9/422. paras. 116. 119 and 122–123.
A/CN.9/433. paras. 110–114.
A/CN.9/435. paras. 17–23.

A4–073   *Article 20. Effects of recognition of a foreign main proceeding*

1. Upon recognition of a foreign proceeding that is a foreign main proceeding,

    (a) Commencement or continuation of individual actions or individual proceedings concerning the debtor's assets, rights, obligations or liabilities is stayed;
    (b) Execution against the debtor's assets is stayed; and
    (c) The right to transfer, encumber or otherwise dispose of any assets of the debtor is suspended.

2. The scope, and the modification or termination, of the stay and suspension referred to in paragraph 1 of this article are subject to [*refer to any provisions of law of the enacting State relating to insolvency that apply to exceptions, limitations, modifications or termination in respect of the stay and suspension referred to in paragraph 1 of this article*].

3. Paragraph 1(a) of this article does not affect the right to commence individual actions or proceedings to the extent necessary to preserve a claim against the debtor.

4. Paragraph 1 of this article does not affect the right to request the commencement of a proceeding under [*identify laws of the enacting State relating to insolvency*] or the right to file claims in such a proceeding.

141. While relief under articles 19 and 21 is discretionary, the effects provided by article 20 are not, for they flow automatically from recognition of the foreign main proceeding. Another difference between discretionary relief under articles 19 and 21 and the effects under article 20 is that discretionary relief may be issued in favour of main and non-main proceedings, while the automatic effects apply only to main proceedings.

142. In States where an appropriate court order is needed for the effects of article 20 to become operative, the enacting State, in order to achieve the purpose of the article, should include (perhaps in the opening words of paragraph 1) language directing the court to issue an order putting into effect the consequences specified in subparagraphs *(a)*, *(b)* and *(c)* of that paragraph.

143. The automatic consequences envisaged in article 20 are necessary to allow steps to be taken to organize an orderly and fair cross-border insolvency proceeding. In order to achieve those benefits, it is justified to impose on the insolvent debtor the consequences of article 20 in the enacting State (i.e. the country where it maintains a limited business presence), even if the State where the center of the debtor's main interests is situated poses different (possibly less stringent) conditions for the commencement of insolvency proceedings or even if the automatic effects of the insolvency proceeding in the country of origin are different from the effects of article 20 in the enacting State. This approach reflects a basic principle underlying the Model Law according to which recognition of foreign proceedings by the court of the enacting State grants effects that are considered necessary for an orderly and fair conduct of a cross-border insolvency.

Recognition, therefore, has its own effects rather than importing the consequences of the foreign law into the insolvency system of the enacting State. If recognition should in a given case produce results that would be contrary to the legitimate interests of an interested party, including the debtor, the law of the enacting State should provide possibilities for protecting those interests, as indicated in article 20, paragraph 2 (and discussed in paragraph 149 below).

144. By virtue of article 2, subparagraph *(a)*, the effects of recognition extend also to foreign "interim proceedings". That solution is necessary since, as explained in paragraph 69 above, interim proceedings (provided they meet the requisites of article 2, subparagraph *(a)*), should not be distinguished from other insolvency proceedings merely because they are of an interim nature. If after recognition the foreign "interim proceeding" ceases to have a sufficient basis for the automatic effects of article 20, the automatic stay could be terminated pursuant to the law of the enacting State, as indicated in article 20, paragraph 2. (See also article 18, which deals with the obligation of the foreign representative "to inform the court promptly of any substantial change in the status of the recognized foreign proceeding or the status of the foreign representative's appointment".)

145. Subparagraph 1*(a)*, by not distinguishing between various kinds of individual actions, also covers actions before an arbitral tribunal. Thus, article 20 establishes a mandatory limitation to the effectiveness of an arbitration agreement. This limitation is added to other possible limitations restricting the freedom of the parties to agree to arbitration that may exist under national law (e.g. limits as to arbitrability or as to the capacity to conclude an arbitration agreement). Such limitations are not contrary to the Convention on the Recognition and Enforcement of Foreign Arbitral Awards (1958).[16] However, bearing in mind the particularities of international arbitration, in particular its relative independence from the legal system of the State where the arbitral proceeding takes place, it might not always be possible, in practical terms, to implement the automatic stay of arbitral proceedings. For example, if the arbitration does not take place in the enacting State and perhaps also not in the State of the main proceeding, it may be difficult to enforce the stay of the arbitral proceedings. Apart from that, the interests of the parties may be a reason for allowing an arbitral proceeding to continue, a possibility that is envisaged in paragraph 2 and left to the provisions of law of the enacting State.

146. Subparagraph 1*(a)* refers not only to "individual actions" but also to "individual proceedings" in order to cover, in addition to "actions" instituted by creditors in a court against the debtor or its assets, also enforcement measures initiated by creditors outside the court system, measures that creditors are allowed to take under certain conditions in some States. Subparagraph 1*(b)* has been added to make it abundantly clear that executions against the assets of the debtor are covered by the stay.

147. The Model Law does not deal with sanctions that might apply to acts performed in defiance of the suspension of transfers of assets provided under article 20, subparagraph 1*(c)*. Those sanctions vary, depending on the legal system; they might include criminal sanctions, penalties and fines or the acts themselves might be void or capable of being set aside. From the viewpoint of creditors, the main purpose of such sanctions is to facilitate recovery for the insolvency proceeding of any assets improperly transferred by the debtor and, for that purpose, the setting aside of such transactions is preferable to the imposition of criminal or administrative sanctions on the debtor.

[16] United Nations, *Treaty Series*, vol. 330. No.4739.

Paragraph 2

148. Notwithstanding the "automatic" or "mandatory" nature of the effects under article 20, it is expressly provided that the scope of those effects depends on exceptions or limitations that may exist in the law of the enacting State. Those exceptions may be, for example, the enforcement of claims by secured creditors, payments by the debtor in the ordinary course of business, initiation of court action for claims that have arisen after the commencement of the insolvency proceeding (or after recognition of a foreign main proceeding), or completion of open financial-market transactions.

149. Sometimes it may be desirable for the court to modify or terminate the effects of article 20. The rules governing the power of the court to do so vary. In some legal systems the courts are authorized to make individual exceptions upon request by an interested party, under conditions prescribed by local law, while in others the courts do not have that power, in line with the principle that, in general, courts do not have the power to set aside the application of a statutory rule of law. If courts are to be given such a power, some legal systems would normally require setting out grounds on which the court could modify or terminate the mandatory effects of recognition under article 20, paragraph 1. In view of that situation, article 20, paragraph 2, provides that the modification or termination of the stay and the suspension provided in the article is subject to the provisions of law of the enacting State relating to insolvency.

150. Generally, it is useful for persons that are adversely affected by the stay or suspension under article 20, paragraph 1, to have an opportunity to be heard by the court, which should then be allowed to modify or terminate those effects. It would be consistent with the objectives of the Model Law if the enacting State would spell out, or refer to, the provisions that govern this question.

Paragraph 3

151. The Model Law does not cover the question of whether the limitation period for a claim ceases to run when the claimant is unable to commence individual proceedings as a result of article 20, subparagraph 1*(a)*, A harmonized rule on that question would not be feasible; however, since it is necessary to protect creditors from losing their claims because of a stay pursuant to that subparagraph, paragraph 3 has been added to authorize the commencement of individual action to the extent necessary to preserve claims against the debtor. Once the claim has been preserved, the action continues to be covered by the stay.

152. Paragraph 3 might seem unnecessary in a State where a demand for payment or performance served by the creditor on the debtor causes the cessation of the running of the limitation period or where the stay of the kind envisaged in subparagraph 1*(a)* triggers such cessation. However, paragraph 3 may still be useful even in such States because the question of the cessation of the running of the limitation period might, pursuant to rules concerning conflict of laws, be governed by the law of a State other than the enacting State; furthermore, the paragraph would be useful as assurance to foreign claimants that their claims would not be prejudiced in the enacting State.

Paragraph 4

153. Paragraph 4 merely clarifies that the automatic stay and suspension pursuant to article 20 do not prevent anyone, including the foreign representative or foreign creditors, from requesting the commencement of a local insolvency proceeding and from participating in that proceeding. The right to apply to commence a local insolvency proceeding and to participate in it is in a general way dealt with in articles 11, 12 and

13. If a local proceeding is indeed initiated, article 29 deals with the coordination of the foreign and the local proceedings.

Discussion in UNCITRAL and in the Working Group

A/52/17, paras. 47–60.
A/CN.9/419. paras. 137–143.
A/CN.9/422. paras. 94–110.
A/CN.9/433, paras. 115–126.
A/CN.9/435. paras. 24–48.

Article 21. Relief that may be granted upon recognition of a foreign proceeding   **A4–074**

1. Upon recognition of a foreign proceeding, whether main or non-main, where necessary to protect the assets of the debtor or the interests of the creditors, the court may, at the request of the foreign representative, grant any appropriate relief, including:

   (a) Staying the commencement or continuation of individual actions or individual proceedings concerning the debtor's assets, rights, obligations or liabilities, to the extent they have not been stayed under paragraph 1(a) of article 20;
   (b) Staying execution against the debtor's assets to the extent it has not been stayed under paragraph 1(b) of article 20;
   (c) Suspending the right to transfer, encumber or otherwise dispose of any assets of the debtor to the extent this right has not been suspended under paragraph 1(c) of article 20;
   (d) Providing for the examination of witnesses, the taking of evidence or the delivery of information concerning the debtor's assets, affairs, rights, obligations or liabilities;
   (e) Entrusting the administration or realization of all or part of the debtor's assets located in this State to the foreign representative or another person designated by the court;
   (f) Extending relief granted under paragraph 1 of article 19;
   (g) Granting any additional relief that may be available to [*insert the title of a person or body administering a reorganization or liquidation under the law of the enacting State*] under the laws of this State.

2. Upon recognition of a foreign proceeding, whether main or non-main, the court may, at the request of the foreign representative, entrust the distribution of all or part of the debtor's assets located in this State to the foreign representative or another person designated by the court, provided that the court is satisfied that the interests of creditors in this State are adequately protected.

3. In granting relief under this article to a representative of a foreign non-main proceeding, the court must be satisfied that the relief relates to assets that, under the law of this State, should be administered in the foreign non-main proceeding or concerns information required in that proceeding.

154. Post-recognition relief under article 21 is discretionary, as is pre-recognition relief under article 19. The types of relief listed in article 21, paragraph 1, are typical or most frequent in insolvency proceedings; however, the list is not exhaustive and the court is not restricted unnecessarily in its ability to grant any type of relief that is available under the law of the enacting State and needed in the circumstances of the case.

155. The explanation relating to the use of the expressions "individual actions" and "individual proceedings" in article 20, subparagraph 1*(a)* and to coverage of

execution proceedings (see paragraphs 145–146 above) applies also to article 21, subparagraph 1*(a)*.

156. It is in the nature of discretionary relief that the court may tailor it to the case at hand. This idea is reinforced by article 22, paragraph 2, according to which the court may subject the relief granted to conditions that it considers appropriate.

Paragraph 2

157. The "turnover" of assets to the foreign representative (or another person), as envisaged in paragraph 2, is discretionary. It should be noted that the Model Law contains several safeguards designed to ensure the protection of local interests before assets are turned over to the foreign representative. Those safeguards include the following: the general statement of the principle of protection of local interests in article 22, paragraph 1; the provision in article 21, paragraph 2, that the court should not authorize the turnover of assets until it is assured that the local creditors' interests are protected; and article 22, paragraph 2, according to which the court may subject the relief that it grants to conditions it considers appropriate.

Paragraph 3

158. One salient factor to be taken into account in tailoring the relief is whether it is for a foreign main or non-main proceeding. The interests and the authority of a representative of a foreign non-main proceeding are typically narrower than the interests and the authority of a representative of a foreign main proceeding, who normally seeks to gain control over all assets of the insolvent debtor. Paragraph 3 reflects that idea by providing *(a)* that relief granted to a foreign non-main proceeding should be limited to assets that are to be administered in that non-main proceeding and *(b)* that, if the foreign representative seeks information concerning the debtor's assets or affairs, the relief must concern information required in that proceeding. The objective is to admonish the court that relief in favour of a foreign non-main proceeding should not give unnecessarily broad powers to the foreign representative and that such relief should not interfere with the administration of another insolvency proceeding, in particular the main proceeding.

159. The proviso "under the law of this State" reflects the principle underlying the Model Law that recognition of a foreign proceeding does not mean extending the effects of the foreign proceeding as they may be prescribed by the law of the foreign State. Instead, recognition of a foreign proceeding entails attaching to the foreign proceeding consequences envisaged by the law of the enacting State.

160. The idea underlying article 21, paragraph 3, has been reflected also in article 19, paragraph 4 (prerecognition relief), article 29, subparagraph *(c)* (coordination of a foreign proceeding with a local proceeding) and article 30 (coordination of more than one foreign proceeding).

Discussion in UNCITRAL and in the Working Group

A/52/17, paras. 61–73.
A/CN.9/419. paras. 148–152 and 154–166.
A/CN.9/422, paras. 111–113.
A/CN.9/433, paras. 127–134 and 138–139.
A/CN.9/435, paras. 49–61.

Article 22. Protection of creditors and other interested persons   **A4–075**

1. In granting or denying relief under article 19 or 21, or in modifying or terminating relief under paragraph 3 of this article, the court must be satisfied that the interests of the creditors and other interested persons, including the debtor, are adequately protected.

2. The court may subject relief granted under article 19 or 21 to conditions it considers appropriate.

3. The court may at the request of the foreign representative or a person affected by relief granted under article 19 or 21, or at its own motion, modify or terminate such relief.

161. The idea underlying article 22 is that there should be a balance between relief that may be granted to the foreign representative and the interests of the persons that may be affected by such relief. This balance is essential to achieve the objectives of cross-border insolvency legislation.

162. The reference to the interests of creditors, the debtor and other interested parties in article 22, paragraph 1, provides useful elements to guide the court in exercising its powers under article 19 or 21. In order to allow the court to tailor the relief better, the court is clearly authorized to subject the relief to conditions (paragraph 2) and to modify or terminate the relief granted (paragraph 3). An additional feature of paragraph 3 is that it expressly gives standing to the parties who may be affected by the consequences of articles 19 and 21 to petition the court to modify and terminate those consequences.

Apart from that, article 22 is intended to operate in the context of the procedural system of the enacting State.

163. In many cases the affected creditors will be "local" creditors. Nevertheless, in enacting article 22, it is not advisable to attempt to limit it to local creditors. Any express reference to local creditors in paragraph 1 would require a definition of those creditors. An attempt to draft such a definition (and to establish criteria according to which a particular category of creditors might receive special treatment) would not only show the difficulty of crafting such a definition but would also reveal that there is no justification for discriminating creditors on the basis of criteria such as place of business or nationality.

164. Protection of all interested persons is linked to provisions in national laws on notification requirements; those may be general publicity requirements, designed to apprise potentially interested persons (e.g. local creditors or local agents of a debtor) that a foreign proceeding has been recognized, or there may be requirements for individual notifications that the court, under its own procedural rules, has to issue to persons that would be directly affected by recognition or relief granted by the court. National laws vary as to the form, time and content of notice required to be given of the recognition of foreign proceedings, and the Model Law does not attempt to modify those laws (see also paragraph 132 above).

Discussion in UNCITRAL and in the Working Group

A/52/17, paras. 82–93.
A/CN.9/422, paragraph 113.
A/CN.9/433, paras. 140–146.
A/CN.9/435, paras. 72–78.

A4–076   *Article 23. Actions to avoid acts detrimental to creditors*

1. Upon recognition of a foreign proceeding, the foreign representative has standing to initiate [*refer to the types of actions to avoid or otherwise render ineffective acts detrimental to creditors that are available in this State to a person or body administering a reorganization or liquidation*].

2. When the foreign proceeding is a foreign non-main proceeding, the court must be satisfied that the action relates to assets that, under the law of this State, should be administered in the foreign non-main proceeding.

165. Under many national laws both individual creditors and insolvency administrators have a right to bring actions to avoid or otherwise render ineffective acts detrimental to creditors. Such a right, insofar as it pertains to individual creditors, is often not governed by insolvency law but by general provisions of law (such as the civil code); the right is not necessarily tied to the existence of an insolvency proceeding against the debtor so that the action may be instituted prior to the commencement of such a proceeding. The person having such a right is typically only an affected creditor and not another person such as the insolvency administrator. Furthermore, the conditions for these individual creditor actions are different from the conditions applicable to similar actions that might be initiated by an insolvency administrator. The procedural standing conferred by article 23 extends only to actions that are available to the local insolvency administrator in the context of an insolvency proceeding, and the article does not equate the foreign representative with individual creditors who may have similar rights under a different set of conditions. Such actions of individual creditors fall outside the scope of article 23.

166. The Model Law expressly provides that a foreign representative has "standing" (a concept in some systems referred to as "active procedural legitimation", "active legitimation" or "legitimation") to initiate actions to avoid or otherwise render ineffective legal acts detrimental to creditors. The provision is drafted narrowly in that it does not create any substantive right regarding such actions and also does not provide any solution involving conflict of laws. The effect of the provision is that a foreign representative is not prevented from initiating such actions by the sole fact that the foreign representative is not the insolvency administrator appointed in the enacting State.

167. Granting procedural standing to the foreign representative to institute such actions is not without difficulty. In particular, such actions might not be looked upon favourably because of their potential for creating uncertainty about concluded or performed transactions. However, since the right to commence such actions is essential to protect the integrity of the assets of the debtor and is often the only realistic way to achieve such protection, it has been considered important to ensure that such right would not be denied to a foreign representative on the sole ground that he or she has not been locally appointed.

Discussion in UNCITRAL and in the Working Group

A/52/17, paras. 210–216.
A/CN.9/433. para. 134.
A/CN.9/435. paras. 62–66.

A4–077   *Article 24. Intervention by a foreign representative in proceedings in this State*

Upon recognition of a foreign proceeding, the foreign representative may, provided the requirements of the law of this State are met, intervene in any proceedings in which the debtor is a party.

168. The purpose of article 24 is to avoid the denial of standing to the foreign representative to intervene in proceedings merely because the procedural legislation may not have contemplated the foreign representative among those having such standing. The article applies to foreign representatives of both main and non-main proceedings.

169. The word "intervene" in the context of article 20 is intended to refer to cases where the foreign representative appears in court and makes representations in proceedings, whether those proceedings be individual court actions or other proceedings (including extrajudicial proceedings) instituted by the debtor against a third party or proceedings instituted by a third party against the debtor. The proceedings where the foreign representative might intervene could only be those that have not been stayed under article 20, subparagraph 1(a), or article 21, subparagraph 1*(a)*.

170. Article 24, which is limited to providing procedural standing, makes it clear (by stating "provided the requirements of the law of this State are met") that all other conditions of the local law for a person to be able to intervene remain intact.

171. Many if not all national procedural laws contemplate cases where a party (the foreign representative in this article) who demonstrates a legal interest in the outcome of a dispute between two other parties may be permitted by the court to be heard in the proceedings. Those procedural laws use different expressions to refer to such situations, the expression "intervention" being frequently used. If the enacting State uses another expression for that concept, the use of such other expression in enacting article 24 would be appropriate.

172. The word "participate" as used in the context of article 12 refers to cases where the foreign representative makes representations in a collective insolvency proceeding (see paragraph 102 above), whereas the word "intervene" as used in article 24 covers cases where the foreign representative takes part in proceedings concerning an individual action by or against the debtor.

Discussion in UNCITRAL and in the Working Group

A/52/17, paras. 117–123.
A/CN.9/422. paras. 148–149.
A/CN.9/433, paras. 51,58.
A/CN.9/435. paras. 79–84.

Chapter IV. Cooperation with foreign courts and foreign representatives **A4–078**

173. Chapter IV (articles 25–27), on cross-border cooperation, is a core element of the Model Law. Its objective is to enable courts and insolvency administrators from two or more countries to be efficient and achieve optimal results. Cooperation as described in the chapter is often the only realistic way, for example, to prevent dissipation of assets, to maximize the value of assets (e.g. when items of production equipment located in two States are worth more if sold together than if sold separately or to find the best solutions for the reorganization of the enterprise.

174. Articles 25 and 26 not only authorize cross-border cooperation, they also mandate it by providing that the court and the insolvency administrator "shall cooperate to the maximum extent possible". The articles are designed to overcome the widespread problem of national laws lacking rules providing a legal basis for cooperation by local courts with foreign courts in dealing with cross-border insolvencies.

Enactment of such a legal basis would be particularly helpful in legal systems in which the discretion given to judges to operate outside areas of express statutory authorization is limited. However, even in jurisdictions in which there is a tradition of wider judicial latitude, enactment of a legislative framework for cooperation has proved to be useful.

175. To the extent that cross-border judicial cooperation in the enacting State is based on the principle of comity among nations, the enactment of articles 25–27 offers an opportunity for making that principle more concrete and adapted to the particular circumstances of cross-border insolvencies.

176. In the States in which the proper legal basis for international cooperation in the area of cross-border insolvency is not the principle of comity, but an international agreement (e.g. a bilateral or multilateral treaty or an exchange of letters between the cooperating authorities) based on the principle of reciprocity, chapter IV of the Model Law may serve as a model for the elaboration of such international cooperation agreements.

177. The articles in chapter IV leave certain decisions, in particular when and how to cooperate, to the courts and, subject to the supervision of the courts, to the insolvency administrators. For a court (or a person or body referred to in articles 25 and 26) to cooperate with a foreign court or a foreign representative regarding a foreign proceeding, the Model Law does not require a previous formal decision to recognize that foreign proceeding.

178. The importance of granting the courts flexibility and discretion in cooperating with foreign courts or foreign representatives was emphasized at the Second UNCITRAL-INSOL Multinational Judicial Colloquium on Cross-Border Insolvency. At that Colloquium, reports of a number of cases in which judicial cooperation in fact occurred were given by the judges involved in the cases. From those reports a number of points emerged that might be summarized as follows: *(a)* communication between courts is possible but should be done carefully and with appropriate safeguards for the protection of substantive and procedural rights of the parties; *(b)* communication should be done openly, in the presence of the parties involved (except in extreme circumstances), who should be given advance notice; *(c)* communications that might be exchanged are various and include: e.g. exchanges of formal court orders or judgements; supply of informal writings of general information, questions and observations; and transmission of transcripts of court proceedings; *(d)* means of communication include, for example, telephone, facsimile, electronic mail facilities and video; and *(e)* where communication is necessary and is intelligently used, there could be considerable benefits for the persons involved in, and affected by, the cross-border insolvency.

A4–079   *Article 25. Cooperation and direct communication between a court of this State and foreign courts or foreign representatives*

1. In matters referred to in article 1, the court shall cooperate to the maximum extent possible with foreign courts or foreign representatives, either directly or through a [*insert the title of a person or body administering a reorganization or liquidation under the law of the enacting State*].

2. The court is entitled to communicate directly with, or to request information or assist-ance directly from, foreign courts or foreign representatives.

179. The ability of courts, with appropriate involvement of the parties, to communicate "directly" and to request information and assistance "directly" from foreign courts or foreign representatives is intended to avoid the use of time-consuming procedures tradi-tionally in use, such as letters rogatory. This ability is critical when the courts consider that they should act with urgency. In order to emphasize the flexible and potentially urgent character of cooperation, the enacting State may find it useful to

include in the enactment of the Model Law an express provision that would authorize the courts, when they engage in cross-border communications under article 25, to forgo use of the formalities (e.g. communication via higher courts, letters rogatory or other diplomatic or consular channels) that are inconsistent with the policy behind the provision.

Article 26. Cooperation and direct communication between the [insert the title of a person or body administering a reorganization or liquidation under the law of the enacting State] *and foreign courts or foreign representatives* **A4–080**

1. In matters referred to in article 1, a [*insert the title of a person or body administering a reorganization or liquidation under the law of the enacting State*] shall, in the exercise of its functions and subject to the supervision of the court, cooperate to the maximum extent possible with foreign courts or foreign representatives.

2. The [*insert the title of a person or body administering a reorganization or liquidation under the law of the enacting State*] is entitled, in the exercise of its functions and subject to the supervision of the court, to communicate directly with foreign courts or foreign representatives.

180. Article 26 on international cooperation between persons who are appointed to administer assets of insolvent debtors reflects the important role that such persons can play in devising and implementing cooperative arrangements, within the parameters of their authority. The provision makes it clear that an insolvency administrator acts under the overall supervision of the competent court (by stating "in the exercise of its functions and subject to the supervision of the court"). The Model Law does not modify the rules already existing in the insolvency law of the enacting State on the supervisory functions of the court over the activities of the insolvency administrator. Generally, a certain degree of latitude and initiative on the part of administrators, within the broad confines of judicial supervision, are mainstays of cooperation in practical terms; it is therefore advisable that the enacting State does not change that in enacting the Model Law. In particular, there should be no suggestion that ad hoc authorization would be needed for each communication between the administrator and a foreign body.

Article 27. Forms of cooperation **A4–081**

Cooperation referred to in articles 25 and 26 may be implemented by any appropriate means, including:

   (a)   Appointment of a person or body to act at the direction of the court;
   (b)   Communication of information by any means considered appropriate by the court;
   (c)   Coordination of the administration and supervision of the debtor's assets and affairs;
   (d)   Approval or implementation by courts of agreements concerning the coordination of proceedings;
   (e)   Coordination of concurrent proceedings regarding the same debtor;
   (f)   [*The enacting State may wish to list additional forms or examples of cooperation*].

181. Article 27 is suggested to be used by the enacting State to provide courts with an indicative list of the types of cooperation that are authorized by articles 25 and 26. Such an indicative listing may be particularly helpful in States with a limited tradition of direct cross-border judicial cooperation and in States where judicial discretion has traditionally been limited. Any listing of forms of possible cooperation should not

purport to be exhaustive, as this might inadvertently preclude certain forms of appropriate cooperation.

182. The implementation of cooperation would be subject to any mandatory rules applicable in the enacting State; for example, in the case of requests for information, rules restricting the communication of information (e.g. for reasons of protection of privacy) would apply.

183. Subparagraph *(f)* of article 27 offers the enacting State the possibility to include additional forms of possible cooperation. Those might include, for example, suspension or termination of existing proceedings in the enacting State.

Discussion in UNCITRAL and in the Working Group

A/52/17, paras. 124–129.
A/CN.9/419. paras. 75–76, 80–83 and 118–133.
A/CN.9/422, paras 129–143.
A/CN.9/433. paras. 164–172.
A/CN.9/435. paras. 85–94.

A4–082   Chapter V. Concurrent proceedings

Article 28. Commencement of a proceeding under [identify laws of the enacting State relating to insolvency] *after recognition of a foreign main proceeding*

After recognition of a foreign main proceeding, a proceeding under [*identify laws of the enacting State relating to insolvency*] may be commenced only if the debtor has assets in this State; the effects of that proceeding shall be restricted to the assets of the debtor that are located in this State and, to the extent necessary to implement cooperation and coordination under articles 25, 26 and 27, to other assets of the debtor that, under the law of this State, should be administered in that proceeding.

184. Article 28, in conjunction with article 29, provides that recognition of a foreign main proceeding will not prevent the commencement of a local insolvency proceeding concerning the same debtor as long as the debtor has assets in the State.

185. The position taken in article 28 is in substance the same as the position taken in a number of States. In some States, however, for the court to have jurisdiction to commence a local insolvency proceeding, the mere presence of assets in the State is not sufficient. For such jurisdiction to exist, the debtor must be engaged in an economic activity in the State (to use the terminology of the Model Law, the debtor must have an "establishment" in the State, as defined in article 2, subparagraph *(f)*). In article 28, the less restrictive solution was opted for in a context where the debtor is already involved in a foreign main proceeding. While the solution leaves a broad ground for commencing a local proceeding after recognition of a foreign main proceeding, it serves the purpose of indicating that, if the debtor has no assets in the State, there is no jurisdiction for commencing an insolvency proceeding.

186. Nevertheless, the enacting State may wish to adopt the more restrictive solution of allowing the initiation of the local proceeding only if the debtor has an establishment in the State. The rationale may be that, when the assets in the enacting State are not part of an establishment, the commencement of a local proceeding would typically not be the most efficient way to protect the creditors, including local creditors. By tailoring relief to be granted to the foreign main proceeding and cooperating with the foreign court and foreign representative, the court in the enacting State would have sufficient

opportunities to ensure that the assets in the State would be administered in such a way that local interests would be adequately protected. Therefore, the enacting State would act in line with the philosophy of the Model Law if it enacts the article by replacing the words "only if the debtor has assets in this State", as they currently appear in article 28, with the words "only if the debtor has an establishment in this State".

187. Ordinarily, the local proceeding of the kind envisaged in article 28 would be limited to the assets located in the State. In some situations, however, a meaningful administration of the local insolvency proceeding may have to include certain assets abroad, especially when there is no foreign proceeding necessary or available in the State where the assets are situated (for example, where the local establishment would have an operating plant in a foreign jurisdiction, where it would be possible to sell the debtor's assets in the enacting State and the assets abroad as a "going concern", or where assets were fraudulently transferred abroad from the enacting State). In order to allow such limited cross-border reach of a local proceeding, the article includes the words "and . . . to other assets of the debtor that . . . should be administered in that proceeding". Two restrictions have been included in the article concerning the possible extension of effects of a local proceeding to assets located abroad: firstly, the extension is permissible "to the extent necessary to implement cooperation and coordination under articles 25, 26 and 27"; and. secondly, those foreign assets must be subject to administration in the enacting State "under the law of [the enacting State]". Those restrictions are useful in order to avoid creating an open-ended faculty to extend the effects of a local proceeding to assets located abroad, a faculty that would generate uncertainty as to the application of the provision and that might lead to conflicts of jurisdiction.

Discussion in UNCITRAL and in the Working Group

A/52/17, paras. 94–101.
A/CN.9/422, paras. 192–197.
A/CN.9/433, paras. 173–181.
A/CN.9/435. paras. 180–183.

Article 29. Coordination of a proceeding under [identify laws of the enacting State   **A4–083**
relating to insolvency] *and a foreign proceeding*

Where a foreign proceeding and a proceeding under [*identify laws of the enacting State relating to insolvency*] are taking place concurrently regarding the same debtor, the court shall seek cooperation and coordination under articles 25, 26 and 27, and the following shall apply:

    (a) When the proceeding in this State is taking place at the time the application for recognition of the foreign proceeding is filed,

        (i) Any relief granted under article 19 or 21 must be consistent with the proceeding in this State; and

        (ii) If the foreign proceeding is recognized in this State as a foreign main proceeding, article 20 does not apply;

    (b) When the proceeding in this State commences after recognition, or after the filing of the application for recognition, of the foreign proceeding,

        (i) Any relief in effect under article 19 or 21 shall be reviewed by the court and shall be modified or terminated if inconsistent with the proceeding in this State; and

        (ii) If the foreign proceeding is a foreign main proceeding, the stay and suspension referred to in paragraph 1 of article 20 shall be modified or terminated pursuant to paragraph 2 of article 20 if inconsistent with the proceeding in this State;

(c) In granting, extending or modifying relief granted to a representative of a foreign non-main proceeding, the court must be satisfied that the relief relates to assets that, under the law of this State, should be administered in the foreign non-main proceeding or concerns information required in that proceeding.

188. Article 29 gives guidance to the court that deals with cases where the debtor is subject to a foreign proceeding and a local proceeding at the same time. The opening words of the provision direct the court that in all such cases it must seek cooperation and coordination pursuant to chapter IV (articles 25, 26 and 27) of the Model Law.

189. The salient principle embodied in article 29 is that the commencement of a local proceeding does not prevent or terminate the recognition of a foreign proceeding. This principle is essential for achieving the objectives of the Model Law in that it allows the court in the enacting State in all circumstances to provide relief in favour of the foreign proceeding.

190. However, the article maintains a pre-eminence of the local proceeding over the foreign proceeding. This has been done in the following ways: firstly, any relief to be granted to the foreign proceeding must be consistent with the local proceeding (article 29, subparagraph *(a)*(i)); secondly, any relief that has already been granted to the foreign proceeding must be reviewed and modified or terminated to ensure consistency with the local proceeding (article 29, subparagraph *(b)*(i)); thirdly, if the foreign proceeding is a main proceeding, the automatic effects pursuant to article 20 are to be modified and terminated if inconsistent with the local proceeding (those automatic effects do not terminate automatically since they may be beneficial, and the court may wish to maintain them) (article 29, subparagraph *(b)*(ii)); and fourthly, where a local proceeding is pending at the time a foreign proceeding is recognized as a main proceeding, the foreign proceeding does not enjoy the automatic effects of article 20 (article 29, subparagraph *(a)*(ii)). Article 29 avoids establishing a rigid hierarchy between the proceedings since that would unnecessarily hinder the ability of the court to cooperate and exercise its discretion under articles 19 and 21. It is desirable not to restrict that latitude of the court when article 29 is enacted.

191. Article 29, subparagraph *(c)*, incorporates the principle that relief granted to a foreign non-main proceeding should be limited to assets that are to be administered in that non-main proceeding or must concern information required in that proceeding. That principle is expressed in article 21, paragraph 3, which deals in a general way with the type of relief that may be granted to a foreign representative, and is restated in article 29, which deals with coordination of local and foreign proceedings. Article 19, paragraph 4, on pre-recognition relief, and article 30, on coordination of more than one foreign proceeding, are inspired by the same principle (see also the comments in paragraph 140 above).

Discussion in UNCITRAL and in the Working Group

A/52/17, paras. 106–110.
A/CN.9/435, paras. 190–191.

A4–084 *Article 30. Coordination of more than one foreign proceeding*

In matters referred to in article 1, in respect of more than one foreign proceeding regarding the same debtor, the court shall seek cooperation and coordination under articles 25, 26 and 27, and the following shall apply:

(a)   Any relief granted under article 19 or 21 to a representative of a foreign non-main proceeding after recognition of a foreign main proceeding must be consistent with the foreign main proceeding;

(b)   If a foreign main proceeding is recognized after recognition, or after the filing of an application for recognition, of a foreign non-main proceeding, any relief in effect under article 19 or 21 shall be reviewed by the court and shall be modified or terminated if inconsistent with the foreign main proceeding;

(c)   If after recognition of a foreign non-main proceeding, another foreign non-main proceeding is recognized, the court shall grant, modify or terminate relief for the purpose of facilitating coordination of the proceedings.

192. Article 30 deals with cases where the debtor is subject to insolvency proceedings in more than one foreign State and foreign representatives of more than one foreign proceeding seek recognition or relief in the enacting State. The provision applies whether or not an insolvency proceeding is pending in the enacting State. If, in addition to two or more foreign proceedings, there is a proceeding in the enacting State, the court will have to act pursuant to both article 29 and article 30.

193. The objective of article 30 is similar to the objective of article 29 in that the key issue in the case of concurrent proceedings is to promote cooperation, coordination and consistency of relief granted to different proceedings. Such consistency will be achieved by appropriate tailoring of relief to be granted or by modifying or terminating relief already granted. Unlike article 29 (which, as a matter of principle, gives primacy to the local proceeding), article 30 gives preference to the foreign main proceeding if there is one. In the case of more than one foreign non-main proceeding, the provision does not *a priori* treat any foreign proceeding preferentially. Priority for the foreign main proceeding is reflected in the requirement that any relief in favour of a foreign non-main proceeding (whether already granted or to be granted) must be consistent with the foreign main proceeding (article 30, subparagraphs *(a)* and *(b)*).

Discussion in UNCITRAL

A/52/17, paras. 111–112.

Article 31. Presumption of insolvency based on recognition of a foreign main proceeding   **A4–085**

In the absence of evidence to the contrary, recognition of a foreign main proceeding is, for the purpose of commencing a proceeding under [*identify laws of the enacting State relating to insolvency*], proof that the debtor is insolvent.

194. In some jurisdictions, proof that the debtor is insolvent is required for the commencement of insolvency proceedings. In other jurisdictions, insolvency proceedings may be commenced under specific circumstances defined by law that do not necessarily mean that the debtor is in fact insolvent; those circumstances may be, for example, cessation of payments by the debtor or certain actions of the debtor such as a corporate decision, dissipation of its assets or abandonment of its establishment.

195. In jurisdictions where insolvency is a condition for commencing insolvency proceedings, article 31 establishes, upon recognition of a foreign main proceeding, a rebuttable presumption of insolvency of the debtor for the purposes of commencing an insolvency proceeding in the enacting State. The presumption does not apply if the foreign proceeding is a non-main proceeding. The reason is that an insolvency proceeding commenced in a State other than the State where the debtor has the centre

of its main interests does not necessarily mean that the debtor is to be subject to laws relating to insolvency in other States.

196. For the national laws where proof that the debtor is insolvent is not required for the commencement of insolvency proceedings, the presumption established in article 31 may be of little practical significance and the enacting State may decide not to enact it.

197. Article 31 would have particular significance when proving insolvency as the prerequisite for an insolvency proceeding would be a time-consuming exercise and of little additional benefit bearing in mind that the debtor is already in an insolvency proceeding in the State where it has the centre of its main interests and the commencement of a local proceeding may be urgently needed for the protection of local creditors. Nonetheless, the court of the enacting State is not bound by the decision of the foreign court, and local criteria for demonstrating insolvency remain operative, as is clarified by the words "in the absence of evidence to the contrary".

Discussion in UNCITRAL and in the Working Group

A/52/17, paras. 94 and 102–105.
A/CN.9/422, para. 196.
A/CN.9/433, paras. 173 and 180–189.
A/CN.9/435, paras. 180 and 184.

A4–086   *Article 32. Rule of payment in concurrent proceedings*

Without prejudice to secured claims or rights *in rem*, a creditor who has received part payment in respect of its claim in a proceeding pursuant to a law relating to insolvency in a foreign State may not receive a payment for the same claim in a proceeding under [*identify laws of the enacting State relating to insolvency*] regarding the same debtor, so long as the payment to the other creditors of the same class is proportionately less than the payment the creditor has already received.

198. The rule set forth in article 32 (sometimes referred to as the hotchpotch rule) is a useful safeguard in a legal regime for coordination and cooperation in the administration of cross-border insolvency proceedings. It is intended to avoid situations in which a creditor might obtain more favourable treatment than the other creditors of the same class by obtaining payment of the same claim in insolvency proceedings in different jurisdictions. For example, an unsecured creditor has received 5 per cent of its claim in a foreign insolvency proceeding; that creditor also participates in the insolvency proceeding in the enacting State, where the rate of distribution is 15 per cent; in order to put the creditor in the equal position as the other creditors in the enacting State, the creditor would receive 10 per cent of its claim in the enacting State.

199. Article 32 does not affect the ranking of claims as established by the law of the enacting State and is solely intended to establish the equal treatment of creditors of the same class. To the extent claims of secured creditors or creditors with rights *in rem* are paid in full (a matter that depends on the law of the State where the proceeding is conducted), those claims are not affected by the provision.

200. The words "secured claims" are used to refer generally to claims guaranteed by particular assets, while the words "rights in rem" are intended to indicate rights relating to a particular property that are enforceable also against third parties. A given right may fall within the ambit of both expressions, depending on the classification and terminology of the applicable law. The enacting State may use another term or terms for expressing those concepts.

Discussion in UNCITRAL and in the Working Group

A/52/17, paras. 130–134.
A/CN.9/419, paras. 89–93.
A/CN.9/422, paras. 198–199.
A/CN.9/433, paras. 182–183.
A/CN.9/435. paras. 96 and 197–198.

VI. ASSISTANCE FROM THE UNCITRAL SECRETARIAT A4–087

Assistance in drafting legislation

201. The UNCITRAL secretariat assists States with technical consultations for the preparation of legislation based on the Model Law. Further information may be obtained from the UNCITRAL secretariat (mailing address: Vienna International Centre, P.O. Box 500, A-1400 Vienna, Austria: telephone: (43-1) 26060–4060; facsimile: (43-1) 26060–5813; electronic mail: uncitral@unov.un.or.at; Internet home page: *http://www.un.or.at/uncitral*).

Information on the interpretation of legislation based on the Model Law

202. Once enacted, the Model Law will be included in the CLOUT information system, which is used for collecting and disseminating information on case law relating to the conventions and model laws that have emanated from the work of UNCITRAL. The purpose of the system is to promote international awareness of the legislative texts formulated by UNCITRAL and to facilitate their uniform interpretation and application. The secretariat publishes, in the six official languages of the United Nations, abstracts of decisions and makes available, against reimbursement of copying expenses, the decisions on the basis of which the abstracts were prepared. The system is explained in a user's guide that is available from the secretariat in hard copy (A/CN.9/SER.C/GUTDE/1) and on the above-mentioned Internet home page of UNCITRAL.

Annex A4–088

General Assembly resolution 52/158 of 15 December 1997

52/158. Model Law on Cross-Border Insolvency of the United Nations Commission on International Trade Law

The General Assembly,

Recalling its resolution 2205 (XXI) of 17 December 1966, by which it created the United Nations Commission on International Trade Law with a mandate to further the progressive harmonization and unification of the law of international trade and in that respect to bear in mind the interests of all peoples, in particular those of developing countries, in the extensive development of international trade. *Noting* that increased cross-border trade and investment leads to greater incidence of cases where enterprises and individuals have assets in more than one State, *Noting* also that when a debtor with assets in more than one State becomes subject to an insolvency proceeding, there often exists an urgent need for cross-border cooperation and coordination in the supervision and administration of the insolvent debtor's assets and affairs, *Considering* that inadequate coordination and cooperation in cases of cross-border insolvency reduce the possibility of rescuing financially troubled but viable businesses, impede a fair and efficient administration of cross-border insolvencies, make it more likely that the debtor's assets would be concealed or dissipated and hinder reorganizations or liquidations of debtors' assets and affairs that would be the most advantageous for the creditors and other interested persons, including the debtors and the debtors' employees, *Noting* that many States lack a legislative framework that would make possible or facilitate effective cross-border coordination and cooperation, *Commenced* that fair and internationally harmonized legislation on cross-border insolvency that respects the national procedural and judicial systems and is acceptable to States with different legal, social and economic systems would contribute to the development of international trade and investment. *Considering* that a set of internationally harmonized model legislative provisions on crossborder insolvency is needed to assist States in modernizing their legislation governing cross-border insolvency.

1. *Expresses its appreciation* to the United Nations Commission on International Trade Law for completing and adopting the Model Law on Cross-Border Insolvency contained in the annex to the present resolutions

2. *Requests* the Secretary-General to transmit the text of the Model Law. together with the Guide to Enactment of the Model Law prepared by the Secretariat, to Governments and interested bodies;

3. *Recommends* that all States review their legislation on cross-border aspects of insolvency to determine whether the legislation meets the objectives of a modern and efficient insolvency system and, in that review, give favourable consideration to the Model Law, bearing in mind the need for an internationally harmonized legislation governing instances of cross-border insolvency;

4. *Recommends also* that all efforts be made to ensure that the Model Law. together with the Guide, become generally known and available.

72nd plenary meeting 15 December 1997

APPENDIX 5

Chapter 15—US Bankruptcy Code s.256

Bankruptcy Abuse Prevention and Consumer Protection Act of 2005 (Enrolled as Agreed to or Passed by Both House and Senate)

SUBCHAPTER IV—COOPERATION WITH FOREIGN COURTS AND FOREIGN REPRESENTATIVES

SUBCHAPTER V—CONCURRENT PROCEEDINGS

A5–001   **Sec. 802. Other Amendments to Titles 11 and 28, United States Code.**

(a) APPLICABILITY OF CHAPTERS—Section 103 of title 11, United States Code, is amended—

(1)   in subsection (a), by inserting before the period the following: ", and this chapter, sections 307, 362(n), 555 through 557, and 559 through 562 apply in a case under chapter 15"; and

(2)   by adding at the end the following:

"(k) Chapter 15 applies only in a case under such chapter, except that—

(1)   sections 1505, 1513, and 1514 apply in all cases under this title; and

(2)   section 1509 applies whether or not a case under this title is pending.".

(b) DEFINITIONS—Section 101 of title 11, United States Code, is amended by striking paragraphs (23) and (24) and inserting the following:

"(23) 'foreign proceeding' means a collective judicial or administrative proceeding in a foreign country, including an interim proceeding, under a law relating to insolvency or adjustment of debt in which proceeding the assets and affairs of the debtor are subject to control or supervision by a foreign court, for the purpose of reorganization or liquidation;

(24) 'foreign representative' means a person or body, including a person or body appointed on an interim basis, authorized in a foreign proceeding to administer the reorganization or the liquidation of the debtor's assets or affairs or to act as a representative of such foreign proceeding;".

(c) AMENDMENTS TO TITLE 28, UNITED STATES CODE—

(1)   PROCEDURES—Section 157(b)(2) of title 28, United States Code, is amended—

(A)   in subparagraph (N), by striking "and" at the end;

(B)   in subparagraph (0), by striking the period at the end and inserting "; and"; and

(C)   by adding at the end the following:

"(P) recognition of foreign proceedings and other matters under chapter 15 of title 11.".

(2) BANKRUPTCY CASES AND PROCEEDINGS—Section 1334(c) of title 28, United States Code, is amended by striking "Nothing in" and inserting "Except with respect to a case under chapter 15 of title 11, nothing in".

(3) DUTIES OF TRUSTEES—Section 586(a)(3) of title 28, United States Code, is amended by striking "or 13" and inserting "13, or 15".

(4) VENUE OF CASES ANCILLARY TO FOREIGN PROCEEDINGS— Section 1410 of title 28, United States Code, is amended to read as follows:

"Sec. 1410. Venue of cases ancillary to foreign proceedings   A5–002

A case under chapter 15 of title 11 may be commenced in the district court of the United States for the district—

(1) in which the debtor has its principal place of business or principal assets in the United States;

(2) if the debtor does not have a place of business or assets in the United States, in which there is pending against the debtor an action or proceeding in a Federal or State court; or

(3) in a case other than those specified in paragraph (1) or (2), in which venue will be consistent with the interests of justice and the convenience of the parties, having regard to the relief sought by the foreign representative.".

(d) OTHER SECTIONS OF TITLE 11—Title 11 of the United States Code is amended—

(1) in section 109 (b), by striking paragraph (3) and inserting the following:

"(3) (A) a foreign insurance company, engaged in such business in the United States; or

(B) a foreign bank, savings bank, cooperative bank, savings and loan association, building and loan association, or credit union, that has a branch or agency (as defined in section 1(b) of the International Banking Act of 1978 in the United States.";

(2) in section 303, by striking subsection (k);

(3) by striking section 304;

(4) in the table of sections for chapter 3 by striking the item relating to section 304;

(5) in section 306 by striking ", 304," each place it appears;

(6) in section 305(a) by striking paragraph (2) and inserting the following:

"(2) (A) a petition under section 1515 for recognition of a foreign proceeding has been granted; and

(B) the purposes of chapter 15 of this title would be best served by such dismissal or suspension."; and

(7) in section 508—

(A) by striking subsection (a); and

(B) in subsection (b), by striking "(b)".

Sec. 1501. Purpose and scope of application   A5–003

(a) The purpose of this chapter is to incorporate the Model Law on Cross-Border Insolvency so as to provide effective mechanisms for dealing with cases of cross-border insolvency with the objectives of—

(1) cooperation between—

(A) courts of the United States, United States trustees, trustees, examiners, debtors, and debtors in possession; and

(B) the courts and other competent authorities of foreign countries involved in cross-border insolvency cases;

(2) greater legal certainty for trade and investment;

(3) fair and efficient administration of cross-border insolvencies that protects the interests of all creditors, and other interested entities, including the debtor;

(4) protection and maximization of the value of the debtor's assets; and

(5) facilitation of the rescue of financially troubled businesses, thereby protecting investment and preserving employment.

(b) This chapter applies where—

(1) assistance is sought in the United States by a foreign court or a foreign representative in connection with a foreign proceeding;

(2) assistance is sought in a foreign country in connection with a case under this title;

(3) a foreign proceeding and a case under this title with respect to the same debtor are pending concurrently; or

(4) creditors or other interested persons in a foreign country have an interest in requesting the commencement of, or participating in, a case or proceeding under this title.

(c) This chapter does not apply to—

(1) a proceeding concerning an entity, other than a foreign insurance company, identified by exclusion in section 109(b);

(2) an individual, or to an individual and such individual's spouse, who have debts within the limits specified in section 109(e) and who are citizens of the United States or aliens lawfully admitted for permanent residence in the United States; or

(3) an entity subject to a proceeding under the Securities Investor Protection Act of 1970, a stockbroker subject to subchapter III of chapter 7 of this title, or a commodity broker subject to subchapter IV of chapter 7 of this title.

(d) The court may not grant relief under this chapter with respect to any deposit, escrow, trust fund, or other security required or permitted under any applicable State insurance law or regulation for the benefit of claim holders in the United States.

A5–004 SUBCHAPTER I—GENERAL PROVISIONS

Sec. 1502. Definitions

For the purposes of this chapter, the term—

(1) "debtor" means an entity that is the subject of a foreign proceeding;

(2) "establishment" means any place of operations where the debtor carries out a nontransitory economic activity;

(3) "foreign court" means a judicial or other authority competent to control or supervise a foreign proceeding;

(4) "foreign main proceeding" means a foreign proceeding pending in the country where the debtor has the center of its main interests;

(5) "foreign non-main proceeding" means a foreign proceeding, other than a foreign main proceeding, pending in a country where the debtor has an establishment;

(6) "trustee" includes a trustee, a debtor in possession in a case under any chapter of this title, or a debtor under chapter 9 of this title;

(7) "recognition" means the entry of an order granting recognition of a foreign main proceeding or foreign non-main proceeding under this chapter; and

(8) "within the territorial jurisdiction of the United States", when used with reference to property of a debtor, refers to tangible property located within the territory of the United States and intangible property deemed under applicable nonbankruptcy law to be located within that territory, including any property subject to attachment or garnishment that may properly be seized or garnished by an action in a Federal or State court in the United States.

Sec. 1503. International obligations of the United States   A5–005

To the extent that this chapter conflicts with an obligation of the United States arising out of any treaty or other form of agreement to which it is a party with one or more other countries, the requirements of the treaty or agreement prevail.

Sec. 1504. Commencement of ancillary case   A5–006

A case under this chapter is commenced by the filing of a petition for recognition of a foreign proceeding under section 1515.

Sec. 1505. Authorization to act in a foreign country   A5–007

A trustee or another entity (including an examiner) may be authorized by the court to act in a foreign country on behalf of an estate created under section 541. An entity authorized to act under this section may act in any way permitted by the applicable foreign law

Sec. 1506. Public policy exception   A5–008

Nothing in this chapter prevents the court from refusing to take an action governed by this chapter if the action would be manifestly contrary to the public policy of the United States.

Sec. 1507. Additional assistance   A5–009

(a) Subject to the specific limitations stated elsewhere in this chapter the court, if recognition is granted, may provide additional assistance to a foreign representative under this title or under other laws of the United States.

(b) In determining whether to provide additional assistance under this title or under other laws of the United States, the court shall consider whether such additional assistance, consistent with the principles of comity, will reasonably assure—

(1) just treatment of all holders of claims against or interests in the debtor's property;

(2) protection of claim holders in the United States against prejudice and inconvenience in the processing of claims in such foreign proceeding;

(3) prevention of preferential or fraudulent dispositions of property of the debtor;

(4) distribution of proceeds of the debtor's property substantially in accordance with the order prescribed by this title; and

(5) if appropriate, the provision of an opportunity for a fresh start for the individual that such foreign proceeding concerns.

A5–010   Sec. 1508. Interpretation

In interpreting this chapter, the court shall consider its international origin, and the need to promote an application of this chapter that is consistent with the application of similar statutes adopted by foreign jurisdictions.

CHAPTER II—ACCESS OF FOREIGN REPRESENTATIVES AND CREDITORS TO THE COURT

A5–011   Sec. 1509. Right of direct access

(a)   A foreign representative may commence a case under section 1504 by filing directly with the court a petition for recognition of a foreign proceeding under section 1515.

(b)   If the court grants recognition under section 1517, and subject to any limitations that the court may impose consistent with the policy of this chapter—

(1)   the foreign representative has the capacity to sue and be sued in a court in the United States;

(2)   the foreign representative may apply directly to a court in the United States for appropriate relief in that court; and

(3)   a court in the United States shall grant comity or cooperation to the foreign representative.

(c)   A request for comity or cooperation by a foreign representative in a court in the United States other than the court which granted recognition shall be accompanied by a certified copy of an order granting recognition under section 1517.

(d)   If the court denies recognition under this chapter, the court may issue any appropriate order necessary to prevent the foreign representative from obtaining comity or cooperation from courts in the United States.

(e)   Whether or not the court grants recognition, and subject to sections 306 and 1510, a foreign representative is subject to applicable nonbankruptcy law.

(f)   Notwithstanding any other provision of this section, the failure of a foreign representative to commence a case or to obtain recognition under this chapter does not affect any right the foreign representative may have to sue in a court in the United States to collect or recover a claim which is the property of the debtor.

A5–012   Sec. 1510. Limited jurisdiction

The sole fact that a foreign representative files a petition under section 1515 does not subject the foreign representative to the jurisdiction of any court in the United States for any other purpose.

A5–013   Sec. 1511. Commencement of case under section 301 or 303

(a)   Upon recognition, a foreign representative may commence—

(1)   an involuntary case under section 303; or

(2)   a voluntary case under section 301 or 302, if the foreign proceeding is a foreign main proceeding.

(b)   The petition commencing a case under subsection (a) must be accompanied by a certified copy of an order granting recognition. The court where the petition for recognition has been filed must be advised of the foreign representative's intent to commence a case under subsection (a) prior to such commencement.

Sec. 1512. Participation of a foreign representative in a case under this title   A5–014

Upon recognition of a foreign proceeding, the foreign representative in the recognized proceeding is entitled to participate as a party in interest in a case regarding the debtor under this title.

Sec. 1513. Access of foreign creditors to a case under this title   A5–015

    (a)   Foreign creditors have the same rights regarding the commencement of, and participation in, a case under this title as domestic creditors.

    (b)   (1)   Subsection (a) does not change or codify present law as to the priority of claims under section 507 or 726, except that the claim of a foreign creditor under those sections shall not be given a lower priority than that of general unsecured claims without priority solely because the holder of such claim is a foreign creditor.

           (2) (A) Subsection (a) and paragraph (1) do not change or codify present law as to the allowability of foreign revenue claims or other foreign public law claims in a proceeding under this title.

                 (B) Allowance and priority as to a foreign tax claim or other foreign public law claim shall be governed by any applicable tax treaty of the United States, under the conditions and circumstances specified therein.

Sec. 1514. Notification to foreign creditors concerning a case under this title   A5–016

    (a)   Whenever in a case under this title notice is to be given to creditors generally or to any class or category of creditors, such notice shall also be given to the known creditors generally, or to creditors in the notified class or category, that do not have addresses in the United States. The court may order that appropriate steps be taken with a view to notifying any creditor whose address is not yet known.

    (b)   Such notification to creditors with foreign addresses described in subsection (a) shall be given individually, unless the court considers that, under the circumstances, some other form of notification would be more appropriate. No letter or other formality is required.

    (c)   When a notification of commencement of a case is to be given to foreign creditors, such notification shall—

           (1)   indicate the time period for filing proofs of claim and specify the place for filing such proofs of claim;

           (2)   indicate whether secured creditors need to file proofs of claim; and

           (3)   contain any other information required to be included in such notification to creditors under this title and the orders of the court.

    (d)   Any rule of procedure or order of the court as to notice or the filing of a proof of claim shall provide such additional time to creditors with foreign addresses as is reasonable under the circumstances.

SUBCHAPTER III—RECOGNITION OF A FOREIGN PROCEEDING AND RELIEF

Sec. 1515. Application for recognition   A5–017

    (a)   A foreign representative applies to the court for recognition of a foreign proceeding in which the foreign representative has been appointed by filing a petition for recognition.

(b) A petition for recognition shall be accompanied by—

(1) a certified copy of the decision commencing such foreign proceeding and appointing the foreign representative;

(2) a certificate from the foreign court affirming the existence of such foreign proceeding and of the appointment of the foreign representative; or

(3) in the absence of evidence referred to in paragraphs (1) and (2), any other evidence acceptable to the court of the existence of such foreign proceeding and of the appointment of the foreign representative.

(c) A petition for recognition shall also be accompanied by a statement identifying all foreign proceedings with respect to the debtor that are known to the foreign representative.

(d) The documents referred to in paragraphs (1) and (2) of subsection (b) shall be translated into English. The court may require a translation into English of additional documents.

A5–018   Sec. 1516. Presumptions concerning recognition

(a) If the decision or certificate referred to in section 1515(b) indicates that the foreign proceeding is a foreign proceeding and that the person or body is a foreign representative, the court is entitled to so presume.

(b) The court is entitled to presume that documents submitted in support of the petition for recognition are authentic, whether or not they have been legalized.

(c) In the absence of evidence to the contrary, the debtor's registered office, or habitual residence in the case of an individual, is presumed to be the center of the debtor's main interests.

A5–019   Sec. 1517. Order granting recognition

(a) Subject to section 1506, after notice and a hearing, an order recognizing a foreign proceeding shall be entered if—

(1) such foreign proceeding for which recognition is sought is a foreign main proceeding or foreign non-main proceeding within the meaning of section 1502;

(2) the foreign representative applying for recognition is a person or body; and

(3) the petition meets the requirements of section 1515.

(b) Such foreign proceeding shall be recognized—

(1) as a foreign main proceeding if it is pending in the country where the debtor has the center of its main interests; or

(2) as a foreign non-main proceeding if the debtor has an establishment within the meaning of section 1502 in the foreign country where the proceeding is pending.

(c) A petition for recognition of a foreign proceeding shall be decided upon at the earliest possible time. Entry of an order recognizing a foreign proceeding constitutes recognition under this chapter.

(d) The provisions of this subchapter do not prevent modification or termination of recognition if it is shown that the grounds for granting it were fully or partially lacking or have ceased to exist, but in considering such action the court shall give due weight to possible prejudice to parties that have relied upon the order granting recognition. A case under this chapter may be closed in the manner prescribed under section 350.

Sec. 1518. Subsequent information   A5–020

From the time of filing the petition for recognition of a foreign proceeding, the
foreign representative shall file with the court promptly a notice of change of status
concerning—

    (1) any substantial change in the status of such foreign proceeding or the status
          of the foreign representative's appointment; and

    (2) any other foreign proceeding regarding the debtor that becomes known to the
          foreign representative.

See. 1519. Relief that may be granted upon filing petition for recognition   A5–021

    (a) From the time of filing a petition for recognition until the court rules on the
         petition, the court may, at the request of the foreign representative, where
         relief is urgently needed to protect the assets of the debtor or the interests of
         the creditors, grant relief of a provisional nature, including—

         (1) staying execution against the debtor's assets;

         (2) entrusting the administration or realization of all or part of the debtor's
             assets located in the United States to the foreign representative or
             another person authorized by the court, including an examiner, in order
             to protect and preserve the value of assets that, by their nature or
             because of other circumstances, are perishable, susceptible to devalua-
             tion or otherwise in jeopardy; and

         (3) any relief referred to in paragraph (3), (4), or (7) of section 1521(a).

    (b) Unless extended under section 1521(a)(6), the relief granted under this
         section terminates when the petition for recognition is granted.

    (c) It is a ground for denial of relief under this section that such relief would
         interfere with the administration of a foreign main proceeding.

    (d) The court may not enjoin a police or regulatory act of a governmental unit,
         including a criminal action or proceeding, under this section.

    (e) The standards, procedures, and limitations applicable to an injunction shall
         apply to relief under this section.

    (f) The exercise of rights not subject to the stay arising under section 362(a)
         pursuant to paragraph (6), (7), (17), or (27) of section 362(b) or pursuant to
         section 362(n) shall not be stayed by any order of a court or administrative
         agency in any proceeding under this chapter.

Sec. 1520. Effects of recognition of a foreign main proceeding   A5–022

    (a) Upon recognition of a foreign proceeding that is a foreign main
         proceeding—

         (1) sections 361 and 362 apply with respect to the debtor and the property
             of the debtor that is within the territorial jurisdiction of the United
             States;

         (2) sections 363, 549, and 552 apply to a transfer of an interest of the
             debtor in property that is within the territorial jurisdiction of the United
             States to the same extent that the sections would apply to property of
             an estate;

         (3) unless the court orders otherwise, the foreign representative may
             operate the debtor's business and may exercise the rights and powers
             of a trustee under and to the extent provided by sections 363 and 552;
             and

         (4) section 552 applies to property of the debtor that is within the territo-
             rial jurisdiction of the United States.

(b) Subsection (a) does not affect the right to commence an individual action or proceeding in a foreign country to the extent necessary to preserve a claim against the debtor.

(c) Subsection (a) does not affect the right of a foreign representative or an entity to file a petition commencing a case under this title or the right of any party to file claims or take other proper actions in such a case.

A5–023   Sec. 1521.   Relief that may be granted upon recognition

(a) Upon recognition of a foreign proceeding, whether main or non-main, where necessary to effectuate the purpose of this chapter and to protect the assets of the debtor or the interests of the creditors, the court may, at the request of the foreign representative, grant any appropriate relief, including—

   (1) staying the commencement or continuation of an individual action or proceeding concerning the debtor's assets, rights, obligations or liabilities to the extent they have not been stayed under section 1520(a);

   (2) staying execution against the debtor's assets to the extent it has not been stayed under section 1520(a);

   (3) suspending the right to transfer, encumber or otherwise dispose of any assets of the debtor to the extent this right has not been suspended under section 1520(a);

   (4) providing for the examination of witnesses, the taking of evidence or the delivery of information concerning the debtor's assets, affairs, rights, obligations or liabilities;

   (5) entrusting the administration or realization of all or part of the debtor's assets within the territorial jurisdiction of the United States to the foreign representative or another person, including an examiner, authorized by the court;

   (6) extending relief granted under section 1519(a); and

   (7) granting any additional relief that may be available to a trustee, except for relief available under sections 522, 544, 545, 547, 548, 550, and 724(a).

(b) Upon recognition of a foreign proceeding, whether main or non-main, the court may, at the request of the foreign representative, entrust the distribution of all or part of the debtor's assets located in the United States to the foreign representative or another person, including an examiner, authorized by the court, provided that the court is satisfied that the interests of creditors in the United States are sufficiently protected.

(c) In granting relief under this section to a representative of a foreign non-main proceeding, the court must be satisfied that the relief relates to assets that, under the law of the United States, should be administered in the foreign non-main proceeding or concerns information required in that proceeding.

(d) The court may not enjoin a police or regulatory act of a governmental unit, including a criminal action or proceeding, under this section.

(e) The standards, procedures, and limitations applicable to an injunction shall apply to relief under paragraphs (1), (2), (3), and (6) of subsection (a).

(f) The exercise of rights not subject to the stay arising under section 362(a) pursuant to paragraph (6), (7), (17), or (27) of section 362(b) or pursuant to section 362(n) shall not be stayed by any order of a court or administrative agency in any proceeding under this chapter.

A5–024   Sec. 1522.   Protection of creditors and other interested persons

(a) The court may grant relief under section 1519 or 1521, or may modify or terminate relief under subsection (c), only if the interests of the creditors and other interested entities, including the debtor, are sufficiently protected.

(b) The court may subject relief granted under section 1519 or 1521, or the operation of the debtor's business under section 1520(a)(3), to conditions it considers appropriate, including the giving of security or the filing of a bond.

(c) The court may, at the request of the foreign representative or an entity affected by relief granted under section 1519 or 1521, or at its own motion, modify or terminate such relief.

(d) Section 1104(d) shall apply to the appointment of an examiner under this chapter. Any examiner shall comply with the qualification requirements imposed on a trustee by section 322.

Sec. 1523. Actions to avoid acts detrimental to creditors   A5–025

(a) Upon recognition of a foreign proceeding, the foreign representative has standing in a case concerning the debtor pending under another chapter of this title to initiate actions under sections 522, 544, 545, 547, 548, 550, 553, and 724(a).

(b) When a foreign proceeding is a foreign non-main proceeding, the court must be satisfied that an action under subsection (a) relates to assets that, under United States law, should be administered in the foreign non-main proceeding.

Sec. 1524. Intervention by a foreign representative   A5–026

Upon recognition of a foreign proceeding, the foreign representative may intervene in any proceedings in a State or Federal court in the United States in which the debtor is a party.

SUBCHAPTER IV—COOPERATION WITH FOREIGN COURTS AND FOREIGN REPRESENTATIVES

Sec. 1525. Cooperation and direct communication between the court and foreign   A5–027
courts or foreign representatives

(a) Consistent with section 1501, the court shall cooperate to the maximum extent possible with a foreign court or a foreign representative, either directly or through the trustee.

(b) The court is entitled to communicate directly with, or to request information or assistance directly from, a foreign court or a foreign representative, subject to the rights of a party in interest to notice and participation.

Sec. 1526. Cooperation and direct communication between the trustee and foreign   A5–028
courts or foreign representatives

(a) Consistent with section 1501, the trustee or other person, including an examiner, authorized by the court, shall, subject to the supervision of the court, cooperate to the maximum extent possible with a foreign court or a foreign representative.

(b) The trustee or other person, including an examiner, authorized by the court is entitled, subject to the supervision of the court, to communicate directly with a foreign court or a foreign representative.

Sec. 1527. Forms of cooperation   A5–029

Cooperation referred to in sections 1525 and 1526 may be implemented by any appropriate means, including—

(1) appointment of a person or body, including an examiner, to act at the direction of the court;

(2) communication of information by any means considered appropriate by the court;

(3) coordination of the administration and supervision of the debtor's assets and affairs;

(4) approval or implementation of agreements concerning the coordination of proceedings; and

(5) coordination of concurrent proceedings regarding the same debtor.

SUBCHAPTER V—CONCURRENT PROCEEDINGS

A5–030 **Sec. 1528. Commencement of a case under this title after recognition of a foreign main proceeding**

After recognition of a foreign main proceeding, a case under another chapter of this title may be commenced only if the debtor has assets in the United States. The effects of such case shall be restricted to the assets of the debtor that are within the territorial jurisdiction of the United States and, to the extent necessary to implement cooperation and coordination under sections 1525, 1526, and 1527, to other assets of the debtor that are within the jurisdiction of the court under sections 541(a) of this title, and 1334(e) of title 28, to the extent that such other assets are not subject to the jurisdiction and control of a foreign proceeding that has been recognized under this chapter.

A5–031 **Sec. 1529. Coordination of a case under this title and a foreign proceeding**

If a foreign proceeding and a case under another chapter of this title are pending concurrently regarding the same debtor, the court shall seek cooperation and coordination under sections 1525, 1526, and 1527, and the following shall apply:

(1) If the case in the United States pending at the time the petition for recognition of such foreign proceeding is filed—

    (A) any relief granted under section 1519 or 1521 must be consistent with the relief granted in the case in the United States; and

    (B) section 1520 does not apply even if such foreign proceeding is recognized as a foreign main proceeding.

(2) If a case in the United States under this title commences after recognition, or after the date of the filing of the petition for recognition, of such foreign proceeding—

    (A) any relief in effect under section 1519 or 1521 shall be reviewed by the court and shall be modified or terminated if inconsistent with the case in the United States; and

    (B) if such foreign proceeding is a foreign main proceeding, the stay and suspension referred to in section 1520(a) shall be modified or terminated if inconsistent with the relief granted in the case in the United States.

(3) In granting, extending, or modifying relief granted to a representative of a foreign non-main proceeding, the court must be satisfied that the relief relates to assets that, under the laws of the United States, should be administered in the foreign non-main proceeding or concerns information required in that proceeding.

(4) In achieving cooperation and coordination under sections 1528 and 1529, the court may grant any of the relief authorized under section 305.

Sec. 1530. Coordination of more than 1 foreign proceeding   A5–032

In matters referred to in section 1501, with respect to more than 1 foreign proceeding regarding the debtor, the court shall seek cooperation and coordination under sections 1525, 1526, and 1527, and the following shall apply:

(1) Any relief granted under section 1519 or 1521 to a representative of a foreign non-main proceeding after recognition of a foreign main proceeding must be consistent with the foreign main proceeding.

(2) If a foreign main proceeding is recognized after recognition, or after the filing of a petition for recognition, of a foreign non-main proceeding, any relief in effect under section 1519 or 1521 shall be reviewed by the court and shall be modified or terminated if inconsistent with the foreign main proceeding.

(3) If, after recognition of a foreign non-main proceeding, another foreign non-main proceeding is recognized, the court shall grant, modify, or terminate relief for the purpose of facilitating coordination of the proceedings.

Sec. 1531. Presumption of insolvency based on recognition of a foreign main   A5–033
proceeding

In the absence of evidence to the contrary, recognition of a foreign main proceeding is, for the purpose of commencing a proceeding under section 303, proof that the debtor is generally not paying its debts as such debts become due.

Sec. 1532. Rule of payment in concurrent proceedings   A5–034

Without prejudice to secured claims or rights in rem, a creditor who has received payment with respect to its claim in a foreign proceeding pursuant to a law relating to insolvency may not receive a payment for the same claim in a case under any other chapter of this title regarding the debtor, so long as the payment to other creditors of the same class is proportionately less than the payment the creditor has already received.

INDEX

This index has been prepared using Sweet and Maxwell's Legal Taxonomy. Main index entries conform to keywords provided by the Legal Taxonomy except where references to specific documents or non-standard terms (denoted by quotation marks) have been included. These keywords provide a means of identifying similar concepts in other Sweet & Maxwell publications and online services to which keywords from the Legal Taxonomy have been applied. Readers may find some minor differences between terms used in the text and those which appear in the index. Suggestions to *sweetandmaxwell.taxonomy@thomson.com.*

(all references are to paragraph number)

Accounting periods
tax
  administration, 5–017—5–028
  administrative receivership, 5–047
  winding-up, 15–056
Administration
accounting periods, 5–017—5–028
capital gains, 5–030
conflict of laws
  foreign appointments, 30–025—30–026
  generally, 30–021
  powers of English courts,
    30–022—30–024
corporate recovery
  continuation of business,
    10–003—10–004
  rescue and realisation, 10–001
disposals, 11–001—11–007
expenses
  conclusion, 4–038
  general principles, 4–020—4–036
  priorities, 4–037
groups of companies, 5–038—5–041
interest, 5–036
liens
  enforceability, 23–006
  generally, 23–005
  inquiry into company dealings,
    23–007
  moratorium on security enforcement,
    23–008—23–011
national insurance contributions, 5–037
PAYE, 5–037
pensions, effect on, 17–002—17–004
pre-pack administrations, 5–042
rates
  distress, 19–016—19–017
rent, 5–035
set-off
  discounting, 22–045—22–051
  distribution, meaning of,
    22–042—22–043

expenses, 22–044
impact of other forms of set-off,
  22–035—22–036
introduction, 22–032—22–033
liquidation, differing rules for, 22–038
moratoriums, 22–035—22–036
practical implications for creditors,
  22–041
reform proposals, 22–052
schemes of arrangement, 22–037
set-off and cut-off dates,
  22–039—22–040
voluntary arrangements, 22–037
wording of rule, 22–034
tax
  accounting periods, 5–017—5–028
  capital gains, 5–030
  groups of companies, 5–038—5–041
  interest, 5–036
  international issues, 5–067—5–068
  national insurance contributions, 5–037
  PAYE, 5–037
  pre-appointment taxes, 5–015—5–016
  pre-pack administrations, 5–042
  rental income, 5–035
  status of administrator, 5–012—5–014
  trading income, 5–033—5–034
  VAT, 5–059—5–066
termination
  automatic, 27–019   27 020
  court application by administrator,
    27–024—27–025
  court application by creditor, 27–028
  dissolution following, 27–046—27–047
  extension of term, 27–021—27–023
  liquidation following, 27–029—27–045
  methods, 27–048
  objective achieved, 27–026—27–027
  trading income, 5–033—5–034
Administration orders
appointment of administrator under,
  6–003—6–005

Displacement
removal of receivers, 28–005
Disposals
company names
prohibition on re-use of,
11–091—11–097
contracts of sale
apportionment of liabilities, 11–052
book debts, 11–071—11–072
completion, 11–038—11–042
definitions, 11–033—11–034
employees, 11–055—11–069
exclusions, 11–075—11–076
existing contracts, 11–070
goodwill, 11–073—11–074
intellectual property, 11–050—11–051
introduction, 11–025
parties, 11–026—11–030
payment, 11–038—11–042
pre-payments, 11–052
price, 11–037
properties, 11–077—11–080
recitals, 11–031—11–032
records, 11–053—11–054
risk, 11–043
third party assets, 11–044—11–045
third party stock, 11–046—11–049
title, 11–035—11–036
conveyancing
administrators, 11–113—11–115
court orders for sale, 11–121
generally, 11–110—11–111
over-reaching, 11–114, 11–120
receivers post winding-up, 11–123
receivers pre winding-up,
11–116—11–122
statutory powers, 11–112
warranties, 11–122
decisions
administration, 11–001—11–007
receivership, 11–008
forced sale of assets, 11–100—11–101
hive downs
concept, 11–081—11–082
employees, 11–088—11–090
legality, 11–083—11–084
method, 11–085—11–087
leases, 11–105—11–109
manner of, 11–009—11–010
reconstructions, 11–099
sales at valuation, 11–102—11–104
schemes of arrangements, 11–099
secured property, 11–098
transfer of going concern, 11–011—11–024
winding-up, 15–045—15–047
Dissipation of assets
continuation of business, 10–021
Dissolution
administration
distributions, 27–018
following termination of,
27–046—27–047

Distress
leases as security, 18–017
rates
administration, 19–016—19–017
introduction, 19–015
receivership, 19–018—19–023
unsecured creditors, 14–022—14–032
Distributions
administrators
dissolution, 27–018
dividends, 27–016
generally, 27–010
leave of court, 27–011
notice, 27–012
proving, 27–013
ranking of creditors, 27–017
set-off, 27–014—27–015
meaning, 22–042—22–043
receivers
fixed charges, 28–023—28–035
floating charges, 28–036—28–063
introduction, 28–022
missing debenture holders, 28–064
redemption, 28–065—28–066
Dividends
administrators, 27–016
Duty of care
receivers, 13–015—13–034,
13–039—13–043
Duty to account
receivers, 13–069—13–070
Employees
construction contracts, 25–034—25–036
contracts of employment
continuance and adoption,
16–009—16–019
direct government payment, 16–008
dismissal, 16–007
re-employment, 16–020—16–021
redundancy, 16–022—16–023
survival of existing, 16–002—16–006
disposals
contracts of sale, 11–055—11–069
hive downs, 11–088—11–090
introduction, 16–001
transfer of undertakings
consequences, 16–026
general principle, 16–024
information and consultation, 16–035
meaning, 16–025
scope, 16–027—16–028
unfair dismissal, 16–034
voidable transfers, 16–029—16–033
Enforcement
securities
liens, 23–006
moratoriums, 9–009—9–011
Environment Agency
role of, 26–007—26–008
Environmental law
administrators
generally, 26–009

human rights, 13–063—13–064
rates
  distress for, 19–024
  occupied property, 19–002—19–007
  unoccupied property, 19–008—19–014
torts, 13–059—13–061
trespass, 13–057
wrongful interference with contract, 13–056
wrongful trading, 13–065
Receivers' powers and duties
court-appointed receivers, 29–014—29–015
duty to account, 13–069—13–070
debenture-holders, to, 13–072—13–072
introduction, 13–001
release, 13–077
third parties
  duty of care, 13–015—13–034,
      13–039—13–043
  fair dealing, 13–044—13–046
  fairness, 13–035—13–038
  generally, 13–002—13–004
  good faith, 13–005—13–010
  mortgagees in possession,
      13–011—13–013
  self-dealing, 13–044—13–046
waiver, 13–077
Receivership
corporate recovery
  continuation of business, 10–005
  realisation, 10–002
disposals, 11–008
liens, 23–012—23–014
moratoriums, 9–008
rates
  distress, 19–018—19–023
set-off
  contracts, 22–062
  Crown debts, 22–063
  floating charges, 22–060—22–061
  generally, 22–053
  notice of creation of security interests,
      22–054—22–059
  practical lessons, 22–066—22–067
  pro-rata sharing clause, 22–064—22–065
Recognition of judgments
EU law, 31–021—31–022
UNCITRAL Model Law
  consequences of, 32–011—32–013
  interim relief pending, 32–010
  introduction, 32–009
  reliefs, 32–024
Reconstructions
disposals, 11–099
Rectification
registration of charges, 3–122—3–127
Redemption
distributions by receivers,
    28–065—28–066
Redundancy
contracts of employment, 16–022—16–023
Re-engagement
contracts of employment, 16–020—16–021

Registrar of Companies
notice of appointment of receiver, 7–054
Registration
charges
  certificates, 3–128—3–131
  extensions of time, 3–122—3–127
  introduction, 3–106
  non-registration, consequences of,
      3–118—3–120
  priorities, 3–121
  rectification, 3–122—3–127
  registrability, 3–107—3–116
  required particulars, 3–117
liens, 23–003
Release
receivers' powers and duties, 13–077
Reliefs
forfeiture
  breach of condition against liquidation,
      18–015
  chargee's application, 18–012
  discretion, 18–014
  construction contracts, 25–008—25–010
  leases as security, 18–011—18–016
  tenant's application, 18–011
  time limits, 18–013
UNCITRAL Model Law
  discretionary relief, 32–026
  interim relief, 32–010
  recognition, and, 32–024
Remediation notices
environmental law
  appeals, 26–040
  appropriate person, 26–038
  generally, 26–037
  penalties for non-compliance, 26–041
  timing, 26–039
Removal
administrators
  by court, 27–002—27–003
  by creditors' meeting, 27–004
  by qualifying floating charge holder,
      27–005
receivers
  administration orders, 28–007
  courts, 28–003—28–004
  death, 28–008
  debenture holders, 28–001—28–002
  displacement, 28–005
  qualifications, 28–006
Remuneration
Court-appointed receivers, 29–017
receivers, 15–051
Rent
non-payment
  forfeiture, 18–006
tax
  administration, 5–035
  administrative receivership, 5–055
Repossession
goods
  moratoriums, 9–012—9–013